FOREWORD

The "USAF Statistical Digest", (Short Title USAFSD-53) summarizes in one document the volume of statistical data collected and published by various offices in Headquarters, United States Air Force and certain major commands. It is to be used as the official basic reference document for the period and areas covered.

The Fiscal Year 1953 edition is the eighth edition of the series. Original editions - Army Air Force Statistical Digest (World War II) and supplement Number 1, 1945 were followed by AAF Statistical Digest, 1946 and USAF Statistical Digest 1947. The 1946 and 1947 editions made Air Force Statistics available in summarized form,available as far back as possible, with the exception of Combat Operations. This data is found only in the 1945 edition. The 1948 issue was the first strictly annual publication. The present issue, and the 1949, 1950, 1951, and 1952 editions are organized on a Fiscal Year basis.

Immediately following this introductory statement is a Major Air Command Directory, containing information which is appropriate to all data included in this issue. Definitions appropriate to only one area will be found in an introductory statement preceding the Part in question.

Sources of the majority of the data are the published and unpublished records of the Directorate of Statistical Services. The balance of the data was furnished by other agencies as noted in source reference data.

Correspondence relative to the content of this document as well as recommendation for new material for inclusion should be addressed to Director of Statistical Services, Headquarters United States Air Force, Washington 25, D. C.

AIR STAFF–DEPARTMENT OF THE AIR FORCE
MAJOR AIR COMMANDS & SEPARATE OPERATING AGENCIES

CHIEF OF STAFF
VICE CHIEF OF STAFF
ASS'T VICE CHIEF OF STAFF

SURGEON GENERAL
THE INSPECTOR GENERAL
THE JUDGE ADVOCATE GENERAL
SCIENTIFIC ADVISORY BOARD
SPECIAL ASS'T FOR RESERVE FORCES

AIR ADJUTANT GENERAL
SECRETARY OF THE AIR STAFF

DEPUTY CHIEF OF STAFF COMPTROLLER
ASSISTANT DEPUTY CHIEF OF STAFF
- ASSISTANT FOR PLANS AND INTERNATIONAL AFFAIRS
- AUDITOR GENERAL
- DIRECTOR OF ACCOUNTING
- DIRECTOR OF STATISTICAL SERVICES
- DIRECTOR OF BUDGET
- DIRECTOR OF MANAGEMENT ANALYSIS SERVICE
- DIRECTOR OF FINANCE

DEPUTY CHIEF OF STAFF PERSONNEL
ASSISTANT DEPUTY CHIEF OF STAFF
- ASSISTANT FOR GROUND SAFETY
- DIRECTOR, WAF
- CHIEF OF AF CHAPLAINS
- DIRECTOR OF PERSONNEL PLANNING
- DIRECTOR OF MILITARY PERSONNEL
- DIRECTOR OF CIVILIAN PERSONNEL
- DIRECTOR OF TRAINING

DEPUTY CHIEF OF STAFF DEVELOPMENT
ASSISTANT DEPUTY CHIEF OF STAFF
- ASSISTANT FOR DEVELOPMENT PLANNING
- ASSISTANT FOR DEVELOPMENT PROGRAMMING
- DIRECTOR OF REQUIREMENTS
- DIRECTOR OF RESEARCH & DEVELOPMENT

DEPUTY CHIEF OF STAFF OPERATIONS
ASSISTANT DEPUTY CHIEFS OF STAFF
- ASSISTANT FOR [illegible]
- ASSISTANT FOR PROGRAMMING
- DIRECTOR OF INSTALLATIONS
- DIRECTOR OF INTELLIGENCE
- DIRECTOR OF PLANS
- DIRECTOR OF COMMUNICATIONS
- DIRECTOR OF MANPOWER AND ORGANIZATION
- DIRECTOR OF OPERATIONS

DEPUTY CHIEF OF STAFF MATERIEL
ASSISTANT DEPUTY CHIEF OF STAFF
- ASSISTANT FOR MATERIEL PROGRAM CONTROL
- ASSISTANT FOR LOGISTICS PLANS
- ASSISTANT FOR MUTUAL SECURITY
- DIRECTOR OF MAINTENANCE ENGINEERING
- DIRECTOR OF SUPPLY & SERVICES
- DIRECTOR OF INDUSTRIAL RESOURCES
- DIRECTOR OF TRANSPORTATION
- DIRECTOR OF PROCUREMENT AND PRODUCTION ENGINEERING

MAJOR COMMANDS

- STRATEGIC AIR COMMAND
- AIR UNIVERSITY
- CONTINENTAL AIR COMMAND
- AIR DEFENSE COMMAND
- TACTICAL AIR COMMAND
- MILITARY AIR TRANSPORT SERVICE
- AIR MATERIEL COMMAND
- AIR PROVING GROUND COMMAND
- AIR TRAINING COMMAND
- AIR R & D COMMAND
- HQS COMMAND
- USAF SECURITY SERVICE
- USAFE
- CARIBBEAN AIR COMMAND
- FAR EAST AIR FORCES
- ALASKAN AIR COMMAND
- NORTHEAST AIR COMMAND

SEPARATE OPERATING AGENCY

- AIR FORCE FINANCE DIVISION

30 JUNE 1953

FEAF - Korea Summary

Part I

STATISTICAL SUMMARY OF USAF COMBAT OPERATIONS IN KOREA 26 JUNE 1950 THROUGH 27 JULY 1953

The tables included in this section provide official USAF statistics pertaining to USAF Combat Operations in Korea and selected data for Far East Air Forces during the period 26 June 1950 through 27 July 1953.

The sources of all data in this section, unless otherwise noted, were statistical and intelligence reports submitted to Headquarters USAF by FEAF and the various statistical publications of FEAF.

DEFINITIONS

AIRCRAFT INVENTORY - ACTIVE
Those aircraft designated as "active" by the utilization codes in Attachment 1 to AFR 65-110. Normally all aircraft except those receiving depot modification or reconditioning, those in storage, those on project, those awaiting reclamation, or those considered excess to the requirements of the command.

AIRCRAFT LOSS - OPERATIONAL
Any loss of an aircraft sustained while carrying out a combat mission or performing direct combat support.

AIRCRAFT LOSS TO ENEMY ACTION
An aircraft known to be lost to an exact type of enemy action (i.e. Enemy Aircraft or Ground Fire).

AIRCRAFT LOSS TO ENEMY ACTION - CAUSE UNKNOWN
An aircraft known to be lost due to enemy action, but the exact type of enemy action causing the loss is unknown.

AIRCRAFT LOSS - NOT ENEMY ACTION
An aircraft known to be lost to an exact cause of any type except that due to enemy action.

AIRCRAFT LOSS - CAUSE UNKNOWN
An aircraft known to be lost but for which no information is available to indicate the exact cause of loss.

AIRCRAFT LOSS - NON-OPERATIONAL
Any loss of an aircraft sustained while performing any type of mission other than combat or combat support.

AIRCRAFT POSSESSED
An aircraft is "possessed" by an organization when that organization is physically using the aircraft in the accomplishment of its mission. Specifically, an aircraft is considered "possessed" if the aircraft can be included in the definition contained in paragraph 10f, AFR 65-110, 15 January 1952.

CASUALTY
Any person who is dead (from any cause) or whose services are lost to his unit for 24 hours or more because of involuntary absence (missing), capture, internment, or wounds, or injuries requiring admission to a medical treatment facility. Any person undergoing treatment for wounds or injuries as of 2400 local time, is considered as having been lost to his unit for 24 hours or longer. Mental disorders, psychoneurotic cases, colds and other diseases (not causing death) are not included as casualties. Casualties are divided into "battle" and "nonbattle" categories.

CASUALTY, BATTLE
A person in a theater of operations who becomes a casualty as defined herein, as a result of an outside force or agent of the enemy, in the face of the enemy, or as a result of going to or returning from a combat mission; provided that the incident is directly related to enemy action. Where evidence is not readily available that the casualty was due to nonbattle factors, the person is counted as a battle casualty.

COMBAT MISSION
The dispatch of one or more aircraft for the purpose of accomplishing a particular task of combat operations. Types are as follows:

INTERDICTION AND ARMED RECONNAISSANCE
A mission with the primary purpose of penetrating enemy lines and interdicting traffic, communications, and movement significant to the enemy's military operations in a given area.

CLOSE SUPPORT
A mission with the primary purpose of direct close support of friendly surface forces in the accomplishment of their immediate objective and/or preventing front line enemy forces from carrying out their objectives and which require close coordination of air and surface activities prior to and/or during the mission.

COUNTER AIR-OFFENSIVE
A mission with the purpose of seeking out and destroying enemy air forces or escorting friendly aircraft on missions over enemy territory.

COUNTER AIR-DEFENSIVE
A mission with the purpose of defending friendly forces from attack by enemy air forces.

RECONNAISSANCE
A mission which is carried out to obtain information concerning enemy resources, terrain, activities, and targets, or information on the results of other air operations.

CARGO
A mission with the primary purpose of transporting troops and their equipment and/or supplies to specified landing areas or to furnish logistical support in the form of personnel and/or supplies and equipment to friendly forces in the field.

STATISTICAL SUMMARY OF USAF COMBAT OPERATIONS IN KOREA
26 JUNE 1950 THROUGH 27 JULY 1953 — CONTINUED

SEARCH AND RESCUE

A mission for the purpose of locating, rescueing, or assisting personnel in distress on land or at sea, or for the purpose of providing "Standby" rescue service such as orbit missions or escort for distressed aircraft.

TACTICAL CONTROL

A mission flown with the primary purpose of directing, controlling, or otherwise coordinating attacks of other friendly aircraft.

OTHER

All missions which do not fall under one of the above categories.

COMBAT READY AIRCRAFT

An aircraft is "Combat Ready" when, without additional maintenance, the aircraft can fly safely and carry out the current mission of the unit. Loading bombs, ammunition, cameras, classified equipment, or any additional equipment necessary for operations in abnormal climatic zones, which is on hand/or can readily be installed will not be considered in determining the "Combat Ready" status of the aircraft.

COMBAT READY CREW

An aircrew is "Combat Ready" when the unit commander considers it capable of performing the type of flying operations required by the unit's current mission.

COMMITTED (UNIT, AIRCRAFT, CREW)

A unit, aircraft, or tactical crew designated by the appropriate command to participate in flying operations against enemy forces or in direct support of friendly forces.

DEAD

Includes those persons killed outright (or dying before reaching a medical treatment facility): those wounded or injured persons who subsequently died of their wounds or injuries (after being admitted to a medical treatment facility): those persons reported as missing who were either subsequently conclusively determined to have been killed, or who, having been in a missing status for a year or more, were presumed to be no longer living; whether or not these incidents occurred "in action" or under "battle" or "nonbattle" conditions.

ENEMY AIRCRAFT DESTROYED

An enemy aircraft definitely known to have been destroyed. One seen to crash, burn, explode, or be otherwise destroyed.

ENEMY AIRCRAFT PROBABLY DESTROYED

An enemy aircraft seen to break off combat under circumstances which lead to the conclusion that it must be a loss, although it was not actually seen to crash, burn, explode, or be otherwise destroyed.

IN ACTION

A person is "in action" when going to or returning from a combat mission, if in contact with a force, element or agent of the enemy; when directly engaging the enemy; when participating in a combat mission strike against the enemy (if in contact with a force, element, or agent of the enemy); when in contact with a force, element, or agent of the enemy while engaged in firefighting; search and rescue or ground activities in connection with a combat mission; or while under attack by a force, element or agent of the enemy.

MISSING

Any person is missing who is involuntarily absent or who fails to return from a scheduled flight or mission, and who is not known to be dead, AWOL, in a hospital, in confinement, on leave, or in any other absent category.

OPERATIONAL FLYING HOURS

All hours flown on combat missions or on missions in support of combat operations.

PRISONERS OF WAR

Persons, previously listed as missing, who are verified by the International Red Cross, State Department, or other international organization as being in the hands of the enemy.

RETIREMENT

Retired from combat flying upon completion of tour. For the purpose of this report only those personnel who have completed a tour of duty and are withdrawn from combat flying and are not expected to perform any additional combat duty on the current tour are to be considered as retirements.

RETURNS TO MILITARY CONTROL

Persons, previously reported as missing, who have returned to military control from a missing status.

SORTIE

One aircraft airborne on a mission against the enemy or in direct support of combat operations.

EFFECTIVE SORTIE

A sortie which carries out the purpose of its mission.

NON-EFFECTIVE SORTIE

A sortie which fails for any reason to carry out the purpose of the mission. Non-effective sorties include aborts, sorties forced to turn back due to enemy action, or lost prior to accomplishing the purpose of the mission.

TACTICAL AIR CREW

A stipulated number of tactical air crew personnel locally organized as a crew to operate primary tactical unit aircraft.

STATISTICAL SUMMARY OF USAF COMBAT OPERATIONS IN KOREA 26 JUNE 1950 THROUGH 27 JULY 1953 — CONTINUED

TACTICAL AIR CREW PERSONNEL

Personnel whose current principal duty is the occupancy of an air crew position in a primary tactical unit aircraft.

TACTICAL UNIT

A unit designated for direct accomplishment of combat or for operations in direct support thereof. Primarily a tactical unit (for purposes of AFR 55-83) is the type of unit listed in parts A, C, and D, table II, AFL 150-10, 2 February 1953. However, provisional and/or Table of Distribution units organized for participation in or direct support of combat operations, for example the 6147th Tactical Control Group of Far East Air Forces, are also included.

WOUNDED OR INJURED

Persons suffering physical harm or damage from causes other than disease, whether or not the harm or damage was caused by force or violence; was accompanied by external bleeding; resulted in the tearing, piercing, laceration or breaking of the skin or mucous membrane; or happened under "battle" or "nonbattle" conditions. Includes all persons reported as wounded or injured, but who later returned to duty, were evacuated to U. S., or were separated; excludes those persons reported as wounded or injured who subsequently died of their wounds or injuries.

MAP I – DEPLOYMENT OF COMMITTED TACTICAL UNITS – 2 JULY 1950

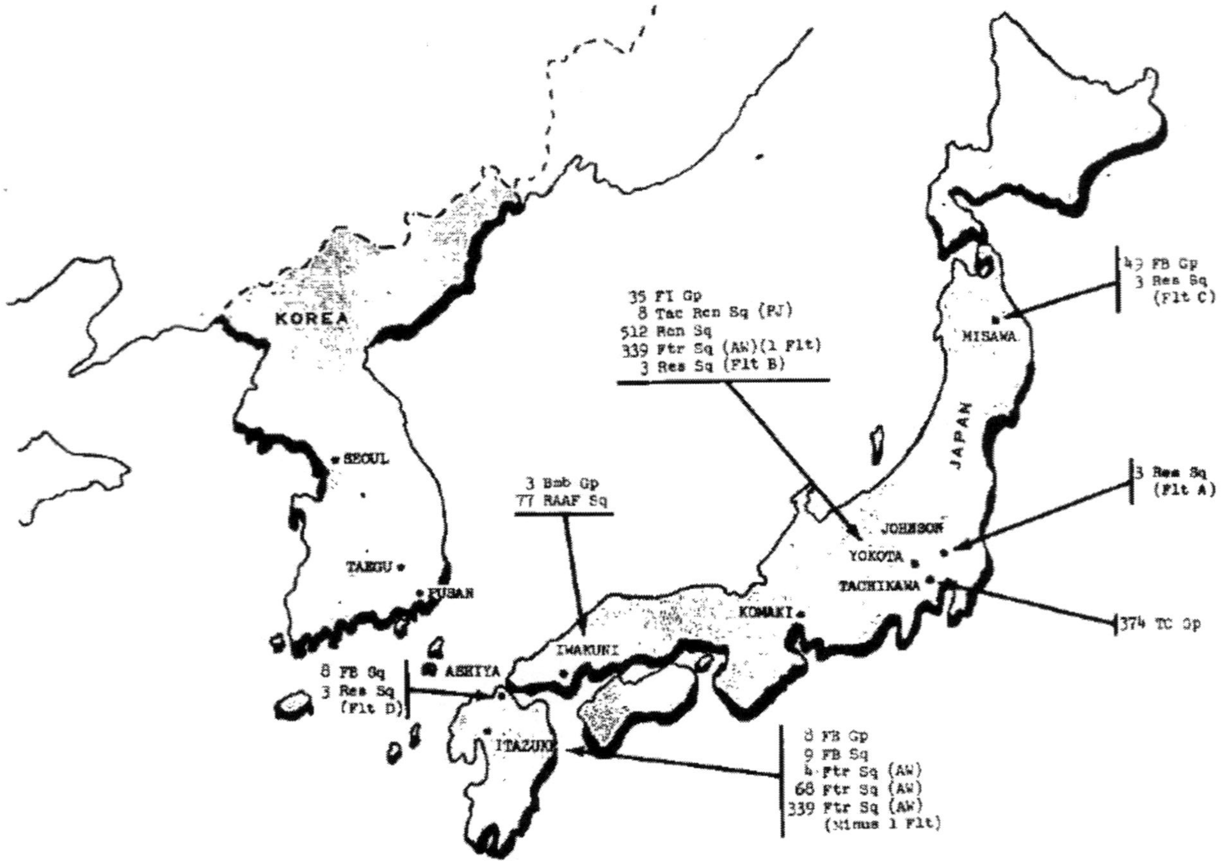

KOREA
SEOUL
TAEGU
PUSAN
JAPAN
MISAWA
JOHNSON
YOKOTA
TACHIKAWA
KOMAKI
IWAKUNI
ASHIYA
ITAZUKE

49 FB Gp
3 Res Sq
(Flt C)

3 Res Sq
(Flt A)

374 TC Gp

35 FI Gp
8 Tac Ren Sq (PJ)
512 Ren Sq
339 Ftr Sq (AW)(1 Flt)
3 Res Sq (Flt B)

3 Bmb Gp
77 RAAF Sq

8 FB Sq
3 Res Sq
(Flt D)

8 FB Gp
9 FB Sq
4 Ftr Sq (AW)
68 Ftr Sq (AW)
339 Ftr Sq (AW)
(Minus 1 Flt)

MAP II — DEPLOYMENT OF COMMITTED TACTICAL UNITS — 27 JULY 1953

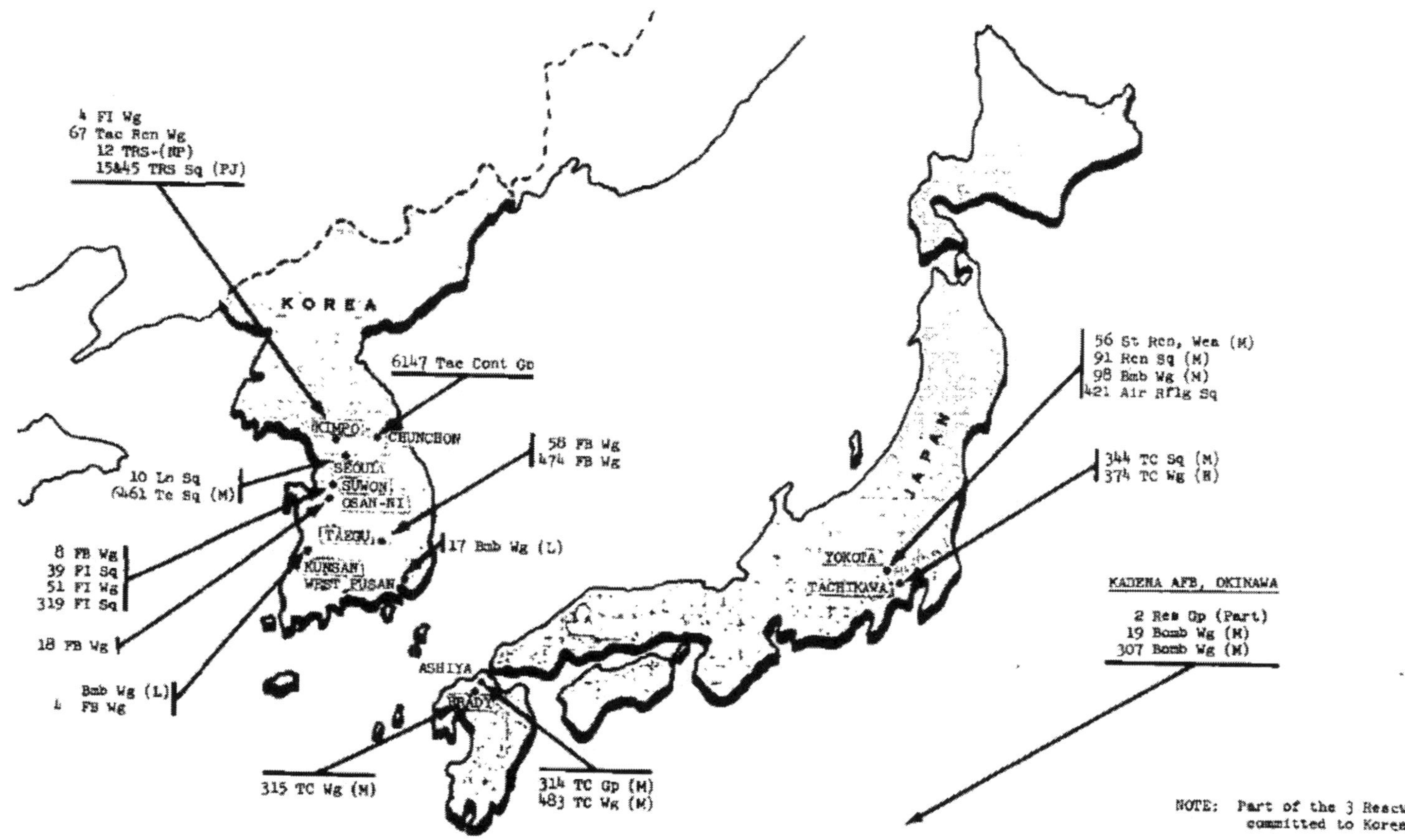

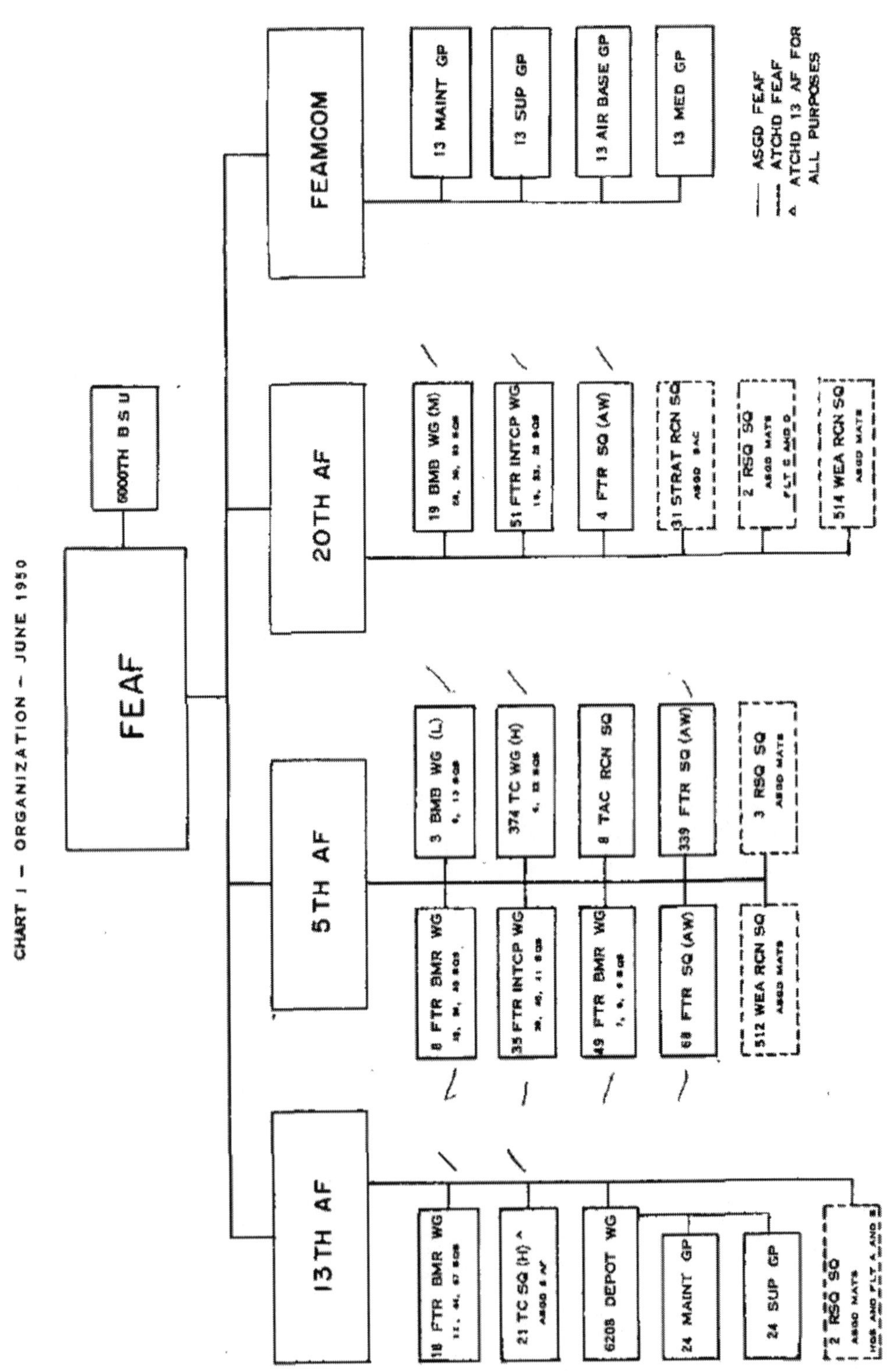
CHART I — ORGANIZATION — JUNE 1950
FEAF
5000TH B S U
FEAMCOM
13 MAINT GP
13 SUP GP
13 AIR BASE GP
13 MED GP
ASGD FEAF
ATCHD FEAF
ATCHD 13 AF FOR ALL PURPOSES
20TH AF
19 BMB WG (M)
28, 30, 93 SQS
51 FTR INTCP WG
16, 25, 26 SQS
4 FTR SQ (AW)
31 STRAT RCN SQ
ASGD SAC
2 RSQ SQ
ASGD MATS
FLT C AND D
514 WEA RCN SQ
ASGD MATS
5TH AF
3 BMB WG (L)
8, 13 SQS
374 TC WG (H)
6, 22 SQS
8 TAC RCN SQ
339 FTR SQ (AW)
3 RSQ SQ
ASGD MATS
8 FTR BMR WG
35, 36, 80 SQS
35 FTR INTCP WG
39, 40, 41 SQS
49 FTR BMR WG
7, 8, 9 SQS
68 FTR SQ (AW)
512 WEA RCN SQ
ASGD MATS
13TH AF
18 FTR BMR WG
12, 44, 67 SQS
21 TC SQ (H)
ASGD 5 AF
6208 DEPOT WG
24 MAINT GP
24 SUP GP
2 RSQ SQ
ASGD MATS
HQS AND FLT A AND B

TABLE 1 – FEAF ORGANIZATION – 23 JUNE 1950

23 JUNE 1950	
13th Air Force 18 Fighter Bomber Wing. 21 Troop Carrier Squadron. a/ 6208 Depot Wing. 24 Maintenance Group. 24 Supply Group. 2 Air Rescue Squadron, Headquarters and Flights A and B. Assigned MATS, Attached FEAF. 5th Air Force 8 Fighter Bomber Wing, 35, 36 and 80 Squadrons. 3 Bombardment Wing, Light, 8 and 13 Squadrons. 35 Fighter Interceptor Wing, 39, 40, and 41 Squadrons 374 Troop Carrier Wing, Heavy, 6 and 22 Squadrons. 49 Fighter Bomber Wing, 7, 8, and 9 Squadrons. 8 Tactical Reconnaissance Squadron. 68 Fighter Squadron (All Weather). 339 Fighter Squadron (All Weather). 3 Air Rescue Squadron. Assigned MATS, Attached FEAF.	5th Air Force - Continued 512 Weather Reconnaissance Squadron (Very Long Range). Assigned MATS, Attached FEAF. 20th Air Force 19 Bombardment Wing, Medium, 28, 30, and 93 Squadrons. 51 Fighter Interceptor Wing, 16, 25, and 26 Squadrons. 4 Fighter Squadron (All Weather). 31 Strategic Reconnaissance Squadron. Assigned SAC, Attached FEAF. 2 Air Rescue Squadron, Flights C and D. Assigned MATS, Attached FEAF. 514 Weather Reconnaissance Squadron (Very Long Range). Assigned MATS, Attached FEAF. FEAMCOM 13 Maintenance Group. 13 Supply Group. 13 Medical Group. 13 Air Base Group.

a/ Assigned 5th Air Force, Attached 13th Air Force for all purposes.

Source: Operations Statistics Division, Directorate of Statistical Services, DCS/C.

CHART II — ORGANIZATION — JULY 1953

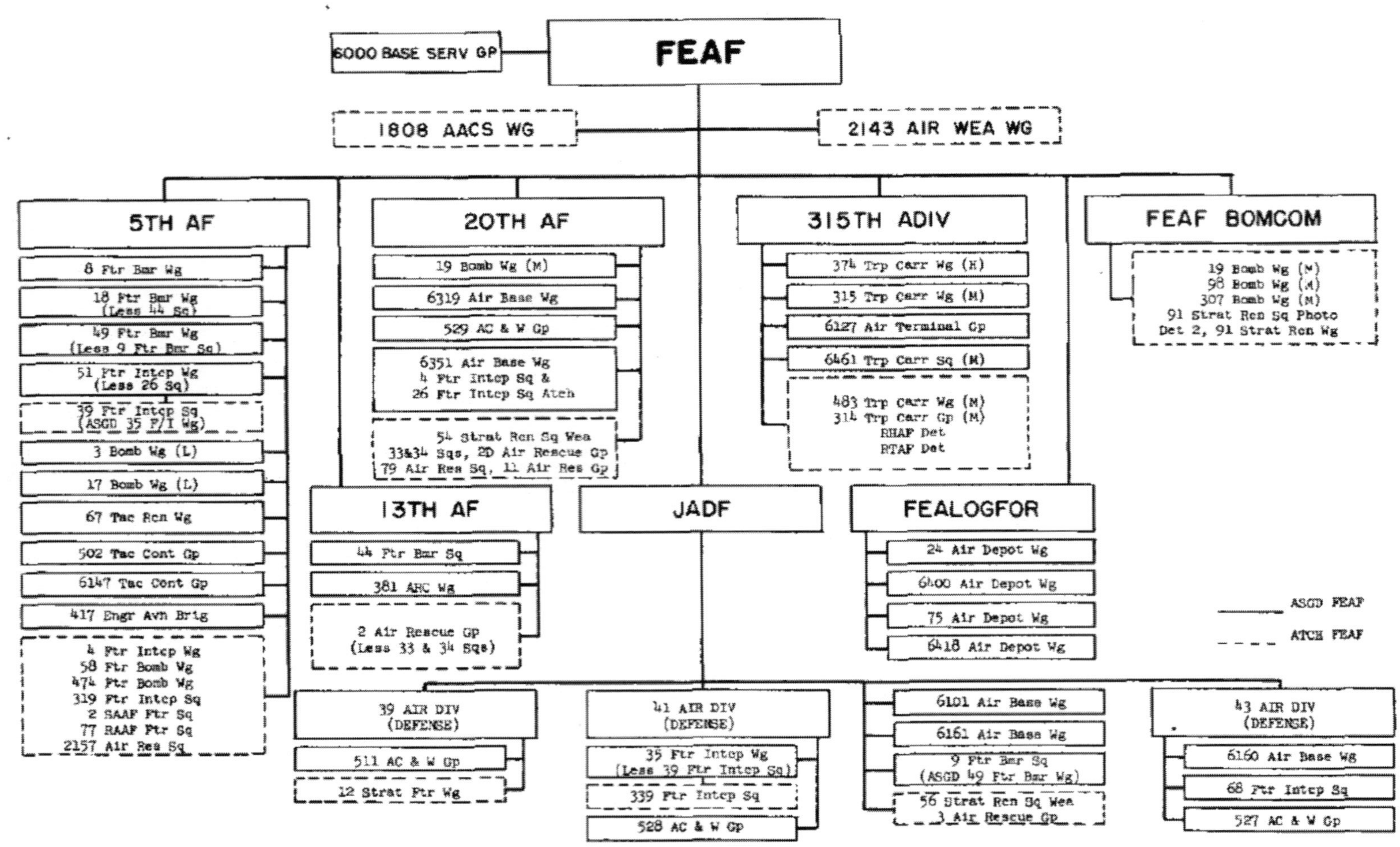
FEAF
6000 BASE SERV GP
1808 AACS WG
2143 AIR WEA WG
5TH AF
8 Ftr Bmr Wg
18 Ftr Bmr Wg (Less 44 Sq)
49 Ftr Bmr Wg (Less 9 Ftr Bmr Sq)
51 Ftr Intcp Wg (Less 26 Sq)
39 Ftr Intcp Sq (ASGD 35 F/I Wg)
3 Bomb Wg (L)
17 Bomb Wg (L)
67 Tac Rcn Wg
502 Tac Cont Gp
6147 Tac Cont Gp
417 Engr Avn Brig
4 Ftr Intcp Wg
58 Ftr Bomb Wg
474 Ftr Bomb Wg
319 Ftr Intcp Sq
2 SAAF Ftr Sq
77 RAAF Ftr Sq
2157 Air Res Sq
20TH AF
19 Bomb Wg (M)
6319 Air Base Wg
529 AC & W Gp
6351 Air Base Wg
4 Ftr Intcp Sq &
26 Ftr Intcp Sq Atch
54 Strat Rcn Sq Wea
33&34 Sqs, 2D Air Rescue Gp
79 Air Res Sq, 11 Air Res Gp
315TH ADIV
374 Trp Carr Wg (H)
315 Trp Carr Wg (M)
6127 Air Terminal Gp
6461 Trp Carr Sq (M)
483 Trp Carr Wg (M)
314 Trp Carr Gp (M)
RHAF Det
RTAF Det
FEAF BOMCOM
19 Bomb Wg (M)
98 Bomb Wg (M)
307 Bomb Wg (M)
91 Strat Rcn Sq Photo
Det 2, 91 Strat Rcn Wg
13TH AF
44 Ftr Bmr Sq
381 ARC Wg
2 Air Rescue Gp
(Less 33 & 34 Sqs)
JADF
FEALOGFOR
24 Air Depot Wg
6400 Air Depot Wg
75 Air Depot Wg
6418 Air Depot Wg
ASGD FEAF
ATCH FEAF
39 AIR DIV
(DEFENSE)
511 AC & W Gp
12 Strat Ftr Wg
41 AIR DIV
(DEFENSE)
35 Ftr Intcp Wg
(Less 39 Ftr Intcp Sq)
339 Ftr Intcp Sq
528 AC & W Gp
6101 Air Base Wg
6161 Air Base Wg
9 Ftr Bmr Sq
(ASGD 49 Ftr Bmr Wg)
56 Strat Rcn Sq Wea
3 Air Rescue Gp
43 AIR DIV
(DEFENSE)
6160 Air Base Wg
68 Ftr Intcp Sq
527 AC & W Gp

TABLE 2 — FEAF ORGANIZATION — 27 JULY 1953

27 JULY 1953

5th Air Force

- 8 Fighter Bomber Wing, 35, 36 and 80 Squadrons.
- 18 Fighter Bomber Wing, 12 and 67 Squadrons.
- 49 Fighter Bomber Wing, 7 and 8 Squadrons.
- 51 Fighter Interceptor Wing, 16 and 25 Squadrons.
- 39 Fighter Interceptor Squadron (35 Wg), attached.
- 3 Bombardment Wing, Light, 8, 13 and 90 Squadrons.
- 17 Bombardment Wing, Light, 34, 37 and 95 Squadrons.
- 67 Tactical Reconnaissance Wing, 12, 15 and 45 Squadrons.
- 502 Tactical Control Group, 605 Squadron. Also 606, 607 and 608 AC&W Squadrons.
- 6147 Tactical Control Group, 6148 and 6149 Squadrons.
- 417 Engineering Aviation Brigade.
- 4 Fighter Interceptor Wing, 334, 335 and 336 Squadrons. Attached FEAF.
- 58 Fighter Bomber Wing, 69, 310 and 311 Squadrons. Attached FEAF.
- 474 Fighter Bomber Wing, 428, 429 and 430 Squadrons. Attached FEAF.
- 319 Fighter Interceptor Squadron. Attached FEAF.
- 2 South African Air Force (SAAF) Fighter Squadron. Attached FEAF.
- 77 Royal Australian Air Force (RAAF) Fighter Squadron. Attached FEAF.
- 2157 Air Rescue Squadron. Attached FEAF.

13th Air Force

- 44 Fighter Bomber Squadron (18 Wg).
- 581 Air Resupply and Communications Wing.
- 2 Air Rescue Group, 31 and 32 Squadrons. Attached FEAF.

20th Air Force

- 19 Bombardment Wing, Medium, 28, 30 and 93 Squadrons.
- 6319 Air Base Wing.
- 529 AC&W Group, 623, 624, 851 and 852 Squadrons.
- 6351 Air Base Wing, 4 and 26 Fighter Interceptor Squadrons attached.
- 54 Strategic Reconnaissance Squadron (Weather). Attached FEAF.
- 2 Air Rescue Group, 33 and 34 Squadrons. Attached FEAF.
- 11 Air Rescue Group, 79 Squadron. Attached FEAF.

FEAF Logistical Forces

- 24 Air Depot Wing.
- 6400 Air Depot Wing.
- 75 Air Depot Wing.
- 6418 Air Depot Wing.

Japan Air Defense Force

- 39 Air Division (Defense)
  - 511 AC&W Group, 613, 847 and 848 Squadrons.
  - 12 Strategic Fighter Wing. Attached FEAF.
- 41 Air Division (Defense)
  - 35 Fighter Interceptor Wing, 40 and 41 Squadrons.
  - 339 Fighter Interceptor Squadron. Attached FEAF.
  - 528 AC&W Group, 611, 621 and 849 Squadrons.
- 6101 Air Base Wing.
- 6161 Air Base Wing.
- 9 Fighter Bomber Squadron, assigned 49 Fighter Bomber Wing.
- 56 Strategic Reconnaissance Squadron (Weather). Attached FEAF.
- 3 Air Rescue Group. Attached FEAF.
- 43 Air Division (Defense)
  - 6160 Air Base Wing.
  - 68 Fighter Interceptor Squadron.
  - 527 AC&W Group, 610, 618, 620 and 850 Squadrons.

315th Air Division

- 374 Troop Carrier Wing, Heavy, 6, 21 and 22 Squadrons.
- 315 Troop Carrier Wing, Medium, 19, 34, 43 and 344 Squadrons.
- 6127 Air Terminal Group.
- 6461 Troop Carrier Squadron, Medium.
- 483 Troop Carrier Wing, Medium, 815, 816 and 817 Squadrons. Attached FEAF.
- 314 Troop Carrier Group, Medium, 50 61 and 62 Squadrons. Attached FEAF.
- Royal Hellenic Air Force (RHAF) Detachment (C-47). Attached FEAF.
- Royal Thailand Air Force (RTAF) Detachment (C-47). Attached FEAF.

FEAF Bomber Command

- 19 Bombardment Wing, Medium, 28, 30 and 93 Squadrons. Assigned 20th Air Force.
- 98 Bombardment Wing, Medium, 343, 344 and 345 Squadrons. Attached FEAF.
- 307 Bombardment Wing, Medium, 370, 371 and 372 Squadrons. Attached FEAF.
- 91 Strategic Reconnaissance Squadron (Photo), Detachment 2, attached FEAF, 91 Strategic Reconnaissance Wing.

Source: Operations Statistics Division, Directorate of Statistical Services, DCS/C.

TABLE 3 — FEAF AIRBASE FACILITIES AS OF 31 JULY 1953

AIRFIELDS				ACTIVE RUNWAYS						HARDSTANDS		APRONS			
NAME	MAXIMUM TYPE ACFT	CLASS	STATUS	NO	LENGTH (FT)	WIDTH (FT)	SURFACE	GROSS LOAD (1000 lbs)	CONDITION	NO	SURFACE	WARMUP (SQ YDS)	SERVICE & PARKING (SQ YDS)	AVN FUEL BULK STOR CAP BBLS	REMARKS
JAPAN															
Ashiya.	C-119,C-54	AB	A	1	6,000	165	CCON	80	GOOD	64 4	CCON PSP	18,336	138,474	41,500	PSP Overruns 200' SE 150' NW
Atsugi.	F2V,C-54,F9F	NAS	A	1	6,000	150	CCON	80	EXC	-	-	30,000	207,502	22,000	Transferred to Navy
Bofu.	F-80,C-54	AB	A	1	5,300	147	CCON	80	GOOD	-	-	4,444	52,336	-	Hills & Mts Near Fld
Brady	C-45	AB	A	2	4,191 3,781	150 264	PSP	60	FAIR	22	PSP	7,777	44,666	2,000	REUAJ
Chitose #1. . . .	C-54,F-84	AAB	A	1	7,000	150	CCON	82	FAIR	-	-	1,112	47,309	47,749	
Chitose #2. . . .		AAB	I	1	8,200	-	CCON	40	POOR	-	-	-	-	-	REUAJ
Hachinohe	C-46	AAB	I	1	3,935	328	CCON	60	POOR	-	-	-	78,480	14,000	REUAJ
Hamamatsu	B-17	AB	I	1	4,593	328	CCON	60	POOR	-	-	-	78,534	-	
Haneda.	C-97	AB	A	2	7,000 5,300	150 150	ACON ACON	140 80	FAIR GOOD	5	PSP	20,000	66,711 60,451	22,500	MATS International
Hanshin	C-54	AAB	I	2	5,226 4,226	328 328	CCON CCON	37	GOOD GOOD	-	-	-	74,511	-	
Hitoyoshi		AAB	I	1	4,920	164	CCON	6	FAIR	-	-	-	-	-	Released
Itami	C-54,AD-3,F9F	AB	A	2	6,000 4,225	328 328	CCON CCON	80	GOOD GOOD	14	CCON	-	133,178	25,000	
Itazuke	C-124,F-84	AB	A	1	9,000	150	ACON CCON	140	EXC	37 3	GRAVEL CCON	19,888	266,832	97,213	Overruns 100' N Side CCON 1000' S Side Gravel
Iwakuni	C-54	AB	A	1	5,000	150	CCON	80	GOOD	-	-	-	23,300	2,520	
Jimmachi.	C-46	AAB	I	1	4,920	164	CCON	30	FAIR	-	-	-	-	-	Released
Johnson	C-54,F-80,F-94	AB	A	1	6,000	150	CCON	70	EXC	10 48	PSP ACON	19,013	80,666	67,571	
Kabayama.	B-25	AAB	I	1	3,838	258	CCON	35	GOOD	-	-	-	-	-	Released
Kanoya.	B-25	AAB	I	1	5,670	164	CCON	35	POOR	-	-	-	900,000	-	Released
Kisarazu.	F-86,84,80,94	AB	A	1	6,000	150	ACON CCON	60	POOR	-	-	17,000	64,200	14,385	200 ASPH Overrun Each End

TABLE 3 — FEAF AIRBASE FACILITIES AS OF 31 JULY 1953 — CONTINUED

AIRFIELDS				ACTIVE RUNWAYS						HARDSTANDS		APRONS		AVN FUEL BULK STOR CAP BBLS	REMARKS
NAME	MAXIMUM TYPE ACFT	CLASS	STA-TUS	NO	LENGTH (FT)	WIDTH (FT)	SURFACE	GROSS LOAD (1000 lbs)	CONDI-TION	NO	SUR-FACE	WARMUP (SQ YDS)	SERVICE & PARKING (SQ YDS)		
JAPAN (Cont'd)															
Kochi	C-47	AAB	A	1	4,133	197	CCON	35	UNK	-	-	-	1,429,974	-	Released
Komaki.	C-54	AB	A	1	7,500	150	CCON	82	EXC	a/ 1	CCON	40,148	113,556	35,071	a/ GCA
Komatsu	F-51	AAB	TE	1	5,635	328	CCON	15	FAIR	-	-	-	-	-	
Konoike	F-51	AAB	I	2	5,237 4,948	262 262	CCON CCON	- -	POOR POOR	- -	- -	- -	- -	- -	Released
Matsushima. . . .	C-46	AAB	A	2	6,000 5,000	150 263	A&CCON CCON	80 55	GOOD FAIR	- -	- -	27,236 -	89,653 -	53,000 -	REUAJ. Airborne Training Field.
Miho.	C-54,B-26	AB	A	2	4,053 6,000	262 150	ACON CCON	35 80	POOR POOR	- -	- -	17,776 -	268,172 -	5,040 -	
Mineyama.	T-6	AAB	E	1	2,000	80	GRAVEL	6	POOR	-	-	-	-	-	
Misawa.	B-29,F-84	AB	A	1	8,500	150	CCON	140	GOOD	101	-	49,300	168,550	178,714	
Mito East	T-6	AAB	I	1	3,155	238	CCON PSP	30	POOR	37,494 Sq Yds	-	-	39,372	-	
Miyazaki.	T-6	AAB	I	2	5,254 4,950	328 262	CCON CCON	6 6	POOR POOR	- -	- -	- -	93,841 -	- -	Encroachment
Niigata	C-54,F-86	AAB	I	1	6,000	150	CCON	80	GOOD	25	CCON	14,888	16,666	11,000	
Omura	L-5	AAB	I	1	2,970	100	CCON	6	POOR	-	-	-	-	-	Released
Ozuki	T-6	AAB	I	1	3,960	198	CCON	30	POOR	-	-	-	-	-	Released
Shiroi.	T-6	AAB	A	1	4,950	328	CCON	6	POOR	-	-	-	-	-	
Sone.	F-51	AAB	TE	1	4,940	198	CCON	15	FAIR	-	-	-	-	-	
Tachikawa	C-124	AB	A	1	a/ 5,000	150	ACON	150	EXC	1	CCON	-	293,738	72,500	a/ PSP Overruns 850'N 950'S
Takamatsu	F-51	AAB	I	1	4,100	200	ACON	12	POOR	-	-	-	19,760	-	Released
Tojimbara		AAB	I	1	1,800	151	SOD	-	POOR	-	-	-	-	-	Being Released
Tsuiki.	C-54,F-86	AAB	A	1	7,000	130	PSP	60	FAIR	59	PSP	-	279,038	16,000	
Yaizu	B-26	AAB	I	1	4,921	262	CCON	35	GOOD	-	-	-	17,927	-	Encroachment

TABLE 3 — FEAF AIRBASE FACILITIES AS OF 31 JULY 1953 — CONTINUED

AIRFIELDS				ACTIVE RUNWAYS						HARDSTANDS		APRONS		AVN FUEL BULK STOR CAP BBLS	REMARKS
NAME	MAXIMUM TYPE ACFT	CLASS	STA-TUS	NO	LENGTH (FT)	WIDTH (FT)	SURFACE	GROSS LOAD (1000 lbs)	CONDI-TION	NO	SUR-FACE	WARMUP (SQ YDS)	SERVICE & PARKING (SQ YDS)		
JAPAN (Cont'd)															
Yakumo.	C-54,F-84	AAB	I	1	6,000	150	CCON	80	EXC	-	-	17,444	26,666	11,000	
Yokota.	B-29,F-94	AB	A	1	8,000	150	CCON	140	GOOD	39 21 40	PSP CCON SST	17,150	210,831	181,054	Concrete Overruns 1000' Each End
IWO JIMA															
Central	B-29	AB	A	1	9,800	200	ACON	140	FAIR	-	-	-	305,000	20,000	
GUAM															
Anderson.	B-29,F-84	AFB	A	2	8,500 8,500	200 180	ACON ACON	140	GOOD GOOD	72 84	ACON CORAL	135,940 -	604,550 -	40,000 -	Coral Overruns 1000' Each End
Harmon.		AFB	I	1	7,000	200	SST	140	GOOD	82	SST	-	606,100	13,000	
N. W. Guam. . . .		AAB	I	2	8,503 8,519	180 150	ACON ACON	140	GOOD GOOD	25 2	CORAL ACON	- -	876,183 -	- -	
PHILIPPINE ISLANDS															
Clark	B-29,F-80	AFB	A	1	8,500	150	CCON	140	GOOD	87 2	ACON	15,811	208,488	50,000	
RYUKYUS															
Hirara.	C-47	AAB	I	1	4,700	150	CORAL	30	POOR	-	-	-	-	-	
Ie Shima.		AAB	I	3	7,000 7,000 6,600	150 100 150	COWB COWB COWB	80	FAIR	200	COWB	-	101,777	-	
OKINAWA															
Awase		AAB	I	1	5,000	160	ACON	80	GOOD	67	COWB	-	40,555	-	
Bolo.		AAB	I	1	a/	-	-	-	-	b/	-	-	-	-	a/ A/F Redesignated b/ 52 Hardstands Prog.
Futema.	B-29	AAB	I	1	8,000	200	ACON	140	EXC	24	ACON	3,500	26,600	20,000	CSAP Overruns 500'SW, 600'NE.
Kadena.	B-29,B-36	AB	A	2	9,500 9,900	300 200	ACON A&ACON	357 140	EXC	89	ACON	-	108,333	150,000	
Motobu.		AAB	I	1	7,000	100	CORAL	40	FAIR	51	COWB	-	191,072	-	Coral Overruns 50'SW, 300'NE
Naha.		AB	-	1	-	-	-	-	-	-	-	-	146,881	70,000	R/W To Be Opnl 1Jan54
Yonabaru.		NAS	-	1	7,000	150	ACON	40	-	86	COWB	-	495,800	-	Transferred to Navy
Yontan.	B-29,F-84	AAB	1/ A	1	7,000	150	ACON	140	GOOD	24	ACON	-	608,700	14,000	1/ Limited Active

TABLE 3 – FEAF AIRBASE FACILITIES AS OF 31 JULY 1953 – CONTINUED

AIRFIELDS				ACTIVE RUNWAYS						HARDSTANDS		APRONS			
NAME	MAXIMUM TYPE ACFT	CLASS	STA-TUS	NO	LENGTH (FT)	WIDTH (FT)	SURFACE	GROSS LOAD (1000 lbs)	CONDI-TION	NO	SUR-FACE	WARMUP (SQ YDS)	SERVICE & PARKING (SQ YDS)	AVN FUEL BULK STOR CAP BBLS	REMARKS
KOREA															
Pusan West. . . .	B-26,C-47,F-86	AB	A	1	7,000	150	ASPH	100	GOOD	-	-	-	61,111	12,000	
Taegu #1.	F-84,C-124,B-26	AB	E A	2	8,100 9,000	100 150	PSP CCON	82 100	GOOD EXC	a/ 29	-	-	98,000	44,000 5,000	a/ Revetments
Pohang-Dong . . .	C-47,F3D	AB	A	1	6,007	150	CCON ASPH	82	GOOD	-	-	-	48,666	6,000 20,000	
Sachon.	C-54,F-51	AB	A	a/1	4,923	197	CCON	30	GOOD	-	-	-	7,111	-	a/ Limited Opnl
Taejon.	F-51	AB	E	1	3,850	115	GRAVEL	-	EXC	-	-	-	GRAVEL AREA	-	
Pyongtaek	F-86,B-17,C-54	AB	A	2	4,900 8,000	100 150	PSP CCON	82	FAIR EXC	-	-	-	110,000	15,000	
Kwanju.	C-47	AB	E	1	3,825	100	ASPH	30	POOR	-	-	-	-	-	
Kunsan.	B-26,F-86,F3D C-47	AB	A	1	a/ 9,000 9,000	150 150	ACON CCON	100 100	GOOD	- b/ 67	- -	- -	120,466	11,000 20,000	a/ New Strip Under Constr. b/ Revetments.
Pusan East. . . .	B-26,C-54,F-51	AB	A	1	6,490	150	ASPH	60	GOOD	-	-	-	45,555	8,000	
Chinhae	C-47	AB	A	1	4,155	150	PSP	80	GOOD	-	-	-	24,222	13,000	
Ulsan		AB	E	1	2,000	50	CCON & EARTH	LIASON ONLY	GOOD	-	-	-	-	-	
Mangun.		AB	E	1	6,900	400	a/		-	-	-	-	-	-	a/ Reverting to Farm-land
Suwon	B-26,F-86,C-47	AB	A	1	9,000	150	ASPH	82	GOOD	c/131	-	-	56,333	a/ 4,000 b/51,000	a/ AVGAS. b/ JP4. c/ Revetments.
Kimpo	F-86,B-26,C-54	AB	A	1	d/6,200	150	ASPH	82	GOOD	c/ 86	-	-	102,777	a/ 8,000 b/50,000	a/ AVGAS. b/ JP4 c/ Revetments. d/R/W Being Ext 2000'.
Seoul	F-86,B-26,C-54, C-124	AB	A	1	5,650	120	ASPH	82	GOOD	-	-	-	71,111	6,000	
Kangnung.	F-51,C-47	AB	A	1	5,693	100	PSP	30	POOR	-	-	-	19,111	2,000	ROK AF
Taegu #2.	F-86,B-26,F-51, C-54,C-47	AB	a/	1	4,335	140	ASPH	82	GOOD	-	-	-	21,622	-	a/ Limited Operations.
Wonju		AB	E	1	2,700	100	GRAVEL	-	GOOD	-	-	-	SOD AREA	-	

TABLE 3 — FEAF AIRBASE FACILITIES AS OF 31 JULY 1953 — CONTINUED

AIRFIELDS				ACTIVE RUNWAYS						HARDSTANDS		APRONS		AVN FUEL BULK STOR CAP BBLS	REMARKS
NAME	MAXIMUM TYPE ACFT	CLASS	STATUS	NO	LENGTH (FT)	WIDTH (FT)	SURFACE	GROSS LOAD (1000 lbs)	CONDITION	NO	SURFACE	WARMUP (SQ YDS)	SERVICE & PARKING (SQ YDS)		
KOREA (Cont'd)															
Mosulpo	C-47	AB	E	1	4,000	3,000	SOD	70	GOOD	-	-	-	SOD AREA	-	
Cheju	C-47	AB	a/	2	5,050 6,075	870 570	SOD SOD	70 70	GOOD GOOD	-	-	-	SOD AREA	-	a/ Limited Operations.
Chungju	C-47	AB	E	1	3,200	100	GRAVEL	-	GOOD	-	-	-	SOD AREA	-	Glide Angles: SW6: 1, NE 10: 1 Limited Operations
Andong.		AB	E	1	3,250	100	GRAVEL	-	VERY POOR	-	-	-	SOD AREA	-	
Kyongju		AB	E	1	3,620	100	GRAVEL	-	GOOD	-	-	-	SOD AREA	-	Limited Operations
Yoju.	C-47	AB	E	1	3,700	140	GRAVEL	30	FAIR	-	-	-	1,115	-	Limited Operations
Hoengsong	C-47	AB	A	1	4,800	100	ASPH & PSP	37	EXC	-	-	-	11,111	2,000	
Chunchon.	C-47,LT-6	AB	A	1	4,190	130	ASPH	80	GOOD	a/ 54	-	-	16,111	2,000	a/ Revetments
Iri		AB	E	1	3,000	100	DECOMP GRANITE	-	POOR	-	-	-	-	-	Old Japanese R/W.
Seoul East. . . .		SITE	-	-	-	-	-	-	-	-	-	-	-	-	
Sokcho-Ri		AB	E	1	4,377	120	DECOMP GRANITE	80	FAIR	-	-	-	SOD AREA	-	
Inji.		AB	E	1	4,000	150	ASPH	30	GOOD	-	-	-	32,200	-	
Yanggu.		AB	E	1	6,000	150	GRAVEL	80	EXC	-	-	-	60,333	-	
Paengyong	C-47	AB	E	1	4,000	100	BEACH	BEACH	FAIR	-	-	-	BEACH AREA	-	Usable Only at Low Tide
Cho-Do.	C-47	AB	E	1	3,500	100	BEACH	BEACH	FAIR	-	-	-	BEACH AREA	-	Usable Only at Low Tide
Osan-Ni	C-124,B-26,F-84	AB	A	1	9,000	150	CCON	100	EXC	-	-	-	94,444	a/ 6,000 b/44,000	Airfield Under Constr. a/ AVGAS. b/ JP4.

NOTE:
AFB - Air Force Base
AB - Air Base
AAB - Auxiliary Air Base
ACON - Asphalt Concrete
CCON - Cement Concrete
COWB - Coral Water Bound
CSAP - Crushed Stone Asphalt Penetrated
DAST - Double Asphaltic Surface Treatment
SST - Single Asphaltic Surface Treatment
NAS - Naval Air Station
CSWB - Crushed Stone Waterbound
GRAP - Gravel Asphalt Penetrated
PSP - Pierced Steel Plank
REUAJ - Real Estate Under Army Jurisdiction
A - Active
I - Inactive
E - Emergency

Source: Operations Statistics Division, Directorate of Statistical Services, DCS/C.

TABLE 4 – SUMMARY OF FEAF OPERATIONS, BY QUARTER – JULY 1950 THROUGH 27 JULY 1953
(USAF, USMC AND FRIENDLY FOREIGN)

TYPE OPERATION	TOTAL a/	JUL-SEP 1950	OCT-DEC	JAN-MAR 1951	APR-JUN	JUL-SEP	OCT-DEC	JAN-MAR 1952	APR-JUN	JUL-SEP	OCT-DEC	JAN-MAR 1953	APR-JUN	1 - 27 JUL
Number Groups/Squadrons	19/62	16/44	19/57	19/59	19/59	18/59	18/62	18/63	19/66	20/70	19/68	19/67	19/68	19/69
Aircraft Possessed	1,248	657	1,040	1,133	1,156	1,215	1,230	1,272	1,261	1,441	1,505	1,454	1,516	1,536
Combat Ready	839	412	621	740	756	832	804	796	842	988	1,045	1,009	1,130	1,140
Crews Possessed	N/A	N/A	N/A	N/A	N/A	N/A	N/A	N/A	N/A	N/A	N/A	N/A	N/A	N/A
Combat Ready	N/A	N/A	N/A	N/A	N/A	N/A	N/A	N/A	N/A	N/A	N/A	N/A	N/A	N/A
Sorties - Total	864,011	42,778	59,838	72,817	81,249	64,441	74,999	69,380	78,086	67,805	76,215	66,835	86,050	23,518
Close Support	N/A	N/A	N/A	N/A	N/A	5,915	6,514	3,854	7,133	9,822	11,592	8,029	19,380	7,532
Interdiction and Armed Reconnaissance	N/A	N/A	N/A	N/A	N/A	N/A	N/A	N/A	N/A	N/A	N/A	N/A	N/A	N/A
Counter Air Offensive	N/A	N/A	N/A	N/A	N/A	N/A	N/A	N/A	N/A	N/A	N/A	N/A	N/A	N/A
Counter Air Defensive	N/A	N/A	N/A	N/A	N/A	1,588	1,570	2,863	3,135	1,877	1,765	2,823	3,418	680
Cargo	N/A	N/A	N/A	N/A	N/A	15,299	14,710	14,844	13,106	13,398	12,837	13,059	14,371	3,773
Other	N/A	N/A	N/A	N/A	N/A	10,659	12,147	12,436	15,310	11,801	12,827	13,072	16,480	3,736
Aircraft Losses - Total	1,986	142	177	170	255	208	205	182	160	133	107	89	117	41
Enemy Action	1,041	82	54	62	140	113	138	106	95	72	63	50	51	15
Air-to-Air	147	5	4	4	11	11	34	14	18	16	15	7	5	3
Ground Fire	816	73	47	52	123	96	98	84	64	46	43	35	44	11
Cause Unknown	78	4	3	6	6	6	6	8	13	10	5	8	2	1
Not Enemy Action	945	60	123	108	115	95	67	76	65	61	44	39	66	26
Expenditures														
Bombs - Tons	N/A	N/A	N/A	N/A	N/A	30,250	37,832	41,908	42,013	38,751	46,069	42,801	54,809	18,698
Napalm - Tons	N/A	N/A	N/A	N/A	N/A	3,549	3,647	942	2,050	2,293	3,638	902	2,149	605
Rockets - Number	N/A	N/A	N/A	N/A	N/A	36,656	42,988	25,714	24,647	19,593	11,259	4,375	10,345	929
Ammunition - 100's Rounds	N/A	N/A	N/A	N/A	N/A	183,145	249,670	108,244	100,668	60,163	55,039	38,825	37,760	10,309

a/ Averages computed on 37 month basis.
Source: Operations Statistics Division, Directorate of Statistical Services, DCS/C.

TABLE — 5 — SUMMARY OF ROYAL AUSTRALIAN AIR FORCE OPERATIONS, BY QUARTER — JULY 1950 THROUGH 27 JULY 1953

(RAAF converted from F-51 type aircraft to Meteor MK-8 type aircraft during May 1951.)

TYPE OPERATION	TOTAL c/	JUL-SEP 1950	OCT-DEC	JAN-MAR 1951	APR-JUN	JUL-SEP	OCT-DEC	JAN-MAR 1952	APR-JUN	JUL-SEP	OCT-DEC	JAN-MAR 1953	APR-JUN	1 - 27 JUL
Number Groups/Squadrons	0/1	0/1	0/1	0/1	0/1	0/1	0/1	0/1	0/1	0/1	0/1	0/1	0/1	0/1
Aircraft Possessed	26	24	19	19	a/ 27	24	20	24	25	39	37	34	24	22
Combat Ready	17	8	13	15	a/ 24	16	13	16	23	18	19	20	20	21
Crews Possessed	27	29	21	19	a/ 27	30	29	29	29	25	27	28	27	26
Combat Ready	23	29	21	19	a/ 27	21	20	24	18	23	25	22	27	26
Sorties - Total	18,688	1,629	868	1,212	104	943	1,326	2,595	2,510	1,665	2,034	1,834	1,748	220
Close Support	N/A	N/A	N/A	N/A	N/A	12	-	-	2	-	-	-	18	4
Interdiction and Armed Reconnaissance	N/A	N/A	N/A	N/A	N/A	8	-	171	1,053	1,258	1,341	1,279	1,561	206
Counter Air Offensive	N/A	N/A	N/A	N/A	N/A	853	710	176	4	359	612	449	6	-
Counter Air Defensive	N/A	N/A	N/A	N/A	N/A	58	559	1,649	1,254	12	10	4	-	-
Cargo	N/A	N/A	N/A	N/A	N/A	-	-	-	-	-	-	-	-	-
Other	N/A	N/A	N/A	N/A	N/A	12	57	599	197	6	71	102	163	10
Aircraft Losses - Total	52	6	1	8	-	4	5	7	5	3	2	5	5	1
Enemy Action	30	3	1	5	-	1	3	6	3	1	2	1	4	-
Air-to-Air	5	-	-	-	-	1	3	-	-	-	1	-	-	-
Ground Fire	21	2	1	4	-	-	-	6	2	-	1	1	4	-
Cause Unknown	4	1	-	1	-	-	-	-	1	1	-	-	-	-
Not Enemy Action	22	3	-	3	-	3	2	1	2	2	-	4	1	1
Expenditures														
Bombs - Tons	N/A	b/ 405	b/ 277	N/A	-	-	-	-	-	-	-	-	-	-
Napalm - Tons	N/A			N/A	-	-	-	28	-	-	-	-	768	294
Rockets - Number	N/A	5,892	2,553	N/A	-	-	-	5,174	4,930	4,453	4,478	2,069	8,734	822
Ammunition - 100's Rounds	N/A	17,406	7,055	N/A	-	17	63	315	131	-	-	2,367	112	-

a/ These figures are for the first 10 days of the Quarter. RAAF ceased operations during April 1951.
b/ Separate breakdown of Bombs and Napalm not available during this period.
c/ Averages computed on 37 month basis.
Source: Operations Statistics Division, Directorate of Statistical Services, DCS/C.

TABLE 6 — SUMMARY OF SOUTH AFRICAN AIR FORCE OPERATIONS, BY QUARTER — JULY 1950 THROUGH 27 JULY 1953

(SAAF ceased operations with F-51 type aircraft in December 1952. Operations with F-86 type aircraft began in March 1953.)

TYPE OPERATION	TOTAL b/	JUL-SEP 1950	OCT-DEC	JAN-MAR 1951	APR-JUN	JUL-SEP	OCT-DEC	JAN-MAR 1952	APR-JUN	JUL-SEP	OCT-DEC	JAN-MAR 1953	APR-JUN	1 - 27 JUL
Number Groups/Squadrons	0/1	0/0	0/1	0/1	0/1	0/1	0/1	0/1	0/1	0/1	0/1	0/1	0/1	0/1
Aircraft Possessed	20	-	13	24	19	41	22	14	27	25	23	18	17	17
Combat Ready	14	-	11	17	17	35	13	10	18	20	16	7	10	9
Crews Possessed	27	-	23	33	32	45	27	30	23	23	30	31	24	24
Combat Ready	22	-	23	33	32	38	25	28	23	11	17	20	18	24
Sorties - Total	12,610	-	413	1,582	1,690	1,539	1,600	1,216	1,239	953	951	77	1,040	310
Close Support	N/A	-	N/A	N/A	N/A	340	460	39	221	201	436	-	287	109
Interdiction and Armed Reconnaissance	N/A	-	N/A	N/A	N/A	1,044	1,068	1,051	823	682	363	-	461	115
Counter Air Offensive	N/A	-	N/A	N/A	N/A	11	8	-	-	-	-	77	273	77
Counter Air Defensive	N/A	-	N/A	N/A	N/A	8	14	24	-	4	24	-	8	-
Cargo	N/A	-	N/A	N/A	N/A	-	-	-	-	-	-	-	-	-
Other	N/A	-	N/A	N/A	N/A	136	50	102	195	66	128	-	11	9
Aircraft Losses - Total	63	-	-	10	7	18	12	7	2	2	3	-	1	1
Enemy Action	45	-	-	8	5	13	8	6	-	2	1	-	1	1
Air-to-Air	2	-	-	-	-	-	-	1	-	-	1	-	-	-
Ground Fire	40	-	-	6	4	13	8	5	-	2	-	-	1	1
Cause Unknown	3	-	-	2	1	-	-	-	-	-	-	-	-	-
Not Enemy Action	18	-	-	2	2	5	4	1	2	-	2	-	-	-
Expenditures														
Bombs - Tons	N/A	-	a/ 267	N/A	a/966	524	N/A	N/A	N/A	N/A	N/A	N/A	N/A	N/A
Napalm - Tons	N/A	-		N/A		327	N/A	N/A	N/A	N/A	N/A	N/A	N/A	N/A
Rockets - Number	N/A	-	1,590	N/A	8,499	4,370	N/A	N/A	N/A	N/A	N/A	N/A	N/A	N/A
Ammunition - 100's Rounds	N/A	-	2,049	N/A	11,449	9,464	N/A	N/A	N/A	N/A	N/A	N/A	N/A	N/A

a/ Separate breakdown of Bombs and Napalm not available during this period. b/ Averages computed on 37 month basis.

Source: Operations Statistics Division, Directorate of Statistical Services, DCS/C.

TABLE 7 — SUMMARY OF FRIENDLY FOREIGN OPERATIONS, BY QUARTER — JULY 1950 THROUGH 27 JULY 1953
(RAAF, SAAF, ROKAF, RHAF, AND TAF)

TYPE OPERATION	TOTAL b/	JUL-SEP 1950	OCT-DEC	JAN-MAR 1951	APR-JUN	JUL-SEP	OCT-DEC	JAN-MAR 1952	APR-JUN	JUL-SEP	OCT-DEC	JAN-MAR 1953	APR-JUN	1 - 27 JUL
Number Groups/Squadrons	0/3	0/1	0/2	0/2	0/2	0/2	0/3	0/3	0/4	0/4	0/4	0/4	0/4	0/4
Aircraft Possessed	72	24	49	51	30	74	66	56	78	98	106	97	121	120
Combat Ready	49	8	35	38	19	56	42	40	60	67	66	61	80	87
Crews Possessed	97	29	62	60	36	85	99	111	119	129	137	149	121	162
Combat Ready	81	29	62	60	36	69	79	87	83	102	113	126	113	123
Sorties - Total	45,186	1,718	1,442	3,521	2,552	3,177	4,039	4,859	5,186	4,074	5,268	3,618	4,672	1,060
Close Support	N/A	N/A	N/A	N/A	N/A	352	532	89	244	228	786	862	1,571	409
Interdiction and Armed Reconnaissance	N/A	N/A	N/A	N/A	N/A	1,052	1,656	1,675	2,631	2,897	2,918	1,635	2,180	402
Counter Air Offensive	N/A	N/A	N/A	N/A	N/A	864	718	176	4	359	612	526	279	77
Counter Air Defensive	N/A	N/A	N/A	N/A	N/A	65	573	1,673	1,254	16	34	4	8	-
Cargo	N/A	N/A	N/A	N/A	N/A	695	396	471	656	502	719	489	460	153
Other	N/A	N/A	N/A	N/A	N/A	148	164	775	397	72	199	102	174	19
Aircraft Losses - Total	152	10	1	19	11	26	23	16	9	8	9	8	10	2
Enemy Action	101	7	1	13	7	17	14	14	5	5	6	4	7	1
Air-to-Air	7	-	-	-	-	1	3	1	-	-	2	-	-	-
Ground Fire	84	6	1	10	6	16	11	13	3	2	4	4	7	1
Cause Unknown	10	1	-	3	1	-	-	-	2	3	-	-	-	-
Not Enemy Action	51	3	-	6	4	9	9	2	4	3	3	4	3	1
Expenditures														
Bombs - Tons	a/12,742	a/405	a/544	a/1,570	a/966	524	868	735	898	859	1,148	605	1,267	385
Napalm - Tons						327	379	87	43	2	65	-	771	294
Rockets - Number	83,538	5,892	4,143	11,270	8,499	4,370	7,146	9,661	6,784	7,957	5,285	2,975	8,734	822
Ammunition - 100's Rounds	127,912	17,406	9,104	19,333	11,449	9,481	17,896	7,434	4,884	7,201	9,685	9,426	3,306	1,307

a/ Separate breakdown of Bombs and Napalm not available during this period.
b/ Averages computed on 37 month basis.
Source: Operations Statistics Division, Directorate of Statistical Services, DCS/C.

TABLE 8 — SUMMARY OF USMC OPERATIONS, BY QUARTER — JULY 1950 THROUGH 27 JULY 1953

TYPE OPERATION	TOTAL d/	JUL-SEP 1950	OCT-DEC	JAN-MAR 1951	APR-JUN	JUL-SEP	OCT-DEC	JAN-MAR 1952	APR-JUN	JUL-SEP	OCT-DEC	JAN-MAR 1953	APR-JUN	1 - 27 JUL
Number Groups/Squadrons	2/7	2/0	2/4	2/4	2/6	2/5	2/5	2/6	2/6	2/7	2/8	2/7	2/8	2/9
Aircraft Possessed	136	24	129	133	136	125	132	126	134	167	164	175	179	173
Combat Ready	92	a/11	a/32	66	98	94	93	91	93	124	120	130	138	140
Crews Possessed	N/A	N/A	N/A	N/A	N/A	N/A	N/A	N/A	N/A	N/A	N/A	N/A	N/A	N/A
Combat Ready	N/A	N/A	N/A	N/A	N/A	N/A	N/A	N/A	N/A	N/A	N/A	N/A	N/A	N/A
Sorties - Total	107,939	1,136	5,462	6,426	11,202	8,583	10,579	9,315	10,769	9,829	11,035	9,703	11,112	2,788
Close Support	37,385	884	3,441	1,846	3,295	2,799	3,544	2,128	3,237	3,836	3,668	3,217	4,227	1,263
Other Offensive b/	59,042	153	1,708	4,445	7,302	4,987	5,890	6,023	6,007	4,694	6,080	5,043	5,437	1,273
Interdiction and Armed Reconnaissance	N/A	N/A	N/A	N/A	N/A	N/A	N/A	N/A	N/A	N/A	N/A	N/A	N/A	N/A
Counter Air Offensive	N/A	N/A	N/A	N/A	N/A	N/A	N/A	N/A	N/A	N/A	N/A	N/A	N/A	N/A
Counter Air Defensive	5,652	-	78	89	513	689	566	687	720	797	588	375	453	97
Cargo	-	-	-	-	-	-	-	-	-	-	-	-	-	-
Other	5,860	99	235	46	92	108	579	477	805	502	699	1,068	995	155
Aircraft Losses - Total	368	8	31	21	58	37	50	19	40	44	20	16	18	6
Enemy Action	183	2	8	9	36	20	32	8	19	22	12	9	5	1
Air-to-Air	1	-	-	-	-	-	-	-	-	-	-	-	-	1
Ground Fire	182	2	8	9	36	20	32	8	19	22	12	9	5	-
Cause Unknown	-	-	-	-	-	-	-	-	-	-	-	-	-	-
Not Enemy Action	185	6	23	12	22	17	18	11	21	22	8	7	13	5
Expenditures c/														
Bombs - Tons	N/A	N/A	N/A	N/A	N/A	2,466	4,937	7,180	7,677	7,553	8,969	8,624	9,705	3,027
Napalm - Tons	N/A	N/A	N/A	N/A	N/A	1,265	1,529	320	1,409	1,844	2,460	794	1,193	169
Rockets - Number	N/A	N/A	N/A	N/A	N/A	12,648	17,455	6,254	7,566	3,861	1,084	1,035	1,424	91
Ammunition - 100's Rounds	N/A	N/A	N/A	N/A	N/A	21,629	31,451	2,909	-	8	28	-	91	124

a/ Figures are estimated.
b/ Includes Interdiction and Armed Reconnaissance, Counter Air and Escort.
c/ Breakdown not available from Navy Sources. Data extracted from RCS: 2AF-V4 (Monthly Combat Operations Report).
d/ Averages computed on 37 month basis.
Source: Operations Statistics Division, Directorate of Statistical Services, DCS/C.

TABLE 9 – STATISTICAL SUMMARY OF USAF OPERATIONS,

TYPE OPERATION	TOTAL KOREAN AIR WAR	OPERATIONS DURING					
		JUN & JUL 1950	AUG	SEP	OCT	NOV	DEC
Aircraft Losses							
Total Theater	2,015	65	59	68	66	63	83
Committed Forces	1,747	56	44	54	59	52	69
Operational	1,466	36	38	50	48	46	51
Enemy Action	757	25	23	25	18	17	10
Air-to-Air	139	4	1	-	1	1	2
Ground Fire	550	20	21	24	16	15	7
Cause Unknown	68	1	1	1	1	1	1
Not Enemy Action	472	5	11	17	19	24	28
Unknown or Missing	237	6	4	8	11	5	13
Non-Operational	281	20	6	4	11	6	18
Flying Accidents	235	12	5	4	11	6	8
Other	46	8	1	-	-	-	10
Pilot Claims - Enemy Acft							
Destroyed - Total	953	45	29	4	-	9	10
Air-to-Ground	53	15	27	3	-	-	2
Air-to-Air	900	29	2	1	-	9	8
MIG-15	823	-	-	-	-	-	8
Other	77	29	2	1	-	9	-
Probable - Total	193	20	9	2	-	5	7
Air-to-Ground	25	12	7	1	-	1	2
Air-to-Air	168	8	2	1	-	4	5
MIG-15	145	-	-	-	-	-	2
Other	23	8	2	1	-	4	3
Damaged - Total	1,009	16	10	8	-	7	7
Air-to-Ground	36	7	10	8	-	-	1
Air-to-Air	973	9	-	-	-	7	6
MIG-15	946	-	-	-	-	7	6
Other	27	9	-	-	-	-	-
Sorties							
By Category							
Total Korean Operations	710,886	8,499	15,586	15,839	16,634	18,116	18,184
Effective	699,030	8,039	15,328	15,504	16,128	17,669	17,631
Non-Effective	11,856	460	258	335	506	447	553
Day	595,086	8,440	15,063	15,219	16,347	17,847	17,206
Night	115,800	59	523	620	287	269	978
By Type Aircraft							
Total Korean Operations	710,886	8,499	15,586	15,839	16,634	18,116	18,184
Medium Bomber	20,448	572	1,280	1,334	719	715	727
Light Bomber	60,096	727	970	980	535	1,112	1,660
Jet Fighter	276,796	4,445	3,693	3,256	4,327	4,083	5,612
Prop Fighter	64,475	1,000	5,060	4,334	2,427	2,868	2,559
Reconnaissance	45,839	328	642	658	545	612	564
Cargo	185,528	1,256	2,618	3,155	6,079	6,685	5,282
Other	57,704	171	1,323	2,122	2,002	2,041	1,780
By Type Mission							
Total All Operations	751,672	8,499	15,586	16,499	17,598	19,146	19,641
Intra Japan Cargo	40,786	-	-	660	964	1,030	1,457
Korean Operations	710,886	8,499	15,586	15,839	16,634	18,116	18,184
Total Combat	461,554	7,080	11,662	10,580	8,573	9,442	11,306
Close Support	92,603	3,942	6,774	6,250	3,340	3,652	3,336
Interdiction and Armed Reconnaissance	220,168	2,199	3,299	3,281	4,474	4,210	6,462
Strategic	994	57	613	247	77	-	-
Counter Air Offensive	73,887	457	242	39	107	750	672
Counter Air Defensive	12,931	89	75	87	10	166	88
Reconnaissance	60,971	336	659	676	565	664	748
Total Combat Support	249,332	1,419	3,924	5,259	8,061	8,674	6,878
Rescue	15,192	-	136	260	217	173	102
Cargo	176,503	1,279	2,717	3,301	6,275	6,772	5,310
Tactical Control	34,836	137	1,025	1,463	1,282	1,473	1,259
Other	22,801	3	46	235	287	256	207

BY MONTH – 25 JUNE 1950 THROUGH 27 JULY 1953

FISCAL YEAR 1951 JAN 1951	FEB	MAR	APR	MAY	JUN	TYPE OPERATION
						Aircraft Losses
53	63	62	88	63	75	Total Theater
44	54	55	84	63	68	Committed Forces
34	45	51	73	54	59	Operational
7	12	21	42	24	31	Enemy Action
2	-	2	4	-	7	Air-to-Air
5	11	17	36	23	22	Ground Fire
-	1	2	2	1	2	Cause Unknown
24	24	16	14	20	18	Not Enemy Action
3	9	14	17	10	10	Unknown or Missing
10	9	4	11	9	9	Non-Operational
8	8	4	9	6	6	Flying Accidents
2	1	-	2	3	3	Other
						Pilot Claims - Enemy Acft
7	1	9	14	9	18	Destroyed - Total
-	-	-	-	1	-	Air-to-Ground
7	1	9	14	8	18	Air-to-Air
4	-	9	14	6	14	MIG-15
3	1	-	-	2	4	Other
3	-	4	4	1	2	Probable - Total
-	-	-	-	-	-	Air-to-Ground
3	-	4	4	1	2	Air-to-Air
2	-	4	4	1	1	MIG-15
1	-	-	-	-	1	Other
15	3	14	41	18	36	Damaged - Total
3	-	-	-	2	-	Air-to-Ground
12	3	14	41	16	36	Air-to-Air
9	-	14	41	15	34	MIG-15
3	3	-	-	1	2	Other
						Sorties
						By Category
20,374	18,710	23,786	22,611	23,489	21,395	Total Korean Operations
19,892	18,164	23,222	22,063	23,181	21,127	Effective
482	546	564	548	308	268	Non-Effective
19,318	17,409	21,023	19,802	21,186	18,691	Day
1,056	1,301	2,763	2,809	2,303	2,704	Night
						By Type Aircraft
20,374	18,710	23,786	22,611	23,489	21,395	Total Korean Operations
794	717	786	565	547	447	Medium Bomber
1,470	1,248	1,425	1,617	1,711	1,554	Light Bomber
6,941	5,896	8,961	7,342	7,381	6,239	Jet Fighter
2,136	1,856	3,036	3,689	3,773	3,201	Prop Fighter
898	787	1,052	1,117	944	945	Reconnaissance
6,529	6,574	6,832	6,357	7,528	7,328	Cargo
1,606	1,632	1,694	1,924	1,605	1,681	Other
						By Type Mission
22,176	19,568	24,949	23,441	24,457	22,360	Total All Operations
1,802	858	1,163	830	968	965	Intra Japan Cargo
20,374	18,710	23,786	22,611	23,489	21,395	Korean Operations
12,663	11,048	15,194	14,676	14,398	12,324	Total Combat
2,671	3,002	5,405	2,598	2,824	2,030	Close Support
7,794	6,178	7,371	8,655	8,224	7,037	Interdiction and Armed Reconnaissance
-	-	-	-	-	-	Strategic
826	466	990	1,202	1,353	1,330	Counter Air Offensive
50	70	169	374	395	269	Counter Air Defensive
1,322	1,332	2,259	1,847	1,602	1,658	Reconnaissance
7,711	7,662	7,592	7,935	9,091	9,071	Total Combat Support
100	171	163	173	116	296	Rescue
6,517	6,600	6,551	6,006	7,183	7,136	Cargo
862	819	369	1,162	1,462	1,482	Tactical Control
232	72	509	594	330	157	Other

TABLE 9 – STATISTICAL SUMMARY OF USAF OPERATIONS,

TYPE OPERATION	OPERATIONS DURING					
	JUL 1951	AUG	SEP	OCT	NOV	DEC
Aircraft Losses						
Total Theater	63	71	63	75	46	51
Committed Forces	59	59	53	68	39	46
Operational	49	50	46	58	34	40
Enemy Action	21	28	27	38	23	31
Air-to-Air	1	3	6	14	8	9
Ground Fire	16	23	21	23	11	21
Cause Unknown	4	2	-	1	4	1
Not Enemy Action	17	13	11	16	9	4
Unknown or Missing	11	9	8	4	2	5
Non-Operational	10	9	7	10	5	6
Flying Accidents	9	9	6	10	5	6
Other	1	-	1	-	-	-
Pilot Claims - Enemy Acft						
Destroyed - Total	12	4	14	32	31	29
Air-to-Ground	-	-	-	-	4	-
Air-to-Air	12	4	14	32	27	29
MIG-15	9	4	14	32	16	29
Other	3	-	-	-	11	-
Probable - Total	1	-	2	8	9	5
Air-to-Ground	-	-	-	-	2	-
Air-to-Air	1	-	2	8	7	5
MIG-15	1	-	2	8	7	5
Other	-	-	-	-	-	-
Damaged - Total	7	3	34	48	56	38
Air-to-Ground	-	-	-	-	5	-
Air-to-Air	7	3	34	48	51	38
MIG-15	6	3	34	48	50	35
Other	1	-	-	-	1	3
Sorties						
By Category						
Total Korean Operations	15,914	17,456	19,311	21,887	19,166	19,328
Effective	15,553	17,098	19,063	21,683	18,952	19,110
Non-Effective	361	358	248	204	214	218
Day	13,287	13,979	15,891	18,342	15,373	15,716
Night	2,627	3,477	3,420	3,545	3,793	3,612
By Type Aircraft						
Total Korean Operations	15,914	17,456	19,311	21,887	19,166	19,328
Medium Bomber	499	477	520	509	430	424
Light Bomber	1,499	1,710	1,962	1,956	1,868	1,698
Jet Fighter	4,351	4,836	6,704	8,082	7,030	7,481
Prop Fighter	2,445	2,358	2,946	3,320	2,157	1,593
Reconnaissance	851	965	1,152	1,356	1,383	1,730
Cargo	5,072	5,546	4,790	5,156	5,058	5,218
Other	1,197	1,564	1,237	1,508	1,240	1,184
By Type Mission						
Total All Operations	17,103	18,802	20,581	23,132	20,217	20,408
Intra Japan Cargo	1,189	1,346	1,270	1,245	1,051	1,080
Korean Operations	15,914	17,456	19,311	21,887	19,166	19,328
Total Combat	9,503	10,204	14,056	15,953	13,678	13,641
Close Support	1,084	818	862	1,000	1,136	302
Interdiction and Armed Reconnaissance	5,939	6,565	8,686	9,753	8,735	8,347
Strategic	-	-	-	-	-	-
Counter Air Offensive	799	855	1,263	1,814	1,019	2,126
Counter Air Defensive	212	293	298	167	99	165
Reconnaissance	1,469	1,673	2,947	3,219	2,689	2,701
Total Combat Support	6,411	7,252	5,255	5,934	5,488	5,687
Rescue	394	393	358	694	347	328
Cargo	4,904	5,255	4,445	4,813	4,655	4,846
Tactical Control	851	969	22	-	-	-
Other	262	635	430	427	486	513

BY MONTH — 26 JUNE 1950 THROUGH 27 JULY 1953 — CONTINUED

FISCAL YEAR 1952						
JAN 1952	FEB	MAR	APR	MAY	JUN	TYPE OPERATION
						Aircraft Losses
68	59	48	53	65	39	Total Theater
65	51	44	43	52	36	Committed Forces
59	48	40	36	47	28	Operational
37	24	23	24	31	16	Enemy Action
5	4	4	5	9	4	Air-to-Air
28	19	16	15	17	10	Ground Fire
4	1	3	4	5	2	Cause Unknown
12	17	11	8	11	9	Not Enemy Action
10	7	6	4	5	3	Unknown or Missing
6	3	4	7	5	8	Non-Operational
6	3	3	6	4	6	Flying Accidents
-	-	1	1	1	2	Other
						Pilot Claims - Enemy Acft
31	17	39	45	32	20	Destroyed - Total
-	-	-	-	-	-	Air-to-Ground
31	17	39	45	32	20	Air-to-Air
31	17	39	44	27	20	MIG-15
-	-	-	1	5	-	Other
3	4	9	7	3	2	Probable - Total
-	-	-	-	-	-	Air-to-Ground
3	4	9	7	3	2	Air-to-Air
3	4	9	7	3	2	MIG-15
-	-	-	-	-	-	Other
19	43	76	52	24	6	Damaged - Total
-	-	-	-	-	-	Air-to-Ground
19	43	76	52	24	6	Air-to-Air
19	43	76	52	24	4	MIG-15
-	-	-	-	-	2	Other
						Sorties
						By Category
18,581	16,972	19,653	18,541	23,954	19,636	Total Korean Operations
18,264	16,663	19,359	18,195	23,644	19,356	Effective
317	309	294	346	310	280	Non-Effective
14,690	13,273	15,676	14,835	19,503	15,389	Day
3,891	3,699	3,977	3,706	4,451	4,247	Night
						By Type Aircraft
18,581	16,972	19,653	18,541	23,954	19,636	Total Korean Operations
515	407	475	382	406	378	Medium Bomber
1,653	1,520	1,552	1,472	1,825	1,791	Light Bomber
6,563	6,344	8,240	8,582	11,337	7,430	Jet Fighter
1,434	1,271	1,172	1,082	1,421	1,216	Prop Fighter
1,549	1,589	1,604	1,706	2,443	2,102	Reconnaissance
5,333	4,805	5,392	4,001	4,682	5,065	Cargo
1,534	1,036	1,218	1,316	1,840	1,654	Other
						By Type Mission
19,799	18,058	20,795	19,302	25,193	20,513	Total All Operations
1,218	1,086	1,142	761	1,239	877	Intra Japan Cargo
18,581	16,972	19,653	18,541	23,954	19,636	Korean Operations
11,953	10,690	12,620	12,628	16,736	12,565	Total Combat
394	162	1,081	711	1,031	1,910	Close Support
6,805	6,268	6,437	6,288	8,126	5,603	Interdiction and Armed Reconnaissance
-	-	-	-	-	-	Strategic
2,288	2,441	3,270	3,624	4,728	2,391	Counter Air Offensive
163	183	157	246	423	492	Counter Air Defensive
2,303	1,636	1,675	1,759	2,428	2,169	Reconnaissance
6,628	6,282	7,033	5,913	7,218	7,071	Total Combat Support
527	458	504	665	518	609	Rescue
4,920	4,451	5,002	3,595	4,210	4,645	Cargo
533	720	840	964	1,303	1,088	Tactical Control
648	653	687	689	887	729	Other

TABLE 9 – STATISTICAL SUMMARY OF USAF OPERATIONS,

TYPE OPERATION	OPERATIONS DURING FISCAL YEAR					
	JUL 1952	AUG	SEP	OCT	NOV	DEC
Aircraft Losses						
Total Theater	42	42	41	47	32	36
Committed Forces	34	32	37	42	30	31
Operational	25	27	29	34	22	22
Enemy Action	13	15	17	21	15	9
Air-to-Air	4	2	10	5	5	3
Ground Fire	8	10	4	13	8	6
Cause Unknown	1	3	3	3	2	-
Not Enemy Action	7	8	6	8	5	10
Unknown or Missing	5	4	6	5	2	3
Non-Operational	9	5	8	8	8	9
Flying Accidents	9	4	8	7	8	5
Other	-	1	-	1	-	4
Pilot Claims - Enemy Acft						
Destroyed - Total	19	34	63	27	28	28
Air-to-Ground	-	-	-	-	-	-
Air-to-Air	19	34	63	27	28	28
MIG-15	19	33	63	27	28	28
Other	-	1	-	-	-	-
Probable - Total	5	4	8	1	6	8
Air-to-Ground	-	-	-	-	-	-
Air-to-Air	5	4	8	1	6	8
MIG-15	5	4	7	1	5	8
Other	-	-	1	-	1	-
Damaged - Total	11	35	61	26	18	29
Air-to-Ground	-	-	-	-	-	-
Air-to-Air	11	35	61	26	18	29
MIG-15	11	35	61	26	18	29
Other	-	-	-	-	-	-
SORTIES						
By Category						
Total Korean Operations	16,634	18,337	18,931	22,971	17,746	19,195
Effective	16,352	18,027	18,590	22,707	17,509	18,893
Non-Effective	282	310	341	264	237	302
Day	12,730	14,761	15,488	18,440	13,392	14,882
Night	3,904	3,576	3,443	4,531	4,354	4,313
By Type Aircraft						
Total Korean Operations	16,634	18,337	18,931	22,971	17,746	19,195
Medium Bomber	441	387	448	494	416	465
Light Bomber	1,783	1,507	1,741	2,250	1,818	1,606
Jet Fighter	6,013	7,652	7,716	10,389	7,727	9,260
Prop Fighter	889	669	1,161	1,263	1,011	712
Reconnaissance	1,462	1,762	1,726	1,758	1,544	1,391
Cargo	4,636	4,882	4,441	4,990	3,863	4,147
Other	1,410	1,478	1,698	1,827	1,367	1,614
By Type Mission						
Total All Operations	17,485	19,296	20,036	24,273	19,239	20,044
Intra Japan Cargo	851	959	1,105	1,302	1,493	849
Korean Operations	16,634	18,337	18,931	22,971	17,746	19,195
Total Combat	10,255	11,478	12,246	15,629	11,990	12,474
Close Support	2,082	1,854	1,822	3,009	2,416	1,713
Interdiction and Armed Reconnaissance	4,104	4,978	5,120	6,357	5,330	5,650
Strategic	-	-	-	-	-	-
Counter Air Offensive	2,287	2,595	3,299	4,093	2,400	2,856
Counter Air Defensive	386	328	350	228	214	701
Reconnaissance	1,396	1,723	1,655	1,942	1,630	1,554
Total Combat Support	6,379	6,859	6,685	7,342	5,756	6,721
Rescue	578	475	619	599	498	413
Cargo	4,305	4,535	4,056	4,559	3,606	3,953
Tactical Control	869	1,101	1,255	1,437	1,070	1,180
Other	627	748	755	747	582	1,175

Source: Operations Statistics Division, Directorate of Statistical Services, DCS/C.

BY MONTH — 26 JUNE 1950 THROUGH 27 JULY 1953 — CONTINUED

1953 AND 1 THROUGH 27 JULY							
JAN 1953	FEB	MAR	APR	MAY	JUN	1 THRU 27 JUL	TYPE OPERATION
							Aircraft Losses
40	32	35	29	35	49	46	Total Theater
34	25	27	27	29	44	38	Committed Forces
30	16	19	24	27	38	33	Operational
16	11	10	12	9	18	13	Enemy Action
3	2	2	4	1	-	2	Air-to-Air
10	5	7	6	8	18	10	Ground Fire
3	4	1	2	-	-	1	Cause Unknown
11	4	6	7	13	14	15	Not Enemy Action
3	1	3	5	5	6	5	Unknown or Missing
4	9	8	3	2	6	5	Non-Operational
4	8	8	3	2	6	3	Flying Accidents
-	1	-	-	-	-	2	Other
							Pilot Claims - Enemy Acft
39	25	34	27	58	78	32	Destroyed - Total
-	-	-	-	-	-	-	Air-to-Ground
39	25	34	27	58	78	32	Air-to-Air
37	25	34	27	56	78	31	MIG-15
2	-	-	-	2	-	1	Other
9	6	10	8	5	11	2	Probable - Total
-	-	-	-	-	-	-	Air-to-Ground
9	6	10	8	5	11	2	Air-to-Air
9	5	10	8	5	11	2	MIG-15
-	1	-	-	-	-	-	Other
47	41	39	33	30	42	16	Damaged - Total
-	-	-	-	-	-	-	Air-to-Ground
47	41	39	33	30	42	16	Air-to-Air
47	40	39	33	30	42	15	MIG-15
-	1	-	-	-	-	1	Other
							Sorties
							By Category
18,890	16,583	18,041	23,094	23,264	23,908	19,670	Total Korean Operations
18,625	16,433	17,880	22,909	23,067	23,684	19,466	Effective
265	150	161	185	197	224	204	Non-Effective
14,089	12,166	13,597	18,273	18,336	19,453	15,974	Day
4,801	4,417	4,444	4,821	4,928	4,455	3,696	Night
							By Type Aircraft
18,890	16,583	18,041	23,094	23,264	23,908	19,670	Total Korean Operations
443	359	466	453	513	501	437	Medium Bomber
1,817	1,807	1,688	1,924	2,036	2,325	2,279	Light Bomber
8,908	7,881	8,291	11,959	12,027	13,063	10,754	Jet Fighter
416	-	-	-	-	-	-	Prop Fighter
1,236	1,074	1,068	1,389	1,602	1,293	1,012	Reconnaissance
4,507	4,006	4,830	4,922	5,093	4,901	3,969	Cargo
1,563	1,456	1,698	2,447	1,993	1,825	1,219	Other
							By Type Mission
19,833	17,387	19,666	24,754	24,936	25,339	21,561	Total All Operations
943	804	1,625	1,660	1,672	1,431	1,891	Intra Japan Cargo
18,890	16,583	18,041	23,094	23,264	23,908	19,670	Korean Operations
12,104	10,574	10,852	14,904	15,078	16,203	13,594	Total Combat
1,218	1,545	1,187	2,617	3,887	7,078	5,860	Close Support
5,714	4,858	4,264	5,310	4,706	3,450	3,591	Interdiction and Armed Reconnaissance
-	-	-	-	-	-	-	Strategic
2,901	2,000	2,911	3,927	3,645	3,467	2,454	Counter Air Offensive
678	936	830	1,028	1,186	743	583	Counter Air Defensive
1,593	1,235	1,660	2,022	1,654	1,465	1,106	Reconnaissance
6,786	6,009	7,189	8,190	8,186	7,705	6,076	Total Combat Support
498	446	662	793	762	568	279	Rescue
4,292	3,754	4,524	4,625	4,765	4,521	3,620	Cargo
1,103	1,000	1,009	1,498	1,208	1,145	876	Tactical Control
893	809	994	1,274	1,451	1,471	1,301	Other

TABLE 10 — STATISTICAL SUMMARY OF USAF OPERATIONS, BY TYPE MODEL — 26 JUNE 1950 THROUGH 27 JULY 1953

OPERATION	TOTAL	B-26	B-29	F-51	F-80	F-82	F-84	F-86	F-94	RB/WB-26	RB/WB-29
AIRCRAFT											
Average (EOM) Theater Inventory	2,000	161	109	167	270	16	247	184	56	27	36
Average (EOM) Active Inventory	1,857	147	109	136	247	15	226	164	56	26	36
Average (EOM) Inactive Inventory	143	14	-	31	23	1	21	20	-	1	-
Average Active On Hand	N/A	146	108	120	245	14	229	169	57	N/A	N/A
Average Possessed In Committed Units	1,038	105	99	72	107	4	121	107	12	20	25
Average Combat Ready In Committed Units	698	74	68	45	67	2	86	79	8	15	11
CREWS											
Average (EOM) Theater Inventory	1,767	144	101	121	268	18	263	203	66	34	36
Average Possessed In Committed Units	1,435	145	97	97	153	6	201	185	19	32	25
Average Combat Ready In Committed Units	1,168	113	87	82	126	6	144	138	13	23	24
HOURS AND FUEL CONSUMPTION											
Total Hours Flown	3,163,018	323,223	235,552	171,293	287,619	15,273	272,280	168,400	60,513	40,681	68,887
Operational Hours	1,842,571	232,044	183,250	134,213	162,848	5,137	159,387	121,735	7,656	34,114	18,759
Non-Operational Hours	1,320,447	91,179	52,302	37,080	124,771	10,136	112,893	46,665	52,857	6,567	50,128
Fuel Consumed (Thousands of Gallons)	764,396	49,964	109,343	11,545	111,975	2,403	110,065	66,873	23,880	a/	a/
SORTIES											
By Category											
Total Korean Operations	710,886	60,096	20,448	62,607	98,515	1,868	86,408	87,179	4,694	11,944	2,535
Effective	699,030	59,318	19,768	60,821	97,126	1,817	85,035	86,027	4,592	11,774	2,421
Non-Effective	11,856	778	680	1,786	1,389	51	1,373	1,152	102	170	114
Day	595,086	11,207	10,125	62,495	97,865	1,334	84,367	87,078	99	2,999	1,685
Night	115,800	48,889	10,323	112	650	534	2,041	101	4,595	8,945	850
Total Korean Operations	710,886	60,096	20,448	62,607	98,515	1,868	86,408	87,179	4,694	11,944	2,535
Total Combat	379,201	49,063	12,741	39,280	64,489	872	79,188	84,547	4,688	8,692	1,663
Close Support	59,636	9,030	2,106	9,837	11,765	-	21,038	5,718	-	115	-
Interdiction & Armed Recon.	189,271	39,798	10,624	24,180	48,113	6	55,505	3,935	-	57	38
Strategic	-	-	-	-	-	-	-	-	-	-	-
Counter Air-Offensive	70,328	-	-	283	817	-	1,467	67,582	134	-	-
Counter Air-Defensive	12,296	35	-	468	597	422	894	5,387	4,482	-	-
Reconnaissance	54,670	200	11	4,512	3,177	444	284	1,925	72	8,520	1,625
Total Combat Support	199,571	2,331	849	1,979	864	104	2,578	2,183	6	2,194	113
Tactical Control	26,516	21	-	-	-	-	-	8	-	5	-
Rescue	14,033	3	21	1,830	607	-	1,517	912	2	1	4
Cargo	137,731		-	-	-	-	-	-	-	-	-
Other	21,291	2,307	828	149	257	104	1,061	1,263	4	2,188	109
Unknown b/	132,114	8,702	6,858	21,348	33,162	892	4,642	449	-	1,058	759
EXPENDITURES											
Bombs (Tons)	386,037	112,215	168,368	12,909	33,266	122	50,427	7,508	-	977	231
Napalm (Tons)	32,357	3,101	-	15,221	8,327	-	5,560	148	-	-	-
Rockets, H.E. (Number)	313,600	25,065	-	183,034	80,935	1,892	22,154	270	-	120	-
Rockets, Smoke (Number)	55,797	-	-	-	-	-	-	-	-	-	-
Machine Gun Ammunitions (100's of Rounds)	1,668,531	310,494	44,631	435,630	588,344	3,478	212,891	58,173	67	1	6,091

TABLE 10 — STATISTICAL SUMMARY OF USAF OPERATIONS, BY TYPE MODEL — 26 JUNE 1950 THROUGH 27 JULY 1953 — CONTINUED

OPERATION	RF-51	RF-80	C-46	C/VC-47	C-54	C-119	C-124	T/LT-6	H-5 YH/H-19	SA-16 SB-29 TB-29	MISC
AIRCRAFT											
Average (EOM) Theater Inventory	18	39	70	123	47	87	9	105	27	33	169
Average (EOM) Active Inventory	16	35	68	116	47	85	9	103	25	33	158
Average (EOM) Inactive Inventory	2	4	2	7	-	2	-	2	2	-	11
Average Active On Hand	15	35	N/A	110	46	83	10	N/A	N/A	N/A	N/A
Average Possessed In Committed Units	10	26	56	37	43	76	8	47	12	15	36
Average Combat Ready In Committed Units	7	18	41	25	32	43	4	35	8	9	23
CREWS											
Average (EOM) Theater Inventory	26	39	72	46	71	83	8	79	14	17	58
Average Possessed In Committed Units	25	38	71	49	71	82	9	73	14	11	32
Average Combat Ready In Committed Units	22	30	65	46	66	74	8	47	13	11	30
HOURS AND FUEL CONSUMPTION											
Total Hours Flown	20,884	28,573	218,947	324,567	262,093	155,636	22,023	178,305	18,281	42,992	246,996
Operational Hours	19,019	24,491	125,914	112,853	203,311	105,824	15,690	110,641	10,701	12,607	41,377
Non-Operational Hours	1,865	4,082	93,033	211,714	58,782	49,812	5,333	67,664	7,580	30,385	205,619
Fuel Consumed (Thousands of Gallons)	a/	a/	33,655	31,902	45,642	38,996	11,116	a/	a/	a/	117,037
SORTIES											
By Category											
Total Korean Operations	10,570	19,843	43,567	46,291	57,841	34,124	3,705	39,955	9,400	2,984	6,312
Effective	10,441	18,957	43,312	45,870	57,433	33,639	3,688	38,645	9,310	2,897	6,139
Non-Effective	129	886	255	421	408	485	17	1,310	90	87	173
Day	10,523	19,791	32,202	39,195	46,166	27,837	2,089	39,897	9,363	2,657	6,112
Night	47	52	11,365	7,096	11,675	6,287	1,616	58	37	327	200
Total Korean Operations	10,570	19,843	43,567	46,291	57,841	34,124	3,705	39,955	9,400	2,984	6,312
Total Combat	10,064	17,153	1	268	-	-	-	5,467	42	16	967
Close Support	-	-	-	-	-	-	-	-	-	-	7
Interdiction & Armed Recon	2	-	-	-	-	-	-	-	-	-	13
Strategic	-	-	-	-	-	-	-	-	-	-	-
Counter Air-Offensive	-	-	-	-	-	-	-	-	-	-	45
Counter Air-Defensive	-	-	-	-	-	-	-	11	-	-	-
Reconnaissance	10,062	17,153	1	268	-	-	-	5,456	42	16	902
Total Combat Support	25	3	36,211	36,064	47,834	23,267	3,705	25,200	8,571	2,753	2,737
Tactical Control	-	-	-	1,706	-	-	-	24,749	-	-	27
Rescue	3	3	-	46	-	-	-	9	6,440	2,554	81
Cargo	-	-	35,185	27,641	47,834	23,267	3,705	-	19	1	83
Other	22	-	1,026	6,671	-	-	-	442	2,116	198	2,546
Unknown b/	481	2,687	7,355	9,959	10,007	10,857	-	9,288	787	215	2,608
EXPENDITURES											
Bombs (Tons)	-	8	-	-	-	-	-	-	-	-	6
Napalm (Tons)	-	-	-	-	-	-	-	-	-	-	-
Rockets, H.E. (Number)	130	-	-	-	-	-	-	-	-	-	-
Rockets, Smoke (Number)	-	-	-	-	-	-	-	55,797	-	-	-
Machine Gun Ammunitions (100's of rounds)	7,941	-	-	-	-	-	-	-	-	284	506

TABLE 10 — STATISTICAL SUMMARY OF USAF OPERATIONS, BY TYPE MODEL — 26 JUNE 1950 THROUGH 27 JULY 1953 — CONTINUED

OPERATION	TOTAL	B-26	B-29	F-51	F-80	F-82	F-84	F-86	F-94	RB/WB-26	RB/WB-29
CASUALTIES											
Total	2,721	670	714	305	362	37	230	118	12	5	10
Killed	1,144	283	280	131	160	23	98	47	6	4	5
Missing	1,261	324	343	133	164	13	121	65	6	-	-
Wounded	316	63	91	41	38	1	11	6	-	1	5
CREW LOSSES											
Total c/	7,620	913	368	462	749	35	1,247	958	115	231	74
Operational	400	32	20	42	57	-	116	79	7	3	-
Retired	3,753	558	295	189	422	-	529	528	56	133	37
AIRCRAFT LOSSES d/											
Theater --Total	2,015	210	72	351	373	24	335	224	28	16	10
Committed Units - Total	1,747	203	69	322	324	17	305	218	12	16	6
Operational	1,466	166	57	300	277	11	249	184	9	7	3
Enemy Action	757	56	24	194	143	4	153	110	1	1	-
Air-to-Air	139	-	17	10	14	-	18	78	1	-	-
Ground Fire	550	48	5	172	113	4	122	19	-	-	-
Cause Unknown	68	8	2	12	16	-	13	13	-	1	-
Not Enemy Action	472	41	27	74	96	4	63	61	6	5	1
Unknown or Missing	237	71	6	32	38	3	33	13	2	1	2
Non-Operational	281	35	12	22	47	6	56	34	3	9	3
Flying Accidents	235	25	9	10	44	5	53	32	3	8	1
Other	46	10	3	12	3	1	3	2	-	1	2
Non-Committed Units - Total	268	7	3	29	49	7	30	6	16	-	4
Flying Accidents	216	3	3	26	39	4	29	6	16	-	4
Other	52	4	-	3	10	3	1	-	-	-	-
PILOT CLAIMS - ENEMY AIRCRAFT											
Destroyed - Total	953	7	18	37	58	4	9	814	4	-	1
Air-to-Ground	53	-	-	28	21	-	-	4	-	-	-
Air-to-Air	900	7	18	9	37	4	9	810	4	-	1
MIG-15	823	-	16	-	6	-	8	792	1	-	-
Other	77	7	2	9	31	4	1	18	3	-	1
Probable - Total	193	-	11	11	37	2	13	119	-	-	-
Air-to-Ground	25	-	-	8	15	-	1	1	-	-	-
Air-to-Air	168	-	11	3	22	2	12	118	-	-	-
MIG-15	145	-	7	-	9	-	11	118	-	-	-
Other	23	-	4	3	13	2	1	-	-	-	-
Damaged - Total	1,009	7	15	27	57	-	83	818	2	-	-
Air-to-Ground	36	-	-	15	16	-	1	4	-	-	-
Air-to-Air	973	7	15	12	41	-	82	814	2	-	-
MIG-15	946	3	11	9	32	-	82	808	1	-	-
Other	27	4	4	3	9	-	-	6	1	-	-

TABLE 10 — STATISTICAL SUMMARY OF USAF OPERATIONS, BY TYPE MODEL — 26 JUNE 1950 THROUGH 27 JULY 1953 — CONTINUED

OPERATION	RF-51	RF-80	C-46	C/VC-47	C-54	C-119	C-124	T/LT-6	H-5 H/YH-19	SA-16 SB-29 TB-29	MISC
CASUALTIES											
Total	17	23	16	15	24	26	-	100	10	13	14
Killed	5	12	3	9	14	15	-	33	5	3	8
Missing	10	11	7	6	5	8	-	35	4	-	6
Wounded	2	-	6	-	5	3	-	32	1	10	-
CREW LOSSES											
Total c/	174	235	346	232	234	262	48	631	134	50	122
Operational	10	6	1	3	-	-	1	20	-	-	3
Retired	109	120	98	129	54	107	26	261	35	10	57
AIRCRAFT LOSSES d/											
Theater-Total b/	24	27	34	41	16	21	1	96	32	7	73
Committed Units - Total	23	25	23	21	15	19	1	76	25	3	24
Operational	22	22	16	13	9	11	1	68	21	2	16
Enemy Action	19	3	-	2	-	2	-	39	5	-	1
Air-to-Air	-	1	-	-	-	-	-	-	-	-	-
Ground Fire	17	1	-	2	-	2	-	39	5	-	1
Cause Unknown	2	1	-	-	-	-	-	-	-	-	-
Not Enemy Action	1	9	14	8	8	9	1	13	16	2	13
Unknown or Missing	2	10	2	3	1	-	-	16	-	-	2
Non-Operational	1	3	7	8	6	8	-	8	4	1	8
Flying Accidents	1	3	7	7	2	8	-	4	4	1	8
Other	-	-	-	1	4	-	-	4	-	-	-
Non-Committed Units - Total	1	2	11	20	1	2	-	20	7	4	49
Flying Accidents	1	1	8	12	1	2	-	14	7	4	36
Other	-	1	3	8	-	-	-	6	-	-	13
PILOT CLAIMS - ENEMY AIRCRAFT											
Destroyed - Total	1	-	-	-	-	-	-	-	-	-	-
Air-to-Ground	-	-	-	-	-	-	-	-	-	-	-
Air-to-Air	1	-	-	-	-	-	-	-	-	-	-
MIG-15	-	-	-	-	-	-	-	-	-	-	-
Other	1	-	-	-	-	-	-	-	-	-	-
Probable - Total	-	-	-	-	-	-	-	-	-	-	-
Air-to-Ground	-	-	-	-	-	-	-	-	-	-	-
Air-to-Air	-	-	-	-	-	-	-	-	-	-	-
MIG-15	-	-	-	-	-	-	-	-	-	-	-
Other	-	-	-	-	-	-	-	-	-	-	-
Damaged - Total	-	-	-	-	-	-	-	-	-	-	-
Air-to-Ground	-	-	-	-	-	-	-	-	-	-	-
Air-to-Air	-	-	-	-	-	-	-	-	-	-	-
MIG-15	-	-	-	-	-	-	-	-	-	-	-
Other	-	-	-	-	-	-	-	-	-	-	-

a/ Included in Miscellaneous.
b/ The breakdown by type mission for these sorties is unavailable due to it not being required the first 8 months of combat.
c/ Includes all casualties including those listed as other.
d/ Does not include Q-14 or G-4 losses nor any loss due to "Transfer or Division".
Source: Operations Statistics Division, Directorate of Statistical Services, DCS/C.

TABLE 11 — USAF END-OF-MONTH AIRCRAFT INVENTORY, BY TYPE MODEL, BY MONTH — JULY 1950 THROUGH JULY 1953

(Overall Theater Inventory Including Non-Committed Units)

MONTH	TOTAL	B-26	B-29	F-51	F-80	F-82	F-84	F-86	F-94	RB/ WB-25	RB/ WB-29	RF-51	RF-80	C-46	VC/ C-47	C-54	C-119	C-124	LT/ T-6	B-5 YH/ H-19	SA-16 SB-29 TB-29	MISC
Average	2,000	161	109	167	270	16	247	184	56	27	36	18	39	70	123	47	87	9	105	27	33	169
July - 1950	1,389	79	87	190	528	37	-	-	-	-	4	-	35	41	84	31	-	-	135	-	-	138
August	1,648	77	149	213	522	37	-	-	-	16	31	-	50	40	91	30	73	-	127	13	8	171
September	1,633	76	145	192	507	35	-	-	-	25	35	-	48	39	98	29	99	-	121	12	8	164
October	1,621	136	98	175	486	34	-	-	-	22	34	12	51	38	105	28	95	-	116	16	10	165
November	1,699	131	96	161	429	33	76	26	-	22	35	12	51	86	118	25	95	-	110	17	15	161
December	1,812	122	99	248	403	31	72	74	-	22	34	12	56	83	103	62	93	-	104	16	20	158
January - 1951	1,801	111	98	249	384	28	97	86	-	20	36	11	40	77	116	61	92	-	101	18	19	157
February	1,809	99	99	300	364	26	107	84	-	20	37	10	40	75	112	64	91	-	97	17	17	150
March	1,846	117	100	317	342	24	106	102	15	20	36	9	39	75	111	64	90	-	94	17	20	148
April	1,798	118	92	301	321	24	102	100	14	23	36	8	39	75	111	68	89	-	87	21	20	149
May	1,766	139	100	268	290	22	100	95	14	27	39	8	38	74	115	65	90	-	87	25	23	147
June	1,828	158	102	246	267	23	173	89	14	26	39	7	36	74	128	63	67	-	85	27	24	160
July	1,793	157	104	227	254	24	175	93	14	24	38	7	36	72	129	64	66	-	81	28	24	156
August	1,846	149	106	204	236	22	236	112	32	24	36	19	35	70	128	65	66	-	80	28	24	154
September	1,808	140	105	180	231	22	227	105	32	24	36	34	35	68	133	66	86	1	75	27	27	154
October	1,776	132	99	170	220	23	220	99	44	23	39	33	34	67	134	67	85	1	75	26	27	158
November	1,824	140	107	147	215	22	225	167	44	23	38	33	34	67	135	66	85	-	69	25	28	154
December	1,852	137	105	132	222	22	216	165	55	27	38	32	34	67	129	66	79	-	109	25	32	160
January - 1952	1,907	155	107	123	224	22	208	169	80	33	39	31	34	66	130	65	78	-	123	25	33	162
February	1,892	165	115	114	215	22	189	155	105	32	38	26	30	65	129	65	79	-	122	28	35	163
March	1,982	191	115	139	221	22	195	175	105	32	37	25	30	68	128	65	77	-	124	30	36	167
April	2,037	204	113	167	214	22	210	175	104	32	37	24	30	70	131	67	76	-	124	29	37	171
May	1,954	187	107	156	212	-	189	167	101	28	38	23	42	73	132	65	75	6	121	28	41	163
June	1,997	178	98	147	214	-	224	181	100	30	40	22	42	76	131	65	74	13	118	27	42	175
July	2,210	190	118	150	224	-	353	177	100	30	40	22	40	76	134	64	95	13	117	36	49	182
August	2,327	194	117	133	227	-	450	210	98	31	37	20	39	77	129	57	100	25	117	37	48	181
September	2,358	232	121	131	223	-	418	248	98	32	36	20	39	76	130	48	99	26	116	36	51	178
October	2,392	232	116	118	219	-	474	253	98	32	36	32	25	75	132	44	99	26	114	39	51	177
November	2,291	227	114	113	206	-	465	234	96	32	35	32	25	74	128	20	88	26	113	39	52	172
December	2,365	216	113	128	204	-	475	302	94	37	36	30	25	74	127	20	66	26	111	39	50	172
January - 1953	2,347	207	109	126	188	-	486	291	90	37	39	30	26	74	131	15	87	26	111	35	51	188
February	2,415	194	107	124	179	-	490	373	90	35	38	22	29	74	132	16	102	26	110	35	49	190
March	2,469	189	114	107	184	-	475	448	89	35	38	22	33	74	128	15	104	26	107	33	48	200
April	2,399	190	118	86	161	-	438	453	89	32	38	14	52	73	128	14	100	26	104	33	49	201
May	2,428	197	119	74	161	-	441	476	87	31	37	10	53	73	136	17	104	26	99	33	49	205
June	2,361	193	118	69	157	-	406	479	83	31	35	-	56	73	134	19	103	25	98	32	50	200
July	2,314	194	117	65	152	-	410	439	82	30	37	-	57	73	133	21	104	25	96	34	49	196

Source: Operations Statistics Division, Directorate of Statistical Services, DCS/C.

TABLE 12 – USAF END-OF-MONTH CREW INVENTORY, BY TYPE MODEL, BY MONTH – JULY 1950 THROUGH JULY 1953

(Overall Theater Inventory Including Non-Committed Units)

MONTH	TOTAL	B-26	B-29	F-51	F-80	F-82	F-84	F-86	F-94	RB/WB-26	RB/WB-29	RF-51	RF-80	C-46	VC/C-47	C-54	C-119	C-124	LT/T-6	H-5/YH/H-19	SA-16/SB-29/TB-29	MISC
Average	1,767	144	101	121	268	18	263	203	66	34	36	26	39	72	46	71	83	8	79	N/A	N/A	89
July - 1950	735	40	81	70	368	25	-	-	-	-	29	-	15	6	38	23	-	-	8	N/A	N/A	32
August	966	56	143	180	297	30	-	-	-	12	36	-	26	16	63	16	-	-	34	N/A	N/A	57
September	1,110	60	140	179	300	29	-	-	-	16	39	-	24	19	57	10	97	-	45	N/A	N/A	95
October	1,044	79	86	171	324	32	-	-	-	14	38	-	12	11	32	16	99	-	50	N/A	N/A	80
November	1,079	146	89	196	273	35	-	-	-	16	37	-	18	31	26	22	74	-	38	N/A	N/A	78
December	1,316	155	86	106	306	42	85	92	-	25	36	18	30	50	25	36	95	-	37	N/A	N/A	92
January - 1951	1,315	139	89	107	325	49	92	91	-	19	34	12	16	56	18	42	99	-	45	N/A	N/A	82
February	1,312	126	92	122	378	50	84	80	-	23	36	6	17	15	35	38	99	-	46	N/A	N/A	65
March	1,257	109	84	120	380	46	74	87	-	23	35	-	17	7	32	41	98	-	38	N/A	N/A	66
April	1,272	111	75	105	374	47	88	89	7	24	32	23	16	6	27	38	97	-	43	N/A	N/A	70
May	1,475	116	86	115	344	41	133	100	14	30	34	36	28	55	36	65	95	-	65	N/A	N/A	82
June	1,677	120	97	126	314	36	178	111	21	36	35	49	40	103	45	91	93	-	87	N/A	N/A	95
July	1,691	105	86	122	349	29	217	121	16	39	33	50	44	82	47	91	86	-	90	N/A	N/A	84
August	1,787	103	89	152	275	27	288	110	15	38	34	46	56	94	43	157	89	-	88	N/A	N/A	83
September	1,865	148	91	146	307	30	278	115	18	37	36	43	40	103	44	168	100	-	91	N/A	N/A	70
October	1,789	99	89	159	307	25	290	112	22	30	38	44	34	97	44	119	100	1	96	N/A	N/A	83
November	1,860	94	83	178	300	23	294	163	29	31	36	47	34	102	46	127	96	-	102	N/A	N/A	75
December	1,914	101	94	188	248	24	283	216	27	41	36	48	39	107	48	127	87	-	128	N/A	N/A	72
January - 1952	1,941	105	97	176	266	19	284	202	37	45	35	53	42	102	61	138	88	-	125	25	26	15
February	1,898	111	100	170	228	10	298	215	45	43	33	43	40	115	61	117	70	-	116	24	26	33
March	1,999	146	104	181	224	-	306	174	81	55	37	48	50	116	63	116	86	-	131	19	33	29
April	2,079	157	117	179	220	-	315	192	83	56	36	60	45	111	64	120	82	-	144	23	33	42
May	2,010	169	117	138	216	-	320	223	93	44	37	54	38	95	62	116	75	-	114	23	28	48
June	1,924	186	100	133	200	-	304	223	91	40	35	55	29	80	58	125	77	-	90	22	32	44
July	1,934	174	112	118	222	-	303	216	103	39	34	49	33	73	60	133	80	-	88	18	40	39
August	2,008	185	126	117	223	-	350	224	113	29	34	43	47	86	62	105	80	3	88	22	31	38
September	1,981	158	115	117	233	-	351	230	111	28	35	34	53	89	61	85	77	4	107	23	37	33
October	2,033	184	110	156	243	-	394	237	120	27	36	21	41	64	54	73	72	15	84	27	32	43
November	2,052	191	105	144	254	-	399	248	130	34	37	24	52	76	43	33	78	19	85	25	34	41
December	2,038	191	102	121	250	-	416	256	127	31	37	20	52	71	42	28	80	33	78	30	34	39
January - 1953	2,080	214	102	115	234	-	395	321	130	36	37	14	51	76	45	35	84	34	62	30	30	35
February	2,202	230	103	31	229	-	405	438	148	41	38	11	49	90	41	36	97	38	74	31	30	42
March	2,240	225	77	36	206	-	440	457	165	48	36	1	52	89	43	32	90	37	83	35	31	57
April	2,352	199	114	-	201	-	484	541	177	57	36	-	50	91	40	25	90	35	85	44	31	52
May	2,422	199	114	-	176	-	522	591	179	47	36	-	65	88	46	19	93	33	86	36	38	54
June	2,363	202	119	-	166	-	513	550	168	54	39	-	68	88	43	25	92	31	74	37	36	58
July	2,319	191	109	-	158	-	554	489	165	55	38	-	69	90	57	21	91	31	73	34	34	60

Note: Not available. Included in Miscellaneous.

Source: Operations Statistics Division, Directorate of Statistical Services, DCS/C.

TABLE 13 — AVERAGE AIRCRAFT POSSESSED IN COMMITTED UNITS BY TYPE MODEL BY MONTH — 26 JUNE 1950 THROUGH 27 JULY 1953

MONTH	TOTAL	B-26	B-29	F-51	F-80	F-82	F-84	F-86	F-94	RB/ WB-26	RB/ WB-29	RF-51	RF-80	C-46	VC/ C-47	C-54	C-119	C-124	LT/ T-6	H-5 YH/ H-19	SA-16 SB-29 TB-29	MISC
Average. . . .	1,040	105	99	72	107	4	121	107	12	20	25	10	26	56	37	43	76	8	47	N/A	N/A	65
July - 1950 a/. .	398	49	63	20	145	14	-	-	-	-	18	-	17	3	19	26	-	-	11	N/A	N/A	13
August.	626	47	130	141	128	8	-	-	-	10	20	-	18	6	38	26	2	-	27	N/A	N/A	25
September	804	46	141	139	138	9	-	-	-	15	22	-	20	52	28	24	75	-	36	N/A	N/A	59
October	840	45	133	144	187	7	-	-	-	19	24	-	25	29	26	23	88	-	39	N/A	N/A	51
November.	822	89	90	131	169	6	-	-	-	19	23	-	25	48	27	22	86	-	35	N/A	N/A	52
December.	925	98	86	104	151	9	b/ 69	c/ 19	-	18	24	g/ 1	21	65	27	60	84	-	38	N/A	N/A	51
January - 1951. .	925	92	88	99	172	9	69	4	-	16	25	10	15	70	21	58	85	-	38	N/A	N/A	54
February.	939	78	91	107	203	8	70	-	-	13	25	7	15	62	17	59	87	-	42	N/A	N/A	55
March	984	79	90	110	195	7	77	37	-	11	26	6	17	64	18	60	87	-	46	N/A	N/A	54
April	964	83	86	102	169	6	78	46	-	11	25	7	20	55	25	61	83	-	56	N/A	N/A	51
May	1,007	96	88	124	165	5	80	47	-	13	26	8	18	49	28	61	82	-	57	N/A	N/A	60
June.	999	102	93	123	147	4	85	44	-	14	27	7	20	49	30	60	80	-	51	N/A	N/A	63
July.	990	103	95	95	136	5	103	41	-	17	27	5	21	55	52	59	78	-	54	15	17	12
August.	1,021	109	97	112	124	4	126	39	-	21	25	5	28	56	49	58	76	-	51	14	16	11
September	1,038	104	97	110	118	6	137	44	-	22	25	6	30	59	46	59	80	h/ 1	52	13	16	13
October	1,027	99	93	115	111	5	135	42	-	22	26	7	31	60	46	59	78	1	49	13	15	20
November.	1,004	97	89	96	98	6	125	56	-	22	26	20	29	61	46	58	77	-	48	13	18	19
December.	1,064	99	97	76	79	6	127	127	-	21	24	32	31	61	46	58	73	-	45	18	21	23
January - 1952. .	1,101	104	96	71	69	10	123	133	d/ 15	21	26	31	33	60	51	61	68	-	60	20	18	31
February.	1,084	102	92	70	69	e/ 10	109	133	20	21	26	26	30	58	53	63	66	-	68	20	18	30
March	1,086	106	105	60	81	-	88	133	36	22	25	23	27	65	51	62	67	-	63	25	18	29
April	1,050	109	109	54	82	-	85	129	25	24	25	23	26	57	37	62	69	-	66	20	18	30
May	1,031	107	102	47	79	-	87	131	23	25	26	22	25	54	42	63	66	-	57	19	22	34
June.	1,067	106	93	51	87	-	103	135	24	24	26	21	25	55	42	62	69	-	55	19	27	43
July.	1,148	106	94	53	82	-	181	138	23	24	26	20	30	55	43	63	68	14	54	18	24	32
August.	1,190	117	96	53	87	-	164	150	23	23	27	18	31	64	46	59	83	14	51	18	23	43
September	1,191	123	98	54	86	-	173	151	24	24	26	16	25	64	49	49	75	27	50	16	23	40
October	1,255	134	101	55	89	-	213	163	25	24	25	15	25	68	40	40	91	25	49	17	23	33
November.	1,237	136	97	52	90	-	215	165	25	24	25	14	24	66	39	32	84	25	47	19	25	33
December.	1,212	134	100	51	98	-	207	161	22	25	26	14	24	67	36	15	84	25	47	18	26	32
January - 1953. .	1,193	140	99	39	101	-	202	163	20	26	26	9	23	67	36	12	81	25	47	22	24	31
February.	1,166	134	95	f/ 1	101	-	215	179	20	25	26	i/ 5	22	66	38	10	81	25	47	22	23	31
March	1,188	139	98	-	78	-	207	224	22	25	27	-	22	66	33	10	83	25	46	22	27	34
April	1,216	138	107	-	40	-	201	265	21	25	26	-	36	64	33	11	96	25	45	21	28	34
May	1,225	152	109	-	7	-	213	277	21	25	25	-	42	64	36	10	87	25	43	20	26	43
June.	1,208	140	109	-	6	-	213	273	19	25	25	-	48	59	39	12	92	25	40	19	25	39
July(thru the 27)	1,243	136	104	-	5	-	215	297	20	25	25	-	47	63	50	14	95	24	37	19	25	42

a/ Includes 27 through 30 June 1950.
b/ F-84 type acft began operations Dec 50.
c/ F-86 type acft began operations Dec 50.
d/ F-94 type acft began operations Jan 52.
e/ F-82 type acft removed from combat status Feb 52.
f/ F-51 type acft removed from combat status Jan 53.
g/ RF-51 type acft began operations Dec 50.
h/ C-124 type acft began operations Sep 51.
i/ RF-51 type acft removed from combat status Feb 53.
N/A Not available. Included in Miscellaneous.
Source: Operations Statistics Division, Directorate of Statistical Services, DCS/C.

TABLE – 14 – AVERAGE CREWS POSSESSED IN COMMITTED UNITS, BY TYPE MODEL, BY MONTH – 26 JUNE 1950 THROUGH 27 JULY 1953

MONTH	TOTAL	B-26	B-29	F-51	F-80	F-82	F-84	F-86	F-94	RB/WB-26	RB/WB-29	RF-51	RF-80	C-46	VC/C-47	C-54	C-119	C-124	LT/T-6	H-5 YH/H-19	SA-16 SB-29 TB-29	MISC
Average	1,435	145	97	97	153	6	201	185	19	32	25	25	38	71	49	71	82	9	73	N/A	N/A	57
July - 1950 a/	387	45	59	21	140	11	-	-	-	-	20	-	17	5	23	25	-	-	8	N/A	N/A	13
August	631	45	130	163	120	8	-	-	-	7	23	-	22	5	49	11	-	-	24	N/A	N/A	24
September	819	55	140	164	136	8	-	-	-	15	25	-	24	21	58	12	61	-	35	N/A	N/A	65
October	915	58	135	168	212	8	-	-	-	14	28	-	20	15	39	14	97	-	37	N/A	N/A	70
November	905	119	84	172	187	12	-	-	-	14	27	-	16	24	26	20	95	-	46	N/A	N/A	63
December	1,064	144	84	167	220	18	b/54	c/26	-	16	27	g/1	18	43	29	33	85	-	37	N/A	N/A	62
January - 1951	1,084	134	88	110	222	22	95	6	-	22	24	17	21	52	23	39	100	-	48	N/A	N/A	61
February	1,019	132	97	104	217	19	84	-	-	21	25	9	17	35	25	39	101	-	44	N/A	N/A	50
March	1,062	120	91	118	280	14	75	41	-	20	24	1	17	8	33	32	99	-	45	N/A	N/A	44
April	1,020	109	79	95	254	9	88	58	-	22	23	13	17	7	30	38	94	-	39	N/A	N/A	45
May	1,191	113	86	104	225	15	92	57	-	27	25	28	22	62	34	101	96	-	50	N/A	N/A	54
June	1,402	131	98	118	254	11	137	59	-	33	26	38	36	94	43	92	93	h/	71	N/A	N/A	68
July	1,462	107	89	116	236	11	185	88	-	37	25	50	43	87	66	100	89	-	88	18	16	11
August	1,496	113	87	121	191	9	211	82	-	38	25	50	52	89	66	147	89	-	81	18	18	9
September	1,591	138	89	115	207	13	225	90	-	36	25	45	49	100	66	160	98	1	90	16	18	10
October	1,550	125	89	109	233	10	227	85	-	37	25	45	36	94	63	130	98	1	97	14	18	14
November	1,534	100	86	118	221	6	231	116	-	29	26	48	31	100	64	120	89	-	100	14	18	17
December	1,627	109	96	139	138	8	233	201	-	38	24	48	38	103	65	127	92	-	115	17	20	16
January - 1952	1,630	103	93	139	127	9	205	217	d/12	36	25	54	42	104	66	130	89	-	122	23	20	14
February	1,631	103	88	127	135	e/7	226	210	25	36	24	45	41	109	66	129	85	-	118	23	20	14
March	1,613	131	97	128	120	-	221	201	25	45	24	49	50	119	67	115	85	-	93	17	12	14
April	1,598	155	104	133	118	-	201	178	25	48	24	56	47	113	62	120	87	-	83	17	7	20
May	1,613	179	106	101	118	-	218	202	25	44	26	58	41	98	65	119	76	-	89	18	7	23
June	1,571	186	100	99	116	-	206	223	24	35	24	55	28	77	49	126	77	-	93	18	7	28
July	1,604	174	100	85	122	-	230	216	35	39	23	49	33	73	61	133	76	-	88	14	21	32
August	1,674	185	106	87	123	-	290	224	35	29	24	43	47	86	63	105	76	3	88	18	13	29
September	1,655	158	103	89	127	-	293	230	30	28	25	34	53	89	62	85	74	4	107	18	20	26
October	1,667	184	94	119	138	-	314	237	32	27	25	21	41	64	55	73	69	15	84	24	19	32
November	1,697	191	97	107	142	-	320	248	40	34	26	24	52	76	44	46	75	19	85	22	18	31
December	1,661	191	95	86	140	-	313	256	49	31	27	20	52	71	42	28	80	33	76	25	17	29
January	1,695	214	98	f/80	126	-	299	307	46	36	26	14	51	76	45	35	84	34	62	23	15	24
February	1,791	230	99	-	126	-	297	423	51	41	26	i/10	49	90	41	36	95	38	74	24	15	26
March	1,823	225	100	1	103	-	336	441	50	48	24	-	52	89	44	32	87	37	83	27	16	28
April	1,900	199	107	-	59	-	381	528	51	59	22	-	50	91	40	25	87	35	85	34	19	28
May	1,953	199	107	-	21	-	419	576	52	47	24	-	65	88	45	19	89	33	86	28	22	33
June	1,888	202	108	-	6	-	415	535	45	54	27	-	63	88	43	25	88	31	74	31	21	32
July	1,792	263	98	-	5	-	322	489	47	55	26	-	59	90	58	21	87	31	73	26	14	28

a/ Includes 26 through 30 June 1950.
d/ F-94 type acft began operations Jan 52.
g/ RF-51 type acft began operations Dec 50.
N/A Not Available and included in Misc.

b/ F-84 type acft began operations Dec 50.
e/ F-82 type acft removed from combat status Feb 52.
h/ C-124 type acft began operations Sep 51.

c/ F-86 type acft began operations Dec 50.
f/ F-51 type acft removed from combat status Jan 53.
i/ RF-51 type acft removed from combat status Feb 53.

Source: Operations Statistics Division, Directorate of Statistical Services, DCS/C.

TABLE 15 — AVERAGE AIRCRAFT COMBAT READY IN COMMITTED UNITS BY TYPE MODEL, BY MONTH — 26 JUNE 1950 THROUGH 27 JULY 1953

MONTH	TOTAL	B-26	B-29	F-51	F-80	F-82	F-84	F-86	F-94	RB/ WB-26	RB/ WB-29	RF-51	RF-80	C-46	VC/ C-47	C-54	C-119	C-124	LT/ T-6	H-5 YH/ H-19	SA-16 SB-29 TB-29	MISC
Average	698	74	68	45	67	2	86	79	8	15	11	7	18	41	25	32	43	4	35	N/A	N/A	40
July - 1950 a/	252	30	49	14	69	10	-	-	-	-	12	-	10	3	14	22	-	-	9	N/A	N/A	10
August	404	29	89	93	75	6	-	-	-	1	11	-	12	4	29	21	1	-	21	N/A	N/A	12
September	523	38	109	82	94	6	-	-	-	11	9	-	13	19	23	22	41	-	24	N/A	N/A	32
October	555	29	102	76	128	4	-	-	-	14	12	-	19	18	23	16	56	-	26	N/A	N/A	32
November	515	60	69	83	107	3	-	-	-	13	9	-	15	26	15	14	42	-	24	N/A	N/A	35
December	593	65	63	71	118	6	b/ 27	c/ 15	-	10	10	g/	9	44	9	38	47	-	25	N/A	N/A	36
January - 1951	606	56	69	57	115	5	47	3	-	14	11	8	11	44	9	46	48	-	26	N/A	N/A	37
February	621	45	70	65	117	4	49	-	-	12	11	4	12	47	13	46	64	-	23	N/A	N/A	39
March	682	50	72	66	123	5	51	28	-	10	12	4	14	57	15	50	61	-	28	N/A	N/A	36
April	601	45	68	61	95	3	50	37	-	9	10	4	15	46	20	49	13	-	40	N/A	N/A	36
May	668	52	70	73	98	3	48	41	-	10	11	3	13	36	23	46	61	-	39	N/A	N/A	41
June	647	58	68	67	94	2	50	37	-	12	13	3	13	36	20	43	53	-	32	N/A	N/A	46
July	685	70	74	65	73	2	64	35	-	15	12	3	16	43	47	47	55	-	32	10	12	10
August	669	78	75	70	66	2	50	31	-	17	13	4	21	42	42	48	52	-	29	9	13	7
September	693	76	71	61	59	2	74	33	-	17	14	3	19	51	38	47	64	h/ 1	34	8	13	8
October	685	75	66	66	58	2	73	34	-	15	12	4	19	43	40	48	58	1	35	9	12	15
November	668	75	59	53	56	1	73	33	-	14	12	12	21	47	40	45	60	-	32	8	12	15
December	654	73	57	38	47	2	70	58	-	14	8	21	23	46	38	47	39	-	30	11	16	16
January - 1952	653	75	65	48	34	3	61	61	d/ 5	15	12	18	21	45	32	45	29	-	37	14	16	17
February	674	83	61	44	35	e/ 2	54	85	9	13	10	23	18	41	44	44	11	-	51	14	14	18
March	667	78	72	35	49	-	48	80	18	16	11	16	18	35	31	45	30	-	48	12	11	14
April	687	77	64	43	49	-	47	93	16	19	10	19	16	39	28	45	35	-	50	12	10	15
May	664	71	58	41	49	-	46	90	14	18	12	14	19	42	22	50	27	-	42	14	15	20
June	716	69	64	28	54	-	80	108	14	16	11	14	19	44	23	47	27	-	43	15	17	23
July	794	69	66	30	61	-	132	110	14	17	11	17	22	50	23	45	21	6	48	13	18	21
August	783	81	65	35	62	-	112	114	17	19	12	15	20	50	23	41	14	4	44	14	17	24
September	814	90	60	36	60	-	135	107	16	19	12	12	18	48	26	30	45	8	42	11	17	22
October	866	102	47	40	61	-	166	119	18	20	10	11	18	51	19	26	52	13	44	13	17	19
November	874	98	49	40	62	-	172	127	18	20	11	11	19	49	22	21	46	15	43	14	15	22
December	838	98	54	34	74	-	159	117	17	20	12	8	17	50	18	10	45	14	43	14	17	17
January - 1953	812	102	58	20	73	-	156	126	14	20	12	5	15	45	19	7	49	9	43	16	7	16
February	801	97	59	f/	67	-	167	130	13	19	11	i/ 3	14	45	23	7	48	15	42	16	8	17
March	840	102	63	-	53	-	170	174	16	20	13	-	15	47	20	7	46	18	39	10	8	19
April	887	113	73	-	33	-	163	206	16	18	13	-	22	46	21	7	56	18	38	16	8	20
May	920	117	75	-	7	-	185	229	16	18	9	-	31	47	22	6	60	17	37	17	8	19
June	930	107	76	-	5	-	195	222	15	20	13	-	37	49	24	8	65	15	36	11	8	24
July(thru the 27)	913	111	76	-	3	-	191	223	12	15	9	-	41	46	20	10	63	10	33	11	6	33

a/ Includes 27 through 30 June 1950.
b/ F-84 type acft began operations Dec 50.
c/ F-86 type acft began operations Dec 50.
d/ F-94 type acft began operations Jan 52.
e/ F-82 type acft removed from combat status Feb 52.
f/ F-51 type acft removed from combat status Jan 53.
g/ RF-51 type acft began operations Dec 50.
h/ C-124 type acft began operations Sep 51.
i/ RF-51 type acft removed from combat status Feb 53.
N/A Not Available. Included in Miscellaneous.

Source: Operations Statistics Division, Directorate of Statistical Services, DCS/C.

TABLE 16 — AVERAGE CREWS COMBAT READY IN COMMITTED UNITS, BY TYPE MODEL, BY MONTH — 26 JUNE 1950 THROUGH 27 JULY 1953

MONTH	TOTAL	B-26	B-29	F-51	F-80	F-82	F-84	F-86	F-94	RB/ WB-26	RB/ WB-29	RF-51	RF-80	C-46	VC/ C-47	C-54	C-119	C-124	LT/ T-6	H-5 YH/ H-19	SA-16 SB-29 TB-29	MISC
Average	1,168	113	87	82	126	6	144	138	13	23	24	22	30	65	46	66	74	8	47	N/A	N/A	54
July - 1950 a/	375	45	59	21	130	11	-	-	-	-	20	-	16	5	22	25	-	-	8	N/A	N/A	13
August	613	45	127	162	110	8	-	-	-	7	23	-	22	5	45	11	-	-	24	N/A	N/A	24
September	776	55	138	161	130	7	-	-	-	14	25	-	24	10	41	12	61	-	32	N/A	N/A	66
October	876	57	135	160	203	7	-	-	-	12	28	-	20	14	39	13	86	-	33	N/A	N/A	69
November	871	115	84	169	182	9	-	-	-	12	27	-	16	24	26	20	81	-	43	N/A	N/A	63
December	1,008	142	84	156	202	17	b/54	c/26	-	13	27	g/	16	43	29	33	68	-	36	N/A	N/A	62
January - 1951	1,016	132	88	109	204	19	84	6	-	15	24	16	19	52	23	39	82	-	44	N/A	N/A	60
February	934	120	88	103	198	18	67	-	-	16	25	9	17	35	25	39	85	-	40	N/A	N/A	49
March	973	102	89	114	260	14	58	41	-	18	24	1	17	8	33	31	83	-	37	N/A	N/A	43
April	958	105	76	94	239	9	72	58	-	21	23	10	17	7	30	38	77	-	37	N/A	N/A	45
May	1,013	96	74	96	205	9	84	57	-	24	25	26	21	19	33	76	80	-	41	N/A	N/A	47
June	1,120	97	91	88	191	10	99	52	-	23	25	32	26	75	42	79	76	-	53	N/A	N/A	61
July	1,217	90	88	89	189	11	141	82	-	23	24	37	31	80	64	87	78	-	62	15	16	10
August	1,242	96	85	89	159	9	155	69	-	24	24	45	34	81	61	131	79	-	62	12	18	9
September	1,294	116	88	90	133	9	174	75	-	29	24	39	34	91	62	149	87	h/1	52	13	18	10
October	1,256	110	85	90	152	8	200	62	-	25	22	38	32	83	61	117	86	1	41	11	18	14
November	1,235	85	79	90	148	6	205	74	-	18	24	43	28	97	62	108	82	-	40	12	17	17
December	1,269	81	86	103	108	8	183	133	-	24	23	43	30	96	62	122	82	-	33	16	20	16
January - 1952	1,235	75	83	103	77	9	153	156	d/9	22	25	42	26	99	63	123	83	-	38	19	20	10
February	1,243	75	82	105	75	e/7	145	170	9	22	24	36	27	105	64	124	80	-	42	21	19	11
March	1,249	90	85	103	85	-	145	162	17	29	24	42	26	113	65	106	80	-	38	17	11	11
April	1,285	113	79	104	94	-	144	140	23	25	24	50	36	109	60	116	83	-	46	15	7	17
May	1,303	132	88	79	92	-	171	148	18	26	24	54	30	92	63	114	72	-	57	15	7	21
June	1,268	136	86	73	91	-	152	173	18	24	23	48	20	75	48	115	73	-	69	15	7	22
July	1,272	132	86	51	94	-	166	172	17	27	21	44	23	67	56	121	73	-	62	12	20	28
August	1,331	134	87	54	103	-	203	185	16	22	23	36	34	78	58	99	73	2	68	18	13	25
September	1,334	127	84	63	104	-	216	191	21	23	22	28	36	81	57	80	72	-	69	16	20	24
October	1,376	151	82	89	116	-	231	194	20	22	22	18	32	57	52	73	67	15	61	24	19	31
November	1,339	129	78	96	105	-	249	196	21	26	23	21	37	70	41	33	68	18	62	20	18	28
December	1,273	118	82	72	120	-	213	196	26	25	22	19	34	56	39	28	76	31	51	21	17	27
January - 1953	1,247	127	79	f/41	106	-	191	218	30	26	26	14	34	60	41	35	78	32	48	23	15	23
February	1,307	153	79	-	102	-	189	247	33	37	25	i/10	40	79	41	35	86	37	50	24	15	25
March	1,274	171	79	1	79	-	201	226	39	30	21	-	44	87	43	32	74	36	48	23	16	24
April	1,380	148	83	-	50	-	208	347	41	45	21	-	46	87	39	24	75	35	57	32	18	24
May	1,520	152	86	-	15	-	259	459	44	37	22	-	60	86	43	19	81	33	50	25	20	29
June	1,443	140	89	-	6	-	254	408	42	37	25	-	53	82	42	25	78	31	50	31	20	30
July (through the 27th)	1,512	197	87	-	5	-	280	398	43	42	26	-	52	89	43	21	79	30	56	23	13	28

a/ Includes 26 through 30 June 1950.
b/ F-84 type acft began operations Dec 50.
c/ F-86 type acft began operations Dec 50.
d/ F-94 type acft began operations Jan 52.
e/ F-82 type acft removed from combat status Feb 52.
f/ F-51 type acft removed from combat status Jan 53.
g/ RF-51 type acft began operations Dec 50.
h/ C-124 type acft began operations Sep 51.
i/ RF-51 type acft removed from combat status Feb 53.
N/A Not Available. Included in Miscellaneous.

Source: Operations Statistics Division, Directorate of Statistical Services, DCS/C.

TABLE 17 — AIRBORNE SORTIES BY MONTH, BY TYPE MODEL — 26 JUNE 1950 THROUGH 27 JULY 1953

MONTH	TOTAL	B-26	B-29	F-51	F-80	F-82	F-84	F-86	F-94	RB/WB-26	RB/WB-29
Total	710,886	60,096	20,448	62,607	98,515	1,868	86,408	87,179	4,694	11,944	2,535
July - 1950 a/	8,499	727	572	713	4,445	287	-	-	-	-	81
August	15,586	970	1,280	4,933	3,693	127	-	-	-	21	107
September	15,839	980	1,334	4,282	3,256	52	-	-	-	168	105
October	16,634	535	719	2,395	4,327	32	-	-	-	142	116
November	18,116	1,112	715	2,818	4,083	50	-	-	-	122	81
December	18,184	1,660	727	2,400	4,394	159	b/ 982	c/ 236	-	168	96
January - 1951	20,374	1,470	794	2,024	4,637	112	2,092	212	-	215	93
February	18,710	1,248	717	1,783	4,327	73	1,568	1	-	222	80
March	23,786	1,425	786	3,018	5,608	18	2,449	904	-	287	73
April	22,611	1,617	565	3,632	4,090	57	2,179	1,073	-	312	65
May	23,489	1,711	547	3,702	4,036	71	1,985	1,360	-	359	75
June	21,395	1,554	447	3,152	3,446	49	1,543	1,250	-	356	56
July	15,914	1,499	499	2,370	2,289	75	1,328	734	-	358	71
August	17,456	1,710	477	2,227	2,308	131	1,588	940	-	438	70
September	19,311	1,962	520	2,811	2,777	135	2,808	1,119	-	467	86
October	21,887	1,956	509	3,181	3,106	139	3,354	1,622	-	446	91
November	19,166	1,868	430	2,070	2,678	87	3,349	1,003	-	343	77
December	19,328	1,698	424	1,545	2,362	48	3,053	2,066	-	358	63
January - 1952	18,581	1,653	515	1,333	1,600	101	2,577	2,340	d/ 46	190	61
February	16,972	1,520	407	1,206	1,612	e/ 65	2,140	2,500	92	366	63
March	19,653	1,552	475	1,172	2,438	-	2,289	3,359	154	429	75
April	18,541	1,472	382	1,082	2,629	-	1,978	3,783	192	438	70
May	23,954	1,825	406	1,421	3,460	-	2,418	5,190	269	498	94
June	19,636	1,791	378	1,216	2,414	-	1,932	2,778	306	406	59
July	16,634	1,783	441	889	1,593	-	1,713	2,423	284	398	31
August	18,337	1,507	387	669	2,160	-	2,461	3,010	21	370	24
September	18,931	1,741	448	1,161	1,785	-	2,338	3,586	7	412	29
October	22,971	2,250	494	1,263	2,214	-	3,831	4,320	24	336	18
November	17,746	1,818	416	1,011	1,865	-	3,126	2,635	101	330	12
December	19,195	1,606	465	712	2,117	-	3,403	3,418	322	311	28
January - 1953	18,890	1,817	443	f/ 416	1,993	-	3,129	3,429	357	355	71
February	16,583	1,807	359	-	1,844	-	3,004	2,652	381	333	61
March	18,041	1,688	466	-	1,465	-	2,807	3,632	387	351	70
April	23,094	1,924	453	-	1,194	-	4,909	5,346	510	455	66
May	23,264	2,036	513	-	138	-	4,697	6,721	471	496	69
June	23,908	2,325	501	-	109	-	4,795	7,696	463	380	69
July (through the 27th)	19,670	2,279	437	-	23	-	4,583	5,841	307	308	79

a/ Includes 27 through 30 Jun 50.
b/ F-84 type acft began operations Dec 50.
c/ F-86 type acft began operations Dec 50.
d/ F-94 type acft began operations Jan 52.
e/ F-82 type acft removed from combat status Feb 52.
f/ F-51 type acft removed from combat status Jan 53.

TABLE 17 — AIRBORNE SORTIES BY MONTH • BY TYPE MODEL — 26 JUNE 1950 THROUGH 27 JULY 1953 — CONTINUED

MONTH	RF-51	RF-80	C-46	VC/C-47	C-54	C-119	C-124	T/LT-6	H-5 H/YH-19	SA-16 SB/TB-29	MISC
Total	10,570	19,843	43,567	46,291	57,841	34,124	3,705	39,955	9,400	2,984	6,312
July - 1950 a/	-	247	111	1,060	85	-	-	137	-	-	34
August	-	514	59	2,422	107	30	-	1,025	128	2	168
September	-	385	238	1,700	497	720	-	1,463	150	39	470
October	-	267	548	1,253	1,525	2,753	-	1,282	140	32	548
November	-	390	1,638	905	1,413	2,729	-	1,473	127	26	434
December	g/ 10	280	1,415	570	1,502	1,795	-	1,399	42	51	298
January - 1951	257	320	1,961	889	2,160	1,519	-	1,286	51	44	238
February	214	264	1,385	1,160	2,718	1,311	-	1,223	149	21	246
March	314	365	1,349	1,519	2,720	1,244	-	1,348	131	29	199
April	233	492	1,132	1,881	3,076	268	-	1,524	68	31	316
May	108	393	1,496	1,686	2,957	1,389	-	1,421	83	46	64
June	87	435	1,313	1,576	2,985	1,454	-	1,401	158	81	52
July	93	320	850	993	2,379	850	-	833	286	66	21
August	85	367	1,145	1,152	2,209	1,040	-	969	495	92	13
September	98	500	535	1,303	2,548	400	h/ 4	942	193	100	3
October	115	691	872	1,261	2,298	705	20	1,000	399	107	15
November	411	544	1,041	1,217	2,335	465	-	945	196	99	8
December	764	532	1,094	1,163	2,193	768	-	845	223	78	51
January - 1952	775	515	1,110	1,374	2,298	551	-	1,009	379	75	79
February	662	470	1,106	1,265	2,168	266	-	636	302	67	59
March	624	447	966	1,671	2,256	499	-	769	298	97	83
April	636	539	527	1,449	1,598	427	-	893	245	88	113
May	988	815	887	1,192	2,015	588	-	1,210	430	99	149
June	824	719	1,325	1,074	2,428	233	-	1,012	545	55	136
July	558	422	1,434	992	2,053	129	28	794	528	48	93
August	714	594	1,354	1,131	2,060	277	60	1,024	301	93	120
September	497	721	1,201	1,238	1,127	684	191	1,176	337	125	127
October	510	847	1,386	1,136	967	1,228	273	1,344	289	133	108
November	396	767	951	926	871	885	230	982	227	93	104
December	359	663	1,271	920	440	1,212	304	1,078	191	129	246
January - 1953	196	579	1,333	987	347	1,484	356	1,005	264	124	205
February	1/ 42	611	1,303	852	262	1,220	369	913	266	96	208
March	-	605	1,663	1,213	217	1,230	507	961	377	118	284
April	-	805	2,198	1,261	239	783	441	1,557	471	182	300
May	-	991	2,206	1,363	217	919	488	1,187	415	174	263
June	-	818	1,813	1,389	254	1,189	256	1,074	362	141	274
July (through the 27th)	-	589	1,351	1,148	317	975	178	815	154	103	183

g/ RF-51 type acft began operations Dec 50.
h/ C-124 type acft began operations Sep 51.
1/ RF-51 type acft removed from combat status Feb 53.
Source: Operations Statistics Division, Directorate of Statistical Services, DCS/C.

TABLE 18 – EFFECTIVE SORTIES BY TYPE MODEL, BY MONTH – 26 JUNE 1950 THROUGH 27 JULY 1953

MONTH	TOTAL	B-26	B-29	F-51	F-80	F-82	F-84	F-86	F-94	RB/WB-26	RB/WB-29
Total.	699,030	59,318	19,768	60,821	97,126	1,817	85,035	86,027	4,592	11,774	2,421
July - 1950 a/.	8,039	684	547	695	4,198	256	-	-	-	-	78
August.	15,328	958	1,247	4,837	3,608	125	-	-	-	19	103
September	15,504	954	1,300	4,176	3,172	51	-	-	-	160	103
October	16,128	492	706	2,197	4,232	31	-	-	-	132	115
November.	17,669	1,045	673	2,675	4,013	50	-	-	-	117	76
December.	17,631	1,591	710	2,246	4,326	153	b/ 926	c/ 229	-	163	92
January - 1951.	19,892	1,429	775	1,909	4,561	111	2,059	207	-	210	87
February.	18,164	1,188	708	1,681	4,241	66	1,512	1	-	214	76
March	23,222	1,394	760	2,914	5,508	17	2,399	858	-	275	72
April	22,063	1,583	551	3,558	4,002	56	2,151	1,057	-	303	63
May	23,181	1,698	534	3,627	3,964	71	1,958	1,354	-	358	73
June.	21,127	1,542	433	3,112	3,396	49	1,476	1,244	-	354	56
July.	15,553	1,486	487	2,335	2,266	75	1,278	728	-	349	70
August.	17,098	1,697	464	2,168	2,288	131	1,536	930	-	431	69
September	19,063	1,955	509	2,778	2,768	135	2,744	1,108	-	464	82
October	21,683	1,951	486	3,148	3,101	139	3,317	1,613	-	445	86
November.	18,952	1,860	405	2,045	2,670	87	3,316	999	-	338	72
December.	19,110	1,694	406	1,517	2,348	48	3,021	2,044	-	356	63
January - 1952.	18,264	1,642	486	1,296	1,588	101	2,530	2,296	d/ 46	190	61
February.	16,663	1,517	391	1,170	1,596	e/ 65	2,094	2,460	92	356	61
March	19,359	1,542	455	1,137	2,430	-	2,253	3,330	151	414	70
April	18,195	1,468	367	1,034	2,574	-	1,953	3,742	183	430	66
May	23,644	1,812	396	1,377	3,451	-	2,376	5,138	264	497	88
June.	19,356	1,781	364	1,181	2,404	-	1,896	2,742	301	402	49
July.	16,352	1,760	432	872	1,581	-	1,678	2,379	277	386	26
August.	18,027	1,474	367	655	2,144	-	2,404	2,971	21	368	22
September	18,590	1,714	420	1,130	1,775	-	2,271	3,536	7	408	26
October	22,707	2,223	483	1,252	2,207	-	3,787	4,261	24	333	15
November.	17,509	1,805	397	1,005	1,857	-	3,088	2,615	99	326	9
December.	18,893	1,583	437	694	2,109	-	3,362	3,361	309	304	28
January - 1953.	18,625	1,797	424	f/ 400	1,991	-	3,090	3,344	330	354	69
February.	16,433	1,793	344	-	1,840	-	2,973	2,624	369	329	56
March	17,880	1,687	446	-	1,464	-	2,782	3,574	380	351	66
April	22,909	1,921	439	-	1,183	-	4,871	5,271	508	455	64
May	23,067	2,022	500	-	138	-	4,640	6,649	468	496	66
June.	23,684	2,313	493	-	109	-	4,757	7,598	460	380	66
July (through the 27th)	19,466	2,263	426	-	23	-	4,537	5,764	303	307	77

a/ Includes 27 through 30 June 50.
d/ F-94 type acft began operations Jan 52.
b/ F-84 type acft began operations Dec 50.
e/ F-82 type acft removed from combat status Feb 52.
c/ F-86 type acft began operations Dec 50.
f/ F-51 type acft removed from combat status Jan 53.

TABLE 18 – EFFECTIVE SORTIES BY TYPE MODEL, BY MONTH – 26 JUNE 1950 THROUGH 27 JULY 1953 (CONTINUED)

MONTH	RF-51	RF-80	C-46	VC/C-47	C-54	C-119	C-124	T/LT-6	H-5 YH/H-19	SA-16 SB/TB-29	MISC
Total	10,441	18,957	43,312	45,870	57,433	33,639	3,688	38,645	9,310	2,897	6,139
July - 1950 a/	-	241	107	998	67	-	-	135	-	-	33
August	-	509	58	2,407	107	30	-	1,024	127	2	167
September	-	381	237	1,681	480	703	-	1,458	148	38	462
October	-	281	546	1,238	1,494	2,712	-	1,259	130	32	531
November	-	368	1,627	902	1,394	2,706	-	1,437	127	26	433
December	g/ 8	249	1,400	568	1,484	1,776	-	1,327	42	51	290
January - 1951	238	281	1,945	882	2,143	1,475	-	1,251	51	41	237
February	197	239	1,381	1,146	2,694	1,249	-	1,158	149	19	245
March	295	335	1,343	1,509	2,709	1,212	-	1,266	130	29	197
April	227	489	1,128	1,875	3,038	245	-	1,329	67	27	314
May	106	384	1,496	1,682	2,948	1,369	-	1,367	83	46	63
June	84	423	1,313	1,571	2,983	1,447	-	1,356	158	79	51
July	89	317	837	977	2,333	839	-	724	279	64	20
August	85	364	1,126	1,149	2,193	1,009	-	861	494	90	13
September	98	497	519	1,300	2,524	389	h/ 4	901	187	98	3
October	115	684	858	1,259	2,286	700	20	965	390	105	15
November	404	544	1,026	1,210	2,326	462	-	889	193	98	8
December	757	527	1,082	1,151	2,175	765	-	806	221	78	51
January - 1952	763	477	1,085	1,351	2,289	544	-	987	379	75	78
February	660	425	1,086	1,252	2,157	265	-	610	291	62	53
March	619	389	960	1,644	2,252	497	-	748	297	95	76
April	636	479	518	1,428	1,594	418	-	867	241	88	109
May	984	750	886	1,189	2,008	573	-	1,193	430	93	139
June	824	656	1,324	1,066	2,423	233	-	986	544	53	127
July	554	377	1,432	975	2,052	125	28	766	528	47	77
August	706	523	1,347	1,113	2,055	273	60	1,017	301	93	113
September	497	637	1,196	1,226	1,126	682	190	1,168	336	124	121
October	510	801	1,375	1,117	967	1,218	273	1,334	289	131	107
November	396	714	943	910	865	867	229	970	227	92	95
December	355	645	1,268	912	430	1,184	303	1,066	187	124	232
January - 1953	194	578	1,331	977	338	1,475	355	998	259	121	200
February	i/ 40	611	1,303	851	260	1,210	368	904	263	93	202
March	-	603	1,663	1,209	215	1,228	505	944	374	114	275
April	-	798	2,198	1,260	239	782	440	1,545	465	178	292
May	-	986	2,206	1,359	216	817	487	1,175	414	167	261
June	-	808	1,813	1,382	254	1,185	253	1,055	358	132	268
July (through the 27th)	-	587	1,349	1,144	315	975	173	799	151	92	181

g/ RF-51 type acft began operations Dec 50. h/ C-124 type acft began operations Sep 51. i/ RF-51 type acft removed from combat status Feb 53.
Source: Operations Statistics Division, Directorate Statistical Services, DCS/C

TABLE 19 — NONEFFECTIVE SORTIES BY TYPE MODEL, BY MONTH — 26 JUNE 1950 THROUGH 27 JULY 1953

MONTH	TOTAL	B-26	B-29	F-51	F-80	F-82	F-84	F-86	F-94	RB/WB-26	RB/WB-29
Total	11,856	778	680	1,786	1,389	51	1,373	1,152	102	170	114
July - 1950 a/	460	43	25	18	247	31	-	-	-	-	3
August	258	12	33	96	85	2	-	-	-	2	4
September	335	26	34	106	84	1	-	-	-	8	2
October	506	43	13	198	95	1	-	-	-	10	1
November	447	67	42	143	70	-	-	-	-	5	5
December	553	69	17	154	68	6	b/ 56	c/ 7	-	5	4
January - 1951	482	41	19	115	76	1	33	5	-	5	6
February	546	60	9	102	86	7	56	-	-	8	4
March	564	31	26	104	100	1	50	46	-	12	1
April	548	34	14	74	88	1	28	16	-	9	2
May	308	13	13	75	72	-	27	6	-	1	2
June	268	12	14	40	50	-	67	6	-	2	-
July	361	13	12	35	23	-	50	6	-	9	1
August	358	13	13	59	20	-	52	10	-	7	1
September	248	7	11	33	9	-	64	11	-	3	4
October	204	5	23	33	5	-	37	9	-	1	5
November	214	8	25	25	8	-	33	4	-	5	5
December	218	4	18	28	14	-	32	22	-	2	-
January - 1952	317	11	29	37	12	-	47	44	d/	-	-
February	309	3	16	36	16	e/	46	40	-	10	2
March	294	10	20	35	8	-	36	29	3	15	5
April	346	4	15	48	55	-	25	41	9	8	4
May	310	13	10	44	9	-	42	52	5	1	6
June	280	10	14	35	10	-	36	36	5	4	10
July	282	23	9	17	12	-	35	44	7	12	5
August	310	33	20	14	16	-	57	39	-	2	2
September	341	27	28	31	10	-	67	50	-	4	3
October	264	27	11	11	7	-	44	59	-	3	3
November	237	13	19	6	8	-	38	20	2	4	3
December	302	23	28	18	8	-	41	57	13	7	-
January - 1953	265	20	19	f/ 16	2	-	39	85	27	1	2
February	150	14	15	-	4	-	31	28	12	4	5
March	161	1	20	-	1	-	25	58	7	-	4
April	185	3	14	-	11	-	38	75	2	-	2
May	197	14	13	-	-	-	57	72	3	-	3
June	224	12	8	-	-	-	38	98	3	-	3
July (through the 27th)	204	16	11	-	-	-	46	77	4	1	2

a/ Includes 27 through 30 Jun 50.
d/ F-94 type acft began operations Jan 52.
b/ F-84 type acft began operations Dec 50.
e/ F-82 type acft removed from combat status Feb 52.
c/ F-86 type acft began operations Dec 50.
f/ F-51 type acft removed from combat status Jan 53.

TABLE 19 — NON EFFECTIVE SORTIES BY TYPE MODEL, BY MONTH — 26 JUNE 1950 THROUGH 27 JULY 1953 — Continued

MONTH	RF-51	RF-80	C-46	VC/C-47	C-54	C-119	C-124	T/LT-6	H-5 YH/H-19	SA-16 SB/TB-29	MISC
Total	129	886	255	421	408	485	17	1,310	90	87	173
July - 1950 a/	-	6	4	62	18	-	-	2	-	-	1
August	-	5	1	15	-	-	-	1	1	-	1
September	-	4	1	19	17	17	-	5	2	1	8
October	-	6	2	15	31	41	-	23	10	-	17
November	-	22	11	3	19	23	-	36	-	-	1
December	g/ 2	31	15	2	18	19	-	72	-	-	8
January - 1951	19	39	16	7	17	44	-	35	-	3	1
February	17	25	4	14	24	62	-	65	-	2	1
March	19	30	6	10	11	32	-	82	1	-	2
April	6	3	4	6	38	23	-	195	1	4	2
May	2	9	-	4	9	20	-	54	-	-	1
June	3	12	-	5	2	7	-	45	-	2	1
July	4	3	13	16	46	11	-	109	7	2	1
August	-	3	19	3	16	31	-	108	1	2	-
September	-	3	16	3	24	11	h/	41	6	2	-
October	-	7	14	2	12	5	-	35	9	2	-
November	7	-	15	7	9	3	-	56	3	1	-
December	7	5	12	12	18	3	-	39	2	-	-
January - 1952	12	38	25	23	9	7	-	22	-	-	1
February	2	45	20	13	11	1	-	26	11	5	6
March	5	58	6	27	4	2	-	21	1	2	7
April	-	60	9	21	4	9	-	26	4	-	4
May	4	65	1	3	7	15	-	17	-	6	10
June	-	63	1	8	5	5	-	26	1	2	9
July	4	45	2	17	1	4	-	28	-	1	16
August	8	71	7	18	5	4	-	7	-	-	7
September	-	84	5	12	1	2	1	8	1	1	6
October	-	46	11	19	-	10	-	10	-	2	1
November	-	53	8	16	6	18	1	12	-	1	9
December	4	18	3	8	10	28	1	12	4	5	14
January - 1953	2	1	2	10	9	9	1	7	5	3	5
February	1/ 2	-	-	1	2	10	1	9	3	3	6
March	-	2	-	4	2	2	2	17	3	4	9
April	-	7	-	1	-	1	1	12	6	4	8
May	-	5	-	4	1	2	1	12	1	7	2
June	-	10	-	7	-	4	3	19	4	9	6
July (through the 27th)	-	2	2	4	2	-	5	16	3	11	2

g/ RF-51 type acft began operations Dec 50.
h/ C-124 type acft began operations Sep 51.
1/ RF-51 type acft removed from combat status Feb 53.
Source: Operations Statistics Division, Directorate of Statistical Services, DCS/C.

TABLE 20 — NIGHT SORTIES BY TYPE MODEL, BY MONTH — 26 JUNE 1950 THROUGH 27 JULY 1953

MONTH	TOTAL	B-26	B-29	F-51	F-80	F-82	F-84	F-86	F-94	RB/WB-26	RB/WB-29
Total	115,800	48,889	10,323	112	650	534	2,041	101	4,595	8,945	850
July - 1950 a/	59	36	-	-	-	23	-	-	-	-	-
August	523	458	-	22	4	29	-	-	-	7	-
September	620	437	43	-	-	18	-	-	-	122	-
October	287	229	14	-	-	-	-	-	-	44	-
November	269	188	-	-	-	-	-	-	-	81	-
December	978	838	24	-	-	-	b/	c/	-	116	-
January - 1951	1,056	783	29	-	-	11	-	-	-	199	-
February	1,301	662	45	3	-	-	-	-	-	204	12
March	2,763	840	72	-	114	6	-	-	-	215	17
April	2,809	816	107	71	123	33	164	99	-	231	3
May	2,303	1,088	233	-	6	18	-	-	-	202	2
June	2,704	1,256	165	-	-	12	-	2	-	317	4
July	2,627	1,394	127	16	-	13	-	-	-	279	21
August	3,477	1,642	70	-	-	27	-	-	-	362	34
September	3,420	1,922	151	-	-	48	36	-	-	371	31
October	3,545	1,882	210	-	4	73	-	-	-	337	37
November	3,793	1,822	329	-	-	36	-	-	-	260	32
December	3,612	1,664	403	-	-	24	-	-	-	273	32
January - 1952	3,891	1,606	499	-	-	100	-	-	d/ 36	166	31
February	3,699	1,511	407	-	-	e/ 63	-	-	89	302	34
March	3,977	1,543	475	-	-	-	-	-	154	353	37
April	3,706	1,467	382	-	-	-	-	-	192	350	40
May	4,451	1,819	395	-	-	-	-	-	257	386	63
June	4,247	1,689	378	-	-	-	-	-	267	311	35
July	3,904	1,337	441	-	-	-	24	-	273	254	24
August	3,576	1,229	387	-	-	-	20	-	21	286	19
September	3,443	1,322	407	-	-	-	8	-	7	282	22
October	4,531	2,084	482	-	-	-	8	-	24	244	16
November	4,354	1,645	416	-	74	-	261	-	101	237	12
December	4,313	1,502	465	-	51	-	215	-	320	221	28
January - 1953	4,801	1,755	443	f/	96	-	230	-	357	275	40
February	4,417	1,701	359	-	78	-	184	-	381	236	31
March	4,444	1,607	463	-	100	-	203	-	387	233	39
April	4,821	1,893	452	-	-	-	212	-	510	363	35
May	4,928	1,984	512	-	-	-	225	-	471	372	36
June	4,455	1,670	501	-	-	-	181	-	459	255	38
July (through the 27th)	3,696	1,568	437	-	-	-	70	-	289	199	45

a/ Includes 27 through 30 Jun 50.
b/ F-84 type acft began operations Dec 50.
c/ F-86 type acft began operations Dec 50.
d/ F-94 type acft began operations Jan 52.
e/ F-82 type acft removed from combat status Feb 52.
f/ F-51 type acft removed from combat status Jan 53.

TABLE 20 — NIGHT SORTIES BY TYPE MODEL, BY MONTH — 26 JUNE 1950 THROUGH 27 JULY 1953 — CONTINUED

MONTH	RF-51	RF-80	C-46	VC/C-47	C-54	C-119	C-124	LT/T-6	H-5 YH/H-19	SA-16 SB/TB-29	MISC
Total	47	52	11,365	7,096	11,675	6,287	1,616	58	37	327	200
July - 1950 g/	-	-	-	-	-	-	-	-	-	-	-
August	3	-	-	-	-	-	-	-	-	-	-
September	-	-	-	-	-	-	-	-	-	-	-
October	-	-	-	-	-	-	-	-	-	-	-
November	-	-	-	-	-	-	-	-	-	-	-
December	g/	-	-	-	-	-	-	-	-	-	-
January - 1951	-	-	-	34	-	-	-	-	-	-	-
February	-	-	183	97	94	1	-	-	-	-	-
March	16	9	453	277	509	217	-	15	-	-	3
April	-	-	86	277	731	65	-	-	-	-	3
May	-	7	120	65	353	209	-	-	-	-	-
June	-	-	236	174	399	135	-	-	-	-	4
July	-	-	213	195	260	107	-	-	-	-	2
August	-	-	384	406	329	223	-	-	-	-	-
September	-	11	123	299	347	79	h/	-	-	1	1
October	-	25	185	257	368	167	-	-	-	-	-
November	-	-	293	326	553	142	-	-	-	-	-
December	-	-	249	279	457	231	-	-	-	-	-
January - 1952	-	-	373	357	531	192	-	-	-	-	-
February	28	-	401	292	499	73	-	-	-	-	-
March	-	-	354	346	585	128	-	-	-	-	2
April	-	-	281	309	526	155	-	-	-	-	4
May	-	-	331	259	632	305	-	-	-	-	4
June	-	-	518	214	746	87	-	-	-	-	2
July	-	-	522	202	736	67	15	-	-	-	9
August	-	-	631	199	624	110	28	-	-	19	3
September	-	-	461	166	457	212	79	-	-	20	-
October	-	-	522	154	452	397	125	-	-	22	1
November	-	-	540	123	314	470	138	-	-	20	3
December	-	-	454	98	264	494	152	-	6	32	11
January - 1953	-	-	473	101	202	629	152	-	1	31	16
February	i/	-	503	120	145	430	196	-	4	23	26
March	-	-	554	226	112	242	219	-	2	28	29
April	-	-	556	295	110	107	178	30	18	31	31
May	-	-	474	355	114	139	180	10	1	37	18
June	-	-	480	300	102	314	98	3	5	34	15
July (through the 27th)	-	-	412	294	124	160	56	-	-	29	13

g/ RF-51 type acft began operations Dec 50. h/ C-124 type acft began operations Sep 51. i/ RF-51 type acft removed from combat status Feb 53.
Source: Operations Statistics Division, Directorate of Statistical Services, DCS/C.

TABLE 21 — AIRBORNE SORTIES BY TYPE MISSION, BY MONTH — 26 JUNE 1950 THROUGH 27 JULY 1953

MONTH	CLOSE SUPPORT	INTERDICTION AND ARMED RECON	COUNTER AIR OFFENSIVE	COUNTER AIR DEFENSIVE	STRATEGIC	RECON	TOTAL COMBAT	TACTICAL CONTROL	SEARCH AND RESCUE	COMBAT CARGO	MISC a/	TOTAL COMBAT SUPPORT	TOTAL KOREAN OPERATIONS	INTRA JAPAN CARGO	TOTAL USAF IN SUPPORT OF KAW
Total	92,603	220,168	73,887	12,931	994	60,971	461,554	34,836	15,192	176,503	22,801	249,332	710,886	40,786	751,672
July - 1950 b/	3,942	2,199	457	89	57	336	7,080	137	-	1,279	3	1,419	8,499	-	8,499
August	6,774	3,299	242	75	613	659	11,662	1,025	136	2,717	46	3,924	15,586	-	15,586
September	6,250	3,281	39	87	247	676	10,580	1,463	260	3,301	235	5,259	15,839	660	16,499
October	3,340	4,474	107	10	77	565	8,573	1,282	217	6,275	287	8,061	16,634	964	17,598
November	3,652	4,210	750	166	-	664	9,442	1,473	173	6,772	256	8,674	18,116	1,030	19,146
December	3,336	6,462	672	88	-	748	11,306	1,259	102	5,310	207	6,878	18,184	1,457	19,641
January - 1951	2,671	7,794	826	50	-	1,322	12,663	862	100	6,517	232	7,711	20,374	1,802	22,176
February	3,002	6,178	466	70	-	1,332	11,048	819	171	6,600	72	7,662	18,710	858	19,568
March	5,405	7,371	990	169	-	2,259	16,194	369	163	6,551	509	7,592	23,786	1,163	24,949
April	2,598	8,655	1,202	374	-	1,847	14,676	1,162	173	6,006	594	7,935	22,611	830	23,441
May	2,824	8,224	1,353	395	-	1,602	14,398	1,462	116	7,183	330	9,091	23,489	968	24,457
June	2,030	7,037	1,330	269	-	1,658	12,324	1,482	296	7,136	157	9,071	21,395	965	22,360
July	1,084	5,939	799	212	-	1,469	9,503	851	394	4,904	262	6,411	15,914	1,189	17,103
August	818	6,565	855	293	-	1,673	10,204	969	393	5,255	635	7,252	17,456	1,346	18,802
September	862	8,686	1,263	298	-	2,947	14,056	22	358	4,445	430	5,255	19,311	1,270	20,581
October	1,000	9,753	1,814	167	-	3,219	15,953	-	694	4,813	427	5,934	21,887	1,245	23,132
November	1,136	8,735	1,019	99	-	2,689	13,676	-	347	4,655	486	5,488	19,166	1,051	20,217
December	302	8,347	2,126	165	-	2,701	13,641	-	328	4,846	513	5,687	19,328	1,080	20,408
January - 1952	394	6,805	2,288	163	-	2,303	11,953	533	527	4,920	648	6,628	18,581	1,218	19,799
February	162	6,268	2,441	183	-	1,636	10,690	720	458	4,451	653	6,282	16,972	1,086	18,058
March	1,081	6,437	3,270	157	-	1,675	12,620	840	504	5,002	687	7,033	19,653	1,142	20,795
April	711	6,288	3,624	246	-	1,759	12,628	964	665	3,595	689	5,913	18,541	761	19,302
May	1,031	8,126	4,728	423	-	2,428	16,736	1,303	818	4,210	887	7,218	23,954	1,239	25,193
June	1,910	5,603	2,391	492	-	2,169	12,565	1,088	609	4,645	729	7,071	19,636	877	20,513
July	2,082	4,104	2,287	386	-	1,396	10,255	869	578	4,305	627	6,379	16,634	851	17,485
August	1,854	4,978	2,595	328	-	1,723	11,478	1,101	475	4,535	748	6,859	18,337	959	19,296
September	1,822	5,120	3,299	350	-	1,655	12,246	1,255	619	4,056	755	6,685	18,931	1,105	20,036
October	3,009	6,357	4,093	228	-	1,942	15,629	1,437	599	4,559	747	7,342	22,971	1,302	24,273
November	2,416	5,330	2,400	214	-	1,630	11,990	1,070	498	3,606	582	5,756	17,746	1,493	19,239
December	1,713	5,650	2,856	701	-	1,554	12,474	1,180	413	3,953	1,175	6,721	19,195	849	20,044
January - 1953	1,218	5,714	2,901	678	-	1,593	12,104	1,103	498	4,292	893	6,786	18,890	943	19,833
February	1,545	4,858	2,000	936	-	1,235	10,574	1,000	446	3,754	809	6,009	16,583	804	17,387
March	1,187	4,264	2,911	830	-	1,660	10,852	1,009	662	4,524	994	7,189	18,041	1,625	19,666
April	2,617	5,310	3,927	1,028	-	2,022	14,904	1,498	793	4,625	1,274	8,190	23,094	1,660	24,754
May	3,887	4,706	3,645	1,186	-	1,654	15,078	1,208	762	4,765	1,451	8,186	23,264	1,672	24,936
June	7,078	3,450	3,467	743	-	1,465	16,203	1,145	568	4,521	1,471	7,705	23,908	1,431	25,339
July (thru the 27th)	5,860	3,591	2,454	583	-	1,106	13,594	876	279	3,620	1,301	6,076	19,670	1,891	21,561

a/ Miscellaneous includes, Refueling, Liaison, etc type missions. b/ Includes 27 through 30 June 1950.
Source: Operations Statistics Division, Directorate of Statistical Services, DCS/C.

TABLE 22 — TONS OF BOMBS EXPENDED BY TYPE MODEL, BY MONTH — 26 JUNE 1950 THROUGH 27 JULY 1953

MONTH	TOTAL	B-26	B-29	F-51	F-80	F-82	F-84	F-86	RECON
Total	386,037	112,215	168,368	12,909	33,266	122	50,427	7,508	1,222
July - 1950 a/.	5,715	997	4,432	211	32	43	-	-	-
August.	12,135	1,308	9,840	938	1	48	-	-	-
September	12,374	961	10,905	464	21	23	-	-	-
October	6,385	514	5,765	52	2	-	-	-	52
November.	6,490	1,021	5,319	69	45	-	-	-	36
December.	7,583	1,358	5,509	126	347	-	b/ 170	c/	73
January - 1951.	9,054	1,424	6,875	78	323	-	272	-	82
February.	8,130	1,104	6,449	19	479	8	24	-	47
March	9,100	1,933	6,334	68	632	-	80	-	53
April	7,545	2,041	4,333	654	502	-	15	-	-
May	8,584	2,683	4,579	623	604	-	95	-	-
June.	7,438	2,348	3,657	821	434	-	178	-	-
July.	8,311	2,175	4,068	689	1,180	-	199	-	-
August.	8,356	2,779	3,765	379	988	-	445	-	-
September	10,593	3,671	3,879	592	1,269	-	1,047	-	135
October	11,290	3,367	3,724	802	1,610	-	1,754	-	33
November.	10,180	3,451	3,054	568	1,357	-	1,695	-	55
December.	10,557	3,631	3,501	512	1,355	-	1,523	-	35
January - 1952.	11,685	3,571	4,602	470	1,175	-	1,832	-	35
February.	10,494	3,714	3,718	380	1,139	d/	1,542	-	1
March	11,814	3,814	4,253	420	1,654	-	1,673	-	-
April	10,303	3,529	3,417	393	1,900	-	1,052	-	12
May	11,677	3,965	3,542	535	2,421	-	1,140	13	61
June.	11,258	3,916	3,413	505	1,987	-	1,400	-	37
July.	9,965	3,056	3,799	387	1,242	-	1,475	-	6
August.	9,657	2,602	3,170	289	1,601	-	1,965	-	30
September	10,717	3,294	3,497	504	1,360	-	2,013	-	49
October	12,401	4,310	4,155	546	1,248	-	2,094	-	48
November.	10,916	3,641	3,530	380	1,415	-	1,925	-	25
December.	12,635	3,601	4,061	290	1,480	-	3,089	-	114
January - 1953.	12,188	4,145	3,876	e/ 145	1,284	-	2,688	-	50
February.	10,836	4,305	3,005	-	1,119	-	2,384	-	23
March	10,548	3,864	3,923	-	578	-	2,157	-	26
April	12,554	4,268	3,929	-	482	-	3,521	323	31
May	14,563	4,914	4,467	-	-	-	3,441	1,705	36
June.	16,720	5,592	4,160	-	-	-	3,913	3,044	11
July (through the 27th) .	15,286	5,348	3,863	-	-	-	3,626	2,423	26

a/ Includes 27 through 30 June 1950.

b/ F-84 type acft began operations December 1950.

c/ F-86 type acft began operations December 1950.

d/ F-82 type acft removed from combat status February 1952.

e/ F-51 type acft removed from combat status January 1953.

Source: Operations Statistics Division, Directorate of Statistical Services, DCS/C.

TABLE 23 — TONS OF NAPALM EXPENDED BY TYPE MODEL - BY MONTH —
26 JUNE 1950 THROUGH 27 JULY 1953

MONTH	TOTAL	B-26	B-29	F-51	F-80	F-84	F-86
Total	32,357	3,101	-	15,221	8,327	5,560	148
July - 1950 a/	3	-	-	1	2	-	-
August	614	1	-	610	3	-	-
September	1,712	98	-	1,601	13	-	-
October	671	-	-	647	24	-	-
November	1,548	260	-	1,180	108	-	-
December	1,964	554	-	1,004	356	b/ 50	c/
January - 1951	2,498	489	-	1,023	763	223	-
February	2,927	727	-	914	857	429	-
March	3,833	163	-	1,776	886	1,008	-
April	3,854	412	-	1,171	1,209	1,056	6
May	3,681	151	-	1,476	1,303	751	-
June	2,228	53	-	645	1,411	119	-
July	516	5	-	377	94	40	-
August	672	6	-	553	87	26	-
September	769	-	-	589	146	34	-
October	758	106	-	552	96	4	-
November	573	-	-	439	128	6	-
December	408	3	-	219	68	118	-
January - 1952	196	-	-	141	33	22	-
February	132	4	-	32	93	3	-
March	207	8	-	19	175	5	-
April	29	-	-	-	14	15	-
May	385	-	-	71	202	112	-
June	184	-	-	55	32	97	-
July	183	-	-	34	29	120	-
August	202	1	-	6	91	104	-
September	62	14	-	-	5	43	-
October	211	-	-	12	33	166	-
November	886	12	-	74	64	736	-
December	16	11	-	-	-	5	-
January - 1953	18	4	-	d/	-	14	-
February	14	1	-	-	1	12	-
March	76	9	-	-	1	3	63
April	12	5	-	-	-	7	-
May	56	4	-	-	-	52	-
June	117	-	-	-	-	111	6
July (thru the 27th)	142	-	-	-	-	69	73

a/ Includes 27 through 30 June 1950.

b/ F-84 type acft began operations December 1950.

c/ F-86 type acft began operations December 1950.

d/ F-51 type acft removed from combat status January 1953.

Source: Operations Statistics Division, Directorate of Statistical Services, DCS/C.

TABLE 24 — ROCKET EXPENDITURES, BY TYPE MODEL, BY MONTH — 26 JUNE 1950 THROUGH 27 JULY 1953

(55,797 Smoke Rockets fired by LT/T-6 aircraft not included in the following table.)

MONTH	TOTAL	B-26	B-29	F-51	F-80	F-82	F-84	F-86	RECON
Total	313,600	25,065	-	183,034	80,935	1,892	22,154	270	250
July - 1950 a/	11,933	606	-	2,894	7,761	672	-	-	-
August	23,277	75	-	15,687	6,732	783	-	-	-
September	24,030	2,066	-	13,861	7,959	144	-	-	-
October	16,064	720	-	6,820	8,524	-	-	-	-
November	22,363	2,280	-	10,412	9,621	-	-	-	50
December	23,539	6,475	-	7,949	7,157	-	b/1,958	c/	-
January - 1951	22,575	5,078	-	8,941	5,787	245	2,362	162	-
February	20,118	3,526	-	7,864	7,658	8	992	-	70
March	26,139	523	-	15,100	8,709	40	1,767	-	-
April	17,935	694	-	13,973	3,104	-	164	-	-
May	20,392	1,426	-	16,119	2,829	-	18	-	-
June	13,881	44	-	12,597	1,139	-	101	-	-
July	7,414	13	-	6,835	316	-	250	-	-
August	4,960	-	-	3,788	550	-	622	-	-
September	7,264	43	-	5,510	1,325	-	386	-	-
October	7,801	122	-	7,122	238	-	319	-	-
November	6,221	269	-	5,931	5	-	16	-	-
December	4,365	121	-	3,944	12	-	288	-	-
January - 1952	3,749	263	-	3,354	15	-	117	-	-
February	2,122	63	-	1,952	63	d/	20	24	-
March	3,928	98	-	1,884	217	-	1,729	-	-
April	1,864	28	-	760	57	-	1,019	-	-
May	4,321	38	-	1,871	-	-	2,412	-	-
June	4,112	36	-	1,658	-	-	2,418	-	-
July	3,681	-	-	2,001	437	-	1,243	-	-
August	2,111	45	-	735	200	-	1,131	-	-
September	1,983	8	-	1,837	-	-	138	-	-
October	3,835	14	-	1,238	299	-	2,227	-	57
November	450	129	-	207	12	-	62	-	40
December	605	57	-	170	189	-	99	60	30
January - 1953	287	123	-	e/ 20	8	-	133	-	3
February	78	66	-	-	12	-	-	-	-
March	-	-	-	-	-	-	-	-	-
April	141	-	-	-	-	-	141	-	-
May	-	-	-	-	-	-	-	-	-
June	46	-	-	-	-	-	22	24	-
July (through the 27th)	16	16	-	-	-	-	-	-	-

a/ Includes 27 through 30 June 1950.

b/ F-84 type acft began operations December 1950.

c/ F-86 type acft began operations December 1950.

d/ F-82 type acft removed from combat status February 1952.

e/ F-51 type acft removed from combat status January 1953.

Source: Operations Statistics Division, Directorate of Statistical Services, DCS/C.

TABLE 25 — AMMUNITION EXPENDITURES, BY TYPE MODEL, BY MONTH — 26 JUNE 1950 THROUGH 27 JULY 1953

(Figures in the following table indicate hundreds of rounds of .50 caliber ammunition.)

MONTH	TOTAL	B-26	B-29	F-51	F-80	F-82	F-84	F-86	F-94	RECON	MISC
Total . . .	1,668,531	310,494	44,631	435,630	588,344	3,478	212,891	58,173	67	14,375	448
July - 1950 a/ . .	35,957	2,361	1,154	7,188	24,494	745	-	-	-	15	-
August	86,086	5,221	2,061	46,587	30,700	1,384	-	-	-	131	2
September.	78,854	11,251	2,594	38,477	25,869	452	-	-	-	128	83
October.	50,591	6,713	1,243	16,816	25,646	-	-	-	-	166	7
November	64,895	15,522	813	19,832	28,624	-	-	-	-	103	1
December	93,750	29,703	1,049	17,869	38,186	128	b/ 6,576	c/ 114	-	125	-
January - 1951 . .	94,612	22,439	818	14,371	40,310	464	14,722	1,092	-	395	1
February	83,011	15,449	710	14,471	37,515	245	13,683	-	-	938	-
March.	114,972	8,998	1,129	29,751	52,443	57	20,218	563	-	1,813	-
April.	88,610	7,013	1,151	32,354	31,377	-	15,977	580	-	54	104
May.	90,732	8,978	437	29,235	36,383	-	15,421	182	-	86	10
June	69,498	8,132	493	20,582	32,376	-	7,017	794	-	104	-
July	44,215	7,671	1,410	13,676	16,085	-	3,989	242	-	1,107	35
August	47,350	8,641	2,485	11,032	20,208	-	4,232	261	-	468	23
September.	60,470	15,739	559	15,286	23,958	3	4,304	480	-	139	2
October.	70,138	18,493	1,233	19,277	25,104	-	3,577	1,358	-	966	130
November	72,035	17,924	540	20,597	29,315	-	2,314	1,070	-	225	50
December	58,150	17,596	552	10,478	21,455	-	5,674	1,397	-	998	-
January - 1952 . .	39,218	14,398	314	6,890	10,413	-	4,512	1,672	d/	1,019	-
February	28,040	11,873	271	4,829	5,421	e/	3,451	1,882	-	313	-
March.	30,643	7,715	379	4,966	6,886	-	7,066	3,359	-	272	-
April.	27,196	6,291	526	4,087	4,825	-	7,165	3,569	-	733	-
May.	35,808	12,264	1,990	6,454	5,312	-	6,024	3,232	5	527	-
June	32,780	10,895	2,567	6,639	3,224	-	7,292	1,150	-	1,013	-
July	20,698	5,573	2,847	4,111	2,505	-	4,457	1,032	22	151	-
August	17,608	2,238	2,740	2,560	2,482	-	5,208	2,210	-	170	-
September.	14,648	89	2,080	4,699	1,151	-	3,191	3,308	-	130	-
October.	18,631	329	2,791	5,286	934	-	5,824	3,213	-	254	-
November	14,529	767	997	4,240	736	-	6,096	1,625	-	108	-
December	12,166	829	923	1,798	2,026	-	3,841	2,471	3	275	-
January - 1953 . .	11,851	1,973	708	f/ 1,192	311	-	4,880	2,592	10	185	-
February	9,101	1,663	854	-	269	-	4,008	2,180	2	125	-
March.	8,447	953	898	-	566	-	3,635	2,139	-	256	-
April.	11,765	985	1,100	-	1,2[illegible]	-	5,795	2,167	-	483	-
May.	9,718	1,508	771	-	-	-	4,459	2,842	10	128	-
June	12,880	1,168	774	-	-	-	5,324	5,516	15	83	-
July (thru the 27)	8,878	1,139	670	-	-	-	2,999	3,881	-	189	-

a/ Includes 27 through 30 June 1950.

b/ F-84 type acft began operations December 1950.

c/ F-86 type acft began operations December 1950.

d/ F-94 type acft began operations January 1952.

e/ F-82 type acft removed from combat status February 1952.

f/ F-51 type acft removed from combat status January 1953.

Source: Operations Statistics Division, Directorate of Statistical Services, DCS/C.

TABLE 26 — BOMB AND NAPALM EXPENDITURES BY TYPE MISSION, BY MONTH — 26 JUNE 1950 THROUGH 27 JULY 1953

MONTH	BOMBS						
	TOTAL EXPENDITURES	CLOSE SUPPORT	INTERDICTION & ARMED RECON	COUNTER AIR OFFENSIVE	COUNTER AIR DEFENSIVE	RECON	MISC
Total.	a/ 386,037	61,469	218,448	27	99	958	4,503
July - 1950 b/. . . .	5,715						
August.	12,135						
September	12,374						
October	6,385						
November.	6,490						
December.	7,583						
January - 1951. . . .	9,054		NOT AVAILABLE				
February.	8,130						
March	9,100						
April	7,545						
May	8,584						
June.	7,438						
July.	8,311	1,588	6,630	8	10	8	67
August.	8,356	689	7,576	-	-	11	80
September	10,593	770	9,570	-	36	141	76
October	11,290	823	10,332	2	-	33	100
November.	10,180	1,293	8,698	-	2	55	132
December.	10,557	956	9,456	-	-	54	81
January - 1952. . . .	11,685	1,408	10,101	-	-	37	139
February.	10,494	755	9,636	-	-	13	90
March	11,814	1,285	10,451	-	-	-	78
April	10,303	1,034	9,182	-	-	12	75
May	11,677	983	10,504	13	-	65	112
June.	11,258	2,504	8,599	-	-	37	118
July.	9,965	2,820	7,036	-	-	8	101
August.	9,657	2,274	7,183	-	-	20	180
September	10,717	2,406	8,129	-	47	45	90
October	12,401	3,153	9,047	-	-	20	181
November.	10,916	2,650	8,061	-	-	67	138
December.	12,635	2,490	9,763	-	-	77	305
January - 1953. . . .	12,188	1,773	9,916	-	-	137	362
February.	10,836	2,268	8,393	2	-	28	145
March	10,548	1,785	8,564	-	-	11	188
April	12,554	2,941	9,231	-	4	62	316
May	14,563	4,556	9,630	2	-	9	366
June.	16,720	10,225	6,071	-	-	-	424
July (thru the 27th).	15,286	8,040	6,679	-	-	8	559

MONTH	NAPALM						
	TOTAL EXPENDITURES	CLOSE SUPPORT	INTERDICTION & ARMED RECON	COUNTER AIR OFFENSIVE	COUNTER AIR DEFENSIVE	RECON	MISC
Total.	a/ 32,357	2,858	3,815	61	10	27	53
July - 1950 b/. . . .	3						
August.	614						
September	1,712						
October	671						
November.	1,548						
December.	1,964						
January - 1951. . . .	2,498		NOT AVAILABLE				
February.	2,927						
March	3,833						
April	3,854						
May	3,681						
June.	2,228						
July.	516	276	238	2	-	-	-
August.	672	375	293	-	-	4	-
September	769	468	295	3	-	3	-
October	758	455	289	2	-	-	12
November.	573	504	66	-	-	-	3
December.	408	41	333	-	-	3	31
January - 1952. . . .	196	84	110	2	-	-	-
February.	132	5	125	-	-	-	2
March	207	16	191	-	-	-	-
April	29	11	18	-	-	-	-
May	385	42	331	-	-	12	-
June.	184	43	141	-	-	-	-
July.	183	54	129	-	-	-	-
August.	202	83	118	-	-	-	1
September	62	-	62	-	-	-	-
October	211	33	178	-	-	-	-
November.	886	103	777	-	-	4	2
December.	16	3	13	-	-	-	-
January - 1953. . . .	18	-	17	-	-	-	1
February.	14	-	13	-	-	1	-
March	76	4	9	52	10	-	1
April	12	7	5	-	-	-	-
May	56	9	47	-	-	-	-
June.	117	107	10	-	-	-	-
July (thru the 27th).	142	135	7	-	-	-	-

a/ Totals do not cross check.
b/ Includes 27 through 30 June 1950.
Source: Operations Statistics Division, Directorate of Statistical Services, DCS/C.

TABLE 27 — ROCKET AND AMMUNITION EXPENDITURES BY TYPE MISSION, BY MONTH — 26 JUNE 1950 THROUGH 27 JULY 1953

MONTH	ROCKETS a/							AMMUNITION						
	TOTAL EXPENDITURES	CLOSE SUPPORT	INTERDICTION & ARMED RECON	COUNTER AIR OFFENSIVE	COUNTER AIR DEFENSIVE	RECON	MISC	TOTAL EXPENDITURES	CLOSE SUPPORT	INTERDICTION & ARMED RECON	COUNTER AIR OFFENSIVE	COUNTER AIR DEFENSIVE	RECON	MISC
Total	b/ 313,600	49,299	97,885	557	334	563	1,063	b/ 1,668,531	254,729	733,575	52,927	6,883	17,382	15,279
July - 1950 c/	11,933	NOT AVAILABLE						35,957	NOT AVAILABLE					
August	23,277							86,086						
September	24,030							78,854						
October	16,064							50,591						
November	22,363							64,895						
December	23,539							93,750						
January - 1951	22,575							94,612						
February	20,118							83,011						
March	26,139	11,897	14,058	160	-	24	-	114,972	51,046	57,982	3,344	438	2,161	1
April	17,935	4,084	13,663	146	30	12	-	88,610	24,459	62,163	1,137	266	412	173
May	20,392	3,189	16,684	52	304	99	64	90,732	25,331	63,598	439	825	427	112
June	13,881	2,644	10,946	107	-	-	184	69,498	19,436	48,056	1,415	-	256	335
July	7,414	3,073	4,246	43	-	28	24	44,215	8,746	32,377	442	363	1,133	1,154
August	4,960	2,039	2,897	-	-	24	-	47,350	7,374	39,112	281	5	187	391
September	7,264	2,029	5,159	8	-	44	24	60,470	8,436	49,040	738	843	1,045	368
October	7,801	2,977	4,703	8	-	-	113	70,138	20,942	44,224	1,727	366	1,330	1,549
November	6,221	2,760	3,423	-	-	-	38	72,035	12,875	56,753	1,142	452	383	430
December	4,365	525	3,610	-	-	93	137	58,150	2,294	52,253	1,590	32	1,343	638
January - 1952	3,749	576	3,125	9	-	-	39	39,218	2,274	33,973	1,750	-	1,021	200
February	2,122	139	1,906	24	-	-	53	28,040	840	24,415	1,876	25	441	443
March	3,928	2,619	1,304	-	-	1	4	30,643	10,179	16,360	3,305	35	485	279
April	1,864	1,578	244	-	-	8	34	27,196	6,337	15,268	3,480	52	885	1,174
May	4,321	1,786	2,515	-	-	-	20	35,808	6,598	24,267	2,971	159	776	1,037
June	4,112	2,506	1,606	-	-	-	-	32,780	6,587	22,911	908	145	1,229	1,000
July	3,681	1,246	2,385	-	-	26	24	20,698	3,750	14,809	985	58	408	688
August	2,111	1,212	851	-	-	6	42	17,608	4,463	9,654	1,807	339	444	901
September	1,983	1,085	875	-	-	-	23	14,648	4,048	6,233	3,082	643	177	465
October	3,835	1,262	2,502	-	-	65	6	18,631	6,141	7,889	3,104	214	321	962
November	450	14	385	-	-	40	11	14,529	5,378	7,168	1,459	105	112	307
December	605	59	309	-	-	90	147	12,166	2,602	5,032	3,077	149	570	736
January - 1953	287	-	228	-	-	3	56	11,851	1,638	7,140	2,305	190	322	256
February	78	-	78	-	-	-	-	9,101	1,640	4,896	1,841	290	126	308
March	-	-	-	-	-	-	-	8,447	787	5,020	1,840	212	294	294
April	141	-	141	-	-	-	-	11,765	1,383	7,520	1,743	201	524	394
May	-	-	-	-	-	-	-	9,718	1,941	5,103	1,785	298	145	446
June	46	-	26	-	-	-	20	12,880	3,804	6,358	2,253	99	178	188
July (through the 27th)	16	-	16	-	-	-	-	8,878	3,400	4,001	1,101	79	247	50

a/ Does not include 55,797 Smoke Rockets expended by LT/T-6 type acft on Tactical Missions.
Source: Operations Statistics Division, Directorate of Statistical Services, DCS/C.

b/ Totals do not cross check.

c/ Includes 27 through 30 June 1950.

TABLE 28 — FEAF COMBAT CLAIMS BY USAF, USMC, AND FRIENDLY FOREIGN — 26 JUNE 1950 THROUGH 27 JULY 1953

TYPE CLAIM	DESTROYED					DAMAGED				
	TOTAL	JUN 50 JUN 51	JUL 51 JUN 52	JUL 52 JUN 53	JUL 53	TOTAL	JUN 50 JUN 51	JUL 51 JUN 52	JUL 52 JUN 53	JUL 53
FEAF - TOTAL										
Aircraft	976	159	312	470	35	1,218	234	465	501	18
Tanks	1,327	1,181	91	43	12	1,367	1,225	91	35	16
Vehicles	82,920	19,393	37,786	24,249	1,492	33,131	13,729	17,746	1,434	222
Locomotives	963	512	293	154	4	1,171	589	384	197	1
Railroad Cars	10,407	3,956	4,364	1,827	260	22,674	11,615	8,445	2,401	213
Railroad Cuts	-	-	-	-	-	28,621	1,235	24,251	3,029	106
Bridges	1,153	387	393	321	52	3,049	1,132	1,214	572	131
Buildings	118,231	85,781	16,321	15,476	653	88,461	61,497	23,006	3,862	96
Tunnels	65	29	29	7	-	939	623	259	56	1
Gun Positions	8,663	2,318	3,713	2,611	21	7,568	1,311	1,101	4,799	357
Bunkers	8,839	13	4,349	4,477	-	7,214	23	953	5,699	539
Oil Storage Tanks	16	16	-	-	-	3	2	-	1	-
Barges & Boats	593	316	225	51	1	821	435	284	102	-
Troops	184,808	156,524	23,179	5,020	85	-	-	-	-	-
USAF										
Aircraft	953	155	306	460	32	1,202	232	459	493	18
Tanks	1,156	1,087	46	13	10	1,208	1,103	67	23	15
Vehicles	74,589	14,705	34,827	23,583	1,474	29,597	11,247	17,041	1,100	209
Locomotives	869	444	272	149	4	1,085	549	346	189	1
Railroad Cars	9,358	3,578	3,899	1,642	239	21,090	11,029	7,711	2,148	202
Railroad Cuts	-	-	-	-	-	22,858	996	19,308	2,454	100
Bridges	827	279	249	252	47	2,256	851	855	439	111
Buildings	88,839	69,224	10,242	9,170	203	75,406	52,605	20,416	2,308	77
Tunnels	49	22	22	5	-	752	508	213	31	-
Gun Positions	5,163	1,906	1,906	1,342	9	4,259	1,110	709	2,239	201
Bunkers	3,702	1	1,601	2,100	-	3,205	8	197	2,774	226
Oil Storage Tanks	16	16	-	-	-	1	1	-	-	-
Barges & Boats	399	242	119	38	-	726	419	231	76	-
Troops	145,416	130,495	13,606	1,250	65	-	-	-	-	-
USMC										
Aircraft	20	4	3	10	3	8	2	-	6	-
Tanks	142	68	44	28	2	130	96	22	11	1
Vehicles	5,943	4,134	1,560	232	17	2,824	2,317	385	116	6
Locomotives	77	59	15	3	-	82	38	38	6	-
Railroad Cars	753	265	344	143	1	1,012	464	414	128	6
Railroad Cuts	-	-	-	-	-	4,762	196	4,077	488	1
Bridges	316	106	144	61	5	717	253	327	117	20
Buildings	19,290	10,722	3,747	4,486	335	8,125	5,475	1,565	1,085	-
Tunnels	13	6	6	1	-	151	91	40	20	-
Gun Positions	3,370	377	1,761	1,220	12	2,896	128	350	2,329	89
Bunkers	4,872	11	2,647	2,214	-	3,275	14	661	2,470	130
Oil Storage Tanks	-	-	-	-	-	2	1	-	1	-
Barges & Boats	149	50	86	12	1	63	11	33	19	-
Troops	35,451	22,699	9,152	3,580	20	-	-	-	-	-
FRIENDLY FOREIGN										
Aircraft	3	-	3	-	-	8	-	6	2	-
Tanks	29	26	1	2	-	29	26	2	1	-
Vehicles	2,388	554	1,399	434	1	710	165	320	218	7
Locomotives	17	9	6	2	-	4	2	-	2	-
Railroad Cars	296	113	121	42	20	572	122	320	125	5
Railroad Cuts	-	-	-	-	-	1,001	43	866	87	5
Bridges	10	2	-	8	-	76	28	32	16	-
Buildings	10,102	5,835	2,332	1,820	115	4,930	3,417	1,025	469	19
Tunnels	3	1	1	1	-	36	24	6	5	1
Gun Positions	130	35	46	49	-	413	73	42	231	67
Bunkers	265	1	101	163	-	734	1	95	455	183
Oil Storage Tanks	-	-	-	-	-	-	-	-	-	-
Barges & Boats	45	24	20	1	-	32	5	20	7	-
Troops	3,941	3,330	421	190	-	-	-	-	-	-

Source: Operations Statistics Division, Directorate of Statistical Services, DCS/C.

TABLE 29 — USAF CLAIMS OF ENEMY AIRCRAFT BY TYPE AIRCRAFT — 26 JUNE 1950 THROUGH 27 JULY 1953

TYPE CLAIM & TYPE ENEMY AIRCRAFT	TOTAL AIR TO AIR & AIR TO GROUND	AIR-TO-AIR - BY TYPE MODEL USAF AIRCRAFT										TOTAL AIR TO GROUND
		TOTAL	B-26	B-29	F-51	F-80	F-82	F-84	F-86	F-94	RB-29	
Destroyed - All Types	953	a/900	7	18	9	37	4	9	810	4	1	53
TU-2	9	9	-	-	-	-	-	-	9	-	-	-
YAK-3, 9 & 11	40	24	3	-	3	10	2	1	5	-	-	16
LA-5, 7 & 9	6	6	-	-	1	1	-	-	3	1	-	-
IL-2 & 10	5	a/ 5	-	-	4	-	-	-	-	-	-	-
MIG-15 & All Types	827	823	-	16	-	6	-	8	792	1	-	4
IL-12	1	1	-	-	-	-	-	-	1	-	-	-
PO-2	5	5	4	-	-	-	-	-	-	1	-	-
Ftr Unidentified	59	26	-	2	1	20	2	-	-	-	1	33
Unidentified	1	1	-	-	-	-	-	-	-	1	-	-
Probable - All Types	193	168	-	11	3	21	2	12	118	1	-	25
TU-2	1	1	-	-	1	-	-	-	-	-	-	-
YAK-3, 9 & 11	16	7	-	-	1	6	-	-	-	-	-	9
LA-5, 7 & 9	-	-	-	-	-	-	-	-	-	-	-	-
IL-2 & 10	1	1	-	-	1	-	-	-	-	-	-	-
MIG-15 & All Types	148	145	-	7	-	8	-	11	118	1	-	3
IL-12	-	-	-	-	-	-	-	-	-	-	-	-
PO-2	-	-	-	-	-	-	-	-	-	-	-	-
Ftr Unidentified	27	14	-	4	-	7	2	1	-	-	-	13
Unidentified	-	-	-	-	-	-	-	-	-	-	-	-
Damaged - All Types	1,009	973	7	15	12	41	-	82	814	2	-	36
TU-2	4	4	-	-	-	-	-	-	4	-	-	-
YAK-3, 9 & 11	33	15	3	3	1	8	-	-	-	-	-	18
LA-5, 7 & 9	8	4	1	-	-	-	-	-	2	1	-	4
IL-2 & 10	3	3	-	-	2	1	-	-	-	-	-	-
MIG-15 & All Types	951	946	3	11	9	32	-	82	808	1	-	5
IL-12	-	-	-	-	-	-	-	-	-	-	-	-
PO-2	-	-	-	-	-	-	-	-	-	-	-	-
Ftr Unidentified	9	-	-	-	-	-	-	-	-	-	-	9
Unidentified	1	1	-	1	-	-	-	-	-	-	-	-

a/ Includes an IL-10 destroyed by an RF-51.
Source: Operations Statistics Division, Directorate of Statistical Services, DCS/C.

TABLE 30 — TOTAL AIR-TO-AIR CLAIMS BY TYPE MODEL USAF AIRCRAFT, BY MONTH — 26 JUNE 1950 THROUGH 27 JULY 1953

MONTH	ALL TYPES ENEMY AIRCRAFT										MIG - 15					
	TOTAL CLAIMS	B-26	B-29	F-51	F-80	F-82	F-84	F-86	F-94	RB-29	TOTAL CLAIMS	B-29	F-80	F-84	F-86	F-94
Total	a/ 900	7	18	9	37	4	9	810	4	1	823	16	6	8	792	1
July - 1950 b/	29	2	-	4	19	4	-	-	-	-	-	-	-	-	-	-
August	2	-	-	-	2	-	-	-	-	-	-	-	-	-	-	-
September	1	-	-	-	1	-	-	-	-	-	-	-	-	-	-	-
October	-	-	-	-	-	-	-	-	-	-	-	-	-	-	-	-
November	9	-	1	-	7	-	-	-	-	1	-	-	-	-	-	-
December	8	-	-	-	-	-	c/	d/ 8	-	-	8	-	-	c/	d/ 8	-
January - 1951	7	1	-	1	-	-	5	-	-	-	4	-	-	4	-	-
February	1	-	-	1	-	-	-	-	-	-	-	-	-	-	-	-
March	9	-	3	-	3	-	-	3	-	-	9	3	3	-	3	-
April	14	-	-	-	-	-	-	14	-	-	14	-	-	-	14	-
May	8	-	1	-	2	-	-	5	-	-	6	1	-	-	5	-
June	18	1	2	3	1	-	1	10	-	-	14	2	1	1	10	-
July	12	3	2	-	-	-	-	7	-	-	9	2	-	-	7	-
August	4	-	-	-	-	-	-	4	-	-	4	-	-	-	4	-
September	14	-	-	-	-	-	1	13	-	-	14	-	-	1	13	-
October	32	-	7	-	-	-	1	24	-	-	32	7	-	1	24	-
November	27	-	-	-	2	-	-	25	-	-	16	-	2	-	14	-
December	29	-	-	-	-	-	1	28	-	-	29	-	-	1	28	-
January - 1952	31	-	-	-	-	-	-	31	e/	-	31	-	-	-	31	-
February	17	-	-	-	-	f/	-	17	-	-	17	-	-	-	17	-
March	39	-	-	-	-	-	-	39	-	-	39	-	-	-	39	-
April	a/ 45	-	-	-	-	-	-	44	-	-	44	-	-	-	44	-
May	32	-	-	-	-	-	-	32	-	-	27	-	-	-	27	-
June	20	-	-	-	-	-	-	20	-	-	20	-	-	-	20	-
July	19	-	1	-	-	-	-	18	-	-	19	1	-	-	18	-
August	34	-	1	-	-	-	-	33	-	-	33	-	-	-	33	-
September	63	-	-	-	-	-	-	63	-	-	63	-	-	-	63	-
October	27	-	-	-	-	-	-	27	-	-	27	-	-	-	27	-
November	28	-	-	-	-	-	-	28	-	-	28	-	-	-	28	-
December	28	-	-	-	-	-	-	28	-	-	28	-	-	-	28	-
January - 1953	39	-	-	g/	-	-	-	38	1	-	37	-	-	-	37	-
February	25	-	-	-	-	-	-	25	-	-	25	-	-	-	25	-
March	34	-	-	-	-	-	-	34	-	-	34	-	-	-	34	-
April	27	-	-	-	-	-	-	27	-	-	27	-	-	-	27	-
May	58	-	-	-	-	-	-	56	2	-	56	-	-	-	56	-
June	78	-	-	-	-	-	-	77	1	-	78	-	-	-	77	1
July (through the 27th)	32	-	-	-	-	-	-	32	-	-	31	-	-	-	31	-

a/ Includes an IL-10 destroyed by an RF-51.
b/ Includes 26 through 30 Jun 50.
c/ F-84 type acft began operations Dec 50.
d/ F-86 type acft began operations Dec 50.
e/ F-94 type acft began operations Jan 52.
f/ F-82 type acft removed from combat status Feb 52.
g/ F-51 type acft removed from combat status Jan 53.

Source: Operations Statistics Division, Directorate of Statistical Services, DCS/C.

TABLE 31 — USAF CLAIMS OF ENEMY AIRCRAFT — AIR TO AIR — BY TYPE MISSION — 26 JUNE 1950 THROUGH 27 JULY 1953

MONTH	DESTROYED								PROBABLE						DAMAGED						
	TOTAL	ARMED RECON AND INTER-DICTION	COUNTER AIR OFFENSIVE			COUNTER AIR DE-FENSIVE	OTHER	UN-KNOWN	TOTAL	ARMED RECON AND INTER-DICTION	COUNTER AIR OFFENSIVE			OTHER AND UN-KNOWN	TOTAL	COUNTER AIR OFFENSIVE			COUNTER AIR DE-FENSIVE	OTHER	UNKNOWN
			TOTAL	PA-TROL	ES-CORT						TOTAL	PA-TROL	ES-CORT			TOTAL	PA-TROL	ES-CORT			
Total	900	55	787	722	65	30	22	6	168	34	126	121	5	8	973	612	554	58	18	18	325
July - 1950 a/	29	18	-	-	-	-	7	4	8	5	-	-	-	3	9	-	-	-	-	-	9
August	2	-	2	2	-	-	-	-	2	-	2	2	-	-	-	-	-	-	-	-	-
September	1	1	-	-	-	-	-	-	1	1	-	-	-	-	-	-	-	-	-	-	-
October	-	-	-	-	-	-	-	-	-	-	-	-	-	-	-	-	-	-	-	-	-
November	9	4	4	4	-	-	1	-	4	4	-	-	-	-	7	-	-	-	-	-	7
December	8	-	8	8	-	-	-	-	5	3	2	2	-	-	6	-	-	-	-	-	6
January - 1951	7	2	5	5	-	-	-	-	3	1	2	2	-	-	12	-	-	-	-	-	12
February	1	1	-	-	-	-	-	-	-	-	-	-	-	-	3	-	-	-	-	-	3
March	9	6	3	3	-	-	-	-	4	4	-	-	-	-	14	-	-	-	-	-	14
April	14	-	14	14	-	-	-	-	4	-	4	4	-	-	41	-	-	-	-	-	41
May	8	2	5	-	5	-	1	-	1	-	1	1	-	-	16	-	-	-	-	-	16
June	18	4	14	11	3	-	-	-	2	-	2	1	1	-	36	-	-	-	-	-	36
July	12	5	7	3	4	-	-	-	1	1	-	-	-	-	7	-	-	-	-	-	7
August	4	-	4	4	-	-	-	-	-	-	-	-	-	-	3	-	-	-	-	-	3
September	14	1	13	13	-	-	-	-	2	2	-	-	-	-	34	-	-	-	-	-	34
October	32	7	25	24	1	-	-	-	8	7	1	-	1	-	48	-	-	-	-	-	48
November	27	2	25	25	-	-	-	-	7	4	3	3	-	-	51	-	-	-	-	-	51
December	29	1	28	27	1	-	-	-	5	-	5	5	-	-	38	-	-	-	-	-	38
January - 1952	31	-	29	29	-	-	2	-	3	-	3	3	-	-	19	17	17	-	-	2	-
February	17	-	17	17	-	-	-	-	4	-	3	3	-	1	43	42	42	-	-	1	-
March	39	-	39	33	6	-	-	-	9	-	9	9	-	-	76	76	73	3	-	-	-
April	45	1	44	40	4	-	-	-	7	-	7	7	-	-	52	52	50	2	-	-	-
May	32	-	32	32	-	-	-	-	3	-	3	3	-	-	24	20	16	4	-	4	-
June	20	-	19	19	-	1	-	-	2	-	1	1	-	1	6	6	4	2	-	-	-
July	19	-	18	18	-	-	-	1	5	-	4	4	-	1	11	11	10	1	-	-	-
August	34	-	22	20	2	10	1	1	4	-	4	4	-	-	35	33	23	10	2	-	-
September	63	-	61	55	6	2	-	-	8	1	7	7	-	-	61	56	48	8	3	2	-
October	27	-	27	25	2	-	-	-	1	-	1	1	-	-	26	26	19	7	-	-	-
November	28	-	25	20	5	3	-	-	6	1	5	5	-	-	18	16	15	1	2	-	-
December	28	-	23	19	4	1	4	-	8	-	7	7	-	1	29	24	22	2	3	2	-
January - 1953	39	-	37	33	4	2	-	-	9	-	9	9	-	-	47	42	39	3	4	1	-
February	25	-	21	21	-	4	-	-	6	-	5	5	-	1	41	39	35	4	2	-	-
March	34	-	32	28	4	2	-	-	10	-	10	9	1	-	39	37	36	1	1	1	-
April	27	-	27	27	-	-	-	-	8	-	8	8	-	-	33	30	29	1	-	3	-
May	58	-	54	50	4	4	-	-	5	-	5	5	-	-	30	29	28	1	-	1	-
June	78	-	77	68	9	1	-	-	11	-	11	9	2	-	42	41	33	8	1	-	-
July (thru the 27th)	32	-	26	25	1	-	6	-	2	-	2	2	-	-	16	15	15	-	-	1	-

a/ Includes 26 through 30 June 1950.
Source: Operations Statistics Division, Directorate of Statistical Services, DCS/C.

TABLE 32 – USAF AIRCRAFT CLAIMS OF ENEMY AIRCRAFT, BY TYPE MISSION, BY MONTH – 26 JUNE 1950 THROUGH 27 JULY 1953

MONTH	TOTAL	CLOSE SUPPORT	INTERDICTION AND ARMED RECON	COUNTER AIR OFFENSIVE	COUNTER AIR DEFENSIVE	RECON	RESCUE	MISC
Total	900	7	55	791	30	8	4	5
July - 1950 a/	29	6	18	4	-	1	-	-
August	2	-	-	2	-	-	-	-
September	1	-	1	-	-	-	-	-
October	-	-	-	-	-	-	-	-
November	9	-	4	4	-	1	-	-
December	8	-	-	8	-	-	-	-
January - 1951	7	-	2	5	-	-	-	-
February	1	-	1	-	-	-	-	-
March	9	-	6	3	-	-	-	-
April	14	-	-	14	-	-	-	-
May	8	1	2	5	-	-	-	-
June	18	-	4	14	-	-	-	-
July	12	-	5	7	-	-	-	-
August	4	-	-	4	-	-	-	-
September	14	-	1	13	-	-	-	-
October	32	-	7	25	-	-	-	-
November	27	-	2	25	-	-	-	-
December	29	-	1	28	-	-	-	-
January - 1952	31	-	-	29	-	-	2	-
February	17	-	-	17	-	-	-	-
March	39	-	-	39	-	-	-	-
April	45	-	1	44	-	-	-	-
May	32	-	-	32	-	-	-	-
June	20	-	-	19	1	-	-	-
July	19	-	-	18	-	-	-	1
August	34	-	-	22	10	-	-	2
September	63	-	-	61	2	-	-	-
October	27	-	-	27	-	-	-	-
November	28	-	-	25	3	-	-	-
December	28	-	-	23	1	-	2	2
January - 1953	39	-	-	37	2	-	-	-
February	25	-	-	21	4	-	-	-
March	34	-	-	32	2	-	-	-
April	27	-	-	27	-	-	-	-
May	58	-	-	54	4	-	-	-
June	78	-	-	77	1	-	-	-
July (through the 27th)	32	-	-	26	-	6	-	-

a/ Includes 26 through 30 June 1950.
Source: Operations Statistics Division, Directorate of Statistical Services, DCS/C.

TABLE 33 — TOTAL USAF AIRCRAFT LOSSES BY TYPE OF LOSS, BY MONTH — 26 JUNE 1950 THROUGH 27 JULY 1953

MONTH	TOTAL LOSSES	OPERATIONAL							NON-OPERATIONAL						
		TOTAL OPNL LOSSES	ENEMY ACTION				NOT ENEMY ACTION	* UNKNOWN	TOTAL NON-OPNL LOSSES	ENEMY ACTION	ABANDONMENT ENEMY ACTION	FLYING ACCIDENT	GROUND ACCIDENT	FAIR WEAR & TEAR	RECLAMATION SALVAGE
			* TOTAL	AIR TO AIR	GROUND FIRE	CAUSE/ UNKNOWN									
Total	1,747	1,466	757	139	550	68	472	237	281	9	14	235	15	3	5
July - 1950 a/	56	36	25	4	20	1	5	6	20	5	-	12	1	1	1
August	44	38	23	1	21	1	11	4	6	1	-	5	-	-	-
September	54	50	25	-	24	1	17	8	4	-	-	4	-	-	-
October	59	48	18	1	16	1	19	11	11	-	-	11	-	-	-
November	52	46	17	1	15	1	24	5	6	-	-	6	-	-	-
December	69	51	10	2	7	1	28	13	18	-	10	8	-	-	-
January - 1951	44	34	7	2	5	-	24	3	10	-	2	8	-	-	-
February	54	45	12	-	11	1	24	9	9	-	-	8	1	-	-
March	55	51	21	2	17	2	16	14	4	-	-	4	-	-	-
April	84	73	42	4	36	2	14	17	11	-	2	9	-	-	-
May	63	54	24	-	23	1	20	10	9	-	-	6	2	1	-
June	68	59	31	7	22	2	18	10	9	1	-	6	1	-	1
July	59	49	21	1	16	4	17	11	10	-	-	9	-	1	-
August	59	50	28	3	23	2	13	9	9	-	-	9	-	-	-
September	53	46	27	6	21	-	11	8	7	1	-	6	-	-	-
October	68	58	38	14	23	1	16	4	10	-	-	10	-	-	-
November	39	34	23	8	11	4	9	2	5	-	-	5	-	-	-
December	46	40	31	9	21	1	4	5	6	-	-	6	-	-	-
January - 1952	65	59	37	5	28	4	12	10	6	-	-	6	-	-	-
February	51	48	24	4	19	1	17	7	3	-	-	3	-	-	-
March	44	40	23	4	16	3	11	6	4	-	-	3	1	-	-
April	43	36	24	5	15	4	8	4	7	-	-	6	1	-	-
May	52	47	31	9	17	5	11	5	5	-	-	4	-	-	1
June	36	28	16	4	10	2	9	3	8	-	-	6	1	-	1
July	34	25	13	4	8	1	7	5	9	-	-	9	-	-	-
August	32	27	15	2	10	3	8	4	5	-	-	4	1	-	-
September	37	29	17	10	4	3	6	6	8	-	-	8	-	-	-
October	42	34	21	5	13	3	8	5	8	1	-	7	-	-	-
November	30	22	15	5	8	2	5	2	8	-	-	8	-	-	-
December	31	22	9	3	6	-	10	3	9	-	-	5	4	-	-
January - 1953	34	30	16	3	10	3	11	3	4	-	-	4	-	-	-
February	25	16	11	2	5	4	4	1	9	-	-	8	-	-	1
March	27	19	10	2	7	1	6	3	8	-	-	8	-	-	-
April	27	24	12	4	6	2	7	5	3	-	-	3	-	-	-
May	29	27	9	1	8	-	13	5	2	-	-	2	-	-	-
June	44	38	18	-	18	-	14	6	6	-	-	6	-	-	-
July (through the 27th)	38	33	13	2	10	1	15	5	5	-	-	3	2	-	-

a/ Includes 26 through 30 June 1950.
Source: Operations Statistics Division, Directorate of Statistical Services, DCS/C.

TABLE 34 – TOTAL USAF AIRCRAFT LOSSES BY TYPE MODEL, BY MONTH–26 JUNE 1950 THROUGH 27 JULY 1953

MONTH	TOTAL	B-26	B-29	F-51	F-80	F-82	F-84	F-86	F-94	RB/ WB-26	RB/ WB-29	RF-51	RF-80	C-46	VC/ C-47	C-54	C-119	C-124	LT/ T-6	H-5 YH/H-19	SA-16 SB-29	MISC
Total	1,747	203	69	322	324	17	305	218	12	16	6	23	25	23	21	15	19	1	76	25	3	a/ 24
July - 1950 b/	56	12	1	76	21	4	-	-	-	-	1	-	-	-	1	5	-	-	2	1	-	2
August	44	2	-	28	4	1	-	-	-	-	-	-	-	1	2	-	-	-	6	-	-	-
September	54	3	4	23	9	2	-	-	-	-	-	-	2	-	1	2	1	-	3	2	-	2
October	59	3	2	21	20	-	-	-	-	4	-	-	1	-	1	-	2	-	3	-	-	2
November	52	5	2	16	13	-	-	-	-	-	1	-	1	1	2	2	1	-	4	2	-	2
December	69	7	1	20	19	3	c/ 4	d/ 1	-	-	-	h/	1	2	2	1	1	-	5	-	-	2
January - 1951	44	9	-	4	10	1	2	-	-	1	-	-	2	6	2	2	-	-	3	-	2	-
February	54	13	-	10	20	-	1	2	-	-	-	1	-	-	-	1	-	-	3	1	-	2
March	55	5	1	16	20	1	2	-	-	-	-	1	1	-	-	2	2	-	2	2	-	-
April	84	10	8	27	21	-	3	3	-	-	-	1	-	1	3	-	-	-	6	1	-	-
May	63	7	1	14	27	2	2	4	-	-	-	-	1	-	-	-	1	-	1	-	-	3
June	68	7	1	16	20	-	7	6	-	3	-	1	1	1	-	-	2	-	2	1	-	-
July	59	7	-	17	12	1	11	4	-	2	-	-	-	1	-	-	-	-	3	-	-	1
August	59	8	1	15	15	1	10	1	-	-	-	1	1	2	1	-	-	-	1	1	-	1
September	53	11	2	10	8	-	6	6	-	-	-	-	-	1	2	-	1	i/	4	2	-	-
October	68	10	9	8	10	-	14	8	-	3	-	1	1	-	-	-	-	-	3	1	-	-
November	39	2	3	7	8	1	11	4	-	-	-	-	-	-	-	-	-	-	2	1	-	-
December	46	3	1	9	7	-	14	9	-	-	-	1	-	-	-	-	1	-	1	-	-	-
January - 1952	65	6	4	9	9	-	18	12	e/	-	-	2	1	1	-	-	1	-	1	1	-	-
February	51	3	3	7	3	f/	18	5	1	1	-	5	3	2	-	-	-	-	-	-	-	-
March	44	6	2	7	1	-	20	5	-	-	-	1	-	-	-	-	-	-	1	1	-	-
April	43	7	2	10	8	-	8	5	-	-	-	-	1	-	1	-	1	-	-	-	-	-
May	52	8	-	8	4	-	15	11	-	1	-	2	-	-	-	-	-	-	2	1	-	-
June	36	7	6	3	2	-	4	6	1	-	1	-	1	-	-	-	-	-	1	1	-	3
July	34	3	1	1	3	-	12	8	-	-	1	-	1	-	-	-	1	-	1	1	-	1
August	32	5	2	2	3	-	8	7	-	-	-	2	1	-	-	-	-	-	1	-	-	1
September	37	1	3	1	3	-	14	12	-	-	-	-	-	1	-	-	-	-	-	1	-	1
October	42	3	-	3	3	-	16	8	-	-	1	2	1	1	-	-	1	-	2	1	-	-
November	30	2	3	2	4	-	8	7	1	-	-	-	-	1	-	-	1	-	1	-	-	-
December	31	10	1	1	2	-	6	7	1	-	-	2	-	-	-	-	-	-	1	-	-	-
January - 1953	34	3	4	g/ 1	5	-	10	6	3	-	-	-	1	-	-	-	-	-	-	-	1	-
February	25	4	-	-	4	-	10	6	-	-	1	j/	-	-	-	-	-	-	-	-	-	-
March	27	1	-	-	4	-	12	7	-	-	-	-	-	-	-	-	1	-	1	1	-	-
April	27	3	-	-	1	-	9	8	-	-	-	-	1	1	-	-	-	-	3	1	-	-
May	29	2	-	-	-	-	10	11	1	-	-	-	1	-	-	-	-	-	4	-	-	-
June	44	-	-	-	-	-	8	27	3	-	-	-	-	-	1	-	1	1	1	1	-	1
July (through the 27th)	38	5	1	-	1	-	12	12	1	1	-	-	1	-	2	-	-	-	2	-	-	-

a/ Includes 1 RB-45, Dec 50; 1 RB-45,Jun 52; 1 RF-86,Jun 52; 1 RF-86,Sep 52; 1 RF-86,Jun 53; 1 C-45;Dec 50; 1 C-45,Feb 51; 1 L-5,Jun 50; 1 L-5,Sep 50; 2 L-5,Oct 50; 1 L-5, Nov 50; 1 L-5,May 51; 1 L-5,Jul 51; 1 L-5,Jun 52; 1 L-5,Aug 52; 1 T-33,Jul 50; 1 T-33,Sep 50; 1 T-33,Nov 50; 1 T-33,Feb 51; 2 T-33,May 51; 1 T-33,Aug 51; 1 T-33,Jul 52.
b/ Includes 26 through 30 Jun 50.
c/ F-84 type acft began operations Dec 50.
d/ F-86 type acft began operations Dec 50.
e/ F-94 type acft began operations Jan 52.
f/ F-82 type acft removed from combat status Feb 52.
g/ F-51 type acft removed from combat status Jan 53.
h/ RF-51 type acft began operations Dec 50.
i/ C-124 type acft began operations Sep 51.
j/ RF-51 type acft removed from combat status Feb 53.
Source: Operations Statistics Division, Directorate of Statistical Services, DCS/C.

TABLE 35 – TOTAL USAF AIRCRAFT OPERATIONAL LOSSES BY TYPE MODEL, BY MONTH – 26 JUNE 1950 THROUGH 27 JULY 1953

MONTH	TOTAL	B-26	B-29	F-51	F-80	F-82	F-84	F-86	F-94	RB/ WB-26	RB/ WB-29	RF-51	RF-80	C-46	VC/ C-47	C-54	C-119	C-124	LT/ T-6	H-5 YH/H-19	SA-16 SB-29	MISC
Total	1,466	168	57	300	277	11	249	184	9	7	3	22	22	16	13	9	11	1	68	21	2	a/16
July - 1950 b/	36	11	1	5	12	2	-	-	-	-	-	-	-	-	1	1	-	-	1	1	-	1
August	38	2	-	25	3	1	-	-	-	-	-	-	-	-	2	-	-	-	5	-	-	-
September	50	3	4	22	9	1	-	-	-	-	-	-	2	-	1	1	-	-	3	2	-	2
October	48	3	2	20	15	-	-	-	-	-	-	-	1	-	1	-	1	-	3	-	-	2
November	46	5	2	16	9	-	-	-	-	-	1	-	1	1	1	2	1	-	4	2	-	1
December	51	7	-	13	17	1	c/ 2	d/ 1	-	-	-	h/	1	2	1	1	1	-	2	-	-	2
January - 1951	34	7	-	4	7	1	2	-	-	1	-	-	1	4	1	2	-	-	3	-	1	-
February	45	10	-	10	19	-	1	-	-	-	-	1	-	-	-	1	-	-	3	-	-	-
March	51	4	1	16	19	1	2	-	-	-	-	1	1	-	-	1	2	-	2	1	-	-
April	73	9	8	26	18	-	3	2	-	-	-	1	-	-	1	-	-	-	4	1	-	-
May	54	5	1	12	27	1	1	3	-	-	-	-	1	-	-	-	-	-	1	-	-	2
June	59	6	1	16	16	-	6	5	-	2	-	1	1	1	-	-	2	-	2	-	-	-
July	49	7	-	14	10	1	11	2	-	-	-	-	-	-	-	-	-	-	3	-	-	1
August	50	6	1	15	15	1	6	1	-	-	-	1	1	1	-	-	-	-	1	1	-	-
September	46	11	2	9	6	-	5	6	-	-	-	-	-	1	-	-	-	i/	4	2	-	-
October	58	6	7	8	9	-	13	8	-	1	-	1	1	-	-	-	-	-	3	1	-	-
November	34	2	3	6	6	1	10	3	-	-	-	-	-	-	-	-	-	-	2	1	-	-
December	40	3	1	9	6	-	12	7	-	-	-	1	-	-	-	-	-	-	1	-	-	-
January - 1952	59	5	4	9	9	-	16	11	e/	-	-	2	1	-	-	-	-	-	1	1	-	-
February	48	3	2	7	3	f/	16	5	1	1	-	5	3	2	-	-	-	-	-	-	-	-
March	40	6	1	7	-	-	19	4	-	-	-	1	-	-	-	-	-	-	1	1	-	-
April	36	4	1	10	7	-	7	5	-	-	-	-	-	-	1	-	1	-	-	-	-	-
May	47	6	-	8	4	-	14	10	-	1	-	1	-	-	-	-	-	-	2	1	-	-
June	28	5	2	3	2	-	3	6	-	-	1	-	1	-	-	-	-	-	1	1	-	3
July	25	3	1	1	2	-	8	6	-	-	1	-	1	-	-	-	-	-	1	1	-	-
August	27	4	2	2	3	-	7	6	-	-	-	2	-	-	-	-	-	-	-	-	-	1
September	29	-	1	1	3	-	10	12	-	-	-	-	-	1	-	-	-	-	-	1	-	-
October	34	2	-	2	3	-	14	7	-	-	-	2	1	1	-	-	-	-	2	-	-	-
November	22	2	3	2	4	-	4	4	-	-	-	-	-	1	-	-	1	-	1	-	-	-
December	22	6	1	1	2	-	3	5	1	-	-	2	-	-	-	-	-	-	1	-	-	-
January - 1953	30	3	4	g/ 1	4	-	9	4	3	-	-	-	1	-	-	-	-	-	-	-	1	-
February	16	2	-	-	3	-	6	5	-	-	-	j/	-	-	-	-	-	-	-	-	-	-
March	19	1	-	-	3	-	7	5	-	-	-	-	-	-	-	-	1	-	1	1	-	-
April	24	3	-	-	1	-	7	7	-	-	-	-	1	1	-	-	-	-	3	1	-	-
May	27	2	-	-	-	-	8	11	1	-	-	-	1	-	-	-	-	-	4	-	-	-
June	38	-	-	-	-	-	7	23	2	-	-	-	-	-	1	-	1	1	1	1	-	1
July (thru the 27th)	33	4	1	-	1	-	10	10	1	1	-	-	1	-	2	-	-	-	2	-	-	-

a/ Includes: 1 RB-45, Dec 50; 1 RB-45, Jun 52; 1 RF-86, Jun 52; 1 RF-86, Jun 53; 1 C-45, Dec 50; 1 L-5, Jun 50; 1 L-5, Sep 50; 2 L-5, Oct 50; 1 L-5, Nov 50; 1 L-5, May 51; 1 L-5, Jul 51; 1 L-5, Jun 52; 1 L-5, Aug 52; 1 T-33, Sep 50; 1 T-33, May 51

b/ Includes 26 through 30 June 1950.

c/ F-84 type acft began operations Dec 50.

d/ F-86 type acft began operations Dec 50.

e/ F-94 type acft began operations Jan 52.

f/ F-82 type acft removed from combat status Feb 52.

g/ F-51 type acft removed from combat status Jan 53.

h/ RF-51 type acft began operations Dec 50.

i/ C-124 type acft began operations Sep 51.

j/ RF-51 type acft removed from combat status Feb 53.

Source: Operations Statistics Division, Directorate of Statistical Services, DCS/C.

TABLE 36 — TOTAL USAF AIRCRAFT LOSSES TO ENEMY ACTION BY TYPE MODEL, BY MONTH — 26 JUNE 1950 THROUGH 27 JULY 1953

MONTH	TOTAL	B-26	B-29	F-51	F-80	F-82	F-84	F-86	F-94	WB-26	RF-51	RF-80	VC/C-47	C-119	LT/T-6	H-5 YH/H-19	MISC
Total	757	56	24	194	143	4	153	110	1	1	19	3	2	2	39	5	a/ 1
July - 1950 b/	25	7	1	4	10	1	-	-	-	-	-	-	-	-	1	1	-
August	23	1	-	18	2	1	-	-	-	-	-	-	-	-	1	-	-
September	25	1	-	13	5	1	-	-	-	-	-	-	1	-	3	1	-
October	18	-	-	11	6	-	-	-	-	-	-	-	-	-	1	-	-
November	17	4	1	8	2	-	-	-	-	-	-	-	-	-	2	-	-
December	10	1	-	3	3	-	c/	d/ 1	-	-	h/	-	-	1	1	-	-
January - 1951	7	2	-	1	1	-	1	-	-	-	-	-	1	-	1	-	-
February	12	2	-	4	3	-	-	-	-	-	1	-	-	-	2	-	-
March	21	1	-	7	9	-	1	-	-	-	1	-	-	1	1	-	-
April	42	4	5	17	12	-	2	-	-	-	-	-	-	-	2	-	-
May	24	4	1	8	11	-	-	-	-	-	-	-	-	-	-	-	-
June	31	2	1	14	9	-	2	2	-	-	1	-	-	-	-	-	-
July	21	2	-	7	7	1	2	1	-	-	-	-	-	-	1	-	-
August	28	1	1	11	8	-	4	-	-	-	1	1	-	-	1	-	-
September	27	3	-	8	4	-	4	3	-	-	-	-	-	-	4	1	-
October	38	2	5	5	6	-	7	7	-	-	1	1	-	-	3	1	-
November	23	-	2	4	6	-	7	3	-	-	-	-	-	-	1	-	-
December	31	1	-	8	5	-	9	7	-	-	1	-	-	-	-	-	-
January - 1952	37	1	-	9	6	-	13	5	e/	-	2	-	-	-	1	-	-
February	24	-	-	5	2	f/	9	2	1	-	5	-	-	-	-	-	-
March	23	2	-	5	-	-	12	3	-	-	1	-	-	-	-	-	-
April	24	-	-	9	6	-	5	4	-	-	-	-	-	-	-	-	-
May	31	1	-	5	3	-	13	6	-	1	1	-	-	-	1	-	-
June	16	2	1	3	1	-	2	4	-	-	-	-	-	-	1	1	1
July	13	-	-	1	2	-	4	5	-	-	-	-	-	-	1	-	-
August	15	2	-	1	3	-	4	4	-	-	1	-	-	-	-	-	-
September	17	-	1	1	1	-	5	9	-	-	-	-	-	-	-	-	-
October	21	1	-	1	1	-	9	5	-	-	2	-	-	-	2	-	-
November	15	2	1	2	2	-	3	4	-	-	-	-	-	-	1	-	-
December	9	2	1	-	-	-	2	2	-	-	1	-	-	-	1	-	-
January - 1953	16	-	3	g/ 1	4	-	6	2	-	-	-	-	-	-	-	-	-
February	11	2	-	-	1	-	4	4	-	-	i/	-	-	-	-	-	-
March	10	-	-	-	-	-	7	3	-	-	-	-	-	-	-	-	-
April	12	1	-	-	1	-	3	5	-	-	-	-	-	-	2	-	-
May	9	1	-	-	-	-	5	1	-	-	-	-	-	-	2	-	-
June	18	-	-	-	-	-	3	14	-	-	-	-	-	-	1	-	-
July (thru the 27th)	13	1	-	-	1	-	5	4	-	-	-	1	-	-	1	-	-

a/ 1 RF-86, June 1952.
b/ Includes 26 through 30 June 1950.
c/ F-84 type acft began operations Dec 50.
d/ F-86 type acft began operations Dec 50.
e/ F-94 type acft began operations Jan 52.
f/ F-82 type acft removed from combat status Feb 52.
g/ F-51 type acft removed from combat status Jan 53.
h/ RF-51 type acft began operations Dec 50.
i/ RF-51 type acft removed from combat status Feb 53.

Source: Operations Statistics Division, Directorate of Statistical Services, DCS/C.

TABLE 37 – USAF AIRCRAFT LOSSES (AIR – TO – AIR AND ENEMY ACTION CAUSE UNKNOWN) BY TYPE MODEL, BY MONTH – 26 JUNE 1950 THROUGH 27 JULY 1953

MONTH	AIR - TO - AIR								ENEMY ACTION CAUSE UNKNOWN									
	TOTAL	B-29	F-51	F-80	F-84	F-86	F-94	RF-80	TOTAL	B-26	B-29	F-51	F-80	F-84	F-86	RB/ WB-26	RF-51	RF-80
Total	139	17	10	14	18	78	1	1	68	8	2	12	16	13	13	1	2	1
July - 1950 a/	4	1	-	3	-	-	-	-	1	1	-	-	-	-	-	-	-	-
August	1	-	1	-	-	-	-	-	1	-	-	1	-	-	-	-	-	-
September	-	-	-	-	-	-	-	-	1	-	-	1	-	-	-	-	-	-
October	1	-	1	-	-	-	-	-	1	-	-	-	1	-	-	-	-	-
November	1	1	-	-	-	-	-	-	1	-	-	1	-	-	-	-	-	-
December	2	-	-	1	b/	c/ 1	-	-	1	-	-	-	1	b/	c/	-	f/	-
January - 1951	2	-	-	1	1	-	-	-	-	-	-	-	-	-	-	-	-	-
February	-	-	-	-	-	-	-	-	1	-	-	-	1	-	-	-	-	-
March	2	-	-	2	-	-	-	-	2	-	-	-	2	-	-	-	-	-
April	4	4	-	-	-	-	-	-	2	-	-	2	-	-	-	-	-	-
May	-	-	-	-	-	-	-	-	1	-	-	-	1	-	-	-	-	-
June	7	1	2	2	-	2	-	-	2	1	-	-	1	-	-	-	-	-
July	1	-	1	-	-	-	-	-	4	1	-	1	1	-	1	-	-	-
August	3	-	3	-	-	-	-	-	2	-	-	-	2	-	-	-	-	-
September	6	-	1	1	1	3	-	-	-	-	-	-	-	-	-	-	-	-
October	14	4	-	-	2	7	-	1	1	-	-	-	-	-	-	-	1	-
November	8	1	-	1	3	3	-	-	4	-	-	1	1	2	-	-	-	-
December	9	-	-	2	1	6	-	-	1	-	-	-	-	-	1	-	-	-
January - 1952	5	-	-	-	-	5	d/	-	4	-	-	-	-	3	-	-	1	-
February	4	-	-	-	1	2	1	-	1	-	-	-	1	-	-	-	-	-
March	4	-	-	-	2	2	-	-	3	-	-	-	-	2	1	-	-	-
April	5	-	-	1	-	4	-	-	4	-	-	1	3	-	-	-	-	-
May	9	-	1	-	3	5	-	-	5	1	-	1	-	1	1	1	-	-
June	4	1	-	-	-	3	-	-	2	1	-	1	-	-	-	-	-	-
July	4	-	-	-	-	4	-	-	1	-	-	-	-	-	1	-	-	-
August	2	-	-	-	-	2	-	-	3	-	-	-	-	1	2	-	-	-
September	10	-	-	-	3	7	-	-	3	-	1	-	-	1	1	-	-	-
October	5	-	-	-	1	4	-	-	3	-	-	-	1	1	1	-	-	-
November	5	1	-	-	-	4	-	-	2	1	-	1	-	-	-	-	-	-
December	3	1	-	-	-	2	-	-	-	-	-	-	-	-	-	-	-	-
January - 1953	3	2	e/	-	-	1	-	-	3	-	1	e/ 1	-	-	1	-	-	-
February	2	-	-	-	-	2	-	-	4	2	-	-	-	-	2	-	g/	-
March	2	-	-	-	-	2	-	-	1	-	-	-	-	1	-	-	-	-
April	4	-	-	-	-	4	-	-	2	-	-	-	-	1	1	-	-	-
May	1	-	-	-	-	1	-	-	-	-	-	-	-	-	-	-	-	-
June	-	-	-	-	-	-	-	-	-	-	-	-	-	-	-	-	-	-
July (Thru the 27th)	2	-	-	-	-	2	-	-	1	-	-	-	-	-	-	-	-	1

a/ Includes 26 through 30 Jun 50.
b/ F-84 type acft began operations Dec 50.
c/ F-86 type acft began operations Dec 50.
d/ F-94 type acft began operations Jan 52.
e/ F-51 type acft removed from combat status Jan 53.
f/ RF-51 type acft began operations Dec 50.
g/ RF-51 type acft removed from combat status Feb 53.
Source: Operations Statistics Division, Directorate of Statistical Services, DCS/C.

TABLE 38 — USAF AIRCRAFT LOSSES TO ENEMY AIRCRAFT — 26 JUNE 1950 THROUGH 27 JULY 1953

ALL TYPES ENEMY AIRCRAFT	TOTAL AIR TO AIR LOSSES	B-26	B-29	F-51	F-80	F-84	F-86	F-94	RF-80
Destroyed - All Types	139	-	17	10	14	18	78	1	1
MIG-15.	118	-	15	3	8	15	76	-	1
YAK-9	1	-	1	-	-	-	-	-	-
Unidentified. . .	20	-	1	7	6	3	2	1	-
Major Damage - All Types	78	1	9	2	3	7	56	-	-
MIG-15.	73	-	9	2	2	7	53	-	-
LA-9.	1	-	-	-	-	-	1	-	-
Unidentified. . .	4	1	-	-	1	-	2	-	-
Minor Damage - All Types	8	-	1	-	-	3	4	-	-
MIG-15.	7	-	1	-	-	3	3	-	-
Unidentified. . .	1	-	-	-	-	-	1	-	-

Source: Operations Statistics Division, Directorate of Statistical Services, DCS/C.

308700 O - 54 - 6

TABLE 39 — USAF AIRCRAFT LOSSES (ENEMY GROUND FIRE) BY TYPE MODEL - BY MONTH — 26 JUNE 1950 THROUGH 27 JULY 1953

MONTH	TOTAL	B-26	B-29	F-51	F-80	F-82	F-84	F-86	RF-51	RF-80	VC/C-47	C-119	LT/T-6	H-5 YH/H-19	MISC
Total	550	48	5	172	113	4	122	19	17	1	2	2	39	5	a/ 1
July - 1950 b/	20	6	-	4	7	1	-	-	-	-	-	-	1	1	-
August	21	1	-	16	2	1	-	-	-	-	-	-	1	-	-
September	24	1	-	12	5	1	-	-	-	-	1	-	3	1	-
October	16	-	-	10	5	-	-	-	-	-	-	-	1	-	-
November	15	4	-	7	2	-	-	-	-	-	-	-	2	-	-
December	7	1	-	3	1	-	c/	d/	-	-	-	1	1	-	-
January - 1951	5	2	-	1	-	-	-	-	-	-	1	-	1	-	-
February	11	2	-	4	2	-	-	-	1	-	-	-	2	-	-
March	17	1	-	7	5	-	1	-	1	-	-	1	1	-	-
April	36	4	1	15	12	-	2	-	-	-	-	-	2	-	-
May	23	4	1	8	10	-	-	-	-	-	-	-	-	-	-
June	22	1	-	12	6	-	2	-	1	-	-	-	-	-	-
July	16	1	-	5	6	1	2	-	-	-	-	-	1	-	-
August	23	1	1	8	6	-	4	-	1	1	-	-	1	-	-
September	21	3	-	7	3	-	3	-	-	-	-	-	4	1	-
October	23	2	1	5	6	-	5	-	-	-	-	-	3	1	-
November	11	-	1	3	4	-	2	-	-	-	-	-	1	-	-
December	21	1	-	8	3	-	8	-	1	-	-	-	-	-	-
January - 1952	28	1	-	9	6	-	10	-	1	-	-	-	1	-	-
February	19	-	-	5	1	e/	8	-	5	-	-	-	-	-	-
March	16	2	-	5	-	-	8	-	1	-	-	-	-	-	-
April	15	-	-	8	2	-	5	-	-	-	-	-	-	-	-
May	17	-	-	3	3	-	9	-	1	-	-	-	1	-	-
June	10	1	-	2	1	-	2	1	-	-	-	-	1	1	1
July	8	-	-	1	2	-	4	-	-	-	-	-	1	-	-
August	10	2	-	1	3	-	3	-	1	-	-	-	-	-	-
September	4	-	-	1	1	-	1	1	-	-	-	-	-	-	-
October	13	1	-	1	-	-	7	-	2	-	-	-	2	-	-
November	8	1	-	1	2	-	3	-	-	-	-	-	1	-	-
December	6	2	-	-	-	-	2	-	1	-	-	-	1	-	-
January - 1953	10	-	-	f/	4	-	6	-	-	-	-	-	-	-	-
February	5	-	-	-	1	-	4	-	g/	-	-	-	-	-	-
March	7	-	-	-	-	-	6	1	-	-	-	-	-	-	-
April	6	1	-	-	1	-	2	-	-	-	-	-	2	-	-
May	8	1	-	-	-	-	5	-	-	-	-	-	2	-	-
June	18	-	-	-	-	-	3	14	-	-	-	-	1	-	-
July (thru the 27th)	10	1	-	-	1	-	5	2	-	-	-	-	1	-	-

a/ 1 RF-86, June 1952.
b/ Includes 26 through 30 Jun 50.
c/ F-84 type acft began operations Dec 50.
d/ F-86 type acft began operations Dec 50.
e/ F-82 type acft removed from combat status Feb 52.
f/ F-51 type acft removed from combat status Jan 53.
g/ RF-51 type acft removed from combat status Feb 53.

Source: Operations Statistics Division, Directorate of Statistical Services, DCS/C.

TABLE 40 — USAF AIRCRAFT LOSSES (OPERATIONAL NON-ENEMY ACTION) BY TYPE MODEL, BY MONTH — 26 JUNE 1950 THROUGH 27 JULY 1953

MONTH	TOTAL	B-26	B-29	F-51	F-80	F-82	F-84	F-86	F-94	RB/WB-26	RB/WB-29	RF-51	RF-80	C-46	VC/C-47	C-54	C-119	C-124	LT/T-6	H-5 YH/H-19	SA-16 SB-29	MISC
Total	472	41	27	74	96	4	63	61	6	5	1	1	9	14	8	8	9	1	13	16	2	a/ 13
July - 1950 b/	5	1	-	-	2	1	-	-	-	-	-	-	-	-	1	-	-	-	-	-	-	-
August	11	1	-	6	1	-	-	-	-	-	-	-	-	-	2	-	-	-	1	-	-	-
September	17	1	4	6	2	-	-	-	-	-	-	-	-	-	-	1	-	-	-	1	-	2
October	19	-	2	7	5	-	-	-	-	-	-	-	-	-	-	-	1	-	2	-	-	2
November	24	1	1	7	5	-	-	-	-	-	1	-	1	1	-	2	1	-	1	2	-	1
December	28	2	-	8	11	1	c/	d/	-	-	-	h/	1	2	1	1	-	-	-	-	-	1
January - 1951	24	3	-	3	6	-	1	-	-	1	-	-	1	4	-	2	-	-	2	-	1	-
February	24	2	-	6	14	-	1	-	-	-	-	-	-	-	-	1	-	-	-	-	-	-
March	16	-	1	4	8	-	-	-	-	-	-	-	-	-	-	1	1	-	-	1	-	-
April	14	2	3	1	6	-	-	1	-	-	-	-	-	-	-	-	-	-	-	1	-	-
May	20	-	-	3	11	-	-	3	-	-	-	-	1	-	-	-	-	-	-	-	-	2
June	18	1	-	1	5	-	3	1	-	2	-	-	-	1	-	-	2	-	2	-	-	-
July	17	2	-	4	2	-	7	1	-	-	-	-	-	-	-	-	-	-	-	-	-	1
August	13	3	-	1	4	1	1	1	-	-	-	-	-	1	-	-	-	i/	-	1	-	-
September	11	3	1	1	1	-	1	2	-	-	-	-	-	1	-	-	-	-	-	1	-	-
October	16	2	2	2	2	-	6	1	-	1	-	-	-	-	-	-	-	-	-	-	-	-
November	9	-	1	2	-	1	3	-	-	-	-	-	-	-	-	-	-	-	1	1	-	-
December	4	-	1	1	-	-	2	-	-	-	-	-	-	-	-	-	-	-	-	-	-	-
January - 1952	12	1	2	-	1	-	2	5	e/	-	-	-	-	-	-	-	-	-	-	1	-	-
February	17	-	2	2	1	f/	6	3	-	-	-	-	2	1	-	-	-	-	-	-	-	-
March	11	1	1	2	-	-	6	-	-	-	-	-	-	-	-	-	-	-	-	1	-	-
April	8	2	1	1	-	-	1	1	-	-	-	-	-	-	1	-	1	-	-	-	-	-
May	11	2	-	3	1	-	-	3	-	-	-	-	-	-	-	-	-	-	1	1	-	-
June	9	2	-	-	1	-	1	2	-	-	-	-	1	-	-	-	-	-	-	-	-	2
July	7	-	-	-	-	-	4	1	-	-	-	-	1	-	-	-	-	-	-	1	-	-
August	8	1	2	1	-	-	-	2	-	-	-	1	-	-	-	-	-	-	-	-	-	1
September	6	-	-	-	-	-	2	2	-	-	-	-	-	1	-	-	-	-	-	1	-	-
October	8	-	-	1	2	-	2	2	-	-	-	-	1	-	-	-	-	-	-	-	-	-
November	5	-	1	-	1	-	1	-	-	-	-	-	-	1	-	-	1	-	-	-	-	-
December	10	3	-	1	1	-	1	3	1	-	-	-	-	-	-	-	-	-	-	-	-	-
January - 1953	11	2	1	g/	-	-	2	2	3	-	-	-	-	-	-	-	-	-	-	-	1	-
February	4	-	-	-	1	-	2	1	-	-	-	j/	-	-	-	-	-	-	-	-	-	-
March	6	-	-	-	2	-	-	2	-	-	-	-	-	-	-	-	1	-	-	1	-	-
April	7	1	-	-	-	-	1	2	-	-	-	-	-	1	-	-	-	-	1	1	-	-
May	13	1	-	-	-	-	1	9	-	-	-	-	-	-	-	-	-	-	2	-	-	-
June	14	-	-	-	-	-	2	6	1	-	-	-	-	-	1	-	1	1	-	1	-	1
July (through the 27th)	15	1	1	-	-	-	4	5	1	1	-	-	-	-	2	-	-	-	-	-	-	-

a/ Includes 1 RB-45, Jun 52; 1 RF-86, Jun 53; 1 C-45, Dec 50; 1 L-5, Sep 50; 2 L-5, Oct 50; 1 L-5, Nov 50; 1 L-5, May 51; 1 L-5, Jul 51; 1 L-5, Jun 52; 1 L-5, Aug 52; 1 T-33, Sep 50; 1 T-33, May 51.
b/ Includes 26 June through 30 June 1950.
c/ F-84 type acft began operations Dec 50.
d/ F-86 type acft began operations Dec 50.
e/ F-94 type acft began operations Jan 52.
f/ F-82 type acft removed from combat status Feb 52.
g/ F-51 type acft removed from combat status Jan 53.
h/ RF-51 type acft began operations Dec 50.
i/ C-124 type acft began operations Sep 51.
j/ RF-51 type acft removed from combat status Feb 53.

Source: Operations Statistics Division, Directorate of Statistical Services, DCS/C.

TABLE 41 — USAF AIRCRAFT OPERATIONAL LOSSES (MISSING OR UNKNOWN CAUSE) BY TYPE MODEL, BY MONTH — 26 JUNE 1950 THROUGH 27 JULY 1953

MONTH	TOTAL	B-26	B-29	F-51	F-80	F-82	F-84	F-86	F-94	RB/WB-26	RB/WB-29	RF-51	RF-80	C-46	VC/C-47	C-54	LT/T-6	MISC
Total	237	71	6	32	38	3	33	13	2	1	2	2	10	2	3	1	16	a/ 2
July - 1950 b/	6	3	-	1	-	-	-	-	-	-	-	-	-	-	-	1	-	1
August	4	-	-	1	-	-	-	-	-	-	-	-	-	-	-	-	3	-
September	8	1	-	3	2	-	-	-	-	-	-	-	2	-	-	-	-	-
October	11	3	-	2	4	-	-	-	-	-	-	-	1	-	1	-	-	-
November	5	-	-	1	2	-	-	-	-	-	-	-	-	-	1	-	1	-
December	13	4	-	2	3	-	c/ 2	d/	-	-	-	h/	-	-	-	-	1	1
January - 1951	3	2	-	-	-	1	-	-	-	-	-	-	-	-	-	-	-	-
February	9	6	-	-	2	-	-	-	-	-	-	-	-	-	-	-	1	-
March	14	3	-	5	2	1	1	-	-	-	-	-	1	-	-	-	1	-
April	17	3	-	8	-	-	1	1	-	-	-	1	-	-	1	-	2	-
May	10	1	-	1	5	1	1	-	-	-	-	-	-	-	-	-	1	-
June	10	3	-	1	2	-	1	2	-	-	-	-	1	-	-	-	-	-
July	11	3	-	3	1	-	2	-	-	-	-	-	-	-	-	-	2	-
August	9	2	-	3	3	-	1	-	-	-	-	-	-	-	-	-	-	-
September	8	5	1	-	1	-	-	1	-	-	-	-	-	-	-	-	-	-
October	4	2	-	1	1	-	-	-	-	-	-	-	-	-	-	-	-	-
November	2	2	-	-	-	-	-	-	-	-	-	-	-	-	-	-	-	-
December	5	2	-	-	1	-	1	-	-	-	-	-	-	-	-	-	1	-
January - 1952	10	3	2	-	2	-	1	1	e/	-	-	-	1	-	-	-	-	-
February	7	3	-	-	-	f/	1	-	-	1	-	-	1	1	-	-	-	-
March	6	3	-	-	-	-	1	1	-	-	-	-	-	-	-	-	1	-
April	4	2	-	-	1	-	1	-	-	-	-	-	-	-	-	-	-	-
May	5	3	-	-	-	-	1	1	-	-	-	-	-	-	-	-	-	-
June	3	1	1	-	-	-	-	-	-	-	1	-	-	-	-	-	-	-
July	5	3	1	-	-	-	-	-	-	-	1	-	-	-	-	-	-	-
August	4	1	-	-	-	-	3	-	-	-	-	-	-	-	-	-	-	-
September	6	-	-	-	2	-	3	1	-	-	-	-	-	-	-	-	-	-
October	5	1	-	-	-	-	3	-	-	-	-	-	-	1	-	-	-	-
November	2	-	1	-	1	-	-	-	-	-	-	-	-	-	-	-	-	-
December	3	1	-	-	1	-	-	-	-	-	-	1	-	-	-	-	-	-
January - 1953	3	1	-	g/	-	-	1	-	-	-	-	-	1	-	-	-	-	-
February	1	-	-	-	1	-	-	-	-	-	-	i/	-	-	-	-	-	-
March	3	1	-	-	1	-	-	-	-	-	-	-	-	-	-	-	1	-
April	5	1	-	-	-	-	3	-	-	-	-	-	1	-	-	-	-	-
May	5	-	-	-	-	-	2	1	1	-	-	-	1	-	-	-	-	-
June	6	-	-	-	-	-	2	3	1	-	-	-	-	-	-	-	-	-
July (through the 27th)	5	2	-	-	-	-	1	1	-	-	-	-	-	-	-	-	1	-

a/ Includes 1 RB-45, Dec 50; 1 L-5, Jun 50.
b/ Includes 26 through 30 June 1950.
c/ F-84 type acft began operations Dec 50.
d/ F-86 type acft began operations Dec 50.
e/ F-94 type acft began operations Jan 52.
f/ F-82 type acft removed from combat status Feb 52.
g/ F-51 type acft removed from combat status Jan 53.
h/ RF-51 type acft began operations Dec 50.
i/ RF-51 type acft removed from combat status Feb 53.

Source: Operations Statistics Division, Directorate of Statistical Services, DCS/C.

TABLE 42 — USAF AIRCRAFT NON-OPERATIONAL LOSSES BY TYPE MODEL, BY MONTH — 26 JUNE 1950 THROUGH 27 JULY 1953

MONTH	TOTAL	B-26	B-29	F-51	F-80	F-82	F-84	F-86	F-94	RB/ WB-26	RB/ WB-29	RF-51	RF-80	C-46	VC/ C-47	C-54	C-119	LT/ T-6	H-5 YH/H-19	SA-16 SB-29	MISC
Total	281	35	12	22	47	6	56	34	3	9	3	1	3	7	8	6	8	8	4	1	a/ 8
July - 1950 b/	20	1	-	1	9	2	-	-	-	-	1	-	-	-	-	4	-	1	-	-	1
August	6	-	-	3	1	-	-	-	-	-	-	-	-	1	-	-	-	1	-	-	-
September	4	-	-	1	-	1	-	-	-	-	-	-	-	-	-	1	1	-	-	-	-
October	11	-	-	1	5	-	-	-	-	4	-	-	-	-	-	-	1	-	-	-	-
November	6	-	-	-	4	-	-	-	-	-	-	-	-	-	1	-	-	-	-	-	1
December	18	-	1	7	2	2	c/ 2	d/	-	-	-	h/	-	-	1	-	-	3	-	-	-
January - 1951	10	2	-	-	3	-	-	-	-	-	-	-	1	2	1	-	-	-	-	1	-
February	9	3	-	-	1	-	-	2	-	-	-	-	-	-	-	-	-	-	1	-	2
March	4	1	-	-	1	-	-	-	-	-	-	-	-	-	-	1	-	-	1	-	-
April	11	1	-	1	3	-	-	1	-	-	-	-	-	1	2	-	-	2	-	-	-
May	9	2	-	2	-	1	1	1	-	-	-	-	-	-	-	-	1	-	-	-	1
June	9	1	-	-	4	-	1	1	-	1	-	-	-	-	-	-	-	-	1	-	-
July	10	-	-	3	2	-	-	2	-	2	-	-	-	1	-	-	-	-	-	-	-
August	9	2	-	-	-	-	4	-	-	-	-	-	-	1	1	-	-	-	-	-	1
September	7	-	-	1	2	-	1	-	-	-	-	-	-	-	2	-	1	-	-	-	-
October	10	4	2	-	1	-	1	-	-	2	-	-	-	-	-	-	-	-	-	-	-
November	5	-	-	1	2	-	1	1	-	-	-	-	-	-	-	-	-	-	-	-	-
December	6	-	-	-	1	-	2	2	-	-	-	-	-	-	-	-	1	-	-	-	-
January - 1952	6	1	-	-	-	-	2	1	e/	-	-	-	-	1	-	-	1	-	-	-	-
February	3	-	1	-	-	f/	2	-	-	-	-	-	-	-	-	-	-	-	-	-	-
March	4	-	1	-	1	-	1	1	-	-	-	-	-	-	-	-	-	-	-	-	-
April	7	3	1	-	1	-	1	-	-	-	-	-	1	-	-	-	-	-	-	-	-
May	5	2	-	-	-	-	1	1	-	-	-	1	-	-	-	-	-	-	-	-	-
June	8	2	4	-	-	-	1	-	1	-	-	-	-	-	-	-	-	-	-	-	-
July	9	-	-	-	1	-	4	2	-	-	-	-	-	-	-	-	1	-	-	-	1
August	5	1	-	-	-	-	1	1	-	-	-	-	1	-	-	-	-	1	-	-	-
September	8	1	2	-	-	-	4	-	-	-	-	-	-	-	-	-	-	-	-	-	1
October	8	1	-	1	-	-	2	1	-	-	1	-	-	-	-	-	1	-	1	-	-
November	8	-	-	-	-	-	4	3	1	-	-	-	-	-	-	-	-	-	-	-	-
December	9	4	-	-	-	-	3	2	-	-	-	-	-	-	-	-	-	-	-	-	-
January - 1953	4	-	-	g/	1	-	1	2	-	-	-	-	-	-	-	-	-	-	-	-	-
February	9	2	-	-	1	-	4	1	-	-	1	i/	-	-	-	-	-	-	-	-	-
March	8	-	-	-	1	-	5	2	-	-	-	-	-	-	-	-	-	-	-	-	-
April	3	-	-	-	-	-	2	1	-	-	-	-	-	-	-	-	-	-	-	-	-
May	2	-	-	-	-	-	2	-	-	-	-	-	-	-	-	-	-	-	-	-	-
June	6	-	-	-	-	-	1	4	1	-	-	-	-	-	-	-	-	-	-	-	-
July (through the 27th)	5	1	-	-	-	-	2	2	-	-	-	-	-	-	-	-	-	-	-	-	-

a/ Includes 1 RF-86, Sep 52; 1 C-45, Feb 51; 1 T-33, Jul 50; 1 T-33, Nov 50; 1 T-33, Feb 51; 1 T-33, May 51; 1 T-33, Aug 51; 1 T-33, Jul 52.
b/ Includes 26 through 30 Jun 50.
c/ F-84 type acft began operations Dec 50.
d/ F-86 type acft began operations Dec 50.
e/ F-94 type acft began operations Jan 52.
f/ F-82 type acft removed from combat status Feb 52.
g/ F-51 type acft removed from combat status Jan 53.
h/ RF-51 type acft began operations Dec 50.
i/ RF-51 type acft removed from combat status Feb 53.

Source: Operations Statistics Division, Directorate of Statistical Services, DCS/C.

TABLE 43 — USAF AIRCRAFT LOSSES (NON—OPERATIONAL FLYING ACCIDENT) BY TYPE MODEL, BY MONTH — 26 JUNE 1950 THROUGH 27 JULY 1953

MONTH	TOTAL	B-26	B-29	F-51	F-80	F-82	F-84	F-86	F-94	RB/WB-26	RB/WB-29	RF-51	RF-80	C-46	VC/C-47	C-54	C-119	LT/T-6	H-5 YH/H-19	SA-16 SB-29	MISC
Total	235	25	9	10	44	5	53	32	3	8	1	1	3	7	7	2	8	4	4	1	a/ 8
July - 1950 b/	12	1	-	-	8	1	-	-	-	-	-	-	-	-	-	-	-	1	-	-	1
August	5	-	-	2	1	-	-	-	-	-	-	-	-	1	-	-	-	1	-	-	-
September	4	-	-	1	-	1	-	-	-	-	-	-	-	-	-	1	1	-	-	-	-
October	11	-	-	1	5	-	-	-	-	4	-	-	-	-	-	-	1	-	-	-	-
November	6	-	-	-	4	-	-	-	-	-	-	-	-	-	1	-	-	-	-	-	1
December	8	-	1	-	2	2	c/ 2	d/	-	-	-	h/	-	-	-	-	-	1	-	-	-
January - 1951	8	2	-	-	1	-	-	-	-	-	-	-	1	2	1	-	-	-	-	1	-
February	8	2	-	-	1	-	-	2	-	-	-	-	-	-	-	-	-	-	1	-	2
March	4	1	-	-	1	-	-	-	-	-	-	-	-	-	-	1	-	-	1	-	-
April	9	1	-	1	3	-	-	1	-	-	-	-	-	1	2	-	-	-	-	-	-
May	6	1	-	1	-	1	-	1	-	-	-	-	-	-	-	-	1	-	-	-	1
June	6	-	-	-	4	-	1	-	-	-	-	-	-	-	-	-	-	-	1	-	-
July	9	-	-	2	2	-	-	2	-	2	-	-	-	1	-	-	-	-	-	-	-
August	9	2	-	-	-	-	4	-	-	-	-	-	-	1	1	-	-	-	-	-	1
September	6	-	-	-	2	-	1	-	-	-	-	-	-	-	2	-	1	-	-	-	-
October	10	4	2	-	1	-	1	-	-	2	-	-	-	-	-	-	-	-	-	-	-
November	5	-	-	1	2	-	1	1	-	-	-	-	-	-	-	-	-	-	-	-	-
December	6	-	-	-	1	-	2	2	-	-	-	-	-	-	-	-	1	-	-	-	-
January - 1952	6	1	-	-	-	-	2	1	e/	-	-	-	-	1	-	-	1	-	-	-	-
February	3	-	1	-	-	f/	2	-	-	-	-	-	-	-	-	-	-	-	-	-	-
March	3	-	-	-	1	-	1	1	-	-	-	-	-	-	-	-	-	-	-	-	-
April	6	3	-	-	1	-	1	-	-	-	-	-	1	-	-	-	-	-	-	-	-
May	4	1	-	-	-	-	1	1	-	-	-	1	-	-	-	-	-	-	-	-	-
June	6	2	3	-	-	-	-	-	1	-	-	-	-	-	-	-	-	-	-	-	-
July	9	-	-	-	1	-	4	2	-	-	-	-	-	-	-	-	1	-	-	-	1
August	4	-	-	-	-	-	1	1	-	-	-	-	1	-	-	-	-	1	-	-	-
September	8	1	2	-	-	-	4	-	-	-	-	-	-	-	-	-	-	-	-	-	1
October	7	1	-	1	-	-	2	1	-	-	-	-	-	-	-	-	1	-	1	-	-
November	8	-	-	-	-	-	4	3	1	-	-	-	-	-	-	-	-	-	-	-	-
December	5	-	-	-	-	-	3	2	-	-	-	-	-	-	-	-	-	-	-	-	-
January - 1953	4	-	-	g/	1	-	1	2	-	-	-	-	-	-	-	-	-	-	-	-	-
February	8	1	-	-	1	-	4	1	-	-	1	i/	-	-	-	-	-	-	-	-	-
March	8	-	-	-	1	-	5	2	-	-	-	-	-	-	-	-	-	-	-	-	-
April	3	-	-	-	-	-	2	1	-	-	-	-	-	-	-	-	-	-	-	-	-
May	2	-	-	-	-	-	2	-	-	-	-	-	-	-	-	-	-	-	-	-	-
June	6	-	-	-	-	-	1	4	1	-	-	-	-	-	-	-	-	-	-	-	-
July (through the 27th)	3	1	-	-	-	-	1	1	-	-	-	-	-	-	-	-	-	-	-	-	-

a/ Includes 1 RF-86, Sep 52; 1 C-45, Feb 51; 1 T-33, Jul 50; 1 T-33, Nov 50; 1 T-33, Feb 51; 1 T-33, May 51; 1 T-33, Aug 51; 1 T-33, Jul 52.
b/ Includes 26 through 30 Jun 50.
c/ F-84 type acft began operations Dec 50.
d/ F-86 type acft began operations Dec 50.
e/ F-94 type acft began operations Jan 52.
f/ F-82 type acft removed from combat status Feb 52.
g/ F-51 type acft removed from combat status Jan 53.
h/ RF-51 type acft began operations Dec 50.
i/ RF-51 type acft removed from combat status Feb 53.

Source: Operations Statistics Division, Directorate of Statistical Services, DCS/C.

TABLE 44 — USAF AIRCRAFT LOSSES (OPERATIONAL AND ENEMY ACTION) BY TYPE MISSION, BY MONTH — 26 JUNE 1950 THROUGH 27 JULY 1953

MONTH	OPERATIONAL LOSSES							ENEMY ACTION LOSSES						
	TOTAL	INTERDICTION	CLOSE SUPPORT	COUNTER AIR OFFENSIVE	COUNTER AIR DEFENSIVE	RECON	OTHER	TOTAL	INTERDICTION	CLOSE SUPPORT	COUNTER AIR OFFENSIVE	COUNTER AIR DEFENSIVE	RECON	OTHER
Total	1,466	749	261	164	17	99	176	757	415	139	96	5	47	55
July - 1950 a/	36	17	9	2	-	-	8	25	12	7	2	-	-	4
August	38	24	6	-	-	-	8	23	17	4	-	-	-	2
September	50	17	20	-	-	2	11	25	7	13	-	-	-	5
October	48	16	24	-	-	1	7	18	5	12	-	-	-	1
November	46	17	15	-	-	2	12	17	9	6	-	-	-	2
December	51	29	11	1	-	2	8	10	3	4	1	-	-	2
January - 1951	34	15	6	-	-	2	11	7	4	1	-	-	-	2
February	45	23	17	-	-	1	4	12	5	4	-	-	1	2
March	51	17	21	-	-	6	7	21	7	11	-	-	1	2
April	73	32	29	3	-	2	7	42	20	19	-	-	1	2
May	54	40	5	3	1	3	2	24	22	2	-	-	-	-
June	59	34	5	8	1	5	6	31	24	-	4	-	3	-
July	49	33	2	3	1	4	6	21	15	-	-	1	3	2
August	50	33	5	1	1	5	5	28	19	3	-	-	4	2
September	46	29	3	7	-	4	3	27	16	2	4	-	4	1
October	58	36	4	9	-	6	3	38	21	2	8	-	5	2
November	34	23	4	3	-	3	1	23	16	3	3	-	1	-
December	40	28	3	7	-	2	-	31	20	3	7	-	1	-
January - 1952	59	40	2	11	-	4	2	37	27	1	5	-	3	1
February	48	26	2	5	1	10	4	24	13	-	2	1	7	1
March	40	28	4	4	-	1	3	23	16	3	3	-	1	-
April	36	22	3	5	-	-	6	24	14	3	4	-	-	3
May	47	29	-	10	-	2	6	31	21	-	6	-	2	2
June	28	10	4	5	1	4	4	16	5	3	3	1	1	3
July	25	12	3	6	-	2	2	13	5	2	5	-	-	1
August	27	6	12	6	-	2	1	15	2	8	4	-	1	-
September	29	12	2	13	-	-	2	17	6	2	9	-	-	-
October	34	18	2	7	-	4	3	21	10	1	5	-	3	2
November	22	11	3	2	2	1	3	15	7	2	2	2	1	1
December	22	7	3	5	2	4	1	9	3	2	2	-	1	1
January - 1953	30	18	1	4	3	1	3	16	11	1	2	-	-	2
February	16	7	3	5	-	1	-	11	5	2	4	-	-	-
March	19	7	2	4	-	3	3	10	5	2	3	-	-	-
April	24	7	1	7	-	1	8	12	4	-	5	-	-	3
May	27	6	5	8	1	1	6	9	4	2	1	-	-	2
June	38	11	11	6	2	2	6	18	10	6	1	-	-	1
July (through the 27th)	33	9	9	4	1	6	4	13	5	3	1	-	3	1

a/ Includes 26 through 30 June 1950.

Source: Operations Statistics Division, Directorate of Statistical Services, DCS/C.

TABLE 45 – USAF AIRCRAFT OPERATIONAL LOSSES (AIR – TO – AIR, GROUND FIRE, AND ENEMY ACTION CAUSE UNKNOWN) BY TYPE MISSION, BY MONTH – 26 JUNE 1950 THROUGH 27 JULY 1953

MONTH	AIR - TO - AIR							GROUND FIRE							ENEMY ACTION CAUSE UNKNOWN						
	TOTAL	INTER-DICTION	CLOSE SUPPORT	COUNTER AIR OFFENSIVE	COUNTER AIR DEFENSIVE	RECON	OTHER	TOTAL	INTER-DICTION	CLOSE SUPPORT	COUNTER AIR OFFENSIVE	COUNTER AIR DEFENSIVE	RECON	OTHER	TOTAL	INTER-DICTION	CLOSE SUPPORT	COUNTER AIR OFFENSIVE	COUNTER AIR DEFENSIVE	RECON	OTHER
Total	139	46	6	80	4	2	1	550	332	124	4	-	40	50	68	37	9	12	1	5	4
July - 1950 a/	4	1	-	2	-	-	1	20	10	7	-	-	-	3	1	1	-	-	-	-	-
August	1	1	-	-	-	-	-	21	15	4	-	-	-	2	1	1	-	-	-	-	-
September	-	-	-	-	-	-	-	24	7	12	-	-	-	5	1	-	1	-	-	-	-
October	1	1	-	-	-	-	-	16	3	12	-	-	-	1	1	1	-	-	-	-	-
November	1	1	-	-	-	-	-	15	8	5	-	-	-	2	1	-	1	-	-	-	-
December	2	1	-	1	-	-	-	7	1	4	-	-	-	2	1	1	-	-	-	-	-
January - 1951	2	1	1	-	-	-	-	5	3	-	-	-	-	2	-	-	-	-	-	-	-
February	-	-	-	-	-	-	-	11	4	4	-	-	1	2	1	1	-	-	-	-	-
March	2	-	2	-	-	-	-	17	5	9	-	-	1	2	2	2	-	-	-	-	-
April	4	4	-	-	-	-	-	36	16	17	-	-	1	2	2	-	2	-	-	-	-
May	-	-	-	-	-	-	-	23	21	2	-	-	-	-	1	1	-	-	-	-	-
June	7	3	-	4	-	-	-	22	19	-	-	-	3	-	2	2	-	-	-	-	-
July	1	1	-	-	-	-	-	16	12	-	-	-	3	1	4	2	-	-	1	-	1
August	3	3	-	-	-	-	-	23	14	3	-	-	4	2	2	2	-	-	-	-	-
September	6	2	-	4	-	-	-	21	14	2	-	-	4	1	-	-	-	-	-	-	-
October	14	5	-	8	-	1	-	23	16	2	-	-	3	2	1	-	-	-	-	1	-
November	8	4	1	3	-	-	-	11	8	2	-	-	1	-	4	4	-	-	-	-	-
December	9	2	1	6	-	-	-	21	18	2	-	-	1	-	1	-	-	1	-	-	-
January - 1952	5	-	-	5	-	-	-	28	24	1	-	-	2	1	4	3	-	-	-	1	-
February	4	1	-	2	1	-	-	19	11	-	-	-	7	1	1	1	-	-	-	-	-
March	4	2	-	2	-	-	-	16	13	2	-	-	1	-	3	1	1	1	-	-	-
April	5	-	1	4	-	-	-	15	12	1	-	-	-	2	4	2	1	-	-	-	1
May	9	4	-	5	-	-	-	17	14	-	-	-	1	2	5	3	-	1	-	1	-
June	4	1	-	2	1	-	-	10	2	3	1	-	1	3	2	2	-	-	-	-	-
July	4	-	-	4	-	-	-	8	5	2	-	-	-	1	1	-	-	1	-	-	-
August	2	-	-	2	-	-	-	10	2	7	-	-	1	-	3	-	1	2	-	-	-
September	10	3	-	7	-	-	-	4	2	1	1	-	-	-	3	1	1	1	-	-	-
October	5	1	-	4	-	-	-	13	8	1	-	-	2	2	3	1	-	1	-	1	-
November	5	1	-	2	2	-	-	8	5	1	-	-	1	1	2	1	1	-	-	-	-
December	3	1	-	2	-	-	-	6	2	2	-	-	1	1	-	-	-	-	-	-	-
January - 1953	3	2	-	1	-	-	-	10	9	1	-	-	-	-	3	-	-	1	-	-	2
February	2	-	-	2	-	-	-	5	3	2	-	-	-	-	4	2	-	2	-	-	-
March	2	-	-	2	-	-	-	7	4	2	1	-	-	-	1	1	-	-	-	-	-
April	4	-	-	4	-	-	-	6	3	-	-	-	-	3	2	1	-	1	-	-	-
May	1	-	-	1	-	-	-	8	4	2	-	-	-	2	-	-	-	-	-	-	-
June	-	-	-	-	-	-	-	18	10	6	1	-	-	1	-	-	-	-	-	-	-
July b/	2	-	-	1	-	1	-	10	5	3	-	-	1	1	1	-	-	-	-	1	-

a/ Includes 26 through 30 June 1950. b/ 1 July through 27 July 1953.
Source: Operations Statistics Division, Directorate of Statistical Services, DCS/C.

TABLE 46 – USAF AIRCRAFT OPERATIONAL LOSSES (NON – ENEMY ACTION AND CAUSE UNKNOWN) BY TYPE MISSION, BY MONTH – 26 JUNE 1950 THROUGH 27 JULY 1953

MONTH	OPERATIONAL NON ENEMY ACTION							OPERATIONAL CAUSE UNKNOWN						
	TOTAL	INTER-DICTION	CLOSE SUPPORT	COUNTER AIR OFFENSIVE	COUNTER AIR DEFENSIVE	RECON	OTHER	TOTAL	INTER-DICTION	CLOSE SUPPORT	COUNTER AIR OFFENSIVE	COUNTER AIR DEFENSIVE	RECON	OTHER
Total	472	199	85	58	7	28	95	237	135	37	10	5	24	26
July - 1950 a/	5	1	2	-	-	-	2	6	4	-	-	-	-	2
August	11	6	2	-	-	-	3	4	1	-	-	-	-	3
September	17	7	4	-	-	-	6	8	3	3	-	-	2	-
October	19	6	8	-	-	-	5	11	5	4	-	-	1	1
November	24	7	7	-	-	2	8	5	1	2	-	-	-	2
December	28	18	4	-	-	1	5	13	8	3	-	-	1	1
January - 1951	24	8	5	-	-	2	9	3	3	-	-	-	-	-
February	24	11	12	-	-	-	1	9	7	1	-	-	-	1
March	16	6	6	-	-	-	4	14	4	4	-	-	5	1
April	14	7	4	1	-	-	2	17	5	6	2	-	1	3
May	20	12	2	3	-	2	1	10	6	1	-	1	1	1
June	18	5	3	2	1	2	5	10	5	2	2	-	-	1
July	17	10	2	3	-	-	2	11	8	-	-	-	1	2
August	13	8	1	1	-	1	2	9	6	1	-	1	-	1
September	11	6	1	2	-	-	2	8	7	-	1	-	-	-
October	15	12	1	1	-	1	-	4	3	1	-	-	-	-
November	9	5	1	-	-	2	1	2	2	-	-	-	-	-
December	4	4	-	-	-	-	-	5	4	-	-	-	1	-
January - 1952	12	5	1	5	-	-	1	10	8	-	1	-	1	-
February	17	9	2	3	-	2	1	7	4	-	-	-	1	2
March	11	8	1	-	-	-	2	6	4	-	1	-	-	1
April	8	4	-	1	-	-	3	4	4	-	-	-	-	-
May	11	4	-	3	-	-	4	5	4	-	1	-	-	-
June	9	3	1	2	-	2	1	3	2	-	-	-	1	-
July	7	3	1	1	-	1	1	5	4	-	-	-	1	-
August	8	3	1	2	-	1	1	4	1	3	-	-	-	-
September	6	1	-	3	-	-	2	6	5	-	1	-	-	-
October	8	4	1	2	-	1	-	5	4	-	-	-	-	1
November	5	3	-	-	-	-	2	2	1	1	-	-	-	-
December	10	3	1	3	2	1	-	3	1	-	-	-	2	-
January - 1953	11	5	-	2	3	-	1	3	2	-	-	-	1	-
February	4	2	1	1	-	-	-	1	-	-	-	-	1	-
March	6	-	-	1	-	3	2	3	2	-	-	-	-	1
April	7	-	-	2	-	-	5	5	3	1	-	-	1	-
May	14	1	3	6	-	-	4	5	1	-	1	1	1	1
June	14	-	2	5	1	1	5	6	1	3	-	1	1	-
July (through the 27th)	15	2	5	3	-	3	2	5	2	1	-	1	-	1

a/ Includes 26 through 30 June 1950.
Source: Operations Statistics Division, Directorate of Statistical Services, DCS/C.

TABLE 47 — USAF FLYING TIME AND FUEL CONSUMPTION — 26 JUNE 1950 THROUGH 27 JULY 1953

(Overall Theater Figures Including Non-Committed Units)

AIRCRAFT	26 June 1950 thru 30 June 1951				AIRCRAFT	FISCAL YEAR 1952				AIRCRAFT	1 July 1952 thru 27 July 1953			
	HOURS			FUEL CONSUMED (1000's Gals.)		HOURS			FUEL CONSUMED (1000's Gals.)		HOURS			FUEL CONSUMED (1000's Gals.)
	TOTAL	OPN'L	NON-OPN'L			TOTAL	OPN'L	NON-OPN'L			TOTAL	OPN'L	NON-OPN'L	
TOTAL	929,008	620,155	308,853	209,987	TOTAL .	1,061,738	593,772	467,966	242,623	TOTAL .	1,177,366	635,219	542,147	311,786
BOMBERS	180,581	151,311	29,270	55,273	BOMBERS.	185,151	128,940	56,211	48,277	BOMBERS.	195,444	133,360	62,084	55,757
B-26.	85,069	69,649	15,420	12,915	B-26. .	121,587	81,001	40,586	17,683	B-26. .	117,313	81,041	36,272	19,366
B-29.	95,512	81,662	13,850	42,358	B-29. .	63,564	47,939	15,625	30,594	B-29. .	58,133	32,321	25,812	36,391
FIGHTERS. . . .	293,766	221,897	71,869	79,357	FIGHTERS	300,185	179,283	120,902	99,273	FIGHTERS	385,120	190,358	194,762	148,111
F-51.	92,678	86,042	6,636	6,055	F-51. .	57,871	39,202	18,669	3,964	F-51. .	20,772	9,813	10,959	1,526
F-80.	143,669	97,792	45,877	53,353	F-80. .	79,180	41,791	37,389	32,260	F-80. .	66,832	23,746	43,086	26,362
F-82.	10,861	3,462	7,399	1,737	F-82. .	4,825	1,874	2,951	666	F-82. .	-	-	-	-
F-84.	31,048	27,703	3,345	11,999	F-84. .	94,056	57,178	36,878	35,749	F-84. .	147,175	74,507	72,668	61,317
F-86.	14,770	6,898	7,872	5,900	F-86. .	48,931	37,532	11,399	19,452	F-86. .	104,692	76,335	28,357	41,521
F-94.	740	-	740	313	F-94. .	15,322	1,706	13,616	6,182	F-94. .	45,649	5,957	39,692	17,385
TRANSPORTS. . .	290,360	165,219	125,141	47,805	TRANSPORTS	390,897	194,851	196,046	61,875	TRANSPORTS	318,124	196,503	121,621	41,893
C-45.	10,131	945	9,186	408	C-45. .	9,686	96	9,590	416	C-45. .	13,839	841	12,998	554
C-46.	54,310	28,654	25,656	8,705	C-46. .	78,416	30,282	48,134	11,545	C-46. .	84,510	67,007	17,503	13,405
C-47.	92,418	33,138	59,280	8,923	C-47. .	129,314	39,197	90,117	12,656	C-47. .	107,688	43,343	64,345	10,323
C-54.	81,056	63,583	17,473	16,796	C-54. .	133,285	101,183	32,102	27,216	C-54. .	48,932	41,363	7,569	1,630
C-119	52,445	38,899	13,546	12,973	C-119 .	40,196	24,093	16,103	10,042	C-119 .	63,155	43,949	19,206	15,981
Other	164,301	81,728	82,573	27,552	Other .	185,505	90,698	94,807	33,198	Other .	278,678	114,998	163,680	66,025
Recon	56,101	30,194	25,907	16,831	Recon .	74,085	46,489	27,596	21,108	Recon .	76,831	40,444	36,387	24,966
S & R	14,132	3,649	10,483	3,203	S & R .	15,714	2,899	12,815	3,369	S & R .	24,305	8,629	15,676	4,792
Trainer . . .	78,473	43,393	35,080	5,831	Trainer.	63,847	22,521	41,326	5,699	Trainer.	80,634	1,853	78,781	12,497
Misc.	15,595	4,492	11,103	1,687	Misc . .	31,859	18,789	13,070	3,022	Misc . .	96,905	64,069	32,836	23,770

SOURCE: Materiel Statistics Division, D/Statistical Services, DCS/C

TABLE 48 — USAF FLYING TIME BY TYPE MODEL, BY MONTH — 26 JUNE 1950 THROUGH 27 JULY 1953

(Overall Theater Figures Including Non-Committed Units)

MONTH	TOTAL	B-26	B-29	F-51	F-80	F-82	F-84	F-86	F-94	RB/WB-26	RB/WB-29
Total	3,163,099	323,223	235,552	171,293	287,619	15,273	272,280	168,400	60,513	40,681	68,887
July - 1950 a/	43,769	2,942	7,780	1,945	12,019	967	-	-	-	g/	g/
August	67,410	4,630	11,726	13,500	10,676	1,067	-	-	-	g/	g/
September	72,104	5,074	13,050	10,477	9,145	1,069	-	-	-	g/	g/
October	73,024	4,536	7,712	8,687	12,067	947	-	-	-	g/	g/
November	77,359	8,837	7,485	8,339	10,758	887	-	-	-	g/	g/
December	76,520	9,409	7,010	6,539	10,904	996	b/ 2,413	c/ 594	-	g/	g/
January - 1951	79,611	7,604	7,772	5,878	11,787	1,106	4,524	1,632	-	g/	g/
February	74,410	6,119	6,753	5,710	12,117	879	3,626	1,354	-	g/	g/
March	89,542	7,114	7,966	8,910	15,877	709	5,573	2,524	d/ 1	1,359	2,237
April	82,721	8,231	5,777	8,374	12,479	622	4,996	2,796	193	1,487	1,942
May	92,847	9,552	5,554	7,139	12,932	628	5,007	2,834	338	1,737	2,382
June	93,605	10,265	5,290	7,062	11,162	571	4,910	3,016	208	1,685	2,153
July	82,749	10,095	5,481	5,491	6,778	573	4,719	1,796	216	1,596	2,110
August	86,753	10,037	5,438	6,323	6,791	682	6,234	2,260	262	1,786	2,330
September	87,067	10,232	5,942	6,795	7,521	661	9,703	2,280	304	1,808	2,350
October	92,781	9,451	5,645	7,534	7,784	741	9,558	2,668	460	1,640	2,581
November	86,464	8,998	4,794	5,080	6,755	619	9,014	2,031	875	1,189	2,119
December	85,140	9,170	4,714	4,646	6,071	542	8,075	3,578	823	1,287	1,942
January - 1952	85,047	8,128	5,813	3,657	5,244	541	7,959	3,796	998	1,242	2,276
February	79,051	8,620	4,697	3,317	5,098	e/ 390	7,447	4,171	1,200	1,244	2,405
March	92,688	9,874	5,257	3,723	6,280	70	8,270	5,566	2,007	1,520	2,089
April	95,968	10,275	5,355	3,885	6,837	6	8,210	6,421	2,284	1,509	2,249
May	101,643	10,548	5,437	4,247	8,069	-	8,741	8,947	2,770	1,573	2,590
June	86,280	9,435	4,971	3,219	5,636	-	6,126	5,444	3,123	1,344	2,289
July	84,815	8,735	5,831	2,435	4,954	-	7,395	4,455	3,139	1,258	2,670
August	89,141	9,663	5,521	2,857	6,108	-	7,834	5,350	3,024	1,221	2,579
September	92,541	9,870	6,036	3,200	5,500	-	10,067	5,996	3,116	1,276	2,504
October	102,506	12,087	6,810	3,487	5,779	-	11,589	7,346	3,523	1,309	2,865
November	86,563	10,058	5,859	2,988	5,515	-	10,072	5,242	2,931	1,186	2,442
December	85,939	8,047	6,030	2,382	5,979	-	11,377	6,446	3,221	1,213	2,428
January - 1953	86,885	9,264	5,518	f/ 1,912	6,044	-	10,877	6,869	3,359	1,335	2,525
February	78,629	8,781	4,948	898	5,365	-	11,060	6,385	3,017	1,094	2,279
March	91,351	8,967	6,407	554	5,629	-	13,465	8,867	3,996	1,157	2,642
April	100,246	9,858	6,210	59	5,280	-	13,878	11,924	4,554	1,296	2,494
May	98,718	9,696	6,835	20	3,924	-	13,952	12,384	3,904	1,754	2,497
June	91,098	9,775	6,309	19	3,273	-	12,212	12,198	3,430	1,402	2,481
July (through the 27th)	90,114	9,246	5,019	5	3,482	-	13,397	11,230	3,237	1,174	2,437

a/ Includes 26 through 30 Jun 50.
b/ F-84 type acft began operations Dec 50.
c/ F-86 type acft began operations Dec 50.
d/ F-94 type acft arrived in theater Mar 51 and committed to combat Jan 52.
e/ F-82 type acft removed from combat status Feb 52.
f/ F-51 type acft removed from combat status Jan 53.
g/ Breakdown not available and is included in Misc.

TABLE 48 — USAF FLYING TIME BY TYPE MODEL, BY MONTH — 26 JUNE 1950 THROUGH 27 JULY 1953 — CONTINUED

(Overall Theater Figures Including Non-Committed Units)

MONTH	RF-51	RF-80	C-46	VC/C-47	C-54	C-119	C-124	T/LT-6	H-5 YH/H-19	SA-16 SB/TB-29	MISC
Total	20,884	28,573	218,947	324,567	262,093	155,636	22,023	178,305	18,261	42,992	247,077
July - 1950 a/	-	g/	1,731	4,052	3,253	-	-	529	g/	g/	8,551
August	-	g/	1,549	5,515	3,592	460	-	2,876	g/	g/	11,819
September	-	g/	2,934	6,131	3,970	4,127	-	3,982	g/	g/	12,145
October	-	g/	3,535	6,681	4,218	9,068	-	3,624	g/	g/	11,949
November	-	g/	5,503	8,445	4,262	7,841	-	3,694	g/	g/	11,308
December	g/ h/	g/	5,616	7,569	5,696	5,791	-	3,317	g/	g/	10,666
January - 1951	g/	g/	4,982	7,000	7,274	4,716	-	3,939	g/	g/	11,397
February	g/	g/	4,704	6,988	7,810	4,493	-	3,728	g/	g/	10,129
March	54	823	4,658	7,609	8,578	4,140	-	4,953	393	695	5,369
April	593	1,005	5,337	8,425	9,865	841	-	5,412	354	803	3,189
May	342	888	6,803	9,262	10,497	5,332	-	5,556	423	835	4,806
June	307	990	6,836	10,046	10,861	5,481	-	6,128	540	873	5,221
July	284	712	5,852	13,348	9,610	3,374	-	4,879	564	910	4,361
August	265	747	6,613	11,549	10,517	4,408	-	4,473	680	1,027	4,331
September	215	841	2,870	11,307	11,383	2,633	i/ 69	4,274	599	925	4,355
October	321	997	4,950	11,467	11,008	4,817	62	4,274	719	1,186	4,918
November	1,039	750	6,011	11,150	11,064	4,305	-	4,990	444	1,015	4,222
December	1,561	729	7,026	10,930	10,915	3,933	-	3,460	426	1,268	4,044
January - 1952	1,769	786	7,661	10,786	11,201	2,685	-	4,323	474	1,126	4,582
February	1,428	748	9,155	7,493	10,745	1,593	-	3,363	419	1,558	3,960
March	1,375	760	8,506	10,323	11,505	3,215	-	4,711	659	1,543	5,435
April	1,348	871	8,622	9,880	12,234	3,630	-	4,722	528	1,642	5,460
May	1,936	1,109	6,348	9,448	12,071	3,771	108	6,281	663	1,453	5,533
June	1,615	1,013	6,635	9,646	11,032	1,827	523	5,675	695	1,499	4,533
July	1,133	645	6,656	10,677	10,370	1,814	633	5,022	685	1,838	4,470
August	1,422	952	6,685	10,403	9,118	2,414	695	5,472	664	1,643	5,516
September	1,102	1,138	6,177	9,655	6,456	3,400	1,967	5,967	679	1,991	6,444
October	932	1,238	6,508	8,872	5,627	5,316	1,943	6,973	808	2,264	7,230
November	709	1,039	6,306	7,571	3,571	4,274	1,967	5,711	743	2,109	6,270
December	644	964	6,069	7,381	2,328	4,564	1,799	5,790	791	1,948	6,538
January - 1953	342	966	6,675	7,587	1,795	5,676	1,546	5,458	757	1,812	6,568
February	j/ 88	866	5,965	6,425	1,424	4,635	1,808	5,342	759	1,511	5,979
March	25	904	6,423	7,805	1,340	5,287	2,298	5,979	973	1,598	7,035
April	5	1,849	6,710	7,842	1,487	7,100	2,153	7,019	826	1,941	7,761
May	6	1,685	7,070	9,061	1,270	5,063	2,215	6,439	698	1,895	8,350
June	19	1,425	6,506	7,955	1,745	6,738	1,181	5,776	768	1,854	6,032
July (through the 27th)	5	1,133	6,760	8,283	2,401	6,874	1,056	4,194	550	2,230	6,601

h/ RF-51 type acft began operations Dec 50.
i/ C-124 type acft began operations Sep 51.
j/ RF-51 type acft removed from combat status Feb 53.

Source: Operations Statistics Division, Director of Statistical Services, DCS/C.

TABLE 49 - USAF OPERATIONAL FLYING TIME BY TYPE MODEL, BY MONTH - 26 JUNE 1950 THROUGH 27 JULY 1953

MONTH	TOTAL	B-26	B-29	F-51	F-80	F-82	F-84	F-86	F-94	RB/WB-26	RB/WB-29
Total	1,842,468	232,044	183,250	134,213	162,848	5,137	159,387	121,735	7,656	34,114	18,759
July - 1950 a/	22,653	2,780	4,796	1,353	8,070	427	-	-	-	g/	g/
August	44,607	4,275	10,904	12,851	6,327	363	-	-	-	g/	g/
September	45,934	4,585	12,422	10,064	5,498	135	-	-	-	g/	g/
October	46,110	2,972	6,864	8,238	8,860	119	-	-	-	g/	g/
November	49,963	6,646	6,917	7,959	7,666	248	-	-	-	g/	g/
December	53,808	8,755	6,661	6,155	7,847	385	b/ 1,894	c/ 419	-	g/	g/
January - 1951	57,592	6,944	7,047	5,602	8,388	513	4,120	183	-	g/	g/
February	54,014	5,570	6,208	5,211	8,537	378	3,444	-	-	g/	g/
March	64,281	6,110	7,042	8,464	12,440	147	5,097	1,672	-	1,155	854
April	56,146	7,288	5,193	7,825	8,344	159	4,745	1,710	-	1,303	703
May	58,620	7,007	4,752	6,304	8,485	198	4,372	2,034	-	1,405	783
June	59,479	7,070	4,184	6,012	6,849	210	4,030	1,850	-	1,364	750
July	46,242	7,159	4,341	2,918	3,191	176	3,191	1,038	-	1,391	738
August	49,096	7,446	4,365	4,393	3,335	276	3,202	1,314	-	1,473	863
September	51,684	7,760	4,631	5,019	4,266	286	6,051	1,546	-	1,558	946
October	53,840	7,279	4,458	5,920	4,544	292	6,371	2,083	-	1,439	1,011
November	49,346	7,139	3,568	3,472	3,818	219	6,711	1,135	-	1,044	819
December	49,086	6,708	3,829	3,186	3,412	225	5,779	2,742	-	1,090	680
January - 1952	46,190	5,934	4,497	2,039	2,258	223	4,969	3,106	d/ 72	1,109	685
February	42,333	5,530	3,673	2,083	2,293	e/ 158	4,243	3,293	117	1,056	716
March	49,397	6,268	3,929	2,309	3,345	-	4,412	4,723	266	1,225	767
April	49,596	6,019	3,416	2,365	3,640	-	3,924	5,440	298	1,231	737
May	58,814	7,351	3,819	2,737	4,733	-	4,675	7,147	450	1,373	938
June	47,238	6,408	3,413	1,921	2,956	-	3,650	3,965	496	1,165	515
July	46,284	5,457	4,039	1,282	2,033	-	3,225	3,402	444	1,049	248
August	47,353	5,108	3,238	1,068	2,687	-	4,117	4,135	29	957	205
September	48,634	5,544	3,925	1,734	2,285	-	3,995	4,904	6	1,094	272
October	57,857	7,549	4,669	2,045	2,882	-	6,538	6,178	30	971	160
November	46,698	5,845	3,696	1,634	2,436	-	5,418	3,895	214	948	152
December	47,545	5,535	4,154	1,322	2,677	-	5,739	4,924	255	977	237
January - 1953	48,350	6,238	3,969	f/ 726	2,677	-	5,459	5,196	688	1,122	751
February	41,660	5,993	3,436	2	2,487	-	5,151	3,909	625	912	622
March	44,947	5,771	4,238	-	2,023	-	4,740	5,586	633	965	712
April	51,395	6,752	3,973	-	1,219	-	7,863	7,568	850	1,150	649
May	52,487	6,850	4,535	-	153	-	7,390	9,062	790	1,414	695
June	54,756	7,573	4,534	-	151	-	7,569	10,021	794	1,160	754
July (through the 27th)	48,433	6,826	3,915	-	36	-	7,303	7,555	599	1,014	797

a/ Includes 26 through 30 Jun 50.
b/ F-84 type acft began operations Dec 50.
c/ F-86 type acft began operations Dec 50.
d/ F-94 type acft began operations Jan 52.
e/ F-82 type acft removed from combat status Feb 52.
f/ F-51 type acft removed from combat status Jan 53.
g/ Breakdown not available and is included in Misc.

TABLE 49 — USAF OPERATIONAL FLYING TIME BY TYPE MODEL, BY MONTH — 26 JUNE 1950 THROUGH 27 JULY 1953 — CONTINUED

MONTH	RF-51	RF-80	C-46	VC/C-47	C-54	C-119	C-124	T/LT-6	H-5 YH/H-19	SA-16 SB/TB-29	MISC
Total	19,019	24,491	125,914	112,853	203,311	105,824	16,690	110,641	10,701	12,607	41,274
July - 1950 a/	-	g/	991	2,546	494	-	-	529	g/	g/	667
August	-	g/	291	3,696	538	95	-	2,816	g/	g/	2,451
September	-	g/	716	1,877	2,171	1,044	-	3,954	g/	g/	3,468
October	-	g/	1,234	2,041	3,959	4,705	-	3,604	g/	g/	3,514
November	-	g/	2,637	2,265	3,898	5,160	-	3,609	g/	g/	2,958
December	g/ h/	g/	3,388	1,830	4,442	5,539	-	3,271	g/	g/	3,222
January - 1952	g/	g/	4,544	1,882	6,417	4,114	-	3,904	g/	g/	3,934
February	g/	g/	4,158	1,838	7,424	4,023	-	3,610	g/	g/	3,613
March	-	705	3,620	2,005	6,369	3,654	-	3,746	328	398	475
April	552	908	2,697	2,429	6,532	753	-	4,280	287	182	256
May	334	862	910	3,422	9,052	4,053	-	4,145	206	100	196
June	267	788	2,999	3,665	9,469	4,642	-	4,714	350	77	189
July	233	596	2,163	4,991	8,049	2,031	-	3,309	423	187	117
August	212	623	2,759	3,463	8,517	2,937	-	3,314	365	144	95
September	202	709	1,045	3,346	9,193	1,628	i/ 12	3,184	173	48	81
October	256	937	1,621	2,933	8,640	2,357	62	3,040	317	39	241
November	866	667	1,575	3,317	8,727	1,959	-	3,848	122	151	189
December	1,436	638	2,211	3,341	8,131	2,702	-	2,355	115	189	317
January - 1952	1,643	621	2,316	2,964	8,517	2,032	-	2,666	169	93	277
February	1,364	577	2,958	2,570	8,223	1,024	-	1,841	196	205	213
March	1,278	607	3,181	3,431	8,804	1,622	-	2,246	274	364	346
April	1,258	692	2,051	3,113	9,671	1,990	-	2,498	321	436	496
May	1,848	1,000	3,175	2,565	8,918	2,702	-	3,297	521	518	1,047
June	1,534	900	5,667	2,775	5,793	1,109	8	3,038	543	525	857
July	978	523	5,955	3,436	9,430	781	139	2,240	432	537	654
August	1,328	787	5,520	4,180	8,249	814	274	2,695	439	484	1,039
September	900	918	4,858	4,320	5,966	2,104	1,009	2,823	410	623	944
October	895	1,153	5,097	3,723	5,135	3,638	1,306	3,384	488	821	1,195
November	660	969	5,203	2,963	3,279	3,620	1,545	2,358	418	541	904
December	605	841	5,433	2,616	2,035	3,808	1,560	2,515	483	832	997
January - 1953	308	780	5,629	2,763	1,594	4,792	1,403	2,294	455	745	761
February	j/ 62	783	5,180	2,189	1,215	3,567	1,622	2,178	463	478	786
March	-	822	4,975	3,583	893	3,624	2,030	2,278	581	608	885
April	-	1,635	5,071	3,460	760	2,802	1,817	3,301	581	928	1,016
May	-	1,417	5,081	3,773	626	3,500	1,954	2,829	484	916	1,018
June	-	1,158	4,835	3,735	922	5,326	1,080	2,918	514	842	870
July (through the 27th)	-	875	4,170	3,807	1,259	5,573	869	2,010	243	596	986

h/ RF-51 type acft began operations Dec 50.
i/ C-124 type acft began operations Sep 51.
j/ RF-51 type acft removed from combat status Feb 53.

Source: Operations Statistics Division, Directorate of Statistical Services, DCS/C.

TABLE 50 — USAF NON OPERATIONAL FLYING TIME BY TYPE MODEL — BY MONTH — 26 JUNE 1950 THROUGH 27 JULY 1953

(Overall Theater Figures Including Non-Committed Units)

MONTH	TOTAL	B-26	B-29	F-51	F-80	F-82	F-84	F-86	F-94	RB/WB-26	RB/WB-29
Total	1,320,631	91,179	52,302	37,080	124,771	10,136	112,893	46,665	52,857	6,567	50,128
July - 1950 a/	21,116	162	2,984	592	3,949	540	-	-	-	g/	g/
August	22,803	355	822	649	4,349	704	-	-	-	g/	g/
September	26,170	489	628	413	3,647	934	-	-	-	g/	g/
October	26,914	1,564	848	449	3,207	828	-	-	-	g/	g/
November	27,396	2,191	568	380	3,092	639	-	-	-	g/	g/
December	22,712	654	349	384	3,057	611	b/ 519	c/ 175	-	g/	g/
January - 1951	22,019	660	725	276	3,399	593	404	1,449	-	g/	g/
February	20,396	549	545	499	3,580	501	182	1,354	-	g/	g/
March	25,261	1,004	924	446	3,437	562	476	852	d/ 1	204	1,383
April	26,575	943	584	549	4,135	463	251	1,086	193	184	1,239
May	34,227	2,545	802	835	4,447	430	635	800	338	332	1,599
June	34,126	3,195	1,106	1,050	4,313	361	880	1,166	208	321	1,403
July	36,507	2,936	1,140	2,573	3,587	397	1,528	758	216	205	1,372
August	37,657	2,591	1,073	1,930	3,456	406	3,032	946	262	313	1,467
September	35,383	2,472	1,311	1,776	3,255	375	3,652	734	304	250	1,404
October	38,941	2,172	1,187	1,614	3,240	449	3,187	585	460	201	1,570
November	37,118	1,859	1,226	1,608	2,937	400	2,303	896	875	145	1,300
December	36,054	2,462	885	1,460	2,659	317	2,296	836	823	197	1,262
January - 1952	38,857	2,194	1,316	1,618	2,986	318	2,990	690	926	133	1,591
February	36,718	3,090	1,024	1,234	2,805	e/ 232	3,204	878	1,083	188	1,689
March	43,291	3,606	1,328	1,414	2,935	70	3,858	843	1,741	295	1,322
April	46,372	4,256	1,939	1,520	3,197	6	4,286	981	1,986	278	1,512
May	42,829	3,197	1,618	1,510	3,336	-	4,066	1,800	2,320	200	1,652
June	39,042	3,027	1,558	1,298	2,680	-	2,476	1,479	2,627	179	1,774
July	38,531	3,278	1,792	1,153	2,921	-	4,170	1,053	2,695	209	2,422
August	41,788	4,555	2,283	1,789	3,421	-	3,717	1,215	2,995	264	2,374
September	43,907	4,326	2,111	1,466	3,215	-	6,072	1,092	3,110	182	2,232
October	44,649	4,538	2,141	1,442	2,897	-	5,051	1,168	3,493	338	2,705
November	39,865	4,213	2,163	1,354	3,079	-	4,654	1,347	2,717	238	2,290
December	38,394	2,512	1,876	1,060	3,302	-	5,638	1,522	2,966	236	2,191
January - 1953	38,535	3,026	1,549	f/ 1,186	3,367	-	5,418	1,673	2,671	213	1,774
February	36,969	2,788	1,512	896	2,878	-	5,909	2,476	2,392	182	1,657
March	46,404	3,196	2,169	554	3,606	-	8,725	3,281	3,363	192	1,930
April	48,851	3,106	2,237	59	4,061	-	6,015	4,356	3,704	146	1,845
May	46,231	2,846	2,300	20	3,771	-	6,562	3,322	3,114	340	1,802
June	36,342	2,202	1,775	19	3,122	-	4,643	2,177	2,636	242	1,727
July (through the 27th)	41,681	2,420	1,904	5	3,446	-	6,094	3,675	2,638	160	1,640

a/ Includes 26 through 30 June 1950.
b/ F-84 type acft began operations Dec 50.
c/ F-86 type acft began operations Dec 50.
d/ F-94 type acft arrived in theater Mar 51 and committed to combat Jan 52.
e/ F-82 type acft removed from combat status Feb 52.
f/ F-51 type acft removed from combat status Jan 53.
g/ Breakdown not available and is included in Misc.

Source: Operations Statistics Division, Directorate of Statistical Services, DCS/C.

TABLE 50 — USAF NON OPERATIONAL FLYING TIME BY TYPE MODEL, BY MONTH — 26 JUNE 1950 THROUGH 27 JULY 1953 — CONTINUED

(Overall Theater Figures Including Non-Committed Units)

MONTH	RF-51	RF-80	C-46	VC/C-47	C-54	C-119	C-124	LT/T-6	H-5 YH/H-19	SA-16 SB/TB-29	MISC
Total	1,865	4,082	93,033	211,714	58,782	49,812	5,333	67,664	7,580	30,385	205,803
July - 1950 a/	-	g/	740	1,506	2,759	-	-	-	g/	g/	7,884
August	-	g/	1,258	1,819	3,054	365	-	60	g/	g/	9,368
September	-	g/	2,218	4,254	1,799	3,083	-	28	g/	g/	8,677
October	-	g/	2,301	4,640	259	4,363	-	20	g/	g/	8,435
November	-	g/	2,866	6,180	364	2,681	-	85	g/	g/	8,350
December	g/ h/	g/	2,228	5,739	1,254	252	-	46	g/	g/	7,444
January - 1951	g/	g/	438	5,118	857	602	-	35	g/	g/	7,463
February	g/	g/	546	5,150	386	470	-	118	g/	g/	6,516
March	54	118	1,038	5,604	2,209	486	-	1,207	65	297	4,894
April	41	97	2,640	5,996	3,333	88	-	1,132	67	621	2,933
May	8	26	5,893	5,840	1,445	1,279	-	1,411	217	735	4,610
June	40	202	3,837	6,381	1,392	839	-	1,414	190	796	5,032
July	51	116	3,689	8,357	1,561	1,343	-	1,570	141	723	4,244
August	53	124	3,854	8,086	2,000	1,471	-	1,159	315	883	4,236
September	13	132	1,825	7,961	2,190	1,005	i/ 57	1,090	426	877	4,274
October	65	60	3,329	8,534	2,368	2,460	-	1,234	402	1,147	4,677
November	173	83	4,436	7,833	2,337	2,346	-	1,142	322	864	4,033
December	125	91	4,815	7,589	2,784	1,231	-	1,105	311	1,079	3,727
January - 1952	126	165	5,345	7,822	2,684	653	-	1,657	305	1,033	4,305
February	64	171	6,197	4,923	2,522	569	-	1,522	223	1,353	3,747
March	97	153	5,325	6,892	2,701	1,593	-	2,465	385	1,179	5,089
April	90	179	6,571	6,767	2,563	1,640	-	2,224	207	1,206	4,964
May	88	109	3,173	6,883	3,153	1,069	108	2,984	142	935	4,486
June	81	113	968	6,871	5,239	718	515	2,637	152	974	3,676
July	155	122	701	7,241	940	1,033	494	2,782	253	1,301	3,816
August	94	165	1,165	6,223	869	1,600	421	2,777	225	1,159	4,477
September	202	220	1,319	5,335	490	1,296	958	3,144	269	1,368	5,500
October	37	85	1,411	5,149	492	1,678	637	3,589	320	1,443	6,035
November	49	70	1,103	4,608	292	654	422	3,353	325	1,568	5,366
December	39	123	636	4,765	293	756	239	3,275	308	1,116	5,541
January - 1953	34	186	1,046	4,824	201	884	143	3,164	302	1,067	5,807
February	j/ 26	83	785	4,236	209	1,068	186	3,164	296	1,033	5,193
March	25	82	1,448	4,222	447	1,663	268	3,701	392	990	6,150
April	5	214	1,639	4,382	727	4,298	336	3,718	245	1,013	6,745
May	6	268	1,989	5,288	644	1,563	261	3,610	214	979	7,332
June	19	267	1,671	4,220	823	1,412	101	2,858	254	1,012	5,162
July (through the 27th)	5	258	2,590	4,476	1,142	1,301	187	2,184	307	1,634	5,615

h/ RF-51 type acft began operations Dec 50.
i/ C-124 type acft began operations Sep 51.
j/ RF-51 type acft removed from combat status Feb 53.

Source: Operations Statistics Division, Directorate of Statistical Services, DCS/C.

TABLE 51 — FEAF BOMBER COMMAND SORTIES BY TYPE TARGET, BY QUARTER — 26 JUNE 1950 THROUGH 27 JULY 1953

QUARTER	TOTAL SORTIES	EFFECTIVE	PRIMARY TARGETS	SECONDARY AND OTHER TARGETS	CLOSE SUPPORT	ROADS RAILROADS AND BRIDGES	AIRFIELDS	MARSHALLING YARDS	SUPPLY CENTERS	TROOP AREAS	INDUSTRIAL AREAS	OTHER a/	NON-EFFECTIVE
Total	20,277	19,588	16,334	3,254	2,803	4,545	1,251	2,919	4,603	718	1,393	1,356	689
July - September - 1950 b/	3,040	2,954	2,477	477	373	939	23	822	-	-	656	141	86
October - December	2,145	2,072	1,597	475	72	574	8	338	869	-	92	119	73
January - March - 1951	2,268	2,208	1,660	548	28	740	100	293	844	137	11	55	60
April - June	1,584	1,542	1,034	508	412	298	331	84	361	7	1	48	42
July - September	1,511	1,471	1,019	452	273	169	101	494	325	13	2	94	40
October - December	1,390	1,320	1,154	166	392	252	231	230	25	32	30	128	70
January - March - 1952	1,369	1,305	1,200	105	259	622	46	122	133	-	16	107	64
April - June	1,179	1,141	1,030	111	159	751	9	80	-	-	44	98	38
July - September	1,299	1,233	1,117	116	148	56	-	258	352	10	321	88	66
October - December	1,354	1,298	1,198	100	179	20	34	47	440	168	124	286	56
January - March - 1953	1,268	1,216	1,111	105	186	42	13	124	507	185	43	116	52
April - June	1,432	1,401	1,322	79	261	50	219	26	631	96	53	65	31
1 July - 27 July	438	427	415	12	61	32	136	1	116	70	-	11	11

a/ Includes Leaflet and Surveillance Missions; Headquarters and Communications Areas and Miscellaneous Targets. b/ Includes 27 through 30 June 1950.
Source: Operations Statistics Division, Directorate of Statistical Services, DCS/C.

TABLE 52 — FEAF BOMBER COMMAND TONNAGE BY TYPE TARGET, BY QUARTER — 26 JUNE 1950 THROUGH 27 JULY 1953

QUARTER	TOTAL TONS DROPPED	EFFECTIVE	PRIMARY TARGETS	SECONDARY AND OTHER TARGETS	CLOSE SUPPORT	ROADS RAILROADS AND BRIDGES	AIRFIELDS	MARSHALLING YARDS	SUPPLY CENTERS	TROOP AREAS	INDUS-TRIAL AREAS	OTHER	LEAFLETS a/	TONS SALVOED
Total	167,100	159,440	132,649	26,791	26,098	36,096	9,663	24,668	42,793	6,483	12,107	1,532	27,180	7,660
July - September - 1950 b/	24,056	23,142	19,397	3,745	3,288	6,712	183	6,712	-	-	5,540	707	1,311	914
October - December	16,314	15,507	11,645	3,862	636	4,083	64	2,869	6,828	-	749	278	2,256	807
January - March - 1951	19,334	18,571	13,618	4,953	253	5,710	845	2,699	7,736	1,227	101	-	1,114	763
April - June	12,835	12,310	8,296	4,014	4,000	2,020	2,598	704	2,917	48	10	13	1,453	525
July - September	11,694	11,184	7,569	3,615	2,609	989	699	3,955	2,715	102	57	58	2,714	510
October - December	10,293	9,518	8,385	1,133	3,491	1,854	1,624	1,745	204	249	229	122	3,348	775
January - March - 1952	12,172	11,440	10,543	897	2,512	5,916	343	1,137	1,265	-	155	112	2,802	732
April - June	10,263	9,862	8,922	940	1,512	7,035	59	766	-	-	450	40	2,933	401
July - September	10,697	10,073	9,161	912	1,313	510	10	2,341	3,001	76	2,802	20	2,308	624
October - December	11,747	11,167	10,175	992	1,710	133	244	441	5,777	1,516	1,211	135	2,427	580
January - March - 1953	11,370	10,821	9,810	1,011	1,758	391	101	1,090	5,313	1,728	393	47	1,354	549
April - June	12,403	12,039	11,426	613	2,448	463	1,695	202	5,972	849	410	-	2,555	364
1 July - 27 July	3,922	3,806	3,702	104	568	280	1,198	7	1,065	688	-	-	605	116

a/ Figures are number of bombs only and are not included in tonnage. b/ Includes 27 through 30 June 1950.
Source: Operations Statistics Division, Directorate of Statistical Services, DCS/C.

TABLE 53 — 315TH AIR DIVISION COMBAT CARGO OPERATIONS, BY AREA — 10 SEPTEMBER 1950 THROUGH 27 JULY 1953

QUARTER ENDING	TOTAL SORTIES	TONS CARGO	FREIGHT	TOTAL PERSONNEL	PATIENTS	PASSENGERS	TON MILES (IN THOUS)	PERSONNEL MILES (IN THOUS)
	INTO KOREA							
Total	65,334	296,316	203,307	907,299	1,037	906,262	75,609	481,338
September - 1950 a/	1,400	7,932	7,826	7,572	-	7,572		
December	7,279	39,226	38,363	23,280	-	23,280	b/14,027	b/46,678
March - 1951	7,362	35,271	33,234	37,655	-	37,655		
June	8,614	46,209	40,439	54,329	3	54,326	14,445	33,486
September	5,873	23,247	14,058	87,745	-	87,745	6,429	45,995
December	6,372	25,566	15,895	92,190	-	92,190	4,958	44,667
March - 1952	5,263	20,360	10,331	97,695	780	96,915	3,828	51,058
June	4,610	20,043	8,405	105,433	17	105,416	5,140	49,055
September	4,694	18,577	7,968	94,333	-	94,333	6,450	48,010
December	5,413	18,639	8,048	102,868	221	102,647	5,578	46,979
March - 1953	3,668	18,558	6,680	105,587	1	105,586	5,055	57,956
June	3,817	17,958	8,345	89,579	15	89,564	5,797	52,368
July (through the 27th)	969	4,730	3,715	9,033	-	9,033	3,902	5,086
	INTRA KOREA							
Total	58,573	133,755	84,580	551,602	134,916	416,686	12,553	96,911
September - 1950 a/	116	217	134	937	-	937		
December	9,495	42,293	36,419	75,016	17,856	57,160	b/2,343	b/10,856
March - 1951	4,609	13,125	8,213	53,479	18,665	34,814		
June	6,391	13,668	6,966	62,244	20,973	41,271	1,492	9,422
September	4,040	8,987	5,045	44,215	11,550	32,665	975	9,583
December	3,729	7,754	4,621	35,390	9,696	25,694	1,111	6,529
March - 1952	3,579	6,521	3,839	35,278	8,596	26,682	533	6,832
June	4,652	7,188	3,600	38,882	5,780	33,102	441	9,394
September	4,656	6,336	2,796	36,851	5,476	31,375	921	8,582
December	3,813	7,084	3,558	39,894	8,519	31,375	1,672	10,522
March - 1953	5,590	7,956	3,595	46,987	8,223	38,764	1,112	10,230
June	6,213	9,514	4,177	61,660	12,358	49,302	1,510	11,339
July (through the 27th)	1,690	3,112	1,617	20,769	7,224	13,545	443	3,622
	OUT OF KOREA							
Total	45,572	149,039	48,783	1,003,878	135,125	868,753	32,828	516,352
September - 1950 a/	351	747	111	6,453	5,973	480		
December	3,560	8,602	5,079	39,630	22,218	17,412	b/6,447	b/51,015
March - 1951	4,277	12,825	7,067	61,228	22,011	39,217		
June	4,155	9,815	2,320	70,679	15,648	55,031	2,803	37,654
September	4,577	11,802	3,245	88,365	10,827	77,538	1,770	50,416
December	5,175	14,745	4,729	103,882	14,173	89,709	2,356	49,222
March - 1952	4,463	14,358	4,676	100,464	5,979	94,485	1,968	58,949
June	3,739	15,527	4,559	105,220	6,266	98,954	3,684	48,393
September	3,925	14,106	3,960	97,784	7,602	90,182	3,368	48,428
December	3,512	14,913	3,814	107,349	8,504	98,845	3,601	46,910
March - 1953	3,570	14,833	3,483	110,681	5,738	104,943	3,677	59,957
June	3,431	13,603	3,852	96,660	6,034	90,626	2,461	57,383
July (through the 27th)	837	3,163	1,888	15,483	4,152	11,331	693	8,025
	INTRA JAPAN							
Total	40,864	100,526	55,093	450,616	36,726	413,890	37,374	188,766
September - 1950 a/	660	1,866	1,294	6,804	3,376	3,428		
December	3,384	7,211	4,490	30,334	12,898	17,436	b/7,813	b/18,993
March - 1951	3,811	9,631	6,710	32,605	5,387	27,218		
June	2,763	7,339	3,869	33,322	930	32,392	3,591	18,219
September	3,798	9,616	4,540	52,812	1,022	51,790	3,177	22,862
December	3,508	9,542	5,041	45,168	2,121	43,047	3,057	19,448
March - 1952	3,473	8,264	4,378	38,843	1,115	37,728	2,641	16,067
June	2,882	8,403	3,636	44,828	1,161	43,667	2,916	25,980
September	2,915	8,820	3,688	47,669	2,316	45,353	3,072	13,800
December	3,644	9,037	4,431	43,638	2,682	40,956	3,072	14,878
March - 1953	3,372	8,226	4,631	33,611	1,657	31,954	3,215	16,826
June	4,763	9,122	5,897	31,868	1,486	30,382	3,332	17,560
July (through the 27th)	1,891	3,449	2,488	9,114	575	8,539	1,488	4,133

a/ 315th Air Division began Combat Cargo Operations, 10 September 1950.
b/ Cumulative from September 1950 through March 1951. Breakdown by Quarter not available.
Source: Operations Statistics Division, Directorate of Statistical Services, DCS/C.

TABLE 54 — TOTAL 315TH AIR DIVISION COMBAT CARGO OPERATIONS — 10 SEPTEMBER 1950 THROUGH 27 JULY 1953

QUARTER ENDING	AVERAGE POSSESSED	AVERAGE COMBAT READY	TOTAL SORTIES	FLYING HOURS	TONS CARGO	FREIGHT	TOTAL PERSONNEL	PATIENTS	PASSENGERS	TON MILES (IN THOUS)	PERSONNEL MILES (IN THOUS)
Total	210	140	210,343	614,836	679,636	391,763	2,913,395	307,804	2,605,591	158,364	1,283,367
September - 1950 a/	179	105	2,527	11,318	10,762	9,365	21,766	9,349	12,417	2,250	5,262
December	195	116	23,718	61,167	97,332	84,351	168,260	52,972	115,288	14,240	43,920
March - 1951	229	167	20,059	53,672	70,852	55,224	184,967	46,063	138,904	14,140	78,360
June	220	150	21,923	63,874	77,031	53,594	220,574	37,554	183,020	22,331	98,781
September	222	172	18,288	65,265	53,652	26,888	273,137	23,399	249,738	12,351	128,856
December	220	160	18,784	62,042	57,607	30,286	276,630	25,990	250,640	11,482	119,866
March - 1952	211	128	16,778	58,129	49,503	23,224	272,280	16,470	255,810	8,970	132,906
June	204	135	15,883	55,470	51,161	20,200	294,363	13,224	281,139	12,181	132,822
September	220	132	16,190	49,076	47,839	18,412	276,637	15,394	261,243	13,811	118,820
December	216	146	16,382	45,078	49,673	19,851	293,749	19,926	273,823	13,923	119,289
March	200	130	16,200	39,640	49,573	18,389	296,866	15,619	281,247	13,059	144,969
June	200	143	18,224	37,299	50,197	22,271	279,767	19,893	259,874	13,100	138,650
July (through the 27th)	208	137	5,387	12,806	14,454	9,708	54,399	11,951	42,448	6,526	20,866

a/ 315th Air Division began Combat Cargo Operations, 10 September 1950.
Source: Operations Statistics Division, Directorate of Statistical Services, DCS/C.

TABLE 55 — 315TH AIR DIVISION COMBAT CARGO OPERATIONS, BY TYPE MODEL — 10 SEPTEMBER 1950 THROUGH 27 JULY 1953

QUARTER ENDING	AVERAGE POSSESSED	AVERAGE COMBAT READY	TOTAL SORTIES	FLYING HOURS	TONS CARGO	FREIGHT	TOTAL PERSONNEL	PATIENTS	PASSENGERS	TON MILES (IN THOUS)	PERSONNEL MILES (IN THOUS)
	C - 46										
Total	57	41	55,681	170,334	124,216	65,836	581,899	24,379	557,520	31,245	186,428
September - 1950 a/	52	19	721	3,748	2,167	1,834	2,959	-	2,959	280	1,160
December	47	29	5,185	12,985	15,588	13,096	22,147	-	22,147	2,240	6,100
March - 1951	65	50	5,648	13,266	13,393	9,334	36,083	-	36,083	2,460	10,130
June	51	39	4,800	15,791	14,034	9,476	44,524	163	44,361	3,646	10,846
September	57	47	3,508	14,173	7,528	4,128	33,649	-	33,649	2,124	10,918
December	60	46	3,831	14,424	9,592	6,508	31,446	2	31,444	2,657	9,010
March - 1952	57	39	4,398	17,286	9,550	5,618	40,476	1,051	39,425	3,038	12,288
June	54	39	3,064	14,740	7,428	3,412	38,412	25	38,387	1,025	12,588
September	61	48	4,151	16,198	9,277	3,207	54,570	628	53,942	2,644	16,732
December	58	47	4,048	14,526	9,234	2,964	69,672	5,418	64,254	2,553	20,677
March - 1953	61	47	5,271	15,158	10,233	2,241	78,464	7,413	71,051	2,384	29,046
June	59	43	8,726	14,083	13,144	2,695	110,796	6,307	104,489	3,613	40,031
July (through the 27th)	59	41	2,330	3,956	3,048	1,323	18,701	3,372	15,329	2,581	6,902

TABLE 55 — 315TH AIR DIVISION COMBAT CARGO OPERATIONS, BY TYPE MODEL — 10 SEPTEMBER 1950 THROUGH 27 JULY 1953 — Continued

QUARTER ENDING	AVERAGE POSSESSED	AVERAGE COMBAT READY	TOTAL SORTIES	FLYING HOURS	TONS CARGO	FREIGHT	TOTAL PERSONNEL	PATIENTS	PASSENGERS	TON MILES (IN THOUS)	PERSONNEL MILES (IN THOUS)
					C - 47						
Total	24	17	36,814	66,359	54,973	30,021	324,091	120,026	204,065	5,355	51,303
September - 1950 a/	28	23	706	1,437	1,612	1,240	5,877	2,568	3,309	100	1,250
December	27	16	5,126	7,895	8,925	4,980	52,253	17,283	34,970	620	5,340
March - 1951	19	12	2,616	3,939	5,290	3,956	29,420	17,562	11,858	630	5,580
June	27	21	4,410	7,969	7,738	3,767	36,599	13,251	23,348	724	4,950
September	26	20	3,446	8,900	5,809	3,292	32,308	10,960	21,348	780	4,636
December	26	19	2,999	7,594	5,287	2,887	24,432	9,991	14,441	1,248	4,689
March - 1952	27	19	2,177	5,600	3,214	2,268	18,939	8,835	10,104	307	3,198
June	23	15	3,127	4,528	3,322	1,864	19,910	6,441	13,469	171	4,191
September	21	12	2,803	4,113	3,070	1,520	19,987	6,196	13,791	209	4,085
December	23	15	3,027	4,725	2,902	1,322	22,121	8,078	14,043	147	4,654
March - 1953	22	15	2,731	3,768	2,281	1,024	17,837	6,669	11,168	156	3,114
June	23	17	2,876	4,633	4,361	1,472	35,196	9,507	25,689	232	4,858
July (through the 27th)	22	15	770	1,258	1,162	429	9,212	2,685	6,527	31	758
					C - 54						
Total	41	31	71,906	238,078	293,653	146,839	1,488,952	152,511	1,336,441	62,161	765,251
September - 1950 a/	24	22	494	2,761	3,092	2,736	9,942	6,781	3,161	750	2,460
December	35	23	6,419	17,985	35,699	31,398	73,918	35,689	38,229	5,330	29,300
March - 1951	59	47	7,906	23,401	34,007	25,022	108,354	28,501	79,853	6,350	60,300
June	61	46	9,482	30,375	43,112	28,680	135,977	24,140	111,837	14,206	81,671
September	60	46	8,706	31,162	32,209	12,649	199,086	12,439	186,647	7,305	111,574
December	60	46	9,273	30,486	33,888	12,760	215,465	15,649	199,816	4,351	103,918
March - 1952	60	46	8,381	30,251	31,427	10,365	209,666	6,584	203,082	3,800	116,296
June	60	47	7,549	30,308	34,822	9,831	232,316	6,758	225,558	8,354	113,553
September	51	39	7,433	23,644	27,092	7,901	178,137	7,808	170,329	8,106	87,702
December	29	22	3,497	10,436	10,042	2,353	72,304	3,923	68,381	2,098	27,631
March - 1953	10	7	1,216	3,702	3,413	1,174	24,739	791	23,948	916	16,272
June	9	7	1,085	2,308	3,208	1,122	20,284	1,743	18,541	362	11,020
July (through the 27th)	13	10	465	1,259	1,642	848	8,764	1,705	7,059	233	3,554

TABLE 55 — 315TH AIR DIVISION COMBAT CARGO OPERATIONS, BY TYPE MODEL — 10 SEPTEMBER 1950 THROUGH 27 JULY 1953 — Continued

QUARTER ENDING	AVERAGE POSSESSED	AVERAGE COMBAT READY	TOTAL SORTIES	FLYING HOURS	TONS CARGO	FREIGHT	TOTAL PERSONNEL	PATIENTS	PASSENGERS	TON MILES (IN THOUS)	PERSONNEL MILES (IN THOUS)
						C - 119					
Total	79	46	41,367	123,379	151,176	129,375	188,321	-	188,321	45,462	57,688
September - 1950 a/	75	41	606	3,372	3,891	3,555	2,988	-	2,988	1,120	392
December	86	48	6,988	22,302	37,120	34,877	19,942	-	19,942	6,050	3,180
March - 1951	86	58	3,889	13,066	18,162	16,912	11,110	-	11,110	4,700	2,350
June	81	44	3,231	9,739	12,147	11,671	3,474	-	3,474	3,755	1,314
September	79	59	2,624	11,014	8,051	6,769	8,038	-	8,038	2,120	1,716
December	74	49	2,660	9,476	8,551	7,899	4,721	-	4,721	3,132	2,194
March - 1952	67	24	1,822	4,992	5,312	4,973	3,199	-	3,199	1,825	1,124
June	67	34	2,143	5,894	5,589	5,093	3,725	-	3,725	2,631	2,490
September	71	27	1,438	3,699	5,003	3,937	9,417	-	9,417	1,763	2,968
December	81	48	4,717	10,980	14,752	9,210	49,270	-	49,270	5,988	14,371
March - 1953	82	47	5,558	11,957	15,142	7,926	64,146	-	64,146	5,123	19,929
June	84	59	4,114	11,424	11,831	11,267	5,031	-	5,031	4,543	4,347
July (through the 27th)	90	61	1,577	5,464	5,625	5,286	3,260	-	3,260	2,712	1,313
						C - 124					
Total	9	5	4,575	16,686	55,618	19,692	330,132	10,888	319,244	14,141	222,697
September - 1951 b/	-	-	4	16	55	50	56	-	56	22	12
December	-	-	21	62	289	232	566	348	218	94	55
March - 1952	-	-	-	-	-	-	-	-	-	-	-
June	-	-	-	-	-	-	-	-	-	-	-
September	16	6	365	1,422	3,397	1,847	14,526	762	13,764	1,089	7,333
December	25	14	1,093	4,411	12,743	4,002	80,382	2,507	77,875	3,137	51,956
March - 1953	25	14	1,424	5,055	18,504	6,024	111,680	746	110,934	4,480	76,608
June	25	17	1,423	4,851	17,653	5,715	108,460	2,336	106,124	4,350	78,394
July (through the 27th)	24	10	245	869	2,977	1,822	14,462	4,189	10,273	969	8,339

a/ 315th Air Division began Combat Cargo Operations, 10 September 1950.

b/ C-124 type aircraft began operations September 1951.

Source: Operations Statistics Division, Directorate of Statistical Services, DCS/C.

TABLE 56 — MATS OPERATIONS FROM U S (McCHORD AND TRAVIS) TO PACIFIC AREA, INCLUDING TOKYO— FISCAL YEAR 1951

MONTH	DEPARTURES				TONNAGE				PASSENGERS			
	TOTAL	MILITARY CARRIER	CONTRACT CARRIER	UNITED NATIONS	TOTAL	MILITARY CARRIER	CONTRACT CARRIER	UNITED NATIONS	TOTAL	MILITARY CARRIER	CONTRACT CARRIER	UNITED NATIONS
PACIFIC AREA												
FISCAL YEAR 1951 - Total	5,910	1,994	3,500	416	31,096.8	11,586.0	17,676.7	1,834.1	91,764	27,040	57,305	7,419
June through August 1950	850	347	471	32	4,660.7	1,964.9	2,489.6	206.2	21,786	9,560	11,192	1,034
September	618	276	308	34	3,305.4	1,499.0	1,626.6	179.8	13,011	5,229	7,040	742
October	551	252	261	38	2,716.6	1,261.9	1,277.4	177.3	10,536	3,417	6,272	847
November	401	218	145	38	1,869.9	1,059.9	643.3	166.7	6,119	2,829	2,580	710
December	480	178	269	33	2,599.9	1,202.1	1,231.5	166.3	6,118	2,045	3,593	480
January - 1951	566	171	364	31	3,003.9	1,083.8	1,748.7	171.4	6,785	1,294	4,862	629
February	520	101	376	43	2,544.4	533.6	1,851.5	159.3	5,657	464	4,572	621
March	466	89	330	47	2,436.6	590.1	1,670.3	176.2	5,067	527	3,969	571
April	518	124	357	37	2,845.6	851.1	1,866.9	127.6	5,573	233	4,753	587
May	487	134	313	40	2,628.2	867.2	1,616.4	144.6	5,271	737	4,009	525
June	453	104	306	43	2,485.6	672.4	1,654.5	158.7	5,841	705	4,463	673
TOKYO												
FISCAL YEAR 1951 - Total	NOT AVAILABLE	NOT AVAILABLE	NOT AVAILABLE	NOT AVAILABLE	26,094.0	8,046.4	16,222.3	1,825.3	76,864	19,062	50,383	7,419
June through August 1950					4,079.7	1,467.5	2,406.0	206.2	19,717	7,758	10,925	1,034
September					2,957.3	1,161.6	1,615.9	179.8	11,829	4,067	7,020	742
October					2,435.9	987.9	1,270.7	177.3	9,573	2,467	6,259	847
November					1,632.4	837.6	632.4	162.4	5,371	2,116	2,545	710
December					2,237.3	854.9	1,220.6	161.8	4,738	725	3,533	480
January - 1951					2,539.6	631.0	1,737.2	171.4	5,652	188	4,835	629
February					1,986.0	268.8	1,557.9	159.3	4,343	242	3,480	621
March					1,839.6	332.2	1,331.2	176.2	3,339	188	2,580	571
April					2,178.5	434.5	1,616.4	127.6	3,753	184	2,982	587
May					2,091.3	559.2	1,387.5	144.6	3,835	548	2,762	525
June					2,116.4	511.2	1,446.5	158.7	4,714	579	3,462	673

Source: Operations Statistics Division, Directorate of Statistical Services, DCS/C.

TABLE 57 — MATS OPERATIONS FROM U S (McCHORD AND TRAVIS) TO PACIFIC AREA, INCLUDING TOKYO — FISCAL YEAR 1952

MONTH	DEPARTURES				TONNAGE				PASSENGERS			
	TOTAL	MILITARY CARRIER	CONTRACT CARRIER	UNITED NATIONS	TOTAL	MILITARY CARRIER	CONTRACT CARRIER	UNITED NATIONS	TOTAL	MILITARY CARRIER	CONTRACT CARRIER	UNITED NATIONS
PACIFIC AREA												
FISCAL YEAR 1952 - Total	5,678	1,400	3,805	473	28,489.9	7,849.1	18,958.4	1,682.4	70,331	13,641	49,601	7,089
July - 1951	447	99	303	45	2,508.5	732.1	1,609.4	167.0	5,292	439	4,319	534
August	422	67	310	45	2,392.2	531.3	1,691.1	169.8	6,149	571	4,973	605
September	444	63	340	41	2,281.7	410.5	1,729.0	142.2	5,801	98	5,108	595
October	539	118	380	41	3,013.4	888.5	1,975.5	149.4	6,706	801	5,420	485
November	486	58	389	39	2,441.5	376.2	1,927.9	137.4	5,572	258	4,746	568
December	496	95	362	39	2,334.7	462.5	1,732.5	139.7	4,339	268	3,552	519
January - 1952	495	158	296	41	2,183.9	718.0	1,327.9	138.0	5,047	1,593	2,946	508
February	474	145	291	38	2,224.6	708.2	1,380.2	136.2	5,554	1,564	3,485	505
March	505	178	288	39	2,423.3	844.1	1,438.5	140.7	6,737	2,383	3,728	626
April	480	153	289	38	2,274.7	751.1	1,389.7	133.9	6,756	1,914	3,930	912
May	480	162	279	39	2,240.0	819.1	1,282.2	138.7	6,379	2,205	3,481	693
June	410	104	278	28	2,171.4	607.5	1,474.5	89.4	5,999	1,547	3,913	539
TOKYO												
FISCAL YEAR 1952 - Total	NOT AVAILABLE	NOT AVAILABLE	NOT AVAILABLE	NOT AVAILABLE	23,085.3	4,497.5	16,909.8	1,678.0	53,903	4,756	42,058	7,089
July - 1951					2,007.3	533.3	1,307.0	167.0	4,117	389	3,194	534
August					1,952.7	375.1	1,407.8	169.8	4,919	336	3,978	605
September					1,876.7	285.0	1,449.5	142.2	4,698	17	4,086	595
October					2,492.5	685.5	1,657.6	149.4	5,265	571	4,209	485
November					2,101.7	266.9	1,697.4	137.4	4,565	6	3,991	568
December					1,870.5	304.1	1,427.9	138.5	2,889	59	2,311	519
January - 1952					1,818.0	394.3	1,287.6	136.1	3,769	395	2,866	508
February					1,794.1	370.5	1,288.7	134.9	4,315	568	3,242	505
March					1,932.5	387.6	1,404.2	140.7	5,188	929	3,633	626
April					1,826.6	365.8	1,326.9	133.9	5,160	664	3,584	912
May					1,794.4	399.4	1,256.3	138.7	4,888	812	3,383	693
June					1,618.3	130.0	1,398.9	89.4	4,130	10	3,581	539

Source: Operations Statistics Division, Directorate of Statistical Services, DCS/C.

TABLE 58 – MATS OPERATIONS FROM U S (McCHORD AND TRAVIS) TO PACIFIC AREA, INCLUDING TOKYO – FISCAL YEAR 1953 THROUGH 27 JULY 1953

MONTH	DEPARTURES				TONNAGE				PASSENGERS			
	TOTAL	MILITARY CARRIER	CONTRACT CARRIER	UNITED NATIONS	TOTAL	MILITARY CARRIER	CONTRACT CARRIER	UNITED NATIONS	TOTAL	MILITARY CARRIER	CONTRACT CARRIER	UNITED NATIONS
PACIFIC AREA												
FY 1953 and July - Total	5,814	1,907	3,601	306	28,785.8	9,851.2	17,945.5	989.1	77,764	23,886	47,347	6,531
July - 1952	461	154	280	27	2,450.7	886.2	1,476.9	87.6	6,628	2,658	3,427	543
August	461	156	280	25	2,384.9	848.4	1,460.1	76.4	6,615	2,624	3,447	544
September	464	173	266	25	2,293.8	856.0	1,360.6	77.2	6,015	2,072	3,467	476
October	490	185	282	23	2,419.8	1,029.0	1,318.9	71.9	6,524	1,897	4,144	483
November	473	146	303	24	2,214.5	675.8	1,466.7	72.0	5,807	1,416	3,848	543
December	481	153	301	27	2,128.9	719.8	1,324.3	84.8	5,378	1,484	3,342	552
January - 1953	467	143	301	23	2,034.0	644.8	1,323.8	65.4	5,422	1,444	3,587	391
February	460	155	285	20	2,316.3	759.2	1,497.0	60.1	6,603	2,320	3,921	362
March	432	125	279	28	2,033.2	523.4	1,419.6	90.2	5,182	1,118	3,430	634
April	426	126	279	21	2,084.4	612.8	1,395.6	76.0	5,582	1,409	3,658	515
May	406	146	238	22	2,142.8	888.4	1,176.0	78.4	6,082	1,940	3,638	504
June	393	117	256	20	2,068.7	640.7	1,356.6	71.4	5,762	1,579	3,760	423
July (through the 27th)	400	128	251	21	2,213.8	766.7	1,369.4	77.7	6,164	1,925	3,678	561
TOKYO												
FY 1953 and July - Total	NOT AVAILABLE	NOT AVAILABLE	NOT AVAILABLE	NOT AVAILABLE	21,774.7	3,582.0	17,203.6	989.1	56,422	5,714	44,177	6,531
July - 1952					1,974.4	445.8	1,441.0	87.6	5,164	1,325	3,296	543
August					1,645.3	142.6	1,426.3	76.4	4,134	234	3,356	544
September					1,604.2	192.2	1,334.8	77.2	4,070	190	3,404	476
October					1,787.9	433.0	1,283.0	71.9	5,153	593	4,077	483
November					1,733.4	238.2	1,423.2	72.0	4,501	323	3,635	543
December					1,597.9	266.2	1,246.9	84.8	3,947	310	3,085	552
January - 1953					1,601.4	236.8	1,299.2	65.4	4,003	126	3,486	391
February					1,853.0	387.6	1,405.3	60.1	5,070	1,311	3,397	362
March					1,499.3	91.4	1,317.7	90.2	3,719	18	3,067	634
April					1,620.5	225.0	1,319.5	76.0	4,176	244	3,417	515
May					1,667.2	452.8	1,136.0	78.4	4,496	546	3,446	504
June					1,548.6	211.7	1,265.5	71.4	3,811	166	3,222	423
July (through the 27th)					1,641.6	258.7	1,305.2	77.7	4,178	328	3,289	561

Source: Operations Statistics Division, Directorate of Statistical Services, DCS/C.

TABLE 59 — ENGINES REMOVED AND AVERAGE HOURS FLOWN ON SELECTED AIRCRAFT IN FEAF - 26 JUNE 1950 THROUGH 31 JULY 1953

(Average hours flown represents average hours flown on engines since manufacture or last major overhaul.)

TYPE OF ENGINE AND AIRCRAFT	FY - 51 (26 June 1950 - 30 June 1951)		FY - 52 (1 July 1951 - 30 June 1952)		FY - 53 (1 July 1952 - 31 July 1953)	
	No. of Engines Removed	Average Hours Flown	No. of Engines Removed	Average Hours Flown	No. of Engines Removed	Average Hours Flown
B-26						
R-2800-71	10	439	-	-	-	-
R-2800-79	204	674	274	625	325	539
B-29						
R-3350-57AM	37	340	362	293	573	312
R-3350-57M	1,117	309	926	310	606	301
R-3350-83	-	-	-	-	5	192
C-46						
R-2800-75	133	610	196	783	197	764
C-47						
R-1830-90	-	-	-	-	2	941
R-1830-90D	156	705	246	649	176	702
R-1830-92	39	769	96	607	89	740
C-54						
R-2000-9	153	759	158	804	35	849
R-2000-11	398	614	594	701	213	621
C-119/124						
R-4360-20A/B	43	486	26	575	11	675
R-4360-20W/WA	90	459	91	624	219	703
F-51D						
V-1650-3	4	346	11	246	1	37
V-1650-7	291	198	330	171	224	167
V-1650-9D	7	235	-	-	-	-
F-80, RF-80						
J33-A-9B	10	137	19	104	35	77
J33-GE-11B	-	-	-	-	8	231
J33-A-17	18	185	19	101	-	-
J33-A-17A	15	158	47	99	15	61
J33-A-17B	-	-	15	81	1	33
J33-A-21/A	7	145	46	113	40	87
J33-A-23	632	152	445	238	167	327
J33-A-35	292	214	611	257	335	275
F-82						
V-1710-143	34	295	13	237	-	-
V-1710-145	38	266	19	289	-	-
F-84E						
J35-A-17A	301	116	412	108	19	122
J35-A-17B	2	34	1,018	108	722	99
J35-A-29	-	-	-	-	792	115
F-86A/E/D/G						
J47-GE-7	1	135	29	53	24	94
J47-GE-13	107	101	589	99	760	126
F-86F						
J47-GE-27	-	-	-	-	341	104
F-94						
J33-A-33	2	40	94	160	179	296

SOURCE: Materiel Statistics Division, Directorate of Statistical Services, DCS/C.

TABLE 60 — FEAF FLYING ACCIDENTS BY TYPE ACCIDENT AND CAUSE FACTORS, BY QUARTER — JULY 1950 THROUGH JULY 1953

(Figures in this table are corrected totals and differ slighly from Type, Model breakdown shown in Table 61, Page 87, for which corrected data not available.)

TYPE ACCIDENT AND CAUSE	TOTAL	JUL-SEP 1950	OCT-DEC 1950	JAN-MAR 1951	APR-JUN 1951	JUL-SEP 1951	OCT-DEC 1951	JAN-MAR 1952	APR-JUN 1952	JUL-SEP 1952	OCT-DEC 1952	JAN-MAR 1953	APR-JUN 1953	JUL 1953
Total Accidents	N/A	88	184	192	192	204	153	161	172	158	147	124	154	N/A
Total Flying Hours	3,164,763	181,969	226,951	245,131	272,295	256,914	264,389	256,786	283,891	265,317	274,079	256,865	290,062	90,114
Number Major Accidents	1,579	76	168	161	155	174	120	122	126	122	110	94	110	41
Rate	50	42	74	66	57	68	45	48	44	46	40	37	38	60
Number Aircraft Destroyed	N/A	49	105	71	61	76	58	59	46	50	43	57	53	N/A
Rate	N/A	27	46	29	22	30	22	23	16	19	16	22	18	N/A
Number Fatal Accidents	N/A	18	24	28	23	24	19	21	23	22	24	22	23	N/A
Rate	N/A	10	11	11	8	9	7	8	8	8	9	9	8	N/A
Fatalities	984	95	49	59	51	86	59	84	55	74	138	38	171	25
Producing Factors - Major Accidents														
Cause Factors														
Pilot Error	720	34	58	73	74	82	52	53	60	64	55	48	43	24
Other Air Crew Error	15	2	2	-	2	2	-	2	1	2	1	-	1	-
Supervision Error	156	7	10	11	6	17	15	19	23	15	26	1	2	4
Maintenance Error	125	5	9	9	10	10	15	16	14	15	10	3	7	2
Material Failure	592	24	52	51	73	72	60	43	47	56	39	25	37	13
Airbase and Airways	193	4	13	20	39	35	9	20	14	18	14	-	4	3
Undetermined	149	9	12	23	7	15	10	14	12	5	11	16	15	-
Other	80	2	13	7	6	6	9	11	8	4	5	1	1	7
Involved Factors														
Fire Before Crash	N/A	3	10	6	9	5	12	9	8	11	7	N/A	N/A	N/A
Fire After Crash	N/A	8	10	14	20	16	28	18	23	21	25	N/A	N/A	N/A
Weather	N/A	11	27	24	27	36	17	16	16	22	21	N/A	N/A	N/A
Non-Compliance W/TO	N/A	4	1	3	2	2	3	-	-	5	1	N/A	N/A	N/A
Violations	N/A	6	13	7	6	6	6	5	16	7	20	N/A	N/A	N/A
Forced Landing	N/A	10	13	18	21	21	16	16	16	17	10	N/A	N/A	N/A
Out of Fuel	N/A	-	6	6	1	3	3	7	1	2	3	N/A	N/A	N/A

Source: Operations Statistics Division, Directorate of Statistical Services, DCS/C.

TABLE 61 — TOTAL FEAF AIRCRAFT ACCIDENTS AND ACCIDENT RATES, BY TYPE MODEL - 1 JULY 1950 THROUGH 31 JULY 1953

(Rates are expressed in Accidents per 100,000 hours.)

TYPE MODEL	TOTAL: MAJOR ACCIDENTS NO.	RATE	NO. DESTROYED	FATALITIES	JUL - SEP 50: MAJOR ACCIDENTS NO.	RATE	NO. DESTROYED	FATALITIES	OCT - DEC 50: MAJOR ACCIDENTS NO.	RATE	NO. DESTROYED	FATALITIES	JAN - MAR 51: MAJOR ACCIDENTS NO.	RATE	NO. DESTROYED	FATALITIES
Total .	1,579	50	NOT AVAILABLE	NOT AVAILABLE	76	42	47	91	168	74	105	49	153	63	67	59
A-16 . . .	11	N/A			-	-	-	-	-	-	-	-	2	124	1	-
B-17 . . .	7	29			2	53	1	-	3	74	-	-	-	-	-	-
B-26 . . .	154	48			4	26	1	1	13	49	9	1	16	63	8	17
B-29 . . .	63	27			7	18	3	17	9	30	3	10	3	10	2	15
B-45 . . .	1	N/A			-	-	-	-	-	-	-	-	-	-	-	-
C-45 . . .	14	36			1	27	1	-	1	30	-	-	2	62	2	3
C-46 . . .	62	28			3	48	1	-	8	54	1	-	10	69	5	5
C-47 . . .	48	15			4	23	4	25	7	30	6	9	6	25	3	2
C-54 . . .	25	10			2	18	2	34	4	28	3	3	6	25	3	4
C-119. . .	46	30			2	44	3	4	6	26	2	3	6	45	1	1
C-124. . .	4	18			-	-	-	-	-	-	-	-	-	-	-	-
F-51 . . .	192	112			15	58	9	-	39	162	26	4	15	68	10	2
F-80(T-33)	374	115			22	62	14	6	54	142	36	14	60	135	22	7
F-82 . . .	19	124			3	97	2	2	5	177	4	4	4	149	2	1
F-84 . . .	192	71			-	-	-	-	5	207	3	-	7	51	1	-
F-86 . . .	163	97			-	-	-	-	4	673	1	-	5	91	2	-
F-94 . . .	58	96			-	-	-	-	-	-	-	-	-	-	-	-
H-5. . . .	24	190			1	165	1	-	2	230	2	-	1	83	1	-
H-19 . . .	9	160			-	-	-	-	-	-	-	-	-	-	-	-
L-5. . . .	26	461			2	222	1	-	1	71	1	-	2	188	1	-
L-17 . . .	1	N/A			-	-	-	-	-	-	1	1	-	-	-	-
L-20 . . .	5	53			-	-	-	-	-	-	-	-	-	-	-	-
T-6. . . .	71	40			8	56	4	2	6	37	6	-	8	55	3	2
T-7. . . .	10	67			-	-	-	-	1	535	1	-	-	-	-	-
Non-USAF .	-	-			-	-	-	-	-	-	-	-	-	-	-	-

TYPE MODEL	APR - JUN 51: MAJOR ACCIDENTS NO.	RATE	NO. DESTROYED	FATALITIES	JUL - SEP 51: MAJOR ACCIDENTS NO.	RATE	NO. DESTROYED	FATALITIES	OCT - DEC 51: MAJOR ACCIDENTS NO.	RATE	NO. DESTROYED	FATALITIES	JAN - MAR 52: MAJOR ACCIDENTS NO.	RATE	NO. DESTROYED	FATALITIES
Total .	154	57	59	51	174	68	76	86	129	49	64	59	122	48	59	84
A-16 . . .	1	57	-	-	-	-	-	-	-	-	-	-	2	80	-	-
B-17 . . .	1	27	1	-	-	-	-	-	1	34	-	-	-	-	-	-
B-26 . . .	15	42	5	2	23	61	8	10	15	45	4	4	7	22	2	3
B-29 . . .	6	25	3	4	2	8	2	28	8	35	6	28	9	37	7	48
B-45 . . .	-	-	-	-	-	-	-	-	-	-	-	-	-	-	-	-
C-45 . . .	-	-	-	-	1	35	-	-	1	36	-	-	1	33	-	-
C-46 . . .	3	16	2	-	11	72	4	14	-	-	-	-	4	17	2	-
C-47 . . .	2	7	1	-	9	25	5	7	3	9	2	6	1	3	-	-
C-54 . . .	3	10	-	-	2	6	-	3	1	3	1	-	1	3	-	-
C-119. . .	5	42	3	10	3	29	1	5	3	23	1	4	2	27	1	3
C-124. . .	-	-	-	-	-	-	-	-	-	-	-	-	-	-	-	-
F-51 . . .	16	67	5	-	27	139	12	2	29	144	13	2	14	92	5	-
F-80(T-33)	64	151	24	28	43	167	14	9	23	92	10	12	19	89	8	5
F-82 . . .	2	97	-	-	3	157	1	-	2	105	1	-	-	-	-	-
F-84 . . .	9	60	4	3	22	107	16	5	22	83	16	3	31	131	21	21
F-86 . . .	12	139	5	2	11	174	5	1	9	109	5	-	17	125	10	4
F-94 . . .	2	271	1	2	2	256	-	-	1	46	-	-	5	119	2	-
H-5. . . .	1	78	1	-	3	173	2	-	4	260	3	-	4	310	1	-
H-19 . . .	-	-	-	-	-	-	-	-	1	1,887	-	-	-	-	-	-
L-5. . . .	4	279	3	-	5	495	3	-	1	50	1	-	2	91	-	-
L-17 . . .	-	-	-	-	-	-	-	-	1	-	-	-	-	-	-	-
L-20 . . .	-	-	-	-	-	-	-	-	-	-	-	-	-	-	-	-
T-6. . . .	7	41	1	-	7	51	3	2	4	31	1	-	3	24	-	-
T-7. . . .	1	129	-	-	-	-	-	-	-	-	-	-	-	-	-	-
Non-USAF .	-	-	-	-	-	-	-	-	-	-	-	-	-	-	-	-

TABLE 61 — TOTAL FEAF AIRCRAFT ACCIDENTS AND ACCIDENT RATES, BY TYPE MODEL
1 JULY 1950 THROUGH 31 JULY 1953 — Continued

TYPE MODEL	MAJOR ACCIDENTS		NO. DESTROYED	FATALITIES	MAJOR ACCIDENTS		NO. DESTROYED	FATALITIES	MAJOR ACCIDENTS		NO. DESTROYED	FATALITIES
	NO.	RATE			NO.	RATE			NO.	RATE		
	APR - JUN 52				JUL - SEP 52				OCT - DEC 52			
Total. .	127	45	47	56	122	46	50	74	109	40	45	137
A-16. . . .	-	-	-	-	1	27	-	-	2	51	-	-
B-17. . . .	-	-	-	-	-	-	-	-	-	-	-	-
B-26. . . .	16	44	6	12	5	15	1	4	14	40	5	5
B-29. . . .	6	24	4	10	7	26	5	41	2	7	2	21
B-45. . . .	1	495	1	-	-	-	-	-	-	-	-	-
C-45. . . .	-	-	-	-	3	91	1	-	1	27	-	-
C-46. . . .	5	23	1	4	4	20	1	-	5	26	2	36
C-47. . . .	2	7	1	8	3	10	2	-	5	21	1	-
C-54. . . .	2	6	-	-	2	8	-	-	2	17	-	-
C-119 . . .	5	54	1	4	5	66	2	8	3	21	2	44
C-124 . . .	-	-	-	-	1	30	-	-	-	-	-	-
F-51. . . .	23	142	9	4	9	74	4	2	4	36	2	-
F-80(T-33).	17	65	4	2	20	88	6	1	16	62	6	2
F-82. . . .	-	-	-	-	-	-	-	-	-	-	-	-
F-84. . . .	10	43	4	4	18	71	15	9	22	67	11	8
F-86. . . .	13	62	6	1	15	94	6	2	16	84	9	4
F-94. . . .	9	110	5	6	11	119	1	1	8	83	4	4
H-5	2	137	1	-	2	162	-	-	1	90	-	-
H-19. . . .	1	234	-	-	4	503	1	-	-	-	-	-
L-5	3	120	1	-	2	136	1	-	3	301	-	-
L-17. . . .	-	-	-	-	-	-	-	-	-	-	-	-
L-20. . . .	-	-	-	-	2	131	1	1	-	-	-	-
T-6	9	53	2	-	6	36	1	-	4	22	-	-
T-7	3	186	-	-	2	126	1	4	1	49	-	-
Non-USAF. .	-	-	1	1	-	-	1	1	-	-	1	13
	JAN - MAR 53				APR - JUN 53				JULY 1953			
Total. .	94	37	57	38	110	38	53	171	41	60	NOT AVAILABLE	NOT AVAILABLE
A-16. . . .	2	68	2	7	1	26	1	-	-	-		
B-17. . . .	-	-	-	-	-	-	-	-	-	-		
B-26. . . .	9	28	3	5	13	37	2	2	4	37		
B-29. . . .	2	7	2	3	1	3	-	-	1	11		
B-45. . . .	-	-	-	-	-	-	-	-	-	-		
C-45. . . .	-	-	-	-	1	24	-	-	2	N/A		
C-46. . . .	3	16	-	-	4	20	1	-	2	30		
C-47. . . .	2	9	-	-	2	8	-	-	2	24		
C-54. . . .	-	-	-	-	-	-	-	-	-	-		
C-119 . . .	2	13	1	-	4	21	1	7	-	-		
C-124 . . .	-	-	-	-	3	54	1	129	-	-		
F-51. . . .	1	26	2	-	-	-	-	-	-	-		
F-80(T-33).	20	78	9	3	12	47	4	4	4	58		
F-82. . . .	-	-	-	-	-	-	-	-	-	-		
F-84. . . .	20	56	20	7	17	42	9	6	9	67		
F-86. . . .	17	76	10	7	35	96	23	13	9	80		
F-94. . . .	8	77	5	5	7	59	4	4	5	154		
H-5	1	84	1	1	2	171	1	-	-	-		
H-19. . . .	-	-	-	-	3	267	2	2	-	-		
L-5	1	120	1	-	-	-	-	-	-	-		
L-17. . . .	-	-	-	-	-	-	-	-	-	-		
L-20. . . .	2	130	-	-	1	32	1	4	-	-		
T-6	4	24	1	-	4	21	3	-	1	24		
T-7	-	-	-	-	-	-	-	-	2	N/A		
Non-USAF. .	-	-	-	-	-	-	-	-	-	-		

Source: Operations Statistics Division, Directorate of Statistical Services, DCS/C.

TABLE 62 — USAF CREWS COMMITTED TO THE KOREAN WAR — JUL 1950 THROUGH JUL 1953

Type and Model Aircraft	FY 1951		FY 1952	FY 1953				FY 1954
	31 Jul (1950)	30 Jun (1951)	30 Jun (1952)	30 Sep (1952)	31 Dec	31 Mar (1953)	30 Jun	31 Jul (1953)
TOTAL	797	1,371	1,566	1,692	1,662	1,801	1,940	1,750
Fighter - Total	498	575	650	840	834	885	1,023	876
F-51	48	118	83	117	83	1	-	-
F-80	424	209	115	138	134	55	6	4
F-82	26	9	-	-	-	-	-	-
F-84	-	158	194	314	306	339	450	328
F-86	-	81	221	239	266	440	514	499
F-94	-	-	36	32	45	50	53	45
Bombardment - Total	130	233	268	262	291	317	308	296
B-26	49	135	166	162	191	212	207	201
B-29	81	98	102	100	100	105	101	95
Reconnaissance - Total	49	124	170	131	140	141	171	146
RF-51	-	37	55	24	15	-	-	-
RF-80	19	24	25	42	52	53	70	57
RF-86	-	-	9	4	4	3	5	6
RB-17	1	-	-	-	-	-	-	-
RB-26	-	36	51	32	37	56	48	37
RB-29	29	12	11	11	14	12	13	13
RB-45	-	2	3	2	2	2	4	4
RB-50	-	-	3	3	3	3	3	4
WB-26	-	-	-	-	-	-	15	12
WB-29	-	13	13	13	13	12	13	13
Transport and Troop Carrier - Total	71	317	327	297	266	310	279	299
C-45	6	-	-	-	-	-	-	-
C-46	7	81	65	76	70	96	91	102
C-47	32	46	62	63	52	56	50	53
C-54	26	118	123	70	29	30	24	21
C-119	-	72	77	75	80	90	86	87
C-124	-	-	-	13	35	38	28	36
Rescue - Total	28	32	38	45	40	44	52	43
H-5	12	15	11	17	10	15	20	15
H-19	-	-	4	7	13	11	10	11
SA-16	-	8	14	12	11	11	14	9
SB-17	16	5	-	-	-	-	-	-
SB-29	-	4	8	8	6	6	7	6
SC-47	-	-	1	1	-	1	1	2
Tanker - Total	-	-	9	9	6	9	8	8
KB-29	-	-	9	9	6	9	8	8
Other - Total	21	90	104	108	85	95	99	82
L-5	-	1	12	-	-	-	-	-
L-20	21	86	91	15	12	13	15	11
T-6	-	-	-	92	72	82	83	70
VC-47	-	2	1	1	1	-	1	1
VH-19	-	1	-	-	-	-	-	-

Source: Personnel Statistics Division, DCS/Comptroller, Headquarters USAF.

TABLE 63 — TACTICAL AIR CREW PERSONNEL RETIRED BY NUMBER OF SORTIES FLOWN AT COMPLETION OF TOUR OF DUTY — JAN 1951 THROUGH JUL 1953

Crew Position By Type and Model of Aircraft	Total	50 and Below	51 through 60	61 through 70	71 throuth 80	81 through 90	91 through 100	101 through 150	Over 150
Retired - Total	15,869	8,672	2,633	1,042	340	464	737	1,860	121
Fighter - Total	2,220	329	55	61	73	102	454	1,127	19
F-51 Pilot	331	30	13	8	9	25	152	90	4
F-80 Pilot	659	45	7	15	17	17	145	406	7
F-84 Pilot	616	117	14	18	26	30	102	309	-
F-86 Pilot	512	60	18	13	21	19	55	322	4
F-94									
Pilot	54	39	1	5	-	6	-	-	3
Aircraft Observer Radar Interceptor	48	38	2	2	-	5	-	-	1
Bomber - Total	8,141	5,370	1,968	687	93	13	8	2	-
B-26 - Total	2,790	544	1,663	509	63	10	1	-	-
Pilot	797	135	498	147	13	4	-	-	-
Aircraft Observer Navigator	634	70	428	121	15	-	-	-	-
Aircraft Observer Navigator Bombardier	439	58	264	104	13	-	-	-	-
Aircraft Observer Radar Operator	11	2	5	4	-	-	-	-	-
Aircraft Observer Bombardier	71	15	47	5	4	-	-	-	-
Turret Systems Mechanic Gunner	792	231	408	128	18	6	1	-	-
Aircraft Mechanic	46	33	13	-	-	-	-	-	-
B-29 - Total	5,351	4,826	305	178	30	3	7	2	-
Pilot	935	816	71	36	6	2	3	1	-
Aircraft Observer Navigator	412	366	27	15	2	-	1	1	-
Aircraft Observer Bombardier	528	471	35	19	1	-	2	-	-
Aircraft Observer Navigator Bombardier	123	91	15	14	2	-	1	-	-
Aircraft Observer Radar Operator	322	314	8	-	-	-	-	-	-
Aircraft Radio Operator	556	499	37	17	2	1	-	-	-
Turret Systems Mechanic Gunner	1,981	1,821	86	63	11	-	-	-	-
Flight Engineer Technician	491	445	26	14	6	-	-	-	-
Aerial Photographer	3	3	-	-	-	-	-	-	-
Reconnaissance - Total	1,370	521	406	139	20	31	88	164	1
RF-51 Pilot	122	4	2	3	4	9	45	54	1
RF-80 Pilot	146	13	-	3	1	7	30	92	-
RB-26 - Total	689	134	382	130	15	15	12	1	-
Pilot	193	29	108	36	6	5	9	-	-
Aircraft Observer Navigator	225	51	143	25	5	1	-	-	-
Aircraft Observer Navigator Bombardier	204	38	99	54	1	9	3	-	-
Weather Officer Reconnaissance	9	1	1	5	2	-	-	-	-
Senior Aircraft Radio Operator	49	11	29	8	-	-	-	1	-
Air Traffic Control Technician	3	-	-	2	1	-	-	-	-
Meteorological Technician	6	4	2	-	-	-	-	-	-
RB-29 - Total	413	370	22	3	-	-	1	17	-
Pilot	74	68	4	1	-	-	-	1	-
Aircraft Observer Navigator	41	38	3	-	-	-	-	-	-
Aircraft Observer Radar Operator	33	31	1	1	-	-	-	-	-
Aircraft Observer Bombardier	4	4	-	-	-	-	-	-	-
Flight Engineer	3	2	-	-	-	-	1	-	-
Electronic Countermeasure Officer	9	9	-	-	-	-	-	-	-
Flight Engineer Technician	36	30	2	-	-	-	-	4	-
Aircraft Radio Operator	36	31	1	-	-	-	-	4	-
Turret Systems Mechanic Gunner	126	118	7	1	-	-	-	-	-
Aerial Photographer	45	34	3	-	-	-	-	8	-
Aerial Photographer Technician	6	5	1	-	-	-	-	-	-
Other Reconnaissance - Total	325	203	46	41	10	2	1	14	8
Transports - Total	2,996	1,899	112	89	104	274	103	344	71
Other - Total	817	350	46	25	40	42	83	209	22

Source: Personnel Statistics Division, DCS/Comptroller, Headquarters USAF.

TABLE 64 — CREW PERSONNEL RETIRED FROM

(Bracketed inclosures indicate combined figures

Line Number	Date	TOTAL	Fighter Total	F-51	F-80	F-84	F-86	F - 94		Bombard-ment Total	B - 29	
								Pilot	Obser-ver		Pilot	Other
1	Total	15,844	2,188	331	645	598	512	52	50	8,147	941	4,416
2	Last Half FY 1951											
3	January (1951)	(	29	12	17	-	-	-	-	(		
4	February	853	30	5	25	-	-	-	-	595	131	383
5	March		49	14	35	-	-	-	-			
6	April	)	76	25	51	-	-	-	-	)		
7	May	184	71	28	41	2	-	-	-	58	-	2
8	June	140	90	11	26	53	-	-	-	32	-	-
9	FY 1952											
10	July (1951)	(	38	19	11	4	4	-	-	(		
11	August	1,014	33	6	23	4	-	-	-	773	79	429
12	September	)	36	26	9	1	-	-	-	)		
13	October	594	35	14	10	-	11	-	-	300	26	108
14	November	629	58	16	11	22	9	-	-	268	31	131
15	December	947	105	12	52	37	2	-	2	516	67	309
16	January (1952)	519	76	26	11	18	20	-	1	213	24	110
17	February	507	114	23	45	37	9	-	-	184	12	76
18	March	633	97	4	17	29	47	-	-	247	28	152
19	April	467	57	5	24	18	10	-	-	250	31	137
20	May	849	69	7	16	10	36	-	-	343	47	212
21	June	391	40	-	11	7	22	-	-	181	16	121
22	FY 1953											
23	July (1952)	420	53	-	25	10	23	-	-	271	20	96
24	August	731	106	19	29	28	23	5	2	245	14	135
25	September	628	42	6	8	-	21	5	2	286	41	199
26	October	895	98	11	18	28	27	5	9	407	51	224
27	November	555	95	13	16	27	39	-	-	279	28	118
28	December	823	124	18	21	36	25	11	13	348	45	197
29	January (1953)	600	109	7	17	51	26	4	4	307	34	166
30	February	546	74	4	21	28	15	3	3	218	24	126
31	March	709	75	-	22	23	18	6	6	452	54	215
32	April	481	70	-	13	38	18	-	1	295	29	172
33	May	561	95	-	17	28	47	2	1	315	34	166
34	June	568	78	-	2	31	32	8	5	390	30	186
35	July	600	61	-	1	28	28	3	1	374	45	246

Source: Personnel Statistics Division, DCS/Comptroller, Hq USAF.

FEAF — 1 JAN 1951 THROUGH JUL 1953

for which breakdowns by month were not available.)

B - 26		Recon-naissance Total	RF-51	RF-80	RF-86	RB - 26		RB - 29		Other Pilot	Tanker	Trans-port	Rescue	Other	Line Number
Pilot	Other					Pilot	Other	Pilot	Other						
797	1,993	1,694	122	149	2	192	497	74	339	312	152	3,005	310	348	1
															2
			-		-										3
35	46	21	-	3	-	1	-	-	17	-	-	-	-	53	4
			-		-										5
			-		-										6
11	45	49	2	3	-	15	29	-	-	-	-	2	1	3	7
19	13	8	3	2	-	-	3	-	-	-	-	-	-	10	8
															9
			-	-	-									5	10
89	176	85	-	-	-	14	53	-	-	-	-	16	-	16	11
			8	10	-									12	12
47	119	55	8	8	-	7	23	-	5	4	-	177	15	12	13
43	63	55	6	-	-	13	22	-	-	14	-	223	24	1	14
41	99	66	11	4	-	5	17	2	7	20	-	233	17	10	15
23	56	34	6	4	-	8	12	1	2	1	-	177	8	11	16
23	73	35	8	3	-	4	18	-	-	2	-	150	7	17	17
19	48	108	8	6	-	11	17	7	36	23	-	149	21	11	18
17	65	64	2	6	-	5	13	4	20	14	-	83	7	6	19
22	62	126	8	5	-	13	45	8	35	12	-	286	9	16	20
-	44	28	-	1	-	2	13	-	9	3	-	134	8	-	21
															22
32	123	43	9	7	-	9	18	-	-	-	-	37	1	10	23
36	60	102	8	11	-	15	26	5	8	29	19	204	9	46	24
1	45	86	7	9	2	6	16	4	22	20	46	156	7	5	25
31	101	91	7	7	1	9	24	7	21	15	-	261	17	21	26
49	84	50	3	4	1	1	5	3	17	16	-	100	19	12	27
36	70	109	7	10	-	12	33	6	23	18	-	207	30	5	28
30	77	55	2	11	1	5	10	2	12	12	25	87	14	3	29
21	47	97	3	2	-	7	21	6	26	32	-	133	15	9	30
37	146	83	6	9	1	8	9	3	21	26	44	28	13	14	31
31	63	67	-	4	1	9	19	4	11	19	-	21	19	9	32
38	77	86	-	11	1	12	28	8	17	9	1	34	9	21	33
37	137	51	-	6	1	1	13	4	14	12	-	42	4	3	34
29	54	40	-	3	-	-	10	-	16	11	17	65	36	7	35

TABLE 65 — EXPERIENCE INDEX OF TACTICAL AIR CREW PERSONNEL IN FEAF — AS OF 27 JUL 1953

Type and Model of Aircraft	Assigned	Experience Index a/																
		0	1 thru 10	11 thru 20	21 thru 30	31 thru 40	41 thru 50	51 thru 60	61 thru 70	71 thru 80	81 thru 90	91 thru 100	101 thru 110	111 thru 120	121 thru 130	131 thru 140	141 thru 150	151 and Over
Total . . .	7,081	784	706	913	732	625	716	438	328	326	346	240	124	160	59	57	48	479
COMMITTED - TOTAL	5,817	638	626	746	647	565	625	376	290	301	314	194	96	99	29	23	30	218
Fighter - Total	895	114	82	77	77	91	78	115	76	55	60	40	14	10	1	3	2	-
F-80	4	-	1	2	-	-	-	-	-	-	1	-	-	-	-	-	-	-
F-84	303	26	19	31	29	44	32	37	17	20	24	16	6	2	-	-	-	-
F-86	499	78	49	34	34	30	39	67	55	32	35	24	8	8	1	3	2	-
F-94	89	10	13	10	14	17	7	11	4	3	-	-	-	-	-	-	-	-
Bombardment - Total. . . .	2,155	395	302	431	395	268	283	48	9	2	1	2	13	1	1	-	-	4
B-26	862	224	180	163	129	61	100	2	2	1	-	-	-	-	-	-	-	-
B-29	1,293	171	122	268	266	207	183	46	7	1	1	2	13	1	1	-	-	4
Recon - Total.	652	47	96	78	73	77	75	63	9	11	7	9	5	24	6	8	15	49
RB-26. . . .	117	3	52	20	23	10	9	-	-	-	-	-	-	-	-	-	-	-
RB-29. . . .	160	21	26	28	29	23	15	18	-	-	-	-	-	-	-	-	-	-
RB-45. . . .	16	-	-	-	-	16	-	-	-	-	-	-	-	-	-	-	-	-
RB-50. . . .	60	-	-	-	-	-	36	24	-	-	-	-	-	-	-	-	-	-
RF-80. . . .	57	6	8	11	5	4	5	4	5	2	2	5	-	-	-	-	-	-
RF-86. . . .	6	-	-	2	1	-	1	1	1	-	-	-	-	-	-	-	-	-
WB-26. . . .	61	11	7	13	10	9	8	3	-	-	-	-	-	-	-	-	-	-
WB-29. . . .	175	6	3	4	5	15	1	13	3	9	5	4	5	24	6	8	15	49
Tanker - Total	73	-	23	-	-	-	48	-	-	-	-	-	-	1	-	-	-	1
KB-29. . . .	73	-	23	-	-	-	48	-	-	-	-	-	-	1	-	-	-	1
Transport - Total. . . .	1,705	56	100	137	84	107	120	116	170	208	235	132	54	56	20	10	11	89
C-46	527	7	22	32	17	29	43	31	63	100	128	16	7	1	-	2	4	25
C-47	228	15	17	32	14	14	17	28	24	26	22	13	-	-	-	-	1	5
C-54	140	8	13	18	5	1	7	7	13	1	23	18	3	7	1	1	3	11
C-119. . . .	494	16	28	31	28	41	40	32	52	67	45	47	18	22	13	2	2	10
C-124. . . .	316	10	20	24	20	22	13	18	18	14	17	38	26	26	6	5	1	38
Rescue - Total	251	4	18	22	15	19	16	16	10	15	10	10	9	7	1	2	2	75
H-5.	27	4	5	4	1	1	1	1	1	2	-	-	1	1	-	-	1	4
H-19	22	-	2	2	1	3	5	3	3	3	-	-	-	-	-	-	-	-
SA-16. . . .	99	-	5	12	5	13	4	5	1	3	3	5	2	-	-	-	-	41
SB-29. . . .	90	-	5	2	7	1	4	7	4	7	7	5	5	6	1	2	1	26
SC-47. . . .	13	-	1	2	1	1	2	-	1	-	-	-	1	-	-	-	-	4
Other - Total.	86	22	5	1	3	3	5	18	16	10	1	1	1	-	-	-	-	-
L-20	11	3	-	-	1	-	-	1	4	1	-	1	-	-	-	-	-	-
LT-6	70	19	5	-	2	3	5	15	11	9	1	-	-	-	-	-	-	-
VC-47. . . .	5	-	-	1	-	-	-	2	1	-	-	-	1	-	-	-	-	-
NOT COMMITTED - TOTAL.	1,264	146	80	167	85	60	91	62	38	25	32	46	28	61	30	34	18	261
Fighter - Total	654	134	28	86	31	20	49	25	16	4	14	24	22	31	9	22	12	127
F-80	160	7	28	8	26	-	17	4	8	-	8	1	3	1	2	4	-	43
F-84	230	126	-	73	-	-	-	-	-	-	-	8	5	13	-	2	1	2
F-86	16	-	-	-	-	2	8	-	-	-	-	2	-	-	1	-	-	3
F-94	248	1	-	5	5	18	24	21	8	4	6	13	14	17	6	16	11	79
Bomber - Total	190	8	18	30	34	18	20	15	4	7	10	9	-	3	5	-	2	7
B-26	21	8	3	-	4	2	-	3	-	-	1	-	-	-	-	-	-	-
B-29	169	-	15	30	30	16	20	12	4	7	9	9	-	3	5	-	2	7
Recon - Total.	158	2	5	4	5	3	3	5	5	3	4	7	2	7	12	11	2	78
RC-45. . . .	6	-	-	-	1	-	-	-	-	-	-	-	-	-	-	-	-	5
RF-80. . . .	5	-	-	-	-	2	-	-	-	-	-	-	-	2	1	-	-	-
WB-29. . . .	147	2	5	4	4	1	3	5	5	3	4	7	2	5	11	11	2	73
Transport - Total. . . .	47	2	7	10	1	8	2	12	2	1	-	1	-	-	-	-	-	1
C-47	20	2	1	1	1	1	-	11	1	-	-	1	-	-	-	-	-	1
C-119. . . .	27	-	6	9	-	7	2	1	1	1	-	-	-	-	-	-	-	-

(Continued)

TABLE 65 — EXPERIENCE INDEX OF TACTICAL AIR CREW PERSONNEL IN FEAF — AS OF 27 JUL 1953
(CONTINUED)

Type and Model of Aircraft	Assigned	Experience Index a/ 0	1 thru 10	11 thru 20	21 thru 30	31 thru 40	41 thru 50	51 thru 60	61 thru 70	71 thru 80	81 thru 90	91 thru 100	101 thru 110	111 thru 120	121 thru 130	131 thru 140	141 thru 150	151 and Over
Rescue - Total	137	-	17	33	9	5	13	5	8	9	3	3	3	4	3	-	1	21
H-5.	2	-	-	1	-	1	-	-	-	-	-	-	-	-	-	-	-	-
H-19	17	-	-	5	-	-	5	-	-	3	-	1	-	1	-	-	-	2
SA-16. . . .	79	-	12	20	8	3	6	4	5	6	3	2	3	3	-	-	-	4
SB-29. . . .	27	-	2	6	-	1	-	1	3	-	-	-	-	-	3	-	1	10
SC-47. . . .	12	-	3	1	1	-	2	-	-	-	-	-	-	-	-	-	-	5
Other - Total.	78	-	5	4	5	6	4	-	3	1	1	2	1	16	1	1	1	27
L-20	16	-	4	3	4	3	2	-	-	-	-	-	-	-	-	-	-	-
T-7.	6	-	-	-	-	-	1	-	-	-	1	-	-	-	-	-	-	4
TB-29. . . .	56	-	1	1	1	3	1	-	3	1	-	2	1	16	1	1	1	23

a/ Based on Number of Sorties or Hours flown and/or Length of Tour in Theater.

Source: Personnel Statistics Division, DCS/Comptroller, Headquarters USAF.

TABLE 66 — USAF MILITARY PERSONNEL BY SEX BASED ON OPERATING LOCATIONS —

Personnel by Location	June (1950)	September	December	March (1951)	June	September	December
GUAM - TOTAL	5,698	4,806	4,073	4,244	4,186	4,139	3,972
Officer - Total	504	370	323	346	354	344	383
Male	504	369	322	345	353	343	381
Female	-	1	1	1	1	1	2
Warrant Officer - Total	13	17	15	13	17	16	10
Male	13	17	15	13	17	16	10
Female	-	-	-	-	-	-	-
Enlisted - Total	5,181	4,419	3,735	3,885	3,815	3,779	3,579
Male	5,181	4,419	3,735	3,885	3,815	3,779	3,579
Female	-	-	-	-	-	-	-
KOREA - TOTAL	1	4,904	10,063	11,582	20,908	26,776	34,895
Officer - Total	1	546	1,218	1,397	2,623	3,517	4,159
Male	1	546	1,218	1,397	2,623	3,517	4,153
Female	-	-	-	-	-	-	6
Warrant Officer - Total	-	11	41	37	66	62	102
Male	-	11	41	37	66	62	102
Female	-	-	-	-	-	-	-
Enlisted - Total	-	4,347	8,804	10,148	18,219	23,197	30,634
Male	-	4,347	8,804	10,148	18,219	23,196	30,634
Female	-	-	-	-	-	1	-
JAPAN - TOTAL	21,324	30,768	34,923	36,466	35,059	37,250	43,468
Officer - Total	2,700	3,741	4,556	5,012	5,007	5,305	5,636
Male	2,663	3,688	4,484	4,882	4,861	5,133	5,451
Female	37	53	72	130	146	172	185
Warrant Officer - Total	96	124	127	149	163	155	127
Male	95	123	125	146	160	152	124
Female	1	1	2	3	3	3	3
Enlisted - Total	18,528	26,903	30,240	31,305	29,889	31,790	37,705
Male	18,528	26,903	30,192	31,257	29,837	31,747	37,659
Female	-	-	48	48	52	43	46
OKINAWA - TOTAL	9,339	10,257	10,389	11,856	8,383	8,865	8,913
Officer - Total	689	846	912	1,101	820	849	941
Male	685	840	905	1,095	813	845	939
Female	4	6	7	6	7	4	2
Warrant Officer - Total	16	23	22	41	38	31	19
Male	16	23	22	41	38	31	19
Female	-	-	-	-	-	-	-
Enlisted - Total	8,634	9,388	9,455	10,714	7,525	7,985	7,953
Male	8,634	9,388	9,455	10,714	7,525	7,985	7,953
Female	-	-	-	-	-	-	-
PHILIPPINE ISLANDS - TOTAL	5,293	5,608	5,659	6,610	5,097	5,923	5,635
Officer - Total	572	534	573	708	531	550	557
Male	547	502	544	692	501	516	523
Female	25	32	29	16	30	34	34
Warrant Officer - Total	24	30	31	39	35	32	23
Male	24	30	31	39	35	32	23
Female	-	-	-	-	-	-	-
Enlisted - Total	4,697	5,044	5,055	5,863	4,531	5,341	5,055
Male	4,697	5,044	5,055	5,863	4,531	5,341	5,055
Female	-	-	-	-	-	-	-

Source: Personnel Statistics Division, DCS Comptroller, Headquarters USAF.

IN MAJOR FAR EASTERN COUNTRIES — JUN 1950 THROUGH JUL 1953

March (1952)	June	September	December	March (1953)	June	July	Personnel by Location
4,766	4,849	5,078	6,585	5,431	5,416	5,399	GUAM - TOTAL
377	357	393	585	364	378	372	Officer - Total
375	355	391	583	363	375	369	Male
2	2	2	2	1	3	3	Female
8	14	13	14	17	20	22	Warrant Officer - Total
8	14	13	14	17	20	22	Male
-	-	-	-	-	-	-	Female
4,381	4,478	4,672	5,986	5,050	5,018	5,005	Enlisted - Total
4,381	4,478	4,672	5,986	5,050	5,018	5,005	Male
-	-	-	-	-	-	-	Female
36,012	42,376	42,963	46,388	46,351	44,650	43,791	KOREA - TOTAL
4,301	4,685	4,689	4,485	4,720	5,101	4,928	Officer - Total
4,289	4,668	4,671	4,467	4,695	5,068	4,896	Male
12	17	18	18	25	33	32	Female
77	128	134	117	140	158	162	Warrant Officer - Total
77	128	134	117	140	158	162	Male
-	-	-	-	-	-	-	Female
31,634	37,563	38,140	41,786	41,491	39,391	38,701	Enlisted - Total
31,634	37,563	38,140	41,786	41,491	39,391	38,700	Male
-	-	-	-	-	-	1	Female
44,870	46,543	50,098	54,418	56,167	60,297	60,299	JAPAN - TOTAL
6,319	6,108	6,204	6,211	6,452	7,338	7,494	Officer - Total
6,129	5,878	5,971	5,985	6,215	7,069	7,234	Male
190	230	233	226	237	269	260	Female
139	186	198	186	198	231	225	Warrant Officer - Total
137	184	196	183	195	229	223	Male
2	2	2	3	3	2	2	Female
38,412	40,249	43,696	48,021	49,517	52,728	52,580	Enlisted - Total
38,361	40,174	43,573	47,812	49,264	52,410	52,270	Male
51	75	123	209	253	318	310	Female
11,097	10,550	10,577	9,736	11,436	10,520	10,532	OKINAWA - TOTAL
1,240	1,083	1,013	734	1,023	1,116	1,090	Officer - Total
1,238	1,078	1,005	726	1,013	1,107	1,078	Male
2	5	8	8	10	9	12	Female
16	32	28	29	34	36	37	Warrant Officer - Total
16	32	28	29	34	36	37	Male
-	-	-	-	-	-	-	Female
9,841	9,435	9,536	8,973	10,379	9,368	9,405	Enlisted - Total
9,841	9,435	9,536	8,973	10,379	9,368	9,405	Male
-	-	-	-	-	-	-	Female
5,216	5,120	7.608	7,369	7,744	7,807	8,036	PHILIPPINE ISLANDS - TOTAL
600	656	897	832	831	828	848	Officer - Total
566	622	863	798	804	798	812	Male
34	34	34	34	27	30	36	Female
16	21	22	14	15	14	13	Warrant Officer - Total
16	21	22	14	15	14	13	Male
-	-	-	-	-	-	-	Female
4,600	4,443	6,689	6,523	6,898	6,965	7,175	Enlisted - Total
4,600	4,443	6,689	6,523	6,898	6,965	7,175	Male
-	-	-	-	-	-	-	Female

128,690

TABLE 67 — USAF PERSONNEL (ASSIGNED, OPERATIONAL, AND OTHER) ON DUTY IN FEAF — JUN 1950 THROUGH JUN 1953

Personnel	June (1950)	June (1951)	June (1952)	July	August	September	October	November
Personnel - Total	54,477	92,549	124,551	128,137	131,922	132,494	136,109	138,218
Officer - Total	5,067	11,117	13,915	14,178	14,595	14,346	14,283	14,178
Enlisted - Total	39,618	70,232	98,823	101,914	105,124	105,918	109,608	111,998
Civilian Assigned to FEAF - Total	9,792	11,200	11,813	12,045	12,203	12,230	12,218	12,042
Military Assigned to FEAF - Total	35,122	62,555	86,347	89,765	92,998	92,928	96,436	99,664
Officer	3,733	8,157	10,055	10,414	10,670	10,372	10,410	10,465
Enlisted	31,389	54,398	76,292	79,351	82,328	82,556	86,026	89,199
Operational Control FEAF - Total	2,178	10,336	15,117	15,094	16,155	16,920	17,187	16,601
Officer	393	1,946	2,520	2,464	2,711	2,792	2,740	2,616
Enlisted	1,785	8,390	12,597	12,630	13,444	14,128	14,447	13,985
FEAF - Other - Total	7,385	8,458	11,274	11,233	10,566	10,416	10,268	9,911
Officer	941	1,014	1,340	1,300	1,214	1,182	1,133	1,097
Enlisted	6,444	7,444	9,934	9,933	9,352	9,234	9,135	8,814

Personnel	December	January (1953)	February	March	April	May	June
Personnel - Total	139,571	140,369	141,355	143,150	141,052	143,175	140,500
Officer - Total	13,781	14,143	14,495	14,804	15,041	15,407	15,429
Enlisted - Total	113,792	114,332	115,366	117,016	114,714	116,612	114,039
Civilian Assigned to FEAF - Total	11,998	11,894	11,494	11,330	11,297	11,156	11,032
Military Assigned to FEAF - Total	101,249	101,912	102,410	102,646	102,363	105,939	104,643
Officer	10,228	10,460	10,704	10,854	11,281	11,685	11,738
Enlisted	91,021	91,452	91,706	91,792	91,082	94,254	92,905
Operational Control FEAF - Total	16,059	16,093	17,063	20,447	18,641	16,730	14,893
Officer	2,441	2,516	2,641	2,946	2,774	2,745	2,706
Enlisted	13,618	13,577	14,422	17,501	15,867	13,985	12,187
FEAF - Other - Total	10,265	10,470	10,388	8,727	8,751	9,350	9,932
Officer	1,112	1,167	1,150	1,004	986	977	985
Enlisted	9,153	9,303	9,238	7,723	7,765	8,373	8,947

Source: Personnel Statistics Division, DCS/Comptroller, Headquarters, USAF.

TABLE 68 — USAF CIVILIAN PERSONNEL BASED ON DUTY LOCATION IN MAJOR FAR EASTERN COUNTRIES- JUN 1950 THROUGH JUL 1953

Personnel by Duty Location	Jun (1950)	Sep	Dec	Mar (1951)	Jun	Sep	Dec
Guam - Total.	938	760	786	782	784	825	915
Continental US Citizens	a/	a/	a/	a/	a/	264	266
Citizens of US Territories and Possessions	a/	a/	a/	a/	a/	58	53
Non-US Citizens	a/	a/	a/	a/	a/	503	596
Korea - Total	1	1	137	4	56	56	63
Continental US Citizens	a/	a/	a/	a/	a/	54	62
Citizens of US Territories and Possessions	a/	a/	a/	a/	a/	-	1
Non-US Citizens	a/	a/	a/	a/	a/	2	-
Japan - Total	1,438	1,726	1,513	1,723	1,865	1,807	1,868
Continental US Citizens	a/	a/	a/	a/	a/	1,613	1,682
Citizens of US Territories and Possessions	a/	a/	a/	a/	a/	178	173
Non-US Citizens	a/	a/	a/	a/	a/	16	13
Okinawa - Total	687	498	741	746	791	808	825
Continental US Citizens	a/	a/	a/	a/	a/	457	482
Citizens of US Territories and Possessions	a/	a/	a/	a/	a/	107	114
Non-US Citizens	a/	a/	a/	a/	a/	244	229
Philippine Islands - Total.	6,884	7,414	7,593	8,012	7,867	7,959	8,196
Continental US Citizens	a/	a/	a/	a/	a/	340	345
Citizens of US Territories and Possessions	a/	a/	a/	a/	a/	-	-
Non-US Citizens	a/	a/	a/	a/	a/	7,619	7,851
	Mar (1952)	**Jun**	**Sep**	**Dec**	**Mar (1953)**	**Jun**	**Jul**
Guam - Total.	1,260	1,059	1,511	1,479	1,441	1,303	1,351
Continental US Citizens	280	225	311	293	274	259	249
Citizens of US Territories and Possessions	111	28	98	77	91	90	79
Non-US Citizens	869	806	1,102	1,109	1,076	954	1,023
Korea - Total	52	68	70	86	83	72	82
Continental US Citizens	45	64	65	83	79	76	79
Citizens of US Territories and Possessions	-	-	-	-	1	1	1
Non-US Citizens	7	4	5	3	3	2	2
Japan - Total	1,784	1,807	1,933	1,906	1,857	1,874	1,762
Continental US Citizens	1,584	1,596	1,717	1,697	1,651	1,606	1,564
Citizens of US Territories and Possessions	182	130	210	203	200	201	195
Non-US Citizens	18	81	6	6	6	67	3
Okinawa - Total	806	781	737	754	754	691	682
Continental US Citizens	466	448	417	429	432	382	377
Citizens of US Territories and Possessions	117	112	108	115	114	107	103
Non-US Citizens	223	221	212	210	208	202	202
Philippine Islands - Total.	8,226	8,339	8,140	7,933	7,363	7,240	7,202
Continental US Citizens	322	343	292	320	314	298	279
Citizens of US Territories and Possessions	-	-	-	-	-	13	-
Non-US Citizens	7,904	7,996	7,848	7,613	7,049	6,929	6,923

a/ Data not required prior to August 1951.

Source: Personnel Statistics Division, DCS/Comptroller, Hq USAF

TABLE 69 — EMPLOYED CIVILIAN PERSONNEL IN FEAF — JUN 1950 THROUGH JUL 1953

Personnel	June (1950)		September		December		March (1951)		June		September		December	
	Male	Female	Male	Female	Male	Female	Male	Female	Male	Female	Male	Female	Male	Female
	US CITIZENS, TERRITORIAL CITIZENS, NON CITIZENS a/													
Employment - Total	8,365	1,427	8,616	1,631	8,751	1,867	9,171	1,947	9,171	2,029	9,511	1,780	9,648	2,136
Continental US Citizens	1,250	888	1,208	1,011	1,196	1,233	1,228	1,274	1,355	1,345	1,353	1,328	1,370	1,418
Citizens of US Territories and Possessions	62	30	145	49	130	52	124	50	127	52	232	89	235	84
Non-US Citizens	7,053	509	7,263	571	7,425	582	7,819	623	7,689	632	7,926	363	8,043	634
	INDIGENOUS PERSONNEL b/													
Employment - Total	1,882	278	3,235	282	3,419	339	4,484		3,474	574	49,284	4,268	47,707	4,116
Japanese	c/	c/	c/	c/	c/	c/	c/ d/	c/ d/	a/	a/	46,095	3,651	44,582	3,538
Okinawans	1,882	278	3,235	282	3,419	339			3,474	574	3,189	617	3,125	578

Personnel	March (1952)		June		September		December		March (1953)		June		July	
	Male	Female	Male	Female	Male	Female	Male	Female	Male	Female	Male	Female	Male	Female
	US CITIZENS, TERRITORIAL CITIZENS, NON CITIZENS a/													
Employment - Total	10,068	2,053	9,821	1,992	10,037	2,193	9,833	2,165	9,268	2,062	9,018	2,014	8,971	1,952
Continental US Citizens	1,328	1,303	1,285	1,282	1,339	1,416	1,315	1,409	1,292	1,348	1,223	1,307	1,209	1,251
Citizens of US Territories and Possessions	251	133	224	82	249	133	258	116	260	119	258	114	254	107
Non-US Citizens	8,489	617	8,312	628	8,449	644	8,260	640	7,716	595	7,537	593	7,508	594
	INDIGENOUS PERSONNEL b/													
Employment - Total	45,157	3,892	43,510	3,820	41,723	3,619	43,219	3,673	44,832	3,834	44,770	3,802	44,859	3,758
Japanese	42,163	3,255	40,532	3,166	38,658	2,919	40,084	2,979	41,872	3,066	41,792	3,112	41,754	3,109
Okinawans	2,994	637	2,978	654	3,065	700	3,135	694	2,960	768	2978	690	3,105	649

a/ Employees who are paid from 01, "Personal Services" funds.
b/ Employees who are paid from 07, "Other Contractual Services" funds.
c/ Japanese strength not required prior to 31 August 1951.
d/ Sex break was not available.

Source: Personnel Statistics Division, DCS/Comptroller, Hq USAF

TABLE 70 — USAF KOREAN BATTLE CASUALTIES RESULTING FROM AIR AND GROUND OPERATIONS, BY TYPE OF PERSONNEL — 25 JUN 1950 THROUGH 27 JUN 1953 (25 JUN — 30 JUN 1950 INCLUDED IN SEP 1950)

(These data are based on date of occurrence and include USAF military personnel only (air and ground). Adjustments have been completed through 30 June 1954. KIA - Killed in Action; MIA - Missing in Action; DOW - Died of Wounds Received in Action; POW - Prisoner of War.)

Date End of Period	Total	Dead				Wounded			Missing						
		Total	KIA	MIA to KIA	DOW	Total	Died of Wounds	Returned to Duty, Evacuated, Etc.	Total	Missing to Killed in Action	Returned to Military Control			POW	Current Missing
											To Duty	With Wounds	From POW		
	a/	b/		c/	c/	b/	c/	d/	b/	c/		c/			
	(1)	(2)	(3)	(4)	(5)	(6)	(7)	(8)	(9)	(10)	(11)	(12)	(13)	(14)	(15)
CASUALTIES RESULTING FROM AIR AND GROUND OPERATIONS - OFFICERS AND AIRMEN															
TOTAL . .	1,841	1,180	165	1004	11	379	11	368	1,303	1,004	38	6	220	-	35
FY 1951-Total.	674	423	88	326	2	233	2	224	357	326	27	4	-	-	-
Sep (1950) . .	163	106	12	93	1	47	1	46	106	93	11	2	-	-	-
Dec.	182	109	41	65	3	71	3	68	72	65	5	2	-	-	-
Mar (1951) . .	138	82	22	56	4	55	4	51	61	56	5	-	-	-	-
Jun.	191	126	13	112	1	60	1	59	118	112	6	-	-	-	-
FY 1952-Total.	330	218	47	171	-	102	-	102	181	171	10	-	-	-	-
Sep (1951) . .	83	59	15	44	-	22	-	22	46	44	2	-	-	-	-
Dec.	126	70	16	54	-	49	-	49	61	54	7	-	-	-	-
Mar (1952) . .	65	52	10	42	-	13	-	13	42	42	-	-	-	-	-
Jun.	56	37	6	31	-	18	-	18	32	31	1	-	-	-	-
FY 1953-Total.	155	90	11	79	-	42	-	42	104	79	1	2	3	-	19
Sep (1952) . .	47	42	-	42	-	4	-	4	43	42	-	-	-	-	1
Dec.	29	17	2	15	-	11	-	11	18	15	-	2	-	-	1
Mar (1953) . .	37	13	1	12	-	8	-	8	28	12	1	-	-	-	15
Jun.	42	18	8	10	-	19	-	19	15	10	-	-	3	-	2
FY 1954-Total.	682	449	19	428	2	2	2	-	661	428	-	-	217	-	16
Sep (1953) . .	257	24	19	3	2	2	2	-	236	3	-	-	217	-	16
Dec.	246	246	-	246	-	-	-	-	246	246	-	-	-	-	-
Mar (1954) . .	152	152	-	152	-	-	-	-	152	152	-	-	-	-	-
Jun.	27	27	-	27	-	-	-	-	27	27	-	-	-	-	-
CASUALTIES RESULTING FROM AIR AND GROUND OPERATIONS - OFFICERS ONLY															
TOTAL . .	1,330	894	124	764	6	243	6	237	964	764	21	1	152	-	26
FY 1951-Total.	449	303	64	234	5	137	5	132	249	234	14	1	-	-	-
Sep (1950) . .	103	74	9	65	-	25	-	25	69	65	4	-	-	-	-
Dec.	102	72	27	43	2	30	2	28	46	43	2	1	-	-	-
Mar (1951) . .	99	61	17	42	2	36	2	34	46	42	4	-	-	-	-
Jun.	145	96	11	84	1	46	1	45	88	84	4	-	-	-	-
FY 1952-Total.	27[illegible]	183	37	146	-	81	-	81	153	146	7	-	-	-	-
Sep (1951) . .	76	54	12	42	-	21	-	21	43	42	1	-	-	-	-
Dec.	91	53	11	42	-	33	-	33	47	42	5	-	-	-	-
Mar (1952) . .	59	47	10	37	-	12	-	12	37	37	-	-	-	-	-
Jun.	45	29	4	25	-	15	-	15	26	25	1	-	-	-	-
FY 1953-Total.	114	76	11	65	-	24	-	24	79	65	-	-	1	-	13
Sep (1952) . .	33	29	-	29	-	3	-	3	30	29	-	-	-	-	1
Dec.	22	16	2	14	-	5	-	5	15	14	-	-	-	-	1
Mar (1953) . .	26	13	1	12	-	4	-	4	21	12	-	-	-	-	9
Jun.	33	18	8	10	-	12	-	12	13	10	-	-	1	-	2
FY 1954-Total.	496	332	12	319	1	1	1	-	483	319	-	-	151	-	13
Sep (1953) . .	180	16	12	3	1	1	1	-	167	3	-	-	151	-	13
Dec.	182	182	-	182	-	-	-	-	182	182	-	-	-	-	-
Mar (1954) . .	110	110	-	110	-	-	-	-	110	110	-	-	-	-	-
Jun.	24	24	-	24	-	-	-	-	24	24	-	-	-	-	-

(Continued)

TABLE 70 — USAF KOREAN BATTLE CASUALTIES RESULTING FROM AIR AND GROUND OPERATIONS, BY TYPE OF PERSONNEL — 25 JUN 1950 THROUGH 27 JUL 1953 (CONTINUED)

(These data are based on date of occurrence and include USAF military personnel only (air and ground). Adjustments have been completed through 30 June 1954.. KIA - Killed in Action; MIA - Missing in Action; DOW - Died of Wounds Received in Action; POW - Prisoner of War.)

Date End of Period	Total a/	Dead: Total b/	Dead: KIA	Dead: MIA to KIA c/	Dead: DOW c/	Wounded: Total b/	Wounded: Died of Wounds c/	Wounded: Returned to Duty, Evacuated, Etc. d/	Missing: Total b/	Missing: Missing to Killed in Action c/	Missing: Returned to Military Control: To Duty	Missing: Returned to Military Control: With Wounds c/	Missing: Returned to Military Control: From POW	Missing: POW	Missing: Current Missing
	(1)	(2)	(3)	(4)	(5)	(6)	(7)	(8)	(9)	(10)	(11)	(12)	(13)	(14)	(15)
	CASUALTIES RESULTING FROM AIR AND GROUND OPERATIONS - AIRMEN ONLY														
TOTAL . .	511	286	41	240	5	136	5	131	339	240	17	5	68	-	9
FY 1951-Total.	225	120	24	92	4	96	4	92	108	92	13	3	-	-	-
Sep (1950) . .	60	32	3	28	1	22	1	21	37	28	7	2	-	-	-
Dec.	80	37	14	22	1	41	1	40	26	22	3	1	-	-	-
Mar (1951) . .	39	21	5	14	2	19	2	17	15	14	1	-	-	-	-
Jun.	46	30	2	28	-	14	-	14	30	28	2	-	-	-	-
FY 1952-Total.	59	35	10	25	-	21	-	21	28	25	3	-	-	-	-
Sep (1951) . .	7	5	3	2	-	1	-	1	3	2	1	-	-	-	-
Dec.	35	17	5	12	-	16	-	16	14	12	2	-	-	-	-
Mar (1952) . .	6	5	-	5	-	1	-	1	5	5	-	-	-	-	-
Jun.	11	8	2	6	-	3	-	3	6	6	-	-	-	-	-
FY 1953-Total.	41	14	-	14	-	18	-	18	25	14	1	2	2	-	6
Sep (1952) . .	14	13	-	13	-	1	-	1	13	13	-	-	-	-	-
Dec.	7	1	-	1	-	6	-	6	3	1	-	2	-	-	-
Mar (1953) . .	11	-	-	-	-	4	-	4	7	-	1	-	-	-	6
Jun.	9	-	-	-	-	7	-	7	2	-	-	-	2	-	-
FY 1954-Total.	186	117	7	109	1	1	1	-	178	109	-	-	66	-	3
Sep (1953) . .	77	8	7	-	1	1	1	-	69	-	-	-	66	-	3
Dec.	64	64	-	64	-	-	-	-	64	64	-	-	-	-	-
Mar (1954) . .	42	42	-	42	-	-	-	-	42	42	-	-	-	-	-
Jun.	3	3	-	3	-	-	-	-	3	3	-	-	-	-	-
	CASUALTIES RESULTING FROM AIR OPERATIONS - OFFICERS AND AIRMEN														
TOTAL . .	1,729	1,144	155	979	10	316	10	306	1,262	979	30	4	214	-	35
FY 1951-Total.	588	397	81	307	9	180	9	171	329	307	20	2	-	-	-
Sep (1950) . .	146	100	10	89	1	36	1	35	101	89	11	1	-	-	-
Dec.	139	94	38	53	3	46	3	43	56	53	2	1	-	-	-
Mar (1951) . .	130	79	21	54	4	51	4	47	58	54	4	-	-	-	-
Jun.	173	124	12	111	1	47	1	46	114	111	3	-	-	-	-
FY 1952-Total.	320	214	44	170	-	97	-	97	179	170	9	-	-	-	-
Sep (1951) . .	80	58	14	44	-	21	-	21	45	44	1	-	-	-	-
Dec.	122	69	16	53	-	46	-	46	60	53	7	-	-	-	-
Mar (1952) . .	65	52	10	42	-	13	-	13	42	42	-	-	-	-	-
Jun.	53	35	4	31	-	17	-	17	32	31	1	-	-	-	-
FY 1953-Total.	151	90	11	79	-	38	-	38	104	79	1	2	3	-	19
Sep (1952) . .	47	42	-	42	-	4	-	4	43	42	-	-	-	-	1
Dec.	28	17	2	15	-	10	-	10	18	15	-	2	-	-	1
Mar (1953) . .	37	13	1	12	-	8	-	8	28	12	1	-	-	-	15
Jun.	39	18	8	10	-	16	-	16	15	10	-	-	3	-	2
FY 1954-Total.	670	443	19	423	1	1	1	-	650	423	-	-	211	-	16
Sep (1953) . .	250	23	19	3	1	1	1	-	230	3	-	-	211	-	16
Dec.	245	245	-	245	-	-	-	-	245	245	-	-	-	-	-
Mar (1954) . .	148	148	-	148	-	-	-	-	148	148	-	-	-	-	-
Jun.	27	27	-	27	-	-	-	-	27	27	-	-	-	-	-

(Continued)

TABLE 70 — USAF KOREAN BATTLE CASUALTIES RESULTING FROM AIR AND GROUND OPERATIONS, BY TYPE OF PERSONNEL — 25 JUN 1950 THROUGH 27 JUL 1953 (CONTINUED)

(These data are based on date of occurrence and include USAF military personnel only (air and ground). Adjustments have been completed through 30 June 1954. KIA - Killed in Action; MIA - Missing in Action; DOW - Died of Wounds Received in Action; POW - Prisoner of War.)

Date End of Period	Total	Dead				Wounded			Missing						
		Total	KIA	MIA to KIA	DOW	Total	Died of Wounds	Returned to Duty, Evacuated, Etc.	Total	Missing to Killed in Action	Returned to Military Control: To Duty	Returned to Military Control: With Wounds	Returned to Military Control: From POW	POW	Current Missing
	a/	b/		c/	c/	b/	c/	d/	b/	c/		c/			
	(1)	(2)	(3)	(4)	(5)	(6)	(7)	(8)	(9)	(10)	(11)	(12)	(13)	(14)	(15)
CASUALTIES RESULTING FROM AIR OPERATIONS - OFFICERS ONLY															
TOTAL . .	1,302	887	121	760	6	226	6	220	956	760	20	1	149	-	26
FY 1951-Total.	429	297	61	231	5	124	5	119	245	231	13	1	-	-	-
Sep (1950) . .	100	72	8	64	-	24	-	24	68	64	4	-	-	-	-
Dec.	95	70	26	42	2	25	2	23	45	42	2	1	-	-	-
Mar (1951) . .	98	60	17	41	2	36	2	34	45	41	4	-	-	-	-
Jun.	136	95	10	84	1	39	1	38	87	84	3	-	-	-	-
FY 1952-Total.	270	183	37	146	-	80	-	80	153	146	7	-	-	-	-
Sep (1951) . .	76	54	12	42	-	21	-	21	43	42	1	-	-	-	-
Dec.	90	53	11	42	-	32	-	32	47	42	5	-	-	-	-
Mar (1952) . .	59	47	10	37	-	12	-	12	37	37	-	-	-	-	-
Jun.	45	29	4	25	-	15	-	15	26	25	1	-	-	-	-
FY 1953-Total.	111	76	11	65	-	21	-	21	79	65	-	-	1	-	13
Sep (1952) . .	33	29	-	29	-	3	-	3	30	29	-	-	-	-	1
Dec.	21	16	2	14	-	4	-	4	15	14	-	-	-	-	1
Mar (1953) . .	26	13	1	12	-	4	-	4	21	12	-	-	-	-	9
Jun.	31	18	8	10	-	10	-	10	13	10	-	-	1	-	2
FY 1954-Total.	492	331	12	318	1	1	1	-	479	318	-	-	148	-	13
Sep (1953) . .	177	16	12	3	1	1	1	-	164	3	-	-	148	-	13
Dec.	182	182	-	182	-	-	-	-	182	182	-	-	-	-	-
Mar (1954) . .	109	109	-	109	-	-	-	-	109	109	-	-	-	-	-
Jun.	24	24	-	24	-	-	-	-	24	24	-	-	-	-	-
CASUALTIES RESULTING FROM AIR OPERATIONS - AIRMEN ONLY															
TOTAL . .	427	257	34	219	4	90	4	86	306	219	10	3	65	-	9
FY 1951-Total.	159	100	20	76	4	56	4	52	84	76	7	1	-	-	-
Sep (1950) . .	46	28	2	25	1	12	1	11	33	25	7	1	-	-	-
Dec.	44	24	12	11	1	21	1	20	11	11	-	-	-	-	-
Mar (1951) . .	32	19	4	13	2	15	2	13	13	13	-	-	-	-	-
Jun.	37	29	2	27	-	8	-	8	27	27	-	-	-	-	-
FY 1952-Total.	54	31	7	24	-	21	-	21	26	24	2	-	-	-	-
Sep (1951) . .	18	4	2	2	-	14	-	14	2	2	-	-	-	-	-
Dec.	19	16	5	11	-	1	-	1	13	11	2	-	-	-	-
Mar (1952) . .	7	5	-	5	-	2	-	2	5	5	-	-	-	-	-
Jun.	10	6	-	6	-	4	-	4	6	6	-	-	-	-	-
FY 1953-Total.	36	14	-	14	-	13	-	13	25	14	1	2	2	-	6
Sep (1952) . .	14	13	-	13	-	1	-	1	13	13	-	-	-	-	-
Dec.	7	1	-	1	-	6	-	6	3	1	-	2	-	-	-
Mar (1953) . .	13	-	-	-	-	6	-	6	7	-	1	-	-	-	6
Jun.	2	-	-	-	-	-	-	-	2	-	-	-	2	-	-
FY 1954-Total.	178	112	7	105	-	-	-	-	171	105	-	-	63	-	3
Sep (1953) . .	73	7	7	-	-	-	-	-	66	-	-	-	63	-	3
Dec.	63	63	-	63	-	-	-	-	63	63	-	-	-	-	-
Mar (1954) . .	39	39	-	39	-	-	-	-	39	39	-	-	-	-	-
Jun.	3	3	-	3	-	-	-	-	3	3	-	-	-	-	-

(Continued)

TABLE 70 – USAF KOREAN BATTLE CASUALTIES RESULTING FROM AIR AND GROUND OPERATIONS, BY TYPE OF PERSONNEL – 25 JUN 1950 THROUGH 27 JUL 1953 (CONTINUED)

(These data are based on date of occurrence and include USAF military personnel only (air and ground). Adjustments have been completed through 30 June 1954.. KIA - Killed in Action; MIA - Missing in Action; DOW - Died of Wounds Received in Action; POW - Prisoner of War.)

Date End of Period	Total a/	Dead				Wounded			Missing						
		Total b/	KIA	MIA to KIA c/	DOW c/	Total b/	Died of Wounds c/	Returned to Duty, Evacuated, Etc. d/	Total b/	Missing to Killed in Action c/	Returned to Military Control: To Duty	Returned to Military Control: With Wounds c/	Returned to Military Control: From POW	POW	Current Missing
	(1)	(2)	(3)	(4)	(5)	(6)	(7)	(8)	(9)	(10)	(11)	(12)	(13)	(14)	(15)
CASUALTIES RESULTING FROM GROUND OPERATIONS - OFFICERS AND AIRMEN															
TOTAL . .	112	36	10	25	1	63	1	62	41	25	8	2	6	-	-
FY 1951-Total.	85	26	7	19	-	52	-	52	28	19	7	2	-	-	-
Sep (1950) . .	17	6	2	4	-	11	-	11	5	4	-	1	-	-	-
Dec.	42	15	3	12	-	24	-	24	16	12	3	1	-	-	-
Mar (1951) . .	8	3	1	2	-	4	-	4	3	2	1	-	-	-	-
Jun.	18	2	1	1	-	13	-	13	4	1	3	-	-	-	-
FY 1952-Total.	11	4	3	1	-	6	-	6	2	1	1	-	-	-	-
Sep (1951) . .	4	1	1	-	-	2	-	2	1	-	1	-	-	-	-
Dec.	4	1	-	1	-	3	-	3	1	1	-	-	-	-	-
Mar (1952) . .	-	-	-	-	-	-	-	-	-	-	-	-	-	-	-
Jun.	3	2	2	-	-	1	-	1	-	-	-	-	-	-	-
FY 1953-Total.	4	-	-	-	-	4	-	4	-	-	-	-	-	-	-
Sep (1952) . .	-	-	-	-	-	-	-	-	-	-	-	-	-	-	-
Dec.	1	-	-	-	-	1	-	1	-	-	-	-	-	-	-
Mar (1953) . .	-	-	-	-	-	-	-	-	-	-	-	-	-	-	-
Jun.	3	-	-	-	-	3	-	3	-	-	-	-	-	-	-
FY 1954-Total.	12	6	-	5	1	1	1	-	11	5	-	-	6	-	-
Sep (1952) . .	7	1	-	-	1	1	1	-	6	-	-	-	6	-	-
Dec.	1	1	-	1	-	-	-	-	1	1	-	-	-	-	-
Mar (1953) . .	4	4	-	4	-	-	-	-	4	4	-	-	-	-	-
Jun.	-	-	-	-	-	-	-	-	-	-	-	-	-	-	-
CASUALTIES RESULTING FROM GROUND OPERATIONS - OFFICERS ONLY															
TOTAL . .	29	7	3	4	-	18	-	18	8	4	1	-	3	-	-
FY 1951-Total.	20	6	3	3	-	13	-	13	4	3	1	-	-	-	-
Sep (1950) . .	3	2	1	1	-	1	-	1	1	1	-	-	-	-	-
Dec.	7	2	1	1	-	5	-	5	1	1	-	-	-	-	-
Mar (1951) . .	1	1	-	1	-	-	-	-	1	1	-	-	-	-	-
Jun.	9	1	1	-	-	7	-	7	1	-	1	-	-	-	-
FY 1952-Total.	2	-	-	-	-	2	-	2	-	-	-	-	-	-	-
Sep (1951) . .	1	-	-	-	-	1	-	1	-	-	-	-	-	-	-
Dec.	1	-	-	-	-	1	-	1	-	-	-	-	-	-	-
Mar (1952) . .	-	-	-	-	-	-	-	-	-	-	-	-	-	-	-
Jun.	-	-	-	-	-	-	-	-	-	-	-	-	-	-	-
FY 1953-Total.	3	-	-	-	-	3	-	3	-	-	-	-	-	-	-
Sep (1952) . .	-	-	-	-	-	-	-	-	-	-	-	-	-	-	-
Dec.	1	-	-	-	-	1	-	1	-	-	-	-	-	-	-
Mar (1953) . .	-	-	-	-	-	-	-	-	-	-	-	-	-	-	-
Jun.	2	-	-	-	-	2	-	2	-	-	-	-	-	-	-
FY 1954-Total.	4	1	-	1	-	-	-	-	4	1	-	-	3	-	-
Sep (1953) . .	3	-	-	-	-	-	-	-	3	-	-	-	3	-	-
Dec.	-	-	-	-	-	-	-	-	-	-	-	-	-	-	-
Mar (1954) . .	1	1	-	1	-	-	-	-	1	1	-	-	-	-	-
Jun.	-	-	-	-	-	-	-	-	-	-	-	-	-	-	-

(Continued)

TABLE 70 — USAF KOREAN BATTLE CASUALTIES RESULTING FROM AIR AND GROUND OPERATIONS, BY TYPE OF PERSONNEL — 25 JUN 1950 THROUGH 27 JUL 1953 (CONTINUED)

(These data are based on date of occurrence and include USAF military personnel only (air and ground). Adjustments have been completed through 30 June 1954. KIA - Killed in Action; MIA - Missing in Action; DOW - Died of Wounds Received in Action; POW - Prisoner of War.)

Date End of Period	Total a/	Dead				Wounded			Missing						
		Total b/	KIA	MIA to KIA c/	DOW c/	Total b/	Died of Wounds c/	Returned to Duty, Evacuated, Etc. d/	Total b/	Missing to Killed in Action c/	Returned To Military Control: To Duty	Returned To Military Control: With Wounds c/	Returned To Military Control: From POW	POW	Current Missing
	(1)	(2)	(3)	(4)	(5)	(6)	(7)	(8)	(9)	(10)	(11)	(12)	(13)	(14)	(15)
	CASUALTIES RESULTING FROM GROUND OPERATIONS - AIRMEN ONLY														
TOTAL . .	83	29	7	21	1	45	1	44	33	21	7	2	3	-	-
FY 1951-Total.	65	20	4	16	-	39	-	39	24	16	6	2	-	-	-
Sep (1950) . .	14	4	1	3	-	10	-	10	4	3	-	1	-	-	-
Dec.	35	13	2	11	-	19	-	19	15	11	3	1	-	-	-
Mar (1951) . .	7	2	1	1	-	4	-	4	2	1	1	-	-	-	-
Jun.	9	1	-	1	-	6	-	6	3	1	2	-	-	-	-
FY 1952-Total.	9	4	3	1	-	4	-	4	2	1	1	-	-	-	-
Sep (1951) . .	3	1	1	-	-	1	-	1	1	-	1	-	-	-	-
Dec.	3	1	-	1	-	2	-	2	1	1	-	-	-	-	-
Mar (1952) . .	-	-	-	-	-	-	-	-	-	-	-	-	-	-	-
Jun.	3	2	2	-	-	1	-	1	-	-	-	-	-	-	-
FY 1953-Total.	1	-	-	-	-	1	-	1	-	-	-	-	-	-	-
Sep (1952) . .	-	-	-	-	-	-	-	-	-	-	-	-	-	-	-
Dec.	-	-	-	-	-	-	-	-	-	-	-	-	-	-	-
Mar (1953) . .	-	-	-	-	-	-	-	-	-	-	-	-	-	-	-
Jun.	1	-	-	-	-	1	-	1	-	-	-	-	-	-	-
FY 1954-Total.	8	5	-	4	1	1	1	-	7	4	-	-	3	-	-
Sep (1953) . .	4	1	-	-	1	1	1	-	3	-	-	-	3	-	-
Dec.	1	1	-	1	-	-	-	-	1	1	-	-	-	-	-
Mar (1954) . .	3	3	-	3	-	-	-	-	3	3	-	-	-	-	-
Jun.	-	-	-	-	-	-	-	-	-	-	-	-	-	-	-
	OFFICER CASUALTIES - PILOTS														
TOTAL . .	1,029	697	99	592	6	192	6	186	739	592	12	1	114	-	20
FY 1951-Total.	358	249	50	194	5	105	5	100	204	194	9	1	-	-	-
Sep (1950) . .	85	62	7	55	-	21	-	21	57	55	2	-	-	-	-
Dec.	81	60	22	36	2	21	2	19	39	36	2	1	-	-	-
Mar (1951) . .	80	49	12	35	2	31	2	29	37	35	2	-	-	-	-
Jun.	112	78	9	68	1	32	1	31	71	68	3	-	-	-	-
FY 1952-Total.	223	154	30	124	-	66	-	66	127	124	3	-	-	-	-
Sep (1951) . .	67	48	11	37	-	18	-	18	38	37	1	-	-	-	-
Dec.	63	40	6	34	-	22	-	22	35	34	1	-	-	-	-
Mar (1952) . .	53	41	9	32	-	12	-	12	32	32	-	-	-	-	-
Jun.	40	25	4	21	-	14	-	14	22	21	1	-	-	-	-
FY 1953-Total.	96	66	10	56	-	20	-	20	66	56	-	-	1	-	9
Sep (1952) . .	24	21	-	21	-	2	-	2	22	21	-	-	-	-	1
Dec.	20	14	1	13	-	5	-	5	14	13	-	-	-	-	1
Mar (1953) . .	22	13	1	12	-	4	-	4	17	12	-	-	-	-	5
Jun.	30	18	8	10	-	9	-	9	13	10	-	-	1	-	2
FY 1954-Total.	352	228	9	218	1	1	1	-	342	218	-	-	113	-	11
Sep (1953) . .	24	13	9	3	1	1	1	-	14	3	-	-	-	-	11
Dec.	237	124	-	124	-	-	-	-	237	124	-	-	113	-	-
Mar (1954) . .	72	72	-	72	-	-	-	-	72	72	-	-	-	-	-
Jun.	19	19	-	19	-	-	-	-	19	19	-	-	-	-	-

(Continued)

TABLE 70 — USAF KOREAN BATTLE CASUALTIES RESULTING FROM AIR AND GROUND OPERATIONS, BY TYPE OF PERSONNEL — 25 JUN 1950 THROUGH 27 JUL 1953 (CONTINUED)

(These data are based on date of occurrence and include USAF military personnel only (air and ground). Adjustments have been completed through 30 June 1954. KIA - Killed in Action; MIA - Missing in Action; DOW - Died of Wounds Received in Action; POW - Prisoner of War.)

Date End of Period	Total a/	Dead				Wounds			Missing						
		Total b/	KIA	MIA to KIA c/	DOW c/	Total b/	Died of Wounds c/	Returned to Duty, Evacuated, Etc. d/	Total b/	Missing to Killed in Action c/	Returned to Military Control: To Duty	Returned to Military Control: With Wounds c/	Returned to Military Control: From POW	POW	Current Missing
	(1)	(2)	(3)	(4)	(5)	(6)	(7)	(8)	(9)	(10)	(11)	(12)	(13)	(14)	(15)
OFFICER CASUALTIES - OTHER RATED															
TOTAL . .	288	191	23	168	-	44	-	44	221	168	9	-	38	-	6
FY 1951-Total.	82	50	13	37	-	27	-	27	42	37	5	-	-	-	-
Sep (1950) . .	16	10	1	9	-	4	-	4	11	9	2	-	-	-	-
Dec.	16	11	5	6	-	5	-	5	6	6	-	-	-	-	-
Mar (1951) . .	19	12	5	7	-	5	-	5	9	7	2	-	-	-	-
Jun.	31	17	2	15	-	13	-	13	16	15	1	-	-	-	-
FY 1952-Total.	46	28	7	21	-	14	-	14	25	21	4	-	-	-	-
Sep (1951) . .	7	5	1	4	-	2	-	2	4	4	-	-	-	-	-
Dec.	28	13	5	8	-	11	-	11	12	8	4	-	-	-	-
Mar (1952) . .	6	6	1	5	-	-	-	-	5	5	-	-	-	-	-
Jun.	5	4	-	4	-	1	-	1	4	4	-	-	-	-	-
FY 1953-Total.	16	9	-	9	-	3	-	3	13	9	-	-	-	-	4
Sep (1952) . .	9	8	-	8	-	1	-	1	8	8	-	-	-	-	-
Dec.	1	1	-	1	-	-	-	-	1	1	-	-	-	-	-
Mar (1953) . .	4	-	-	-	-	-	-	-	4	-	-	-	-	-	4
Jun.	2	-	-	-	-	2	-	2	-	-	-	-	-	-	-
FY 1954-Total.	144	104	3	101	-	-	-	-	141	101	-	-	38	-	2
Sep (1953) . .	43	3	3	-	-	-	-	-	40	-	-	-	38	-	2
Dec.	58	58	-	58	-	-	-	-	58	58	-	-	-	-	-
Mar (1954) . .	38	38	-	38	-	-	-	-	38	38	-	-	-	-	-
Jun.	5	5	-	5	-	-	-	-	5	5	-	-	-	-	-
OFFICER CASUALTIES - NON RATED															
TOTAL . .	13	6	2	4	-	7	-	7	4	4	-	-	-	-	-
FY 1951-Total.	9	4	1	3	-	5	-	5	3	3	-	-	-	-	-
Sep (1950) . .	2	2	1	1	-	-	-	-	1	1	-	-	-	-	-
Dec.	5	1	-	1	-	4	-	4	1	1	-	-	-	-	-
Mar (1951) . .	-	-	-	-	-	-	-	-	-	-	-	-	-	-	-
Jun.	2	1	-	1	-	1	-	1	1	1	-	-	-	-	-
FY 1952-Total.	2	1	-	1	-	1	-	1	1	1	-	-	-	-	-
Sep (1951) . .	2	1	-	1	-	1	-	1	1	1	-	-	-	-	-
Dec.	-	-	-	-	-	-	-	-	-	-	-	-	-	-	-
Mar (1952) . .	-	-	-	-	-	-	-	-	-	-	-	-	-	-	-
Jun.	-	-	-	-	-	-	-	-	-	-	-	-	-	-	-
FY 1953-Total.	2	1	1	-	-	1	-	1	-	-	-	-	-	-	-
Sep (1952) . .	-	-	-	-	-	-	-	-	-	-	-	-	-	-	-
Dec.	1	1	1	-	-	-	-	-	-	-	-	-	-	-	-
Mar (1953) . .	-	-	-	-	-	-	-	-	-	-	-	-	-	-	-
Jun.	1	-	-	-	-	1	-	1	-	-	-	-	-	-	-
FY 1954-Total.	-	-	-	-	-	-	-	-	-	-	-	-	-	-	-
Sep (1953) . .	-	-	-	-	-	-	-	-	-	-	-	-	-	-	-
Dec.	-	-	-	-	-	-	-	-	-	-	-	-	-	-	-
Mar (1954) . .	-	-	-	-	-	-	-	-	-	-	-	-	-	-	-
Jun.	-	-	-	-	-	-	-	-	-	-	-	-	-	-	-

(Continued)

TABLE 70 – USAF KOREAN BATTLE CASUALTIES RESULTING FROM AIR AND GROUND OPERATIONS, BY TYPE OF PERSONNEL – 25 JUN 1950 THROUGH 27 JUL 1953 (CONTINUED)

(These data are based on date of occurrence and include USAF military personnel only (air and ground). Adjustments have been completed through 30 June 1954. KIA - Killed in Action; MIA - Missing in Action; DOW - Died of Wounds Received in Action; POW - Prisoner of War.)

Date End of Period	Total a/	Dead				Wounded			Missing						
		Total b/	KIA	MIA to KIA c/	DOW c/	Total b/	Died of Wounds c/	Returned to Duty, Evacuated, Etc d/	Total b/	Missing to Killed in Action c/	Returned to Military Control			POW	Current Missing
											To Duty	With Wounds c/	From POW		
	(1)	(2)	(3)	(4)	(5)	(6)	(7)	(8)	(9)	(10)	(11)	(12)	(13)	(14)	(15)
	AIRMAN CASUALTIES - AIRCREW														
TOTAL . .	423	254	33	217	4	90	4	86	303	217	10	3	64	-	9
FY 1951-Total.	157	98	20	74	4	56	4	52	82	74	7	1	-	-	-
Sep (1950) . .	45	27	2	24	1	12	1	11	32	24	7	1	-	-	-
Dec.	43	23	12	10	1	21	1	20	10	10	-	-	-	-	-
Mar (1951) . .	32	19	4	13	2	15	2	13	13	13	-	-	-	-	-
Jun.	37	29	2	27	-	8	-	8	27	27	-	-	-	-	-
FY 1952-Total.	49	30	6	24	-	17	-	17	26	24	2	-	-	-	-
Sep (1951) . .	3	3	1	2	-	-	-	-	2	2	-	-	-	-	-
Dec.	32	16	5	11	-	14	-	14	13	11	2	-	-	-	-
Mar (1952) . .	6	5	-	5	-	1	-	1	5	5	-	-	-	-	-
Jun.	8	6	-	6	-	2	-	2	6	6	-	-	-	-	-
FY 1953-Total.	40	14	-	14	-	17	-	17	25	14	1	2	2	-	6
Sep (1952) . .	14	13	-	13	-	1	-	1	13	13	-	-	-	-	-
Dec.	7	1	-	1	-	6	-	6	3	1	-	2	-	-	-
Mar (1953) . .	11	-	-	-	-	4	-	4	7	-	1	-	-	-	6
Jun.	8	-	-	-	-	6	-	6	2	-	-	-	2	-	-
FY 1954-Total.	177	112	7	105	-	-	-	-	170	105	-	-	62	-	3
Sep (1953) . .	72	7	7	-	-	-	-	-	65	-	-	-	62	-	3
Dec.	63	63	-	63	-	-	-	-	63	63	-	-	-	-	-
Mar (1954) . .	39	39	-	39	-	-	-	-	39	39	-	-	-	-	-
Jun.	3	3	-	3	-	-	-	-	3	3	-	-	-	-	-
	AIRMAN CASUALTIES - NON AIRCREW														
TOTAL . .	88	32	8	23	1	46	1	45	36	23	7	2	4	-	-
FY 1951-Total.	68	22	4	18	-	40	-	40	26	18	6	2	-	-	-
Sep (1950) . .	15	5	1	4	-	10	-	10	5	4	-	1	-	-	-
Dec.	37	14	2	12	-	20	-	20	16	12	3	1	-	-	-
Mar (1951) . .	7	2	1	1	-	4	-	4	2	1	1	-	-	-	-
Jun.	9	1	-	1	-	6	-	6	3	1	2	-	-	-	-
FY 1952-Total.	10	5	4	1	-	4	-	4	2	1	1	-	-	-	-
Sep (1951) . .	4	2	2	-	-	1	-	1	1	-	1	-	-	-	-
Dec.	3	1	-	1	-	2	-	2	1	1	-	-	-	-	-
Mar (1952) . .	-	-	-	-	-	-	-	-	-	-	-	-	-	-	-
Jun.	3	2	2	-	-	1	-	1	-	-	-	-	-	-	-
FY 1953-Total.	1	-	-	-	-	1	-	1	-	-	-	-	-	-	-
Sep (1952) . .	-	-	-	-	-	-	-	-	-	-	-	-	-	-	-
Dec.	-	-	-	-	-	-	-	-	-	-	-	-	-	-	-
Mar (1953) . .	-	-	-	-	-	-	-	-	-	-	-	-	-	-	-
Jun.	1	-	-	-	-	1	-	1	-	-	-	-	-	-	-
FY 1954-Total.	9	5	-	4	1	1	1	-	8	4	-	-	4	-	-
Sep (1953) . .	5	1	-	-	1	1	1	-	4	-	-	-	4	-	-
Dec.	1	1	-	1	-	-	-	-	1	1	-	-	-	-	-
Mar (1954) . .	3	3	-	3	-	-	-	-	3	3	-	-	-	-	-
Jun.	-	-	-	-	-	-	-	-	-	-	-	-	-	-	-

(Continued)

TABLE 71 – USAF KOREAN BATTLE CASUALTIES BY TYPE AND BY GRADE OF PERSONNEL – 25 JUN 1950 THROUGH 27 JUL 1953

(These data are based on date of occurrence and adjustments have been completed through 30 June 1954. Data include both air and ground operations.)

Date	Total	Officer							Airman							
		Total	Col	Lt Col	Maj	Capt	1st Lt	2nd Lt	Total	MSGT	TSGT	SSGT	A/1c	A/2c	A/3c	A/B
TOTAL CASUALTIES																
TOTAL	1,841	1,330	13	26	63	316	677	235	511	26	29	124	124	150	50	8
FY 1951-Total	686	454	3	9	22	119	232	69	232	13	17	71	46	59	21	5
Sep (1950)	166	103	-	1	5	22	60	15	63	4	3	25	11	11	7	2
Dec.	205	109	1	1	8	31	51	17	96	6	3	30	13	29	12	3
Mar (1951)	126	97	1	2	4	25	57	8	29	-	6	3	9	9	2	-
Jun.	189	145	1	5	5	41	64	29	44	3	5	13	13	10	-	-
FY 1952-Total	329	270	4	5	10	60	144	47	59	2	2	10	16	16	11	2
Sep (1951)	81	74	1	-	2	23	33	15	7	-	-	1	1	4	1	-
Dec.	126	91	1	-	5	20	54	11	35	2	2	6	8	8	8	1
Mar (1952)	65	59	-	2	3	12	28	14	6	-	-	2	2	1	1	-
Jun.	57	46	2	3	-	5	29	7	11	-	-	1	5	3	1	1
FY 1953-Total	140	103	-	2	9	17	52	23	37	3	-	2	10	19	2	1
Sep (1952)	49	35	-	1	3	7	15	a/ 9	14	2	-	-	6	6	-	-
Dec.	30	21	-	1	3	4	10	3	9	-	-	2	1	5	1	-
Mar (1953)	22	17	a/ -	a/ -	a/ 1	a/ 2	a/ 12	a/ 2	5	1	a/ -	-	a/ -	a/ 3	-	1
Jun.	39	30	-	-	2	a/ 4	15	a/ 9	9	-	-	-	3	5	1	-
FY 1954-Total	668	484	5	11	20	111	243	94	184	7	9	44	53	56	15	-
Sep (1953)	243	168	2	6	a/ 7	a/ 28	a/ 95	a/ 30	75	4	1	19	a/ 21	27	a/ 3	-
Dec.	245	181	2	4	8	45	83	39	64	2	6	15	17	18	6	-
Mar (1954)	153	111	-	-	4	36	56	15	42	1	2	10	13	10	6	-
Jun.	27	24	1	1	1	2	9	10	3	-	-	-	2	1	-	-
DEATHS b/																
TOTAL	1,180	894	8	19	42	213	444	168	286	14	20	80	69	73	27	3
FY 1951-Total	422	302	2	7	15	72	150	49	120	7	10	49	21	25	6	2
Sep (1950)	106	74	-	1	5	15	40	13	32	2	2	17	5	3	2	1
Dec.	127	76	1	-	6	19	35	15	51	3	3	19	6	15	4	1
Mar (1951)	63	56	1	1	1	18	32	3	7	-	2	1	1	3	-	-
Jun.	126	96	-	5	3	27	43	18	30	2	3	12	9	4	-	-
FY 1952-Total	217	182	3	5	7	36	96	35	35	2	2	6	7	8	9	1
Sep (1951)	57	52	1	-	2	13	25	11	5	-	-	1	-	3	1	-
Dec.	70	53	1	-	2	10	32	8	17	2	2	2	3	2	6	-
Mar (1952)	52	47	-	2	3	9	22	11	5	-	-	2	1	1	1	-
Jun.	38	30	1	3	-	4	17	5	8	-	-	1	3	2	1	1
FY 1953-Total	92	78	-	1	6	12	42	17	14	2	-	-	6	6	-	-
Sep (1952)	45	32	-	1	3	7	14	7	13	2	-	-	6	5	-	-
Dec.	17	16	-	-	3	2	8	3	1	-	-	-	-	1	-	-
Mar (1953)	13	13	-	-	-	1	10	2	-	-	-	-	-	-	-	-
Jun.	17	17	-	-	-	2	10	5	-	-	-	-	-	-	-	-
FY 1954-Total	449	332	3	6	14	86	156	67	117	3	8	25	35	34	12	-
Sep (1953)	24	16	-	1	1	3	8	3	8	-	-	-	3	5	-	-
Dec.	245	181	2	4	8	45	83	39	64	2	6	15	17	18	6	-
Mar (1954)	153	111	-	-	4	36	56	15	42	1	2	10	13	10	6	-
Jun.	27	24	1	1	1	2	9	10	3	-	-	-	2	1	-	-

(Continued)

TABLE 71 — USAF KOREAN BATTLE CASUALTIES BY TYPE AND BY GRADE OF PERSONNEL — 25 JUN 1950 THROUGH 27 JUL 1953 (Continued)

(These data are based on date of occurrence and adjustments have been completed through 30 June 1954. Data include both air and ground operations.)

Date	Total	Officer							Airman							
		Total	Col	Lt Col	Maj	Capt	1st Lt	2nd Lt	Total	MSGT	TSGT	SSGT	A/1c	A/2c	A/3c	A/B
WOUNDED OR INJURED																
TOTAL . .	379	243	1	3	13	63	129	34	136	6	6	25	35	44	17	3
FY 1951-Total.	233	137	1	2	7	38	73	16	96	5	6	19	23	28	13	2
Sep (1950) . .	47	25	-	-	-	6	17	2	22	1	1	6	4	c/ 6	4	-
Dec.	71	30	-	1	2	11	c/14	2	41	3	-	10	7	c/11	8	2
Mar (1951) . .	55	36	-	1	3	7	c/21	4	19	-	3	c/ 2	8	c/ 5	1	-
Jun.	60	46	1	-	2	14	c/21	8	14	1	2	1	4	6	-	-
FY 1952-Total.	102	81	-	-	3	21	45	12	21	-	-	4	8	6	2	1
Sep (1951) . .	22	21	-	-	-	9	8	4	1	-	-	-	1	-	-	-
Dec.	49	33	-	-	3	8	19	3	16	-	-	4	4	5	2	1
Mar (1952) . .	13	12	-	-	-	3	6	3	1	-	-	-	1	-	-	-
Jun.	18	15	-	-	-	1	12	2	3	-	-	-	2	1	-	-
FY 1953-Total.	42	24	-	1	3	4	10	6	18	1	-	2	4	9	2	-
Sep (1952) . .	4	3	-	-	-	-	1	2	1	-	-	-	-	1	-	-
Dec.	11	5	-	1	-	2	2	-	6	-	-	2	1	2	1	-
Mar (1953) . .	8	4	-	-	1	1	2	-	4	1	-	-	-	3	-	-
Jun.	19	12	-	-	2	1	5	4	7	-	-	-	3	3	1	-
FY 1954-Total.	2	1	-	-	-	-	1	-	1	-	-	-	-	1	-	-
Sep (1953) . .	2	1	-	-	-	-	c/1	-	1	-	-	-	-	c/ 1	-	-
Dec.	-	-	-	-	-	-	-	-	-	-	-	-	-	-	-	-
Mar (1954) . .	-	-	-	-	-	-	-	-	-	-	-	-	-	-	-	-
Jun.	-	-	-	-	-	-	-	-	-	-	-	-	-	-	-	-
RETURNED TO MILITARY CONTROL																
TOTAL . .	264	174	3	5	6	31	98	31	90	5	2	22	21	33	5	2
FY 1951-Total.	31	15	-	-	-	2	9	4	16	1	1	3	2	6	2	1
Sep (1950) . .	13	4	-	-	-	1	3	-	9	1	-	2	2	2	1	1
Dec.	7	3	-	-	-	1	2	-	4	-	-	1	-	3	-	-
Mar (1951) . .	8	5	-	-	-	-	4	1	3	-	1	-	-	1	1	-
Jun.	3	3	-	-	-	-	-	3	-	-	-	-	-	-	-	-
FY 1952-Total.	10	7	1	-	-	3	3	-	3	-	-	-	1	2	-	-
Sep (1951) . .	2	1	-	-	-	1	-	-	1	-	-	-	-	1	-	-
Dec.	7	5	-	-	-	2	3	-	2	-	-	-	1	1	-	-
Mar (1952) . .	-	-	-	-	-	-	-	-	-	-	-	-	-	-	-	-
Jun.	1	1	1	-	-	-	-	-	-	-	-	-	-	-	-	-
FY 1953-Total.	6	1	-	-	-	1	-	-	5	-	-	-	-	4	-	1
Sep (1952) . .	-	-	-	-	-	-	-	-	-	-	-	-	-	-	-	-
Dec.	2	-	-	-	-	-	-	-	2	-	-	-	-	2	-	-
Mar (1953) . .	1	-	-	-	-	-	-	-	1	-	-	-	-	-	-	1
Jun.	3	1	-	-	-	1	-	-	2	-	-	-	-	2	-	-
FY 1954-Total.	217	151	2	5	6	25	86	27	66	4	1	19	18	21	3	-
Sep (1953) . .	217	151	2	5	6	25	86	27	66	4	1	19	18	21	3	-
Dec.	-	-	-	-	-	-	-	-	-	-	-	-	-	-	-	-
Mar (1954) . .	-	-	-	-	-	-	-	-	-	-	-	-	-	-	-	-
Jun.	-	-	-	-	-	-	-	-	-	-	-	-	-	-	-	-

a/ Includes 35 personnel still carried missing-in-action.
b/ Includes 11 personnel died of wounds received in action.
c/ Includes 11 personnel, who subsequently died of wounds, also reported in total deaths.

308700 O - 54 - 9

TABLE 72 — USAF KOREAN BATTLE CASUALTIES RESULTING FROM AIR OPERATIONS ONLY, BY TYPE OF AIRCRAFT — 25 JUN 1950 THROUGH 27 JUL 1953

(These data are based on date of occurrence and include USAF military personnel only. Adjustments have been completed through 30 June 1954.

Casualties By Type Aircraft	Total	FY 1951				FY 1952				FY 1953				FY 1954 a/			
		Sep (1950)	Dec	Mar (1951)	Jun	Sep (1951)	Dec	Mar (1952)	Jun	Sep (1952)	Dec	Mar (1953)	Jun	Sep (1953)	Dec	Mar (1954)	Jun
DEATHS																	
TOTAL	1,144	100	93	78	125	59	69	54	33	42	18	11	18	23	245	149	27
B-26	283	19	15	17	3	12	5	3	1	2	4	2	-	-	116	75	9
B-29	280	21	14	14	56	2	30	7	12	24	3	1	-	13	49	34	-
F-51	131	23	15	10	16	15	10	6	7	-	1	-	-	-	18	10	-
F-80	160	17	17	14	29	14	13	8	5	5	2	4	-	1	23	7	1
F-82	23	6	4	-	7	-	-	-	-	-	-	-	-	-	4	2	-
F-84	98	-	2	1	1	9	6	18	6	5	5	3	9	2	16	8	7
F-86	47	-	-	1	1	2	3	2	2	4	2	-	7	3	10	5	5
F-94	6	-	-	-	-	-	-	2	-	-	-	-	-	-	-	-	4
C-46	3	-	1	-	-	-	-	2	-	-	-	-	-	-	-	-	-
C-47	9	-	5	-	-	-	-	-	-	-	-	-	-	-	-	4	-
C-54	14	5	3	6	-	-	-	-	-	-	-	-	-	-	-	-	-
C-119	15	-	3	3	8	-	-	1	-	-	-	-	-	-	-	-	-
T-6	33	7	2	3	1	3	2	-	-	1	1	-	1	3	5	3	1
T-33	2	-	-	-	2	-	-	-	-	-	-	-	-	-	-	-	-
H-5	5	-	2	-	-	2	-	1	-	-	-	-	-	-	-	-	-
L-5	1	-	1	-	-	-	-	-	-	-	-	-	-	-	-	-	-
RF-51	5	-	-	1	1	-	-	-	-	1	-	-	-	-	1	1	-
RF-80	12	2	-	1	-	-	-	3	-	-	-	1	1	1	3	-	-
RB-26	4	-	-	4	-	-	-	-	-	-	-	-	-	-	-	-	-
RB-29	5	-	5	-	-	-	-	-	-	-	-	-	-	-	-	-	-
RB-45	4	-	4	-	-	-	-	-	-	-	-	-	-	-	-	-	-
SB-29	3	-	-	3	-	-	-	-	-	-	-	-	-	-	-	-	-
SA-16	-	-	-	-	-	-	-	-	-	-	-	-	-	-	-	-	-
Other	1	-	-	-	-	-	-	1	-	-	-	-	-	-	-	-	-
WOUNDED IN ACTION																	
TOTAL	316	35	47	51	50	20	46	13	15	6	8	10	15	-	-	-	-
B-26	63	8	3	9	9	8	4	2	1	2	3	4	10	-	-	-	-
B-29	91	11	22	3	19	-	28	1	2	2	-	3	-	-	-	-	-
F-51	41	9	3	3	12	4	3	4	1	-	2	-	-	-	-	-	-
F-80	38	3	7	13	4	3	3	2	1	-	1	-	1	-	-	-	-
F-82	1	1	-	-	-	-	-	-	-	-	-	-	-	-	-	-	-
F-84	11	-	-	-	2	1	2	2	1	-	-	2	1	-	-	-	-
F-86	6	-	-	-	-	-	-	-	4	1	1	-	-	-	-	-	-
F-94	-	-	-	-	-	-	-	-	-	-	-	-	-	-	-	-	-
C-46	6	-	6	-	-	-	-	-	-	-	-	-	-	-	-	-	-
C-47	-	-	-	-	-	-	-	-	-	-	-	-	-	-	-	-	-
C-54	5	-	1	4	-	-	-	-	-	-	-	-	-	-	-	-	-
C-119	3	-	-	3	-	-	-	-	-	-	-	-	-	-	-	-	-
T-6	32	-	2	7	3	3	6	1	5	1	-	1	3	-	-	-	-
T-33	-	-	-	-	-	-	-	-	-	-	-	-	-	-	-	-	-
H-5	1	1	-	-	-	-	-	-	-	-	-	-	-	-	-	-	-
L-5	-	-	-	-	-	-	-	-	-	-	-	-	-	-	-	-	-
RF-51	2	-	-	-	-	1	-	1	-	-	-	-	-	-	-	-	-
RF-80	-	-	-	-	-	-	-	-	-	-	-	-	-	-	-	-	-
RB-26	1	-	-	-	-	-	-	-	-	-	1	-	-	-	-	-	-
RB-29	5	2	3	-	-	-	-	-	-	-	-	-	-	-	-	-	-
RB-45	-	-	-	-	-	-	-	-	-	-	-	-	-	-	-	-	-
SB-29	9	-	-	9	-	-	-	-	-	-	-	-	-	-	-	-	-
SA-16	1	-	-	-	1	-	-	-	-	-	-	-	-	-	-	-	-
Other	-	-	-	-	-	-	-	-	-	-	-	-	-	-	-	-	-

(Continued)

TABLE 72 – USAF KOREAN BATTLE CASUALTIES RESULTING FROM AIR OPERATIONS ONLY, BY TYPE OF AIRCRAFT – 25 JUN 1950 THROUGH 27 JUL 1953 (CONTINUED)

(These data are based on date of occurrence and include USAF military personnel only. Adjustments have been completed through 30 June 1954.

Casualties By Type Aircraft	Total	FY 1951				FY 1952				FY 1953				FY 1954			
		Sep (1950)	Dec	Mar (1951)	Jun	Sep (1951)	Dec	Mar (1952)	Jun	Sep (1952)	Dec	Mar (1953)	Jun	Sep (1953)	Dec	Mar (1954)	Jun
	MISSING IN ACTION																
TOTAL	1,261	117	99	100	184	109	118	125	100	93	80	72	45	19	-	-	-
B-26	324	17	34	43	31	43	21	36	30	21	21	10	9	8	-	-	-
B-29	342	40	12	12	65	12	43	18	27	37	36	41	-	-	-	-	-
F-51	122	23	17	11	22	19	14	13	11	1	2	-	-	-	-	-	-
F-80	164	18	18	17	34	22	15	12	8	8	4	7	1	-	-	-	-
F-82	13	6	1	4	2	-	-	-	-	-	-	-	-	-	-	-	-
F-84	121	-	1	3	8	8	17	20	13	16	10	7	12	6	-	-	-
F-86	65	-	2	1	4	2	5	8	6	8	4	5	15	5	-	-	-
F-94	6	-	-	-	-	-	-	2	-	-	-	-	4	-	-	-	-
C-46	7	-	-	-	-	-	-	7	-	-	-	-	-	-	-	-	-
C-47	6	-	2	-	4	-	-	-	-	-	-	-	-	-	-	-	-
C-54	5	5	-	-	-	-	-	-	-	-	-	-	-	-	-	-	-
C-119	8	-	-	-	8	-	-	-	-	-	-	-	-	-	-	-	-
T-6	35	6	4	5	2	3	3	3	3	1	1	1	3	-	-	-	-
T-33	2	-	-	-	2	-	-	-	-	-	-	-	-	-	-	-	-
H-5	4	-	2	-	-	-	-	-	2	-	-	-	-	-	-	-	-
L-5	-	-	-	-	-	-	-	-	-	-	-	-	-	-	-	-	-
FR-51	10	-	-	1	1	-	-	5	-	1	2	-	-	-	-	-	-
RF-80	11	2	2	3	1	-	-	1	-	-	-	1	1	-	-	-	-
RB-26	-	-	-	-	-	-	-	-	-	-	-	-	-	-	-	-	-
RB-29	-	-	-	-	-	-	-	-	-	-	-	-	-	-	-	-	-
RB-45	4	-	4	-	-	-	-	-	-	-	-	-	-	-	-	-	-
SB-29	-	-	-	-	-	-	-	-	-	-	-	-	-	-	-	-	-
SA-16	-	-	-	-	-	-	-	-	-	-	-	-	-	-	-	-	-
Other	-	-	-	-	-	-	-	-	-	-	-	-	-	-	-	-	-

TABLE 73 — USAF KOREAN BATTLE CASUALTIES BY COMMAND — 25 JUN 1950 THROUGH 27 JUL 1953

(These data are based on date of occurrence and include USAF military personnel only (air and ground). Adjustments have been completed through 30 June 1954. - KIA - Killed in Action; MIA - Missing in Action; DOW - Died of Wounds Received in Action; POW - Prisoner of War.)

Date End of Period	Total a/	Dead				Wounded			Missing						
		Total b/	KIA	MIA to KIA c/	DOW c/	Total b/	Died of Wounds c/	Returned to Duty, Evacuated, Etc d/	Total b/	Missing to Killed in Action c/	Returned to Military Control: To Duty	Returned to Military Control: With Wounds c/	Returned to Military Control: From POW	POW	Current Missing
	(1)	(2)	(3)	(4)	(5)	(6)	(7)	(8)	(9)	(10)	(11)	(12)	(13)	(14)	(15)
	FAR EAST AIR FORCE														
TOTAL . .	1,382	892	111	774	7	296	7	289	981	774	33	6	139	-	29
FY 1951-Total.	525	318	54	258	6	186	6	180	289	258	27	4	-	-	-
Sep (1950) . .	132	84	9	74	1	38	1	37	87	74	11	2	-	-	-
Dec.	145	85	25	57	3	58	3	55	64	57	5	2	-	-	-
Mar (1951) . .	110	66	13	52	1	40	1	39	57	52	5	-	-	-	-
Jun.	138	83	7	75	1	50	1	49	81	75	6	-	-	-	-
FY 1952-Total.	236	161	29	132	-	70	-	70	137	132	5	-	-	-	-
Sep (1951) . .	71	48	12	36	-	21	-	21	38	36	2	-	-	-	-
Dec.	63	37	2	35	-	24	-	24	37	35	2	-	-	-	-
Mar (1952) . .	55	43	9	34	-	12	-	12	34	34	-	-	-	-	-
Jun.	47	33	6	27	-	13	-	13	28	27	1	-	-	-	-
FY 1953-Total.	109	47	10	37	-	39	-	39	62	37	1	2	3	-	19
Sep (1952) . .	16	12	-	12	-	3	-	3	13	12	-	-	-	-	1
Dec.	21	9	2	7	-	11	-	11	10	7	-	2	-	-	1
Mar (1953) . .	35	13	1	12	-	6	-	6	28	12	1	-	-	-	15
Jun.	37	13	7	6	-	19	-	19	11	6	-	-	3	-	2
FY 1954-Total.	512	366	18	347	1	1	1	-	493	347	-	-	136	-	10
Sep (1953) . .	167	21	18	2	1	1	1	-	148	2	-	-	136	-	10
Dec.	202	202	-	202	-	-	-	-	202	202	-	-	-	-	-
Mar (1954) . .	118	118	-	118	-	-	-	-	118	118	-	-	-	-	-
Jun.	25	25	-	25	-	-	-	-	25	25	-	-	-	-	-
	STRATEGIC AIR COMMAND														
TOTAL . .	298	183	30	153	-	51	-	51	217	153	5	-	59	-	-
FY 1951-Total.	97	73	19	54	-	24	-	24	54	54	-	-	-	-	-
Sep (1950) . .	26	19	1	18	-	7	-	7	18	18	-	-	-	-	-
Dec.	25	15	12	3	-	10	-	10	3	3	-	-	-	-	-
Mar (1951) . .	5	4	1	3	-	1	-	1	3	3	-	-	-	-	-
Jun.	41	35	5	30	-	6	-	6	30	30	-	-	-	-	-
FY 1952-Total.	63	31	11	20	-	27	-	27	25	20	5	-	-	-	-
Sep (1951) . .	4	4	-	4	-	-	-	-	4	4	-	-	-	-	-
Dec.	56	27	11	16	-	24	-	24	21	16	5	-	-	-	-
Mar (1952) . .	2	-	-	-	-	2	-	2	-	-	-	-	-	-	-
Jun.	1	-	-	-	-	1	-	1	-	-	-	-	-	-	-
FY 1953-Total.	27	27	-	27	-	-	-	-	27	27	-	-	-	-	-
Sep (1952) . .	24	24	-	24	-	-	-	-	24	24	-	-	-	-	-
Dec.	3	3	-	3	-	-	-	-	3	3	-	-	-	-	-
Mar (1953) . .	-	-	-	-	-	-	-	-	-	-	-	-	-	-	-
Jun.	-	-	-	-	-	-	-	-	-	-	-	-	-	-	-
FY 1954-Total.	111	52	-	52	-	-	-	-	111	52	-	-	59	-	-
Sep (1953) . .	59	-	-	-	-	-	-	-	59	-	-	-	59	-	-
Dec.	28	28	-	28	-	-	-	-	28	28	-	-	-	-	-
Mar (1954) . .	24	24	-	24	-	-	-	-	24	24	-	-	-	-	-
Jun.	-	-	-	-	-	-	-	-	-	-	-	-	-	-	-

(Continued)

TABLE 73 — USAF KOREAN BATTLE CASUALTIES BY COMMAND — 25 JUN 1950 THROUGH 27 JUL 1953 (Continued)

(These data are based on date of occurrence and include USAF military personnel only (air and ground). Adjustments have been completed through 30 June 1954. KIA - Killed in Action; MIA - Missing in Action; DOW - Died of Wounds Received in Action; POW - Prisoner of War.)

Date End of Period	Total a/	Dead				Wounded			Missing						
		Total b/	KIA	MIA to KIA c/	DOW c/	Total b/	Died of Wounds c/	Returned to Duty, Evacuated, Etc. d/	Total b/	Missing to Killed in Action c/	Returned To Military Control: To Duty	Returned To Military Control: With Wounds c/	Returned To Military Control: From POW	POW	Current Missing
	(1)	(2)	(3)	(4)	(5)	(6)	(7)	(8)	(9)	(10)	(11)	(12)	(13)	(14)	(15)
MILITARY AIR TRANSPORT SERVICE															
TOTAL . .	38	21	7	11	3	19	3	16	12	11	-	-	1	-	-
FY 1951-Total.	31	15	5	7	3	19	3	16	7	7	-	-	-	-	-
Sep (1950) . .	2	-	-	-	-	2	-	2	-		-	-	-	-	-
Dec.	6	3	1	2	-	3	-	3	2	2	-	-	-	-	-
Mar (1951) . .	17	7	4	-	3	13	3	10	-	-	-	-	-	-	-
Jun.	6	5	-	5	-	1	-	1	5	5	-	-	-	-	-
FY 1952-Total.	3	3	2	1	-	-	-	-	1	1	-	-	-	-	-
Sep (1951) . .	2	2	2	-	-	-	-	-	-	-	-	-	-	-	-
Dec.	-	-	-	-	-	-	-	-	-	-	-	-	-	-	-
Mar (1952) . .	-	-	-	-	-	-	-	-	-	-	-	-	-	-	-
Jun.	1	1	-	1	-	-	-	-	1	1	-	-	-	-	-
FY 1953-Total.	-	-	-	-	-	-	-	-	-	-	-	-	-	-	-
Sep (1952) . .	-	-	-	-	-	-	-	-	-	-	-	-	-	-	-
Dec.	-	-	-	-	-	-	-	-	-	-	-	-	-	-	-
Mar (1953) . .	-	-	-	-	-	-	-	-	-	-	-	-	-	-	-
Jun.	-	-	-	-	-	-	-	-	-	-	-	-	-	-	-
FY 1954-Total.	4	3	-	3	-	-	-	-	4	3	-	-	1	-	-
Sep (1953) . .	1	-	-	-	-	-	-	-	1	-	-	-	1	-	-
Dec.	3	3	-	3	-	-	-	-	3	3	-	-	-	-	-
Mar (1954) . .	-	-	-	-	-	-	-	-	-	-	-	-	-	-	-
Jun.	-	-	-	-	-	-	-	-	-	-	-	-	-	-	-
TACTICAL AIR COMMAND															
TOTAL . .	77	59	12	47	-	4	-	4	61	47	-	-	10	-	4
FY 1951-Total.	15	14	8	6	-	1	-	1	6	6	-	-	-	-	-
Sep (1950) . .	3	3	2	1	-	-	-	-	1	1	-	-	-	-	-
Dec.	6	6	3	3	-	-	-	-	3	3	-	-	-	-	-
Mar (1951) . .	4	3	3	-	-	1	-	1	-	-	-	-	-	-	-
Jun.	2	2	-	2	-	-	-	-	2	2	-	-	-	-	-
FY 1952-Total.	21	18	2	16	-	3	-	3	16	16	-	-	-	-	-
Sep (1951) . .	5	4	-	4	-	1	-	1	4	4	-	-	-	-	-
Dec.	4	3	1	2	-	1	-	1	2	2	-	-	-	-	-
Mar (1952) . .	9	8	1	7	-	1	-	1	7	7	-	-	-	-	-
Jun.	3	3	-	3	-	-	-	-	3	3	-	-	-	-	-
FY 1953-Total.	13	13	1	12	-	-	-	-	12	12	-	-	-	-	-
Sep (1952) . .	4	4	-	4	-	-	-	-	4	4	-	-	-	-	-
Dec.	5	5	-	5	-	-	-	-	5	5	-	-	-	-	-
Mar (1953) . .	-	-	-	-	-	-	-	-	-	-	-	-	-	-	-
Jun.	4	4	1	3	-	-	-	-	3	3	-	-	-	-	-
FY 1954-Total.	28	14	1	13	-	-	-	-	27	13	-	-	10	-	4
Sep (1953) . .	16	2	1	1	-	-	-	-	15	1	-	-	10	-	4
Dec.	5	5	-	5	-	-	-	-	5	5	-	-	-	-	-
Mar (1954) . .	5	5	-	5	-	-	-	-	5	5	-	-	-	-	-
Jun.	2	2	-	2	-	-	-	-	2	2	-	-	-	-	-

(Continued)

TABLE 73 – USAF KOREAN BATTLE CASUALTIES BY COMMAND – 25 JUN 1950 THROUGH 27 JUL 1953 (CONTINUED)

(These data are based on date of occurrence and include USAF military personnel only (air and ground). Adjustments have been completed through 30 June 1954. KIA - Killed in Action; MIA - Missing in Action; DOW - Died of Wounds Received in Action; POW - Prisoner of War.)

Date End of Period	Total a/	Dead: Total b/	Dead: KIA	Dead: MIA to KIA c/	Dead: DOW c/	Wounds: Total b/	Wounds: Died of Wounds c/	Wounds: Returned to Duty, Evacuated, Etc. d/	Missing: Total b/	Missing: Missing to Killed in Action c/	Missing: Returned to Military Control: To Duty	Missing: Returned to Military Control: With Wounds c/	Missing: Returned to Military Control: From POW	Missing: POW	Missing: Current Missing
	(1)	(2)	(3)	(4)	(5)	(6)	(7)	(8)	(9)	(10)	(11)	(12)	(13)	(14)	(15)
	AIR DEFENSE COMMAND														
TOTAL . .	46	25	5	19	1	9	1	8	32	19	-	-	11	-	2
FY 1951-Total.	6	3	2	1	-	3	-	3	1	1	-	-	-	-	-
Sep (1950) . .	-	-	-	-	-	-	-	-	-	-	-	-	-	-	-
Dec.	-	-	-	-	-	-	-	-	-	-	-	-	-	-	-
Mar (1951) . .	2	2	1	1	-	-	-	-	1	1	-	-	-	-	-
Jun.	4	1	1	-	-	3	-	3	-	-	-	-	-	-	-
FY 1952-Total.	9	5	3	2	-	4	-	4	2	2	-	-	-	-	-
Sep (1951) . .	1	1	1	-	-	-	-	-	-	-	-	-	-	-	-
Dec.	3	3	2	1	-	-	-	-	1	1	-	-	-	-	-
Mar (1952) . .	1	1	-	1	-	-	-	-	1	1	-	-	-	-	-
Jun.	4	-	-	-	-	4	-	4	-	-	-	-	-	-	-
FY 1953-Total.	4	3	-	3	-	1	-	1	3	3	-	-	-	-	-
Sep (1952) . .	3	2	-	2	-	1	-	1	2	2	-	-	-	-	-
Dec.	-	-	-	-	-	-	-	-	-	-	-	-	-	-	-
Mar (1953) . .	-	-	-	-	-	-	-	-	-	-	-	-	-	-	-
Jun.	1	1	-	1	-	-	-	-	1	1	-	-	-	-	-
FY 1954-Total.	27	14	-	13	1	1	1	-	26	13	-	-	11	-	2
Sep (1953) . .	14	1	-	-	1	1	1	-	13	-	-	-	11	-	2
Dec.	8	8	-	8	-	-	-	-	8	8	-	-	-	-	-
Mar (1954) . .	5	5	-	5	-	-	-	-	5	5	-	-	-	-	-
Jun.	-	-	-	-	-	-	-	-	-	-	-	-	-	-	-

a/ Total casualties consist of "total deaths," persons "wounded, but who returned to duty, etc,", persons "missing, but returned to duty," "prisoners of war," "prisoners of war returned to military control," and "current missing."

b/ Represents all persons ever reported (for periods specified) under the respective categories (dead, wounded, and missing).

c/ Columns (4) and (10), and (5) and (7) are duplicated in order to show source and eventual disposition of certain sub-categories and to add to totals - columns (2) and (6); however, duplication of figures is not reflected in "total" column (1).

d/ Figures shown in column (12) are also included in column (8), but only column (8) is included in column (1) - "total".

Source: Personnel Statistics Division, Directorate of Statistical Services, DCS/Comptroller

TABLE 74 — USAF KOREAN BATTLE CASUALTIES BY STATE OF RESIDENCE — 25 JUN 1950 THROUGH 27 JUL 1953

(These data are based on date of occurrence and include USAF military personnel only (air and ground). Adjustments have been completed through 30 June 1954. KIA - Killed in Action; MIA - Missing in Action; DOW - Died of Wounds Received in Action; POW - Prisoner of War.)

State of Residence	Total	Dead				Wounded			Missing						
		Total	KIA	MIA to KIA	DOW	Total	Died of Wounds	Returned to Duty, Evacuated, Etc.	Total	Missing to Killed in Action	Returned To Military Control: To Duty	Returned To Military Control: With Wounds	Returned To Military Control: From POW	POW	Current Missing
	a/	b/		c/	c/	b/	c/	d/	b/	c/		c/			
	(1)	(2)	(3)	(4)	(5)	(6)	(7)	(8)	(9)	(10)	(11)	(12)	(13)	(14)	(15)
	TOTAL CASUALTIES - OFFICER AND AIRMAN														
TOTAL . .	1,841	1,180	165	1004	11	379	11	368	1,303	1,004	38	6	220	-	35
Alabama. . . .	28	19	3	16	-	3	-	3	22	16	1	-	4	-	1
Arizona. . . .	18	14	2	12	-	1	-	1	15	12	-	-	3	-	-
Arkansas . . .	17	12	1	11	-	2	-	2	14	11	-	-	3	-	-
California . .	232	165	16	147	2	30	2	28	186	147	3	-	33	-	3
Colorado . . .	21	13	1	11	1	5	1	4	15	11	3	-	1	-	-
Connecticut. .	19	16	2	14	-	1	-	1	16	14	-	-	2	-	-
Delaware . . .	5	3	-	3	-	-	-	-	5	3	-	-	2	-	-
District of Columbia . .	15	11	2	9	-	3	-	3	10	9	-	-	1	-	-
Florida. . . .	54	42	4	38	-	7	-	7	43	38	1	-	3	-	1
Georgia. . . .	28	23	-	23	-	3	-	3	25	23	-	-	2	-	-
Idaho.	14	7	1	6	-	2	-	2	11	6	-	-	4	-	1
Illinois . . .	76	52	8	43	1	12	1	11	56	43	2	-	7	-	4
Indiana. . . .	33	22	3	19	-	4	-	4	27	19	-	1	7	-	-
Iowa	31	22	3	19	-	3	-	3	25	19	-	-	4	-	2
Kansas	24	14	3	11	-	1	-	1	20	11	-	-	9	-	-
Kentucky . . .	23	15	3	12	-	6	-	6	15	12	-	1	2	-	-
Louisiana. . .	27	22	3	19	-	3	-	3	22	19	-	1	2	-	-
Maine.	18	14	2	12	-	1	-	1	15	12	-	-	3	-	-
Maryland . . .	34	19	1	18	-	7	-	7	26	18	1	-	6	-	1
Massachusetts.	33	26	4	20	2	9	2	7	20	20	-	-	-	-	-
Michigan . . .	50	35	5	30	-	4	-	4	42	30	-	1	10	-	1
Minnesota. . .	37	30	6	24	-	2	-	2	29	24	1	-	2	-	2
Mississippi. .	18	13	2	11	-	1	-	1	15	11	-	-	3	-	1
Missouri . . .	37	23	8	15	-	3	-	3	26	15	3	-	6	-	2
Montana. . . .	7	5	2	3	-	-	-	-	5	3	-	-	1	-	1
Nebraska . . .	22	15	2	13	-	4	-	4	16	13	-	-	1	-	2
Nevada	4	3	-	3	-	-	-	-	4	3	-	-	1	-	-
New Hampshire.	2	2	-	2	-	-	-	-	2	2	-	-	-	-	-
New Jersey . .	48	34	7	27	-	8	-	8	34	27	1	1	5	-	-
New Mexico . .	13	11	1	10	-	-	-	-	12	10	-	-	1	-	1
New York . . .	111	75	9	65	1	18	1	17	84	65	5	-	11	-	3
North Carolina	23	16	3	13	-	4	-	4	16	13	1	-	2	-	-
North Dakota .	10	6	1	5	-	2	-	2	7	5	-	-	2	-	-
Ohio	68	46	3	43	-	10	-	10	55	43	2	-	10	-	-
Oklahoma . . .	44	30	2	27	1	9	1	8	33	27	-	-	6	-	-
Oregon	22	16	2	13	1	2	1	1	18	13	-	-	5	-	-
Pennsylvania .	85	60	7	53	-	12	-	12	66	53	1	-	9	-	3
Rhode Island .	11	8	-	8	-	1	-	1	10	8	-	-	2	-	-
South Carolina	14	9	1	8	-	3	-	3	10	8	-	-	1	-	1
South Dakota .	7	4	-	4	-	1	-	1	6	4	-	-	1	-	1

(Continued)

TABLE 74 — USAF KOREAN BATTLE CASUALTIES BY STATE OF RESIDENCE — 25 JUN 1950 THROUGH 27 JUL 1953 (CONTINUED)

(These data are based on date of occurrence and include USAF military personnel only (air and ground). Adjustments have been completed through 30 June 1954. KIA - Killed in Action; MIA - Missing in Action; DOW - Died of Wounds Received in Action; POW - Prisoner of War.)

State of Residence	Total a/	Dead				Wounded			Missing						
		Total b/	KIA	MIA to KIA c/	DOW c/	Total b/	Died of Wounds c/	Returned to Duty, Evacuated, Etc. d/	Total b/	Missing to Killed in Action c/	Returned To Military Control: To Duty	Returned To Military Control: With Wounds c/	Returned To Military Control: From POW	POW	Current Missing
	(1)	(2)	(3)	(4)	(5)	(6)	(7)	(8)	(9)	(10)	(11)	(12)	(13)	(14)	(15)
	TOTAL CASUALTIES - OFFICER AND AIRMAN (Continued)														
Tennessee. . .	30	24	9	15	-	2	-	2	19	15	1	-	2	-	1
Texas.	120	86	17	69	-	15	-	15	88	69	3	-	15	-	1
Utah	10	7	1	6	-	-	-	-	9	6	-	-	2	-	1
Vermont. . . .	4	3	1	2	-	-	-	-	3	2	-	-	1	-	-
Virginia . . .	42	28	9	19	-	5	-	5	28	19	1	-	7	-	1
Washington . .	29	20	3	16	1	4	1	3	22	16	-	-	6	-	-
West Virginia.	29	18	-	18	-	4	-	4	26	18	1	1	6	-	-
Wisconsin. . .	15	11	-	11	-	1	-	1	14	11	-	-	3	-	-
Wyoming. . . .	8	7	1	6	-	1	-	1	6	6	-	-	-	-	-
Alaska	-	-	-	-	-	-	-	-	-	-	-	-	-	-	-
Aleutians. . .	-	-	-	-	-	-	-	-	-	-	-	-	-	-	-
Hawaii	1	1	-	1	-	-	-	-	1	1	-	-	-	-	-
U.S. at Large.	1	1	1	-	-	-	-	-	-	-	-	-	-	-	-
Canada	2	1	-	1	-	-	-	-	2	1	-	-	1	-	-
Undetermined .	167	1	-	-	1	160	1	159	7	-	7	-	-	-	-

a/ Total casualties consist of "total deaths", persons "wounded, but who returned to duty, etc.", persons "missing" but returned to duty," "prisoners of war returned to military control", and current missing".

b/ Represents all persons ever reported (for periods specified) under the respective categories (dead, wounded and missing).

c/ Categories (4) and (10), and (5) and (7) are duplicated in order to show source and eventual disposition of certain sub-categories and to add to totals - columns (2) and (6); however, duplication of figures is not reflected in "total", column (1).

d/ Figures shown in column (12) are also included in column (8), but only column (8) is included in column (1) - "total".

Source: Personnel Statistics Division, Directorate of Statistical Services, DCS/Comptroller.

ORGANIZATIONS — COMBAT AND AIRLIFT UNITS

The tables included in this section provide a summary of active USAF Organizations and summary data pertaining to composition, status, deployment, aircraft, crews and operational readiness of the USAF Combat and Airlift Units, including supporting flying units, during the Fiscal Year 1953.

In addition to information reflecting the status and deployment of the USAF Combat and Airlift Units, the tables contain the following data by type of unit: Total units activated, equipped units by type and model of aircraft possessed; authorized, on hand and combat ready aircraft and crews in units by type and model of aircraft and composition of squadrons by Table of Organization reflecting authorization of aircraft, crews, crew personnel and military personnel.

DEFINITIONS

COMBAT AND AIRLIFT UNIT

A classification of military force having an organization prescribed by the Department of the Air Force, the primary mission of which is one or more of the following:

1. Destruction of enemy forces, resources, and/or installations, for example, bombardment and fighter units and Troop Carrier Units which have a mission of providing airlift for combat elements.

2. Furnishing operational assistance to combat elements, for example, reconnaissance, troop carrier, and supporting flying units.

A Combat Unit is said to be combat ready when it is manned, equipped and fully prepared to perform its combat mission.

COMBAT MISSION

The combat mission of an organization is the specific combat task assigned or, if no specific combat task is assigned the task ordinarily performed by that type of organizations under combat conditions. In the latter case, the mission may be limited by the weapon in the possession of a unit. For example, a unit authorized jet fighters but actually possessing F-51's will consider as its mission the type of operation ordinarily performed by F-51's.

SUPPORT FORCES

Support Forces as shown in the following tables are those flying units consisting of designated types other than those comprising a Combat Group or Wing structure and having a mission of furnishing operational assistance to combat elements.

TABLE 75 – SUMMARY OF ACTIVE USAF ORGANIZATIONS – AS OF 30 JUNE 1953

UNIT	TOTAL	MAJOR COMMANDS a/																
		SAC	AU	CONAC	ADC	TAC	MATS	AMC	APGC	ATRC	ARDC	HEDCOM	USAFSS	USAFE	CAIRC	FEAF	AAC	NEAC
Sub Commands - Total																		
T/O	3	-	-	-	-	-	-	-	-	-	-	-	-	-	-	3	-	-
T/D	38	3	1	5	3	2	7	6	-	3	-	-	-	3	-	2	1	-
Air Forces																		
T/O	3	-	-	-	-	-	-	-	-	-	-	-	-	-	-	3	-	-
T/D	16	3	1	4	-	2	-	-	-	3	-	-	-	3	-	-	-	-
Defense Forces																		
T/D	5	-	-	-	3	-	1	-	-	-	-	-	-	-	-	1	-	-
Services																		
T/D	6	-	-	-	-	-	6	-	-	-	-	-	-	-	-	-	-	-
Areas																		
T/D	8	-	-	-	-	-	-	8	-	-	-	-	-	-	-	-	-	-
Misc b/																		
T/D	3	-	-	1	-	-	-	-	-	-	-	-	-	-	-	1	1	-
Divisions																		
T/O	21	16	-	-	-	-	-	-	-	-	-	-	-	2	-	1	2	-
T/D	21	2	-	-	11	-	4	-	-	-	-	-	-	-	-	3	-	1
Districts																		
T/D	10	-	-	4	-	-	-	6	-	-	-	-	-	-	-	-	-	-
Wings																		
T/O - Total	90	40	-	-	1	18	1	-	-	-	-	-	-	16	-	14	-	-
Combat	81	40	-	-	1	18	-	-	-	-	-	-	-	11	-	11	-	-
Non-Combat	9	-	-	-	-	-	1	-	-	-	-	-	-	5	-	3	-	-
T/D	94	2	1	1	8	-	13	8	4	35	3	2	-	5	-	9	3	-
Reserve	25	-	-	25	-	-	-	-	-	-	-	-	-	-	-	-	-	-
Groups																		
T/O - Total	336	66	-	5	28	80	21	-	-	-	-	-	-	72	-	62	1	1
Combat	43	-	-	-	1	21	-	-	-	-	-	-	-	11	-	10	-	-
Non-Combat	293	66	-	5	27	59	21	-	-	-	-	-	-	61	-	52	1	1
T/D	376	12	5	9	3	3	51	28	4	144	35	13	5	21	1	28	7	7
Reserve	200	-	-	200	-	-	-	-	-	-	-	-	-	-	-	-	-	-
Squadrons																		
T/O	1,634	463	-	4	284	230	138	16	-	-	2	7	15	230	-	212	25	8
T/D	1,427	97	14	36	19	15	193	15	18	645	54	52	4	100	4	97	38	26
Reserve	729	-	-	729	-	-	-	-	-	-	-	-	-	-	-	-	-	-
Flights																		
T/O	73	16	-	-	5	11	9	4	-	2	1	1	-	13	1	10	-	-
T/D	20	1	-	-	-	2	-	-	1	1	-	-	6	5	2	2	-	-
Reserve	2	-	-	2	-	-	-	-	-	-	-	-	-	-	-	-	-	-
Misc																		
T/O	173	14	1	19	23	8	5	5	1	37	4	2	-	21	1	25	4	3
T/D	71	-	7	44	-	-	2	-	2	-	12	2	-	-	1	-	1	-

a/ Excludes Air Force Finance Division which is a separate operating agency.
b/ Includes FEAF Logistic Force, Alaskan Air Force Depot and Aviation Engineering Force.
Source: Operations Statistics Division, Directorate of Statistical Services, DCS/C.

TABLE 76 — COMPOSITION OF COMBAT AND AIRLIFT SQUADRONS — AS OF 30 JUNE 1953

(The usual composition of the various Combat and Airlift Squadrons and the Supporting (Flying) Units are shown below for 30 June 1953.)

TYPE OF SQUADRON	TABLE OF ORGANIZATION a/			AIRCRAFT		CREWS		RATIO C/A AUTHORIZED	PERSONNEL AUTHORIZED		
	NUMBER	MONTH	YEAR	MAJOR TYPE	AUTHORIZED NUMBER	AUTHORIZED NUMBER	NUMBER OF PERSONNEL IN CREW		TOTAL	OFFICERS	AIRMEN
COMBAT											
Bombardment, Heavy.	1-1176P	Mar	53	B-36	10	12	16	1.25	362	109	253
Bombardment, Medium	1-1172P	Mar	53	B-29	10	10	11	1.0	280	88	192
	1-1173P	Mar	53	B-50D	15	18	10	1.25	295	85	210
	1-1173P	Mar	53	B-50A	15	18	11	1.25	310	100	210
	1-1180P	May	52	B-29	10	10	11	1.0	198	61	137
	1-1180P	Mar	53	B-29	10	10	12	1.0	209	62	147
Bombardment, Medium Jet	1-1178P	Mar	53	B-47	15	18	3	1.25	172	66	106
Bombardment, Light.	1-1123P	Apr	52	B-26	16	16	3	1.0	194	55	139
Bombardment, Light Night Intruder	1-1123W	Apr	52	B-26	16	24	3	1.5	270	82	188
	1-1177W	Mar	52	B-26	24	36	4	1.5	369	118	251
Bombardment, Light Jet.	1-1143P	Dec	51	B-45	16	16	4	1.0	264	56	208
	1-1143	Mar	52	B-45	16	20	4	1.25	296	71	225
Strategic Fighter, Jet.	1-1259P	Mar	53	F-84G	25	30	1	1.25	92	36	56
Fighter Bomber.	1-1253P	Aug	52	F-84/86	25	24	1	1.0	160	31	129
	1-1253W	Dec	51	F-80/84/86	25	36	1	1.5	188	43	145
Fighter Bomber/Interceptor.	1-1253P	Dec	51	F-84/86	25	24	1	1.0	162	31	131
Fighter Interceptor	1-1253P	Aug	52	F-80/84/86	25	36	1	1.5	189	44	145
	1-1253W	Dec	51	F-80/86	25	36	1	1.5	195	43	152
	1-1254P	Dec	51	F-94A/C	12	12	2	1.0	206	57	149
	1-1255P	Aug	52	F-94B	25	48	2	2.0	337	107	230
	1-1255P	Nov	52	F-94B	25	36	2	1.5	313	83	230
	1-1255W	Dec	51	F-94B	25	48	2	2.0	380	109	271
	1-1256P	Aug	52	F-51	25	36	1	1.5	178	43	135
	1-1257	Jan	52	F-86D	25	50	1	2.0	302	60	242
	1-1257	Jan	52	F-94C	25	50	2	2.0	352	110	242
	1-1257A	Sep	52	F-94C	12	24	2	2.0	189	57	132
	1-1258	Jan	52	F-89	25	50	2	2.0	375	110	265
Strategic Reconnaissance, Heavy	1-1473P	Mar	53	RB-36	10	12	22	1.25	434	133	301
Strategic Reconnaissance, Medium.	1-1475P	Mar	53	RB-50	15	18	13	1.25	316	104	212
	1-1478P	May	52	RB-29	10	10	10	1.0	199	52	147
	1-1479P	Mar	53	RB-47	15	18	3	1.25	172	66	106
Strategic Recon, Medium Electronics . . .	1-1477P	Mar	53	RB-50	15	22	11	1.5	492	146	346

TABLE 76 — COMPOSITION OF COMBAT AND AIRLIFT SQUADRONS —AS OF 30 JUNE 1953 (CONTINUED)

(See first page of this table for headnote)

TYPE OF SQUADRON	TABLE OF ORGANIZATION b/			AIRCRAFT		CREWS		RATIO C/A AUTHORIZED	PERSONNEL AUTHORIZED		
	NUMBER	MONTH	YEAR	MAJOR TYPE	AUTHORIZED NUMBER	AUTHORIZED NUMBER	NUMBER OF PERSONNEL IN CREW		TOTAL	OFFICERS	AIRMEN
Strategic Recon, Medium Photo	1-1480	Mar	53	RB-29 RB-29	10 2	b/ 10 c/ 2	11 14	1.0 1.0	429 -	70 -	359 -
Strategic Recon, Medium Photo Mapping . .	1-1476P	Mar	53	RB-50 YC-97	15 5	d/ 18 e/ 5	11 5	1.25 1.0	494 -	129 -	365 -
Tactical Reconnaissance Night Photo . . .	1-1433P 1-1433W	Dec Dec	51 51	RB-26 RB-26	18 18	18 24	3 3	1.0 1.3	218 301	64 86	154 213
Tactical Reconnaissance, Photo Jet. . . .	1-1423P 1-1423W	Dec Dec	51 51	RF-80 RF-80	18 18	18 24	1 1	1.0 1.3	143 218	28 40	115 178
AIRLIFT											
Troop Carrier, Heavy.	1-1360P 1-1360W 1-1360W	Dec Dec Dec	51 51 51	C-124 C-54 C-124	12 12 12	12 20 20	7 6 7	1.0 1.7 1.7	235 275 358	43 68 68	192 207 290
Troop Carrier, Medium	1-1361P 1-1361P 1-1361W 1-1361W	Dec Dec Dec Dec	51 51 51 51	C-119 C-119 C-46 C-119	16 16 16 16	16 16 24 32	f/ 4 f/ 4 f/ 4 f/ 4	1.0 1.0 1.5 2.0	188 198 266 312	43 43 62 83	145 155 204 229
Troop Carrier Assault Light (FW).	1-1533P	Dec	51	C-122	16	16	g/ 4	1.0	186	44	142
Troop Carrier Assault (RW).	1-1363P	Dec	51	H-19	16	16	3	1.0	142	40	102
SUPPORT (FLYING)											
Air Transport, Heavy.	1-1552P 1-1552W 1-1553P 1-1553W	Dec Dec Dec Dec	51 51 51 51	C-74, C-124 C-118 C-97 C-97	8 12 8 12	12 18 12 18	h/ 7 h/ 7 h/ 7 h/ 7	1.5 1.5 1.5 1.5	274 407 274 407	46 67 46 67	228 340 228 340
Air Transport, Medium	1-1551P 1-1551W	Dec Dec	51 51	C-54 C-54	8 12	12 18	6 6	1.5 1.5	201 296	45 66	156 230
Air Refueling, Medium..	1-1274P 1-1174P 1-1174P	Mar Mar Mar	53 53 53	KB-29 KB-29 KC-97	20 20 20	20 25 25	8 8 7	1.0 1.25 1.25	299 339 314	90 110 85	209 229 229
Strategic Reconnaissance, Medium Weather.	1-1724P 1-1724W 1-1724W	Dec Dec Dec	51 51 51	WB-29 WB-29 WB-29	12 12 12	12 16 16	10 10 11	1.0 1.3 1.3	458 567 583	76 99 115	382 468 468

TABLE 76 — COMPOSITION OF COMBAT AND AIRLIFT SQUADRONS — AS OF 30 JUNE 1953 (CONTINUED)

(See first page of this table for headnote)

TYPE OF SQUADRON	TABLE OF ORGANIZATION b/			AIRCRAFT		CREWS		RATIO C/A AUTHORIZED	PERSONNEL AUTHORIZED		
	NUMBER	MONTH	YEAR	MAJOR TYPE	AUTHORIZED NUMBER	AUTHORIZED NUMBER	NUMBER OF PERSONNEL IN CREW		TOTAL	OFFICERS	AIRMEN
Air Rescue	1-1614	May	52	SA-16,C-47,H-19	4, 1, 2	4, 1, 2	7, 6, 2	1.0	128	27	101
	1-1614	May	52	SA-16,C-47,H-21	4, 1, 2	4, 1, 2	7, 6, 2	1.0	129	27	102
	1-1614	May	52	SB-29,C-47,H-19	4, 1, 2	4, 1, 2	9, 6, 2	1.0	156	31	125
Air Resupply	1-1941	May	51	B-29,A-16	12, 4	12, 4	10, 6	1.0	425	97	328
				H-19,C-119	4, 4	4, 4	2, 5	1.0	-	-	-
	1-1941	Jan	52	B-29,A-16	12, 4	12, 4	10, 6	1.0	433	97	336
				H-19,C-119	4, 4	4, 4	2, 5	1.0	-	-	-
Liaison	1-1923P	Jan	52	L-20	15	16	1	1.0	99	21	78
	1-1923P	Jan	52	L-20,H-19	15, 4	16, 4	1	1.0	117	25	92
	1-1923P	Jan	52	L-20,H-19	15, 8	16, 8	1	1.0	135	29	106
Logistics Support	1-1535	Sep	52	C-124	12	18	6	1.5	441	84	357
Strategic Support	1-1534P	Mar	53	C-124	12	18	6	1.5	323	64	259
Tow Target	1-1961	Jan	52	B-26,B-45	20, 4	20, 4	3	1.0	304	47	257
				B-29	4	4	7	1.0	-	-	-
Pilotless Bomber, Light	1-1950P	Aug	52	B-61	-	-	-	-	467	41	416
Air Transport (Air Evacuations)	MATS T/D			C-47/54	6	10	4	1.7	131	42	89
Mapping & Charting	SAC T/D			RC-45	15	-	-	-	191	43	148

Note: The table above includes Supporting Flying Units.

a/ P - Peace W - War
b/ Photograph Crews
c/ Electronic Crews
d/ Combat Crews
e/ Transport Crews
f/ Plus 1 Navigator per 4 Crews.
g/ Plus 1 Acft Observer per 4 Crews.
h/ Plus 1 Flt Stewart per 2 Crews.

Source: Operations Statistics Division, Directorate of Statistical Services, DCS/C.

TABLE 77 – COMBAT AND AIRLIFT WINGS AND SQUADRONS, BY TYPE, WORLDWIDE, CONTINENTAL US, AND OVERSEAS – FY 1953

Statistics on the number of Combat and Airlift Wings and Squadrons (including Flying Supporting Units) presented in the following tables include only those units which were actually activated and/or organized prior to or on the dates shown, and for which inactivation or discontinuance orders had not been actually accomplished by the dates shown. The units are listed by the number of wing headquarters (with certain exceptions) and squadrons of Bomber, Fighter, and Reconnaissance as the Combat types and the Troop Carrier as the Airlift type. The Flying Supporting units are Troop Carrier Assault, MATS Air Transport and Air Refueling Squadrons as the Support Forces and Air Rescue Groups and Air Resupply, Liaison, Logistic Support, Mapping and Charting, Strategic Reconnaissance, Medium Weather, Air Transport (Air Evacuation) Strategic Support, Tow Target and Pilotless Bomber Squadrons as Separate Units. The exception in concept of a Wing referred to above are those squadrons which have no wing headquarters but are considered as equivalent of a wing on the basis of three squadrons comprising one wing and are so included in these tables. Figures within parentheses represent the number of squadrons of the type corresponding to the wing. Activated units presented in these tables are defined in AFR 20-38, 17 November 1950.

Units located within the continental limits of the United States are shown within their respective assigned commands. Units located outside the continental limits of the United States are shown in the major commands in which they are located.

TYPE OF UNIT	31 JUL (1952)	31 AUG	30 SEP	31 OCT	30 NOV	31 DEC	31 JAN (1953)	28 FEB	31 MAR	30 APR	31 MAY	30 JUN
						WORLDWIDE						
Combat and Airlift - Total	96 (290)	96 (290)	96 (290)	97 (293)	98 (297)	98 (299)	99 (302)	102 (310)	103 (314)	106 (322)	106 (322)	106 (322)
Combat Wing - Total	81 (244)	81 (244)	81 (244)	82 (247)	83 (251)	83 (251)	84 (254)	87 (262)	88 (266)	91 (274)	91 (274)	90 (271)
Strategic - Total	38 (115)	38 (115)	38 (115)	39 (118)	39 (118)	39 (118)	40 (121)	41 (124)	41 (124)	41 (124)	41 (124)	41 (124)
Bomb Heavy	4 (12)	4 (12)	4 (12)	4 (12)	5 (15)	5 (15)	5 (15)	6 (18)	6 (18)	6 (18)	6 (18)	6 (18)
Bomb Medium	22 (66)	22 (66)	22 (66)	23 (69)	22 (66)	22 (66)	22 (66)	22 (66)	22 (66)	22 (66)	22 (66)	22 (66)
Strategic Rcn Heavy	3 (9)	3 (9)	3 (9)	4 (12)	4 (12)	4 (12)	4 (12)	4 (12)	4 (12)	4 (12)	4 (12)	4 (12)
Strategic Rcn Medium	5 (16)	5 (16)	5 (16)	4 (13)	4 (13)	4 (13)	4 (13)	4 (13)	4 (13)	4 (13)	4 (13)	4 (13)
Strategic Fighter	4 (12)	4 (12)	4 (12)	4 (12)	4 (12)	4 (12)	5 (15)	5 (15)	5 (15)	5 (15)	5 (15)	5 (15)
Air Defense - Total	20 (60)	20 (60)	20 (60)	20 (60)	21 (64)	21 (64)	21 (64)	23 (69)	24 (73)	26 (78)	26 (78)	26 (78)
Fighter Interceptor	20 60	20 60	20 60	20 60	21 64	21 64	21 64	23 69	24 73	26 78	26 78	26 78
Tactical - Total	23 (69)	23 (69)	23 (69)	23 (69)	23 (69)	23 (69)	23 (69)	23 (69)	23 (69)	24 (72)	24 (72)	23 (69)
Bomb Light	4 (12)	4 (12)	4 (12)	4 (12)	4 (12)	4 (12)	4 (12)	4 (12)	4 (12)	4 (12)	4 (12)	4 (12)
Fighter Bomber	15 (45)	15 (45)	15 (45)	15 (45)	15 (45)	15 (45)	15 (45)	15 (45)	15 (45)	16 (48)	16 (48)	15 (45)
Tactical Recon.	4 (12)	4 (12)	4 (12)	4 (12)	4 (12)	4 (12)	4 (12)	4 (12)	4 (12)	4 (12)	4 (12)	4 (12)
Airlift Wing - Total	15 (46)	15 (46)	15 (46)	15 (46)	15 (46)	15 (48)	15 (48)	15 (48)	15 (48)	15 (48)	15 (48)	16 (51)
Troop Carrier Heavy	3 (9)	3 (9)	3 (9)	3 (9)	3 (9)	3 (10)	3 (10)	3 (10)	3 (10)	3 (10)	3 (10)	4 (13)
Troop Carrier Medium	12 (37)	12 (37)	12 (37)	12 (37)	12 (37)	12 (38)	12 (38)	12 (38)	12 (38)	12 (38)	12 (38)	12 (38)
Support Forces												
Airlift Squadron - Total	1	1	1	1	1	2	2	2	2	2	2	2
Troop Carr Aslt (FW)	1	1	1	1	1	1	1	1	1	1	1	1
Troop Carr Aslt (RW)	-	-	-	-	-	1	1	1	1	1	1	1
MATS Squadron - Total	29	29	31	31	31	31	34	34	34	35	35	35
Air Transport, Heavy	12	12	13	13	13	13	14	14	14	14	14	14
Air Transport, Medium	17	17	18	18	18	18	20	20	20	21	21	21
Air Refueling Sq - Total	17	17	17	19	19	19	20	21	21	22	22	22
Air Rflg (MB & RCN)	17	17	17	19	19	19	20	21	21	22	22	22

TABLE 77 — COMBAT AND AIRLIFT WINGS AND SQUADRONS, BY TYPE, WORLDWIDE, CONTINENTAL US, AND OVERSEAS — FY 1953 (CONTINUED)

(See first page of the table for headnote.)

TYPE OF UNIT	31 JUL (1952)	31 AUG	30 SEP	31 OCT	30 NOV	31 DEC	31 JAN (1953)	28 FEB	31 MAR	30 APR	31 MAY	30 JUN
WORLDWIDE (Continued)												
Separate Unit - Total. . .	41	41	44	47	47	47	48	49	49	50	52	52
Air Rescue Group	12	12	12	12	12	12	12	12	12	12	13	13
Air Resupply Sq.	2	2	3	3	3	3	3	3	3	3	3	3
Liaison Sq	5	5	6	8	8	8	9	9	9	10	10	10
Logistics Spt Sq	-	-	1	1	1	1	1	1	1	1	1	1
Mapp & Chart Sq.	-	-	-	1	1	1	1	1	1	1	1	1
Strat Rcn Sq, M Wea. . .	6	6	6	6	6	6	6	6	6	6	6	6
Air Trans Sq (AE). . . .	6	6	6	6	6	6	6	6	6	6	6	6
Strategic Spt Sq	3	3	3	3	3	3	3	4	4	4	4	4
Tow Target Sq.	5	5	5	5	5	5	5	5	5	5	6	6
Plts Bomb Sq, L (Matador)	2	2	2	2	2	2	2	2	2	2	2	2
²CONTINENTAL US												
Combat and Airlift - Total	60 (178)	60 (178)	60 (177)	61 (179)	64 (188)	64 (190)	64 (190)	67 (199)	69 (206)	71 (213)	71 (213)	70 (211)
Combat Wing - Total. . .	52 (155)	52 (155)	52 (154)	53 (156)	55 (163)	55 (163)	55 (163)	58 (172)	60 (179)	62 (186)	62 (186)	60 (181)
Strategic - Total. . .	31 (93)	31 (93)	31 (93)	32 (96)	33 (99)	33 (99)	33 (99)	34 (103)	35 (105)	35 (105)	35 (105)	35 (105)
Bomb Heavy	4 (12)	4 (12)	4 (12)	4 (12)	5 (15)	5 (15)	5 (15)	6 (18)	6 (18)	6 (18)	6 (18)	6 (18)
Bomb Medium.	18 (54)	18 (54)	18 (54)	18 (54)	18 (54)	18 (54)	17 (51)	17 (52)	18 (54)	18 (54)	18 (54)	18 (54)
Strategic Rcn Heavy.	2 (6)	2 (6)	2 (6)	3 (9)	3 (9)	3 (9)	3 (9)	3 (9)	3 (9)	3 (9)	3 (9)	3 (9)
Strategic Rcn Medium	4 (12)	4 (12)	4 (12)	4 (12)	4 (12)	4 (12)	4 (12)	4 (12)	4 (12)	4 (12)	4 (12)	4 (12)
Strategic Fighter. .	3 (9)	3 (9)	3 (9)	3 (9)	3 (9)	3 (9)	4 (12)	4 (12)	4 (12)	4 (12)	4 (12)	4 (12)
Air Defense - Total. .	14 (40)	14 (40)	14 (40)	14 (39)	15 (43)	15 (43)	15 (43)	17 (48)	18 (52)	19 (56)	19 (56)	18 (54)
Fighter Interceptor.	14 (40)	14 (40)	14 (40)	14 (39)	15 (43)	15 (43)	15 (43)	17 (48)	18 (52)	19 (56)	19 (56)	18 (54)
Tactical - Total . . .	7 (22)	7 (22)	7 (21)	7 (21)	7 (21)	7 (21)	7 (21)	7 (21)	7 (22)	8 (25)	8 (25)	7 (22)
Bomb Light	0 (1)	0 (1)	0 (1)	0 (1)	0 (1)	0 (1)	0 (1)	0 (1)	0 (1)	0 (1)	0 (1)	0 (1)
Fighter Bomber . . .	5 (15)	5 (15)	5 (14)	5 (14)	5 (14)	5 (14)	5 (14)	5 (14)	5 (15)	6 (18)	6 (18)	5 (15)
Tactical Recon . . .	2 (6)	2 (6)	2 (6)	2 (6)	2 (6)	2 (6)	2 (6)	2 (6)	2 (6)	2 (6)	2 (6)	2 (6)
Airlift Wing - Total . .	8 (23)	8 (23)	8 (23)	8 (23)	9 (25)	9 (27)	9 (27)	9 (27)	9 (27)	9 (27)	9 (27)	10 (30)
Troop Carrier Heavy. .	1 (3)	1 (3)	1 (3)	1 (3)	2 (5)	2 (6)	2 (6)	2 (6)	2 (6)	2 (6)	2 (6)	3 (9)
Troop Carrier Medium .	7 (20)	7 (20)	7 (20)	7 (20)	7 (20)	7 (21)	7 (21)	7 (21)	7 (21)	7 (21)	7 (21)	7 (21)
Support Forces												
Airlift Squadron - Total	1	1	1	1	1	2	2	2	2	2	2	2
Troop Carrier Aslt (FW)	1	1	1	1	1	1	1	1	1	1	1	1
Troop Carrier Aslt (RW)	-	-	-	-	-	1	1	1	1	1	1	1
MATS Squadron - Total. .	19	19	21	21	21	21	24	24	24	25	25	25
Air Transport Heavy. .	11	11	12	12	12	12	13	13	13	13	13	13
Air Transport Medium .	8	8	9	9	9	9	11	11	11	12	12	12

TABLE 77 — COMBAT AND AIRLIFT WINGS AND SQUADRONS, BY TYPE, WORLDWIDE, CONTINENTAL US, AND OVERSEAS — FISCAL YEAR 1953 (CONTINUED)

(See first page of the table for headnote.)

TYPE OF UNIT	31 JUL (1952)	31 AUG	30 SEP	31 OCT	30 NOV	31 DEC	31 JAN (1953)	28 FEB	31 MAR	30 APR	31 MAY	30 JUN
CONTINENTAL US (Continued)												
Support Forces (Cont'd)												
Air Refueling Sq - Total	15	15	14	16	17	17	19	20	20	21	21	21
Air Rflg (MB & RCN)	15	15	14	16	17	17	19	20	20	21	21	21
Separate Unit - Total	24	24	27	30	29	29	30	30	29	29	30	30
Air Rescue Group	4	4	3	4	3	3	3	3	3	3	4	4
Air Resupply Sq	1	1	2	1	1	1	1	1	1	1	1	1
Liaison Sq	3	3	5	7	7	7	8	7	6	6	6	6
Logistics Support Sq	-	-	1	1	1	1	1	1	1	1	1	1
Mapping & Charting Sq	-	-	-	1	1	1	1	1	1	1	1	1
Strat Rcn Sq, M Wea	1	1	1	1	1	1	1	1	1	1	1	1
Air Trans Sq (AE)	6	6	6	6	6	6	6	6	6	6	6	6
Strategic Support Sq	3	3	3	3	3	3	3	4	4	4	4	4
Tow Target Sq	4	4	4	4	4	4	4	4	4	4	4	4
Plts Bomb Sq, L (Matador)	2	2	2	2	2	2	2	2	2	2	2	2
OVERSEAS												
Combat and Airlift - Total	36 (112)	36 (112)	36 (113)	36 (114)	34 (109)	34 (109)	35 (112)	35 (111)	34 (108)	35 (109)	35 (109)	36 (111)
Combat Wing - Total	29 (89)	29 (89)	29 (90)	29 (91)	28 (88)	28 (88)	29 (91)	29 (90)	28 (87)	29 (88)	29 (88)	30 (90)
Strategic - Total	7 (22)	7 (22)	7 (22)	7 (22)	6 (19)	6 (19)	7 (22)	7 (21)	6 (19)	6 (19)	6 (19)	6 (19)
Bomb Medium	4 (12)	4 (12)	4 (12)	5 (15)	4 (12)	4 (12)	5 (15)	5 (14)	4 (12)	4 (12)	4 (12)	4 (12)
Strategic Rcn Heavy	1 (3)	1 (3)	1 (3)	1 (3)	1 (3)	1 (3)	1 (3)	1 (3)	1 (3)	1 (3)	1 (3)	1 (3)
Strategic Rcn Medium	1 (4)	1 (4)	1 (4)	0 (1)	0 (1)	0 (1)	0 (1)	0 (1)	0 (1)	0 (1)	0 (1)	0 (1)
Strategic Fighter	1 (3)	1 (3)	1 (3)	1 (3)	1 (3)	1 (3)	1 (3)	1 (3)	1 (3)	1 (3)	1 (3)	1 (3)
Air Defense - Total	6 (20)	6 (20)	6 (20)	6 (21)	6 (21)	6 (21)	6 (21)	6 (21)	6 (21)	7 (22)	7 (22)	8 (24)
Fighter Interceptor	6 (20)	6 (20)	6 (20)	6 (21)	6 (21)	6 (21)	6 (21)	6 (21)	6 (21)	7 (22)	7 (22)	8 (24)
Tactical - Total	16 (47)	16 (47)	16 (48)	16 (48)	16 (48)	16 (48)	16 (48)	16 (48)	16 (47)	16 (47)	16 (47)	16 (47)
Bomb Light	4 (11)	4 (11)	4 (11)	4 (11)	4 (11)	4 (11)	4 (11)	4 (11)	4 (11)	4 (11)	4 (11)	4 (11)
Fighter Bomber	10 (30)	10 (30)	10 (31)	10 (31)	10 (31)	10 (31)	10 (31)	10 (31)	10 (30)	10 (30)	10 (30)	10 (30)
Tactical Recon.	2 (6)	2 (6)	2 (6)	2 (6)	2 (6)	2 (6)	2 (6)	2 (6)	2 (6)	2 (6)	2 (6)	2 (6)
Airlift Wing - Total	7 (23)	7 (23)	7 (23)	7 (23)	6 (21)	6 (21)	6 (21)	6 (21)	6 (21)	6 (21)	6 (21)	6 (21)
Troop Carr Heavy	2 (6)	2 (5)	2 (6)	2 (6)	1 (4)	1 (4)	1 (4)	1 (4)	1 (4)	1 (4)	1 (4)	1 (4)
Troop Carr Medium	5 (17)	5 (17)	5 (17)	5 (17)	5 (17)	5 (17)	5 (17)	5 (17)	5 (17)	5 (17)	5 (17)	5 (17)
Support Forces												
MATS Squadron - Total	10	10	10	10	10	10	10	10	10	10	10	10
Air Transport, Heavy	1	1	1	1	1	1	1	1	1	1	1	1
Air Transport, Medium	9	9	9	9	9	9	9	9	9	9	9	9
Air Refueling Sq - Total	2	2	3	3	2	2	1	1	1	1	1	1
Air Rflg (MB & RCN)	2	2	3	3	2	2	1	1	1	1	1	1
Separate Unit - Total	17	17	17	17	18	18	18	19	20	21	22	22
Air Rescue Group	8	8	9	8	9	9	9	9	9	9	9	9
Air Resupply	1	1	1	2	2	2	2	2	2	2	2	2
Liaison Sq	2	2	1	1	1	1	1	2	3	4	4	4
Strat Rcn Sq, M Wea	5	5	5	5	5	5	5	5	5	5	5	5
Tow Target Sq	1	1	1	1	1	1	1	1	1	1	2	2

Source: Operations Statistics Division, Directorate of Statistical Services, DCS/C.

TABLE 78 — COMBAT AND AIRLIFT WINGS AND SQUADRONS, BY TYPE, BY COMMAND— FISCAL YEAR 1953

(Includes Flying Supporting Units. Units located within the continental limits of the United States are shown within their respective assigned commands. Units located outside the continental limits of the United States are shown in the major commands in which they are located.)

TYPE OF UNIT	31 JUL (1952)	31 AUG	30 SEP	31 OCT	30 NOV	31 DEC	31 JAN (1953)	28 FEB	31 MAR	30 APR	31 MAY	30 JUN
AIR DEFENSE COMMAND												
Combat and Airlift - Total.	14 (40)	14 (40)	14 (40)	14 (39)	15 (43)	15 (43)	15 (43)	17 (48)	18 (52)	19 (56)	19 (56)	18 (54)
Combat Wing - Total	14 (40)	14 (40)	14 (40)	14 (39)	15 (43)	15 (43)	15 (43)	17 (48)	18 (52)	19 (56)	19 (56)	18 (54)
Air Defense - Total	14 (40)	14 (40)	14 (40)	14 (39)	15 (43)	15 (43)	15 (43)	17 (48)	18 (52)	19 (56)	19 (56)	18 (54)
Fighter Interceptor	14 (40)	14 (40)	14 (40)	14 (39)	15 (43)	15 (43)	15 (43)	17 (48)	18 (52)	19 (56)	19 (56)	18 (54)
Separate Units - Total	-	-	-	1	1	1	2	2	2	2	2	2
Liaison Squadron	-	-	-	1	1	1	2	2	2	2	2	2
AIR MATERIEL COMMAND												
Separate Units - Total	-	-	1	1	1	1	1	1	1	1	1	1
Logistics Support Sq.	-	-	1	1	1	1	1	1	1	1	1	1
AIR RESEARCH AND DEVELOPMENT COMMAND												
Separate Units - Total	2	2	2	2	2	2	2	2	2	2	2	2
Plts Bmr Sq, L(Matador)	2	2	2	2	2	2	2	2	2	2	2	2
MILITARY AIR TRANSPORT SERVICE												
Support Forces												
MATS Squadrons - Total	19	19	21	21	21	21	24	24	24	25	25	25
Air Transport, Heavy	11	11	12	12	12	12	13	13	13	13	13	13
Air Transport, Medium	8	8	9	9	9	9	11	11	11	12	12	12
Separate Units - Total	11	11	12	11	10	10	10	10	10	10	11	11
Air Rescue Gp	3	3	3	3	2	2	2	2	2	2	3	3
Air Resupply Sq	1	1	2	1	1	1	1	1	1	1	1	1
Strat Rcn Sq, M Wea	1	1	1	1	1	1	1	1	1	1	1	1
Air Trans Sq (AE)	6	6	6	6	6	6	6	6	6	6	6	6
STRATEGIC AIR COMMAND												
Combat and Airlift - Total.	31 (93)	31 (93)	31 (93)	32 (96)	33 (99)	33 (99)	33 (99)	34 (103)	35 (105)	35 (105)	35 (105)	35 (105)
Combat Wing - Total	31 (93)	31 (93)	31 (93)	32 (96)	33 (99)	33 (99)	33 (99)	34 (103)	35 (105)	35 (105)	35 (105)	35 (105)
Strategic - Total	31 (93)	31 (93)	31 (93)	32 (96)	33 (99)	33 (99)	33 (99)	34 (103)	35 (105)	35 (105)	35 (105)	35 (105)
Bomb Heavy	4 (12)	4 (12)	4 (12)	4 (12)	5 (15)	5 (15)	5 (15)	6 (18)	6 (18)	6 (18)	6 (18)	6 (18)
Bomb Medium	18 (54)	18 (54)	18 (54)	18 (54)	18 (54)	18 (54)	17 (51)	17 (52)	18 (54)	18 (54)	18 (54)	18 (54)
Strategic Rcn, H.	2 (6)	2 (6)	2 (6)	3 (9)	3 (9)	3 (9)	3 (9)	3 (9)	3 (9)	3 (9)	3 (9)	3 (9)
Strategic Rcn, M.	4 (12)	4 (12)	4 (12)	4 (12)	4 (12)	4 (12)	4 (12)	4 (12)	4 (12)	4 (12)	4 (12)	4 (12)
Strategic Fighter	3 (9)	3 (9)	3 (9)	3 (9)	3 (9)	3 (9)	4 (12)	4 (12)	4 (12)	4 (12)	4 (12)	4 (12)

TABLE 78 — COMBAT AND AIRLIFT WINGS AND SQUADRONS, BY TYPE, BY COMMAND — FISCAL YEAR 1953 (Continued)

TYPE OF UNIT	31 JUL (1952)	31 AUG	30 SEP	31 OCT	30 NOV	31 DEC	31 JAN (1953)	28 FEB	31 MAR	30 APR	31 MAY	30 JUN
					STRATEGIC AIR COMMAND Continued							
Support Forces												
Air Refueling Sqs - Total	15	15	14	16	17	17	19	20	20	21	21	21
Air Rflg (MB&RCN)	15	15	14	16	17	17	19	20	20	21	21	21
Separate Units - Total	4	4	3	5	5	5	5	6	6	6	6	6
Air Rescue Group	1	1	-	1	1	1	1	1	1	1	1	1
Mapping & Chart Sq.	-	-	-	1	1	1	1	1	1	1	1	1
Strategic Spt Sq.	3	3	3	3	3	3	3	4	4	4	4	4
					TACTICAL AIR COMMAND							
Combat and Airlift - Total	15 (45)	15 (45)	15 (44)	15 (44)	16 (46)	16 (48)	16 (48)	16 (48)	16 (49)	17 (52)	17 (52)	17 (52)
Combat Wing - Total	7 (22)	7 (22)	7 (21)	7 (21)	7 (21)	7 (21)	7 (21)	7 (21)	7 (22)	8 (25)	8 (25)	7 (22)
Tactical - Total	7 (22)	7 (22)	7 (21)	7 (21)	7 (21)	7 (21)	7 (21)	7 (21)	7 (22)	8 (25)	8 (25)	7 (22)
Bomb Light	0 (1)	0 (1)	0 (1)	0 (1)	0 (1)	0 (1)	0 (1)	0 (1)	0 (1)	0 (1)	0 (1)	0 (1)
Fighter Bomber	5 (15)	5 (15)	5 (14)	5 (14)	5 (14)	5 (14)	5 (14)	5 (14)	5 (15)	6 (18)	6 (18)	5 (15)
Tactical Recon.	2 (6)	2 (6)	2 (6)	2 (6)	2 (6)	2 (6)	2 (6)	2 (6)	2 (6)	2 (6)	2 (6)	2 (6)
Airlift Wing - Total	8 (23)	8 (23)	8 (23)	8 (23)	9 (25)	9 (27)	9 (27)	9 (27)	9 (27)	9 (27)	9 (27)	10 (30)
Troop Carr, Heavy	1 (3)	1 (3)	1 (3)	1 (3)	2 (5)	2 (6)	2 (6)	2 (6)	2 (6)	2 (6)	2 (6)	3 (9)
Troop Carr, Medium	7 (20)	7 (20)	7 (20)	7 (20)	7 (20)	7 (21)	7 (21)	7 (21)	7 (21)	7 (21)	7 (21)	7 (21)
Support Forces												
Airlift Squadrons - Total	1	1	1	1	1	2	2	2	2	2	2	2
Troop Carr Aslt FW.	1	1	1	1	1	1	1	1	1	1	1	1
Troop Carr Aslt RW.	-	-	-	-	-	1	1	1	1	1	1	1
Separate Units - Total	7	7	9	10	10	10	10	9	8	8	8	8
Liaison Sq.	3	3	5	6	6	6	6	5	4	4	4	4
Tow Target Sq	4	4	4	4	4	4	4	4	4	4	4	4
					ALASKAN AIR COMMAND							
Combat and Airlift - Total	1 (5)	1 (5)	1 (5)	1 (5)	1 (5)	1 (5)	1 (5)	1 (5)	1 (5)	1 (5)	1 (5)	1 (5)
Combat Wing - Total	1 (4)	1 (4)	1 (4)	1 (4)	1 (4)	1 (4)	1 (4)	1 (4)	1 (4)	1 (4)	1 (4)	1 (4)
Air Defense - Total	1 (4)	1 (4)	1 (4)	1 (4)	1 (4)	1 (4)	1 (4)	1 (4)	1 (4)	1 (4)	1 (4)	1 (4)
Fighter Interceptor	1 (4)	1 (4)	1 (4)	1 (4)	1 (4)	1 (4)	1 (4)	1 (4)	1 (4)	1 (4)	1 (4)	1 (4)
Airlift Wing - Total	0 (1)	0 (1)	0 (1)	0 (1)	0 (1)	0 (1)	0 (1)	0 (1)	0 (1)	0 (1)	0 (1)	0 (1)
Troop Carrier, H.	0 (1)	0 (1)	0 (1)	0 (1)	0 (1)	0 (1)	0 (1)	0 (1)	0 (1)	0 (1)	0 (1)	0 (1)

TABLE 78 — COMBAT AND AIRLIFT WINGS AND SQUADRONS, BY TYPE, BY COMMAND — FISCAL YEAR 1953 — (CONTINUED)

TYPE OF UNIT	31 JUL (1952)	31 AUG	30 SEP	31 OCT	30 NOV	31 DEC	31 JAN (1953)	28 FEB	31 MAR	30 APR	31 MAY	30 JUN
ALASKAN AIR COMMAND - Continued												
Separate Units - Total	2	2	2	2	2	2	2	2	2	3	3	3
Air Rescue Group	1	1	1	1	1	1	1	1	1	1	1	1
Liaison Sq.	-	-	-	-	-	-	-	-	-	1	1	1
Strat Rcn Sq, M, Wea.	1	1	1	1	1	1	1	1	1	1	1	1
CARIBBEAN AIR COMMAND												
Combat and Airlift - Total	2 (6)	2 (6)	2 (6)	1 (3)	1 (3)	1 (3)	1 (3)	1 (3)	1 (3)	1 (3)	1 (3)	1 (3)
Combat Wing - Total	2 (6)	2 (6)	2 (6)	1 (3)	1 (3)	1 (3)	1 (3)	1 (3)	1 (3)	1 (3)	1 (3)	1 (3)
Strategic - Total	2 (6)	2 (6)	2 (6)	1 (3)	1 (3)	1 (3)	1 (3)	1 (3)	1 (3)	1 (3)	1 (3)	1 (3)
Strat Rcn, Heavy	1 (3)	1 (3)	1 (3)	1 (3)	1 (3)	1 (3)	1 (3)	1 (3)	1 (3)	1 (3)	1 (3)	1 (3)
Strat Rcn, Medium	1 (3)	1 (3)	1 (3)	- -	- -	- -	- -	- -	- -	- -	- -	- -
Support Forces												
MATS Squadrons - Total	1	1	1	1	1	1	1	1	1	1	1	1
Air Transport, M.	1	1	1	1	1	1	1	1	1	1	1	1
Air Refueling Sqs - Total	1	1	1	1	1	1	-	-	-	-	-	-
Air Rflg (M&RCN)	1	1	1	1	1	1	-	-	-	-	-	-
Separate Units - Total	3	3	2	2	2	2	2	2	2	2	2	2
Air Rescue Group	1	1	1	1	1	1	1	1	1	1	1	1
Liaison Sq.	1	1	-	-	-	-	-	-	-	-	-	-
Strat Rcn Sq, M Wea	1	1	1	1	1	1	1	1	1	1	1	1
FAR EAST AIR FORCES												
Combat and Airlift - Total	21 (66)	21 (66)	21 (66)	21 (66)	20 (64)	20 (64)	20 (64)	20 (64)	20 (64)	20 (64)	20 (64)	20 (64)
Combat Wing - Total	16 (50)	16 (50)	16 (50)	16 (50)	16 (50)	16 (50)	16 (50)	16 (50)	16 (50)	16 (50)	16 (50)	16 (50)
Strategic - Total	4 (13)	4 (13)	4 (13)	4 (13)	4 (13)	4 (13)	4 (13)	4 (13)	4 (13)	4 (13)	4 (13)	4 (13)
Bomb Medium	3 (9)	3 (9)	3 (9)	3 (9)	3 (9)	3 (9)	3 (9)	3 (9)	3 (9)	3 (9)	3 (9)	3 (9)
Strat Rcn Medium	0 (1)	0 (1)	0 (1)	0 (1)	0 (1)	0 (1)	0 (1)	0 (1)	0 (1)	0 (1)	0 (1)	0 (1)
Strategic Fighter	1 (3)	1 (3)	1 (3)	1 (3)	1 (3)	1 (3)	1 (3)	1 (3)	1 (3)	1 (3)	1 (3)	1 (3)
Air Defense - Total	4 (13)	4 (13)	4 (13)	4 (13)	4 (13)	4 (13)	4 (13)	4 (13)	4 (13)	4 (13)	4 (13)	4 (13)
Fighter Interceptor	4 (13)	4 (13)	4 (13)	4 (13)	4 (13)	4 (13)	4 (13)	4 (13)	4 (13)	4 (13)	4 (13)	4 (13)
Tactical - Total	8 (24)	8 (24)	8 (24)	8 (24)	8 (24)	8 (24)	8 (24)	8 (24)	8 (24)	8 (24)	8 (24)	8 (24)
Bomb Light	2 (6)	2 (6)	2 (6)	2 (6)	2 (6)	2 (6)	2 (6)	2 (6)	2 (6)	2 (6)	2 (6)	2 (6)
Fighter Bomber	5 (15)	5 (15)	5 (15)	5 (15)	5 (15)	5 (15)	5 (15)	5 (15)	5 (15)	5 (15)	5 (15)	5 (15)
Tactical Recon.	1 (3)	1 (3)	1 (3)	1 (3)	1 (3)	1 (3)	1 (3)	1 (3)	1 (3)	1 (3)	1 (3)	1 (3)

TABLE 78 — COMBAT AND AIRLIFT WINGS AND SQUADRONS, BY TYPE, BY COMMAND — FISCAL YEAR 1953 — (Continued)

TYPE OF UNIT	31 JUL (1952)	31 AUG	30 SEP	31 OCT	30 NOV	31 DEC	31 JAN (1953)	28 FEB	31 MAR	30 APR	31 MAY	30 JUN
FAR EAST AIR FORCE - Continued												
Airlift Wing - Total	5 (16)	5 (16)	5 (16)	5 (16)	4 (14)	4 (14)	4 (14)	4 (14)	4 (14)	4 (14)	4 (14)	4 (14)
Troop Carrier, Heavy	2 (5)	2 (5)	2 (5)	2 (5)	1 (3)	1 (3)	1 (3)	1 (3)	1 (3)	1 (3)	1 (3)	1 (3)
Troop Carrier, Medium	3 (11)	3 (11)	3 (11)	3 (11)	3 (11)	3 (11)	3 (11)	3 (11)	3 (11)	3 (11)	3 (11)	3 (11)
Support Forces												
MATS Squadrons - Total	7	7	7	7	7	7	7	7	7	7	7	7
Air Transport, Heavy	1	1	1	1	1	1	1	1	1	1	1	1
Air Transport, Medium	6	6	6	6	6	6	6	6	6	6	6	6
Air Refueling - Total	-	-	1	1	-	-	-	-	-	-	-	-
Air Rflg (MB & RCN)	-	-	1	1	-	-	-	-	-	-	-	-
Separate Units - Total	9	9	9	9	9	9	9	9	10	10	10	10
Air Rescue Group	3	3	3	3	3	3	3	3	3	3	3	3
Air Resupply Sqs	1	1	1	1	1	1	1	1	1	1	1	1
Liaison Sqs	1	1	1	1	1	1	1	1	2	2	2	2
Strat Rcn Sq, M Wea	3	3	3	3	3	3	3	3	3	3	3	3
Tow Target Sqs	1	1	1	1	1	1	1	1	1	1	1	1
NORTHEAST AIR COMMAND												
Combat and Airlift - Total	- -	- -	0 (1)	0 (2)	0 (2)	0 (2)	0 (2)	0 (2)	0 (1)	1 (2)	1 (2)	1 (2)
Combat Wing - Total	- -	- -	0 (1)	0 (2)	0 (2)	0 (2)	0 (2)	0 (2)	0 (1)	1 (2)	1 (2)	1 (2)
Air Defense - Total	- -	- -	- -	0 (1)	0 (1)	0 (1)	0 (1)	0 (1)	0 (1)	1 (2)	1 (2)	1 (2)
Fighter Interceptor	- -	- -	- -	0 (1)	0 (1)	0 (1)	0 (1)	0 (1)	0 (1)	1 (2)	1 (2)	1 (2)
Tactical - Total	- -	- -	0 (1)	0 (1)	0 (1)	0 (1)	0 (1)	0 (1)	- -	- -	- -	- -
Fighter Bomber	- -	- -	0 (1)	0 (1)	0 (1)	0 (1)	0 (1)	0 (1)	- -	- -	- -	- -
Separate Units - Total	1	1	1	1	1	1	1	1	1	1	1	1
Air Rescue Group	1	1	1	1	1	1	1	1	1	1	1	1
UNITED STATES AIR FORCES IN EUROPE												
Combat and Airlift - Total	12 (35)	12 (35)	12 (35)	13 (38)	12 (35)	12 (35)	13 (38)	13 (37)	12 (35)	12 (35)	12 (35)	13 (37)
Combat Wing - Total	10 (29)	10 (29)	10 (29)	11 (32)	10 (29)	10 (29)	11 (32)	11 (31)	10 (29)	10 (29)	10 (29)	11 (31)
Strategic - Total	1 (3)	1 (3)	1 (3)	2 (6)	1 (3)	1 (3)	2 (6)	2 (5)	1 (3)	1 (3)	1 (3)	1 (3)
Bomb Medium	1 (3)	1 (3)	1 (3)	2 (6)	1 (3)	1 (3)	2 (6)	2 (5)	1 (3)	1 (3)	1 (3)	1 (3)
Air Defense - Total	1 (3)	1 (3)	1 (3)	1 (3)	1 (3)	1 (3)	1 (3)	1 (3)	1 (3)	1 (3)	1 (3)	2 (5)
Fighter Interceptor	1 (3)	1 (3)	1 (3)	1 (3)	1 (3)	1 (3)	1 (3)	1 (3)	1 (3)	1 (3)	1 (3)	2 (5)

TABLE 78 — COMBAT AND AIRLIFT WINGS AND SQUADRONS, BY TYPE, BY COMMAND — FISCAL YEAR 1953 — (CONTINUED)

TYPE OF UNIT	31 JUL (1952)	31 AUG	30 SEP	31 OCT	30 NOV	31 DEC	31 JAN (1953)	28 FEB	31 MAR	30 APR	31 MAY	30 JUN
UNITED STATES AIR FORCES IN EUROPE - Continued												
Tactical - Total	8 (23)	8 (23)	8 (23)	8 (23)	8 (24)	8 (23)	8 (23)	8 (23)	8 (23)	8 (23)	8 (23)	8 (23)
Bomb Light	2 (5)	2 (5)	2 (5)	2 (5)	2 (5)	2 (5)	2 (5)	2 (5)	2 (5)	2 (5)	2 (5)	2 (5)
Fighter Bomber	5 (15)	5 (15)	5 (15)	5 (15)	5 (15)	5 (15)	5 (15)	5 (15)	5 (15)	5 (15)	5 (25)	5 (15)
Tactical Recon.	1 (3)	1 (3)	1 (3)	1 (3)	1 (3)	1 (3)	1 (3)	1 (3)	1 (3)	1 (3)	1 (3)	1 (3)
Airlift Wing - Total	2 (6)	2 (6)	2 (6)	2 (6)	2 (6)	2 (6)	2 (6)	2 (6)	2 (6)	2 (6)	2 (6)	2 (6)
Troop Carrier, M.	2 (6)	2 (6)	2 (6)	2 (6)	2 (6)	2 (6)	2 (6)	2 (6)	2 (6)	2 (6)	2 (6)	2 (6)
Support Forces												
MATS Squadrons - Total	2	2	2	2	2	2	2	2	2	2	2	2
Air Transport, M.	2	2	2	2	2	2	2	2	2	2	2	2
Air Refueling Sqs - Total	1	1	1	1	1	1	1	1	1	1	1	1
Air Rflg (MB & RCN)	1	1	1	1	1	1	1	1	1	1	1	1
Separate Units - Total	2	2	3	3	4	4	4	5	5	5	6	6
Air Rescue Group	2	2	3	2	3	3	3	3	3	3	3	3
Air Resupply Sq	-	-	-	1	1	1	1	1	1	1	1	1
Liaison Squadron	-	-	-	-	-	-	-	1	1	1	1	1
Tow Target Squadron	-	-	-	-	-	-	-	-	-	-	1	1

Source: Operations Statistics Division, Directorate of Statistical Services, DCS/C.

TABLE 79 — NUMBER OF ACTIVATED USAF COMBAT WINGS AND AIRLIFT UNITS CLASSIFIED BY TYPE OF AIRCRAFT POSSESSED — FISCAL YEAR 1953

(Combat and Airlift Wings and Airlift Support Squadrons are indicated by open figures. Figures within the parenthesis represent the number of Squadrons of the type corresponding to the Wing.)

TYPE OF ACFT POSSESSED BY TYPE OF UNIT	30 SEP 52		31 DEC 52		31 MAR 53		30 JUN 53	
Combat Airlift Wing & Squadron - Total a/								
Activated	96	(291)	98	(301)	103	(316)	106	(324)
Unequipped	10	(31)	13	(41)	12	(41)	11	(35)
Equipped b/	86	(260)	85	(260)	91	(275)	95	(289)
Combat Wing & Squadron - Total								
Activated	81	(244)	83	(251)	88	(266)	90	(271)
Unequipped	10	(31)	12	(37)	12	(39)	10	(32)
Equipped b/	71	(213)	71	(214)	76	(227)	80	(239)
Bomber - Total	28	(83)	28	(83)	28	(85)	28	(83)
B - 36	3	(10)	4	(12)	4	(12)	5	(14)
B - 47	1	(3)	2	(4)	3	(9)	4	(13)
B - 50	5	(15)	5	(15)	5	(15)	5	(15)
B - 29	15	(43)	13	(40)	12	(37)	10	(29)
B - 45	1	(2)	1	(2)	1	(2)	1	(2)
B - 26	3	(10)	3	(10)	3	(10)	3	(10)
Fighter - Total	34	(103)	35	(107)	38	(113)	42	(124)
F - 94	4	(10)	4	(12)	5	(16)	7	(21)
F - 89	0	(1)	0	(1)	1	(2)	1	(2)
F - 86	6	(19)	7	(22)	10	(29)	16	(49)
F - 84	12	(36)	13	(39)	13	(40)	14	(42)
F - 80	2	(7)	2	(7)	2	(5)	2	(5)
F - 51	8	(23)	7	(20)	5	(16)	2	(5)
F - 47	2	(7)	2	(6)	2	(6)	-	-
Reconnaissance - Total	9	(27)	8	(24)	10	(29)	10	(32)
RB - 36	2	(5)	3	(7)	4	(12)	4	(12)
RB - 50	1	(3)	1	(3)	1	(3)	1	(3)
RB - 47	-	-	-	-	-	-	1	(2)
RB - 29	1	(3)	0	(1)	1	(2)	0	(2)
RB - 45	1	(3)	0	(1)	0	(1)	0	(1)
RB - 26	1	(4)	1	(4)	1	(4)	1	(4)
RF - 80	3	(7)	3	(7)	3	(7)	3	(8)
RF - 51	0	(1)	0	(1)	-	-	-	-
Airlift Wing & Squadron - Total a/								
Activated	15	(47)	15	(50)	15	(50)	16	(53)
Unequipped	-	-	1	(4)	0	(2)	1	(3)
Equipped b/	15	(47)	14	(46)	15	(48)	15	(50)
Troop Carrier - Total	15	(47)	14	(46)	15	(48)	15	(50)
C - 124	2	(5)	2	(6)	3	(9)	3	(9)
C - 54	1	(4)	0	(1)	0	(1)	0	(1)
C - 122	0	(1)	0	(1)	-	-	0	(1)
C - 119	6	(17)	7	(21)	8	(24)	9	(27)
C - 82	2	(6)	2	(6)	1	(4)	1	(2)
C - 47	0	(1)	0	(1)	0	(1)	0	(1)
C - 46	4	(13)	3	(10)	3	(9)	2	(8)
H - 19	-	-	-	-	-	-	0	(1)
Airlift Support Squadrons								
MATS Air Transport Squadron - Total								
Activated	33		33		34		35	
Unequipped	6		2		1		1	
Equipped b/	27		31		33		34	
C - 124	5		5		7		7	
C - 118	-		1		1		1	
C - 97	5		5		5		5	
C - 74	1		1		1		1	
C - 54	16		19		19		20	
Air Refueling Squadron, Medium - Total								
Activated	17		19		21		22	
Unequipped	4		4		4		4	
Equipped b/	13		15		17		18	
KC - 97	4		6		8		10	
KB - 29	9		9		9		8	

a/ Does not include Aircraft Support Squadrons.
b/ Equipped includes all units possessing 50% or more of authorized number of aircraft.
Source: Operations Statistics Division, Directorate Statistical Services, DCS/C.

TABLE 80 — AIRCRAFT AND CREWS IN COMBAT AND AIRLIFT UNITS – BY QUARTERS – FY 1953

BY TYPE AND MODEL OF AIRCRAFT	30 SEPTEMBER 1952						31 DECEMBER 1952					
	AIRCRAFT			CREWS			AIRCRAFT			CREWS		
	AUTH	ON HAND	COMBAT READY	AUTH	ON HAND	COMBAT READY	AUTH	ON HAND	COMBAT READY	AUTH	ON HAND	COMBAT READY
Combat and Airlift - Total.	6,678	5,681	3,403	8,152	6,476	5,038	6,903	5,845	3,541	8,912	6,703	4,725
Combat - Total.	4,668	3,846	2,229	5,685	4,630	3,422	4,774	3,951	2,433	6,394	4,936	3,207
Bomber - Total.	1,146	1,020	603	1,214	1,111	874	1,191	1,091	641	1,259	1,077	699
B-26.	168	186	139	228	197	165	168	187	120	228	219	120
B-29.	450	465	253	450	499	365	420	475	276	420	385	274
B-36.	120	85	42	120	99	83	150	118	64	150	120	57
B-45.	48	49	21	56	40	39	48	41	20	56	51	50
B-47.	135	32	2	135	26	-	180	59	30	180	73	-
B-50.	225	203	146	225	250	222	225	211	131	225	229	198
Fighter - Total	2,937	2,397	1,427	3,853	3,042	2,161	2,998	2,429	1,574	4,517	3,358	2,135
F-47.	150	139	70	180	127	88	50	122	66	72	82	60
F-51.	525	515	326	612	573	394	200	480	307	288	514	373
F-80.	200	190	106	288	275	243	200	205	136	288	261	219
F-82.	-	5	1	-	4	-	-	6	2	-	3	3
F-84.	950	779	459	1,035	905	748	1,025	810	512	1,107	1,028	716
F-86A/E/F	525	398	242	720	547	422	775	455	329	1,386	936	463
F-86D	-	-	-	-	-	-	225	-	-	450	-	-
F-89.	125	75	28	250	157	-	125	73	45	250	30	-
F-94.	462	296	195	768	454	266	398	278	177	676	504	301
Reconnaissance - Total.	585	429	199	618	477	387	585	431	218	618	501	373
RB-26	72	78	25	78	65	40	72	93	51	78	68	50
RB-29	72	31	10	72	33	23	42	18	7	42	72	19
RB-36	90	70	19	90	73	66	120	104	35	120	73	50
RB-45	45	22	5	45	32	32	45	10	6	45	33	31
RB-47	45	-	-	45	-	-	45	-	-	45	-	-
YRB-47.	-	-	-	-	-	-	-	-	-	-	-	-
RB-50	45	34	24	48	44	35	45	23	2	48	27	27
RF-51	18	19	14	24	24	22	18	13	6	24	15	14
RF-80	126	107	65	132	137	103	126	103	75	132	142	112
RF-86	-	3	2	-	4	3	-	2	1	-	4	3
WB-26	-	-	-	-	-	-	-	-	-	-	-	-
WB-29	72	65	35	84	65	63	72	65	35	84	67	67
Airlift - Total a/. . . .	1,052	961	620	1,509	1,026	964	1,100	1,023	612	1,497	983	921
C-46.	208	203	133	272	190	172	160	165	86	224	138	127
C-47.	42	51	44	75	73	72	42	45	39	59	60	60
C-54.	190	180	129	380	259	259	170	180	132	310	227	227
C-74.	8	10	9	26	17	17	8	9	8	26	13	13
C-82.	96	81	47	96	65	48	96	85	42	96	63	49
C-97.	44	46	35	90	74	74	44	46	31	90	73	73
C-118	8	-	-	12	-	-	8	10	5	12	7	7
C-119	272	255	147	304	215	200	336	315	192	368	233	217
C-122	16	9	6	16	7	7	16	8	5	16	11	7
C-124	168	126	70	238	126	115	204	154	68	280	154	137
H-19.	-	-	-	-	-	-	16	6	4	16	4	4
Airlift Support												
Air Refueling - Total . .	340	275	172	340	258	199	380	298	128	380	250	184
KB-29	200	176	134	200	189	182	200	159	103	200	178	144
KC-97	140	99	38	140	69	17	180	139	25	180	72	40
Miscellaneous - Total b/.	618	599	382	618	562	453	649	573	368	641	534	413

TABLE 80 — AIRCRAFT AND CREWS IN COMBAT AND AIRLIFT UNITS — BY QUARTERS — FY 1953 — CONTINUED

BY TYPE AND MODEL OF AIRCRAFT	31 MARCH 1953						30 JUNE 1953					
	AIRCRAFT			CREWS			AIRCRAFT			CREWS		
	AUTH	ON HAND	COMBAT READY	AUTH	ON HAND	COMBAT READY	AUTH	ON HAND	COMBAT READY	AUTH	ON HAND	COMBAT READY
Combat and Airlift - Total.	7,349	6,070	3,787	9,041	6,674	4,747	7,648	6,477	3,898	9,870	7,016	4,754
Combat - Total.	5,106	4,129	2,642	6,485	4,884	3,203	5,233	4,351	2,703	7,072	5,179	3,234
Bomber - Total.	1,236	1,111	639	1,304	1,113	668	1,206	1,102	589	1,409	1,080	703
B-26.	168	185	137	228	249	164	168	196	146	228	246	156
B-29.	390	406	228	390	369	210	315	319	177	315	267	148
B-36.	180	129	72	180	122	80	180	135	51	216	140	114
B-45.	48	38	17	56	36	34	48	37	16	56	38	31
B-47.	225	144	48	225	121	-	270	211	62	324	180	61
B-50.	225	209	137	225	216	180	225	204	137	270	209	193
Fighter - Total	3,285	2,598	1,796	4,563	3,299	2,164	3,397	2,757	1,803	4,939	3,554	2,074
F-47.	-	84	56	-	62	9	-	17	13	-	42	14
F-51.	100	361	233	144	400	255	50	197	148	72	179	112
F-80.	125	175	107	180	182	157	100	136	92	144	195	116
F-82.	-	7	3	-	2	-	-	11	1	-	7	-
F-84.	1,200	964	710	1,351	1,167	832	1,125	932	689	1,369	1,287	806
F-86A/E/F	950	673	471	1,188	919	591	1,175	967	612	1,532	1,193	721
F-86D	375	6	-	750	-	-	375	143	40	750	85	34
F-89.	100	39	24	200	9	-	100	31	20	200	37	-
F-94.	435	289	192	750	558	320	472	323	188	872	529	271
Reconnaissance - Total.	585	420	207	618	472	371	630	492	311	724	545	457
RB-26	72	86	41	78	92	74	72	83	48	78	89	82
RB-29	42	23	15	42	23	13	42	19	9	42	18	11
RB-36	120	112	34	120	79	54	120	105	52	144	98	73
RB-45	-	11	3	-	32	18	-	18	5	-	23	21
RB-47	90	-	-	90	-	-	-	-	-	-	-	-
YRB-47.	-	-	-	-	-	-	135	24	12	162	8	-
RB-50	45	29	16	48	44	38	45	35	23	58	46	36
RF-51	-	-	-	-	-	-	-	-	-	-	-	-
RF-80	144	93	64	156	142	118	144	133	114	156	174	149
RF-86	-	-	-	-	-	-	-	2	2	-	5	5
WB-26	-	-	-	-	-	-	-	6	2	-	17	15
WB-29	72	66	34	84	60	56	72	67	44	84	67	65
Airlift - Total a/.	1,156	1,051	681	1,475	1,029	957	1,199	1,099	573	1,485	1,032	906
C-46.	64	146	93	128	136	131	64	121	91	96	134	122
C-47.	42	44	36	59	63	61	40	45	31	56	55	53
C-54.	198	189	149	302	223	223	208	187	114	310	207	178
C-74.	8	8	7	12	9	9	8	8	4	12	11	11
C-82.	64	54	28	64	31	18	32	32	9	32	19	12
C-97.	50	47	27	66	56	56	49	46	23	79	52	47
C-118	12	12	6	18	9	9	12	8	6	18	9	9
C-119	464	358	230	496	295	278	496	403	250	528	325	306
C-122	16	7	5	16	7	7	16	8	6	16	7	7
C-124	222	180	95	298	194	159	258	220	33	322	205	153
H-19.	16	6	5	16	6	6	16	21	6	16	8	8
Airlift Support												
Air Refueling - Total	420	338	144	420	273	180	440	376	227	540	290	180
KB-29	200	158	108	200	153	133	180	153	107	215	157	119
KC-97	220	180	36	220	120	47	260	223	120	325	133	61
Miscellaneous - Total b/.	667	552	320	661	488	407	776	651	395	773	515	434

a/ Includes Troop Carrier, Logistic Support, Military Air Transport Service and Strategic Support Units.

b/ Includes Air Resupply, Liaison, Mapping and Charting and Tow Target Units.

Source: Operations Statistics Division, Directorate of Statistical Services, DCS/C.

TABLE 81 — OPERATIONAL READINESS OF COMBAT AND AIRLIFT WINGS — FISCAL YEAR 1953

Readiness is based on the Commanding Officers Overall Index representing the operational capability of the unit. Indexes are based on the percentages shown below:

INDEX	PERCENTAGE OF READINESS	
10 - 7	100 - 66	High degree of capability
6 - 4	65 - 36	Medium degree of capability
3 - 0	35 - 0	Little or no degree of capability

TYPE WING	10 DECEMBER 1952			
	TOTAL	10 - 7	6 - 4	3 - 0
Total	98	49	25	24
Heavy Bomber	5	2	1	2
Medium Bomber	22	14	1	7
Light Bomber	4	3	0	1
Fighter Escort	4	1	3	0
Fighter Bomber	15	5	7	3
Fighter Interceptor	21	10	5	6
Strategic Reconnaissance, Heavy	4	2	0	2
Strategic Reconnaissance, Medium	4	3	0	1
Tactical Reconnaissance	4	2	1	1
Troop Carrier, Heavy	3	2	0	1
Troop Carrier, Medium	12	5	7	0

Effective 30 June 1953, unit capabilities are expressed as "C" ratings (see below). These evaluations are prepared by Headquarters USAF after considering all known factors affecting unit readiness.

C - 1 High degree of relative capability. Adequately manned, equipped and trained to perform assigned mission with latest UE (first line aircraft or equipment).

C - 2 Same as above with second line equipment (F-51, B-29, etc.) or aircraft or equipment not designed to perform the primary mission of the unit.

C - 3 A lesser degree of capability than indicated above on either first or second line equipment. Shortages of personnel, facilities, etc., exist.

C - 4 A very low degree of capability. Extreme shortages in equipment, personnel and facilities exist.

TYPE WING	30 JUNE 1953				
	TOTAL	C - 1	C - 2	C - 3	C - 4
Total	106	39	25	33	9
Heavy Bomber	6	4	0	1	1
Medium Bomber	22	6	6	6	4
Light Bomber	4	1	2	1	0
Strategic Fighter	5	4	0	1	0
Fighter Bomber	15	9	0	5	1
Fighter Interceptor	26	3	11	11	1
Strategic Reconnaissance, Heavy	4	3	0	1	0
Strategic Reconnaissance, Medium	4	1	1	1	1
Tactical Reconnaissance	4	0	4	0	0
Troop Carrier, Heavy	4	2	0	1	1
Troop Carrier, Medium	12	6	1	5	0

Source: Operations Statistics Division, Directorate of Statistical Services, DCS/C.

Flight Operation

Part III

FLIGHT OPERATIONS

Aircraft flight operations data included in this section are based on statistics submitted on AF Form 110A, in accordance with AFR 65-110 as revised. The 110A report is compiled on a physical possession basis with the various activity categories determined by the assigned purposes of the status of the aircraft rather than actual use.

The tables provide summary data covering flight operations on "Operating Active", "Other Active", and "Inactive" USAF aircraft and include aircraft utilization, flying hours, fuel consumption, etc., during the Fiscal Year 1953. The data are segregated into the following types of activity: Administrative, Minimum Individual Training, Unit Training, Unit Support, Flying and Technical Training, Mutual Defense Assistance Program, Combat Crew Training, MATS Transport, MATS Air Evacuation, Test (except "X" models), Test Support, Special Missions, Command Support, Project, En Route, and Inactive. These various categories of USAF operations are defined as follows:

a. Administrative: Aircraft assigned for administrative or staff work as outlined in AFL 150-10A. (AD)

b. Minimum Individual Training: Aircraft assigned for the primary purpose of providing minimum individual training as outlined in AFL 150-10. (CI)

c. Primary Tactical Unit: Aircraft assigned as primary unit equipment for the direct accomplishment of the tactical unit operations in accordance with appropriate authorizations as shown in AFL 150-10A. (CC)

d. Unit Support: Aircraft which are authorized and assigned as tactical unit support aircraft, as indicated in AFL 150-10A. (CP)

e. Flying and Technical Training: Aircraft assigned for the flying and technical training activities of the Air Training Command, as outlined in AFL 150-10. (CU)

f. MDAP Aircraft Temporarily Diverted to USAF: Those aircraft programmed for foreign countries under the Mutual Defense Assistance Program for which delivery to the ultimate recipient foreign countries has been deferred in order to divert temporarily those aircraft to the Air Force. (CX)

g. Combat Crew Training: Aircraft authorized and assigned specifically to combat crew training. (TC)

h. MATS Transport: Aircraft assigned to MATS for transport and related uses (Divisions and Base Commands only), in accordance with AFL 150-10A. (CT)

i. MATS Air Evacuations: Aircraft assigned for the accomplishment of air evacuation operations within MATS, in accordance with appropriate authorizations as shown in AFL 150-10A. (CE)

j. Test: Aircraft assigned for testing, research and development (except "X" models and aircraft on bailment contract for test), as authorized in AFL 150-10A. (EX)

k. Test Support: Aircraft assigned to support organized tests of aircraft and allied equipment, authorized in AFL 150-10A. (Except aircraft on bailment contract for test support.) (ES)

l. Special Mission: Aircraft assigned as special mission aircraft in accordance with AFL 150-10A, and such other special missions as required to support the primary missions of the USAF. (CM)

m. Operating Active: The total of the above categories - (AD, CI, CC, CP, CU, CX, TC, CT, CE, EX, ES, and CM).

n. Other Active (Command Support and En route): Aircraft of one command undergoing organizational or field maintenance in a unit of a different major air command, aircraft undergoing depot maintenance, and aircraft in an en route status. (RF, RT, RR)

o. Other Active (Project): Aircraft on project established to effect assignment or reassignment of USAF aircraft to fulfill active requirements as ordered by the Aircraft Distribution Office of Headquarters Air Materiel Command. (PA)

p. Inactive: Storage aircraft, aircraft on a project to be assigned to an inactive category or a non-USAF activity, flyable inactive aircraft, aircraft undergoing modification; aircraft on loan, "X" model aircraft, aircraft declared excess to the Department of the Air Force requirements, aircraft reported to the Aircraft Distribution Office as excess to the requirements of an Air Force or command, new production, and aircraft recommended for reclamation. (SS, SC, SI, PI, PN, PI, RM, AL, all "X" models, XP, XS, XG, MP, RS, SO, and XJ).

TABLE 82 – USAF FLIGHT OPERATIONS WORLD-WIDE SUMMARY BY TYPE & MODEL OF AIRCRAFT

TYPE AND MODEL	FIRST QUARTER FISCAL YEAR 1953				SECOND QUARTER FISCAL YEAR 1953			
	HOURS FLOWN	AVERAGE AIRCRAFT		LANDINGS	HOURS FLOWN	AVERAGE AIRCRAFT		LANDINGS
		ON HAND	IN COM.			ON HAND	IN COM.	
TOTAL	2,140,440			1,912,876	1,922,809			1,683,909
OPERATING ACTIVE	2,123,698	14,119	9,626	1,905,387	1,908,543	14,875	10,020	1,676,540
OTHER ACTIVE	12,845	1,429	157	4,848	10,633	1,180	143	4,165
INACTIVE	3,897			2,641	3,633			3,204
OPERATING ACTIVE								
TOTAL	2,123,698	14,119	9,626	1,905,387	1,908,543	14,875	10,020	1,676,540
BOMBER	176,862	1,369	926	69,665	164,766	1,466	976	67,621
B-17	2,388	29	20	1,464	2,400	31	20	1,388
B-25	557	8	6	291	521	8	6	299
B-26	49,608	282	201	25,668	47,273	316	217	23,776
B-29	78,003	615	425	28,191	70,588	634	434	26,019
B-36	11,550	85	58	1,426	12,279	114	80	2,092
B-45	4,157	64	34	2,438	2,075	56	25	1,090
B-47	3,644	69	26	4,280	6,452	88	42	7,457
B-50	26,955	217	156	5,907	23,178	219	152	5,500
TANKER	25,875	284	213	8,928	26,221	305	222	8,573
KB-29	17,376	180	135	5,538	16,267	171	126	4,529
KC-97	8,499	104	78	3,390	9,954	134	96	4,044
FIGHTER	295,436	3,221	2,110	235,790	261,742	3,370	2,103	208,230
F-47	10,478	138	91	7,950	4,992	90	61	3,779
F-51	55,656	610	426	39,424	45,833	617	428	32,281
F-80	47,276	450	271	42,788	40,132	421	252	36,960
F-82	475	10	3	223	253	9	3	146
F-84	79,633	978	662	58,565	76,312	1,113	666	55,458
F-86	55,593	574	377	48,575	59,190	661	425	51,931
F-89	4,044	93	32	3,148	331	105	39	325
F-94	42,281	368	248	35,117	34,699	354	229	27,350
RECONNAISANCE	62,308	491	318	23,980	55,400	480	295	20,999
RB-17	1,183	12	6	532	1,237	11	5	650
RB-25	313	3	2	151	209	3	2	119
RB-26	10,510	84	61	4,918	9,433	90	65	4,259
RB-29	3,897	32	19	819	3,396	26	17	743
WB-29	14,824	70	36	3,236	15,020	68	38	2,967
RB-36	8,340	71	42	1,006	8,237	95	56	1,306
RB-45	2,176	24	14	642	1,092	15	9	683
RB-47	-	-	-	-	43	1	-	28
RB-50	4,292	34	24	862	2,577	28	15	542
RC-45	459	4	3	411	615	5	4	420
RC-47	955	7	6	550	826	6	5	547
RF-51	3,770	22	19	2,271	2,335	19	13	1,450
RF-80	11,362	123	83	8,343	10,288	109	65	7,197
RF-86	227	5	3	239	92	4	1	88
SEARCH AND RESCUE	26,467	212	133	23,024	23,812	216	147	17,404
SA-10	639	6	4	455	265	2	2	336
SA-16	16,290	126	74	18,595	15,569	144	84	13,596
SB-17	5,203	43	31	2,128	3,504	30	34	1,426
SB-29	3,263	26	16	848	3,619	30	19	935
SC-47	483	4	3	269	348	3	3	335
SC-54	347	3	3	173	359	3	2	170
SH-5	242	4	2	556	148	4	3	606
CARGO	549,764	2,683	1,864	279,695	477,496	2,703	1,836	232,046
CB-17	3,947	34	26	1,618	3,668	37	27	1,434
CB-25	7,727	49	35	3,794	4,487	36	27	1,988
CB-26	383	2	2	254	281	2	1	237
C-45	67,156	400	276	41,586	56,914	427	295	35,458
C-46	34,984	223	163	23,165	31,632	200	129	21,881
C-47/53	250,265	1,087	816	134,748	207,740	1,040	769	105,686
C-54	102,067	272	190	34,777	81,894	270	173	25,695
C-74	3,778	9	5	769	3,481	9	5	610
C-82	9,774	110	61	5,559	6,098	110	61	3,315
C-97	18,298	61	25	5,115	16,086	62	27	4,586
C-117	1,530	12	9	919	1,632	14	11	833
C-118	191	1	1	62	1,692	9	4	428
C-119	26,016	271	160	17,357	31,740	313	211	19,799

TABLE 82 — USAF FLIGHT OPERATIONS WORLD-WIDE SUMMARY BY TYPE & MODEL OF AIRCRAFT — Continued

TYPE AND MODEL	FIRST QUARTER FISCAL YEAR 1953				SECOND QUARTER FISCAL YEAR 1953			
	HOURS FLOWN	AVERAGE AIRCRAFT		LANDINGS	HOURS FLOWN	AVERAGE AIRCRAFT		LANDINGS
		ON HAND	IN COM.			ON HAND	IN COM.	
	OPERATING ACTIVE Continued							
CARGO - Continued								
C-121	2,078	10	8	806	2,268	9	6	717
C-122	511	10	8	568	412	9	7	466
C-124	21,055	131	78	8,593	27,470	155	83	8,912
C-125	4	1	1	5	1	1	-	1
TRAINER	929,683	5,205	3,585	1,107,223	839,327	5,685	3,975	963,014
TB-17	2,481	30	20	1,417	2,288	32	19	1,371
TB-25	137,828	742	495	84,818	133,198	823	573	86,090
TB-26	28,107	252	157	21,789	23,973	242	150	19,310
TB-29	6,992	56	33	8,119	8,259	81	52	6,722
TB-45	163	4	3	118	398	9	6	286
TB-50	2,282	14	10	1,175	3,946	32	21	1,081
TC-45	6,978	62	40	4,908	10,637	95	67	5,643
TC-47	13,990	51	40	6,699	13,263	49	39	6,003
TC-54	1,162	6	3	246	1,270	6	5	306
TF-47	26	2	1	13	3	-	-	1
TF-51	17,546	126	74	15,126	13,329	123	71	9,998
TF-80	4,440	43	21	4,191	4,638	46	19	4,058
TH-5	78	1	-	344	60	1	1	141
T-6	464,032	2,234	1,758	723,520	380,818	2,341	1,841	586,494
T-7	21,046	162	94	12,855	15,207	136	76	9,519
T-11	40,265	324	195	27,858	29,042	264	184	18,637
T-28	55,883	328	184	58,450	58,118	389	230	57,266
T-29	12,757	69	47	4,495	14,859	93	61	5,542
T-33	112,795	693	408	129,999	126,015	898	560	144,538
T-34	544	2	1	678	5	2	-	5
T-35	288	4	1	405	1	3	-	3
COMMUNICATION	56,282	627	459	156,126	58,770	622	447	157,281
LC-126	411	5	4	672	375	3	2	292
L-5	7,566	107	73	9,721	5,468	112	79	7,030
L-13	2,102	48	29	6,180	1,158	36	15	3,983
L-16	263	73	70	620	659	50	42	2,233
L-17	15	1	1	17	11	-	-	12
L-19	28	2	1	54	16	2	1	37
L-20	6,058	71	61	9,032	9,636	105	84	14,190
L-21	21,886	145	106	54,816	22,772	148	109	52,796
LT-6	8,567	51	46	5,792	9,442	44	42	6,277
H-5	3,425	45	30	20,217	3,084	45	29	19,790
H-12	38	3	-	84	66	4	3	173
H-13	3,169	26	14	35,675	3,002	26	13	34,805
H-18	53	1	1	131	11	1	-	73
H-19	2,516	37	19	11,414	3,015	41	25	15,252
H-23	184	11	4	1,690	42	4	2	285
H-24	1	1	-	11	-	1	1	-
H-25	-	-	-	-	13	-	-	53
TARGET	1,021	27	18	956	1,009	28	19	1,372
QB-17	875	15	10	765	702	15	11	711
QF-80	40	2	1	41	181	4	2	421
Q-14	22	8	5	27	8	7	5	9
QT-33	84	2	2	123	118	2	1	231
	OTHER ACTIVE							
TOTAL	12,845	1,429	157	4,848	10,633	1,180	143	4,165
BOMBER	3,964	219	63	1,169	2,992	144	37	712
B-17	9	2	-	5	1	-	-	1
B-25	3	-	-	1	-	-	-	-
B-26	2,696	115	51	824	1,940	56	24	406
B-29	1,037	63	11	247	826	46	10	191
B-36	2	12	-	1	5	12	-	1
B-45	3	1	-	2	-	3	-	-
B-47	19	1	-	1	39	3	1	20
B-50	195	25	1	88	181	24	2	93
TANKER	2	2	-	2	-	-	-	-
KB-29	2	2	-	2	-	-	-	-
FIGHTER	2,542	701	32	1,242	3,401	540	45	1,570
F-47	30	9	2	31	19	19	5	30

TABLE 82 — USAF FLIGHT OPERATIONS WORLD-WIDE SUMMARY BY TYPE & MODEL OF AIRCRAFT — CONTINUED

TYPE AND MODEL	FIRST QUARTER FISCAL YEAR 1953				SECOND QUARTER FISCAL YEAR 1953			
	HOURS FLOWN	AVERAGE AIRCRAFT		LANDINGS	HOURS FLOWN	AVERAGE AIRCRAFT		LANDINGS
		ON HAND	IN COM.			ON HAND	IN COM.	
	OTHER ACTIVE Continued							
FIGHTER - Continued								
F-51	88	110	4	106	70	72	3	87
F-80	73	77	4	76	65	38	3	62
F-82	-	4	-	-	-	3	-	-
F-84	2,226	353	20	898	2,769	264	29	1,014
F-86	119	131	2	127	318	130	4	276
F-89	-	1	-	-	-	1	-	-
F-94	6	16	-	4	160	13	1	101
RECONNAISSANCE	516	51	7	139	638	61	14	165
RB-17	-	-	-	-	-	1	-	-
RB-26	55	8	3	19	213	12	6	46
RB-29	52	3	-	17	129	6	1	22
WB-29	348	10	1	61	241	13	1	55
RB-36	28	6	-	13	-	-	-	-
RB-45	-	1	-	-	-	1	1	-
RB-50	5	6	1	6	7	6	1	8
RC-45	4	1	-	4	-	-	-	-
RF-51	10	5	1	5	35	12	1	24
RF-80	14	11	1	14	12	8	3	9
RC-54	-	-	-	-	-	1	-	-
RF-86	-	-	-	-	-	-	-	-
RC-47	-	-	-	-	1	1	-	1
SEARCH AND RESCUE	184	21	5	40	112	25	3	37
SA-10	4	3	2	4	-	2	1	1
SA-16	72	10	2	15	17	15	1	22
SB-17	6	4	-	6	1	3	1	1
SB-29	102	4	1	15	92	4	-	11
SC-47	-	-	-	-	2	1	-	2
CARGO	4,381	147	16	1,186	2,307	161	12	633
CB-17	6	2	-	6	63	1	-	15
CB-25	135	3	1	122	5	2	-	6
C-45	68	20	1	81	33	20	-	35
C-46	138	13	2	35	12	4	-	12
C-47	566	63	3	346	595	70	3	287
C-54	1,793	16	3	311	860	19	3	174
C-82	77	10	-	24	9	10	-	6
C-97	39	1	-	6	-	2	-	-
C-117	4	1	-	3	2	-	-	1
C-119	929	15	4	153	718	23	5	93
C-124	626	3	2	99	9	8	1	3
CB-29	-	-	-	-	1	-	-	1
C-74	-	-	-	-	-	1	-	-
C-122	-	-	-	-	-	1	-	-
TRAINER	1,113	187	32	847	1,047	151	29	915
T-6	27	24	-	28	19	19	1	26
T-7	141	4	2	62	138	3	1	48
T-11	11	10	-	23	8	10	1	14
T-28	1	2	-	1	17	4	-	36
T-29	-	1	1	-	-	-	-	-
T-33	428	49	7	225	271	35	6	182
TB-17	13	2	-	9	140	1	-	41
TB-25	334	44	11	419	351	43	11	489
TB-26	11	13	2	13	18	12	1	25
TB-29	124	14	2	39	73	7	2	34
TB-50	-	1	1	-	-	-	-	-
TC-45	-	1	-	-	2	1	-	6
TC-46	1	1	-	1	-	-	-	-
TC-47	1	1	-	1	4	2	-	3
TC-54	2	-	-	2	-	-	-	-
TF-47	5	2	-	8	-	-	-	-
TF-51	14	17	5	18	6	14	6	11
TF-80	-	1	1	-	-	-	-	-
TB-45	-	-	-	-	-	-	-	-
COMMUNICATION	143	101	2	223	134	96	3	132
L-4	15	20	1	21	12	15	-	18
L-5	31	46	-	36	46	30	-	40
L-13	16	2	1	34	-	1	-	-
L-16	12	9	-	19	17	31	2	25

TABLE 82 — USAF FLIGHT OPERATIONS WORLD-WIDE SUMMARY BY TYPE & MODEL OF AIRCRAFT — CONTINUED

TYPE AND MODEL	FIRST QUARTER FISCAL YEAR 1953				SECOND QUARTER FISCAL YEAR 1953			
	HOURS FLOWN	AVERAGE AIRCRAFT		LANDINGS	HOURS FLOWN	AVERAGE AIRCRAFT		LANDINGS
		ON HAND	IN COM.			ON HAND	IN COM.	
	OTHER ACTIVE Continued							
COMMUNICATION-Cont'd								
L-17	-	-	-	-	-	-	-	-
L-19	-	-	-	-	-	-	-	-
L-20	34	8	-	37	38	9	-	16
LT-6	17	2	-	9	12	2	-	12
H-5	4	5	-	25	2	4	1	8
H-12	-	1	-	-	-	-	-	-
H-13	-	-	-	-	-	1	-	-
H-19	14	8	-	42	7	3	-	13
TARGET	-	-	-	-	2	2	-	1
QF-80	-	-	-	-	2	2	-	1
	INACTIVE							
TOTAL	3,897			2,641	3,633			3,204
BOMBER	1,081			569	769			681
B-17	142			51	79			30
B-25	27			31	59			84
B-26	300			232	199			263
B-29	574			219	405			276
B-36	2			1	-			-
B-43	12			9	18			19
B-45	21			24	8			8
B-50	3			2	1			1
TANKER	23			27	22			28
KB-29	23			27	22			28
FIGHTER	380			367	698			687
F-47	226			156	484			329
F-51	15			14	28			41
F-80	8			12	4			6
F-84	103			145	1,78			307
F-86	20			28	2			2
F-94	8			12	1			1
F-92	-			-	1			1
RECONNAISANCE	142			120	108			79
RB-26	59			53	25			25
RB-36	45			24	56			30
RB-50	2			2	-			-
RF-51	11			15	4			7
RF-80	25			26	-			-
RB-29	-			-	21			14
RB-45	-			-	2			3
SEARCH AND RESCUE	1			5	7			13
SA-16	1			5	6			11
SB-17	-			-	1			2
CARGO	1,677			829	1,382			655
CB-25	2			3	2			2
CB-26	59			40	16			10
C-46	592			355	312			170
C-47	563			301	420			319
C-54	1			1	-			-
C-82	34			30	7			7
XC-99	352			45	406			50
C-117	3			4	-			-
C-119	12			29	14			13
C-124	59			21	199			78
CB-17	-			-	6			6
TRAINER	368			442	392			519
TB-25	211			239	207			182
TB-26	8			8	52			54
TB-29	63			78	9			9
TC-54	3			5	2			4
TF-47	9			6	21			13
TRF-51	15			17	-			-
T-6	57			87	77			237

TABLE 82 — USAF FLIGHT OPERATIONS WORLD-WIDE SUMMARY BY TYPE & MODEL OF AIRCRAFT — CONTINUED

TYPE AND MODEL	FIRST QUARTER FISCAL YEAR 1953				SECOND QUARTER FISCAL YEAR 1953			
	HOURS FLOWN	AVERAGE AIRCRAFT		LANDINGS	HOURS FLOWN	AVERAGE AIRCRAFT		LANDINGS
		ON HAND	IN COM.			ON HAND	IN COM.	
	INACTIVE Continued							
TRAINER - Continued								
T-33	-			-	4			2
T-28	2			2	14			14
TB-45	-			-	4			3
T-11	-			-	2			1
COMMUNICATION	223			280	255			542
L-13	7			15	1			6
XL-17	41			42	72			96
L-20	175			223	114			250
XL-26	-			-	63			175
H-13	-			-	5			15
TARGET	2			2	-			-
QB-17	2			2	-			-
	THIRD QUARTER FISCAL YEAR 1953				FOURTH QUARTER FISCAL YEAR 1953			
TOTAL	1,941,968		1/	1,610,610	2,169,279		1/	1,978,758
OPERATING ACTIVE	1,929,476	15,231		1,601,051	2,152,509	15,480		1,966,962
OTHER ACTIVE	7,221	1,429		4,395	11,177	1,420		6,456
INACTIVE	5,271			5,164	5,593			5,340
	OPERATING ACTIVE							
TOTAL	1,929,476	15,231		1,601,051	2,152,509	15,480		1,966,962
BOMBER	162,650	1,514		69,684	156,812	1,506		67,861
B-17	2,015	31		1,488	2,421	29		1,574
B-25	556	8		317	690	8		380
B-26	47,836	314		24,601	50,889	308		25,863
B-29	62,196	574		25,405	46,166	493		17,099
B-36	12,771	125		2,137	14,115	143		2,420
B-45	671	48		372	2,550	46		1,308
B-47	13,473	184		9,845	17,293	254		13,207
B-50	23,107	229		5,503	22,635	224		5,988
JD-1	25	1		16	53	1		22
TANKER	23,916	319		8,390	25,307	360		11,133
KB-29	13,183	161		4,405	11,399	154		4,779
KC-97	10,733	158		3,985	13,908	206		6,354
FIGHTER	290,241	3,491		230,503	351,595	3,663		280,350
F-47	1,589	60		1,282	1,449	27		1,063
F-51	30,341	508		21,339	19,861	317		13,502
F-80	44,709	444		40,335	43,993	428		42,217
F-82	200	7		101	481	11		308
F-84	102,917	1,232		72,332	129,663	1,279		93,421
F-86	75,528	810		67,838	113,619	1,183		96,708
F-89	6	82		9	1,746	40		1,290
F-94	34,851	348		27,287	40,783	378		31,841
RECONNAISSANCE	51,586	471		19,311	59,604	507		24,394
RB-17	1,096	10		387	660	9		288
RB-25	218	3		155	200	3		149
RB-26	9,588	90		4,438	9,145	83		4,670
RB-29	2,609	20		629	3,110	26		823
WB-29	13,730	68		3,353	14,947	69		4,339
RB-36	8,810	113		1,211	12,316	112		1,286
RB-45	960	12		324	1,081	18		416
RB-47	44	1		26	412	10		586
RB-50	3,370	34		618	3,525	34		649
RC-45	438	5		457	595	6		358
RC-47	611	5		428	688	5		610
RF-51	492	9		355	87	1		80
RF-80	9,506	99		6,827	11,279	122		9,601
RF-86	114	2		103	122	3		106
WB-26	-	-		-	1,437	6		433

TABLE 82 — USAF FLIGHT OPERATIONS WORLD-WIDE SUMMARY BY TYPE & MODEL OF AIRCRAFT — CONTINUED

TYPE AND MODEL	THIRD QUARTER FISCAL YEAR 1953				FOURTH QUARTER FISCAL YEAR 1953			
	HOURS FLOWN	AVERAGE AIRCRAFT		LANDINGS	HOURS FLOWN	AVERAGE AIRCRAFT		LANDINGS
		ON HAND	IN COM. a/			ON HAND	IN COM. a/	
OPERATING ACTIVE Continued								
SEARCH AND RESCUE	22,389	221		19,432	28,105	232		24,900
SA-16	16,817	156		16,874	22,628	185		22,279
SB-17	1,556	16		745	1,379	12		909
SB-29	3,069	31		962	3,252	29		1,103
SC-47	536	4		370	599	5		463
SC-54	333	2		172	247	1		146
SH-5	78	2		309	-	-		-
CARGO	451,381	2,742		237,948	512,943	2,871		274,079
CB-17	3,969	36		1,507	3,741	34		1,612
CB-25	4,531	34		2,002	4,168	30		1,900
CB-26	332	2		232	289	2		234
CB-29	9	-		2	-	-		-
C-45	62,499	482		42,837	77,822	553		50,301
C-46	25,396	158		19,307	29,441	147		21,440
C-47/53	197,321	1,029		105,648	216,267	1,029		120,425
C-54	68,920	261		21,519	73,743	271		24,387
C-74	2,571	8		537	2,483	8		852
C-82	5,155	100		2,694	2,449	65		1,616
C-97	14,820	61		4,722	15,412	61		5,441
C-117	1,168	12		655	3,344	21		1,934
C-118	2,288	13		630	3,482	16		1,060
C-119	35,228	357		24,849	48,539	416		29,515
C-121	1,228	7		679	1,304	8		613
C-122	330	7		390	454	7		496
C-124	25,616	174		9,738	30,005	202		12,253
C-125	-	1		-	-	1		-
TRAINER	865,309	5,837		858,974	940,287	5,599		1,081,949
TB-17	2,945	35		1,489	3,057	32		1,828
TB-25	147,070	855		90,939	148,866	845		94,043
TB-26	23,300	218		19,501	24,920	228		20,621
TB-29	13,662	100		9,299	12,472	115		7,010
TB-45	167	8		137	505	8		327
TB-47	-	-		-	1,671	13		2,380
TB-50	3,099	44		824	7,349	46		2,725
TC-45	6,854	93		6,389	12,234	94		9,246
TC-47	10,424	48		6,409	11,262	38		7,157
TC-54	1,416	7		358	2,048	8		427
TF-51	7,079	108		4,611	5,972	83		3,929
TF-80	4,842	63		4,126	2,486	32		2,062
TH-5	46	1		303	-	-		-
T-6	348,905	2,252		398,868	331,737	1,874		524,441
T-7	11,846	98		7,796	9,270	71		6,089
T-11	21,680	219		14,856	20,433	179		13,579
T-28	67,267	476		83,082	110,710	540		142,538
T-29	22,495	111		9,696	29,580	130		11,013
T-33	172,205	1,096		200,275	205,715	1,260		232,533
T-34	5	2		10	-	2		1
T-35	2	3		6	-	1		-
COMMUNICATION	60,913	608		155,283	76,473	710		200,911
L-5	5,555	112		6,870	5,777	108		7,059
L-13	628	24		1,564	384	21		1,148
L-16	880	50		2,623	1,453	49		4,184
L-17	9	1		6	-	-		-
L-19	20	2		30	39	2		57
L-20	9,773	101		13,033	16,093	156		20,967
L-21	25,913	142		51,585	29,118	146		64,119
L-23	9	-		7	83	1		84
LT-6	8,151	46		5,851	9,916	43		6,225
H-5	2,875	45		17,515	2,476	45		10,113
H-12	44	2		87	50	2		115
H-13	3,430	31		39,131	5,542	50		61,717
H-18	18	1		112	-	1		-
H-19	3,362	46		16,184	5,114	78		23,495
H-21	51	1		41	223	3		520
H-23	1	2		4	102	3		731
H-25	194	2		640	103	2		377

TABLE 82 — USAF FLIGHT OPERATIONS WORLD-WIDE SUMMARY BY TYPE & MODEL OF AIRCRAFT — Continued

TYPE AND MODEL	THIRD QUARTER FISCAL YEAR 1953				FOURTH QUARTER FISCAL YEAR 1953			
	HOURS FLOWN	AVERAGE AIRCRAFT		LANDINGS	HOURS FLOWN	AVERAGE AIRCRAFT		LANDINGS
		ON HAND	IN COM. a/			ON HAND	IN COM. a/	
OPERATING ACTIVE Continued								
TARGET	1,091	28		1,526	1,383	32		1,385
QB-17	781	16		985	1,099	22		1,030
QF-80	246	6		457	227	7		281
Q-14	31	5		31	1	2		1
QT-33	33	1		53	56	1		73
OTHER ACTIVE								
TOTAL	7,221	1,429		4,395	11,177	1,419		6,456
BOMBER	842	159		363	1,784	175		543
B-17	-	1		-	1	3		1
B-25	2	1		2	-	1		-
B-26	348	54		204	974	59		342
B-29	395	67		107	758	79		180
B-36	30	12		11	16	4		7
B-45	-	4		-	-	9		-
B-47	8	7		4	34	7		12
B-50	59	13		35	1	13		1
TANKER	7	6		3	40	12		36
KB-29	4	6		2	40	12		35
KC-97	3	-		1	-	-		-
FIGHTER	1,713	676		1,673	2,717	678		2,648
F-47	20	17		21	12	8		16
F-51	65	84		75	242	126		242
F-80	38	27		45	217	34		103
F-84	912	289		945	914	272		1,192
F-86	567	222		499	1,106	174		834
F-89	23	21		28	141	38		195
F-94	88	16		60	85	25		66
FV-5	-	-		-	-	1		-
RECONNAISSANCE	595	73		157	577	67		206
RB-17	-	4		-	3	6		3
WB-17	-	-		-	-	1		-
RB-26	10	9		8	211	9		70
RB-29	100	8		25	3	3		3
WB-29	279	12		53	236	11		49
RB-36	5	5		2	17	8		8
RB-45	53	1		11	29	-		5
RB-47	-	-		-	-	1		-
RB-50	98	6		22	31	5		28
RC-45	-	1		-	-	1		-
RC-47	1	1		1	2	-		3
RC-54	-	1		-	-	1		-
RF-51	9	9		11	29	10		26
RF-80	35	14		19	10	9		6
RF-86	5	2		5	6	2		5
SEARCH AND RESCUE	316	28		128	347	20		88
SA-10	-	-		-	-	-		-
SA-16	125	15		87	277	12		59
SB-17	6	6		4	-	-		-
SB-29	123	5		26	66	6		20
SC-47	61	-		10	-	-		-
SC-54	1	1		1	4	1		9
SH-5	-	1		-	-	1		-
CARGO	2,493	197		798	3,427	206		1,058
CB-17	16	3		10	158	6		38
CB-25	5	2		12	-	1		-
CB-26	-	-		-	-	-		-
CB-29	1	1		1	-	-		-
C-45	105	13		53	114	15		80
C-46	19	8		13	197	11		21
C-47	721	76		342	692	68		372
C-54	345	24		107	623	16		158
C-74	2	1		2	9	2		7
C-82	4	20		4	14	42		16
C-97	5	4		4	52	4		37

TABLE 82 —USAF FLIGHT OPERATIONS WORLD-WIDE SUMMARY BY TYPE & MODEL OF AIRCRAFT — CONTINUED

TYPE AND MODEL	THIRD QUARTER FISCAL YEAR 1953				FOURTH QUARTER FISCAL YEAR 1953			
	HOURS FLOWN	AVERAGE AIRCRAFT		LANDINGS	HOURS FLOWN	AVERAGE AIRCRAFT		LANDINGS
		ON HAND	IN COM. a/			ON HAND	IN COM. a/	
OTHER ACTIVE Continued								
CARGO - Continued								
C-117	-	-		-	4	-		6
C-119	1,266	33		246	1,438	24		274
C-121	-	-		-	-	-		-
C-122	-	1		-	2	1		2
C-124	4	11		4	124	16		47
TRAINER	1,102	151		1,055	2,017	164		1,655
TB-17	9	4		8	6	4		6
TB-25	180	30		188	45	11		40
TB-26	57	14		29	208	28		104
TB-29	8	6		5	33	4		11
TB-45	-	1		-	-	1		-
TB-47	-	-		-	-	1		-
TB-50	-	-		-	-	-		-
TC-45	2	-		3	1	-		1
TC-47	3	-		4	3	-		3
TC-54	-	-		-	8	1		5
TF-51	30	11		17	11	9		20
TF-80	-	1		-	-	-		-
TH-5	-	-		-	-	1		-
T-6	53	17		62	79	22		53
T-7	90	3		44	41	2		24
T-11	13	4		22	-	2		-
T-28	2	7		4	76	11		101
T-33	627	53		663	759	65		793
MK-4	28	-		6	747	2		494
COMMUNICATION	146	138		215	263	95		216
L-4	14	17		17	16	19		18
L-5	27	19		32	11	13		15
L-13	1	-		1	-	-		-
L-16	40	61		77	51	39		76
L-17	-	-		-	-	-		-
L-19	-	-		-	55	-		15
L-20	56	32		40	10	6		8
L-21	-	-		-	2	1		4
L-23	-	-		-	109	6		56
LT-6	-	1		-	5	1		5
H-5	2	4		8	3	4		15
H-12	-	1		-	-	1		-
H-13	4	1		22	-	1		-
H-19	2	2		18	1	4		4
TARGET	7	1		3	5	2		6
QF-80	7	1		3	4	1		5
QB-17	-	-		-	1	1		1
INACTIVE								
TOTAL	5,271			5,164	5,593			5,340
BOMBER	1,188			705	556			480
B-17	74			29	85			43
B-25	18			21	19			28
B-26	456			390	221			212
XB-26	53			25	63			41
B-29	476			191	58			54
XB-29	69			19	20			7
B-45	2			2	17			15
B-47	-			-	20			7
XB-43	30			20	19			14
XB-51	10			8	34			56
TANKERS	27			32	30			43
KB-29	27			32	30			43
FIGHTER	766			559	1,145			1,068
F-47	433			187	175			77
F-51	53			63	226			177

TABLE 82 — USAF FLIGHT OPERATIONS WORLD-WIDE SUMMARY BY TYPE & MODEL OF AIRCRAFT — Continued

TYPE AND MODEL	THIRD QUARTER FISCAL YEAR 1953				FOURTH QUARTER FISCAL YEAR 1953			
	HOURS FLOWN	AVERAGE AIRCRAFT		LANDINGS	HOURS FLOWN	AVERAGE AIRCRAFT		LANDINGS
		ON HAND	IN COM.			ON HAND	IN COM.	
	INACTIVE Continued							
FIGHTER - Continued								
F-80	7			7	-			-
F-82	7			5	12			10
F-84	111			132	130			161
F-86	116			111	458			507
F-89	38			52	124			102
XF-92	1			2	8			12
F-94	-			-	1			1
XF-88	-			-	11			21
RECONNAISSANCE	108			88	108			101
RB-26	49			36	48			45
RB-29	5			9	-			-
WB-29	-			-	1			1
RB-36	10			5	-			-
RB-45	16			14	10			8
RC-47	2			1	-			-
RF-51	7			7	9			17
RF-80	19			16	40			30
SEARCH AND RESCUE	28			44	35			105
SA-16	5			13	18			84
SB-17	23			31	17			21
CARGO	1,275			643	1,526			767
CB-26	17			11	15			7
C-46	405			237	440			256
C-47	307			246	372			288
XC-99	372			49	424			58
C-119	7			5	115			97
C-124	161			88	132			37
XC-120	6			7	28			24
TRAINER	1,291			1,468	1,471			1,273
TB-25	178			151	250			178
TB-26	171			109	60			56
TB-29	26			17	50			45
TB-45	-			-	2			3
TF-47	29			32	-			-
TF-51	8			6	3			2
T-6	739			1,018	575			589
T-7	27			13	174			73
T-11	15			11	273			243
XT-28	82			94	41			59
T-29	1			4	-			-
T-33	15			13	33			25
COMMUNICATION	581			1,616	610			1,433
L-13	3			10	-			-
L-17	-			-	35			41
XL-17	338			1,030	117			152
L-20	68			128	91			162
L-21	38			82	43			139
L-23	17			45	145			270
H-12	4			8	-			-
H-13	1			3	26			204
H-19	112			310	152			460
H-21	-			-	1			5
TARGET	7			9	112			70
QB-17	7			9	112			70

a/ In Commission data for Third and Fourth Quarter not available.

SOURCE: Materiel Statistics Division, D/Statistical Services, DCS/C

TABLE 83 — USAF AIRCRAFT FLYING TIME — BY COMMAND

COMMAND	FISCAL YEAR 1953												
	TOTAL	JULY (1952)	AUGUST	SEPTEMBER	OCTOBER	NOVEMBER	DECEMBER	JANUARY (1953)	FEBRUARY	MARCH	APRIL	MAY	JUNE
TOTAL USAF	8,178,254	717,245	705,806	717,389	736,591	610,554	579,523	616,603	612,010	713,254	703,870	717,163	748,246
TOTAL CONTINENTAL US.	6,215,584	554,381	533,053	541,661	561,971	458,297	437,805	477,847	469,678	544,626	524,995	533,334	577,936
Air Defense	472,603	44,303	44,595	41,287	39,755	33,934	31,079	32,247	34,833	42,340	41,204	41,933	45,093
Air Materiel	169,907	14,423	14,843	15,031	15,300	12,654	12,368	13,326	13,996	14,295	14,367	14,379	14,925
Air Proving Ground	47,171	3,975	4,282	3,860	4,358	3,394	3,868	3,788	3,549	4,066	3,973	4,071	3,987
Air Research & Development	143,900	12,637	12,768	12,897	13,102	10,624	9,819	10,300	10,407	12,809	12,162	12,943	13,432
Air Training	3,524,368	308,651	295,505	304,923	326,740	252,718	248,662	282,301	269,892	311,100	298,093	296,961	329,822
Air University	87,547	6,759	6,862	8,318	7,479	6,987	5,519	5,936	7,191	8,088	8,277	9,016	7,115
Civil Air Patrol	16,179	1,455	1,842	1,279	1,423	1,094	1,137	932	1,163	1,507	1,640	1,251	1,456
Continental Air	48,697	3,774	3,623	3,258	3,371	3,746	3,734	4,031	4,490	4,630	4,668	4,574	4,798
Headquarters	108,635	15,512	9,823	9,683	10,520	6,365	6,166	7,062	7,959	9,130	8,893	9,112	8,410
Inspector General	6,142	1,840	1,190	1,022	1,190	900	a/	-	-	-	-	-	-
M A T S	439,340	35,530	39,180	38,887	38,160	35,169	33,636	33,442	33,642	37,208	36,980	39,694	37,812
Strategic Air	683,272	62,075	58,129	57,376	55,581	56,994	49,643	52,905	51,968	60,580	56,112	58,002	63,907
USAF Security Service	1,685	65	241	170	139	203	156	125	204	137	78	90	77
Tactical Air	466,138	43,382	40,170	43,670	44,853	33,515	32,018	32,452	30,384	38,736	38,548	41,308	47,102
TOTAL OVERSEAS	1,962,670	162,864	172,753	175,728	174,620	152,257	141,718	136,756	142,332	168,628	178,875	183,829	170,310
Alaskan Air	83,911	6,990	8,256	7,529	6,878	5,556	4,586	3,732	5,089	8,096	8,521	9,731	8,947
Air Attaches	6,076	1,132	1,169	1,198	1,638	939	b/	-	-	-	-	-	-
Air Materiel	2,104	376	156	212	194	81	151	89	123	214	185	209	114
Air Research & Development	5,077	356	459	835	1,611	-	209	221	299	367	266	193	261
Caribbean Air	12,806	705	607	548	756	760	1,356	949	1,435	980	1,646	1,571	1,493
Civil Air Patrol	306	35	45	11	51	21	22	1	2	14	-	30	74
USAF In Europe	339,525	35,086	35,577	35,008	24,034	16,664	15,887	17,635	24,253	32,165	33,272	35,629	34,315
Far East Air Forces	1,087,151	83,635	89,141	92,541	102,506	86,563	85,939	86,828	78,585	91,351	100,246	98,718	91,098
Headquarters	14,053	-	-	-	-	-	2,264	1,470	2,010	2,163	2,141	2,405	1,600
Joint Brazil-US Mil. Comm.	4,663	343	437	347	482	367	415	327	344	563	297	418	323
Latin American Mission	3,121	730	474	504	318	1,095	b/	-	-	-	-	-	-
M A T S.	271,828	24,334	24,670	23,818	22,134	23,649	21,971	19,574	19,909	22,230	23,402	23,993	22,144
Military Aviation Miss	1,408	426	151	94	384	353	a/	-	-	-	-	-	-
M D A P.	1,958	259	510	382	471	336	a/	-	-	-	-	-	-
Northeast Air	30,643	2,465	2,620	1,919	2,229	2,136	2,422	1,970	2,237	3,400	3,015	3,361	2,869
Strategic Air	91,689	5,992	8,481	10,478	8,359	11,421	6,242	5,844	7,755	6,966	5,846	7,571	6,734
Tactical Air	5,985	-	-	304	2,377	2,148	254	116	291	119	38	-	338
Turkish Foreign Aid Gp	366	-	-	-	198	168	a/	-	-	-	-	-	-

a/ Included in Headquarters
b/ Included in Caribbean Air

NOTE: Due to changes in reporting procedures as of 1 December 1952, components of Headquarters and Caribbean Air Command could not be broken out.

SOURCE: Materiel Statistics Division - Director of Statistical Services DCS/C

TABLE 84 — SUMMARY OF USAF FLIGHT OPERATIONS BY TYPE OF ACTIVITY — FY 1953

TYPE OF ACTIVITY	FISCAL YEAR 1953			
	HOURS FLOWN	AVERAGE AIRCRAFT		LANDINGS
		ON HAND	IN COMMISSION	
WORLD-WIDE - TOTAL (Excluding Air Force Reserve)	8,174,496			7,185,076
OPERATING ACTIVE	8,114,226	59,705	19,646	7,148,863
Administrative	42,050	290	120	15,340
Minimum Individual Training	1,271,358	8,345	2,764	781,671
Unit Training	2,305,967	22,604	7,633	1,379,910
Unit Support	293,884	1,886	623	219,514
Student Training	3,277,632	19,633	6,449	4,240,412
MATS: Transport	318,962	1,065	264	99,348
Air Evacuation	48,894	145	53	27,539
Combat Crew Training	61,335	317	100	31,711
Test	81,688	1,776	423	68,427
Test Support	54,600	574	162	40,894
Special Missions	314,946	2,658	894	210,705
MDAP	42,910	412	161	33,392
OTHER ACTIVE	41,876	5,458	301	19,864
Command Support	10,363	4,243	117	9,496
Project	2,495	680	68	2,213
Enroute	29,018	535	116	8,155
INACTIVE	18,394			16,349
CONTINENTAL U.S. - TOTAL	6,214,173			5,933,944
OPERATING ACTIVE	6,184,128	45,497	14,723	5,908,988
Administrative	22,564	161	64	6,974
Minimum Individual Training	1,013,456	7,009	2,305	591,306
Unit Training	1,052,866	12,340	4,079	578,682
Unit Support	206,438	1,330	447	145,015
Student Training	3,277,632	19,633	6,449	4,240,412
MATS: Transport	183,081	700	159	63,969
Air Evacuation	48,894	145	53	27,639
Combat Crew Training	61,335	317	100	31,711
Test	80,562	1,756	411	67,639
Test Support	48,129	515	146	30,076
Special Missions	159,936	1,350	440	100,788
MDAP	29,235	241	70	24,777
OTHER ACTIVE	15,438	3,532	179	11,792
Command Support	6,541	2,750	98	6,049
Project	2,494	675	68	2,212
En Route	6,403	107	13	3,531
INACTIVE	14,607			13,264
OVERSEAS - TOTAL	1,961,880			1,251,132
OPERATING ACTIVE	1,931,655	14,208	4,923	1,239,975
Administrative	19,486	129	56	8,366
Minimum Individual Training	257,902	1,336	459	190,365
Unit Training	1,253,101	10,264	3,554	801,228
Unit Support	89,003	556	176	74,499
MATS: Transport	135,881	365	105	35,379
Test	1,126	20	12	788
Test Support	6,471	59	16	10,818
Special Missions	155,010	1,308	454	109,917
MDAP	13,675	171	91	8,615
OTHER ACTIVE	26,438	1,926	122	8,072
Command Support	3,822	1,493	19	3,447
Project	1	5	-	1
En Route	22,615	428	103	4,624
INACTIVE	3,787			3,085

SOURCE: Materiel Statistics Division - D/Statistical Services - DCS/C

TABLE 85 — USAF FLIGHT OPERATIONS BY TYPE OF ACTIVITY – QUARTERLY FY 1953

TYPE OF ACTIVITY	FIRST QUARTER FISCAL YEAR 1953				SECOND QUARTER FISCAL YEAR 1953			
	HOURS FLOWN	AVERAGE A/C		LANDINGS	HOURS FLOWN	AVERAGE A/C		LANDINGS
		ON HAND	IN COM.			ON HAND	IN COM.	
WORLD-WIDE TOTAL-(Excl-AFR)	2,140,440			1,912,876	1,922,809			1,682,832
OPERATING ACTIVE	2,123,698	14,119	9,626	1,905,387	1,908,543	14,875	10,020	1,675,463
Administrative	12,820	78	62	4,674	9,915	71	58	3,518
Minimum Individual Tng	353,990	2,036	1,365	215,414	293,662	2,083	1,399	175,587
Unit Training.	604,420	5,417	3,837	356,503	530,760	5,456	3,796	305,472
Unit Support	73,899	428	296	53,559	72,985	474	327	52,227
Student Training . . .	841,427	4,579	3,100	1,143,111	764,629	4,919	3,349	1,010,366
MATS: Transport . . .	85,832	229	130	26,186	79,523	262	134	23,452
Air Evac. . . .	12,919	36	26	7,549	12,669	37	27	6,864
Combat Crew Training .	15,032	70	48	7,499	13,186	78	52	6,524
Test	21,926	429	211	18,573	19,909	451	212	15,664
Test Support	13,682	125	82	9,498	13,241	137	80	11,396
Special Missions . . .	77,475	588	420	53,782	76,309	669	474	48,802
MDAP	10,276	104	49	9,039	21,755	238	112	15,591
OTHER ACTIVE	12,845	1,429	157	4,848	10,633	1,180	143	4,165
Command Support. . . .	2,484	984	59	2,279	2,026	967	58	1,815
Project.	603	269	37	602	700	115	30	642
En route	9,758	176	61	1,967	7,907	98	55	1,708
INACTIVE	3,897			2,641	3,633			3,204
CONTINENTAL U.S. - TOTAL (Excl. AFR)	1,629,095			1,590,975	1,455,103			1,396,104
OPERATING ACTIVE	1,622,455	10,703	7,227	1,586,674	1,448,421	11,197	7,496	1,391,178
Administrative	4,320	31	29	542	6,352	43	35	2,104
Minimum Individual Tng	281,300	1,694	1,129	162,160	236,746	1,762	1,176	135,344
Unit Training.	284,901	2,926	2,072	155,743	238,962	2,889	2,007	126,726
Unit Support	51,848	295	206	35,833	52,476	334	241	35,476
Student Training . . .	841,427	4,579	3,100	1,143,111	764,629	4,919	3,349	1,010,366
MATS: Transport . . .	48,725	149	79	16,794	46,417	168	80	15,176
Air Evac. . . .	12,919	36	26	7,549	12,669	37	27	6,864
Combat Crew Training .	15,032	70	48	7,499	13,186	78	52	6,524
Test	21,721	427	210	18,306	19,147	436	201	15,231
Test Support	12,366	117	77	7,235	11,106	122	69	6,802
Special Mission. . . .	39,381	291	213	24,069	36,890	326	227	22,383
MDAP	8,515	88	38	7,833	9,841	83	32	8,182
OTHER ACTIVE	3,664	906	89	2,315	3,760	725	90	2,375
Command Support. . . .	1,466	618	48	1,376	1,273	584	50	1,098
Project.	603	268	37	602	699	113	31	641
En route	1,595	20	4	337	1,788	28	9	636
INACTIVE	2,976			1,986	2,922			2,551
OVERSEAS - TOTAL	511,345			321,901	467,706			286,728
OPERATING ACTIVE	501,243	3,417	2,402	318,713	460,122	3,676	2,521	284,285
Administrative	8,500	47	33	4,132	3,563	28	23	1,414
Minimum Individual Tng	72,690	342	237	53,254	56,916	321	222	40,243
Unit Training.	319,519	2,491	1,765	200,760	291,798	2,567	1,789	178,746
Unit Support	22,051	134	90	17,726	20,509	139	86	16,751
MATS: Transport . . .	37,107	80	52	9,392	33,106	93	53	8,276
Test	205	2	1	267	762	15	11	433
Test Support	1,316	8	5	2,263	2,135	15	11	4,594
Special Missions . . .	38,094	297	207	29,713	39,419	343	247	26,419
MDAP	1,761	16	12	1,206	11,914	155	79	7,409
OTHER ACTIVE	9,181	523	68	2,533	6,873	455	54	1,790
Command Support. . . .	1,018	366	11	903	753	383	8	717
Project.	-	1	-	-	1	2	-	1
En route	8,163	156	57	1,630	6,119	70	46	1,072
INACTIVE	921			655	711			653

TABLE 85 — USAF FLIGHT OPERATIONS BY TYPE OF ACTIVITY — QUARTERLY FY 1953 — CONTINUED

TYPE OF ACTIVITY	THIRD QUARTER FISCAL YEAR 1953				FOURTH QUARTER FISCAL YEAR 1953			
	HOURS FLOWN	AVERAGE A/C		LANDINGS	HOURS FLOWN	AVERAGE A/C		LANDINGS
		ON HAND	IN COM. a/			ON HAND	IN COM. a/	
WORLD-WIDE TOTAL-(Excl-AFR)	1,941,968			1,610,610	2,169,279			1,978,758
OPERATING ACTIVE	1,929,476	15,231		1,601,051	2,152,509	15,480		1,966,962
Administrative	8,965	69		3,261	10,350	72		3,887
Minimum Individual Tng	293,091	2,097		184,382	330,615	2,129		206,288
Unit Training.	538,197	5,711		320,908	632,590	6,020		397,027
Unit Support	71,288	488		53,588	75,712	496		60,140
Student Training . . .	812,140	5,193		928,344	859,436	4,942		1,158,591
MATS: Transport . . .	74,272	281		22,967	79,335	293		26,743
Air Evac. . . .	11,395	37		6,263	11,911	35		6,863
Combat Crew Training .	13,835	74		7,151	19,282	95		10,537
Test	18,329	447		15,812	21,524	449		18,378
Test Support	13,148	148		8,931	14,529	164		11,069
Special Missions . . .	74,816	686		49,444	86,346	715		58,677
MDAP	-	-		-	10,879	70		8,762
OTHER ACTIVE	7,221	1,429		4,395	11,177	1,420		6,456
Command Support. . . .	2,408	1,102		2,256	3,445	1,190		3,146
Project.	772	200		591	420	96		378
En route	4,041	127		1,548	7,312	134		2,932
INACTIVE	5,271			5,164	5,593			5,340
CONTINENTAL U.S. - TOTAL (Excl. AFR)	1,492,151			1,321,362	1,637,824			1,625,503
OPERATING ACTIVE	1,484,442	11,706		1,314,067	1,628,810	11,891		1,616,969
Administrative	5,609	43		2,014	6,283	44		2,314
Minimum Individual Tng	235,715	1,765		140,806	259,695	1,788		152,996
Unit Training.	246,163	3,137		132,458	282,840	3,388		163,755
Unit Support	50,523	351		35,929	51,591	350		37,777
Student Training . . .	812,140	5,193		928,344	859,436	4,942		1,158,591
MATS: Transport . . .	41,694	184		14,545	46,245	199		17,454
Air Evac. . . .	11,395	37		6,263	11,911	35		6,863
Combat Crew Training .	13,835	74		7,151	19,282	95		10,537
Test	18,170	444		15,724	21,524	449		18,378
Test Support	11,693	131		6,990	12,964	145		9,049
Special Mission. . . .	37,505	347		23,843	46,160	386		30,493
MDAP	-	-		-	10,879	70		8,762
OTHER ACTIVE	3,455	925		2,924	4,559	976		4,178
Command Support. . . .	1,449	700		1,327	2,353	848		2,248
Project.	772	199		591	420	95		378
En route	1,234	26		1,006	1,786	33		1,552
INACTIVE	4,254			4,371	4,455			4,356
OVERSEAS - TOTAL.	449,817			289,248	533,012			353,255
OPERATING ACTIVE	445,034	3,525		286,984	525,256	3,590		349,993
Administrative	3,356	26		1,247	4,067	28		1,573
Minimum Individual Tng	57,376	332		43,576	70,920	341		53,292
Unit Training.	292,034	2,574		188,450	349,750	2,632		233,272
Unit Support	20,765	137		17,659	25,678	146		22,363
MATS: Transport . . .	32,578	97		8,422	33,090	95		9,289
Test	159	3		88	-	-		-
Test Support	1,455	17		1,941	1,565	19		2,020
Special Missions . . .	37,311	339		25,601	40,186	329		28,184
OTHER ACTIVE	3,766	504		1,471	6,618	444		2,278
Command Support. . . .	959	402		929	1,092	342		898
Project.	-	1		-	-	1		-
En route	2,807	101		542	5,526	101		1,380
INACTIVE	1,017			793	1,138			984

a/ In Commission data for Third and Fourth Quarter not available.

SOURCE: Materiel Statistics Division, D/Statistical Services, DCS/C.

TABLE 86 — UTILIZATION OF USAF AIRPLANES BY COMMAND (OPERATING ACTIVE)

SUMMARY FISCAL YEAR 1953

COMMAND	OPERATING ACTIVE-COMBAT AIRPLANES: BOMBER			TANKER			FIGHTER			RECONNAISSANCE a/		
	Hours Flown	Av A/C On Hand Per Month	Av Hrs Flown Per A/C on Hand Per Month	Hours Flown	Av A/C On Hand Per Month	Av Hrs Flown Per A/C on Hand Per Month	Hours Flown	Av A/C On Hand Per Month	Av Hrs Flown Per A/C on Hand Per Month	Hours Flown	Av A/C On Hand Per Month	Av Hrs Flown Per A/C on Hand Per Month
TOTAL USAF	661,090	1,462	38	101,319	316	27	1,199,943	3,436	29	329,702	707	39
Air Defense	1,527	2	55	-	-	-	249,855	725	29	315	1	24
Air Materiel	974	2	36	146	-	36	818	4	18	-	-	-
Air Proving Ground	9,874	34	24	1,040	3	32	5,285	36	12	1,610	6	21
Air Research&Development	17,356	107	14	445	3	11	14,930	130	10	3,332	16	17
Air Training	63,271	111	48	-	-	-	320,974	756	35	2,812	8	30
Air University	-	-	-	-	-	-	-	-	-	-	-	-
Continental Air	-	-	-	-	-	-	-	-	-	-	-	-
Headquarters b/	-	-	-	-	-	-	-	-	-	1,977	4	37
Strategic Air	297,409	751	33	97,270	302	27	56,789	201	23	58,795	150	33
Tactical Air	63,469	99	54	-	-	-	61,019	294	17	41,638	90	38
Mil Air Transport Serv.	2,424	11	18	-	-	-	852	3	21	113,379	208	45
Alaskan Air	72	-	12	-	-	-	31,281	86	30	113	-	28
Caribbean Air	269	1	34	-	-	-	-	-	-	3	-	1
Far East Air Forces	180,152	252	60	2,418	8	25	347,253	799	36	90,761	162	47
US Air Forces in Europe	24,283	94	22	-	-	-	106,848	395	23	14,309	60	20
Northeast Air							4,039	7	45	658	2	25

COMMAND	OPERATING ACTIVE NON-COMBAT AIRPLANES: CARGO			TRAINER			COMMUNICATIONS		
	Hours Flown	Av A/C On Hand Per Month	Av Hrs Flown Per A/C on Hand Per Month	Hours Flown	Av A/C On Hand Per Month	Av Hrs Flown Per A/C on Hand Per Month	Hours Flown	Av A/C On Hand Per Month	Av Hrs Flown Per A/C on Hand Per Month
TOTAL USAF	1,992,710	2,750	60	3,575,756	5,578	53	252,960	644	33
Air Defense	93,598	122	64	122,694	264	39	4,569	16	24
Air Materiel	115,710	137	70	28,648	46	52	313	5	5
Air Proving Ground	12,735	19	55	11,343	32	29	852	3	22
Air Research&Development	73,212	136	45	29,727	95	26	7,314	39	16
Air Training	85,620	116	61	2,913,510	4,059	60	136,386	290	39
Air University	53,435	65	69	34,038	69	41	-	-	-
Continental Air	29,633	45	55	18,992	36	43	30	-	-
Headquarters	110,732	201	46	47,746	74	54	983	6	15
Strategic Air	160,574	224	60	103,299	279	31	162	-	-
Tactical Air	189,454	458	34	96,185	259	31	19,611	76	21
Mil Air Transport Serv.	517,865	537	80	69,974	142	41	5,428	25	18
Alaskan Air	43,398	54	67	2,747	7	32	6,133	11	48
Caribbean Air	14,806	28	45	509	2	27	260	2	11
Far East Air Forces	312,845	326	80	74,886	135	46	57,114	113	42
US Air Forces in Europe	157,359	255	51	20,588	76	22	11,154	53	17
Northeast Air	21,734	27	67	870	3	24	2,651	5	45

a/ Includes Search and Rescue.
b/ Includes Air Attaches, Civil Air Patrol, Military Aviation Missions, MDAP, and Joint Brazil U. S. Commissions.

TABLE 87 — USAF FLYING TIME, FUEL CONSUMPTION, AND RATE BY TYPE AND MODEL

Type and Model	Hours Flown	Fuel Issued (Gallons)	Rate Per Hour
TOTAL	8,173,597	1,644,979,582	-
Bomber - Total	675,194	322,887,419	-
B-17	9,614	2,030,545	211
B-26	202,934	30,182,333	149
B-29	262,500	111,412,356	424
B-36	50,770	54,163,741	1,067
B-45	9,504	11,686,644	1,230
B-47	40,982	62,022,458	1,513
B-50	96,315	50,919,939	529
Other	2,575	469,403	-
Tanker - Total	101,470	44,944,366	-
KB-29	58,373	25,238,966	432
KC-97	43,097	19,705,400	457
Fighter - Total	1,212,378	422,325,232	-
F-47	20,007	2,210,814	110
F-51	152,478	10,408,041	68
F-80	176,524	66,727,112	378
F-82	1,428	188,579	132
F-84	395,868	156,777,060	396
F-86	306,636	122,414,484	399
F-89	6,453	5,592,146	867
F-94	152,963	57,986,435	379
Other	21	20,561	-
Reconnaissance - Total	231,671	112,569,324	-
RB-17	4,179	966,779	231
RB-25	940	137,253	146
RB-26	39,346	5,625,054	143
WB-26	1,437	209,563	146
RB-29	13,322	5,592,119	420
WB-29	59,626	30,258,737	507
RB-36	37,864	38,865,288	1,026
RB-45	5,419	6,121,768	1,130
RB-47	499	678,850	1,360
RB-50	13,907	7,405,498	532
RF-51	6,798	475,041	70
RF-80	42,571	15,538,002	365
RF-86	566	303,953	537
RC-45	2,111	91,099	43
RC-47	3,086	297,737	96
Other	-	2,583	-
Search & Rescue - Total	101,803	17,429,455	-
SA-10	908	84,907	94
SA-16	71,825	8,668,128	121
SB-17	11,696	2,581,291	221
SB-29	13,586	5,644,015	415
SC-47	2,029	183,998	91
SC-54	1,291	256,002	198
SH-5	468	11,114	24
Cargo - Total	2,011,653	318,720,828	-
CB-17	15,574	3,380,177	217
CB-25	21,062	2,937,486	139
CB-26	1,392	191,760	138
C-45	266,135	10,248,292	38
C-46	123,568	19,005,694	154
C-47/53	875,830	80,502,758	92
C-54	330,197	65,947,104	200
C-74	12,324	5,704,522	463
C-82	23,621	4,260,399	180
C-97	64,712	31,575,594	488
XC-99	1,554	1,271,800	818
C-117	7,687	715,045	93
C-118	7,552	2,759,639	365
C-119	146,022	35,867,404	246
C-121	6,878	2,717,319	395
C-122	1,709	196,694	115
C-124	105,460	51,366,472	487
Other	376	72,669	-
Trainer - Total	3,594,556	402,254,947	-
T-6	1,537,039	38,285,906	25
T-7	57,980	2,243,326	39
T-11	111,741	4,131,822	37
T-28	292,213	10,877,382	37
T-29	79,366	12,699,077	160
T-33	618,867	197,600,118	319
TB-17	10,939	2,525,447	231
TB-25	570,283	72,638,358	127
TB-26	100,886	14,905,229	148
TB-29	41,771	17,646,208	422
TB-45	1,239	1,594,286	1,287
TB-47	1,671	2,607,414	1,560
TB-50	16,676	8,850,277	531
TF-51	44,013	2,688,221	61
TF-80	16,406	5,768,513	352
TC-45	36,708	1,510,293	41
TC-47	48,950	4,496,388	92
TC-54	5,911	1,141,255	193
Other	1,898	45,427	-
Communication - Total	244,872	3,848,011	-
L-5	24,481	240,609	10
L-13	4,427	46,670	11
L-16	3,248	13,036	4
L-17	638	8,593	13
L-20	42,146	781,380	19
L-21	99,772	600,154	6
LT-6	26,189	1,097,413	42
H-5	11,871	315,543	27
H-13	15,179	177,274	12
H-19	14,295	511,501	36
Other	2,626	55,838	-

SOURCE: Materiel Statistics Division, D/Statistical Services DCS/C

TABLE 88 — UTILIZATION AND FUEL CONSUMPTION RATE — USAF JET AIRCRAFT BY TYPE AND MODEL

TYPE AND MODEL	OPERATING ACTIVE: HOURS FLOWN	Av. A/C On Hand	Av. Hours Flown Per A/C On Hand (Per Month)	Fuel Consumed	Rate Per Hour
SUMMARY - FY 1953					
TOTAL	1,764,373	4,220	35	706,972,927	-
B-45 . .	9,453	54	15	11,618,193	1,229
B-47 . .	40,862	149	23	60,558,685	1,482
F-80 . .	177,022	436	34	66,610,989	376
F-84 . .	388,525	1,150	28	154,016,728	396
F-86 . .	303,930	808	31	121,305,019	399
F-89 . .	6,127	80	6	5,004,609	817
F-94 . .	152,614	362	35	57,894,282	379
RB-45. .	5,309	17	26	5,973,341	1,125
RB-47. .	499	3	14	678,850	1,360
RF-80. .	42,435	113	31	15,514,996	366
RF-86. .	555	4	12	299,868	540
T-33 . .	616,730	986	52	197,193,186	320
TB-45. .	1,233	7	15	1,583,876	1,285
TB-47. .	1,671	3	43	2,607,414	1,560
TF-80. .	16,406	41	33	5,768,513	352
QF-80. .	711	5	12	2,238,524	335
QT-33. .	291	2	12	105,854	364
FIRST QUARTER - FY 1953					
TOTAL	367,915	3,492	35	145,069,584	-
B-45 . .	4,157	64	22	5,306,313	1,276
B-47 . .	3,644	69	18	4,937,400	1,355
F-80 . .	47,276	450	35	17,638,913	373
F-84 . .	79,633	978	27	32,008,400	402
F-86 . .	55,593	574	32	21,917,079	394
F-89 . .	4,044	93	15	3,328,579	823
F-94 . .	42,281	368	38	15,512,295	367
RB-45. .	2,176	24	30	2,294,902	1,055
RF-80. .	11,362	123	31	4,258,959	375
RF-86. .	227	5	16	117,877	519
T-33 . .	112,795	693	54	36,001,451	319
TB-45. .	163	4	15	205,036	1,258
TF-80. .	4,440	43	34	1,501,389	338
QF-80. .	40	2	8	11,485	287
QT-33. .	84	2	12	29,506	351
SECOND QUARTER - FY 1953					
TOTAL	362,985	3,887	31	142,797,849	-
B-45 . .	2,075	56	12	2,551,156	1,229
B-47 . .	6,452	88	24	10,344,692	1,603
F-80 . .	41,061	421	32	15,734,049	383
F-84 . .	76,312	1,114	23	30,292,623	397
F-86 . .	59,190	661	30	23,486,411	397
F-89 a/.	331	105	-	220,640	-
F-94 . .	34,699	354	33	12,824,487	370
RB-45. .	1,092	15	24	1,306,281	1,196
RB-47. .	43	1	14	83,876	1,951
RF-80. .	10,288	109	31	3,737,835	363
RF-86. .	92	4	8	48,457	527
T-33 . .	126,015	898	47	39,957,678	317
TB-45. .	398	9	15	518,632	1,303
TF-80. .	4,638	46	33	1,587,429	342
QF-80. .	181	4	14	61,199	338
QT-33. .	118	2	20	42,404	359
THIRD QUARTER - FY 1953					
TOTAL	460,272	4,421	35	181,466,894	-
B-45 . .	671	48	5	840,460	1,253
B-47 . .	13,473	184	24	18,823,158	1,397
F-80 . .	44,692	444	34	17,078,600	382
F-84 . .	102,917	1,232	28	40,033,819	389
F-86 . .	75,528	811	31	29,831,616	395
F-89 a/.	6	83	-	41,174	-
F-94 . .	34,851	349	33	13,314,834	382
RB-45. .	960	12	26	1,100,312	1,146
RB-47. .	44	1	15	76,744	1,744
RF-80. .	9,506	99	32	3,412,249	359
RF-86. .	114	3	14	56,817	498
T-33 . .	172,205	1,096	52	54,755,940	318
TB-45. .	167	8	7	230,093	1,378
TF-80. .	4,842	44	37	1,773,012	366
QF-80. .	263	6	14	85,414	325
QT-33. .	33	1	8	12,652	383
FOURTH QUARTER - FY 1953					
TOTAL	573,201	5,080	38	237,638,600	-
B-45 . .	2,550	46	19	2,920,264	1,145
B-47 . .	17,293	254	23	26,453,435	1,530
F-80 . .	43,993	429	34	16,159,427	367
F-84 . .	129,663	1,277	34	51,681,886	399
F-86 . .	113,619	1,184	32	46,069,913	405
F-89 . .	1,746	39	15	1,414,216	810
F-94 . .	40,783	378	36	16,242,666	398
RB-45. .	1,081	18	20	1,271,846	1,177
RB-47. .	412	10	14	518,230	1,258
RF-80. .	11,279	122	31	4,105,953	364
RF-86. .	122	3	15	76,717	629
T-33 . .	205,715	1,259	54	66,478,117	323
TB-45. .	505	8	21	630,115	1,248
TB-47. .	1,671	13	43	2,607,414	1,560
TF-80. .	2,486	32	26	906,683	365
QF-80. .	227	7	11	80,426	354
QT-33. .	56	1	19	21,292	380

a/ Rates for F-89 not computed. Rates would be unrealistic as F-89's were grounded during this period because of malfunction.

SOURCE: Materiel Statistics Division, D/Statistical Services, DCS/C

TABLE 89 — USAF AVIATION FUEL CONSUMPTION

COMMAND	FISCAL YEAR 1953												
	TOTAL	JUL '52	AUGUST	SEPTEMBER	OCTOBER	NOVEMBER	DECEMBER	JAN '53	FEBRUARY	MARCH	APRIL	MAY	JUNE
TOTAL	1,646,085,083	131,434,711	132,107,332	131,771,924	136,341,795	121,146,228	114,422,288	124,011,078	124,622,633	149,774,948	152,781,616	156,920,052	170,750,478
CONT'L US.	1,143,878,984	91,664,557	90,780,694	89,482,017	94,444,416	82,120,410	78,813,949	89,670,528	88,933,630	106,346,440	106,266,363	108,026,604	117,329,376
ADC	104,451,092	9,583,668	9,897,411	8,537,124	7,804,335	6,753,210	6,443,331	7,035,910	7,938,428	9,672,595	9,736,663	9,670,567	11,377,850
AMC	25,127,530	2,002,319	1,976,494	2,140,582	2,124,558	1,771,037	1,855,332	1,870,044	2,018,609	2,119,355	2,471,237	2,320,785	2,457,178
APGC	12,639,374	1,057,998	1,070,852	883,483	1,130,868	852,570	1,122,723	1,074,468	1,074,049	1,166,643	1,114,208	1,087,631	1,003,881
ARDC	29,994,007	2,650,208	2,424,225	2,479,243	2,688,700	2,129,203	1,877,102	2,184,542	2,396,642	2,864,556	2,613,025	2,657,582	3,028,979
ATRC	471,621,083	32,654,354	33,583,500	34,374,626	39,145,493	31,959,358	32,512,220	40,687,850	37,590,610	46,535,544	47,642,947	46,157,658	48,776,923
AU	5,526,902	436,793	449,357	503,186	496,586	476,051	347,493	485,104	363,510	487,321	511,939	509,595	459,967
CAP	784,172	72,997	78,054	62,626	63,009	53,242	56,503	44,649	57,517	81,066	80,776	61,550	72,183
CONAC	4,338,476	340,531	336,162	308,158	317,370	358,801	335,167	365,962	385,507	400,928	391,895	403,341	394,654
HQC	10,240,497	1,438,735	861,119	793,489	910,544	517,905	594,321	700,104	771,394	1,069,545	857,094	905,037	821,210
IG	743,551	203,963	154,319	129,035	144,890	111,344	a/	-	-	-	-	-	-
MATS	94,917,168	8,155,805	8,950,565	8,596,060	8,160,256	7,592,970	7,877,110	6,648,324	7,379,907	7,851,470	7,289,932	8,436,471	7,978,298
SAC	300,420,613	26,316,035	24,597,221	24,114,994	23,826,061	23,824,927	20,098,791	22,709,824	23,856,305	27,024,050	25,973,660	27,298,120	30,780,625
USAFSS	175,828	7,394	24,793	17,096	14,092	20,508	15,316	11,568	21,168	14,477	9,497	11,292	8,627
TAC	82,898,691	6,743,757	6,376,622	6,542,315	7,617,654	5,699,284	5,678,540	5,852,179	5,079,984	7,058,890	7,573,490	8,506,975	10,169,001
OVERSEAS	502,206,099	39,770,154	41,326,638	42,289,907	41,897,379	39,025,818	35,608,339	34,340,550	35,689,003	43,428,508	46,515,253	48,893,448	53,421,102
AAC	19,490,524	1,289,877	1,962,911	1,469,949	1,314,042	1,352,658	1,269,169	833,519	1,203,131	2,107,708	2,152,367	2,353,608	2,181,585
AAT	604,435	119,746	110,654	114,422	158,319	101,294	b/	-	-	-	-	-	-
AMC	225,798	42,571	16,581	19,222	14,544	7,320	17,627	10,713	14,653	27,244	23,159	21,052	11,112
ARD	190,818	5,860	5,695	20,250	65,851	-	11,354	12,328	12,348	16,479	12,386	11,401	16,866
CAIRC	1,468,735	69,546	70,491	71,447	91,590	93,595	161,075	120,245	164,203	108,873	180,453	172,435	164,782
CAP	12,989	1,673	2,002	499	1,808	847	1,618	131	75	688	-	898	2,750
EUROPE	83,775,031	9,917,117	9,585,215	8,956,322	5,461,507	4,076,153	3,752,184	3,679,906	5,313,391	7,364,279	8,377,353	8,832,176	8,459,428
FEAF	285,015,639	20,337,737	21,242,416	23,025,136	25,533,829	22,314,421	22,593,421	22,730,855	21,412,098	25,132,460	27,448,168	27,785,906	25,459,192
HQC	1,362,461	-	-	-	-	-	223,543	139,045	190,378	226,272	201,982	229,134	152,107
JBUSDC	744,648	53,332	74,091	56,286	75,508	63,459	67,766	53,515	51,496	102,920	32,262	65,494	48,519
LAM	309,279	71,398	43,397	54,721	32,442	107,321	c/	-	-	-	-	-	-
MATS	63,789,756	5,102,625	5,086,478	4,947,597	4,739,258	4,958,756	4,644,138	4,017,358	4,173,961	4,630,747	4,850,395	5,015,046	11,623,397
MILMIS	125,066	40,094	14,801	7,025	33,700	29,446	b/	-	-	-	-	-	-
MDAP	197,858	26,418	53,070	41,495	44,576	32,299	b/	-	-	-	-	-	-
NEAC	5,388,624	329,890	402,900	250,980	331,040	377,188	459,217	370,499	480,040	636,877	578,877	659,148	511,968
SAC	38,264,497	2,362,270	2,655,936	3,234,415	3,480,412	4,982,778	2,369,422	2,364,295	2,654,206	3,064,061	2,654,404	3,747,150	4,695,148
TAC	1,203,100	-	-	20,141	499,810	510,585	37,805	8,141	19,023	9,900	3,447	-	94,248
TURKISH	36,841	-	-	-	19,143	17,698	b/	-	-	-	-	-	-

a/ Included in Headquarters Command
b/ Included in Headquarters Command
c/ Included in CAIRC

SOURCE: Materiel Statistics Division, D/Statistical Services, DCS/C

FLYING SAFETY

The content of this section presents aircraft accident data for the Fiscal Year 1953. This presentation includes data for Air National Guard, Air Force Reserve, Military Air Transport Service Navy units and Civil Air Patrol in all tables.

During the fiscal year 1953, all accidents, major and minor, totaled 3,472. These accident statistics are reflected by command, by type and model of aircraft involved, by phase of operation in which the accident occurred, by the factors causing the accident and by the conditions affecting the accident. All rates are expressed in accidents per 100,000 flying hours.

It should be noted that accidents in aircraft which were on bailment contract and/or loan, are included in total numbers of accidents shown in all tables. However, bailment/loan accidents are not included in rate computations as flying time is not available for these aircraft. All other computations and dollar loss data include bailment/loan accidents.

The dollar losses, presented herein, represent the investment cost of airplanes destroyed, plus the average cost of labor, materiel and indirect expenses required to repair airplanes sustaining substantial damage as the result of accidents. Dollar losses do not include the cost of lives lost, injuries, property damage, search and rescue, minor aircraft damage or other losses resulting from aircraft accidents.

Same as Navy

Data in this section prepared by the Directorate of Flight Safety Research, Office of The Inspector General, Norton Air Force Base, California.

TABLE 90 — USAF AND ANG AIRCRAFT ACCIDENTS RATES AND DOLLAR LOSS — BY COMMAND — FY 1953
(Includes hours and accidents in the Air Force Reserve, MATS Navy Units, and Civil Air Patrol Aircraft in the USAF inventory. Rates are expressed in accidents per 100,000 hours.)

COMMAND	FLYING HOURS a/	MAJOR ACCIDENTS		FATAL ACCIDENTS b/		FATALITIES c/		AIRCRAFT DESTROYED d/		MINOR ACCIDENTS		DOLLAR LOSS
		No.	Rate	No.	Rate	No.	Rate	No.	Rate	No.	Rate	
F.Y. 1953 - TOTAL	8,488,654	2,188	26	430	5	1,274	15	893	11	1,284	15	$ 245,656,671
1st Quarter	2,208,438	626	28	110	5	227	10	242	11	305	14	62,641,732
2nd Quarter	1,984,104	547	28	106	5	509	26	181	9	287	14	52,400,504
3rd Quarter	2,015,319	466	23	101	5	234	12	219	11	319	16	72,369,388
4th Quarter	2,280,793	549	24	113	5	304	13	251	11	373	16	58,245,047
AIR DEFENSE COMMAND	472,603	220	47	37	8	56	12	91	19	122	26	22,954,239
1st Quarter	130,185	74	57	9	7	11	8	32	25	19	15	9,881,458
2nd Quarter	104,768	48	46	7	7	22	21	14	13	22	21	3,916,328
3rd Quarter	109,420	46	42	9	8	10	9	20	18	38	35	3,683,423
4th Quarter	128,230	52	41	12	9	13	10	25	19	43	34	5,473,030
AIR MATERIEL COMMAND	169,089	34	18	3	1	5	2	8	4	42	23	6,491,883
1st Quarter	45,041	14	27	3	4	5	7	4	7	11	20	5,620,156
2nd Quarter	37,818	14	34	-	-	-	-	2	5	11	29	491,343
3rd Quarter	42,043	1	2	-	-	-	-	1	2	10	21	24,876
4th Quarter	44,187	5	9	-	-	-	-	1	2	10	23	355,508
AIR PROVING GROUND	47,410	15	32	2	4	8	17	7	15	17	36	2,704,310
1st Quarter	12,117	1	8	1	8	6	50	1	8	2	17	228,438
2nd Quarter	11,620	3	26	-	-	-	-	-	-	2	17	51,637
3rd Quarter	11,403	5	44	-	-	-	-	3	26	4	35	561,965
4th Quarter	12,270	6	49	1	8	2	16	3	24	9	73	1,862,270
AIR RESEARCH & DEVELOPMENT	148,980	44	30	4	3	12	8	10	7	36	23	3,889,941
1st Quarter	39,952	12	30	-	-	-	-	3	8	13	33	565,116
2nd Quarter	35,365	15	42	2	6	8	23	3	8	6	17	2,660,549
3rd Quarter	34,403	9	26	2	6	4	12	2	6	11	29	303,680
4th Quarter	39,260	8	20	-	-	-	-	2	5	6	13	360,596
AIR TRAINING COMMAND	3,524,368	901	26	189	5	254	7	352	10	496	14	64,552,361
1st Quarter	909,079	240	26	49	5	67	7	93	10	122	13	13,685,792
2nd Quarter	828,120	225	27	41	5	56	7	68	8	123	15	12,088,868
3rd Quarter	862,293	194	22	38	4	47	5	77	9	124	14	18,295,656
4th Quarter	924,876	242	26	61	7	84	9	114	12	127	14	20,482,045
AIR UNIVERSITY	87,547	6	7	-	-	-	-	1	1	7	8	134,819
1st Quarter	21,939	3	14	-	-	-	-	-	-	1	5	34,034
2nd Quarter	19,985	1	5	-	-	-	-	-	-	1	5	17,017
3rd Quarter	21,215	2	9	-	-	-	-	1	5	3	14	83,768
4th Quarter	24,408	-	-	-	-	-	-	-	-	2	8	-
ALASKAN AIR COMMAND	83,911	30	36	8	10	13	15	14	17	31	37	3,490,980
1st Quarter	22,775	10	44	3	13	5	22	5	22	11	48	1,102,011
2nd Quarter	17,020	6	35	2	12	3	18	2	12	6	35	574,778
3rd Quarter	16,917	8	47	2	12	3	18	5	30	5	30	1,330,749
4th Quarter	27,199	6	22	1	4	2	7	2	7	9	33	483,442
CARIBBEAN AIR COMMAND	15,927	2	13	-	-	-	-	2	13	2	13	103,967
1st Quarter	3,568	1	28	-	-	-	-	1	28	1	28	29,845
2nd Quarter	4,285	-	-	-	-	-	-	-	-	1	23	-
3rd Quarter	3,364	-	-	-	-	-	-	-	-	-	-	-
4th Quarter	4,710	1	21	-	-	-	-	1	21	-	-	74,122
CIVIL AIR PATROL	16,485	3	18	-	-	-	-	-	-	4	24	47,262
1st Quarter	4,667	-	-	-	-	-	-	-	-	-	-	-
2nd Quarter	3,748	1	27	-	-	-	-	-	-	-	-	17,017
3rd Quarter	3,619	1	28	-	-	-	-	-	-	2	55	13,796
4th Quarter	4,451	1	22	-	-	-	-	-	-	2	45	16,449
CONTINENTAL AIR COMMAND	121,584	16	13	4	3	5	4	6	5	47	39	664,364
1st Quarter	19,653	1	5	-	-	-	-	1	5	6	31	95,458
2nd Quarter	25,136	3	12	1	4	1	4	-	-	12	48	4,563
3rd Quarter	32,959	3	9	2	6	3	9	3	9	13	39	303,605
4th Quarter	43,836	9	21	1	2	1	2	2	5	16	36	260,738
FAR EAST AIR FORCES	1,086,323	437	40	91	8	421	39	204	19	147	14	52,563,123
1st Quarter	265,317	121	46	22	8	74	28	49	18	37	14	13,197,164
2nd Quarter	274,079	111	40	24	9	138	50	45	16	36	13	12,250,978
3rd Quarter	256,865	94	37	22	9	38	15	57	22	30	12	13,175,236
4th Quarter	290,062	111	38	23	8	171	59	53	18	44	15	13,939,745
HEADQUARTERS COMMAND	138,638	15	11	4	3	15	11	3	2	12	9	690,724
1st Quarter	44,391	6	14	2	5	10	23	1	2	4	9	227,572
2nd Quarter	31,892	2	6	-	-	-	-	-	-	4	13	95,115
3rd Quarter	29,794	5	17	1	3	3	10	1	3	3	10	328,420
4th Quarter	32,561	2	6	1	3	2	6	1	3	1	3	39,617

TABLE 90 — USAF AND ANG AIRCRAFT ACCIDENTS, RATES AND DOLLAR LOSS—BY COMMAND FY 1953 — (Continued)

COMMAND	FLYING HOURS a/	MAJOR ACCIDENTS No.	MAJOR ACCIDENTS Rate	FATAL ACCIDENTS b/ No.	FATAL ACCIDENTS b/ Rate	FATALITIES c/ No.	FATALITIES c/ Rate	AIRCRAFT DESTROYED d/ No.	AIRCRAFT DESTROYED d/ Rate	MINOR ACCIDENTS No.	MINOR ACCIDENTS Rate	DOLLAR LOSS
MILITARY AIR TRANSPORT SERVICE a/	804,929	54	7	8	1	124	15	17	2	46	6	7,941,271
1st Quarter	210,877	18	9	1	-	1	-	4	2	15	7	1,713,353
2nd Quarter	198,706	16	8	3	2	102	51	5	3	11	6	2,681,925
3rd Quarter	188,306	8	4	2	1	11	6	3	2	11	6	1,379,423
4th Quarter	207,040	12	6	2	1	10	5	5	2	9	4	2,166,570
NORTHEAST AIR COMMAND	30,643	10	33	1	3	14	46	6	20	11	36	1,778,391
1st Quarter	7,004	1	14	-	-	-	-	1	14	4	57	95,458
2nd Quarter	6,787	3	44	-	-	-	-	2	29	2	29	656,098
3rd Quarter	7,607	3	39	1	13	14	184	1	13	1	13	406,784
4th Quarter	9,245	3	32	-	-	-	-	2	22	4	43	620,051
STRATEGIC AIR COMMAND	774,961	94	12	26	3	132	17	43	6	61	8	47,810,190
1st Quarter	202,531	20	10	4	2	24	12	7	3	12	6	9,136,434
2nd Quarter	188,240	28	15	9	5	27	14	13	7	15	8	8,316,376
3rd Quarter	186,018	25	13	8	4	75	40	13	7	14	8	25,534,009
4th Quarter	198,172	21	11	5	3	6	3	10	5	20	10	4,823,371
TACTICAL AIR COMMAND	472,123	111	24	18	4	159	34	39	8	100	21	9,017,172
1st Quarter	127,526	34	27	5	4	8	6	11	9	25	20	1,477,117
2nd Quarter	115,165	36	31	7	6	138	120	10	9	18	16	4,302,990
3rd Quarter	102,098	16	16	6	6	13	13	9	9	21	21	1,588,053
4th Quarter	127,334	25	20	-	-	-	-	9	7	36	28	1,649,012
U.S. AIR FORCES IN EUROPE	339,525	136	40	25	7	46	14	62	18	59	17	17,394,866
1st Quarter	105,671	52	49	9	9	14	13	19	18	16	15	4,862,156
2nd Quarter	56,585	26	46	6	11	10	18	13	23	12	21	3,957,334
3rd Quarter	74,053	29	39	5	7	10	14	15	20	17	23	3,623,743
4th Quarter	103,216	29	28	5	5	12	12	15	15	14	14	4,951,633
MISCELLANEOUS e/	6,348	-	-	-	-	-	-	-	-	-	-	-
1st Quarter	1,603	-	-	-	-	-	-	-	-	-	-	-
2nd Quarter	1,762	-	-	-	-	-	-	-	-	-	-	-
3rd Quarter	1,700	-	-	-	-	-	-	-	-	-	-	-
4th Quarter	1,283	-	-	-	-	-	-	-	-	-	-	-
AIR NATIONAL GUARD	147,260	49	33	7	5	7	5	20	14	37	25	1,552,119
1st Quarter	34,542	18	52	2	6	2	6	10	29	6	17	690,170
2nd Quarter	23,023	9	39	4	17	4	17	4	17	5	22	317,588
3rd Quarter	31,242	9	29	-	-	-	-	2	6	9	29	227,518
4th Quarter	58,453	13	22	1	2	1	2	4	7	17	29	316,843
USAF-AT-LARGE f/	-	11	-	3	-	3	-	8	-	7	-	1,874,689
1st Quarter												
2nd Quarter												
3rd Quarter	-	8	-	3	-	3	-	6	-	3	-	1,504,684
4th Quarter	-	3	-	-	-	-	-	2	-	4	-	370,005

a/ Flying hours include 93,761 hours flown by Navy for MATS.
b/ More than one fatality may occur as the result of any one fatal accident.
c/ Fatalities include all persons killed and/or missing as the result of major accidents.
d/ Aircraft destroyed includes missing aircraft.
e/ USAF Security Service, Joint Brazil-US Mil. Comm.
f/ USAF-at-Large - For statistical purposes, accidents during ferrying in aircraft possessed by one command but operated by another are not charged to a specific command, but are included in the USAF totals.

Accidents in aircraft which were on bailment contract and/or on loan are included in the above and succeeding tabulations of USAF Aircraft Accidents. However, flying time is not available for B/L aircraft, and accidents in these planes are not included in rate computations. The B/L accidents are listed below.

TABLE 91 — USAF BAILMENT/LOAN ACCIDENTS — FY 1953

COMMAND	MAJOR ACCIDENTS	FATAL ACCIDENTS	FATALITIES	AIRCRAFT DESTROYED	MINOR ACCIDENTS
F.Y. 1953 - TOTAL	4	1	2	1	6
1st Quarter	2	1	2	1	2
2nd Quarter	1	-	-	-	-
3rd Quarter	-	-	-	-	3
4th Quarter	1	-	-	-	1
AIR MATERIEL COMMAND	4	1	2	1	3
1st Quarter	2	1	2	1	2
2nd Quarter	1	-	-	-	-
3rd Quarter	-	-	-	-	1
4th Quarter	1	-	-	-	-
AIR RESEARCH & DEVELOPMENT	-	-	-	-	2
3rd Quarter	-	-	-	-	1
4th Quarter	-	-	-	-	1
USAF-AT-LARGE f/	-	-	-	-	1
3rd Quarter	-	-	-	-	1

TABLE 92 — USAF AND ANG AIRCRAFT ACCIDENTS, RATES AND DOLLAR LOSS — BY TYPE AND MODEL — FY 1953

(Includes hours and accidents in the Air Force Reserve, MATS Navy Units, and Civil Air Patrol Aircraft in the USAF Inventory. Rates are expressed in accidents per 100,000 hours.)

TYPE AND MODEL	FLYING HOURS a/	MAJOR ACCIDENTS		FATAL ACCIDENTS b/		FATALITIES c/		AIRCRAFT DESTROYED d/		MINOR ACCIDENTS		DOLLAR LOSS
		No.	Rate	No.	Rate	No.	Rate	No.	Rate	No.	Rate	
FY 1953 - TOTAL	8,488,654	2,188	26	430	5	1,274	15	893	11	1,284	15	$ 245,656,671
FIRST QUARTER - TOTAL	2,208,438	626	28	110	5	227	10	242	11	305	14	62,641,732
BOMBER	446,231	63	14	16	3	92	20	22	5	38	9	20,371,284
Non-Jet (Sub Total)	435,975	52	12	14	3	83	19	20	4	35	8	14,194,912
B-17	16,255	2	12	1	6	7	43	2	12	4	25	467,697
B-25	147,137	8	5	2	1	8	5	2	1	3	2	381,492
B-26	92,202	19	21	3	3	10	11	5	5	11	12	1,239,426
B-29	126,680	19	15	7	6	56	44	10	8	14	11	7,302,704
B-36	19,967	3	10	1	-	2	-	1	-	1	5	4,784,835
B-50	33,734	1	3	-	-	-	-	-	-	2	6	18,758
Jet (Sub Total)	10,256	11	107	2	20	9	88	2	20	3	29	6,176,372
B-43	12	-	-	-	-	-	-	-	-	-	-	-
B-45	6,581	5	76	-	-	-	-	-	-	1	15	84,060
B-47	3,663	6	164	2	55	9	246	2	55	2	55	6,092,312
CARGO a/	540,333	41	8	3	-	15	2	11	2	44	8	2,898,113
C-46	41,287	4	10	-	-	-	-	1	2	5	12	289,190
C-47/53 (C-117) a/	277,546	18	6	2	1	7	3	7	3	24	9	852,837
C-54 a/	127,495	3	2	-	-	-	-	-	-	5	4	146,997
C-74	3,778	-	-	-	-	-	-	-	-	-	-	-
C-82	9,885	1	10	-	-	-	-	1	10	4	40	370,252
C-97	26,836	4	15	-	-	-	-	-	-	1	4	87,528
C-118 a/	1,864	-	-	-	-	-	-	-	-	-	-	-
C-119	26,957	8	30	1	4	8	30	2	7	5	19	1,063,010
C-121 a/	2,078	-	-	-	-	-	-	-	-	-	-	-
C-124	21,740	3	14	-	-	-	-	-	-	-	-	88,299
Other	867	-	-	-	-	-	-	-	-	-	-	-
FIGHTER	469,255	366	78	76	16	90	19	163	35	98	20	34,332,763
Non-Jet (Sub Total)	108,450	76	70	11	10	12	11	36	33	25	23	2,801,739
F-47	11,577	17	147	2	17	2	17	6	52	3	26	714,827
F-51	96,398	59	61	9	9	10	10	30	31	21	22	2,086,912
F-82	475	-	-	-	-	-	-	-	-	1	735	-
Jet (Sub Total)	360,805	290	80	65	18	78	22	127	35	73	20	31,531,024
F-80	63,238	60	95	12	19	11	17	27	43	15	24	4,220,337
T-33	113,307	55	49	16	14	21	19	22	19	16	14	3,407,200
F-84	81,962	74	90	19	23	23	28	41	50	16	20	10,337,507
F-86	55,959	42	75	8	14	8	14	19	34	15	23	5,974,022
F-89	4,044	8	198	2	49	3	74	3	74	-	-	3,504,929
F-94	42,295	51	118	8	19	12	28	15	35	11	26	4,087,029
TRAINER	687,207	120	17	12	2	24	3	37	5	100	15	3,125,819
C-45	74,840	12	16	-	-	-	-	4	5	15	20	394,683
T-6	481,429	85	18	8	2	13	3	23	5	75	16	1,058,389
T-7	21,187	3	14	1	5	4	19	1	5	3	14	216,634
T-11	40,276	8	20	-	-	-	-	-	-	2	5	294,704
T-28	55,886	11	20	3	5	7	13	9	16	4	7	1,158,472
T-29	12,757	-	-	-	-	-	-	-	-	1	8	-
T-34	544	-	-	-	-	-	-	-	-	-	-	-
T-35	288	1	347	-	-	-	-	-	-	-	-	2,937
LIAISON	38,660	13	34	2	5	3	8	5	13	16	41	181,431
HELICOPTER	9,724	15	154	1	10	2	21	3	31	4	41	929,016
MISCELLANEOUS	17,028	8	47	-	-	1	6	1	6	5	29	803,306
SECOND QUARTER - TOTAL	1,984,104	547	28	106	5	509	26	181	9	287	14	52,400,504
BOMBER	416,665	58	14	12	3	65	16	20	5	45	11	14,453,776
Non-Jet (Sub Total)	406,534	50	12	9	2	57	14	15	4	40	10	8,950,837
B-17	14,090	1	7	-	-	-	-	-	-	1	7	15,022
B-25	139,039	8	6	-	-	-	-	-	-	11	8	237,991
B-26	83,970	25	30	5	6	9	11	8	10	12	14	1,969,247
B-29	118,968	8	7	2	2	32	27	4	3	13	11	2,705,947
B-36	20,577	3	15	-	-	-	-	-	-	2	10	239,076
B-50	29,890	5	17	2	7	15	54	3	10	1	3	3,793,554

TABLE 92 – USAF AND ANG AIRCRAFT ACCIDENTS, RATES AND DOLLAR LOSS BY TYPE AND MODEL – FY 1953 – CONTINUED)

TYPE AND MODEL	FLYING HOURS a/	MAJOR ACCIDENTS		FATAL ACCIDENTS b/		FATALITIES c/		AIRCRAFT DESTROYED d/		MINOR ACCIDENTS		DOLLAR LOSS
		No.	Rate	No.	Rate	No.	Rate	No.	Rate	No.	Rate	
SECOND QUARTER - Cont'd												
BOMBER - Cont'd												
Jet (Sub Total)	10,131	8	79	3	30	8	79	5	49	5	49	$ 5,472,939
B-43	18	-	-	-	-	-	-	-	-	-	-	-
B-45	3,579	5	140	3	84	8	224	5	140	2	56	5,300,779
B-47	6,534	3	46	-	-	-	-	-	-	3	46	172,160
CARGO	480,456	58	12	14	3	327	68	17	4	42	9	8,894,849
C-46	39,873	7	18	3	8	36	90	2	5	7	18	1,037,150
C-47/53 (C-117) a/	233,986	23	10	4	2	23	10	6	3	23	10	918,353
C-54 a/	102,689	6	6	1	1	37	36	2	2	1	1	881,444
C-74	3,481	-	-	-	-	-	-	-	-	-	-	-
C-82	6,114	3	49	-	-	-	-	-	-	1	16	120,591
C-97	26,040	1	4	-	-	-	-	-	-	2	8	24,456
C-118 a/	5,036	-	-	-	-	-	-	-	-	1	20	-
C-119	32,472	13	40	4	12	92	283	5	15	3	9	2,604,243
C-121 a/	2,268	-	-	-	-	-	-	-	-	-	-	-
C-124	27,678	4	14	2	7	139	502	2	7	4	14	3,276,389
C-122	412	1	243	-	-	-	-	-	-	-	-	32,223
Other	407	-	-	-	-	-	-	-	-	-	-	-
FIGHTER	433,085	311	72	67	15	79	18	125	29	83	19	26,972,425
Non-Jet (Sub Total)	77,302	63	81	9	12	9	12	19	25	29	38	2,041,500
F-47	6,029	6	100	1	17	1	17	3	50	4	66	349,318
F-51	71,020	57	80	8	11	8	11	16	23	25	35	1,692,182
F-82	253	-	-	-	-	-	-	-	-	-	-	-
Jet (Sub Total)	355,783	248	69	58	16	70	20	106	30	54	15	24,930,925
F-80	55,322	45	81	9	16	9	16	17	31	12	22	2,474,324
T-33	126,408	37	29	11	9	19	15	20	16	14	11	3,276,829
F-84	79,259	80	101	23	29	23	29	39	49	8	10	9,978,592
F-86	59,602	52	87	10	17	12	20	21	35	15	25	6,584,629
Other	332	-	-	-	-	-	-	-	-	-	-	-
F-94	34,860	34	95	5	14	7	20	9	26	5	14	2,616,551
TRAINER	588,120	103	18	13	2	24	4	19	3	103	18	1,797,926
C-45	68,241	17	25	1	1	3	4	2	3	4	6	450,255
T-6	402,468	65	16	11	3	18	4	15	4	88	22	796,374
T-7	15,345	2	13	1	7	3	20	1	7	4	26	87,450
T-11	29,052	5	17	-	-	-	-	1	3	4	14	295,000
T-28	58,149	13	22	-	-	-	-	-	-	2	3	168,847
T-29	14,859	1	7	-	-	-	-	-	-	1	7	-
Other	6	-	-	-	-	-	-	-	-	-	-	-
LIAISON	40,458	6	15	-	-	-	-	-	-	10	25	37,990
HELICOPTER	9,455	8	85	-	-	-	-	-	-	3	32	178,464
MISCELLANEOUS	15,865	3	19	-	-	14	88	-	-	1	6	65,074
THIRD QUARTER - TOTAL	2,015,319	466	23	101	5	234	12	219	11	319	16	72,369,388
BOMBER	425,213	50	12	16	4	105	25	24	6	38	9	34,520,428
Non-Jet (Sub Total)	409,779	41	10	15	4	102	25	22	5	33	8	28,925,281
B-17	12,497	1	8	-	-	-	-	-	-	2	16	15,022
B-25	152,758	4	3	1	1	3	2	2	1	6	4	314,482
B-26	83,203	21	25	5	6	14	17	7	8	10	12	1,763,826
B-29	109,962	6	5	4	4	34	31	5	5	11	10	3,405,544
B-36	21,626	4	18	2	9	25	116	4	18	1	5	18,426,242
B-50	29,733	5	17	3	10	26	87	4	13	3	10	5,000,165
Jet (Sub Total)	15,434	9	58	1	6	3	19	2	13	5	32	5,595,147
B-45	1,869	2	107	-	-	-	-	-	-	-	-	56,896
B-47	13,525	7	52	1	7	3	22	2	15	5	37	5,538,251
Other	40	-	-	-	-	-	-	-	-	-	-	-
CARGO	448,782	23	5	3	1	22	5	10	2	27	6	4,024,246
C-46	36,710	4	11	-	-	-	-	1	3	2	5	287,028
C-47/53 (C-117) a/	221,133	9	4	1	-	3	1	2	1	14	6	327,365
C-54 a/	83,627	2	2	1	1	14	17	2	2	-	-	815,839

TABLE 92 — USAF AND ANG AIRCRAFT ACCIDENTS, RATES AND DOLLAR LOSS BY TYPE AND MODEL — FY 1953 — CONTINUED

TYPE AND MODEL	FLYING HOURS a/	MAJOR ACCIDENTS		FATAL ACCIDENTS b/		FATALITIES c/		AIRCRAFT DESTROYED d/		MINOR ACCIDENTS		DOLLAR LOSS
		No.	Rate	No.	Rate	No.	Rate	No.	Rate	No.	Rate	
THIRD QUARTER - Cont'd												
CARGO - Cont'd												
C-82	5,159	2	39	-	-	-	-	1	19	-	-	$ 410,449
C-97	25,561	-	-	-	-	-	-	-	-	3	12	-
C-118 a/	9,746	-	-	-	-	-	-	-	-	1	10	-
C-119	36,501	5	14	1	3	5	14	4	11	5	14	2,159,488
C-124	25,781	1	4	-	-	-	-	-	-	2	8	24,077
Other	4,564	-	-	-	-	-	-	-	-	-	-	-
FIGHTER	501,194	280	56	65	13	76	15	150	30	151	30	30,108,937
Non-Jet (Sub Total)	53,628	42	78	9	17	9	17	23	43	35	65	1,658,982
F-47	2,952	3	102	2	68	2	68	2	68	4	136	174,671
F-51	50,469	38	75	7	14	7	14	21	42	31	61	1,467,750
F-82	207	1	483	-	-	-	-	-	-	-	-	16,561
Jet (Sub Total)	447,566	238	53	56	13	67	15	127	28	116	26	28,449,955
F-80	59,409	38	64	7	12	7	12	15	25	16	27	2,065,211
T-33	172,880	45	26	8	5	11	6	16	9	26	15	2,763,366
F-84	103,940	73	70	21	20	22	21	52	50	25	23	12,309,802
F-86	76,330	57	75	13	17	16	21	30	39	36	47	7,384,049
F-89	67	-	-	-	-	-	-	-	-	1	-	-
F-92	1	-	-	-	-	-	-	-	-	-	-	-
F-94	34,939	25	72	7	20	11	31	14	40	12	34	3,927,527
TRAINER	569,514	89	16	13	2	18	3	28	5	87	15	2,366,058
C-45	69,947	7	10	-	-	-	-	1	1	7	10	168,853
T-6	375,692	60	16	10	3	14	4	17	5	70	19	847,578
T-7	11,963	2	17	-	-	-	-	1	8	1	8	86,714
T-11	21,707	3	14	-	-	-	-	-	-	3	14	71,826
T-28	67,665	17	25	3	4	4	6	9	13	6	9	1,191,087
Other	35	-	-	-	-	-	-	-	-	-	-	-
T-29	22,505	-	-	-	-	-	-	-	-	-	-	-
LIAISON	43,389	13	30	2	5	5	12	3	7	11	25	156,093
HELICOPTER	10,224	7	68	1	10	1	10	2	20	3	29	234,918
MISCELLANEOUS	17,003	4	24	1	6	7	41	2	12	2	6	958,708
FOURTH QUARTER - TOTAL	2,280,793	549	24	113	5	304	13	251	11	373	16	58,245,047
BOMBER	434,263	49	11	5	1	24	6	11	3	43	10	5,426,920
Non-Jet (Sub Total)	410,586	39	9	5	1	24	6	11	3	39	9	5,016,749
B-17	12,740	-	-	-	-	-	-	-	-	2	16	-
B-25	154,248	6	4	-	-	-	-	2	1	4	3	382,717
B-26	90,713	25	28	1	1	2	2	5	6	15	17	1,356,394
B-29	92,880	4	4	3	3	20	22	3	3	13	14	1,921,012
B-36	26,464	2	8	-	-	-	-	-	-	3	11	192,808
B-50	33,541	2	6	1	3	2	6	1	3	2	6	1,163,818
Jet (Sub Total)	23,677	10	38	-	-	-	-	-	-	4	17	410,171
B-45	4,194	5	119	-	-	-	-	-	-	1	24	151,427
B-47	19,430	5	21	-	-	-	-	-	-	3	15	258,744
Other	53	-	-	-	-	-	-	-	-	-	-	-
CARGO	507,264	32	6	3	1	145	29	9	2	43	8	6,511,032
C-46	43,762	5	11	-	-	-	-	1	2	5	11	296,604
C-47/53 (C-117) a/	243,719	11	5	1	-	1	-	2	1	17	7	324,558
C-54 a/	87,042	1	1	-	-	-	-	1	1	4	3	386,258
C-82	2,463	1	41	-	-	-	-	-	-	-	-	40,197
C-97	29,372	1	3	-	-	-	-	-	-	1	3	24,456
C-119	50,092	7	14	1	2	15	30	3	6	10	20	2,209,164
C-124	30,261	6	20	1	3	129	426	2	7	6	20	3,229,795
Other	20,553	-	-	-	-	-	-	-	-	-	-	-
FIGHTER	609,086	339	56	83	14	99	16	180	30	161	26	40,457,945
Non-Jet (Sub Total)	55,310	34	61	5	9	5	9	18	33	28	51	1,311,143
F-47	2,904	4	138	1	34	1	34	2	69	6	207	177,995
F-51	51,913	30	58	4	8	4	8	16	31	22	42	1,133,148
F-82	493	-	-	-	-	-	-	-	-	-	-	-

TABLE 92 — USAF AND ANG AIRCRAFT ACCIDENTS, RATES AND DOLLAR LOSS BY TYPE AND MODEL — FY 1953 — CONTINUED

TYPE AND MODEL	FLYING HOURS a/	MAJOR ACCIDENTS		FATAL ACCIDENTS b/		FATALITIES c/		AIRCRAFT DESTROYED d/		MINOR ACCIDENTS		DOLLAR LOSS
		No.	Rate	No.	Rate	No.	Rate	No.	Rate	No.	Rate	
FOURTH QUARTER - Cont'd												
FIGHTER - Cont'd												
Jet (Sub Total). . .	553,776	305	55	78	14	94	17	162	29	133	24	$ 39,146,802
F-80	58,256	37	64	10	17	10	17	19	33	21	36	2,648,976
T-33	206,603	83	40	24	12	31	15	39	19	26	13	6,341,648
F-84	130,707	70	54	21	16	21	16	42	32	13	10	10,605,776
F-86	115,311	90	78	18	16	22	19	52	45	55	48	15,507,402
F-89	2,011	-	-	-	-	-	-	-	-	1	50	-
F-94	40,869	25	61	5	12	10	24	10	24	17	42	4,043,000
Other.	19	-	-	-	-	-	-	-	-	-	-	-
TRAINER.	639,756	108	17	18	3	28	4	41	6	110	17	3,366,476
C-45	90,766	11	12	-	-	-	-	2	2	15	17	258,279
T-6.	373,252	64	17	11	3	19	5	24	6	73	20	1,204,320
T-7.	9,485	3	32	-	-	-	-	2	21	3	32	160,428
T-11	20,706	2	10	1	5	1	5	2	10	4	19	177,522
T-28	115,220	28	24	6	5	8	7	11	10	14	12	1,565,927
T-29	29,580	-	-	-	-	-	-	-	-	1	3	-
MK-4	747	-	-	-	-	-	-	-	-	-	-	-
LIAISON.	53,654	7	13	2	4	5	9	2	4	12	22	98,769
HELICOPTER	13,793	10	73	1	7	2	15	4	29	3	22	578,198
MISCELLANEOUS.	22,977	4	17	1	4	1	4	4	17	1	4	1,805,707

Accidents in aircraft which were on bailment contract and/or on loan are included in the above and succeeding tabulations of USAF Aircraft Accidents. However, flying time is not available for B/L aircraft, and accidents in these planes are not included in rate computations. The B/L accidents are listed below.

TABLE 93 — USAF BAILMENT/LOAN ACCIDENTS — FISCAL YEAR 1953

MODEL	MAJOR ACCIDENTS	FATAL ACCIDENTS b/	FATALITIES c/	AIRCRAFT DESTROYED d/	MINOR ACCIDENTS
FISCAL YEAR - TOTAL. .	4	1	2	1	6
B-36.	1	1	2	1	-
B-47.	1	-	-	-	-
C-47.	-	-	-	-	1
C-54.	-	-	-	-	1
F-84.	-	-	-	-	1
F-86.	-	-	-	-	2
F-94.	2	-	-	-	-
X-5	-	-	-	-	1

NOTE: The footnotes below apply to both tables 92 and 93.

a/ Flying Hours include hours flown by Navy for MATS.
b/ More than one fatality may occur as the result of any one fatal accident.
c/ Fatalities include all persons killed and/or missing as the result of major accidents.
d/ Aircraft destroyed includes missing aircraft.

SOURCE: D/Flight Safety Research - The Inspector General

TABLE 94 — USAF AND ANG MAJOR AIRCRAFT ACCIDENTS — BY PHASE OF OPERATIONS

(Includes Air Force Reserve and Civil Air Patrol)

TYPE AND MODEL	MAJOR ACCIDENTS	TAXIING	TAKE-OFF	IN FLIGHT	GO AROUND	LANDING	MISCELLANEOUS a/	UNDETERMINED
TOTAL FY 1953	2,188	65	277	722	92	946	71	15
FIRST QUARTER - TOTAL	626	24	75	192	32	272	26	5
BOMBER	63	3	5	22	2	21	10	-
Non-Jet (Sub Total)	52	3	5	17	2	18	7	-
B-17	2	-	1	1	-	-	-	-
B-25	8	1	-	1	-	4	2	-
B-26	19	-	3	7	-	5	4	-
B-29	19	2	1	7	2	7	-	-
B-36	3	-	-	1	-	1	1	-
B-50	1	-	-	-	-	1	-	-
Jet (Sub Total)	11	-	-	5	-	3	3	-
B-45	5	-	-	2	-	1	2	-
B-47	6	-	-	3	-	2	1	-
CARGO	41	6	2	14	3	14	2	-
C-46	4	2	-	2	-	-	-	-
C-47/53 (C-117)	18	2	1	5	2	7	1	-
C-54	3	-	-	2	-	1	-	-
C-82	1	-	-	-	-	1	-	-
C-97	4	-	-	2	-	2	-	-
C-119	8	2	1	3	1	1	-	-
C-124	3	-	-	-	-	2	1	-
FIGHTER	366	6	42	131	17	158	9	3
Non-Jet (Sub Total)	76	5	8	25	3	35	-	-
F-47	17	2	6	4	1	4	-	-
F-51	59	3	2	21	2	31	-	-
Jet (Sub Total)	290	1	34	106	14	123	9	3
F-80	60	-	6	24	1	27	2	-
T-33	55	-	9	18	4	22	1	1
F-84	74	-	9	33	3	26	3	-
F-86	42	-	6	15	5	14	2	-
F-89	8	-	-	4	-	3	1	-
F-94	51	1	4	12	1	31	-	2
TRAINER	120	7	17	22	10	62	-	2
C-45	12	1	5	3	-	3	-	-
T-6	85	6	7	11	10	49	-	2
T-7	3	-	2	1	-	-	-	-
T-11	8	-	2	-	-	6	-	-
T-28	11	-	1	7	-	3	-	-
T-35	1	-	-	-	-	1	-	-
HELICOPTER	15	-	2	1	-	8	4	-
LIAISON	13	2	5	2	-	4	-	-
MISCELLANEOUS b/	8	-	2	-	-	5	1	-
SECOND QUARTER - TOTAL	547	17	69	155	15	259	25	7
BOMBER	58	5	5	20	-	24	3	1
Non-Jet (Sub Total)	50	5	4	15	-	22	2	1
B-17	1	-	-	1	-	-	-	-
B-25	8	1	-	1	-	5	1	-
B-26	25	2	3	10	-	10	-	-
B-29	8	1	-	1	-	5	-	1
B-36	3	-	1	2	-	-	-	-
B-50	5	1	-	1	-	2	1	-
Jet (Sub Total)	8	-	1	4	-	2	1	-
B-45	5	-	1	3	-	-	1	-
B-47	3	-	-	1	-	2	-	-
CARGO	58	2	10	12	1	29	1	3
C-46	7	-	2	1	-	3	-	1
C-47/53 (C-117)	23	2	5	4	-	11	1	-
C-54	6	-	-	1	1	4	-	-
C-82	3	-	-	1	-	1	-	1
C-97	1	-	-	-	-	1	-	-
C-119	13	-	2	4	-	6	-	1
C-122	1	-	-	-	-	1	-	-
C-124	4	-	1	1	-	2	-	-

TABLE 94 – USAF AND ANG MAJOR AIRCRAFT ACCIDENTS – BY PHASE OF OPERATIONS –(CONTINUED)

TYPE AND MODEL	MAJOR ACCIDENTS	TAXIING	TAKE-OFF	IN FLIGHT	GO AROUND	LANDING	MISCELLANEOUS a/	UNDETERMINED
SECOND QUARTER - Cont'd								
FIGHTER	311	6	36	105	11	136	15	2
Non-Jet (Sub Total)	63	3	8	17	2	30	3	-
F-47	6	1	1	1	-	2	1	-
F-51	57	2	7	16	2	28	2	-
Jet (Sub Total)	248	3	28	88	9	106	12	2
F-80	45	1	8	13	-	19	3	1
T-33	37	-	4	11	1	21	-	-
F-84	80	1	12	31	2	31	3	-
F-86	52	1	1	25	5	14	6	-
F-94	34	-	3	8	1	21	-	1
TRAINER	103	4	16	17	3	58	4	1
C-45	17	1	4	-	-	12	-	-
T-6	65	3	4	14	3	38	2	1
T-7	2	-	2	-	-	-	-	-
T-11	5	-	2	1	-	2	-	-
T-28	13	-	4	2	-	6	1	-
T-29	1	-	-	-	-	-	1	-
HELICOPTER	8	-	-	-	-	6	2	-
LIAISON	6	-	1	-	-	5	-	-
MISCELLANEOUS b/	3	-	1	1	-	1	-	-
THIRD QUARTER - TOTAL	466	10	63	171	16	199	7	-
BOMBER	50	-	10	19	1	20	-	-
Non-Jet (Sub Total)	41	-	9	16	1	15	-	-
B-17	1	-	-	-	-	1	-	-
B-25	4	-	1	-	1	2	-	-
B-26	21	-	5	7	-	9	-	-
B-29	6	-	2	4	-	-	-	-
B-36	4	-	-	3	-	1	-	-
B-50	5	-	1	2	-	2	-	-
Jet (Sub Total)	9	-	1	3	-	5	-	-
B-45	2	-	1	1	-	-	-	-
B-47	7	-	-	2	-	5	-	-
CARGO	23	1	3	6	-	13	-	-
C-46	4	1	-	1	-	2	-	-
C-47/53 (C-117)	9	-	3	1	-	5	-	-
C-54	2	-	-	-	-	2	-	-
C-82	2	-	-	1	-	1	-	-
C-119	5	-	-	2	-	3	-	-
C-124	1	-	-	1	-	-	-	-
FIGHTER	280	4	31	112	10	119	4	-
Non-Jet (Sub Total)	42	3	4	21	1	12	1	-
F-47	3	-	-	3	-	-	-	-
F-51	38	3	4	17	1	12	1	-
F-82	1	-	-	1	-	-	-	-
Jet (Sub Total)	238	1	27	91	9	107	3	-
F-80	38	-	7	14	-	17	-	-
T-33	45	-	4	14	4	22	1	-
F-84	73	-	6	34	3	30	-	-
F-86	57	1	6	20	2	26	2	-
F-94	25	-	4	9	-	12	-	-
TRAINER	89	5	11	28	5	39	1	-
C-45	7	-	2	2	-	3	-	-
T-6	60	4	5	16	4	30	1	-
T-7	2	-	-	-	-	2	-	-
T-11	3	-	1	-	-	2	-	-
T-28	17	1	3	10	1	2	-	-
HELICOPTER	7	-	2	2	-	2	1	-
LIAISON	13	-	4	3	-	5	1	-
MISCELLANEOUS b/	4	-	2	1	-	1	-	-

TABLE 94 — USAF AND ANG MAJOR AIRCRAFT ACCIDENTS — BY PHASE OF OPERATIONS — Continued

TYPE AND MODEL	MAJOR ACCIDENTS	TAXIING	TAKE-OFF	IN FLIGHT	GO AROUND	LANDING	MISCELLANEOUS a/	UNDETERMINED
FOURTH QUARTER - TOTAL. .	549	14	70	204	29	216	13	3
BOMBER.	49	2	5	9	2	28	3	-
Non-Jet (Sub Total). .	39	2	4	6	2	25	-	-
B-25	6	1	2	-	1	2	-	-
B-26	25	-	1	2	1	21	-	-
B-29	4	-	1	2	-	1	-	-
B-36	2	1	-	1	-	-	-	-
B-50	2	-	-	1	-	1	-	-
Jet (Sub Total). .	10	-	1	3	-	3	3	-
B-45	5	-	1	1	-	-	3	-
B-47	5	-	-	2	-	3	-	-
CARGO	32	3	5	6	-	16	2	-
C-46	5	-	1	2	-	2	-	-
C-47/53 (C-117). . .	11	1	2	-	-	7	1	-
C-54	1	-	-	-	-	1	-	-
C-82	1	-	-	-	-	1	-	-
C-97	1	-	-	-	-	-	1	-
C-119.	7	1	2	1	-	3	-	-
C-124.	6	1	-	3	-	2	-	-
FIGHTER	339	7	47	137	14	130	3	1
Non-Jet (Sub Total). .	34	4	5	10	1	14	-	-
F-47	4	-	1	2	-	1	-	-
F-51	30	4	4	8	1	13	-	-
Jet (Sub Total). .	305	3	42	127	13	116	3	1
F-80	37	-	5	18	1	12	1	-
T-33	83	2	7	27	2	44	-	1
F-84	70	1	8	34	4	23	-	-
F-86	90	-	16	38	4	30	2	-
F-94	25	-	6	10	2	7	-	-
TRAINER	108	1	9	42	12	38	4	2
C-45	11	1	3	1	-	4	2	-
T-6.	64	-	4	21	9	27	2	1
T-7.	3	-	-	2	1	-	-	-
T-11	2	-	-	1	-	-	-	1
T-28	28	-	2	17	2	7	-	-
HELICOPTER.	10	-	1	6	-	2	1	-
LIAISON	7	1	2	1	1	2	-	-
MISCELLANEOUS a/. . . .	4	-	1	3	-	-	-	-

a/ Other phases not listed.

b/ All other types aircraft.

SOURCE: D/Flight Safety Research - The Inspector General

TABLE 95 — FACTORS CAUSING USAF AND ANG MAJOR AIRCRAFT ACCIDENTS

(Includes Air Force Reserve and Civil Air Patrol)

TYPE AND MODEL	MAJOR a/ ACCIDENTS	PILOT ERROR	SUPERVISORY ERROR	MAINTENANCE	AIRBASE & AIRWAYS	MATERIEL FAILURE	OTHER b/
TOTAL F.Y. 1953. . .	2,188	1,299	370	195	170	763	472
FIRST QUARTER - TOTAL. .	626	358	76	65	53	230	88
BOMBER	63	27	8	9	8	35	12
Non-Jet (Sub Total) .	52	24	8	7	8	32	9
B-17.	2	2	-	-	-	-	1
B-25.	8	5	3	1	3	4	-
B-26.	19	5	2	4	1	12	1
B-29.	19	10	3	1	4	13	4
B-36.	3	1	-	1	-	3	.3
B-50.	1	1	-	-	-	-	-
Jet (Sub Total) . . .	11	3	-	2	-	3	3
B-45.	5	1	-	2	-	1	1
B-47.	6	2	-	-	-	2	2
CARGO.	41 ·	22	7	6	10	12	12
C-46.	4	3	2	1	1	1	1
C-47/53 (C-117) . .	18	11	4	1	5	5	4
C-54.	3	2	-	-	1	1	1
C-82.	1	1	-	-	1	-	-
C-97.	4	1	-	1	1	2	3
C-119	8	2	1	2	-	3	3
C-124	3	2	-	1	1	-	-
FIGHTER - TOTAL. . . .	366	194	38	30	27	148	54
Non-Jet (Sub Total) .	76	38	8	7	4	35	5
F-47.	17	5	2	1	1	12	2
F-51.	59	33	6	6	3	23	3
Jet (Sub Total) .	290	156	30	23	23	113	49
F-80.	60	37	5	7	3	23	6
T-33.	55	30	4	5	7	10	14
F-84.	74	29	10	3	2	39	18
F-86.	42	22	5	4	4	17	3
F-89.	8	2	-	1	-	5	3
F-94.	51	36	6	3	7	19	5
TRAINER.	120	98	22	10	3	20	7
C-45.	12	8	1	1	1	4	-
T-6	85	74	17	4	2	9	4
T-7	3	2	1	-	-	-	1
T-11.	8	5	-	4	-	4	1
T-28.	11	9	3	1	-	2	1
T-35.	1	-	-	-	-	1	-
HELICOPTER	15	8	-	4	4	7	1
LIAISON.	13	7	-	3	1	4	1
MISCELLANEOUS c/ . . .	8	2	1	3	-	4	1
SECOND QUARTER - TOTAL .	547	383	86	52	35	185	82
BOMBER	58	20	12	8	4	24	15
Non-Jet (Sub Total) .	50	19	11	8	4	19	12
B-17.	1	-	-	1	-	-	-
B-25.	8	3	2	-	-	4	2
B-26.	25	11	9	4	4	6	7
B-29.	8	4	-	2	-	5	1
B-36.	3	-	-	-	-	2	1
B-50.	5	1	-	1	-	2	1
Jet (Sub Total) .	8	1	1	-	-	5	3
B-45.	5	-	-	-	-	3	2
B-47.	3	1	1	-	-	2	1
CARGO.	58	38	16	7	9	18	14
C-46.	7	3	1	-	1	1	3
C-47/53 (C-117) . .	23	18	5	3	4	4	2
C-54.	6	5	2	-	1	3	1
C-82.	3	1	-	1	-	1	1
C-97.	1	1	1	-	-	-	-
C-119	13	6	4	2	-	6	5
C-122	1	-	-	-	1	-	-
C-124	4	4	3	1	2	3	2
FIGHTER - TOTAL. . . .	311	175	37	26	17	114	43
Non-Jet (Sub Total) .	63	31	7	6	-	26	7
F-47.	6	3	1	1	-	2	2
F-51.	57	28	6	5	-	24	5

TABLE 95 – FACTORS CAUSING USAF AND ANG MAJOR AIRCRAFT ACCIDENTS – CONTINUED

TYPE AND MODEL	MAJOR ACCIDENTS a/	PILOT ERROR	SUPERVISORY ERROR	MAINTENANCE	AIRBASE & AIRWAYS	MATERIEL FAILURE	OTHER b/
SECOND QUARTER - Cont'd.							
FIGHTER - Continued							
Jet (Sub Total)	248	144	30	20	17	88	36
F-80	45	27	4	2	2	19	4
T-33	37	28	6	3	-	10	8
F-84	80	40	13	7	7	27	16
F-86	52	26	5	6	2	26	6
F-94	34	23	2	2	6	6	2
TRAINER	103	78	19	10	3	23	8
C-45	17	13	4	1	1	7	2
T-6	65	55	12	4	2	5	4
T-7	2	1	1	-	-	-	1
T-11	5	4	1	2	-	3	-
T-28	13	5	1	2	-	8	1
T-29	1	-	-	1	-	-	-
HELICOPTER	8	6	1	-	1	4	-
LIAISON	6	4	1	1	-	1	-
MISCELLANEOUS c/	3	2	-	-	1	1	2
THIRD QUARTER - TOTAL	466	302	108	40	34	142	130
BOMBER	50	23	11	7	1	22	22
Non-Jet (Sub Total)	41	19	9	6	1	17	20
B-17	1	-	-	-	-	1	-
B-25	4	3	1	1	-	2	1
B-26	21	9	4	4	1	6	14
B-29	6	2	-	1	-	5	1
B-36	4	1	2	-	-	1	2
B-50	5	4	2	-	-	2	2
Jet (Sub Total)	9	4	2	1	-	5	2
B-45	2	1	-	-	-	2	1
B-47	7	3	2	1	-	3	1
CARGO	23	17	8	2	5	9	10
C-46	4	4	4	-	1	1	2
C-47/53 (C-117)	9	8	3	-	2	2	4
C-54	2	2	-	-	-	-	2
C-82	2	1	1	1	-	1	-
C-119	5	2	-	1	2	4	2
C-124	1	-	-	-	-	1	-
FIGHTER - TOTAL	280	182	55	22	24	85	73
Non-Jet (Sub Total)	42	27	8	4	2	15	11
F-47	3	1	-	1	-	1	2
F-51	38	26	8	3	2	13	9
F-82	1	-	-	-	-	1	-
Jet (Sub Total)	238	155	47	18	22	70	62
F-80	38	27	5	4	4	9	7
T-33	45	38	12	3	2	8	12
F-84	73	49	17	4	10	20	20
F-86	57	29	10	5	3	26	13
F-94	25	12	3	2	3	7	10
TRAINER	89	63	23	9	2	18	19
C-45	7	4	2	2	1	3	2
T-6	60	49	19	1	1	4	15
T-7	2	-	-	1	-	2	-
T-11	3	1	-	2	-	-	-
T-28	17	9	2	3	-	9	2
HELICOPTER	7	4	1	-	1	2	2
LIAISON	13	9	8	-	1	4	2
MISCELLANEOUS c/	4	4	2	-	-	2	2
FOURTH QUARTER - TOTAL	549	316	100	38	48	206	172
BOMBER	49	27	11	5	4	28	14
Non-Jet (Sub Total)	39	25	10	3	4	20	14
B-25	6	4	2	-	1	1	5

TABLE 95 – FACTORS CAUSING USAF AND ANG MAJOR AIRCRAFT ACCIDENTS – CONTINUED

TYPE AND MODEL	MAJOR a/ ACCIDENTS	PILOT ERROR	SUPERVISORY ERROR	MAINTENANCE	AIRBASE & AIRWAYS	MATERIEL FAILURE	OTHER b/
FOURTH QUARTER - Cont'd.							
BOMBER - Continued							
B-26	25	16	5	1	3	14	7
B-29	4	4	2	2	-	2	1
B-36	2	1	1	-	-	1	1
B-50	2	-	-	-	-	2	-
Jet (Sub Total)	10	2	1	2	-	8	-
B-45	5	1	-	-	-	5	-
B-47	5	1	1	2	-	3	-
CARGO	32	19	8	4	5	8	16
C-46	5	3	1	2	2	1	3
C-47/53 (C-117)	11	9	4	1	3	1	8
C-54	1	1	-	-	-	-	1
C-82	1	1	-	-	-	-	-
C-97	1	-	-	-	-	1	-
C-119	7	2	2	1	-	1	4
C-124	6	3	1	-	-	4	-
FIGHTER - TOTAL	339	188	50	19	35	124	109
Non-Jet (Sub Total)	34	23	7	1	2	14	6
F-47	4	4	3	-	-	1	2
F-51	30	19	4	1	2	13	4
Jet (Sub Total)	305	165	43	18	33	110	103
F-80	37	22	3	1	4	17	11
T-33	83	54	12	4	8	21	35
F-84	70	33	10	1	5	30	24
F-86	90	41	12	9	11	38	24
F-94	25	15	6	3	5	4	9
TRAINER	108	68	24	9	3	38	24
C-45	11	9	4	1	-	7	4
T-6	64	46	13	5	2	9	14
T-7	3	3	1	-	1	2	1
T-11	2	1	1	-	-	1	1
T-28	28	9	5	3	-	19	4
HELICOPTER	10	6	4	-	1	4	3
LIAISON	7	5	2	-	-	1	4
MISCELLANEOUS c/	4	3	1	1	-	3	2

a/ Total Cause Factors may exceed total accidents since many accidents have multiple causes.

b/ Other crew member error, other personnel, miscellaneous unsafe conditions, and undetermined.

c/ All other types.

SOURCE: D/Flight Safety Research - The Inspector General

TABLE 96 — SELECTED CONDITIONS AFFECTING USAF/ANG MAJOR AIRCRAFT ACCIDENTS

(Includes Air Force Reserve and Civil Air Patrol)

TYPE AND MODEL	MAJOR ACCIDENTS a/	INVOLVED FACTORS a/						
		FIRE BEFORE ACCIDENT	FIRE AFTER ACCIDENT	WEATHER	NON-COMPLIANCE WITH T/O	VIOLATIONS	FORCED LANDING	OUT OF FUEL
TOTAL FY 1953 . . .	2,188	178	468	282	29	208	323	75
FIRST QUARTER - TOTAL .	626	71	140	73	12	53	95	10
BOMBER.	63	18	13	6	-	6	-	-
Non-Jet (Sub Total).	52	14	11	6	-	6	-	-
B-17	2	1	1	-	-	-	-	-
B-25	8	2	-	1	-	2	-	-
B-26	19	4	3	1	-	2	-	-
B-29	19	7	5	4	-	2	-	-
B-36	3	-	2	-	-	-	-	-
B-50	1	-	-	-	-	-	-	-
Jet (Sub Total).	11	4	2	-	-	-	-	-
B-45	5	3	1	-	-	-	-	-
B-47	6	1	1	-	-	-	-	-
CARGO	41	2	6	14	2	5	6	-
C-46	4	-	1	1	-	1	-	-
C-47/53 (C-117). .	18	2	3	7	1	1	4	-
C-54	3	-	-	1	-	1	-	-
C-82	1	-	1	-	-	-	-	-
C-97	4	-	-	2	-	1	-	-
C-119.	8	-	1	2	1	1	2	-
C-124.	3	-	-	1	-	-	-	-
FIGHTER	366	51	103	34	10	25	62	8
Non-Jet (Sub Total).	76	8	15	6	-	8	18	-
F-47	17	5	4	1	-	3	4	-
F-51	59	3	11	5	-	5	14	-
Jet (Sub Total).	290	43	88	28	10	17	44	8
F-80	60	9	16	3	3	3	13	2
T-33	55	4	22	10	3	5	9	2
F-84	74	14	20	3	-	3	12	-
F-86	42	10	16	3	3	5	5	3
F-89	8	2	4	-	-	-	-	-
F-94	51	4	10	9	1	1	5	1
TRAINER	120	-	16	12	-	14	17	2
C-45	12	-	2	2	-	1	2	1
T-6.	85	-	7	8	-	11	11	-
T-7.	3	-	1	2	-	-	1	-
T-11	8	-	-	-	-	-	-	-
T-28	11	-	5	-	-	2	3	1
T-35	1	-	1	-	-	-	-	-
HELICOPTER.	15	-	1	4	-	-	4	-
LIAISON	13	-	1	3	-	3	4	-
MISCELLANEOUS b/. . .	8	-	-	-	-	-	2	-
SECOND QUARTER - TOTAL.	547	38	100	87	2	66	79	20
BOMBER.	58	6	12	11	1	10	4	3
Non-Jet (Sub Total).	50	5	9	10	1	9	4	3
B-17	1	1	-	-	-	-	-	-
B-25	8	-	1	-	-	1	1	-
B-26	25	1	5	5	1	5	-	3
B-29	8	1	-	4	-	2	2	-
B-36	3	1	1	-	-	-	-	-
B-50	5	1	2	1	-	1	1	-
Jet (Sub Total).	8	1	3	1	-	1	-	-
B-45	5	1	3	-	-	-	-	-
B-47	3	-	-	1	-	1	-	-
CARGO	58	1	11	23	-	12	3	-
C-46	7	-	-	2	-	1	1	-
C-47/53 (C-117). .	23	-	3	10	-	6	1	-
C-54	6	-	2	4	-	3	-	-
C-82	3	-	-	-	-	-	-	-
C-97	1	-	-	-	-	1	-	-
C-119.	13	1	4	5	-	1	1	-
C-122.	1	-	-	-	-	-	-	-
C-124.	4	-	2	2	-	-	-	-

TABLE 96 — SELECTED CONDITIONS AFFECTING USAF ANG MAJOR AIRCRAFT ACCIDENTS — Continued

TYPE AND MODEL	MAJOR ACCIDENTS a/	INVOLVED FACTORS a/						
		FIRE BEFORE ACCIDENT	FIRE AFTER ACCIDENT	WEATHER	NON-COMPLIANCE WITH T/O	VIOLATIONS	FORCED LANDING	OUT OF FUEL
SECOND QUARTER - Cont'd								
FIGHTER	311	31	74	34	1	25	47	14
Non-Jet (Sub Total)	63	5	10	2	-	6	8	1
F-47	6	1	3	-	-	1	2	-
F-51	57	4	7	2	-	5	6	1
Jet (Sub Total)	248	26	64	32	1	19	39	13
F-80	45	4	9	3	-	4	6	-
T-33	37	-	11	7	-	1	9	4
F-84	80	7	27	9	1	9	14	4
F-86	52	12	14	6	-	4	9	4
F-94	34	3	3	7	-	1	1	1
TRAINER	103	-	3	17	-	18	20	3
C-45	17	-	1	4	-	3	4	-
T-6	65	-	2	10	-	10	7	2
T-7	2	-	-	1	-	-	-	-
T-11	5	-	-	2	-	2	1	-
T-28	13	-	-	-	-	3	8	1
T-29	1	-	-	-	-	-	-	-
HELICOPTER	8	-	-	1	-	1	4	-
LIAISON	6	-	-	-	-	-	1	-
MISCELLANEOUS b/	3	-	-	1	-	-	-	-
THIRD QUARTER - TOTAL	466	28	98	58	4	47	61	25
BOMBER	50	4	16	8	1	7	3	1
Non-Jet (Sub Total)	41	3	13	8	1	7	3	1
B-17	1	-	-	-	-	-	-	-
B-25	4	-	-	1	-	1	2	-
B-26	21	-	5	4	1	4	-	-
B-29	6	3	2	-	-	-	1	-
B-36	4	-	4	2	-	1	-	1
B-50	5	-	2	1	-	1	-	-
Jet (Sub Total)	9	1	3	-	-	-	-	-
B-45	2	1	-	-	-	-	-	-
B-47	7	-	3	-	-	-	-	-
CARGO	23	1	5	8	-	6	2	1
C-46	4	-	-	2	-	2	-	1
C-47/53 (C-117)	9	-	1	2	-	3	2	-
C-54	2	-	2	2	-	-	-	-
C-82	2	-	-	-	-	-	-	-
C-119	5	-	2	2	-	1	-	-
C-124	1	1	-	-	-	-	-	-
FIGHTER	280	21	71	30	2	19	43	18
Non-Jet (Sub Total)	42	4	10	5	-	3	11	2
F-47	3	-	2	1	-	-	-	-
F-51	38	4	8	4	-	3	11	2
F-82	1	-	-	-	-	-	-	-
Jet (Sub Total)	238	17	61	25	2	16	32	16
F-80	38	2	7	3	2	-	3	1
T-33	45	-	8	7	-	5	5	6
F-84	73	8	23	8	-	4	10	2
F-86	57	6	15	5	-	5	11	7
F-94	25	1	8	2	-	2	3	-
TRAINER	89	2	5	10	1	12	9	3
C-45	7	-	-	2	-	1	2	-
T-6	60	1	3	8	-	9	1	3
T-7	2	-	-	-	-	-	1	-
T-11	3	-	-	-	1	-	-	-
T-28	17	1	2	-	-	2	5	-
HELICOPTER	7	-	-	-	-	-	2	1
LIAISON	13	-	-	1	-	2	2	1
MISCELLANEOUS b/	4	-	1	1	-	1	-	-

TABLE 96 — SELECTED CONDITIONS AFFECTING USAF ANG MAJOR AIRCRAFT ACCIDENTS — Continued

TYPE AND MODEL	MAJOR ACCIDENTS a/	INVOLVED FACTORS a/						
		FIRE BEFORE ACCIDENT	FIRE AFTER ACCIDENT	WEATHER	NON-COMPLIANCE WITH T/O	VIOLATIONS	FORCED LANDING	OUT OF FUEL
FOURTH QUARTER - TOTAL.	549	41	130	64	11	42	88	20
BOMBER.	49	3	11	6	2	7	4	-
Non-Jet (Sub Total).	39	3	6	6	1	7	4	-
B-25	6	1	-	2	-	-	1	-
B-26	25	1	3	4	-	6	1	-
B-29	4	1	2	-	1	1	1	-
B-36	2	-	-	-	-	-	-	-
B-50	2	-	1	-	-	-	1	-
Jet (Sub Total).	10	-	5	-	1	-	-	-
B-45	5	-	4	-	-	-	-	-
B-47	5	-	1	-	1	-	-	-
CARGO	32	6	2	9	-	5	3	1
C-46	5	1	-	2	-	1	1	-
C-47/53 (C-117). .	21	1	1	6	-	2	2	1
C-54	1	-	-	1	-	-	-	-
C-82	1	-	-	-	-	-	-	-
C-97	1	1	-	-	-	-	-	-
C-119.	7	-	-	-	-	1	-	-
C-124.	6	3	1	-	-	1	-	-
FIGHTER	339	30	106	37	6	19	53	14
Non-Jet (Sub Total).	34	1	7	3	-	2	5	-
F-47	4	-	-	2	-	1	1	-
F-51	30	1	7	1	-	1	4	-
Jet (Sub Total).	305	29	99	34	6	17	48	14
F-80	37	5	8	4	2	3	9	-
T-33	83	3	28	11	1	5	12	6
F-84	70	4	27	10	-	5	10	3
F-86	90	15	32	5	-	4	14	5
F-94	25	2	4	4	3	-	3	-
TRAINER	108	2	8	7	2	10	24	4
C-45	11	-	-	2	1	-	1	-
T-6.	64	2	3	4	1	7	8	2
T-7.	3	-	-	-	-	-	2	1
T-11	2	-	-	1	-	-	1	-
T-28	28	-	5	-	-	3	12	1
HELICOPTER.	10	-	1	2	-	-	3	-
LIAISON	7	-	1	2	-	1	-	-
MISCELLANEOUS b/. . .	4	-	1	1	1	-	1	1

a/ None, one or more than one, factor may be involved in any one aircraft accident.
b/ All other types.

SOURCE: D/Flight Safety Research - The Inspector General

TABLE 97 — USAF AND ANG MAJOR ACCIDENTS AND DOLLAR LOSS BY PRIMARY CAUSE FACTORS OF ACCIDENTS — FY 1953

Since multi-plane accidents are analyzed statistically as single accidents and are tabulated by responsible aircraft, the dollar losses shown may include losses in models other than the model listed in the line total. The line totals indicate accident dollar loss for which each model was responsible.

TYPE AND MODEL	TOTAL USAF/ANG		PILOT ERROR		SUPERVISORY ERROR		MAINTENANCE		MATERIEL FAILURE		AIRBASE & AIRWAYS		OTHER a/	
	Number	Dollar Loss	Number	Dollar Loss	Number	Dollar Loss	Number	Dollar Loss	Number	Dollar Loss	Number	Dollar Loss	Number	Dollar Loss
TOTAL FY 1953	2,188	$ 245,656,671	1,126	$ 92,402,225	57	$ 15,177,310	124	$ 8,968,799	595	$ 79,247,480	14	$ 1,117,239	272	$ 48,743,618
FIRST QUARTER - TOTAL	626	62,641,732	323	20,821,900	10	1,655,917	42	2,948,044	180	24,406,477	3	45,566	68	12,763,828
BOMBER	63	20,159,863	25	5,694,274	-	-	6	292,773	27	8,252,788	1	19,335	4	5,900,693
Non-Jet (Sub Total)	52	13,983,491	22	5,566,966	-	-	4	259,149	24	8,125,480	1	19,335	1	12,561
B-17	2	239,259	2	239,259	-	-	-	-	-	-	-	-	-	-
B-25	8	398,509	3	174,244	-	-	1	38,670	3	166,260	1	19,335	-	-
B-26	19	1,239,426	5	463,665	-	-	3	220,479	10	542,721	-	-	1	12,561
B-29	19	7,302,704	10	4,591,348	-	-	-	-	9	2,711,356	-	-	-	-
B-36	3	4,784,835	1	79,692	-	-	-	-	2	4,705,143	-	-	-	-
B-50	1	18,758	1	18,758	-	-	-	-	-	-	-	-	-	-
Jet (Sub Total)	11	6,176,372	3	127,308	-	-	2	33,624	3	127,308	-	-	3	5,888,132
B-45	5	84,060	1	16,812	-	-	2	33,624	1	16,812	-	-	1	16,812
B-47	6	6,092,312	2	110,496	-	-	-	-	2	110,496	-	-	2	5,871,320
CARGO	41	2,898,113	21	1,413,775	1	14,717	4	922,295	7	358,548	-	-	8	188,778
C-46	4	369,061	3	277,229	-	-	-	-	1	91,832	-	-	-	-
C-47/53 (C-117)	18	758,249	11	540,826	1	14,717	-	-	4	202,706	-	-	2	-
C-54	3	146,997	2	97,998	-	-	-	-	-	-	-	-	1	48,999
C-82	1	370,252	1	370,252	-	-	-	-	-	-	-	-	-	-
C-97	4	87,528	1	21,882	-	-	1	21,882	-	-	-	-	2	43,764
C-119	8	1,077,727	1	46,722	-	-	2	870,980	2	64,010	-	-	3	96,015
C-124	3	88,299	2	58,866	-	-	1	29,433	-	-	-	-	-	-
FIGHTER	366	34,561,201	169	11,291,676	8	1,598,261	21	1,153,726	119	14,333,780	-	-	49	6,183,758
Non-Jet (Sub Total)	76	2,801,739	32	1,113,763	2	57,982	5	148,574	32	1,230,745	-	-	5	250,675
F-47	17	714,827	4	176,047	1	7,806	-	-	10	443,727	-	-	2	87,247
F-51	59	2,086,912	28	937,716	1	50,176	5	148,574	22	787,018	-	-	3	163,428
Jet (Sub Total)	290	31,759,462	137	10,177,913	6	1,540,279	16	1,005,152	87	13,103,035	-	-	44	5,933,083
F-80	60	4,220,337	30	1,926,514	1	18,452	5	240,465	19	1,500,219	-	-	5	534,687
T-33	55	3,407,200	28	1,218,983	-	-	3	57,990	10	693,749	-	-	14	1,436,478
F-84	74	10,337,507	26	2,923,617	1	398,553	2	421,002	29	4,001,402	-	-	16	2,592,933
F-86	42	6,202,460	17	1,843,652	3	915,167	3	228,524	16	2,920,734	-	-	3	294,383
F-89	8	3,504,929	2	35,424	-	-	-	-	5	3,469,505	-	-	1	-
F-94	51	4,087,029	34	2,229,723	1	208,107	3	57,171	8	517,426	-	-	5	1,074,602
TRAINER	120	3,108,802	93	2,216,916	1	42,939	4	196,752	16	385,596	-	-	6	266,599
C-45	12	377,666	8	191,905	-	-	1	97,167	3	88,594	-	-	-	-
T-6	85	1,058,389	71	817,982	1	42,939	2	29,439	7	92,880	-	-	4	75,149
T-7	3	216,634	2	143,716	-	-	-	-	-	-	-	-	1	72,918
T-11	8	294,704	4	152,732	-	-	1	70,146	3	71,826	-	-	-	-
T-28	11	1,158,472	8	910,581	-	-	-	-	2	129,359	-	-	1	118,532
T-35	1	2,937	-	-	-	-	-	-	1	2,937	-	-	-	-
HELICOPTER	15	929,016	6	70,916	-	-	3	305,502	4	317,050	1	11,548	1	224,000
LIAISON	13	181,431	7	69,269	-	-	2	44,459	3	53,020	1	14,683	-	-
MISCELLANEOUS	8	803,306	2	65,074	-	-	2	32,537	-	705,695	-	-	-	-

TABLE 97 – USAF AND ANG MAJOR ACCIDENTS AND DOLLAR LOSS BY PRIMARY CAUSE FACTORS OF ACCIDENTS – FY 1953 – CONTINUED

TYPE AND MODEL	TOTAL USAF/ANG		PILOT ERROR		SUPERVISORY ERROR		MAINTENANCE		MATERIEL FAILURE		AIRBASE & AIRWAYS		OTHER a/	
	Number	Dollar Loss	Number	Dollar Loss	Number	Dollar Loss	Number	Dollar Loss	Number	Dollar Loss	Number	Dollar Loss	Number	Dollar Loss
SECOND QUARTER - TOTAL	547	$ 52,400,504	282	$ 22,276,102	19	$ 2,106,926	32	$ 1,112,223	144	$ 14,696,558	8	$ 953,985	62	$ 11,254,710
BOMBER	58	13,827,265	18	1,903,532	4	624,954	5	90,221	17	6,318,195	1	191,916	13	4,698,447
Non-Jet (Sub Total)	50	8,354,326	17	1,848,284	4	624,954	5	90,221	13	3,156,024	1	191,916	10	2,442,927
B-17	1	15,022	-	-	-	-	1	15,022	-	-	-	-	-	-
B-25	8	237,991	3	38,670	-	-	-	-	3	176,576	-	-	2	22,745
B-26	25	1,989,247	9	481,137	4	624,954	3	37,683	3	222,975	1	191,916	5	430,582
B-29	8	2,079,436	4	120,656	-	-	-	-	3	1,295,195	-	-	1	663,585
B-36	3	239,076	-	-	-	-	-	-	2	159,384	-	-	1	79,692
B-50	5	3,793,554	1	1,207,821	-	-	1	37,516	2	1,301,894	-	-	1	1,246,323
Jet (Sub Total)	8	5,472,939	1	55,248	-	-	-	-	4	3,162,171	-	-	3	2,255,520
B-45	5	5,300,779	-	-	-	-	-	-	3	3,106,923	-	-	2	2,193,856
B-47	3	172,160	1	55,248	-	-	-	-	1	55,248	-	-	1	61,664
CARGO	58	8,933,509	34	6,585,181	2	29,434	3	56,646	9	689,253	2	471,867	8	1,101,128
C-46	7	1,037,150	3	506,614	-	-	-	-	1	11,961	-	-	3	518,575
C-47/53 (C-117)	23	957,013	17	879,964	2	29,434	2	16,449	2	31,166	-	-	-	-
C-54	6	881,444	4	441,800	-	-	-	-	-	-	1	439,644	1	-
C-82	3	120,591	-	-	-	-	1	40,197	1	40,197	-	-	1	40,197
C-97	1	24,456	1	24,456	-	-	-	-	-	-	-	-	-	-
C-119	13	2,604,243	5	1,455,958	-	-	-	-	5	605,929	-	-	3	542,356
C-122	1	32,223	-	-	-	-	-	-	-	-	1	32,223	-	-
C-124	4	3,276,389	4	3,276,389	-	-	-	-	-	-	-	-	-	-
FIGHTER	311	27,560,276	150	12,401,696	8	1,364,954	17	893,781	96	7,274,618	5	290,202	35	5,335,025
Non-Jet (Sub Total)	63	2,026,348	28	862,903	1	15,152	5	149,077	24	699,273	-	-	5	299,943
F-47	6	349,318	3	174,437	-	-	1	84,897	1	4,877	-	-	1	85,107
F-51	57	1,677,030	25	688,466	1	15,152	4	64,180	23	694,396	-	-	4	214,836
Jet (Sub Total)	248	25,533,928	122	11,538,793	7	1,349,802	12	744,704	72	6,575,345	5	290,202	30	5,035,082
F-80	45	2,549,498	24	1,342,248	-	-	2	130,111	17	823,976	-	-	2	253,163
T-33	37	3,238,169	23	1,984,222	2	154,229	-	-	6	548,009	-	-	6	551,709
F-84	80	9,978,592	32	3,293,315	3	493,391	5	307,822	23	2,832,684	1	24,330	16	3,027,050
F-86	52	6,524,607	20	2,650,519	2	702,182	4	105,034	22	2,273,556	-	-	4	793,316
F-94	34	3,243,062	23	2,268,489	-	-	1	201,737	4	97,120	4	265,872	2	409,844
TRAINER	103	1,797,926	70	1,169,475	4	80,642	6	68,503	18	359,196	-	-	5	120,110
C-45	17	450,255	10	250,653	-	-	-	-	6	182,585	-	-	1	17,017
T-6	65	796,374	52	657,985	4	80,642	2	9,436	4	18,872	-	-	3	29,439
T-7	2	87,450	1	13,796	-	-	-	-	-	-	-	-	1	73,654
T-11	5	295,000	3	200,912	-	-	1	23,942	1	70,146	-	-	-	-
T-28	13	168,847	4	46,129	-	-	2	35,125	7	87,593	-	-	-	-
T-29	1	-	-	-	-	-	1	-	-	-	-	-	-	-
HELICOPTER	8	178,464	4	126,180	1	6,942	-	-	3	45,342	-	-	-	-
LIAISON	5	37,990	4	24,964	-	-	1	3,072	1	9,954	-	-	-	-
MISCELLANEOUS	3	65,074	2	65,074	-	-	-	-	-	-	-	-	1	-

TABLE 97 — USAF AND ANG MAJOR ACCIDENTS AND DOLLAR LOSS BY PRIMARY CAUSE FACTORS OF ACCIDENTS — FY 1953 — CONTINUED

TYPE AND MODEL	TOTAL USAF/ANG		PILOT ERROR		SUPERVISORY ERROR		MAINTENANCE		MATERIEL FAILURE		AIRBASE & AIRWAYS		OTHER a/	
	Number	Dollar Loss	Number	Dollar Loss	Number	Dollar Loss	Number	Dollar Loss	Number	Dollar Loss	Number	Dollar Loss	Number	Dollar Loss
THIRD QUARTER - TOTAL	466	$ 72,369,388	254	$ 25,678,935	17	$ 10,236,625	24	$ 2,171,569	107	$ 20,471,686	1	$ 52,942	63	$ 13,757,631
BOMBER	50	34,520,428	14	6,529,344	2	9,077,418	3	702,650	16	11,333,709	-	-	15	6,877,307
Non-Jet (Sub Total)	41	28,925,281	10	4,061,369	2	9,077,418	2	640,986	13	8,296,649	-	-	14	6,848,859
B-17	1	15,022	-	-	-	-	-	-	1	15,022	-	-	-	-
B-25	4	314,482	1	22,745	-	-	-	-	2	157,241	-	-	1	134,496
B-26	21	1,763,826	6	303,540	-	-	1	13,809	4	55,236	-	-	10	1,391,241
B-29	6	3,405,544	-	-	-	-	1	627,177	4	1,980,523	-	-	1	797,844
B-36	4	18,426,242	-	-	2	9,077,418	-	-	1	4,842,304	-	-	1	4,506,520
B-50	5	5,000,165	3	3,735,084	-	-	-	-	1	1,246,323	-	-	1	18,758
Jet (Sub Total)	9	5,595,147	4	2,467,975	-	-	1	61,664	3	3,037,060	-	-	1	28,448
B-45	2	56,896	1	28,448	-	-	-	-	-	-	-	-	1	28,448
B-47	7	5,538,251	3	2,439,527	-	-	1	61,664	3	3,037,060	-	-	-	-
CARGO	23	3,972,015	15	2,184,203	-	-	2	475,453	5	1,295,910	-	-	1	16,449
C-46	4	287,028	4	287,028	-	-	-	-	-	-	-	-	-	-
C-47/53 (C-117)	9	327,365	7	294,467	-	-	-	-	1	16,449	-	-	1	16,449
C-54	2	763,608	2	763,608	-	-	-	-	-	-	-	-	-	-
C-82	2	410,449	1	370,252	-	-	1	40,197	-	-	-	-	-	-
C-119	5	2,159,488	1	468,848	-	-	1	435,256	3	1,255,384	-	-	-	-
C-124	1	24,077	-	-	-	-	-	-	1	24,077	-	-	-	-
FIGHTER	280	30,161,168	156	14,607,332	8	1,111,888	14	691,763	64	7,127,434	1	52,942	37	6,569,809
Non-Jet (Sub Total)	42	1,658,982	23	1,026,543	-	-	1	16,938	14	370,244	1	52,942	3	192,315
F-47	3	174,671	1	84,897	-	-	-	-	1	4,877	-	-	1	84,897
F-51	38	1,467,750	22	941,646	-	-	1	16,938	12	348,806	1	52,942	2	107,418
F-82	1	16,561	-	-	-	-	-	-	1	16,561	-	-	-	-
Jet (Sub Total)	238	28,502,186	133	13,580,789	8	1,111,888	13	674,825	50	6,757,190	-	-	34	6,377,494
F-80	38	2,065,211	24	1,049,562	-	-	3	206,501	8	528,480	-	-	3	280,358
F-84	73	12,285,472	41	6,042,733	4	988,846	3	288,673	15	2,757,771	-	-	10	2,207,449
T-33	45	2,763,366	34	2,118,503	2	45,232	2	45,232	3	67,848	-	-	4	486,551
F-86	57	7,384,049	24	3,033,486	1	27,459	3	82,377	19	2,223,394	-	-	10	2,017,333
F-94	25	4,004,088	10	1,336,205	1	50,351	2	52,042	5	1,179,697	-	-	7	1,385,793
TRAINER	89	2,366,058	56	1,197,910	4	24,365	5	301,703	16	607,679	-	-	8	234,401
C-45	7	168,853	3	100,785	-	-	1	17,617	3	51,051	-	-	-	-
T-6	60	847,578	45	546,983	4	24,365	-	-	4	54,946	-	-	7	221,284
T-7	2	86,714	-	-	-	-	-	-	2	86,714	-	-	-	-
T-11	3	71,826	1	23,942	-	-	2	47,884	-	-	-	-	-	-
T-28	17	1,191,087	7	526,200	-	-	2	236,802	7	414,968	-	-	1	13,117
HELICOPTER	7	234,918	3	118,270	1	17,960	-	-	2	80,728	-	-	1	17,960
LIAISON	13	156,093	7	83,168	2	4,994	-	-	3	26,226	-	-	1	41,705
MISCELLANEOUS	4	958,708	3	958,708	-	-	-	-	1	-	-	-	-	-

TABLE 97 — USAF AND ANG MAJOR ACCIDENTS AND DOLLAR LOSS BY PRIMARY CAUSE FACTORS OF ACCIDENTS — FY 1953 — CONTINUED

TYPE AND MODEL	TOTAL USAF/ANG		PILOT ERROR		SUPERVISORY ERROR		MAINTENANCE		MATERIEL FAILURE		AIRBASE & AIRWAYS		OTHER a/	
	Number	Dollar Loss	Number	Dollar Loss	Number	Dollar Loss	Number	Dollar Loss	Number	Dollar Loss	Number	Dollar Loss	Number	Dollar Loss
FOURTH QUARTER - TOTAL	549	$ 58,245,047	267	$ 23,625,288	11	$ 1,177,842	26	$ 2,736,963	164	$ 19,672,759	2	$ 64,746	79	$ 10,967,449
BOMBER	49	5,426,920	20	2,087,666	2	261,372	2	257,021	21	2,690,471	-	-	4	130,390
Non-Jet (Sub Total)	39	5,016,749	19	2,038,396	2	261,372	1	195,357	13	2,391,234	-	-	4	130,390
B-25	6	382,717	3	179,986	1	45,490	-	-	1	134,496	-	-	1	22,745
B-26	25	1,356,394	13	564,575	1	215,882	1	195,357	8	352,627	-	-	2	27,953
B-29	4	1,921,012	3	1,293,835	-	-	1	-	1	627,177	-	-	-	-
B-36	2	192,808	-	-	-	-	-	-	1	113,116	-	-	1	79,692
B-50	2	1,163,818	-	-	-	-	-	-	2	1,163,818	-	-	-	-
Jet (Sub Total)	10	410,171	1	49,270	-	-	1	61,664	8	299,237	-	-	-	-
B-45	5	151,427	-	-	-	-	-	-	5	151,427	-	-	-	-
B-47	5	258,744	1	49,270	-	-	1	61,664	3	147,810	-	-	-	-
CARGO	32	4,884,952	17	2,012,530	1	24,638	3	288,483	6	1,970,060	-	-	5	589,241
C-46	5	296,604	3	32,759	-	-	2	263,845	-	-	-	-	-	-
C-47/53 (C-117)	11	324,558	8	195,211	-	-	-	-	-	-	-	-	3	129,347
C-54	1	386,258	1	386,258	-	-	-	-	-	-	-	-	-	-
C-82	1	40,197	1	40,197	-	-	-	-	-	-	-	-	-	-
C-97	1	24,456	-	-	-	-	-	-	1	24,456	-	-	-	-
C-119	7	583,084	2	49,276	1	24,638	1	24,638	1	24,638	-	-	2	459,894
C-124	6	3,229,795	2	1,308,829	-	-	-	-	4	1,920,966	-	-	-	-
FIGHTER	339	42,084,025	160	16,784,780	6	747,840	13	1,626,395	102	13,367,284	2	64,746	56	9,492,980
Non-Jet (Sub Total)	34	1,311,143	22	848,941	-	-	-	-	10	357,550	-	-	2	104,652
F-47	4	177,995	4	177,995	-	-	-	-	-	-	-	-	-	-
F-51	30	1,133,148	18	670,946	-	-	-	-	10	357,550	-	-	2	104,652
Jet (Sub Total)	305	40,772,882	138	15,935,839	6	747,840	13	1,626,395	92	13,009,734	2	64,746	54	9,388,328
F-80	37	2,523,205	17	857,542	-	-	1	18,623	15	1,267,251	-	-	4	379,789
T-33	83	6,341,648	48	2,838,334	3	296,542	1	137,017	12	732,046	-	-	19	2,337,709
F-84	70	12,231,856	27	5,849,101	1	48,660	1	240,673	28	3,519,099	1	30,778	12	2,543,545
F-86	90	15,633,173	33	4,435,949	-	-	8	1,170,038	33	7,202,412	1	33,968	15	2,790,806
F-94	25	4,043,000	13	1,954,913	2	402,638	2	60,044	4	288,926	-	-	14	1,336,479
TRAINER	108	3,366,476	57	1,455,486	2	143,992	7	143,290	30	883,623	-	-	12	740,085
C-45	11	258,279	5	120,793	-	-	1	17,017	4	67,500	-	-	1	52,969
T-6	64	1,204,320	44	620,602	1	25,591	4	100,039	8	192,837	-	-	7	265,251
T-7	3	160,428	2	90,245	-	-	-	-	1	70,183	-	-	-	-
T-11	2	177,522	-	-	-	-	-	-	1	89,037	-	-	1	88,485
T-28	28	1,565,927	6	623,846	1	118,401	2	26,234	16	464,066	-	-	3	333,380
HELICOPTER	10	578,198	6	278,186	-	-	-	-	4	300,010	-	-	-	-
LIAISON	7	98,769	5	84,016	-	-	-	-	-	-	-	-	2	14,753
MISCELLANEOUS	4	1,805,707	2	922,622	-	-	1	421,774	1	461,311	-	-	-	-

a/ Other crew member error, other personnel, miscellaneous unsafe conditions, and undetermined.

SOURCE: D/Flight Safety Research - The Inspector General

TABLE 98 — FLYING HOURS, NUMBER AND RATES OF MAJOR ACCIDENTS, FATAL ACCIDENTS AND FATALITIES 1921 THROUGH 1953

(Rates computed on the basis of 100,000 Flying Hours)

YEAR	FLYING HOURS	MAJOR ACCIDENTS		FATAL ACCIDENTS		FATALITIES	
		Number	Rate	Number	Rate	Number	Rate
Fiscal Years:	WORLD WIDE USAF						
1921	77,351	361	467	45	58	73	94
1922	65,214	330	506	24	37	44	68
1923	65,750	283	430	33	50	58	88
1924	97,834	275	281	23	24	34	35
1925	150,319	311	207	30	20	40	27
1926	158,402	334	211	27	17	43	27
1927	140,906	227	161	28	20	43	31
1928	182,903	249	136	25	14	27	15
1929	263,381	390	148	43	16	62	24
1930	325,223	468	144	37	11	52	16
1931	396,961	456	115	21	5	26	7
1932	371,254	423	114	32	9	49	13
1933	432,966	442	102	28	7	46	11
1934	374,235	412	110	35	9	54	14
1935	449,583	453	101	33	7	47	11
1936	518,749	430	83	42	8	59	11
1937	520,493	358	69	27	5	48	9
1938	598,907	375	63	38	6	62	10
1939	729,225	389	53	32	4	52	7
1940	937,922	478	51	46	5	90	10
1941	2,368,046	1515	63	143	6	252	11
	CONTINENTAL USAF a/						
Calendar Years:							
1942	14,246,366	10090	71	1116	8	2384	17
1943	32,064,789	20389	64	2264	7	5603	17
1944	35,503,205	16128	45	1936	5	4973	14
1945	15,052,224	6661	44	804	5	2174	14
	WORLD WIDE USAF						
1946	3,624,792	2194	61	274	8	879	24
1947 b/. . . .	3,516,141	1555	44	205	6	584	17
1948	4,437,509	1783	40	243	5	619	14
1949	4,699,897	1731	37	245	5	577	12
1950	4,780,949	1744	36	267	6	781	16
1951	6,660,848	2184	33	370	6	1015	15
1952	7,972,482	2274	29	399	5	1214	15
1953	8,498,019	2075	24	433	5	949	11

a/ Overseas Accidents were not reported during war years.

b/ Accident data for the Air National Guard are included since 1947. This tabulation may, therefore, not necessarily agree with data published in prior years which excluded the ANG.

SOURCE: D/Flight Safety Research - The Inspector General.

308700 O - 54 - 13

GROUND SAFETY

Ground Accident statistics were approved and directed by Air Force Regulation 32-1, dated 24 August 1948. (See Paragraph 4a(6).) In establishing the reporting system, standardized cost factors and definitions have been approved. The present standard accidents costs for injuries and fatalities were estalbished by Air Force Regulation 32-2, dated 24 June 1953.

FISCAL YEAR 1953

Injury	Military	Civilian
Non-Disabling	$ 7.00	$ 7.00
Temporary Total	30.00/Day	14.00/Day
Permanent Partial	43,000.00	10,500.00
Permanent Total	63,500.00	70,000.00
Fatal	31,500.00	25,000.00

Quarterly estimates can be made by dividing the total by 4, as the quarterly experience was approximately equal. Frequency rates were computed to the following formulas:

a. Civilian Injury Rate = $\frac{\text{Number of Civilian disabling and fatal injuries} \times 1{,}000{,}000}{\text{Total hours of civilian employment}}$

b. Military Injury Rate (On Duty) = $\frac{\text{Number of Military disabling and fatal injuries "On Duty"} \times 100{,}000}{\text{Total Military Man-days of exposure} \times 1/3}$

c. Military Injury Rate (Off Duty) = $\frac{\text{Number of Military disabling and fatal injuries "Off Duty"} \times 100{,}000}{\text{Total Military Man-days of exposure} \times 2/3}$

d. USAF Motor Vehicle Accident Rate = $\frac{\text{Number of USAF Motor Vehicle Accidents} \times 100{,}000}{\text{Total USAF Motor Vehicle Mileage}}$

Cost Per Capita was computed by the following formula per month or per annum:

$$\frac{\text{Cost of Injuries} + \text{Cost of Fatalities} + \text{Cost of Property Damage}}{\text{Total Command Strength (Average Military and Average Civilian)}}$$

The strength figures employed were based on exposure (man-days for military and man-hours for civilians) as reported by the Major Air Commands.

The "USAF Statistical Digest" reports accidents and accident rates on a fiscal year basis. The following reductions and increase were noted for fiscal year 1953 over fiscal year 1952:

Military Accident rates - Continental US - 8.74 per cent increase
Military Accident rates - Overseas - 14.61 per cent decrease
Civilian Accident rates - Continental US - 24.46 per cent decrease
Civilian Accident rates - Overseas - 3.38 per cent decrease

The following definitions were used in developing the tables in this section of the book:

DISABLING INJURY - An injury which results in death, permanent total, permanent partial injury, or an injury, which in the opinion of competent medical authority makes it impossible for the injured to return to work or duty at any time during the next calendar day following date of injury.

TORT CLAIM - Any wrong, injury, or damage, not including a breach of contract, for which a civil suit can be brought.

USAF MOTOR VEHICLE ACCIDENT - An incident involving the operation of an Air Force motor vehicle which results in either disabling or non-disabling injury to Air Force personnel and/or non-USAF persons and/or damage aggregating $25.00 or more to Air Force motor vehicles, or to other vehicles or property without regard to ownership.

USAF PROPERTY DAMAGE ACCIDENT - An incident resulting from Air Force Ground operation wherein Air Force property is accidently damaged in amount of $25.00 or more.

TABLE 99 — USAF MILITARY PERSONNEL INJURIES, WORLDWIDE — FY 1953

Nomenclature	Worldwide	Continental US	Overseas
Average Strength	974,683	722,560	252,123
Man Days Exposure	355,759,240	263,734,309	92,024,931
Injuries - Total	110,911	76,684	34,227
Non-Disabling - Total	90,556	61,928	28,628
Disabling - Total	19,300	13,875	5,425
On Duty	6,394	4,076	2,318
Off Duty	12,906	9,799	3,107
Permanent Impairment - Total	67	49	18
On Duty	20	7	13
Off Duty	47	42	5
Fatalities - Total	988	832	156
On Duty	153	92	61
Off Duty	835	740	95
Man Days Lost - Total	333,631	247,566	86,065
On Duty	88,152	54,820	33,332
Off Duty	245,479	192,746	52,733
Injury Rate	5.72	5.60	6.08

Source: Assistant for Ground Safety, DCS/Personnel, Hq. USAF.

TABLE 100 — USAF CIVILIAN PERSONNEL INJURIES, WORLDWIDE — FY 1953

Nomenclature	Worldwide	Continental US	Overseas
Average Strength	321,917	263,214	58,703
Man Hours Exposure	656,710,449	536,956,062	119,754,387
Injuries - Total	122,456	114,242	8,214
Non-Disabling	119,283	111,787	7,496
Disabling	3,079	2,380	699
Permanent Impairment	73	61	12
Fatal	21	14	7
Man Days Lost	37,580	28,090	9,490
Injury Rate	4.83	4.57	6.00

Source: Assistant for Ground Safety, DCS/ Personnel, Hq. USAF.

TABLE 101 — SUMMARY AND COST ANALYSIS OF USAF MOTOR VEHICLE ACCIDENTS, WORLDWIDE — FY 1953

Nomenclature	Worldwide	Continental US	Overseas
Total Accidents	6,824	4,014	2,810
Miles Operated	523,249,846	276,014,392	247,235,454
Accident Rate	1.30	1.45	1.14
Personnel Injuries - Total	1,572	736	836
Non-Disabling	654	328	326
Disabling	860	380	480
Permanent Impairment	4	3	1
Fatal	54	25	29
Cost of Injuries - Total	$ 2,300,829	$ 1,048,020	$ 1,252,809
Cost of Vehicle Damaged in Vehicle Accidents - Total	$ 932,245	$ 508,826	$ 423,419
Cost of Aircraft Damaged by Vehicle Accidents - Total	$ 397,857	$ 156,564	$ 241,293
Cost of Other AF Property Damaged By Vehicle Accidents - Total	$ 162,760	$ 68,828	$ 93,932
Days Vehicles Out of Service - Total	42,209	23,269	18,940
Days Aircraft Out Of Service - Total	1,473	974	499

Source: Assistant for Ground Safety, DCS/Personnel, Hq. USAF.

TABLE 102 – COST ANALYSIS OF USAF GROUND ACCIDENTS, WORLDWIDE – FY 1953

Cost and Strength	WORLDWIDE	CONTINENTAL US	OVERSEAS
Cost Per Capita Per Annum	$ 40.16	$ 41.07	$ 37.25
Military Cost Per Capita Per Annum	$ 46.18	$ 50.49	$ 33.84
Civilian Cost Per Capita Per Annum	$ 7.86	$ 8.23	$ 6.21
Accident Cost - Total a/	$ 52,066,021	$ 40,487,700	$ 11,578,321
Cost of Military Injuries - Total	45,014,822	36,482,976	8,531,846
Non-Disabling - Total	633,892	433,496	200,396
Disabling - Total	10,008,933	7,426,980	2,581,950
On Duty	2,644,560	1,644,600	999,960
Off Duty	7,364,370	5,782,380	1,581,990
Permanent Impairment - Total	3,250,000	2,414,500	835,500
On Duty	942,000	342,000	600,000
Off Duty	2,308,000	2,072,500	235,500
Fatalities - Total	31,122,000	26,208,000	4,914,000
On Duty	4,819,500	2,898,000	1,921,500
Off Duty	26,302,500	23,310,000	2,992,500
Cost of Civilian Injuries - Total	b/ 2,530,938	2,166,269	b/ 364,669
Non-Disabling	834,981	782,509	52,472
Disabling	518,958	393,260	125,698
Permanent Impairment	717,299	640,500	76,799
Fatalities	459,700	350,000	109,700
Total Cost of Vehicles Damaged - by all Causes	957,985	517,919	440,066
Total Cost of Aircraft Damage - by all Causes	2,917,575	1,005,138	1,912,437
Total Cost of Other Property Damage - by all Causes	$ 644,701	$ 315,398	$ 329,303
Average Strength - Total	1,296,600	985,774	310,826
Military	974,683	722,560	252,123
Civilian	321,917	263,214	58,703

a/ Excludes cost of tort claims.
b/ Included in the Overseas Commands are injuries to Foreign National civilian employees. Cost yardsticks for this class of personnel are different than for American civilians.

Source: Assistant for Ground Safety, DCS/Personnel, Hq USAF.

TABLE 103 - USAF GROUND ACCIDENT COST ANALYSIS BY COST PER CAPITA CONTINENTAL US AND OVERSEAS - FY 1953

Month	CONTINENTAL US						
	Total	Air Defense Command	Air Materiel Command	Air Proving Ground Command	Air Research and Development Command	Air Training Command	Air University
July (1952)	$ 4.24	$ 6.72	$ 1.67	$ 6.44	$ 5.09	$ 5.13	$ 4.01
August	3.71	6.44	.62	6.85	2.65	4.08	.49
September	2.95	5.49	2.34	4.55	2.95	3.35	.37
October	3.24	5.22	1.68	7.74	1.27	3.41	1.41
November	3.43	6.94	2.15	1.39	3.70	3.31	5.32
December	4.53	6.34	.98	.90	2.74	5.14	.36
January (1953)	2.09	2.11	.85	3.95	3.16	1.41	2.96
February	2.36	.81	.70	.82	1.36	2.84	.26
March	3.59	2.33	1.05	3.58	2.26	1.99	.61
April	3.35	5.02	1.76	.97	1.50	2.93	2.35
May	3.68	3.42	.79	4.31	2.66	4.33	3.69
June	3.24	3.02	.93	9.71	1.93	4.09	2.48

	CONTINENTAL US (Continued)						
	Continental Air Command	Headquarters Command	Military Air Transport Service	Strategic Air Command	Tactical Air Command	USAF Security Service	Misc Organizations a/
July (1952)	$ 3.31	$ 2.00	$ 5.18	$ 3.83	$ 4.91	$ 3.48	$ 14.63
August	5.15	.31	3.79	4.88	6.28	.37	7.38
September	3.97	1.82	3.59	3.84	4.47	3.63	.47
October	2.06	4.11	4.57	3.34	3.90	3.80	10.74
November	1.89	1.89	3.70	3.28	4.81	1.19	3.57
December	10.31	.21	2.74	5.20	7.88	5.82	6.83
January (1953)	2.04	.47	3.27	3.74	2.62	5.79	.40
February	5.37	.30	3.37	3.76	2.20	2.39	.60
March	1.87	1.69	4.47	4.47	3.14	2.79	b/ 107.83
April	7.46	2.92	3.42	4.06	4.92	.97	3.78
May	3.74	3.81	3.23	4.55	7.62	2.02	10.59
June	4.62	2.35	3.01	3.34	4.62	.41	15.22

	OVERSEAS						
	Total	Alaskan Air Command	Caribbean Air Command	Far East Air Forces	Military Air Transport Service	Northeast Air Command	US Air Forces in Europe
July (1952)	$ 4.70	$ 2.06	$ .40	$ 4.55	$ 4.34	$ 1.95	$ 6.06
August	3.21	5.06	.34	3.57	3.34	2.33	2.12
September	2.60	.63	.34	2.82	2.14	.82	3.08
October	2.55	1.88	.30	2.02	2.43	.56	3.70
November	2.33	1.04	14.49	2.89	1.61	1.19	2.13
December	6.88	8.91	.14	11.50	1.64	2.02	4.00
January (1953)	2.09	2.98	.05	2.96	.73	.99	1.64
February	2.57	.50	.21	2.15	1.45	1.13	4.29
March	2.63	4.31	.61	1.74	1.63	.97	4.03
April	4.29	4.47	.12	6.63	1.00	.89	3.11
May	1.90	.79	.09	2.37	1.62	.49	1.90
June	1.97	.62	.33	1.79	1.25	.42	2.94

a/ Includes Headquarters USAF, Air Force Finance Division, and Special Weapons Projects.
b/ Includes 30 fatalities who were passengers in a chartered commercial aircraft which crashed near DeCota, Calif.

Source: Assistant for Ground Safety, DCS/ Personnel, Hq. USAF.

AIRCRAFT — MATERIEL

The tables included in this section provide summary data pertaining to the procurement, production, inventory, status, deployment and disposition of USAF aircraft, and similar information and other major items of materiel in the USAF during the Fiscal Year 1953.

In addition to information reflecting the status of aircraft procurement and production, the data contain the following information by type and model of aircraft: Total aircraft inventory, active and inactive aircraft inventory, planned program, aircraft in and out of commission, aircraft in storage, aircraft excess to all military requirements, aircraft production gains and losses to the aircraft inventory, and a summary of active and inactive aircraft by functional distribution.

The classification of aircraft herein is in accordance with AF Regulation 65-60, dated 9 May 1949, and changes A and B, Aeronautical Board Memorandum, dated 21 October 1947, and the latest AF Technical Orders and other authorizations. The type classification is generally based upon the basic type designator or the prefix preceding the basic type designator of each aircraft model. A prefix is assigned an aircraft model when the aircraft is modified to perform a function (indicated by the prefix) other than its basically designated purpose. The classification into FIRST and SECOND-LINE categories is in accordance with HOI 150-9, dated 14 August 1951 and as specified in Table VIII, AFL 150-10, dated 2 February 1953.

DEFINITIONS: The following definitions apply to the terms herein -

AIRCRAFT: The term aircraft and all type, model and series designations including prefixes are synonymous with the terminology of heavier-than-air aircraft as shown in AF Regulation 65-60, dated 9 May 1949, as amended, 30 August 1950 and 7 December 1950. All aircraft which have been accepted by the USAF and USAF Reserve Forces and which are currently in the accountable inventory are included, except Class 01Z aircraft which are shown separately.

AIRPLANES: All aircraft except aerial target type aircraft.

ACTIVE AIRCRAFT INVENTORY: The number of aircraft provided an organization in the accomplishment of its mission - aircraft undergoing maintenance, administrative aircraft, test aircraft (excluding those test aircraft on bailment and X-prefixed models), aircraft provided for minimum individual training, active project aircraft and en-route aircraft.

INACTIVE AIRCRAFT INVENTORY: Storage aircraft, flyable inactive aircraft, aircraft undergoing modification, aircraft on loan, bailment contract (except those bailed for maintenance), X-prefixed aircraft, aircraft declared excess to requirements, aircraft recommended for reclamation, aircraft on project for assignment to a non-USAF activity, inactive project aircraft, and aircraft accepted by USAF but not delivered to recipient.

FIRST and SECOND-LINE AIRCRAFT: The classification of aircraft into first and second-line categories is in accordance with the provisions of HOI 150-9 dated 14 August 1951, and the first-line life specified in Table VIII of AFL 150-10, dated 2 February 1953.

ACCEPTANCE: Aircraft which have been shop-assembled and fully inspected by constituted USAF or Navy production authorities; and the title, responsibility, and accountability assumed by the contracting agency or recipient.

IN COMMISSION: In commission means that an aircraft, without additional repair or maintenance, is safe and capable of normal flight operations. This does not necessarily indicate that the aircraft is capable of performing a specific mission such as combat, photo, etc., but merely that the aircraft is flyable and that the Form 1 and the Form 41B do not bear a red cross. Weather, runway conditions, shortages of operation personnel, or other factors not relating to the aircraft itself will not cause an aircraft to be reported "out of commission".

A O C P: "Aircraft Out of Commission Awaiting Parts" are those aircraft not flyable as indicated by a red cross on Form 1 and Form 41B, solely due to lack of parts. Aircraft will not be reported as awaiting parts unless the required parts have been requisitioned from the normal supply source at the station where the aircraft is located and notification has been received from the normal supply source that the parts are not available. This category does not include those aircraft awaiting parts required for the performance of modifications defined in AF Regulation 65-60.

AIRFRAME WEIGHT: The weight of the assembled principal structural components of an airplane. It includes hull or fuselage, wings, stabilizers, vertical fins, control surfaces, landing gear, and nacelles.

* * * * * * * * * * * *

PILOTLESS AIRCRAFT AND GUIDED AIRCRAFT ROCKETS: The table shows complete production data for the Fiscal Year 1953. All contracts, including those that have been completed and those currently in production are reflected in this report. The data also include the quarterly cumulative total on contract and the quarterly cumulative deliveries. The data were obtained from the latest procurement schedule - Air Materiel Command. The target drones shown in this report are used for training purposes only.

USAF AMMUNITION: A semi-annual worldwide inventory of selected USAF ammunition in possession of USAF bases and depots during Fiscal Year 1953. The table is shown by area and also includes reserve stockages of the Air Force in zone of interior depots under control of Department of Defense activities other than Air Force. The data presented herein is based upon reports prepared and submitted to Headquarters USAF by each major air command.

TABLE 104 — U. S. MILITARY AIRPLANE PRODUCTION BY RECIPIENT — QUARTERLY — FY 1953

(MDAP includes Grant and Reimbursable Aid. Navy production excludes experimental models)

TYPE, MODEL, SERIES AND MANUFACTURER	TOTAL ACCEPTANCES		JUL 52 THRU SEP 52		OCT 52 THRU DEC 52		JAN 53 THRU MAR 53		APR 53 THRU JUN 53	
	UNITS	AIRFRAME WEIGHT (000,S)	UNITS	AIRFRAME WEIGHT (000,S)	UNITS	AIRFRAME WEIGHT (000,S)	UNITS	AIRFRAME WEIGHT (000,S)	UNITS	AIRFRAME WEIGHT (000,S)
TOTAL MILITARY PRODUCTION	10,802	131,191.7	2,372	30,041.5	2,698	29,789.0	2,755	34,368.7	2,977	36,992.5
RECIPIENT:										
USAF	4,729	83,487.2	936	20,550.0	1,059	18,401.9	1,251	21,092.2	1,483	23,443.1
NAVY	2,519	26,646.9	550	4,402.4	590	5,349.9	700	8,212.3	679	8,682.3
COAST GUARD	16	116.3	10	40.2	-	-	1	14.5	5	61.6
MDAP	2,062	18,836.5	490	4,533.4	577	5,187.7	506	4,749.9	489	4,365.5
ARMY	1,311	1,667.3	330	465.1	405	500.2	269	274.6	307	427.4
NATIONAL GUARD, ARMY DIVISION	155	139.5	56	50.4	57	51.3	28	25.2	14	12.6
SOLD FOR CASH (NAVY PROD.)	10	298.0	-	-	10	298.0	-	-	-	-
	U. S. AIR FORCE									
BOMBER	364	23,015.8	122	7,593.2	45	3,001.6	91	5,818.6	106	6,602.4
B-36H . . Convair	43	4,929.0	15	1,684.4	9	1,016.2	10	1,168.2	9	1,060.2
B-47B . . Boeing, Doug., Lock.	190	10,535.1	107	5,908.8	36	1,985.4	33	1,845.5	14	795.4
YB-47C . Boeing	1	55.8	-	-	-	-	1	55.8	-	-
B-47E . . Boeing	128	7,266.1	-	-	-	-	46	2,634.2	82	4,631.9
XB-52 . . Boeing	1	114.9	-	-	-	-	-	-	1	114.9
YB-52 a/. Boeing	1	114.9	-	-	-	-	1	114.9	-	-
FIGHTER	2,109	17,619.1	292	2,598.3	425	3,555.6	603	4,889.4	789	6,575.8
F-84F . . Republic & Gen.Motors	49	500.2	-	-	2	23.3	8	82.0	39	394.9
F-84G . . Republic	342	2,963.7	88	756.8	129	1,109.4	107	940.0	18	157.5
F-86D . . N. American	448	3,969.8	23	204.7	34	302.6	115	1,023.5	276	2,439.0
F-86E . . N. Amer. & Canadair	98	730.0	92	685.3	6	44.7	-	-	-	-
F-86F . . N. American	971	7,305.0	52	392.7	215	1,623.2	329	2,474.1	375	2,815.0
YF-86H . N. American	2	18.2	-	-	-	-	2	18.2	-	-
F-89C . . Northrop	35	633.5	22	398.2	13	235.3	-	-	-	-
F-89D . . Northrop	10	202.8	3	60.3	-	-	-	-	7	142.5
F-94C . . Lockheed	153	1,283.6	12	100.3	26	217.1	42	351.6	73	614.6
F-100A . N. American	1	12.3	-	-	-	-	-	-	1	12.3
RECONNAISSANCE	42	4,676.8	13	1,446.4	11	1,212.6	9	1,002.6	9	1,015.2
RB-36H . Convair	42	4,676.8	13	1,446.4	11	1,212.6	9	1,002.6	9	1,015.2
SEARCH AND RESCUE	100	1,420.0	20	284.0	34	482.8	27	383.4	19	269.8
SA-16A . Grumman	100	1,420.0	20	284.0	34	482.8	27	383.4	19	269.8
TANKER	148	8,467.8	32	1,821.4	36	1,945.8	37	2,156.8	43	2,543.8
KC-97F . Boeing	120	6,803.8	32	1,821.4	36	1,945.8	37	2,156.8	15	879.8
KC-97G . Boeing	28	1,664.0	-	-	-	-	-	-	28	1,664.0
CARGO	380	18,118.8	91	4,501.1	109	5,029.6	96	4,526.4	84	4,061.7
C-118A . Douglas	18	703.8	9	349.6	8	314.8	1	39.4	-	-
C-119C . Fairchild	41	1,188.6	-	-	4	115.6	37	1,073.0	-	-
C-119F . Fairchild & Kaiser	175	5,028.0	47	1,342.7	61	1,750.7	25	719.6	42	1,215.0
C-119G . Fairchild	11	315.5	-	-	-	-	-	-	11	315.5
YC-119H . Fairchild	1	39.7	-	-	1	39.7	-	-	-	-
C-124A . Douglas	70	5,617.6	35	2,808.8	35	2,808.8	-	-	-	-
C-124C . Douglas	64	5,225.6	-	-	-	-	33	2,694.4	31	2,531.2
TRAINER	1,357	9,529.4	322	2,215.4	371	3,105.4	325	2,111.0	339	2,097.6
T-28A . . N. American	362	1,438.9	90	360.0	90	360.0	92	363.4	90	355.5
T-29B . . Convair	72	1,496.9	17	349.3	19	390.4	18	378.0	18	379.2
T-33A . . Lockheed	899	5,310.6	210	1,239.0	245	1,445.5	213	1,263.2	231	1,362.9
TB-50H . Boeing	24	1,283.0	5	267.1	17	909.5	2	106.4	-	-
HELICOPTER	85	359.7	1	3.6	4	19.3	33	133.2	47	203.6
YH-12B . Bell	1	3.6	1	3.6	-	-	-	-	-	-
H-19B . . Sikorsky	71	284.6	-	-	-	-	30	120.0	41	164.6
YH-20 . . McDonnell	2	0.6	-	-	1	0.3	1	0.3	-	-
YH-21 . . Piasecki	11	70.9	-	-	3	19.0	2	12.9	6	39.0
LIAISON	142	266.3	43	86.6	24	49.2	28	57.3	47	73.2
L-19A . . Cessna	20	18.0	-	-	-	-	-	-	20	18.0
L-20A . . DeHavilland	122	248.3	43	86.6	24	49.2	28	57.3	27	55.2
SPECIAL RESEARCH	2	13.5	-	-	-	-	2	13.5	-	-
X-1A . . Bell	1	7.1	-	-	-	-	1	7.1	-	-
X-1B . . Bell	1	6.4	-	-	-	-	1	6.4	-	-

TABLE 104 — U. S. MILITARY AIRPLANE PRODUCTION BY RECIPIENT — QUARTERLY — FY 1953 — CONTINUED

(MDAP includes Grant and Reimbursable Aid. Navy production excludes experimental models)

TYPE, MODEL, SERIES AND MANUFACTURER	TOTAL ACCEPTANCES		JUL 52 THRU SEP 52		OCT 52 THRU DEC 52		JAN 53 THRU MAR 53		APR 53 THRU JUN 53	
	UNITS	AIRFRAME WEIGHT (000'S)	UNITS	AIRFRAME WEIGHT (000'S)	UNITS	AIRFRAME WEIGHT (000'S)	UNITS	AIRFRAME WEIGHT (000'S)	UNITS	AIRFRAME WEIGHT (000'S)
	NAVY									
BOMBER	777	10,222.7	247	2,518.7	190	2,149.8	184	2,717.6	156	2,836.6
P2V-5 . . Lockheed	68	2,025.8	12	357.0	11	327.8	17	506.6	28	834.4
P2V-6 . . Lockheed	34	1,020.0	-	-	7	210.0	20	600.0	7	210.0
P5M-1 . . Martin	54	1,776.6	10	329.0	5	164.5	14	460.6	25	822.5
AD-4B . . Douglas	166	1,212.5	4	29.9	29	211.7	69	503.7	64	467.2
AD-4N . . Douglas	194	1,465.6	116	868.8	65	497.3	13	99.5	-	-
AD-4W . . Douglas	42	315.6	18	133.2	24	182.4	-	-	-	-
AD-5N . . Douglas	4	33.2	-	-	-	-	2	16.6	2	16.6
AD-6 . . Douglas	1	7.6	-	-	-	-	-	-	1	7.6
AU-1 . . Chance Vought	39	241.8	39	241.8	-	-	-	-	-	-
A2D-1 . . Douglas	2	19.6	-	-	-	-	-	-	2	19.6
AF-2S . . Grumman	70	717.8	27	276.9	29	297.3	14	143.6	-	-
AF-2W . . Grumman	46	461.5	15	151.5	15	150.0	16	160.0	-	-
AF-3S . . Grumman	25	256.3	-	-	-	-	16	164.1	9	92.2
AJ-2 . . N. American	20	419.0	-	-	-	-	3	62.9	17	356.1
AJ-2P . . N. American	11	239.4	6	130.6	5	108.8	-	-	-	-
S2F-1 . . Grumman	1	10.4	-	-	-	-	-	-	1	10.4
FIGHTER	1,054	9,220.3	182	1,437.6	257	2,249.9	288	2,603.8	327	2,929.0
F2H-2P . McDonnell	14	121.1	14	121.1	-	-	-	-	-	-
F2H-3 . . McDonnell	175	1,600.2	24	218.4	56	512.5	85	777.8	10	91.5
F2H-4 . . McDonnell	95	869.2	-	-	-	-	-	-	95	869.2
F3D-2 . . Douglas	157	1,632.0	8	82.4	44	457.6	53	551.2	52	540.8
F3D-3 . . Douglas	5	51.5	5	51.5	-	-	-	-	-	-
F7U-1 . . Chance Vought	1	11.4	-	-	1	11.4	-	-	-	-
F7U-3 . . Chance Vought	26	321.8	1	12.1	5	61.8	11	135.8	9	112.1
F9F-5 . . Grumman	161	1,180.3	118	855.6	43	324.7	-	-	-	-
F9F-5P . Grumman	3	23.1	3	23.1	-	-	-	-	-	-
F9F-6 . . Grumman	341	2,779.4	9	73.4	104	847.7	117	953.6	111	904.7
F9F-6P . Grumman	19	157.7	-	-	3	24.9	10	83.0	6	49.8
F9F-7 . . Grumman	50	407.5	-	-	-	-	8	65.2	42	342.3
FJ-2 . . N. American	7	65.1	-	-	1	9.3	4	37.2	2	18.6
CARGO	132	4,846.6	3	117.5	11	488.3	58	2,038.8	60	2,202.0
R4Q-2 . . Fairchild	58	1,620.4	-	-	-	-	28	780.4	30	840.0
R6D-1 . . Douglas	54	2,244.2	3	117.5	7	291.9	29	1,209.3	15	625.5
R7V-1 . . Lockheed	20	982.0	-	-	4	196.4	1	49.1	15	736.5
TRAINER	174	1,027.5	10	59.0	40	234.1	70	415.8	54	318.6
TV-2 . . Lockheed	174	1,027.5	10	59.0	40	234.1	70	415.8	54	318.6
HELICOPTER	336	955.7	99	261.5	89	225.1	76	241.5	72	227.6
HO5S-1&2 Sikorsky	55	79.1	17	23.8	30	43.6	8	11.7	-	-
HOK-1 . . Kaman	2	5.0	-	-	-	-	-	-	2	5.0
HRS-1 . . Sikorsky	12	43.2	12	43.2	-	-	-	-	-	-
HRS-2 . . Sikorsky	38	136.8	24	86.4	14	50.4	-	-	-	-
HRS-3 . . Sikorsky	69	255.3	-	-	-	-	48	177.6	21	77.7
HTK-1 . . Kaman	23	38.9	5	8.3	6	10.2	7	11.9	5	8.5
HTL-5 . . Bell	13	14.3	13	14.3	-	-	-	-	-	-
HUP-2 . . Piasecki	124	383.1	28	85.5	39	120.9	13	40.3	44	136.4
LIAISON	25	22.5	9	8.1	3	2.7	13	11.7	-	-
OE-1 . . Cessna	25	22.5	9	8.1	3	2.7	13	11.7	-	-
UTILITY	19	275.5	-	-	-	-	10	145.0	9	130.5
UF-1 . . Grumman	19	275.5	-	-	-	-	10	145.0	9	130.5
LIGHTER-THAN-AIR	2	76.1	-	-	-	-	1	38.1	1	38.0
ZP2N . . Goodyear	2	75.1	-	-	-	-	1	38.1	1	38.0
	COAST GUARD									
HELICOPTER	9	14.8	8	11.2	-	-	-	-	1	3.6
HO4S-3 . Sikorsky	1	3.6	-	-	-	-	-	-	1	3.6
HO5S-1 . Sikorsky	8	11.2	8	11.2	-	-	-	-	-	-
UTILITY	7	101.5	2	29.0	-	-	1	14.5	4	58.0
UF-1 . . Grumman	7	101.5	2	29.0	-	-	1	14.5	4	58.0

TABLE 104 — U. S. MILITARY AIRPLANE PRODUCTION BY RECIPIENT — QUARTERLY — FY 1953 — CONTINUED

MDAP includes Grant and Reimbursable Aid. Navy production excludes experimental models

TYPE, MODEL, SERIES AND MANUFACTURER	TOTAL ACCEPTANCES		JUL 52 THRU SEP 52		OCT 52 THRU DEC 52		JAN 53 THRU MAR 53		APR 53 THRU JUN 53	
	UNITS	AIRFRAME WEIGHT (000'S)	UNITS	AIRFRAME WEIGHT (000'S)	UNITS	AIRFRAME WEIGHT (000'S)	UNITS	AIRFRAME WEIGHT (000'S)	UNITS	AIRFRAME WEIGHT (000'S)
	MUTUAL DEFENSE ASSISTANCE PROGRAM									
BOMBER	74	1,900.1	-	-	19	365.2	27	686.3	28	848.6
P2V-5 . . Lockheed	46	1,443.7	-	-	10	298.0	20	634.5	16	511.2
P2V-6 . . Lockheed	11	330.0	-	-	-	-	-	-	11	330.0
AD-4W . . Douglas	17	126.4	-	-	9	67.2	7	51.8	1	7.4
FIGHTER	1,625	13,843.2	444	3,786.2	529	4,415.0	389	3,383.3	263	2,258.7
F-84G . . Republic	1,505	13,043.1	429	3,689.4	465	3,999.0	374	3,285.8	237	2,068.9
F-86E . . Canadair	26	189.8	-	-	-	-	-	-	26	189.8
F4U-7 . . Chance Vought	94	610.3	15	96.8	64	416.0	15	97.5	-	-
SEARCH AND RESCUE	2	28.4	-	-	-	-	2	28.4	-	-
SA-16A . . Grumman	2	28.4	-	-	-	-	2	28.4	-	-
CARGO	69	1,985.0	21	599.7	12	345.2	13	375.3	23	664.8
C-119F . Fairchild	18	514.2	18	514.2	-	-	-	-	-	-
C-119F b/ Fairchild	28	806.5	3	85.5	8	229.6	6	173.2	11	318.2
C-119G . . Fairchild	23	664.3	-	-	4	115.6	7	202.1	12	346.6
TRAINER	239	951.1	25	147.5	4	23.6	66	266.4	144	513.6
T-33A . . Lockheed	91	537.6	25	147.5	4	23.6	27	160.0	35	206.5
T-35A b/. Temco	7	5.4	-	-	-	-	-	-	7	5.4
Mark IV . Canadian Car	115	310.5	-	-	-	-	38	102.6	77	207.9
SNB-5 . . Beech	26	97.6	-	-	-	-	1	3.8	25	93.8
HELICOPTER	47	123.3	-	-	10	36.0	6	7.5	31	79.8
H-19B . . Sikorsky	3	12.0	-	-	-	-	-	-	3	12.0
HO4S-3 . Sikorsky	14	50.4	-	-	-	-	-	-	14	50.4
HRS-2 . . Sikorsky	10	36.0	-	-	10	36.0	-	-	-	-
HTE-2 . . Hiller	20	24.9	-	-	-	-	6	7.5	14	17.4
LIAISON	6	5.4	-	-	3	2.7	3	2.7	-	-
L-19A . . Cessna	3	2.7	-	-	3	2.7	-	-	-	-
L-19A b/. Cessna	3	2.7	-	-	-	-	3	2.7	-	-
	ARMY									
HELICOPTER	629	1,021.8	184	331.0	190	313.1	121	153.1	134	224.6
H-13E . . Bell	334	383.2	86	115.1	97	102.0	89	97.9	62	68.2
H-13G . . Bell	16	17.6	-	-	-	-	-	-	16	17.6
H-19C . . Sikorsky	65	251.6	35	136.0	30	115.6	-	-	-	-
H-23B c/. Hiller	157	202.1	63	79.9	55	71.5	24	31.2	15	19.5
H-25A c/. Piasecki	55	165.0	-	-	8	24.0	8	24.0	39	117.0
YH-30 . . McCulloch	2	2.3	-	-	-	-	-	-	2	2.3
LIAISON	682	645.5	146	134.1	215	187.1	148	121.5	173	202.8
L-18C d/. Piper	164	82.0	60	30.0	104	52.0	-	-	-	-
L-19A . . Cessna	296	266.4	61	54.9	63	56.7	82	73.8	90	81.0
L-20A . . DeHavilland	52	106.1	23	46.6	29	59.5	-	-	-	-
L-21B . . Piper	47	28.2	-	-	-	-	-	-	47	28.2
L-21B d/. Piper	75	37.5	-	-	16	8.0	59	29.5	-	-
L-23A . . Beech	43	111.8	-	-	-	-	7	18.2	36	93.6
YL-26 . . Aero Design	3	10.9	-	-	3	10.9	-	-	-	-
LC-126 d/ Cessna	2	2.6	2	2.6	-	-	-	-	-	-
	NATIONAL GUARD, ARMY DIVISIONS									
LIAISON	155	139.5	56	50.4	57	51.3	28	25.2	14	12.6
L-19A . . Cessna	155	139.5	56	50.4	57	51.3	28	25.2	14	12.6
	SOLD FOR CASH (NAVY PRODUCTION)									
BOMBER	10	298.0	-	-	10	298.0	-	-	-	-
P2V-5 . . Lockheed	10	298.0	-	-	10	298.0	-	-	-	-

a/ Accepted from experimental program.
b/ Reimbursable Aid.
c/ Navy for Army.
d/ Army for MDAP.
SOURCE: Materiel Statistics Division, Directorate of Statistical Services, DCS/C

TABLE 105 — PRODUCTION AND DELIVERIES OF USAF PILOTLESS AIRCRAFT, GUIDED AIRCRAFT ROCKETS AND TARGET DRONES — QUARTERLY FY 1953

POPULAR NAME	TYPE	QUANTITY ON CONTRACT	ACCEPTED AS OF 30 JUN 52	SCHEDULE AS OF 30 JUN 52	DELIVERIES-FISCAL YEAR 1953				SCHEDULE AS OF 30 JUN 53	ACCEPTED AS OF 30 JUN 53
					1st Quarter	2nd Quarter	3rd Quarter	4th Quarter		
	PILOTLESS BOMBERS (TAC)									
Matador .	YB-61A	52	40	37	4	2	5	1	52	52
	B-61A	144	1	1	-	10	4	21	59	36
	PILOTLESS BOMBERS (SAC)									
Snark . .	XB-62	65	-	-	-	-	1	1	9	2
Rascal .	XB-63	82	6	6	2	1	1	1	19	11
Shrike .	X-9 (RTV-A-4) . .	31	20	21	3	6	2	-	31	31
	PILOTLESS FIGHTER INTERCEPTORS									
Bomarc .	XF-99	48	-	-	2	-	1	2	7	5
	GUIDED AIRCRAFT ROCKETS									
Falcon .	X-GAR-1	65	31	33	15	1	2	4	59	53
	Y-GAR-1	80	-	-	2	15	28	30	75	75
	TARGET DRONE									
	OQ-19D USAF . . .	1,675	384	725	636	655	-	-	1,675	1,675
	AFF . . .	6,410	4,647	4,939	10	243	700	650	6,250	6,250
	NG(G) . .	400	-	-	-	-	-	-	-	-
	YQ-1	6	-	-	-	-	-	-	4	-

SOURCE: MATERIEL STATISTICS DIVISION, DIRECTORATE OF STATISTICAL SERVICES, DCS/C

TABLE 106 — USAF AIRPLANE ACCEPTANCES — UNITS AND AIRFRAME WEIGHT BY RECIPIENT — FISCAL YEARS 1951 1952 1953

(Airframe Weight in thousands of pounds. Excludes experimental, used, and remanufactured airplanes. MDAP includes Grant Aid and Reimbursable Aid.)

MONTH AND YEAR	TOTAL		USAF		USAF for MDAP		USAF for Navy		USAF for Army	
	Units	Airframe Weight	Units	Airframe Weight	Units	Airframe Weight	Units	Airframe Weight	Units	Airframe Weight
FY 51 - Total	2,596	29,385.5	1,756	27,800.7	107	737.0	16	89.5	717	758.3
July 1950 . .	119	1,517.3	116	1,491.3	-	-	2	11.3	1	14.7
August . . .	136	2,619.7	131	2,591.5	-	-	5	28.2	-	-
September . .	211	3,236.7	157	3,046.3	14	98.7	3	17.0	37	74.7
October . . .	189	2,676.2	135	2,572.9	9	63.4	-	-	45	39.9
November . .	132	2,043.0	126	1,996.9	2	14.1	-	-	4	32.0
December . .	145	2,054.3	129	2,041.2	-	-	-	-	16	13.1
January 1951.	201	1,560.0	114	1,475.6	-	-	-	-	87	84.4
February . .	234	2,085.4	153	2,015.2	-	-	-	-	81	70.2
March	317	3,263.5	206	3,150.8	-	-	-	-	111	112.7
April	269	2,653.2	174	2,545.6	2	11.0	-	-	93	96.6
May	315	3,235.2	184	3,046.1	13	82.2	-	-	118	107.9
June	328	2,440.0	131	1,827.3	67	467.6	6	33.0	124	112.1
FY 52 - Total	5,617	63,798.4	2,814	54,239.5	798	6,429.2	156	1,398.9	1,849	1,667.8
July 1951 . .	372	3,255.4	232	3,063.6	8	48.5	6	33.9	126	109.4
August . . .	332	3,597.1	119	3,328.8	7	38.5	13	39.5	193	190.3
September . .	395	3,701.5	208	3,408.8	11	109.6	14	40.3	162	142.8
October . . .	462	4,305.5	211	3,905.4	25	107.2	11	37.9	215	192.0
November . .	362	4,174.8	189	3,722.6	9	51.8	19	281.9	145	118.5
December . .	468	5,040.8	224	4,102.6	51	383.9	25	427.3	168	127.0
January 1952.	471	4,994.0	222	4,291.3	39	289.7	21	266.5	189	146.5
February . .	514	5,471.0	233	4,491.7	101	800.9	7	39.6	173	138.8
March	579	6,634.6	256	5,265.7	150	1,187.9	10	56.5	163	124.5
April	520	6,920.8	256	5,453.7	148	1,296.8	10	58.5	106	111.8
May	576	7,651.9	324	6,300.5	137	1,164.7	10	58.5	105	128.2
June	566	8,051.0	340	6,904.8	112	949.7	10	58.5	104	138.0
FY 53 - Total .	8,104	104,914.3	4,723	83,243.3	1,870	17,560.9	257	2,670.4	1,254	1,439.7
July 1952	608	8,355.5	349	6,791.0	160	1,362.5	10	59.0	89	143.0
August . . .	546	8,546.5	348	7,284.5	101	1,123.9	-	-	97	138.2
September . .	599	8,587.2	239	6,474.5	214	1,950.2	9	8.1	137	154.4
October . . .	658	8,179.6	363	6,606.5	156	1,413.4	4	8.6	135	151.1
November . .	666	7,779.6	338	5,940.6	167	1,540.0	23	134.6	138	164.4
December . .	670	7,803.7	357	5,854.5	171	1,715.1	16	93.6	126	140.5
January 1953	682	8,872.8	397	7,204.9	159	1,464.1	20	119.0	106	84.8
February . .	699	8,849.5	395	6,750.0	168	1,554.7	58	474.3	78	70.5
March	719	9,283.0	455	7,008.6	150	1,570.5	33	614.6	81	89.3
April	753	9,703.2	446	7,178.0	163	1,680.9	55	744.4	89	99.9
May	752	9,368.1	475	7,639.6	137	1,191.1	29	414.2	111	123.2
June.	752	9,585.5	561	8,510.6	124	994.5	-	-	67	80.4

SOURCE: Materiel Statistics Division, Directorate of Statistical Services, DCS/C

TABLE 107 — USAF AIRCRAFT ACCEPTANCE SUMMARY — MONTHLY — FISCAL YEAR 1953

TYPE, MODEL AND SERIES	MANUFACTURER	QUANTITY ON PROGRAM	ACCEPTED PRIOR TO 1 JULY 1952	ACCEPTANCES - FISCAL YEAR 1953												FISCAL YEAR TOTAL	TOTAL ACCEPTED TO DATE
				1952 JUL	AUG	SEP	OCT	NOV	DEC	1953 JAN	FEB	MAR	APR	MAY	JUN		
USAF (Excludes Experimental Models)																	
TOTAL			3,397	349	348	239	363	338	357	397	395	455	446	475	561	4,723	8,120
Bomber			238	40	45	37	20	12	13	29	30	31	34	36	35	362	600
B-36H	Convair	83	32	4	4	7	3	4	2	4	3	3	3	3	3	43	75
B-47B	Boeing	379	206	36	41	30	17	8	11	25	5	-	-	-	-	173	379
B-47B	Douglas	10	-	-	-	-	-	-	-	-	1	1	3	3	2	10	10
B-47B	Lockheed	8	-	-	-	-	-	-	-	-	-	1	1	2	3	7	7
B-47E	Boeing	701	-	-	-	-	-	-	-	-	20	26	27	28	27	128	128
YB-47C	Boeing	1	-	-	-	-	-	-	-	-	1	-	-	-	-	1	1
Fighter			1,024	116	116	60	144	138	143	175	194	234	244	258	287	2,109	3,133
F-84F	Gen. Motors	237	-	-	-	-	-	-	-	-	-	-	-	-	1	1	1
F-84F	Republic	2,015	-	-	-	-	-	2	-	-	2	6	8	16	14	48	48
F-84G	Republic	789	447	37	45	5	52	40	37	43	31	33	18	-	-	342	789
F-86D	N. American	2,504	29	10	6	7	9	11	14	27	33	55	70	90	116	448	477
F-86E	N. American	336	243	13	46	28	6	-	-	-	-	-	-	-	-	93	336
F-86E	Canadair	60	55	5	-	-	-	-	-	-	-	-	-	-	-	5	60
F-86F	N. American, Col.	700	5	2	9	11	23	14	26	28	50	55	60	60	60	398	403
F-86F	N. American, Ing.	1,259	106	29	-	1	40	55	57	65	65	66	65	65	65	573	679
YF-86H	N. American	2	-	-	-	-	-	-	-	1	-	1	-	-	-	2	2
F-89C	Northrop	163	128	8	7	7	7	6	-	-	-	-	-	-	-	35	163
F-89D	Northrop	605	2	3	-	-	-	-	-	-	-	-	1	3	3	10	12
F-94C	Lockheed	387	9	9	3	-	7	10	9	11	13	18	22	24	27	153	162
YF-100A	No. American	2	-	-	-	-	-	-	-	-	-	-	-	-	1	1	1
Reconnaissance			23	4	4	5	4	3	4	3	3	3	3	3	3	42	65
RB-36H	Convair	73	23	4	4	5	4	3	4	3	3	3	3	3	3	42	65
Search & Rescue			143	8	10	2	10	12	12	12	6	9	6	7	6	100	243
SA-16A	Grumman	302	143	8	10	2	10	12	12	12	6	9	6	7	6	100	243
Tanker			38	6	12	14	12	12	12	12	12	13	14	13	16	148	186
KC-97F	Boeing	158	38	6	12	14	12	12	12	12	12	13	14	1	-	120	158
KC-97G	Boeing	600	-	-	-	-	-	-	-	-	-	-	-	12	16	28	28
Cargo			401	36	24	31	38	41	30	46	30	20	20	26	38	380	781
C-118A	Douglas	101	-	2	4	3	4	4	-	1	-	-	-	-	-	18	18
C-119C	Fairchild	303	262	-	-	-	-	-	4	26	11	-	-	-	-	41	303
C-119F	Fairchild	121	1	20	5	16	21	21	14	-	1	2	2	9	9	120	121
C-119F	Kaiser	71	4	3	3	-	-	4	1	7	7	8	7	7	8	55	59
C-119G	Fairchild	308	-	-	-	-	-	-	-	-	-	-	1	-	10	11	11
YC-119H	Fairchild	1	-	-	-	-	1	-	-	-	-	-	-	-	-	1	1
C-124A	Douglas	204	134	11	12	12	12	12	11	-	-	-	-	-	-	70	204
C-124C	Douglas	243	-	-	-	-	-	-	-	12	11	10	10	10	11	64	64

TABLE 107 — USAF AIRCRAFT ACCEPTANCE SUMMARY — MONTHLY — FISCAL YEAR 1953 — Continued

TYPE, MODEL AND SERIES	MANUFACTURER	QUANTITY ON PROGRAM	ACCEPTED PRIOR TO 1 JULY 1952	ACCEPTANCES - FISCAL YEAR 1953												FISCAL YEAR TOTAL	TOTAL ACCEPTED TO DATE
				JUL	AUG	SEP	OCT	NOV	DEC	JAN	FEB	MAR	APR	MAY	JUN		
USAF FOR ARMY (Cont'd)																	
Liaison (Cont'd)																	
L-21B	Cessna	62	-	-	-	-	-	-	-	-	-	-	16	24	7	47	47
L-23A	Beech	95	-	-	-	-	-	-	-	-	1	6	12	14	10	43	43
YL-26	Aero Design	3	-	-	-	-	-	2	1	-	-	-	-	-	-	3	3
LC-126C a/	Cessna	2	-	-	-	2	-	-	-	-	-	-	-	-	-	2	2
USAF FOR MDAP																	
TOTAL			784	160	101	214	156	167	171	159	168	150	163	137	124	1,870	2,654
Grant Aid			784	160	98	214	154	165	164	156	165	147	158	131	117	1,829	2,613
Bomber			6	-	-	-	2	3	5	6	4	10	15	1	-	46	52
P2V-5	Lockheed	52	6	-	-	-	2	3	5	6	4	10	15	1	-	46	52
Fighter			710	155	70	204	148	162	155	139	128	107	97	50	76	1,531	2,241
F-84G	Republic	2,236	710	155	70	204	148	162	155	139	128	107	97	50	50	1,505	2,215
F-86E	Canadair	60	-	-	-	-	-	-	-	-	-	-	-	-	26	26	26
Search & Rescue			1	-	-	-	-	-	-	-	2	-	-	-	-	2	3
SA-16A	Grumman	3	1	-	-	-	-	-	-	-	2	-	-	-	-	2	3
Cargo			-	-	12	6	-	-	4	-	3	4	4	4	4	41	41
C-119F	Fairchild	18	-	-	12	6	-	-	-	-	-	-	-	-	-	18	18
C-119G	Fairchild	62	-	-	-	-	-	-	4	-	3	4	4	4	4	23	23
Trainer			67	5	16	4	4	-	-	11	28	26	42	34	36	206	273
T-33A	Lockheed	628	67	5	16	4	4	-	-	6	8	13	11	12	12	91	158
Mark IV	Canadian Car	285	-	-	-	-	-	-	-	5	20	13	31	22	24	115	115
Helicopter			-	-	-	-	-	-	-	-	-	-	-	2	1	3	3
H-19B	Sikorsky	20	-	-	-	-	-	-	-	-	-	-	-	2	1	3	3
Reimbursable Aid			-	-	3	-	2	2	7	3	3	3	5	6	7	41	41
Cargo			-	-	3	-	2	2	4	-	3	3	3	4	4	28	28
C-119F	Fairchild	35	-	-	3	-	2	2	4	-	3	3	3	4	4	28	28
Trainer			-	-	-	-	-	-	-	-	-	-	2	2	3	7	7
T-35A	Temco	10	-	-	-	-	-	-	-	-	-	-	2	2	3	7	7
Liaison			-	-	-	-	-	-	3	3	-	-	-	-	-	6	6
L-19A	Cessna	6	-	-	-	-	-	-	3	3	-	-	-	-	-	6	6

TABLE 107 — USAF AIRCRAFT ACCEPTANCE SUMMARY — MONTHLY — FISCAL YEAR 1953 — CONTINUED

TYPE, MODEL AND SERIES	MANUFACTURER	QUANTITY ON PROGRAM	ACCEPTED PRIOR TO 1 JULY 1952	ACCEPTANCES - FISCAL YEAR 1953												FISCAL YEAR TOTAL	TOTAL ACCEPTED TO DATE
				1952 JUL	AUG	SEP	OCT	NOV	DEC	1953 JAN	FEB	MAR	APR	MAY	JUN		
USAF (Cont'd)																	
Trainer			1,460	118	127	77	127	112	132	111	93	121	99	106	134	1,357	2,817
T-28A	N. American	1,194	693	30	30	30	30	30	30	30	30	32	30	30	30	362	1,055
T-29B	Convair	105	25	4	6	7	6	7	6	6	6	6	6	6	6	72	97
T-33A	Lockheed	3,308	742	84	89	37	84	72	89	74	56	83	63	70	98	899	1,641
TB-50H	Boeing	24	-	-	2	3	7	3	7	1	1	-	-	-	-	24	24
Helicopter			9	-	1	-	-	-	3	-	18	14	17	17	13	83	92
YH-12B	Bell	10	9	-	1	-	-	-	-	-	-	-	-	-	-	1	10
H-19B	Sikorsky	244	-	-	-	-	-	-	-	-	17	13	16	14	11	71	71
YH-21	Piasecki	18	-	-	-	-	-	-	3	-	1	1	1	3	2	11	11
Liaison			61	21	9	13	8	8	8	9	9	10	9	9	29	142	203
L-20A	DeHavilland	212	61	21	9	13	8	8	8	9	9	10	9	9	9	122	183*
L-19A	Cessna	20	-	-	-	-	-	-	-	-	-	-	-	-	20	20	20
	USAF - EXPERIMENTAL ACFT																
TOTAL			2	-	-	-	-	-	1	2	-	2	1	-	-	6	8
Bomber			-	-	-	-	-	-	-	-	-	1	1	-	-	2	2
YB-52	Boeing	1	-	-	-	-	-	-	-	-	-	1	-	-	-	1	1
XB-52	Boeing	1	-	-	-	-	-	-	-	-	-	-	1	-	-	1	1
Helicopter			-	-	-	-	-	-	1	1	-	-	-	-	-	2	2
XH-20	McDonnell	2	-	-	-	-	-	-	1	1	-	-	-	-	-	2	2
Special Research			2	-	-	-	-	-	-	1	-	1	-	-	-	2	4
X-1A	Bell	4	2	-	-	-	-	-	-	-	-	1	-	-	-	1	3
X-1B	Bell	1	-	-	-	-	-	-	-	1	-	-	-	-	-	1	1
	USAF FOR ARMY																
TOTAL			2,268	89	97	137	135	138	126	106	78	81	89	111	67	1,254	3,522
Helicopter			163	40	39	42	42	50	35	27	31	31	21	33	26	417	580
H-13E	Bell	490	156	27	28	31	31	39	27	27	31	31	21	31	10	334	490
H-13G	Bell	214	-	-	-	-	-	-	-	-	-	-	-	-	16	16	16
H-19C	Sikorsky	72	7	13	11	11	11	11	8	-	-	-	-	-	-	65	72
YH-30	McCulloch	3	-	-	-	-	-	-	-	-	-	-	-	2	-	2	2
Liaison			2,105	49	58	95	93	88	91	79	47	50	68	78	41	837	2,942
L-18C a/	Piper	798	450	-	11	49	42	38	24	-	-	-	-	-	-	164	614
L-19A b/	Cessna	2,300	1,595	42	42	33	43	38	39	39	27	44	40	40	24	451	2,046
L-20A	DeHavilland	205	60	7	5	11	8	10	11	-	-	-	-	-	-	52	112
L-21B a/	Piper	151	-	-	-	-	-	-	16	40	19	-	-	-	-	75	75

TABLE 107 — USAF AIRCRAFT ACCEPTANCE SUMMARY — MONTHLY — FISCAL YEAR 1953 — CONTINUED

TYPE, MODEL AND SERIES	MANUFACTURER	QUANTITY ON PROGRAM	ACCEPTED PRIOR TO 1 JULY 1952	ACCEPTANCES - FISCAL YEAR 1953												FISCAL YEAR TOTAL	TOTAL ACCEPTED TO DATE
				1952 JUL	AUG	SEP	OCT	NOV	DEC	1953 JAN	FEB	MAR	APR	MAY	JUN		
				USAF FOR NAVY													
TOTAL			157	10	-	9	4	23	16	20	58	33	55	29	-	257	414
Cargo R4Q-2	Fairchild	58	- -	- -	- -	- -	- -	- -	- -	- -	9 9	19 19	19 19	11 11	- -	58 58	58 58
Trainer TV-2	Lockheed	554	122 122	10 10	- -	- -	1 1	23 23	16 16	20 20	36 36	14 14	36 36	18 18	- -	174 174	296 296
Liaison OE-1	Cessna	60	35 35	- -	- -	9 9	3 3	- -	- -	- -	13 13	- -	- -	- -	- -	25 25	60 60
				SPECIAL ITEMS													
C-45G	Beech (Remfg.for USAF)	372	57	-	14	25	56	22	26	16	32	21	31	26	26	295	352
T-6G	N. Amer., Col. (Remfg. for USAF) . . .	824	496	91	132	66	39	-	-	-	-	-	-	-	-	328	824
T-6G	N. Amer., Fresno (Remfg. for USAF) . . .	11	-	-	2	3	5	-	-	-	-	-	-	-	-	11	11
T-6G	N. Amer., Fresno (Remfg. for ANG) . . .	110	-	-	-	-	-	-	4	5	9	30	2	-	-	50	50
TC-45G	Beech (Remfg. for USAF)	96	36	30	30	-	-	-	-	-	-	-	-	-	-	60	96
H-23B	Hiller (Navy for Army)	273	40	16	24	23	21	19	15	5	8	11	-	7	8	157	197
H-25A	Piasecki (Navy for Army)	70	-	-	-	-	2	1	5	2	6	-	-	39	-	55	55
B-57	Martin (Pur. for USAF)	2	-	-	-	1	-	-	-	1	-	-	-	-	-	2	2

a/ Army for MDAP

b/ Includes 487 L-19A's accepted to date for National Guard, Army Division

SOURCE: Materiel Statistics Division, Directorate of Statistical Services, DCS/C.

TABLE 108 — USAF AIRPLANE ACCEPTANCES, JET AND PISTON — MONTHLY-FISCAL YEAR 1953

(Excludes experimental, used and remanufactured airplanes.)
"USAF FOR OTHER" includes MDAP, Army and Navy.

MONTH AND YEAR	JET			PISTON		
	TOTAL	USAF	USAF FOR OTHER	TOTAL	USAF	USAF FOR OTHER
TOTAL - FY 53	5,123	3,327	1,796	2,981	1,396	1,585
July - 1952	406	236	170	202	113	89
August	332	246	86	214	102	112
September	335	127	208	264	112	152
October	398	245	153	260	118	142
November	403	218	185	263	120	143
December	414	243	171	256	114	142
January - 1953	439	274	165	243	123	120
February	449	277	172	250	118	132
March	479	345	134	240	110	130
April	482	338	144	271	108	163
May	481	361	120	271	114	157
June	505	417	88	247	144	103

SOURCE: Materiel Statistics Division, Directorate of Statistical Services, DCS/C.

TABLE 109 — AIRPLANES AUTHORIZED FOR USAF PROCUREMENT BY TYPE, MODEL AND SERIES — FY 51, 52, 53

(Excludes experimental, used, and remanufactured aircraft) Program data as of 30 September 1953.)

TYPE, MODEL AND SERIES	FISCAL YEAR 1951	FISCAL YEAR 1952	FISCAL YEAR 1953
Total	8,431	6,659	5,569
Heavy Bomber	44	60	-
B-36H	44	24	-
B-36J	-	33	-
B-52A	-	3	-
Medium Bomber	532	625	500
B-47B	306	5	-
B-47E	226	620	500
Light Bomber	-	110	217
B-57A	-	8	-
B-57B	-	102	191
B-66B	-	-	26
Fighter	3,993	3,361	2,510
F-84E	215	-	-
F-84F	719	663	870
YF-84F	2	-	-
F-84G	652	137	-
F-86D	826	901	624
F-86E	225	60	-
F-86F	576	1,226	157
F-86H	-	173	300
YF-86H	-	2	-
F-89C	100	-	-
F-89D	193	172	240
F-94B	206	-	-
F-94C	279	-	-
YF-100A	-	2	-
F-100A	-	23	250
F-101A	-	-	29
YF-102	-	2	-
F-102A	-	-	40
Reconnaissance	232	426	291
RB-36H	39	26	-
RB-47E	52	168	65
RB-52B	-	17	43
RB-57A	-	67	-
RB-66A	-	5	-
RB-66B	-	-	73
RF-84F	130	128	80
YRF-84F	1	-	-
RC-121C	10	-	-
RC-121D	-	15	30
Search & Rescue	222	17	-
SA-16A	222	17	-

TYPE, MODEL AND SERIES	FISCAL YEAR 1951	FISCAL YEAR 1952	FISCAL YEAR 1953
Tanker	230	318	262
KC-97E	60	-	-
KC-97F	158	-	-
KC-97G	12	318	262
Cargo	592	459	418
YC-47F	1	-	-
C-118A	18	-	83
C-119C	169	-	-
C-119F	192	-	88
C-119G	45	117	146
YC-119H	1	-	-
C-123B	-	165	-
C-124A	125	-	-
YC-124B	1	-	-
C-124C	40	151	52
C-130A	-	-	7
C-131A	-	26	-
C-131B	-	-	36
YC-130	-	-	2
YC-135	-	-	2
YC-139	-	-	2
Trainer	2,293	1,025	1,158
T-28A	744	59	-
T-29B	105	-	-
T-29C	-	85	34
T-29D	-	40	52
T-33A	1,420	747	866
T-34A	-	94	206
TB-50H	24	-	-
Helicopter	182	155	193
H-13G	-	-	51
H-19A	50	-	-
H-19B	73	110	61
H-21A	32	-	-
H-21B	27	45	81
Liaison	111	103	20
L-19A	-	-	20
YL-20A	2	-	-
L-20A	109	103	-

SOURCE: Materiel Statistics Division, Directorate of Statistical Services, DCS/C.

TABLE 110 — USAF AND RESERVE FORCES FIRST AND SECOND LINE AIRPLANE INVENTORY SUMMARY — FY 1953

As of End of Month

STATUS AND CLASSIFICATION	JUL-52	AUG	SEP	OCT	NOV	DEC	JAN-53	FEB	MAR	APR	MAY	JUN
TOTAL	21,012	21,309	21,391	21,612	21,857	22,045	22,286	22,659	22,803	23,082	23,155	23,548
FIRST-LINE	8,079	8,539	8,717	8,966	9,103	9,316	9,605	10,051	10,334	10,709	11,053	11,364
USAF	7,857	8,252	8,310	8,693	8,582	8,938	9,293	9,604	9,944	10,261	10,575	10,873
Active	6,547	6,819	7,039	7,269	7,276	7,570	8,022	8,367	8,450	8,700	8,984	9,280
Inactive	1,310	1,433	1,271	1,424	1,306	1,368	1,271	1,237	1,494	1,561	1,591	1,593
AIR NATIONAL GUARD	40	40	49	50	51	52	59	75	100	100	100	106
Active	40	40	49	50	51	50	56	64	85	100	100	106
Inactive	-	-	-	-	-	2	3	11	15	-	-	-
AIR FORCE RESERVE	-	-	-	-	-	-	-	1	23	23	25	49
Active	-	-	-	-	-	-	-	-	23	23	23	48
Inactive	-	-	-	-	-	-	-	1	-	-	2	1
CIVIL AIR PATROL	129	138	123	97	72	25	22	22	-	-	-	-
Active	129	138	123	97	72	25	22	22	-	-	-	-
Inactive	-	-	-	-	-	-	-	-	-	-	-	-
MDAP	53	109	235	126	259	219	103	225	186	187	263	256
Active	2	7	8	5	39	35	10	17	23	29	79	75
Inactive	51	102	227	121	220	184	93	208	163	158	184	181
U. S. ARMY	-	-	-	-	128	75	126	96	56	102	88	80
Active	-	-	-	-	-	5	-	1	-	-	5	18
Inactive	-	-	-	-	128	70	126	95	56	102	83	62
U. S. NAVY	-	-	-	-	-	1	2	28	1	34	2	-
Active	-	-	-	-	-	1	1	1	1	-	-	-
Inactive	-	-	-	-	-	-	1	27	-	34	2	-
NATIONAL GUARD BUREAU ARMY DIVISION	-	-	-	-	11	6	-	-	24	2	-	-
Active	-	-	-	-	-	-	-	-	-	-	-	-
Inactive	-	-	-	-	11	6	-	-	24	2	-	-
SECOND-LINE	12,933	12,770	12,674	12,646	12,754	12,729	12,681	12,608	12,469	12,373	12,102	12,184
USAF	12,233	11,984	11,748	11,714	11,630	11,498	11,410	11,270	11,007	10,663	10,440	10,434
Active	9,261	9,116	9,008	8,950	8,868	8,855	8,728	8,610	8,394	8,139	7,921	7,794
Inactive	2,972	2,868	2,740	2,764	2,762	2,643	2,682	2,660	2,613	2,524	2,519	2,640
AIR NATIONAL GUARD	378	400	424	420	461	461	465	508	641	861	850	914
Active	376	398	423	418	461	446	453	480	602	742	819	883
Inactive	2	2	1	2	-	15	12	28	39	119	31	31
AIR FORCE RESERVE	72	103	143	144	158	178	214	229	244	277	274	272
Active	72	103	143	144	158	175	211	226	241	273	271	267
Inactive	-	-	-	-	-	3	3	3	3	4	3	5
CIVIL AIR PATROL	151	180	236	268	358	449	502	498	521	519	516	519
Active	150	179	235	267	354	447	493	497	519	519	515	519
Inactive	1	1	1	1	4	2	9	1	2	-	1	-
MDAP	99	103	123	100	116	91	85	100	55	52	20	40
Active	10	10	20	15	20	11	8	8	1	-	-	21
Inactive	89	93	103	85	96	80	77	92	54	52	20	19
U. S. ARMY	-	-	-	-	11	4	3	1	1	1	2	4
Active	-	-	-	-	1	3	2	-	-	-	-	2
Inactive	-	-	-	-	10	1	1	1	1	1	2	2
U. S. NAVY	-	-	-	-	-	1	1	1	-	-	-	1
Active	-	-	-	-	-	-	-	-	-	-	-	-
Inactive	-	-	-	-	-	1	1	1	-	-	-	1
NATIONAL GUARD BUREAU ARMY DIVISION	-	-	-	-	20	47	1	1	-	-	-	-
Active	-	-	-	-	20	40	1	1	-	-	-	-
Inactive	-	-	-	-	-	7	-	-	-	-	-	-

SOURCE: Materiel Statistics Division, Directorate of Statistical Services, DCS/C

TABLE 111 — USAF AND RESERVE FORCES AIRCRAFT INVENTORY BY COMMAND — SEMI-ANNUAL — FY 1953

COMMAND	31 DECEMBER 1952		30 JUNE 1953	
	CONTINENTAL	OVERSEAS	CONTINENTAL	OVERSEAS
TOTAL	17,663	4,420	19,029	4,575
USAF - TOTAL	16,113	4,361	16,859	4,504
Air Defense	1,107	-	1,420	-
Air Materiel	4,650	75	5,122	47
Air Proving Ground	161	-	161	-
Air Research and Development	542	23	581	21
Air University	148	-	173	-
Air Training	5,500	-	5,226	-
Continental Air	99	-	113	-
Headquarters, USAF	201	77	204	63
Military Air Transport Service	641	345	635	349
Strategic Air	1,775	128	1,922	157
Tactical Air	1,286	25	1,299	2
USAF Security Service	3	-	3	-
Alaskan Air	-	198	-	171
Caribbean Air	-	32	-	30
Far East Air Forces	-	2,365	-	2,361
Northeast Air	-	53	-	78
US Air Forces in Europe	-	1,031	-	1,212
Joint Brazil-US Military Commission	-	9	-	6
RESERVE FORCES - TOTAL	1,106	59	1,789	71
Air National Guard	466	47	970	50
Air Force Reserve	178	-	321	-
Civil Air Patrol	462	12	498	21
EARMARKED FOR NON-USAF AGENCIES - TOTAL	444	-	381	-
Mutual Defense Assistance Program	310	-	296	-
U. S. Army	79	-	84	-
U. S. Navy	2	-	1	-
National Guard Bureau, Army Division	53	-	-	-

SOURCE: Materiel Statistics Division, Directorate of Statistical Services, DCS/C

TABLE 112 — FUNCTIONAL DISTRIBUTION OF USAF AIRCRAFT BY TYPE — QUARTERLY, FISCAL YEAR 1953

TYPE OF AIRCRAFT	TOTAL AIRCRAFT INVENTORY	ACTIVE									INACTIVE					
		TOTAL	TACTICAL AND TRANSPORT	TRAINING	MINIMUM INDIVIDUAL TRAINING	ADMINI-STRATIVE	SPECIAL MISSION	TEST	MAINTE-NANCE	PROJECT	TOTAL	STORAGE	MODIFI-CATION	BAILMENT AND X-MODEL	OTHER	EXCESS AND RECOMMENDED RECLAMATION
30 SEPTEMBER 1952																
USAF - TOTAL	20,096	16,074	6,218	4,974	2,066	80	621	573	1,247	295	4,022	1,963	1,175	435	426	23
Bomber	2,934	1,665	1,050	179	24	3	13	138	176	82	1,269	666	513	55	34	1
Tanker	325	297	287	-	-	-	-	7	2	1	28	-	13	2	13	-
Fighter	4,735	3,949	2,428	732	20	-	1	171	479	118	786	219	298	74	186	9
Reconnaissance	649	536	435	7	2	1	16	20	42	13	113	45	63	2	3	-
Search and Rescue	268	245	187	-	-	-	17	6	27	8	23	11	2	-	9	1
Special Research	4	-	-	-	-	-	-	-	-	-	4	-	-	4	-	-
Cargo	3,282	2,976	1,218	20	902	66	352	91	279	48	306	10	90	170	30	6
Trainer	6,924	5,663	395	3,768	1,107	10	113	81	175	14	1,261	897	189	115	57	3
Communication	937	716	218	268	11	-	109	32	67	11	221	115	1	8	94	3
Glider	1	-	-	-	-	-	-	-	-	-	1	-	-	1	-	-
Aerial Target	37	27	-	-	-	-	-	27	-	-	10	-	6	4	-	-
31 DECEMBER 1952																
USAF - TOTAL	20,474	16,456	6,407	5,197	2,110	68	673	582	1,126	293	4,018	1,759	1,231	451	549	28
Bomber	2,856	1,666	1,140	192	26	3	11	149	133	12	1,190	611	494	58	27	-
Tanker	360	302	292	-	-	-	-	7	3	-	58	-	33	4	21	-
Fighter	4,993	4,014	2,417	781	15	-	1	166	441	193	979	145	417	89	317	11
Reconnaissance	652	550	447	7	1	1	14	17	47	16	102	39	45	2	14	2
Search and Rescue	293	252	199	-	-	-	16	5	29	3	41	11	6	-	23	1
Special Research	4	-	-	-	-	-	-	-	-	-	4	-	-	4	-	-
Cargo	3,385	3,043	1,277	18	877	52	382	97	319	21	342	21	100	192	24	5
Trainer	7,099	5,945	435	3,937	1,176	12	154	77	133	21	1,154	852	133	87	80	2
Communication	794	653	200	262	15	-	95	35	19	27	141	80	1	10	43	7
Glider	1	-	-	-	-	-	-	-	-	-	1	-	-	1	-	-
Aerial Target	37	31	-	-	-	-	-	29	2	-	6	-	2	4	-	-

TABLE 112 — FUNCTIONAL DISTRIBUTION OF USAF AIRCRAFT BY TYPE — QUARTERLY, FISCAL YEAR 1953 — CONTINUED

TYPE OF AIRCRAFT	TOTAL AIRCRAFT INVENTORY	ACTIVE									INACTIVE					
		TOTAL	TACTICAL AND TRANSPORT	TRAINING	MINIMUM INDIVIDUAL TRAINING	ADMINI-STRATIVE	SPECIAL MISSION	TEST	MAINTE-NANCE	PROJECT	TOTAL	STORAGE	MODIFI-CATION	BAILMENT AND X-MODEL	OTHER	EXCESS AND RECOMMENDED RECLAMATION
31 MARCH 1953																
USAF - TOTAL	20,989	16,873	6,605	5,239	2,152	75	701	592	1,170	339	4,116	1,675	1,110	434	873	24
Bomber	2,815	1,695	1,141	176	23	4	19	140	162	30	1,120	512	406	61	140	1
Tanker	393	349	335	-	-	-	-	4	9	1	44	-	26	2	16	-
Fighter	5,423	4,232	2,583	819	17	-	-	173	417	223	1,191	264	437	92	393	5
Reconnaissance	660	534	430	7	-	1	16	13	54	13	126	37	58	3	26	2
Search and Rescue	295	256	204	-	-	-	21	5	23	3	39	-	28	-	10	1
Special Research	5	-	-	-	-	-	-	-	-	-	5	-	-	5	-	-
Cargo	3,495	3,166	1,276	23	968	55	377	100	323	44	329	44	61	188	34	2
Trainer	7,032	5,919	414	3,926	1,131	15	166	90	162	15	1,113	740	87	64	218	4
Communication	833	693	222	288	13	-	102	40	18	10	140	78	3	14	36	9
Glider	1	-	-	-	-	-	-	-	-	-	1	-	-	1	-	-
Aerial Target	37	29	-	-	-	-	-	27	2	-	8	-	4	4	-	-
30 JUNE 1953																
USAF - TOTAL	21,363	17,108	7,067	4,948	2,083	67	684	614	1,334	311	4,255	2,024	1,018	429	759	25
Bomber	2,716	1,644	1,134	149	12	3	17	135	163	31	1,072	585	264	60	163	-
Tanker	435	385	367	-	-	-	-	6	12	-	50	-	27	4	19	-
Fighter	5,533	4,379	2,751	748	13	-	8	167	490	202	1,154	228	408	84	419	15
Reconnaissance	703	600	489	20	1	1	10	13	49	17	103	26	45	3	29	-
Search and Rescue	285	256	209	-	-	-	15	6	21	5	29	-	21	-	7	1
Special Research	5	-	-	-	-	-	-	-	-	-	5	-	-	5	-	-
Cargo	3,643	3,275	1,328	19	1,031	51	378	107	339	22	368	106	61	178	22	1
Trainer	7,107	5,750	481	3,703	1,020	12	168	105	230	31	1,357	1,040	178	79	56	4
Communication	880	785	308	309	6	-	88	44	27	3	95	26	8	13	44	4
Glider	-	-	-	-	-	-	-	-	-	-	-	-	-	-	-	-
Aerial Target	56	34	-	-	-	-	-	31	3	-	22	13	6	3	-	-

SOURCE: Materiel Statistics Division, Directorate of Statistical Services, DCS/C

TABLE 113 - FUNCTIONAL DISTRIBUTION OF USAF AIRCRAFT INVENTORY BY COMMAND - QUARTERLY FISCAL YEAR 1953

COMMAND	TOTAL INVENTORY	ACTIVE									INACTIVE					
		TOTAL	TACTICAL TRANSPORT UNITS	TRAINING UNITS	MINIMUM INDIV TRAINING	ADMINI-STRATIVE	SPECIAL MISSION	TEST	MAINTE-NANCE	PROJECT	TOTAL	STORAGE	MODIFI-CATION	RAILMENT X-MODELS	OTHER	EXCESS & REC. RECL.
30 SEPTEMBER 1952																
USAF - TOTAL	20,096	16,074	6,218	4,974	2,066	80	621	573	1,247	295	4,022	1,963	1,175	435	426	23
CONTINENTAL US	15,683	11,903	3,397	4,974	1,715	42	284	550	805	136	3,780	1,869	1,151	331	414	15
Air Training	5,303	5,303	-	4,903	358	3	16	-	23	-	-	-	-	-	-	-
Air Materiel	4,730	1,027	7	-	174	5	9	2	697	133	3,703	1,868	1,151	311	367	6
Strategic Air	1,661	1,560	1,328	-	291	12	7	1	20	1	1	-	-	-	1	-
Air Defense	1,008	1,004	769	-	178	5	34	-	18	-	4	-	-	-	-	4
Tactical Air	1,325	1,295	1,030	70	166	2	15	-	12	-	30	-	-	-	28	2
Military Air Transport Service	562	544	263	1	191	5	77	-	5	2	18	1	-	-	17	-
Air Research and Development	536	516	-	-	80	5	2	414	15	-	20	-	-	20	-	-
Headquarters, USAF	226	223	-	-	101	1	119	-	2	-	3	-	-	-	-	3
Air Proving Ground	161	160	-	-	23	-	-	133	4	-	1	-	-	-	1	-
Air University	106	106	-	-	99	2	1	-	4	-	-	-	-	-	-	-
Continental Air	62	62	-	-	54	2	1	-	5	-	-	-	-	-	-	-
USAF Security Service	3	3	-	-	-	-	3	-	-	-	-	-	-	-	-	-
OVERSEAS	4,413	4,171	2,821	-	351	38	337	23	442	159	242	94	24	104	12	8
Alaskan Air	217	195	120	-	33	-	16	6	15	5	22	-	22	-	-	-
Caribbean Air	34	33	6	-	9	2	16	-	-	-	1	-	-	-	-	1
Far East Air Forces	2,358	2,264	1,597	-	116	13	86	-	341	111	94	93	-	-	-	1
US Air Forces In Europe	1,032	1,023	682	-	138	5	66	-	79	33	9	1	1	5	-	2
Northeast Air	39	37	-	-	8	12	12	-	5	-	2	-	1	-	-	1
Joint Brazil-US Mil.Com	10	9	-	-	-	-	9	-	-	-	1	-	-	-	-	1
Air Materiel	109	-	-	-	-	-	-	-	-	-	109	-	-	97	12	-
Strategic Air	180	180	145	-	13	3	1	17	1	-	-	-	-	-	-	-
Tactical Air	27	27	25	-	-	-	-	-	-	2	-	-	-	-	-	-
Military Air Transport Service	310	308	246	-	34	3	21	-	1	3	2	-	-	-	-	2
Air Research and Development	23	22	-	-	-	-	18	-	-	4	1	-	-	1	-	-
Headquarters, USAF	74	73	-	-	-	-	72	-	-	1	1	-	-	1	-	-
31 DECEMBER 1952																
USAF - TOTAL	20,474	16,456	6,407	5,197	2,110	68	673	582	1,126	293	4,018	1,759	1,231	451	549	28
CONTINENTAL US	16,113	12,343	3,568	5,197	1,777	44	334	562	703	158	3,770	1,651	1,203	358	537	21
Air Training	5,500	5,500	-	5,113	351	4	15	-	15	2	-	-	-	-	-	-
Air Materiel	4,650	978	11	-	169	6	7	4	626	155	3,672	1,651	1,202	336	474	9
Strategic Air	1,775	1,775	1,448	-	284	11	13	-	19	-	-	-	-	-	-	-
Air Defense	1,107	1,099	832	-	187	6	62	-	12	-	8	-	-	-	-	8
Tactical Air	1,286	1,231	972	84	151	3	14	-	7	-	55	-	-	-	54	1
Military Air Transport Service	641	632	302	-	212	6	110	-	2	-	9	-	-	-	8	1
Air Research and Development	542	518	3	-	78	3	2	423	9	-	24	-	1	22	-	1
Headquarters, USAF	201	200	-	-	115	1	79	-	5	-	1	-	-	-	-	1
Air Proving Ground	161	160	-	-	21	-	-	135	4	-	1	-	-	-	1	-
Air University	148	148	-	-	139	2	3	-	3	1	-	-	-	-	-	-

TABLE 113 – FUNCTIONAL DISTRIBUTION OF USAF AIRCRAFT INVENTORY BY COMMAND – QUARTERLY, FISCAL YEAR 1953 – CONTINUED

COMMAND	TOTAL INVENTORY	ACTIVE										INACTIVE					
		TOTAL	TACTICAL TRANSPORT UNITS	TRAINING UNITS	MINIMUM PROFY TRAINING	ADMINI-STRATIVE	SPECIAL MISSION	TEST	MAINTE-NANCE	PROJECT	TOTAL	STORAGE	MODIFI-CATION	BAILMENT X-MODELS	OTHER	EXCESS & REC. RECL.
31 DECEMBER 1952-Cont'd CONTINENTAL US-Cont'd																
Continental Air	99	99	-	-	70	2	26	-	1	-	-	-	-	-	-	-
USAF Security Service	3	3	-	-	-	-	3	-	-	-	-	-	-	-	-	-
OVERSEAS	4,361	4,113	2,839	-	333	24	339	20	423	135	248	108	28	93	12	7
Alaskan Air	198	171	109	-	21	-	14	11	14	2	27	-	26	-	-	1
Caribbean Air	32	31	-	-	9	2	19	-	1	-	1	-	-	-	-	1
Far East Air Forces	2,365	2,238	1,626	-	102	14	73	-	305	118	127	100	-	20	6	1
US Air Forces in Europe	1,031	1,027	683	-	149	4	91	-	93	7	4	-	-	2	-	2
Northeast Air	53	49	14	-	10	-	23	-	2	-	4	-	2	-	-	2
Joint Brazil-US Mil. Com	9	9	-	-	-	-	9	-	-	-	-	-	-	-	-	-
Air Materiel	75	-	-	-	-	-	-	-	-	-	75	-	-	69	6	-
Strategic Air	128	128	109	-	13	3	1	-	1	1	-	-	-	-	-	-
Tactical Air	25	25	25	-	-	-	-	-	-	-	-	-	-	-	-	-
Military Air Transport Service	345	345	273	-	29	1	30	-	7	5	-	-	-	-	-	-
Air Research and Development	23	14	-	-	-	-	3	9	-	2	9	8	-	1	-	-
Headquarters, USAF	77	76	-	-	-	-	76	-	-	-	1	-	-	1	-	-
31 MARCH 1953																
USAF - TOTAL	20,989	16,873	6,605	5,239	2,152	75	701	592	1,170	339	4,116	1,675	1,110	434	873	24
CONTINENTAL US	16,445	12,828	3,792	5,238	1,794	44	353	570	880	157	3,617	1,472	1,086	363	677	19
Air Training	5,705	5,536	-	5,169	333	5	18	-	10	1	169	-	-	-	165	4
Air Materiel	4,539	1,172	11	-	173	6	8	3	822	149	3,367	1,472	1,086	340	462	7
Strategic Air	1,931	1,930	1,618	-	271	10	14	-	13	4	1	-	-	-	-	1
Air Defense	1,247	1,244	965	-	204	5	61	-	9	-	3	-	-	-	-	3
Tactical Air	1,202	1,162	890	69	171	4	19	-	9	-	40	-	-	-	39	1
Military Air Transport Service	672	665	305	-	232	7	114	-	5	2	7	-	-	-	7	-
Air Research and Development	543	518	3	-	70	4	-	437	4	-	25	-	-	23	-	2
Headquarters, USAF	199	199	-	-	107	1	90	-	1	-	-	-	-	-	-	-
Air Proving Ground	160	155	-	-	23	-	-	130	2	-	5	-	-	-	4	1
Air University	151	151	-	-	147	1	1	-	1	1	-	-	-	-	-	-
Continental Air	93	93	-	-	63	1	25	-	4	-	-	-	-	-	-	-
USAF Security Service	3	3	-	-	-	-	3	-	-	-	-	-	-	-	-	-
OVERSEAS	4,534	4,038	2,811	-	358	31	347	21	268	182	496	201	24	71	196	4
Alaskan Air	194	169	102	-	23	-	18	8	13	5	25	-	24	-	-	1
Caribbean Air	29	29	-	-	9	2	18	-	-	-	-	-	-	-	-	-
Far East Air Forces	2,469	2,061	1,608	-	98	12	83	-	140	120	408	196	-	21	191	-
US Air Forces in Europe	1,123	1,118	671	-	168	4	104	-	127	44	5	-	-	2	-	3
Northeast Air	62	62	14	-	14	2	26	-	3	3	-	-	-	-	-	-
Joint Brazil-US Mil. Com	11	11	-	-	-	-	11	-	-	-	-	-	-	-	-	-
Air Materiel	51	-	-	-	-	-	-	-	-	-	51	-	-	46	5	-

TABLE 113 – FUNCTIONAL DISTRIBUTION OF USAF AIRCRAFT INVENTORY BY COMMAND – QUARTERLY, FISCAL YEAR 1953 – CONTINUED

COMMAND	TOTAL INVENTORY	ACTIVE									INACTIVE					
		TOTAL	TACTICAL TRANSPORT UNITS	TRAINING UNITS	MINIMUM INDIV TRAINING	ADMINI-STRATIVE	SPECIAL MISSION	TEST	MAINTE-NANCE	PROJECT	TOTAL	STORAGE	MODIFI-CATION	BAILMENT X-MODELS	OTHER	EXCESS & REC. RECL.
31 MARCH 1953-Cont'd CONTINENTAL US-Cont'd																
Strategic Air	131	131	110	-	14	4	1	1	1	-	-	-	-	-	-	-
Tactical Air	25	25	25	-	-	-	-	-	-	-	-	-	-	-	-	-
Military Air Transport Service	354	354	281	-	31	7	21	-	4	10	-	-	-	-	-	-
Air Research and Development	21	15	-	-	-	-	3	12	-	-	6	5	-	1	-	-
Headquarters, USAF	64	63	-	-	1	-	62	-	-	-	1	-	-	1	-	-
Accountability Terminated *	10	7	2	1	-	-	1	1	2	-	3	2	-	-	-	1
30 JUNE 1953																
USAF - TOTAL	21,363	17,108	7,067	4,948	2,083	67	684	614	1,334	311	4,255	2,024	1,018	429	759	25
CONTINENTAL US	16,859	12,975	4,104	4,948	1,745	40	373	596	987	182	3,884	1,871	1,015	361	617	20
Air Training	5,226	5,210	-	4,861	285	2	42	-	20	-	16	-	-	-	7	9
Air Materiel	5,122	1,289	11	-	170	6	8	6	906	182	3,833	1,871	1,015	340	603	4
Strategic Air	1,922	1,918	1,604	-	273	11	13	1	16	-	4	-	-	-	1	3
Air Defense	1,420	1,418	1,134	-	206	4	68	-	6	-	2	-	-	-	-	2
Tactical Air	1,299	1,299	1,021	87	163	3	19	-	6	-	-	-	-	-	-	-
Military Air Transport Service	635	629	331	-	181	7	106	-	4	-	6	-	-	-	6	-
Air Research and Development	581	561	3	-	90	3	-	453	12	-	20	-	-	19	-	1
Headquarters, USAF	204	203	-	-	111	2	86	-	4	-	1	-	-	1	-	-
Air Proving Ground	161	159	-	-	21	-	-	136	2	-	2	-	-	1	-	1
Air University	173	173	-	-	165	1	2	-	5	-	-	-	-	-	-	-
Continental Air	113	113	-	-	80	1	26	-	6	-	-	-	-	-	-	-
USAF Security Service	3	3	-	-	-	-	3	-	-	-	-	-	-	-	-	-
OVERSEAS	4,504	4,133	2,963	-	338	27	311	18	347	129	371	153	3	68	142	5
Alaskan Air	171	168	113	-	22	-	9	4	17	3	3	-	3	-	-	-
Caribbean Air	30	30	-	-	9	1	18	-	1	1	-	-	-	-	-	-
Far East Air Forces	2,361	2,051	1,648	-	88	10	64	-	190	51	310	150	-	18	141	1
US Air Forces in Europe	1,212	1,205	764	-	155	2	103	-	124	57	7	-	-	3	-	4
Northeast Air	78	78	15	-	14	2	26	-	5	16	-	-	-	-	-	-
Joint Brazil-US Mil. Com	6	6	-	-	-	-	6	-	-	-	-	-	-	-	-	-
Air Materiel	47	-	-	-	-	-	-	-	-	-	47	-	-	46	1	-
Strategic Air	157	157	132	-	16	5	1	-	2	1	-	-	-	-	-	-
Tactical Air	9	9	9	-	-	-	-	-	-	-	-	-	-	-	-	-
Military Air Transport Service	349	349	282	-	32	7	20	-	8	-	-	-	-	-	-	-
Air Research and Development	21	17	-	-	-	-	3	14	-	-	4	3	-	1	-	-
Headquarters, USAF	63	63	-	-	2	-	61	-	-	-	-	-	-	-	-	-

* Possessing units recommended accountability termination of these aircraft, but did not receive disposal instructions by 31 March 1953.

SOURCE: Materiel Statistics Division, Directorate of Statistical Services, DCS/C

TABLE 114 — USAF AND RESERVE FORCES AIRPLANE INVENTORY — MONTHLY, FISCAL YEAR 1953

Note: Reserve stock includes airplanes in storage, undergoing modification, in flyable inactive status, on inactive and non-USAF projects, excess to commands, and airplanes accepted but not delivered.

	TOTAL	USAF	Air National Guard	Air Force Reserve	Civil Air Patrol	EARMARKED			
						MDAP	US Army	US Navy	National Guard, Army Division
31 July 1952 TOTAL	21,012	20,090	418	72	280	152	-	-	-
ACTIVE	16,587	15,808	416	72	279	12	-	-	-
First-Line Combat	3,170	3,170	-	-	-	-	-	-	-
Second-Line Combat	3,866	3,574	290	-	-	2	-	-	-
Non-Combat	9,551	9,064	126	72	279	10	-	-	-
INACTIVE	4,425	4,282	2	-	1	140	-	-	-
Reserve Stock	3,968	3,828	-	-	-	140	-	-	-
First-Line Combat	547	507	-	-	-	40	-	-	-
Second-Line Combat	1,577	1,489	-	-	-	88	-	-	-
Non-Combat	1,844	1,832	-	-	-	12	-	-	-
Experimental, Loan and Bailment	425	425	-	-	-	-	-	-	-
First-Line Combat	76	76	-	-	-	-	-	-	-
Second-Line Combat	57	57	-	-	-	-	-	-	-
Non-Combat	292	292	-	-	-	-	-	-	-
Excess and Recommended Reclamation	32	29	2	-	1	-	-	-	-
First-Line Combat	5	5	-	-	-	-	-	-	-
Second-Line Combat	10	8	2	-	-	-	-	-	-
Non-Combat	17	16	-	-	1	-	-	-	-
31 August 1952 TOTAL	21,309	20,236	440	103	318	212	-	-	-
ACTIVE	16,810	15,935	438	103	317	17	-	-	-
First-Line Combat	3,226	3,226	-	-	-	-	-	-	-
Second-Line Combat	3,775	3,483	290	-	-	2	-	-	-
Non-Combat	9,809	9,226	148	103	317	15	-	-	-
INACTIVE	4,499	4,301	2	-	1	195	-	-	-
Reserve Stock	4,040	3,852	-	-	-	188	-	-	-
First-Line Combat	643	574	-	-	-	69	-	-	-
Second-Line Combat	1,619	1,526	-	-	-	93	-	-	-
Non-Combat	1,778	1,752	-	-	-	26	-	-	-
Experimental, Loan and Bailment	434	427	-	-	-	7	-	-	-
First-Line Combat	77	77	-	-	-	-	-	-	-
Second-Line Combat	55	55	-	-	-	-	-	-	-
Non-Combat	302	295	-	-	-	7	-	-	-
Excess and Recommended Reclamation	25	22	2	-	1	-	-	-	-
First-Line Combat	-	-	-	-	-	-	-	-	-
Second-Line Combat	8	6	2	-	-	-	-	-	-
Non-Combat	17	16	-	-	1	-	-	-	-
30 September 1952 TOTAL	21,391	20,058	473	143	359	358	-	-	-
ACTIVE	17,046	16,047	470	143	358	28	-	-	-
First-Line Combat	3,290	3,286	-	-	-	4	-	-	-
Second-Line Combat	3,696	3,406	290	-	-	-	-	-	-
Non-Combat	10,060	9,355	180	143	358	24	-	-	-
INACTIVE	4,345	4,011	3	-	1	330	-	-	-
Reserve Stock	3,889	3,558	1	-	-	330	-	-	-
First-Line Combat	712	518	-	-	-	194	-	-	-
Second-Line Combat	1,652	1,557	-	-	-	95	-	-	-
Non-Combat	1,525	1,483	1	-	-	41	-	-	-
Experimental, Loan and Bailment	430	430	-	-	-	-	-	-	-
First-Line Combat	78	78	-	-	-	-	-	-	-
Second-Line Combat	55	55	-	-	-	-	-	-	-
Non-Combat	297	297	-	-	-	-	-	-	-
Excess and Recommended Reclamation	26	23	2	-	1	-	-	-	-
First-Line Combat	-	-	-	-	-	-	-	-	-
Second-Line Combat	13	11	2	-	-	-	-	-	-
Non-Combat	13	12	-	-	1	-	-	-	-

TABLE 114 — USAF AND RESERVE FORCES AIRPLANE INVENTORY — MONTHLY, FISCAL YEAR 1953 — CONTINUED

	TOTAL	USAF	Air National Guard	Air Force Reserve	Civil Air Patrol	EARMARKED			
						MDAP	US Army	US Navy	National Guard, Army Division
31 October 1952 TOTAL	21,612	20,407	470	144	365	226	-	-	-
ACTIVE	17,215	16,219	468	144	364	20	-	-	-
First-Line Combat	3,319	3,316	-	-	-	3	-	-	-
Second-Line Combat	3,644	3,353	284	-	-	7	-	-	-
Non-Combat	10,252	9,550	184	144	364	10	-	-	-
INACTIVE	4,397	4,188	2	-	1	206	-	-	-
Reserve Stock	3,917	3,711	-	-	-	206	-	-	-
First-Line Combat	759	661	-	-	-	98	-	-	-
Second-Line Combat	1,654	1,577	-	-	-	77	-	-	-
Non-Combat	1,504	1,473	-	-	-	31	-	-	-
Experimental, Loan and Bailment	453	453	-	-	-	-	-	-	-
First-Line Combat	80	80	-	-	-	-	-	-	-
Second-Line Combat	56	56	-	-	-	-	-	-	-
Non-Combat	317	317	-	-	-	-	-	-	-
Excess and Recommended Reclamation	27	24	2	-	1	-	-	-	-
First-Line Combat	3	3	-	-	-	-	-	-	-
Second-Line Combat	10	8	2	-	-	-	-	-	-
Non-Combat	14	13	-	-	1	-	-	-	-
30 November 1952 TOTAL	21,857	20,212	512	158	430	375	139	-	31
ACTIVE	17,320	16,144	512	158	426	59	1	-	20
First-Line Combat	3,347	3,309	-	-	-	38	-	-	-
Second-Line Combat	3,599	3,297	295	-	-	7	-	-	-
Non-Combat	10,374	9,538	217	158	426	14	1	-	20
INACTIVE	4,537	4,068	-	-	4	316	138	-	11
Reserve Stock	4,079	3,610	-	-	4	316	138	-	11
First-Line Combat	877	674	-	-	-	203	-	-	-
Second-Line Combat	1,690	1,605	-	-	-	76	9	-	-
Non-Combat	1,512	1,331	-	-	4	37	129	-	11
Experimental, Loan and Bailment	432	432	-	-	-	-	-	-	-
First-Line Combat	85	85	-	-	-	-	-	-	-
Second-Line Combat	57	57	-	-	-	-	-	-	-
Non-Combat	290	290	-	-	-	-	-	-	-
Excess and Recommended Reclamation	26	26	-	-	-	-	-	-	-
First-Line Combat	2	2	-	-	-	-	-	-	-
Second-Line Combat	9	9	-	-	-	-	-	-	-
Non-Combat	15	15	-	-	-	-	-	-	-
31 December 1952 TOTAL	22,045	20,436	513	178	474	310	79	2	53
ACTIVE	17,663	16,425	496	175	472	46	8	1	40
First-Line Combat	3,478	3,444	-	-	-	34	-	-	-
Second-Line Combat	3,649	3,340	292	8	-	6	3	-	-
Non-Combat	10,536	9,641	204	167	472	6	5	1	40
INACTIVE	4,382	4,011	17	3	2	264	71	1	13
Reserve Stock	3,883	3,537	2	3	-	263	71	1	6
First-Line Combat	858	702	-	-	-	156	-	-	-
Second-Line Combat	1,570	1,501	1	-	-	68	-	-	-
Non-Combat	1,455	1,334	1	3	-	39	71	1	6
Experimental, Loan and Bailment	461	446	14	-	-	1	-	-	-
First-Line Combat	87	86	-	-	-	1	-	-	-
Second-Line Combat	67	67	-	-	-	-	-	-	-
Non-Combat	307	293	14	-	-	-	-	-	-
Excess and Recommended Reclamation	38	28	1	-	2	-	-	-	7
First-Line Combat	4	4	-	-	-	-	-	-	-
Second-Line Combat	11	10	1	-	-	-	-	-	-
Non-Combat	23	14	-	-	2	-	-	-	7

TABLE 114 —USAF AND RESERVE FORCES AIRPLANE INVENTORY – MONTHLY, FISCAL YEAR 1953 – CONTINUED

	TOTAL	USAF	Air National Guard	Air Force Reserve	Civil Air Patrol	EARMARKED			
						MDAP	US Army	US Navy	National Guard, Army Division
31 January 1953 TOTAL	22,286	20,703	524	214	524	188	129	3	1
ACTIVE	18,007	16,750	509	211	515	18	2	1	1
First-Line Combat	3,739	3,738	-	-	-	1	-	-	-
Second-Line Combat	3,595	3,266	289	31	-	7	2	-	-
Non-Combat	10,673	9,746	220	180	515	10	-	1	1
INACTIVE	4,279	3,953	15	3	9	170	127	2	-
Reserve Stock	3,793	3,489	3	3	-	169	127	2	-
First-Line Combat	733	650	-	-	-	83	-	-	-
Second-Line Combat	1,614	1,552	-	-	-	62	-	-	-
Non-Combat	1,446	1,287	3	3	-	24	127	2	-
Experimental, Loan and Bailment	454	442	11	-	-	1	-	-	-
First-Line Combat	79	79	-	-	-	-	-	-	-
Second-Line Combat	66	65	-	-	-	1	-	-	-
Non-Combat	309	298	11	-	-	-	-	-	-
Excess and Recommended Reclamation	32	22	1	-	9	-	-	-	-
First-Line Combat	3	3	-	-	-	-	-	-	-
Second-Line Combat	8	7	1	-	-	-	-	-	-
Non-Combat	21	12	-	-	9	-	-	-	-
28 February 1953 TOTAL	22,659	20,874	583	230	520	325	97	29	1
ACTIVE	18,294	16,977	544	226	519	25	1	1	1
First-Line Combat	3,957	3,948	-	-	-	8	1	-	-
Second-Line Combat	3,564	3,227	299	36	-	2	-	-	-
Non-Combat	10,773	9,802	245	190	519	15	-	1	1
INACTIVE	4,365	3,897	39	4	1	300	96	28	-
Reserve Stock	3,916	3,464	26	4	-	299	95	28	-
First-Line Combat	763	592	-	-	-	171	-	-	-
Second-Line Combat	1,612	1,530	2	-	-	80	-	-	-
Non-Combat	1,541	1,342	24	4	-	48	95	28	-
Experimental, Loan and Bailment	428	414	12	-	-	1	1	-	-
First-Line Combat	83	82	-	-	-	-	1	-	-
Second-Line Combat	68	67	-	-	-	1	-	-	-
Non-Combat	277	265	12	-	-	-	-	-	-
Excess and Recommended Reclamation	21	19	1	-	1	-	-	-	-
First-Line Combat	4	4	-	-	-	-	-	-	-
Second-Line Combat	6	5	1	-	-	-	-	-	-
Non-Combat	11	10	-	-	1	-	-	-	-
31 March 1953 TOTAL	22,803	20,951	741	267	521	241	57	1	24
ACTIVE	18,339	16,844	687	264	519	24	-	1	-
First-Line Combat	3,950	3,938	-	-	-	12	-	-	-
Second-Line Combat	3,513	3,128	344	40	-	1	-	-	-
Non-Combat	10,876	9,778	343	224	519	11	-	1	-
INACTIVE	4,464	4,107	54	3	2	217	57	-	24
Reserve Stock	4,007	3,654	53	3	-	216	57	-	24
First-Line Combat	949	830	-	-	-	119	-	-	-
Second-Line Combat	1,568	1,523	-	-	-	45	-	-	-
Non-Combat	1,490	1,301	53	3	-	52	57	-	24
Experimental, Loan and Bailment	431	429	1	-	-	1	-	-	-
First-Line Combat	89	89	-	-	-	-	-	-	-
Second-Line Combat	70	69	-	-	-	1	-	-	-
Non-Combat	272	271	1	-	-	-	-	-	-
Excess and Recommended Reclamation	26	24	-	-	2	-	-	-	-
First-Line Combat	3	3	-	-	-	-	-	-	-
Second-Line Combat	6	6	-	-	-	-	-	-	-
Non-Combat	17	15	-	-	2	-	-	-	-

TABLE 114 —USAF AND RESERVE FORCES AIRPLANE INVENTORY – MONTHLY, FISCAL YEAR 1953 — CONTINUED

	TOTAL	USAF	Air National Guard	Air Force Reserve	Civil Air Patrol	EARMARKED			
						MDAP	US Army	US Navy	National Guard, Army Division
30 April 1953 TOTAL	23,082	20,924	961	300	519	239	103	34	2
ACTIVE	18,525	16,839	842	296	519	29	-	-	-
First-Line Combat	4,054	4,038	-	-	-	16	-	-	-
Second-Line Combat	3,468	2,997	402	69	-	-	-	-	-
Non-Combat	11,003	9,804	440	227	519	13	-	-	-
INACTIVE	4,557	4,085	119	4	-	210	103	34	2
Reserve Stock	4,116	3,645	119	4	-	209	103	34	2
First-Line Combat	1,013	940	-	-	-	73	-	-	-
Second-Line Combat	1,524	1,388	89	1	-	46	-	-	-
Non-Combat	1,579	1,317	30	3	-	90	103	34	2
Experimental, Loan and Bailment	413	412	-	-	-	1	-	-	-
First-Line Combat	92	92	-	-	-	-	-	-	-
Second-Line Combat	56	55	-	-	-	1	-	-	-
Non-Combat	265	265	-	-	-	-	-	-	-
Excess and Recommended Reclamation	28	28	-	-	-	-	-	-	-
First-Line Combat	2	2	-	-	-	-	-	-	-
Second-Line Combat	14	14	-	-	-	-	-	-	-
Non-Combat	12	12	-	-	-	-	-	-	-
31 May 1953 TOTAL	23,155	21,015	950	299	516	283	90	2	-
ACTIVE	18,717	16,905	919	294	515	79	5	-	-
First-Line Combat	4,260	4,191	-	-	-	69	-	-	-
Second-Line Combat	3,442	2,947	428	67	-	-	-	-	-
Non-Combat	11,015	9,767	491	227	515	10	5	-	-
INACTIVE	4,438	4,110	31	5	1	204	85	2	-
Reserve Stock	3,993	3,669	31	5	-	201	85	2	-
First-Line Combat	1,055	953	-	-	-	102	-	-	-
Second-Line Combat	1,371	1,363	7	-	-	-	1	-	-
Non-Combat	1,567	1,353	24	5	-	99	84	2	-
Experimental, Loan and Bailment	424	421	-	-	-	3	-	-	-
First-Line Combat	92	91	-	-	-	1	-	-	-
Second-Line Combat	61	61	-	-	-	-	-	-	-
Non-Combat	271	269	-	-	-	2	-	-	-
Excess and Recommended Reclamation	21	20	-	-	1	-	-	-	-
First-Line Combat	2	2	-	-	-	-	-	-	-
Second-Line Combat	11	11	-	-	-	-	-	-	-
Non-Combat	8	7	-	-	1	-	-	-	-
30 June 1953 TOTAL	23,548	21,307	1,020	321	519	296	84	1	-
ACTIVE	19,013	17,074	989	315	519	96	20	-	-
First-Line Combat	4,416	4,350	-	-	-	66	-	-	-
Second-Line Combat	3,464	2,914	477	65	-	6	2	-	-
Non-Combat	11,133	9,810	512	250	519	24	18	-	-
INACTIVE	4,535	4,233	31	6	-	200	64	1	-
Reserve Stock	4,081	3,782	30	6	-	199	64	-	-
First-Line Combat	992	920	-	-	-	72	-	-	-
Second-Line Combat	1,350	1,321	13	2	-	13	1	-	-
Non-Combat	1,739	1,541	17	4	-	114	63	-	-
Experimental, Loan and Bailment	427	426	-	-	-	1	-	-	-
First-Line Combat	89	89	-	-	-	-	-	-	-
Second-Line Combat	63	62	-	-	-	1	-	-	-
Non-Combat	275	275	-	-	-	-	-	-	-
Excess and Recommended Reclamation	27	25	1	-	-	-	-	1	-
First-Line Combat	6	6	-	-	-	-	-	-	-
Second-Line Combat	11	10	1	-	-	-	-	-	-
Non-Combat	10	9	-	-	-	-	-	1	-

SOURCE: Materiel Statistics Division, Directorate of Statistical Services, DCS/C

TABLE 115 — CUMULATIVE AGE DISTRIBUTION OF THE USAF AIRPLANE INVENTORY — QUARTERLY, FY 1953

AGE IN MONTHS	TOTAL AIRPLANES	BOMBER			FIGHTER			CARGO			TRAINER	OTHER TYPES a/
		HEAVY	MEDIUM	LIGHT	FIGHTER-BOMBER		INTERCEPTOR JET	HEAVY	MEDIUM	LIGHT		
					JET	PISTON						
	30 September 1952											
Under 6	2969	27	206	-	429	-	382	62	112	86	1332	333
" 12	4612	80	290	1	640	-	684	98	156	93	1956	614
" 18	5876	130	308	1	844	-	933	138	222	95	2429	776
" 24	6759	148	337	1	952	-	1097	173	259	102	2852	838
" 30	7588	158	420	3	1084	-	1250	214	312	105	3157	885
" 36	8135	159	489	48	1279	-	1352	221	353	105	3230	899
" 42	8487	159	512	63	1391	-	1445	223	355	105	3267	967
" 48	8883	159	539	70	1582	27	1479	224	365	105	3294	1039
" 54	9176	160	563	80	1769	33	1483	224	365	129	3306	1064
" 60	9425		572	80	1876	34		227	365	153	3316	1159
" 66	9576		572	80	1948	34		234	365	188	3338	1173
" 72	9761		572	80	1998	34		241	366	225	3346	1256
" 78	9868		597	80	2012	34		244	366	239	3353	1300
" 84	10091		609	81	2063	49		245	385	278	3391	1347
" 90	14265		1509	448	2082	733			669	712	4374	1850
" 96	17627		1881	841	2083	1156			749	1369	5588	2072
" 102	18986		1891	880		1169			749	2021	6214	2091
" 108	19485			883					750	2186	6525	2110
" 114	19763								750	2268	6709	2122
" 120	19890								751	2281	6819	2125
" 126	19995									2285	6915	2130
" 132	20038									2286	6957	
" 138	20056										6975	
" 144	20058										6977	
	31 December 1952											
Under 6	2706	24	143	-	407	-	494	70	132	143	1070	223
" 12	4921	51	298	1	681	-	803	120	212	198	2106	451
" 18	6321	114	335	1	937	-	1073	146	264	200	2554	697
" 24	7362	152	344	1	1058	-	1275	189	307	205	3040	791
" 30	8162	168	391	1	1110	-	1425	225	346	211	3435	850
" 36	8795		463	32	1292	-	1549	244	390	211	3578	868
" 42	9260		541	55	1466	-	1633	256	422	211	3618	890
" 48	9661		549	67	1595	7	1719	257	431	211	3654	1003
" 54	9985		588	72	1796	32	1723	258	435	223	3677	1013
" 60	10258		600	76	1928	33	1725	261	435	248	3692	1092
" 66	10466		601	76	2035	33		263	436	278	3712	1139
" 72	10553		601	76	2046	33		274	436	312	3715	1167
" 78	10743		601	76	2101	33		278	436	343	3726	1256
" 84	10839		630	76	2124	35		278	436	346	3737	1284
" 90	12692		1021	147	2166	324		279	588	613	4159	1502
" 96	17055		1775	656	2175	995			811	1044	5488	1939
" 102	19063		1881	797		1091			811	1751	6378	2007
" 108	19785			807		1092			812	2148	6677	2021
" 114	20168			808					812	2250	6943	2035
" 120	20273								812	2287	7006	2040
" 126	20340								813	2289	7070	
" 132	20395									2293	7121	
" 138	20413										7139	
" 144	20421										7147	

TABLE 116 — CUMULATIVE AGE DISTRIBUTION OF THE USAF AIRPLANE INVENTORY — QUARTERLY, FISCAL YEAR 1953 — Continued

AGE IN MONTHS	TOTAL AIRPLANES	BOMBER			FIGHTER			CARGO			TRAINER	OTHER TYPES a/
		HEAVY	MEDIUM	LIGHT	FIGHTER-BOMBER JET	FIGHTER-BOMBER PISTON	INTERCEPTOR JET	HEAVY	MEDIUM	LIGHT		
	31 March 1953											
Under 6	2752	20	116	1	496	-	752	67	139	173	710	278
" 12	5495	45	322	1	854	-	1104	128	248	261	2007	525
" 18	7040	97	402	2	1055	-	1379	164	290	268	2617	766
" 24	8252	147	418	2	1248	-	1613	203	354	269	3082	916
" 30	9103	166	446	2	1337	-	1773	240	390	276	3499	974
" 36	9856	176	519	3	1440	-	1917	273	435	279	3795	1019
" 42	10363		580	43	1625	-	2011	286	463	279	3868	1032
" 48	10746		618	61	1740	-	2101	290	482	279	3906	1093
" 54	11112		644	67	1912	27	2133	291	492	279	3934	1157
" 60	11373		667	75	2074	32	2137	291	492	303	3948	1178
" 66	11576		673	75	2157	33		294	492	327	3960	1252
" 72	11722		673	75	2227	33		301	493	361	3981	1265
" 78	11897		673	75	2275	33		308	493	398	3989	1340
" 84	11996		690	75	2290	33		311	493	413	3993	1385
" 90	12197		706	76	2337	38		312	512	450	4027	1426
" 96	15944		1547	384	2355	575			786	852	4924	1896
" 102	18964		1879	725	2356	925		866		1444	6051	2093
" 108	20160		1886	750		930			866	2060	6575	2112
" 114	20579			753					867	2220	6816	2126
" 120	20790								867	2299	6939	2135
" 126	20864								868	2310	6998	2138
" 132	20918									2311	7051	
" 138	20942									2315	7071	
" 144	20950										7079	
" 150	20951										7080	
	30 June 1953											
Under 6	2942	21	174	1	255	-	1195	64	115	152	608	357
" 12	5553	43	295	1	673	-	1620	133	244	295	1638	611
" 18	7665	70	399	2	918	-	1898	183	322	352	2671	850
" 24	9000	133	400	2	1155	-	2147	209	374	353	3134	1093
" 30	10005	170	405	2	1264	-	2339	252	416	357	3615	1185
" 36	10785	186	451	2	1314	-	2485	289	454	363	4001	1240
" 42	11384		522	32	1470	-	2603	308	495	363	4140	1265
" 48	11828		598	55	1636	-	2683	320	526	363	4179	1282
" 54	12165		606	67	1752	4	2764	321	535	363	4215	1352
" 60	12410		644	71	1886	13	2768	322	539	375	4236	1370
" 66	12562		656	75	1932	14	2770	324	539	400	4246	1420
" 72	12719		657	75	2024	14		326	540	429	4252	1445
" 78	12803		657	75	2036	14		337	540	463	4252	1473
" 84	12981		657	75	2089	14		341	540	494	4255	1560
" 90	13073		686	75	2115	15		341	540	497	4262	1586
" 96	14660		1064	142	2155	139		342	692	759	4624	1787
" 102	18408		1757	565	2164	553			912	1177	5806	2176
" 108	20199		1849	671		599			912	1863	6606	2237
" 114	20844			680					913	2244	6848	2249
" 120	21141			681					913	2344	7031	2262
" 126	21221								913	2381	7069	2267
" 132	21259								914	2383	7104	
" 138	21295									2387	7136	
" 144	21304										7145	
" 150	21307										7148	

a/ Includes Tanker, Reconnaissance, Search & Rescue, Special Research, and Communication.

SOURCE: Materiel Statistics Division, Directorate of Statistical Services, DCS/C.

TABLE 117 — CALENDAR AGE DISTRIBUTION OF THE USAF AIRPLANE INVENTORY — QUARTERLY, FY 1953

AGE IN MONTHS		NUMBER OF AIRPLANES			
		30 SEPTEMBER 1952	31 DECEMBER 1952	31 MARCH 1953	30 JUNE 1953
0	2.9	1,544	1,273	1,469	1,559
3.0	5.9	1,425	1,433	1,283	1,383
6.0	8.9	854	1,383	1,394	1,257
9.0	11.9	789	832	1,349	1,354
12.0	14.9	683	740	823	1,310
15.0	17.9	581	660	722	802
18.0	20.9	487	568	650	700
21.0	23.9	396	473	562	635
24.0	26.9	396	391	462	550
27.0	29.9	433	409	389	455
30.0	32.9	316	367	402	386
33.0	35.9	231	266	351	394
36.0	38.9	164	257	254	348
39.0	41.9	188	208	253	251
42.0	44.9	227	186	202	253
45.0	47.9	169	215	181	191
48.0	50.9	165	166	207	154
51.0	53.9	128	158	159	183
54.0	56.9	153	125	147	133
57.0	59.9	96	148	114	112
60.0	62.9	115	86	134	73
63.0	65.9	36	122	69	79
66.0	68.9	51	36	110	38
69.0	71.9	134	51	36	119
72.0	74.9	59	126	51	34
75.0	77.9	48	64	124	50
78.0	80.9	59	38	62	118
81.0	83.9	164	58	37	60
84.0	86.9	1,754	157	56	37
87.0	89.9	2,420	1,696	145	55
90.0	92.9	2,097	2,340	1,553	138
93.0	95.9	1,265	2,023	2,194	1,449
96.0	98.9	878	1,185	1,893	2,011
99.0	101.9	481	823	1,127	1,737
102.0	104.9	284	459	762	1,041
105.0	107.9	215	263	434	750
108.0	110.9	202	201	243	418
111.0	113.9	76	182	176	227
114.0	116.9	70	57	160	160
117.0	119.9	57	48	51	137
120.0	122.9	47	38	41	48
123.0	125.9	58	29	33	32
126.0	128.9	26	36	25	24
129.0	131.9	17	19	29	14
132.0	134.9	11	12	17	24
135.0	137.9	7	6	7	12
138.0	140.9	2	6	6	5
141.0	143.9		2	2	4
144.0	146.9			1	2
147.0	149.9				1
Average Age in Months		56.8	55.7	53.7	51.7

SOURCE: Materiel Statistics Division, Directorate of Statistical Services, DCS/C

TABLE 118 — USAF AIRCRAFT IN STORAGE BY MODEL — QUARTERLY, FISCAL YEAR 1953

TYPE AND MODEL	30 SEPTEMBER 1952	31 DECEMBER 1952	31 MARCH 1953	30 JUNE 1953
TOTAL	1,963	1,759	1,675	2,024
BOMBER	666	611	512	598
B-17	8	7	2	15
B-25	35	8	-	-
B-26	106	89	42	23
B-29	517	507	468	560
FIGHTER	219	145	264	228
F-47	174	105	102	100
F-51	6	6	78	55
F-80	19	7	9	9
F-84	14	21	69	37
F-86	6	6	5	27
F-94	-	-	1	-
RECONNAISSANCE	45	39	37	26
RB-17	7	6	-	-
WB-17	-	1	-	-
RB-26	3	1	4	1
RB-29	20	20	19	19
RB-49	1	1	1	1
RC-45	1	1	-	-
RF-51	-	8	12	-
RF-80	13	-	1	2
RF-86	-	1	-	3
SEARCH AND RESCUE	11	11	-	-
SB-17	11	11	-	-
CARGO	10	21	44	106
C-46	1	10	29	33
C-47	-	1	-	2
C-54	1	1	1	1
C-82	4	4	13	70
C-119	2	4	-	-
CB-25	1	-	-	-
CB-26	1	1	1	-
TRAINER	897	852	740	1,040
T-6	119	119	120	445
T-28	388	387	387	368
T-33	-	1	-	-
TB-17	2	2	-	-
TB-25	3	2	-	-
TB-26	28	23	6	1
TB-29	251	250	211	213
TF-47	106	68	16	13
COMMUNICATION	115	80	78	26
L-13	65	74	77	10
LT-6	1	2	-	-
H-13	-	-	1	16
H-19	3	4	-	-
H-23	46	-	-	-

SOURCE: Materiel Statistics Division, Directorate of Statistical Services, DCS/C.

308700 O - 54 - 15

TABLE 119 — INVENTORY OF STORED USAF AIRCRAFT BY LOCATION — QUARTERLY, FISCAL YEAR 1953

LOCATION	TOTAL		BOMBER		FIGHTER		CARGO		TRAINER		OTHER TYPES a/	
	STORAGE	COCOONED STORAGE	STORAGE	COCOONED STORAGE	STORAGE	COCOONED STORAGE	STORAGE	COCOONED STORAGE	STORAGE	COCOONED STORAGE	STORAGE	COCOONED STORAGE
	30 September 1952											
TOTAL	1,691	272	522	144	192	27	10	-	810	87	157	14
Dv Monthan AFB . .	59	136	26	81	-	-	-	-	33	55	-	-
Hill AFB	98	-	77	-	-	-	-	-	12	-	9	-
Kelly AFB	442	-	23	-	-	-	-	-	398	-	21	-
McClellan AFB . .	101	14	51	11	-	-	-	-	1	3	49	-
Mt. Home AFB . . .	1	-	1	-	-	-	-	-	-	-	-	-
Norton AFB	176	-	1	-	-	-	-	-	115	-	60	-
Olmsted AFB . . .	1	-	-	-	-	-	1	-	-	-	-	-
Ontario AFB . . .	1	-	-	-	-	-	-	-	-	-	1	-
Pyote AFB	396	-	261	-	-	-	2	-	133	-	-	-
Robins AFB	42	72	21	43	-	-	5	-	7	29	9	-
Tinker AFB	330	-	44	-	174	-	-	-	111	-	1	-
Erding AD	1	-	-	-	-	-	-	-	-	-	1	-
Feamcom AB	43	-	17	-	18	-	2	-	-	-	6	-
Kisarazu AF . . .	-	50	-	9	-	27	-	-	-	-	-	14
	31 December 1952											
TOTAL	1,519	240	463	148	132	13	21	-	782	70	121	9
Dv Monthan AFB . .	114	81	26	81	-	-	-	-	88	-	-	-
Hill AFB	89	-	73	-	-	-	-	-	7	-	9	-
Kelly AFB	450	-	23	-	-	-	9	-	397	-	21	-
McClellan AFB . .	78	11	26	11	-	-	-	-	3	-	49	-
Norton AFB	131	-	1	-	-	-	-	-	115	-	15	-
Olmsted AFB . . .	3	-	-	-	-	-	3	-	-	-	-	-
Ontario AFB . . .	1	-	-	-	-	-	-	-	-	-	1	-
Pyote AFB	353	-	221	-	-	-	1	-	131	-	-	-
Robins AFB	70	43	21	43	-	-	5	-	35	-	9	-
Tinker AFB	159	68	48	-	105	-	-	-	5	68	1	-
Eniwetok IS. . . .	8	-	-	-	-	-	-	-	-	-	8	-
Feamcom AB	63	-	24	-	27	-	3	-	1	-	8	-
Kisarazu AF . . .	-	37	-	13	-	13	-	-	-	2	-	9
	31 March 1953											
TOTAL	1,380	295	378	134	207	57	44	-	652	88	99	16
Dv Monthan AFB . .	59	136	26	81	-	-	-	-	33	55	-	-
Hill AFB	96	5	70	-	-	-	25	-	-	5	1	-
Kelly AFB	440	-	21	-	-	-	10	-	397	-	12	-
McClellan AFB . .	61	-	13	-	-	-	-	-	-	-	48	-
Norton AFB	121	-	1	-	-	-	-	-	115	-	5	-
Ontario AFB . . .	1	-	-	-	-	-	-	-	-	-	1	-
Pyote AFB	268	-	180	-	-	-	1	-	87	-	-	-
Robins AFB	52	71	19	43	-	-	5	-	2	28	26	-
Tinker AFB	162	-	43	-	102	-	-	-	17	-	-	-
Eniwetok IS. . . .	5	-	-	-	-	-	-	-	-	-	5	-
Feamcom AB	25	-	3	-	18	-	2	-	1	-	1	-
Hanshin AB	-	1	-	-	-	1	-	-	-	-	-	-
Iwakuni AB	2	-	2	-	-	-	-	-	-	-	-	-
Kisarazu AF . . .	87	82	-	10	87	56	-	-	-	-	-	16
Komacki AB	1	-	-	-	-	-	1	-	-	-	-	-
	30 June 1953											
TOTAL	1,774	250	478	120	184	44	106	-	956	84	50	2
Dv Monthan AFB . .	137	136	102	81	-	-	-	-	35	55	-	-
Hill AFB	119	-	70	-	-	-	43	-	5	-	1	-
Kelly AFB	821	-	23	-	-	-	53	-	718	-	27	-
McClellan AFB . .	6	-	6	-	-	-	-	-	-	-	-	-
Norton AFB	106	-	1	-	-	-	-	-	100	-	5	-
Ontario AFB . . .	1	-	-	-	-	-	-	-	-	-	1	-
Pyote AFB	257	-	175	-	-	-	-	-	82	-	-	-
Robins AFB	29	64	14	36	-	-	5	-	1	28	9	-
Tinker AFB	194	1	81	-	100	-	-	-	13	1	-	-
Eniwetok Is. . . .	3	-	-	-	-	-	-	-	-	-	3	-
Feamcom AB	42	-	3	-	30	-	5	-	1	-	3	-
Iwakuni AB	6	-	3	-	1	-	-	-	1	-	1	-
Kisarazu AF . . .	53	49	-	3	53	44	-	-	-	-	-	2

a/ Includes Reconnaissance, Search and Rescue, and Communication

SOURCE: Materiel Statistics Division, Directorate of Statistical Services, DCS/C

TABLE 120 — USAF AND RESERVE FORCES CLASS 01Z INVENTORY BY MODEL — QUARTERLY, FISCAL YEAR 1953

TYPE AND MODEL	30 SEPTEMBER 1952	31 DECEMBER 1952	31 MARCH 1953	30 JUNE 1953
TOTAL	288	303	343	387
B-25	10	10	10	10
B-26	3	3	3	3
EB-26	1	1	1	-
B-29	20	27	29	28
EB-29	1	1	1	1
B-47	3	4	5	2
XB-47	1	1	1	1
B-50	3	3	3	3
F-47	1	1	1	1
F-51	-	-	-	8
F-80	5	5	5	6
F-84	67	70	99	113
YF-84	1	1	-	-
F-86	15	16	17	17
F-89	3	3	2	2
F-94	3	4	4	4
RB-36	1	1	1	1
C-46	-	-	-	6
C-47	1	1	1	1
C-54	6	5	5	5
ZC-54	1	1	1	1
C-97	-	-	-	1
C-119	-	-	1	2
C-124	1	1	1	2
YC-125	21	21	21	-
T-6	11	11	11	11
T-29	-	-	-	1
TB-25	16	16	16	16
TB-26	3	3	3	4
TB-29	1	1	1	1
TB-47	-	-	-	6
TRF-51	1	1	-	-
TF-80	8	8	8	8
L-5	7	7	7	7
L-16	44	44	44	44
L-17	3	3	3	3
L-19	4	4	13	23
H-5	3	3	3	3
YH-5	1	1	1	1
H-13	7	8	8	26
YH-13	6	8	8	8
YH-21	-	-	-	2
YH-23	5	5	5	5

SOURCE: Materiel Statistics Division, Directorate of Statistical Services, DCS/C.

TABLE 121 — USAF AND RESERVE FORCES AIRCRAFT INVENTORY GAINS AND

LINE NUMBER	TYPE, MODEL AND LINE CLASSIFICATION	AIRCRAFT INVENTORY 1 JULY 1952	GAINS: PRODUCTION: USAF	GAINS: PRODUCTION: NON-USAF AGENCIES	GAINS: CONVERSION	GAINS: FIRST LINE	GAINS: SALVAGE	GAINS: CLASS 01Z	GAINS: OTHER a/
1	AIRCRAFT - TOTAL	20,665	4,729	3,539	1,363	1,103	389	10	362
2	First-Line	7,605	4,706	3,534	504	21	13	6	162
3	Second-Line	13,060	23	5	859	1,082	376	4	200
4	AIRPLANE - TOTAL	20,633	4,729	3,539	1,318	1,103	389	10	362
5	First-Line	7,605	4,706	3,534	504	21	13	6	162
6	Second-Line	13,028	23	5	814	1,082	376	4	200
7	COMBAT - TOTAL	9,107	2,763	1,579	434	643	23	8	35
8	BOMBER	2,914	364	46	104	94	1	1	4
9	First-Line	703	361	46	18	-	-	-	3
10	Second-Line	2,211	3	-	86	94	1	1	1
11	TANKER	295	148	-	-	-	-	-	-
12	First-Line	100	148	-	-	-	-	-	-
13	Second-Line	195	-	-	-	-	-	-	-
14	FIGHTER	4,994	2,109	1,531	204	540	19	7	31
15	First-Line	2,469	2,106	1,531	40	-	11	6	6
16	Second-Line	2,525	-3	-	164	540	8	1	25
17	RECONNAISSANCE	649	42	-	117	7	1	-	-
18	First-Line	161	42	-	16	-	-	-	-
19	Second-Line	488	-	-	101	7	1	-	-
20	SEARCH AND RESCUE	255	100	2	9	2	2	-	-
21	First-Line	137	100	2	-	2	-	-	-
22	Second-Line	118	-	-	9	-	2	-	-
23	NON-COMBAT - TOTAL	11,526	1,966	1,960	884	460	366	2	327
24	SPECIAL RESEARCH	4	2	-	-	-	-	-	-
25	First-Line	-	-	-	-	-	-	-	-
26	Second-Line	4	2	-	-	-	-	-	-
27	CARGO	3,354	380	127	79	133	301	-	12
28	First-Line	653	379	127	9	-	-	-	1
29	Second-Line	2,701	1	-	70	133	301	-	11
30	TRAINER	6,862	1,357	388	790	54	60	1	42
31	First-Line	2,655	1,357	388	414	-	-	-	16
32	Second-Line	4,207	-	-	376	54	60	1	26
33	COMMUNICATION	1,306	227	1,445	15	273	5	1	273
34	First-Line	727	213	1,440	7	19	2	-	136
35	Second-Line	579	14	5	8	254	3	1	137
36	GLIDER	1	-	-	-	-	-	-	-
37	Second-Line	1	-	-	-	-	-	-	-
38	AERIAL TARGET	31	-	-	45	-	-	-	-
39	Second-Line	31	-	-	45	-	-	-	-

LOSSES BY TYPE, MODEL, AND LINE CLASSIFICATION – FISCAL YEAR 1953

LOSSES								ENDING INVENTORY 30 JUNE 1953						
				TRANSFERS										
CON-VERSION	SECOND LINE	SALVAGE SURVEY RCLM	CLASS 01Z	FOREIGN GOV'TS (STOCK)	OTHER NON-USAF (STOCK)	NEW PRODUCTION	GAINED IN ERROR	TOTAL	USAF	ANG	AFR	CAP	EAR-MARKED	LINE NUMBER
1,363	1,103	2,190	250	498	46	3,099	7	23,604	21,363	1,020	321	519	381	1
151	1,082	763	61	24	11	3,093	2	11,364	10,873	106	49	-	336	2
1,212	21	1,427	189	474	35	6	5	12,240	10,490	914	272	519	45	3
1,356	1,103	2,176	250	498	46	3,099	7	23,548	21,307	1,020	321	519	381	4
151	1,082	763	61	24	11	3,093	2	11,364	10,873	106	49	-	336	5
1,205	21	1,413	189	474	35	6	5	12,184	10,434	914	272	519	45	6
627	643	1,110	190	438	25	1,168	-	10,391	9,672	491	67	-	161	7
435	94	169	16	8	15	46	-	2,745	2,716	27	-	-	2	8
69	94	23	3	-	2	46	-	894	893	-	-	-	1	9
366	-	146	13	8	13	-	-	1,851	1,823	27	-	-	1	10
5	-	3	-	-	-	-	-	435	435	-	-	-	-	11
3	-	-	-	-	-	-	-	245	245	-	-	-	-	12
2	-	3	-	-	-	-	-	190	190	-	-	-	-	13
109	540	867	174	415	7	1,120	-	6,203	5,533	450	67	-	153	14
54	540	490	11	21	1	1,120	-	3,932	3,795	-	-	-	137	15
55	-	377	163	394	6	-	-	2,271	1,738	450	67	-	16	16
30	7	40	-	13	3	-	-	723	703	14	-	-	6	17
3	7	7	-	-	-	-	-	202	202	-	-	-	-	18
27	-	33	-	13	3	-	-	521	501	14	-	-	6	19
48	2	31	-	2	-	2	-	285	285	-	-	-	-	20
1	-	8	-	-	-	2	-	230	230	-	-	-	-	21
47	2	23	-	2	-	-	-	55	55	-	-	-	-	22
729	460	1,066	60	60	21	1,931	7	13,157	11,635	529	254	519	220	23
-	-	1	-	-	-	-	-	5	5	-	-	-	-	24
-	-	-	-	-	-	-	-	-	-	-	-	-	-	25
-	-	1	-	-	-	-	-	5	5	-	-	-	-	26
98	133	149	11	14	11	117	1	3,852	3,643	86	113	-	10	27
4	133	20	5	-	3	117	-	887	878	-	-	-	9	28
94	-	129	6	14	8	-	1	2,965	2,765	86	113	-	1	29
620	54	696	2	41	8	312	6	7,815	7,107	441	141	-	126	30
11	54	181	1	3	4	312	2	4,262	4,001	106	49	-	106	31
609	-	515	1	38	4	-	4	3,553	3,106	335	92	-	20	32
11	273	220	47	5	2	1,502	-	1,485	880	2	-	519	84	33
6	254	34	41	-	1	1,496	-	712	629	-	-	-	83	34
5	19	186	6	5	1	6	-	773	251	2	-	519	1	35
-	-	1	-	-	-	-	-	-	-	-	-	-	-	36
-	-	1	-	-	-	-	-	-	-	-	-	-	-	37
7	-	13	-	-	-	-	-	56	56	-	-	-	-	38
7	-	13	-	-	-	-	-	56	56	-	-	-	-	39

TABLE 121 – USAF AND RESERVE FORCES AIRCRAFT INVENTORY GAINS AND LOSSES

LINE NUMBER	TYPE, MODEL AND LINE CLASSIFICATION	AIRCRAFT INVENTORY 1 JULY 1952	GAINS						
			PRODUCTION		CON-VERSION	FIRST LINE	SALVAGE	CLASS 01Z	OTHER a/
			USAF	NON-USAF AGENCIES					
1	BOMBER	2,914	364	46	104	94	1	1	4
2	FIRST-LINE	703	361	46	18	-	-	-	3
3	B-36	144	43	-	6	-	-	-	-
4	B-45	85	-	-	2	-	-	-	-
5	B-47	205	318	-	10	-	-	-	-
6	B-50	269	-	-	-	-	-	-	-
7	B-57	-	-	-	-	-	-	-	2
8	P2V-5	-	-	46	-	-	-	-	1
9	SECOND-LINE	2,211	3	-	86	94	1	1	1
10	B-17	43	-	-	7	-	-	-	-
11	B-24	1	-	-	-	-	-	-	-
12	B-25	181	-	-	3	-	-	-	-
13	B-26	644	-	-	36	-	1	-	-
14	XB-26	1	-	-	-	-	-	-	-
15	B-29	1,328	-	-	36	-	-	1	-
16	YB-29	1	-	-	2	-	-	-	-
17	XB-29	2	-	-	1	-	-	-	-
18	XB-36	1	-	-	-	-	-	-	-
19	XB-43	1	-	-	-	-	-	-	-
20	B-45	3	-	-	1	21	-	-	-
21	XB-45	1	-	-	-	-	-	-	-
22	B-47	-	-	-	-	73	-	-	-
23	YB-47	-	1	-	-	-	-	-	-
24	XB-47	1	-	-	-	-	-	-	-
25	XB-51	1	-	-	-	-	-	-	-
26	YB-52	-	1	-	-	-	-	-	-
27	XB-52	-	1	-	-	-	-	-	-
28	YB-60	2	-	-	-	-	-	-	-
29	JD-1	-	-	-	-	-	-	-	1
30	TANKER	295	148	-	-	-	-	-	-
31	FIRST-LINE	100	148	-	-	-	-	-	-
32	KC-97	100	148	-	-	-	-	-	-
33	SECOND-LINE	195	-	-	-	-	-	-	-
34	KB-29M	82	-	-	-	-	-	-	-
35	KB-29J	1	-	-	-	-	-	-	-
36	KB-29P	112	-	-	-	-	-	-	-
37	FIGHTER	4,994	2,109	1,531	204	540	19	7	31
38	FIRST-LINE	2,469	2,106	1,531	40	-	11	6	6
39	F9F	-	-	-	-	-	-	-	1
40	F-80	156	-	-	3	-	-	-	-
41	F-84	1,069	391	1,505	11	-	9	1	4
42	F-86	666	1,517	26	10	-	1	1	1
43	F-89	164	45	-	8	-	-	4	-
44	YF-89	-	-	-	1	-	-	-	-
45	F-94	424	153	-	7	-	1	-	-
46	SECOND-LINE	2,525	3	-	164	540	8	1	25
47	F9F	1	-	-	-	1	-	-	-
48	F-47	546	-	-	90	-	-	-	4
49	F-51	1,052	-	-	13	-	4	-	20
50	F-80	461	-	-	46	128	1	1	-
51	F-82	40	-	-	1	-	-	-	1
52	F-84	318	-	-	5	211	1	-	-
53	YF-84	2	-	-	-	-	-	-	-
54	F-86	90	-	-	6	196	2	-	-
55	YF-86	2	2	-	-	-	-	-	-
56	XF-86	3	-	-	-	-	-	-	-
57	XF-88	2	-	-	1	-	-	-	-
58	YF-89	1	-	-	-	1	-	-	-
59	XF-90	1	-	-	-	-	-	-	-
60	XF-91	1	-	-	-	-	-	-	-
61	XF-92	1	-	-	-	-	-	-	-
62	EF-94	-	-	-	1	3	-	-	-
63	YF-94	4	-	-	1	-	-	-	-
64	YF-100	-	1	-	-	-	-	-	-

BY TYPE, MODEL, AND LINE CLASSIFICATION – FISCAL YEAR 1953 – CONTINUED

LOSSES								ENDING INVENTORY 30 JUNE 1953						
				TRANSFERS										
CON-VERSION	SECOND LINE	SALVAGE SURVEY RCLM	CLASS 01Z	FOREIGN GOV'TS (STOCK)	OTHER NON-USAF (STOCK)	NEW PRODUCTION	GAINED IN ERROR	TOTAL	USAF	ANG	AFR	CAP	EAR-MARKED	LINE NUMBER
435	94	169	16	8	15	46	-	2,745	2,716	27	-	-	2	1
69	94	23	3	-	2	46	-	894	893	-	-	-	1	2
4	-	5	-	-	-	-	-	184	184	-	-	-	-	3
9	21	4	-	-	-	-	-	53	53	-	-	-	-	4
45	73	6	3	-	2	-	-	404	404	-	-	-	-	5
11	-	7	-	-	-	-	-	251	251	-	-	-	-	6
-	-	1	-	-	-	-	-	1	1	-	-	-	-	7
-	-	-	-	-	-	46	-	1	-	-	-	-	1	8
366	-	146	13	8	13	-	-	1,851	1,823	27	-	-	1	9
5	-	4	-	-	-	-	-	41	41	-	-	-	-	10
-	-	-	-	-	-	-	-	1	1	-	-	-	-	11
149	-	-	-	-	-	-	-	35	35	-	-	-	-	12
62	-	53	-	8	3	-	-	555	528	27	-	-	-	13
-	-	-	-	-	-	-	-	1	1	-	-	-	-	14
70	-	87	12	-	9	-	-	1,187	1,186	-	-	-	1	15
-	-	-	-	-	-	-	-	3	3	-	-	-	-	16
-	-	-	-	-	-	-	-	3	3	-	-	-	-	17
-	-	1	-	-	-	-	-	-	-	-	-	-	-	18
-	-	-	-	-	-	-	-	1	1	-	-	-	-	19
6	-	-	-	-	-	-	-	19	19	-	-	-	-	20
-	-	1	-	-	-	-	-	-	-	-	-	-	-	21
72	-	-	1	-	-	-	-	-	-	-	-	-	-	22
-	-	-	-	-	-	-	-	1	1	-	-	-	-	23
-	-	-	-	-	-	-	-	1	1	-	-	-	-	24
-	-	-	-	-	-	-	-	1	1	-	-	-	-	25
-	-	-	-	-	-	-	-	1	1	-	-	-	-	26
-	-	-	-	-	-	-	-	1	1	-	-	-	-	27
2	-	-	-	-	-	-	-	-	-	-	-	-	-	28
-	-	-	-	-	1	-	-	-	-	-	-	-	-	29
5	-	3	-	-	-	-	-	435	435	-	-	-	-	30
3	-	-	-	-	-	-	-	245	245	-	-	-	-	31
3	-	-	-	-	-	-	-	245	245	-	-	-	-	32
2	-	3	-	-	-	-	-	190	190	-	-	-	-	33
-	-	1	-	-	-	-	-	81	81	-	-	-	-	34
-	-	1	-	-	-	-	-	-	-	-	-	-	-	35
2	-	1	-	-	-	-	-	109	109	-	-	-	-	36
109	540	867	174	415	7	1,120	-	6,203	5,533	450	67	-	153	37
54	540	490	11	21	1	1,120	-	3,932	3,795	-	-	-	137	38
-	1	-	-	-	-	-	-	-	-	-	-	-	-	39
10	128	18	-	-	1	-	-	2	2	-	-	-	-	40
12	211	228	-	-	-	1,097	-	1,442	1,308	-	-	-	134	41
15	196	182	5	21	-	23	-	1,770	1,767	-	-	-	3	42
9	-	8	3	-	-	-	-	201	201	-	-	-	-	43
-	1	-	-	-	-	-	-	-	-	-	-	-	-	44
8	3	54	3	-	-	-	-	517	517	-	-	-	-	45
55	-	377	163	394	6	-	-	2,271	1,738	450	67	-	16	46
-	-	-	-	-	1	-	-	1	1	-	-	-	-	47
2	-	136	-	305	-	-	-	197	149	35	-	-	13	48
3	-	81	8	89	-	-	-	908	435	406	67	-	-	49
37	-	76	1	-	-	-	-	523	514	9	-	-	-	50
1	-	24	-	-	2	-	-	15	15	-	-	-	-	51
4	-	41	154	-	-	-	-	336	333	-	-	-	3	52
-	-	-	-	-	-	-	-	2	2	-	-	-	-	53
6	-	16	-	-	-	-	-	272	272	-	-	-	-	54
-	-	-	-	-	2	-	-	2	2	-	-	-	-	55
-	-	2	-	-	1	-	-	-	-	-	-	-	-	56
1	-	-	-	-	-	-	-	2	2	-	-	-	-	57
-	-	-	-	-	-	-	-	2	2	-	-	-	-	58
-	-	1	-	-	-	-	-	-	-	-	-	-	-	59
-	-	-	-	-	-	-	-	1	1	-	-	-	-	60
-	-	-	-	-	-	-	-	1	1	-	-	-	-	61
-	-	-	-	-	-	-	-	4	4	-	-	-	-	62
1	-	-	-	-	-	-	-	4	4	-	-	-	-	63
-	-	-	-	-	-	-	-	1	1	-	-	-	-	64

TABLE 121 — USAF AND RESERVE FORCES AIRCRAFT INVENTORY GAINS AND LOSSES

LINE NUMBER	TYPE, MODEL AND LINE CLASSIFICATION	AIRCRAFT INVENTORY 1 JULY 1952	GAINS						
			PRODUCTION		CON-VERSION	FIRST LINE	SALVAGE	CLASS 012	OTHER a/
			USAF	NON-USAF AGENCIES					
1	RECONNAISSANCE	649	42	-	117	7	1	-	-
2	FIRST-LINE	161	42	-	16	-	-	-	-
3	RB-36	92	42	-	-	-	-	-	-
4	RB-45	25	-	-	-	-	-	-	-
5	RB-47	-	-	-	1	-	-	-	-
6	RB-50	42	-	-	-	-	-	-	-
7	RF-80	-	-	-	10	-	-	-	-
8	RF-86	2	-	-	5	-	-	-	-
9	SECOND-LINE	488	-	-	101	7	1	-	-
10	RB-17	17	-	-	-	-	-	-	-
11	WB-17	1	-	-	-	-	-	-	-
12	RB-25	3	-	-	-	-	-	-	-
13	RB-26	104	-	-	25	-	-	-	-
14	WB-26	-	-	-	6	-	-	-	-
15	RB-29	59	-	-	-	-	-	-	-
16	WB-29	83	-	-	-	-	-	-	-
17	RB-47	-	-	-	36	-	-	-	-
18	RB-49	1	-	-	-	-	-	-	-
19	RC-45	8	-	-	2	-	-	-	-
20	RC-47	7	-	-	10	-	-	-	-
21	RC-54	-	-	-	1	-	-	-	-
22	RF-51	45	-	-	-	-	-	-	-
23	RF-80	153	-	-	21	6	1	-	-
24	XRF-80	1	-	-	-	-	-	-	-
25	RF-84	2	-	-	-	-	-	-	-
26	RF-86	3	-	-	-	1	-	-	-
27	XR-12	1	-	-	-	-	-	-	-
28	SEARCH AND RESCUE	255	100	2	9	2	2	-	-
29	FIRST-LINE	137	100	2	-	2	-	-	-
30	SA-16	137	100	2	-	-	-	-	-
31	SH-5	-	-	-	-	2	-	-	-
32	SECOND-LINE	118	-	-	9	-	2	-	-
33	SA-10	13	-	-	-	-	-	-	-
34	SB-17	62	-	-	1	-	1	-	-
35	SB-29	29	-	-	7	-	-	-	-
36	SC-47	5	-	-	1	-	-	-	-
37	SC-54	3	-	-	-	-	-	-	-
38	SH-5	6	-	-	-	-	1	-	-
39	SPECIAL RESEARCH	4	2	-	-	-	-	-	-
40	SECOND-LINE	4	2	-	-	-	-	-	-
41	X-1	1	2	-	-	-	-	-	-
42	X-4	2	-	-	-	-	-	-	-
43	X-5	1	-	-	-	-	-	-	-
44	CARGO	3,354	380	127	79	133	301	-	12
45	FIRST-LINE	653	379	127	2	-	-	-	1
46	C-74	11	-	-	-	-	-	-	-
47	C-82	134	-	-	-	-	-	-	-
48	C-97	61	-	-	3	-	-	-	-
49	YC-97	7	-	-	1	-	-	-	-
50	C-118	-	18	-	-	-	-	-	-
51	VC-118	1	-	-	1	-	-	-	-
52	C-119	298	227	69	2	-	-	-	-
53	C-121	8	-	-	-	-	-	-	-
54	VC-121	2	-	-	-	-	-	-	-
55	C-124	130	134	-	-	-	-	-	-
56	VT-29	-	-	-	2	-	-	-	-
57	R4Q	1	-	58	-	-	-	-	1
58	SECOND-LINE	2,701	1	-	70	133	301	-	11
59	C-45	422	-	-	4	-	299	-	-
60	C-46	421	-	-	1	-	-	-	-
61	C-47	1,058	-	-	18	-	1	-	9
62	AC-47	-	-	-	8	-	-	-	-
63	VC-47	280	-	-	22	-	-	-	-
64	YC-47	1	-	-	-	-	-	-	-
65	VC-53	2	-	-	-	-	-	-	-

BY TYPE, MODEL, AND LINE CLASSIFICATION – FISCAL YEAR 1953 – CONTINUED

LOSSES								ENDING INVENTORY 30 JUNE 1953						
				TRANSFERS										
CON-VERSION	SECOND LINE	SALVAGE SURVEY RCLM	CLASS 01Z	FOREIGN GOV'TS (STOCK)	OTHER NON-USAF (STOCK)	NEW PRODUCTION	GAINED IN ERROR	TOTAL	USAF	ANG	AFR	CAP	EAR-MARKED	LINE NUMBER
30	7	40	-	13	3	-	-	723	703	14	-	-	6	1
3	7	7	-	-	-	-	-	202	202	-	-	-	-	2
-	-	2	-	-	-	-	-	132	132	-	-	-	-	3
-	-	1	-	-	-	-	-	24	24	-	-	-	-	4
-	-	-	-	-	-	-	-	1	1	-	-	-	-	5
-	-	1	-	-	-	-	-	41	41	-	-	-	-	6
3	6	1	-	-	-	-	-	-	-	-	-	-	-	7
-	1	2	-	-	-	-	-	4	4	-	-	-	-	8
27	-	33	-	13	3	-	-	521	501	14	-	-	6	9
-	-	-	-	2	-	-	-	15	15	-	-	-	-	10
-	-	-	-	-	-	-	-	1	1	-	-	-	-	11
-	-	-	-	-	-	-	-	3	3	-	-	-	-	12
7	-	3	-	-	-	-	-	119	109	10	-	-	-	13
-	-	-	-	-	-	-	-	6	6	-	-	-	-	14
6	-	4	-	-	-	-	-	49	49	-	-	-	-	15
-	-	3	-	-	-	-	-	80	80	-	-	-	-	16
-	-	-	-	-	-	-	-	36	36	-	-	-	-	17
-	-	-	-	-	-	-	-	1	1	-	-	-	-	18
-	-	2	-	-	-	-	-	8	8	-	-	-	-	19
10	-	-	-	-	-	-	-	7	7	-	-	-	-	20
-	-	-	-	-	-	-	-	1	1	-	-	-	-	21
-	-	6	-	11	2	-	-	26	16	4	-	-	6	22
4	-	15	-	-	-	-	-	162	162	-	-	-	-	23
-	-	-	-	-	-	-	-	1	1	-	-	-	-	24
-	-	-	-	-	-	-	-	2	2	-	-	-	-	25
-	-	-	-	-	-	-	-	4	4	-	-	-	-	26
-	-	-	-	-	1	-	-	-	-	-	-	-	-	27
48	2	31	-	2	-	2	-	285	295	-	-	-	-	28
1	-	8	-	-	-	2	-	230	230	-	-	-	-	29
-	-	7	-	-	-	2	-	230	230	-	-	-	-	30
1	-	1	-	-	-	-	-	-	-	-	-	-	-	31
47	2	23	-	2	-	-	-	55	55	-	-	-	-	32
-	-	13	-	-	-	-	-	-	-	-	-	-	-	33
43	-	6	-	2	-	-	-	11	11	-	-	-	-	34
-	-	1	-	-	-	-	-	35	35	-	-	-	-	35
1	-	-	-	-	-	-	-	5	5	-	-	-	-	36
-	-	-	-	-	-	-	-	3	3	-	-	-	-	37
3	2	1	-	-	-	-	-	1	1	-	-	-	-	38
-	-	1	-	-	-	-	-	5	5	-	-	-	-	39
-	-	1	-	-	-	-	-	5	5	-	-	-	-	40
-	-	1	-	-	-	-	-	2	2	-	-	-	-	41
-	-	-	-	-	-	-	-	2	2	-	-	-	-	42
-	-	-	-	-	-	-	-	1	1	-	-	-	-	43
98	133	149	11	14	11	117	1	3,852	3,643	66	113	-	10	44
4	133	20	5	-	3	117	-	887	878	-	-	-	9	45
-	-	-	-	-	-	-	-	11	11	-	-	-	-	46
-	131	3	-	-	-	-	-	-	-	-	-	-	-	47
1	-	-	1	-	-	-	-	62	62	-	-	-	-	48
-	-	-	-	-	-	-	-	8	8	-	-	-	-	49
1	-	-	-	-	2	-	-	15	15	-	-	-	-	50
-	-	-	-	-	-	-	-	2	2	-	-	-	-	51
2	-	14	2	-	-	58	-	520	511	-	-	-	9	52
-	-	-	-	-	-	-	-	8	8	-	-	-	-	53
-	-	-	-	-	-	-	-	2	2	-	-	-	-	54
-	-	3	2	-	-	-	-	259	259	-	-	-	-	55
-	2	-	-	-	-	-	-	-	-	-	-	-	-	56
-	-	-	-	-	1	59	-	-	-	-	-	-	-	57
94	-	129	6	14	8	-	1	2,965	2,765	86	113	-	1	58
6	-	86	-	-	-	-	-	633	633	-	-	-	-	59
2	-	9	6	-	-	-	-	405	283	9	113	-	-	60
41	-	19	-	13	2	-	1	1,010	947	63	-	-	-	61
-	-	-	-	-	-	-	-	8	8	-	-	-	-	62
18	-	6	-	-	-	-	-	278	265	13	-	-	-	63
-	-	-	-	-	-	-	-	1	-	-	-	-	1	64
-	-	-	-	-	-	-	-	2	1	1	-	-	-	65

TABLE 121 — USAF AND RESERVE FORCES AIRCRAFT INVENTORY GAINS AND LOSSES

LINE NUMBER	TYPE, MODEL AND LINE CLASSIFICATION	AIRCRAFT INVENTORY 1 JULY 1952	GAINS						
			PRODUCTION		CON-VERSION	FIRST LINE	SALVAGE	CLASS 01Z	OTHER a/
			USAF	NON-USAF AGENCIES					
1	CARGO - Cont'd								
2	SECOND-LINE - Cont'd								
3	C-54	374	-	-	1	-	-	-	2
4	VC-54	10	-	-	-	-	-	-	-
5	ZC-54	1	-	-	-	-	-	-	-
6	C-82	4	-	-	1	131	1	-	-
7	XC-99	1	-	-	-	-	-	-	-
8	C-117	15	-	-	11	-	-	-	-
9	YC-119	-	1	-	-	-	-	-	-
10	XC-120	1	-	-	-	-	-	-	-
11	YC-122	10	-	-	-	-	-	-	-
12	YC-124	1	-	-	-	-	-	-	-
13	YC-125	1	-	-	-	-	-	-	-
14	VB-17	39	-	-	2	-	-	-	-
15	CB/VB-25	56	-	-	1	-	-	-	-
16	CB/VB-26	3	-	-	-	-	-	-	-
17	CB-29	1	-	-	-	-	-	-	-
18	VT-29	-	-	-	1	2	-	-	-
19	TRAINER	6,862	1,357	388	790	54	60	1	42
20	FIRST-LINE	2,655	1,357	388	414	-	-	-	16
21	T-6	1,197	-	-	395	-	-	-	2
22	T-28	684	362	-	5	-	-	-	-
23	T-29	73	72	-	1	-	-	-	-
24	T-33	701	899	266	2	-	-	-	-
25	T-35	-	-	7	-	-	-	-	-
26	TB-50	-	24	-	11	-	-	-	-
27	MK-4	-	-	115	-	-	-	-	14
28	SECOND-LINE	4,207	-	-	376	54	60	1	26
29	T-6	1,620	-	-	3	42	-	-	4
30	T-7	170	-	-	-	-	-	-	-
31	T-11	425	-	-	-	-	-	-	-
32	T-28	-	-	-	1	-	-	-	-
33	XT-28	2	-	-	-	-	-	-	-
34	T-29	-	-	-	-	1	-	-	-
35	YT-34	3	-	-	-	-	-	-	-
36	YT-35	3	-	-	-	-	-	-	-
37	TB-17	39	-	-	15	-	-	-	-
38	TB-25	816	-	-	177	-	-	-	-
39	TB-26	323	-	-	34	-	-	-	-
40	TB-29	343	-	-	61	-	-	-	-
41	TB-45	-	-	-	11	-	-	-	-
42	TB-47	-	-	-	70	-	-	-	-
43	TB-50	11	-	-	-	11	-	-	-
44	TC-45	36	-	-	-	-	60	-	-
45	TC-46	1	-	-	1	-	-	-	-
46	TC-47	53	-	-	-	-	-	-	-
47	TC-54	8	-	-	-	-	-	-	-
48	TF-47	141	-	-	1	-	-	-	21
49	TF-51	151	-	-	1	-	-	-	1
50	TRF-51	2	-	-	-	-	-	1	-
51	TF-80	59	-	-	1	-	-	-	-
52	TH-5	1	-	-	-	-	-	-	-
53	COMMUNICATION	1,306	227	1,445	15	273	5	1	273
54	FIRST-LINE	727	213	1,440	7	19	2	-	136
55	L-16	199	-	-	-	-	-	-	54
56	L-17	1	-	-	-	-	-	-	-
57	L-18	-	-	164	-	-	-	-	-
58	L-19	71	20	482	1	-	-	-	19
59	L-20	68	122	52	2	-	-	-	-
60	L-21	125	-	122	-	-	-	-	24
61	L-23	-	-	43	-	-	-	-	10
62	LC-126	6	-	2	-	-	-	-	-
63	LT-6	55	-	-	-	-	1	-	-
64	H-5	6	-	-	1	19	-	-	-
65	H-13	51	-	350	-	-	-	-	18
66	H-19	56	71	68	3	-	1	-	2
67	H-23	89	-	141	-	-	-	-	8
68	H-25	-	-	16	-	-	-	-	1

BY TYPE, MODEL, AND LINE CLASSIFICATION – FISCAL YEAR 1953 – Continued

LOSSES								ENDING INVENTORY 30 JUNE 1953						
				TRANSFERS										
CON-VERSION	SECOND LINE	SALVAGE SURVEY RCLM	CLASS 01Z	FOREIGN GOV'TS (STOCK)	OTHER NON-USAF (STOCK	NEW PRODUCTION	GAINED IN ERROR	TOTAL	USAF	ANG	AFR	CAP	EAR-MARKED	LINE NUMBER
														1
														2
2	-	6	-	1	6	-	-	362	362	-	-	-	-	3
-	-	-	-	-	-	-	-	10	10	-	-	-	-	4
-	-	-	-	-	-	-	-	1	1	-	-	-	-	5
1	-	1	-	-	-	-	-	135	135	-	-	-	-	6
-	-	-	-	-	-	-	-	1	1	-	-	-	-	7
-	-	-	-	-	-	-	-	26	26	-	-	-	-	8
-	-	-	-	-	-	-	-	1	1	-	-	-	-	9
-	-	-	-	-	-	-	-	1	1	-	-	-	-	10
-	-	1	-	-	-	-	-	9	9	-	-	-	-	11
-	-	-	-	-	-	-	-	1	1	-	-	-	-	12
-	-	-	-	-	-	-	-	1	1	-	-	-	-	13
-	-	1	-	-	-	-	-	40	40	-	-	-	-	14
24	-	-	-	-	-	-	-	33	33	-	-	-	-	15
-	-	-	-	-	-	-	-	3	3	-	-	-	-	16
-	-	-	-	-	-	-	-	1	1	-	-	-	-	17
-	-	-	-	-	-	-	-	3	3	-	-	-	-	18
620	54	696	2	41	8	312	6	7,815	7,107	441	141	-	126	19
11	54	181	1	3	4	312	2	4,262	4,001	106	45	-	106	20
1	42	42	-	-	2	-	2	1,505	1,405	100	-	-	-	21
5	-	33	-	-	2	-	-	1,011	962	-	49	-	-	22
3	1	-	1	-	-	-	-	141	141	-	-	-	-	23
2	-	105	-	3	-	262	-	1,496	1,469	6	-	-	21	24
-	-	-	-	-	-	6	-	1	-	-	-	-	1	25
-	11	-	-	-	-	-	-	24	24	-	-	-	-	26
-	-	1	-	-	-	44	-	84	-	-	-	-	84	27
609	-	515	1	38	4	-	4	3,553	3,106	335	92	-	20	28
397	-	39	-	-	-	-	3	1,230	860	304	61	-	5	29
-	-	105	-	-	-	-	-	65	65	-	-	-	-	30
-	-	262	-	-	-	-	-	163	163	-	-	-	-	31
-	-	-	-	-	-	-	-	1	1	-	-	-	-	32
1	-	-	-	-	-	-	-	1	1	-	-	-	-	33
1	-	-	-	-	-	-	-	-	-	-	-	-	-	34
-	-	-	-	-	-	-	-	3	3	-	-	-	-	35
-	-	3	-	-	-	-	-	-	-	-	-	-	-	36
6	-	-	-	1	3	-	-	44	44	-	-	-	-	37
8	-	6	-	15	-	-	1	963	948	-	-	-	15	38
32	-	5	-	-	-	-	-	320	313	7	-	-	-	39
29	-	39	-	-	-	-	-	336	336	-	-	-	-	40
-	-	-	-	-	-	-	-	11	11	-	-	-	-	41
-	-	-	1	-	-	-	-	69	69	-	-	-	-	42
-	-	-	-	-	-	-	-	22	22	-	-	-	-	43
-	-	1	-	-	-	-	-	95	95	-	-	-	-	44
-	-	-	-	-	-	-	-	2	-	1	1	-	-	45
-	-	1	-	-	-	-	-	52	52	-	-	-	-	46
-	-	-	-	-	-	-	-	8	8	-	-	-	-	47
89	-	39	-	22	-	-	-	13	13	-	-	-	-	48
11	-	11	-	-	1	-	-	130	80	20	30	-	-	49
-	-	-	-	-	-	-	-	3	2	1	-	-	-	50
35	-	4	-	-	-	-	-	21	19	2	-	-	-	51
-	-	-	-	-	-	-	-	1	1	-	-	-	-	52
11	273	220	47	5	2	1,502	-	1,485	880	2	-	519	84	53
6	254	34	41	-	1	1,496	-	712	629	-	-	-	83	54
-	247	1	4	-	1	-	-	-	-	-	-	-	-	55
-	-	-	-	-	-	-	-	1	-	-	-	-	1	56
-	-	-	-	-	-	164	-	-	-	-	-	-	-	57
1	-	3	19	-	-	548	-	22	18	-	-	-	4	58
2	-	4	-	-	-	58	-	180	180	-	-	-	-	59
-	-	2	-	-	-	122	-	147	147	-	-	-	-	60
-	-	-	-	-	-	29	-	24	1	-	-	-	23	61
-	-	1	-	-	-	2	-	5	5	-	-	-	-	62
-	-	15	-	-	-	-	-	41	41	-	-	-	-	63
-	7	1	-	-	-	-	-	18	18	-	-	-	-	64
-	-	1	18	-	-	261	-	139	97	-	-	-	42	65
3	-	6	-	-	-	73	-	119	116	-	-	-	3	66
-	-	-	-	-	-	224	-	14	4	-	-	-	10	67
-	-	-	-	-	-	15	-	2	2	-	-	-	-	68

TABLE 122 — USAF AND RESERVE FORCES AIRCRAFT INVENTORY GAINS AND LOSSES

LINE NUMBER	TYPE, MODEL AND LINE CLASSIFICATION	AIRCRAFT INVENTORY 1 JULY 1952	GAINS						
			PRODUCTION		CON-VERSION	FIRST LINE	SALVAGE	CLASS 01Z	OTHER a/
			USAF	NON-USAF AGENCIES					
1	COMMUNICATION - Cont'd								
2	SECOND-LINE	579	14	5	8	254	3	1	137
3	L-4	151	-	-	1	-	-	-	-
4	L-5	231	-	-	-	-	-	-	-
5	L-13	130	-	-	1	-	-	-	-
6	L-16	-	-	-	-	247	-	1	136
7	XL-17	3	-	-	-	-	-	-	-
8	YL-20	1	-	-	-	-	-	-	-
9	YL-26	-	-	3	-	-	-	-	-
10	H-5	44	-	-	4	7	2	-	-
11	YH-12	8	1	-	2	-	-	-	-
12	H-13	4	-	-	-	-	1	-	-
13	YH-18	2	-	-	-	-	-	-	1
14	YH-19	4	-	-	-	-	-	-	-
15	XH-20	-	2	-	-	-	-	-	-
16	YH-21	-	11	-	-	-	-	-	-
17	YH-24	1	-	-	-	-	-	-	-
18	YH-30	-	-	2	-	-	-	-	-
19	GLIDER	1	-	-	-	-	-	-	-
20	SECOND-LINE	1	-	-	-	-	-	-	-
21	XG-18	1	-	-	-	-	-	-	-
22	AERIAL TARGET	31	-	-	45	-	-	-	-
23	SECOND-LINE	31	-	-	45	-	-	-	-
24	Q-14	10	-	-	7	-	-	-	-
25	QB-17	16	-	-	29	-	-	-	-
26	QF-80	2	-	-	8	-	-	-	-
27	QT-33	3	-	-	-	-	-	-	-
28	QB-45	-	-	-	1	-	-	-	-

a/ Includes gains due to reallocation of USAF aircraft from non-USAF agencies and miscellaneous inventory adjustments.

SOURCE: Materiel Statistics Division, Directorate of Statistical Services, DCS/C.

BY TYPE, MODEL, AND LINE CLASSIFICATION — FISCAL YEAR 1953

LOSSES								ENDING INVENTORY 30 JUNE 1953						
				TRANSFERS										
CON- VERSION	SECOND LINE	SALVAGE SURVEY RCLM	CLASS 01Z	FOREIGN GOV'TS (STOCK)	OTHER NON-USAF (STOCK)	NEW PRODUCTION	GAINED IN ERROR	TOTAL	USAF	ANG	AFR	CAP	EAR- MARKED	LINE NUMBER
														1
5	19	186	6	5	1	6	-	773	251	2	-	519	1	2
1	-	24	-	-	-	-	-	127	-	-	-	127	-	3
-	-	43	-	5	-	-	-	183	117	-	-	66	-	4
1	-	98	-	-	-	-	-	32	32	-	-	-	-	5
-	-	11	1	-	-	-	-	372	44	2	-	326	-	6
-	-	-	-	-	-	-	-	3	3	-	-	-	-	7
-	-	-	-	-	-	-	-	1	1	-	-	-	-	8
-	-	-	-	-	-	3	-	-	-	-	-	-	-	9
1	19	5	-	-	1	-	-	31	31	-	-	-	-	10
2	-	3	-	-	-	-	-	6	6	-	-	-	-	11
-	-	-	3	-	-	-	-	2	2	-	-	-	-	12
-	-	-	-	-	-	-	-	3	2	-	-	-	1	13
-	-	1	-	-	-	-	-	3	3	-	-	-	-	14
-	-	1	-	-	-	-	-	1	1	-	-	-	-	15
-	-	-	2	-	-	-	-	9	9	-	-	-	-	16
-	-	-	-	-	-	1	-	-	-	-	-	-	-	17
-	-	-	-	-	-	2	-	-	-	-	-	-	-	18
-	-	1	-	-	-	-	-	-	-	-	-	-	-	19
-	-	1	-	-	-	-	-	-	-	-	-	-	-	20
-	-	1	-	-	-	-	-	-	-	-	-	-	-	21
7	-	13	-	-	-	-	-	56	56	-	-	-	-	22
7	-	13	-	-	-	-	-	56	56	-	-	-	-	23
7	-	7	-	-	-	-	-	3	3	-	-	-	-	24
-	-	4	-	-	-	-	-	41	41	-	-	-	-	25
-	-	1	-	-	-	-	-	9	9	-	-	-	-	26
-	-	1	-	-	-	-	-	2	2	-	-	-	-	27
-	-	-	-	-	-	-	-	1	1	-	-	-	-	28

TABLE 123 — USAF AND RESERVE FORCES AIRCRAFT LOSSES BY CAUSE – FISCAL YEAR 1953

Basic model includes prefixed versions except those which change the aircraft type. Adjustments have been made for those aircraft which were reported lost during Fiscal Year 1953 and subsequently regained.

TYPE AND MODEL	TOTAL	BEYOND ECONOMICAL REPAIR: TOTAL	ENEMY ACTION a/	FLYING ACCIDENT	GROUND ACCIDENT	NATURAL PHENOMENA	TESTED TO DESTRUCTION	FAIR WEAR AND TEAR	ABNORMAL DETERIORATION IN USE	ABNORMAL STORAGE DETERIORATION	NORMAL STORAGE DETERIORATION	DESTROYED OR IMPOUNDED IN NON-ENEMY COUNTRY	NOT BEYOND ECONOMICAL REPAIR: TOTAL	RECLAMATION SALVAGE AND SURVEY	CLASS 01Z	CLASS 26 AND 32	TRANSFERS FROM STOCK	TRANSFERS FROM NEW PRODUCTION
TOTAL	5990	1346	315	886	29	24	40	44	4	2	1	1	4644	807	234	10	517	3076
BOMBER	251	109	41	51	11	1	4	1	-	-	-	-	142	59	16	-	22	45
B-17	4	4	-	2	1	-	1	-	-	-	-	-	-	-	-	-	-	-
B-26	63	51	29	15	7	-	-	-	-	-	-	-	12	1	-	-	11	-
B-29	107	29	12	15	-	-	1	1	-	-	-	-	78	58	12	-	8	-
B-36	6	6	-	3	1	1	1	-	-	-	-	-	-	-	-	-	-	-
B-45	5	5	-	4	-	-	1	-	-	-	-	-	-	-	-	-	-	-
B-47	12	6	-	4	2	-	-	-	-	-	-	-	6	-	4	-	2	-
B-50	7	7	-	7	-	-	-	-	-	-	-	-	-	-	-	-	-	-
B-57	1	1	-	1	-	-	-	-	-	-	-	-	-	-	-	-	-	-
P2V-5	45	-	-	-	-	-	-	-	-	-	-	-	45	-	-	-	-	45
JD-1	1	-	-	-	-	-	-	-	-	-	-	-	1	-	-	-	1	-
TANKER	3	3	-	2	-	-	1	-	-	-	-	-	-	-	-	-	-	-
KB-29	3	3	-	2	-	-	1	-	-	-	-	-	-	-	-	-	-	-
FIGHTER	2546	714	230	454	11	-	13	4	1	-	-	1	1832	131	160	6	418	1117
F9F	1	-	-	-	-	-	-	-	-	-	-	-	1	-	-	-	1	-
F-47	437	36	-	22	3	-	9	2	-	-	-	-	401	99	-	1	301	-
F-51	176	78	10	67	-	-	-	1	-	-	-	-	98	1	8	-	89	-
F-80	95	91	28	63	-	-	-	-	-	-	-	-	4	1	1	1	1	-
F-82	26	1	-	-	-	-	-	-	1	-	-	-	25	23	-	-	2	-
F-84	1495	252	90	154	6	-	-	1	-	-	-	1	1243	4	142	3	-	1094
F-86	249	197	95	98	2	-	2	-	-	-	-	-	52	1	4	-	24	23
F-89	10	5	-	4	-	-	1	-	-	-	-	-	5	2	2	1	-	-
F-90	1	1	-	-	-	-	1	-	-	-	-	-	-	-	-	-	-	-
F-94	56	53	7	46	-	-	-	-	-	-	-	-	3	-	3	-	-	-
RECONNAISSANCE	55	38	14	21	2	-	-	1	-	-	-	-	17	1	-	-	16	-
RB-17	2	-	-	-	-	-	-	-	-	-	-	-	2	-	-	-	2	-
RB-26	3	3	-	3	-	-	-	-	-	-	-	-	-	-	-	-	-	-
RB-29	4	4	2	1	1	-	-	-	-	-	-	-	-	-	-	-	-	-
WB-29	3	3	-	3	-	-	-	-	-	-	-	-	-	-	-	-	-	-
RB-36	2	2	-	2	-	-	-	-	-	-	-	-	-	-	-	-	-	-
RB-45	1	1	-	1	-	-	-	-	-	-	-	-	-	-	-	-	-	-
RB-50	1	1	-	1	-	-	-	-	-	-	-	-	-	-	-	-	-	-
RC-45	2	1	-	-	-	-	-	1	-	-	-	-	1	1	-	-	-	-
RF-51	19	6	6	-	-	-	-	-	-	-	-	-	13	-	-	-	13	-
RF-80	15	15	5	9	1	-	-	-	-	-	-	-	-	-	-	-	-	-
RF-86	2	2	1	1	-	-	-	-	-	-	-	-	-	-	-	-	-	-
XR-12	1	-	-	-	-	-	-	-	-	-	-	-	1	-	-	-	1	-

TABLE 123 – USAF AND RESERVE FORCES AIRCRAFT LOSSES BY CAUSE – FISCAL YEAR 1953 – Continued

TYPE AND MODEL	TOTAL	BEYOND ECONOMICAL REPAIR											NOT BEYOND ECONOMICAL REPAIR					
		TOTAL	ENEMY ACTION a/	FLYING ACCIDENT	GROUND ACCIDENT	NATURAL PHENOMENA	TESTED TO DESTRUCTION	FAIR WEAR AND TEAR	ABNORMAL DETERIORATION IN USE	ABNORMAL STORAGE DETERIORATION	NORMAL STORAGE DETERIORATION	DESTROYED OR IMPOUNDED IN NON-ENEMY COUNTRY	TOTAL	RECLAMATION SALVAGE AND SURVEY	CLASS 01Z	CLASS 26 AND 32	TRANSFERS FROM STOCK	TRANSFERS FROM NEW PRODUCTION
SEARCH & RESCUE	34	17	2	9	-	1	5	-	-	-	-	-	17	13	-	-	2	2
SA-10 . . .	13	-	-	-	-	-	-	-	-	-	-	-	13	13	-	-	-	-
SA-16 . . .	9	7	1	5	-	1	-	-	-	-	-	-	2	-	-	-	-	2
SB-17 . . .	10	8	-	3	-	-	5	-	-	-	-	-	2	-	-	-	2	-
SB-29 . . .	1	1	-	1	-	-	-	-	-	-	-	-	-	-	-	-	-	-
SH-5 . . .	1	1	1	-	-	-	-	-	-	-	-	-	-	-	-	-	-	-
SPECIAL RESEARCH	1	1	-	1	-	-	-	-	-	-	-	-	-	-	-	-	-	-
X-1	1	1	-	1	-	-	-	-	-	-	-	-	-	-	-	-	-	-
CARGO	296	65	8	52	3	-	-	-	-	2	-	-	231	78	10	1	25	117
C-45 . . .	82	5	-	5	-	-	-	-	-	-	-	-	77	77	-	-	-	-
C-46 . . .	14	9	4	4	1	-	-	-	-	-	-	-	5	-	5	-	-	-
C-47 . . .	40	24	-	20	2	-	-	-	-	2	-	-	16	-	-	-	16	-
C-54 . . .	12	6	-	6	-	-	-	-	-	-	-	-	6	-	-	-	6	-
C-82 . . .	4	3	-	3	-	-	-	-	-	-	-	-	1	1	-	-	-	-
C-97 . . .	1	-	-	-	-	-	-	-	-	-	-	-	1	-	1	-	-	-
C-118 . . .	2	-	-	-	-	-	-	-	-	-	-	-	2	-	-	-	2	-
C-119 . . .	74	14	3	11	-	-	-	-	-	-	-	-	60	-	2	-	-	58
C-122 . . .	1	1	-	1	-	-	-	-	-	-	-	-	-	-	-	-	-	-
C-124 . . .	5	3	1	2	-	-	-	-	-	-	-	-	2	-	2	-	-	-
VB-17 . . .	1	-	-	-	-	-	-	-	-	-	-	-	1	-	-	1	-	-
R4Q (C-119C)	60	-	-	-	-	-	-	-	-	-	-	-	60	-	-	-	1	59
TRAINER	1023	274	1	260	-	3	7	2	1	-	-	-	749	421	2	1	27	298
T-6	81	81	1	79	-	-	-	1	-	-	-	-	-	-	-	-	-	-
T-7	105	7	-	5	-	2	-	-	-	-	-	-	98	98	-	-	-	-
T-11 . . .	262	11	-	9	-	1	-	1	-	-	-	-	251	251	-	-	-	-
T-28 . . .	35	32	-	32	-	-	-	-	-	-	-	-	3	1	-	-	2	-
T-29 . . .	1	-	-	-	-	-	-	-	-	-	-	-	1	-	1	-	-	-
T-33 . . .	370	104	-	104	-	-	-	-	-	-	-	-	266	1	-	-	3	262
T-35 . . .	9	-	-	-	-	-	-	-	-	-	-	-	9	3	-	-	-	6
TB-17 . . .	4	-	-	-	-	-	-	-	-	-	-	-	4	-	-	-	4	-
TB-25 . . .	22	6	-	6	-	-	-	-	-	-	-	-	16	-	-	-	16	-
TB-26 . . .	5	5	-	4	-	-	-	-	1	-	-	-	-	-	-	-	-	-
TB-29 . . .	39	3	-	3	-	-	-	-	-	-	-	-	36	36	-	-	-	-
TB-47 . . .	1	-	-	-	-	-	-	-	-	-	-	-	1	-	1	-	-	-
TC-45 . . .	1	1	-	1	-	-	-	-	-	-	-	-	-	-	-	-	-	-
TC-47 . . .	1	1	-	1	-	-	-	-	-	-	-	-	-	-	-	-	-	-
TF-47 . . .	40	8	-	1	-	-	-	-	-	-	-	-	32	31	-	-	1	-
TF-51 . . .	12	10	-	10	-	-	-	-	-	-	-	-	2	-	-	1	1	-
TF-80 . . .	4	4	-	4	-	-	-	-	-	-	-	-	-	-	-	-	-	-
MARK IV	31	1	-	1	-	-	-	-	-	-	-	-	30	-	-	-	-	30

TABLE 123 — USAF AND RESERVE FORCES AIRCRAFT LOSSES BY CAUSE — FISCAL YEAR 1953 — CONTINUED

TYPE AND MODEL	TOTAL	BEYOND ECONOMICAL REPAIR											NOT BEYOND ECONOMICAL REPAIR					
		TOTAL	ENEMY ACTION a/	FLYING ACCIDENT	GROUND ACCIDENT	NATURAL PHENOMENA	TESTED TO DESTRUCTION	FAIR WEAR AND TEAR	ABNORMAL DETERIORATION IN USE	ABNORMAL STORAGE DETERIORATION	NORMAL STORAGE DETERIORATION	DESTROYED OR IMPOUNDED IN NON-ENEMY COUNTRY	TOTAL	RECLAMATION SALVAGE AND SURVEY	CLASS 01Z	CLASS 26 AND 32	TRANSFERS FROM STOCK	TRANSFERS FROM NEW PRODUCTION
COMMUNICATION	1767	112	19	34	2	19	-	36	2	-	-	-	1655	104	46	1	7	1497
L-4	24	23	-	6	1	9	-	5	2	-	-	-	1	1	-	-	-	-
L-5	48	39	1	6	-	2	-	30	-	-	-	-	9	4	-	-	5	-
L-13	98	1	-	1	-	-	-	-	-	-	-	-	97	97	-	-	-	-
L-16	16	11	-	5	1	5	-	-	-	-	-	-	5	-	4	-	1	-
L-18	164	-	-	-	-	-	-	-	-	-	-	-	164	-	-	-	-	164
L-19	570	3	-	-	-	3	-	-	-	-	-	-	567	-	19	-	-	548
L-20	62	4	-	4	-	-	-	-	-	-	-	-	58	-	-	-	-	58
L-21	124	2	-	2	-	-	-	-	-	-	-	-	122	-	-	-	-	122
L-23	27	-	-	-	-	-	-	-	-	-	-	-	27	-	-	-	-	27
YL-26	3	-	-	-	-	-	-	-	-	-	-	-	3	-	-	-	-	3
LC-126	3	1	-	1	-	-	-	-	-	-	-	-	2	-	-	-	-	2
LT-6	14	14	13	1	-	-	-	-	-	-	-	-	-	-	-	-	-	-
H-5	7	5	2	3	-	-	-	-	-	-	-	-	2	1	-	-	1	-
H-12	3	2	-	1	-	-	-	1	-	-	-	-	1	1	-	-	-	-
H-13	283	1	-	1	-	-	-	-	-	-	-	-	282	-	21	-	-	261
H-19	79	6	3	3	-	-	-	-	-	-	-	-	73	-	-	-	-	73
XH-20	1	-	-	-	-	-	-	-	-	-	-	-	1	-	-	1	-	-
YH-21	2	-	-	-	-	-	-	-	-	-	-	-	2	-	2	-	-	-
H-23	221	-	-	-	-	-	-	-	-	-	-	-	221	-	-	-	-	221
YH-24	1	-	-	-	-	-	-	-	-	-	-	-	1	-	-	-	-	1
H-25	15	-	-	-	-	-	-	-	-	-	-	-	15	-	-	-	-	15
YH-30	2	-	-	-	-	-	-	-	-	-	-	-	2	-	-	-	-	2
GLIDER	1	1	-	-	-	-	-	-	-	-	1	-	-	-	-	-	-	-
G-18	1	1	-	-	-	-	-	-	-	-	1	-	-	-	-	-	-	-
AERIAL TARGET	13	12	-	2	-	-	10	-	-	-	-	-	1	-	-	1	-	-
Q-14	7	6	-	1	-	-	5	-	-	-	-	-	1	-	-	1	-	-
QB-17	4	4	-	-	-	-	4	-	-	-	-	-	-	-	-	-	-	-
QF-80	1	1	-	-	-	-	1	-	-	-	-	-	-	-	-	-	-	-
QT-33	1	1	-	1	-	-	-	-	-	-	-	-	-	-	-	-	-	-

a/ Includes aircraft lost in FEAF for the following reasons: Lost on Combat Mission Due to Enemy Action, Lost on Combat Mission Not Due to Enemy Action, Missing on Combat Mission or Unknown, Lost Due to Enemy Action Not on Combat Mission, and Aircraft Abandoned.

SOURCE: Materiel Statistics Division, Directorate of Statistical Services, DCS/C.

TABLE 124 — STATUS AND LINE CLASSIFICATION OF USAF AIRCRAFT BY TYPE AND MODEL — QUARTERLY, FISCAL YEAR 1953

TYPE AND MODEL	TOTAL			ACTIVE			INACTIVE		
	TOTAL	FIRST LINE	SECOND LINE	TOTAL	FIRST LINE	SECOND LINE	TOTAL	FIRST LINE	SECOND LINE
	30 September 1952								
AIRCRAFT - TOTAL	20096	8310	11786	16074	7039	9035	4022	1271	2751
BOMBERS	2934	797	2137	1665	509	1156	1269	288	981
B-17	41	-	41	27	-	27	14	-	14
B-24	1	-	1	-	-	-	1	-	1
B-25	140	-	140	9	-	9	131	-	131
B-26	621	-	621	403	-	403	218	-	218
B-29	1319	-	1319	710	-	710	609	-	609
B-36	158	157	1	129	129	-	29	28	1
B-43	1	-	1	-	-	-	1	-	1
B-45	78	69	9	68	61	7	10	8	2
B-47	311	310	1	73	73	-	238	237	1
B-50	261	261	-	246	246	-	15	15	-
B-51	1	-	1	-	-	-	1	-	1
B-60	2	-	2	-	-	-	2	-	2
TANKER	325	132	193	297	116	181	28	16	12
KB-29M	81	-	81	80	-	80	1	-	1
KB-29P	112	-	112	101	-	101	11	-	11
KC-97	132	132	-	116	116	-	16	16	-
FIGHTER	4735	2624	2111	3949	2368	1581	786	256	530
F9F	1	-	1	-	-	-	1	-	1
F-47	376	-	376	122	-	122	254	-	254
F-51	757	-	757	729	-	729	28	-	28
F-80	581	116	465	477	101	376	104	15	89
F-82	36	-	36	13	-	13	23	-	23
F-84	1497	1159	338	1368	1117	251	129	42	87
F-86	876	747	129	744	656	88	132	91	41
F-88	2	-	2	-	-	-	2	-	2
F-89	185	184	1	109	109	-	76	75	1
F-91	1	-	1	-	-	-	1	-	1
F-92	1	-	1	-	-	-	1	-	1
F-94	422	418	4	387	385	2	35	33	2
RECONNAISSANCE	649	172	477	536	147	389	113	25	88
RB-17	17	-	17	11	-	11	6	-	6
WB-17	1	-	1	-	-	-	1	-	1
RB-25	3	-	3	3	-	3	-	-	-
RB-26	111	-	111	95	-	95	16	-	16
RB-29	56	-	56	36	-	36	20	-	20
WB-29	82	-	82	82	-	82	-	-	-
RB-36	105	105	-	80	80	-	25	25	-
RB-45	25	25	-	25	25	-	-	-	-
RB-49	1	-	1	-	-	-	1	-	1
RB-50	42	42	-	42	42	-	-	-	-
RC-45	6	-	6	5	-	5	1	-	1
RC-47	7	-	7	7	-	7	-	-	-
RF-51	38	-	38	27	-	27	11	-	11
RF-80	149	-	149	119	-	119	30	-	30
RF-84	2	-	2	-	-	-	2	-	2
RF-86	4	-	4	4	-	4	-	-	-
SEARCH & RESCUE	268	157	111	245	146	99	23	11	12
SA-10	7	-	7	7	-	7	-	-	-
SA-16	157	157	-	146	146	-	11	11	-
SB-17	56	-	56	44	-	44	12	-	12
SB-29	33	-	33	33	-	33	-	-	-
SC-47	6	-	6	6	-	6	-	-	-
SC-54	3	-	3	3	-	3	-	-	-
SH-5	6	-	6	6	-	6	-	-	-
SPECIAL RESEARCH	4	-	4	-	-	-	4	-	4
X-1	1	-	1	-	-	-	1	-	1
X-4	2	-	2	-	-	-	2	-	2
X-5	1	-	1	-	-	-	1	-	1

TABLE 124 - STATUS AND LINE CLASSIFICATION OF USAF AIRCRAFT BY TYPE AND MODEL - QUARTERLY, FISCAL YEAR 1953 - Continued

TYPE AND MODEL	TOTAL			ACTIVE			INACTIVE		
	TOTAL	FIRST LINE	SECOND LINE	TOTAL	FIRST LINE	SECOND LINE	TOTAL	FIRST LINE	SECOND LINE
	30 September 1952 - Continued								
CARGO	3282	728	2554	2976	677	2299	306	51	255
C-45	449	-	449	424	-	424	25	-	25
C-46	340	-	340	222	-	222	118	-	118
C-47	1251	-	1251	1197	-	1197	54	-	54
C-53	1	-	1	1	-	1	-	-	-
C-54	384	-	384	340	-	340	44	-	44
C-74	11	11	-	11	11	-	-	-	-
C-82	135	120	15	121	111	10	14	9	5
C-97	68	68	-	62	62	-	6	6	-
C-99	1	-	1	-	-	-	1	-	1
C-117	15	-	15	14	-	14	1	-	1
C-118	10	10	-	3	3	-	7	7	-
C-119	345	345	-	327	327	-	18	18	-
C-120	1	-	1	-	-	-	1	-	1
C-121	10	10	-	10	10	-	-	-	-
C-122	10	-	10	10	-	10	-	-	-
C-124	165	164	1	153	153	-	12	11	1
C-125	1	-	1	1	-	1	-	-	-
VB-17	40	-	40	38	-	38	2	-	2
CB-25	9	-	9	8	-	8	1	-	1
VB-25	32	-	32	32	-	32	-	-	-
CB-26	1	-	1	-	-	-	1	-	1
VB-26	2	-	2	2	-	2	-	-	-
CB-29	1	-	1	-	-	-	1	-	1
TRAINER	6924	3123	3801	5663	2643	3020	1261	480	781
T-6	2635	1395	1241	2317	1393	924	319	2	317
T-7	163	-	163	161	-	161	2	-	2
T-11	330	-	330	330	-	330	-	-	-
T-28	767	765	2	345	345	-	422	420	2
T-29	90	90	-	82	82	-	8	8	-
T-33	868	868	-	820	820	-	48	48	-
T-34	3	-	3	3	-	3	-	-	-
T-35	3	-	3	3	-	3	-	-	-
TB-17	37	-	37	33	-	33	4	-	4
TB-25	866	-	866	845	-	845	21	-	21
TB-26	310	-	310	262	-	262	48	-	48
TB-29	335	-	335	75	-	75	260	-	260
TB-45	9	-	9	8	-	8	1	-	1
TB-50	24	5	19	22	3	19	2	2	-
TC-45	96	-	96	96	-	96	-	-	-
TC-47	52	-	52	52	-	52	-	-	-
TC-54	8	-	8	7	-	7	1	-	1
TF-47	122	-	122	1	-	1	121	-	121
TF-51	146	-	146	146	-	146	-	-	-
TRF-51	2	-	2	2	-	2	-	-	-
TF-80	56	-	56	52	-	52	4	-	4
TH-5	1	-	1	1	-	1	-	-	-
COMMUNICATION	937	577	360	716	433	283	221	144	77
L-4	17	-	17	17	-	17	-	-	-
L-5	147	-	147	145	-	145	2	-	2
L-13	115	-	115	50	-	50	65	-	65
L-16	68	57	11	67	56	11	1	1	-
L-17	4	1	3	1	1	-	3	-	3
L-19	24	24	-	2	2	-	22	22	-
L-20	109	108	1	97	96	1	12	12	-
L-21	148	148	-	148	148	-	-	-	-
LC-126	7	7	-	5	5	-	2	2	-
LT-6	53	53	-	52	52	-	1	1	-
H-5	49	2	47	48	2	46	1	-	1
H-12	8	-	8	5	-	5	3	-	3
H-13	50	46	4	27	23	4	23	23	-
H-18	2	-	2	2	-	2	-	-	-
H-19	65	61	4	43	42	1	22	19	3
H-23	70	70	-	6	6	-	64	64	-
H-24	1	-	1	1	-	1	-	-	-
GLIDER	1	-	1	-	-	-	1	-	1
G-18	1	-	1	-	-	-	1	-	1

TABLE 124 — STATUS AND LINE CLASSIFICATION OF USAF AIRCRAFT BY TYPE AND MODEL — QUARTERLY, FISCAL YEAR 1953 — CONTINUED

TYPE AND MODEL	TOTAL			ACTIVE			INACTIVE		
	TOTAL	FIRST LINE	SECOND LINE	TOTAL	FIRST LINE	SECOND LINE	TOTAL	FIRST LINE	SECOND LINE
	30 September 1952 - Continued								
AERIAL TARGET	37	-	37	27	-	27	10	-	10
Q-14	8	-	8	7	-	7	1	-	1
QB-17	15	-	15	14	-	14	1	-	1
QB-45	1	-	1	-	-	-	1	-	1
QF-80	10	-	10	4	-	4	6	-	6
QT-33	3	-	3	2	-	2	1	-	1
	31 December 1952								
AIRCRAFT - TOTAL	20474	8938	11536	16456	7570	8886	4018	1368	2650
BOMBER	2856	832	2024	1666	564	1102	1190	268	922
B-17	44	-	44	31	-	31	13	-	13
B-24	1	-	1	-	-	-	1	-	1
B-25	91	-	91	9	-	9	82	-	82
B-26	595	-	595	369	-	369	226	-	226
B-29	1280	-	1280	689	-	689	591	-	591
B-36	166	166	-	147	147	-	19	19	-
B-43	1	-	1	-	-	-	1	-	1
B-45	74	66	8	54	50	4	20	16	4
B-47	345	344	1	123	123	-	222	221	1
B-50	256	256	-	244	244	-	12	12	-
B-51	1	-	1	-	-	-	1	-	1
B-60	2	-	2	-	-	-	2	-	2
TANKER	360	168	192	302	143	159	58	25	33
KB-29M	81	-	81	78	-	78	3	-	3
KB-29P	110	-	110	81	-	81	29	-	29
YKB-29P	1	-	1	-	-	-	1	-	1
KC-97	168	168	-	143	143	-	25	25	-
FIGHTER	4993	2862	2131	4014	2401	1613	979	461	518
F9F	1	-	1	-	-	-	1	-	1
F-47	316	-	316	84	-	84	232	-	232
F-51	742	-	742	701	-	701	41	-	41
F-80	559	84	475	479	71	408	80	13	67
F-82	35	-	35	8	-	8	27	-	27
F-84	1611	1230	381	1403	1120	283	208	110	98
F-86	1089	917	172	861	734	127	228	183	45
F-88	2	-	2	-	-	-	2	-	2
F-89	198	197	1	111	111		87	86	1
F-91	1	-	1	-	-	-	1	-	1
F-92	1	-	1	-	-	-	1	-	1
F-94	438	434	4	367	365	2	71	69	2
RECONNAISSANCE	652	182	470	550	165	385	102	17	85
RB-17	17	-	17	11	-	11	6	-	6
VB-17	1	-	1	-	-	-	1	-	1
RB-25	3	-	3	3	-	3	-	-	-
RB-26	114	-	114	103	-	103	11	-	11
RB-29	51	-	51	27	-	27	24	-	24
WB-29	81	-	81	81	-	81	-	-	-
RB-36	116	116	-	110	110	-	6	6	-
RB-45	24	24	-	13	13	-	11	11	-
RB-47	1	1	-	1	1	-	-	-	-
RB-49	1	-	1	-	-	-	1	-	1
RB-50	41	41	-	41	41	-	-	-	-
RC-45	6	-	6	5	-	5	1	-	1
RC-47	9	-	9	7	-	7	2	-	2
RC-54	1	-	1	1	-	1	-	-	-
RF-51	34	-	34	26	-	26	8	-	8
RF-80	146	-	146	118	-	118	28	-	28
RF-84	2	-	2	-	-	-	2	-	2
RF-86	4	-	4	3	-	3	1	-	1
SEARCH & RESCUE	293	192	101	252	171	81	41	21	20
SA-10	3	-	3	3	-	3	-	-	-
SA-16	190	190	-	169	169	-	21	21	-

TABLE 124 — STATUS AND LINE CLASSIFICATION OF USAF AIRCRAFT BY TYPE AND MODEL — QUARTERLY, FISCAL YEAR 1953 — CONTINUED

TYPE AND MODEL	TOTAL			ACTIVE			INACTIVE		
	TOTAL	FIRST LINE	SECOND LINE	TOTAL	FIRST LINE	SECOND LINE	TOTAL	FIRST LINE	SECOND LINE
	31 December 1952 - Continued								
SEARCH & RESCUE (Cont'd)									
SB-17	49	-	49	29	-	29	20	-	20
SB-29	36	-	36	36	-	36	-	-	-
SC-47	6	-	6	6	-	6	-	-	-
SC-54	3	-	3	3	-	3	-	-	-
SH-5	6	2	4	6	2	4	-	-	-
SPECIAL RESEARCH	4	-	4	-	-	-	4	-	4
X-1	1	-	1	-	-	-	1	-	1
X-4	2	-	2	-	-	-	2	-	2
X-5	1	-	1	-	-	-	1	-	1
CARGO	3385	710	2675	3043	662	2381	342	48	294
C-45	510	-	510	464	-	464	46	-	46
C-46	301	-	301	170	-	170	131	-	131
C-47	1238	-	1238	1184	-	1184	54	-	54
C-53	1	-	1	1	-	1	-	-	-
C-54	376	-	376	333	-	333	43	-	43
C-74	11	10	1	11	10	1	-	-	-
C-82	136	-	136	122	-	122	14	-	14
C-97	68	68	-	63	63	-	5	5	-
C-99	1	-	1	-	-	-	1	-	1
C-117	15	-	15	15	-	15	-	-	-
C-118	18	18	-	14	14	-	4	4	-
C-119	407	406	1	383	382	1	24	24	-
C-120	1	-	1	-	-	-	1	-	1
C-121	10	10	-	10	10	-	-	-	-
C-122	10	-	10	10	-	10	-	-	-
C-124	199	198	1	183	183	-	16	15	1
C-125	1	-	1	1	-	1	-	-	-
VB-17	39	-	39	38	-	38	1	-	1
CB-25	7	-	7	6	-	6	1	-	1
VB-25	32	-	32	32	-	32	-	-	-
CB-26	1	-	1	-	-	-	1	-	1
VB-26	2	-	2	2	-	2	-	-	-
CB-29	1	-	1	1	-	1	-	-	-
TRAINER	7099	3501	3598	5945	3024	2921	1154	477	677
T-6	2587	1429	1158	2354	1429	925	233	-	233
T-7	124	-	124	121	-	121	3	-	3
T-11	254	-	254	248	-	248	6	-	6
T-28	851	849	2	425	425	-	426	424	2
T-29	109	109	-	102	102	-	7	7	-
T-33	1092	1092	-	1049	1049	-	43	43	-
T-34	3	-	3	2	-	2	1	-	1
T-35	3	-	3	3	-	3	-	-	-
TB-17	40	-	40	35	-	35	5	-	5
TB-25	911	-	911	889	-	889	22	-	22
TB-26	294	-	294	231	-	231	63	-	63
TB-29	352	-	352	96	-	96	256	-	256
TB-45	10	-	10	9	-	9	1	-	1
TB-50	44	22	22	41	19	22	3	3	-
TC-45	95	-	95	95	-	95	-	-	-
TC-47	52	-	52	52	-	52	-	-	-
TC-54	8	-	8	8	-	8	-	-	-
TF-47	73	-	73	-	-	-	73	-	73
TF-51	138	-	138	136	-	136	2	-	2
TRF-51	2	-	2	2	-	2	-	-	-
TF-80	56	-	56	46	-	46	10	-	10
TH-5	1	-	1	1	-	1	-	-	-
COMMUNICATION	794	491	303	653	440	213	141	51	90
L-5	122	-	122	121	-	121	1	-	1
L-13	109	-	109	35	-	35	74	-	74
L-16	51	26	25	50	26	24	1	-	1
L-17	4	1	3	1	1	-	3	-	3
L-19	14	14	-	2	2	-	12	12	-
L-20	130	129	1	123	122	1	7	7	-
L-21	148	148	-	148	148	-	-	-	-
LC-126	5	5	-	-	-	-	5	5	-
LT-6	49	49	-	47	47	-	2	2	-

TABLE 124 — STATUS AND LINE CLASSIFICATION OF USAF AIRCRAFT BY TYPE AND MODEL — QUARTERLY, FISCAL YEAR 1953 — CONTINUED

TYPE AND MODEL	TOTAL			ACTIVE			INACTIVE		
	TOTAL	FIRST LINE	SECOND LINE	TOTAL	FIRST LINE	SECOND LINE	TOTAL	FIRST LINE	SECOND LINE
	31 December 1952 - Continued								
COMMUNICATION (Cont'd)									
H-5	49	25	24	48	25	23	1	-	1
H-12	6	-	6	4	-	4	2	-	2
H-13	28	26	2	24	23	1	4	3	1
H-18	2	-	2	2	-	2	-	-	-
H-19	53	49	4	46	45	1	7	4	3
H-20	1	-	1	-	-	-	1	-	1
H-21	3	-	3	-	-	-	3	-	3
H-23	14	14	-	1	1	-	13	13	-
H-24	1	-	1	1	-	1	-	-	-
H-25	5	5	-	-	-	-	5	5	-
GLIDER	1	-	1	-	-	-	1	-	1
G-18	1	-	1	-	-	-	1	-	1
AERIAL TARGET	37	-	37	31	-	31	6	-	6
Q-14	8	-	8	7	-	7	1	-	1
QB-17	15	-	15	15	-	15	-	-	-
QB-45	1	-	1	-	-	-	1	-	1
QF-80	10	-	10	7	-	7	3	-	3
QT-33	3	-	3	2	-	2	1	-	1
	31 March 1953								
AIRCRAFT - TOTAL	20989	9944	11045	16873	8450	8423	4116	1494	2622
BOMBER	2815	904	1911	1695	660	1035	1120	244	876
B-17	44	-	44	33	-	33	11	-	11
B-24	1	-	1	-	-	-	1	-	1
B-25	67	-	67	9	-	9	58	-	58
B-26	565	-	565	353	-	353	212	-	212
B-29	1213	-	1213	633	-	633	580	-	580
B-36	173	173	-	141	141	-	32	32	-
B-43	1	-	1	-	-	-	1	-	1
B-45	72	59	13	53	47	6	19	12	7
B-47	421	419	2	231	231	-	190	188	2
B-50	252	252	-	241	241	-	11	11	-
B-51	1	-	1	-	-	-	1	-	1
B-52	1	-	1	-	-	-	1	-	1
B-57	1	1	-	-	-	-	1	1	-
B-60	2	-	2	-	-	-	2	-	2
JD-1	1	-	1	1	-	1	-	-	-
TANKER	393	203	190	349	182	167	44	21	23
KB-29M	81	-	81	75	-	75	6	-	6
KB-29P	109	-	109	92	-	92	17	-	17
KC-97	203	203	-	182	182	-	21	21	-
FIGHTER	5423	3348	2075	4232	2720	1512	1191	628	563
F9F	1	-	1	-	-	-	1	-	1
F-47	252	-	252	60	-	60	192	-	192
F-51	644	-	644	514	-	514	130	-	130
F-80	538	38	500	465	31	434	73	7	66
F-82	34	-	34	9	-	9	25	-	25
F-84	1813	1398	415	1530	1213	317	283	185	98
F-86	1471	1253	218	1183	1009	174	288	244	44
F-88	2	-	2	-	-	-	2	-	2
F-89	198	196	2	87	87	-	111	109	2
F-91	1	-	1	-	-	-	1	-	1
F-92	1	-	1	-	-	-	1	-	1
F-94	468	463	5	384	380	4	84	83	1
RECONNAISSANCE	660	191	469	534	180	354	126	11	115
RB-17	17	-	17	17	-	17	-	-	-
WB-17	1	-	1	1	-	1	-	-	-
RB-25	3	-	3	3	-	3	-	-	-
RB-26	114	-	114	94	-	94	20	-	20
RB-29	50	-	50	30	-	30	20	-	20
WB-29	80	-	80	79	-	79	1	-	1
RB-36	123	123	-	122	122	-	1	1	-

TABLE 124 – STATUS AND LINE CLASSIFICATION OF USAF AIRCRAFT BY TYPE AND MODEL – QUARTERLY, FISCAL YEAR 1953 – CONTINUED

TYPE AND MODEL	TOTAL			ACTIVE			INACTIVE		
	TOTAL	FIRST LINE	SECOND LINE	TOTAL	FIRST LINE	SECOND LINE	TOTAL	FIRST LINE	SECOND LINE
	31 March 1953 - Continued								
RECONNAISSANCE (Cont'd)									
RB-45	24	24	-	14	14	-	10	10	-
RB-47	1	1	-	1	1	-	-	-	-
RB-49	1	-	1	-	-	-	1	-	1
RB-50	41	41	-	41	41	-	-	-	-
RC-45	6	-	6	6	-	6	-	-	-
RC-47	17	-	17	9	-	9	8	-	8
RC-54	1	-	1	1	-	1	-	-	-
RF-51	30	-	30	6	-	6	24	-	24
RF-80	143	-	143	104	-	104	39	-	39
RF-84	2	-	2	-	-	-	2	-	2
RF-86	6	2	4	6	2	4	-	-	-
SEARCH & RESCUE	295	214	81	256	196	60	39	18	21
SA-16	214	214	-	196	196	-	18	18	-
SB-17	35	-	35	14	-	14	21	-	21
SB-29	36	-	36	36	-	36	-	-	-
SC-47	6	-	6	6	-	6	-	-	-
SC-54	3	-	3	3	-	3	-	-	-
SH-5	1	-	1	1	-	1	-	-	-
AERIAL TARGET	5	-	5	-	-	-	5	-	5
X-1	2	-	2	-	-	-	2	-	2
X-4	2	-	2	-	-	-	2	-	2
X-5	1	-	1	-	-	-	1	-	1
CARGO	3495	800	2695	3166	743	2423	329	57	272
C-45	563	-	563	537	-	537	26	-	26
C-46	293	-	293	167	-	167	126	-	126
C-47	1223	-	1223	1166	-	1166	57	-	57
C-53	1	-	1	1	-	1	-	-	-
C-54	374	-	374	330	-	330	44	-	44
C-74	11	10	1	11	10	1	-	-	-
C-82	135	-	135	122	-	122	13	-	13
C-97	70	70	-	67	67	-	3	3	-
C-99	1	-	1	-	-	-	1	-	1
C-117	15	-	15	15	-	15	-	-	-
C-118	17	17	-	14	14	-	3	3	-
C-119	465	464	1	448	447	1	17	17	-
C-120	1	-	1	-	-	-	1	-	1
C-121	10	10	-	10	10	-	-	-	-
C-122	9	-	9	8	-	8	1	-	1
C-124	230	229	1	195	195	-	35	34	1
C-125	1	-	1	1	-	1	-	-	-
VB-17	40	-	40	40	-	40	-	-	-
VB-25	32	-	32	32	-	32	-	-	-
CB-26	1	-	1	-	-	-	1	-	1
VB-26	2	-	2	2	-	2	-	-	-
CB-29	1	-	1	-	-	-	1	-	1
TRAINER	7032	3768	3264	5919	3297	2622	1113	471	642
T-6	2392	1421	971	2085	1421	664	307	-	307
T-7	97	-	97	95	-	95	2	-	2
T-11	217	-	217	207	-	207	10	-	10
T-28	912	910	2	513	513	-	399	397	2
T-29	127	127	-	120	120	-	7	7	-
T-33	1286	1286	-	1219	1219	-	67	67	-
T-34	3	-	3	2	-	2	1	-	1
T-35	3	-	3	3	-	3	-	-	-
TB-17	44	-	44	39	-	39	5	-	5
TB-25	933	-	933	902	-	902	31	-	31
TB-26	291	-	291	257	-	257	34	-	34
TB-29	331	-	331	111	-	111	220	-	220
TB-45	11	-	11	8	-	8	3	-	3
TB-50	46	24	22	46	24	22	-	-	-
TC-45	95	-	95	95	-	95	-	-	-
TC-47	52	-	52	52	-	52	-	-	-
TC-54	8	-	8	8	-	8	-	-	-
TF-47	22	-	22	-	-	-	22	-	22

TABLE 124 —STATUS AND LINE CLASSIFICATION OF USAF AIRCRAFT BY TYPE AND MODEL — QUARTERLY, FISCAL YEAR 1953 — CONTINUED

TYPE AND MODEL	TOTAL			ACTIVE			INACTIVE		
	TOTAL	FIRST LINE	SECOND LINE	TOTAL	FIRST LINE	SECOND LINE	TOTAL	FIRST LINE	SECOND LINE
	31 March 1953 - Continued								
TRAINER (Cont'd)									
TF-51	105	-	105	105	-	105	-	-	-
TRF-51	3	-	3	2	-	2	1	-	1
TF-80	53	-	53	49	-	49	4	-	4
TH-5	1	-	1	1	-	1	-	-	-
COMMUNICATION	833	516	317	693	472	221	140	44	96
L-5	119	-	119	118	-	118	1	-	1
L-13	98	-	98	20	-	20	78	-	78
L-16	50	-	50	49	-	49	1	-	1
L-17	4	1	3	1	1	-	3	-	3
L-19	2	2	-	2	2	-	-	-	-
L-20	156	155	1	144	143	1	12	12	-
L-21	148	148	-	148	148	-	-	-	-
L-23	2	2	-	-	-	-	2	2	-
LC-126	5	5	-	-	-	-	5	5	-
LT-6	48	48	-	48	48	-	-	-	-
H-5	50	24	26	50	24	26	-	-	-
H-12	6	-	6	2	-	2	4	-	4
H-13	53	51	2	49	48	1	4	3	1
H-18	2	-	2	1	-	1	1	-	1
H-19	79	76	3	55	54	1	24	22	2
H-20	2	-	2	-	-	-	2	-	2
H-21	5	-	5	2	-	2	3	-	3
H-23	2	2	-	2	2	-	-	-	-
H-25	2	2	-	2	2	-	-	-	-
GLIDER	1	-	1	-	-	-	1	-	1
G-18	1	-	1	-	-	-	1	-	1
AERIAL TARGET	37	-	37	29	-	29	8	-	8
Q-14	4	-	4	3	-	3	1	-	1
QB-17	21	-	21	17	-	17	4	-	4
QB-45	1	-	1	-	-	-	1	-	1
QF-80	9	-	9	8	-	8	1	-	1
QT-33	2	-	2	1	-	1	1	-	1
	30 June 1953								
AIRCRAFT - TOTAL	21363	10873	10490	17108	9280	7828	4255	1593	2662
BOMBER	2716	893	1823	1644	692	952	1072	201	871
B-17	41	-	41	31	-	31	10	-	10
B-24	1	-	1	-	-	-	1	-	1
B-25	35	-	35	9	-	9	26	-	26
B-26	529	-	529	370	-	370	159	-	159
B-29	1192	-	1192	527	-	527	665	-	665
B-36	184	184	-	151	151	-	33	33	-
B-43	1	-	1	-	-	-	1	-	1
B-45	72	53	19	54	39	15	18	14	4
B-47	406	404	2	262	262	-	144	142	2
B-50	251	251	-	240	240	-	11	11	-
B-51	1	-	1	-	-	-	1	-	1
B-52	2	-	2	-	-	-	2	-	2
B-57	1	1	-	-	-	-	1	1	-
TANKER	435	245	190	385	221	164	50	24	26
KB-29M	81	-	81	78	-	78	3	-	3
KB-29P	109	-	109	86	-	86	23	-	23
KC-97	245	245	-	221	221	-	24	24	-
FIGHTER	5533	3795	1738	4379	3048	1331	1154	747	407
F9F	1	-	1	-	-	-	1	-	1
F-47	149	-	149	18	-	18	131	-	131
F-51	435	-	435	343	-	343	92	-	92
F-80	516	2	514	464	2	462	52	-	52
F-82	15	-	15	11	-	11	4	-	4
F-84	1643	1308	335	1398	1142	256	245	166	79
F-86	2041	1767	274	1651	1414	237	390	353	37
F-88	2	-	2	-	-	-	2	-	2
F-89	203	201	2	60	60	-	143	141	2
F-91	1	-	1	-	-	-	1	-	1

TABLE 124 – STATUS AND LINE CLASSIFICATION OF USAF AIRCRAFT BY TYPE AND MODEL – QUARTERLY, FISCAL YEAR 1953 – CONTINUED

TYPE AND MODEL	TOTAL			ACTIVE			INACTIVE		
	TOTAL	FIRST LINE	SECOND LINE	TOTAL	FIRST LINE	SECOND LINE	TOTAL	FIRST LINE	SECOND LINE
	30 June 1953 - Continued								
FIGHTER (Cont't)									
F-92	1	-	1	-	-	-	1	-	1
F-94	525	517	8	434	430	4	91	87	4
F-100	1	-	1	-	-	-	1	-	1
RECONNAISSANCE	703	202	501	600	186	414	103	16	87
RB-17	15	-	15	10	-	10	5	-	5
WB-17	1	-	1	1	-	1	-	-	-
RB-25	3	-	3	3	-	3	-	-	-
RB-26	109	-	109	91	-	91	18	-	18
WB-26	6	-	6	6	-	6	-	-	-
RB-29	49	-	49	29	-	29	20	-	20
WB-29	80	-	80	80	-	80	-	-	-
RB-36	132	132	-	120	120	-	12	12	-
RB-45	24	24	-	20	20	-	4	4	-
RB-47	37	1	36	34	1	33	3	-	3
RB-49	1	-	1	-	-	-	1	-	1
RB-50	41	41	-	41	41	-	-	-	-
RC-45	8	-	8	8	-	8	-	-	-
RC-47	7	-	7	7	-	7	-	-	-
RC-54	1	-	1	1	-	1	-	-	-
RC-51	16	-	16	1	-	1	15	-	15
RF-80	163	-	163	144	-	144	19	-	19
RF-84	2	-	2	-	-	-	2	-	2
RF-86	8	4	4	4	4	-	4	-	4
SEARCH & RESCUE	285	230	55	256	203	53	29	27	2
SA-16	230	230	-	203	203	-	27	27	-
SB-17	11	-	11	10	-	10	1	-	1
SB-29	35	-	35	34	-	34	1	-	1
SC-47	5	-	5	5	-	5	-	-	-
SC-54	3	-	3	3	-	3	-	-	-
SH-5	1	-	1	1	-	1	-	-	-
SPECIAL RESEARCH	5	-	5	-	-	-	5	-	5
X-1	2	-	2	-	-	-	2	-	2
X-4	2	-	2	-	-	-	2	-	2
X-5	1	-	1	-	-	-	1	-	1
CARGO	3643	878	2765	3275	830	2445	368	48	320
C-45	633	-	633	614	-	614	19	-	19
C-46	283	-	283	157	-	157	126	-	126
C-47	1220	-	1220	1169	-	1169	51	-	51
C-53	1	-	1	1	-	1	-	-	-
C-54	373	-	373	330	-	330	43	-	43
C-74	11	11	-	11	11	-	-	-	-
C-82	135	-	135	64	-	64	71	-	71
C-97	70	70	-	62	62	-	8	8	-
C-99	1	-	1	-	-	-	1	-	1
C-117	26	-	26	23	-	23	3	-	3
C-118	17	17	-	16	16	-	1	1	-
C-119	512	511	1	494	494	-	18	17	1
C-120	1	-	1	-	-	-	1	-	1
C-121	10	10	-	10	10	-	-	-	-
C-122	9	-	9	9	-	9	-	-	-
C-124	260	259	1	237	237	-	23	22	1
C-125	1	-	1	1	-	1	-	-	-
VB-17	40	-	40	39	-	39	1	-	1
VB-25	33	-	33	33	-	33	-	-	-
CB-26	1	-	1	-	-	-	1	-	1
VB-26	2	-	2	2	-	2	-	-	-
CB-29	1	-	1	-	-	-	1	-	1
VT-29	3	-	3	3	-	3	-	-	-
TRAINER	7107	4001	3106	5750	3537	2213	1357	464	893
T-6	2265	1405	860	1722	1405	317	543	-	543
T-7	65	-	65	63	-	63	2	-	2
T-11	163	-	163	159	-	159	4	-	4

TABLE 124 — STATUS AND LINE CLASSIFICATION OF USAF AIRCRAFT BY TYPE AND MODEL — QUARTERLY, FISCAL YEAR 1953 — CONTINUED

TYPE AND MODEL	TOTAL			ACTIVE			INACTIVE		
	TOTAL	FIRST LINE	SECOND LINE	TOTAL	First Line	SECOND LINE	TOTAL	FIRST LINE	SECOND LINE
	30 June 1953 - Continued								
TRAINER (Cont'd)									
T-28	964	962	2	567	566	1	397	396	1
T-29	141	141	-	138	138	-	3	3	-
T-33	1469	1469	-	1404	1404	-	65	65	-
T-34	3	-	3	2	-	2	1	-	1
TB-17	44	-	44	33	-	33	11	-	11
TB-25	948	-	948	898	-	898	50	-	50
TB-26	313	-	313	280	-	280	33	-	33
TB-29	336	-	336	121	-	121	215	-	215
TB-45	11	-	11	10	-	10	1	-	1
TB-47	69	-	69	55	-	55	14	-	14
TB-50	46	24	22	45	24	21	1	-	1
TF-47	13	-	13	-	-	-	13	-	13
TF-51	80	-	80	76	-	76	4	-	4
TRF-51	2	-	2	2	-	2	-	-	-
TF-80	19	-	19	19	-	19	-	-	-
TC-45	95	-	95	95	-	95	-	-	-
TC-47	52	-	52	52	-	52	-	-	-
TC-54	8	-	8	8	-	8	-	-	-
TH-5	1	-	1	1	-	1	-	-	-
COMMUNICATION	880	629	251	785	563	222	95	66	29
L-5	177	-	117	116	-	116	1	-	1
L-13	32	-	32	21	-	21	11	-	11
L-16	44	-	44	43	-	43	1	-	1
L-17	3	-	3	-	-	-	3	-	3
L-19	18	18	-	4	4	-	14	14	-
L-20	181	180	1	179	178	1	2	2	-
L-21	147	147	-	147	147	-	-	-	-
L-23	1	1	-	1	1	-	-	-	-
LC-126	5	5	-	-	-	-	5	5	-
LT-6	41	41	-	41	41	-	-	-	-
H-5	49	18	31	49	18	31	-	-	-
H-12	6	-	6	3	-	3	3	-	3
H-13	99	97	2	66	65	1	33	32	1
H-18	2	-	2	1	-	1	1	-	1
H-19	119	116	3	104	103	1	15	13	2
H-20	1	-	1	-	-	-	1	-	1
H-21	9	-	9	4	-	4	5	-	5
H-23	4	4	-	4	4	-	-	-	-
H-25	2	2	-	2	2	-	-	-	-
AERIAL TARGET	56	-	56	34	-	34	22	-	22
Q-14	3	-	3	2	-	2	1	-	1
QB-17	41	-	41	23	-	23	18	-	18
QB-45	1	-	1	-	-	-	1	-	1
QF-80	9	-	9	8	-	8	1	-	1
QT-33	2	-	2	1	-	1	1	-	-

SOURCE: Materiel Statistics Division, Directorate of Statistical Services, DCS/C.

TABLE 125 -- WORLD-WIDE SUMMARY USAF ACTIVE AIRCRAFT OUT OF COMMISSION BY COMMAND -- FY 1953

MAJOR AIR COMMAND	AVERAGE AIRCRAFT ON HAND DURING MONTH	AVERAGE AIRCRAFT IN COMMISSION	AVERAGE AIRCRAFT OUT OF COMMISSION						
			TOTAL		Awaiting Parts	Technical Order Compliance	MAINTENANCE		Other Reasons
			Average Number AOC	% Of AOH			Periodic	Malfunction, Defect, Damage	
USAF - TOTAL. . . .	16,291	10,278	6,013	37	945	295	1,861	2,161	751
CONTINENTAL - TOTAL. . .	12,262	7,736	4,526	37	647	253	1,422	1,692	512
Air Defense Command	1,143	790	353	31	92	14	125	93	29
Air Materiel Command.	992	227	765	77	14	113	67	410	161
Air Proving Ground Command. . .	158	93	65	41	10	8	22	18	7
Air Research & Development Com.	529	268	261	49	38	10	79	54	80
Air University.	137	109	28	20	5	2	12	7	2
Continental Air Command	88	64	24	27	4	2	11	6	1
Headquarters Command.	212	153	59	28	10	1	22	23	3
Military Air Transport Service.	609	349	260	43	53	5	108	76	18
Strategic Air Command	1,767	1,212	555	31	117	20	204	187	27
Tactical Air Command.	1,263	866	397	31	78	15	178	98	28
Air Training Command.	5,361	3,602	1,759	33	226	63	594	720	156
USAF Security Service	3	3	-	-	-	-	-	-	-
OVERSEAS - TOTAL . . .	4,029	2,542	1,487	37	298	42	439	469	239
Alaskan Air Command	178	97	81	46	18	1	21	39	2
US Air Forces in Europe	1,057	661	396	37	121	26	127	106	16
Joint Brazil-US Military Comm .	10	6	4	40	-	-	2	1	1
Caribbean Air Command	32	22	10	31	1	-	6	1	2
Far East Air Forces	2,120	1,338	782	37	102	10	199	263	208
Headquarters Command.	56	47	9	16	-	1	7	1	-
Military Air Transport Service.	332	196	136	41	36	3	54	37	6
Northeast Air Command	50	28	22	44	8	1	7	5	1
Strategic Air Command	154	116	38	25	10	-	13	13	2
Air Research & Development Com.	15	10	5	33	1	-	2	1	1
Tactical Air Command.	25	21	4	16	1	-	1	2	-

SOURCE: Materiel Statistics Division, Directorate of Statistical Services, DCS/C

TABLE 126 —WORLD-WIDE SUMMARY USAF AVERAGE ACTIVE AIRCRAFT OUT OF COMMISSION BY CAUSE — BY TYPE AND MODEL — FISCAL YEAR 1953

TYPE AND MODEL OF AIRCRAFT	AVERAGE AIRCRAFT ON HAND DURING MONTH	AVERAGE AIRCRAFT IN COMMISSION	AVERAGE AIRCRAFT OUT OF COMMISSION						
			TOTAL		Awaiting Parts	Technical Order Compliance	MAINTENANCE		Other Reasons
			Average Number AOC	% Of ACH			Periodic	Malfunction, Defect, Damage	
TOTAL USAF	16,291	10,278	6,013	37	945	295	1,861	2,161	751
BOMBER	1,638	1,005	633	39	95	42	192	254	50
B-17	32	20	12	38	1	-	7	2	2
B-25	9	6	3	33	-	-	1	1	1
B-26	377	239	138	37	23	4	53	50	8
B-29	642	401	241	38	26	14	70	115	16
B-36	127	81	46	36	8	1	14	21	2
B-45	58	25	33	57	8	6	7	10	2
B-47	153	75	78	51	14	6	14	32	12
B-50	240	158	82	34	15	11	26	23	7
TANKER	321	220	101	31	28	3	27	38	5
KB-29	171	120	51	30	11	1	13	24	2
KC-97	150	100	50	33	17	2	14	14	3
FIGHTER	4,085	2,302	1,783	44	260	102	427	617	377
F-47	91	57	34	37	6	1	7	17	3
F-51	611	372	239	39	28	43	64	67	37
F-80	479	267	212	44	37	12	46	88	29
F-82	11	4	7	64	1	-	1	4	1
F-84	1,446	792	654	45	81	26	159	233	155
F-86	972	544	428	44	71	8	91	132	126
F-89	95	30	65	68	5	6	18	22	14
F-94	380	236	144	38	31	6	41	54	12
RECONNAISSANCE	549	323	226	41	46	4	66	91	19
RB-17	13	5	8	62	2	-	2	3	1
RB-25	3	2	1	33	-	-	1	-	-
RB-26	96	66	30	31	8	-	13	7	2
WB-26	1	1	-	-	-	-	-	-	-
RB-29	31	18	13	42	1	1	3	7	1
WB-29	80	38	42	52	4	-	13	23	2
RB-36	102	59	43	42	9	-	15	18	1
RB-45	18	10	8	44	2	-	3	3	-
RB-47	3	2	1	33	-	-	-	1	-
RB-50	39	21	18	46	3	-	4	11	-
RC-45	6	4	2	33	-	-	1	1	-
RC-47	6	5	1	17	-	-	1	-	-
RF-51	22	11	11	50	1	-	1	4	5
RF-80	124	79	45	36	16	3	8	11	7
RF-86	4	2	2	50	-	-	1	1	-
RC-54	1	-	1	100	-	-	-	1	-
SEARCH & RESCUE	244	141	103	42	26	6	30	35	6
SA-10	3	3	-	-	-	-	-	-	-
SA-16	168	94	74	44	23	6	20	20	5
SB-17	29	19	10	34	1	-	4	4	1
SB-29	33	19	14	42	2	-	4	8	-
SC-47	5	3	2	40	-	-	1	1	-
SC-54	3	1	2	67	-	-	1	1	-
SH-5	3	2	1	33	-	-	-	1	-
CARGO	2,931	1,872	1,059	36	186	51	434	331	57
C-45	482	320	162	34	33	8	68	44	9
C-46	192	123	69	36	7	2	33	22	5
C-47/53	1,115	765	350	31	44	28	171	92	15
C-54	288	176	112	39	13	3	47	43	6
C-74	9	5	4	44	-	-	3	1	-
C-82	118	51	67	57	13	2	15	32	5
C-97	64	27	37	58	10	-	12	14	1
C-117	15	12	3	20	-	-	2	1	-
C-118	10	4	6	60	2	-	2	2	-
C-119	364	229	135	37	37	4	39	43	12
C-121	9	7	2	22	-	-	1	1	-
C-122	9	7	2	22	1	-	-	1	-
C-124	176	91	85	48	23	4	32	24	2
C-125	1	-	1	100	-	-	-	-	1
VB-17	38	26	12	32	2	-	4	5	1
CB-25	7	5	2	29	-	-	1	1	-
VB-25	32	23	9	28	1	-	4	4	-
VB-26	2	1	1	50	-	-	-	1	-

TABLE 126 – WORLD-WIDE SUMMARY USAF AVERAGE ACTIVE AIRCRAFT OUT OF COMMISSION BY CAUSE – BY TYPE AND MODEL – FISCAL YEAR 1953 – CONTINUED

TYPE AND MODEL OF AIRCRAFT	AVERAGE AIRCRAFT ON HAND DURING MONTH	AVERAGE AIRCRAFT IN COMMISSION	AVERAGE AIRCRAFT OUT OF COMMISSION: TOTAL: Average Number AOC	TOTAL: % of AOH	Awaiting Parts	Technical Order Compliance	MAINTENANCE: Periodic	MAINTENANCE: Malfunction, Defect, Damage	Other Reasons
TRAINER	5,745	3,935	1,810	32	257	68	616	680	187
T-6	2,195	1,757	438	20	40	8	153	140	97
T-7	120	71	49	41	10	1	22	14	2
T-11	258	164	94	36	18	4	43	24	5
T-28	440	270	170	39	22	9	29	85	25
T-29	100	66	34	34	6	-	14	14	-
T-33	1,038	618	420	40	70	26	123	181	20
T-34	2	-	2	100	-	-	-	-	2
TB-17	35	20	15	43	2	-	6	4	3
TB-25	848	564	284	33	30	3	128	111	12
TB-26	253	148	105	42	20	4	41	37	3
TB-29	96	32	44	46	6	1	15	16	6
TB-50	34	15	19	56	4	1	4	7	3
TC-45	86	56	30	35	7	1	9	11	2
TB-45	8	5	3	38	-	1	2	-	-
TB-47	4	1	3	75	1	-	1	1	-
TC-47	50	37	13	26	1	2	4	6	-
TC-54	7	5	2	28	-	-	1	1	-
TF-47	1	1	-	-	-	-	-	-	-
TF-51	124	64	60	48	16	5	15	20	4
TF-80	42	19	23	55	6	2	6	8	1
TH-5	1	1	-	-	-	-	-	-	-
MK-4	1	1	-	-	-	-	-	-	-
COMMUNICATIONS	750	460	290	39	45	18	67	111	49
Liaison	601	377	224	37	29	17	54	85	39
L-4	25	5	20	80	3	-	7	8	2
L-5	130	69	61	47	11	4	17	19	10
L-13	33	18	15	45	3	-	3	4	5
L-16	91	39	52	57	1	13	10	25	3
L-19	2	1	1	50	-	-	-	-	1
L-20	122	89	33	27	6	-	7	10	10
L-21	146	112	34	23	3	-	8	17	6
L-23	2	-	2	100	-	-	-	-	2
LT-6	48	42	6	12	2	-	2	2	-
LC-126	2	2	-	-	-	-	-	-	-
Helicopter	149	83	66	44	16	1	13	26	10
H-5	49	29	20	41	6	-	4	7	3
H-12	4	2	2	50	1	-	-	1	-
H-13	34	18	16	47	1	-	4	10	1
H-18	1	1	-	-	-	-	-	-	-
H-19	54	29	25	46	8	-	5	7	5
H-21	1	1	-	-	-	-	-	-	-
H-23	5	2	3	60	-	1	-	1	1
H-25	1	1	-	-	-	-	-	-	-
TARGET	28	20	8	28	-	1	2	4	1
QB-17	17	12	5	29	-	-	2	3	-
QF-80	5	3	2	40	-	1	-	1	-
QT-33	1	1	-	-	-	-	-	-	-
Q-14	5	4	1	20	-	-	-	-	1

SOURCE: Materiel Statistics Division, D/Statistical Services, DCS/C

TABLE 127 – INVENTORY OF USAF AMMUNITION – WORLDWIDE (SEMI-ANNUAL) – FY 1953

TYPE OF MUNITIONS	ARSENAL STOCKS ON HAND Z/I	TOTAL Z/I	TOTAL O/S	FEAF	CAIRC	AAC	USAFE England	USAFE Europe	MEDITERRANEAN	NEAC	ATLANTIC
	DECEMBER 1952										
ARMOR PIERCING BOMBS											
1,000 lbs	-	-	1,159	-	-	-	1,159	-	-	-	-
1,600 lbs	-	-	-	-	-	-	-	-	-	-	-
SEMI-ARMOR PIERCING BOMBS											
500 lbs	84,680	818	285	203	-	82	-	-	-	-	-
1,000 lbs	16,420	4,169	15,820	204	-	7,982	1,200	6,434	-	-	-
FRAGMENTATION BOMBS											
260 lbs	198,029	438	60,342	45,629	-	4,357	6,682	3,674	-	-	-
FRAGMENTATION CLUSTERS											
20 lbs x 6	181,295	482	205	-	-	205	-	-	-	-	-
23 lbs x 3	-	-	2,324	-	-	20		2,304	-	-	
20 lbs x 20	161,490	35	19,842	18,234	-	1,608	-	-	-	-	-
1,000 lb HEAT T-27	-	1,600	100	-	-	-	-	-	-	100	-
GENERAL PURPOSE BOMBS											
100 lbs	45,891	9,037	68,491	64,662	-	304	425	3,100	-	-	-
250 lbs	-	-	2	-	-	-	2	-	-	-	-
500 lbs	939,012	17,489	193,082	162,345	-	16,517	10,344	3,876	-	-	-
1,000 lbs	132,131	1,595	34,446	22,853	-	3,510	6,827	1,256	-	-	-
2,000 lbs	49,354	458	29,557	24,914	-	793	2,686	1,164	-	-	-
4,000 lbs	701	5	7,423		-	4	739	-	-	-	-
INCENDIARY BOMBS											
100 lbs	-	-	62,043	24,502	12	18,529	1,424	17,517	-	59	-
500 lbs	-	7,146	54,327	1,043	-	754	6,329	2,461	43,740	-	-
INCENDIARY CLUSTERS											
4 lbs x 110	-	129	-	-	-	-	-	-	-	-	-
CARTRIDGES (M rds)											
50 Cal.	168,906	667,343	660,530	594,186	-	8,142	37,044	2,837	14,192	196	3,933
20 MM Percus. Pr.	4,341	254,931	528,360	36,787	-	309,060	41,940	-	206	140,198	169
ROCKETS											
5" HVAR	101	32,933	148,593	110,915	2	7,705	22,938	7,033	-	-	-
6.5" ATAR Heads	37	10,521	121,623	85,268	2	8,331	13,089	14,901	-	-	32
UNIT - JATO	23,270	5,774	32,799	17,552	-	580	13,840	386	138	303	-
PYROTECHNIC SIGNALS											
AN M37 - M45	1,375	174,337	297,666	97,022	107	136,263	13,281	27,913	19,385	2,704	991
AN M53 - M58	1,108	69,277	152,228	52,660	137	27,904	10,993	43,710	12,526	3,128	1,170
Drift - Day	130,000	131,229	55,572	17,774	-	155	3,016	30,361	300	3,894	72
Drift - Night	300,000	115	999	-	-	879	-	-	120	-	-
Distress - All Types	80,000	96,410	24,207	6,230	1,590	1,026	7,990	6,452	-	919	-
Bomb - Photoflash	8,663	4,319	17,385	16,305	-	-	1,080	-	-	-	-

TABLE 127 — INVENTORY OF USAF AMMUNITION — WORLDWIDE (SEMI-ANNUAL) — FY 1953 (CONTINUED)

TYPE OF MUNITIONS	ARSENAL STOCKS ON HAND Z/I	TOTAL Z/I	TOTAL O/S	FEAF	CAIRC	AAC	ENG-LAND	EUR-OPE	MEDIT-TERRAN-EAN	NEAC	AT-LANTIC
	DECEMBER 1952 (Cont'd)										
PYROTECHNIC SIGNALS (Cont'd)											
Flare, Parachute	-	-	-	-	-	-	-	-	-	-	-
FIRE BOMB MATERIEL											
Igniter WP M15	78,757	1,923	3,983	-	-	-	1,182	2,795	-	6	-
Igniter NA M15	-	249	1,429	-	-	10	600	819	-	-	-
Igniter WP M16	88,061	1,692	3,460	-	-	1,192	2,262	-	-	6	-
Igniter NA M16	6,248	306	600	-	-	-	600	-	-	-	-
100 Gal. Tank	-	-	764	-	-	-	-	764	-	-	-
NAPALM	4,568	4,731	46,694	-	-	97	43	43,625	-	-	2,929
RAZON BOMB TAIL	-	6,869	118,084	114,607	-	3,102	-	375	-	-	-
	JUNE 1953										
ARMOR PIERCING BOMBS											
1,000 lbs	7,445	-	-	-	-	-	-	-	-	-	-
1,600 lbs	170	-	-	-	-	-	-	-	-	-	-
SEMI-ARMOR PIERCING BOMBS											
500 lbs	190,351	795	2,602	2,515	-	87	-	-	-	-	-
1,000 lbs	423,968	4,454	64,832	47,452	-	8,198	2,300	6,882	-	-	-
FRAGMENTATION BOMBS											
260 lbs	143,571	440	110,135	93,041	-	4,357	9,306	3,431	-	-	-
FRAGMENTATION CLUSTERS											
20 lbs x 6	436,183	79,282	39,641	38,022	-	205	50	1,364	-	-	-
23 lbs x 3	241,070	2,766	1,383	-	-	20	-	1,363	-	-	-
20 lbs x 20	149,079	57,960	28,980	27,374	-	1,606	-	-	-	-	-
1,000 lbs HEAT T-27	-	-	-	-	-	-	-	-	-	-	-
GENERAL PURPOSE BOMBS											
100 lbs	8,871	3,713	147,559	145,574	-	304	402	1,209	-	70	-
250 lbs	-	-	4	-	-	-	4	-	-	-	-
500 lbs	739,671	83,921	203,744	158,485	-	20,559	18,742	5,958	-	-	-
1,000 lbs	7,113	904	69,577	56,425	-	4,277	7,401	1,474	-	-	-
2,000 lbs	16,490	383	22,231	18,773	-	772	2,686	-	-	-	-
4,000 lbs	380	28	2,818	2,075	-	4	739	-	-	-	-
INCENDIARY BOMBS											
100 lbs	117	123,445	43,896	26,766	12	3,933	5,269	7,906	-	-	10
500 lbs	710,184	17,743	7,581	799	-	-	6,183	599	-	-	-

TABLE 127 — INVENTORY OF USAF AMMUNITION — WORLDWIDE (SEMI-ANNUAL) — FY 1953 — CONTINUED

TYPE OF MUNITIONS	ARSENAL STOCKS ON HAND Z/I	TOTAL Z/I	TOTAL O/S	FEAF	CAIRC	AAC	ENG-LAND	EUR-OPE	MEDIT-TERRAN-EAN	NEAC	AT-LANTIC
	JUNE 1953 (Cont'd)										
INCENDIARY CLUSTERS											
4 lbs x 110	-	-	-	-	-	-	-	-	-	-	-
CARTRIDGES (M rds)											
50 Cal.	166,634	39,507	171,205	92,591	-	16,881	32,683	14,251	7,261	484	6,854
20 MM	3,775	22,402	16,321	738	-	13,259	389	276	838	237	584
ROCKETS											
5" HVAR	314,343	27,736	213,737	115,202	2	7,708	44,561	45,132	-	-	1,132
6.5" ATAR Heads	213,240	17,446	245,310	202,601	2	7.894	18,782	14,898	-	-	1,133
UNIT - JATO	41,629	5,249	29,414	18,576	-	441	6,664	3,063	108	562	-
PYROTECHNIC SIGNALS											
AN M37 - M45	1,437,421	187,762	291,553	75,306	1,612	140,914	19,839	25,270	20,258	3,708	4,646
AN M53 - M58	1,019,541	70,173	131,141	45,375	681	32,679	14,005	20,178	12,347	3,866	2,010
Drift - Day	185,066	156,726	52,770	25,674	-	696	2,151	22,592	280	1,211	166
Drift - Night	21,921	926	1,828	2	-	1,650	176	-	-	-	-
Distress - All Types	95,877	100,480	2,830	9,897	1,946	688	8,000	6,257	78	1,134	300
Bomb - Photoflash	40,371	6,878	2,360	-	-	200	2,160	-	-	-	-
Flare, Parachute	-	-	-	-	-	-	-	-	-	-	-
FIRE BOMB MATERIEL											
Igniter WP M15	73,279	1,010	83,338	79,117	-	1,382	1,182	1,561	96	-	-
Igniter NA M15	-	23	7,591	6,746	-	20	600	225	-	-	-
Igniter WP m16	82,176	606	79,829	74,688	-	1,382	2,262	1,401	96	-	-
Igniter NA M16	6,208	56	9,939	9,147	-	-	600	192	-	-	-
100 Gal. Tank	-	-	14,360	12,988	-	-	-	972	-	-	400
NAPALM	3,887	5,692	862,008	792,588	-	96	45	69,279	-	-	-
RAZON BOMB TAIL	1,554	6,631	151,015	123,137	-	5,502	22,001	375	-	-	-

SOURCE: MATERIEL STATISTICS DIVISION, DIRECTORATE OF STATISTICAL SERVICES, DCS/C

Aircraft Engines

Part VI

TABLE 128 – FACTORY ACCEPTANCES OF AIRCRAFT ENGINES BY THE USAF QUARTERLY – FY 1953

(INCLUDES ALL ENGINES ACCEPTED BY THE USAF FOR THE USAF, ARMY, NAVY, MDAP AND RCAF)

MANUFACTURER MODEL AND ENGINE SERIES	Unit Power (pounds thrust or horsepower)	QUARTERLY - FISCAL YEAR 1953							
		1st QUARTER		2nd QUARTER		3rd QUARTER		4th QUARTER	
		Number	Average Unit Cost	Number	Average Unit Cost	Number	Average Unit Cost	Number	Average Unit Cost
T O T A L		5,856		7,412		8,295		7,728	
AIRCOOLED MOTORS Total		255		331		240		161	
O-335-4 a/	200 HP	22	$ 2,145	55	$ 2,145	-	$ -	-	$ -
O-335-4 b/	200 HP	-	-	1	2,145	-	-	-	-
YO-335-5 a/	200 HP	160	2,343	160	2,438	120	2,438	95	2,438
O-335-6 a/	200 HP	48	2,140	79	2,315	96	2,477	57	2,477
O-425-1 b/	245 HP	25	7,801	36	7,801	24	7,801	9	7,801
ALLISON DIVISION GMC Total		1,805		1,547		1,581		1,434	
J33-A-10/10A b/	4,600 lbs	8	20,740	17	20,740	18	21,775	3	21,775
J33-A-16/16A b/	6,150 lbs	-	-	3	33,850	65	32,415	120	32,415
J33-A-35	4,600 lbs	409	19,455	454	19,455	520	21,450	543	21,450
J33-A-35 b/	4,600 lbs	93	19,455	94	19,455	-	-	-	-
J33-A-35 c/	4,600 lbs	-	-	-	-	20	21,450	37	21,450
J33-A-37	4,600 lbs	42	14,370	45	15,352	45	15,830	50	15,830
J35-A-27	5,000 lbs	-	-	-	-	5	37,385	3	37,385
J35-A-29	5,600 lbs	450	34,445	88	34,445	86	34,445	203	34,445
J35-A-29 b/	5,600 lbs	-	-	-	-	2	34,445	-	-
J35-A-29 c/	5,600 lbs	533	40,792	825	34,350	755	34,675	454	34,675
J35-A-33	5,400 lbs	113	40,450	-	-	-	-	-	-
J35-A-33A	5,400 lbs	142	41,380	-	-	-	-	-	-
J35-A-41	5,450 lbs	-	-	41	41,790	54	43,565	3	43,565
J71-A-3	9,700 lbs	2	233,280	-	-	10	248,700	18	248,700
T-40-A-6 b/	1,225 lbs	11	462,500	-	-	-	-	-	-
T-40-A-10 b/	1,225 lbs	2	462,500	-	-	1	462,500	-	-
BUICK - Total		-		-		8		77	
J65-B-3	7,220 lbs	-	-	1	224,670	8	224,670	77	224,670
CHEVROLET - Total		-		123		300		381	
R-3350-26W b/	2,700 HP	-	-	123	157,305	300	129,101	225	53,571
R-3350-85	3,250 HP	-	-	-	-	-	-	60	362,000
R-3350-85 c/	3,250 HP	-	-	-	-	-	-	63	62,200
R-3350-85 d/	3,250 HP	-	-	-	-	-	-	3	62,200
CONTINENTAL A & E Total		55		87		45		31	
R-975-34/42 a/	525 HP	-	-	-	-	8	20,113	-	-
R-975-34/42 b/	525 HP	52	22,635	87	22,635	35	21,050	21	20,113
R-975-40 b/	420 HP	3	21,794	-	-	2	20,113	10	20,113
CONTINENTAL MOTORS Total		253		264		274		253	
O-470-11 a/	213 HP	253	3,000	264	3,068	274	3,013	251	2,887
O-470-13	225 HP	-	-	-	-	-	-	2	3,456
FAIRCHILD - Total		4		10		10		15	
J44-R-1	950 lbs	4	17,500	10	17,300	10	17,000	15	17,000
FORD MOTOR COMPANY Total		66		13		187		384	
R-4360-53	3,500 HP	65	326,365	-	-	56	326,365	108	326,365
R-4360-59/59B	3,250 HP	-	-	-	-	2	261,356	33	261,356
R-4360-63	3,400 HP	1	272,745	13	272,745	129	272,745	243	272,745
GENERAL ELECTRIC (EVENDALE & WEST-LYNN) - Total		2,010		2,18[illegible]		2,141		1,699	
J47-GE-2 (27) b/	5,910 lbs	-	-	26	54,948	-	-	-	-
J47-GE-2 b/	5,910 lbs	-	-	-	-	4	52,189	46	45,530
J47-GE-13	5,200 lbs	168	48,976	-	-	2	43,087	-	-
J47-GE-13 c/	5,200 lbs	-	-	180	43,087	18	43,087	-	-
J47-GE-13 d/	5,200 lbs	342	43,087	86	43,087	-	-	-	-
J47-GE-17	5,425 lbs	173	66,710	269	65,609	370	64,834	437	64,806
J47-GE-19	5,200 lbs	74	40,388	206	46,455	74	48,890	27	48,890
J47-GE-23	5,620 lbs	647	53,508	166	53,508	9	53,508	-	-
J47-GE-25	5,670 lbs	181	41,853	711	44,813	794	49,362	321	52,376
J47-GE-27	5,910 lbs	424	42,705	544	43,888	864	48,364	867	46,387
J47-GE-27 d/	5,910 lbs	1	42,705	-	-	-	-	-	-
J73-GE-3	8,920 lbs	-	-	-	-	6	272,520	1	272,520

TABLE 128 – FACTORY ACCEPTANCES OF AIRCRAFT ENGINES BY THE USAF QUARTERLY – FY 1953 – CONTINUED

(INCLUDES ALL ENGINES ACCEPTED BY THE USAF FOR THE USAF, ARMY, NAVY, MDAP AND RCAF)

MANUFACTURER, MODEL AND ENGINE SERIES	Unit Power (pounds thrust or Horsepower)	QUARTERLY - FISCAL YEAR 1953							
		1st QUARTER		2nd QUARTER		3rd QUARTER		4th QUARTER	
		Number	Average Unit Cost	Number	Average Unit Cost	Number	Average Unit Cost	Number	Average Unit Cost
KAISER - Total		-		90		296		447	
R-1300-1/1A	800 HP	-	$ -	66	$145,505	172	$131,708	227	$ 26,853
R-1300-3	800 HP	-	-	7	25,535	56	25,535	108	25,535
R-1300-3 b/	800 HP	-	-	17	114,070	68	25,535	112	25,535
BRIDGEPORT-LYCOMING Total		105		203		269		263	
R-1820-76A/B	1,425 HP	94	46,075	138	46,075	69	46,075	59	46,075
R-1820-76A/B b/	1,425 HP	11	114,736	62	114,736	19	114,736	-	-
R-1820-76A/B c/	1,425 HP	-	-	-	-	18	46,075	-	-
R-1820-82 b/	1,525 HP	-	-	-	-	61	146,909	137	73,615
R-1820-103	1,425 HP	-	-	3	40,528	72	40,528	38	40,124
R-1820-103 a/	1,425 HP	-	-	-	-	30	40,528	23	40,528
R-1820-86 b/	1,425 HP	-	-	-	-	-	-	6	25,610
LYCOMING-SPENCER DIVISION - Total		50		68		73		7	
O-435-17 a/	255 HP	50	3,148	68	3,148	73	3,148	7	3,148
NASH - KELVINATOR Total		-		5		33		72	
R-2800-52W	2,200 HP	-	-	5	96,855	3	64,434	12	69,346
R-2800-52W b/	2,200 HP	-	-	-	-	13	64,434	21	69,346
R-2800-99	2,200 HP	-	-	-	-	17	97,169	39	97,169
PACKARD - Total		10		265		620		549	
J47-PM-25	5,670 lbs	10	128,264	265	128,182	620	69,689	549	36,489
PRATT & WHITNEY Total		735		826		918		768	
YT-34-P-1	1,275 lbs	-	-	1	306,036	4	306,036	1	306,036
J48-P-5	6,350 lbs	69	71,139	87	71,139	184	71,139	60	71,139
J48-P-5A	6,350 lbs	-	-	-	-	-	-	112	71,384
J57-P-1	9,500 lbs	-	-	-	-	3	156,279	13	156,279
J57-P-3	8,700 lbs	20	278,088	13	278,088	5	278,088	-	-
J57-P-7	8,450 lbs	-	-	1	195,052	5	195,052	-	-
J57-P-11	9,220 lbs	-	-	-	-	-	-	2	195,052
J57-P-13	9,220 lbs	-	-	-	-	-	-	1	195,052
R-1340-57 e/	600 HP	42	-	74	-	45	-	13	-
R-2800-97	2,100 HP	43	36,182	71	36,182	24	36,182	19	36,182
R-4360-20/W/WA	3,250 HP	133	55,649	160	55,649	151	55,649	45	55,649
R-4360-35/35B	3,250 HP	113	45,029	23	45,029	-	-	-	-
R-4360-53	3,500 HP	176	75,178	218	75,178	207	75,178	198	75,178
R-4360-59/59B	3,250 HP	135	61,083	178	61,083	290	61,083	304	61,083
R-4360-63	3,400 HP	4	51,535	-	-	-	-	-	-
STUDEBAKER - Total		135		744		658		581	
J47-ST-25	5,670 lbs	135	72,357	744	71,488	658	47,379	581	38,975
WRIGHT AERONAUTICAL Total		373		647		642		606	
YJ65-W-1	7,220 lbs	5	219,584	30	219,584	72	188,898	57	89,620
R-1300-1/1A	800 HP	83	19,663	38	19,726	1	19,760	-	-
R-1820-76A/B	1,425 HP	7	21,197	9	21,197	-	-	-	-
R-1820-80 b/	1,475 HP	7	22,402	5	22,539	-	-	-	-
R-1820-82 b/	1,525 HP	2	26,560	8	28,809	3	29,130	-	-
R-1820-103	1,425 HP	-	-	8	20,591	8	22,365	-	-
R-3350-26W c/	2,700 HP	80	43,052	12	43,052	-	-	-	-
R-3350-30W/WA b/	3,250 HP	56	61,819	200	65,239	237	66,289	233	64,608
R-3350-30W/WA c/	3,250 HP	33	61,819	31	65,735	21	67,097	3	67,097
R-3350-34	3,250 HP	1	74,134	-	-	-	-	40	72,822
R-3350-34 b/	3,250 HP	4	74,134	5	75,051	45	75,051	31	72,822
R-3350-85	3,250 HP	95	61,319	301	65,443	255	67,093	242	65,074

a/ USAF for Army

b/ USAF for Navy

c/ USAF for MDAP

d/ USAF for RCAF

e/ These R-1340-57 were modified from R-1340-AN-1's furnished as G.F.P. Overhaul and modification was accomplished on an individual basis, at varying costs.

TABLE 129 — RECAPITULATION OF FACTORY ACCEPTANCES OF AIRCRAFT ENGINES

MANUFACTURER, MODEL AND ENGINE SERIES	UNIT POWER (Pounds Thrust or Horsepower)	QUARTERLY - FISCAL YEAR 1953							
		1st QUARTER		2nd QUARTER		3rd QUARTER		4th QUARTER	
		Number	Total Pounds Thrust or Horsepower	Number	Total Pounds Thrust or Horsepower	Number	Total Pounds Thrust or Horsepower	Number	Total Pounds Thrust or Horsepower
JET ENGINES - TOTAL.	5,552	4,058	22,080,010	4,887	26,925,020	5,291	29,666,060	4,601	25,902,820
For USAF.	5,571	3,068	16,830,375	3,656	20,239,110	4,408	24,732,620	3,941	22,166,560
For ARMY.	-	-	-	-	-	-	-	-	-
For NAVY.	5,276	114	480,525	140	682,710	90	519,840	169	1,023,660
For MDAP.	5,552	533	2,984,800	1,005	5,556,000	793	4,413,600	491	2,712,600
For RCAF.	5,202	343	1,784,310	86	447,200	-	-	-	-
RECIPROCATING ENGINES - TOTAL	2,085	1,798	3,431,199	2,525	4,917,242	3,004	6,364,822	3,127	7,080,830
For USAF.	2,685	992	2,736,575	1,312	3,477,150	1,557	4,144,525	1,790	4,816,775
For ARMY.	241	533	112,639	626	132,372	593	162,927	433	118,400
For NAVY.	2,263	160	258,735	544	1,174,570	807	1,959,270	835	1,917,205
For MDAP.	2,930	113	323,250	43	133,150	39	93,900	66	214,500
For RCAF.	1,650	-	-	-	-	8	4,200	3	13,950

SOURCE: Materiel Statistics Division, Directorate of Statistical Services, DCS/C

TABLE 130 — NUMBER OF SELECTED AIRPLANE ENGINES REMOVED FOR MAJOR OVERHAUL WITH AVERAGE OPERATING HOURS SINCE MANUFACTURE OR MAJOR OVERHAUL QUARTERLY FY 1953 — BY TYPE OF ENGINE

TYPE OF ENGINE	30 SEPTEMBER 1952		31 DECEMBER 1952		31 MARCH 1953		30 JUNE 1953	
	Engines Removed	Average Operating Hours Per Engine	Engines Removed	Average Operating Hours Per Engine	Engines Removed	Average Operating Hours Per Engine	Engines Removed	Average Operating Hours Per Engine
J 33.	783	220.7	1,247	222.5	1,165	216.1	1,339	243.1
J 34.	a/	a/	a/	a/	a/	a/	3	29.7
J 35.	740	89.9	1,120	99.3	1,129	104.6	1,334	117.7
J 47.	684	107.8	974	125.7	1,135	135.0	1,741	132.3
J 48.	1	13.0	9	30.6	11	45.9	43	85.5
J 57.	a/	a/	2	26.5	a/	a/	17	78.2
J 65	a/	a/	a/	a/	a/	a/	27	11.4
R-755	2	271.0	a/	a/	a/	a/	1	765.0
R-985	204	1,045.7	281	879.3	116	808.3	128	901.0
R-1300. . . .	41	284.4	82	346.3	94	423.7	199	410.4
R-1340. . . .	300	1,039.8	310	970.5	285	940.4	252	939.4
R-1820. . . .	105	592.0	110	569.3	149	641.3	151	557.3
R-1830. . . .	584	817.6	568	813.5	514	799.9	559	811.9
R-2000. . . .	544	765.4	512	800.3	412	796.4	367	754.3
R-2600. . . .	359	634.1	405	700.5	358	708.9	398	705.5
R-2800. . . .	397	637.3	541	503.0	400	657.9	418	644.1
R-3350. . . .	1,537	327.5	1,441	320.1	1,255	332.6	1,400	296.4
R-4360	832	370.9	789	415.7	994	431.1	1,233	428.3
V-32.	27	117.4	a/	a/	a/	a/	a/	a/
V-1650. . . .	444	200.2	376	203.1	273	202.5	271	184.5
V-1710. . . .	2	104.0	3	209.3	2	287.5	3	212.7
O-170	3	599.0	3	388.0	3	538.3	1	475.0
O-190	a/	a/	a/	a/	2	577.0	3	699.0
O-205	a/	a/	a/	a/	1	170.0	1	541.0
O-290	1	396.0	6	357.5	34	707.1	63	692.6
O-335	3	310.3	10	336.8	9	291.0	1	99.0
O-425	9	130.3	3	94.7	1	187.0	1	217.0
O-435	12	456.2	13	470.4	12	462.8	14	411.2
O-470	15	269.3	6	321.6	6	302.3	1	333.0
E-225	2	331.5	a/	a/	a/	a/	a/	a/
T-49.	a/	a/	3	30.0	a/	a/	a/	a/

a/ No removals reported

SOURCE: Materiel Statistics Division, Directorate of Statistical Services, DCS/C

TABLE 131 — AVERAGE MANHOURS EXPENDED PER MAJOR AIRPLANE ENGINE OVERHAUL AT AIR MATERIEL COMMAND AIR DEPOT IN CONTINENTAL U. S. FY 1953 — BY TYPE OF ENGINE

TYPE OF ENGINE	30 SEPTEMBER 1952		31 DECEMBER 1952		31 MARCH 1953		30 JUNE 1953	
	Engines Overhauled	Average Man-Hours Per Engine	Engines Overhauled	Average Man-Hours Per Engine	Engines Overhauled	Average Man-Hours Per Engine	Engines Overhauled	Average Man-Hours Per Engine
J33	505	548.2	1,000	511.5	454	441.4	714	420.6
J35	1,177	639.5	155	633.3	1,059	653.6	721	665.0
J47	532	685.5	522	670.9	604	686.3	866	616.7
R-1300.	a/	a/	17	439.2	a/	a/	a/	a/
R-1340.	1	169.0	76	264.6	3	355.5	196	292.1
R-2000.	242	511.2	576	533.3	1,026	510.1	657	469.8
R-2600.	518	458.1	398	561.5	a/	a/	a/	a/
R-2800.	219	508.5	691	531.7	1,065	508.2	841	425.1
R-3350.	908	667.0	3,412	672.3	1,415	667.7	2,867	609.6
R-4360.	422	1,532.1	816	1,404.7	1,059	1,271.3	622	1,287.0
V-1650.	250	503.3	101	504.6	172	459.2	290	416.6
O-425	a/	a/	a/	a/	6	147.7	a/	a/

a/ No overhauls during quarter

SOURCE: Materiel Statistics Division, Directorate of Statistical Services, DCS/C

TABLE 132 — INVENTORY AND STATUS OF SPARE AIRCRAFT ENGINES IN CONTINENTAL U. S. QUARTERLY — FY 1953

TYPE OF ENGINE	30 SEPTEMBER 1952			31 DECEMBER 1952			31 MARCH 1953			30 JUNE 1953		
	Total	Service-able	Repar-able	Total	Service-able	Repar-able	Total	Service-able	Repar-able	Total	Service-able	Repar-able
TOTAL	62,052	24,549	37,503	55,785	21,909	33,876	57,640	25,600	32,040	58,407	25,513	32,894
I-16	1	-	1	-	-	-	-	-	-	-	-	-
J30	-	-	-	2	2	-	-	-	-	-	-	-
J31	13	6	7	3	2	1	3	2	1	3	-	3
T-31	-	-	-	5	-	5	5	-	5	5	-	5
J33	3,984	2,051	1,933	3,534	1,795	1,739	3,632	2,130	1,502	3,870	2,272	1,598
J34	4	2	2	2	-	2	2	-	2	3	-	3
J35	3,919	2,090	1,829	3,823	1,980	1,843	3,663	2,243	1,420	3,453	2,301	1,152
J47	5,109	3,586	1,523	5,664	4,141	1,523	7,566	6,261	1,305	8,223	6,796	1,427
J48	40	29	11	8	1	7	48	44	4	159	140	19
J57	3	3	-	-	-	-	-	-	-	-	-	-
J65	-	-	-	11	11	-	2	2	-	77	27	50
J71	2	2	-	1	-	1	-	-	-	-	-	-
T-40	-	-	-	1	-	1	-	-	-	-	-	-
0-170	501	264	237	500	253	247	513	241	272	508	198	310
0-190	297	100	197	245	24	221	348	86	262	353	72	281
0-200	20	14	6	20	14	6	20	14	6	20	14	6
0-205	63	36	27	82	39	43	80	35	45	82	34	48
0-225	-	-	-	1	-	1	-	-	-	-	-	-
0-290	91	71	20	108	93	15	124	86	38	59	26	33
0-300	62	45	17	63	46	17	64	46	18	64	46	18
0-335	728	568	160	83	61	22	40	22	18	43	26	17
0-405	95	88	7	96	88	8	96	88	8	96	88	8
0-425	159	7	152	193	4	189	216	22	194	206	21	185
0-435	1,309	333	976	1,249	292	957	461	330	131	1,158	261	897
0-440	-	-	-	109	106	3	110	106	4	2	-	2
0-470	746	214	532	47	3	44	192	45	147	362	25	337
R-670	64	56	8	64	56	8	64	56	8	64	56	8
R-680	256	216	40	254	214	40	254	212	42	256	212	44
R-755	42	17	25	14	-	14	6	1	5	21	2	19
R-975	2	-	2	-	-	-	-	-	-	-	-	-
R-985	2,931	980	1,951	3,260	714	2,546	3,219	790	2,429	3,220	953	2,267
R-1300	123	66	57	531	48	483	604	154	450	708	252	456
R-1340	1,129	601	528	1,709	485	1,224	1,178	659	519	1,620	629	991
R-1820	1,736	267	1,469	1,613	242	1,371	1,885	387	1,498	1,626	372	1,254
R-1830	3,861	1,180	2,681	3,630	1,083	2,547	3,738	1,373	2,365	3,308	915	2,393
R-2000	1,584	966	618	1,336	648	688	1,532	829	703	1,547	900	647
R-2180	8	8	-	-	-	-	-	-	-	-	-	-
R-2600	2,527	1,693	834	2,511	1,454	1,057	2,450	1,123	1,327	2,304	920	1,384
R-2800	9,856	3,940	5,916	9,372	3,774	5,598	9,648	3,063	6,585	9,443	2,741	6,702
R-3350	12,158	2,641	9,517	7,704	2,338	5,366	7,701	3,021	4,680	8,168	3,038	5,130
R-4360	3,140	1,365	1,775	2,845	1,239	1,606	3,088	1,419	1,669	3,040	1,708	1,332
V-770	15	15	-	-	-	-	-	-	-	-	-	-
V-1650	4,703	657	4,046	4,520	435	4,085	4,530	503	4,027	4,269	464	3,805
V-1710	605	259	346	571	224	347	556	207	349	64	4	60
V-3420	2	1	1	1	-	1	1	-	1	1	-	1
E-005	54	6	48	-	-	-	-	-	-	-	-	-
E-225	1	-	1	-	-	-	1	-	1	2	-	2
L-440	109	106	3	-	-	-	-	-	-	-	-	-

SOURCE: Materiel Statistics Division, Directorate of Statistical Services, DCS/C.

TABLE 133 — INVENTORY AND STATUS OF SPARE AIRCRAFT ENGINES IN OVERSEAS COMMANDS
QUARTERLY — FY 1953

COMMAND AND TYPE OF ENGINE	30 SEPTEMBER 1952			31 DECEMBER 1952			31 MARCH 1953			30 JUNE 1953		
	TOTAL	Service-able	Repar-able	TOTAL	Service-able	Repar-able	TOTAL	Service-able	Repar-able	TOTAL	Service-able	Repar-able
TOTAL	7,330	6,054	1,276	6,545	5,134	1,411	7,205	5,723	1,482	6,240	4,577	1,663
ALASKAN AIR COMMAND	596	491	105	317	278	39	420	381	39	408	368	40
J33	127	113	14	50	36	14	102	83	19	76	64	12
J35	-	-	-	-	-	-	-	-	-	12	12	-
J47	-	-	-	6	5	1	4	3	1	-	-	-
O-190	-	-	-	-	-	-	-	-	-	1	1	-
O-335	6	6	-	6	6	-	6	6	-	6	6	-
O-425	3	2	1	2	1	1	1	-	1	-	-	-
O-435	5	5	-	2	2	-	2	1	1	1	1	-
O-470	13	13	-	4	4	-	4	4	-	3	3	-
R-755	14	12	2	3	3	-	3	3	-	-	-	-
R-985	26	23	3	17	15	2	11	10	1	13	13	-
R-1340	-	-	-	-	-	-	-	-	-	1	1	-
R-1820	39	33	6	32	32	-	29	29	-	24	21	3
R-1830	137	82	55	37	26	11	39	35	4	70	63	7
R-2000	79	62	17	28	25	3	34	34	-	24	24	-
R-2800	21	20	1	12	11	1	5	5	-	7	7	-
R-3350	78	77	1	26	25	1	73	65	8	34	21	13
R-4360	10	10	-	12	11	1	23	21	2	50	50	-
V-1710	38	33	5	80	76	4	84	82	2	86	81	5
AIR MATERIEL COMMAND-OVERSEAS	-	-	-	2	-	2	2	-	2	35	33	2
R-985	-	-	-	-	-	-	-	-	-	33	33	-
R-2800	-	-	-	2	-	2	2	-	2	2	-	2
ANG, PUERTO RICO	-	-	-	9	8	1	-	-	-	-	-	-
R-1340	-	-	-	2	2	-	-	-	-	-	-	-
R-1830	-	-	-	3	3	-	-	-	-	-	-	-
R-2800	-	-	-	4	3	1	-	-	-	-	-	-
CARIBBEAN AIR COMMAND	108	46	62	65	46	19	86	48	38	62	51	11
O-425	11	10	1	6	-	6	-	-	-	-	-	-
O-435	5	3	2	3	2	1	3	-	3	3	3	-
O-470	6	1	5	6	4	2	6	2	4	3	3	-
R-985	3	1	2	3	3	-	4	2	2	4	4	-
R-1820	14	5	9	8	6	2	18	11	7	15	14	1
R-1830	48	17	31	30	22	8	34	17	17	18	11	7
R-2000	14	5	9	5	5	-	13	11	2	12	11	1
R-2800	7	4	3	4	4	-	8	5	3	7	5	2
FAR EAST AIR FORCES COMMAND	3,822	3,015	807	3,378	2,418	960	4,007	3,029	978	2,854	1,839	1,015
J33	525	389	136	462	279	183	433	277	156	351	213	138
J35	496	399	97	448	341	107	482	334	148	312	199	113
J47	432	365	67	325	236	89	700	649	51	296	207	89
O-170	10	10	-	5	2	3	10	5	5	5	5	-
O-190	16	14	2	13	13	-	14	6	8	9	1	8
O-205	4	4	-	4	4	-	4	-	4	4	-	4
O-335	16	15	1	42	31	11	41	32	9	40	33	7
O-405	1	1	-	-	-	-	-	-	-	-	-	-
O-435	59	56	3	57	54	3	20	17	3	56	47	9
O-470	58	35	23	274	129	145	402	179	223	363	70	293
R-985	50	39	11	40	34	6	71	54	17	56	43	13
R-1340	86	72	14	67	56	11	124	99	25	86	67	19
R-1820	110	94	16	66	56	10	93	53	40	71	43	28
R-1830	189	148	41	166	128	38	241	184	57	173	117	56
R-2000	271	200	71	248	168	80	165	141	24	105	91	14
R-2600	-	-	-	-	-	-	-	-	-	8	8	-
R-2800	290	246	44	253	178	75	352	273	79	290	221	69
R-3350	435	213	222	571	449	122	553	439	94	348	231	117
R-4360	71	65	6	106	90	16	201	194	7	219	193	26
V-1650	703	650	53	231	170	61	121	93	28	62	50	12
JOINT BRAZIL US-MILITARY COMM.	20	16	4	15	-	15	-	-	-	9	6	3
R-1820	16	12	4	12	-	12	-	-	-	4	2	2
R-1830	4	4	-	3	-	3	-	-	-	5	4	1

TABLE 133 — INVENTORY AND STATUS OF SPARE AIRCRAFT ENGINES IN OVERSEAS COMMANDS QUARTERLY – FY 1953 — Continued

COMMAND AND TYPE OF ENGINE	30 SEPTEMBER 1952			31 DECEMBER 1952			31 MARCH 1953			30 JUNE 1953		
	TOTAL	Serviceable	Reparable	TOTAL	Serviceable	Reparable	TOTAL	Serviceable	Reparable	TOTAL	Serviceable	Reparable
MILITARY AIR TRANSPORT SERVICE OVERSEAS	295	259	36	403	282	121	382	294	88	358	296	62
J33	-	-	-	-	-	-	-	-	-	8	6	2
J35	5	5	-	6	5	1	5	-	5	-	-	-
J47	-	-	-	-	-	-	-	-	-	2	2	-
O-190	1	1	-	1	1	-	1	1	-	1	1	-
O-435	5	5	-	2	2	-	1	1	-	1	1	-
R-985	5	5	-	5	4	1	4	4	-	3	3	-
R-1340	3	3	-	2	2	-	2	2	-	2	2	-
R-1820	32	27	5	26	21	5	20	12	8	33	22	11
R-1830	33	32	1	39	29	10	28	21	7	31	23	8
R-2000	99	82	17	161	109	52	133	86	47	119	92	27
R-2800	8	6	2	12	11	1	5	5	-	21	19	2
R-3350	76	71	5	123	75	48	148	131	17	95	86	9
R-4360	17	11	6	22	19	3	35	31	4	42	39	3
O-030	2	2	-	-	-	-	-	-	-	-	-	-
V-1650	9	9	-	4	4	-	-	-	-	-	-	-
NORTHEAST AIR COMMAND	62	60	2	123	114	9	169	136	33	217	199	18
J33	-	-	-	43	41	2	79	75	4	100	96	4
J35	-	-	-	-	-	-	-	-	-	4	4	-
J47	-	-	-	-	-	-	-	-	-	1	1	-
R-985	4	4	-	3	2	1	5	4	1	5	5	-
R-1820	16	15	1	7	7	-	18	14	4	16	15	1
R-1830	11	11	-	10	10	-	10	7	3	28	25	3
R-2000	17	16	1	40	34	6	36	17	19	43	35	8
R-2600	-	-	-	-	-	-	3	3	-	3	3	-
R-2800	12	12	-	11	11	-	7	7	-	4	4	-
R-3350	1	1	-	7	7	-	9	7	2	8	8	-
R-4360	1	1	-	2	2	-	2	2	-	5	3	2
STRATEGIC AIR COMMAND-OVERSEAS	61	53	8	189	114	75	178	147	31	390	324	66
J33	-	-	-	-	-	-	-	-	-	4	4	-
J35	-	-	-	40	20	20	-	-	-	28	12	16
J47	-	-	-	2	2	-	35	32	3	125	121	4
O-190	2	2	-	-	-	-	2	2	-	2	2	-
O-470	4	4	-	-	-	-	-	-	-	-	-	-
R-985	2	2	-	-	-	-	4	4	-	4	4	-
R-1340	2	2	-	-	-	-	-	-	-	-	-	-
R-1820	2	2	-	-	-	-	4	4	-	3	1	2
R-1830	7	6	1	5	1	4	9	9	-	6	6	-
R-2000	2	1	1	2	2	-	3	3	-	6	6	-
R-2800	16	13	3	-	-	-	9	9	-	9	9	-
R-3350	7	7	-	87	65	22	42	28	14	67	43	24
R-4360	17	14	3	53	24	29	70	56	14	131	112	19
V-1650	-	-	-	-	-	-	-	-	-	5	4	1
U. S. AIR FORCES IN EUROPE	2,366	2,114	252	2,044	1,874	170	1,961	1,688	273	1,907	1,461	446
J33	137	128	9	267	255	12	151	127	24	142	130	12
J35	925	864	61	493	455	38	340	222	118	322	226	96
J47	145	125	20	176	169	7	202	181	21	273	131	142
O-335	11	10	1	2	2	-	2	2	-	2	2	-
O-435	104	82	22	91	87	4	175	170	5	38	36	2
O-470	52	19	33	38	34	4	-	-	-	5	5	-
R-985	19	19	-	23	21	2	24	22	2	27	25	2
R-1340	23	22	1	25	22	3	15	14	1	37	37	-
R-1820	44	33	11	37	31	6	45	45	-	63	52	11
R-1830	218	156	62	188	126	62	230	194	36	286	232	54
R-2000	131	125	6	176	159	17	217	189	28	218	191	27
R-2800	164	143	21	171	161	10	194	187	7	148	138	10
R-3350	251	248	3	236	232	4	226	196	30	221	146	75
R-4360	142	140	2	121	120	1	140	139	1	125	110	15

SOURCE: Materiel Statistics Division, Directorate of Statistical Services, DCS/C.

AVIATION FUEL AND OIL

The information contained in this section summarizes USAF aviation fuel and oil, world-wide, for Fiscal Year 1953.

The data shown in Tables 1 through 7 include fuel and oil inventories, issues and receipts. Storage capacity is not included as a new reporting system was started in September 1953 to improve the accuracy of storage capacity figures. A storage capacity table will be included in the Statistical Digest for Fiscal Year 1954.

Base and Terminal fuel inventories, both jet and avgas, increased during the fiscal year by 8,249,486 barrels or 61%. Total inventory as of 30 June 1953 was 21,696,842 barrels of which 8,245,293 barrels (38%) were jet fuel. Cumulative fuel issues as of 30 June 1953 totaled 50,744,926 barrels of which 20,494,377 barrels (40%) were jet. Total issues during FY 53 increased by 14,630,280 barrels, or 41%, over the FY 52 figures of 36,114,646 barrels. For the first time jet issues totaled more than anyone of the avgas grades. Total oil inventory as of 30 June 1953 was 160,477 barrels. Oil issues during the year totaled 438,936 barrels. This is 1 barrel of oil issued for every 116 barrels of fuel.

The tables in this section were developed by the Directorate of Statistical Services based on the World-Wide Aviation Fuel Inventory and Issues Report, RCS: SS-AU-26.

TABLE 134 — INVENTORIES OF USAF AVIATION FUEL — FY 51, 52, 53

LOCATION	BARRELS OF 42 US GALLONS								
	FISCAL YEAR 1953			FISCAL YEAR 1952			FISCAL YEAR 1951		
	TOTAL	JET	AVGAS	TOTAL	JET	AVGAS	TOTAL	JET	AVGAS
WORLD-WIDE	21,696,842	8,245,293	13,451,549	13,447,356	3,920,241	9,527,115	12,639,571	3,514,282	9,125,289
Zone of Interior	10,196,418	4,729,066	5,467,352	3,944,475	1,101,130	2,843,345	4,721,466	1,293,169	3,428,297
Base	2,205,817	1,188,675	1,017,142	1,217,691	374,643	843,048	1,307,986	245,805	1,062,181
Terminal	7,550,632	3,264,437	4,286,195	2,695,928	710,359	1,985,569	3,250,480	934,364	2,316,116
In Transit	439,969	275,954	164,015	30,856	16,128	14,728	163,000	113,000	50,000
Overseas	11,500,424	3,516,227	7,984,197	9,502,881	2,819,111	6,683,770	7,918,105	2,221,113	5,696,992
Base	4,419,594	1,247,138	3,172,456	3,016,604	945,290	2,071,314	1,749,508 a/	399,251	1,350,257 a/
Terminal	6,645,830	2,120,089	4,525,741	5,181,503	1,550,618	3,630,885	5,341,597	1,329,862	4,011,735
In Transit	435,000	149,000	286,000	1,304,774	323,203	981,571	827,000	492,000	335,000

a/ Includes 3,288 barrels in caches.

SOURCE: Materiel Statistics Division, D/Statistical Services, DCS/C

TABLE 135 — CUMULATIVE BASE ISSUES OF USAF OWNED FUEL — FY 51, 52, 53

ISSUED TO	BARRELS OF 42 US GALLONS								
	FISCAL YEAR 1953			FISCAL YEAR 1952			FISCAL YEAR 1951		
	TOTAL	JET	AVGAS	TOTAL	JET	AVGAS	TOTAL	JET	AVGAS
WORLD-WIDE ISSUES & LOSSES	50,744,926	20,494,377	30,250,549	36,114,646	11,600,015	24,514,631	26,224,672	7,291,385	18,933,287
Net Issues	50,379,060	20,382,226	29,996,834	35,300,409	11,458,719	23,841,690	25,700,968	7,157,276	18,543,692
Losses	365,866	112,151	253,715	814,237	141,296	672,941	523,704	134,109	389,595
A/C of USAF Commands	42,289,943	18,525,157	23,764,786	32,696,326	10,907,804	21,788,522	22,607,234	6,692,301	15,914,933
Reserve Components A/C	229,974	8,928	221,046	250,650	36,589	214,061	1,147,368	194,997	952,371
Aircraft Other than USAF	1,937,251	288,170	1,649,081	1,531,874	182,282	1,349,592	1,320,891	66,058	1,254,833
Other than Aircraft	1,040,663	490,938	549,725	821,559	332,044	489,515	625,475	203,920	421,555
Cash Issues a/	6,451	60	6,391	-	-	-	-	-	-
Sales to Other than USAF	4,874,778	1,068,973	3,805,805	-	-	-	-	-	-

a/ Cash issues reporting effective September 1952.

SOURCE: Materiel Statistics Division, D/Statistical Services, DCS/C

TABLE 136 — SUMMARY WORLD-WIDE USAF FUEL INVENTORY — END OF QUARTER — FY 1953

LOCATION	BARRELS OF 42 US GALLONS				
	TOTAL	GRADE OF FUEL			
		JET	115/145	100/130	91/96-80
	30 SEPTEMBER 1952				
WORLD-WIDE - TOTAL	14,251,813	4,628,864	5,490,071	3,909,219	223,659
Zone of Interior	3,800,792	1,282,695	986,051	1,317,325	214,721
Overseas	9,189,021	2,742,169	4,146,020	2,291,894	8,938
In Transit	1,262,000	604,000	[illegible]	300,000	
	31 DECEMBER 1952				
WORLD-WIDE - TOTAL	16,331,091	6,695,355	5,436,266	3,880,753	318,717
Zone of Interior	5,821,571	2,921,819	896,084	1,723,993	279,675
Overseas	9,213,826	3,223,812	4,257,182	1,725,893	6,939
In Transit	1,295,694	549,724	283,000	430,867	32,103
	31 MARCH 1953				
WORLD-WIDE - TOTAL	18,162,214	7,031,647	6,380,863	4,503,524	246,180
Zone of Interior	6,770,173	3,336,523	1,117,730	2,089,255	226,665
Overseas	10,026,704	3,137,029	4,739,815	2,143,396	6,464
In Transit	1,365,337	558,095	523,318	270,873	13,051
	30 JUNE 1953				
WORLD-WIDE - TOTAL	21,696,842	8,245,293	8,615,131	4,528,834	307,584
Zone of Interior	9,756,449	4,453,112	2,974,242	2,083,679	245,416
Overseas	11,065,424	3,367,227	5,391,660	2,300,751	5,786
In Transit	874,969	424,954	249,229	144,404	56,382

SOURCE: Materiel Statistics Division, D/Statistical Services, DCS/C

TABLE 137 — AVIATION FUEL RECEIPTS FROM INDUSTRY — FY 1953

TYPE	BARRELS OF 42 US GALLONS					
	TOTAL	GRADE OF FUEL				
		JET	115/145	100/130	91/96	80
GRAND TOTAL	59,029,667	25,823,289	14,782,920	15,817,386	2,558,003	48,069
Bulk.	55,289,240	25,036,709	13,553,433	14,218,041	2,433,580	47,477
Contractor-Owned Into-Plane Issues.	1,962,154	375,556	305,300	1,168,493	112,213	592
Purchases From Other than USAP. . .	1,778,273	411,024	924,187	430,852	12,210	-

SOURCES: USAF POL Accounting Division, MAAMA

Fuels and Lubricants Division, MASEA

TABLE 138 — WORLD-WIDE USAF AVIATION FUEL INVENTORY — END OF QUARTER — FY 1953

(USAF Owned Aviation Fuel On Hand - Does not include fuel in transit or contractor owned stocks on USAF Installations)

AREA	AND COUNTRY	BARRELS OF 42 U.S. GALLONS: TOTAL			JET		115/145		100/130		91/96-80	
		TOTAL	BASE	TERMINAL	BASE	TERMINAL	BASE	TERMINAL	BASE	TERMINAL	BASE	TERMINAL
AS OF 30 SEPTEMBER 1952												
WORLD-WIDE - TOTAL		12,989,813	5,071,079	7,918,734	1,527,463	2,497,401	2,314,816	2,817,255	1,153,438	2,455,781	75,362	148,297
ZONE OF INTERIOR		3,800,792	1,521,987	2,278,805	558,646	724,049	492,650	493,401	403,642	913,683	67,049	147,672
OVERSEAS		9,189,021	3,549,092	5,639,929	968,817	1,773,352	1,822,166	2,323,854	749,796	1,542,098	8,313	625
OVERSEAS												
CINCAL	Alaska	532,664	318,350	214,314	45,463	70,203	77,732	26,858	192,633	117,253	2,522	-
CINCARIB	Canal Zone	37,488	37,488	-	-	-	124	-	37,065	-	299	-
	Puerto Rico	36,257	36,257	-	-	-	24,269	-	11,939	-	49	-
CINCUSAREUR	Austria	1,181	1,181	-	-	-	-	-	1,168	-	13	-
	France	285,105	285,105	-	225,480	-	42,809	-	16,695	-	121	-
	Germany	408,737	59,158	349,579	38,943	113,154	12,800	129,443	6,977	106,982	438	-
	Netherlands	276,620	-	276,620	-	94,882	-	64,595	-	117,143	-	-
CINCFE	Formosa	6,538	6,538	-	3,037	-	-	-	3,501	-	-	-
	Japan	2,699,150	356,224	2,342,926	171,745	981,185	40,752	482,357	142,251	879,364	1,476	-
	Korea	309,182	137,697	171,485	72,687	88,947	8,352	29,826	54,609	52,712	2,049	-
	Okinawa	195,766	120,292	75,474	26,040	32,479	42,990	-	51,262	42,995	-	-
CINCLANT	Azores	101,785	101,785	-	2,520	-	98,681	-	-	-	584	-
	Iceland	222,411	84,218	138,193	11,465	-	72,753	138,193	-	-	-	-
CINCNE	Greenland	1,029,417	1,029,417	-	253,461	-	775,956	-	-	-	-	-
	Labrador	282,494	282,494	-	30,886	-	251,228	-	-	-	380	-
	Newfoundland	94,553	94,553	-	16,780	-	77,451	-	-	-	322	-
CINCNELM Medit'n	Libya	19,819	19,819	-	4,276	-	15,543	-	-	-	-	-
	Morocco	213,031	208,823	4,208	24,490	3,157	184,333	1,051	-	-	-	-
U. Kingdom	England	1,822,868	57,832	1,765,036	25,770	306,466	26,476	1,378,326	5,586	80,244	-	-
CINCPAC	Guam	34,785	34,785	-	-	-	34,785	-	-	-	-	-
	Hawaii	247,114	159,036	88,078	13	-	12,858	-	146,119	88,078	46	-
	Iwo Jima	19,819	19,819	-	-	-	-	-	19,819	-	-	-
	Johnston Is.	50,844	50,844	-	-	-	13,951	-	36,893	-	-	-
	Philippine Is.	261,393	47,377	214,016	15,761	82,879	8,323	73,205	23,279	57,307	14	625
AS OF 31 DECEMBER 1952												
WORLD-WIDE - TOTAL		15,035,397	6,273,939	8,761,458	2,303,490	3,842,141	2,653,064	2,500,202	1,227,193	2,222,693	90,192	196,422
ZONE OF INTERIOR		5,821,571	2,017,869	3,803,702	968,435	1,953,384	443,697	452,387	521,966	1,202,027	83,771	195,904
OVERSEAS		9,213,826	4,256,070	4,957,756	1,335,055	1,888,757	2,209,367	2,047,815	705,227	1,020,666	6,421	518
OVERSEAS												
CINCAL	Alaska	552,162	306,096	246,066	53,150	81,740	87,882	50,931	163,943	113,395	1,121	-
CINCARIB	Canal Zone	61,734	61,734	-	-	-	261	-	61,190	-	283	-
	Puerto Rico	55,958	55,958	-	-	-	28,412	-	27,513	-	33	-
CINCUSAREUR	Austria	859	859	-	-	-	-	-	811	-	48	-
	France	310,195	310,195	-	248,253	-	46,764	-	14,918	-	260	-

TABLE 138 — WORLD-WIDE USAF AVIATION FUEL INVENTORY — END OF QUARTER — FY 1953 — CONTINUED

(USAF Owned Aviation Fuel on Hand - Does not include fuel in transit or contractor owned stocks on USAF Installations)

AREA	AND COUNTRY	BARRELS OF 42 U. S. GALLONS										
		TOTAL			JET		115/145		100/130		91/96-80	
		TOTAL	BASE	TERMINAL	BASE	TERMINAL	BASE	TERMINAL	BASE	TERMINAL	BASE	TERMINAL
		AS OF 31 DECEMBER 1952 (Continued)										
CINCUSAREUR - Cont'd												
	Germany. . . .	467,351	66,397	400,954	42,485	173,121	16,789	130,123	6,715	97,710	408	-
	Netherlands. .	221,524	-	221,524		170,120	-	31,571	-	19,833	-	-
CINCFE	Formosa. . . .	6,126	6,126	-	2,686	-	-	-	3,440	-	-	-
	Japan.	2,097,949	559,357	1,538,591	230,444	758,373	88,653	231,004	238,370	549,214	1,890	-
	Korea.	229,509	128,773	100,736	77,250	69,419	9,539	10,555	40,580	20,762	1,404	-
	Okinawa. . . .	133,964	94,474	39,490	21,120	21,099	28,179	10,490	45,171	7,901	4	-
CINCLANT	Azores	101,785	101,785	-	2,520	-	98,681	-	-	-	584	-
	Iceland. . . .	219,735	84,218	135,517	11,465	-	72,753	135,517	-	-	-	-
CINCNE	Greenland. . .	1,108,559	1,108,559	-	353,989	-	754,570	-	-	-	-	-
	Labrador . . .	778,427	778,427	-	169,222	-	609,205	-	-	-	-	-
	Newfoundland .	125,575	125,575	-	54,434	-	70,819	-	-	-	322	-
CINCNELM												
Medit'n	Libya.	8,414	-	8,414	-	-	-	8,414	-	-	-	-
	Morocco. . . .	248,490	175,649	72,841	17,805	-	157,844	72,841	-	-	-	-
U. Kingdom	England. . . .	2,007,661	60,308	1,947,353	22,773	557,313	32,094	1,330,437	5,441	59,603	-	-
CINCPAC	Guam	64,811	64,811	-	-	-	64,811	-	-	-	-	-
	Hawaii	134,681	43,909	90,772	3,174	-	19,749	-	20,946	90,772	40	-
	Iwo Jima . . .	13,341	13,341	-	-	-	-	-	13,341	-	-	-
	Johnston Is. .	54,886	54,886	-	-	-	15,071	-	39,815	-	-	-
	Philippine Is.	210,131	54,633	155,498	24,285	57,572	7,291	35,932	23,033	61,476	24	518
		AS OF 31 MARCH 1953										
WORLD-WIDE - TOTAL .		16,796,877	6,614,530	10,182,347	2,436,545	4,037,007	2,835,140	3,022,405	1,219,949	3,012,702	122,896	110,233
ZONE OF INTERIOR. . .		6,770,173	2,122,171	4,648,002	1,036,677	2,299,846	471,669	646,061	497,393	1,591,862	116,432	110,233
OVERSEAS.		10,026,704	4,492,359	5,534,345	1,399,868	1,737,161	2,363,471	2,376,344	722,556	1,420,840	6,464	-
OVERSEAS												
CINCAL	Alaska	482,380	238,680	243,700	40,157	80,000	82,086	76,900	115,146	86,800	1,291	-
CINCARIB	Canal Zone . .	52,992	52,992	-	-	-	882	-	52,110	-	-	-
	Puerto Rico. .	58,815	58,815	-	-	-	25,881	-	32,906	-	28	-
a/CINCUSAREUR	Austria. . . .	966	966	-	-	-	-	-	924	-	42	-
	France	298,832	298,832	-	246,392	-	41,664	-	10,430	-	346	-
	Germany. . . .	419,648	104,734	314,914	73,219	107,750	22,393	117,530	8,684	89,634	438	-
b/CINCFE	Formosa. . . .	6,126	6,126	-	2,686	-	-	-	3,440	-	-	-
	Japan.	(	587,624	(	220,724	(	92,189	(	272,684	(	2,027	-
	Korea.	(2,709,345	203,417	(1,810,767	134,781	(649,997	13,579	(352,422	53,572	(808,348	1,485	-
	Okinawa. . . .	(	107,537	(	36,451	(	21,988	(	49,098	(	-	-
CINCLANT	Azores	218,485	218,485	-	11,402	-	156,843	-	49,874	-	366	-
	Iceland. . . .	206,015	71,483	134,532	-	-	71,483	134,532	-	-	-	-
CINCNE	Greenland. . .	1,049,284	1,049,284	-	342,977	-	706,307	-	-	-	-	-
	Labrador . . .	719,087	719,087	-	152,173	-	566,914	-	-	-	-	-
	Newfoundland .	192,449	192,449	-	56,016	-	136,111	-	-	-	322	-
CINCNELM												
Medit'n	Libya.	59,358	36,979	22,379	15,168	5,906	21,811	16,473	-	-	-	-
	Morocco. . . .	319,970	264,781	55,189	20,924	29,293	243,857	25,896	-	-	-	-
U. Kingdom	England. . . .	2,380,444	66,775	2,313,669	20,446	864,215	42,102	1,404,642	4,227	44,812	-	-

TABLE 138 — WORLD-WIDE USAF AVIATION FUEL INVENTORY — END OF QUARTER — FY 1953 — CONTINUED

(USAF Owned Aviation Fuel on Hand - Does not include fuel in transit or contractor owned stocks on USAF Installations)

AREA	AND COUNTRY	TOTAL			JET		115/145		100/130		91/96-80	
		TOTAL	BASE	TERMINAL	BASE	TERMINAL	BASE	TERMINAL	BASE	TERMINAL	BASE	TERMINAL
		BARRELS OF 42 U. S. GALLONS										
		AS OF 31 MARCH 1953 (Continued)										
CINCPAC	Guam	64,811	64,811	-	-	-	64,811	-	-	-	-	-
	Hawaii	667,870	28,675	639,195	2,473	-	18,922	247,949	7,242	391,246	38	-
	Iwo Jima	12,661	12,661	-	-	-	3,207	-	9,454	-	-	-
	Johnston Is.	50,315	50,315	-	-	-	21,940	-	28,375	-	-	-
	Philippine Is.	56,851	56,851	-	23,879	-	8,501	-	24,390	-	81	-
		AS OF 30 JUNE 1953										
WORLD-WIDE - TOTAL		20,821,873	6,625,411	14,196,462	2,435,813	5,384,526	2,815,922	5,549,980	1,238,466	3,145,964	135,210	115,992
ZONE OF INTERIOR		9,756,449	2,205,817	7,550,632	1,188,675	3,264,437	465,875	2,508,367	421,838	1,661,841	129,429	115,987
OVERSEAS		11,065,424	4,419,594	6,645,830	1,247,138	2,120,089	2,350,047	3,041,613	816,628	1,484,123	5,781	5
OVERSEAS												
CINCAL	Alaska	410,026	299,056	110,970	52,935	20,259	104,503	36,329	139,643	54,382	1,975	-
CINCARIB	Canal Zone	41,789	41,789	-	-	-	824	-	40,965	-	-	-
	Puerto Rico	137,311	137,311	-	-	-	115,622	-	21,662	-	27	-
CINCUSAREUR	Austria	29	29	-	-	-	-	-	-	-	29	-
	France	312,140	28,397	283,743	18,122	36,466	4,809	247,277	4,945	-	521	-
	Germany	555,248	103,436	451,812	80,825	239,466	11,584	123,696	10,394	88,650	633	-
c/CINCFE	Japan	2,514,819	625,842	1,888,977	260,208	447,791	107,457	646,586	256,857	794,600	1,320	-
	Korea	625,489	209,990	415,499	137,383	208,133	12,147	74,022	60,075	133,344	385	-
	Okinawa	202,058	163,944	38,114	32,594	12,846	28,055	-	103,295	25,268	-	-
CINCLANT	Azores	250,882	250,882	-	11,376	-	142,082	-	97,124	-	300	-
	Iceland	204,528	71,131	133,397	-	-	71,131	133,397	-	-	-	-
CINCNE	Greenland	1,052,185	1,052,185	-	341,244	-	710,941	-	-	-	-	-
	Labrador	712,707	712,707	-	144,824	-	567,570	-	196	-	117	-
	Newfoundland	185,657	185,657	-	55,786	-	129,550	-	-	-	321	-
CINCNELM												
Medit'n	Libya	34,082	34,082	-	18,107	-	15,975	-	-	-	-	-
	Morocco	251,614	195,880	55,734	27,257	26,672	168,065	29,062	558	-	-	-
U. Kingdom	England	2,574,393	92,155	2,482,238	40,001	937,840	48,313	1,516,246	3,841	28,152	-	-
CINCPAC	Guam	64,811	64,811	-	-	-	64,811	-	-	-	-	-
	Hawaii	683,147	26,425	656,722	1,799	128,591	19,760	234,998	4,840	293,133	26	-
	Iwo Jima	7,197	7,197	-	-	-	2,421	-	4,776	-	-	-
	Johnston Is.	56,048	56,048	-	-	-	14,729	-	41,319	-	-	-
	Philippine Is.	189,264	60,640	128,624	24,677	62,025	9,698	-	26,138	66,594	127	5

NOTE: The above fuel inventories excluded in transit fuel as follows:
1,262,000 bbls, 30 Sep 52 — 1,365,337 bbls, 31 Mar 53
1,295,694 bbls, 31 Dec 52 — 874,969 bbls, 30 Jun 53

a/ Netherlands dropped, since it had no USAF owned fuel.
b/ Terminal breakdown for CINCFE by country not available.
c/ Formosa dropped since it had no USAF owned fuel.

SOURCE: Materiel Statistics Division, D/Statistical Services, DCS/C

TABLE 139 — BASE ISSUES OF USAF AVIATION FUEL — FY 1953

RECIPIENT	GRADE OF FUEL (Barrels of 42 US Gallons)					Cumulative Since 1 July 1952
	TOTAL	JET	115/145	100/130	91/96-80	
	SUMMARY 1 JULY 1952 - 30 JUNE 1953					
TOTAL NET ISSUES AND LOSSES	50,744,926	20,494,377	12,455,313	15,180,730	2,614,506	
OVERSEAS - TOTAL	18,461,983	6,603,164	5,644,455	5,966,468	247,896	
a/ZONE OF INTERIOR - TOTAL	32,282,943	13,891,213	6,810,858	9,214,262	2,366,610	
ISSUED TO						
a/Aircraft of USAF Commands	42,289,943	18,525,157	9,229,744	12,341,606	2,193,436	
Reserve Components Aircraft	229,974	8,928	531	204,087	16,428	
Aircraft Other Than USAF	1,937,251	288,170	679,646	857,329	112,106	
Other Than Aircraft	1,040,663	490,938	182,019	322,133	45,573	
Cash Issues	6,451	60	4,639	1,640	112	
b/Sales to Others	4,874,778	1,068,973	2,248,968	1,321,136	235,701	
Determinable Losses	365,866	112,151	109,766	132,799	11,150	
	FIRST QUARTER FISCAL YEAR 1953 (JULY-SEPTEMBER 1952)					
TOTAL NET ISSUES AND DET. LOSSES	11,237,164	4,121,137	2,467,368	4,250,289	398,370	11,237,164
Cumulative Since 1 July 1952	11,237,164	4,121,137	2,467,368	4,250,289	398,370	
TOTAL NET ISSUES	11,063,966	4,072,626	2,426,831	4,172,241	392,268	11,063,966
Cumulative Since 1 July 1952	11,063,966	4,072,626	2,426,831	4,172,241	392,268	
DETERMINABLE LOSSES	173,198	48,511	40,537	78,048	6,102	173,198
Cumulative Since 1 July 1952	173,198	48,511	40,537	78,048	6,102	
AIRCRAFT OF USAF COMMANDS						
TOTAL NET ISSUES	10,359,123	3,919,530	2,232,131	3,847,083	360,379	10,359,123
Air Defense Command	650,298	495,117	1,142	147,324	6,715	650,298
Air Materiel Command	220,117	67,261	27,899	122,751	2,206	220,117
Air Proving Ground Command	72,815	31,504	10,037	30,934	340	72,815
Air Research and Development Command	193,551	89,490	17,515	81,318	5,228	193,551
Air Training Command	2,501,457	1,445,964	42,612	729,536	283,345	2,501,457
Air University	22,490	98	13	14,295	8,084	22,490
Continental Air Command	40,074	1,673	637	36,054	1,710	40,074
Headquarters Command	91,455	275	830	87,977	2,373	91,455
Military Air Transport Service	879,220	13,946	404,504	458,216	2,554	879,220
Strategic Air Command	2,247,054	266,629	1,346,728	629,054	4,643	2,247,054
Tactical Air Command	524,701	136,718	112,479	262,517	12,987	524,701
USAF Security Service	1,555	615	-	936	4	1,555
Alaskan Air Command	142,865	83,359	13,619	45,820	67	142,865
Air Forces in Europe	596,129	420,912	40,359	133,935	923	596,129
Caribbean Air Command	4,401	29	-	4,327	55	4,401
Far East Air Forces	1,653,587	772,040	111,081	769,522	944	1,653,587
Northeast Air Command	26,816	21	26,351	444	-	26,816
Into-Plane from contractor owned stocks	490,538	93,889	76,325	292,123	28,201	490,538
Cumulative Since 1 July 1952	10,359,123	3,919,530	2,232,131	3,847,083	360,379	
RESERVE COMPONENTS AIRCRAFT						
TOTAL NET ISSUES	49,968	100	331	48,666	871	49,968
Air Force Reserve	3,605	8	83	3,311	203	3,605
Air National Guard	46,363	92	248	45,355	668	46,363
Cumulative Since 1 July 1952	49,968	100	331	48,666	871	
c/ AIRCRAFT OTHER THAN USAF						
TOTAL NET ISSUES	423,807	57,972	154,086	188,457	23,292	423,807
Canadian Air Force or Navy	16,160	7,537	1,990	6,516	117	16,160
Commercial Air Lines	129,708	745	9,967	109,160	9,836	129,708
Foreign Governments	38,862	19,216	1,792	16,614	1,240	38,862
Mutual Defense Assistance Program	651	42	181	422	6	651
U. S. Army	5,215	68	313	4,302	532	5,215
U. S. Marines	3,343	925	1,113	1,050	255	3,343
U. S. Navy	202,017	10,992	137,957	42,403	10,665	202,017
U. S. Government Agencies	9,370	5,564	526	3,199	81	9,370
Others	18,481	12,883	247	4,791	560	18,481
Cumulative Since 1 July 1952	423,807	57,972	154,086	188,457	23,292	
OTHER THAN AIRCRAFT						
TOTAL NET ISSUES	230,993	95,024	40,283	87,981	7,705	230,993
Crash Boats	4,795	-	-	2,917	1,878	4,795
Emergency Search and Rescue	245	-	-	173	72	245
Engine Block Testing	210,983	92,453	37,028	77,821	3,681	210,983
Miscellaneous	14,970	2,571	3,255	7,070	2,074	14,970
Cumulative Since 1 July 1952	230,993	95,024	40,283	87,981	7,705	
TOTAL CASH ISSUES	75	-	-	54	21	75
Cumulative Since 1 September 1952	75	-	-	54	21	

TABLE 139 — BASE ISSUES OF USAF AVIATION FUEL — FY 1953 — CONTINUED

RECIPIENT	GRADE OF FUEL (Barrels of 42 US Gallons)					Cumulative Since 1 July 1952
	TOTAL	JET	115/145	100/130	91/96-80	
	SECOND QUARTER FISCAL YEAR 1953 (OCTOBER-DECEMBER 1952)					
TOTAL NET ISSUES AND DET. LOSSES	10,366,840	3,986,497	2,448,650	3,586,811	344,882	21,604,004
Cumulative Since 1 July 1952	21,604,004	8,107,634	4,916,018	7,837,100	743,252	
TOTAL NET ISSUES	10,253,480	3,956,789	2,406,564	3,547,099	343,028	21,317,446
Cumulative Since 1 July 1952	21,317,446	8,029,415	4,833,395	7,719,340	735,296	
DETERMINABLE LOSSES	113,360	29,708	42,086	39,712	1,854	286,558
Cumulative Since 1 July 1952	286,558	78,219	82,623	117,760	7,956	
AIRCRAFT OF USAF COMMANDS						
TOTAL NET ISSUES	9,447,904	3,743,720	2,199,823	3,194,864	309,497	19,807,027
Air Defense Command	489,702	375,929	2,688	105,421	5,664	1,140,000
Air Materiel Command	156,615	24,869	30,328	97,397	4,021	376,732
Air Proving Ground Command	77,844	43,018	7,213	27,024	589	150,659
Air Research and Development Command	165,409	69,991	18,265	72,425	4,728	358,960
Air Training Command	2,475,280	1,547,967	55,591	643,850	227,872	4,976,737
Air University	27,997	62	-	18,853	9,082	50,487
Continental Air Command	50,354	1,347	235	46,829	1,943	90,428
Headquarters Command	68,961	649	7,854	58,263	2,195	160,416
Military Air Transport Service	708,437	7,364	336,879	361,389	2,805	1,587,657
Strategic Air Command	2,144,696	307,426	1,307,642	526,660	2,968	4,391,750
Tactical Air Command	515,772	142,877	125,835	230,189	16,871	1,040,473
USAF Security Service	5,519	-	4,388	1,128	3	7,074
Alaskan Air Command	102,572	57,876	11,081	32,966	649	245,437
Air Forces in Europe	303,130	210,458	14,688	77,460	524	899,259
Caribbean Air Command	6,440	-	185	6,237	18	10,841
Far East Air Forces	1,636,526	854,645	185,333	595,186	1,362	3,290,113
Northeast Air Command	22,112	5,353	15,293	1,464	2	48,928
Into-Plane from contractor owned stocks	490,538	93,889	76,325	292,123	28,201	981,076
Cumulative Since 1 July 1952	19,807,027	7,663,250	4,431,954	7,041,947	669,876	
RESERVE COMPONENTS AIRCRAFT						
TOTAL NET ISSUES	40,632	306	14	39,185	1,127	90,600
Air Force Reserve	1,424	28	-	737	659	5,029
Air National Guard	39,208	278	14	38,448	468	85,571
Cumulative Since 1 July 1952	90,600	406	345	87,851	1,998	
e/ AIRCRAFT OTHER THAN USAF						
TOTAL NET ISSUES	487,161	81,394	158,066	222,362	25,339	910,968
Canadian Air Force or Navy	19,957	504	13,147	6,168	138	36,117
Commercial Air Lines	156,675	167	9,594	131,848	15,066	286,383
Foreign Governments	52,935	25,611	3,185	23,696	443	91,797
Mutual Defense Assistance Program	8,030	5,408	1,620	998	4	8,681
U. S. Army	3,114	48	210	2,123	733	8,329
U. S. Marines	12,960	2,010	6,831	3,469	650	16,303
U. S. Navy	185,350	9,675	122,522	44,991	8,162	387,367
U. S. Government Agencies	27,371	24,017	480	2,775	99	36,741
Others	20,769	13,954	477	6,294	44	39,250
Cumulative Since 1 July 1952	910,968	139,366	312,152	410,819	48,631	
OTHER THAN AIRCRAFT						
TOTAL NET ISSUES	277,501	131,355	48,590	90,506	7,050	508,494
Crash Boats	3,661	-	-	2,478	1,183	8,456
Emergency Search and Rescue	437	-	13	353	71	682
Engine Block Testing	223,238	101,969	46,801	73,143	1,325	434,221
Miscellaneous	50,165	29,386	1,776	14,532	4,471	65,135
Cumulative Since 1 July 1952	508,494	226,379	88,873	178,487	14,755	
TOTAL CASH ISSUES	282	14	71	182	15	357
Cumulative Since 1 September 1952	357	14	71	236	36	

TABLE 139 — BASE ISSUES OF USAF AVIATION FUEL — FY 1953 — CONTINUED

RECIPIENT	GRADE OF FUEL (Barrels of 42 US Gallons)					Cumulative Since 1 July 1952
	TOTAL	JET	115/145	100/130	91/96-80	
	THIRD QUARTER FISCAL YEAR 1953 (JANUARY-MARCH 1953)					
TOTAL NET ISSUES AND DET. LOSSES	10,879,379	4,780,279	2,455,707	2,989,782	653,611	32,483,383
Cumulative Since 1 July 1952	32,483,383	12,887,913	7,371,725	10,826,882	1,396,863	
TOTAL NET ISSUES	10,821,391	4,752,052	2,434,811	2,984,085	650,443	32,138,837
Cumulative Since 1 July 1952	32,138,837	12,781,467	7,268,206	10,703,425	1,385,739	
DETERMINABLE LOSSES	57,988	28,227	20,896	5,697	3,168	344,546
Cumulative Since 1 July 1952	344,546	106,446	103,519	123,457	11,124	
AIRCRAFT OF USAF COMMANDS TOTAL NET ISSUES	10,059,661	4,566,467	2,230,027	2,655,796	607,371	29,866,688
Air Defense Command	586,738	457,163	17,772	99,125	12,678	1,726,738
Air Materiel Command	170,530	39,548	36,537	75,822	18,623	547,262
Air Proving Ground Command	78,434	42,200	9,921	24,769	1,544	229,093
Air Research and Development Command	188,353	96,621	20,780	58,217	12,735	547,313
Air Training Command	3,122,917	2,152,112	40,097	475,900	454,808	8,099,654
Air University	28,610	36	29	7,852	20,693	79,097
Continental Air Command	59,573	986	130	52,255	6,202	150,001
Headquarters Command	58,497	1,024	775	44,340	12,358	218,913
Military Air Transport Service	812,012	20,441	379,638	398,614	13,319	2,399,669
Strategic Air Command	2,274,239	573,083	1,279,737	405,804	15,615	6,665,989
Tactical Air Command	486,127	152,705	135,021	189,088	9,313	1,526,600
USAF Security Service	1,111	10	-	980	121	8,185
Alaskan Air Command	89,931	43,707	10,141	35,862	221	335,368
Air Forces in Europe	356,135	237,122	32,159	86,368	486	1,255,394
Caribbean Air Command	6,317	6	63	5,976	272	17,158
Far East Air Forces	1,203,526	635,478	166,968	400,932	148	4,493,639
Northeast Air Command	46,073	20,336	23,934	1,769	34	95,001
Into-Plane from contractor owned stocks	490,538	93,869	76,325	292,123	28,201	1,471,614
Cumulative Since 1 July 1952	29,866,688	12,229,717	6,661,981	9,697,743	1,277,247	
RESERVE COMPONENTS AIRCRAFT TOTAL NET ISSUES	51,453	761	79	47,296	3,317	142,053
Air Force Reserve	1,878	2	8	1,150	718	6,987
Air National Guard	49,575	759	71	46,146	2,599	135,146
Cumulative Since 1 July 1952	142,053	1,167	424	135,147	5,315	
c/ AIRCRAFT OTHER THAN USAF TOTAL NET ISSUES	435,755	58,176	148,414	201,930	27,235	1,346,723
Canadian Air Force or Navy	16,706	3,826	3,086	9,693	101	52,823
Commercial Air Lines	127,549	18	4,162	110,529	12,840	413,932
Foreign Governments	36,831	26,322	1,010	9,398	101	128,628
Mutual Defense Assistance Program	6,881	5,118	730	1,026	7	15,562
U. S. Army	3,987	164	304	2,495	1,024	12,316
U. S. Marine	36,532	5,603	12,372	17,093	1,464	52,835
U. S. Navy	189,370	7,689	126,261	44,070	11,350	576,737
U. S. Government Agencies	12,487	6,273	393	5,503	318	49,228
Others	5,412	3,163	96	2,123	30	44,662
Cumulative Since 1 July 1952	1,346,723	197,542	460,566	612,749	75,866	
OTHER THAN AIRCRAFT TOTAL NET ISSUES	271,922	126,614	54,475	78,356	12,477	780,416
Crash Boats	4,217	-	68	3,190	959	12,673
Emergency Search and Rescue	465	-	- 5	342	128	1,147
Engine Block Testing	233,438	118,971	53,476	57,357	3,634	667,659
Miscellaneous	33,802	7,643	936	17,467	7,756	98,937
Cumulative Since 1 July 1952	780,416	352,993	143,348	256,843	27,232	
TOTAL CASH ISSUES	2,600	34	1,816	707	43	2,957
Cumulative Since 1 September 1952	2,957	48	1,887	943	79	

TABLE 139 — BASE ISSUES OF USAF AVIATION FUEL — FY 1953 — CONTINUED

RECIPIENT	GRADE OF FUEL (Barrels of 42 US Gallons)					Cumulative Since 1 July 1952
	TOTAL	JET	115/145	100/130	91/96-80	
	FOURTH QUARTER FISCAL YEAR 1953 (APRIL-JUNE 1953)					
TOTAL NET ISSUES AND DET. LOSSES	18,261,543	7,606,464	5,083,588	4,353,848	1,217,643	50,744,926
Cumulative Since 1 July 1952	50,744,926	20,494,377	12,455,313	15,180,730	2,614,506	
TOTAL NET ISSUES	18,240,223	7,600,759	5,077,341	4,344,506	1,217,617	50,379,060
Cumulative Since 1 July 1952	50,379,060	20,382,226	12,345,547	15,047,931	2,603,356	
DETERMINABLE LOSSES	21,320	5,705	6,247	9,342	26	365,866
Cumulative Since 1 July 1952	365,866	112,151	109,766	132,799	11,150	
AIRCRAFT OF USAF COMMANDS TOTAL NET ISSUES	12,423,255	6,295,440	2,567,763	2,643,863	916,189	42,289,943
Air Defense Command	747,973	614,833	4,015	97,606	31,519	2,474,711
Air Materiel Command	233,341	75,738	56,917	49,600	51,086	780,603
Air Proving Ground Command	78,433	43,076	7,070	23,375	4,912	307,526
Air Research and Development Command	243,675	139,073	23,944	59,228	21,430	790,988
Air Training Command	3,562,312	2,588,439	86,910	327,076	559,887	11,661,966
Air University	33,514	49	9	4,603	28,853	112,611
Continental Air Command	74,314	439	294	53,853	19,728	224,315
Headquarters Command	66,717	1,129	208	17,287	48,093	285,630
Military Air Transport Service	855,897	27,257	395,021	384,331	49,288	3,255,566
Strategic Air Command	2,687,048	828,387	1,406,034	415,881	36,746	9,353,037
Tactical Air Command	716,962	309,157	201,600	171,991	34,214	2,243,562
USAF Security Service	841	12	-	519	310	9,026
Alaskan Air Command	177,148	116,482	25,310	34,841	515	512,516
Air Forces in Europe	546,897	372,111	54,659	119,671	456	1,802,291
Caribbean Air Command	7,216	41	210	6,260	705	24,374
Far East Air Forces	1,852,790	1,068,746	199,719	584,143	182	6,346,429
Northeast Air Command	47,637	16,582	29,518	1,474	63	142,638
Into-Plane from contractor owned stocks	490,540	93,889	76,325	292,124	28,202	1,962,154
Cumulative Since 1 July 1952	42,289,943	18,525,157	9,229,744	12,341,606	2,193,436	
RESERVE COMPONENTS AIRCRAFT TOTAL NET ISSUES	87,921	7,761	107	68,940	11,113	229,974
Air Force Reserve	1,703	20	-	1,234	449	8,610
Air National Guard	86,218	7,741	107	67,706	10,664	221,364
Cumulative Since 1 July 1952	229,974	8,928	531	204,087	16,428	
c/ AIRCRAFT OTHER THAN USAF TOTAL NET ISSUES	590,528	90,628	219,080	244,580	36,240	1,937,251
Canadian Air Force or Navy	18,116	4,334	4,036	9,624	122	70,939
Commercial Air Lines	155,967	357	15,087	129,894	10,629	569,899
Foreign Governments	61,717	45,902	856	14,703	256	190,345
Mutual Defense Assistance Program	11,044	5,441	4,631	953	19	26,606
U. S. Army	5,570	1	508	3,709	1,352	17,886
U. S. Marines	62,031	10,976	15,742	29,627	5,686	114,866
U. S. Navy	256,358	14,743	177,374	46,386	17,855	833,095
U. S. Government Agencies	9,782	787	812	7,901	282	59,010
Others	9,943	8,087	34	1,783	39	54,605
Cumulative Since 1 July 1952	1,937,251	288,170	679,646	857,329	112,106	
OTHER THAN AIRCRAFT TOTAL NET ISSUES	260,247	137,945	38,671	65,290	18,341	1,040,663
Crash Boats	4,594	-	-	3,102	1,492	17,267
Emergency Search and Rescue	428	10	- 9	253	174	1,575
Engine Block Testing	212,169	127,722	36,299	43,485	4,663	879,828
Miscellaneous	43,056	10,213	2,381	18,450	12,012	141,993
Cumulative Since 1 July 1952	1,040,663	490,938	182,019	322,133	45,573	
TOTAL CASH ISSUES	3,494	12	2,752	697	33	6,451
Cumulative Since 1 September 1952	6,451	60	4,639	1,640	112	
d/ TOTAL SALES TO OTHER THAN USAF	4,874,778	1,068,973	2,248,968	1,321,136	235,701	4,874,778
Cumulative Since 1 July 1952	4,874,778	1,068,973	2,248,968	1,321,136	235,701	

a/ Includes into-plane deliveries from contractor owned stocks.
b/ Figures as reported by USAF POL Accounting Division, MAAMA. The total is reported in overseas total as breakdown by ZI and OS is not available.
c/ Breakdown of Aircraft Other Than USAF:

Foreign Governments (excluding MDAP)
- All foreign air forces, except Royal Canadian AF or Navy.
- Danish government
- All foreign governments except Canada.

U. S. Government Agencies
- American Republics Program
- Atomic Energy Commission
- Civil Aeronautics Authority
- Coast Guard

U. S. Army
- Army Field Forces
- Ground National Guard

Others
- Joint Brazil - U.S. Military Commission
- Joint U. S. Military Advisory Group
- National Advisory Committee
- United Nations

d/ Figures as obtained from USAF POL Accounting Division, MAAMA are reported for the fourth quarter only as breakdown by month or quarter not available.

SOURCE: Materiel Statistics Division, D/Statistical Services, DCS/C

TABLE 140 — WORLD-WIDE AVIATION OIL INVENTORY – END OF QUARTER – FY 1953

	TOTAL	BARRELS OF 42 US GALLONS						
		AVLUBE				JET OIL		
		1120	1100	1080	1065	1015	1010	1005
	END OF QUARTER - 30 SEPTEMBER 1952							
WORLD-WIDE - TOTAL	184,729	7,451	138,085	1,903	4,395	-	27,075	5,820
Zone of Interior	76,429	2,735	46,350	1,258	2,646	-	20,468	2,972
Overseas	108,300	4,716	91,735	645	1,749	-	6,607	2,848
	END OF QUARTER - 31 DECEMBER 1952							
WORLD-WIDE - TOTAL	189,804	5,846	143,809	1,745	5,007	-	27,151	6,246
Zone of Interior	82,466	2,334	52,306	1,240	2,730	-	20,691	3,165
Overseas	107,338	3,512	91,503	505	2,277	-	6,460	3,081
	END OF QUARTER - 31 MARCH 1953							
WORLD-WIDE - TOTAL	186,656	4,764	143,359	1,567	4,683	-	25,416	6,867
Zone of Interior	77,701	2,064	50,136	1,058	2,168	-	18,960	3,315
Overseas	108,955	2,700	93,223	509	2,515	-	6,456	3,552
	END OF QUARTER - 30 JUNE 1953							
WORLD-WIDE - TOTAL	160,477	3,782	120,040	1,446	4,210	19	24,051	6,929
Zone of Interior	71,208	1,590	45,594	994	2,280	-	17,641	3,109
Overseas	89,269	2,192	74,446	452	1,930	19	6,410	3,820

Note: The above excludes re-used product.

TABLE 141 — WORLD-WIDE AVIATION OIL ISSUES – BY QUARTER – FY 1953

	TOTAL	BARRELS OF 42 US GALLONS							
		AVLUBE				JET OIL			CUMULATIVE SINCE 1 JULY 1952
		1120	1100	1080	1065	1015	1010	1005	
	FIRST QUARTER, JULY - SEPTEMBER 1952								
WORLD-WIDE - TOTAL	120,373	3,378	110,114	330	1,141	-	4,706	704	120,373
Zone of Interior	80,524	1,419	75,652	305	645	-	2,119	384	80,524
Overseas	39,849	1,959	34,462	25	496	-	2,587	320	39,849
Cumulative Since 1 July 1952	120,373	3,378	110,114	330	1,141	-	4,706	704	
	SECOND QUARTER, OCTOBER - DECEMBER 1952								
WORLD-WIDE - TOTAL	99,937	2,588	92,930	322	770	-	2,847	480	220,310
Zone of Interior	71,431	398	67,866	167	681	-	1,844	475	151,955
Overseas	28,506	2,190	25,064	155	89	-	1,003	5	68,355
Cumulative Since 1 July 1952	220,310	5,966	203,044	652	1,911	-	7,553	1,184	
	THIRD QUARTER, JANUARY - MARCH 1953								
WORLD-WIDE - TOTAL	109,881	2,902	102,091	170	913	-	3,268	537	330,191
Zone Of Interior	72,723	293	69,117	163	713	-	1,924	513	224,678
Overseas	37,158	2,609	32,974	7	200	-	1,344	24	105,513
Cumulative Since 1 July 1952	330,191	8,868	305,135	822	2,824	-	10,821	1,721	
	FOURTH QUARTER, APRIL - JUNE 1953								
WORLD-WIDE - TOTAL	108,745	855	103,129	99	574	-	3,301	787	438,936
Zone of Interior	79,773	241	76,008	98	435	-	2,311	680	304,451
Overseas	28,972	614	27,121	1	139	-	990	107	134,485
Cumulative Since 1 July 1952	438,936	9,723	408,264	921	3,398	-	14,122	2,508	

Note: Actual issues include losses, and exclude re-used product.

SOURCE: Materiel Statistics Division, D/Statistical Services, DCS/C

Part VIII

Stockpiling

STATUS OF THE USAF STRATEGIC MATERIALS STOCKPILING PROGRAM

This part of the USAF Statistical Digest on the "USAF Strategic Materials Stockpiling", contains data for Fiscal Years 1950-1953, and is shown as follows: summary of the utilization of storage space by depot; total storage requirement apportioned to the Air Force; storage space allocated; storage space earmarked; storage space occupied; total tons on hand.

These materials are for the consumption of private industry as well as the United States government. Normally, these materials will flow into private industry for fabrication of the final product.

TABLE 142 — STATUS OF THE STRATEGIC MATERIALS STOCKPILING PROGRAM

MATERIEL	SQUARE FEET — TOTAL STORAGE REQUIREMENT APPORTIONED TO DEPARTMENT OF AIR FORCE								STORAGE SPACE OCCUPIED AS OF 30 JUNE 1953		BALANCE OF SPACE AVAILABLE FOR STORAGE AS OF 30 JUNE '53		TONS — EST. TONNAGE WHICH CAN BE ACCOM. IN AVAILABLE SPACE AS OF 30 JUNE 1953	
	30 JUNE 1950		30 JUNE 1951		30 JUNE 1952		30 JUNE 1953							
	OPEN	WARE-HOUSE	OPEN	WARE-HOUSE	OPEN	WARE-HOUSE	OPEN	WARE-HOUSE	OPEN	WARE-HOUSE	OPEN	WARE-HOUSE	OPEN	WARE-HOUSE
TOTAL	583,800	1,613,030	535,500	1,877,169	535,600	1,596,869	498,750	1,521,831	403,200	1,514,556	95,550	76,265	2,117.5	359.0
Aluminum	-	-	-	-	5,000	-	4,235	-	4,235	-	-	-	-	-
Antimony	-	21,000	-	21,000	-	20,760	8,650	7,950	8,650	7,950	-	-	-	-
Asbestos	-	-	-	32,000	-	32,000	-	-	-	-	-	-	-	-
Bismuth	-	-	-	-	-	-	-	-	-	-	-	-	-	-
Beryllium	-	-	-	1,160	-	240	-	800	-	600	-	-	-	-
Brass	-	-	-	-	-	-	8,500	1,200	8,500	1,200	-	-	-	-
Copper	390,500	-	443,600	-	443,600	-	320,292	-	240,392	-	79,900	-	1,997.5	-
Cordage Fiber	-	152,000	-	172,320	-	-	-	-	-	-	-	-	-	-
Graphite	-	23,000	-	20,000	-	20,300	-	24,000	-	24,000	-	-	-	-
Hog Bristles	-	-	-	2,000	-	4,000	-	7,050	-	7,050	-	-	-	-
Kyanite	12,600	-	-	-	-	-	-	-	-	-	-	-	-	-
Lead	129,500	-	91,900	-	87,000	-	84,373	-	80,773	-	3,600	-	120.0	-
Magnesium	-	61,000	-	29,000	-	29,000	28,000	-	28,000	-	-	-	-	-
Manganese	51,200	-	-	(STORAGE PROGRAM CANCELLED)										
Mercury	-	10,000	-	23,400	-	23,400	-	11,700	-	11,700	-	-	-	-
Mica	-	102,500	-	84,000	-	82,000	-	88,042	-	88,042	-	68,000	-	680.0
Molybdenum	-	10,000	-	10,000	-	10,000	-	1,800	-	1,800	-	-	-	-
Narcotics	-	5,200	-	-	-	-	-	-	-	29,200	-	-	-	-
Nickel Oxide	-	18,100	-	18,100	-	23,600	-	25,200	-	-	-	-	-	-
Pepper	-	1,400	-	1,400	-	1,400	-	1,600	-	1,600	-	-	-	-
Quartz Crystal	-	2,000	-	3,608	-	3,608	-	3,608	-	3,608	-	-	-	-
Quebracho	-	-	-	-	-	-	-	-	-	-	-	-	-	-
Quinine	-	7,500	-	-	-	-	-	-	-	-	-	-	-	-
Rubber	-	1,032,950	-	683,231	-	647,831	-	658,131	-	655,786	-	2,335	-	259.0
Shellac	-	15,000	-	-	-	-	-	-	-	-	-	-	-	-
Tin	-	25,000	-	25,000	-	25,000	25,000	-	25,000	-	-	-	-	-
Tungsten	-	49,180	-	49,180	-	49,180	-	66,180	-	61,250	-	4,930	-	100.0
Zinc	-	-	-	-	-	-	19,700	-	7,650	-	12,050	-	-	-
General	-	77,200	-	701,770	-	624,570	-	624,570	-	624,570	-	-	-	-

TABLE 143—STATUS OF STORAGE SPACE OCCUPIED FOR THE STRATEGIC MATERIALS STOCKPILING PROGRAM — FY 1953

MATERIEL	DEPOT	STORAGE SPACE OCCUPIED - SQUARE FEET							
		30 JUNE 1950		30 JUNE 1951		JUNE 1952		30 JUNE 1953	
		OPEN	WARE-HOUSE	OPEN	WARE-HOUSE	OPEN	WARE-HOUSE	OPEN	WARE-HOUSE
TOTAL		286,200	1,317,200	333,700	1,522,118	342,000	1,506,849	403,200	1,514,556
Aluminum	Maywood	-	-	-	-	400	-	4,235	-
Antimony	Rome	-	17,000	-	15,840	-	16,000	8,650	3,950
	San Antonio	-	4,000	-	4,000	-	4,000	-	4,000
Asbestos	San Antonio	-	-	-	-	-	-	-	-
Bismuth	Rome	-	-	-	-	-	-	-	-
Beryllium	Rome	-	-	-	-	-	240	-	800
Brass	Rome	-	-	-	-	-	-	8,500	1,200
Copper	Binghamton a/	-	-	-	-	-	-	-	-
	Rome	182,600	500	221,200	500	232,700	500	229,700	-
	Maywood	23,500	-	25,500	-	25,500	-	10,692	-
Cordage Fiber	Binghamton a/	-	172,320	-	-	-	-	-	-
Graphite	Rome	-	15,000	-	20,300	-	20,300	-	24,000
Hog Bristles	Rome	-	-	-	1,500	-	4,000	-	7,050
Kyanite	Rome	-	-	-	-	-	-	-	-
Lead	Rome	51,700	-	51,900	-	48,300	-	48,300	-
	Maywood	28,400	-	35,100	-	35,100	-	32,473	-
Magnesium	San Antonio	-	29,000	-	29,000	-	29,000	28,000	-
Manganese	Rome	-	-	-	-	-	-	-	-
Mercury	Rome	-	11,700	-	23,400	-	23,400	-	11,700
	Binghamton a/	-	5,000	-	-	-	-	-	-
Mica	Middletown	-	25,000	-	25,000	-	25,000	-	28,042
	Rome	-	43,400	-	52,400	-	53,000	-	60,000
	Binghamton a/	-	31,000	-	-	-	-	-	-
Molybdenum	Middletown	-	1,000	-	1,000	-	1,000	-	1,800
Narcotics	Binghamton a/	-	1,600	-	-	-	-	-	-
Nickel Oxide	Middletown	-	8,100	-	8,100	-	8,100	-	8,300
	Rome	-	10,000	-	15,500	-	15,500	-	16,900
Pepper	Rome	-	1,400	-	1,400	-	1,400	-	1,600
Quartz Crystals	Dayton	-	1,700	-	3,608	-	3,608	-	3,608
Quebracho	Rome	-	-	-	-	-	-	-	-
Quinine	Binghamton a/	-	6,100	-	-	-	-	-	-
Rubber	Binghamton a/	-	385,900	-	-	-	-	-	-
	Rome	-	199,500	-	199,700	-	199,700	-	210,000
	Maywood	-	116,700	-	220,600	-	185,000	-	185,000
	Shreveport	-	17,800	-	-	-	-	-	-
	Topeka	-	4,400	-	129,300	-	133,531	-	132,586
	Shelby	-	129,600	-	78,100	-	89,000	-	128,200
Shellac	Binghamton a/	-	13,900	-	-	-	-	-	-
Tin	Rome	-	-	-	-	-	-	-	-
	Shreveport	-	25,000	-	25,000	-	25,000	25,000	-
Tungsten	Rome	-	40,580	-	43,300	-	45,000	-	61,250
Zinc	Dayton	-	-	-	-	-	-	7,650	-
General	Shreveport	-	-	-	-	-	-	-	-
	Binghamton a/	-	-	-	624,570	-	624,570	-	624,570

TABLE 144—STATUS OF UTILIZED DEPOT STORAGE SPACE FOR THE STRATEGIC MATERIALS STOCKPILING PROGRAM — FY 1953

SUMMARY - UTILIZATION OF DEPOT STORAGE SPACE - SQUARE FEET

DATE AND ACTION	TOTAL		MAYWOOD		ROME		SAN ANTONIO		BINGHAMTON	
	OPEN	WARE-HOUSE	OPEN	WARE-HOUSE	OPEN	WARE-HOUSE	OPEN	WARE-HOUSE	OPEN	WARE-HOUSE
30 JUNE 1950										
Allocated . . .	310,000	1,428,150	50,000	150,000	266,000	341,060	-	65,000	-	624,750
Occupied . . .	286,200	1,317,200	51,900	116,700	222,600	339,080	-	33,000	-	615,820
Earmarked . . .	222,600	2,732,200	-	30,000	234,300	163,700	-	-		35,500
Tons	226,344.06		23,327.79		115,358.19		3,369.62		58,839.56	
30 JUNE 1951										
Allocated . . .	435,500	1,633,149	370,000	220,600	65,500	388,140	-	65,000	-	-
Occupied . . .	333,700	1,522,118	35,100	220,600	289,600	373,840	-	33,000	-	-
Earmarked . . .	100,000	-	-	-	100,000	-	-	-	-	-
Tons	289,862.90		34,221.71		161,642.32		3,339.62		-	
30 JUNE 1952										
Allocated . . .	435,600	1,596,889	65,600	185,000	370,000	387,480	-	65,000	a/	a/
Occupied . . .	342,000	1,506,849	61,000	185,000	281,000	379,040	-	33,000	a/	a/
Earmarked . . .	100,000	-	-	-	100,000	-	-	-	a/	a/
Tons	289,901.58		33,736.39		162,879.45		3,339.62		a/	
30 JUNE 1953										
Allocated . . .	498,750	1,521,831	47,400	185,000	378,650	403,380	28,000	4,000	a/	a/
Occupied . . .	403,200	1,514,556	47,400	185,000	295,150	376,950	28,000	4,000	a/	a/
Earmarked . . .	100,000	-	-	-	100,000	-	-	-	a/	a/
Tons			34,434.98		162,629.60		3,339.62		a/	

DATE AND ACTION	MIDDLETOWN		DAYTON		SHREVEPORT		TOPEKA		SHELBY		GENERAL	
	OPEN	WARE-HOUSE	OPEN	WARE-HOUSE	OPEN	WARE-HOUSE	OPEN	WARE-HOUSE	OPEN	WARE-HOUSE	OPEN	WARE-HOUSE
30 JUNE 1950												
Allocated . .	-	43,100	-	2,000	-	42,800	-	25,000	-	129,600	-	-
Occupied . .	-	34,100	-	1,700	-	42,800	-	4,400	-	129,600	-	-
Earmarked . .	-	-	-	-	-	77,200	-	90,000	-	-	-	-
Tons . . .	4,698.55		195.81		7,485.21		482.30		13,067.09		-	
30 JUNE 1951												
Allocated . .	-	43,100	-	3,608	-	25,000	-	133,531	-	129,600	-	624,570
Occupied . .	-	34,100	-	3,608	-	25,000	-	129,300	-	78,100	-	624,570
Earmarked . .	-	-	-	-	-	-	-	-	-	-	-	-
Tons . . .	4,416.01		200.97		6,008.48		13,697.04		7,497.23		58,389.50	
30 JUNE 1952												
Allocated . .	-	43,100	-	3,608	-	25,000	-	133,531	-	129,600	-	624,570
Occupied . .	-	34,100	-	3,608	-	25,000	-	133,531	-	80,000	-	624,570
Earmarked . .	-	-	-	-	-	-	-	-	-	-	-	-
Tons . . .	4,416.01		200.97		6,008.48		14,496.29		6,434.87		58,389.50	
30 JUNE 1953												
Allocated . .	-	38,142	19,700	3,608	25,000	-	-	133,531	-	129,600	-	624,570
Occupied . .	-	12,942	7,650	3,608	25,000	-	-	132,586	-	128,200	-	624,570
Earmarked . .	-	-	-	-	-	-	-	-	-	-	-	-
Tons . . .	4,416.01		4,100.97		6,008.48		14,314.98		9,855.89		58,389.50	

TABLE 145—STATUS OF STORAGE SPACE ALLOCATED FOR THE STRATEGIC MATERIALS STOCKPILING PROGRAM — FY 1953

MATERIEL	DEPOT	STORAGE SPACE ALLOCATED - SQUARE FEET							
		30 JUNE 1950		30 JUNE 1951		30 JUNE 1952		30 JUNE 1953	
		OPEN	WARE-HOUSE	OPEN	WARE HOUSE	OPEN	WARE-HOUSE	OPEN	WARE-HOUSE
TOTAL		310,000	1,428,150	435,500	1,633,149	435,600	1,596,889	498,750	1,521,831
Aluminum . . .	Maywood . . .	-	-	-	-	5,000	-	4,235	-
Antimony . . .	Rome	-	17,000	-	17,000	-	16,760	8,650	3,950
	San Antonio	-	4,000	-	4,000	-	4,000	-	4,000
Asbestos . . .	San Antonio	-	-	-	32,000	-	32,000	-	-
Bismuth . . .	Rome	-	-	-	-	-	-	-	-
Beryllium . .	Rome	-	-	-	1,160	-	240	-	800
Copper	Binghamton a/	-	-	-	-	-	-	-	-
	Rome	200,000	-	318,100	-	318,100	-	309,600	-
	Maywood . .	22,500	-	25,500	-	25,000	-	10,692	-
Cordage Fiber .	Binghamton a/	-	172,320	-	-	-	-	-	-
Graphite . . .	Rome	-	20,000	-	20,000	-	20,300	-	24,000
Hog Bristles .	Rome	-	-	-	2,000	-	4,000	-	7,050
Kyanite	Rome	-	-	-	-	-	-	-	-
Lead	Rome	60,000	-	51,900	-	51,900	-	51,900	-
	Maywood . .	27,500	-	40,000	-	35,100	-	32,473	-
Magnesium . . .	San Antonio	-	61,000	-	29,000	-	29,000	28,000	-
Manganese . . .	Rome	-	-	-	-	-	-	-	-
Mercury	Rome	-	5,000	-	23,400	-	23,400	-	11,700
	Binghamton a/	-	5,000	-	-	-	-	-	-
Mica	Middletown .	-	25,000	-	25,000	-	25,000	-	28,042
	Rome	-	44,000	-	59,000	-	57,000	-	60,000
	Binghamton a/	-	33,500	-	-	-	-	-	-
Molybdenum . .	Middletown .	-	10,000	-	10,000	-	10,000	-	1,800
Narcotics . . .	Binghamton a/	-	5,200	-	-	-	-	-	-
Nickel Oxide .	Middletown .	-	8,100	-	8,100	-	8,100	-	8,300
	Rome	-	10,000	-	15,500	-	15,500	-	16,900
Pepper.	Rome. . . .	-	1,400	-	1,400	0	1,400	-	1,600
Quartz Crystals	Dayton . .	-	2,000	-	3,608	-	3,608	-	3,608
Quebracho . . .	Rome. . . .	-	-	-	-	-	-	-	-
Quinine	Binghamton a/	-	7,500	-	-	-	-	-	-
Rubber.	Binghamton a/	-	386,050	-	-	-	-	-	-
	Rome. . . .	-	199,500	-	199,500	-	199,700	-	210,000
	Maywood . .	-	150,000	-	220,600	-	185,000	-	185,000
	Shreveport.	-	17,800	-	-	-	-	-	-
	Topeka. . .	-	25,000	-	133,531	-	133,531	-	133,531
	Shelby. . .	-	129,600	-	129,600	-	129,600	-	129,600
Shellac	Binghamton a/	-	15,000	-	-	-	-	-	-
Tin	Rome.	-	-	-	-	-	-	-	-
	Shreveport . .	-	25,000	-	25,000	-	25,000	25,000	-
Tungsten . . .	Rome	-	49,180	-	49,180	-	49,180	-	66,180
Zinc	Dayton . . .	-	-	-	-	-	-	19,700	-
General	Shreveport .	-	-	-	-	-	-	-	-
	Binghamton a/	-	-	-	624,570	-	624,570	-	624,570
Brass	Rome	-	-	-	-	-	-	8,500	1,200

TABLE 146—STATUS OF STORAGE SPACE EARMARKED FOR THE STRATEGIC MATERIALS STOCKPILING PROGRAM — FY 1953

MATERIEL	DEPOT	STORAGE SPACE EARMARKED - SQUARE FEET							
		30 JUNE 1950		30 JUNE 1951		30 JUNE 1952		30 JUNE 1953	
		OPEN	WARE-HOUSE	OPEN	WARE-HOUSE	OPEN	WARE-HOUSE	OPEN	WARE-HOUSE
TOTAL		222,600	202,200	100,000	77,200	100,000	-	100,000	-
Antimony . . .	Rome	-	-	-	-	-	-	-	-
Bismuth	Rome	-	-	-	-	-	-	-	-
Copper	Binghamton a/	168,000	-	100,000	-	100,000	-	100,000	-
	Rome	-	-	-	-	-	-	-	-
Cordage Fiber .	Binghamton a/	-	-	-	-	-	-	-	-
Graphite . . .	Rome	-	-	-	-	-	-	-	-
Kyanite	Rome	12,600	-	-	-	-	-	-	-
Lead	Rome	42,000	-	-	-	-	-	-	-
Manganese . . .	Rome	-	-	-	-	-	-	-	-
Mercury	Binghamton a/	-	-	-	-	-	-	-	-
Mica	Rome	-	-	-	-	-	-	-	-
Narcotics . . .	Binghamton a/	-	-	-	-	-	-	-	-
Nickel Oxide .	Rome	-	-	-	-	-	-	-	-
Pepper	Rome	-	-	-	-	-	-	-	-
Quebracho . . .	Rome	-	-	-	-	-	-	-	-
Rubber	Binghamton a/	-	-	-	-	-	-	-	-
	Rome	-	-	-	-	-	-	-	-
	Maywood . .	-	35,000	-	-	-	-	-	-
	Topeka . .	-	90,000	-	-	-	-	-	-
Shellac	Binghamton a/	-	-	-	-	-	-	-	-
Tin	Rome	-	-	-	-	-	-	-	-
General	Shreveport .	-	77,200	-	77,200	-	-	-	-

TABLE 147—MATERIEL ON HAND FOR THE STRATEGIC MATERIALS STOCKPILING PROGRAM FY 1953

MATERIEL	DEPOT	TOTAL TONS ON HAND			
		30 JUNE 1950	30 JUNE 1951	30 JUNE 1952	30 JUNE 1953
TOTAL		224,083.58	287,593.06	287,631.74	301,130.03
Aluminum	Maywood	-	-	111.83	971.36
Antimony	Rome	3,169.10	3,193.05	3,235.75	3,235.75
	San Antonio	943.07	943.07	943.07	943.07
Asbestos	San Antonio	-	-	-	-
Bismuth	Rome	-	-	-	-
Beryllium	Rome	-	-	-	19.76
Brass	Rome	-	-	-	1,742.04
Copper	Binghamton a/	-	-	-	-
	Rome	63,877.98	107,591.31	109,979.92	109,497.77
	Maywood	5,355.35	6,188.17	6,188.17	6,188.17
Cordage Fiber	Binghamton	14,692.50	-	-	-
Graphite	Rome	1,462.09	1,789.04	1,789.04	1,789.04
Hog Bristles	Rome	-	44.02	318.92	318.92
Kyanite	Rome	-	-	-	-
Lead	Rome	12,617.28	12,634.04	10,088.41	10,088.41
	Maywood	9,231.63	13,406.06	13,087.50	13,087.50
Magnesium	San Antonio	2,396.55	2,396.55	2,396.55	2,396.55
Manganese	Rome	-	-	-	-
Mercury	Rome	1,748.22	1,748.22	1,748.22	1,748.22
	Binghamton a/	1,700.00	-	-	-
Mica	Middletown	2,555.36	2,272.82	2,272.82	2,272.82
	Rome	3,963.26	5,286.60	5,407.82	5,664.56
	Binghamton a/	5,157.00	-	-	-
Molybdenum	Middletown	248.50	248.50	248.50	248.50
Narcotics	Binghamton a/	129.00	-	-	-
Nickel Oxide	Middletown	1,894.69	1,894.69	1,894.69	1,894.69
	Rome	-	-	-	2,369.84
Pepper	Rome	82.80	82.80	82.80	82.80
Quartz Crystals	Dayton	195.81	200.97	200.97	200.97
Quebracho	Rome	-	-	-	-
Quinine	Binghamton a/	323.00	-	-	-
Rubber	Binghamton a/	35,614.00	-	-	-
	Rome	16,683.29	16,663.31	16,663.31	16,663.31
	Maywood	8,751.81	14,627.48	14,348.89	14,187.95
	Shreveport	1,476.73	-	-	-
	Topeka	482.30	13,697.04	14,496.29	14,314.98
	Shelby	13,067.09	7,947.23	6,434.87	9,855.89
Shellac	Binghamton a/	783.00	-	-	-
Tin	Rome	-	-	-	-
	Shreveport	6,008.48	6,008.48	6,008.48	6,008.48
Tungsten	Rome	9,484.69	10,340.11	11,295.42	13,049.18
Zinc	Dayton	-	-	-	3,900.00
General	Shreveport	-	-	-	-
	Binghamton	-	58,389.50	58,389.50	58,389.50

a/ The Binghamton AFSPD was transferred on 1 July 1950 to GSA for operation as a stockpile depot exclusively, and the commodities are classified herein under "General" - as of that date.

USAF Industrial Reserve

Part IX

USAF INDUSTRIAL RESERVE

This part of the USAF Statistical Digest on the USAF Industrial Reserve includes two tables. The first table titled - "USAF Departmental Industrial Reserve", includes information on industrial facilities for which the Air Force has custody, jurisdiction and accountability. These facilities are listed in order of plant number and show the location, product, and any appropriate remarks regarding the present status of the plant.

Table number 2 - "USAF Production Expansion Projects", includes all facilities in the USAF Industrial Reserve which are producing airframes, engines, engine components, and guided missiles, and shows code, total programmed funds, cumulative obligations, unobligated remainder of programmed funds, military product, and appropriate remarks.

TABLE 148 — USAF DEPARTMENTAL INDUSTRIAL RESERVE

AFP NUMBER	OPERATOR	LOCATION	PRODUCT	REMARKS
1		Omaha, Nebraska		Inactive - Used by Hq SAC also Machine Tool Storage
2	BOP, GM	Kansas City, Kansas	F-84F	GM has notified USAF of intention to exercise option to purchase. Plant is currently leased.
3	Douglas Aircraft Co.	Tulsa, Oklahoma	B-47	
4	Convair	Ft. Worth, Texas	B-36, B-58	Planned 2nd source F-102
6 8	Lockheed Aircraft Corp.	Marietta, Georgia Orchard Place, Illinois	B-47	Inactive - Storage, ANG, ADC
9	North American Aviation, Inc.	Inglewood, California	F-86, F-100	Sale to NAA, Inc., pending
10	Northrop Aircraft, Inc.	Hawthorne, California	F-89 - Snark	Scrambled Facility
11	Fairchild Airplane & Eng. Co.	Hagerstown, Maryland	C-119	Scrambled Facility
13	Boeing Aircraft Corp.	Wichita, Kansas	B-47	Second source for B-52
14	Lockheed Aircraft Corp.	Burbank, California	C-121, T-33, F-94	
15	Douglas Aircraft Corp.	Long Beach, California	C-124, RB-66	Scrambled Facility
16	North American Aviation, Inc.	Downey, California	T-28 Navaho Missile	
17	Boeing Aircraft Co.	Seattle, Washington	B-52, KC-97	Scrambled Facility
18	Bell Aircraft Corp.	Kenmore, New York	B-47 Power Packs	
26	Allison Division, GMC	Indianapolis, Indiana	J-33-35-71 Engines	Scrambled Facility
27	A. O. Smith	Toledo, Ohio	B-47 Landing Gear	Part leased
28	General Electric	Everett, Mass.	J-47 Components	
29	General Electric	West Lynn, Mass.	J-47	
30	Allison Division, GMC	Indianapolis, Indiana	Engine Flight Testing	Consists of a hanger and office
31	Smith-Hinchman & Cryllis	Willow Run, Michigan	R & D	Consists of hangar, boiler room, 3 story administration building
32	Lycoming Division, AVCO	Williamsport, Pa.	J-47 Components	Scrambled Facility
33	Wright-Aero	Woodridge, New Jersey	J-65 - R-3350	Scrambled Facility

TABLE 148 — USAF DEPARTMENTAL INDUSTRIAL RESERVE (CONTINUED)

AFP NUMBER	OPERATOR	LOCATION	PRODUCT	REMARKS
35	Emerson Electric Co.	Washington Park, Illinois	A-2 Fire Control System	
36	General Electric	Evendale, Ohio	J-47	Formerly called Lockland, Ohio
38	Bell Aircraft Co.	Modeltown, New York	Missile Test	Parts of the premises occupied by AEC, ADC & Navy
39	Ford Motor Co.	Chicago, Illinois	J-57, R-4360 Engines	
40	Chevrolet Division, GMC	Tonawanda	R-3350 Engines	
41	Champion Machine & Forging	Cleveland, Ohio	Forgings	Scrambled Facility
42	NAA - Lockheed- Northrop	Palmdale, California	Flight Test	
43	Bridgeport -Lycoming Div., AVCO	Stratford, Connecticut	R-1820 Engines	
44	Hughes Tool Company	Tucson, Arizona	Missiles	
45	Heppenstall - Eddystone Corp.	Eddystone, Pa.	Storage Site	
46	Haynes - Stellite	Alexandria, Ind	Buckets & Blades	
47	ALCOA	Cleveland, Ohio	Heavy Press	Under Construction
48	Kaiser Aluminum Co.	Newark, Ohio	Storage	Heavy Press site - To be inactive
49	Curtiss-Wright (Metals Proc. Div)	Buffalo, New York	Heavy Press	Under Construction
50	Kaiser Aluminum Co.	Halethorpe, Md	Heavy Press	Under construction
51	A. O. Smith	Greece, New York	B-52 Weldments	
66	Phillips Petroleum Co.	McGregor, Texas	ATO Units	Under Construction
	General Electric	Johnson City, New York	Fire Control Systems	In process of transfer to AF from GSA
	A. C. Spark Plug Div., GM	Milwaukee, Wisconsin	Gun Sights - Nav Systems	In process of transfer to AF from GSA
	Bohn-Aluminum	Adrian, Michigan	Forgings - Extrusions	In process of transfer to AF from GSA
	Wyman-Gordon	N. Grafton, Mass.	Heavy Press	In process of transfer to AF from GSA
	Studebaker Co.	Chicago, Illinois	J-47 Engines	Plancor 40 now on lease from National Tea Co. To be acquired.

TABLE 149 — USAF PRODUCTION EXPANSION PROJECTS — FY 1953

(In thousands of dollars.)

SPECIAL FACILITY CONTRACTOR	CODE	TOTAL PROGRAMMED FUNDS	CUMULATIVE OBLIGATIONS	UNOBLIGATED REMAINDER OF PROG. FUNDS	MILITARY PRODUCT	REMARKS
			AIRFRAMES			
Boeing Airplane Co. Seattle, Wash.	C-P a/	39,192	37,692	1,500	B-52 KC-97 Bomarc	Bomarc R & D
Boeing Airplane Co. Wichita, Kansas	C b/	22,951	22,951	-	B-47 RB-47	
Buick-Olds-Pontiac Div. Kansas City, Kans.	C	23,256	23,256	-	F-84	
Consolidated Vultee Fort Worth, Texas	C	9,371	9,371	-	B-36 RB-36	
Consolidated Vultee Forth Worth, Texas	C	-	1,000	-	MX-1589	
Consolidated Vultee Fort Worth, Texas	C	-	-	3,766	MX-1964	
Consolidated Vultee San Diego, Calif.	P c/	-	3,650	-	T-29	
Consolidated Vultee San Diego, Calif.	P	27,185	13,585	13,600	F-102	
Douglas Aircraft Long Beach, Calif.	C-P	27,500	22,000	5,500	C-124 RB-66 B-66	
Douglas Aircraft Tulsa, Oklahoma	C	38,022	36,022	2,000	B-47 Prod. RB-66C Prod.	
Fairchild Acft. Div. Hagerstown, Md.	C	(Being Re-programmed)	7,708	860	C-119	
Fairchild Acft. Div. Seattle, Wash.	C	-	-	13,167	B-52 Flt. Test	
Grand Central Acft. Co. Tucson Ariz.	P	5,100	5,100	-	B-47 Modif.	
Hayes Acft. Corp. Birmingham, Ala.	C	4,771	4,373	398	B-25 Modif. C-119 Modif. C-124 Modif.	
Lockheed Acft. Corp. Palmdale, Calif.	C	21,774	21,774	-	F-94 Flt. Test T-33 Flt. Test	
Lockheed Acft. Corp. Burbank, Calif.	C-P	5,694	5,446	248	T-33 F-94	
Lockheed Acft. Corp. Marietta, Ga.	C	40,733	40,733	-	B-47 C-130A	
Lockheed Acft. Corp. Marietta, Ga.	C	1,000	-	1,000	C-130A	
Martin, Glenn L. Baltimore, Md.	C-P	-	10,000	-	B-57	
McDonnell Acft. Corp. St. Louis, Mo.	C-P	11,500	10,000	1,500	F-101	
North American Aviation Corp. Los Angeles, Calif.	P	11,868	11,868	-	T-28 F-86 F-100	

TABLE 149 — USAF PRODUCTION EXPANSION PROJECTS — FY 1953 (Continued)

(In thousands of dollars.)

SPECIAL FACILITY CONTRACTOR	CODE	TOTAL PROGRAMMED FUNDS	CUMULATIVE OBLIGATIONS	UNOBLIGATED REMAINDER OF PROG. FUNDS	MILITARY PRODUCT	REMARKS.
			AIRFRAMES			
North American Aviation Palmdale, Calif.	C	4,835	4,835	-	Flt. Test	
Northrop Acft. Inc. Hawthorne Calif.	C-P	3,360	3,360	-	F-89	
Northrop Acft. Inc. Ontario, Calif.	P	1,021	1,021	-	F-89 Flt. Test	
Northrop Acft, Inc. Palmdale, Calif	C	4,400	-	-	F-89 Flt. Test	
Republic Aviation Corp. Farmingdale, N. Y.	P	11,776	11,776	-	F-84 RF-84F F-105 RF-105	
Sikorsky Acft. Div. United Acft. Bridgeport, Conn.	P	-	-	10,000	Helicopters & Helicopter Parts	
			ENGINES			
Air Cooled Motors, Inc. Syracuse, N. Y.	P	981	981	-	Helicopter Eng.	
Allison Division, GMC Indianapolis, Ind.	C-P	46,000	46,000	-	J-35 & J-33 Eng.	
Allison Division, GMC Indianapolis, Ind.	C-P	10,800	10,800	-	J-71-A3 Eng.	
Allison Division, GMC Indianapolis, Ind.	C-P	6,300	6,300	-	T-56 Eng.	
Bridgeport-Lycoming Div. AVCO, Stratford, Conn	C	32,439	25,866	6,573	R-1820 Eng.	
Buick Motor Div., GMC Flint, Mich.	P	107,000	107,000	-	J-65 Eng.	
Buick Motor Div., GMC Willow Springs, Ill.	C-P	-	2,532	-	J-65 Eng.	
Chevrolet Div., GMC Tonawanda, N. Y.	C	50,000	50,000	-	R-3350 Eng.	
Continental Motors Corp. Muskegon, Mich.	P	-	2,885	-	C-470-11 & 13 Eng.	
Fairchild Engine Div. Farmingdale, N. Y.	P	-	520	-	Andover Eng.	
Foote Bros., Gear & Machine Chicago, Ill.	P	180	180	-	B-36 & R-4360 Eng.	
Ford Motor Co. Chicago, Ill.	C	47,000	40,000	7,000	J-57 Eng.	
Ford Motor Co. Chicago, Ill.	C	103,500	103,500	-	R-4360 Eng.	
General Electric Co. Lockland, Ohio	C-P	77,219	77,219	-	J-47 & J-73 Eng.	
General Electric Co. Lockland, Ohio	C-P	-	5,000	-	MX-1589	
General Electric Co. West Lynn, Mass.	C-P	-	600	-	Fuel Storage	

TABLE 149 — USAF PRODUCTION EXPANSION PROJECTS — FY 1953 (CONTINUED)

(In thousands of dollars.)

SPECIAL FACILITY CONTRACTOR	CODE	TOTAL PROGRAMMED FUNDS	CUMULATIVE OBLIGATIONS	UNOBLIGATED REMAINDER OF PROG. FUNDS	MILITARY PRODUCT	REMARKS
			ENGINES (Cont'd)			
General Electric Co. West Lynn, Mass.	C-P	406	-	-	J-47 Eng. Parts	
Kaiser Mfg. Corp. (Willys Motors Inc.) Detroit, Mich.	P	15,140	15,140	-	R-1300 Eng.	
Nash-Kelvinator Kenosha, Wis.	P	-	36,725	-	R-2800 Eng.	
Packard Motor Car Co. Detroit, Mich.	P	-	48,000	-	J-47 Eng.	
Packard Motor Car Co. Detroit Mich.	P	-	11,000	-	J-47 Buckets & blades	
Pratt & Whitney Aircraft Southington Plant, East Hartford, Conn.	C-P	-	26,000	-	R-4360 Eng.	
Studebaker Corporation South Bend, Ind.	P	-	42,150	8,000	J-47 Eng.	R&D Proj.
Wright Aero Corporation Woodridge, N. J.	C-P	-	5,180	-	Ram jet Test Facility	
Wright Aero Corporation Woodridge, N. J.	C-P	7,000	5,000	2,000	Y6-67-W1, Turbo Jet Eng.	
Wright Aero Corporation Woodridge, N. J.	C-P	138,450	138,450	-	R-3350 & J-65 Eng.	
			ENGINE COMPONENTS			
Allison Division, GMC Indianapolis, Ind.	P	-	13,000	-	Development Facility	
Ahlberg Company Chicago, Ill.	P	-	160	-	High Precision Bearings	
Allegheny Ludlum Steel Watervliet, N. Y.	P	-	-	352	Titanium Prod.	
American Bosch Corp. Springfield, Mass.	P	430	430	-	Jet Eng, Nozzle Trim Tab, Over-speed Governor	
American Metal Prod. Detroit, Mich.	P	-	978	-	J-47 Components	
American Welding Mfg. Co. Warren, Idaho	P	-	4,160	-	J-47 Casing Jet Rings	
Bardon Corporation Danbury, Conn.	P	-	250	-	Bearings	
Bingham-Herbrand Corp. Fremont, Ohio	P	-	5,300	-	J-47 Buckets & Blades	
Boston Gear Works Div. Quincy, Mass	P	-	817	-	H-13D Trans. Assembly	
Bridgeport-Lycoming Div. Stratford, Conn.	C	16,034	15,400	634	J-47 Rotor Ass'y. Vane, Stator, Turbine & Wheel Frame Ass'y.	
Budd Mfg. Co. Philadelphia, Pa.	P	-	6,000	-	J-47 Parts, Nozzle Liners	
Case, J. I. Co. Racine, Wisc.	P	-	1,500	-	R-2800 Prop. Shaft Ass'y.	

TABLE 149 — USAF PRODUCTION EXPANSION PROJECTS — FY 1953 (CONTINUED)

(In thousands of dollars.)

SPECIAL FACILITY CONTRACTOR	CODE	TOTAL PROGRAMMED FUNDS	CUMULATIVE OBLIGATIONS	UNOBLIGATED REMAINDER OF PROG. FUNDS	MILITARY PRODUCT	REMARKS
	ENGINE COMPONENTS					
Cleveland Graphite-Bronze Cleveland, Ohio	P	-	2,500	-	Bearings	
Cleveland Industrial Tool Cleveland, Ohio	P	-	90	-	Bearing Shells	
Delevan Mfg. Co.	P	-	128	-	J-57 Fuel Noz.	
Deepfreeze Appliance Div. Chicago, Ill.	P	-	75	-	R-4360 Parts	
Deepfreeze Appliance Div. North Chicago, Ill.	P	-	2,075	-	R-2800 Pump & Regulator Ass'y.	
Delco Remy Division, GMC Anderson, Ind.	P	3,831	3,575	256	T- 56 & J-71 Comp., Rotor Blades	
Eaton Mfg. Co. Battle Creek, Mich.	P	4,102	4,102	-	J-47 & J-73 Rotor Blades	
Eaton Mfg. Co. Marshall, Mich.	P	-	74	-	R-4360 Suction Pumps	
Eaton Mfg. Co. Battle Creek, Mich.	P	-	2,000	-	R-4360 Valves	
Eaton Mfg. Co. Battle Creek, Mich.	P	-	730	-	R-3350 Valves	
Eaton Mfg. Co. Cleveland, Ohio	P	-	136	-	R-4360 Bearings Ret. Plates	
Eaton Mfg. Co. Battle Creek, Mich.	P	-	121	-	R-1300 Exhaust Intake	
Eaton Mfg. Co. Saginaw, Mich.	P	-	735	-	R-4360 Valve Seats, Rotors & Suction Pumps	
Eclipse Mach. Div. Elmira, N. Y.	P	-	680	-	J-47 Fuel Nozzles	
Excello Corporation Detroit, Mich.	P	-	1,200	-	R-4360 Parts	
Excello Corporation, Lima, Ohio	P	1,047	886	161	J-57 Parts	
Fairchild Eng. Div. Farmingdale, N. Y.	P	-	865	-	J-47 Frames and Drives	
Fairchild Eng. Div. Valley Stream, N. Y.	C	-	5,100	-	J-47 Component	
Firestone Steel Prod. Akron, Ohio	P	-	2,710	-	J-47 & 57 Comp.	
Frigidaire Division, GMC Dayton, Ohio	P	-	3,000	-	Fuel Cartridge Starting Cart.	
General Electric Co. Everett, Mass.	C-P	-	350	-	J-47 Cornice Couplings	
Heintz Mfg. Co. Philadelphia, Pa.	P	777	777	-	J-47 Exhaust Units	
Heli-Coil Corp. Danbury, Conn.	P	-	438	-	Inserts	

TABLE 149 — USAF PRODUCTION EXPANSION PROJECTS — FY 1953 (Continued)

(In thousands of dollars.)

SPECIAL FACILITY CONTRACTOR	CODE	TOTAL PROGRAMMED FUNDS	CUMULATIVE OBLIGATIONS	UNOBLIGATED REMAINDER OF PROG. FUNDS	MILITARY PRODUCT	REMARKS
			ENGINE COMPONENTS			
Hotpoint, Inc. Milwaukee, Wisc.	P	3,908	3,908	-	Turbos	
Handaille-Hershey Corp. Decatur, Ill.	P	-	3,600	-	R-2800, Rod Ass'y, Rod Plates	
Hudson Motor Car Co. Detroit, Mich,	P	-	88	-	Crankshaft, Prop shaft & Rocker Arm	
ITE Circuit Breaker Co. Philadelphia, Pa.	P	-	1,430	-	J-47 Corp.	
Kelsey-Hayes Wheel Co. Detroit, Mich.	P	-	241	-	J-57 Eng. Pts	
Lycoming-Spencer Div. Williamsport, Pa.	C-P	-	600	-	J-47 Gear Boxes, Scav-enger Pump	
Lycoming-Spencer Div. Williamsport, Pa.	C-P	-	15	-	V-1650 Parts	
Muskegon Motor Spec. Jackson, Mich,	P	-	67	-	O-335-1 H Crankshaft	
National Radiator Co. Johnstown, Pa,	P	-	143	-	J-57 Mani-folds	
New Hampshire Ball Bearings Peterborough, N. H.	P	-	450	-	Ball Bearings	
Norma Hoffman Bearings Stamford, Conn.	P	-	1,100	-	Bearings	
Parker Appliance Co. Cleveland, Ohio	P	-	2,200	-	Eng. Valves	
Perfect Circle Corp. Richmond, Ind,	P	-	600	-	Comp. Rings	
Ryan Aeronautical Co. San Diego, Calif.	P	-	35	-	C-119 Exhaust Hoods	
Solar Acft. Co. Des Moines, Ia.	P	-	4,000	-	J-47 Comp.	
Solar Acft Co. San Diego, Calif.	P	2,335	2,275	60	J-47 Comp. B-31 & B-36 Comp.	
Solar Acft. Co. Des Moines, Ia.	P	-	1,548	-	J-57 Comp.	
Stainless Ware Co. of Amer. Walled Lake, Mich.	P	-	200	-	Machine Studs	
Steel Improvement & Forge Cleveland, Ohio	P	-	2,350	-	J-33-35-37 Buckets, Blade Nozzles	
Sunstrand Machine Tool Co. Rockford, Ill.	P	8,852	3,852	5,000	Alt. Drive. Alt. Pump	
Thompson Prod. Inc. Cleveland, Ohio	P	-	4,000	-	R-4360 Valves and Seats	
Thompson Prod. Inc. Cleveland, Ohio	P	-	186	-	R-2800 Dup. Ind. Ass'y.	
Thompson Prod. Inc. Cleveland, Ohio	P	-	580	-	R-1820 Imp. Ass'y. Valves	

TABLE 149 — USAF PRODUCTION EXPANSION PROJECTS — FY 1953 (CONTINUED)

(In thousands of dollars.)

SPECIAL FACILITY CONTRACTOR	CODE	TOTAL PROGRAMMED FUNDS	CUMULATIVE OBLIGATIONS	UNOBLIGATED REMAINDER OF PROG. FUNDS	MILITARY PRODUCT	REMARKS
			ENGINE COMPONENTS			
Thompson Products Inc. Cleveland, Ohio	P	-	17,950	-	J-47	
Thompson Products Inc. Cleveland, Ohio	P	-	5,000	-	Jet Eng. Components	
Thompson Products Inc. Cleveland, Ohio	P	-	1,590	-	R-3350V Inserts, S. W. Ass'y	
Thompson Products Inc. Cleveland, Ohio	P	-	170	-	R-1300 Exhaust & Intake valve	
Thompson Products Inc. St. Catherines, Ont. Canada	P	-	2,100	-	J-65 Comp.	Rotors & blades
Thompson Products Inc. Cleveland, Ohio	P	2,708	2,708	-	J-57 Blades	
Thompson Products Inc. Harrisburg, Pa.	P	-	500	-	J-47 Comp.	
Thompson Products Inc. Cleveland, Ohio	P	-	5,240	-	J-47 Buckets Blades & Stator blades	
Thompson Products inc. Cleveland, Ohio	P	-	2,091	-	J-65 & 71 Components	R-3350 Super Impeller
Tube Turns Inc. Louisville, Ky.	P	-	475	-	R-3350 & 4360 Alum. Heads	
Utica Drop Forge & Tool Utica, N. Y.	P	925	925	-	J-47 Blades	
Utica Drop Forge & Tool Yorkville, N. Y.	P	-	1,302	-	J-42-47-48-57 Turbine Blades	
Utica Drop Forge & Tool Clayville, N. Y.	P	-	650	-	Props	
Utica Drop Forge & Tool Utica, N. Y.	P	1,196	1,196	-	J-65 Blades & Buckets	
Warner Gear Division Borg-Warner Corporation Muncie, Ind.	P	-	1,000	-	J-65 Gear Box	
Willys Overland Motors Inc. Anderson, Ind.	P	-	6,076	-	J-47 Frames & Gears	
Wright Aeronautical Corp. Woodridge, N. J.	C-P	-	5,300	-	J-47 Comp.	
Ryan Aeronautical Co. San Diego, Calif.	P	-	1,780	-	J-47 Comp.	
			PROPELLERS			
Aeroproducts Operations Allison Div. GMC Dayton, Ohio	P	-	6,572	-	C-119 Prop.	
Aeroproducts Operations Allison Div. GMC Indianapolis, Ind.	P	-	77	-	C-8 Prop.	
Curtiss-Wright Corp. Caldwell, N. J.	P	-	110	-	Prop. Blades	

TABLE 149 — USAF PRODUCTION EXPANSION PROJECTS — FY 1953 (CONTINUED)

(In thousands of dollars.)

SPECIAL FACILITY CONTRACTOR	CODE	TOTAL PROGRAMMED FUNDS	CUMULATIVE OBLIGATIONS	UNOBLIGATED REMAINDER OF PROG. FUNDS	MILITARY PRODUCT	REMARKS
	MISSILES					
Hughes Aircraft Co. Tucson, Ariz.	C	25,726	22,576	3,150	Missiles	
Bell Aircraft Corp Niagara Falls, N. Y.	P	3,663	3,663	-	Rascal	
Bell Aircraft Corp. Buffalo, N. Y.	C	1,471	1,471	-	-	
Hughes Aircraft Co. Culver City, Calif.	P	1,411	-	-	Falcon	
North America Aviation Co. Downey, Calif.	C	12,392	1,423	10,969	Navaho	
Northrop Aircraft, Inc. Hawthorne, Calif.	C-P	-	2,376	-	Snark	
Northrop Aircraft, Inc. Hawthorne, Calif.	C-P	1,500	1,500	-	-	
Northrop Aircraft Inc. Hawthorne, Calif.	C-P	-	3,000	-	Guidance Sys	
Martin, Glenn L. Baltimore, Md.	C-P	3,636	3,636	-	Matador	

Notes: C - P - Portions are government owned contractor operated, and portions are privately owned.

C - Government owned, contractor operated.

P - Privately owned.

TABLE 150 — STATUS OF USAF RESEARCH AND DEVELOPMENT FUNDS — FISCAL YEARS 1950 THROUGH 1953 AS OF 30 JUNE 1953

(Excludes reimbursements. In millions of dollars. Figures in parentheses indicate minus amounts.)

FISCAL YEAR	APPROPRIATION	ADJUSTMENTS	OBLIGATIONS	EXPENDITURES	UNLIQUIDATED OBLIGATIONS
Appropriation - Total. . .	$1480.6	$88.8	$1483.7	$1046.5	$437.2
1950.	a/b/ 233.0	(17.6)	213.7	206.4	7.3
1951.	a/c/d/ 297.6	72.3	365.4	325.3	40.1
1952.	d/ 425.0	26.1	430.3	321.8	108.5
1953.	d/ 525.0	8.0	474.3	193.0	281.3

Note: Fiscal Years 1948 and 1949 are not reported, inasmuch as the Research and Development Programs for these years were included in the Annual Appropriation "Department of the Air Force, 1948" and "General Expenses, 1949" both of which appropriations lapsed for obligation and expenditure purposes as of 30 June 1952, and were not available to the Air Force during Fiscal Year 1953.

a/ Reflects $22.6 million which was appropriated during FY 1950 but was held in reserve and applied to the FY 1951 Program.

b/ Reflects transfer of $5.0 million from "Aircraft and Related Procurement, Air Force" for research portion of Joint Long Range Proving Ground, authorized by PL 358-81st Congress.

c/ Reflects transfer of $.7 million to "Signal Service of the Army" for "Armed Forces Security Service".

d/ Includes transfers from "Emergency Fund, Office, Secretary of Defense" as follows:

Total	84.5
1951	50.4
1952	26.1
1953	8.0

Source: Financial Management Division, Directorate of Budget, DCS/C.

TABLE 151 — DEPARTMENT OF THE AIR FORCE RESEARCH AND DEVELOPMENT APPROPRIATION CUMULATIVE OBLIGATIONS BY COMMAND-AS OF 30 JUNE 1953

COMMAND	PROGRAM YEAR - 1950								
	TOTAL ALL PROGRAMS	PROJECT 601 FIRST DESTINATION TRANS	PROJECT 610 RESEARCH	PROJECT 620 MAJOR WEAPONS COMPONENTS DEV	PROJECT 640 WEAPONS SYS DEVELOPMENT	PROJECT 650 OPERATIONAL ENGINEERING	PROJECT 660 HUMAN FACTORS DEVELOPMENT	PROJECT 670 SPECIAL PROJECTS	PROJECT 680 MANAGEMENT & OPERATIONS
U. S. AIR FORCE - TOTAL a/	$213,794,073	$85,000	$25,487,707	$54,667,809	$80,732,319	$ 6,850,049	$2,160,360	$8,009,075	$35,801,754
Continental U. S. - Total	$213,674,485	$85,000	$25,487,707	$54,598,252	$80,732,319	$ 6,850,049	$2,159,897	$7,979,248	$35,782,013
Overseas - Total	$ 119,588	$ -	$ -	$ 69,557	$ -	$ -	$ 463	$ 29,827	$ 19,741
Headquarters, USAF	8,318,304	-	679,807	300,000	-	6,550,000	25,000	761,461	2,036
Air Research and Development Command	45,052,881	-	11,381,592	27,610,122	-	64,766	85,469	4,584,828	1,326,104
Air Materiel Command	154,213,328	85,000	12,838,674	26,688,130	80,635,405	149,152	44,519	999,204	32,773,244
Air Training Command	1,158,098	-	352,499	-	-	-	422,432	-	383,167
Air University	2,137,259	-	143,000	-	-	-	1,335,981	-	658,278
Alaskan Air Command	110,424	-	-	69,557	-	-	463	20,663	19,741
Air Proving Ground Command	96,914	-	-	-	96,914	-	-	-	-
Air Force Special Weapons Center	97,701	-	-	-	-	86,131	-	-	11,570
Arnold Air Development Center	91,362	-	-	-	-	-	-	-	91,362
Military Air Transport Service	133,585	-	-	-	-	-	-	133,585	-
Air Force Missile Test Center	1,639,864	-	-	-	-	-	-	1,464,928	174,936
Far East Air Force	9,164	-	-	-	-	-	-	9,164	-
Headquarters Command USAF	735,189	-	92,135	-	-	-	246,496	35,242	361,316

COMMAND	PROGRAM YEAR - 1951							
	TOTAL ALL PROGRAMS	PROJECT 601 FIRST DESTINATION TRANS	PROJECT 610 RESEARCH	PROJECT 620 MAJOR WEAPONS COMPONENTS DEV	PROJECT 640 WEAPONS SYS DEVELOPMENT	PROJECT 660 HUMAN FACTORS DEVELOPMENT	PROJECT 680 SPECIAL PROJECTS	PROJECT 690 LABORATORY OPERATIONS
U. S. Air Force - Total b/	$365,541,627	$153,883	$51,904,262	$86,291,377	$164,640,901	$4,614,322	$14,447,701	$43,489,181
Continental U. S. - Total	$365,403,464	$153,883	$51,904,262	$86,291,377	$164,640,901	$4,510,396	$14,447,701	$43,454,944
Overseas - Total	$ 138,163	$ -	$ -	$ -	$ -	$ 103,926	$ -	$ 34,237
Headquarters, USAF	6,284,394	-	922,414	400,000	-	69,971	4,892,009	-
Air Research and Development Command	294,361,829	-	44,027,074	81,815,502	148,920,689	264,861	2,404,784	16,928,919
Air Materiel Command	48,623,415	153,883	6,435,957	4,075,875	15,625,292	32,362	309,960	21,990,086
Secretary of Air Staff	1,243,480	-	176,429	-	-	425,372	-	641,679
Air Training Command	1,669,708	-	227,388	-	-	729,866	-	712,454
Air University	3,945,915	-	115,000	-	-	2,987,964	-	842,951
Alaskan Air Command	138,163	-	-	-	-	103,926	-	34,237
Air Proving Ground Command	221,191	-	-	-	94,920	-	-	126,271
Air Force Special Weapons Center	190,667	-	-	-	-	-	-	190,667
Arnold Air Development Center	781,871	-	-	-	-	-	-	781,871
Military Air Transport Service	40,389	-	-	-	-	-	40,389	-
Air Force Missile Test Center	8,040,605	-	-	-	-	-	6,800,559	1,240,046

TABLE 151 — DEPARTMENT OF THE AIR FORCE RESEARCH AND DEVELOPMENT APPROPRIATION CUMULATIVE OBLIGATIONS BY COMMAND AS OF 30 JUNE 1953 — CONTINUED

COMMAND	PROGRAM YEAR - 1952									
	TOTAL ALL PROGRAMS	PROJECT 610 AIRCRAFT	PROJECT 620 GUIDED MISSILES	PROJECT 630 PROPULSION	PROJECT 640 ELECTRONICS	PROJECT 650 ARMAMENT	PROJECT 660 EQUIPMENT	PROJECT 670 SCIENCE	PROJECT 680 SPECIAL PROJECTS	PROJECT 690 LABORATORY OPERATIONS
U. S. Air Force - Total c/	$430,677,174	$55,230,841	$103,235,377	$51,834,773	$42,750,306	$24,885,914	$27,278,637	$50,780,411	$16,574,484	$58,106,431
Continental U. S. - Total	$430,395,968	$55,230,841	$103,235,377	$51,834,773	$42,750,306	$24,885,914	$27,278,637	$50,556,159	$16,574,484	$58,049,477
Overseas - Total	$ 281,206	$ -	$ -	$ -	$ -	$ -	$ -	$ 224,252	$ -	$ 56,954
Headquarters, USAF	3,512,956	-	-	-	-	-	350,000	809,286	2,353,670	-
Air Research and Development Command	413,325,458	55,210,841	103,205,377	51,814,773	42,730,306	24,872,914	26,691,341	42,476,773	11,486,765	54,836,368
Air Materiel Command	128,000	20,000	30,000	20,000	20,000	13,000	15,000	5,000	5,000	-
Secretary of Air Staff	4,470,328	-	-	-	-	-	112,403	1,012,158	2,729,049	616,718
Air Training Command	2,792,795	-	-	-	-	-	-	1,691,048	-	1,101,747
Air University	5,689,216	-	-	-	-	-	109,893	4,561,894	-	1,017,429
Alaskan Air Command	281,206	-	-	-	-	-	-	224,252	-	56,954
Air Proving Ground Command	309,389	-	-	-	-	-	-	-	-	309,389
Air Force Special Weapons Center	167,826	-	-	-	-	-	-	-	-	167,826

COMMAND	PROGRAM YEAR - 1953									
	TOTAL ALL PROGRAMS	PROJECT 610 AIRCRAFT	PROJECT 620 GUIDED MISSILES	PROJECT 630 PROPULSION	PROJECT 640 ELECTRONICS	PROJECT 650 ARMAMENT	PROJECT 660 EQUIPMENT	PROJECT 670 SCIENCE	PROJECT 680 SPECIAL PROJECTS	PROJECT 690 LABORATORY OPERATIONS
U. S. Air Force - Total d/	$474,284,650	$38,974,964	$126,568,698	$60,785,586	$74,278,903	$24,446,485	$21,451,881	$46,128,725	$14,798,406	$66,851,002
Continental U. S. - Total	$473,921,822	$38,974,964	$126,568,698	$60,785,586	$74,278,903	$24,446,485	$21,451,881	$45,828,836	$14,798,406	$66,788,063
Overseas - Total	$ 362,828	$ -	$ -	$ -	$ -	$ -	$ -	$ 299,889	$ -	$ 62,939
Headquarters, USAF	5,000,000	-	-	-	5,000,000	-	-	-	-	-
Air Research and Development Command	458,771,668	38,959,964	126,559,698	60,710,586	69,268,903	24,426,485	20,992,053	40,491,188	13,088,682	64,274,109
Air Materiel Command	149,000	15,000	9,000	75,000	10,000	20,000	15,000	5,000	-	-
Secretary of Air Staff	3,594,355	-	-	-	-	-	444,828	1,015,811	1,709,724	423,992
Air Training Command	1,926,289	-	-	-	-	-	-	966,582	-	959,707
Air University	4,480,510	-	-	-	-	-	-	3,350,255	-	1,130,255
Alaskan Air Command	362,828	-	-	-	-	-	-	299,889	-	62,939

a/ There were no reimbursement collections during Fiscal Year 1953 for Fiscal Year 1950 Programs.
b/ Includes Total Reimbursement Collections of $137,433.
c/ Includes Total Reimbursement Collections of $342,571.
d/ Includes Total Reimbursement Collections of $37,761.

Source: Financial Management Division, Directorate of Budget, DCS/C.

Fiscal

Part XI

Fiscal

FISCAL

The Fiscal area covers the major portion of tables relating to financial matters. Subjects covered are: Budget, Procurement, Bonds.

BUDGET

DEFINITIONS

The Budget Section of this area reflects the funding operations of the various Air Force Appropriations and/or funds with the respective major programs for the fiscal years indicated in the title of each table. Some of the related Budget tables are to be found in other areas of the publication such as reports on Air National Guard, Reserve Forces, Mutual Defense Assistance Program, and Research and Development.

The report on Reserve Officer Training Corps does not appear as a separate table in this publication but is combined with the Reserve table inasmuch as the ROTC and AF Reserve Programs were merged in FY 1951 under the Reserve Personnel Requirements Appropriation in so far as pay is concerned while the Reserve procurement was abolished in other Air Force appropriations.

ANNUAL BUDGET AUTHORIZATION

The annual amount authorized for the purpose of executing an approved annual financial plan and which it is expected will be allocated to a Command or allotted to an installation during the fiscal year for the project covered by the authorization. The amount of the annual budget authorization is not available for obligation until the funds are allotted.

APPROPRIATION ACCOUNT

An account established to make amounts available for obligation and expenditure from the Treasury. (AFM 172-1).

APPROPRIATIONS OR CASH APPROPRIATIONS

An authorization by an act of Congress to make payments out of the Treasury for specified purposes within a prescribed amount. (AFM 172-1).

APPROPRIATION REIMBURSEMENT

A collection, other than an expenditure refund, for commodities work, or service furnished, or to be furnished, to an individual, firm, corporation, or federal agency, or for the benefit of other appropriations of the Department of the Air Force, which collection lawfully may be covered into the Treasury of the United States as repayment to an appropriation. (AFM 172-1).

BUDGET PROGRAM

The classifications of contemplated or actual obligations and expenditures by related projects within a major program; e.g. Aircraft and Related Material, Electronics Equipment, etc. (AFM 172-1).

CONTRACT AUTHORIZATION

Statutory authorization under which contracts or other obligations may be entered into prior to appropriations for the payment of such obligations. (AFM 172-1).

EXPENDITURES

The amount of vouchers, or other documents (less refunds received) which have been entered in fiscal accounts as final charges against an appropriation or fund. (AFM 172-1).

FUND

A sum of money or other resources authorized by law to be set aside and to be used or expended only for authorized purposes. (AFM 172-1).

MAJOR PROGRAM

The broadest divisions or classifications of contemplated or actual obligations and expenditures according to function or activity; e.g. Procurement, Construction, Maintenance, Administration, etc. (AFM 172-1).

OBLIGATION

The amount of an order placed, a contract awarded, a service received, or any other transaction which legally reserve an appropriation or fund during a given period of time. (AFM 172-1).

OBLIGATIONS INCURRED

Represent the total amount of obligations which have been established against an appropriation or fund during a given period of time. (AFM 172-1).

PROJECT

The classification of actual or contemplated obligations and expenditures in terms of the specific function or activity within the related budget program. (AFM 172-1).

REAL PROPERTY

Representing the fixed capital assets of the Air Force, consists of lands and interests therein, such as ownership, leases, permits, easements, licenses, or rights-of-way; ground and structural facilities; utility systems (except those communications systems and installed technical equipment which are not the responsibility of the air installation officer); and permanently attached or installed appurtenances thereto other than "P" property. ("P" property is that nonexpendable property which is permanently attached to or integrated into real property in such a manner that it cannot be removed without causing substantial physical damage or changing the designed standard and only as listed in the attachment. See paragraph 7, AFR 93-1. "P" property will be recorded in the real property accountable record.) Real property includes, but is not limited to, runways, taxiways, aprons, roads, walks, railroads, towers, bridges, piers, docks, drainage systems, utility systems (lighting, heating, water, gas, power, sewage disposal, liquid fuel distribution, and the like), storage facilities, structural or training aids and recreational facilities, housing facilities, hospital, operational, technical, and other buildings and structures.

RESERVE
That portion of an appropriation (or contract authorization) held or set aside for further operations, contingencies, or other purposes, and in respect of which authorization to incur obligations has been withheld. (AFM 172-1).

UNLIQUIDATED OBLIGATION
Is that portion of an obligation for which expenditure is yet to be made. (AFM 172-1).

UNOBLIGATED BALANCE
Is that portion of a budgetary authorization which has not been obligated. The term refers to appropriations, apportionments, allocations, and allotments. (AFM 172-1).

MISCELLANEOUS

DEFINITIONS

CONTRACTS
(Ref: ASPrl 1-201.6 Sec 15 Appendix A). All types of agreements and orders for the procurement of supplies or services. It includes, by way of description and without limitation, awards and preliminary notices of award; contracts of a fixed-price, cost, cost plus a fixed fee, or incentive type; contracts providing for the issuance of job orders, task orders or task letters thereunder; letter contracts, letters of intent, and purchase orders. It also includes amendments, modifications, and supplemental agreements with respect to any of the foregoing.

PROCUREMENT
The term "procurement" includes by way of description and without limitation, purchasing, renting, leasing, or otherwise obtaining supplies or services.

TABLE 152 — DEPARTMENT OF THE AIR FORCE USAF APPROPRIATIONS AND NEW OBLIGATING AUTHORITY FOR FY 1953

(In thousands of dollars. Figures in parentheses indicate minus amounts.)

APPROPRIATION TITLES AND CITATION OF PUBLIC LAWS	OBLIGATING AUTHORITY ENACTED			CASH TRANSFERS	NET OBLIGATING AUTHORITY
	TOTAL	CASH APPROPRIATED	CONTRACT AUTHOR-IZATIONS		
All Appropriations - Total a/ b/	$ 17,787,983	$ 17,787,983	$ -	$ (242,142)	$ 17,545,841
Aircraft and Related Procurement (Continuing) a/ - Total	8,200,000	8,200,000	-	(142)	8,199,858
PL 488, 82nd Congress	8,200,000	8,200,000	-	-	8,200,000
Net Transfers In or (Out)	-	-	-	c/(142)	(142)
Major Procurement Other Than Aircraft (Continuing) - Total	900,000	900,000	-	-	900,000
PL 488, 82nd Congress	900,000	900,000	-	-	900,000
Acquisition and Construction of Real Property (Continuing) - Total	1,200,000	1,200,000	-	-	1,200,000
PL 547, 82nd Congress	1,200,000	1,200,000	-	-	1,200,000
Maintenance and Operations, 1953 - Total	3,600,000	3,600,000	-	(398,852)	3,201,148
PL 488, 82nd Congress	3,600,000	3,600,000	-	-	3,600,000
PL 11, 83rd Congress	-	-	-	d/(250,000)	(250,000)
Net Transfers In or (Out)	-	-	-	d/(148,852)	(148,852)
Military Personnel Requirements, 1953 - Total	3,200,000	3,200,000	-	148,852	3,348,852
PL 488, 82nd Congress	3,200,000	3,200,000	-	-	3,200,000
Net Transfers In or (Out)	-	-	-	e/ 148,852	148,852
Research and Development (Continuing) - Total	525,000	525,000	-	8,000	533,000
PL 488, 82nd Congress	525,000	525,000	-	-	525,000
Net Transfers In or (Out)	-	-	-	f/ 8,000	8,000
Reserve Personnel Requirements, 1953 and 1954 - Total	26,196	26,196	-	-	26,196
PL 488, 82nd Congress	g/26,196	g/26,196	-	-	26,196
Air National Guard, 1953 - Total	106,000	106,000	-	-	106,000
PL 488, 82nd Congress	106,000	106,000	-	-	106,000
Contingencies, 1953 - Total	30,787	30,787	-	-	30,787
PL 488, 82nd Congress	30,787	30,787	-	-	30,787

a/ Excludes $ 2,800,000 thousand appropriated in FY 1953 to finance the deferred portion of the FY 1952 program.

b/ Excludes $ 1,685,000 thousand in "Aircraft and Related Procurement" Appropriation, and $ 45,335 thousand in "Acquisition and Construction of Real Property" Appropriation, of cash appropriated to finance prior years contract authorizations.

c/ Transfer authorized by PL 784, 81st Congress: To General Services Administration, $142 thousand.

d/ Transfers as authorized by PL 11, 83rd Congress:
To Military Requirements, Army $ 250,000 thousand
To Military Personnel Requirements, Air Force $ 73,852 thousand
Transfers as authorized by PL 604, 82nd Congress:
To Military Personnel Requirements, Air Force $ 75,000 thousand
$ 398,852 thousand

e/ Transfers from Maintenance and Operations, Air Force, $ 148,852 thousand. (See footnote d/ above.)

f/ Transfers authorized by PL 488, 82nd Congress: From Emergency Fund, Office of the Secretary of Defense $ 8,000 thousand.

g/ Includes amounts in reserve for application to the FY 1954 program.

Source: Financial Management Division, Directorate of Budget, DCS/C.

TABLE 153 — OBLIGATIONS AND EXPENDITURES DURING FY 1953

(In thousands of dollars. Figures

Line No	PROGRAM NUMBER	APPROPRIATION AND PROGRAM TITLE	NET OBLIGATING AUTHORITY
1		All Appropriations - Total a/ b/	$ 17,828,952
2		Aircraft and Related Procurement, (Continuing) - Total a/ b/	$ 8,206,318
3	110	Aircraft, Complete	4,839,998
4	120	Initial Aircraft Component Spares and Spare Parts	1.587.739
5	130	Related Aircraft Procurement	780,093
6	140	Modification of In-Service Aircraft and Component Equipment	224,500
7	150	Guided Missiles - Complete	480,200
8	180	Industrial Mobilization	6,923
9	190	Procurement and Production-Administration	69,850
10		Undistributed	217,015
11		Major Procurement Other Than Aircraft (Continuing) - Total a/	$ 1,182,470
12	210	Weapons and Ammunition	448,846
13	220	Ground Powered and Marine Equipment	72,827
14	230	Electronics and Communications Equipment	405,551
15	250	Training Equipment	59,562
16	270	Other Major Equipment	138,847
17	299	Classified Project	38,313
18		Undistributed	18,524
19		Acquisition and Construction of Real Property (Continuing) - Total	$ 1,200,000
20		Maintenance and Operations - Total	$ 3,201,148
21	410	Operation of Aircraft	950,128
22	420	Organization, Base and Maintenance Equipment and Supplies	243,715
23	430	Logistical Support	1,022,176
24	440	Training Support	207,450
25	450	Operational Support	488,286
26	460	Research and Test Support	72,771
27	470	Medical Support	85,671
28	480	Service Wide Support	130,951
29		Military Personnel Requirements - Total	$ 3,348,852
30	510	Pay and Allowances Air Force	2,872,000
31	530	Movements Permanent Change of Station	162,700
32	550	Subsistence	3[illegible]4,200
33	560	Civilian Clothing	455
34	590	Other Military Personnel Requirements	9,497
35		Research and Development (Continuing) - Total	$ 533,000
36	610	Aircraft	42,857
37	620	Guided Missiles	129,544
38	630	Propulsion	74,940
39	640	Electronics	81,649
40	650	Armament	40,283
41	660	Equipment	28,158
42	670	Sciences	49,790
43	680	Special Projects	16,248
44	690	Laboratory Operations	67,943
45		Undistributed	1,588
46		Reserve Personnel Requirements - (Multiple Year) - Total a/	$ 20,377
47	520	Pay and Allowances, Air Force Reserve and Air Force ROTC	14,470
48	540	Travel, Air Force Reserve and Air Force ROTC - Training Duty	781
49	550	Subsistence	82
50	560	Individual Clothing	5,044
51		Air National Guard - Total	$ 106,000
52		Contingencies - Total	$ 30,787

a/ Includes funds appropriated in prior years which were applied to Fiscal Year 1953 Programs.
b/ Excludes $2,800,000 thousand appropriated in Fiscal Year 1953 to finance the deferred portion of the Fiscal Year 1952 Program.
c/ Less than $500.

Source: Financial Management Division, Directorate of Budget, DCS/C.

AGAINST NET OBLIGATING AUTHORITY FOR THE FY 1953 PROGRAM

in parentheses indicate minus amounts.)

OBLIGATIONS							
TOTAL NET OBLIGATIONS	REIMBURSEMENTS COLLECTED	TOTAL GROSS OBLIGATIONS	FIRST QUARTER	SECOND QUARTER	THIRD QUARTER	FOURTH QUARTER	Line No.
$ 14,624,824	$ 312,913	$ 14,937,737	$ 5,261,818	$ 3,641,046	$ 3,366,082	$ 2,668,791	1
$ 6,374,929	$ 13,233	$ 6,388,162	$ 3,223,740	$ 1,775,978	$ 927,539	$ 460,905	2
4,242,255	11,988	4,254,243	2,704,428	876,764	440,623	232,428	3
1,271,314	1,006	1,272,320	427,318	539,155	302,395	3,452	4
435,957	-	435,957	60,515	185,672	92,586	97,184	5
128,206	-	128,206	2,065	25,886	41,610	58,645	6
221,112	-	221,112	11,386	129,406	30,763	49,557	7
6,306	154	6,460	1,104	1,085	2,065	2,206	8
69,779	85	69,864	16,924	18,010	17,497	17,433	9
-	-	-	-	-	-	-	10
$ 800,372	$ 139,918	$ 940,290	$ 61,244	$ 160,231	$ 468,913	$ 249,902	11
331,798	132,875	464,673	54,666	64,909	283,816	61,282	12
20,426	3,940	24,366	-	12,904	(9,241)	20,703	13
321,338	1,838	323,176	50	50,850	150,498	121,778	14
41,467	76	41,543	6,114	13,712	18,218	3,499	15
48,393	1,189	49,582	414	1,177	5,867	42,124	16
36,950	-	36,950	-	16,679	19,755	516	17
-	-	-	-	-	-	-	18
$ 313,920	$ -	$ 313,920	$ -	$ 89,949	$ 126,474	$ 97,497	19
$ 3,177,650	$ 158,548	$ 3,336,198	$ 876,325	$ 655,286	$ 869,528	$ 935,059	20
939,708	82,727	1,022,435	312,910	138,773	290,413	280,339	21
241,911	22,239	264,150	23,882	13,739	77,457	149,072	22
1,019,564	9,992	1,029,556	283,474	244,781	249,344	251,957	23
206,635	18,691	225,326	63,118	63,952	47,778	50,478	24
482,275	10,998	493,273	116,745	118,504	127,877	130,147	25
72,593	917	73,510	18,672	17,170	19,192	18,476	26
85,849	12,938	98,787	24,213	25,355	25,147	24,072	27
129,115	46	129,161	33,311	33,012	32,320	30,518	28
$ 3,340,086	$ 909	$ 3,340,995	$ 948,172	$ 773,889	$ 846,758	$ 772,176	29
2,871,746	204	2,871,950	725,542	727,122	705,990	713,296	30
158,580	548	159,128	36,181	41,336	38,036	43,575	31
300,663	1	300,664	184,848	3,306	100,083	12,427	32
377	2	379	94	90	98	97	33
8,720	154	8,874	1,507	2,035	2,551	2,781	34
$ 474,248	$ 37	$ 474,285	$ 111,307	$ 161,177	$ 96,649	$ 105,152	35
38,975	-	38,975	1,851	9,422	10,437	17,265	36
126,569	-	126,569	54,180	46,356	10,550	15,483	37
60,786	-	60,786	1,183	32,891	15,354	11,358	38
74,279	c/	74,279	16,046	15,060	16,959	26,214	39
24,446	-	24,446	7,129	18,276	5,091	(6,050)	40
21,452	-	21,452	2,055	4,828	7,500	7,069	41
46,129	-	46,129	10,131	12,026	11,638	12,334	42
14,798	c/	14,798	2,417	3,963	1,985	6,433	43
66,814	37	66,851	16,315	18,355	17,135	15,046	44
-	-	-	-	-	-	-	45
$ 20,174	$ 1	$ 20,175	$ 5,532	$ 4,368	$ 5,086	$ 5,189	46
14,305	-	14,305	2,351	3,496	4,265	4,193	47
762	-	762	138	34	117	473	48
82	-	82	32	28	29	(7)	49
5,025	1	5,026	3,011	810	675	530	50
$ 93,847	$ 266	$ 94,113	$ 10,202	$ 19,653	$ 22,939	$ 41,319	51
$ 29,598	$ 1	$ 29,599	$ 25,296	$ 515	$ 2,196	$ 1,592	52

TABLE 153 — OBLIGATIONS AND EXPENDITURES DURING FY 1953 AGAINST NET OBLIGATING AUTHORITY FOR THE FY 1953 PROGRAM — CONTINUED

(In thousands of dollars. Figures in parentheses indicate minus amounts.)

APPROPRIATION AND PROGRAM TITLE	EXPENDITURES						
	TOTAL NET EXPENDI-TURES	REIMBURSE-MENTS COLLECTED	TOTAL GROSS EXPENDI-TURES	FIRST QUARTER	SECOND QUARTER	THIRD QUARTER	FOURTH QUARTER
All Appropriations - Total a/b/	$5,781,698	$312,913	$6,094,611	$1,220,798	$1,331,409	$1,595,934	$1,946,470
Acft & Related Proc, (Continuing) - Total a/b/	$ 341,495	$ 13,233	$ 354,728	$ 105,189	$ 20,274	$ 46,142	$ 183,123
Aircraft, Complete	235,070	11,988	247,058	92,085	1,418	18,548	135,007
Initial Acft Comp Spares and Spare Parts	10,148	1,006	11,154	1	712	4,340	6,101
Related Aircraft Procurement	11,949	-	11,949	c/	139	2,614	9,196
Modification of In-Service Acft & Comp Equipment	4,479	-	4,479	c/	c/	872	3,607
Guided Missiles - Complete	10,580	-	10,580	29	(29)	1,123	9,457
Industrial Mobilization	3,263	154	3,417	213	566	1,073	1,565
Proc & Production Admin	66,006	85	66,091	12,861	17,468	17,572	18,190
Undistributed	-	-	-	-	-	-	-
Major Proc Other Than Acft (Continuing) - Total a/	$ (87,913)	$139,918	$ 52,005	$ 6	$ 14,255	$ 12,386	$ 25,358
Weapons and Ammunition	(111,461)	132,875	21,414	c/	107	986	20,321
Ground Powered & Marine Equip	(3,520)	3,940	420	1	2	61	356
Electronics & Comm Equip	2,267	1,838	4,105	4	30	914	3,157
Training Equipment	294	76	370	-	-	350	20
Other Major Equipment	915	1,189	2,104	1	115	484	1,504
Classified Project	23,592	-	23,592	-	14,001	9,591	-
Undistributed	-	-	-	-	-	-	-
Acquisition & Construction of Real Property (Continuing) - Total	$ 55,283	$ -	$ 55,283	$ -	$ -	$ 66,570	$ (11,287)
Maint and Oprs - Total	$1,991,960	$158,548	$2,150,508	$ 300,396	$ 527,849	$ 583,882	$ 738,381
Operation of Aircraft	347,581	82,727	430,308	51,102	102,702	111,975	164,529
Org, Base and Maint Equip and Supplies	52,322	22,239	74,561	9,540	9,298	15,537	40,186
Logistical Support	827,532	9,992	837,524	124,110	215,167	228,735	269,512
Training Support	171,468	18,691	190,159	30,022	47,624	53,470	59,043
Operational Support	365,830	10,998	376,828	45,829	94,925	106,526	129,548
Research and Test Support	63,170	917	64,087	12,131	16,706	17,159	18,091
Medical Support	50,598	12,938	63,536	7,175	14,174	18,290	23,897
Service Wide Support	113,459	46	113,505	20,487	27,253	32,190	33,575
Military Pers Rqmts - Total	$3,194,501	$ 909	$3,195,410	$ 772,999	$ 719,403	$ 803,355	$ 899,653
Pay and Allowances Air Force	2,765,334	204	2,765,538	572,653	676,591	666,929	849,365
Movements - PCS	125,971	548	126,519	18,473	37,286	35,511	35,249
Subsistence	296,645	1	296,646	180,857	3,804	98,960	13,025
Civilian Clothing	256	2	258	32	59	84	83
Other Military Pers Rqmts	6,295	154	6,449	984	1,663	1,871	1,931
Research & Development (Continuing) - Total	$ 193,035	$ 37	$ 193,072	$ 10,998	$ 33,689	$ 63,977	$ 84,408
Aircraft	10,170	-	10,170	555	(22)	1,627	8,010
Guided Missiles	82,589	-	82,589	651	14,510	30,681	36,747
Propulsion	7,104	-	7,104	76	279	2,330	4,419
Electronics	16,966	c/	16,966	21	247	8,542	8,156
Armament	9,136	-	9,136	53	2,536	1,925	4,622
Equipment	2,460	-	2,460	105	265	1,042	1,048
Sciences	11,021	-	11,021	706	2,344	3,289	4,682
Special Projects	2,093	c/	2,093	164	329	541	1,059
Laboratory Operations	51,496	37	51,533	8,667	13,201	14,000	15,665
Undistributed	-	-	-	-	-	-	-
Res Pers Rqmts - (Multiple Year) - Total a/	$ 18,358	$ 1	$ 18,359	$ 1,402	$ 5,840	$ 5,039	$ 6,078
Pay & Allowances, Air Force Reserve & Air Force ROTC	12,787	-	12,787	1,280	3,353	3,804	4,350
Travel, AF Reserve & AF ROTC - Training Duty	753	-	753	129	38	34	552
Subsistence	20	-	20	-	c/	14	6
Individual Clothing	4,798	1	4,799	(7)	2,449	1,187	1,170
Air National Guard - Total	$ 48,366	$ 266	$ 48,632	$ 5,192	$ 9,496	$ 14,043	$ 19,901
Contingencies - Total	$ 26,613	$ 1	$ 26,614	$ 24,616	$ 603	$ 540	$ 855

TABLE 154 - EXPENDITURES AGAINST FISCAL YEAR 1952 PROGRAMS DURING FISCAL YEAR 1953

(In thousands of dollars. Figures in parentheses indicate minus amounts.)

PROGRAM NUMBER	APPROPRIATION AND PROGRAM TITLE	EXPENDITURES						
		TOTAL NET EXPENDITURES	REIMBURSEMENTS COLLECTED	TOTAL GROSS EXPENDITURES	FIRST QUARTER	SECOND QUARTER	THIRD QUARTER	FOURTH QUARTER
	Appropriations - Total a/	$4,619,069	$34,062	$4,653,131	$1,130,032	$1,038,009	$1,082,623	$1,402,467
	Aircraft and Related Procurement - Total a/	$2,026,806	$23,099	$2,049,905	$204,917	$407,276	$532,246	$905,466
110	Aircraft Complete	1,426,455	23,359	1,449,814	194,269	333,784	359,860	561,901
120	Initial Aircraft Component Spares & Spare Parts	415,484	(286)	415,198	9,783	33,295	122,385	249,735
130	Related Aircraft Procurement	92,331	c/	92,331	(12,713)	17,274	31,084	56,686
140	Major Modification/Modernization of Aircraft	43,418	-	43,418	7,269	11,101	8,269	16,779
150	Guided Missiles	43,433	-	43,433	3,697	11,104	10,101	18,531
180	Industrial Mobilization	1,663	c/	1,663	(1,175)	571	448	1,819
190	Procurement and Production Administration	4,022	26	4,048	3,787	147	99	15
	Major Procurement Other Than Aircraft - Total	$160,502	-	$160,502	$33,125	$28,331	$34,437	$64,609
210	Weapons and Ammunition	83,321	-	83,321	16,940	14,729	17,777	33,875
220	Ground Powered and Marine Equipment	14,207	-	14,207	3,822	1,193	4,401	4,791
230	Electronics and Communications Equipment	22,612	-	22,612	5,437	4,230	3,510	9,435
250	Training Equipment	15,945	-	15,945	2,881	4,415	2,364	6,285
270	Other Major Equipment	23,491	-	23,491	3,927	3,603	5,918	10,043
299	Classified Project	926	-	926	118	161	467	180
	Acquisition and Construction of Real Property - Total	b/ $944,075	$552	$944,627	$276,908	$255,442	$238,555	$173,722
	Maintenance and Operations - Total	$1,061,727	$8,359	$1,070,086	$414,643	$239,979	$208,176	$207,288
410	Operation of Aircraft	430,670	1,046	431,716	120,608	93,341	102,503	115,264
420	Organization, Base and Maintenance Supplies and Equipment	244,548	1,401	245,949	65,602	58,863	62,693	58,791
430	Logistical Support	160,026	1,746	161,772	101,713	32,480	13,788	13,791
440	Training Support	45,521	1,066	46,587	26,279	12,434	4,538	3,336
450	Operational Support	103,049	2,088	105,137	65,959	22,871	9,874	6,433
460	Research and Test Support	6,318	150	6,468	5,075	990	302	101
470	Medical Support	57,555	844	58,399	19,608	16,167	13,734	8,890
480	Service-Wide Support	14,040	18	14,058	9,799	2,833	744	682
	Military Personnel Requirements - Total	$198,523	$1,383	$199,906	$139,982	$35,854	$16,598	$7,472
510	Pay and Allowances, Air Force	166,076	351	166,427	116,985	29,305	14,451	5,686
530	Movements, Permanent Change of Station	25,728	879	26,607	18,967	4,703	1,742	1,195
550	Subsistence	2,998	10	3,008	2,128	342	62	476
560	Individual Clothing	88	(4)	84	71	10	2	1
590	Other Military Personnel Requirements	3,633	147	3,780	1,831	1,494	341	114

TABLE 154 — EXPENDITURES AGAINST FISCAL YEAR 1952 PROGRAMS DURING FISCAL YEAR 1953 — CONTINUED

(In thousands of dollars. Figures in parentheses indicate minus amounts.)

PROGRAM NUMBER	APPROPRIATION AND PROGRAM TITLE	EXPENDITURES						
		TOTAL NET EXPENDITURES	REIMBURSEMENTS COLLECTED	TOTAL GROSS EXPENDITURES	FIRST QUARTER	SECOND QUARTER	THIRD QUARTER	FOURTH QUARTER
	Research and Development - Total	$189,191	$301	$189,492	$50,803	$57,957	$44,010	$36,722
610	Aircraft	33,197	-	33,197	13,722	2,573	9,732	7,170
620	Guided Missiles	45,167	-	45,167	18,261	20,975	2,543	3,388
630	Propulsion	24,837	-	24,837	3,866	5,220	9,079	6,672
640	Electronics	24,388	225	24,613	4,146	10,327	5,580	4,560
650	Armament	15,162	-	15,162	3,495	3,472	5,061	3,134
660	Equipment	10,030	-	10,030	1,646	2,134	3,068	3,182
670	Sciences	23,399	-	23,399	4,705	4,993	6,495	7,206
680	Special Projects	4,195	-	4,195	1,039	896	1,246	1,014
690	Laboratory Operations	8,816	76	8,892	(77)	7,367	1,206	396
	Reserve Personnel Requirements - Total	$5,826	c/	$5,826	$2,302	$3,376	$304	$(156)
520	Pay and Allowances, Air Force Reserve and Air Force ROTC	2,747	-	2,747	1,665	309	(22)	795
540	Travel, Air Force Reserve & Air Force ROTC - Training Duty	504	-	504	470	26	26	(18)
550	Subsistence	297	-	297	-	-	297	-
560	Individual Clothing	2,278	c/	2,278	167	3,041	3	(933)
	Air National Guard - Total	$30,479	$367	$30,846	$6,536	$9,465	$7,784	$7,061
	Contingencies - Total	$1,940	$1	$1,941	$816	$329	$513	$283

a/ Includes expenditures against funds which were appropriated during FY 1951 but applied to finance the deferred portion of the FY 1952 Programs.

b/ Includes expenditures during FY 1953 from funds appropriated during FY 1950 and 1951.

c/ Less than $500.

Source: Financial Management Division, Directorate of Budget, DCS/C.

TABLE 155 — EXPENDITURES AGAINST FISCAL YEAR 1951 PROGRAMS DURING FISCAL YEAR 1953

(In thousands of dollars. Figures in parentheses indicate minus amounts.)

PROGRAM NUMBER	APPROPRIATION AND PROGRAM TITLE	EXPENDITURES						
		TOTAL NET EXPENDITURES	REIMBURSEMENTS COLLECTED	TOTAL GROSS EXPENDITURES	FIRST QUARTER	SECOND QUARTER	THIRD QUARTER	FOURTH QUARTER
	Appropriations - Total a/	$4,798,128	$29,310	$4,827,438	$1,155,927	$1,280,952	$1,204,884	$1,185,675
	Aircraft and Related Procurement (Continuing) - Total a/	$3,928,352	$28,973	$3,957,325	$910,267	$1,057,966	$996,971	$992,121
101	First Destination Transportation	37	-	37	13	63	(13)	(26)
110	Aircraft, Complete	1,984,186	28,935	2,013,121	484,342	534,282	576,140	418,357
120	Initial Aircraft Component Spares & Spare Parts	1,136,042	38	1,136,080	209,799	304,796	231,963	389,522
130	Related Aircraft Procurement	541,258	-	541,258	136,536	149,957	124,596	130,169
140	Major Modification/Modernization of Aircraft	81,666	-	81,666	28,372	18,046	18,276	16,972
150	Guided Missiles	51,722	-	51,722	13,527	16,662	14,179	7,354
180	Industrial Mobilization	15,343	c/	15,343	6,006	4,261	3,716	1,360
190	Procurement and Production Administration	115	-	115	57	60	5	(7)
230	Electronics and Communications Equipment	117,983	-	117,983	31,615	29,839	28,109	28,420
	Major Procurement Other Than Aircraft (Continuing) - Total a/	$549,444	-	$549,444	$ 138,001	$137,133	$149,530	$124,780
201	First Destination Transportation	880	-	880	696	169	11	4
210	Weapons and Ammunition	106,669	-	106,669	27,659	20,451	37,842	20,717
220	Ground Powered and Marine Equipment	229,913	-	229,913	63,973	67,373	53,123	45,444
230	Electronics and Communications Equipment	81,738	-	81,738	14,321	19,559	25,278	22,580
250	Training Equipment	36,674	-	36,674	8,182	6,693	9,473	12,326
270	Other Major Equipment	91,945	-	91,945	22,393	22,342	23,768	23,442
299	Classified Project	1,625	-	1,625	777	546	35	267
	Acquisition and Construction of Real Property (Continuing) - Total	b/	b/	b/	b/	b/	b/	b/
	Maintenance and Operations - Total	$239,100	$613	$239,713	$81,051	$66,878	$40,609	$51,175
401	First Destination Transportation	120	-	120	45	30	25	20
410	Operation of Aircraft	122,825	297	123,122	29,441	36,305	24,714	32,662
420	Organization, Base and Maintenance Supplies and Equipment	86,948	(121)	86,827	40,750	23,578	11,066	11,433
430	Logistical Support	10,394	353	10,747	4,120	3,888	1,250	1,489
440	Training Support	5,009	(18)	4,991	1,962	1,043	1,257	729
450	Operational Support	7,245	120	7,365	2,783	883	900	2,799
460	Research and Test Support	313	(17)	296	156	13	108	19
470	Medical Support	4,870	(1)	4,869	1,406	1,058	659	1,746
480	Service-Wide Support	1,376	c/	1,376	388	80	630	278
	Military Personnel Requirements - Total	$3,860	$14	$3,874	$956	$503	$448	$1,967
510	Pay and Allowances, Air Force	2,948	(5)	2,943	453	335	319	1,835
530	Movements, Permanent Change of Station	823	16	839	414	161	97	167
550	Subsistence	56	-	56	36	(2)	20	2
560	Individual Clothing	(1)	-	(1)	c/	(1)	c/	c/
590	Other Military Personnel Requirements	34	3	37	53	9	12	(37)

TABLE 155 — EXPENDITURES AGAINST FISCAL YEAR 1951 PROGRAM DURING FISCAL YEAR 1953 - CONTINUED

(In thousands of dollars. Figures in parentheses indicate minus amounts.)

PROGRAM NUMBER	APPROPRIATION AND PROGRAM TITLE	EXPENDITURES						
		TOTAL NET EXPENDITURES	REIMBURSEMENTS COLLECTED	TOTAL GROSS EXPENDITURES	FIRST QUARTER	SECOND QUARTER	THIRD QUARTER	FOURTH QUARTER
	Research and Development (Continuing) - Total	$65,777	$75	$65,852	$22,875	$16,070	$14,637	$12,270
601	First Destination Transportation	2	-	2	c/	(4)	c/	6
610	Research	10,757	-	10,757	22,049	(15,485)	2,139	2,054
620	Major Weapons Components Development	27,567	-	27,567	1	13,474	7,687	6,405
640	Weapons Systems Development	24,227	75	24,302	29	16,157	4,010	4,106
660	Human Factors Development	1,370	-	1,370	-	878	257	235
680	Special Projects	1,135	-	1,135	789	741	359	(754)
690	Laboratory Operations	719	-	719	7	309	185	218
	Reserve Personnel Requirements - Total	$235	$(1)	$234	$(77)	$192	$7	$112
520	Pay and Allowances, Reserve and ROTC	(56)	-	(56)	(67)	(106)	7	110
540	Travel, Reserve and ROTC	3	-	3	(2)	2	1	2
550	Training Duty	-	-	-	c/	-	c/	c/
560	Individual Clothing	288	(1)	287	(8)	296	(1)	c/
	Air National Guard - Total	$11,157	$(364)	$10,793	$2,724	$2,165	$2,663	$3,241
	Contingencies - Total	$203	-	$203	$130	$45	$19	$9

a/ Includes expenditures against funds which were appropriated during FY 1952 but applied to finance the deferred portion of the FY 1951 programs.

b/ Expenditures during FY 1953 out of funds appropriated for "Acquisition and Construction of Real Property" for FY 1951 are not maintained in Air Force accounting records on a basis which will provide information by year of appropriation. Amounts expended out of FY 1950-52 funds are included in amounts shown on Table 154, "Expenditures against Fiscal Year 1952 Programs During Fiscal Year 1953."

c/ Less than $500.

Source: Financial Management Division, Directorate of Budget, DCS/C.

TABLE 156 — EXPENDITURES AGAINST FY 1950 AND PRIOR YEARS PROGRAMS DURING FISCAL YEAR 1953

(In thousands of dollars. Figures in parentheses indicate minus amounts.)

PROJECT NUMBER	PROJECT TITLE	TOTAL NET EXPENDITURES DURING FY 1953	REIMBURSEMENTS COLLECTED DURING FY 1953	GROSS EXPENDITURES DURING FY 1953				
				TOTAL	FIRST QUARTER	SECOND QUARTER	THIRD QUARTER	FOURTH QUARTER
	All Appropriations - Total a/	$ 187,978	-	$ 187,978	$ 59,123	$ 54,815	$ 36,032	$ 38,008
	Aircraft and Related Procurement - Total	175,535	-	175,535	55,492	52,199	33,409	34,435
110	Aircraft and Related Material	148,204	-	148,204	48,082	44,553	25,571	29,998
170	Electronics Equipment	25,161	-	25,161	7,329	7,077	6,871	3,884
180	Guided Missiles and Special Material	2,618	-	2,618	946	682	601	389
190	Industrial Mobilization	2,009	-	2,009	601	618	351	439
151	Personal Services	(2,084)	-	(2,084)	(1,089)	(735)	-	(260)
152	Temporary Duty Travel	(400)	-	(400)	(400)	-	-	-
101&442	Transportation to First Destination	27	-	27	23	4	15	(15)
	Acquisition and Construction of Real Property - Total	b/	b/	b/	b/	b/	b/	b/
	Research and Development - Total	12,443	-	12,443	3,631	2,616	2,623	3,573
610	Research	3,689	-	3,689	2,672	(1,832)	501	2,348
620	Major Weapons Components Development	4,367	-	4,367	-	2,284	1,091	992
640	Weapons Systems Development	3,853	-	3,853	2	1,515	821	1,515
650	Operational Engineering	17	-	17	-	52	(101)	66
660	Human Factors Development	263	-	263	-	101	16	146
670	Special Projects	171	-	171	941	488	289	(1,547)
680	Management and Operations	83	-	83	16	8	6	53

a/ Other Air Force Appropriations for FY 1950 and prior years are not reported inasmuch as these funds lapsed for expenditure purposes on 30 June 1952 and were not available for expenditure during FY 1953.

b/ Expenditures during FY 1953 out of funds appropriated for "Acquisition and Construction of Real Property" during FY 1950 are not maintained in Air Force accounting records on a basis which will provide information by year of appropriation. Amounts expended out of FY 1950-52 funds are included in amounts shown on Table 154, "Expenditures against Fiscal Year 1952 Programs During Fiscal Year 1953."

Source: Financial Management Division, Directorate of Budget, DCS/C.

TABLE 157 — DEPARTMENT OF THE AIR FORCE STATUS OF UNLIQUIDATED OBLIGATIONS AT BEGINNING AND END OF FY 1949 SHOWING OBLIGATIONS AND EXPENDITURES DURING FY 1949

(Includes reimbursements. In thousands of dollars. Figures in parentheses indicate minus amounts.)

REVISED ORDER OF APPROP.	APPROPRIATION	FISCAL OR PROGRAM YEAR	UNLIQUIDATED OBLIGATIONS 1 JULY 1948	GROSS OBLIGATIONS DURING FY 1949	TOTAL	GROSS EXPENDITURES DURING FY 1949	UNLIQUIDATED OBLIGATIONS TRANSFERRED TO CERTIFIED CLAIMS	UNLIQUIDATED OBLIGATIONS CARRIED FORWARD INTO FY 1950
1	Aircraft and Related Procurement							
		1948	628,700	(1,850)	626,850	372,738	-	254,112
		1949	1,040,125	701,500	1,741,625	168,830	-	1,572,795
	Total		1,668,825	699,650	2,368,475	541,568	-	1,826,907
2	General Expenses, USAF							
	Total	1949	-	960,571	980,571	592,802	-	387,769
3	Salaries, Office, Chief of Staff, USAF							
		1948	a/ 26	-	a/ 26	a/ 26	-	-
		1949	-	6,501	6,501	6,195	-	306
	Total		26	6,501	6,527	6,221	-	306
4	Salaries, Office of the Secretary of the AF							
	Total	1949	-	825	825	779	-	46
5	Department of the Air Force							
	Total	1948	243,747	(5,888)	237,859	163,561	-	74,298
6	Air Corps, Army							
		1942-46	268,000	-	268,000	259,484	8,516	-
		1947	350,342	(3,701)	346,641	266,311	-	80,330
	Total		618,342	(3,701)	614,641	525,795	8,516	80,330
	Grand Total		2,530,940	1,677,958	4,208,898	1,830,726	8,516	2,369,656

a/ Not reported on USAFSD-48/49. Source: Financial Management Division, Directorate of Budget, DCS/C

TABLE 158 — DEPARTMENT OF THE AIR FORCE STATUS OF UNLIQUIDATED OBLIGATIONS AT BEGINNING AND END OF FY 1950 SHOWING OBLIGATIONS AND EXPENDITURES DURING FY 1950

(Includes reimbursements. In thousands of dollars. Figures in parentheses indicate minus amounts.)

REVISED ORDER OF APPROP.	APPROPRIATION	FISCAL OR PROGRAM YEAR	UNLIQUIDATED OBLIGATIONS 1 JULY 1949	GROSS OBLIGATIONS DURING FY 1950	TOTAL	GROSS EXPENDITURES DURING FY 1950	UNLIQUIDATED OBLIGATIONS TRANSFERRED TO CERTIFIED CLAIMS	UNLIQUIDATED OBLIGATIONS CARRIED FORWARD INTO FY 1951
1	Aircraft and Related Procurement							
		1942-46	a/ 75,000	-	75,000	58,975	16,025	-
		1948	254,112	2,870	256,982	168,737	-	88,245
		1949	1,572,795	305,545	1,878,340	903,121	-	975,219
		1950	-	1,348,636	1,348,636	68,005	-	1,280,631
	Total		a/ 1,901,907	1,657,051	3,558,958	1,198,838	16,025	2,344,095
2	Special Procurement							
	Total	1950	-	124,962	124,962	20,463	-	104,499
3	Acquisition and Construction of Real Property							
	Total	1950	-	49,774	49,774	2,902	-	46,872

TABLE 158 — DEPARTMENT OF THE AIR FORCE STATUS OF UNLIQUIDATED OBLIGATIONS AT BEGINNING AND END OF FY 1950 SHOWING OBLIGATIONS AND EXPENDITURES DURING FY 1950 — CONTINUED

(Includes reimbursements. In thousands of dollars. Figures in parentheses indicate minus amounts.)

REVISED ORDER OF APPROP.	APPROPRIATION	FISCAL OR PROGRAM YEAR	UNLIQUIDATED OBLIGATIONS 1 JULY 1949	GROSS OBLIGATIONS DURING FY 1950	TOTAL	GROSS EXPENDITURES DURING FY 1950	UNLIQUIDATED OBLIGATIONS TRANSFERRED TO CERTIFIED CLAIMS	UNLIQUIDATED OBLIGATIONS CARRIED FORWARD INTO FY 1951
4	Maintenance and Operations Total	1950	-	1,138,060	1,138,060	669,474	-	468,586
5	Military Personnel Requirements Total	1950	-	1,293,948	1,293,948	1,144,102	-	149,846
6	Research and Development Total	1950	-	201,734	201,734	62,359	-	139,375
10	Air Force Reserve Total	1950	-	72,767	72,767	46,948	-	25,819
11	Air Force Reserve Officers Training Corps Total	1950	-	7,410	7,410	5,409	-	2,001
12	Air National Guard Total	1950	-	110,683	110,683	68,643	-	42,040
8	Contingencies Total	1950	-	13,572	13,572	13,188	-	384
7	Salaries and Expenses Administration Total	1950	-	58,340	58,340	52,051	-	6,289
9	Claims Total	1950	-	1,316	1,316	1,178	-	138
13	General Expenses, USAF Total	1949	387,769	(3,246)	384,523	272,938	-	111,585
14	Salaries, Office, Chief of Staff, USAF Total	1949	306	-	306	306	-	-
15	Salaries, Office of the Secretary of the AF Total	1949	46	-	46	46	-	-
16	Department of the Air Force Total	1948	74,298	(992)	73,306	44,000	-	29,306
17	Air Corps, Army Total	1947	80,330	3,302	77,028	66,743	-	10,285
	Grand Total		a/ 2,444,656	4,722,077	7,166,733	3,669,588	16,025	3,481,120

a/ Includes $75 million unliquidated obligations under the Aircraft and Related Procurement 1942/46 Program authorized for expenditure in Fiscal Year 1950.
Source: Financial Management Division, Directorate of Budget, DCS/C.

TABLE 159 — DEPARTMENT OF THE AIR FORCE STATUS OF UNLIQUIDATED OBLIGATIONS AT BEGINNING AND END OF FY 1951 SHOWING OBLIGATIONS AND EXPENDITURES DURING FY 1951

(Includes reimbursements. In thousands of dollars. Figures in parentheses indicate minus amounts.

REVISED ORDER OF APPROP.	APPROPRIATION	FISCAL OR PROGRAM YEAR	UNLIQUIDATED OBLIGATIONS 1 JULY 1950	GROSS OBLIGATIONS DURING FY 1951	TOTAL	GROSS EXPENDITURES DURING FY 1951	UNLIQUIDATED OBLIGATIONS TRANSFERRED TO CERTIFIED CLAIMS	UNLIQUIDATED OBLIGATIONS CARRIED FORWARD INTO FY 1952
1	Aircraft and Related Procurement							
		1942-46	-	-	-	a/ (2,220)	-	a/ 2,220
		1948	88,245	(4,118)	84,127	66,174	-	17,953
		1949	975,219	2	975,221	735,903	-	239,318
		1950	1,280,631	27,605	1,308,236	737,232	-	571,004
		1951	-	7,382,009	7,382,009	402,661	-	6,979,348
	Total.		2,344,095	7,405,498	9,749,593	1,939,750	-	7,809,843
2	Major Procurement Other Than Aircraft Total.	1951	-	1,456,498	1,456,498	196,075	-	1,260,423
3	Acquisition and Construction of Real Property Total.	All Yrs	46,872	923,134	970,006	234,925	-	735,081
4	Maintenance and Operations							
		1950	468,586	11,028	479,614	363,856	-	115,758
		1951	-	3,101,851	3,101,851	1,449,797	-	1,652,054
	Total.		468,586	3,112,879	3,581,465	1,813,653	-	1,767,812
5	Military Personnel Requirements							
		1950	149,846	22,027	171,873	165,288	-	6,585
		1951	-	1,882,070	1,882,070	1,607,115	-	274,955
	Total.		149,846	1,904,097	2,053,943	1,772,403	-	281,540
6	Research and Development							
		1950	139,375	5,496	144,871	85,381	-	59,490
		1951	-	324,598	324,598	91,805	-	232,793
	Total.		139,375	330,094	469,469	177,186	-	292,283
7	Reserve Personnel Requirements Total.	1951	-	30,308	30,308	22,906	-	7,402
8	Air National Guard							
		1950	42,040	3,169	45,209	34,195	-	11,014
		1951	-	96,932	96,932	62,551	-	34,381
	Total.		42,040	100,101	142,141	96,746	-	45,395
9	Contingencies							
		1950	384	(5)	379	327	-	52
		1951	-	38,020	38,020	35,893	-	2,127
	Total.		384	38,015	38,399	36,220	-	2,179
10	Special Procurement Total.	1950	104,499	(1,910)	102,589	48,024	-	54,565
12	Air Force Reserve Total.	1950	25,819	453	26,272	19,453	-	6,819

TABLE 159 — DEPARTMENT OF THE AIR FORCE STATUS OF UNLIQUIDATED OBLIGATIONS AT BEGINNING AND END OF FY 1951 SHOWING OBLIGATIONS AND EXPENDITURES DURING FY 1951 — CONTINUED

(Includes reimbursements. In thousands of dollars. Figures in parentheses indicate minus amounts.)

REVISED ORDER OF APPROP.	APPROPRIATION	FISCAL OR PROGRAM YEAR	UNLIQUIDATED OBLIGATIONS 1 JULY 1950	GROSS OBLIGATIONS DURING FY 1951	TOTAL	GROSS EXPENDITURES DURING FY 1951	UNLIQUIDATED OBLIGATIONS TRANSFERRED TO CERTIFIED CLAIMS	UNLIQUIDATED OBLIGATIONS CARRIED FORWARD INTO FY 1952
13	Air Force Reserve Officers Training Corps							
	Total.	1950	2,001	161	2,162	1,865	-	297
11	Salaries and Expenses Administration							
	Total.	1950	6,289	42	6,331	6,017	-	314
14	Claims							
	Total.	1950	138	12	150	141	-	9
15	General Expenses, USAF							
	Total.	1949	111,585	(3,940)	107,645	70,905	-	36,740
16	Department of the Air Force							
	Total.	1948	29,306	(12,463)	16,843	14,859	-	1,984
17	Air Corps, Army							
	Total.	1947	10,285	(2,033)	8,252	8,252	-	-
	Grand Total.		3,481,120	15,280,946	18,762,066	6,459,380	-	12,302,686

a/ Represents expenditure refunds against Air Corps, Army 1942/46 unliquidated obligations paid by the Air Force. (These were not reported on USAFSD/51.)
Source: Financial Management Division, Directorate of Budget, DCS/C.

TABLE 160 — DEPARTMENT OF THE AIR FORCE STATUS OF UNLIQUIDATED OBLIGATIONS AT BEGINNING AND END OF FY 1952 SHOWING OBLIGATIONS AND EXPENDITURES DURING FY 1952

(Includes reimbursements. In thousands of dollars. Figures in parentheses indicate minus amounts.)

REVISED ORDER OF APPROP.	APPROPRIATION	FISCAL OR PROGRAM YEAR	UNLIQUIDATED OBLIGATIONS 1 JULY 1951	GROSS OBLIGATIONS DURING FY 1952	TOTAL	GROSS EXPENDITURES DURING FY 1952	UNLIQUIDATED OBLIGATIONS TRANSFERRED TO CERTIFIED CLAIMS	UNLIQUIDATED OBLIGATIONS CARRIED FORWARD INTO FY 1953
1	Aircraft and Related Procurement							
		1942-46	a/ 2,220	-	a/ 2,220	a/ 514	a/ 1,706	-
		1948	17,953	3,726	21,679	9,581	-	12,098
		1949	239,318	-	239,318	157,578	-	81,740
		1950	571,004	73,535	644,539	437,855	-	206,684
		1951	6,979,348	3,325,794	10,305,142	3,513,276	-	6,791,866
		1952	-	7,150,373	7,150,373	270,178	-	6,880,195
	Total.		7,809,843	10,553,428	18,363,271	4,388,982	1,706	13,972,583
2	Major Procurement Other Than Aircraft							
		1951	1,260,423	473,887	1,734,310	474,239	-	1,260,071
		1952	-	938,082	938,082	38,315	-	899,767
	Total.		1,260,423	1,411,969	2,672,392	512,554	-	2,159,838
3	Acquisition and Construction of Real Property							
	Total	All Yrs	735,081	1,080,989	1,816,070	1,092,119	-	723,951

TABLE 160 — DEPARTMENT OF THE AIR FORCE STATUS OF UNLIQUIDATED OBLIGATIONS AT BEGINNING AND END OF FY 1952 SHOWING OBLIGATIONS AND EXPENDITURES DURING FY 1952 — CONTINUED

(Includes reimbursements. In thousands of dollars. Figures in parentheses indicate minus amounts.)

REVISED ORDER OF APPROP.	APPROPRIATION	FISCAL OR PROGRAM YEAR	UNLIQUIDATED OBLIGATIONS 1 JULY 1951	GROSS OBLIGATIONS DURING FY 1952	TOTAL	GROSS EXPENDITURES DURING FY 1952	UNLIQUIDATED OBLIGATIONS TRANSFERRED TO CERTIFIED CLAIMS	UNLIQUIDATED OBLIGATIONS CARRIED FORWARD INTO FY 1953
4	Maintenance and Operations	1950	115,758	(8,007)	107,751	74,061	33,690	
		1951	1,652,054	6,884	1,658,938	1,311,764	-	347,174
		1952	-	3,527,035	3,527,035	1,900,696	-	1,626,339
	Total.		1,767,812	3,525,912	5,293,724	3,286,521	33,690	1,973,513
5	Military Personnel Requirements	1950	6,585	(204)	6,381	5,904	477	
		1951	274,955	(8,752)	266,203	255,155	-	11,048
		1952	-	2,937,660	2,937,660	2,748,644	-	189,016
	Total.		281,540	2,928,704	3,210,244	3,009,703	477	200,064
6	Research and Development	1950	59,490	7,148	66,638	46,282	-	20,356
		1951	232,793	43,332	276,125	167,756	-	108,369
		1952	-	408,520	408,520	132,607	-	275,913
	Total.		292,283	459,000	751,283	346,645	-	404,638
7	Reserve Personnel Requirements	1951	7,402	(356)	7,046	6,933	-	113
		1952	-	19,264	19,264	14,223	-	5,041
	Total.		7,402	18,908	26,310	21,156	-	5,154
8	Air National Guard	1950	11,014	(745)	10,269	7,860	2,409	-
		1951	34,381	3,509	37,890	21,900	-	15,990
		1952	-	84,560	84,560	27,715	-	56,845
	Total.		45,395	87,324	132,719	57,475	2,409	72,835
9	Contingencies	1950	52	(14)	38	26	12	-
		1951	2,127	(89)	2,038	1,482	-	556
		1952	-	38,409	38,409	36,068	-	2,341
	Total.		2,179	38,306	40,485	37,576	12	2,897
10	Special Procurement Total.	1950	54,565	(3,701)	50,864	35,084	15,780	-
12	Air Force Reserve Total.	1950	6,819	(1,105)	5,714	4,344	1,370	-
13	Air Force Reserve Officers Training Corps Total.	1950	297	(41)	256	194	62	-
11	Salaries and Expenses, Administration Total.	1950	314	35	349	378	(29)	-

TABLE 160 — DEPARTMENT OF THE AIR FORCE STATUS OF UNLIQUIDATED OBLIGATIONS AT BEGINNING AND END OF FY 1952 SHOWING OBLIGATIONS AND EXPENDITURES DURING FY 1952 — CONTINUED

(Includes reimbursements. In thousands of dollars. Figures in parentheses indicate minus amounts.)

REVISED ORDER OF APPROP.	APPROPRIATION	FISCAL OR PROGRAM YEAR	UNLIQUIDATED OBLIGATIONS 1 JULY 1951	GROSS OBLIGATIONS DURING FY 1952	TOTAL	GROSS EXPENDITURES DURING FY 1952	UNLIQUIDATED OBLIGATIONS TRANSFERRED TO CERTIFIED CLAIMS	UNLIQUIDATED OBLIGATIONS CARRIED FORWARD INTO FY 1953
14	Claims							
	Total.	1950	9	(7)	2	11	(9)	-
15	General Expenses, USAF							
	Total.	1949	36,740	(1,030)	35,710	20,383	15,327	-
16	Department of the Air Force							
	Total.	1948	1,984	7,268	9,252	5,430	3,822	-
	Grand Total.		12,302,586	20,105,959	32,408,645	12,818,555	74,617	19,515,473

a/ Activity against unliquidated obligations incurred under Air Corps, Army 1942/46 appropriation not previously reported on USAFSD-52.
Source: Financial Management Division, Directorate of Budget, DCS/C.

TABLE 161 — DEPARTMENT OF THE AIR FORCE STATUS OF UNLIQUIDATED OBLIGATIONS AT BEGINNING AND END OF FY 1953 SHOWING OBLIGATIONS AND EXPENDITURES DURING FY 1953

(Includes reimbursements. In thousands of dollars. Figures in parentheses indicate minus amounts.)

REVISED ORDER OF APPROP.	APPROPRIATION	FISCAL OR PROGRAM YEAR	UNLIQUIDATED OBLIGATIONS 1 JULY 1952	GROSS OBLIGATIONS DURING FY 1953	TOTAL	GROSS EXPENDITURES DURING FY 1953	UNLIQUIDATED OBLIGATIONS TRANSFERRED TO CERTIFIED CLAIMS	UNLIQUIDATED OBLIGATIONS CARRIED FORWARD INTO FY 1954
1	Aircraft and Related Procurement							
		1948	12,098	(4,749)	7,349	(810)	-	8,159
		1949	81,740	(9,272)	72,468	28,098	-	44,370
		1950	206,684	70,937	277,621	148,247	-	129,374
		1951	6,791,866	481,259	7,273,125	3,957,325	-	3,315,800
		1952	6,880,195	2,369,762	9,249,957	2,049,905	-	7,200,052
		1953	-	6,388,162	6,388,162	354,728	-	6,033,434
	Total.		13,972,583	9,296,099	23,268,682	6,537,493	-	16,731,189
2	Major Procurement Other Than Aircraft							
		1951	1,260,071	(34,654)	1,225,417	549,444	-	675,973
		1952	899,767	30,037	929,804	160,502	-	769,302
		1953	-	940,290	940,290	52,005	-	888,285
	Total.		2,159,838	935,673	3,095,511	761,951	-	2,333,560
3	Acquisition and Construction of Real Property							
	Total.	All Yrs	723,951	1,200,339	1,924,290	999,910	-	924,380

TABLE 161 — DEPARTMENT OF THE AIR FORCE STATUS OF UNLIQUIDATED OBLIGATIONS AT BEGINNING AND END OF FY 1953 SHOWING OBLIGATIONS AND EXPENDITURES DURING FY 1953 — CONTINUED

(Includes reimbursements. In thousands of dollars. Figures in parentheses indicate minus amounts.)

REVISED ORDER OF APPROP.	APPROPRIATION	FISCAL OR PROGRAM YEAR	UNLIQUIDATED OBLIGATIONS 1 JULY 1952	GROSS OBLIGATIONS DURING FY 1953	TOTAL	GROSS EXPENDITURES DURING FY 1953	UNLIQUIDATED OBLIGATIONS TRANSFERRED TO CERTIFIED CLAIMS	UNLIQUIDATED OBLIGATIONS CARRIED FORWARD INTO FY 1954
4	Maintenance and Operations	1951	347,174	(24,646)	322,528	239,713	82,815	-
		1952	1,626,339	(81,794)	1,544,545	1,070,086	-	474,459
		1953	-	3,336,198	3,336,198	2,150,508	-	1,185,690
	Total.		1,973,513	3,229,758	5,203,271	3,460,307	82,815	1,660,149
5	Military Personnel Requirements	1951	11,048	(2,167)	8,881	3,874	5,007	-
		1952	189,016	22,865	211,881	199,906	-	11,975
		1953	-	3,340,995	3,340,995	3,195,410	-	145,585
	Total.		200,064	3,361,693	3,561,757	3,399,190	5,007	157,560
6	Research and Development	1950	20,356	(585)	19,771	12,443	-	7,328
		1951	108,369	(2,389)	105,980	65,852	-	40,128
		1952	275,913	22,158	298,071	189,492	-	108,579
		1953	-	474,285	474,285	193,072	-	281,213
	Total.		404,638	493,469	898,107	400,859	-	437,248
7	Reserve Personnel Requirements	1951	113	(26)	87	234	-	(147)
		1952	5,041	947	5,988	5,826	-	162
		1953	-	20,175	20,175	18,359	-	1,816
	Total.		5,154	21,096	26,250	24,419	-	1,831
8	Air National Guard	1951	15,990	(752)	15,238	10,793	4,445	-
		1952	56,845	(369)	56,476	30,846	-	25,630
		1953	-	94,113	94,113	48,632	-	45,481
	Total.		72,835	92,992r	165,827	90,271	4,445	71,111
9	Contingencies	1951	556	(128)	428	203	225	-
		1952	2,341	(297)	2,044	1,941	-	103
		1953	-	29,599	29,599	26,614	-	2,985
	Total.		2,897	29,174	32,071	28,758	225	3,088
	Grand Total.		19,515,473	18,660,293	38,175,766	15,763,158	92,492	22,320,116

Source: Financial Management Division, Directorate of Budget, DCS/C.

TABLE 162 — STATUS OF CONTRACT AUTHORITY ENACTED BY CONGRESS SHOWING CASH SUBSEQUENTLY APPROPRIATED TO LIQUIDATE OBLIGATIONS THEREUNDER AS OF 30 JUNE 1953

TITLE OF APPROPRIATION AND FISCAL YEAR	CONTRACT AUTHORITY ENACTED		APPROPRIATED CASH TO LIQUIDATE CONTRACT AUTHORITY						UNFINANCED CONTRACT AUTHORITY 30 JUN 53
	PUBLIC LAW	AMOUNT	TOTAL	FY 1949 PL 547/80	FY 1950 PL 434/81	FY 1951 PL 759/81	FY 1952 PL 179/82	FY 1953 PL 488/82	
Total		$5,040,378,770	$5,040,378,770	$250,000,000	$800,000,000	$1,550,000,000	$710,000,000	$1,730,378,770	-
Aircraft and Related Procurement - Total		4,885,044,000	4,885,044,000	250,000,000	800,000,000	1,525,000,000	625,000,000	1,685,044,000	-
1948	PL 267; 80th Congress	430,000,000	430,000,000	250,000,000	180,000,000	-	-	-	-
1949	PL 547; 80th Congress	1,687,000,000	1,687,000,000	-	620,000,000	1,067,000,000	-	-	-
1950	PL 434; 81st Congress	a/1,957,755,000	1,957,755,000	-	-	458,000,000	625,000,000	874,755,000	-
1951	PL 759; 81st Congress	b/ 810,289,000	810,289,000	-	-	-	-	810,289,000	-
Acquisition and Construction of Real Property - Total		155,334,770	155,334,770	-	-	25,000,000	85,000,000	45,334,770	-
1950	PL 430; 81st Congress	52,834,770	52,834,770	-	-	25,000,000	27,834,770	-	-
1950	PL 434; 81st Congress	a/ 35,000,000	35,000,000	-	-	-	35,000,000	-	-
1950	PL 583; 81st Congress	35,000,000	35,000,000	-	-	-	22,165,230	12,834,770	-
1951	PL 843; 81st Congress	32,500,000	32,500,000	-	-	-	-	32,500,000	-

a/ $ 35,000,000 transferred from "Aircraft and Related Procurement" to "Acquisition and Construction of Real Property" pursuant to authority granted in PL 434, 81st Congress.

b/ Excludes $726,151,000 contract authority enacted in Fiscal Year 1950 but applied to Fiscal Year 1951 Program, pursuant to authority granted in PL 759, 81st Congress.

Source: Financial Management Division, Directorate of Budget, DCS/C.

TABLE 163 — ANALYSIS OF ACQUISITION AND CONSTRUCTION OF REAL PROPERTY APPROPRIATION AS OF 30 JUNE 1953

(In Millions of Dollars.)

PROGRAM	STATUS OF ENABLING AUTHORITY AND OBLIGATING AUTHORITY ENACTED				
	ENABLING AUTHORITY			OBLIGATING AUTHORITY	
	PUBLIC LAW a/	CONGRESS	AMOUNT	ENACTED	NOT ENACTED
Program - Totals			6,911.2	5,023.4	1,887.8
Aircraft Control and Warning System - Total b/			449.4	419.0	30.4
	30	81st	85.5		
	c/ 703	76th	39.8		
	910	81st	188.3		
	155	82nd	34.4		
	534	82nd	101.4		
Arnold Engineering Development Center - Total			169.5	169.5	-
	415	81st	100.0		
	799	81st	57.5		
	534	82nd	12.0		
Regular Programs - Total			6,292.3	4,434.9	1,857.4
	c/ 703	76th	119.2		
	626	80th	1.1		
	60	81st	75.0		
	420	81st	59.2		
	564	81st	225.5		
	838	81st	3.1		
	910	81st	697.3		
	155	82nd	d/3,411.9		
	534	82nd	d/1,700.0		

PROGRAM	SOURCE OF FUNDS			OBLIGATED			UNOBLIGATED BALANCE 30 JUN 53 e/
	OBLIGATING AUTHORITY ENACTED						
	PUBLIC LAW	CONGRESS	AMOUNT	TOTAL	CUMULATIVE THROUGH 30 JUN 52	DURING FY 53	
Program - Totals			5,023.4	3,253.4	2,053.7	1,199.7	1,770.0
Aircraft Control and Warning System - Total b/			419.0	283.3	196.2	87.1	135.7
	434	81st	54.3				
	759	81st	31.2				
	843	81st	39.8				
	911	81st	76.0				
	179	82nd	29.5				
	254	82nd	117.2				
	547	82nd	71.0				
Arnold Engineering Development Center - Total			169.5	148.5	109.5	39.0	21.0
	430	81st	30.0				
	583	81st	55.0				
	759	81st	15.0				
	843	81st	57.5				
	547	82nd	12.0				
Regular Programs - Total			4,434.9	2,821.6	1,748.0	1,073.6	1,613.3
	358	81st	5.0				
	430	81st	48.8				
	434	81st	1.1				
	759	81st	93.6				
	843	81st	129.9				
	911	81st	731.0				
	43	82nd	281.7				
	179	82nd	72.8				
	254	82nd	1,954.0				
	547	82nd	1,117.0				

a/ Public Law Citations on this table relate only to Enabling Authority. Public Law Citations relating to Obligating Authority will be found in lower part of table.
b/ Includes Tactical Air Control.
c/ Act of 2 July 1940 (54 Stat 712 U.S.C. App. 1171).
d/ Does not reflect recissions enacted in Public Law 209, 83rd Congress, 8 August 1953, as follows:
PL 155 - 82nd Congress $377.7 million
PL 534 - 82nd Congress $ 23.7 million
e/ Available for obligation in subsequent years.
Source: Financial Management Division, Directorate of Budget, DCS/C.

ACTIVITY IN AIR FORCE MANAGEMENT FUNDS DURING FISCAL YEAR 1953

(The Air Force Management Fund was established pursuant to Section 406 of Public Law 216, 81st Congress; approved 10 August 1949. This fund was established for the purpose of facilitating the economical and efficient conduct of operations in the Department of Defense which are financed by two or more appropriations where the costs of the operations are not susceptible to immediate distribution as charges to such appropriations. Figures in parentheses indicate minus amounts.)

LINE NO.		TOTAL DURING FY 1953	PROGRAM YEAR 1953	PROGRAM YEAR 1952	PROGRAM YEAR 1951
1	Unobligated Balances, 1 July 1952	4,883,000	-	4,322,462	560,538
2	Unliquidated Obligations, 1 July 1952	18,166,588	-	18,086,326	80,262
3	Unexpended Balances, 1 July 1952	23,049,588	-	22,408,788	640,800
4	Transfer of Corpus (Reappropriated Each Year)	-	1,000,000	(1,000,000)	-
5	Deposits By Source:				
6	Department of the Army	558,000	558,000	-	-
7	Department of the Navy	5,045,000	5,045,000	-	-
8	Department of the Air Force	129,487,700	129,487,700	-	-
9	Department of Defense (MDAP Program)	66,030,000	66,030,000	-	-
10	Department of Defense (Other)	10,000,000	10,000,000	-	-
11	Miscellaneous Reimbursements	100,253	85,759	15,442	(948)
12	Total Deposits By Source	211,220,953	211,206,459	15,442	(948)
13	Total Available for Obligation (Lines 1, 4 and 12)	216,103,953	212,206,459	3,337,904	559,590
14	Obligational Activity During FY 1953	209,902,485	210,225,165	(181,692)	(140,988)
15	Total Available for Expenditure (Lines 3, 4 and 12)	234,270,541	212,206,459	21,424,230	639,852
16	Expenditure Activity During FY 1953	87,357,682	70,768,441	16,755,153	(165,912)
17	Return of Prior Year Deposits	3,875,000	-	a/3,240,000	b/635,000
18	Unobligated Balances, 30 Jun 53 (Line 13, Less Lines 14 and 17)	2,326,468	1,981,294	279,596	65,578
19	Unliquidated Obligations, 30 Jun 53	140,711,391	139,456,724	1,149,481	105,186
20	Unexpended Balances, 30 Jun 53 (Line 15, Less Lines 16 and 17)	143,037,859	141,438,018	1,429,077	170,764

a/ Returned to: Army, $909,900; Navy, $564,300; Air Force, $1,765,800.
b/ Returned to Air Force, $635,000.
Source: Financial Management Division, Directorate of Budget, DCS/C.

Housing and Installations

Part XII

HOUSING AND INSTALLATIONS

This area covers the following subject matter:
1. Housing and Occupancy
2. Installations

HOUSING

DEFINITIONS

The following definitions are applicable:

Authorized Normal Capacity: Defined in AFR 93-8. Includes capacities of only those buildings constructed for or permanently converted to housing under proper authority (see AFR 85-5).

Spaces Occupied and Received: Includes all personnel spaces (military and civilian) to which the housing is assigned whether such personnel are on TDY, confined, on leave, sick in hospital etc., and transient personnel for which space is reserved.

Authorized AF Housing: All housing under the jurisdiction of the Department of the Air Force or reserved for Air Force use including facilities purchased, leased, constructed by or for the military department, occupied under agreement, and commandeered or requisitioned in areas of military occupation.

TROOP HOUSING

This type of housing includes all buildings designed and planned for troop (officers, enlisted men and civilians) housing, or that which had been converted to housing. Spaces in the following types of housing are included: permanent, semi-permanent (MOB), semi-permanent (other), temporary (T/O), temporary (other), and leased.

FAMILY HOUSING

This includes all buildings designed and planned for family type housing, or that which had been converted to family housing. Included are spaces in the following types of housing:

1. AF Appropriated Funds
   a. Permanent
   b. Semi-permanent (MOB conv.)
   c. Semi-permanent (other)
   d. Temporary (T/O conv.)
   e. Temporary (other)

2. FHA
   a. Permanent
   b. Semi-permanent
   c. Temporary

3. FHA
   a. Permanent
   b. Semi-permanent

OTHER

Troop and family housing not under the real property jurisdiction of the AF but furnished for the use of AF personnel by contract, by other military services or by foreign governments; or family housing that may be assigned to Department of the Air Force by Public Law 475 or by any other existing or future public law.

INSTALLATIONS

DEFINITIONS

Definitions used in connection with Installations are listed below:

AIR FORCE INSTALLATION

This is a defined area of real property in which the Department of the Air Force exercises a real property interest or, where the Department of the Air Force has jurisdiction over real property by agreement, expressed or implied, with foreign governments, or by rights of occupation.

1. Major Type Installations: Installations classified primary, secondary, industrial, Air Force Reserve Crew Training centers, permanent off-base Aircraft Control and Warning Stations and all other installations considered by Headquarters, USAF as important in the current USAF program.

2. Regular Air Force Installations: (Other than Reserve Forces Installations and Industrial Installations) are divided into:

a. Primary Installation (Class 1): An Air Force installation capable of supporting one or more major Air Force activities such as wings or depots and classified as a primary installation by Headquarters, USAF.

b. Secondary Installation (Class 2): An Air Force installation located separate and apart from a primary installation, capable of supporting one or more Air Force activities such as squadrons, or capable of providing sustained support to one or more major activities of a primary installation; and classified as a secondary installation by Headquarters USAF.

c. Minor Installation (Class 3): An Air Force installation such as an auxiliary airfield located separate and apart from either a primary or secondary installation, excluded from the definitions of a primary or secondary installation, and classified as a minor installation by Headquarters, USAF.

308700 O - 54 - 21

3. Reserve Forces Installation (Class 4): An Air Force installation in which the Department of the Air Force exercises a real property interest primarily for the support of the Reserve Forces of the Air Force of the United States, and classified as a Reserve Forces installation by Headquarters, USAF.

4. Industrial Installation (Class 5): An Air Force Installation designed primarily for manufacturing and/or industrial research and development and classified as an industrial installation by Headquarters, USAF.

AIR FORCE LOCATIONS

Air Force Locations at other than Air Force installations at which the United States Air Force has no real property interest are:

1. Other United States Government Installations (Class 6): Locations at which the United States Air Force personnel may be stationed for duty, where the real property jurisdiction is with a United States Government department or agency other than the Department of the Air Force.

2. Non-United States Government Installations (Class 7): Locations at which United States Air Force personnel may be stationed for duty, where the real property jurisdiction is with an agency, corporation, individuals, or government other than the United States Government.

STATUS OF AIR FORCE LOCATIONS

The status of Air Force installations will be as designated below: ("Active" status will be the only designation for Air Force locations at other than Air Force installations where there exists a United States Air Force activity.)

1. Active: An Air Force installation which has been designated in Air Force orders as active; usually an installation accommodating an Air Force activity or one being prepared for an Air Force activity.

2. Inactive: An Air Force installation which has been designated in Air Force orders as inactive; usually an installation closed to operations, with no Air Force activity except caretaking.

3. Industrial Reserve: An Air Force installation utilized for purposes other than research, development, or manufacture of materiel for the Air Force. (This classification applies only to industrial installations.)

4. Excess: An Air Force installation which has been declared by Headquarters USAF, as excess to the requirements of the Department of the Air Force.

5. Surplus: An excess Air Force installation which has been determined by the Administrator, General Services Administration to be surplus to the requirements of all Federal agencies, and for which the Department of the Air Force has been designated to perform care and handling pending disposition.

TABLE 164 – STATUS OF USAF MILITARY AND CIVILIAN HOUSING AND OCCUPANCY BY COMMAND – MAY 1953

COMMAND	AUTHORIZED NORMAL CAPACITY			SPACES OCCUPIED AND RESERVED		
	Authorized AF Housing		Other (Family & Troop)	Authorized AF Housing		Other (Family & Troop)
	Family	Troop		Family	Troop	
WORLD-WIDE	64,417	887,215	42,819	57,036	627,906	42,979
CONTINENTAL US	47,618	607,874	16,676	41,278	407,654	17,401
Air Defense Command	2,410	63,738	1,040	2,218	37,915	706
Air Materiel Command.	6,003	45,042	-	3,959	16,720	1
Air Proving Ground Command. . .	1,470	7,101	153	1,581	5,907	151
Air Research & Development Com.	3,345	16,519	827	2,932	14,096	648
Air Training Command.	13,499	280,219	40	12,086	193,165	344
Air University.	1,093	4,011	-	822	4,723	-
Continental Air Command	1,617	28,208	10,984	949	16,353	12,107
Headquarters Command.	142	3,779	1,182	130	3,138	1,386
Military Air Transport Service.	2,179	20,167	-	2,236	15,184	-
Strategic Air Command	12,378	100,841	420	11,252	75,339	326
Tactical Air Command.	3,482	38,249	2,030	3,113	25,114	1,732
OVERSEAS.	16,799	279,341	26,143	15,758	220,252	25,578
Alaskan Air Command	1,939	24,206	162	1,806	17,924	159
Caribbean Air Command	643	3,347	121	491	1,442	46
Far East Air Forces	6,377	106,068	3,959	5,990	89,906	5,035
Military Air Transport Service.	2,120	27,200	682	1,788	13,360	547
Northeast Air Command	666	16,721	1,015	666	15,813	1,015
Strategic Air Command	720	3,357	4	751	2,982	4
US Air Forces in Europe	4,334	98,442	20,200	4,266	78,825	18,772

TABLE 165 — USAF MAJOR TYPE INSTALLATIONS — BY COMMAND AND TYPE — AS OF 30 JUNE 1953

COMMAND	INVENTORY AS OF 30 JUNE 1953		INSTALLATIONS				OTHER a/	
			WITH AIRFIELDS		WITHOUT AIRFIELDS			
	ACTIVE	INACTIVE	ACTIVE	INACTIVE	ACTIVE	INACTIVE	ACTIVE	INACTIVE
WORLDWIDE - TOTAL	458	27	273	25	60	1	125	1
CONTINENTAL US - TOTAL	315	15	156	13	34	1	125	1
ADC	106	1	29	1	2	-	75	-
AFFD.	1	-	-	-	1	-	-	-
AMC	70	6	11	4	9	1	50	1
APG	5	1	5	1	-	-	-	-
ARDC.	14	-	7	-	7	-	-	-
ATRC.	47	1	41	1	6	-	-	-
AU.	2	-	2	-	-	-	-	-
CAC	16	1	12	1	4	-	-	-
HQC	3	-	1	-	2	-	-	-
HQ USAF	1	-	-	-	1	-	-	-
MATS.	8	-	7	-	1	-	-	-
SAC	28	2	27	2	1	-	-	-
TAC	14	3	14	3	-	-	-	-
OVERSEAS - TOTAL . . .	143	12	117	12	26	-	-	-
AAC	6	1	6	1	-	-	-	-
CAC	2	3	2	3	-	-	-	-
FEAF.	28	4	22	4	6	-	-	-
MATS.	11	4	11	4	-	-	-	-
NEAC.	9	-	8	-	1	-	-	-
SAC	19	-	17	-	2	-	-	-
USAFE	68	-	51	-	17	-	-	-

a/ Includes AC & W Sites and Industrial Plants.

SOURCE: Director of Installations, Deputy Chief of Staff, Operations, Headquarters, USAF

MUTUAL DEFENSE ASSISTANCE PROGRAM (MDAP)

DEFINITION

MDAP (MUTUAL DEFENSE ASSISTANCE PROGRAM) EMPLOYEES
Category of civilian personnel engaged in activities required in carrying out the Mutual Defense Assistance Program as administered by the Air Force. Employment is thus in terms of work units such as man-month equivalents.

GRANT AID
Military aid granted foreign countries under terms of Mutual Defense Assistance appropriation on a non-reimbursable basis.

OFF-SHORE PROCUREMENT
Purchase of military equipment, components, and supplies from non-domestic sources of production.

USAF SUPPORTED AIRCRAFT
Aircraft in foreign countries under the Mutual Defense Assistance Program for which USAF is committed to provide logistic support.

UTILIZATION RATE
Average number of hours flown on each aircraft per month.

TABLE 156 — USAF SUPPORTED AIRCRAFT IN MDAP COUNTRIES, BY COUNTRY, BY TYPE AND MODEL — QUARTERLY, FISCAL YEAR 1953

COUNTRY TYPE AND MODEL	30 SEPTEMBER 1952			31 DECEMBER 1952			31 MARCH 1953			30 JUNE 1953		
	TOTAL	ACTIVE	IN-ACTIVE	TOTAL	ACTIVE	IN-ACTIVE	TOTAL	ACTIVE	IN-ACTIVE	TOTAL	ACTIVE	IN-ACTIVE
AIRCRAFT-TOTAL	3,974	3,072	902	4,342	3,399	943	4,963	4,016	947	5,398	4,389	1,009
TITLE I TOTAL	1,815	1,433	382	2,089	1,712	377	2,366	1,985	381	2,484	2,095	389
Belgium	177	136	41	229	181	48	268	234	34	282	282	-
F-84	90	84	6	126	106	20	162	155	7	168	168	-
C-119	4	-	4	16	16	-	16	15	1	16	16	-
T-6	58	34	24	58	38	20	58	40	18	58	58	-
T-16	18	12	6	20	13	7	20	13	7	28	28	-
T-33	7	6	1	9	8	1	12	11	1	12	12	-
Denmark	50	50	-	99	99	-	114	114	-	134	117	17
B-17	1	1	-	1	1	-	1	1	-	1	1	-
PBY-5	8	8	-	8	8	-	8	8	-	8	8	-
F-84	41	41	-	90	90	-	105	105	-	121	104	17
T-33	-	-	-	-	-	-	-	-	-	4	4	-
France	636	470	166	746	557	189	819	660	159	774	652	122
F-47	179	95	84	172	95	77	168	98	70	164	98	66
F-51	22	17	5	22	17	5	22	17	5	22	22	-
F-84	159	130	29	222	182	40	303	261	42	323	310	13
C-45	26	21	5	26	22	4	25	22	3	25	22	3
C-47	62	60	2	100	93	7	98	87	11	42	25	17
T-6	155	124	31	153	118	35	153	144	9	148	140	8
T-33	33	23	10	51	30	21	50	31	19	50	35	15
Mark IV (Hvd)	-	-	-	-	-	-	-	-	-	-	-	-
Italy	270	257	13	285	274	11	363	322	41	385	351	34
F-47	52	52	-	50	50	-	47	47	-	45	16	29
F-51	81	80	1	79	78	1	79	79	-	76	75	1
F-84	86	75	11	106	96	10	188	147	41	198	197	1
C-119	-	-	-	-	-	-	-	-	-	7	7	-
T-6	48	48	-	46	46	-	45	43	-	44	41	3
T-33	3	2	1	4	4	-	4	4	-	5	5	-
Mark IV (Hvd)	-	-	-	-	-	-	-	-	-	10	10	-
Netherlands	298	222	76	323	246	77	340	258	82	357	239	118
F-84	101	78	23	128	93	35	145	100	45	170	108	62
C-47	16	4	12	16	4	12	16	5	11	16	9	7
T-7	28	24	4	28	23	5	27	22	5	26	19	7
T-16	149	112	37	147	122	25	147	127	20	139	97	42
T-33	4	4	-	4	4	-	4	4	-	6	6	-
Norway	83	62	21	98	81	17	115	95	20	154	132	22
PB2B	6	3	3	6	4	2	6	3	3	6	2	4
F-84	35	33	2	50	47	3	67	64	3	102	98	4
C-47	10	9	1	10	8	2	10	8	2	10	9	1
T-6	9	3	6	9	5	4	9	3	6	9	6	3
T-16	23	14	9	23	17	6	23	17	6	22	12	10
T-33	-	-	-	-	-	-	-	-	-	5	5	-
Portugal	93	63	30	91	75	16	116	108	8	119	111	8
B-17	-	-	-	-	-	-	4	4	-	4	4	-
F-47	43	27	16	42	38	4	39	39	-	38	38	-
F-84	-	-	-	-	-	-	25	25	-	25	25	-
SA-16	1	1	-	1	-	1	1	1	-	3	2	1
C-54	2	-	2	2	2	-	2	2	-	2	2	-
T-6	46	35	11	45	35	10	44	37	7	44	38	6
T-33	-	-	-	-	-	-	-	-	-	2	2	-
B-19	1	-	1	1	-	1	1	-	1	1	-	1
United Kingdom	92	80	12	98	87	11	109	81	28	133	77	56
B-29	83	71	12	82	71	11	80	52	28	80	36	44
RB-29	3	3	-	3	3	-	3	3	-	3	3	-
P2V-5	6	6	-	13	13	-	26	26	-	50	38	12
Yugoslavia	116	93	23	120	112	8	122	113	9	146	134	12
F-47	116	93	23	120	112	8	120	111	9	118	106	12
F-84	-	-	-	-	-	-	-	-	-	23	23	-
T-33	-	-	-	-	-	-	2	2	-	5	5	-

TABLE 166 — USAF SUPPORTED AIRCRAFT IN MDAP COUNTRIES, BY COUNTRY, BY TYPE AND MODEL — QUARTERLY, FISCAL YEAR 1953 — (CONTINUED)

COUNTRY TYPE AND MODEL	30 SEPTEMBER 1952			31 DECEMBER 1952			31 MARCH 1953			30 JUNE 1953		
	TOTAL	ACTIVE	IN-ACTIVE	TOTAL	ACTIVE	IN-ACTIVE	TOTAL	ACTIVE	IN-ACTIVE	TOTAL	ACTIVE	IN-ACTIVE
TITLE II - TOTAL	941	739	202	967	766	201	1,020	766	254	1,084	799	285
Greece	308	229	79	315	245	70	332	268	64	361	294	67
A-25	38	29	9	31	25	6	25	23	2	24	17	7
F-84	34	32	2	59	58	1	95	95	-	126	126	-
C-47	54	34	20	52	31	21	52	30	22	52	35	17
T-6	78	60	18	78	62	16	78	62	16	77	61	16
T-33	5	4	1	7	6	1	7	6	1	10	9	1
L-17	2	1	1	2	1	1	2	2	-	2	2	-
Auster	-	-	-	-	-	-	-	-	-	-	-	-
Spitfire	78	53	25	67	48	19	54	32	22	51	28	23
Moth	19	16	3	19	14	5	19	18	1	19	16	3
Iran	124	86	38	124	85	39	117	75	42	112	70	42
F-47	39	11	28	39	15	24	32	15	17	28	6	22
C-47	4	3	1	4	3	1	4	3	1	4	3	1
T-6	29	25	4	29	20	9	29	23	6	26	21	5
T-13	15	12	3	15	12	3	15	10	5	17	15	2
L-4	37	35	2	37	35	2	37	24	13	37	25	12
Turkey	509	424	85	528	436	92	571	423	148	611	435	176
B-26	27	17	10	27	19	8	27	18	9	29	12	17
F-47	132	128	4	130	104	26	125	94	31	121	79	42
F-84	71	71	-	90	89	1	137	135	2	174	169	5
C-45	2	2	-	2	2	-	2	1	1	2	1	1
C-47	76	51	25	75	51	24	75	33	42	76	37	39
T-6	88	76	12	86	82	4	87	70	17	87	60	27
T-11	105	71	34	104	76	28	104	59	45	106	62	44
T-33	7	7	-	13	13	-	13	13	-	15	15	-
K-225	1	1	-	1	-	1	1	-	1	1	-	1
TITLE III - TOTAL	1,218	900	318	1,286	921	365	1,341	1,036	305	1,362	1,066	296
China, NGR	610	434	176	654	462	192	702	628	74	791	685	106
B-24	20	10	10	20	18	2	20	19	1	19	18	1
B-25	18	9	9	18	15	3	18	14	4	17	13	4
P4Y-2	-	-	-	3	3	-	3	3	-	9	9	-
F-47	41	34	7	81	72	9	131	111	20	218	182	36
F-51	52	48	4	51	35	16	49	43	6	49	41	8
F-84	-	-	-	-	-	-	-	-	-	11	11	-
RB-25	3	3	-	3	2	1	3	3	-	3	2	1
RF-38	3	3	-	3	2	1	3	3	-	-	-	-
RF-51	-	-	-	3	3	-	8	8	-	8	8	-
C-46	138	88	50	137	97	40	136	129	7	136	131	5
C-47	31	16	15	31	13	18	31	24	7	31	25	6
C-54	1	-	1	1	1	-	1	1	-	-	-	-
T-6	163	138	25	155	113	42	154	132	22	150	127	23
T-7	1	1	-	1	1	-	1	-	1	1	1	-
T-11	13	8	5	13	4	9	11	9	2	11	9	2
T-17	114	70	44	122	76	46	121	120	1	115	101	18
T-33	-	-	-	-	-	-	-	-	-	2	2	-
PA-11	5	2	3	5	2	3	5	4	1	-	-	-
L-5	4	2	2	4	3	1	4	3	1	4	3	1
H-5	2	1	1	2	2	-	2	1	1	2	1	1
H-13	1	1	-	1	-	1	1	1	-	1	1	-
Philippines	183	117	66	179	112	67	177	113	64	110	74	36
F-51	41	38	3	38	31	7	36	29	7	33	27	6
C-47	18	14	4	18	14	4	17	14	3	17	15	2
C-64	2	-	2	2	-	2	2	-	2	-	-	-
T-6	31	17	14	30	18	12	28	17	11	29	15	14
T-13	61	29	32	61	30	31	61	32	29	-	-	-
T-26	1	1	-	1	1	-	1	1	-	-	-	-
L-4	1	-	1	1	-	1	1	-	1	-	-	-
L-5	25	15	10	25	16	9	28	18	10	31	17	14
H-47	3	3	-	3	2	1	3	2	1	-	-	-

TABLE 166 — USAF SUPPORTED AIRCRAFT IN MDAP COUNTRIES, BY COUNTRY, BY TYPE AND MODEL — QUARTERLY, FISCAL YEAR 1953 (CONTINUED)

COUNTRY TYPE AND MODEL	30 SEPTEMBER 1952			31 DECEMBER 1952			31 MARCH 1953			30 JUNE 1953		
	TOTAL	ACTIVE	IN-ACTIVE	TOTAL	ACTIVE	IN-ACTIVE	TOTAL	ACTIVE	IN-ACTIVE	TOTAL	ACTIVE	IN-ACTIVE
TITLE III - Cont'd												
Thailand	244	198	46	269	191	78	275	136	139	242	105	137
A-25	6	-	6	5	2	4	6	-	6	-	-	-
F8F	42	39	3	75	48	27	75	50	25	72	34	38
C-45	6	6	-	6	6	-	6	4	2	6	3	3
C-47	4	4	-	4	4	-	4	2	2	4	2	2
T-6	136	106	30	134	95	39	130	53	77	130	46	84
L-4	25	18	7	25	17	8	30	16	14	30	20	10
L-5	-	-	-	-	-	-	-	-	-	-	-	-
Spitfire	16	16	-	11	11	-	15	8	7	-	-	-
Firefly	9	9	-	8	8	-	9	3	6	-	-	-
Vietnam	181	151	30	184	156	28	187	159	28	219	202	17
B-26	36	35	1	36	35	1	40	39	1	41	39	2
RB-26	4	4	-	4	4	-	4	4	-	4	4	-
F6F	28	21	7	27	15	12	2	-	2	-	-	-
F8F	95	73	22	92	79	13	117	92	25	98	85	13
C-47	18	18	-	25	23	2	24	24	-	76	74	2
TITLE IV - TOTAL	-	-	-	-	-	-	236	229	7	468	429	39
Brazil	-	-	-	-	-	-	-	-	-	161	161	-
B-17	-	-	-	-	-	-	-	-	-	5	5	-
B-25	-	-	-	-	-	-	-	-	-	34	34	-
PBY-5	-	-	-	-	-	-	-	-	-	12	12	-
F-47	-	-	-	-	-	-	-	-	-	50	50	-
T-6	-	-	-	-	-	-	-	-	-	60	60	-
Chile	-	-	-	-	-	-	74	74	-	60	60	-
B-25	-	-	-	-	-	-	8	8	-	8	8	-
PBY-5	-	-	-	-	-	-	5	5	-	5	5	-
F-47	-	-	-	-	-	-	7	7	-	7	7	-
T-6	-	-	-	-	-	-	48	48	-	40	40	-
T-11	-	-	-	-	-	-	6	6	-	-	-	-
Colombia	-	-	-	-	-	-	38	38	-	47	37	10
B-25	-	-	-	-	-	-	2	2	-	2	1	1
F-47	-	-	-	-	-	-	11	11	-	22	19	3
T-6	-	-	-	-	-	-	25	25	-	23	17	6
Cuba	-	-	-	-	-	-	26	19	7	26	16	10
B-25	-	-	-	-	-	-	2	2	-	2	1	1
PBY-5	-	-	-	-	-	-	2	1	1	2	1	1
C-45	-	-	-	-	-	-	1	-	1	1	1	-
C-47	-	-	-	-	-	-	3	3	-	3	3	-
T-6	-	-	-	-	-	-	14	10	4	14	10	4
T-7	-	-	-	-	-	-	2	2	-	2	-	2
T-11	-	-	-	-	-	-	2	1	1	2	-	2
Ecuador	-	-	-	-	-	-	20	20	-	26	26	-
F-47	-	-	-	-	-	-	10	10	-	20	20	-
T-6	-	-	-	-	-	-	10	10	-	6	6	-
Peru	-	-	-	-	-	-	78	78	-	90	90	-
B-25	-	-	-	-	-	-	6	6	-	6	6	-
F-47	-	-	-	-	-	-	30	30	-	42	42	-
T-6	-	-	-	-	-	-	35	36	-	36	36	-
PV-2	-	-	-	-	-	-	6	6	-	6	6	-
Uruguay	-	-	-	-	-	-	-	-	-	58	39	19
B-25	-	-	-	-	-	-	-	-	-	10	6	4
F-51	-	-	-	-	-	-	-	-	-	25	10	15
T-6	-	-	-	-	-	-	-	-	-	15	15	-
T-11	-	-	-	-	-	-	-	-	-	8	8	-

SOURCE: Materiel Statistics Division, Directorate of Statistical Services, DCS/C

TABLE 167 — MDAP AIRCRAFT FLYING HOURS BY COUNTRY, MONTHLY — FY 1953

MDAP COUNTRY	JUL 52	AUG	SEP	OCT	NOV	DEC	JAN 53	FEB	MAR	APR	MAY	JUN
Total	66,505	67,950	70,065	72,827	67,593	56,411	63,764	64,124	80,928	85,285	82,043	84,687
Title I	28,275	25,664	27,409	30,853	26,826	21,985	24,089	28,202	35,590	42,419	40,672	37,720
Belgium	2,215	2,835	2,419	2,289	1,940	1,012	1,426	1,862	2,843	6,218	3,752	4,193
Denmark	233	360	502	452	486	322	602	534	768	895	1,068	1,013
France	11,313	8,447	8,447	13,887	11,634	13,275	12,049	12,510	16,331	17,859	18,197	12,628
Italy	4,559	4,089	4,566	3,673	3,241	2,207	4,007	3,509	5,043	4,682	4,552	4,445
Netherlands . . .	4,165	3,475	5,771	3,991	3,855	1,128	944	3,214	2,769	4,445	4,735	5,146
Norway	1,409	1,402	1,488	1,396	1,460	717	1,372	1,743	1,845	2,480	2,475	3,680
Portugal	685	1,109	819	703	1,029	745	1,177	1,465	1,464	1,403	1,921	1,871
United Kingdom .	2,516	1,609	1,611	2,576	1,732	1,563	1,417	1,543	2,078	1,748	1,894	1,662
Yugoslavia . . .	1,180	2,338	1,786	1,886	1,449	1,016	1,095	1,822	2,449	2,689	2,078	3,082
Title II	18,255	16,162	17,972	17,144	13,776	12,287	11,777	10,800	14,007	16,860	15,736	16,279
Greece	8,780	5,774	8,479	7,613	7,133	5,737	6,525	5,511	7,622	9,283	8,659	8,148
Iran	1,542	797	1,074	1,229	962	1,363	1,846	1,309	1,350	1,088	1,277	1,130
Turkey	7,933	9,591	8,419	8,302	5,681	5,187	3,406	3,980	5,035	6,489	5,800	7,001
Title III	19,975	26,124	24,684	24,830	26,991	22,139	24,890	22,456	29,287	23,723	22,303	27,855
China, N.G.R. . .	9,142	16,076	13,017	13,873	13,590	12,334	14,710	12,376	16,631	13,636	13,491	15,892
Philippines . . .	4,358	3,419	3,883	2,932	4,217	3,151	4,199	3,255	3,680	2,700	2,243	2,150
Thailand	2,865	3,221	3,911	3,764	4,008	2,083	2,312	3,038	4,553	2,481	1,644	2,171
Vietnam	3,610	3,408	3,873	4,261	5,176	4,571	3,669	3,787	4,423	4,906	4,925	7,642
Title IV	-	-	-	-	-	-	3,008	2,666	2,044	2,283	3,332	2,833
Chile	-	-	-	-	-	-	1,244	1,304	701	795	824	754
Colombia	-	-	-	-	-	-	328	591	413	301	329	345
Cuba	-	-	-	-	-	-	690	551	698	741	704	489
Ecuador	-	-	-	-	-	-	280	32	69	69	526	142
Peru	-	-	-	-	-	-	456	188	163	377	949	1,038
Uruguay	-	-	-	-	-	-	-	-	-	-	-	65

SOURCE: Materiel Statistics Division, Directorate of Statistical Services, DCS/C.

TABLE 168 – AIRCRAFT SHIPMENTS TO MDAP COUNTRIES – TITLES I, II, III, AND IV, FISCAL YEAR 1953

(Includes USAF Grant Aid and Offshore Procurement)

AIRCRAFT MODEL AND SERIES	CUMULATIVE SHIPMENTS AS OF 30 JUN 52	SHIPMENTS DURING											
		JUL 52	AUG	SEP	OCT	NOV	DEC	JAN 53	FEB	MAR	APR	MAY	JUN
TITLE I - TOTAL	a/ 1296 a/	77	53	135	165	116	113	106	61	111	85	102	127
Belgium	119	-	7	16	39	33	11	-	-	-	-	1	-
F-84E	21	-	-	-	-	-	-	-	-	-	-	-	-
F-84G	75	-	4	11	27	32	11	-	-	-	-	-	-
C-119F	-	-	-	4	12	-	-	-	-	-	-	-	-
T-6D	16	-	-	-	-	-	-	-	-	-	-	-	-
T-33A	7	-	3	1	-	1	-	-	-	-	-	1	-
Denmark	65	b/ -19b/	-	26	21	18	2	-	-	6	8	-	19
F-84E	6	-	-	-	-	-	-	-	-	-	-	-	-
F-84G	37	-	-	26	21	18	2	-	-	4	6	-	17
PBY-5	2	-	-	-	-	-	-	-	-	-	-	-	-
T-6D	20	b/ -19b/	-	-	-	-	-	-	-	-	-	-	-
T-33A	-	-	-	-	-	-	-	-	-	2	2	-	2
France	347	70	18	67	88	21	49	64	35	13	2	50	46
F-84E	46	-	-	-	-	-	-	-	-	-	-	-	-
F-84G	99	18	18	24	c/53 c/	-	35	64	6	-	2	1	-
C-45	1	-	-	-	-	-	-	-	-	-	-	-	-
C-47	-	-	-	16	4	-	-	-	-	-	-	5	6
T-6D	100	b/ 19b/	-	-	-	-	-	-	-	-	-	-	-
T-6G	48	-	-	-	-	-	-	-	-	-	-	-	-
T-33A	35	-	-	10	2	7	-	-	-	-	-	1	-
Mark IV (Hvd) .	-	-	-	-	-	-	-	-	-	-	-	1	8
MD-450	-	11	-	2	5	6	14	-	7	13	-	34	32
Vampire 5	13	8	-	4	19	1	-	-	1	-	-	-	-
Vampire 53 . . .	5	14	-	11	5	7	-	-	21	-	-	-	-
Sipa 12	-	-	-	-	-	-	-	-	-	-	-	8	-
Italy	288	13	14	11	10	-	40	6	-	42	31	39	4
F-47D	75	-	-	-	-	-	-	-	-	-	-	-	-
F-51D	100	-	-	-	-	-	-	-	-	-	-	-	-
F-84G	63	12	12	10	10	-	40	6	-	42	23	14	-
C-119G	-	-	-	-	-	-	-	-	-	-	-	3	3
T-6D	20	-	-	-	-	-	-	-	-	-	-	-	-
T-6G	30	-	-	-	-	-	-	-	-	-	-	-	-
T-33A	-	1	2	1	-	-	-	-	-	-	4	4	1
Mark IV (Hvd) .	-	-	-	-	-	-	-	-	-	-	4	18	-
Netherlands	153	6	12	7	-	32	1	2	8	9	5	2	2
F-84E	21	-	-	-	-	-	-	-	-	-	-	-	-
F-84G	102	-	-	7	-	32	1	2	8	9	5	-	-
C-47	-	6	10	-	-	-	-	-	-	-	-	-	-
T-7	28	-	-	-	-	-	-	-	-	-	-	-	-
T-33A	2	-	2	-	-	-	-	-	-	-	-	2	2
Norway	48	-	-	5	6	8	7	6	5	12	19	3	29
F-84E	6	-	-	-	-	-	-	-	-	-	-	-	-
F-84G	32	-	-	5	6	8	7	6	5	9	18	2	29
C-47	10	-	-	-	-	-	-	-	-	-	-	-	-
T-33A	-	-	-	-	-	-	-	-	-	3	1	1	-
Portugal	71	1	-	-	-	-	-	25	-	-	3	1	-
F-47D	50	-	-	-	-	-	-	-	-	-	-	-	-
F-84G	-	-	-	-	-	-	-	25	-	-	-	-	-
SA-16A	1	-	-	-	-	-	-	-	-	-	1	1	-
T-6G	20	-	-	-	-	-	-	-	-	-	-	-	-
T-33A	-	-	-	-	-	-	-	-	-	-	2	-	-
H-19A	-	1	-	-	-	-	-	-	-	-	-	-	-
United Kingdom	90	3	-	-	-	4	3	3	7	3	17	6	26
B-29	84	-	-	-	-	-	-	-	-	-	-	-	-
RB-29	3	-	-	-	-	-	-	-	-	-	-	-	-
P2V-5	3	3	-	-	-	4	3	3	7	3	17	6	2
F-86E	-	-	-	-	-	-	-	-	-	-	-	-	24
Yugoslavia	115	3	2	3	1	-	-	-	6	26	-	-	1
F-47D	115	3	2	3	1	-	-	-	2	-	-	-	-
F-84G	-	-	-	-	-	-	-	-	-	25	-	-	-
T-33A	-	-	-	-	-	-	-	-	4	1	-	-	1

TABLE 168 – AIRCRAFT SHIPMENTS TO MDAP COUNTRIES – TITLES, I, II, III, AND IV, FISCAL YEAR 1953 – Continued

(Includes USAF Grant Aid and Offshore Procurement)

AIRCRAFT MODEL AND SERIES	CUMULATIVE SHIPMENTS AS OF 30 JUN 52	SHIPMENTS DURING JUL 52	AUG	SEP	OCT	NOV	DEC	JAN 53	FEB	MAR	APR	MAY	JUN
TITLE II - TOTAL	122	2	8	16	30	23	59	20	-	6	53	25	15
Greece	35	1	5	7	8	12	29	8	-	6	16	22	13
F-84G	32	-	4	7	7	11	29	8	-	6	16	21	11
T-33A	3	1	1	-	1	1	-	-	-	-	-	1	2
Iran	7	-	-	-	-	-	-	-	-	-	-	-	-
PT-13	2	-	-	-	-	-	-	-	-	-	-	-	-
L-4	5	-	-	-	-	-	-	-	-	-	-	-	-
Turkey	80	1	3	9	22	11	30	12	-	-	37	3	2
F-84G	72	-	2	9	19	10	30	12	-	-	37	-	2
T-33A	8	1	1	-	3	1	-	-	-	-	-	3	-
TITLE III - TOTAL	314	14	-	4	67	14	20	62	16	60	44	75	34
China, NGR	-	-	-	-	25	14	20	28	16	54	44	68	24
P4Y-2	-	-	-	-	-	3	-	-	-	-	-	3	3
F-47N	-	-	-	-	25	8	20	27	12	51	20	27	-
F-84G	-	-	-	-	-	-	-	-	-	-	24	36	17
RF-51	-	-	-	-	-	3	-	1	4	-	-	-	4
T-33A	-	-	-	-	-	-	-	-	-	3	-	2	-
Korea	10	-	-	-	-	-	-	-	-	-	-	-	-
F-51D	10	-	-	-	-	-	-	-	-	-	-	-	-
Philippines	54	-	-	-	-	-	-	4	-	1	-	4	-
F-51D	50	-	-	-	-	-	-	-	-	-	-	-	-
C-47	4	-	-	-	-	-	-	-	-	-	-	-	-
L-5	-	-	-	-	-	-	-	4	-	1	-	4	-
Thailand	80	-	-	-	36	-	-	-	-	-	-	-	-
F8F	50	-	-	-	36	-	-	-	-	-	-	-	-
T-6F	30	-	-	-	-	-	-	-	-	-	-	-	-
Vietnam	170	14	-	4	6	-	-	30	-	5	-	3	10
B-26	41	-	-	-	-	-	-	-	-	5	-	3	-
F8F	106	14	-	-	-	-	-	30	-	-	-	-	10
RB-26	5	-	-	-	-	-	-	-	-	-	-	-	-
C-47	18	-	-	4	6	-	-	-	-	-	-	-	-
TITLE IV - TOTAL	-	-	-	-	-	-	-	-	-	-	17	-	33
Brazil	-	-	-	-	-	-	-	-	-	-	-	-	5
B-17	-	-	-	-	-	-	-	-	-	-	-	-	5
Chile	-	-	-	-	-	-	-	-	-	-	7	-	10
F-47D	-	-	-	-	-	-	-	-	-	-	7	-	10
Colombia	-	-	-	-	-	-	-	-	-	-	10	-	1
F-47D	-	-	-	-	-	-	-	-	-	-	10	-	1
Ecuador	-	-	-	-	-	-	-	-	-	-	-	-	11
F-47D	-	-	-	-	-	-	-	-	-	-	-	-	11
Peru	-	-	-	-	-	-	-	-	-	-	-	-	6
F-47D	-	-	-	-	-	-	-	-	-	-	-	-	6

a/ Cumulative shipments for Title I Countries as of 30 June 1952 have been adjusted to include offshore procurement aircraft not previously reported.

b/ Nineteen T-6D's were transferred from Denmark to France in July 1952.

c/ One F-84G shipped during October 1952 was returned to continental USAF during November 1952.

SOURCE: Materiel Statistics Division, Directorate of Statistical Services, DCS/C

TABLE 169 — USAF SUPPORTED AIRCRAFT IN MDAP COUNTRIES BY TYPE AND MODEL — QUARTERLY — FY 1953

TYPE AND MODEL	30 SEPTEMBER 1952			31 DECEMBER 1952			31 MARCH 1953			30 JUNE 1953		
	TOTAL	ACTIVE	IN-ACTIVE	TOTAL	ACTIVE	IN-ACTIVE	TOTAL	ACTIVE	IN-ACTIVE	TOTAL	ACTIVE	IN-ACTIVE
AIRCRAFT - TOTAL	3974	3072	902	4342	3399	943	4963	4016	947	5392	4383	1009
BOMBER	249	189	60	251	214	37	295	240	55	380	282	98
A-25	44	29	15	37	27	10	31	23	8	24	17	7
B-17	1	1	-	1	1	-	5	5	-	10	10	-
B-24	20	10	10	20	18	2	20	19	1	19	18	1
B-25	18	9	9	18	15	3	36	32	4	79	69	10
B-26	63	52	11	63	54	9	67	57	10	70	51	19
B-29	83	71	12	82	71	11	80	52	28	80	36	44
FBY-5	8	8	-	8	8	-	15	14	1	27	26	1
PB2B	6	3	3	6	4	2	6	3	3	6	2	4
P2V-5	6	6	-	13	13	-	26	26	-	50	38	12
P4Y-2	-	-	-	3	3	-	3	3	-	9	9	-
PV-2	-	-	-	-		-	6	6	-	6	6	-
FIGHTER	1674	1369	305	1967	1609	358	2397	2010	387	2737	2321	416
F-47	602	440	162	634	486	148	720	573	147	873	663	210
F-51	196	183	13	190	161	29	186	168	18	205	175	30
F-84	617	544	73	871	761	110	1228	1087	141	1438	1336	102
F6F	28	21	7	27	15	12	2	-	2	-	-	-
F8F	137	112	25	167	127	40	192	142	50	170	119	51
Spitfire	94	69	25	78	59	19	69	40	29	51	28	23
RECONNAISSANCE	13	13	-	16	14	2	21	21	-	18	17	1
RB-25	3	3	-	3	2	1	3	3	-	3	2	1
RB-26	4	4	-	4	4	-	4	4	-	4	4	-
RB-29	3	3	-	3	3	-	3	3	-	3	3	-
RF-38	3	3	-	3	2	1	3	3	-	-	-	-
RF-51	-	-	-	3	3	-	8	8	-	8	8	-
SEARCH AND RESCUE	1	1	-	1	-	1	1	1	-	3	2	1
SA-16	1	1	-	1	-	1	1	1	-	3	2	1
CARGO	474	330	144	527	390	137	525	407	118	526	420	106
C-45	34	29	5	34	30	4	34	27	7	34	27	7
C-46	138	88	50	137	97	40	136	129	7	136	131	5
C-47	293	213	80	335	244	91	334	233	101	331	237	94
C-54	3	-	3	3	3	-	3	3	-	2	2	-
C-64	2	-	2	2	-	2	2	-	2	-	-	-
C-119	4	-	4	16	16	-	16	15	1	23	23	-
TRAINER	1461	1093	368	1478	1096	382	1614	1270	344	1623	1276	347
T-6	841	666	175	823	632	191	948	755	193	996	797	199
T-7	29	25	4	29	24	5	30	24	6	29	20	9
T-11	118	79	39	117	80	37	123	75	48	127	79	48
T-13	76	41	35	76	42	34	76	42	34	18	16	2
T-16	190	138	52	190	152	38	190	157	33	189	137	52
T-17	114	70	44	122	76	46	121	120	1	119	101	18
T-26	1	1	-	1	1	-	1	1	-	-	-	-
T-33	59	46	13	88	65	23	92	71	21	116	100	16
Mark IV (Hvd)	-	-	-	-	-	-	-	-	-	10	10	-
PA-11	5	2	3	5	2	3	5	4	1	-	-	-
Moth	19	16	3	19	14	5	19	18	1	19	16	3
Firefly	9	9	-	8	8	-	9	3	6	-	-	-
COMMUNICATION	102	77	25	102	76	26	110	67	43	105	65	40
L-4	63	53	10	63	52	11	68	40	28	63	41	22
L-5	29	17	12	29	19	10	32	21	11	35	20	15
L-17	2	1	1	2	1	1	2	2	-	2	2	-
H-5	2	1	1	2	2	-	2	1	1	2	1	1
H-13	1	1	-	1	-	1	1	1	-	1	1	-
H-19	1	-	1	1	-	1	1	-	1	1	-	1
H-47	3	3	-	3	2	1	3	2	1	-	-	-
Auster	-	-	-	-	-	-	-	-	-	-	-	-
K-225	1	1	-	1	-	1	1	-	1	1	-	1

Source: Materiel Statistics Division, Directorate of Statistical Services, DCS/C.

TABLE 170 — MDAP AIRCRAFT LOSSES BY CAUSE — FISCAL YEAR 1953

TYPE AND MODEL	TOTAL	OPERATIONAL	NON-OPERATIONAL	COMBAT	TRANSFER DIVERSION AND CLASS 01Z
TOTAL	676	277	121	16	262
BOMBER	30	7	14	1	8
A-25	21	1	14	-	6
B-24	2	2	-	-	-
B-25	1	1	-	-	-
B-26	3	-	-	1	2
B-29	3	3	-	-	-
FIGHTER	327	192	63	11	61
F-47	94	76	17	-	1
F-51	25	16	9	-	-
F-84	80	77	2	-	1
F6F	29	-	1	-	28
F8F	40	9	3	11	17
Spitfire	59	14	31	-	14
RECONNAISSANCE	3	-	-	-	3
RF-38	3	-	-	-	3
CARGO	100	17	2	2	79
C-45	2	2	-	-	-
C-46	4	4	-	-	-
C-47	91	11	2	2	76
C-54	1	-	-	-	1
C-64	2	-	-	-	2
TRAINER	184	60	16	2	106
T-6	66	45	9	2	10
T-7	2	1	1	-	-
T-11	10	2	1	-	7
T-13	63	-	2	-	61
T-16	13	2	-	-	11
T-17	6	2	2	-	2
T-26	2	-	1	-	1
T-33	7	7	-	-	-
Firefly	10	1	-	-	9
PA-11	5	-	-	-	5
COMMUNICATION	32	1	26	-	5
L-4	6	-	5	-	1
L-5	6	1	5	-	-
L-17	1	-	-	-	1
H-47	3	-	-	-	3
Auster	16	-	16	-	-

SOURCE: Materiel Statistics Division, Directorate of Statistical Services, DCS/C.

TABLE 171 — MDAP AIRCRAFT FLYING HOURS BY TYPE AND MODEL — QUARTERLY, FISCAL YEAR 1953

TYPE AND MODEL	HOURS FLOWN				
	TOTAL	FIRST QUARTER	SECOND QUARTER	THIRD QUARTER	FOURTH QUARTER
TOTAL	862,182	204,520	196,831	208,816	252,015
BOMBER	57,853	13,750	13,407	15,045	15,651
A-25	6,445	1,802	1,253	1,598	1,792
B-17	449	-	17	149	283
B-24	4,781	1,172	555	1,497	1,557
B-25	7,575	1,421	1,658	2,865	1,631
B-26	12,899	2,859	3,477	2,668	3,895
B-29	15,721	5,366	5,093	3,072	2,190
PBY-5	2,353	455	516	840	542
PB2B	932	357	141	216	218
P2V-5	5,810	318	679	1,852	2,961
P4Y-2	613	-	18	215	380
PV-2	275	-	-	73	202
FIGHTER	280,776	63,632	55,687	67,170	94,287
F-47	82,552	19,578	15,456	21,326	26,192
F-51	28,564	9,179	6,882	6,299	6,204
F-84	116,085	21,195	18,534	26,897	49,459
F6F	2,347	1,211	971	162	3
F8F	37,812	8,443	10,042	9,593	9,734
Spitfire	13,416	4,026	3,802	2,893	2,695
RECONNAISSANCE	3,366	597	594	972	1,203
RB-25	585	170	118	162	135
RB-26	1,273	321	318	328	306
RB-29	418	52	99	114	153
RF-38	172	54	59	59	-
RF-51	918	-	-	309	609
SEARCH AND RESCUE	98	37	-	5	56
SA-16	98	37	-	5	56
CARGO	135,367	31,872	32,012	32,605	38,878
C-45	4,966	1,504	1,049	1,066	1,347
C-46	30,731	6,668	6,706	8,252	9,105
C-47	96,777	23,650	23,712	22,446	26,969
C-54	534	-	10	243	281
C-64	50	50	-	-	-
C-119	2,309	-	535	598	1,176
TRAINER	368,987	90,956	91,122	88,811	98,098
T-6	262,437	62,790	65,100	64,389	70,158
T-7	5,270	1,797	914	1,098	1,461
T-11	17,634	5,828	4,363	2,952	4,491
T-13	13,050	4,501	4,148	3,918	483
T-16	26,349	8,322	4,920	4,359	8,748
T-17	21,666	4,340	7,256	6,989	3,081
T-26	95	44	25	23	3
T-33	16,847	2,225	3,096	4,269	7,257
Mark IV (Hvd.)	109	-	-	-	109
PA-11	373	69	88	90	126
Moth	4,849	1,012	1,029	627	2,181
Firefly	308	28	183	97	-
COMMUNICATION	15,735	3,676	4,009	4,208	3,842
L-4	6,808	1,592	1,872	1,833	1,511
L-5	8,206	1,869	1,887	2,168	2,282
L-17	81	55	7	8	11
H-5	240	59	86	57	38
H-13	28	19	4	5	-
H-47	372	82	153	137	-

SOURCE: Materiel Statistics Division, Directorate of Statistical Services, DCS/C.

TABLE 172 — MDAP AIRCRAFT UTILIZATION RATES FOR SELECTED MODELS — QUARTERLY — FY 1953

TYPE AND MODEL	FIRST QUARTER			SECOND QUARTER			THIRD QUARTER			FOURTH QUARTER		
	AVERAGE ACTIVE AIRCRAFT	TOTAL HOURS FLOWN	MONTHLY UTILI-ZATION RATE	AVERAGE ACTIVE AIRCRAFT	TOTAL HOURS FLOWN	MONTHLY UTILI-ZATION RATE	AVERAGE ACTIVE AIRCRAFT	TOTAL HOURS FLOWN	MONTHLY UTILI-ZATION RATE	AVERAGE ACTIVE AIRCRAFT	TOTAL HOURS FLOWN	MONTHLY UTILI-ZATION RATE
A-25	28	1,802	21.4	28	1,253	14.9	25	1,598	21.3	20	1,792	29.8
B-25	11	1,421	43.0	12	1,658	46.0	24	2,865	39.7	50	1,631	10.8
B-26	52	2,859	18.3	53	3,477	21.8	56	2,668	15.8	54	3,895	24.0
B-29	70	5,366	25.5	71	5,093	23.9	62	3,072	16.5	44	2,190	16.5
P2V-5	4	318	26.5	10	679	22.6	20	1,852	30.8	32	2,961	30.8
F-47	419	19,578	15.5	463	15,456	11.1	530	21,326	13.4	618	26,192	14.1
F-51	186	9,179	16.4	172	6,852	13.3	164	6,299	12.8	172	6,204	12.0
F-84	414	21,195	17.0	652	18,534	9.4	924	26,897	9.7	1,212	49,459	13.6
F8F	108	8,443	26.0	120	10,042	27.8	134	9,593	23.8	130	9,734	24.9
C-46	106	6,668	20.9	92	6,706	24.2	113	8,252	24.3	130	9,105	23.3
C-47	214	23,650	36.8	228	23,712	34.6	238	22,446	31.4	235	26,969	38.2
C-119	-	-	-	8	535	22.2	16	598	12.4	19	1,176	20.6
T-6	659	62,790	31.7	649	65,100	33.4	694	64,389	30.9	776	70,158	30.1
T-7/11	107	7,625	23.7	104	5,277	16.9	102	4,050	13.2	99	5,952	20.0
T-16	143	8,322	19.3	145	4,920	11.3	154	4,359	9.4	147	8,748	19.8
T-17	72	4,340	20.0	73	7,256	33.1	98	6,989	23.7	110	3,081	9.3
T-33	36	2,225	20.6	56	3,096	18.4	68	4,269	20.9	86	7,257	28.1
L-4	50	1,592	10.6	52	1,872	12.0	46	1,833	13.2	40	1,511	12.6
L-5	21	1,869	29.6	18	1,887	34.9	20	2,166	36.1	20	2,282	38.0
Other	235	15,278	21.6	229	13,396	19.4	222	13,293	19.9	204	11,718	19.1

SOURCE: Materiel Statistics Division, Directorate of Statistical Services, DCS/C.

TABLE 173— MUTUAL DEFENSE ASSISTANCE PROGRAM
BY COUNTRY—

(In Thousands

TITLE AND COUNTRY	CUMULATIVE FISCAL YEARS 1950 - 1953			SHIPMENTS FROM PORT CUMULATIVE MONTHLY FISCAL YEAR - 1953			
	PROGRAM	SUPPLY ACTIONS 1/ a/	SHIPMENTS FROM PORT	JULY 1952	AUGUST 1952	SEPTEMBER 1952	OCTOBER 1952
	GRANT AID						
TOTAL	4,793,397	4,217,055	1,142,307	402,669	421,948	457,633	575,132
VALUE OF EQUIPMENT-TOTAL	4,415,669	3,972,812	1,142,307	402,669	421,948	457,633	575,132
TITLE I - TOTAL	3,901,689	3,470,035	830,861	313,873	329,265	355,222	450,826
Belgium	316,965	255,771	78,345	29,260	31,749	35,545	43,812
Denmark	131,143	115,455	42,512	14,663	14,874	21,179	26,820
France	688,957	727,550	190,802	68,605	74,221	82,329	107,278
France (Lisbon)	56,400	56,400	47,055	-	-	-	19,305
France (Budgetary Support Program)	56,850	30,655	8,656	-	-	-	-
France (French MD452 Mark IV)	86,540	86,540	-	-	-	-	-
Italy	385,496	384,042	103,515	40,936	44,666	47,709	61,365
Italy (North Am. AWX)	54,500	-	-	-	-	-	-
Netherlands	230,109	192,076	73,894	39,491	41,184	43,772	48,761
Netherlands (Hawker - Hunter)	42,000	42,000	-	-	-	-	-
Norway	150,023	168,262	57,486	17,700	18,505	20,082	22,228
Portugal	86,610	118,788	25,551	7,133	7,134	7,310	12,773
Fed Rep Ger	527,349	334,815	-	-	-	-	-
United Kingdom	435,968	417,745	160,808	83,726	84,301	84,325	86,799
United Kingdom (Hawker-Hunter	140,074	140,074	-	-	-	-	-
Yugoslavia	222,859	181,038	42,237	12,359	12,631	12,971	21,685
Repair & Rehab. of Excess Stocks	39,561	32,444	b/ a/	-	-	-	-
Accessorial & Sundry Charges	250,285	186,380	b/ a/	-	-	-	-
TITLE II - TOTAL	452,444	430,557	136,274	48,159	50,467	54,642	70,094
Greece	148,178	156,032	68,528	22,534	23,893	25,696	35,498
Greece (United Kingdom)	6,074	5,451	3,822	-	-	-	-
Iran	8,012	7,426	1,719	1,128	1,146	1,233	1,374
Turkey	238,784	250,815	62,205	24,497	25,428	27,713	33,222
Repair & Rehab. of Excess Stocks	1,801	42	b/ a/	-	-	-	-
Accessorial & Sundry Charges	49,595	10,791	b/ a/	-	-	-	-
TITLE III - TOTAL	409,167	311,391	169,349	40,637	42,198	47,247	53,551
NORC	178,532	99,034	68,658	2,052	3,035	3,166	6,122
French Indo-China	142,713	145,655	71,077	25,123	25,209	29,710	31,659
French Indo-China (Lisbon)	3,600	3,600	4,346	-	-	-	1,023
Korea	529	529	529	529	529	529	529
Philippines	18,561	21,299	7,342	5,002	5,080	5,267	5,478
Thailand	33,243	26,878	17,397	7,931	8,345	8,575	8,740
Repair & Rehab. of Excess Stocks	11,457	6,802	b/ a/	-	-	-	-
Accessorial & Sundry Charges	20,532	7,594	b/ a/	-	-	-	-
TITLE IV - TOTAL	30,097	5,072	5,823	-	18	522	661
Brazil	8,195	864	-	-	-	-	-
Chile	4,893	694	1,922	-	-	-	-
Columbia	3,400	552	1,469	-	-	246	253
Cuba	1,890	705	253	-	18	147	154
Equador	2,083	557	1,277	-	-	-	125
Peru	3,722	1,033	902	-	-	129	129
Uruguay	1,417	477	-	-	-	-	-
Repair & Rehab. of Excess Stocks	4,100	3	b/ a/	-	-	-	-
Accessorial & Sundry Charges	397	187	b/ a/	-	-	-	-

1/ Represents the Cumulative Supply Actions as of 31 March 1953, since after this date these data were not reported by country.

a/ Not applicable.

SUPPLY ACTIONS AND SHIPMENTS FROM PORTS
— FY 1953
of Dollars)

NOVEMBER 1952	DECEMBER 1952	JANUARY 1953	FEBRUARY 1953	MARCH 1953	APRIL 1953	MAY 1953	JUNE 1953	TITLE AND COUNTRY
SHIPMENTS FROM PORT - CUMULATIVE MONTHLY FISCAL YEAR - 1953								
GRANT AID								
601,416	676,182	781,044	837,336	881,623	978,842	1,075,140	1,142,307	TOTAL
601,416	676,182	781,044	837,336	881,623	978,842	1,075,140	1,142,307	VALUE OF EQUIPMENT - TOTAL
458,404	503,249	586,805	627,410	660,449	728,654	796,413	830,861	TITLE I - TOTAL
48,422	53,891	71,153	72,338	72,548	73,303	76,986	78,345	Belgium
29,651	30,641	32,818	33,789	35,035	36,906	37,488	42,512	Denmark
115,062	129,945	147,381	158,760	162,835	176,357	187,127	190,802	France
19,305	27,543	32,744	34,383	34,382	44,220	46,949	47,055	France (Lisbon)
-	-	-	-	-	-	-	8,656	France (Budgetary Support Program)
-	-	-	-	-	-	-	-	France (French MD452 Mark IV)
52,217	56,210	67,172	71,068	82,512	89,306	100,445	103,515	Italy
-	-	-	-	-	-	-	-	Italy (North Am. AWX)
51,137	56,776	61,230	64,001	67,377	69,284	73,661	73,894	Netherlands
-	-	-	-	-	-	-	-	Netherlands (Hawker-Hunter)
23,412	24,459	31,375	34,841	37,708	42,960	48,739	57,486	Norway
9,517	10,230	13,062	21,540	21,982	23,112	25,396	25,551	Portugal
-	-	-	-	-	-	-	-	Fed Rep Ger
87,856	88,124	101,783	107,296	110,036	135,912	159,369	160,808	United Kingdom
-	-	-	-	-	-	-	-	United Kingdom (Hawker-Hunter)
21,825	25,430	28,087	29,394	36,034	37,294	40,253	42,237	Yugoslavia
-	-	-	-	-	-	-	-	Repair & Rehab. of Excess Stocks
-	-	-	-	-	-	-	-	Accessorial & Sundry Charges
77,716	85,271	96,406	103,642	105,618	120,209	130,821	136,274	TITLE II - TOTAL
38,238	41,752	47,781	50,516	52,165	56,829	64,858	68,528	Greece
-	2,503	2,920	2,920	2,946	3,379	3,436	3,822	Greece (United Kingdom)
1,386	1,389	1,410	1,472	1,536	1,568	1,693	1,719	Iran
38,092	39,627	44,295	48,734	48,971	58,433	60,834	62,205	Turkey
-	-	-	-	-	-	-	-	Repair & Rehab. of Excess Stocks
-	-	-	-	-	-	-	-	Accessorial & Sundry Charges
64,572	86,861	97,007	105,455	114,651	127,389	143,992	169,349	TITLE III - TOTAL
8,890	23,644	28,350	25,700	32,970	43,668	59,299	68,658	NGRC
34,807	40,002	45,073	55,592	56,918	57,317	57,915	71,077	French Indo-China
1,023	1,016	2,238	2,238	2,238	3,229	3,230	4,346	French Ind-China (Lisbon)
529	529	529	529	530	529	529	529	Korea
5,569	5,716	5,900	6,248	6,349	6,877	7,037	7,342	Philippines
13,754	15,954	14,917	15,148	15,646	15,769	15,962	17,397	Thailand
-	-	-	-	-	-	-	-	Repair & Rehab. of Excess Stocks
-	-	-	-	-	-	-	-	Accessorial & Sundry Charges
724	801	826	829	905	2,590	3,914	5,823	TITLE IV - TOTAL
-	-	-	-	-	-	-	-	Brazil
-	-	-	-	-	1,656	1,810	1,922	Chile
256	285	297	298	298	298	343	1,469	Columbia
158	158	160	160	196	198	216	253	Cuba
126	145	151	151	151	151	1,244	1,277	Equador
184	213	218	220	260	287	301	902	Peru
-	-	-	-	-	-	-	-	Uruguay
-	-	-	-	-	-	-	-	Repair & Rehab. of Excess Stocks
-	-	-	-	-	-	-	-	Accessorial & Sunkry Charges

SOURCE: MATERIEL STATISTICS DIVISION, DIRECTORATE OF STATISTICAL SERVICES, DCS/C.

TABLE 174 – MUTUAL DEFENSE ASSISTANCE PROGRAM SUPPLY ACTIONS AND SHIPMENTS FROM PORTS BY MAJOR EQUIPMENT CATEGORY

(In Thousands of Dollars)

MAJOR EQUIPMENT CATEGORY	CUMULATIVE FISCAL YRS. 50 - 53			SHIPMENTS FROM PORT-CUMULATIVE MONTHLY FY 1953			
	PROGRAM	SUPPLY ACTIONS	SHIPMENTS FROM PORT	JULY 1952	AUGUST 1952	SEPTEMBER 1952	OCTOBER 1952
	GRANT AID						
TOTAL	4,793,397	4,356,039	1,142,307	402,669	421,948	457,633	575,132
VALUE OF EQUIPMENT - TOTAL	4,415,669	4,099,140	1,142,307	402,669	421,948	457,633	575,132
Acft. & Aero. Equip.	2,695,017	2,622,593	784,700	331,641	347,816	380,931	466,202
Radios & Radar	378,875	352,978	23,685	5,868	6,359	6,594	9,440
Engineering Equip. & Sup.	122,756	105,871	46,609	9,410	9,861	9,896	17,520
Artillery	76,125	44,958	3,376	313	313	313	1,387
Quartermaster Equip. & Sup.	290,423	190,127	57,526	23,930	25,797	28,047	37,537
Bombs, Rockets, & Misc. Ammo.	359,633	296,242	156,570	29,803	30,065	30,065	40,771
Tng. Equip., Maint. & Sup.	37,640	32,385	5,744	1,546	1,574	1,614	2,075
Petroleum Oil & Lub. for Acft.	5,334	5,165	155	80	80	80	83
Petroleum Oil & Lub. for Other than Acft.	3,828	3,230	63	78	83	93	117
Off-shore Procurement Prog. b/	446,038	445,591	63,879	-	-	-	-
Repair & Rehab. of Excess Stocks	56,919	41,888	a/	-	-	-	-
Accessorial & Sundry Charges	320,809	215,011	a/	-	-	-	-
	REIMBURSABLE MATERIEL						
TOTAL	328,894	316,331	124,529	35,189	70,898	71,215	5,380
Acft. & Aero. Equip.	312,203	303,235	117,883	33,595	69,713	70,025	5,380
Engineering Equip. & Sup.	7,990	6,154	2,828	-	55	55	-
Quartermaster Equip. & Sup.	55	55	55	98	104	104	-
Bombs, Rockets, & Misc. Ammo.	4,371	3,326	3,077	1,383	946	964	-
Tng. Equip., Maint., Parts and Sup.	2,159	1,891	347	11	14	15	-
General Equip., Maint., Parts and Sup. c/	1,902	1,482	268	69	24	30	-
Weapons Maint., Parts & Sup. d/	214	188	71	33	38	22	-

MAJOR EQUIPMENT CATEGORY	NOVEMBER 1952	DECEMBER 1952	JANUARY 1953	FEBRUARY 1953	MARCH 1953	APRIL 1953	MAY 1953	JUNE 1953
	GRANT AID							
TOTAL	601,416	676,182	781,044	837,336	881,623	978,842	1,075,140	1,142,307
VALUE OF EQUIPMENT - TOTAL	601,416	676,182	781,044	837,336	881,623	978,842	1,075,140	1,142,307
Acft. & Aero. Equip.	470,724	497,281	577,162	620,234	654,756	728,488	786,348	784,700
Radios & Radar	10,255	10,678	11,036	12,363	13,554	15,107	21,742	23,685
Engineering Equip. & Sup.	19,851	21,813	25,568	30,283	33,870	37,677	48,611	46,609
Artillery	3,724	4,676	4,696	5,088	5,172	5,215	5,542	3,376
Quartermaster Equip. & Sup.	39,244	42,083	45,150	46,964	50,450	55,205	60,894	57,526
Bombs, Rockets., & Misc. Ammo.	54,991	96,456	114,041	118,936	120,197	132,815	146,485	156,570
Tng. Equip., Maint. & Sup.	2,427	2,986	3,163	3,247	3,407	4,112	5,294	5,744
Petroleum Oil & Lub. for Acft.	83	88	95	160	156	160	161	155
Petroleum Oil & Lub. for Other than Acft.	117	121	133	61	61	63	63	63
Off-shore Procurement Prog. b/	-	-	-	-	-	-	-	63,879
Repair & Rehab. of Excess Stocks	a/	a/	a/	-	-	-	-	-
Accessorial & Sundry Charges	-	-	a/	-	-	-	-	-
	REIMBURSABLE MATERIEL							
TOTAL	5,378	-	5,102	92,238	101,470	117,188	118,845	124,529
Acft. & Aero. Equip.	5,378	-	5,102	88,482	97,236	112,081	112,810	117,883
Engineering Equip. & Sup.	-	-	-	55	55	55	55	55
Quartermaster Equip. & Sup.	-	-	-	193	260	278	283	268
Bombs, Rockets, & Misc. Ammo.	-	-	-	2,519	2,791	3,037	3,053	3,077
Tng. Equip., Maint., Parts and Sup.	-	-	-	23	29	34	295	347
General Equip., Maint., Parts and Sup.	-	-	-	905	1,035	1,634	2,280	2,828
Weapons Maint., Parts & Sup.	-	-	-	61	64	69	69	71

a/ Not applicable.

b/ The Off-Shore Procurement Program was included in MDAP Materiel Report for the first time in June, 1953.

c/ Includes Radios & Radar.

d/ Includes Artillery.

SOURCE: MATERIEL STATISTICS DIVISION, DIRECTORATE OF STATISTICAL SERVICES, DCS/C.

TABLE 175 – USAF CIVILIAN PERSONNEL IN SALARIED AND WAGE BOARD GROUPS EMPLOYED UNDER MUTUAL DEFENSE ASSISTANCE PROGRAM (MDAP) – FY 1953

Group By Location	Jul (1952)	Aug	Sep	Oct	Nov	Dec	Jan (1953)	Feb	Mar	Apr	May	Jun
WORLDWIDE - TOTAL	4,925	4,759	5,025	5,005	5,118	4,985	5,293	5,748	4,857	4,096	3,895	3,918
Salaried	3,063	2,897	3,350	3,380	3,458	3,539	3,711	3,940	3,502	2,916	2,897	2,867
Wage Board	1,862	1,862	1,675	1,625	1,660	1,446	1,582	1,808	1,355	1,180	998	1,051
CONTINENTAL US - TOTAL	3,534	3,304	3,460	3,821	3,910	3,606	3,866	4,357	4,270	3,509	3,301	3,323
Salaried	2,674	2,504	2,587	2,757	2,817	2,778	2,824	3,069	3,130	2,549	2,519	2,488
Wage Board	860	800	873	1,064	1,093	828	1,042	1,288	1,140	960	782	835
Air Materiel Command - Total	3,879	3,148	3,310	3,647	3,735	3,434	3,696	4,188	4,110	3,349	3,140	3,164
Salaried	2,519	2,348	2,437	2,583	2,642	2,608	2,654	2,900	2,970	2,389	2,358	2,329
Wage Board	860	800	873	1,064	1,093	826	1,042	1,288	1,140	960	782	835
Air Training Command - Total	29	29	29	37	37	37	37	32	29	29	28	28
Salaried	29	29	29	37	37	35	37	32	29	29	28	28
Wage Board	-	-	-	-	-	2	-	-	-	-	-	-
Headquarters, USAF - Total	126	127	121	137	138	135	133	137	131	131	133	131
Salaried	126	127	121	137	138	135	133	137	131	131	133	131
Wage Board	-	-	-	-	-	-	-	-	-	-	-	-
OVERSEAS - TOTAL	1,391	1,455	1,565	1,184	1,208	1,379	1,427	1,391	587	587	594	595
Salaried	389	393	763	623	641	761	887	871	372	367	378	379
Wage Board	1,002	1,062	802	561	567	618	540	520	215	220	216	216
Air Materiel Command - Total	-	-	-	-	-	-	-	-	-	-	5	6
Salaried	-	-	-	-	-	-	-	-	-	-	5	6
Wage Board	-	-	-	-	-	-	-	-	-	-	-	-
Caribbean Air Command - Total	-	1	1	1	1	1	1	1	1	1	1	1
Salaried	-	1	1	1	1	1	1	1	1	1	1	1
Wage Board	-	-	-	-	-	-	-	-	-	-	-	-
Far East Air Forces - Total	20	22	19	18	15	15	14	13	13	12	12	12
Salaried	20	22	19	18	15	15	14	13	13	12	12	12
Wage Board	-	-	-	-	-	-	-	-	-	-	-	-
Headquarters Command, USAF - Total	83	80	80	87	87	58	83	26	24	20	25	27
Salaried	22	20	21	27	27	21	24	26	24	20	25	27
Wage Board	61	60	59	60	60	37	59	-	-	-	-	-
US Air Forces, Europe - Total	1,288	1,352	1,465	1,078	1,105	1,305	1,329	1,351	549	554	551	549
Salaried	347	350	722	577	598	724	848	831	334	334	335	333
Wage Board	941	1,002	743	501	507	581	481	520	215	220	216	216

Source: Personnel Statistics Division, DCS/Comptroller, Hq USAF

TABLE 176 — TUITION RATES FOR MDAP FORMAL TRAINING — FY 1953

(In the accomplishment of training of foreign students under the Mutual Defense Assistance Program (MDAP), the USAF charged the MDAP - appropriated funds for specific courses of training. This charge for "tuition" was reimbursed to the regular USAF accounts, from which the expense for MDAP training was funded. The determination of the tuition rates was based on the policy directive issued by the Office of Secretary of Defense to all of the three Services. This policy was predicated on the language of the appropriation legislation.

The policy specifically excluded the pay and allowances of all military personnel from MDAP, therefore, MDAP tuition rates were developed to include those pertinent direct and indirect expenses other than military pay and allowances. The tuition rates were based on the number of entries into training and the experience factor of attrition for each course.)

Course Number	Course Title	Calendar Days	Course Cost
	ADMINISTRATIVE COURSES		
OFFICERS			
22103	Classification & Assignment Officer	48	$ 180
AIRMEN			
73150	Career Guidance	58	225
73250	Personnel Specialist	42	170
75100	Technical Instructor (Armament & Photographic Fields)	47	530
75100	Technical Instructor (Radio)	56	325
75100	Technical Instructor (A & E Field - General)	56	150
75100	Technical Instructor (Automotive, Supply & Wire Maintenance Fields)	47	170
75100	Technical Instructor (Radar & Electronic Fields)	47	135
75100	Technical Instructor (A & E Fields Special)	45	210
75200	General Instructor	56	75
	AIRCRAFT MAINTENANCE COURSES		
OFFICERS			
10281	Flight Engineer Refresher (Ground Phase B-36)	90	525
48230	Aircraft Maintenance Officer	200	1,140
48231	Maintenance Administration	60	350
AIRMEN			
16600	Powerman	140	560
30080	A & E Liaison Mechanic	106	1,005
39950	Rotary Wing Mechanic H-13	48	480
42350	Aircraft Propeller Mechanic	60	310
42450	Mechanical Accessories & Equipment Technician	50	355
42550	Aircraft Hydraulic Mechanic	60	330
43150	Rotary Wing Mechanic H-5	48	475
43151	Aircraft Mechanic General - A & E	163	365
43151-A	Aircraft Mechanic Special B-36	40	120
43151-B	Aircraft Mechanic Special B-29	46	110
43151-J	Aircraft Mechanic Special B-47	46	130
43151-SP	Aircraft Mechanic Special F-89B	23	650
43152-A	Aircraft Reciprocating Mechanic Special R-4360	40	220
43152-B	Aircraft Reciprocating Mechanic Special R-3350	40	220
43152-Z	Engine Analyzer	10	60
43153-1	Aircraft Jet Engine Mechanic Special J-33	35	195
43153-2	Aircraft Jet Engine Mechanic Special J-35	35	190
43153-3	Aircraft Jet Engine Mechanic Special J-47	35	190
43154-A	Aircraft Electrician Special B-36	50	260
43154-B	Aircraft Electrician General	60	320
43156	Aircraft Instrument Mechanic	60	325
43271	Flight Engineer Technician	120	580
53150	Machinist	136	595
53250	Welder	100	545
53450	Airframe Repairman	106	445
	AIR POLICE TRAINING		
AIRMEN			
96130	Air Police Course	49	515
	COMMUNICATIONS COURSES		
OFFICERS			
02050	Communications Officer	315	1,925

(Continued)

TABLE – TUITION RATES FOR MDAP FORMAL TRAINING – FY 1953 (Continued)

(See first page of this table for headnote affecting this page.)

Course Number	Course Title	Calendar Days	Course Cost
	COMMUNICATIONS COURSES (CONTINUED)		
AIRMEN			
27251	Control Tower Operator	82	$ 175
27270	Air Traffic Control Operator	47	105
29150	Teletype Operator	76	215
29250	Cryptographic Operator	56	225
29350	Radio Operator - General	192	380
29352	Radio Intercept Operator	23	100
30120	Radio Fundamentals	154	620
30150	Radio Mechanic - Airborne Equipment	56	285
30151	Radio Mechanic - Ground Equipment	56	255
30171	Radio Maintenance Technician - Airborne Equipment	189	980
30173	Radio Maintenance Technician Ground Equipment	224	1,250
36150	Installer Cableman	140	495
36250	Central Office Equipment Mechanic	99	330
36251	Carrier Repeater Mechanic	111	405
36350	Communications Machine Repairman	158	530
	COMPTROLLER COURSES		
OFFICERS			
24010	Machine Records Officer	53	275
63022	Budget Officer	54	215
64020	Statistical Services Officer	60	260
AIRMEN			
26801	Budget & Fiscal Clerk	41	170
27201	Key Punch Machine Operator	12	90
40001	Tabulating Machine Operator	70	510
62200	Finance Technical Clerk	82	335
81050	Basic-Budget, Accounting & Disbursing Course	88	325
81370	Cost Analysis Technician	58	230
81470	Auditing Technician	117	650
83150	Statistical Specialist	76	325
83250	Machine Accounting	76	365
	ENGINEER COURSES		
AIRMEN			
56150-S	Cummins Generator Operator	18	135
56550-S	Heating Specialist	24	120
	FLYING COURSES		
OFFICERS			
1025	Pilot to Pilot AOB	97	3,690
1035-G	Bombardment - Flexible Gunnery Training	21	184
07888	Staff Officer - ECM Indoctrination	5	15
10140	Aircraft Controller	56	1,345
103100	Radar Bombardier Refresher	48	1,605
103401	Navigation Training for Bombardiers	168	2,990
103403	Navigator Training (To include Refresher)	49	635
103700	Navigator to Navigator - Bombardier	90	3,550
103700	Bombardier to Navigator - Bombardier	66	2,860
103702	K System Training for Navigator - Bombardier	54	1,935
103703	Bombardment Instructor	35	760
105400	Liaison Pilot	120	1,440
105402K	Basic - Pilot Instructor School	40	860
105403K	Single Engine - Pilot Instructor School	40	860
105404K	Multi Engine - Pilot Instructor School	40	860
103404	Navigator Instructor	21	250
105900	A/C Gunnery Instructor Training	76	19,530
105901	Instrument Pilot Instructor (B-26)	56	3,250
105903K	Instrument Pilot Instructor (Jet)	56	3,360
106601	Helicopter Pilot Training - H-5	82	1,330
106602	Helicopter Pilot Training - H-13	34	645
None	All Weather Fighter Interceptor Training	56	2,875
None	Combat Crew Training School (Jet)	56	11,385

(Continued)

TABLE — TUITION RATES FOR MDAP FORMAL TRAINING — FY 1953 (Continued)

(See first page of this table for headnote affecting this page.)

Course Number	Course Title	Calendar Days	Course Cost
	FLYING COURSES (CONTINUED)		
CADETS			
1051	USAF Basic Pilot School M. E.	168	$ 7,055
1054	USAF Pilot School S. E. (Jet)	182	11,600
1054	USAF Pilot School S. E. (Conventional)	171	4,455
105401	USAF Primary Pilot School	205	4,000
AIRMEN			
32351-F	Flexible Gunnery Training B-26	14	65
32351-F	Flexible Gunnery Training B-29	56	610
	GUIDED MISSILES COURSES		
OFFICERS			
10451	Guided Missiles Guidance & Control Officer	147	715
AIRMEN			
31100	Guided Missiles Fundamentals	41	220
31300	Guided Missiles Guidance Technician	99	640
31400	Guided Missiles Attitude Control Technician	64	320
	INTELLIGENCE COURSES		
OFFICERS			
85031	Photo & Radar Interpretation Officer	112	645
95000	Air Intelligence Officer	71	375
AIRMEN			
20450	Intelligence Operations Specialist	64	305
20451	Photo Interpretation Specialist	76	365
	MUNITIONS, WEAPONS MAINTENANCE & ARMAMENT SYSTEMS COURSES		
OFFICERS			
45930	Armament Systems Officer	261	1,180
45931	Armament Systems Officer - Cross Training	170	720
AIRMEN			
32020	Armament Systems Fundamentals	117	595
32150-A	"M" Series Bombsight Mechanic	35	120
32150-E	"K" Series Systems Mechanic	117	600
32171-E	"K" Series Systems Mechanic	158	600
32250-A	"E" Series Systems Mechanic	58	195
32250-B	AN/APG-30 Sight Systems Mechanic	41	140
32250-C	"A & K" Gun, Bomb, & Rocket Sighting Mechanic	29	95
32350-A	Turret Systems Mechanic B-36	76	295
32350-B	Gunlaying Systems Mechanic B-36	76	260
32350-F	Turret Systems Mechanic B-26, B-29 & B-50	111	400
32371-F	Turret Systems Technician B-26, B-29 & B-50	41	160
32440	Weapons Course	48	875
32540	Munitions Course	76	1,180
43151-H	Aircraft Mechanic Specialist F-84C	23	70
43151-H2	Aircraft Mechanic General (Jet)	23	65
46150	Basic Munitions	58	215
46250	Basic Weapons Repair	76	280
95512	Pre K-1 (AN/APS-23)	29	105
	PHOTOGRAPHIC COURSES		
OFFICERS			
85020	Aerial Photographic Officer	95	1,145
AIRMEN			
23150	Aerial Photographer	70	1,215
23250	Photo & Laboratory Technician	99	460
40350	Camera Repairman	70	300

(Continued)

TABLE — TUITION RATES FOR MDAP FORMAL TRAINING — FY 1953 (CONTINUED)

(See first page of this table for headnote affecting this page.)

Course Number	Course Title	Calendar Days	Course Cost
	RADAR COURSES		
OFFICERS			
01106	Electronics Officer - Ground	233	$ 705
01410	Electronics Officer - Air	245	800
7888X	Electronics Counter Measures Officer	280	1,690
AIRMEN			
27272	Aircraft Landing Control Operator	70	200
27350	Aircraft Control & Warning Operator	35	75
30220	Airmen Electronics Fundamentals	134	265
30250	Radar Mechanic - Airborne Equipment	82	250
30251-A	Radar Mechanic - AC&W Equipment	82	265
30271	Radar Technician - Airborne Equipment	106	580
30273-A	Radar Technician - AC&W Equipment	82	1,000
32051-B	Channel I AN/MPM-1	117	575
32150-F	APQ-24 System Mechanic	82	255
32171-F	Q-24 System Technician	87	340
30273-B	Radar Technician - Air Traffic Control Equipment	117	375
30273-C	Radar Technician - AN/MSQ-1	93	320
95307	Radar Technician - GCA	117	520
	SUPPLY COURSES		
OFFICERS			
40000	Supply Officer General	58	215
AIRMEN			
64050	Supply Technician	64	180
	WEATHER COURSES		
OFFICERS			
82053	Weather Equipment Engineering Officer	152	725
82197	High Altitude Forecaster Officer	71	315
AIRMEN			
25000A	Basic Weather Services (Equipment Channel)	130	630
25000B	Basic Weather Services (Observer Channel)	95	415
25100	Advanced Weather Equipment	142	845
25171	Intermediate Weather Equipment (Radar Phase)	99	200
25171	Intermediate Weather Equipment (Weather Phase)	71	470
25200	Advanced Meteorological	200	830
25270	Intermediate Meteorological	237	995
25271	Climatological	237	1,020
	MISCELLANEOUS TECHNICAL COURSES		
OFFICERS			
01000	Electronic Fundamentals - Phase I	128	410
09130	Transportation Officer	58	585
13833	Fire & Aircraft Crash Rescue Officer	88	4,660
48050	Automotive Maintenance & Repair Officer	94	525
73145	Radiological Defense Officer	42	210
AIRMEN			
34130	Instrument Trainer Repairman	60	275
34150	Instrument Trainer Repairman - Special Z-1	80	370
47151	Automotive Mechanic - Senior	105	360
60350	Special Vehicle Operator	58	250
70250	Basic Clerical	76	210
75100	Tech Instructor, San Marcos	47	180
95150	Basic Fire Fighter & Crash Rescueman	47	650
99550	Radiological Specialist	29	65

Source: Procurement and Research Division, Director of Budget, DCS/Comptroller, Hq USAF.

TABLE 177 — STATUS OF DEPARTMENT OF THE AIR FORCE MDAP FUNDS

(In thousands of dollars. Figures in parentheses indicate minus amounts.)

PURPOSE	USAF APPROVED PROGRAMS FOR MDAP	ALLOCATION FROM OSD TO USAF	ALLOCATION TO AF COMMANDS	CUMULATIVE OBLIGATIONS 30 JUN 53	CUMULATIVE OBLIGATIONS 30 JUN 52	OBLIGATIONS DURING FISCAL YEAR 1953				
						TOTAL	FIRST QUARTER	SECOND QUARTER	THIRD QUARTER	FOURTH QUARTER
FY 1950, 1951, 1952 and 1953 - Total	4,806,364	4,771,284	4,741,454	4,388,355	3,258,289	1,130,066	1,976	262,356	159,207	706,527
Title I Countries	3,955,442	3,924,243	3,896,144	3,625,412	2,675,423.	949,989	3,949	170,469	126,306	649,265
Title II Countries	461,662	458,162	456,657	443,812	327,462	116,350	(3,488)	77,786	23,669	18,383
Title III Countries	370,056	369,679	369,493	308,059	252,908	55,151	1,074	13,926	7,847	32,304
Title IV Countries	19,204	19,200	19,160	11,072	2,496	8,576	441	175	1,385	6,575
FY 1953 Program - Total	1,399,467	1,368,226	1,342,372	1,104,385	-	1,104,385	14,058	298,005	165,676	626,646
Title I Countries	1,191,714	1,160,514	1,135,865	949,167	-	949,167	11,706	209,010	136,553	591,898
Title II Countries	119,779	119,755	118,660	113,180	-	113,180	1,202	80,981	19,319	11,678
Title III Countries	76,880	76,867	76,792	35,747	-	35,747	1,105	7,973	9,144	17,525
Title IV Countries	11,094	11,090	11,055	6,291	-	6,291	45	41	660	5,545
FY 1952 Program - Total	1,571,245	1,570,985	1,568,622	1,491,391	1,484,894	6,497	(20,965)	(26,489)	(16,573)	70,524
Title I Countries	1,181,070	1,181,070	1,179,136	1,118,190	1,126,764	(8,574)	(14,759)	(19,297)	(17,465)	42,947
Title II Countries	201,994	201,994	201,658	197,619	199,079	(1,460)	(6,278)	(6,077)	1,553	9,342
Title III Countries	180,071	179,811	179,723	170,801	156,555	14,246	(324)	(1,249)	(1,386)	17,205
Title IV Countries	8,110	8,110	8,105	4,781	2,496	2,285	396	134	725	1,030
FY 1951 Program - Total	1,689,098	1,689,051	1,687,529	1,654,677	1,630,690	23,987	9,036	(7,724)	8,736	13,939
Title I Countries	1,501,065	1,501,135	1,499,656	1,481,805	1,470,881	10,924	7,129	(18,813)	6,615	15,993
Title II Countries	89,634	89,634	89,592	85,144	77,853	7,291	1,581	3,884	2,063	(237)
Title III Countries	98,399	98,282	98,281	87,728	81,956	5,772	326	7,205	58	(1,817)
FY 1950 Program - Total	146,554	143,022	142,931	137,902	142,705	(4,803)	(153)	(1,436)	1,368	(4,582)
Title I Countries	81,593	81,524	81,487	76,250	77,778	(1,528)	(127)	(431)	603	(1,573)
Title II Countries	50,255	46,779	46,747	47,869	50,530	(2,661)	7	(1,002)	734	(2,400)
Title III Countries	14,706	14,719	14,697	13,783	14,397	(614)	(33)	(3)	31	(609)

Source: Financial Management Division, Directorate of Budget, DCS/C.

MILITARY PERSONNEL

DEFINITIONS

AERONAUTICAL STATUS
The general grouping of Air Force personnel with reference to their aeronautical rating, aeronautical designation and flying status. The principal groupings are:

1. Rated Personnel: USAF Officers who have been awarded an aeronautical rating of Pilot or Aircraft Observer on personnel orders per authority AFR 50-7.

2. Non-Rated Personnel: Personnel who do not have an aeronautical rating of Pilot or Aircraft Observer, including personnel who have aeronautical designation, e. g., Flight Surgeon, Aviation Medical Examiner, Flight Nurse, Non-Rated Crew Member and Non-Rated Non-Crew Member, even though such personnel may be on flying status.

AIR CREW
A stipulated number of air crew personnel locally organized to operate an aircraft on an assigned mission. (For single-place aircraft, "air crew" equals "air crew personnel.")

AIR CREW PERSONNEL
Personnel whose current principal duty is occupancy of an air crew position. Included are tactical air crew personnel, instructors, advanced flying students, and administrative crew personnel whose principal duty is flying.

AIR FORCE COMMAND STRENGTH
All military personnel (permanent party and pipeline, USAF, SCARWAF, and Navy) who are assigned to Air Force units. This strength is chargeable against the personnel ceiling of the Department of the Air Force and is under the command jurisdiction of the Chief of Staff, USAF.

1. Command Strength - Continental: The total strength of military personnel who are assigned to units of which the Headquarters have permanent station location in the Continental US or to units which are enroute between Continental and Oversea stations but are assigned to a Continental Command or to the ZI portion of a Global Command.

2. Command Strength - Oversea: The total strength of military personnel who are assigned to units of which the Headquarters have permanent station location outside the Continental US or to units which are enroute between Continental and Oversea stations but are assigned to an Oversea Command or to the oversea portion of a Global Command.

3. Command Strength - Worldwide: The total strength of personnel assigned to Air Force units (USAF and SCARWAF) regardless of location.

AIR FORCE DEPARTMENTAL STRENGTH
The total strength of military personnel commissioned, appointed or enlisted in the United States Air Force, whether or not such personnel have been placed on duty with another Department.

AIR FORCE PERSONNEL
A general term comprising all military personnel (USAF, SCARWAF, or Navy) assigned to Air Force Units.

COMMAND
A major organizational division of the United States Air Force.

1. Continental Command: A Major Air Command whose command headquarters and subordinate units are located within the Continental United States.

2. Oversea Command: A Major Air Command whose command headquarters and subordinate units are located outside the Continental United States.

3. Global Command: A command whose command headquarters is located either inside or outside the Continental US and whose subordinate units are located both inside and outside Continental US.

COMMITTED UNITS
Units specifically designated by competent authority for combat operations or operations in direct support of combat operations; for example, units committed to the Korean air war.

COMPLETE AIR CREW
A crew which is fully manned in accordance with local crew position requirements of the type and model of aircraft in which reported.

DEFINITIONS

DEPARTMENT OF AIR FORCE PERSONNEL
Military Personnel who have been commissioned, appointed, or enlisted in the United States Air Force.

DEPARTMENT OF ARMY PERSONNEL
Military Personnel who have been commissioned, appointed, or enlisted in the United States Army. Such personnel included herein are identified as SCARWAF.

DEPARTMENTAL STATUS
The basic department of the Department of Defense in which an individual is currently commissioned, appointed or enlisted, regardless of whether or not such individual has been placed on duty with another of the departments.

FUNCTIONAL GROUP
The general grouping of personnel according to their status as to permanent party or pipeline.

IMMEDIATE REENLISTMENT
A reenlistment in the Regular Air Force within 24 hours to fill own vacancy.

INDEFINITE TERM OF ENLISTMENT
An unspecified period of time.

INTACT UNIT
A unit with all elements of a unit.

MILITARY USAF DECORATIONS
1. Awards for Heroism - Normally given for a single or a series of related acts for a single act or a series of related acts accomplished over a short period of a few days (not awarded to Civilians or Foreigners).

a. Medal of Honor - Awarded by Department of the Air Force only to any officer, non-commissioned officer or airman in action involving actual conflict with an enemy for conspicuous gallantry and intrepidity at the risk of life above and beyond the call of duty.

b. Distinguished Service Cross - Awarded to persons (military, civilian, foreign) serving in any capacity for extraordinary heroism in connection with military operations against an armed enemy, so extraordinary as to set that individual apart from his comrades. During combat operations awarding is delegated to AF theater commanders.

c. Silver Star - Awarded to persons (military, civilian, foreign) serving in any capacity for gallantry which means heroism of a high degree involving risk of life in action not warranting the award of a Medal of Honor or Distinguished Service Cross. Awarded by Air Force Commanders during combat operations.

d. Distinguished Flying Cross - Awarded for heroism or extraordinary achievement while participating in aerial flight. Awarded by Air Force Commanders for U. S. Personnel during active combat operations to members of military, naval or air forces in any capacity with the Air Force.

e. Soldier's Medal - Awarded to members of military, naval or air forces serving in any capacity with the Air Force for heroism not involving actual conflict with the enemy. The act or acts of heroism must include voluntary risk of life and will not be made purely on the basis of saving a life. Awarding during active combat operations by Air Force Commanders.

f. Bronze Star Medal (Valor) - Awarded to persons (military, civilian, foreign) serving in any capacity with the Air Force for heroic achievement not involving participation in aerial flight in actual combat against an enemy of the United States. The required achievements is less than that required for the Silver Star, but nevertheless must be accomplished with distinction. Awarding during active combat operations is delegated to the Air Force Commanders.

2. Meritorious Service Awards - Decorations for meritorious service are awarded for achievements or services, which are outstanding and exceptional when the individual is compared with others of like rank on similar type duties. Except for the Distinguished Service Medal, the position of the individual should have no relation to the degree of the award. Service as well as heroism decorations are primarily for wartime use.

a. Distinguished Service Medal - Awarded to persons serving in any capacity with the Air Force (The President has directed that no awards be made to civilians). Awarded to foreigners only in most exceptional circumstan-

DEFINITIONS

ces. The awards are made by Department of the Air Force only for exceptional meritorious service to the Government in duty of great responsibility.

b. Legion of Merit - Awards made by the Air Force only to members of the armed forces of the United States and friendly foreign nations for exceptionally meritorious conduct in the performance of outstanding service. Recommendations must show superior performance. It may be awarded for specific accomplishments.

c. Distinguished Flying Cross - Awarding delegated to Air Force commanders for US Personnel to Air Force commanders during combat operations. Awards made to members of the military, naval and air forces serving in any capacity with the Air Force for extraordinary achievement while participating in aerial flights. Results accomplished must be so exceptional and outstanding as to clearly set the individual apart from his comrades who have been so recognized.

d. Bronze Star Medal - Awarded to persons (military, civilian, foreign) serving in any capacity with the Air Force for meritorious achievement or service, not involving participation in aerial flight, in connection with military operations against an enemy of the United States. The required achievement or service is less than that required for the Legion of Merit. Award is limited to active operational area. Awarding delegated to division commanders for US personnel; for foreigners to theater commanders. For acts or services since VE Day in Europe and VJ Day in Pacific, no delegation authorized below theater commander. Not awarded for service in Japan or China after 2 March 1946, other areas after 12 January 1946.

e. Air Medal - Awarded to persons (military, civilian, foreign) serving in any capacity with the Air Force, awarding being delegated to Air Force Commanders for US personnel during active operations; for foreigners to theater commanders and delegated to CG, USAFE, for certain airlift personnel.

f. Commendation Ribbon - Awarded to members of the United States serving in any capacity with the Air Force by Commanding Generals who are Lieutenant Generals or higher and certain other specified commanders to personnel below the grade of major for service longer than six months but authority to award delegated to CG, USAFE, for certain airlift personnel. All other awards made by the Department of the Air Force. Awards are made for service required in less exceptional cases than that required for the Legion of Merit, nevertheless must be accomplished with distinction. Same degree of service required as that for which the Bronze Star Medal or Air Medal is awarded.

g. Purple Heart - Awarded to members of the United States armed forces and American civilians serving with the armed forces for wounds received in action against an enemy of the United States or as a direct result of an act of such enemy provided such wounds necessitated treatment by a medical officer. (Includes frost bite, but excludes trench foot). Commanders of certain medical installations were authorized to award and authority could have been delegated to any officer.

3. To Civilians

a. Purple Heart to certain civilians (accredited war correspondents, Red Cross personnel, etc.) who were citizens of the United States.

b. Medal of Freedom, including palms to foreigners, military or civilian, and without palms to civilian citizens of the United States. (Awarded only by commanders specifically designated.)

c. Distinguished Service Cross, Silver Star, Bronze Star Medal, and Purple Heart to officers and crew members of the US Merchant Marine.

OPERATING LOCATION

A permanent duty station of an individual. A station is considered permanent if the orders specify a period of three months or longer. If no period is specified the duty station is considered permanent.

MILITARY PERSONNEL — Continued

DEFINITIONS

OPERATIONAL CONTROL

Control exercised over the combat or service operation of subordinate or other organizations. Operational control comprises those functions of a command involving the composition of subordinate forces,the assignment of tasks, the designation of objectives, and the authoritative direction necessary to accomplish the mission. Normally it does not include such matters as administration, discipline, or internal organization.

OPERATIONAL READY AIR CREW

A complete air crew, present for duty, which a unit commander considers fully capable of performing the type of flying operation required of it by the tactical unit's combat mission. Complete air crews with other than tactical units will be considered operationally ready if determined by the commander of the unit to which assigned or attached to be qualified, without further training, for immediate assignment to tactical units, in the capacity in which reported.

PERMANENT PARTY PERSONNEL

Those personnel assigned to a unit to perform their principal duty in the furtherance of the missions of the unit and who are properly chargeable against the authorization of the unit. This is to include assigned overstrength.

PIPELINE PERSONNEL

Those USAF, SCARWAF, and Navy personnel who are assigned to an Air Force Unit temporarily for the purpose of administration and enlistment, reenlistment, replacement processing, training or hospitalization, i.e., those that are temporarily ineffective. Such personnel are not chargeable against the specific authorizations of the unit to which they are assigned while in a pipeline status.

The categories of pipeline personnel are defined as follows:

(1) Oversea Replacements. Personnel who are assigned to a unit to be processed for further reassignment and movement to duty with an oversea unit.

(2) Returnees. Personnel who are assigned to be processed for return from overseas for further reassignment and movement to duty with a ZI unit.

(3) Fillers. Personnel assigned to a unit as a result of just having entered extended active duty and who are awaiting reassignment to another unit for duty, further training, or overseas movement.

(4) Patients. Hospitalized personnel assigned to an Air Force unit which administers personnel undergoing inpatient treatment at a medical facility operated by any of the three military departments.

(5) Students. Personnel assigned in a student status to a unit charged with administration of individuals attending a formal course of instruction at a service or civilian school or a basic military training course.

REGULAR AIR FORCE PERSONNEL

Department of the Air Force military personnel who are, by enlistment, appointment, or commission, members of the Regular United States Air Force.

RETIREMENT

Retired from combat flying upon completion of tour. For the tables herein, only those personnel who have completed a tour of duty and are withdrawn from combat flying and are not expected to perform any additional combat duty on the current tour are considered as retirements.

SCARWAF PERSONNEL

Those Department of the Army personnel assigned as permanent party or pipeline to a USAF or SCARWAF unit.

SORTIE

An aircraft airborne on an assigned mission against the enemy or in support of combat operations. Normally, a sortie begins when aircraft is airborne and ends at time of first scheduled or intended landing.

MILITARY PERSONNEL — Continued

DEFINITIONS

SORTIE CREDIT

The credit which an air crew member receives for having flown on a combat mission and which is used as a measure for the determination of a tour of duty.

TACTICAL AIR CREW

A stipulated number of tactical air crew personnel locally organized as a crew to operate primary tactical unit aircraft.

TACTICAL AIR CREW PERSONNEL

Personnel whose current principal duty is the occupancy of an air crew position in a primary tactical unit aircraft.

TACTICAL MISSION

A mission flown by a tactical unit in performing its designated functions.

TACTICAL UNIT

A unit organized for the direct accomplishment of combat mission or for operations in direct support thereof (specifically, those types of units listed in Table 11, parts A, C and D, AFL 150-10, 2 February 1953.)

TOUR OF DUTY

The accomplishment of a variable amount of combat, or combat support activity, which, in the judgment of the theater or major air commander is sufficient to constitute eligibility for retirement of air crew personnel, current operational demands upon the command permitting. Although usually measured in sorties, combat hours, time in theater, or a combination of these factors, the actual retirement point will vary depending upon local conditions, availability of replacements, etc.

TRANSFER

Permanent change in departmental status, regardless of whether or not accompanied by a change of command status and/or unit assignment.

USAF PERSONNEL

Those Department of the Air Force military personnel assigned as permanent party or pipeline to a USAF or SCARWAF unit.

MILITARY PERSONNEL TRAINING

DEFINITIONS

ATTRITION

Attrition includes three groups of students:

1. Those who fail a course because of academic or flying deficiency.

2. Those who are losses from service because of fatality as a direct result of training.

3. Those who are withdrawn from a course because of illness, death, or any reason other than 1 and 2 above and who will not continue that course at a later date.

COURSE LENGTHS

A table showing the approximate length of courses at the Air University, Air War College, Air Command and Staff School, and Joint Service School for FY 1953 is entered below:

Air War College (Top Secret)	10 Months
Field Officer Course (Top Secret)	22 Weeks
Squadron Officer Course (Restricted)	10 Weeks
Communications Electronics Staff Officer Course (Crypto)	22 Weeks
Logistic Staff Officer Course (Top Secret)	22 Weeks
Comptroller Staff Officer Course (Secret)	15 Weeks

MILITARY PERSONNEL TRAINING — Continued

DEFINITIONS

COURSE LENGTHS (Continued)

Judge Advocate General Staff Officer Course (Restricted) . . . . 10 Weeks

Academic Instructor Course (Restricted). . . . . 6 Weeks

Air Weapon Course (Top Secret) . . . . 7 Weeks

Air Weapon Orientation Course (Top Secret) . . . . 5 Days

Intelligence Staff Officer Course (Top Secret) . . . . 22 Weeks

FATALITY
This type of attrition is a student lost from a course by reason of accidental death, occurring as a direct result of training while actually undergoing instruction. (Students becoming fatalities by reason of death from other causes are reported as "Other".)

FOREIGN NATIONALS
Students who are detailed to the school in an attached status from any foreign country, territory, or possession, excluding those possessions and territories of the United States of America.

GRADUATES
Students who have successfully completed a course in which enrolled.

HOLDOVERS
Students who do not graduate when normally scheduled, but are still enrolled in the course. These students are reported as enrolled at the beginning of the ensuing period unless otherwise disposed of.

MDAP TRAINING
Refers to the training of foreign nationals under the Mutual Defense Assistance Program. (They are included in the foreign training statistics of the tables, but a training table on MDAP may be found under that area of the publication.)

STUDENTS (TRAINING)
Training students are those personnel enrolled for the purpose of undergoing standardized courses of instruction at service schools conducted by the US Air Force, Army, Navy, and Civilian Schools and Hospitals. (This group includes USAF, Army, Navy, and Civilian students, or foreign nationals.) In referring to USAF training, students fall under these categories:

1. Assigned - Personnel assigned to the school unit and for whom the school unit is responsible for morning report strength accountability.
2. Attached - Personnel attached to the school unit from other units of the Air Force or other Federal agencies, who are scheduled to return to their respective units upon completion of the course, and for whom strength accountability is at all times maintained by such other units.

TABLE 179 — DEPARTMENTAL STRENGTH OF OFFICER PERSONNEL BY AERONAUTICAL STATUS, BY GRADE IN WHICH SERVING — FY 1953

Month a/	Total	Grade							
		General	Colonel	Lieutenant Colonel	Major	Captain	First Lieutenant	Second Lieutenant	Warrant Officer
	PILOT								
1952									
July	51,418	270	2,328	3,622	9,029	19,404	13,348	3,405	12
August	51,219	267	2,323	3,614	9,094	19,219	13,277	3,411	14
September	51,335	293	2,306	3,649	9,083	19,065	13,239	2,700	-
October	50,979	301	2,287	3,615	9,071	18,984	13,256	3,465	-
November	51,362	308	2,291	3,651	9,036	18,885	13,323	3,868	-
December	50,734	324	2,281	3,658	8,948	18,340	13,138	4,045	-
1953									
January	50,418	323	2,271	3,640	8,943	18,330	13,200	3,711	-
February	50,785	320	2,263	3,633	8,956	18,235	13,418	3,960	-
March	51,170	311	2,262	3,607	8,967	18,181	13,566	4,276	-
April	51,346	307	2,330	3,629	9,704	19,538	11,343	4,495	-
May	51,595	307	2,414	3,681	9,719	19,331	11,504	4,639	-
June	51,991	322	2,461	3,768	9,736	19,105	11,765	4,834	-
	AIRCRAFT OBSERVER b/								
1952									
July	17,219	11	132	401	1,887	6,003	6,635	2,132	18
August	17,045	10	123	408	1,871	5,865	6,579	2,168	21
September	16,908	13	122	403	1,869	5,826	6,456	2,219	-
October	16,907	13	122	407	1,862	5,738	6,472	2,293	-
November	16,955	15	120	399	1,846	5,743	6,514	2,318	-
December	16,667	15	122	429	1,935	5,481	6,285	2,400	-
1953									
January	16,545	15	125	432	1,930	5,395	6,244	2,404	-
February	16,328	15	122	442	1,916	5,282	6,088	2,463	-
March	16,193	14	123	448	1,925	5,195	5,951	2,537	-
April	16,029	14	132	456	2,075	6,001	4,836	2,515	-
May	16,255	14	141	460	2,066	5,944	4,863	2,767	-
June	16,391	15	150	465	2,091	5,853	4,958	2,859	-
	NON-RATED c/								
1952									
July	59,202	38	1,588	4,277	9,429	14,265	9,891	16,397	3,917
August	60,721	39	1,619	4,279	9,494	14,441	9,256	17,638	3,955
September	62,765	40	1,604	4,240	9,281	14,237	9,664	19,653	4,046
October	62,839	45	1,581	4,169	9,162	13,724	10,127	20,068	3,963
November	62,356	43	1,557	4,100	8,992	13,312	10,679	19,528	4,145
December	61,316	43	1,519	4,038	8,787	12,788	11,203	19,046	3,892
1953									
January	60,712	43	1,505	3,972	8,634	12,328	12,854	17,520	3,856
February	60,452	42	1,486	3,928	8,525	11,983	14,571	16,047	3,868
March	61,091	43	1,474	3,882	8,377	11,802	15,470	16,196	3,847
April	60,410	43	1,543	3,939	8,957	12,048	14,695	15,349	3,836
May	60,417	42	1,613	4,021	9,006	11,881	14,933	15,116	3,805
June	60,591	45	1,690	4,037	8,857	11,278	15,004	15,896	3,784

a/ Data are as of the 15th of the month prior to December 1952 and as of the end of the month for the remainder of of the fiscal year.

b/ Includes Aircraft Medical (See Table for Medical strength).

c/ Unknowns were included in the reports for July(1952) through May (1953) and were prorated by Aeronautical Status in June (1953).

Source: Personnel Statistics Division, DCS/Comptroller, Headquarters, USAF.

TABLE 180 — DEPARTMENTAL STRENGTH OF OFFICER PERSONNEL ON FLYING STATUS BY AERONAUTICAL STATUS, BY GRADE IN WHICH SERVING — FY 1953

Month a/	Total	Grade							
		General	Colonel	Lieutenant Colonel	Major	Captain	First Lieutenant	Second Lieutenant	Warrant Officer
	PILOT								
1952									
July	46,569	257	2,245	3,467	8,464	17,369	11,688	3,079	-
August	46,281	251	2,240	3,459	8,530	17,161	11,541	3,099	-
September	46,883	277	2,228	3,491	8,543	17,220	11,644	3,480	-
October	46,417	280	2,201	3,470	8,544	17,071	11,613	3,238	-
November	46,981	289	2,208	3,503	8,510	17,037	11,767	3,667	-
December	46,569	309	2,201	3,514	8,452	16,571	11,670	3,852	-
1953									
January	46,355	308	2,190	3,495	8,444	16,628	11,778	3,512	-
February	46,870	307	2,186	3,490	8,480	16,551	12,030	3,826	-
March	47,239	297	2,178	3,456	8,452	16,513	12,211	4,132	-
April	47,656	292	2,295	3,479	9,183	17,713	10,334	4,410	-
May	48,013	292	2,328	3,532	9,188	17,574	10,525	4,574	-
June	48,469	309	2,371	3,610	9,199	17,410	10,800	4,770	-
	AIRCRAFT OBSERVER b/								
1952									
July	14,222	9	93	313	1,516	4,750	5,557	1,984	-
August	14,038	9	96	317	1,493	4,635	5,480	2,008	-
September	14,187	12	95	313	1,490	4,668	5,494	2,115	-
October	14,135	12	99	321	1,475	4,574	5,476	2,178	-
November	14,261	14	96	289	1,460	4,609	5,570	2,223	-
December	14,122	15	93	334	1,557	4,399	5,407	2,317	-
1953									
January	14,029	15	96	338	1,547	4,298	5,376	2,359	-
February	13,886	15	91	351	1,540	4,232	5,242	2,415	-
March	13,840	14	89	354	1,537	4,168	5,170	2,508	-
April	13,729	14	95	363	1,639	4,867	4,261	2,490	-
May	13,949	14	101	365	1,620	4,819	4,299	2,731	-
June	14,104	15	107	366	1,654	4,762	4,385	2,815	-
	NON-RATED c/								
1952									
July	3,468	4	61	148	225	634	471	1,889	36
August	3,137	5	58	132	218	608	398	1,690	28
September	2,615	3	57	122	171	486	300	1,455	21
October	2,754	3	54	104	136	488	310	1,637	22
November	2,817	3	60	101	123	439	322	1,739	30
December	2,994	2	53	93	126	439	412	1,840	29
1953									
January	2,662	2	53	93	118	392	397	1,585	22
February	2,792	2	52	87	108	367	446	1,714	16
March	3,352	2	55	82	107	352	497	2,225	32
April	3,060	2	63	81	136	357	478	1,911	32
May	2,983	2	65	77	143	344	468	1,857	27
June	3,391	2	67	80	146	301	459	2,305	31

a/ Data are as of the 15th of the month prior to December 1952 and as of the end of the month for the remainder of the fiscal year.

b/ Includes Aircraft Medical (See Table for Medical strength.)

c/ Unknowns were included in the reports for July (1952) through May (1953) and were prorated by Aeronautical Status in June (1953).

Source: Personnel Statistics Division, DCS/Comptroller, Headquarters, USAF.

TABLE 181 — DEPARTMENTAL STRENGTH OF OFFICER AND WARRANT OFFICER PERSONNEL BY AERONAUTICAL RATING, BY AERONAUTICAL DESIGNATION — FY 1953

Rating and Designation	15 September (1952)	31 December	31 March (1953)	30 June
Departmental Strength - Total	131,008	128,717	128,454	128,973
Rated - Total	68,243	67,401	67,363	68,382
Pilot - Total	51,335	50,734	51,170	51,991
Command	950	979	997	1,010
Senior	14,611	15,180	15,983	16,576
Pilot	35,774	34,575	34,190	34,405
Aircraft Observer - Total	16,908	16,667	16,193	16,391
Observer a/	179	655	879	1,311
Bombardment	1,986	1,901	1,859	1,925
Navigator-Bombardier	510	625	929	1,156
Radar All Weather Fighter, Radio Observer I, and Radar Night Fighter	753	962	1,060	1,131
Navigator	6,482	5,897	5,498	5,256
Bombardier	4,110	3,780	3,286	2,919
Radar RCM, Radio Observer C, and Radar Electronic Countermeasure b/	1,344	1,273	1,218	1,098
Radar Bombardier	356	331	309	455
Flight Engineer	863	877	803	799
Flexible Gunner	188	227	207	195
Medical	137	139	145	146
Non-Rated - Total	60,611	60,352	60,460	60,591
Aeronautical Designation - Total	1,259	1,314	1,256	1,220
Flight Surgeon	311	322	316	316
Aviation Medical Examiner	428	405	367	319
Flight Nurse	520	587	573	585
No Rating or Designation - Total	59,352	59,038	59,204	59,371
Rating and Designation Unknown - Total	2,154	964	631	c/

a/ "Aircraft Observer" Rating granted subsequent to 1 July 1952.

b/ Observer Radar RCM, Radio Observer C redesignated Radar Electronic Countermeasure, January 1953.

c/ Unknown Rating and Designation were prorated.

Source: Personnel Statistics Division, DCS/Comptroller, Headquarters USAF.

308700 O - 54 - 23

TABLE 182 — DEPARTMENTAL STRENGTH OF OFFICER PERSONNEL BY AERONAUTICAL STATUS, BY COMMAND — FY 1953

(Other-Rated in the table below are Aircraft Observers including Aircraft Observer-Medical)

Command and Aeronautical Status	15 June (1952)	15 September	31 December	31 March (1953)	30 June
	CONTINENTAL US				
Total	96,535	100,240	98,436	97,255	96,507
Pilot - Total	37,710	37,939	37,455	37,651	38,163
Other-Rated - Total	14,071	13,829	13,800	13,239	13,177
Non-Rated - Total	44,754	48,472	47,181	46,365	45,167
Permanent Party - Total	83,791	85,654	83,673	80,848	79,578
Pilot	33,848	33,534	32,559	32,611	33,757
Other-Rated	11,416	11,054	11,420	10,750	10,651
Non-Rated	38,527	41,066	39,694	37,487	35,170
Air Defense Command - Total	8,298	8,462	7,930	7,400	7,505
Pilot	4,084	4,055	3,619	3,450	3,706
Other-Rated	748	809	929	880	908
Non-Rated	3,466	3,598	3,382	3,070	2,891
Air Force Finance Division - Total	69	74	76	73	62
Pilot	13	15	14	16	16
Other-Rated	4	3	2	1	1
Non-Rated	52	56	60	56	45
Air Materiel Command - Total	5,046	5,422	4,987	4,313	3,830
Pilot	1,429	1,460	1,328	1,187	1,080
Other-Rated	246	242	214	174	154
Non-Rated	3,371	3,720	3,445	2,952	2,596
Air Proving Ground Command - Total	986	1,029	973	951	921
Pilot	427	418	413	416	422
Other-Rated	85	79	78	76	62
Non-Rated	474	532	482	459	437
Air Research and Development Command - Total	4,491	4,906	4,797	4,476	4,400
Pilot	1,476	1,514	1,520	1,492	1,508
Other-Rated	299	265	251	235	247
Non-Rated	2,716	3,127	3,026	2,749	2,645
Air Training Command - Total	16,632	17,438	17,622	17,216	17,065
Pilot	6,359	6,548	6,601	6,720	7,160
Other-Rated	2,189	2,131	2,425	2,274	2,140
Non-Rated	8,084	8,759	8,596	8,222	7,765
Air University - Total	1,574	3,159	3,257	3,227	3,148
Pilot	592	1,335	1,422	1,415	1,419
Other-Rated	82	104	102	98	85
Non-Rated	900	1,720	1,733	1,714	1,644
Continental Air Command - Total	4,334	2,828	2,945	2,960	2,755
Pilot	1,546	773	808	793	747
Other-Rated	213	107	93	86	83
Non-Rated	2,575	1,948	2,044	2,081	1,925
Headquarters Command USAF - Total	5,389	5,447	5,319	5,015	4,356
Pilot	1,571	1,546	1,490	1,494	1,322
Other-Rated	268	254	265	258	213
Non-Rated	3,550	3,647	3,564	3,263	2,821
Headquarters US Air Force - Total	2,942	2,910	2,944	2,927	3,007
Pilot	1,412	1,390	1,432	1,423	1,478
Other-Rated	112	113	117	124	129
Non-Rated	1,418	1,407	1,395	1,380	1,400
Military Air Transport Service - Total	8,102	8,005	7,252	7,111	7,044
Pilot	3,841	3,661	3,327	3,372	3,574
Other-Rated	899	818	687	652	697
Non-Rated	3,362	3,526	3,238	3,087	2,773
Strategic Air Command - Total	18,969	18,871	18,864	18,474	18,789
Pilot	7,446	7,348	7,323	7,557	7,933
Other-Rated	5,775	5,659	5,757	5,445	5,517
Non-Rated	5,748	5,864	5,784	5,472	5,339

(Continued)

TABLE 182 — DEPARTMENTAL STRENGTH OF OFFICER PERSONNEL BY AERONAUTICAL STATUS, BY COMMAND — FY 1953 — (CONTINUED)

Command and Aeronautical Status	15 June (1952)	15 September	31 December	31 March (1953)	30 June
	CONTINENTAL US (Continued)				
Tactical Air Command - Total	6,393	6,275	5,901	5,904	5,887
Pilot	3,501	3,324	3,117	3,125	3,236
Other-Rated	463	438	455	399	369
Non-Rated	2,429	2,513	2,329	2,380	2,282
USAF Security Service - Total	566	828	806	801	809
Pilot	151	147	145	151	156
Other-Rated	33	32	45	48	46
Non-Rated	382	649	616	602	607
Pipeline (Students, Transients, and Patients) - Total	12,744	14,586	14,763	16,407	16,929
Pilot	3,862	4,405	4,896	5,040	4,406
Other-Rated	2,655	2,775	2,380	2,489	2,526
Non-Rated	6,227	7,406	7,487	8,878	9,997
	OVERSEAS				
Total	29,625	30,768	30,281	31,199	32,466
Pilot - Total	13,163	13,390	13,147	13,518	13,820
Other-Rated - Total	3,143	3,022	2,758	2,927	3,190
Non-Rated - Total	13,319	14,356	14,376	14,754	15,456
Alaskan Air Command - Total	1,595	1,711	1,697	1,713	1,714
Pilot	577	608	613	612	617
Other-Rated	124	149	143	202	207
Non-Rated	894	954	941	899	890
Caribbean Air Command - Total	213	212	223	230	230
Pilot	117	111	121	123	124
Other-Rated	3	6	5	5	6
Non-Rated	93	95	97	102	100
Far East Air Forces - Total	9,602	9,990	9,804	10,335	11,134
Pilot	4,278	4,417	4,395	4,617	4,765
Other-Rated	1,049	916	918	1,030	1,170
Non-Rated	4,275	4,657	4,491	4,688	5,199
Headquarters Command USAF - Total	684	708	718	717	941
Pilot	358	339	359	368	502
Other-Rated	15	13	20	22	41
Non-Rated	311	356	339	327	398
Military Air Transport Service - Total	5,331	5,358	5,371	5,053	5,030
Pilot	2,624	2,605	2,615	2,482	2,371
Other-Rated	817	790	762	671	737
Non-Rated	1,890	1,963	1,994	1,900	1,922
Northeast Air Command - Total	1,025	994	1,003	1,005	999
Pilot	355	342	311	349	343
Other-Rated	52	52	54	78	75
Non-Rated	618	600	638	578	581
Strategic Air Command - Total	1,760	1,748	1,398	1,606	1,632
Pilot	607	590	451	516	507
Other-Rated	367	388	179	260	282
Non-Rated	786	770	768	830	843
Tactical Air Command - Total	1,268	1,182	878	961	901
Pilot	830	769	556	605	663
Other-Rated	103	92	31	27	22
Non-Rated	335	321	291	329	216
USAF Security Service - Total	305	359	386	418	444
Pilot	90	106	98	95	109
Other-Rated	22	25	24	21	27
Non-Rated	193	228	264	302	308

(Continued)

TABLE 182 — DEPARTMENTAL STRENGTH OF OFFICER PERSONNEL BY AERONAUTICAL STATUS, BY COMMAND — FY 1953 — (CONTINUED)

Command and Aeronautical Status	15 June (1952)	15 September	31 December	31 March (1953)	30 June
	OVERSEAS (Continued)				
US Air Forces, Europe - Total	7,461	8,124	8,398	8,729	9,001
Pilot	3,107	3,301	3,387	3,505	3,574
Other-Rated	545	547	551	558	564
Non-Rated	3,809	4,276	4,460	4,666	4,863
Air Defense Command - Total	355	349	365	378	398
Pilot	212	190	225	220	229
Other-Rated	46	44	70	51	55
Non-Rated	97	115	70	107	114
Air Research and Development Command - Total	26	33	40	54	42
Pilot	8	12	16	26	16
Other-Rated	-	-	1	2	4
Non-Rated	18	21	23	26	22

Source: Personnel Statistics Division, DCS/Comptroller, Headquarters, USAF.

TABLE 183 – DEPARTMENTAL STRENGTH OF OFFICER PERSONNEL ON FLYING STATUS, BY AERONAUTICAL STATUS, BY COMMAND – FY 1953

(Other-Rated in the table below are Aircraft Observers including Aircraft Observer-Medical)

Command and Aeronautical Status	15 June (1952)	15 September	31 December	31 March (1953)	30 June
	CONTINENTAL US				
Total	49,235	48,828	49,214	49,502	50,409
Pilot - Total	34,425	34,719	34,568	34,897	35,744
Other-Rated - Total	11,774	11,792	11,978	11,542	11,577
Non-Rated - Total	3,036	2,317	2,668	3,063	3,088
Permanent Party - Total	40,954	40,430	40,378	39,897	41,334
Pilot	30,848	30,572	29,908	30,156	31,596
Other-Rated	9,259	9,140	9,713	9,182	9,222
Non-Rated	847	718	757	559	516
Air Defense Command - Total	4,204	4,279	4,251	3,928	4,288
Pilot	3,643	3,617	3,320	3,154	3,467
Other-Rated	516	617	794	741	792
Non-Rated	45	45	137	33	29
Air Force Finance Division - Total	11	13	11	13	13
Pilot	10	12	11	13	13
Other-Rated	1	1	-	-	-
Non-Rated	-	-	-	-	-
Air Materiel Command - Total	1,260	1,222	1,167	1,088	997
Pilot	1,173	1,134	1,064	991	911
Other-Rated	67	63	71	75	68
Non-Rated	20	25	32	22	18
Air Proving Ground Command - Total	446	441	437	451	455
Pilot	384	384	382	396	405
Other-Rated	57	55	52	51	44
Non-Rated	5	2	3	4	6
Air Research and Development Command - Total	1,578	1,576	1,617	1,572	1,627
Pilot	1,312	1,337	1,367	1,371	1,387
Other-Rated	193	163	162	162	172
Non-Rated	73	76	88	39	68
Air Training Command - Total	7,546	7,686	8,085	8,150	8,527
Pilot	5,692	5,883	5,962	6,138	6,635
Other-Rated	1,723	1,715	2,034	1,917	1,815
Non-Rated	131	88	89	95	77
Air University - Total	624	1,360	1,430	1,423	1,415
Pilot	551	1,270	1,342	1,339	1,342
Other-Rated	32	48	46	42	35
Non-Rated	41	42	42	42	38
Continental Air Command - Total	1,438	678	720	684	657
Pilot	1,354	640	685	654	634
Other-Rated	70	19	19	16	10
Non-Rated	14	19	16	14	13
Headquarters Command USAF - Total	1,616	1,612	1,384	1,348	1,207
Pilot	1,351	1,350	1,269	1,254	1,133
Other-Rated	123	118	88	88	63
Non-Rated	142	144	27	6	11
Headquarters US Air Force - Total	1,451	1,417	1,465	1,440	1,499
Pilot	1,360	1,327	1,370	1,349	1,407
Other-Rated	73	73	70	66	68
Non-Rated	18	17	25	25	24
Military Air Transport Service - Total	4,448	4,179	3,770	3,814	4,072
Pilot	3,560	3,393	3,102	3,170	3,386
Other-Rated	765	675	579	545	599
Non-Rated	123	111	89	99	87
Strategic Air Command - Total	12,467	12,338	12,496	12,471	12,956
Pilot	7,025	6,992	6,953	7,215	7,627
Other-Rated	5,250	5,237	5,388	5,114	5,216
Non-Rated	192	109	155	142	113

(Continued)

TABLE 183 — DEPARTMENTAL STRENGTH OF OFFICER PERSONNEL ON FLYING STATUS, BY AERONAUTICAL STATUS, BY COMMAND — FY 1953 — (CONTINUED)

Command and Aeronautical Status	15 June (1952)	15 September	31 December	31 March (1953)	30 June
	CONTINENTAL US (Continued)				
Tactical Air Command - Total	3,745	3,511	3,421	3,368	3,477
Pilot	3,333	3,135	2,984	2,993	3,126
Other-Rated	369	336	383	337	319
Non-Rated	43	40	54	38	32
USAF Security Service - Total	120	118	124	147	144
Pilot	100	98	97	119	123
Other-Rated	20	20	27	28	21
Non-Rated	-	-	-	-	-
Pipeline(Students, Transients, and Patients) - Total	8,281	8,398	8,836	9,605	9,075
Pilot	3,577	4,147	4,660	4,741	4,148
Other-Rated	2,515	2,652	2,265	2,360	2,355
Non-Rated	2,189	1,599	1,911	2,504	2,572
	OVERSEAS				
Total	14,919	14,857	14,471	14,929	15,555
Pilot - Total	12,000	12,164	12,001	12,342	12,725
Other-Rated - Total	2,547	2,395	2,144	2,298	2,527
Non-Rated - Total	372	298	326	289	303
Alaskan Air Command - Total	597	646	662	722	745
Pilot	503	531	542	543	560
Other-Rated	86	109	112	169	174
Non-Rated	8	6	8	10	11
Caribbean Air Command - Total	121	118	127	129	129
Pilot	114	110	119	121	121
Other-Rated	2	2	2	1	1
Non-Rated	5	6	6	7	7
Far East Air Forces - Total	4,943	4,872	4,901	5,137	5,462
Pilot	3,952	4,037	4,037	4,194	4,384
Other-Rated	884	745	761	868	986
Non-Rated	107	90	103	75	92
Headquarters Command USAF - Total	357	331	356	364	502
Pilot	346	324	344	351	477
Other-Rated	8	7	10	12	24
Non-Rated	3	-	2	1	1
Military Air Transport Service - Total	3,253	3,187	3,188	2,995	2,949
Pilot	2,402	2,394	2,431	2,322	2,208
Other-Rated	725	694	661	580	652
Non-Rated	126	99	96	93	89
Northeast Air Command - Total	309	294	291	348	350
Pilot	276	266	260	294	300
Other-Rated	30	22	23	47	46
Non-Rated	3	6	8	7	4
Strategic Air Command - Total	889	884	532	672	688
Pilot	533	521	383	447	441
Other-Rated	315	337	127	199	223
Non-Rated	41	26	22	26	24
Tactical Air Command - Total	900	824	560	601	673
Pilot	798	742	532	580	652
Other-Rated	92	77	20	16	18
Non-Rated	10	5	8	5	3
USAF Security Service - Total	83	96	88	82	100
Pilot	69	82	74	69	84
Other-Rated	12	14	13	13	16
Non-Rated	2	-	1	-	-

(Continued)

TABLE 183 — DEPARTMENTAL STRENGTH OF OFFICER PERSONNEL ON FLYING STATUS, BY AERONAUTICAL STATUS, BY COMMAND — FY 1953 — (CONTINUED)

Command and Aeronautical Status	15 June (1952)	15 September	31 December	31 March (1953)	30 June
	OVERSEAS (Continued)				
US Air Forces, Europe - Total	3,230	3,375	3,466	3,586	3,669
Pilot	2,804	2,968	3,046	3,179	3,264
Other-Rated	360	350	351	343	335
Non-Rated	66	57	69	64	70
Air Defense Command - Total	231	221	285	267	270
Pilot	197	180	218	217	219
Other-Rated	33	38	64	49	49
Non-Rated	1	3	3	1	2
Air Research and Development Command - Total	6	9	15	26	18
Pilot	6	9	15	25	15
Other-Rated	-	-	-	1	3
Non-Rated	-	-	-	-	-

Source: Personnel Statistics Division, DCS/Comptroller, Headquarters USAF.

TABLE 184 — DEPARTMENTAL STRENGTH OF PILOTS ON FLYING STATUS BY AGE — 15 DEC 1948 THROUGH 31 MAY 1953

(Data in table below are based on special reports, therefore information was not available at recurring intervals through August 1950.)

Age Groups	15 December 1948	15 June 1949	15 August 1950	15 November 1951	15 May 1952	15 November 1952	31 May 1953
Total	26,720	28,668	26,573	45,695	46,209	46,981	48,013
Below 24 - Total	1,064	593	1,143	1,379	856	1,931	1,540
19	21	1	2	-	-	-	-
20	142	17	1	-	-	-	2
21	88	154	69	-	3	20	11
22	88	176	602	426	142	550	228
23	725	245	469	953	711	1,361	1,299
24 through 26 - Total	5,960	4,586	3,154	3,787	3,453	4,141	5,342
24	1,514	837	642	761	1,418	1,883	2,057
25	1,888	1,695	954	986	925	1,047	2,147
26	2,558	2,056	1,558	2,040	1,110	1,211	1,138
27 through 29 - Total	9,672	9,876	7,430	12,456	9,754	9,653	6,994
27	3,413	2,696	1,930	3,599	2,119	2,151	1,254
28	3,350	3,600	2,386	4,147	3,539	3,559	2,270
29	2,909	3,580	3,114	4,710	4,096	3,943	3,470
30 through 32 - Total	6,674	8,259	8,281	14,976	15,114	14,820	13,416
30	2,747	3,086	3,089	5,458	4,602	4,532	3,889
31	2,203	2,870	2,689	5,242	5,403	5,295	4,383
32	1,724	2,303	2,503	4,276	5,109	4,993	5,144
33 through 35 - Total	1,870	3,488	4,493	9,143	10,916	10,593	12,383
33	1,130	1,795	1,941	3,822	4,157	4,011	4,924
34	490	1,174	1,541	3,045	3,810	3,703	3,931
35	250	519	1,011	2,276	2,949	2,879	3,528
36 through 38 - Total	492	642	845	2,345	4,257	4,098	6,132
36	166	265	454	1,460	2,262	2,182	2,781
37	188	177	224	586	1,429	1,366	2,050
38	138	200	167	299	566	550	1,301
39 through 41 - Total	310	409	423	575	677	655	985
39	126	148	170	208	290	279	526
40	94	146	125	201	200	195	276
41	90	115	128	166	187	181	183
42 through 44 - Total	266	300	282	387	428	405	467
42	95	96	101	146	160	155	181
43	92	99	78	122	150	145	148
44	79	105	103	119	118	105	138
45 through 47 - Total	145	189	228	290	313	301	291
45	54	83	88	103	105	97	107
46	50	56	80	105	101	96	91
47	41	50	60	82	107	108	93
48 through 50 - Total	92	111	140	164	202	190	226
48	46	40	54	67	81	74	101
49	22	48	47	53	64	63	69
50	24	23	39	44	57	53	56
51 and Older - Total	175	213	154	193	239	194	237

Source: Personnel Statistics Division, DCS/Comptroller, Headquarters USAF.

TABLE 185 — USAF AIR CREWS BY TYPE AND MODEL OF AIRCRAFT — FY 1953

Type and Model Aircraft	30 June (1952)		30 September		31 December		31 March (1953)		30 June	
	Total	Tac-tical	Total	Tac-tical	Total	Tac-tical	Total	Tac-tical	Total	Tac-tical
Total	8,455	6,617	8,971	6,786	9,545	6,903	9,827	7,086	10,669	7,683
Fighter - Total	3,596	3,071	3,970	3,437	4,163	3,563	4,166	3,581	4,622	3,979
F-47	161	161	188	186	158	155	83	80	22	18
F-51	682	570	729	632	682	605	481	448	273	250
F-80	563	270	602	314	594	305	487	237	484	246
F-82	6	6	4	4	3	3	2	2	7	7
F-84	973	932	1,005	953	1,079	981	1,344	1,213	1,595	1,426
F-86	686	652	705	651	851	766	1,116	1,006	1,497	1,383
F-86D	-	-	-	-	15	-	30	-	72	-
F-89	90	78	202	193	120	120	4	4	59	59
F-94	435	402	535	504	661	628	619	591	613	590
Bombardment - Total	1,282	1,195	1,219	1,111	1,172	1,038	1,272	1,130	1,442	1,181
B-17	3	-	13	-	10	-	2	-	-	-
B-25	47	-	59	-	86	-	79	-	194	-
B-26	180	168	172	162	225	220	249	245	248	245
B-29	601	593	507	502	379	378	329	327	262	256
B-36	94	93	112	111	121	120	141	120	162	151
B-45	52	52	55	52	50	50	51	51	38	38
B-47	45	45	43	43	45	45	168	168	264	264
B-50	260	244	258	241	255	225	253	219	274	227
Reconnaissance - Total	573	573	529	529	527	527	539	539	586	586
RB-17	4	4	4	4	3	3	2	2	-	-
RB-26	93	93	79	79	85	85	107	107	82	82
B/RB-29	41	41	79	79	70	70	72	72	63	63
RB-36	58	58	60	60	60	60	67	67	107	107
B/RB-45	32	32	30	30	32	32	32	32	23	23
RB-47	-	-	-	-	-	-	-	-	24	24
RB-50	40	40	43	43	44	44	45	45	48	48
RC-45	1	1	1	1	1	1	1	1	2	2
RF-51	60	60	24	24	15	15	-	-	-	-
RF-80	174	174	139	139	150	150	147	147	149	149
RF-86	9	9	4	4	4	4	3	3	5	5
WB-29	61	61	66	66	63	63	63	63	68	68
WB-26	-	-	-	-	-	-	-	-	15	15
Tanker - Total	270	270	260	260	263	263	293	293	298	298
KB-29	208	208	185	185	183	183	164	164	155	155
KC-97	62	62	75	75	80	80	129	129	143	143
Transport - Total	1,281	1,110	1,135	995	1,157	982	1,242	1,065	1,226	1,041
C-45	2	-	1	-	1	-	1	-	-	-
C-46	176	175	190	189	137	136	141	140	138	137
C-47	210	134	207	118	171	119	184	109	164	111
C-54	381	320	271	232	186	120	254	200	247	172
C-74	12	12	12	12	11	11	10	10	10	10
C-82	83	83	81	81	161	158	50	47	28	28
C-97	103	72	32	24	64	40	77	52	74	48
C-118	-	-	-	-	8	-	7	-	14	-
C-119	216	216	225	225	248	242	312	309	324	320
C-124	98	98	116	114	170	156	206	198	227	215
Rescue - Total	225	193	248	204	276	239	248	207	282	247
H-5	73	41	78	35	88	51	78	39	75	42
H-19	12	12	23	23	34	34	37	36	39	38
H-21	-	-	-	-	-	-	1	-	1	-
SA-10	4	4	5	4	2	2	-	-	-	-
SA-16	71	71	89	89	105	105	90	90	120	120
SB-17	28	28	17	17	11	11	6	6	7	7
SB-29	25	25	27	27	25	25	25	25	28	28
SC-47	2	2	2	2	4	4	4	4	5	5
SC-54	-	-	-	-	-	-	-	-	-	-
YC-97	-	-	-	-	-	-	-	-	-	-
YC-122	10	10	7	7	7	7	7	7	7	7

(Continued)

TABLE 185 — USAF AIR CREWS BY TYPE AND MODEL OF AIRCRAFT — FY 1953 (CONTINUED)

Type and Model Aircraft	30 June (1952)		30 September		31 December		31 March (1953)		30 June	
	Total	Tac-tical	Total	Tac-tical	Total	Tac-tical	Total	Tac-tical	Total	Tac-tical
Other - Total	1,228	205	1,610	250	1,987	291	2,067	271	2,213	351
L-5	97	12	108	-	107	-	107	-	114	-
L-13	12	12	-	-	13	-	-	-	-	-
L-20	4	4	37	37	74	74	63	63	86	86
LC-126	3	3	-	-	-	-	-	-	-	-
T-6	622	92	776	115	802	116	798	124	386	117
T-7	-	-	-	-	-	-	-	-	2	2
T-28	133	-	71	-	212	-	153	-	307	-
T-29	33	-	36	-	51	-	53	-	78	-
T-33	231	-	463	-	590	-	779	-	1,115	61
TB-26	88	77	91	79	86	73	72	62	83	64
TB-29	4	4	27	18	31	27	29	22	26	20
VC-47	1	1	1	1	18	1	13	-	16	1
TB-25	-	-	-	-	3	-	-	-	-	-

Source: Personnel Statistics Division, DCS/Comptroller, Headquarters USAF.

TABLE 186 — USAF AIR CREWS BY TYPE, BY COMMAND — FY 1953

Command and Type	30 June (1952)		30 September		31 December		31 March (1953)		30 June	
	Total	Tactical	Total	Tactical	Total	Tactical	Total	Tactical	Total	Tactical
TOTAL	8,455	6,617	8,971	6,786	9,545	6,903	9,827	7,086	10,669	7,683
Alaskan Air Command - Total	110	109	143	117	152	144	194	189	212	209
Fighter	69	69	91	91	98	98	144	144	153	153
Bombardment	1	-	9	-	4	-	2	-	2	-
Reconnaissance	7	7	10	10	12	12	12	12	11	11
Transport	16	16	18	1	15	11	15	12	9	8
Rescue	14	14	15	15	23	23	21	21	25	25
Other	3	3	-	-	-	-	-	-	12	12
Air Defense Command - Total	1,053	1,044	1,255	1,246	1,323	1,316	1,000	993	1,096	1,090
Fighter	1,044	1,044	1,246	1,246	1,316	1,316	993	993	1,090	1,090
Bombardment	3	-	4	-	-	-	-	-	-	-
Transport	6	-	-	-	-	-	-	-	-	-
Other	-	-	5	-	7	-	7	-	6	-
Air Materiel Command - Total	37	-	38	-	53	-	62	8	68	15
Fighter	1	-	6	-	12	-	14	-	19	-
Bombardment	3	-	1	-	1	-	1	-	4	-
Transport	31	-	28	-	38	-	47	8	45	15
Rescue	-	-	1	-	-	-	-	-	-	-
Other	2	-	2	-	2	-	-	-	-	-
Air Proving Ground Command - Total	33	-	51	-	55	-	68	-	53	-
Fighter	13	-	24	-	32	-	49	-	33	-
Bombardment	10	-	12	-	11	-	3	-	2	-
Transport	2	-	9	-	2	-	2	-	2	-
Rescue	1	-	-	-	2	-	3	-	2	-
Other	7	-	6	-	8	-	11	-	14	-
Air Research and Development Command - Total	17	-	10	-	51	-	42	-	52	-
Fighter	17	-	10	-	37	-	40	-	50	-
Rescue	-	-	-	-	1	-	2	-	2	-
Other	-	-	-	-	13	-	-	-	-	-
Air Training Command - Total	1,589	-	1,937	-	2,303	-	2,378	-	2,605	-
Fighter	493	-	492	-	518	-	473	-	533	-
Bombardment	56	-	65	-	113	-	111	-	231	-
Transport	6	-	7	-	4	-	4	-	5	-
Rescue	31	-	43	-	34	-	36	-	31	-
Other	1,003	-	1,330	-	1,634	-	1,754	-	1,805	-
Caribbean Air Command - Total	17	17	10	-	8	8	7	7	6	6
Transport	2	2	1	-	1	1	-	-	-	-
Rescue	7	7	9	-	7	7	7	7	6	6
Other	8	8	-	-	-	-	-	-	-	-
Continental Air Command - Total	1	-	2	-	19	-	20	-	25	-
Fighter	1	-	1	-	1	-	6	-	8	-
Transport	-	-	-	-	-	-	1	-	1	-
Other	-	-	1	-	18	-	13	-	16	-
Far East Air Force - Total	1,897	1,885	2,054	2,036	2,062	2,051	2,260	2,248	2,441	2,423
Fighter	937	937	1,130	1,130	1,173	1,173	1,262	1,262	1,426	1,426
Bombardment	271	268	278	274	296	296	325	324	321	320
Reconnaissance	186	186	146	146	155	155	156	156	190	190
Tanker	9	9	9	9	6	6	9	9	8	8
Transport	327	327	300	300	266	266	313	313	284	284
Rescue	54	54	69	69	66	66	67	67	73	73
Other	113	104	122	108	100	89	128	117	139	122

(Continued)

TABLE 186 — USAF AIR CREWS BY TYPE, BY COMMAND — FY 1953 (Continued)

Command and Type	30 June (1952)		30 September		31 December		31 March (1953)		30 June	
	Total	Tactical	Total	Tactical	Total	Tactical	Total	Tactical	Total	Tactical
Headquarters Command - Total	36	-	52	-	-	-	-	-	7	-
Bombardment	3	-	6	-	-	-	-	-	7	-
Transport	33	-	46	-	-	-	-	-	-	-
Military Air Transport Service - Total	511	425	368	356	499	407	458	381	512	407
Fighter	-	-	-	-	-	-	-	-	25	25
Bombardment	4	4	1	1	-	-	-	-	-	-
Reconnaissance	30	30	33	33	27	27	27	27	32	32
Transport	409	323	259	247	387	295	373	296	374	269
Rescue	68	68	75	75	85	85	58	58	81	81
Northeast Air Command - Total	17	14	18	14	67	43	61	38	65	43
Fighter	-	-	-	-	29	29	22	22	23	23
Transport	3	-	4	-	25	1	24	1	22	-
Rescue	14	14	14	14	13	13	15	15	20	20
Strategic Air Command - Total	1,585	1,577	1,534	1,528	1,451	1,445	1,694	1,643	1,812	1,782
Fighter	212	212	190	190	225	225	330	330	357	357
Bombardment	866	862	799	796	678	675	756	732	799	785
Reconnaissance	154	154	196	196	187	187	202	202	245	245
Tanker	261	261	251	251	257	257	284	284	290	290
Transport	91	87	93	90	94	91	117	90	112	96
Rescue	1	1	5	5	10	10	5	5	9	9
Tactical Air Command - Total	797	793	804	798	785	781	774	770	879	878
Fighter	284	284	296	296	289	289	297	294	345	345
Bombardment	16	12	7	3	5	3	2	2	-	-
Reconnaissance	142	142	97	97	95	95	106	106	57	57
Transport	260	260	286	284	239	237	257	256	291	290
Rescue	18	18	15	15	17	17	18	18	21	21
Other	77	77	103	103	140	140	94	94	165	165
US Air Force in Europe - Total	688	686	636	632	642	633	657	657	691	685
Fighter	492	492	444	444	404	404	426	426	449	449
Bombardment	39	39	37	37	64	64	69	69	76	76
Reconnaissance	54	54	47	47	51	51	39	39	51	51
Transport	78	78	74	72	86	80	89	89	77	75
Rescue	11	11	16	16	16	16	16	16	16	16
Other	14	12	18	16	21	18	18	18	22	18
USAF AFS Graduates on Hand at End of Month and Pipeline - Total	67	67	59	59	75	75	152	152	145	145
Fighter	33	33	36	36	29	29	110	110	111	111
Bombardment	10	10	-	-	-	-	-	-	-	-
Reconnaissance	-	-	-	-	2	2	-	-	-	-
Transport	17	17	-	-	-	-	-	-	-	-
Rescue	6	6	-	-	-	-	-	-	-	-
Other	1	1	23	23	44	44	42	42	34	34

Source: Personnel Statistics Division, DCS/Comptroller, Headquarters USAF.

TABLE 167 — COMPLETE AIR CREW INVENTORY OF TACTICAL UNITS BY TYPE AND MODEL AIRCRAFT, BY COMMAND — FY 1953

(Excludes transients and Air Crew School Graduates at Advanced Flying Schools.)

Type of Unit	Total	CONTINENTAL US				OVERSEAS				
		ADC	TAC	SAC	MATS	AAC	USAFE	FEAF	NEAC	CAC
Total	7,538	1,090	a/ 893	1,782	407	209	685	2,423	43	6
Fighter - Total	3,868	1,090	345	357	25	153	449	1,426	23	-
F-47	18	18	-	-	-	-	-	-	-	-
F-51	235	158	77	-	-	-	-	-	-	-
F-80	218	54	-	-	-	-	-	164	-	-
F-82	7	-	-	-	-	7	-	-	-	-
F-84	1,409	135	-	357	-	-	359	558	-	-
F-86	1,332	444	268	-	-	-	90	530	-	-
F-89	59	59	-	-	-	-	-	-	-	-
F-94	590	222	-	-	25	146	-	174	23	-
Bombardment - Total	1,233	-	-	828	-	-	76	329	-	-
B-26	254	-	-	-	-	-	38	216	-	-
B-29	299	-	-	186	-	-	-	113	-	-
B-36	151	-	-	151	-	-	-	-	-	-
B-45	38	-	-	-	-	-	38	-	-	-
B-47	264	-	-	264	-	-	-	-	-	-
B-50	227	-	-	227	-	-	-	-	-	-
Reconnaissance - Total	543	-	57	202	32	11	51	190	-	-
RB-26	82	-	19	-	-	-	15	48	-	-
B/RB-29	20	-	-	7	-	-	-	13	-	-
RB-36	107	-	-	107	-	-	-	-	-	-
B/RB-45	23	-	-	19	-	-	-	4	-	-
RB-47	24	-	-	24	-	-	-	-	-	-
RB-50	48	-	-	45	-	-	-	3	-	-
RC-45	2	-	-	-	-	-	-	2	-	-
RF-80	113	-	38	-	-	-	-	75	-	-
RF-86	41	-	-	-	-	-	36	5	-	-
WB-26	15	-	-	-	-	-	-	15	-	-
WB-29	68	-	-	-	32	11	-	25	-	-
Tanker - Total	298	-	-	290	-	-	-	8	-	-
KB-29	155	-	-	147	-	-	-	8	-	-
KC-97	143	-	-	143	-	-	-	-	-	-
Transport - Total	1,041	-	a/ 305	100	269	8	75	284	-	-
C-46	137	-	46	-	-	-	-	91	-	-
C-47	111	-	-	29	31	-	-	51	-	-
C-54	172	-	-	-	146	2	-	24	-	-
C-74	10	-	-	-	10	-	-	-	-	-
C-82	28	-	28	-	-	-	-	-	-	-
C-97	33	-	-	4	29	-	-	-	-	-
C-119	320	-	155	-	-	-	75	90	-	-
C-124	230	-	a/ 76	67	53	6	-	28	-	-
Rescue - Total	238	-	21	5	81	25	16	64	20	6
H-5	42	-	-	1	6	8	-	21	5	1
H-19	29	-	14	-	4	-	4	6	1	-
SA-16	120	-	-	4	58	13	8	25	7	5
SB-17	7	-	-	-	3	4	-	-	-	-
SB-29	28	-	-	-	10	-	4	11	3	-
SC-47	5	-	-	-	-	-	-	1	4	-
YC-122	7	-	7	-	-	-	-	-	-	-
Other - Total	317	-	165	-	-	12	18	122	-	-
L-20	86	-	41	-	-	12	-	33	-	-
T-6	83	-	-	-	-	-	-	83	-	-
T-7	2	-	-	-	-	-	-	2	-	-
T-33	61	-	61	-	-	-	-	-	-	-
TB-26	64	-	54	-	-	-	10	-	-	-
TB-29	20	-	9	-	-	-	8	3	-	-
VC-47	1	-	-	-	-	-	-	1	-	-

a/ Includes 15 C-124 assigned to AMC for Logistical Support.

Source: Personnel Statistics Division, DCS/Comptroller, Headquarters USAF.

TABLE 188 — USAF AIR CREW PERSONNEL BY TYPE AND MODEL OF AIRCRAFT — FY 1953

Type and Model Aircraft	30 June (1952)		30 September		31 December		31 March (1953)		30 June	
	Total	Tac-tical	Total	Tac-tical	Total	Tac-tical	Total	Tac-tical	Total	Tac-tical
TOTAL	42,933	33,880	43,808	34,967	45,633	35,024	45,987	35,381	47,493	36,511
Fighter - Total	4,431	3,798	4,958	4,344	5,161	4,496	5,139	4,489	5,497	4,790
F-47	107	105	189	186	158	155	83	80	22	18
F-51	695	583	729	632	682	605	481	448	274	250
F-80	572	277	612	314	594	305	473	223	485	246
F-82	15	15	19	19	20	20	30	30	28	28
F-84	1,034	988	1,006	953	1,079	981	1,397	1,266	1,604	1,435
F-86	691	652	690	651	851	766	1,190	1,050	1,498	1,379
F-86D	-	-	17	-	15	-	-	-	72	-
F-89	205	169	450	419	274	271	60	59	155	150
F-94	1,112	1,009	1,246	1,170	1,488	1,393	1,425	1,333	1,359	1,284
Bombardment - Total	17,515	13,597	17,777	14,002	17,769	13,533	17,115	12,994	17,326	13,128
B-17	241	-	330	-	322	-	327	-	231	2
B-24	1	-	1	-	1	-	-	-	-	-
B-25	1,965	1	1,851	17	2,073	-	1,687	-	1,742	-
B-26	1,246	930	1,258	919	1,394	1,043	1,462	1,114	1,642	1,254
B-29	8,936	7,835	8,848	7,892	8,303	7,201	7,354	6,267	6,653	5,418
B-36	1,875	1,845	2,051	2,018	2,222	2,174	2,514	2,211	2,685	2,492
B-45	153	139	238	225	246	238	234	222	178	164
B-47	223	143	226	135	239	135	511	396	921	786
B-50	2,875	2,704	2,974	2,796	2,969	2,742	3,026	2,784	3,274	3,012
Reconnaissance - Total	4,369	4,331	3,929	3,887	4,288	4,245	4,664	4,625	5,224	5,186
RB-17	30	30	29	29	28	28	25	25	-	-
RB-25	14	-	15	-	16	-	14	-	15	-
RB-26	309	309	220	220	275	275	320	320	232	232
RB-29	578	578	475	475	323	323	268	268	433	433
RB-36	1,551	1,543	1,628	1,618	1,919	1,908	2,170	2,160	2,673	2,664
RB-45	95	95	90	90	96	96	97	97	73	73
RB-47	-	-	-	-	-	-	-	-	87	87
RB-50	659	659	577	577	669	669	759	759	751	751
RC-45	7	7	5	5	4	4	3	3	7	7
RC-47	16	-	17	-	16	-	15	-	14	-
RF-51	60	60	24	24	15	15	-	-	-	-
RF-80	182	182	139	139	150	150	149	149	149	149
RF-86	9	9	4	4	4	4	3	3	5	5
WB-26	-	-	-	-	-	-	-	-	68	68
WB-29	859	859	706	706	773	773	841	841	717	717
Tanker - Total	2,203	2,181	2,550	2,528	2,663	2,648	3,348	3,335	3,566	3,545
KB-29	1,720	1,720	1,692	1,685	1,648	1,648	1,748	1,748	1,783	1,783
KC-97	483	461	858	843	1,015	1,000	1,600	1,587	1,783	1,762
Transport - Total	10,756	7,791	10,165	7,683	10,954	7,786	10,912	7,836	10,889	7,664
C-45	225	-	260	-	360	-	309	-	327	-
C-46	1,248	1,233	1,189	1,119	1,231	1,152	1,193	1,072	1,098	959
C-47	2,357	711	2,358	751	2,332	755	2,313	761	2,277	730
C-54	2,870	2,167	2,261	1,859	2,182	1,581	2,090	1,493	2,038	1,352
C-74	155	155	191	191	161	161	85	85	83	83
C-82	475	439	489	438	462	416	369	328	194	171
C-97	816	521	509	454	661	381	590	375	598	388
C-118	-	-	-	-	76	-	86	-	95	-
C-119	1,349	1,330	1,217	1,208	1,390	1,337	1,663	1,589	1,918	1,825
C-124	1,261	1,235	1,671	1,663	2,099	2,003	2,214	2,133	2,261	2,156
Rescue - Total	1,734	1,687	1,982	1,917	1,714	1,634	1,580	1,500	1,603	1,513
H-5	119	82	169	122	102	65	119	80	120	83
H-19	28	25	73	68	95	84	111	99	136	125
H-21	-	-	-	-	-	-	-	-	6	-
SA-16	765	760	776	766	792	760	812	783	836	800
SB-17	270	270	428	428	124	124	65	65	68	68
SB-29	432	432	428	428	495	495	423	423	341	341
SC-47	30	30	25	25	22	22	22	22	44	44

(Continued)

TABLE 188 – USAF AIR CREW PERSONNEL BY TYPE AND MODEL OF AIRCRAFT – FY 1953 (CONTINUED)

Type and Model Aircraft	30 June (1952)		30 September		31 December		31 March (1953)		30 June	
	Total	Tac-tical	Total	Tac-tical	Total	Tac-tical	Total	Tac-tical	Total	Tac-tical
Rescue - Total (Continued)										
YC-122	43	43	36	36	71	71	28	28	27	27
YC- 97	-	-	-	-	-	-	-	-	25	25
SA- 10	47	45	47	44	13	13	-	-	-	-
Other - Total	1,925	495	2,447	606	3,084	682	3,229	602	3,388	685
DC-45	1	-	1	-	1	-	-	-	-	-
L-5	97	12	108	-	107	-	107	-	114	-
L-13	23	22	13	-	13	-	-	-	-	-
L-16	-	-	2	-	1	-	-	-	2	-
L-20	7	7	37	37	93	88	95	63	112	86
L-21	-	-	-	-	3	-	3	-	4	-
LC-126	2	2	-	-	-	-	-	-	-	-
T-6	629	92	781	115	809	116	812	126	386	107
T-7	5	-	9	-	6	-	10	-	15	7
T-11	17	-	21	-	25	-	12	-	22	-
T-28	133	-	71	-	212	-	153	-	307	-
T-29	185	-	286	108	321	-	385	-	429	-
T-33	234	-	472	-	602	-	790	-	1,131	61
TB-17	5	-	1	-	2	-	4	-	3	-
TB-25	41	-	58	-	70	-	82	-	51	-
TB-26	392	340	360	304	374	318	327	269	339	273
TB-29	89	16	168	40	284	158	299	140	326	148
VB-17	28	-	28	-	33	-	30	-	24	-
VB-25	-	-	-	-	1	-	1	-	-	-
VC-45	1	-	-	-	-	-	-	-	-	-
VC-47	13	4	10	2	98	2	91	4	92	3
VC-54	13	-	10	-	17	-	13	-	10	-
VC-121	5	-	6	-	7	-	7	-	8	-
XC-99	5	-	5	-	5	-	8	-	11	-
XC-120	-	-	-	-	-	-	-	-	2	-

Source: Personnel Statistics Division, DCS/Comptroller, Headquarters USAF.

TABLE 189 — USAF AIR CREW PERSONNEL BY TYPE OF AIRCRAFT, BY COMMAND — FY 1953

Command and Type	30 June (1952)		30 September		31 December		31 March (1953)		30 June	
	Total	Tactical	Total	Tactical	Total	Tactical	Total	Tactical	Total	Tactical
Total	42,933	33,880	43,808	34,967	45,633	35,024	45,987	35,381	47,493	36,511
Alaskan Air Command - Total	616	566	692	623	715	593	851	693	863	738
Fighter	177	177	209	209	222	222	308	308	310	310
Bombardment	14	1	28	-	19	-	24	-	25	-
Reconnaissance	178	178	-	-	147	147	153	153	162	162
Transport	157	122	140	101	203	105	235	110	215	118
Rescue	85	83	315	313	119	119	122	122	136	136
Other	5	5	-	-	5	-	9	-	15	12
Air Defense Command - Total	1,797	1,503	2,152	1,859	2,213	1,913	1,810	1,456	1,819	1,479
Fighter	1,503	1,503	1,859	1,859	1,913	1,913	1,456	1,456	1,479	1,479
Bombardment	59	-	39	-	41	-	51	-	50	-
Transport	122	-	70	-	71	-	69	-	70	-
Other	113	-	184	-	188	-	234	-	220	-
Air Materiel Command - Total	295	-	268	-	319	-	426	101	419	119
Fighter	10	-	12	-	15	-	17	-	23	-
Bombardment	114	-	99	-	93	-	104	-	101	-
Transport	161	-	148	-	202	-	295	101	292	119
Rescue	2	-	1	-	-	-	-	-	-	-
Other	8	-	8	-	9	-	10	-	3	-
Air Proving Ground Command - Total	321	-	308	-	288	-	310	-	296	-
Fighter	24	-	27	-	35	-	49	-	33	-
Bombardment	216	-	204	-	188	-	188	-	186	-
Transport	63	-	60	-	52	-	56	-	47	-
Rescue	4	-	4	-	2	-	5	-	9	-
Other	14	-	13	-	11	-	12	-	21	-
Air Research and Development Command - Total	361	-	464	-	673	-	665	-	733	-
Fighter	18	-	10	-	41	-	46	-	62	-
Bombardment	184	-	314	-	442	-	445	-	426	-
Tanker	1	-	3	-	2	-	-	-	-	-
Transport	154	-	116	-	148	-	160	-	226	-
Rescue	3	-	8	-	18	-	12	-	15	-
Other	1	-	13	-	22	-	2	-	4	-
Air Training Command - Total	4,786	-	5,088	-	5,748	-	5,562	-	5,943	-
Fighter	580	-	564	-	573	-	529	-	581	-
Bombardment	2,778	-	2,654	-	2,832	-	2,521	-	2,740	-
Reconnaissance	30	-	32	-	32	-	29	-	29	-
Transport	212	-	311	-	358	-	341	-	378	-
Rescue	31	-	43	-	36	-	40	-	36	-
Other	1,155	-	1,484	-	1,917	-	2,102	-	2,179	-
Air University - Total	176	-	156	-	150	-	164	-	176	-
Bombardment	58	-	60	-	63	-	69	-	75	-
Transport	118	-	96	-	87	-	95	-	101	-
Caribbean Air Command - Total	167	72	146	62	150	62	165	62	133	48
Bombardment	19	-	7	-	10	-	11	-	10	-
Transport	75	3	76	5	79	6	90	3	77	2
Rescue	61	61	57	57	56	56	59	59	46	46
Other	12	8	6	-	5	-	5	-	-	-
Continental Air Command - Total	79	-	131	-	236	-	267	-	285	-
Fighter	1	-	1	-	1	-	6	-	8	-
Bombardment	21	-	20	-	21	-	19	-	19	-
Transport	53	-	102	-	111	-	147	-	162	-
Other	4	-	8	-	103	-	95	-	96	-
Far East Air Forces - Total	6,268	5,988	6,776	6,562	6,717	6,525	7,206	6,998	7,332	7,120
Fighter	1,067	1,067	1,276	1,276	1,337	1,337	1,447	1,447	1,613	1,613
Bombardment	1,921	1,864	2,067	2,059	2,136	2,133	2,347	2,336	2,357	2,347
Reconnaissance	739	739	745	745	784	784	765	765	843	843
Tanker	72	72	70	63	69	69	72	72	71	71
Transport	1,879	1,756	1,970	1,860	1,824	1,726	1,946	1,836	1,822	1,709
Rescue	383	383	450	450	393	390	425	423	422	421
Other	207	107	198	109	174	86	204	119	204	116

(Continued)

TABLE 189 – USAF AIR CREW PERSONNEL BY TYPE OF AIRCRAFT, BY COMMAND – FY 1953 (CONTINUED)

Command and Type	30 June (1952)		30 September		31 December		31 March (1953)		30 June	
	Total	Tactical	Total	Tactical	Total	Tactical	Total	Tactical	Total	Tactical
Headquarters Command - Total	530	-	410	-	415	-	224	-	221	-
Bombardment	171	-	107	-	186	-	112	-	124	-
Transport	359	-	303	-	229	-	112	-	97	-
Military Air Transport Service - Total	4,425	3,623	3,614	3,360	3,783	3,010	3,763	3,066	3,815	3,047
Fighter	-	-	-	-	-	-	-	-	52	52
Bombardment	264	264	40	40	-	-	-	-	-	-
Reconnaissance	401	401	353	353	293	293	365	365	383	383
Transport	3,059	2,257	2,542	2,288	2,932	2,159	2,928	2,231	2,849	2,081
Rescue	701	701	679	679	558	558	470	470	531	531
Northeast Air Command - Total	202	107	294	126	371	168	374	171	390	180
Fighter	-	-	8	8	58	58	46	45	48	48
Bombardment	2	-	4	-	3	-	6	-	6	-
Transport	94	6	163	6	201	6	212	20	197	-
Rescue	106	101	119	112	109	104	110	105	137	132
Other	-	-	-	-	-	-	-	-	2	-
Strategic Air Command - Total	16,181	15,841	16,788	16,442	16,709	16,328	17,410	16,780	18,056	17,550
Fighter	213	213	190	190	225	225	330	330	357	357
Bombardment	10,569	10,513	10,872	10,785	10,405	10,310	9,856	9,505	9,659	9,451
Reconnaissance	2,562	2,554	2,418	2,408	2,643	2,632	3,046	3,036	3,597	3,588
Tanker	2,130	2,109	2,477	2,465	2,592	2,579	3,276	3,263	3,495	3,474
Transport	652	416	770	555	787	544	853	612	875	632
Rescue	36	36	39	39	38	38	34	34	48	48
Other	19	-	22	-	19	-	15	-	25	-
Tactical Air Command - Total	2,877	2,691	2,744	2,574	2,924	2,745	2,769	2,587	3,023	2,832
Fighter	298	298	296	296	289	289	297	294	345	345
Bombardment	218	76	185	70	168	58	140	50	138	37
Reconnaissance	241	241	169	169	162	162	163	163	81	81
Transport	1,730	1,686	1,636	1,581	1,732	1,684	1,747	1,679	1,966	1,896
Rescue	56	56	54	54	86	86	45	45	50	50
Other	334	334	404	404	487	466	377	356	443	423
US Air Force in Europe - Total	1,766	1,403	1,783	1,365	1,903	1,361	1,911	1,357	2,025	1,434
Fighter	492	492	444	444	404	404	432	432	449	449
Bombardment	344	316	359	330	409	279	379	260	417	300
Reconnaissance	64	64	31	31	80	80	69	69	81	81
Transport	691	368	748	373	787	405	783	401	806	387
Rescue	123	123	117	117	123	107	126	110	133	117
Other	52	40	84	70	100	86	122	85	139	100
USAF Advanced Flying School Graduates on Hand at End of Month and Pipeline - Total	2,086	2,086	1,994	1,994	2,319	2,319	2,110	2,110	1,964	1,964
Fighter	48	48	62	62	48	48	176	176	137	137
Bombardment	563	563	718	718	753	753	843	843	993	993
Reconnaissance	154	154	146	146	147	147	74	74	48	48
Transport	1,177	1,177	914	914	1,151	1,151	843	843	720	720
Rescue	143	143	131	131	176	176	132	132	32	32
Other	1	1	23	23	44	44	42	42	34	34

Source: Personnel Statistics Division, DCS/Comptroller, Headquarters USAF.

TABLE 190 — AVERAGE COMBAT EXPERIENCE LEVEL OF USAF AIR CREW PERSONNEL IN COMMITTED UNITS, BY SELECTED AIRCRAFT TYPES — JUN 1952 THROUGH JUL 1953

Date	B - 29		B - 26		F - 84		F - 86	
	Number of Personnel	Av Exp Level (Sorties	Number of Personnel	Av Exp Level (Sorties)	Number of Personnel	Av Exp Level (Sorties)	Number of Personnel	Av Exp Level (Sorties)
1952								
June	1,248	10.9	616	22.5	194	34.3	221	42.5
July	1,233	12.7	544	21.2	297	24.6	224	39.6
August	1,335	11.8	565	18.4	287	27.4	221	44.3
September	1,307	13.4	568	20.6	314	27.8	239	43.8
October	1,193	11.9	614	19.1	324	30.2	244	48.6
November	1,266	12.0	674	16.2	334	31.0	241	41.1
December	1,264	11.0	707	14.9	306	30.6	266	37.0
1953								
January	1,329	10.7	790	14.7	293	27.3	296	34.2
February	1,402	10.8	924	15.7	321	25.7	370	35.9
March	1,359	11.1	838	15.0	339	25.3	440	32.7
April	1,346	11.6	854	17.4	373	26.2	520	33.3
May	1,453	11.6	909	17.6	437	26.2	534	44.3
June	1,271	13.9	902	18.2	459	27.4	510	41.6
July	1,293	25.4	862	16.1	303	44.4	499	44.3

Date	F - 80		F - 51		F - 94	
	Number of Personnel	Av Exp Level (Sorties)	Number of Personnel	Av Exp Level (Sorties)	Number of Personnel	Av Exp Level (Sorties)
1952						
June	115	50.9	83	29.9	76	5.3
July	126	35.8	86	30.1	76	7.9
August	121	32.6	74	29.3	70	10.7
September	138	36.8	117	30.2	71	8.6
October	134	45.1	120	33.6	64	7.9
November	147	44.2	100	38.2	111	5.7
December	134	47.8	83	38.2	92	6.3
1953						
January	124	49.8	75	39.4	90	13.6
February	131	41.7	-	-	104	17.0
March	55	49.3	-	-	98	30.1
April	55	51.8	-	-	102	31.2
May	5	58.4	-	-	109	36.7
June	6	20.5	-	-	107	34.2
July	4	30.5	-	-	89	29.3

Source: Personnel Statistics Division, DCS/Comptroller, Headquarters USAF.

TABLE 191 — AVERAGE EXPERIENCE LEVEL OF AIR CREW PERSONNEL RETIRED FROM UNITS COMMITTED TO THE KOREAN WAR BY SELECTED AIRCRAFT TYPES — JUN 1952 THROUGH JUL 1953

Date	B - 29		B - 26		F - 84		F - 86	
	Number of Personnel	Av Exp Level (Sorties)	Number of Personnel	Av Exp Level (Sorties)	Number of Personnel	Av Exp Level (Sorties)	Number of Personnel	Av Exp Level (Sorties)
1952								
June	137	33.2	44	60.5	7	78.4	22	102.7
July	116	30.7	155	60.8	10	86.5	23	99.9
August	149	28.3	96	57.0	28	102.6	23	109.0
September	240	41.0	46	67.7	18	103.3	21	105.0
October	275	31.0	132	50.7	28	55.9	27	82.2
November	146	33.7	133	50.6	27	71.8	39	101.4
December	242	31.8	106	50.0	36	66.3	25	98.3
1953								
January	200	34.7	107	49.9	51	89.4	26	78.7
February	150	31.4	68	41.4	28	68.4	15	100.1
March	269	30.4	183	50.3	23	73.8	18	90.5
April	201	29.9	94	52.0	38	73.4	18	93.3
May	200	32.9	115	52.7	28	106.5	47	97.4
June	216	31.9	174	43.3	31	86.8	32	85.8
July	285	38.1	83	30.1	28	90.1	28	100.5

Date	F - 80		F - 51		F - 94	
	Number of Personnel	Av Exp Level (Sorties)	Number of Personnel	Av Exp Level (Sorties)	Number of Personnel	Av Exp Level (Sorties)
1952						
June	11	105.5	-	-	-	-
July	25	103.9	-	-	-	-
August	29	113.8	19	113.9	7	107.0
September	9	113.3	6	77.2	7	35.6
October	18	74.9	11	60.1	14	22.6
November	16	91.8	13	69.4	-	-
December	21	96.0	18	80.5	24	29.7
1953						
January	17	102.0	7	71.3	8	18.0
February	21	100.1	4	85.5	6	28.8
March	22	94.1	-	-	12	38.8
April	13	97.1	-	-	1	86.0
May	17	91.4	-	-	3	85.6
June	2	105.5	-	-	13	76.3
July	1	106.0	-	-	4	155.5

Source: Personnel Statistics Division, DCS/Comptroller, Headquarters USAF.

TABLE 192 – PEAK STRENGTH OF MILITARY PERSONNEL BY FISCAL YEAR AND CALENDAR YEAR – JUN 1939 THROUGH JUN 1953

(A resume of Worldwide peak strengths covering fiscal years 1940 through 1953 and calendar years 1939 (last half) through 1952 may be of interest to recipients of this publication. Peak strengths for the respective types of military personnel are underscored and other types are shown for the corresponding periods. (The lowest point reached in Worldwide USAF military strength since World War II was in May 1947 with a total of 303,614 personnel - 43,076 Officers and 260,538 Enlisted.)

Date	Total	Officer a/	Enlisted b/
Peak Strength By Fiscal Year			
1940			
June (1940)	51,165	3,361	47,804
1941			
May (1941)	152,641	9,078	143,563
June (1941)	152,125	10,611	141,514
1942			
June (1942)	764,415	55,956	708,459
1943			
June (1943)	2,197,114	205,874	1,991,240
1944			
January (1944). . . .	2,400,151	287,294	2,112,857
March (1944). . . .	2,411,294	306,889	2,104,405
June (1944). . . .	2,372,292	333,401	2,038,891
1945			
July (1944)	2,403,806	342,914	2,060,892
May (1945)	2,310,436	388,295	1,922,141
1946			
July (1945)	2,262,092	371,269	1,890,823
1947			
July (1946).	450,626	72,983	377,643
1948			
June (1948).	387,730	48,957	338,773
1949			
June (1949).	419,347	57,851	361,496
1950			
July (1949).	422,515	59,120	363,395
December (1949). . .	413,286	60,770	352,516
1951			
June (1951).	788,381	107,099	681,282
1952			
June (1952)	973,474	128,401	845,073
1953			
October (1952) . . .	969,566	132,621	836,945
April (1953). . . .	980,205	129,685	850,520

Calendar Year	Total	Officer a/	Enlisted b/
Peak Strength by Calendar Year			
1939 (Last Half)			
November	39,058	3,030	36,028
December	43,118	3,006	40,112
1940			
December	99,993	5,203	94,790
1941			
December	354,161	24,521	329,640
1942			
December	1,597,049	127,267	1,469,782
1943			
November	2,383,370	265,630	2,117,740
December	2,373,882	274,347	2,099,535
1944			
January.	2,400,151	287,294	2,112,857
July	2,403,806	342,914	2,060,892
December	2,359,456	375,973	1,983,483
1945			
January.	2,345,068	377,426	1,967,642
May.	2,310,436	388,295	1,922,141
1946			
January.	733,786	141,643	592,143
1947			
January.	327,404	48,021	279,383
December	339,246	47,021	292,225
1948			
December	412,312	53,948	358,364
1949			
July	422,515	59,120	363,395
December	413,286	60,770	352,516
1950			
December	559,329	69,901	489,428
1951			
December	897,366	121,635	775,731
1952			
June	973,474	128,401	845,073
August	975,603	131,868	843,735
October.	969,566	132,621	836,945

a/ Includes Flight and Warrant Officers.
b/ Includes Aviation Cadets.

Source: Personnel Statistics Division, DCS/Comptroller, Headquarters USAF.

TABLE 193 — COMMAND STRENGTH BASED ON OPERATING LOCATION BY STATE, CONTINENTAL US — FY 1953

State	1952						1953					
	July	August	September	October	November	December	January	February	March	April	May	June
Total. .	714,016	706,621	703,019	698,637	690,314	678,977	678,205	680,610	687,243	690,702	684,772	676,309
Alabama . . .	13,759	16,688	17,043	17,101	16,781	16,977	16,863	16,591	16,575	15,918	15,703	15,498
Arizona . . .	17,885	17,386	17,203	17,431	18,980	17,865	16,789	16,371	16,545	16,711	16,237	16,398
Arkansas. . .	130	118	111	105	109	96	96	92	99	97	105	103
California. .	89,629	87,877	87,879	86,997	89,831	88,651	90,184	90,262	85,925	86,723	81,707	81,391
Colorado . .	18,110	17,699	17,169	16,939	16,204	15,575	15,784	15,905	16,139	16,684	16,852	16,926
Connecticut .	112	55	50	43	58	56	56	54	57	57	59	60
Delaware. . .	3,126	3,168	3,152	3,189	3,080	3,071	3,115	3,069	3,052	3,120	3,147	3,199
District of Columbia. .	11,339	10,621	10,256	10,912	10,107	10,067	10,024	10,038	10,016	9,950	9,952	9,662
Florida . . .	42,452	42,467	42,843	42,379	41,892	41,575	41,822	41,799	41,707	41,593	41,710	39,315
Georgia . . .	24,575	24,228	23,951	24,478	23,959	23,571	22,748	22,581	22,820	22,663	22,643	22,720
Idaho	5,220	4,986	3,111	2,879	2,756	2,831	2,870	2,980	3,014	3,067	3,714	3,962
Illinois. . .	30,486	30,270	28,599	26,779	25,730	23,613	22,928	22,930	22,719	23,349	24,441	26,165
Indiana . . .	1,125	971	959	931	925	924	912	879	894	861	851	841
Iowa.	1,386	1,314	1,229	1,165	1,145	1,200	1,234	1,300	1,289	1,286	1,307	1,388
Kansas. . . .	11,017	11,646	12,614	15,504	15,944	16,611	17,184	17,530	17,992	18,650	18,830	18,877
Kentucky. . .	2,193	2,112	2,259	2,209	2,080	2,023	2,040	2,016	1,913	1,249	1,185	1,153
Louisiana . .	19,238	18,916	18,936	19,205	18,941	19,049	19,183	19,210	19,601	19,747	19,966	20,441
Maine	4,879	4,741	5,097	5,135	5,120	5,147	5,273	5,724	6,042	6,636	7,495	8,334
Maryland. . .	7,915	7,665	7,642	7,006	8,206	8,343	8,595	8,695	8,948	8,987	9,137	9,344
Massachusetts	14,603	14,391	14,043	13,213	13,087	13,229	13,099	13,018	13,280	13,369	13,454	13,320
Michigan. . .	6,933	6,905	6,992	7,117	6,995	7,008	7,042	7,123	7,231	7,292	7,490	7,665
Minnesota . .	3,226	3,209	3,240	3,300	3,141	2,860	3,014	3,009	2,912	2,907	2,974	3,010
Mississippi .	22,413	21,897	21,372	20,518	19,015	19,071	19,573	20,095	20,313	21,748	23,852	24,636
Missouri. . .	2,216	2,274	2,153	2,205	2,228	2,232	2,158	2,241	2,363	2,278	1,857	2,056
Montana . . .	5,095	4,984	5,161	5,018	4,706	4,519	4,450	4,326	4,028	4,244	4,737	4,836
Nebraska. . .	5,545	5,425	5,400	5,442	5,533	5,534	5,426	5,260	5,212	5,189	5,179	5,138
Nevada	6,285	6,295	6,320	6,383	6,179	6,613	6,724	6,900	6,966	6,989	6,971	6,946
New hampshire	1,403	1,566	1,571	1,517	1,386	1,158	897	832	715	690	701	1,149
New Jersey. .	11,442	9,644	11,004	10,772	10,187	10,747	9,893	9,195	9,441	11,410	11,647	11,295
New Mexico. .	19,682	19,457	21,810	23,297	22,464	22,734	22,615	22,235	22,231	22,250	22,038	22,155
New York . .	38,882	38,914	37,198	34,436	34,650	34,021	35,243	37,331	40,265	40,856	34,074	28,548
North Carolina	5,098	5,136	5,069	5,125	4,564	4,630	4,906	4,938	4,984	4,807	4,823	5,135
North Dakota.	423	426	435	430	412	398	380	385	397	389	376	382
Ohio	17,697	17,694	17,757	17,627	17,406	17,303	17,253	17,117	17,173	17,187	17,544	17,264
Oklahoma. . .	9,265	8,968	8,568	8,432	8,340	8,212	8,133	7,824	7,709	7,935	7,755	7,518
Oregon. . . .	2,271	2,086	2,094	2,024	1,929	1,863	2,684	1,746	1,783	1,845	1,959	1,694
Pennsylvania.	3,266	3,171	3,148	3,172	3,048	2,888	2,853	2,796	2,739	2,714	2,728	2,633
Rhode Island.	42	33	30	30	32	33	35	33	33	32	32	33
South Carolina	13,009	12,635	12,277	11,820	9,954	9,897	9,656	9,785	10,094	10,094	10,320	10,524
South Dakota.	7,433	7,515	7,385	7,621	7,275	7,288	7,320	6,992	6,719	6,491	6,513	6,583
Tennessee . .	7,879	7,445	6,870	6,623	6,446	6,658	6,782	7,029	7,242	7,176	7,241	7,322
Texas	151,550	152,089	152,427	152,155	151,050	145,544	142,480	143,148	147,885	146,443	146,082	141,758
Utah	2,449	2,281	2,356	2,421	2,647	2,615	2,736	2,395	2,489	1,670	1,528	1,721
Vermont . . .	1,228	1,166	1,157	1,174	1,108	1,068	1,082	1,061	1,047	1,067	1,062	1,068
Virginia. . .	8,878	9,047	9,388	9,499	9,303	9,226	9,630	9,928	10,124	10,662	10,100	10,294
Washington. .	24,747	24,447	23,720	23,562	23,772	23,083	22,709	22,658	22,608	21,987	22,334	21,236
West Virginia	231	210	209	203	202	194	190	185	180	177	175	174
Wisconsin . .	2,649	2,635	2,675	2,593	2,397	2,427	2,429	2,377	2,400	2,407	2,354	2,391
Wyoming . . .	11,381	11,308	10,612	9,805	8,784	7,951	8,562	9,160	9,636	10,341	11,555	11,583
Unknown . . .	2,219	440	375	716	226	728	551	1,472	1,697	708	276	465

Source: Personnel Statistical Division DCS/Comptroller, Headquarters, USAF

TABLE 194 — COMMAND STRENGTH BASED ON OPERATING LOCATION OUTSIDE CONTINENTAL US BY COUNTRY — FY 1953

Country	1952						1953					
	July	August	September	October	November	December	January	February	March	April	May	June
Total . .	259,542	268,982	268,306	270,929	278,038	278,626	280,504	284,487	286,959	289,503	295,108	301,284
Afghanistan.	3	6	4	4	4	3	3	2	2	2	3	2
Alaska. . .	21,740	22,068	21,798	22,001	22,187	22,145	22,321	22,576	22,376	22,980	23,358	23,127
Arabia . . .	993	1,004	991	1,001	1,030	1,006	890	930	924	959	942	1,003
Argentina. .	5	5	5	5	5	5	5	4	4	4	5	5
Australia. .	3	4	4	4	3	4	3	3	4	3	6	6
Austria. . .	273	282	288	273	278	291	299	280	280	281	289	317
Azores . . .	1,101	1,124	1,130	1,196	1,281	1,262	1,288	1,259	1,289	1,256	1,234	1,210
Belgium. . .	29	30	31	33	32	32	31	30	31	34	37	36
Bermuda. . .	2,333	2,419	2,412	2,448	2,440	2,256	2,340	2,316	2,228	2,163	2,117	2,055
Bolivia . . .	11	10	11	12	12	13	14	14	14	11	13	13
Brazil . . .	112	112	111	114	113	102	113	109	106	104	105	106
Brit.W.Inds.	302	309	322	339	349	327	324	418	370	410	409	402
Burma. . . .	6	7	7	7	7	6	6	6	6	6	6	6
Canada . . .	68	73	64	60	61	319	360	395	581	741	826	816
Canal Zone .	1,998	2,014	1,956	1,935	1,970	1,941	1,948	1,951	1,930	1,978	1,965	1,945
Chile. . . .	13	15	16	20	17	16	16	19	19	19	20	18
China. . . .	3	6	2	2	2	2	2	2	2	2	1	1
Colombia.. .	10	10	9	9	9	9	9	10	10	10	11	11
Cuba	18	18	17	16	16	15	15	15	15	3	16	16
Cyprus . . .	2	2	2	2	1	-	1	1	2	2	2	2
Czechoslovakia	2	2	1	1	1	1	1	1	1	1	1	1
Denmark. . .	21	24	25	23	21	19	19	21	21	22	24	25
Dominican Rep.	2	2	2	2	2	2	2	2	2	2	2	2
Ecuador. . .	18	19	19	19	19	20	19	19	20	20	20	20
Egypt. . . .	8	17	9	12	5	7	7	7	7	7	8	8
El Salvador.	10	9	10	11	10	11	92	11	11	12	11	11
England a/ .	41,658	43,024	40,124	38,962	38,719	38,626	38,832	38,932	38,568	39,248	39,526	41,715
Eritrea. . .	2	1	1	1	1	1	-	-	-	-	-	-
Finland. . .	8	8	8	7	7	6	5	5	5	4	5	5
Formosa. . .	110	125	127	149	172	150	134	136	137	137	147	142
France . . .	10,902	12,886	13,154	13,668	14,370	14,675	14,530	15,318	15,678	17,549	17,073	17,308
French Morocco	6,272	6,369	6,417	6,565	6,873	7,035	7,073	7,154	7,637	8,035	7,957	8,822
Germany. . .	30,557	30,634	30,728	31,164	33,336	33,371	33,983	34,696	34,671	35,975	37,427	37,833
Greece . . .	212	211	211	191	221	227	229	227	240	251	242	241
Greenland. .	2,392	2,502	2,919	3,082	3,441	3,584	3,602	3,936	4,063	4,077	4,379	4,711
Guam	4,989	5,021	5,078	5,256	5,295	6,585	5,181	5,183	5,431	6,856	6,859	5,416
Guatemala. .	16	17	17	17	17	16	17	16	14	14	15	14
Haiti. . . .	9	8	9	9	9	9	9	9	10	10	10	9
Hawaii . . .	6,500	6,413	6,237	5,930	5,705	5,550	5,474	5,509	5,411	5,334	5,251	5,216
Honduras . .	6	7	8	8	9	8	8	8	8	7	8	7
Hungary. . .	3	4	4	4	4	3	3	3	3	3	3	1
Iceland. . .	1,232	1,279	1,273	1,466	1,608	1,579	1,584	1,579	1,548	1,930	1,925	1,979
India. . . .	17	24	18	17	18	15	13	13	7	8	16	14
Indo-China .	24	17	23	25	26	25	24	24	25	24	28	34
Iran	45	47	46	49	46	47	46	42	45	46	48	45
Iraq	9	15	8	8	8	8	8	8	8	7	7	6
Ireland. . .	2	6	2	3	3	6	2	2	2	2	2	2
Israel . . .	4	5	6	6	6	6	6	6	5	5	6	6
Italy. . . .	372	384	519	514	530	532	546	563	581	698	715	739
Iwo Jima . .	287	277	312	314	296	276	290	306	301	300	275	283
Japan	45,888	49,515	50,098	51,888	54,062	54,418	52,680	53,914	56,167	52,959	57,307	60,297
Johnston Is.	672	668	659	647	610	586	595	646	640	669	596	607
Korea. . . .	44,129	43,973	42,963	45,244	45,046	46,388	47,674	47,551	46,351	47,214	46,031	44,650
Labrador . .	1,785	1,838	1,819	1,957	2,196	1,863	2,104	2,198	2,260	2,310	2,430	2,495
Levant Sts b/	7	6	6	6	6	6	6	6	6	6	-	-
Liberia. . .	1	1	1	1	1	1	1	1	1	1	1	1
Libya. . . .	2,218	2,962	4,522	4,487	4,650	4,742	4,913	5,023	5,111	5,262	5,361	5,261
Malay States c/	6	6	6	6	6	6	6	6	6	5	5	5
Marshall Is.	500	1,333	1,522	604	1,367	601	678	672	661	604	646	710
Mexico . . .	9	9	9	9	7	7	8	8	8	8	9	9
Morocco. . .	52	62	33	34	34	7	32	31	31	31	-	-

(CONTINUED)

TABLE 194 — COMMAND STRENGTH BASED ON OPERATING LOCATION OUTSIDE CONTINENTAL US BY COUNTRY — FY 1953 — (Continued)

Country	1952						1953					
	July	August	September	October	November	December	January	February	March	April	May	June
Netherlands. .	22	23	24	23	33	30	35	35	23	22	24	25
Newfoundland .	6,371	6,504	6,532	6,959	6,496	6,346	6,363	6,327	6,282	6,002	6,234	7,175
Nicaragua. . .	-	-	-	-	-	-	-	-	-	3	6	6
Norway	92	103	119	125	123	128	133	136	136	142	143	145
Okinawa. . . .	10,751	10,657	10,577	11,276	11,462	9,736	11,399	11,456	11,436	9,646	9,638	10,520
Pakistan . . .	-	-	-	-	-	-	-	-	6	5	5	5
Paraguay . . .	12	12	12	13	13	13	13	13	13	13	13	13
Peru	33	29	35	36	36	35	36	37	41	40	40	35
Philippine Is.	6,843	7,029	7,608	7,395	7,380	7,369	7,445	7,387	7,744	7,501	7,408	7,807
Poland	2	3	3	3	2	2	2	2	2	2	1	1
Portugal . . .	30	32	33	32	32	34	32	33	43	43	33	31
Puerto Rico. .	4,661	4,477	4,378	2,308	2,901	3,185	3,643	3,879	4,296	4,431	4,652	4,674
Russia	3	3	3	2	3	2	2	4	4	4	6	5
Saint Thomas .	1	1	-	-	-	-	-	-	-	-	-	-
Scotland . . .	371	454	478	523	525	535	557	618	608	634	714	657
Siam d/. . . .	41	55	48	48	48	47	48	48	51	51	47	48
Spain.	9	27	11	11	11	10	10	11	11	14	15	15
Sweden	8	15	12	11	12	12	12	11	11	11	14	14
Switzerland. .	4	4	4	4	3	2	2	2	2	2	2	2
Syria.	-	-	-	-	-	-	-	-	-	-	6	6
Tangier. . . .	-	-	-	-	-	-	-	-	-	-	6	6
Transvaal. . .	7	6	6	6	6	5	4	4	3	3	-	-
Turkey	239	240	233	237	242	249	247	242	246	241	290	289
Union of South Africa . . .	-	-	-	-	-	-	-	-	-	-	4	4
Uruguay. . . .	12	16	13	12	12	12	12	12	11	11	11	11
Venezuela. . .	27	22	27	29	28	26	26	26	27	27	26	26
Yugoslavia . .	14	14	14	15	15	17	17	16	26	26	26	17
Unknown. . . .	10	8	3	14	75	52	42	56	42	8	3	-

a/ England includes Wales.
b/ March 1953 Levant States changed to Lebanon.
c/ March 1953 Malay States changed to Malaya.
d/ March 1953 Siam changed to Thailand.

Source: Personnel Statistics Division, DCS/Comptroller, Headquarters USAF.

TABLE 195 — COMMAND STRENGTH BY TYPE OF PERSONNEL — FY 1953

End of Month	WORLDWIDE				CONTINENTAL US				OVERSEAS			
	Total	Officer	W/O	E/P a/	Total	Officer	W/O	E/P a/	Total	Officer	W/O	E/P
1952												
July	973,558	125,282	4,182	844,094	717,182	95,362	3,162	618,658	256,376	29,920	1,020	225,436
August . . .	975,603	127,693	4,175	843,735	710,547	97,136	3,146	610,265	265,056	30,557	1,029	233,470
September. .	971,325	128,232	4,153	838,940	704,555	97,480	3,076	603,999	266,770	30,752	1,077	234,941
October. . .	969,566	128,469	4,152	836,945	700,005	98,055	3,080	598,870	269,561	30,414	1,072	238,075
November . .	968,352	127,656	4,167	836,529	692,456	97,075	3,086	592,295	275,896	30,581	1,081	244,234
December . .	957,603	126,340	4,115	827,148	680,515	96,265	3,037	581,213	277,088	30,075	1,078	245,935
1953												
January. . .	958,709	125,420	4,073	829,216	679,018	94,934	2,967	581,117	279,691	30,486	1,106	248,099
February . .	965,097	125,315	4,090	835,692	681,487	94,350	2,963	584,174	283,610	30,965	1,127	251,518
March . . .	974,202	126,219	4,072	843,911	688,228	95,198	2,943	590,087	285,974	31,021	1,129	253,824
April . . .	980,205	125,622	4,063	850,520	691,851	93,912	2,912	595,027	288,354	31,710	1,151	255,493
May.	979,880	126,067	4,025	849,788	685,992	93,783	2,877	589,332	293,888	32,284	1,148	260,456
June	977,593	126,769	4,000	846,824	681,978	94,383	2,821	584,774	295,615	32,386	1,179	262,050

a/ Includes Aviation Cadets.

Source: Personnel Statistics Division, DCS/Comptroller, Hq. USAF.

TABLE 196 — COMMAND STRENGTH OF NEGRO PERSONNEL BY TYPE OF PERSONNEL — FY 1953

(For Overall Totals - See Table 195)

End of Month	WORLDWIDE			CONTINENTAL US			OVERSEAS		
	Officer	Warrant Officer	Enlisted a/	Officer	Warrant Officer	Enlisted a/	Officer	Warrant Officer	Enlisted
1952									
July.	804	48	62,830	563	33	46,955	241	15	15,875
August.	836	48	64,911	577	29	47,912	259	19	16,999
September	898	49	65,873	626	31	48,425	272	18	17,448
October	947	51	66,558	688	32	48,370	259	19	18,188
November.	952	55	66,937	692	36	48,296	260	19	18,641
December.	978	58	66,995	725	38	47,877	253	20	19,118
1953									
January	989	58	67,176	729	38	47,588	260	20	19,588
February.	1,015	58	67,694	746	39	47,252	269	19	20,442
March	1,064	62	69,214	787	43	48,171	277	19	21,043
April	1,093	62	70,138	811	42	48,434	282	20	21,704
May	1,140	60	70,176	844	40	47,549	296	20	22,627
June.	1,182	56	69,720	884	37	46,692	298	19	23,028

a/ Includes Aviation Cadets.

Source: Personnel Statistics Division, DCS/Comptroller, Headquarters USAF.

TABLE 197 – COMMAND STRENGTH BY GRADE IN WHICH SERVING – FY 1953

Grade	July (1952)	August	September	October	November	December
Total	973,558	975,603	971,325	969,566	968,352	957,603
Officer and Warrant Officer - Total	129,464	131,868	132,385	132,621	131,823	130,455
Officer - Total	125,282	127,693	128,232	128,469	127,656	126,340
General - Total	319	315	359	366	366	382
General	7	7	7	7	7	7
Lieutenant General	17	17	19	19	19	19
Major General	115	114	124	128	128	135
Brigadier General	180	177	209	212	212	221
Colonel	4,067	4,081	4,009	3,988	3,974	3,938
Lieutenant Colonel	8,380	8,358	8,265	8,242	8,200	8,181
Major	20,580	20,476	20,315	20,128	19,952	19,791
Captain	40,008	39,786	39,185	38,571	38,092	37,024
First Lieutenant	29,609	29,689	29,900	30,622	31,206	31,032
Second Lieutenant	22,319	24,988	26,199	26,552	25,866	25,992
Warrant Officer - Total	4,182	4,175	4,153	4,152	4,167	4,115
Chief Warrant Officer, W-4	137	137	137	134	135	128
Chief Warrant Officer, W-3	288	272	279	287	287	286
Chief Warrant Officer, W-2	1,016	1,098	1,023	1,018	1,015	1,020
Warrant Officer, Junior Grade W-1	2,741	2,668	2,714	2,713	2,730	2,681
Enlisted - Total	836,477	835,704	831,203	828,994	827,846	818,958
Seventh Grade	44,404	44,865	44,427	45,063	44,786	45,161
Sixth Grade	52,655	53,454	52,570	53,289	52,618	53,112
Fifth Grade	119,309	119,263	113,818	116,567	113,390	116,192
Fourth Grade	153,467	156,910	151,509	155,529	151,276	154,013
Third Grade	181,845	182,763	182,883	180,865	182,099	187,077
Second Grade	229,709	223,446	231,167	224,685	231,202	215,028
First Grade	55,088	55,003	54,829	52,996	52,475	48,375
Aviation Cadet - Total	7,617	8,031	7,737	7,951	8,683	8,190

Grade	January (1953)	February	March	April	May	June
Total	958,709	965,097	974,202	980,205	979,880	977,593
Officer and Warrant Officer - Total	129,493	129,405	130,291	129,685	130,092	130,769
Officer - Total	125,420	125,315	126,219	125,622	126,067	126,769
General - Total	381	377	368	364	363	382
General	7	7	7	7	7	7
Lieutenant General	19	19	18	17	20	18
Major General	135	134	128	127	124	134
Brigadier General	220	217	215	213	212	223
Colonel	3,917	3,888	3,874	4,020	4,183	4,314
Lieutenant Colonel	8,102	8,064	7,998	8,080	8,220	8,324
Major	19,633	19,514	19,379	20,855	20,909	20,805
Captain	36,477	35,918	35,593	38,010	37,571	36,649
First Lieutenant	32,707	34,464	35,360	31,264	31,672	32,090
Second Lieutenant	24,203	23,090	23,647	23,029	23,149	24,205
Warrant Officer - Total	4,073	4,090	4,072	4,063	4,025	4,000
Chief Warrant Officer, W-4	123	127	125	130	137	139
Chief Warrant Officer, W-3	284	286	276	345	380	397
Chief Warrant Officer, W-2	1,018	1,011	1,021	1,182	1,257	1,275
Warrant Officer, Junior Grade W-1	2,648	2,666	2,650	2,406	2,251	2,189
Enlisted - Total	819,933	826,538	834,258	840,047	840,019	837,667
Seventh Grade	44,985	45,529	45,108	45,646	45,184	45,176
Sixth Grade	52,758	53,995	53,566	54,573	54,193	54,279
Fifth Grade	114,827	122,118	120,686	129,159	128,581	131,342
Fourth Grade	151,008	157,695	156,290	167,002	166,425	171,893
Third Grade	189,555	199,418	199,409	204,907	205,453	205,478
Second Grade	216,321	192,050	199,872	190,717	203,098	200,638
First Grade	50,479	55,733	59,327	48,043	37,085	28,861
Aviation Cadet - Total	9,283	9,154	9,653	10,473	9,769	9,157

Source: Personnel Statistics Division, DCS/Comptroller, Headquarters USAF.

TABLE 198 — COMMAND STRENGTH OF GENERAL OFFICERS BY GRADE IN WHICH SERVING — FY 1953

End of Month	Total			General			Lieutenant General			Major General			Brigadier General		
	Total	Contl US	O/S	Total	Contl US	O/S	Total	Contl US	O/S	Total	Contl US	O/S	Total	Contl US	O/S
1952															
July	319	255	64	7	5	2	17	14	3	115	99	16	180	137	43
August	315	249	66	7	5	2	17	14	3	114	97	17	177	133	44
September.	359	288	71	7	5	2	19	15	4	124	105	19	209	163	46
October.	366	292	74	7	5	2	19	15	4	128	109	19	212	163	49
November	366	292	74	7	5	2	19	15	4	127	108	19	213	164	49
December	382	305	77	7	5	2	19	15	4	135	114	21	221	171	50
1953															
January.	381	304	77	7	5	2	19	15	4	135	115	20	220	169	51
February	377	296	81	7	5	2	19	15	4	134	114	20	217	162	55
March.	368	287	81	7	5	2	18	14	4	128	109	19	215	159	56
April.	364	284	80	7	5	2	17	13	4	127	107	20	213	159	54
May.	363	284	79	7	5	2	19	15	4	125	103	22	212	161	51
June	382	306	76	7	5	2	18	14	4	134	113	21	223	174	49

Source: Personnel Statistics Division, DCS/Comptroller, Headquarters, USAF

TABLE 199 — COMMAND STRENGTH OF NEGRO PERSONNEL BY GRADE IN WHICH SERVING — FY 1953

Grade	July (1952)	August	September	October	November	December
Total	63,682	65,795	66,820	67,556	67,944	68,031
Officer and Warrant Officer - Total	852	884	947	998	1,007	1,036
Officer - Total	804	836	898	947	952	978
General	-	-	-	-	-	-
Colonel	2	4	4	4	4	4
Lieutenant Colonel	9	9	8	8	8	8
Major	85	85	85	85	83	82
Captain	251	250	255	257	258	256
First Lieutenant	227	244	270	299	308	317
Second Lieutenant	230	244	276	294	291	311
Warrant Officer - Total	48	48	49	51	55	58
Chief Warrant Officer, W-4	-	-	-	-	-	-
Chief Warrant Officer, W-3	-	-	-	-	-	-
Chief Warrant Officer, W-2	9	11	8	11	8	8
Warrant Officer, JG W-1	39	37	41	40	47	50
Enlisted - Total	62,779	64,845	65,798	66,475	66,822	66,862
Master Sergeant	771	783	759	787	805	807
Technical Sergeant & Sergeant 1st Class	1,574	1,622	1,599	1,665	1,673	1,678
Staff Sergeant & Sergeant	6,559	6,831	6,657	6,891	6,726	6,835
Airman 1st Class & Corporal	9,114	9,234	8,946	9,013	8,779	8,603
Airman 2nd Class & Private 1st Class	11,306	12,015	11,979	12,590	12,657	13,840
Airman 3rd Class & Private 2	24,264	24,804	26,642	26,895	27,815	27,288
Basic Airman & Private 1	9,191	9,556	9,206	8,634	8,367	7,811
Aviation Cadet - Total	51	66	75	83	115	133
	January (1953)	February	March	April	May	June
Total	68,223	68,767	70,340	71,293	71,376	70,958
Officer and Warrant Officer - Total	1,047	1,073	1,126	1,155	1,200	1,238
Officer - Total	989	1,015	1,064	1,093	1,140	1,182
General	-	-	-	-	-	-
Colonel	4	5	5	5	5	5
Lieutenant Colonel	8	8	8	7	7	10
Major	78	76	75	94	99	100
Captain	258	263	267	280	290	282
First Lieutenant	334	356	391	379	396	408
Second Lieutenant	307	307	318	328	343	377
Warrant Officer - Total	58	58	62	62	60	56
Chief Warrant Officer, W-4	-	-	-	-	-	-
Chief Warrant Officer, W-3	-	-	-	-	-	-
Chief Warrant Officer, W-2	9	8	9	9	9	8
Warrant Officer, JG W-1	49	50	53	53	51	48
Enlisted - Total	67,017	67,540	69,018	69,938	69,990	69,552
Master Sergeant	794	813	817	841	825	822
Technical Sergeant & Sergeant 1st Class	1,673	1,740	1,754	1,796	1,780	1,815
Staff Sergeant & Sergeant	6,821	7,077	7,031	7,525	7,504	7,345
Airman 1st Class & Corporal	8,228	8,464	8,491	9,069	9,074	9,311
Airman 2nd Class & Private 1st Class	14,059	15,671	15,874	17,532	17,536	17,980
Airman 3rd Class & Private 2	27,547	25,942	26,957	25,958	26,845	26,755
Basic Airman & Private 1	7,895	7,833	8,094	7,217	6,426	5,524
Aviation Cadet - Total	159	154	196	200	186	168

Source: Personnel Statistics Division, DCS/Comptroller, Headquarters USAF.

TABLE 200 — SUMMARY — COMMAND STRENGTH BY PERSONNEL IDENTITY — FY 1953

(WAF - Women in the Air Force; AFNC - Air Force Nurse Corps; WMSC - Women's Medical Specialist Corps).

End of Month	Total	OFFICER			WARRANT OFFICER		Aviation Cadet	ENLISTED	
		Male	WAF	AFNC and WMSC	Male	Female		Male	Female
	WORLDWIDE								
1952									
July	973,558	121,448	951	2,883	4,176	6	7,617	824,931	11,546
August	975,603	123,826	988	2,879	4,169	6	8,031	823,818	11,886
September	971,325	124,346	1,005	2,881	4,147	6	7,737	818,852	12,351
October	969,566	124,582	983	2,904	4,146	6	7,951	816,303	12,691
November	968,352	123,724	987	2,945	4,161	6	8,683	815,060	12,786
December	957,603	122,404	1,000	2,936	4,109	6	8,190	806,542	12,416
1953									
January	958,709	121,419	991	3,010	4,067	6	9,283	807,497	12,436
February	965,097	121,316	986	3,013	4,084	6	9,154	814,212	12,326
March	974,202	122,166	1,013	3,040	4,066	6	9,653	822,058	12,200
April	980,205	121,577	995	3,050	4,057	6	10,473	827,991	12,056
May	979,880	121,962	993	3,112	4,019	6	9,769	828,202	11,817
June	977,593	122,636	1,023	3,110	3,994	6	9,157	825,888	11,779
	CONTINENTAL US								
1952									
July	717,182	92,297	817	2,248	3,158	4	7,617	600,002	11,039
August	710,547	94,090	840	2,206	3,142	4	8,031	590,904	11,330
September	704,555	94,436	855	2,189	3,072	4	7,737	584,519	11,743
October	700,005	95,024	837	2,194	3,076	4	7,951	578,890	12,029
November	692,456	94,020	828	2,227	3,083	3	8,683	571,552	12,060
December	680,515	93,217	840	2,208	3,034	3	8,190	561,419	11,604
1953									
January	679,018	91,851	828	2,255	2,964	3	9,283	560,214	11,620
February	681,487	91,277	814	2,259	2,960	3	9,154	563,612	11,408
March	688,228	92,082	841	2,275	2,941	2	9,653	569,194	11,240
April	691,851	90,836	812	2,264	2,910	2	10,473	573,593	10,961
May	685,992	90,690	783	2,310	2,874	3	9,769	568,866	10,697
June	681,978	91,289	792	2,302	2,818	3	9,157	565,048	10,569
	OVERSEAS								
1952									
July	256,376	29,151	134	635	1,018	2	-	224,929	507
August	265,056	29,736	148	673	1,027	2	-	232,914	556
September	266,770	29,910	150	692	1,075	2	-	234,333	608
October	269,561	29,558	146	710	1,070	2	-	237,413	662
November	275,896	29,704	159	718	1,078	3	-	243,508	726
December	277,088	29,187	160	728	1,075	3	-	245,123	812
1953									
January	279,691	29,568	163	755	1,103	3	-	247,283	816
February	283,610	30,039	172	754	1,124	3	-	250,600	918
March	285,974	30,084	172	765	1,125	4	-	252,864	960
April	288,354	30,741	183	786	1,147	4	-	254,398	1,095
May	293,888	31,272	210	802	1,145	3	-	259,336	1,120
June	295,615	31,347	231	808	1,176	3	-	260,840	1,210

Source: Personnel Statistics Division, DCS/Comptroller, Hq, USAF

TABLE 201 – COMMAND STRENGTH BY PERSONNEL IDENTITY, BY COMMAND – FY 1953

(WAF - Women in the Air Force; AFNC - Air Force Nurse Corps; WMSC - Women's Medical Specialist Corps)

End Of Month	Total	Officer			Warrant Officer		Aviation Cadet	Enlisted	
		Male	WAF	AFNC And WMSC	Male	Female		Male	Female
CONTINENTAL US (PERMANENT PARTY AND STUDENTS)									
Air Defense Command a/									
1952									
July	67,700	7,852	67	92	301	-	-	58,437	951
August	67,681	8,070	70	92	294	-	-	58,138	1,017
September	66,762	7,972	74	87	287	-	-	57,241	1,101
October	65,917	7,869	76	85	288	-	-	56,476	1,123
November	63,443	7,688	72	85	276	-	-	54,205	1,117
December	61,799	7,515	72	85	270	-	-	52,720	1,137
1953									
January	61,655	7,367	69	85	269	-	-	52,735	1,130
February	61,314	7,171	69	88	263	-	-	52,645	1,078
March	61,289	7,001	63	91	260	-	-	52,827	1,047
April	60,884	6,971	58	93	263	-	-	52,451	1,048
May	61,359	7,063	56	92	262	-	-	52,825	1,061
June	62,379	7,113	59	87	260	-	-	53,799	1,061
Air Force Finance Division									
1952									
July	77	77	-	-	-	-	-	-	-
August	77	77	-	-	-	-	-	-	-
September	73	73	-	-	-	-	-	-	-
October	74	74	-	-	-	-	-	-	-
November	73	73	-	-	-	-	-	-	-
December	76	76	-	-	-	-	-	-	-
1953									
January	76	76	-	-	-	-	-	-	-
February	75	75	-	-	-	-	-	-	-
March	73	73	-	-	-	-	-	-	-
April	70	70	-	-	-	-	-	-	-
May	63	63	-	-	-	-	-	-	-
June	62	62	-	-	-	-	-	-	-
Air Force Transients And Patients b/									
1952									
July	34,197	4,584	38	47	100	-	3	29,128	297
August	29,822	4,703	17	57	98	-	2	24,777	168
September	32,272	5,563	43	75	67	-	4	26,272	248
October	32,612	5,455	26	70	72	1	5	26,744	239
November	32,271	5,122	31	63	70	-	5	26,826	154
December	30,417	5,435	36	53	70	-	6	24,728	89
1953									
January	29,946	5,574	24	50	64	-	3	24,071	160
February	30,291	5,159	19	64	77	1	3	24,811	157
March	27,500	5,829	52	54	69	-	5	21,257	234
April	30,241	5,246	24	56	90	-	6	24,687	132
May	27,548	4,727	29	55	117	1	1	22,459	159
June	28,046	4,996	51	68	100	1	1	22,638	191
Air Materiel Command									
1952									
July	23,950	5,001	49	130	208	-	-	18,289	273
August	23,569	5,063	49	129	202	-	-	17,839	287
September	23,628	4,990	52	127	200	-	-	17,969	290
October	23,647	4,869	52	124	197	-	-	18,106	299
November	23,668	4,760	55	124	194	-	-	18,233	302
December	23,896	4,631	55	121	196	-	-	18,531	362
1953									
January	21,110	4,266	55	118	175	-	-	16,119	377
February	17,998	4,094	54	117	172	-	-	13,203	358
March	17,519	3,988	49	121	167	-	-	12,863	331
April	15,951	3,869	44	130	160	-	-	11,432	316
May	15,220	3,752	38	131	147	-	-	10,856	296
June	15,030	3,530	35	131	148	-	-	10,907	279

(CONTINENTAL US - CONTINUED)

TABLE 201 — COMMAND STRENGTH BY PERSONNEL IDENTITY, BY COMMAND — FY 1953 (Continued)

(WAF - Women in the Air Force; AFNC - Air Force Nurse Corps; WMSC - Women's Medical Specialist Corps)

End Of Month	Total	Officer			Warrant Officer		Aviation Cadet	Enlisted	
		Male	WAF	AFNC And WMSC	Male	Female		Male	Female
	Air Proving Ground								
1952									
July	8,943	905	9	44	70	-	-	7,798	117
August	8,762	909	8	44	69	-	-	7,617	115
September	8,630	907	8	46	65	-	-	7,475	129
October	8,161	893	7	44	58	-	-	7,019	140
November	8,113	898	7	46	53	-	-	6,943	166
December	8,192	871	8	45	49	-	-	7,039	180
1953									
January	8,396	856	8	44	47	-	-	7,188	253
February	8,713	849	7	44	45	-	-	7,475	293
March	8,748	855	8	44	44	-	-	7,504	293
April	8,830	841	7	39	46	-	-	7,607	290
May	8,949	844	8	48	41	-	-	7,710	298
June	8,894	830	7	46	40	-	-	7,667	304
	Air Research And Development Command								
1952									
July	19,985	4,504	24	60	118	-	-	15,136	143
August	20,628	4,677	24	61	116	-	-	15,565	185
September	21,087	4,670	32	59	117	-	-	15,986	223
October	21,437	4,600	36	57	118	-	-	16,381	245
November	21,478	4,601	45	49	118	-	-	16,378	287
December	21,630	4,589	38	56	118	-	-	16,500	329
1953									
January	21,558	4,440	40	55	119	-	-	16,538	366
February	21,417	4,328	40	57	120	-	-	16,497	375
March	21,322	4,260	42	62	118	-	-	16,446	394
April	22,078	4,250	53	65	124	-	-	17,110	476
May	21,640	4,192	51	69	125	-	-	16,700	503
June	21,239	4,169	50	67	121	-	-	16,315	517
	Air Training Command a/								
1952									
July	260,938	21,824	271	959	695	-	7,614	224,430	5,145
August	260,459	22,455	307	924	694	-	8,029	222,710	5,340
September	254,424	22,447	266	920	689	-	7,733	217,035	5,334
October	249,065	23,226	267	947	688	-	7,946	210,480	5,511
November	243,530	22,751	226	986	684	-	8,678	204,680	5,525
December	233,832	22,501	230	967	678	-	8,184	196,184	5,088
1953									
January	235,214	21,942	237	971	668	1	9,280	197,156	4,959
February	241,517	22,675	234	958	665	-	9,151	203,173	4,661
March	248,634	23,367	207	970	660	-	9,648	209,389	4,393
April	251,083	23,331	199	943	641	-	0,467	211,328	4,174
May	245,518	23,709	189	970	613	-	9,768	206,386	3,883
June	237,539	24,110	190	989	606	-	9,156	198,714	3,774
	Air University a/								
1952									
July	8,143	3,112	21	122	54	-	-	4,707	127
August	11,353	4,906	23	125	76	-	-	6,078	145
September	11,889	5,314	32	120	76	-	-	6,171	176
October	12,151	5,469	36	127	73	-	-	6,256	190
November	12,164	5,473	38	128	74	-	-	6,250	201
December	12,232	5,448	38	128	74	-	-	6,347	197
1953									
January	12,415	5,460	37	123	72	-	-	6,524	199
February	12,589	5,471	37	128	72	-	-	6,673	208
March	12,593	5,401	37	129	71	-	-	6,752	203
April	12,466	5,456	34	122	72	-	-	6,596	186
May	12,479	5,420	32	112	72	-	-	6,655	188
June	12,353	5,591	35	108	70	-	-	6,364	185

(CONTINENTAL US - CONTINUED)

TABLE 201 — COMMAND STRENGTH BY PERSONNEL IDENTITY, BY COMMAND — FY 1953 (Continued)

(WAF - Women in the Air Force; AFNC - Air Force Nurse Corps; WMSC - Women's Medical Specialist Corps)

End of Month	Total	Officer			Warrant Officer		Aviation Cadet	Enlisted	
		Male	WAF	AFNC and WMSC	Male	Female		Male	Female
	Continental Air Command								
1952									
July	34,819	4,406	79	67	273	-	-	29,330	664
August	31,546	2,901	76	66	240	-	-	27,616	647
September	32,208	2,791	74	62	232	-	-	28,359	690
October	31,665	2,810	73	61	234	-	-	27,823	664
November	35,416	3,147	75	66	288	-	-	31,173	667
December	35,441	3,199	77	66	285	-	-	31,143	671
1953									
January	34,771	3,194	79	65	280	-	-	30,526	627
February	33,674	3,161	78	67	278	-	-	29,447	643
March	33,243	3,155	106	68	276	-	-	28,986	652
April	31,203	3,013	104	65	255	-	-	27,110	656
May	31,073	2,984	101	67	256	-	-	27,012	653
June	30,261	2,844	95	64	242	-	-	26,362	654
	Headquarters Command, USAF a/								
1952									
July	21,138	5,289	58	50	230	1	-	14,393	1,117
August	18,514	5,240	72	40	224	1	-	11,823	1,114
September	18,441	5,165	74	39	227	1	-	11,807	1,128
October	18,966	5,218	65	32	231	-	-	12,266	1,154
November	18,606	5,129	64	33	218	-	-	12,015	1,147
December	18,420	5,102	67	35	214	-	-	11,873	1,129
1953									
January	16,909	5,086	43	47	204	-	-	10,990	539
February	16,857	4,977	42	47	198	-	-	11,047	546
March	16,871	4,887	44	47	199	-	-	11,137	557
April	16,635	4,776	44	49	195	-	-	11,010	561
May	15,922	4,469	38	49	187	-	-	10,617	562
June	15,829	4,439	34	48	180	-	-	10,571	557
	Headquarters USAF								
1952									
July	3,009	2,917	44	8	39	1	-	-	-
August	2,919	2,828	43	8	39	1	-	-	-
September	2,891	2,799	41	8	42	1	-	-	-
October	2,890	2,798	40	8	43	1	-	-	-
November	2,906	2,812	42	8	43	1	-	-	-
December	2,948	2,852	42	8	45	1	-	-	-
1953									
January	2,925	2,828	43	8	46	-	-	-	-
February	2,929	2,830	42	8	49	-	-	-	-
March	2,931	2,832	41	8	50	-	-	-	-
April	2,970	2,871	40	8	51	-	-	-	-
May	2,992	2,892	38	8	54	-	-	-	-
June	3,011	2,907	40	8	56	-	-	-	-
	Military Air Transport Service (Continental US)								
1952									
July	46,454	7,216	59	170	270	2	-	37,930	807
August	49,144	7,526	60	168	298	2	-	40,252	838
September	47,431	7,159	63	162	285	2	-	38,887	873
October	46,398	6,962	62	159	289	2	-	38,036	888
November	45,448	6,812	66	150	286	2	-	37,192	940
December	44,918	6,752	69	150	282	2	-	36,675	988
1953									
January	45,745	6,697	89	165	280	2	-	36,872	1,640
February	45,594	6,598	91	158	283	2	-	36,708	1,754
March	46,150	6,591	89	152	283	2	-	37,173	1,860
April	45,268	6,514	93	156	278	2	-	36,355	1,870
May	45,414	6,536	90	145	274	2	-	36,509	1,858
June	45,796	6,544	84	147	272	2	-	36,926	1,821

(CONTINENTAL US - CONTINUED)

TABLE 201 — COMMAND STRENGTH BY PERSONNEL IDENTITY, BY COMMAND — FY 1953 (CONTINUED)

(WAF - Women in the Air Force; AFNC - Air Force Nurse Corps; WMSC - Women's Medical Specialist Corps)

End of Month	Total	Officer			Warrant Officer		Aviation Cadet	Enlisted	
		Male	WAF	AFNC and WMSC	Male	Female		Male	Female
	Strategic Air Command								
1952									
July	134,763	18,081	60	382	580	-	-	114,772	888
August	134,124	18,103	55	377	569	-	-	114,098	922
September	133,618	17,893	58	362	562	-	-	113,794	949
October	136,906	18,264	56	365	564	-	-	116,704	953
November	137,274	18,236	66	373	557	-	-	117,129	913
December	138,369	17,898	66	388	532	-	-	118,660	825
1953									
January	139,611	17,743	66	408	524	-	-	120,095	775
February	138,733	17,599	63	406	518	-	-	119,401	746
March	139,939	17,508	64	411	519	-	-	120,734	703
April	141,588	17,446	66	412	516	-	-	122,460	688
May	143,778	17,815	67	439	503	-	-	124,290	664
June	145,447	17,833	66	420	499	-	-	126,004	625
	Tactical Air Command								
1952									
July	48,407	5,908	32	117	197	-	-	41,662	491
August	47,078	5,881	30	115	199	-	-	40,319	534
September	46,153	5,890	32	122	201	-	-	39,323	585
October	45,021	5,700	32	115	199	-	-	38,369	606
November	42,731	5,731	34	116	198	-	-	36,028	624
December	42,922	5,574	35	106	196	-	-	36,417	594
1953									
January	43,487	5,571	31	116	191	-	-	36,998	580
February	44,459	5,535	31	117	196	-	-	38,006	574
March	45,865	5,567	30	118	201	-	-	39,388	561
April	46,841	5,404	37	122	198	-	-	40,524	556
May	48,219	5,458	37	125	197	-	-	41,838	564
June	50,294	5,548	38	119	196	-	-	43,802	591
	USAF Security Service								
1952									
July	4,659	621	6	-	23	-	-	3,990	19
August	4,871	751	6	-	24	-	-	4,072	18
September	5,048	803	6	-	22	-	-	4,200	17
October	5,095	817	9	-	22	-	-	4,230	17
November	5,335	787	7	-	24	-	-	4,500	17
December	5,423	774	7	-	25	-	-	4,602	15
1953									
January	5,200	751	7	-	25	-	-	4,402	15
February	5,327	755	7	-	24	-	-	4,526	15
March	5,551	768	9	-	24	-	-	4,738	12
April	5,743	778	9	-	25	-	-	4,923	8
May	5,818	766	9	-	26	-	-	5,009	8
June	5,798	773	8	-	28	-	-	4,979	10
	OVERSEAS (PERMANENT PARTY AND PIPELINE)								
	Air Defense Command c/								
1952									
July	2,641	341	-	-	8	-	-	2,292	-
August	2,540	349	-	-	6	-	-	2,185	-
September	2,540	335	-	-	4	-	-	2,201	-
October	2,757	323	-	-	4	-	-	2,430	-
November	2,612	354	-	-	3	-	-	2,255	-
December	2,807	361	-	-	4	-	-	2,442	-
1953									
January	2,769	362	-	-	6	-	-	2,401	-
February	2,731	393	-	-	8	-	-	2,330	-
March	2,770	370	-	-	8	-	-	2,392	-
April	2,860	395	-	-	7	-	-	2,458	-
May	2,726	376	-	-	8	-	-	2,342	-
June	2,553	387	-	-	11	-	-	2,155	-

(OVERSEAS - CONTINUED)

TABLE 201 — COMMAND STRENGTH BY PERSONNEL IDENTITY, BY COMMAND — FY 1953 (CONTINUED)

(WAF - Women in the Air Force; AFNC - Air Force Nurse Corps; WMSC - Women's Medical Specialist Corps)

End of Month	Total	Officer			Warrant Officer		Aviation Cadet	Enlisted	
		Male	WAF	AFNC and WMSC	Male	Female		Male	Female
	Air Research and Development Command								
1952									
July	297	31	-	-	1	-	-	265	-
August	303	30	-	-	1	-	-	272	-
September	321	33	-	-	1	-	-	287	-
October	341	39	-	-	1	-	-	301	-
November	321	35	-	-	1	-	-	285	-
December	391	39	-	-	1	-	-	351	-
1953									
January	602	57	-	-	3	-	-	542	-
February	612	56	-	-	3	-	-	553	-
March	610	51	-	-	3	-	-	556	-
April	561	44	-	-	2	-	-	515	-
May	592	39	-	-	2	-	-	551	-
June	638	39	-	-	3	-	-	596	-
	Alaskan Air Command								
1952									
July	17,721	1,494	6	73	68	-	-	16,080	-
August	18,023	1,588	10	77	68	-	-	16,280	-
September	17,821	1,607	13	79	76	-	-	16,046	-
October	17,968	1,614	13	79	79	-	-	16,183	-
November	18,178	1,636	12	92	79	-	-	15,359	-
December	18,120	1,586	12	93	78	-	-	16,351	-
1953									
January	18,164	1,632	12	92	75	-	-	16,353	-
February	18,355	1,633	12	91	76	-	-	16,543	-
March	18,108	1,609	12	89	76	-	-	16,322	-
April	18,585	1,660	13	93	77	-	-	16,742	-
May	18,962	1,677	13	87	74	-	-	17,111	-
June	18,726	1,620	13	78	63	-	-	16,952	-
	Caribbean Air Command								
1952									
July	1,659	192	1	2	19	-	-	1,445	-
August	1,642	192	1	2	17	-	-	1,430	-
September	1,633	197	1	2	17	-	-	1,416	-
October	1,628	206	1	2	17	-	-	1,402	-
November	1,619	207	3	-	17	-	-	1,392	-
December	1,592	204	1	2	16	-	-	1,369	-
1953									
January	1,603	208	1	2	17	-	-	1,375	-
February	1,606	209	1	2	17	-	-	1,377	-
March	1,591	211	3	-	16	-	-	1,361	-
April	1,635	212	1	2	17	-	-	1,403	-
May	1,638	216	1	2	16	-	-	1,403	-
June	1,623	211	1	2	16	-	-	1,393	-
	Far East Air Force								
1952									
July	89,765	9,842	42	215	314	1	-	79,265	86
August	92,998	10,085	49	220	315	1	-	82,246	82
September	92,928	9,786	42	224	319	1	-	82,450	106
October	96,436	9,843	42	221	303	1	-	85,889	137
November	99,664	9,912	45	217	289	2	-	89,067	132
December	101,249	9,687	47	209	283	2	-	90,830	191
1953									
January	101,912	9,894	48	214	302	2	-	91,264	188
February	102,410	10,126	51	208	317	2	-	91,472	234
March	102,646	10,256	49	221	326	2	-	91,555	237
April	102,363	10,640	57	245	337	2	-	90,825	257
May	105,939	11,020	65	258	341	1	-	93,968	286
June	104,643	11,047	64	255	371	1	-	92,608	297

(OVERSEAS - CONTINUED)

TABLE 201 — COMMAND STRENGTH BY PERSONNEL IDENTITY, BY COMMAND — FY 1953 (CONTINUED)

(WAF - Women in the Air Force; AFNC - Air Force Nurse Corps; WMSC - Women's Medical Specialist Corps)

End of Month	Total	Officer			Warrant Officer		Aviation Cadet	Enlisted	
		Male	WAF	AFNC and WMSC	Male	Female		Male	Female
	Headquarters Command, USAF								
1952									
July	1,577	645	2	-	38	-	-	890	2
August	1,662	655	2	-	38	-	-	963	4
September	1,699	692	2	-	37	-	-	965	3
October	1,742	712	2	-	37	-	-	988	3
November	1,751	718	2	-	37	-	-	991	3
December	1,685	682	2	-	34	-	-	964	3
1953									
January	1,674	683	2	-	34	-	-	952	3
February	1,663	674	2	-	33	-	-	952	2
March	1,687	683	2	-	32	-	-	968	2
April	1,672	685	3	-	30	-	-	952	2
May	1,899	908	7	-	34	-	-	948	2
June	1,899	900	7	-	34	-	-	956	2
	Military Air Transport Service								
1952									
July	39,294	5,037	16	88	180	1	-	33,838	134
August	39,835	5,044	17	74	180	1	-	34,375	144
September	39,329	5,036	19	74	185	1	-	33,864	150
October	39,637	5,018	21	75	197	1	-	34,162	163
November	40,422	5,173	22	73	201	1	-	34,780	172
December	39,975	5,071	21	74	204	1	-	34,421	183
1953									
January	38,220	4,881	24	64	199	1	-	32,856	195
February	38,435	4,904	27	60	198	1	-	33,035	210
March	37,963	4,780	26	56	189	2	-	32,698	212
April	38,637	4,864	27	56	186	2	-	33,241	261
May	38,196	4,778	29	58	178	2	-	32,889	262
June	38,411	4,750	35	62	181	2	-	33,090	291
	Northeast Air Command								
1952									
July	8,218	943	6	30	31	-	-	7,138	70
August	8,400	925	4	32	30	-	-	7,301	108
September	8,850	941	4	32	34	-	-	7,731	108
October	9,437	964	4	32	33	-	-	8,306	98
November	9,516	971	4	29	39	-	-	8,329	144
December	9,197	944	3	29	43	-	-	8,041	137
1953									
January	9,440	965	4	31	42	-	-	8,264	134
February	9,848	977	4	30	40	-	-	8,668	129
March	9,953	952	4	27	37	-	-	8,809	124
April	9,620	936	4	25	39	-	-	8,497	119
May	10,231	934	4	24	40	-	-	9,118	111
June	11,460	969	6	25	41	-	-	10,315	104
	Strategic Air Command								
1952									
July	15,110	1,637	2	32	59	-	-	13,380	-
August	15,451	1,638	2	36	60	-	-	13,715	-
September	15,081	1,644	2	32	64	-	-	13,339	-
October	14,316	1,267	2	33	59	-	-	12,955	-
November	15,517	1,307	2	35	67	-	-	14,106	-
December	15,985	1,297	3	33	65	-	-	14,587	-
1953									
January	16,611	1,367	2	33	66	-	-	15,143	-
February	16,880	1,444	3	50	71	-	-	15,312	-
March	17,274	1,483	3	49	72	-	-	15,667	-
April	17,490	1,513	3	54	73	-	-	15,847	-
May	17,900	1,513	3	55	76	-	-	16,253	-
June	17,759	1,503	3	52	75	-	-	16,126	-

(OVERSEAS - CONTINUED)

TABLE 201 — COMMAND STRENGTH BY PERSONNEL IDENTITY, BY COMMAND — FY 1953 (CONTINUED)

(WAF - Women in the Air Force; AFNC - Air Force Nurse Corps; WMSC - Women's Medical Specialist Corps)

End of Month	Total	Officer			Warrant Officer		Aviation Cadet	Enlisted	
		Male	WAF	AFNC and WMSC	Male	Female		Male	Female
	Tactical Air Command c/								
1952									
July	7,143	1,090	3	17	16	-	-	6,017	-
August	7,574	1,135	3	17	16	-	-	6,403	-
September	7,741	1,131	3	16	18	-	-	6,573	-
October	7,871	1,120	1	18	18	-	-	6,714	-
November	7,410	936	1	18	16	-	-	6,439	-
December	6,872	843	1	18	16	-	-	5,994	-
1953									
January	7,008	847	1	17	17	-	-	6,126	-
February	7,377	855	1	15	16	-	-	6,490	-
March	8,795	923	2	15	21	-	-	7,834	-
April	5,785	829	1	8	8	-	-	4,939	-
May	5,545	833	1	8	10	-	-	4,693	-
June	5,482	682	3	9	9	-	-	4,579	-
	US Air Forces, Europe								
1952									
July	67,665	7,577	55	178	269	-	-	59,374	212
August	71,161	7,756	58	215	281	-	-	62,636	215
September	73,175	8,159	62	233	304	-	-	64,179	238
October	71,808	8,099	58	250	306	-	-	62,837	258
November	72,884	8,085	66	254	312	-	-	63,895	272
December	73,204	8,106	67	270	315	-	-	64,151	295
1953									
January	75,493	8,295	66	302	326	-	-	66,211	293
February	77,060	8,367	68	298	328	-	-	67,659	340
March	77,748	8,366	69	308	329	-	-	68,293	383
April	81,975	8,545	71	303	355	-	-	72,247	454
May	82,836	8,559	84	310	351	-	-	73,076	456
June	84,602	8,611	97	325	358	-	-	74,698	513
	US Security Service								
1952									
July	5,286	322	1	-	15	-	-	4,945	3
August	5,467	339	2	-	15	-	-	5,108	3
September	5,652	349	2	-	16	-	-	5,282	3
October	5,620	353	2	-	16	-	-	5,246	3
November	6,002	370	2	-	17	-	-	5,610	3
December	6,011	367	3	-	16	-	-	5,622	3
1953									
January	6,195	377	3	-	16	-	-	5,796	3
February	6,633	401	3	-	17	-	-	6,209	3
March	6,829	400	2	-	16	-	-	6,409	2
April	7,171	428	3	-	16	-	-	6,732	2
May	7,424	419	3	-	15	-	-	6,984	3
June	7,819	428	2	-	14	-	-	7,372	3

a/ Includes Students.
b/ These data include all personnel assigned to USAF.
c/ On 15 September 1951 and 15 October 1951 Tactical Air Command (Overseas only) and Air Defense Command (Overseas only) respectively went under the Operational Control of Far East Air Forces.

Source: Personnel Statistics Division, DCS/Comptroller, Headquarters USAF.

TABLE 202 — COMMAND STRENGTH OF NEGRO PERSONNEL BY SEX — FY 1953

End of Month	Worldwide			Continental US			Overseas		
	Total	Male	Female	Total	Male	Female	Total	Male	Female
1952									
July	63,682	62,757	915	47,551	46,690	861	16,131	16,077	54
August	65,795	64,823	972	48,518	47,606	912	17,277	17,217	60
September	66,820	65,733	1,087	49,082	48,058	1,024	17,738	17,675	63
October	67,556	66,414	1,142	49,090	48,010	1,080	18,466	18,404	62
November	67,944	66,763	1,181	49,024	47,910	1,114	18,920	18,853	67
December	68,031	66,874	1,157	48,640	47,554	1,086	19,391	19,320	71
1953									
January	68,223	67,045	1,178	48,355	47,246	1,109	19,868	19,799	69
February	68,767	67,588	1,179	48,037	46,932	1,105	20,730	20,656	74
March	70,340	69,155	1,185	49,001	47,890	1,111	21,339	21,265	74
April	71,293	70,123	1,170	49,287	48,199	1,088	22,006	21,924	82
May	71,376	70,215	1,161	48,433	47,355	1,078	22,943	22,860	83
June	70,958	69,808	1,150	47,613	46,558	1,055	23,345	23,250	95

Source: Personnel Statistics Division, DCS/Comptroller, Headquarters USAF.

TABLE 203 — COMMAND STRENGTH BY DEPARTMENTAL STATUS,

(Naval Officers were included in the USAF in the respective months data as follows: October- 51; November - 97-

Grade	Total	USAF	SCARWAF	Total	USAF	SCARWAF	Total	USAF	SCARWAF
									FIRST HALF
	July (1952)			August			September		
Total	973,558	943,216	30,342	975,603	944,780	30,823	971,325	940,601	30,724
Officer and Warrant Officer-Total	129,464	126,109	1,355	131,868	130,489	1,379	132,385	131,090	1,295
Officer - Total	125,282	124,138	1,144	127,693	126,526	1,167	128,232	127,134	1,098
General - Total	319	319	-	315	315	-	359	359	-
General	7	7	-	7	7	-	7	7	-
Lieutenant General	17	17	-	17	17	-	19	19	-
Major General	115	115	-	114	114	-	124	124	-
Brigadier General	180	180	-	177	177	-	209	209	-
Colonel	4,067	4,051	16	4,081	4,064	17	4,009	3,994	15
Lieutenant Colonel	8,380	8,330	50	8,358	8,307	51	8,265	8,215	50
Major	20,580	20,472	108	20,476	20,365	111	20,315	20,206	109
Captain	40,008	39,651	357	39,786	39,428	358	39,185	38,857	328
First Lieutenant	29,609	29,240	369	29,689	29,307	382	29,900	29,560	340
Second Lieutenant	22,319	22,075	244	24,988	24,740	248	26,199	25,943	256
Warrant Officer - Total	4,182	3,971	211	4,175	3,963	212	4,153	3,956	197
Chief Warrant Officer, W-4	137	132	5	137	135	2	137	135	2
Chief Warrant Officer, W-3	288	284	4	272	270	2	279	277	2
Chief Warrant Officer, W-2	1,016	1,010	6	1,098	1,075	23	1,023	1,016	7
Warrant Officer, JG W-1	2,741	2,545	196	2,668	2,483	185	2,714	2,528	186
Enlisted - Total	836,477	807,490	28,987	835,704	806,260	29,444	831,203	801,774	29,429
Seventh Grade	44,404	43,766	638	44,865	44,227	638	44,427	43,794	633
Sixth Grade	52,655	51,500	1,155	53,454	52,287	1,167	52,570	51,443	1,127
Fifth Grade	119,309	115,267	4,042	119,263	115,091	4,172	113,818	109,828	3,990
Fourth Grade	153,467	143,911	9,556	156,910	147,327	9,583	151,509	142,495	9,014
Third Grade	181,845	174,190	7,655	182,763	175,454	7,309	182,883	175,691	7,192
Second Grade	229,709	224,119	5,590	223,446	217,155	6,291	231,167	224,018	7,149
First Grade	55,088	54,737	351	55,003	54,719	284	54,829	54,505	324
Aviation Cadet - Total	7,617	7,617	-	8,031	8,031	-	7,737	7,737	-
									LAST HALF
	January (1953)			February			March		
Total	958,709	925,081	33,628	965,097	934,572	30,525	974,202	944,362	29,840
Officer and Warrant Officer-Total	129,493	127,800	1,693	129,405	127,697	1,708	130,291	128,592	1,699
Officer - Total	125,420	123,944	1,476	125,315	123,829	1,486	126,219	124,745	1,474
General - Total	381	381	-	377	377	-	368	368	-
General	7	7	-	7	7	-	7	7	-
Lieutenant General	19	19	-	19	19	-	18	18	-
Major General	135	135	-	134	134	-	128	128	-
Brigadier General	220	220	-	217	217	-	215	215	-
Colonel	3,917	3,901	16	3,888	3,873	15	3,874	3,859	15
Lieutenant Colonel	8,102	8,044	58	8,064	8,003	61	7,998	7,937	61
Major	19,633	19,508	125	19,514	19,397	117	19,379	19,269	110
Captain	36,477	36,123	354	35,918	35,579	339	35,593	35,268	325
First Lieutenant	32,707	32,352	355	34,464	34,130	334	35,360	35,035	325
Second Lieutenant	24,203	23,635	568	23,090	22,470	620	23,647	23,009	638
Warrant Officer - Total	4,073	3,856	217	4,090	3,868	222	4,072	3,847	225
Chief Warrant Officer, W-4	123	123	-	127	127	-	125	124	1
Chief Warrant Officer, W-3	284	278	6	286	280	6	276	270	6
Chief Warrant Officer, W-2	1,018	1,007	11	1,011	999	12	1,021	1,007	14
Warrant Officer, JG W-1	2,648	2,448	200	2,666	2,462	204	2,650	2,446	204
Enlisted - Total	819,933	787,998	31,935	826,538	797,721	28,817	834,258	806,117	28,141
Seventh Grade	44,985	44,332	653	45,529	44,915	614	45,108	44,492	616
Sixth Grade	52,758	51,550	1,208	53,995	52,843	1,152	53,566	52,419	1,147
Fifth Grade	114,827	111,393	3,434	122,118	119,159	2,959	120,686	118,010	2,676
Fourth Grade	151,008	143,957	7,051	157,695	151,952	5,743	156,290	151,028	5,262
Third Grade	189,555	177,991	11,564	199,418	187,119	12,299	199,409	187,120	12,289
Second Grade	216,321	208,697	7,624	192,050	186,301	5,749	199,872	194,476	5,396
First Grade	50,479	50,078	401	55,733	55,432	301	59,327	58,572	755
Aviation Cadet - Total	9,283	9,283	-	9,154	9,154	-	9,653	9,653	-

Source: Personnel Statistics Division, DCS/Comptroller, Headquarters USAF.

BY GRADE IN WHICH SERVING — FY 1953

December - 104; January (153) - 125; February - 132; March - 138; April - 143; May - 144; June - 144.

Total	USAF	SCARWAF	Total	USAF	SCARWAF	Total	USAF	SCARWAF	Grade
FY 1953									
October			November			December			
969,566	937,548	32,018	968,352	932,810	35,542	957,603	923,305	34,298	Total
132,621	131,253	1,368	131,823	130,255	1,568	130,455	128,821	1,634	Officer and Warrant Officer-Total
128,469	127,291	1,178	127,656	126,313	1,343	126,340	124,929	1,411	Officer - Total
366	366	-	366	366	-	382	382	-	General - Total
7	7	-	7	7	-	7	7	-	General
19	19	-	19	19	-	19	19	-	Lieutenant General
128	128	-	128	128	-	135	135	-	Major General
212	212	-	212	212	-	221	221	-	Brigadier General
3,988	3,975	13	3,974	3,957	17	3,938	3,922	16	Colonel
8,242	8,191	51	8,200	8,143	57	8,181	8,125	56	Lieutenant Colonel
20,128	20,024	104	19,952	19,837	115	19,791	19,670	121	Major
38,571	38,255	316	38,092	37,738	354	37,024	36,664	360	Captain
30,622	30,301	321	31,206	30,851	355	31,032	30,675	357	First Lieutenant
26,552	26,179	373	25,866	25,421	445	25,992	25,491	501	Second Lieutenant
4,152	3,962	190	4,167	3,942	225	4,115	3,892	223	Warrant Officer - Total
134	132	2	135	135	-	128	128	-	Chief Warrant Officer, W-4
287	284	3	287	281	6	286	280	6	Chief Warrant Officer, W-3
1,018	1,010	8	1,015	1,008	7	1,020	1,013	7	Chief Warrant Officer, W-2
2,713	2,536	177	2,730	2,518	212	2,681	2,471	210	Warrant Officer, JG W-1
828,994	798,344	30,650	827,846	793,872	33,974	818,958	786,294	32,664	Enlisted - Total
45,063	44,443	620	44,786	44,122	664	45,161	44,534	627	Seventh Grade
53,289	52,134	1,155	52,618	51,387	1,231	53,112	51,924	1,188	Sixth Grade
116,567	112,769	3,798	113,390	109,633	3,757	116,192	112,550	3,642	Fifth Grade
155,529	146,777	8,752	151,276	142,989	8,287	154,013	146,364	7,649	Fourth Grade
180,865	173,256	7,609	182,099	173,618	8,481	187,077	176,920	10,157	Third Grade
224,685	216,368	8,317	231,202	220,124	11,078	215,028	206,041	8,987	Second Grade
52,996	52,597	399	52,475	51,999	476	48,375	47,961	414	First Grade
7,951	7,951	-	8,683	8,683	-	8,190	8,190	-	Aviation Cadet - Total

Total	USAF	SCARWAF	Total	USAF	SCARWAF	Total	USAF	SCARWAF	Grade
FY 1953									
April			May			June			
980,205	950,413	29,792	979,880	949,997	29,883	977,593	947,730	29,863	Total
129,685	127,928	1,757	130,092	128,411	1,681	130,769	129,117	1,652	Officer and Warrant Officer-Total
125,622	124,092	1,530	126,067	124,606	1,461	126,769	125,333	1,436	Officer - Total
364	364	-	363	363	-	382	382	-	General - Total
7	7	-	7	7	-	7	7	-	General
17	17	-	20	20	-	18	18	-	Lieutenant General
127	127	-	124	124	-	134	134	-	Major General
213	213	-	212	212	-	223	223	-	Brigadier General
4,020	4,005	15	4,183	4,168	15	4,314	4,301	13	Colonel
8,080	8,024	56	8,220	8,162	58	8,324	8,270	54	Lieutenant Colonel
20,855	20,736	119	20,909	20,791	118	20,805	20,685	120	Major
38,010	37,682	328	37,571	37,253	318	36,649	36,331	318	Captain
31,264	30,922	342	31,672	31,347	325	32,090	31,775	315	First Lieutenant
23,029	22,359	670	23,149	22,522	627	24,205	23,589	616	Second Lieutenant
4,063	3,836	227	4,025	3,805	220	4,000	3,784	216	Warrant Officer - Total
132	131	1	137	136	1	139	136	3	Chief Warrant Officer, W-4
328	321	7	380	372	8	397	385	12	Chief Warrant Officer, W-3
1,139	1,115	24	1,257	1,224	33	1,275	1,244	31	Chief Warrant Officer, W-2
2,464	2,269	195	2,251	2,073	178	2,189	2,019	170	Warrant Officer, JG W-1
840,047	812,012	28,035	840,019	811,817	28,202	837,667	809,456	28,211	Enlisted - Total
45,646	45,027	619	45,184	44,573	611	45,176	44,573	603	Seventh Grade
54,573	53,433	1,140	54,193	53,050	1,143	54,279	53,116	1,163	Sixth Grade
129,159	126,530	2,629	128,581	125,990	2,591	131,342	128,816	2,526	Fifth Grade
167,002	161,654	5,348	166,425	160,882	5,543	171,893	165,267	6,626	Fourth Grade
204,907	192,857	12,050	205,453	193,350	12,103	205,478	194,597	10,881	Third Grade
190,717	185,081	5,636	203,098	197,230	5,868	200,638	194,461	6,177	Second Grade
48,043	47,430	613	37,085	36,742	343	28,861	28,626	235	First Grade
10,473	10,473	-	9,769	9,769	-	9,157	9,157	-	Aviation Cadet

TABLE 204 — COMMAND STRENGTH OF PIPELINE PERSONNEL BY PIPELINE CATEGORY — FY 1953

End of Month	Total	Pipeline Category					
		Students	Transients			Patients	Depot Level Trainees a/
			Fillers	Returnees	Overseas Replacements		
1952							
July - Total	161,213	121,549	4,158	6,242	26,565	2,699	-
Officers	13,668	8,295	626	850	3,529	368	-
Enlisted	147,545	113,254	3,532	5,392	23,036	2,331	-
August - Total	161,496	123,816	2,661	6,031	26,351	2,637	-
Officers	14,656	9,060	1,005	808	3,435	348	-
Enlisted	146,840	114,756	1,656	5,223	22,916	2,289	-
September - Total	159,994	118,833	3,322	7,905	27,369	2,565	-
Officers	15,746	9,436	1,888	781	3,299	342	-
Enlisted	144,248	109,397	1,434	7,124	24,070	2,223	-
October - Total	154,621	114,807	3,393	7,347	26,470	2,604	-
Officers	16,588	10,242	1,547	902	3,517	380	-
Enlisted	138,033	104,565	1,846	6,445	22,953	2,224	-
November - Total	152,207	110,549	2,636	10,563	25,940	2,519	-
Officers	15,370	9,461	1,116	932	3,530	331	-
Enlisted	136,837	101,088	1,520	9,631	22,410	2,188	-
December - Total	137,818	98,698	3,656	9,784	23,168	2,512	-
Officers	15,396	9,229	1,507	1,202	3,133	325	-
Enlisted	122,422	89,469	2,149	8,582	20,035	2,187	-
1953							
January - Total	136,711	100,176	3,529	8,262	22,256	2,488	-
Officers	15,311	8,934	1,392	896	3,748	341	-
Enlisted	121,400	91,242	2,137	7,366	18,508	2,147	-
February - Total	144,242	105,847	4,249	9,402	20,554	2,529	1,661
Officers	16,009	9,765	1,193	1,124	3,571	356	-
Enlisted	128,233	96,082	3,056	8,278	16,983	2,173	1,661
March - Total	148,440	111,807	4,999	8,333	19,019	2,459	1,823
Officers	17,433	10,493	1,595	1,138	3,824	383	-
Enlisted	131,007	101,314	3,404	7,195	15,195	2,076	1,823
April - Total	151,915	115,127	3,522	6,904	22,489	2,354	1,519
Officers	17,319	10,736	1,140	922	4,156	365	-
Enlisted	134,596	104,391	2,382	5,982	18,333	1,989	1,519
May - Total	147,990	109,602	2,427	9,087	23,195	2,350	1,329
Officers	17,186	10,945	511	1,140	4,203	387	-
Enlisted	130,804	98,657	1,916	7,947	18,992	1,963	1,329
June - Total	141,008	101,928	2,920	9,602	23,340	2,239	979
Officers	18,216	11,764	860	1,213	4,005	374	-
Enlisted	122,792	90,164	2,060	8,389	19,335	1,865	979

a/ Category Initiated February 1953
Source: Personnel Statistics Division, DCS/Comptroller, Headquarters USAF.

TABLE 205 — COMMAND STRENGTH BY DEPARTMENTAL STATUS, BY TYPE OF PERSONNEL FY — 1953

End of Month	USAF				SCARWAF				Assigned Navy			
	Total	Officer	W/O	E/P a/	Total	Officer	W/O	E/P	Total	Officer	W/O	E/P
1952												
July	943,216	124,138	3,971	815,107	30,342	1,144	211	28,987	-	-	-	-
August . . .	944,780	126,526	3,963	814,291	30,823	1,167	212	29,444	-	-	-	-
September. .	940,601	127,134	3,956	809,511	30,724	1,098	197	29,429	-	-	-	-
October. . .	937,497	127,240	3,962	806,295	32,018	1,178	190	30,650	51	51	-	-
November . .	932,713	126,216	3,942	802,555	35,542	1,343	225	33,974	97	97	-	-
December . .	923,201	124,825	3,892	794,484	34,298	1,411	223	32,664	104	104	-	-
1953												
January. . .	924,956	123,819	3,856	797,281	33,628	1,476	217	31,935	125	125	-	-
February . .	934,440	123,697	3,868	806,875	30,525	1,486	222	28,817	132	132	-	-
March. . . .	944,224	124,607	3,847	815,770	29,840	1,474	225	28,141	138	138	-	-
April. . . .	950,270	123,949	3,836	822,485	29,792	1,530	227	28,035	143	143	-	-
May.	949,853	124,462	3,805	821,586	29,883	1,461	220	28,202	144	144	-	-
June	947,586	125,189	3,784	818,613	29,863	1,436	216	28,211	144	144	-	-

a/ Includes Aviation Cadets.

Source: Personnel Statistics Division, DCS/Comptroller, Headquarters USAF.

TABLE 206 — DEPARTMENTAL STRENGTH BY TYPE OF PERSONNEL — FY 1953

End of Month	WORLDWIDE				CONTINENTAL US				OVERSEAS			
	Total	Officer	W/O	E/P a/	Total	Officer	W/O	E/P a/	Total	Officer	W/O	E/P
1952												
July	943,216	124,138	3,971	815,107	704,234	94,918	3,079	606,237	238,982	29,220	892	208,870
August . . .	944,780	126,526	3,963	814,291	698,254	96,697	3,065	598,492	246,526	29,829	898	215,799
September. .	940,601	127,134	3,956	809,511	692,055	97,087	3,001	591,967	248,546	30,047	955	217,544
October. . .	937,497	127,240	3,962	806,295	685,735	97,512	2,992	585,231	251,762	29,728	970	221,064
November . .	932,713	126,216	3,942	802,555	676,470	96,393	2,954	577,123	256,243	29,823	988	225,432
December . .	923,201	124,825	3,892	794,484	666,780	95,531	2,905	568,344	256,421	29,294	987	226,140
1953												
January. . .	924,956	123,819	3,856	797,281	665,081	94,174	2,840	568,067	259,875	29,645	1,016	229,214
February . .	934,440	123,697	3,868	806,875	669,666	93,591	2,829	573,246	264,774	30,106	1,039	233,629
March. . . .	944,224	124,607	3,847	815,770	676,424	94,445	2,810	579,169	267,800	30,162	1,037	236,601
April. . . .	950,270	123,949	3,836	822,485	681,579	93,193	2,790	585,596	268,691	30,756	1,046	236,889
May.	949,853	124,462	3,805	821,586	676,152	93,139	2,751	580,262	273,701	31,323	1,054	241,324
June	947,586	125,189	3,784	818,613	672,251	93,801	2,706	575,744	275,335	31,388	1,078	242,869

a/ Includes Aviation Cadets.

Source: Personnel Statistics Division, DCS/Comptroller, Headquarters USAF

TABLE 207 — DEPARTMENTAL STRENGTH OF GENERAL OFFICERS BY PERMANENT GRADE, BY GRADE IN WHICH SERVING — FY 1953

End of Month	Total b/	Permanent Grade a/															
		Major General				Brigadier General				Colonel				Lieutenant Colonel			
		Grade in Which Serving															
		General	Lieutenant General	Major General	Brigadier General	General	Lieutenant General	Major General	Brigadier General	General	Lieutenant General	Major General	Brigadier General	General	Lieutenant General	Major General	Brigadier General
1952																	
July . . .	297	7	17	37	-	-	-	58	25	-	-	15	138	-	-	-	-
August . .	295	7	17	37	-	-	-	57	24	-	-	15	138	-	-	-	-
September.	337	7	19	35	-	-	-	62	17	-	-	20	177	-	-	-	-
October. .	344	7	19	34	-	-	-	63	15	-	-	24	182	-	-	-	-
November .	344	7	19	34	-	-	-	63	15	-	-	24	182	-	-	-	-
December .	360	7	19	34	-	-	-	65	12	-	-	28	195	-	-	-	-
1953																	
January. .	358	7	19	34	-	-	-	64	11	-	-	28	195	-	-	-	-
February .	356	7	19	34	-	-	-	64	10	-	-	28	194	-	-	-	-
March. . .	349	7	18	34	-	-	-	59	10	-	-	28	193	-	-	-	-
April. . .	345	7	17	34	-	-	-	58	10	-	-	28	191	-	-	-	-
May. . . .	345	7	19	32	-	-	-	58	10	-	-	28	191	-	-	-	-
June . . .	364	7	18	32	-	-	-	61	7	-	-	32	207	-	-	-	-

a/ No General Officers in the USAF possess the permanent grade of General or Lieutenant General.
b/ Excludes Air Reserve and Air National Guard Officers.

Source: Personnel Statistics Division, DCS/Comptroller, Headquarters USAF.

TABLE 208 — DEPARTMENTAL STRENGTH OF REGULAR COMMISSIONED OFFICERS BY GRADE IN WHICH SERVING, BY CONTROL BRANCH — FY 1953

Control Branch	Total	General	Colonel	Lieutenant Colonel	Major	Captain	First Lieutenant	Second Lieutenant
1952								
30 September - Total . . .	22,461	337	3,323	4,684	6,791	4,551	1,552	1,223
Air Force Nurse.	411	-	1	7	78	305	19	1
Chaplain	141	1	15	46	54	21	4	-
Dentist	270	1	49	67	96	50	7	-
Medical.	730	15	137	124	237	205	12	-
Medical Service.	263	-	11	56	109	42	23	22
Veterinary	62	-	4	26	19	9	4	-
Women's Medical Specialist . . .	31	-	1	1	4	19	6	-
Women in the Air Force	189	-	-	37	115	30	7	-
All other Air Force.	20,364	320	3,105	4,320	6,079	3,870	1,470	1,200
31 December - Total. . . .	22,658	360	3,290	4,709	6,805	4,636	1,892	966
Air Force Nurse.	400	-	1	7	76	298	18	-
Chaplain	140	1	15	46	54	20	4	-
Dentist.	270	1	48	67	97	51	6	-
Medical.	730	16	136	126	237	206	9	-
Medical Service.	267	-	11	57	109	42	31	17
Veterinary	66	-	4	26	19	13	4	-
Women's Medical Specialist . . .	29	-	1	1	4	17	5	1
Women in the Air Force	187	-	-	37	112	29	9	-
All other Air Force.	20,569	342	3,074	4,342	6,097	3,960	1,806	948
1953								
31 March - Total	22,771	343	3,273	4,722	6,809	4,669	2,210	745
Air Force Nurse	393	-	1	7	76	294	15	-
Chaplain	148	1	15	47	54	24	7	-
Dentist	275	1	48	67	99	56	4	-
Medical.	746	16	136	126	239	223	6	-
Medical Service	267	-	11	57	109	44	41	5
Veterinary	66	-	4	26	19	14	3	-
Women's Medical Specialist . . .	28	-	1	1	4	16	6	-
Women in the Air Force	186	-	-	35	111	28	10	2
All other Air Force.	20,662	325	3,057	4,356	6,098	3,970	2,118	738
30 June - Total.	22,829	364	3,675	4,824	6,878	4,119	2,223	746
Air Force Nurse	387	-	1	13	106	258	9	-
Chaplain	150	1	18	49	52	28	2	-
Dentist.	276	1	56	67	119	29	4	-
Medical.	750	17	155	127	278	171	2	-
Medical Service.	283	-	16	56	108	44	50	9
Veterinary	69	1	6	27	20	9	6	-
Women's Medical Specialist . . .	27	-	1	1	6	14	5	-
Women in the Air Force	182	-	-	39	108	24	10	1
All other Air Force.	20,705	344	3,422	4,445	6,081	3,542	2,135	736

Source: Personnel Statistics Division, DCS/Comptroller, Headquarters USAF.

TABLE 209 — DEPARTMENTAL STRENGTH OF FEMALE PERSONNEL

FIRST HALF

Grade	July (1952) Total	Women in the Air Force	Air Force Nurse Corps	Women's Medical Specialists	August Total	Women in the Air Force	Air Force Nurse Corps	Women's Medical Specialists	September Total	Women in the Air Force	Air Force Nurse Corps	Women's Medical Specialists
Total	15,386	12,503	2,761	122	15,759	12,880	2,752	127	16,243	13,362	2,749	132
Officer and Warrant Officer - Total. .	3,840	957	2,761	122	3,873	994	2,752	127	3,892	1,011	2,749	132
Officer - Total. .	3,834	951	2,761	122	3,867	988	2,752	127	3,886	1,005	2,749	132
Colonel.	3	1	1	1	3	1	1	1	3	1	1	1
Lieutenant Colonel	48	38	9	1	48	37	10	1	48	37	10	1
Major.	236	142	87	7	236	146	82	8	234	142	85	7
Captain.	946	142	760	44	942	147	750	45	936	146	745	45
First Lieutenant	1,372	259	1,081	32	1,436	286	1,116	34	1,460	283	1,141	36
Second Lieutenant	1,229	369	823	37	1,202	371	793	38	1,205	396	767	42
Warrant Officer - Total	6	6	-	-	6	6	-	-	6	6	-	-
WO, W-4	-	-	-	-	-	-	-	-	-	-	-	-
WO, W-3	-	-	-	-	-	-	-	-	-	-	-	-
WO, W-2	5	5	-	-	5	5	-	-	5	5	-	-
WO, W-1	1	1	-	-	1	1	-	-	1	1	-	-
Airman - Total . . .	11,546	11,546	-	-	11,886	11,886	-	-	12,351	12,351	-	-
Master Sergeant. .	123	123	-	-	124	124	-	-	127	127	-	-
Technical Sergeant	339	339	-	-	339	339	-	-	328	328	-	-
Staff Sergeant . .	1,048	1,048	-	-	1,120	1,120	-	-	1,065	1,065	-	-
Airman 1st Class .	1,683	1,683	-	-	1,706	1,706	-	-	1,623	1,623	-	-
Airman 2nd Class .	2,554	2,554	-	-	2,666	2,666	-	-	2,690	2,690	-	-
Airman 3rd Class .	4,137	4,137	-	-	4,493	4,493	-	-	4,682	4,682	-	-
Basic Airman . . .	1,662	1,662	-	-	1,438	1,438	-	-	1,836	1,836	-	-

LAST HALF

Grade	January (1953) Total	Women in the Air Force	Air Force Nurse Corps	Women's Medical Specialists	February Total	Women in the Air Force	Air Force Nurse Corps	Women's Medical Specialists	March Total	Women in the Air Force	Air Force Nurse Corps	Women's Medical Specialists
Total	16,443	13,433	2,844	166	16,331	13,318	2,851	162	16,259	13,219	2,883	157
Officer and Warrant Officer - Total. .	4,007	997	2,844	166	4,005	992	2,851	162	4,059	1,019	2,883	157
Officer - Total. .	4,001	991	2,844	166	3,999	986	2,851	162	4,053	1,013	2,883	157
Colonel.	3	1	1	1	3	1	1	1	3	1	1	1
Lieutenant Colonel	47	36	10	1	46	35	10	1	46	35	10	1
Major	236	139	86	11	231	140	81	10	232	140	82	10
Captain.	898	122	724	52	898	120	725	53	889	120	718	51
First Lieutenant	1,674	323	1,309	42	1,707	322	1,343	42	1,766	337	1,386	43
Second Lieutenant	1,143	370	714	59	1,114	368	691	55	1,117	380	686	51
Warrant Officer - Total.	6	6	-	-	6	6	-	-	6	6	-	-
WO, W-4.	-	-	-	-	-	-	-	-	-	-	-	-
WO, W-3.	-	-	-	-	-	-	-	-	-	-	-	-
WO, W-2.	5	5	-	-	4	4	-	-	5	5	-	-
WO, W-1.	1	1	-	-	2	2	-	-	1	1	-	-
Airman - Total . . .	12,436	12,436	-	-	12,326	12,326	-	-	12,200	12,200	-	-
Master Sergeant. .	134	134	-	-	147	147	-	-	142	142	-	-
Technical Sergeant	329	329	-	-	327	327	-	-	322	322	-	-
Staff Sergeant . .	987	987	-	-	1,027	1,027	-	-	975	975	-	-
Airman 1st Class .	1,560	1,560	-	-	1,723	1,723	-	-	1,677	1,677	-	-
Airman 2nd Class .	2,774	2,774	-	-	3,022	3,022	-	-	2,931	2,931	-	-
Airman 3rd Class .	5,923	5,923	-	-	5,396	5,396	-	-	5,477	5,477	-	-
Basic Airman . . .	729	729	-	-	684	684	-	-	676	676	-	-

Source: Personnel Statistics Division, DCS/Comptroller, Headquarters USAF.

BY GRADE IN WHICH SERVING, BY CONTROL BRANCH — FY 1953

Total	Women in the Air Force	Air Force Nurse Corps	Women's Medical Specialists	Total	Women in the Air Force	Air Force Nurse Corps	Women's Medical Specialists	Total	Women in the Air Force	Air Force Nurse Corps	Women's Medical Specialists	Grade
FY 1953												
October				November				December				
16,584	13,680	2,760	144	16,724	13,779	2,797	148	16,358	13,422	2,793	143	Total
3,893	989	2,760	144	3,938	993	2,797	148	3,942	1,006	2,793	143	Officer and Warrant Officer - Total
3,887	983	2,760	144	3,932	987	2,797	148	3,936	1,000	2,793	143	Officer - Total *
3	1	1	1	3	1	1	1	3	1	1	1	Colonel
48	37	10	1	48	37	10	1	49	38	10	1	Lieutenant Colonel
232	142	83	7	231	143	81	7	228	141	80	7	Major
923	133	744	46	913	135	732	46	904	125	735	44	Captain
1,506	287	1,181	38	1,558	301	1,213	44	1,591	301	1,247	43	First Lieutenant
1,175	383	741	51	1,179	370	760	49	1,161	394	720	47	Second Lieutenant
6	6	-	-	6	6	-	-	6	6	-	-	Warrant Officer - Total
-	-	-	-	-	-	-	-	-	-	-	-	WO, W-4
-	-	-	-	-	-	-	-	-	-	-	-	WO, W-3
5	5	-	-	5	5	-	-	5	5	-	-	WO, W-2
1	1	-	-	1	1	-	-	1	1	-	-	WO, W-1
12,691	12,691	-	-	12,786	12,786	-	-	12,416	12,416	-	-	Airman - Total
134	134	-	-	131	131	-	-	134	134	-	-	Master Sergeant
332	332	-	-	330	330	-	-	329	329	-	-	Technical Sergeant
1,102	1,102	-	-	1,036	1,036	-	-	999	999	-	-	Staff Sergeant
1,653	1,653	-	-	1,581	1,581	-	-	1,650	1,650	-	-	Airman 1st Class
2,816	2,816	-	-	2,809	2,809	-	-	2,830	2,830	-	-	Airman 2nd Class
4,677	4,677	-	-	5,150	5,150	-	-	5,345	5,345	-	-	Airman 3rd Class
1,977	1,977	-	-	1,749	1,749	-	-	1,129	1,129	-	-	Basic Airman
FY 1953												
April				May				June				
16,107	13,057	2,898	152	15,928	12,816	2,969	143	15,918	12,808	2,963	147	Total
4,051	1,001	2,898	152	4,111	999	2,969	143	4,139	1,029	2,963	147	Officer and Warrant Officer - Total
4,045	995	2,898	152	4,105	993	2,969	143	4,133	1,023	2,963	147	Officer - Total
3	1	1	1	3	1	1	1	3	1	1	1	Colonel
50	37	12	1	54	39	14	1	57	41	15	1	Lieutenant Colonel
283	142	131	10	284	143	131	10	280	141	129	10	Major
976	123	807	46	978	122	815	41	967	123	803	41	Captain
1,658	343	1,267	48	1,698	358	1,295	45	1,734	389	1,296	49	First Lieutenant
1,075	349	680	46	1,088	330	713	45	1,092	328	719	45	Second Lieutenant
6	6	-	-	6	6	-	-	6	6	-	-	Warrant Officer - Total
-	-	-	-	-	-	-	-	-	-	-	-	WO, W-4
-	-	-	-	-	-	-	-	-	-	-	-	WO, W-3
5	5	-	-	5	5	-	-	5	5	-	-	WO, W-2
1	1	-	-	1	1	-	-	1	1	-	-	WO, W-1
12,056	12,056	-	-	11,817	11,817	-	-	11,779	11,779	-	-	Airman - Total
149	149	-	-	150	150	-	-	155	155	-	-	Master Sergeant
323	323	-	-	318	318	-	-	326	326	-	-	Technical Sergeant
1,090	1,090	-	-	1,072	1,072	-	-	1,070	1,070	-	-	Staff Sergeant
1,786	1,786	-	-	1,704	1,704	-	-	1,740	1,740	-	-	Airman 1st Class
3,264	3,264	-	-	3,181	3,181	-	-	3,293	3,293	-	-	Airman 2nd Class
4,848	4,848	-	-	4,929	4,929	-	-	4,652	4,652	-	-	Airman 3rd Class
596	596	-	-	463	463	-	-	543	543	-	-	Basic Airman

TABLE 210 — DEPARTMENTAL STRENGTH OF FEMALE MEDICAL OFFICERS BY GRADE IN WHICH SERVING — FY 1953

End of Month	Total	General	Colonel	Lieutenant Colonel	Major	Captain	First Lieutenant	Second Lieutenant	Warrant Officer
1952									
July	2,883	-	2	10	94	804	1,113	860	-
August	2,879	-	2	11	90	795	1,150	831	-
September.	2,881	-	2	11	92	790	1,177	809	-
October.	2,904	-	2	11	90	790	1,219	792	-
November	2,945	-	2	11	88	778	1,257	809	-
December	2,936	-	2	11	87	779	1,290	767	-
1953									
January.	3,010	-	2	11	97	776	1,351	773	-
February	3,013	-	2	11	91	778	1,385	746	-
March.	3,040	-	2	11	92	769	1,429	737	-
April.	3,050	-	2	13	141	853	1,315	726	-
May.	3,112	-	2	15	141	856	1,340	758	-
June	3,110	-	2	16	139	844	1,345	764	-

Source: Personnel Statistics Division, DCS/Comptroller, Headquarters USAF.

TABLE 211 — GAINS AND LOSSES OF MILITARY PERSONNEL TO COMMAND STRENGTH — FY 1953

Gain or Loss	Total	Jul (1952)	Aug	Sep	Oct	Nov	Dec	Jan (1953)	Feb	Mar	Apr	May	Jun
GAIN - TOTAL	212,045	22,139	22,555	20,107	18,916	18,311	14,736	17,402	20,967	22,384	15,893	9,119	9,516
Officer	25,152	2,017	2,931	2,397	1,840	1,081	1,744	1,240	1,977	3,308	2,008	1,722	2,887
Warrant Officer	145	24	7	6	2	50	1	5	14	9	11	5	11
Enlisted	186,748	20,098	19,617	17,704	17,074	17,180	12,991	16,157	18,976	19,067	13,874	7,392	6,618
Commissioned From Civil Life - Total	4,610	824	1,143	519	257	127	181	136	267	456	340	6	354
Officer	4,610	824	1,143	519	257	127	181	136	267	456	340	6	354
Warrant Officer	-	-	-	-	-	-	-	-	-	-	-	-	-
Enlisted	-	-	-	-	-	-	-	-	-	-	-	-	-
Ordered Into Active Military Service From Air Force Reserve Total	12,462	1,110	1,476	976	832	634	324	971	1,069	1,337	1,461	1,084	1,188
Officer	10,259	949	1,378	828	695	482	216	795	886	1,081	1,187	760	1,002
Warrant Officer	-	-	-	-	-	-	-	-	-	-	-	-	-
Enlisted	2,203	161	98	148	137	152	108	176	183	256	274	324	186
No Prior Service Enlistments - Total	130,822	16,314	15,493	12,971	10,730	8,268	9,470	10,445	15,185	14,257	10,167	4,212	3,310
Officer	-	-	-	-	-	-	-	-	-	-	-	-	-
Warrant Officer	-	-	-	-	-	-	-	-	-	-	-	-	-
Enlisted	130,822	16,314	15,493	12,971	10,730	8,268	9,470	10,445	15,185	14,257	10,167	4,212	3,310
Prior Service Enlistments - Total	10,059	999	927	696	793	609	691	1,206	1,082	938	830	635	653
Officer	-	-	-	-	-	-	-	-	-	-	-	-	-
Warrant Officer	-	-	-	-	-	-	-	-	-	-	-	-	-
Enlisted	10,059	999	927	696	793	609	691	1,206	1,082	938	830	635	653
Enlistment For OCS or A/C - Total	3,503	273	331	179	566	491	107	474	363	282	151	108	178
Officer	-	-	-	-	-	-	-	-	-	-	-	-	-
Warrant Officer	-	-	-	-	-	-	-	-	-	-	-	-	-
Enlisted	3,503	273	331	179	566	491	107	474	363	282	151	108	178
Reenlistment Within 30 or 90 Days - Total a/	9,937	262	601	932	1,128	1,106	1,131	1,301	964	848	563	512	589
Officer	-	-	-	-	-	-	-	-	-	-	-	-	-
Warrant Officer	-	-	-	-	-	-	-	-	-	-	-	-	-
Enlisted	9,937	262	601	932	1,128	1,106	1,131	1,301	964	848	563	512	589
Inducted From Civil Life - Total	7	-	-	-	1	3	-	2	-	1	-	-	-
Officer	-	-	-	-	-	-	-	-	-	-	-	-	-
Warrant Officer	-	-	-	-	-	-	-	-	-	-	-	-	-
Enlisted	7	-	-	-	1	3	-	2	-	1	-	-	-

Assigned From Department of Army - Total	21,514	1,450	1,268	2,023	2,966	5,990	722	1,443	506	1,758	1,301	991	1,096
Officer	1,003	33	34	38	135	247	108	60	83	85	85	48	47
Warrant Officer	91	-	1	2	2	49	-	1	6	6	8	5	11
Enlisted	20,420	1,417	1,233	1,983	2,829	5,694	614	1,382	417	1,667	1,208	938	1,038
Commissioned Officer or Appointed Warrant Officer From Active Military Status - Total	986	123	69	74	59	28	18	52	66	113	166	109	109
Officer	935	99	63	70	59	27	18	48	59	110	164	109	109
Warrant Officer	51	24	6	4	-	1	-	4	7	3	2	-	-
Enlisted	-	-	-	-	-	-	-	-	-	-	-	-	-
Commissioned Officer From OCS or A/C - Total	8,281	102	310	938	591	189	1,214	195	674	1,569	226	799	1,374
Officer	8,281	102	310	938	591	189	1,214	195	674	1,569	226	799	1,374
Warrant Officer	-	-	-	-	-	-	-	-	-	-	-	-	-
Enlisted	-	-	-	-	-	-	-	-	-	-	-	-	-
Returned To Military Control From Desertion, General Prisoner, Captured or Missing - Total	9,016	625	865	736	839	785	791	987	727	770	633	626	632
Officer	9	1	2	-	1	2	-	-	1	-	2	-	-
Warrant Officer	2	-	-	-	-	-	-	-	1	-	1	-	-
Enlisted	9,005	624	863	736	838	783	791	987	725	770	630	626	632
Correction of Erroneous Loss - Total	848	57	72	63	54	81	87	190	64	55	55	37	33
Officer	55	9	1	4	2	7	7	6	7	7	4	-	1
Warrant Officer	1	-	-	-	-	-	1	-	-	-	-	-	-
Enlisted	792	48	71	59	52	74	79	184	57	48	51	37	32
LOSS - TOTAL	207,416	21,767	22,630	22,773	21,257	18,999	24,314	15,697	15,577	13,201	10,480	9,396	11,325
Officer	25,999	1,560	1,604	1,870	2,115	2,100	2,563	2,667	2,393	2,615	2,610	1,414	2,488
Warrant Officer	287	15	15	22	11	31	13	50	19	19	24	39	29
Enlisted	181,130	20,192	21,011	20,881	19,131	16,868	21,738	12,980	13,165	10,567	7,846	7,943	8,808
Prior To or Upon Expiration of Term of Service - Total	73,057	10,591	10,404	9,854	8,771	7,473	9,923	5,581	4,296	1,953	1,417	1,204	1,590
Officer	-	-	-	-	-	-	-	-	-	-	-	-	-
Warrant Officer	-	-	-	-	-	-	-	-	-	-	-	-	-
Enlisted	73,057	10,591	10,404	9,854	8,771	7,473	9,923	5,581	4,296	1,953	1,417	1,204	1,590
Reserve Forces Released From Active Military Service - Total	59,256	6,288	6,544	6,391	6,342	6,158	7,565	4,299	3,829	3,456	3,371	1,844	3,169
Officer	22,237	1,135	1,254	1,469	1,787	1,770	2,262	2,382	2,135	2,337	2,369	1,128	2,209
Warrant Officer	74	6	4	3	3	9	4	9	8	8	11	6	3
Enlisted	36,945	5,147	5,286	4,919	4,552	4,379	5,299	1,908	1,686	1,111	991	710	957
Dependency or Hardship - Total	8,070	732	770	668	694	608	679	547	566	696	675	751	684
Officer	214	21	25	24	15	19	27	10	7	15	10	20	21
Warrant Officer	5	-	-	2	-	-	1	-	-	-	-	1	1
Enlisted	7,851	711	745	642	679	589	651	537	559	681	665	730	662

TABLE 211 — GAINS AND LOSSES OF MILITARY PERSONNEL TO COMMAND STRENGTH — FY 1953 (Continued)

Gain or Loss	Total	Jul (1952)	Aug	Sep	Oct	Nov	Dec	Jan (1953)	Feb	Mar	Apr	May	Jun
National Health, Safety or Interest - Total	164	12	22	13	14	19	11	10	8	13	12	12	18
Officer	51	6	8	4	7	9	2	5	1	2	-	2	5
Warrant Officer	4	-	-	-	-	-	-	-	3	-	1	-	-
Enlisted	109	6	14	9	7	10	9	5	4	11	11	10	13
Maximum Age in Grade or Failure of Selection For Promotion (Officer), Convenience of Government (Enl) - Total	922	3	16	14	84	102	38	77	51	147	99	98	193
Officer	83	3	16	14	7	9	4	8	4	6	7	2	3
Warrant Officer	1	-	-	-	-	-	-	-	-	-	-	1	-
Enlisted	838	-	-	-	77	93	34	69	47	141	92	95	190
Medical Reasons or Best Interest of Service - Total	44	8	9	9	1	6	4	1	2	-	2	2	-
Officer	44	8	9	9	1	6	4	1	2	-	2	2	-
Warrant Officer	-	-	-	-	-	-	-	-	-	-	-	-	-
Enlisted	-	-	-	-	-	-	-	-	-	-	-	-	-
Offenders - Total	6,771	503	564	530	570	547	614	550	543	622	564	638	526
Officer	43	7	4	3	1	4	5	3	2	4	2	5	3
Warrant Officer	1	-	-	-	-	1	-	-	-	-	-	-	-
Enlisted	6,727	496	560	527	569	542	609	547	541	618	562	633	523
Substandard Efficiency or Conduct (Officer) Undesirables (Enl) - Total	7,324	615	712	692	731	551	607	557	523	543	568	695	530
Officer	235	42	39	28	25	22	32	21	15	6	2	2	1
Warrant Officer	2	-	1	-	-	-	-	-	1	-	-	-	-
Enlisted	7,087	573	672	664	706	529	575	536	507	537	566	693	529
Disability Discharge - Total	6,946	719	884	776	633	590	512	434	471	478	525	448	476
Officer	354	25	46	45	39	37	23	25	16	16	34	20	28
Warrant Officer	8	1	1	1	-	3	-	-	-	1	-	-	1
Enlisted	6,584	693	837	730	594	550	489	409	455	461	491	428	447
Marriage - Total	1,754	160	172	114	141	114	152	157	152	147	124	169	152
Officer	118	14	9	2	10	4	5	12	14	11	11	10	16
Warrant Officer	-	-	-	-	-	-	-	-	-	-	-	-	-
Enlisted	1,636	146	163	112	131	110	147	145	138	136	113	159	136
Pregnancy - Total	1,120	-	28	69	93	85	98	93	99	143	134	126	152
Officer	108	-	-	5	13	11	10	6	13	13	10	14	13
Warrant Officer	-	-	-	-	-	-	-	-	-	-	-	-	-
Enlisted	1,012	-	28	64	80	74	88	87	86	130	124	112	139

Resignation - Total	3,405	46	53	44	58	121	256	246	324	509	530	618	600
Officer	399	46	49	35	36	26	36	41	25	17	26	37	25
Warrant Officer	19	-	1	-	-	2	2	1	1	2	1	4	5
Enlisted	2,987	-	3	9	22	93	218	204	298	490	503	577	570
Retirement - Total	1,516	44	52	53	57	100	175	104	114	137	194	268	218
Officer	194	13	14	17	13	19	24	11	19	19	21	11	13
Warrant Officer	9	-	3	-	-	2	-	1	1	-	-	1	1
Enlisted	1,313	31	35	36	44	79	151	92	94	118	173	256	204
Deaths - Total	2,323	178	189	171	150	196	274	198	170	210	156	159	272
Officer	677	59	48	58	50	62	74	61	44	58	47	55	61
Warrant Officer	9	-	-	-	1	1	2	1	-	1	-	2	1
Enlisted	1,637	119	141	113	99	133	198	136	126	151	109	102	210
Assigned to Department of Army - Total	13,761	426	633	1,271	989	1,193	1,199	1,504	2,820	1,685	892	692	457
Officer	570	21	22	84	60	53	23	30	62	67	26	76	46
Warrant Officer	66	5	2	14	5	10	2	4	-	3	5	8	8
Enlisted	13,125	400	609	1,173	924	1,130	1,174	1,470	2,758	1,615	861	608	403
To Accept Commission, Appointment as Warrant Officer or Enlist in Other Than Air Force; To Enter USMA or USNA - Total	265	34	26	23	15	17	25	12	20	12	24	27	30
Officer	-	-	-	-	-	-	-	-	-	-	-	-	-
Warrant Officer	-	-	-	-	-	-	-	-	-	-	-	-	-
Enlisted	265	34	26	23	15	17	25	12	20	12	24	27	30
To Accept Commission, Appointment as Warrant Officer or Enlist in Air Force - Total	9,930	226	469	1,076	775	228	1,272	321	817	1,784	466	949	1,547
Officer	31	3	2	2	3	-	2	1	3	4	4	1	6
Warrant Officer	85	3	3	2	2	3	-	34	5	4	5	15	9
Enlisted	9,814	220	464	1,072	770	225	1,270	286	809	1,776	457	933	1,532
Absentee or Deserter - Total	8,599	848	856	780	960	683	725	856	615	531	578	566	601
Officer	22	2	2	2	2	1	2	3	1	5	-	-	2
Warrant Officer	1	-	-	-	-	-	-	-	-	-	1	-	-
Enlisted	8,576	846	854	778	958	682	723	853	614	526	577	566	599
Missing - Total	582	77	82	77	76	69	35	48	30	17	27	13	31
Officer	252	4	20	29	29	35	15	35	17	11	23	11	23
Warrant Officer	1	-	-	-	-	-	1	-	-	-	-	-	-
Enlisted	329	73	62	48	47	34	19	13	13	6	4	2	8
General Prisoner - Total	607	48	43	49	48	49	48	57	55	67	50	45	48
Officer	4	1	-	-	-	-	-	-	2	1	-	-	-
Warrant Officer	-	-	-	-	-	-	-	-	-	-	-	-	-
Enlisted	603	47	43	49	48	49	48	57	53	66	50	45	48
Correction of Erroneous Gain - Total	1,000	209	102	99	55	90	102	45	72	51	72	72	31
Officer	363	150	37	40	17	13	13	12	11	23	16	18	13
Warrant Officer	2	-	-	-	-	-	1	-	-	-	-	1	-
Enlisted	635	59	65	59	38	77	88	33	61	28	56	53	18

a/ Includes reenlistments within 30 days for 1 July 1952 through 28 February 1953 and reenlistments within 90 days for 1 March 1953 through 30 June 1953.

Source: Personnel Statistics Division, DCS/Comptroller, Hq USAF

TABLE 212 — GAINS AND LOSSES OF FEMALE MILITARY PERSONNEL TO COMMAND STRENGTH — FY 1953

(Figures in parenthesis represent WAF Officers only and are included in open figures which include both AN/WS Officers. Data in table below included in Table 211)

Gain or Loss	Total	Jul (1952)	Aug	Sep	Oct	Nov	Dec	Jan (1953)	Feb	Mar	Apr	May	Jun
GAIN - TOTAL	(188) 5,907	(5) 859	(21) 774	(39) 886	(1) 743	(1) 591	(38) 174	(10) 446	(1) 268	(32) 376	(4) 223	(2) 225	(34) 342
Officer AN/WS WAF	(188) 945	(5) 44	(21) 61	(39) 78	(1) 77	(1) 113	(38) 48	(10) 92	(1) 53	(32) 119	(4) 66	(2) 105	(34) 89
Warrant Officer	-	-	-	-	-	-	-	-	-	-	-	-	-
Enlisted	4,962	815	713	808	666	478	126	354	215	257	157	120	253
Commissioned From Civil Life - Total	(31) 55	4	(16) 18	1	6	6	(8) 8	(7) 7	-	1	-	2	2
Officer	(31) 55	4	(16) 18	1	6	6	(8) 8	(7) 7	-	1	-	2	2
Warrant Officer	-	-	-	-	-	-	-	-	-	-	-	-	-
Enlisted	-	-	-	-	-	-	-	-	-	-	-	-	-
Ordered Into Active Service From Air Force Reserve - Total	(26) 748	(2) 37	(1) 37	(6) 42	(1) 68	104	10	(3) 85	(1) 52	86	(4) 66	100	(8) 61
Officer	(26) 742	(2) 37	(1) 37	(6) 42	(1) 68	103	10	(3) 83	(1) 52	86	(4) 65	99	(8) 60
Warrant Officer	-	-	-	-	-	-	-	-	-	-	-	-	-
Enlisted	6	-	-	-	-	1	-	2	-	-	1	1	1
No Prior Service Enlistments - Total	4,813	808	694	779	655	470	114	342	206	235	152	117	241
Officer	-	-	-	-	-	-	-	-	-	-	-	-	-
Warrant Officer	-	-	-	-	-	-	-	-	-	-	-	-	-
Enlisted	4,813	808	694	779	655	470	114	342	206	235	152	117	241
Prior Service Enlistments - Total	40	6	8	3	3	2	4	-	5	4	2	-	3
Officer	-	-	-	-	-	-	-	-	-	-	-	-	-
Warrant Officer	-	-	-	-	-	-	-	-	-	-	-	-	-
Enlisted	40	6	8	3	3	2	4	-	5	4	2	-	3
Enlisted for OCS or A/C - Total	29	-	-	10	-	-	3	3	-	10	-	-	3
Officer	-	-	-	-	-	-	-	-	-	-	-	-	-
Warrant Officer	-	-	-	-	-	-	-	-	-	-	-	-	-
Enlisted	29	-	-	10	-	-	3	3	-	10	-	-	3
Reenlisted Within 30 Days - Total	46	-	5	10	7	4	5	5	3	4	1	-	2
Officer	-	-	-	-	-	-	-	-	-	-	-	-	-
Warrant Officer	-	-	-	-	-	-	-	-	-	-	-	-	-
Enlisted	46	-	5	10	7	4	5	5	3	4	1	-	2
Inducted from Civil Life - Total	-	-	-	-	-	-	-	-	-	-	-	-	-
Officer	-	-	-	-	-	-	-	-	-	-	-	-	-
Warrant Officer	-	-	-	-	-	-	-	-	-	-	-	-	-
Enlisted	-	-	-	-	-	-	-	-	-	-	-	-	-

Assigned From Department of Army - Total	(1) 5	-	(1) 2	1	-	1	-	1	-	-	-	-	-
Officer	(1) 3	-	(1) 2	1	-	-	-	-	-	-	-	-	-
Warrant Officer	-	-	-	-	-	-	-	-	-	-	-	-	-
Enlisted	2	-	-	-	-	1	-	1	-	-	-	-	-
Commissioned Officer or Appointed Warrant Officer From Active Military Status - Total	(7) 20	(1) 1	(3) 3	(1) 1	3	3	-	2	1	-	1	(2) 4	1
Officer	(7) 20	(1) 1	(3) 3	(1) 1	3	3	-	2	1	-	1	(2) 4	1
Warrant Officer	-	-	-	-	-	-	-	-	-	-	-	-	-
Enlisted	-	-	-	-	-	-	-	-	-	-	-	-	-
Commissioned Officer From OCS or A/C - Total	(123) 123	(2) 2	-	(32) 32	-	(1) 1	(30) 30	-	-	(32) 32	-	-	(26) 26
Officer	(123) 123	(2) 2	-	(32) 32	-	(1) 1	(30) 30	-	-	(32) 32	-	-	(26) 26
Warrant Officer	-	-	-	-	-	-	-	-	-	-	-	-	-
Enlisted	-	-	-	-	-	-	-	-	-	-	-	-	-
Returned To Military Control From Desertion, General Prisoner, Captured or Missing - Total	19	1	4	4	-	-	-	1	1	3	1	1	3
Officer	1	-	1	-	-	-	-	-	-	-	-	-	-
Warrant Officer	-	-	-	-	-	-	-	-	-	-	-	-	-
Enlisted	18	1	3	4	-	-	-	1	1	3	1	1	3
Correction of Erroneous Loss	9	-	3	3	1	-	-	-	-	1	-	1	-
Officer	1	-	-	1	-	-	-	-	-	-	-	-	-
Warrant Officer	-	-	-	-	-	-	-	-	-	-	-	-	-
Enlisted	8	-	3	2	1	-	-	-	-	1	-	1	-
LOSS - TOTAL	(124) 4,794	(11) 291	(3) 380	(10) 387	(10) 418	(14) 399	(11) 524	(8) 395	(8) 402	(9) 431	(15) 352	(10) 399	(15) 416
Officer	(124) 724	(11) 61	(3) 47	(10) 53	(10) 67	(14) 60	(11) 57	(8) 47	(8) 57	(9) 76	(15) 70	(10) 63	(15) 66
Warrant Officer	-	-	-	-	-	-	-	-	-	-	-	-	-
Enlisted	4,070	230	333	334	351	339	467	348	345	355	282	336	350
Prior To or Upon Expiration of Term of Service - Total	524	32	67	48	62	75	95	48	50	17	10	10	10
Officer	-	-	-	-	-	-	-	-	-	-	-	-	-
Warrant Officer	-	-	-	-	-	-	-	-	-	-	-	-	-
Enlisted	524	32	67	48	62	75	95	48	50	17	10	10	10
Reserve Forces Released From Active Military Service - Total	(53) 550	(4) 49	42	(8) 54	(8) 48	(5) 41	(6) 72	(1) 36	(2) 45	(3) 50	(5) 44	(3) 32	(8) 37
Officer	(53) 339	(4) 36	25	(8) 38	(8) 32	(5) 31	(6) 32	(1) 24	(2) 27	(3) 45	(5) 42	(3) 31	(8) 36
Warrant Officer	-	-	-	-	-	-	-	-	-	-	-	-	-
Enlisted	151	13	17	16	16	10	40	12	18	5	2	1	1
Dependency or Hardship - Total	(4) 86	3	(1) 11	8	11	(1) 5	6	10	6	(1) 8	(1) 6	7	5
Officer	(4) 14	1	(1) 4	1	1	(1) 1	-	1	-	(1) 2	(1) 1	1	1
Warrant Officer	-	-	-	-	-	-	-	-	-	-	-	-	-
Enlisted	72	2	7	7	10	4	6	9	6	6	5	6	4

TABLE 212 — GAINS AND LOSSES OF FEMALE MILITARY PERSONNEL TO COMMAND STRENGTH — FY 1953 (CONTINUED)

(Figures in parenthesis represent WAF Officers only and are included in open figures which include both AN/WS Officers. Data in table below included in Table 211)

Gain or Loss	Total	Jul (1952)	Aug	Sep	Oct	Nov	Dec	Jan (1953)	Feb	Mar	Apr	May	Jun
National Health, Safety or Interest - Total	1	-	1	-	-	-	-	-	-	-	-	-	-
Officer	1	-	1	-	-	-	-	-	-	-	-	-	-
Warrant Officer	-	-	-	-	-	-	-	-	-	-	-	-	-
Enlisted	-	-	-	-	-	-	-	-	-	-	-	-	-
Maximum Age in Grade or Failure of Selection For Promotion (Officer), Convenience of Government (Enl) - Total	8	-	1	-	2	2	-	2	-	-	-	-	1
Officer	5	-	1	-	1	2	-	1	-	-	-	-	-
Warrant Officer	-	-	-	-	-	-	-	-	-	-	-	-	-
Enlisted	3	-	-	-	1	-	-	1	-	-	-	-	1
Medical Reasons or Best Interest of Service - Total	(1) 3	(1) 1	1	-	-	-	-	-	-	-	-	1	-
Officer	(1) 3	(1) 1	1	-	-	-	-	-	-	-	-	1	-
Warrant Officer	-	-	-	-	-	-	-	-	-	-	-	-	-
Enlisted	-	-	-	-	-	-	-	-	-	-	-	-	-
Offenders - Total	(1) 135	4	9	13	8	19	12	12	7	12	10	(1) 20	9
Officers	(1) 3	1	-	-	-	1	-	-	-	-	-	(1) 1	-
Warrant Officer	-	-	-	-	-	-	-	-	-	-	-	-	-
Enlisted	132	3	9	13	8	18	12	12	7	12	10	19	9
Substandard Efficiency or Conduct (Officer) Undesirables (Enl) - Total	(1) 174	12	13	17	25	15	28	19	(1) 12	2	7	12	12
Officer	(1) 3	-	-	-	1	-	-	1	(1) 1	-	-	-	-
Warrant Officer	-	-	-	-	-	-	-	-	-	-	-	-	-
Enlisted	171	12	13	17	24	15	28	18	11	2	7	12	12
Disability Discharge - Total	(2) 199	18	19	(1) 23	19	26	19	12	17	15	(1) 9	13	9
Officer	(2) 18	2	1	(1) 2	2	2	2	-	1	2	(1) 3	1	-
Warrant Officer	-	-	-	-	-	-	-	-	-	-	-	-	-
Enlisted	181	16	18	21	17	24	17	12	16	13	6	12	9
Marriage - Total	(25) 1,754	(4) 160	(1) 172	114	(1) 141	114	152	(2) 157	(3) 152	(3) 147	(4) 124	(2) 169	(5) 152
Officer	(25) 118	(4) 14	(1) 9	2	(1) 10	4	5	(2) 12	(3) 14	(3) 11	(4) 11	(2) 10	(5) 16
Warrant Officer	-	-	-	-	-	-	-	-	-	-	-	-	-
Enlisted	1,636	146	163	112	131	110	147	145	138	136	113	159	136
Pregnancy - Total	(21) 1,120	-	28	69	93	(5) 85	(2) 98	(3) 93	(1) 99	(2) 143	(3) 134	(3) 126	(2) 152
Officer	(21) 108	-	-	5	13	(5) 11	(2) 10	(3) 6	(1) 13	(2) 13	(3) 10	(3) 14	(2) 13
Warrant Officer	-	-	-	-	-	-	-	-	-	-	-	-	-
Enlisted	1,012	-	28	64	80	74	88	87	86	130	124	112	139

Resignation - Total	(9) 42	(2) 5	3	(1) 3	(1) 5	8	(1) 3	(1) 3	(1) 2	2	(1) 4	(1) 4	-
Officer	(9) 31	(2) 5	3	(1) 3	(1) 5	4	(1) 3	(1) 1	(1) 1	1	(1) 3	(1) 2	-
Warrant Officer	-	-	-	-	-	-	-	-	-	-	-	-	-
Enlisted	11	-	-	-	-	4	-	2	1	1	1	2	-
Retirement - Total	(4) 11	1	(1) 2	-	-	(2) 4	(1) 2	-	1	1	1	2	-
Officer	(4) 8	1	(1) 2	-	-	(2) 3	(1) 1	-	-	1	-	-	-
Warrant Officer	-	-	-	-	-	-	-	-	-	-	-	-	-
Enlisted	3	-	-	-	-	1	1	-	1	-	-	-	-
Deaths - Total	(2) 19	1	1	2	2	(1) 3	(1) 3	1	4	-	-	1	1
Officer	(2) 8	-	-	2	2	(1) 1	(1) 3	-	-	-	-	-	-
Warrant Officer	-	-	-	-	-	-	-	-	-	-	-	-	-
Enlisted	11	1	1	-	-	2	-	1	4	-	-	1	1
Assigned to Department of Army - Total	3	1	-	-	-	1	1	-	-	-	-	-	-
Officer	-	-	-	-	-	-	-	-	-	-	-	-	-
Warrant Officer	-	-	-	-	-	-	-	-	-	-	-	-	-
Enlisted	3	1	-	-	-	1	1	-	-	-	-	-	-
To Accept Commission, Appointment as Warrant Officer or Enlist in Other Than Air Force; To Enter USMA or USNA - Total	2	-	1	1	-	-	-	-	-	-	-	-	-
Officer	-	-	-	-	-	-	-	-	-	-	-	-	-
Warrant Officer	-	-	-	-	-	-	-	-	-	-	-	-	-
Enlisted	2	-	1	1	-	-	-	-	-	-	-	-	-
To Accept Commission, Appointment as Warrant Officer or Enlist in Air Force - Total	132	3	3	33	-	1	30	-	2	32	-	2	26
Officer	-	-	-	-	-	-	-	-	-	-	-	-	-
Warrant Officer	-	-	-	-	-	-	-	-	-	-	-	-	-
Enlisted	132	3	3	33	-	1	30	-	2	32	-	2	26
Absentee or Deserter - Total	(1) 25	1	6	2	1	-	2	(1) 2	4	1	4	-	2
Officer	(1) 1	-	-	-	-	-	-	(1) 1	-	-	-	-	-
Warrant Officer	-	-	-	-	-	-	-	-	-	-	-	-	-
Enlisted	24	1	6	2	1	-	2	1	4	1	4	-	2
Missing - Total	-	-	-	-	-	-	-	-	-	-	-	-	-
Officer	-	-	-	-	-	-	-	-	-	-	-	-	-
Warrant Officer	-	-	-	-	-	-	-	-	-	-	-	-	-
Enlisted	-	-	-	-	-	-	-	-	-	-	-	-	-
General Prisoner - Total	-	-	-	-	-	-	-	-	-	-	-	-	-
Officer	-	-	-	-	-	-	-	-	-	-	-	-	-
Warrant Officer	-	-	-	-	-	-	-	-	-	-	-	-	-
Enlisted	-	-	-	-	-	-	-	-	-	-	-	-	-
Correction of Erroneous Gain - Total	6	-	-	-	1	-	1	-	1	1	-	2	-
Officer	4	-	-	-	-	-	1	-	-	1	-	2	-
Warrant Officer	-	-	-	-	-	-	-	-	-	-	-	-	-
Enlisted	2	-	-	-	1	-	-	-	1	-	-	-	-

TABLE 213 — GAINS OF OFFICER PERSONNEL TO COMMAND STRENGTH BY GRADE — FY 1953

Month	Total	General	Colonel	Lieutenant Colonel	Major	Captain	First Lieutenant	Second Lieutenant	Warrant Officer
FY 1953 - Total . . .	25,297	2	11	135	502	2,178	4,106	18,218	145
July (1952).	2,041	-	-	7	26	135	386	1,463	24
August	2,938	-	2	6	17	69	206	2,631	7
September.	2,403	-	1	4	10	79	225	2,078	6
October.	1,842	-	2	6	16	115	338	1,363	2
November	1,131	-	2	9	20	170	359	521	50
December	1,745	-	1	3	14	74	115	1,537	1
January (1953)	1,245	-	-	7	54	265	368	546	5
February	1,991	-	-	6	56	227	451	1,237	14
March.	3,317	1	2	19	71	365	538	2,312	9
April.	2,019	-	-	15	94	362	517	1,020	11
May.	1,727	1	1	23	50	131	239	1,277	5
June	2,898	-	-	30	74	186	364	2,233	11

Source: Personnel Statistics Division, DCS/Comptroller, Hq USAF

TABLE 214 — GAINS OF ENLISTED PERSONNEL TO COMMAND STRENGTH BY GRADE — FY 1953

Month	Total	Master Sergeant	Technical Sergeant	Staff Sergeant	Airman First Class	Airmen Second Class	Airmen Third Class	Airmen Basic
FY 1953 - Total.	186,748	2,977	3,389	6,235	4,320	3,973	26,566	139,288
July (1952)	20,098	78	102	348	235	168	2,331	16,836
August.	19,617	185	172	451	263	216	2,092	16,238
September	17,704	384	263	486	295	309	2,442	13,525
October	17,074	364	335	654	342	390	3,302	11,687
November	17,180	341	439	850	715	888	4,784	9,163
December.	12,991	291	361	615	302	160	1,266	9,996
January (1953).	16,157	330	450	763	567	413	2,159	11,475
February.	18,976	207	303	505	413	345	1,254	15,949
March	19,067	241	296	483	371	325	2,159	15,192
April	13,874	192	227	358	295	275	1,819	10,708
May	7,392	180	212	391	256	252	1,421	4,680
June.	6,618	184	229	331	266	232	1,537	3,839

Source: Personnel Statistics Division, DCS/Comptroller, Hq USAF

TABLE 215 — LOSSES OF OFFICER PERSONNEL FROM COMMAND STRENGTH BY GRADE — FY 1953

Month	Total	General	Colonel	Lieutenant Colonel	Major	Captain	First Lieutenant	Second Lieutenant	Warrant Officer
FY 1953 - Total . . .	26,286	29	211	747	2,227	9,060	11,388	2,337	287
July (1952).	1,575	2	16	40	116	548	549	289	15
August	1,619	3	15	68	165	556	596	201	15
September.	1,892	2	21	62	160	592	773	260	22
October.	2,126	2	19	57	199	814	840	184	11
November	2,131	1	20	55	211	725	838	250	31
December	2,576	-	17	65	195	879	1,160	247	13
January (1953)	2,717	3	20	110	247	1,026	1,079	182	50
February	2,412	9	20	55	226	831	1,072	180	19
March.	2,634	3	19	79	219	777	1,335	183	19
April.	2,634	3	14	48	175	846	1,384	140	24
May.	1,453	1	12	32	109	433	715	112	39
June	2,517	-	18	76	205	1,033	1,047	109	29

Source: Personnel Statistics Division, DCS/Comptroller, Hq USAF

TABLE 216 — LOSSES OF ENLISTED PERSONNEL FROM COMMAND STRENGTH BY GRADE — FY 1953

Month	Total	Master Sergeant	Technical Sergeant	Staff Sergeant	Airmen First Class	Airmen Third Class	Airmen Third Class	Airmen Basic	Aviation Cadet
FY 1953 - Total	181,130	8,151	11,446	46,735	43,898	24,989	19,808	19,735	6,358
July (1952).	20,192	564	1,082	7,468	5,021	2,318	1,891	1,743	105
August	21,011	687	1,083	7,284	4,911	2,673	2,166	1,890	317
September.	20,881	811	1,120	6,343	5,137	2,919	2,150	1,851	550
October.	19,131	728	1,110	5,019	4,928	2,571	2,132	1,949	694
November	16,868	689	1,046	4,000	4,809	2,612	1,886	1,632	194
December	21,738	885	1,450	5,503	6,180	3,159	2,047	1,787	727
January (1953)	12,980	569	845	2,831	3,642	1,843	1,461	1,592	197
February	13,165	606	876	2,645	3,588	1,922	1,390	1,455	683
March.	10,567	694	804	2,102	1,878	1,417	1,247	1,431	994
April.	7,846	656	660	1,153	1,343	1,173	1,180	1,457	224
May.	7,943	635	623	910	1,193	1,060	1,116	1,596	810
June	8,808	627	747	1,477	1,268	1,322	1,142	1,352	873

Source: Personnel Statistics Division, DCS/Comptroller, Hq USAF

TABLE 217 — ACCESSION STATUS CHANGES OF MILITARY PERSONNEL — FY 1953

(An accession status change is the loss and immediate gain of the same individual and does not affect the strength of the Air Force. Table includes SCARWAF).

Type of Change	Total	Jul (1952)	Aug	Sep	Oct	Nov	Dec	Jan (1953)	Feb	Mar	Apr	May	Jun
Accession Status Changes - Total	39,786	5,366	6,244	6,713	5,111	3,537	3,393	2,316	1,911	1,604	1,131	1,017	1,443
Officer	9,669	278	1,192	1,777	1,593	1,036	918	604	446	384	383	365	693
Warrant Officer	8	-	2	2	-	1	-	-	1	-	-	-	2
Enlisted	30,109	5,088	5,050	4,934	3,518	2,500	2,475	1,712	1,464	1,220	748	652	748
Immediate Reenlistments - Total	21,831	3,026	3,042	3,180	2,464	1,986	2,162	1,476	1,313	1,126	704	620	732
Officer	-	-	-	-	-	-	-	-	-	-	-	-	-
Warrant Officer	-	-	-	-	-	-	-	-	-	-	-	-	-
Enlisted	21,831	3,026	3,042	3,180	2,464	1,986	2,162	1,476	1,313	1,126	704	620	732
Upon Expiration of Unextended Term of Service - Total	13,769	2,068	2,095	2,158	1,453	1,094	1,311	875	769	724	392	374	456
Officer	-	-	-	-	-	-	-	-	-	-	-	-	-
Warrant Officer	-	-	-	-	-	-	-	-	-	-	-	-	-
Enlisted	13,769	2,068	2,095	2,158	1,453	1,094	1,311	875	769	724	392	374	456
Upon Expiration of Extended Term of Service - Total	3,973	354	437	526	541	479	446	326	273	216	155	106	114
Officer	-	-	-	-	-	-	-	-	-	-	-	-	-
Warrant Officer	-	-	-	-	-	-	-	-	-	-	-	-	-
Enlisted	3,973	354	437	526	541	479	446	326	273	216	155	106	114
Prior to Expiration Term of Service - Total	2,152	309	271	298	323	230	138	128	114	86	81	80	94
Officer	-	-	-	-	-	-	-	-	-	-	-	-	-
Warrant Officer	-	-	-	-	-	-	-	-	-	-	-	-	-
Enlisted	2,152	309	271	298	323	230	138	128	114	86	81	80	94
Upon Expiration Term of Service (Non-Reg) - Total	1,054	172	95	71	68	87	211	90	112	62	36	21	29
Officer	-	-	-	-	-	-	-	-	-	-	-	-	-
Warrant Officer	-	-	-	-	-	-	-	-	-	-	-	-	-
Enlisted	1,054	172	95	71	68	87	211	90	112	62	36	21	29
Prior to Expiration Term of Service (Non-Reg) - Total	883	123	144	127	79	96	56	57	45	38	40	39	39
Officer	-	-	-	-	-	-	-	-	-	-	-	-	-
Warrant Officer	-	-	-	-	-	-	-	-	-	-	-	-	-
Enlisted	883	123	144	127	79	96	56	57	45	38	40	39	39
Immediate Recalls - Total	10,034	329	1,222	1,819	1,617	1,099	984	659	456	387	391	368	703
Officer	9,669	278	1,192	1,777	1,593	1,036	918	604	446	384	383	365	693
Warrant Officer	8	-	2	2	-	1	-	-	1	-	-	-	2
Enlisted	357	51	28	40	24	62	66	55	9	3	8	3	8

Retired Transferred to AFRes and Immediatley Ordered to Active Military Service - Total	248	39	20	34	16	46	48	39	2	-	2	2	-
Officer	-	-	-	-	-	-	-	-	-	-	-	-	-
Warrant Officer	-	-	-	-	-	-	-	-	-	-	-	-	-
Enlisted	248	39	20	34	16	46	48	39	2	-	2	2	-
Separated and Immediately Recalled in Volunteer Indefinite Status (AFRes Officers) - Total	9,677	278	1,194	1,779	1,593	1,037	918	604	447	384	383	365	695
Officer	9,669	278	1,192	1,777	1,593	1,036	918	604	446	384	383	365	693
Warrant Officer	8	-	2	2	-	1	-	-	1	-	-	-	2
Enlisted	-	-	-	-	-	-	-	-	-	-	-	-	-
Angus and AFRes Separated and Volunteer for 24 Months Active Military Service - Total	109	12	8	6	8	16	18	16	7	3	6	1	8
Officer	-	-	-	-	-	-	-	-	-	-	-	-	-
Warrant Officer	-	-	-	-	-	-	-	-	-	-	-	-	-
Enlisted	109	12	8	6	8	16	18	16	7	3	6	1	8
Term of Service Extended - Total	7,921	2,011	1,980	1,714	1,030	452	247	181	142	91	36	29	8
Officer	-	-	-	-	-	-	-	-	-	-	-	-	-
Warrant Officer	-	-	-	-	-	-	-	-	-	-	-	-	-
Enlisted	7,921	2,011	1,980	1,714	1,030	452	274	181	142	91	36	29	8

Source: Personnel Statistics Division, DCS/Comptroller, Hq USAF

TABLE 218 — ACCESSION STATUS CHANGES OF FEMALE MILITARY PERSONNEL — FY 1953

(An accession status change is the loss and immediate gain of the same individual and does not affect the strength of the Air Force. Figures in parenthesis represent WAF Officers only and are included in open figures which include both AN/WS and WAF Officers. Data in table below included in Table Table includes SCARWAF).

Type of Change	Total	Jul (1952)	Aug	Sep	Oct	Nov	Dec	Jan (1953)	Feb	Mar	Apr	May	Jun
ACCESSION STATUS CHANGE - TOTAL	(58) 331	31	(3) 57	(11) 59	(13) 38	(4) 23	(2) 27	(6) 21	(1) 19	(2) 31	(3) 8	(1) 1	(12) 16
Officer AN/WS WAF	(58) 62	1	(3) 3	(11) 11	(13) 13	(4) 4	(2) 2	(6) 6	(1) 2	(2) 4	(3) 3	(1) 1	(12) 12
Warrant Officer	-	-	-	-	-	-	-	-	-	-	-	-	-
Enlisted	269	30	54	48	25	19	25	15	17	27	5	-	4
IMMEDIATE REENLISTMENT - TOTAL	214	20	49	26	18	13	22	14	16	27	5	-	4
Officers	-	-	-	-	-	-	-	-	-	-	-	-	-
Warrant Officers	-	-	-	-	-	-	-	-	-	-	-	-	-
Enlisted	214	20	49	26	18	13	22	14	16	27	5	-	4
Upon Expiration of Unextended Term of Service - Total	128	6	27	21	13	8	11	7	10	22	3	-	-
Officers	-	-	-	-	-	-	-	-	-	-	-	-	-
Warrant Officers	-	-	-	-	-	-	-	-	-	-	-	-	-
Enlisted	128	6	27	21	13	8	11	7	10	22	3	-	-
Upon Expiration of Extended Term of Service - Total	40	6	13	5	4	1	5	2	1	-	1	-	2
Officers	-	-	-	-	-	-	-	-	-	-	-	-	-
Warrant Officers	-	-	-	-	-	-	-	-	-	-	-	-	-
Enlisted	40	6	13	5	4	1	5	2	1	-	1	-	2
Prior To Expiration Term of Service - Total	17	4	4	-	1	2	1	2	1	1	-	-	1
Officers	-	-	-	-	-	-	-	-	-	-	-	-	-
Warrant Officers	-	-	-	-	-	-	-	-	-	-	-	-	-
Enlisted	17	4	4	-	1	2	1	2	1	1	-	-	1
Upon Expiration Term of Service (Non-Reg) - Total	17	-	-	-	-	1	3	3	4	4	1	-	1
Officers	-	-	-	-	-	-	-	-	-	-	-	-	-
Warrant Officers	-	-	-	-	-	-	-	-	-	-	-	-	-
Enlisted	17	-	-	-	-	1	3	3	4	4	1	-	1
Prior to Expiration Term of Service (Non-Reg) - Total	12	4	5	-	-	1	2	-	-	-	-	-	-
Officers	-	-	-	-	-	-	-	-	-	-	-	-	-
Warrant Officers	-	-	-	-	-	-	-	-	-	-	-	-	-
Enlisted	12	4	5	-	-	1	2	-	-	-	-	-	-
IMMEDIATE RECALL - TOTAL	(58) 65	1	(3) 3	(11) 12	(13) 13	(4) 4	(2) 3	(6) 7	(1) 2	(2) 4	(3) 3	(1) 1	(12) 12
Officers	(58) 62	1	(3) 3	(11) 11	(13) 13	(4) 4	(2) 2	(6) 6	(1) 2	(2) 4	(3) 3	(1) 1	(12) 12
Warrant Officers	-	-	-	-	-	-	-	-	-	-	-	-	-
Enlisted	3	-	-	1	-	-	1	1	-	-	-	-	-

Retired Transferred to AFRes and Immediately Ordered to Active Duty - Total	-	-	-	-	-	-	-	-	-	-	-	-	-
Officers	-	-	-	-	-	-	-	-	-	-	-	-	-
Warrant Officers	-	-	-	-	-	-	-	-	-	-	-	-	-
Enlisted	-	-	-	-	-	-	-	-	-	-	-	-	-
Separated and Immediately Recalled in Volunteer Indefinite Status (AFR Officers) - Total	(58) 62	1	(3) 3	(11) 11	(13) 13	(4) 4	(2) 2	(6) 6	(1) 2	(2) 4	(3) 3	(1) 1	(12)12
Officers	(58) 62	1	(3) 3	(11) 11	(13) 13	(4) 4	(2) 2	(6) 6	(1) 2	(2) 4	(3) 3	(1) 1	(12)12
Warrant Officer	-	-	-	-	-	-	-	-	-	-	-	-	-
Enlisted	-	-	-	-	-	-	-	-	-	-	-	-	-
ANGUS and AFRes Separated and Volunteer for 24 Months Active Military Service - Total	3	-	-	1	-	-	1	1	-	-	-	-	-
Officers	-	-	-	-	-	-	-	-	-	-	-	-	-
Warrant Officers	-	-	-	-	-	-	-	-	-	-	-	-	-
Enlisted	3	-	-	1	-	-	1	1	-	-	-	-	-
TERM OF SERVICE EXTENDED - TOTAL	52	10	5	21	7	6	2	-	1	-	-	-	-
Officers	-	-	-	-	-	-	-	-	-	-	-	-	-
Warrant Officers	-	-	-	-	-	-	-	-	-	-	-	-	-
Enlisted	52	10	5	21	7	6	2	-	1	-	-	-	-

Source: Personnel Statistics Division, DCS/Comptroller, Hq USAF

TABLE 219 – LOSSES OF OFFICER PERSONNEL FROM COMMAND STRENGTH BY AERONAUTICAL STATUS, BY AGE GROUP – FY 1953

Aeronautical Status	Total	Age Group: Under 24	24 through 26	27 through 29	30 through 32	33 through 35	36 through 38	39 through 41	42 through 44	45 through 47	48 through 50	Over 50
FY 1953 - Total	26,286	1,501	2,918	6,509	6,684	4,518	2,122	770	467	336	176	285
Pilots	7,479	190	419	2,134	2,553	1,481	518	63	29	25	15	52
Other Rated	4,303	51	93	1,474	1,439	899	312	14	3	3	2	13
Non-Rated	14,504	1,260	2,406	2,901	2,692	2,138	1,292	693	435	308	159	220
1952												
July - Total	1,575	37	141	359	436	288	143	62	28	25	12	44
Pilots	442	7	32	117	137	95	34	6	2	3	2	7
Other Rated	297	1	6	90	118	60	18	3	-	-	-	1
Non-Rated	836	29	103	152	181	133	91	53	26	22	10	36
August - Total	1,619	38	98	410	427	347	144	51	44	22	12	26
Pilots	441	9	13	134	143	84	38	5	4	3	2	6
Other Rated	298	1	-	105	100	71	20	-	-	-	-	1
Non-Rated	880	28	85	171	184	192	86	46	40	19	10	19
September - Total	1,892	47	188	507	476	341	185	53	28	33	10	24
Pilots	527	9	47	155	161	102	40	4	2	2	-	5
Other Rated	364	2	8	130	119	78	26	-	-	-	-	1
Non-Rated	1,001	36	133	222	196	161	119	49	26	31	10	18
October - Total	2,126	45	182	575	569	373	203	76	32	28	23	20
Pilots	583	11	41	169	202	109	42	4	2	1	-	2
Other Rated	333	2	9	122	106	65	27	-	-	1	-	1
Non-Rated	1,210	32	132	284	261	199	134	72	30	26	23	17
November - Total	2,131	45	215	549	561	439	152	71	44	25	9	21
Pilots	576	12	25	164	181	139	39	6	2	2	-	6
Other Rated	326	4	7	124	111	65	11	1	1	1	1	-
Non-Rated	1,229	29	183	261	269	235	102	64	41	22	8	15
December - Total	2,576	48	225	736	705	442	246	75	44	27	15	13
Pilots	903	15	29	295	332	157	58	7	3	3	2	2
Other Rated	490	7	13	168	158	96	46	1	1	-	-	-
Non-Rated	1,183	26	183	273	215	189	142	67	40	24	13	11
1953												
January - Total	2,717	66	230	750	748	491	213	79	61	41	18	20
Pilots	835	23	34	239	303	171	48	6	5	1	3	2
Other Rated	416	4	10	151	121	100	28	1	-	1	-	-
Non-Rated	1,466	39	186	360	324	220	137	72	56	39	15	18
February - Total	2,412	95	250	594	677	435	191	54	37	27	16	36
Pilots	708	10	25	200	269	134	48	3	-	3	3	13
Other Rated	439	5	9	148	147	93	34	2	-	-	-	1
Non-Rated	1,265	80	216	246	261	208	109	49	37	24	13	22
March - Total	2,634	238	327	619	644	433	199	76	29	25	20	24
Pilots	770	18	40	223	258	156	58	10	2	3	1	1
Other Rated	480	6	10	176	164	80	35	2	-	-	-	7
Non-Rated	1,384	214	277	220	222	197	106	64	27	22	19	16
April - Total	2,634	330	364	557	638	410	186	48	37	29	17	18
Pilots	779	23	36	202	291	157	56	6	3	1	-	4
Other Rated	510	7	10	165	170	108	45	3	1	-	1	-
Non-Rated	1,345	300	318	190	177	145	85	39	33	28	16	14
May - Total	1,453	212	263	277	282	209	94	41	33	19	7	16
Pilots	371	23	40	92	107	82	21	2	2	-	1	1
Other Rated	135	4	5	40	45	31	9	-	-	-	-	1
Non-Rated	947	185	218	145	130	96	64	39	31	19	6	14
June - Total	2,517	300	435	576	521	310	166	84	50	35	17	23
Pilots	544	30	57	144	169	95	36	4	2	3	1	3
Other Rated	215	8	6	55	80	52	13	1	-	-	-	-
Non-Rated	1,758	262	372	377	272	163	117	79	48	32	16	20

Source: Personnel Statistics Division, DCS/Comptroller, Headquarters, USAF

TABLE 220 — REENLISTMENTS WITH PERMANENT CHANGE OF STATIONS — FY 1953

(Figures in unit column indicate individuals of an intact unit; table includes SCARWAF).

Month	Total			Permanent Party		Pipeline		
	Total	(Individuals)	Units	(Individuals)	Units	Student (Individuals)	Transient (Individuals)	Patient (Individuals)
FY 1953 - Total	1,353,491	1,322,175	31,316	486,294	31,316	326,482	502,346	7,053
Intra	612,698	598,354	14,344	283,435	14,344	182,977	129,320	2,622
Inter	740,793	723,821	16,972	202,859	16,972	143,505	373,026	4,431
July (1952) - Total	125,233	119,735	5,498	42,142	5,498	32,424	44,652	517
Intra	58,434	54,189	4,245	24,799	4,245	17,671	11,622	97
Inter	66,799	65,546	1,253	17,343	1,253	14,753	33,030	420
August - Total	129,085	124,880	4,205	46,245	4,205	33,757	44,453	525
Intra	56,600	54,434	2,166	24,899	2,166	18,557	10,873	105
Inter	72,485	70,446	2,039	21,246	2,039	15,200	33,580	420
September - Total	121,263	121,008	255	43,651	255	34,551	42,224	582
Intra	55,364	55,276	88	24,835	88	18,554	11,776	111
Inter	65,899	65,732	167	18,816	167	15,997	30,448	471
October - Total	115,650	111,651	3,999	41,368	3,999	26,568	43,204	511
Intra	47,626	45,495	2,131	18,866	2,131	13,650	12,919	60
Inter	68,024	66,156	1,868	22,502	1,868	12,918	30,285	451
November - Total	113,395	110,354	3,041	47,090	3,041	22,161	40,724	379
Intra	51,954	51,383	571	29,345	571	11,342	10,618	78
Inter	61,441	58,971	2,470	17,745	2,470	10,819	30,106	301
December - Total	114,208	113,335	873	37,424	873	25,577	48,279	2,055
Intra	45,281	44,807	474	22,404	474	9,694	11,021	1,688
Inter	68,927	68,528	399	15,020	399	15,883	37,258	367
January (1953) - Total	106,898	101,971	4,927	39,581	4,927	21,575	40,335	480
Intra	47,537	46,419	1,118	25,388	1,118	12,190	8,791	50
Inter	59,361	55,552	3,809	14,193	3,809	9,385	31,544	430
February - Total	104,772	102,413	2,359	37,944	2,359	21,615	42,375	479
Intra	49,925	48,157	1,768	24,902	1,768	12,508	10,614	133
Inter	54,847	54,256	591	13,042	591	9,107	31,761	346
March - Total	108,236	107,886	350	38,247	350	23,461	45,758	420
Intra	47,998	47,852	146	22,098	146	13,790	11,873	91
Inter	60,238	60,034	204	16,149	204	9,671	33,885	329
April - Total	107,895	104,637	3,258	37,462	3,258	25,040	41,788	347
Intra	49,300	48,924	376	21,296	376	16,148	11,403	77
Inter	58,595	55,713	2,882	16,166	2,882	8,892	30,385	270
May - Total	107,044	105,589	1,455	37,124	1,455	31,572	36,534	359
Intra	55,318	54,057	1,261	22,057	1,261	21,902	10,026	72
Inter	51,726	51,532	194	15,067	194	9,670	26,508	287
June - Total	99,812	98,716	1,096	38,116	1,096	28,181	32,020	399
Intra	47,361	47,361	-	22,546	-	16,971	7,784	60
Inter	52,451	51,355	1,096	15,570	1,096	11,210	24,236	339

Source: Personnel Statistics Division, DCS/Comptroller, Hq USAF

TABLE 221 — ENLISTMENTS AND REENLISTMENTS BY GRADE — FY 1953

(Excludes Reenlistments in the Army for SCARWAF duty)

Type of Enlistment or Reenlistment by Date	Total	Master Sergeant	Technical Sergeant	Staff Sergeant	Airman First Class	Airman Second Class	Airman Third Class	Basic Airman
FY 1953 - Total	175,567	6,822	6,623	12,183	6,325	2,951	6,642	134,021
No Prior Service Enlistment. . .	130,822	-	3	6	9	45	442	130,317
Enlistment for OCS or Avn Cadet.	3,503	1	1	3	11	16	237	3,234
Prior Service Enlistment	10,059	261	349	869	1,508	1,373	5,383	316
Reenlistment Within 30 or 90 Days	9,906	2,189	2,188	3,561	1,355	451	132	30
Immediate Reenlistment	21,277	4,371	4,082	7,744	3,442	1,066	448	124
1952								
July - Total.	20,805	382	511	1,513	793	284	798	16,524
No Prior Service Enlistment. . . .	16,314	-	1	2	2	6	96	16,207
Enlistment for OCS or Avn Cadet. .	273	1	1	1	-	-	13	257
Prior Service Enlistment	999	18	26	131	105	67	605	47
Reenlistment Within 30 Days. . . .	262	34	30	124	43	20	11	-
Immediate Reenlistment	2,957	329	453	1,255	643	191	73	13
August - Total.	20,297	527	631	1,493	897	332	610	15,807
No Prior Service Enlistment. . . .	15,493	-	-	-	-	13	38	15,442
Enlistment for OCS or Avn Cadet. .	331	-	-	-	-	-	11	320
Prior Service Enlistment	927	28	30	131	119	108	485	26
Reenlistment Within 30 Days. . . .	601	134	93	248	98	20	6	2
Immediate Reenlistment	2,945	365	508	1,114	680	191	70	17
September - Total	17,871	837	703	1,563	871	263	488	13,146
No Prior Service Enlistment. . . .	12,971	-	-	-	1	2	30	12,938
Enlistment for OCS or Avn Cadet. .	179	-	-	-	-	1	7	171
Prior Service Enlistment	696	32	33	85	101	50	377	18
Reenlistment Within 30 Days. . . .	925	303	181	278	115	35	7	6
Immediate Reenlistment	3,100	502	489	1,200	654	175	67	13
October - Total	15,626	852	689	1,381	622	212	604	11,266
No Prior Service Enlistment. . . .	10,730	-	-	2	-	5	43	10,680
Enlistment for OCS or Avn Cadet. .	566	-	-	-	1	1	11	553
Prior Service Enlistment	793	32	46	89	78	54	486	8
Reenlistment Within 30 Days. . . .	1,124	296	221	430	141	26	10	-
Immediate Reenlistment	2,413	524	422	860	402	126	54	25
November - Total.	12,401	794	623	1,113	483	187	480	8,721
No Prior Service Enlistment. . . .	8,268	-	1	-	2	4	43	8,218
Enlistment for OCS or Avn Cadet. .	491	-	-	-	2	1	13	475
Prior Service Enlistment	609	16	28	64	66	43	381	11
Reenlistment Within 30 Days. . . .	1,103	230	240	404	155	56	13	5
Immediate Reenlistment	1,930	548	354	645	258	83	30	12
December - Total.	13,522	774	761	1,244	522	162	498	9,561
No Prior Service Enlistment. . . .	9,470	-	1	1	-	1	26	9,441
Enlistment for OCS or Avn Cadet. .	107	-	-	-	1	-	9	97
Prior Service Enlistment	691	32	37	78	83	41	408	12
Reenlistment Within 30 Days. . . .	1,128	221	278	424	143	39	18	5
Immediate Reenlistment	2,126	521	445	741	295	81	37	6

(CONTINUED)

TABLE 221 – ENLISTMENTS AND REENLISTMENTS BY GRADE – FY 1953 (Continued)

(Excludes Reenlistments in the Army for SCARWAF duty)

Type of Enlistment or Reenlistment by Date	Total	Master Sergeant	Technical Sergeant	Staff Sergeant	Airman First Class	Airman Second Class	Airman Third Class	Basic Airman
1953								
January - Total	14,841	602	675	1,067	511	288	883	10,815
No Prior Service Enlistment	10,445	-	-	1	1	2	41	10,400
Enlistment for OCS or Avn Cadet	474	-	-	1	2	2	112	357
Prior Service Enlistment	1,206	25	41	87	153	156	698	46
Reenlistment Within 30 Days	1,298	223	295	451	214	95	15	5
Immediate Reenlistment	1,418	354	339	527	141	33	17	7
February - Total	18,874	552	577	841	474	283	612	15,535
No Prior Service Enlistment	15,185	-	-	-	2	6	29	15,148
Enlistment for OCS or Avn Cadet	363	-	-	-	-	4	16	343
Prior Service Enlistment	1,082	23	27	67	208	180	540	37
Reenlistment Within 30 Days	960	165	234	343	137	62	15	4
Immediate Reenlistment	1,284	364	316	431	127	31	12	3
March - Total	17,427	483	474	648	383	332	599	14,508
No Prior Service Enlistment	14,257	-	-	-	-	4	36	14,217
Enlistment for OCS or Avn Cadet	282	-	-	-	2	2	22	256
Prior Service Enlistment	938	12	27	51	175	191	454	28
Reenlistment Within 90 Days	848	180	195	287	129	37	19	1
Immediate Reenlistment	1,102	291	252	310	77	98	68	6
April - Total	12,395	367	313	433	273	228	459	10,322
No Prior Service Enlistment	10,167	-	-	-	-	1	32	10,134
Enlistment for OCS or Avn Cadet	151	-	-	-	2	3	8	138
Prior Service Enlistment	830	19	14	32	149	167	402	47
Reenlistment Within 90 Days	560	137	139	172	65	36	10	1
Immediate Reenlistment	687	211	160	229	57	21	7	2
May - Total	6,064	301	305	404	227	193	311	4,323
No Prior Service Enlistment	4,212	-	-	-	-	1	18	4,193
Enlistment for OCS or Avn Cadet	108	-	-	-	1	-	6	101
Prior Service Enlistment	635	12	16	26	126	159	276	20
Reenlistment Within 90 Days	510	123	131	189	48	13	6	-
Immediate Reenlistment	599	166	158	189	52	20	5	9
June - Total	5,444	351	361	483	269	187	300	3,493
No Prior Service Enlistment	3,310	-	-	-	1	-	10	3,299
Enlistment for OCS or Avn Cadet	178	-	-	1	-	2	9	166
Prior Service Enlistment	653	12	24	28	145	157	271	16
Reenlistment Within 90 Days	587	143	151	211	67	12	2	1
Immediate Reenlistment	716	196	186	243	56	16	8	11

Source: Personnel Statistics Division, DCS/Comptroller, Headquarters USAF

308700 O - 54 - 27

TABLE 222 — WAF ENLISTMENTS AND REENLISTMENTS BY GRADE — FY 1953

(Excludes reenlistments in the Army for SCARWAF duty. Figures in parentheses indicate Negro personnel and are included in the open figures. Data in table below is included in Table 221)

Type of Enlistment or Reenlistment by Date	Total Enlistments	Master Sergeant	Technical Sergeant	Staff Sergeant	Airmen First Class	Airmen Second Class	Airmen Third Class	Basic Airmen
FY 1953 - TOTAL . . .	(529) 5,141	(1) 26	59	(6) 120	(3) 45	(1) 35	(1) 35	(517) 4,821
No Prior Service Enlmt .	(516) 4,813	-	-	1	4	4	10	(516) 4,794
Enlmt for OCS or Avn Cadet	(1) 29	-	-	1	-	-	4	(1) 24
Prior Service Enlistment	(1) 40	1	1	5	5	13	(1) 12	3
Reenl Within 30 or 90 Days	46	2	15	23	5	1	-	-
Immediate Reenlistment .	(11) 213	(1) 23	43	(6) 90	(3) 31	(1) 17	9	-
1952								
July - Total.	(106) 834	2	7	(1) 11	5	3	5	(105) 801
No Prior Service Enlmt . .	(105) 808	-	-	-	2	1	4	(105) 801
Enlmt for OCS or Avn Cadet	-	-	-	-	-	-	-	-
Prior Service Enlistment .	6	1	-	1	1	2	1	-
Reenlmt Within 30 Days . .	-	-	-	-	-	-	-	-
Immediate Reenlistment . .	(1) 20	1	7	(1) 10	2	-	-	-
August - Total. . . .	(85) 756	9	13	(4) 26	(2) 5	3	5	(79) 695
No Prior Service Enlmt .	(79) 694	-	-	-	-	-	1	(79) 693
Enlmt for OCS or Avn Cadet	-	-	-	-	-	-	-	-
Prior Service Enlistment .	8	-	-	1	-	2	3	2
Reenlmt Within 30 Days . .	5	1	3	1	-	-	-	-
Immediate Reenlistment . .	(6) 49	8	10	(4) 24	(2) 5	1	1	-
September - Total . .	(123) 828	5	11	13	7	2	2	(123) 788
No Prior Service Enlmt . .	(122) 779	-	-	-	-	-	1	(122) 778
Enlmt for OCS or Avn Cadet	(1) 10	-	-	-	-	-	-	(1) 10
Prior Service Enlistment .	3	-	-	-	1	1	1	-
Reenlmt Within 30 Days . .	10	-	6	4	-	-	-	-
Immediate Reenlistment . .	26	5	5	9	6	1	-	-
October - Total . . .	(72) 682	-	6	(1) 16	2	(1) 4	2	(70) 652
No Prior Service Enlmt . .	(70) 655	-	-	1	-	1	1	(70) 652
Enlmt for OCS or Avn Cadet	-	-	-	-	-	-	-	-
Prior Service Enlistment .	3	-	-	-	-	2	1	-
Reenlmt Within 30 Days . .	7	-	2	5	-	-	-	-
Immediate Reenlistment . .	(2) 17	-	4	(1) 10	2	(1) 1	-	-
November - Total . .	(49) 489	-	6	7	(1) 2	3	2	(48) 469
No Prior Service Enlmt . .	(48) 470	-	-	-	-	1	-	(48) 469
Enlmt for OCS or Avn Cadet	-	-	-	-	-	-	-	-
Prior Service Enlistment .	2	-	-	-	-	-	2	-
Reenlmt Within 30 Days . .	4	-	3	-	1	-	-	-
Immediate Reenlistment . .	(1) 13	-	3	7	(1) 1	2	-	-
December - Total . .	(17) 148	1	7	12	8	2	(1) 1	(16) 117
No Prior Service Enlmt . .	(16) 114	-	-	-	-	-	-	(16) 114
Enlmt for OCS or Avn Cadet	3	-	-	-	-	-	-	3
Prior Service Enlistment .	(1) 4	-	1	-	1	1	(1) 1	-
Reenlmt Within 30 Days . .	5	-	-	3	2	-	-	-
Immediate Reenlistment . .	22	1	6	9	5	1	-	-

(CONTINUED)

TABLE 222 – WAF ENLISTMENTS AND REENLISTMENTS BY GRADE – FY 1953 (Continued)

(Excludes reenlistments in the Army for SCARWAF duty. Figures in parentheses indicate Negro personnel and are included in the open figures. Data in table below is included in Table 221)

Type of Enlistment or Reenlistment, by Date	Total	Master Sergeant	Technical Sergeant	Staff Sergeant	Airman First Class	Airman Second Class	Airman Third Class	Basic Airmen
1953								
January - Total. . .	(34) 364	(1) 2	5	7	4	2	1	(33) 343
No Prior Service Enlmt.	(33) 342	-	-	-	1	-	1	(33) 340
Enlmt for OCS or Avn Cadet	3	-	-	-	-	-	-	3
Prior Service Enlistment	-	-	-	-	-	-	-	-
Reenlmt Within 30 Days.	5	1	-	2	1	1	-	-
Immediate Reenlistment.	(1) 14	(1) 1	5	5	2	1	-	-
February - Total . .	(11) 230	5	-	12	5	2	2	(11) 204
No Prior Service Enlmt. .	(11) 206	-	-	-	1	-	1	(11) 204
Enlmt for OCS or Avn Cadet	-	-	-	-	-	-	-	-
Prior Service Enlistment.	5	-	-	2	-	2	1	-
Reenlmt Within 30 Days. .	3	-	-	3	-	-	-	-
Immediate Reenlistment. .	16	5	-	7	4	-	-	-
March - Total	(11) 280	1	1	8	4	12	13	(11) 241
No Prior Service Enlmt. .	(11) 235	-	-	-	-	1	-	(11) 234
Enlmt for OCS or Avn Cadet	10	-	-	-	-	-	4	6
Prior Service Enlistment.	4	-	-	-	-	1	2	1
Reenlmt Within 90 Days. .	4	-	-	4	-	-	-	-
Immediate Reenlistment. .	27	1	1	4	4	10	7	-
April - Total	(5) 160	1	2	3	-	2	-	(5) 152
No Prior Service Enlmt. .	(5) 152	-	-	-	-	-	-	(5) 152
Enlmt for OCS or Avn Cadet	-	-	-	-	-	-	-	-
Prior Service Enlistment.	2	-	-	-	-	2	-	-
Reenlmt Within 90 Days. .	1	-	1	-	-	-	-	-
Immediate Reenlistment. .	5	1	1	3	-	-	-	-
May - Total	(6) 117	-	-	-	-	-	-	(6) 117
No Prior Service Enlmt. .	(6) 117	-	-	-	-	-	-	(6) 117
Enlmt for OCS or Avn Cadet	-	-	-	-	-	-	-	-
Prior Service Enlistment.	-	-	-	-	-	-	-	-
Reenlmt Within 90 Days. .	-	-	-	-	-	-	-	-
Immediate Reenlistment. .	-	-	-	-	-	-	-	-
June - Total	(10) 253	-	1	5	3	-	2	(10) 242
No Prior Service Enlmt. .	(10) 241	-	-	-	-	-	1	(10) 240
Enlmt for OCS or Avn Cadet	3	-	-	1	-	-	-	2
Prior Service Enlistment.	3	-	-	1	2	-	-	-
Reenlmt Within 90 Days. .	2	-	-	1	1	-	-	-
Immediate Reenlistment. .	4	-	1	2	-	-	1	-

Source: Personnel Statistics Division, DCS/Comptroller, Headquarters USAF

TABLE 223 – NEGRO ENLISTMENTS AND REENLISTMENTS BY GRADE – FY 1953

(Excludes reenlistments in the Army for SCARWAF duty. Data in table below is included in Table 221)

Type of Enlistment or Reenlistment by Date	Total Enlist-ments	Master Sergeant	Technical Sergeant	Staff Sergeant	Airman First Class	Airman Second Class	Airman Third Class	Basic Airman
FY 1953 - Total	18,305	72	186	873	840	449	1,084	14,801
No Prior Service Enlistment. . .	14,691	-	-	-	-	3	48	14,640
Enlistment for OCS or Avn Cadet.	66	-	-	-	-	-	3	63
Prior Service Enlistment .	1,214	2	9	30	76	138	900	59
Reenl Within 30 or 90 Days . . .	591	20	47	235	170	86	28	5
Immediate Reenlistment	1,743	50	130	608	594	222	105	34
1952								
July - Total	3,216	5	21	120	140	60	140	2,730
No Prior Service Enlistment . . .	2,721	-	-	-	-	-	15	2,706
Enlistment for OCS or Avn Cadet. .	1	-	-	-	-	-	-	1
Prior Service Enlistment . . .	134	-	2	5	4	7	98	18
Reenlistment Within 30 Days . . .	17	-	1	5	3	5	3	-
Immediate Reenlistment	343	5	18	110	133	48	24	5
August - Total	2,747	7	15	96	140	46	105	2,338
No Prior Service Enlistment . . .	2,333	-	-	-	-	-	5	2,328
Enlistment for OCS or Avn Cadet. .	2	-	-	-	-	-	-	2
Prior Service Enlistment . . .	98	1	-	2	9	7	74	5
Reenlistment Within 30 Days . . .	34	-	2	13	12	1	5	1
Immediate Reenlistment	280	6	13	81	119	38	21	2
September - Total	2,102	7	23	137	133	43	80	1,679
No Prior Service Enlistment . . .	1,666	-	-	-	-	-	1	1,665
Enlistment for OCS or Avn Cadet. .	5	-	-	-	-	-	1	4
Prior Service Enlistment . . .	74	-	-	2	1	1	65	5
Reenlistment Within 30 Days . . .	39	2	5	18	10	3	1	-
Immediate Reenlistment	318	5	18	117	122	39	12	5
October - Total	1,684	8	19	112	90	34	105	1,316
No Prior Service Enlistment . . .	1,297	-	-	-	-	-	3	1,294
Enlistment for OCS or Avn Cadet. .	8	-	-	-	-	-	-	8
Prior Service Enlistment	102	-	1	4	4	5	88	-
Reenlistment Within 30 Days. . . .	82	3	7	43	21	6	2	-
Immediate Reenlistment	195	5	11	65	65	23	12	14
November - Total	1,205	10	25	90	65	36	66	913
No Prior Service Enlistment. . . .	895	-	-	-	-	-	7	888
Enlistment for OCS or Avn Cadet. .	22	-	-	-	-	-	-	22
Prior Service Enlistment	68	-	-	9	2	4	52	1
Reenlistment Within 30 Days. . . .	72	2	7	22	26	15	-	-
Immediate Reenlistment	148	8	18	59	37	17	7	2
December - Total	1,391	9	23	93	78	30	77	1,081
No Prior Service Enlistment . . .	1,073	-	-	-	-	-	1	1,072
Enlistment for OCS or Avn Cadet. .	8	-	-	-	-	-	-	8
Prior Service Enlistment	77	-	1	4	5	2	64	1
Reenlistment Within 30 Days. . . .	79	2	4	38	20	11	4	-
Immediate Reenlistment	154	7	18	51	53	17	8	-

(CONTINUED)

TABLE 223 —NEGRO ENLISTMENTS AND REENLISTMENTS BY GRADE — FY 1953 — (CONTINUED)

(Excludes reenlistments in the Army for SCARWAF duty. Data in table below is included in Table 221)

Type of Enlistment or Reenlistment by Date	Total Enlist-ments	Master Sergeant	Technical Sergeant	Staff Sergeant	Airman First Class	Airman Second Class	Airman Third Class	Basic Airman
1953								
January - Total	1,170	10	18	72	62	38	126	844
No Prior Service Enlistment. . . .	826	-	-	-	-	1	2	823
Enlistment for OCS or Avn Cadet. .	11	-	-	-	-	-	-	11
Prior Service Enlistment	151	-	2	1	8	13	119	8
Reenlistment Within 30 Days. . . .	92	4	5	33	33	14	2	1
Immediate Reenlistment	90	6	11	38	21	10	3	1
February - Total.	1,471	5	14	47	52	41	110	1,202
No Prior Service Enlistment. . . .	1,198	-	-	-	-	2	6	1,190
Enlistment for OCS or Avn Cadet. .	5	-	-	-	-	-	1	4
Prior Service Enlistment	134	1	-	1	10	20	96	6
Reenlistment Within 30 Days. . . .	67	1	5	18	21	15	5	2
Immediate Reenlistment	67	3	9	28	21	4	2	-
March - Total	1,434	5	10	34	38	47	91	1,209
No Prior Service Enlistment. . . .	1,208	-	-	-	-	-	3	1,205
Enlistment for OCS or Avn Cadet. .	1	-	-	-	-	-	1	-
Prior Service Enlistment	103	-	2	1	12	17	67	4
Reenlistment Within 90 Days. . . .	56	2	5	19	15	10	5	-
Immediate Reenlistment	66	3	3	14	11	20	15	-
April - Total	996	-	4	19	13	29	79	852
No Prior Service Enlistment. . . .	846	-	-	-	-	-	2	844
Enlistment for OCS or Avn Cadet. .	2	-	-	-	-	-	-	2
Prior Service Enlistment	112	-	-	-	9	21	77	5
Reenlistment Within 90 Days. . . .	15	-	2	6	2	4	-	1
Immediate Reenlistment	21	-	2	13	2	4	-	-
May - Total	493	-	7	23	14	19	49	381
No Prior Service Enlistment. . . .	376	-	-	-	-	-	3	373
Enlistment for OCS or Avn Cadet. .	-	-	-	-	-	-	-	-
Prior Service Enlistment	74	-	-	-	7	18	44	5
Reenlistment Within 90 Days. . . .	16	-	1	11	2	1	1	-
Immediate Reenlistment	27	-	6	12	5	-	1	3
June - Total.	396	6	7	30	15	26	56	256
No Prior Service Enlistment. . . .	252	-	-	-	-	-	-	252
Enlistment for OCS or Avn Cadet. .	1	-	-	-	-	-	-	1
Prior Service Enlistment	87	-	1	1	5	23	56	1
Reenlistment Within 90 Days. . . .	22	4	3	9	5	1	-	-
Immediate Reenlistment	34	2	3	20	5	2	-	2

Source: Personnel Statistics Division, DCS/Comptroller, Headquarters USAF

TABLE 224 — ENLISTMENTS AND REENLISTMENTS BY TERM — FY 1953

(Excludes Reenlistments in Army for SCARWAF Duty)

Type of Enlistment or Reenlistment by Date	Total	Term of Enlistment or Reenlistment					
		2 Years	3 Years	4 Years	5 Years	6 Years	Indefinite
FY 1953 - TOTAL	175,567	3,464	22,331	137,576	157	10,290	1,749
No Prior Service Enlistment	130,822	-	4,735	126,079	1	7	-
Enlistment for OCS or Avn Cadet	3,503	3,454	21	27	-	1	-
Prior Service Enlistment	10,059	-	282	9,040	22	709	6
Reenlistment Within 30 or 90 Days	9,906	-	5,889	1,313	51	2,295	358
Immediate Reenlistment	21,277	10	11,404	1,117	83	7,278	1,385
1952							
July - Total	20,805	271	2,251	16,592	13	1,444	234
No Prior Service Enlistment	16,314	-	805	15,508	-	1	-
Enlistment for OCS or Avn Cadet	273	271	-	2	-	-	-
Prior Service Enlistment	999	-	4	911	1	83	-
Reenlistment Within 30 Days	262	-	124	50	-	70	18
Immediate Reenlistment	2,957	-	1,318	121	12	1,290	216
August - Total	20,297	335	2,489	15,752	10	1,435	276
No Prior Service Enlistment	15,493	-	684	14,808	-	1	-
Enlistment for OCS or Avn Cadet	331	331	-	-	-	-	-
Prior Service Enlistment	927	-	38	791	1	97	-
Reenlistment Within 30 Days	601	-	321	61	-	176	43
Immediate Reenlistment	2,945	4	1,446	92	9	1,161	233
September - Total	17,871	171	2,889	13,020	16	1,514	261
No Prior Service Enlistment	12,971	-	749	12,221	-	1	-
Enlistment for OCS or Avn Cadet	179	169	10	-	-	-	-
Prior Service Enlistment	696	-	32	598	-	66	-
Reenlistment Within 30 Days	925	-	583	103	4	201	34
Immediate Reenlistment	3,100	2	1,515	98	12	1,246	227
October - Total	15,626	569	2,647	11,020	15	1,170	205
No Prior Service Enlistment	10,730	-	655	10,074	1	-	-
Enlistment for OCS or Avn Cadet	566	566	-	-	-	-	-
Prior Service Enlistment	793	-	47	685	2	59	-
Reenlistment Within 30 Days	1,124	-	702	140	4	233	45
Immediate Reenlistment	2,413	3	1,243	121	8	878	160
November - Total	12,401	491	2,206	8,569	4	992	139
No Prior Service Enlistment	8,268	-	441	7,827	-	-	-
Enlistment for OCS or Avn Cadet	491	491	-	-	-	-	-
Prior Service Enlistment	609	-	10	541	-	58	-
Reenlistment Within 30 Days	1,103	-	661	119	2	293	28
Immediate Reenlistment	1,930	-	1,094	82	2	641	111
December - Total	13,522	98	2,154	10,110	34	976	150
No Prior Service Enlistment	9,470	-	115	9,354	-	1	-
Enlistment for OCS or Avn Cadet	107	98	3	6	-	-	-
Prior Service Enlistment	691	-	46	553	10	76	6
Reenlistment Within 30 Days	1,128	-	720	89	12	271	36
Immediate Reenlistment	2,126	-	1,270	108	12	628	108

(CONTINUED)

TABLE 224 — ENLISTMENTS AND REENLISTMENTS BY TERM — FY 1953 (CONTINUED)

(Excludes Reenlistments in Army for SCARWAF Duty)

Type of Enlistment or Reenlistment by Date	Total	Term of Enlistment or Reenlistment					
		2 Years	3 Years	4 Years	5 Years	6 Years	Indefinite
1953							
January - Total	14,841	462	2,001	11,491	15	741	131
No Prior Service Enlistment	10,445	-	339	10,106	-	-	-
Enlistment for OCS or Avn Cadet	474	462	3	8	-	1	-
Prior Service Enlistment	1,206	-	28	1,104	4	70	-
Reenlistment Within 30 Days	1,298	-	746	203	7	296	46
Immediate Reenlistment	1,418	-	885	70	4	374	85
February - Total	18,874	362	1,640	16,204	7	571	90
No Prior Service Enlistment	15,185	-	205	14,979	-	1	-
Enlistment for OCS or Avn Cadet	363	362	-	1	-	-	-
Prior Service Enlistment	1,082	-	22	1,001	-	59	-
Reenlistment Within 30 Days	960	-	580	154	3	194	29
Immediate Reenlistment	1,284	-	833	69	4	317	61
March - Total	17,427	272	1,378	15,208	14	473	82
No Prior Service Enlistment	14,257	-	234	14,021	-	2	-
Enlistment for OCS or Avn Cadet	282	271	4	7	-	-	-
Prior Service Enlistment	938	-	15	874	1	48	-
Reenlistment Within 90 Days	848	-	516	122	5	179	26
Immediate Reenlistment	1,102	1	609	184	8	244	56
April - Total	12,395	151	862	10,962	6	343	71
No Prior Service Enlistment	10,167	-	152	10,015	-	-	-
Enlistment for OCS or Avn Cadet	151	151	-	-	-	-	-
Prior Service Enlistment	830	-	18	782	1	29	-
Reenlistment Within 90 Days	560	-	273	121	1	142	23
Immediate Reenlistment	687	-	419	44	4	172	48
May - Total	6,064	108	789	4,817	11	283	56
No Prior Service Enlistment	4,212	-	115	4,097	-	-	-
Enlistment for OCS or Avn Cadet	108	108	-	-	-	-	-
Prior Service Enlistment	635	-	12	594	2	27	-
Reenlistment Within 90 Days	510	-	317	66	5	110	12
Immediate Reenlistment	599	-	345	60	4	146	44
June - Total	5,444	174	1,025	3,831	12	348	54
No Prior Service Enlistment	3,310	-	241	3,069	-	-	-
Enlistment for OCS or Avn Cadet	178	174	1	3	-	-	-
Prior Service Enlistment	653	-	10	606	-	37	-
Reenlistment Within 90 Days	587	-	346	85	8	130	18
Immediate Reenlistment	716	-	427	68	4	181	36

Source: Personnel Statistics Division, DCS/Comptroller, Hq USAF

TABLE 225 – WAF ENLISTMENTS AND REENLISTMENTS BY TERM – FY 1953

(Excludes reenlistments in the Army for SCARWAF duty. Figures in parentheses indicate Negro personnel and are included in the open figures. Data are included in Table 224)

Type of Enlistment or Reenlistment by Date	Total	Term of Enlistment or Reenlistment					
		2 Years	3 Years	4 Years	5 Years	6 Years	Indefinite
FY 1953 - TOTAL	(529) 5,141	-	(521) 4,968	(5) 108	(1) 1	(2) 45	19
No Prior Service Enlistment	(516) 4,813	-	(512) 4,734	(4) 79	-	-	-
Enlmt for OCS or Avn Cadet	(1) 29	-	(1) 20	9	-	-	-
Prior Service Enlistment	(1) 40	-	(1) 37	1	-	2	-
Reenlmt Within 30 or 90 Days	46	-	31	4	-	7	4
Immediate Reenlistment	(11) 213	-	(7) 146	(1) 15	(1) 1	(2) 36	15
1952							
July - Total	(106) 834	-	(104) 821	(1) 8	(1) 1	3	1
No Prior Service Enlistment	(105) 808	-	(104) 805	(1) 3	-	-	-
Enlistment for OCS or Avn Cadet	-	-	-	-	-	-	-
Prior Service Enlistment	6	-	4	1	-	1	-
Reenlistment Within 30 Days	-	-	-	-	-	-	-
Immediate Reenlistment	(1) 20	-	12	4	(1) 1	2	1
August - Total	(85) 756	-	(83) 730	13	-	(2) 7	6
No Prior Service Enlistment	(79) 694	-	(79) 684	10	-	-	-
Enlistment for OCS or Avn Cadet	-	-	-	-	-	-	-
Prior Service Enlistment	8	-	8	-	-	-	-
Reenlistment Within 30 Days	5	-	1	2	-	-	2
Immediate Reenlistment	(6) 49	-	(4) 37	1	-	(2) 7	4
September - Total	(123) 828	-	(122) 786	(1) 30	-	8	4
No Prior Service Enlistment	(122) 779	-	(121) 749	(1) 30	-	-	-
Enlistment for OCS or Avn Cadet	(1) 10	-	(1) 10	-	-	-	-
Prior Service Enlistment	3	-	3	-	-	-	-
Reenlistment Within 30 Days	10	-	10	-	-	-	-
Immediate Reenlistment	26	-	14	-	-	8	4
October - Total	(72) 682	-	(71) 674	(1) 4	-	1	3
No Prior Service Enlistment	(70) 655	-	(70) 655	-	-	-	-
Enlistment for OCS or Avn Cadet	-	-	-	-	-	-	-
Prior Service Enlistment	3	-	3	-	-	-	-
Reenlistment Within 30 Days	7	-	5	1	-	-	1
Immediate Reenlistment	(2) 17	-	(1) 11	(1) 3	-	1	2
November - Total	(49) 489	-	(47) 454	(2) 29	-	5	1
No Prior Service Enlistment	(48) 470	-	(46) 441	(2) 29	-	-	-
Enlistment for OCS or Avn Cadet	-	-	-	-	-	-	-
Prior Service Enlistment	2	-	2	-	-	-	-
Reenlistment Within 30 Days	4	-	3	-	-	1	-
Immediate Reenlistment	(1) 13	-	(1) 8	-	-	4	1
December - Total	(17) 148	-	(17) 142	1	-	4	1
No Prior Service Enlistment	(16) 114	-	(16) 114	-	-	-	-
Enlistment for OCS or Avn Cadet	3	-	3	-	-	-	-
Prior Service Enlistment	(1) 4	-	(1) 4	-	-	-	-
Reenlistment Within 30 Days	5	-	3	1	-	1	-
Immediate Reenlistment	22	-	18	-	-	3	1

(CONTINUED)

TABLE 225 – WAF ENLISTMENTS AND REENLISTMENTS BY TERM – FY 1953 (CONTINUED)

(Excludes reenlistments in the Army for SCARWAF duty. Figures in parentheses indicate Negro personnel and are included in the open figures. Data are included in Table 224)

Type of Enlistment or Reenlistment by Date	Total	Term of Enlistment or Reenlistment					
		2 Years	3 Years	4 Years	5 Years	6 Years	Indefinite
1953							
January - Total	(34) 364	-	(34) 354	4	-	6	-
No Prior Service Enlistment . .	(33) 342	-	(33) 339	3	-	-	-
Enlistment for OCS or Avn Cadet	3	-	3	-	-	-	-
Prior Service Enlistment. . . .	-	-	-	-	-	-	-
Reenlistment Within 30 Days . .	5	-	4	-	-	1	-
Immediate Reenlistment	(1) 14	-	(1) 8	1	-	5	-
February - Total	(11) 230	-	(11) 221	1	-	7	1
No Prior Service Enlistment . .	(11) 206	-	(11) 205	1	-	-	-
Enlistment for OCS or Avn Cadet	-	-	-	-	-	-	-
Prior Service Enlistment. . . .	5	-	4	-	-	1	-
Reenlistment Within 30 Days . .	3	-	1	-	-	2	-
Immediate Reenlistment.	16	-	11	-	-	4	1
March - Total	(11) 280	-	(11) 267	13	-	-	-
No Prior Service Enlistment . .	(11) 235	-	(11) 234	1	-	-	-
Enlistment for OCS or Avn Cadet	10	-	4	6	-	-	-
Prior Service Enlistment. . . .	4	-	4	-	-	-	-
Reenlistment Within 90 Days . .	4	-	4	-	-	-	-
Immediate Reenlistment	27	-	21	6	-	-	-
April - Total	(5) 160	-	(5) 158	-	-	1	1
No Prior Service Enlistment . .	(5) 152	-	(5) 152	-	-	-	-
Enlistment for OCS or Avn Cadet	-	-	-	-	-	-	-
Prior Service Enlistment. . . .	2	-	2	-	-	-	-
Reenlistment Within 90 Days . .	1	-	-	-	-	-	1
Immediate Reenlistment	5	-	4	-	-	1	-
May - Total	(6) 117	-	(6) 115	2	-	-	-
No Prior Service Enlistment . .	(6) 117	-	(6) 115	2	-	-	-
Enlistment for OCS or Avn Cadet	-	-	-	-	-	-	-
Prior Service Enlistment. . . .	-	-	-	-	-	-	-
Reenlistment Within 90 Days . .	-	-	-	-	-	-	-
Immediate Reenlistment	-	-	-	-	-	-	-
June - Total	(10) 253	-	(10) 246	3	-	3	1
No Prior Service Enlistment . .	(10) 241	-	(10) 241	-	-	-	-
Enlistment for OCS or Avn Cadet	3	-	-	3	-	-	-
Prior Service Enlistment. . . .	3	-	3	-	-	-	-
Reenlistment Within 90 Days . .	2	-	-	-	-	2	-
Immediate Reenlistment	4	-	2	-	-	1	1

Source: Personnel Statistics Division, DCS/Comptroller, HQ USAF

TABLE 226 — NEGRO ENLISTMENTS AND REENLISTMENTS BY TERM — FY 1953

(Excludes Reenlistments in Army for SCARWAF duty. Data are included in Table 224)

Type of Enlistment or Reenlistment by Date	Total	Term of Enlistment or Reenlistment					
		2 Years	3 Years	4 Years	5 Years	6 Years	Indefinite
FY 1953 - TOTAL	18,305	65	1,576	15,521	8	1,069	66
No Prior Service Enlistment	14,691	-	512	14,177	-	2	-
Enlistment for OCS or Avn Cadet	66	64	2	-	-	-	-
Prior Service Enlistment	1,214	-	10	1,152	1	51	-
Reenlistment Within 30 or 90 Days	591	-	260	96	5	213	17
Immediate Reenlistment	1,743	1	792	96	2	803	49
1952							
July - Total	3,216	1	234	2,752	1	220	8
No Prior Service Enlistment	2,721	-	104	2,616	-	1	-
Enlistment for OCS or Avn Cadet	1	1	-	-	-	-	-
Prior Service Enlistment	134	-	-	124	-	10	-
Reenlistment Within 30 Days	17	-	5	3	-	9	-
Immediate Reenlistment	343	-	125	9	1	200	8
August - Total	2,747	3	232	2,352	-	155	5
No Prior Service Enlistment	2,333	-	79	2,254	-	-	-
Enlistment for OCS or Avn Cadet	2	2	-	-	-	-	-
Prior Service Enlistment	98	-	1	87	-	10	-
Reenlistment Within 30 Days	34	-	13	5	-	15	1
Immediate Reenlistment	280	1	139	6	-	130	4
September - Total	2,102	4	286	1,628	-	173	11
No Prior Service Enlistment	1,666	-	121	1,545	-	-	-
Enlistment for OCS or Avn Cadet	5	4	1	-	-	-	-
Prior Service Enlistment	74	-	-	72	-	2	-
Reenlistment Within 30 Days	39	-	16	3	-	19	1
Immediate Reenlistment	318	-	148	8	-	152	10
October - Total	1,684	8	193	1,346	-	131	6
No Prior Service Enlistment	1,297	-	70	1,227	-	-	-
Enlistment for OCS or Avn Cadet	8	8	-	-	-	-	-
Prior Service Enlistment	102	-	6	92	-	4	-
Reenlistment Within 30 Days	82	-	38	10	-	32	2
Immediate Reenlistment	195	-	79	17	-	95	4
November - Total	1,205	22	152	923	-	105	3
No Prior Service Enlistment	895	-	46	849	-	-	-
Enlistment for OCS or Avn Cadet	22	22	-	-	-	-	-
Prior Service Enlistment	68	-	-	60	-	8	-
Reenlistment Within 30 Days	72	-	29	14	-	28	1
Immediate Reenlistment	148	-	77	-	-	69	2
December - Total	1,391	8	135	1,141	4	100	3
No Prior Service Enlistment	1,073	-	16	1,057	-	-	-
Enlistment for OCS or Avn Cadet	8	8	-	-	-	-	-
Prior Service Enlistment	77	-	1	71	1	4	-
Reenlistment Within 30 Days	79	-	31	5	2	41	-
Immediate Reenlistment	154	-	87	8	1	55	3

(CONTINUED)

TABLE 226 — NEGRO ENLISTMENTS AND REENLISTMENTS BY TERM — FY 1953 (CONTINUED)

(Excludes Reenlistments in Army for SCARWAF Duty. Data are included in Table 224)

Type of Enlistment or Reenlistment by Date	Total	Term of Enlistment or Reenlistment					
		2 Years	3 Years	4 Years	5 Years	6 Years	Indefinite
1953							
January - Total	1,170	11	128	955	1	59	16
No Prior Service Enlistment	826	-	33	793	-	-	-
Enlistment for OCS or Avn Cadet	11	11	-	-	-	-	-
Prior Service Enlistment	151	-	-	144	-	7	-
Reenlistment Within 30 Days	92	-	50	14	1	21	6
Immediate Reenlistment	90	-	45	4	-	31	10
February - Total	1,471	5	85	1,338	-	36	7
No Prior Service Enlistment	1,198	-	11	1,187	-	-	-
Enlistment for OCS or Avn Cadet	5	5	-	-	-	-	-
Prior Service Enlistment	134	-	-	131	-	3	-
Reenlistment Within 30 Days	67	-	32	19	-	12	4
Immediate Reenlistment	67	-	42	1	-	21	3
March - Total	1,434	1	54	1,341	1	34	3
No Prior Service Enlistment	1,208	-	11	1,196	-	1	-
Enlistment for OCS or Avn Cadet	1	1	-	-	-	-	-
Prior Service Enlistment	103	-	1	102	-	-	-
Reenlistment Within 90 Days	56	-	26	10	1	17	2
Immediate Reenlistment	66	-	16	33	-	16	1
April - Total	996	2	14	959	-	20	1
No Prior Service Enlistment	846	-	5	841	-	-	-
Enlistment for OCS or Avn Cadet	2	2	-	-	-	-	-
Prior Service Enlistment	112	-	1	111	-	-	-
Reenlistment Within 90 Days	15	-	3	4	-	8	-
Immediate Reenlistment	21	-	5	3	-	12	1
May - Total	493	-	26	452	-	14	1
No Prior Service Enlistment	376	-	6	370	-	-	-
Enlistment for OCS or Avn Cadet	-	-	-	-	-	-	-
Prior Service Enlistment	74	-	-	73	-	1	-
Reenlistment Within 90 Days	16	-	7	5	-	4	-
Immediate Reenlistment	27	-	13	4	-	9	1
June - Total	396	-	37	334	1	22	2
No Prior Service Enlistment	252	-	10	242	-	-	-
Enlistment for OCS or Avn Cadet	1	-	1	-	-	-	-
Prior Service Enlistment	87	-	-	85	-	2	-
Reenlistment Within 90 Days	22	-	10	4	1	7	-
Immediate Reenlistment	34	-	16	3	-	13	2

Source: Personnel Statistics Division, DCS/Comptroller, Hq USAF

TABLE 227 — NON-BATTLE AIRCRAFT DEATHS OF USAF AIRMEN, AIRCREW, AND NON-AIRCREW — LAST HALF FY 1952 AND FY 1953

Period	Total	Crew Position							Non Aircrew	
		Photo-grapher	Radar Operator	Radio Operator	Gunner	Engineer	Steward	Medical Specialist	Passen-ger	Student
FY 1952	165	-	4	25	59	34	-	1	29	13
(Last Half FY 52)										
January.	30	-	-	7	5	3	-	-	15	-
February	20	-	1	3	9	6	-	-	-	1
March.	35	-	1	5	17	6	-	-	4	2
April.	35	-	2	6	7	10	-	1	8	1
May.	20	-	-	3	9	4	-	-	2	2
June	25	-	-	1	12	5	-	-	-	7
FY 1953	502	2	5	40	63	65	5	2	272	48
(First Half FY 53)										
July	23	-	1	1	8	6	-	-	4	3
August	15	1	-	2	2	4	-	-	3	3
September.	18	-	-	2	5	3	-	-	2	6
October.	39	-	1	4	10	6	-	-	16	2
November	80	-	1	10	9	11	3	-	39	7
December	97	-	-	4	-	6	-	1	83	3
(Last Half FY 53)										
January.	32	-	1	3	8	8	1	-	8	3
February	24	-	-	4	6	6	-	-	2	6
March.	60	1	1	5	8	6	-	1	35	3
April.	17	-	-	1	5	4	-	-	-	7
May.	8	-	-	2	1	3	-	-	1	1
June	89	-	-	2	1	2	1	-	79	4

Source: Personnel Statistics Division, DCS/Comptroller, Hq USAF.

TABLE 228 – NON-BATTLE DEATHS OF USAF OFFICERS AND AIRMEN BY GRADE IN WHICH SERVING – LAST HALF FY 1952 AND FY 1953

Date	Officer: Total	Gen	Col	Lt Col	Maj	Capt	1st Lt	2nd Lt	W/O	Airmen: Total	M/Sgt	T/Sgt	S/Sgt	A/1c	A/2c	A/3c	A/B	A/C
FY 1952																		
(Last Half FY 1952)-Total	357	2	10	12	40	115	109	67	2	714	49	72	116	122	137	160	44	14
January (1952)	40	-	1	-	7	10	13	9	-	116	6	14	19	19	23	27	8	-
February	65	-	3	3	4	23	19	13	-	108	9	12	12	17	28	22	7	1
March.	68	1	2	5	9	20	20	11	-	131	12	11	26	17	16	39	8	2
April.	98	-	2	3	8	41	26	17	1	112	9	19	19	16	15	28	5	1
May.	39	1	-	-	3	14	15	6	-	118	8	9	19	26	23	21	9	3
June	47	-	2	1	9	7	16	11	1	129	5	7	21	27	32	23	7	7
FY 1953 - Total . .	741	2	14	26	83	200	235	174	7	1,678	115	116	255	327	371	353	69	52
(First Half FY 1953)																		
July (1952).	76	-	2	5	4	23	21	21	-	146	5	11	22	21	31	42	10	4
August	48	1	1	4	6	12	13	11	-	141	6	10	25	25	28	34	10	3
September.	59	-	-	2	7	16	23	11	-	110	8	8	13	16	33	22	4	6
October.	69	-	-	1	9	23	23	12	1	121	4	8	19	32	21	29	6	2
November	76	-	2	-	9	29	20	15	1	177	10	12	34	34	35	30	15	7
December	70	-	-	-	3	14	23	28	2	193	14	9	27	46	48	40	5	4
(Last Half FY 1953)																		
January (1953)	65	-	2	2	7	21	17	16	-	117	17	7	20	20	25	19	6	3
February	44	-	1	-	6	7	16	14	-	113	17	11	10	30	13	20	6	6
March.	64	1	2	5	9	13	21	12	1	164	12	11	21	36	41	33	7	3
April.	52	-	1	-	7	13	18	13	-	114	7	9	21	12	32	21	4	8
May.	55	-	2	3	8	13	17	11	1	100	7	8	20	15	18	23	8	1
June	63	-	1	4	8	16	23	10	1	182	8	12	23	40	46	40	8	5

Source: Personnel Statistics Division, DCS/Comptroller, Hq USAF.

TABLE 229 – NON-BATTLE DEATHS OF USAF OFFICERS BY AERONAUTICAL RATING, BY GRADE IN WHICH SERVING – LAST HALF FY 1952 AND FY 1953

Date	Pilot: Total	Gen	Col	Lt Col	Maj	Capt	1st Lt	2nd Lt	W/O	Observer: Total	Gen	Col	Lt Col	Maj	Capt	1st Lt	2nd Lt	W/O
FY 1952																		
(Last Half FY 1952)-Total	228	2	6	7	19	78	77	39	-	77	-	-	-	6	25	24	22	-
January (1952)	26	-	1	-	2	8	10	5	-	8	-	-	-	1	2	2	3	-
February	45	-	2	1	3	17	15	7	-	15	-	-	-	1	6	3	5	-
March.	42	1	-	3	4	15	12	7	-	12	-	-	-	1	2	6	3	-
April.	62	-	2	2	4	28	17	9	-	22	-	-	-	2	8	7	5	-
May.	23	1	-	-	1	7	9	5	-	9	-	-	-	-	4	4	1	-
June	30	-	1	1	5	3	14	6	-	11	-	-	-	1	3	2	5	-
FY 1953 - Total . .	482	1	4	16	44	140	168	109	-	137	-	-	1	13	38	45	40	-
(First Half FY 1953)																		
July (1952).	55	-	1	3	1	14	19	17	-	13	-	-	-	2	8	2	1	-
August	28	-	-	1	3	7	11	6	-	9	-	-	1	2	2	2	2	-
September.	41	-	-	2	6	10	15	8	-	13	-	-	-	-	5	5	3	-
October.	41	-	-	1	4	16	15	5	-	14	-	-	-	1	5	4	4	-
November	48	-	-	-	5	19	14	10	-	14	-	-	-	1	5	4	4	-
December	37	-	-	-	1	10	13	13	-	14	-	-	-	-	2	4	8	-
(Last Half FY 1953)																		
January (1953)	44	-	1	1	2	16	14	10	-	13	-	-	-	2	3	3	5	-
February	27	-	1	-	2	6	11	7	-	9	-	-	-	1	-	4	4	-
March.	41	1	1	4	4	10	13	8	-	14	-	-	-	2	3	7	2	-
April.	35	-	-	-	4	8	17	6	-	10	-	-	-	2	2	-	6	-
May.	37	-	-	2	6	10	10	9	-	9	-	-	-	-	2	6	1	-
June	48	-	-	2	6	14	16	10	-	5	-	-	-	-	1	4	-	-

Source: Personnel Statistics Division, DCS/Comptroller, Hq USAF.

TABLE 230 – NON-BATTLE DEATHS OF USAF OFFICERS BY AGE GROUPS, BY GRADE IN WHICH SERVING – LAST HALF FY 1952 AND FY 1953

Grade	Total	Age Group							
		20 Through 24	25 Through 29	30 Through 34	35 Through 39	40 Through 44	45 Through 49	50 Through 54	55 and Older
FY 1952									
(Last Half FY 1952) - Total	357	33	112	140	48	11	8	4	1
General	3	-	-	-	-	1	1	-	1
Colonel	10	-	-	2	3	1	2	2	-
Lieutenant Colonel	11	-	-	4	5	1	1	-	-
Major	41	-	3	14	14	4	4	2	-
Captain	116	-	16	78	19	3	-	-	-
First Lieutenant	108	8	51	42	6	1	-	-	-
Second Lieutenant	67	25	42	-	-	-	-	-	-
Warrant Officer	1	-	-	-	1	-	-	-	-
FY 1953 - Total	741	81	232	269	104	26	17	9	3
(First Half FY 1953)									
General	-	-	-	-	-	-	-	-	-
Colonel	5	-	-	-	2	-	1	1	1
Lieutenant Colonel	13	-	-	1	5	2	3	2	-
Major	37	-	1	21	9	3	2	1	-
Captain	116	-	32	66	16	2	-	-	-
First Lieutenant	124	17	68	31	8	-	-	-	-
Second Lieutenant	98	64	31	2	1	-	-	-	-
Warrant Officer	5	-	-	2	1	2	-	-	-
(Last Half FY 1953)									
General	1	-	-	-	-	1	-	-	-
Colonel	9	-	-	-	2	2	1	3	1
Lieutenant Colonel	13	-	-	3	7	-	3	-	-
Major	45	-	2	18	14	4	5	1	1
Captain	80	-	18	42	16	2	1	1	-
First Lieutenant	107	-	20	60	20	6	1	-	-
Second Lieutenant	85	-	60	23	1	1	-	-	-
Warrant Officer	3	-	-	-	2	1	-	-	-

Source: Personnel Statistics Division, DCS/Comptroller, Hq USAF

TABLE 231 – NON-BATTLE DEATHS OF USAF OFFICERS BY CAUSATIVE AGENT BY AGE GROUPS – LAST HALF FY 1952 AND FY 1953

Causative Agent	Total	Age Group							
		20 Through 24	25 Through 29	30 Through 34	35 Through 39	40 Through 44	45 Through 49	50 Through 54	55 and Older
FY 1952									
(Last Half FY 1952) - Total	357	32	115	140	46	10	9	4	1
Aircraft Accident	286	27	101	122	29	2	4	1	-
Vehicle Accident	23	4	5	7	6	1	-	-	-
Disease	31	-	6	4	6	6	5	3	1
Other	17	1	3	7	5	1	-	-	-
FY 1953 - Total	741	158	236	208	91	21	15	11	1
(First Half FY 1953)									
Aircraft Accident	302	69	104	94	29	5	1	-	-
Vehicle Accident	35	9	8	15	2	-	1	-	-
Disease	39	2	10	10	5	4	3	4	1
Other	22	3	6	5	7	1	-	-	-
(Last Half FY 1953)									
Aircraft Accident	270	69	93	70	33	4	1	-	-
Vehicle Accident	14	1	5	4	2	1	1	-	-
Disease	37	1	6	5	9	4	6	6	-
Other	22	4	4	5	4	2	2	1	-

Source: Personnel Statistics Division, DCS/Comptroller, Hq USAF.

TABLE 232 — NON-BATTLE DEATHS OF USAF AIRMEN BY AGE GROUPS, BY GRADE IN WHICH SERVING — LAST HALF FY 1952 AND FY 1953

Grade	Total	Age Group								
		17 Through 19	20 Through 24	25 Through 29	30 Through 34	35 Through 39	40 Through 44	45 Through 49	50 Through 54	55 and Older
FY 1952	714	15	440	103	85	38	21	8	2	2
(Last Half FY 52)										
Master Sergeant	51	-	-	4	20	12	8	4	1	2
Technical Sergeant. . .	72	-	5	16	26	17	5	2	1	-
Staff Sergeant.	114	-	58	25	20	8	1	2	-	-
Airman First Class. . .	126	-	87	28	8	-	3	-	-	-
Airman Second Class . .	139	-	116	21	1	1	-	-	-	-
Airman Third Class. . .	155	10	128	6	7	-	4	-	-	-
Airman Basic.	44	5	33	3	3	-	-	-	-	-
Aviation Cadet.	13	-	13	-	-	-	-	-	-	-
FY 1953	1,678	164	982	222	132	94	46	22	10	6
(First Half FY 53)										
Master Sergeant	45	-	-	2	15	11	11	4	2	-
Technical Sergeant. . .	58	-	4	15	18	13	4	3	1	-
Staff Sergeant.	142	-	68	42	12	10	5	2	2	1
Airman First Class. . .	170	10	122	24	8	2	2	2	-	-
Airman Second Class . .	194	28	149	14	1	1	1	-	-	-
Airman Third Class. . .	202	55	128	13	1	4	1	-	-	-
Airman Basic.	50	19	22	4	4	1	-	-	-	-
Aviation Cadet.	27	-	25	2	-	-	-	-	-	-
(Last Half FY 53)										
Master Sergeant	64	-	-	3	19	22	8	7	2	3
Technical Sergeant. . .	56	-	3	10	22	12	7	2	-	-
Staff Sergeant.	116	-	42	36	18	10	4	2	3	1
Airman First Class. . .	151	-	112	27	8	2	2	-	-	-
Airman Second Class . .	186	9	157	16	1	2	-	-	-	1
Airman Third Class. . .	155	37	105	9	1	2	1	-	-	-
Airman Basic.	36	6	19	5	4	2	-	-	-	-
Aviation Cadet.	26	-	26	-	-	-	-	-	-	-

Source: Personnel Statistics Division, DCS/Comptroller, Hq USAF.

TABLE 233 — NON-BATTLE DEATHS OF USAF AIRMEN BY CAUSATIVE AGENT, BY AGE GROUPS — LAST HALF FY 1952 AND FY 1953

Causative Agent	Total	Age Group								
		17 Through 19	20 Through 24	25 Through 29	30 Through 34	35 Through 39	40 Through 44	45 Through 49	50 Through 54	55 and Older
FY 1952	714	11	436	100	85	38	31	8	3	2
(Last Half FY 52)										
Aircraft Accident . . .	165	1	109	19	28	5	3	-	-	-
Vehicle Accident. . . .	277	6	193	42	18	7	9	1	1	-
Disease	155	-	65	18	22	23	19	6	1	1
Other	117	4	69	21	17	3	-	1	1	1
FY 1953	1,678	63	1,077	224	134	95	47	21	12	5
(First Half FY 53)										
Aircraft Accident . . .	272	7	214	30	12	8	1	-	-	-
Vehicle Accident. . . .	302	22	206	39	15	10	9	1	-	-
Disease	101	3	44	13	11	10	8	7	5	-
Other	213	13	119	36	21	14	6	3	-	1
(Last Half FY 53)										
Aircraft Accident . . .	230	-	177	29	15	5	3	1	-	-
Vehicle Accident. . . .	250	10	167	34	25	10	2	1	1	-
Disease	126	4	44	14	15	22	10	7	6	4
Other	184	4	106	29	20	16	8	1	-	-

Source: Personnel Statistics Division, DCS/Comptroller, Hq USAF.

TABLE 234 – RETIREMENT OF OFFICER AND ENLISTED PERSONNEL BY TYPE OF RETIREMENT – FY 1922 THROUGH FY 1953

(The figures shown in this table represents those individuals who were retired during the fiscal year indicated and remained on Air Force retired list through December 1953).

Fiscal Year Of Retirement	OFFICER				ENLISTED			
	Total	Non Disability	Temporary Disability	Permanent Disability	Total	Non Disability	Temporary Disability	Permanent Disability
Total	7,440	4,248	746	2,446	10,936	2,184	1,081	7,671
1922	-	-	-	-	1	-	-	1
1923	3	3	-	-	10	-	-	10
1924	7	7	-	-	2	1	-	1
1925	6	4	-	2	2	1	-	1
1926	2	2	-	-	6	6	-	-
1927	9	9	-	-	1	1	-	-
1928	-	-	-	-	18	4	-	14
1929	5	5	-	-	16	1	-	15
1930	18	17	-	1	4	2	-	2
1931	12	10	-	2	5	2	-	3
1932	4	4	-	-	6	2	-	4
1933	2	2	-	-	3	2	-	1
1934	12	12	-	-	11	3	-	8
1935	4	4	-	-	25	3	-	22
1936	12	12	-	-	11	6	-	5
1937	12	12	-	-	11	3	-	8
1938	12	12	-	-	4	2	-	2
1939	12	11	-	1	17	6	-	11
1940	24	24	-	-	18	7	-	11
1941	15	14	-	1	12	10	-	2
1942	55	30	-	25	48	32	-	16
1943	90	29	-	61	54	8	-	46
1944	218	44	-	174	311	9	-	302
1945	222	50	-	172	1,564	14	-	1,550
1946	538	330	-	208	2,600	48	-	2,552
1947	1,155	1,016	-	139	1,396	196	-	1,200
1948	765	658	-	107	849	226	-	623
1949	508	425	3	80	370	149	1	220
1950	671	533	20	118	426	247	1	178
1951	1,076	295	150	631	443	207	70	166
1952	1,414	449	417	548	470	245	16	209
1953	557	225	156	176	2,222	741	993	488

Source: Personnel Statistics Division, DCS/Comptroller, Hq. USAF

TABLE 235 – OFFICER RETIREMENTS BY TYPE OF RETIREMENT, BY GRADE OF PERSONNEL – FY 1953

(The figures shown in this table represents those individuals who were retired during month indicated and remained on Air Force retired list through December 1953).

Type of Retirement	Total	Gen	Lt Gen	Maj Gen	Brig Gen	Col	Lt Col	Maj	Capt	1st Lt	2nd Lt	W/O
FY 1953 - Total	557	1	1	17	11	90	94	105	107	67	28	36
Non-Disability	225	-	1	9	5	61	61	54	20	2	-	12
Temporary Disability	156	-	-	-	-	4	10	21	54	40	15	12
Permanent Disability	176	1	-	8	6	25	23	30	33	25	13	12
1952												
July - Total	55	-	-	-	-	9	11	8	10	8	3	6
Non-Disability	14	-	-	-	-	2	4	1	2	-	-	5
Temporary Disability	15	-	-	-	-	1	1	4	4	4	1	-
Permanent Disability	26	-	-	-	-	6	6	3	4	4	2	1
August - Total	38	-	-	2	1	6	7	9	5	6	2	-
Non-Disability	15	-	-	-	1	5	4	5	-	-	-	-
Temporary Disability	11	-	-	-	-	-	1	1	2	5	2	-
Permanent Disability	12	-	-	2	-	1	2	3	3	1	-	-
September - Total	49	-	-	2	-	7	12	8	10	7	2	1
Non-Disability	21	-	-	-	-	6	8	6	1	-	-	-
Temporary Disability	19	-	-	-	-	-	3	1	7	5	2	1
Permanent Disability	9	-	-	2	-	1	1	1	2	2	-	-
October - Total	67	-	-	2	-	10	6	13	19	9	4	4
Non-Disability	25	-	-	1	-	6	3	7	6	1	-	1
Temporary Disability	23	-	-	-	-	-	1	2	10	6	3	1
Permanent Disability	19	-	-	1	-	4	2	4	3	2	1	2
November - Total	51	-	-	-	1	7	9	9	11	7	3	4
Non-Disability	19	-	-	-	1	6	6	4	1	1	-	-
Temporary Disability	15	-	-	-	-	-	1	1	6	3	1	3
Permanent Disability	17	-	-	-	-	1	2	4	4	3	2	1
December - Total	45	-	1	-	1	7	11	15	3	2	4	1
Non-Disability	26	-	1	-	1	4	9	11	-	-	-	-
Temporary Disability	9	-	-	-	-	2	-	3	2	1	-	1
Permanent Disability	10	-	-	-	-	1	2	1	1	1	4	-
1953												
January - Total	26	-	-	-	1	7	3	7	2	4	1	1
Non-Disability	15	-	-	-	-	6	3	5	1	-	-	-
Temporary Disability	4	-	-	-	-	-	-	-	-	2	1	1
Permanent Disability	7	-	-	-	1	1	-	2	1	2	-	-
February - Total	36	-	-	9	2	4	6	5	4	2	2	2
Non-Disability	13	-	-	8	1	-	1	1	1	-	-	1
Temporary Disability	8	-	-	-	-	1	1	1	1	1	2	1
Permanent Disability	15	-	-	1	1	3	4	3	2	1	-	-
March - Total	59	-	-	1	1	8	9	13	12	9	4	2
Non-Disability	24	-	-	-	-	7	8	5	2	-	-	2
Temporary Disability	15	-	-	-	-	-	-	4	5	4	2	-
Permanent Disability	20	-	-	1	1	1	1	4	5	5	2	-
April - Total	34	-	-	-	1	6	10	8	8	-	1	-
Non-Disability	18	-	-	-	-	4	7	5	2	-	-	-
Temporary Disability	6	-	-	-	-	-	-	1	4	-	1	-
Permanent Disability	10	-	-	-	1	2	3	2	2	-	-	-
May - Total	36	-	-	-	1	6	3	2	12	7	1	4
Non-Disability	11	-	-	-	1	4	3	-	2	-	-	1
Temporary Disability	14	-	-	-	-	-	-	1	8	4	-	1
Permanent Disability	11	-	-	-	-	2	-	1	2	3	1	2
June - Total	61	1	-	1	2	13	7	8	11	6	1	11
Non-Disability	24	-	-	-	-	11	5	4	2	-	-	2
Temporary Disability	17	-	-	-	-	-	2	2	5	5	-	3
Permanent Disability	20	1	-	1	2	2	-	2	4	1	1	6

Source: Personnel Statistics Division, DCS/Comptroller, Hq. USAF

308700 O - 54 - 28

TABLE 236 — ENLISTED RETIREMENTS BY TYPE OF RETIREMENT, BY GRADE OF PERSONNEL — FY 1953

(The figures shown in this table represents those individuals who were retired during month indicated and remained on Air Force retired list through December 1953).

Type of Retirement	Total	M/Sgt	T/Sgt	S/Sgt	A/1C	A/2C	A/3C	A3	A/C
FY 1953 - Total	2,222	775	255	344	278	262	247	56	5
Non-Disability	741	595	92	41	7	1	3	2	-
Temporary Disability	993	89	96	216	192	181	175	41	3
Permanent Disability	488	91	67	87	79	80	69	13	2
1952									
July - Total	154	40	19	23	29	24	16	3	-
Non-Disability	28	23	3	2	-	-	-	-	-
Temporary Disability	79	8	7	14	22	13	12	3	-
Permanent Disability	47	9	9	7	7	11	4	-	-
August - Total	183	63	23	31	24	17	16	9	-
Non-Disability	57	48	5	3	1	-	-	-	-
Temporary Disability	85	5	8	21	17	11	15	8	-
Permanent Disability	41	10	10	7	6	6	1	1	-
September - Total	107	34	9	19	14	12	17	2	-
Non-Disability	22	21	-	-	1	-	-	-	-
Temporary Disability	55	4	8	14	9	7	13	-	-
Permanent Disability	30	9	1	5	4	5	4	2	-
October - Total	168	59	18	24	23	21	19	4	-
Non-Disability	62	51	7	3	1	-	-	-	-
Temporary Disability	67	5	5	16	13	13	12	3	-
Permanent Disability	39	3	6	5	9	8	7	1	-
November - Total	243	94	21	36	29	23	32	8	-
Non-Disability	89	71	12	5	-	-	1	-	-
Temporary Disability	96	8	6	24	18	14	22	4	-
Permanent Disability	58	15	3	7	11	9	9	4	-
December - Total	175	61	17	33	25	17	19	2	1
Non-Disability	53	48	3	2	-	-	-	-	-
Temporary Disability	85	7	10	22	18	13	13	2	-
Permanent Disability	37	6	4	9	7	4	6	-	1
1953									
January - Total	81	18	6	13	13	17	9	3	2
Non-Disability	5	4	1	-	-	-	-	-	-
Temporary Disability	57	8	2	9	12	14	8	3	1
Permanent Disability	19	6	3	4	1	3	1	-	1
February - Total	175	69	23	29	12	27	12	3	-
Non-Disability	68	58	6	4	-	-	-	-	-
Temporary Disability	70	5	13	17	6	20	7	2	-
Permanent Disability	37	6	4	8	6	7	5	1	-
March - Total	181	44	26	26	28	23	28	6	-
Non-Disability	34	26	6	-	-	-	1	1	-
Temporary Disability	103	12	13	17	22	17	18	4	-
Permanent Disability	44	6	7	9	6	6	9	1	-
April - Total	237	83	27	32	28	30	29	7	1
Non-Disability	81	65	11	4	1	-	-	-	-
Temporary Disability	107	9	10	21	19	21	21	5	1
Permanent Disability	49	9	6	7	8	9	8	2	-
May - Total	272	107	38	45	27	26	24	4	1
Non-Disability	126	91	23	10	-	1	1	-	-
Temporary Disability	99	11	10	22	20	17	15	3	1
Permanent Disability	47	5	5	13	7	8	8	1	-
June - Total	246	103	28	33	26	25	26	5	-
Non-Disability	116	89	15	8	3	-	-	1	-
Temporary Disability	90	7	4	19	16	21	19	4	-
Permanent Disability	40	7	9	6	7	4	7	-	-

Source: Personnel Statistics Division, DCS/Comptroller, Hq. USAF

TABLE 237 — MILITARY PERSONNEL ARRIVALS BY AIR AND BY WATER FROM OVERSEAS COMMAND — FY 1953

(Table below represents personnel who have debarked from Overseas Commands and includes only those personnel with permanent change of assignment who have been assigned to a Continental US or an Overseas Port Accounting for separation or for further assignment.)

Command From Which Departed	Jul (1952)	Aug	Sep	Oct	Nov	Dec	Jan (1953)	Feb	Mar	Apr	May a/	Jun a/
Total	9,198	9,043	10,817	12,141	10,127	13,840	11,860	13,219	11,009	10,387	6,635	4,014
Officer	1,125	1,080	1,158	1,337	1,433	1,945	2,044	1,621	1,884	1,356	959	812
Enlisted	8,073	7,963	9,659	10,804	8,694	11,895	9,816	11,598	9,125	9,031	5,676	3,202
Alaskan Air Command												
Total	584	740	781	1,008	1,113	1,061	480	584	750	490	572	593
Officer	55	46	62	76	96	125	48	45	112	48	67	44
Enlisted	529	694	719	932	1,017	936	432	539	638	442	505	549
Caribbean Air Command-Total	86	43	36	42	25	32	16	26	39	21	35	54
Officer	13	9	6	9	5	7	3	3	2	2	5	9
Enlisted	73	34	30	33	20	25	13	23	37	19	30	45
Far East Air Forces												
Total	5,051	6,408	5,845	6,122	4,586	7,203	6,879	6,581	6,086	6,614	2,769	1,181
Officer	799	786	724	758	794	1,178	813	884	1,107	888	386	295
Enlisted	4,252	5,622	5,121	5,364	3,792	6,025	6,066	5,697	4,979	5,726	2,383	886
Military Air Transport Services (O/S) - Total	886	714	1,547	1,478	1,557	1,980	1,343	1,662	1,355	938	959	803
Officers	61	67	114	164	132	228	137	212	211	125	137	140
Enlisted	825	647	1,433	1,314	1,425	1,752	1,206	1,450	1,144	813	822	663
Northeast Air Command - Total	442	403	775	1,010	697	1,172	316	877	468	749	520	662
Officer	42	52	36	48	60	85	35	117	83	57	74	88
Enlisted	400	351	739	962	637	1,087	281	760	385	692	446	574
US Air Forces in Europe - Total	2,121	697	1,412	2,174	1,601	1,861	1,002	3,080	2,043	1,403	1,714	644
Officer	145	112	159	251	270	219	152	297	281	207	262	214
Enlisted	1,976	585	1,253	1,923	1,331	1,642	850	2,783	1,762	1,196	1,452	430
Other Areas - Total	28	38	421	307	548	531	1,824	409	268	172	66	77
Officer	10	8	57	31	76	103	856	63	88	29	28	22
Enlisted	18	30	364	276	472	428	968	346	180	143	38	55

a/ Excludes personnel who have just returned from overseas and have elected to be separated at the Port Personnel Processing Squadron or at an Air Force Base nearest individuals home.

Source: Personnel Statistics Division, DCS/Comptroller, Hq. USAF

TABLE 238 — DEPARTURES OF MILITARY PERSONNEL OVERSEAS REPLACEMENTS BY AIR AND BY WATER — FY 1953

(Table below represents personnel who have embarked from Continental US Commands for Overseas during the month and includes only those personnel with permanent change of assignment who have been assigned to a Continental US or Overseas Port Accounting Unit for further assignment to an Overseas unit).

Command Destination	Jul (1952)	Aug	Sep	Oct	Nov	Dec	Jan (1953)	Feb	Mar	Apr	May	Jun
Total	14,123	16,773	13,588	16,650	14,666	15,543	12,300	10,717	12,559	11,499	14,640	11,799
Officers. .	1,416	1,792	1,482	1,385	1,569	1,915	1,730	1,473	1,566	1,553	1,937	1,337
Enlisted. .	12,707	14,981	12,106	15,265	13,097	13,628	10,570	9,244	10,993	9,946	12,703	10,462
Alaskan Air Command												
Total.	927	1,164	1,059	1,212	1,170	883	1,038	654	569	1,330	789	587
Officer.	54	174	133	95	95	54	88	64	47	31	44	48
Enlisted	873	990	926	1,117	1,075	829	950	590	522	1,299	745	539
Caribbean Air. . . Command - Total.	16	13	23	9	10	2	20	20	17	66	29	32
Officer	3	8	6	1	2	2	4	-	2	4	2	1
Enlisted	13	5	17	8	8	-	16	20	15	62	27	31
Far East Air Forces												
Total.	7,078	9,382	7,380	9,746	8,171	9,437	5,541	5,929	7,048	4,037	7,608	5,274
Officer	815	1,138	639	792	975	1,370	983	951	1,099	1,007	1,279	739
Enlisted	6,263	8,244	6,741	8,954	7,196	8,067	4,558	4,978	5,949	3,030	6,329	4,535
Military Air Transport Service (O/S)												
Total	2,023	2,072	1,700	1,588	1,871	1,651	1,712	761	619	904	510	476
Officer.	225	178	194	125	227	154	247	161	96	106	117	100
Enlisted	1,798	1,894	1,506	1,463	1,644	1,497	1,465	600	523	798	393	376
Northeast Air . . Command - Total.	1,340	1,309	1,207	1,509	421	975	901	1,079	618	1,090	1,429	1,499
Officer	35	54	73	61	28	71	112	106	44	64	120	92
Enlisted	1,305	1,255	1,134	1,448	393	904	789	973	574	1,026	1,309	1,407
US Air Forces in . Europe - Total .	2,109	2,364	1,901	2,031	2,207	2,087	2,435	1,927	3,199	3,578	4,080	3,850
Officer	155	149	394	296	206	249	212	167	265	323	355	330
Enlisted	1,954	2,215	1,507	1,735	2,001	1,838	2,223	1,760	2,934	3,255	3,725	3,520
Other Areas - Total	630	469	318	555	816	508	653	347	489	494	195	81
Officer	129	91	43	15	36	15	84	24	13	18	20	27
Enlisted	501	378	275	540	780	493	569	323	476	476	175	54

Source: Personnel Statistics Division, DCS/Comptroller, Hq. USAF

TABLE 239 — REGULAR OFFICERS SELECTED FOR PERMANENT PROMOTIONS — FY 1949 THROUGH FY 1953

(All data indicates officers selected for promotion and not necessarily the number of actual promotions due to resignations, etc. All selections with the exception of lieutenants were made by Selection Boards. Data are based on the dates of the board reports which are not necessarily dates of actual promotions. Promotions for lieutenants were accomplished under Public Law 381, Sec. 508, 1947. According to this law, all second lieutenants were automatically promoted to first lieutenant after completing three (3) years of Promotion List Service. No SCARWAF included.)

Grade to Which Promoted	FY 1949	FY 1950	FY 1951	FY 1952	FY 1953
TOTAL	11,942	4,623	7,759	2,063	1,907
LINE - TOTAL	11,942	4,343	7,349	1,804	1,681
OTHER THAN LINE - TOTAL	-	280	410	259	226
Colonel - Total	-	481	71	-	373
Line	-	431	51	-	362
Other than Line	-	50	20	-	11
Lieutenant Colonel - Total	66	713	2,291	279	87
Line	66	656	2,170	255	51
Other than Line	-	57	121	24	36
Major - Total	3,071	839	3,795	487	220
Line	3,071	783	3,648	435	162
Other than Line	-	56	147	52	58
Captain - Total	8,059	2,421	1,090	607	301
Line	8,059	2,306	991	455	192
Other than Line	-	115	99	152	109
First Lieutenant - Total	746	169	512	690	926
Line	746	167	489	659	914
Other than Line	-	2	23	31	12

Source: Personnel Requirements and Analysis Division, Directorate of Military Personnel, Hq. USAF.

TABLE 240 - TEMPORARY PROMOTIONS OF OFFICERS TO GENERAL OFFICERS BY GRADE TO WHICH PROMOTED - FY 1952 AND FY 1953

(Table indicates the number of actual promotions by month in which promoted for the periods covered. Temporary promotions cover both regular and non regular officers No SCARWAF included.)

Date	Total	General	Lieutenant General	Major General	Brigadier General
FY 1952 - Total.	103	3	4	31	65
July (1951)	32	-	3	8	21
August	-	-	-	-	-
September	-	-	-	-	-
October	31	3	-	9	19
November	-	-	-	-	-
December	1	-	1	-	-
January (1952)	-	-	-	-	-
February	-	-	-	-	-
March	37	-	-	14	23
April	2	-	-	-	2
May	-	-	-	-	-
June	-	-	-	-	-
FY 1953 - Total.	143	3	11	37	92
July (1952)	7	2	a/ 5	-	-
August	-	-	-	-	-
September	62	-	2	14	46
October	15	-	-	6	9
November	-	-	-	-	-
December	25	-	-	8	17
January (1953)	-	-	-	-	-
February	-	-	-	-	-
March	1	-	1	-	-
April	-	-	-	-	-
May	2	-	2	-	-
June	31	1	1	9	20

a/ Included in this total is one Lt General, Authorized as an additional number while serving as deputy director, CIA, UP of P L 15, 83D Congress.

Source: Personnel Requirement and Analysis Division, Directorate of Military Personnel, Hq. USAF

TABLE 241 — OFFICERS SELECTED FOR TEMPORARY PROMOTIONS BY FISCAL YEAR IN WHICH SELECTED-FY 1949 THROUGH FY 1953

(Selections made by Selection Boards do not necessarily mean actual promotions, as cancellations may be made because of resignations, etc. The table includes both regular and non regular officers. The table excludes selections of Captains for promotions accomplished through other than Selection Board actions such as those selected under AFL-35-25 or AFR 36-14. Temporary promotions of Second Lieutenants to First Lieutenants are also excluded as such promotions were not accomplished by action of a Selection Board. Complete data on temporary promotion of lieutenants were not available for this publication. No SCARWAF included).

Grade to which Selected	FY 1949	FY 1950	FY 1951	FY 1952	FY 1953
Total	2,957	2,705	15,097	20,933	9,861
Line - Total	2,957	2,157	14,282	19,595	9,153
Other Than Line - Total	-	548	815	1,338	708
Colonel - Total	251	218	740	1,277	560
Line	251	199	693	1,200	516
Other than Line	-	19	47	77	44
Lieutenant Colonel - Total	400	85	1,499	2,607	1,043
Line	400	66	1,428	2,426	964
Other than Line	-	19	71	181	79
Major - Total	793	665	3,591	8,644	2,741
Line	793	607	3,444	8,008	2,430
Other than Line	-	58	147	636	311
Captain - Total	1,513	1,737	9,267	8,405	5,517
Line	1,513	1,285	8,717	7,961	5,243
Other than Line	-	452	550	444	274

Source: Personnel Requirements and Analysis Division, Directorate of Military Personnel, Hq. USAF

TABLE 242 ESTIMATED PERCENTAGE DISTRIBUTION OF USAF MILITARY PERSONNEL BY AGE AND BY GRADE IN WHICH SERVING — 30 NOV 1952 AND 31 MAY 1953

(Table is based on Departmental Strength)

Grade	Per Cent By Age															
	19 And Under		20 Through 24		25 Through 29		30 Through 34		35 Through 39		40 Through 44		45 Through 49		50 And Older	
	30 Nov 1952	31 May 1953	30 Nov 1952	31 May 1953	30 Nov 1952	31 May 1953	30 Nov 1952	31 May 1953	30 Nov 1952	31 May 1953	30 Nov 1952	31 May 1953	30 Nov 1952	31 May 1953	30 Nov 1952	31 May 1953
Officer - Total			15.3	17.8	20.4	20.8	35.4	34.9	16.9	17.4	7.4	5.0	3.3	2.9	1.3	1.2
Colonel			-	-	-	-	7.1	9.1	35.7	32.9	32.1	24.3	16.1	23.2	9.0	10.5
Lieutenant Colonel			-	-	-	-	31.1	24.6	27.7	41.9	23.4	15.6	12.6	12.1	5.2	5.8
Major	Not Applicable	Not Applicable	-	-	3.5	3.4	50.1	48.1	29.7	32.3	9.4	9.0	4.9	5.5	2.4	1.7
Captain			-	-	16.2	18.5	56.7	57.1	21.7	20.8	5.4	3.6	-	-	-	-
First Lieutenant			10.2	16.2	47.2	46.5	35.4	30.9	7.2	6.4	-	-	-	-	-	-
Second Lieutenant			69.1	77.9	26.2	19.1	4.7	3.0	-	-	-	-	-	-	-	-
Warrant Officer			-	-	7.7	2.7	28.8	30.1	32.8	35.0	19.2	19.4	9.6	8.6	1.9	4.2
Airman - Total	17.3	17.2	59.2	59.3	9.6	10.5	7.9	7.3	3.9	3.9	1.4	1.2	0.5	0.4	0.2	0.2
Master Sergeant	-	-	-	-	10.5	9.2	43.6	42.5	29.3	31.9	10.7	10.7	4.4	4.0	1.5	1.7
Technical Sergeant	-	-	11.7	14.2	25.0	26.9	38.1	36.4	16.9	15.8	6.1	4.8	1.8	1.6	0.4	0.3
Staff Sergeant	-	-	52.1	57.1	23.4	24.6	14.3	11.2	6.4	4.9	2.8	1.6	0.7	0.4	0.3	0.2
Airman First Class	2.9	2.8	82.7	84.4	10.1	9.6	3.4	2.1	0.9	1.1	-	-	-	-	-	-
Airman Second Class	12.0	14.1	80.1	77.7	5.9	6.2	1.5	1.6	0.5	0.4	-	-	-	-	-	-
Airman Third Class	36.7	44.2	58.5	51.4	3.9	3.6	0.9	0.8	-	-	-	-	-	-	-	-
Basic Airman	55.8	59.9	39.7	34.3	2.6	4.4	1.9	1.4	-	-	-	-	-	-	-	-
Aviation Cadet	1.3	5.5	92.8	89.6	5.9	4.9	-	-	-	-	-	-	-	-	-	-

Source: Personnel Statistics Division, DCS/Comptroller, Hq. USAF

TABLE 243 — ESTIMATED PERCENTAGE DISTRIBUTION OF USAF MILITARY PERSONNEL BY MONTHS OF ACTIVE FEDERAL MILITARY SERVICE — 30 NOV 1952 AND 31 MAY 1953

(Table is based on Departmental Strength)

Grade	Total Per Cent	Per Cent Of Military Personnel By Months Of AFMS																			
		0 Through 23		24 Through 47		48 Through 71		72 Through 95		96 Through 119		120 Through 167		168 Through 239		240 Through 299		300 And Over	
		30 Nov 1952	31 May 1953	30 Nov 1952	31 May 1953	30 Nov 1952	31 May 1953	30 Nov 1952	31 May 1953	30 Nov 1952	31 May 1953	30 Nov 1952	31 May 1953	30 Nov 1952	31 May 1953	30 Nov 1952	31 May 1953	30 Nov 1952	31 May 1953
Officer - Total	100.0	15.3	15.0	10.4	11.5	19.1	14.9	11.8	13.1	11.8	9.6	24.5	28.4	4.7	5.1	1.4	1.5	1.0	0.9
Colonel	100.0	-	-	-	-	-	-	3.5	4.1	3.5	4.3	42.1	42.6	38.6	33.3	7.0	11.5	5.3	4.2
Lieutenant Colonel.	100.0	-	-	-	-	5.6	1.3	12.0	10.1	8.8	9.1	55.2	63.5	10.4	9.3	4.0	3.2	4.0	3.5
Major	100.0	1.0	0.5	0.3	0.2	10.3	4.4	14.0	13.9	18.0	13.2	48.4	56.6	5.3	7.5	1.7	2.5	1.0	1.1
Captain	100.0	2.2	1.6	5.8	3.8	22.2	17.0	19.1	21.9	18.2	17.1	27.9	34.2	3.3	3.7	1.3	0.7	-	-
First Lieutenant. .	100.0	9.9	13.8	16.6	21.2	42.8	34.5	11.7	14.2	10.2	6.1	6.4	9.3	2.4	0.9	-	-	-	-
Second Lieutenant .	100.0	62.3	63.3	25.2	29.0	6.4	4.5	1.9	0.8	1.7	0.9	2.5	1.5	-	-	-	-	-	-
Warrant Officer . .	100.0	-	-	3.6	-	3.6	1.0	1.8	1.4	9.1	4.5	45.5	47.9	18.2	29.7	9.1	7.9	9.1	7.6
Airman - Total	100.0	52.3	40.6	19.7	30.8	9.7	9.7	4.8	5.6	4.6	4.7	6.5	6.6	1.6	1.6	0.5	0.3	0.3	0.1
Master Sergeant . .	100.0	-	-	1.2	0.5	3.2	1.7	6.0	5.7	13.1	12.8	49.6	53.7	17.2	20.6	5.7	3.5	4.0	1.5
Technical Sergeant.	100.0	-	-	2.8	1.3	11.0	14.2	16.1	21.2	26.3	24.4	36.8	34.1	5.3	4.2	1.4	0.6	0.3	-
Staff Sergeant . .	100.0	-	-	20.6	33.1	38.7	29.8	17.1	16.9	12.8	10.9	9.0	7.9	1.4	1.2	0.4	0.2	-	-
Airman First Class.	100.0	32.3	13.2	47.3	69.6	12.8	10.3	4.3	3.9	1.6	1.7	1.4	1.2	0.3	0.1	-	-	-	-
Airman Second Class	100.0	68.3	54.6	24.3	37.9	4.7	5.1	1.4	1.3	0.7	0.8	0.6	0.3	-	-	-	-	-	-
Airman Third Class.	100.0	87.2	86.0	8.3	9.8	3.0	2.7	1.5	1.0	-	0.3	-	0.2	-	-	-	-	-	-
Basic Airman . . .	100.0	83.0	78.0	9.8	14.0	4.8	4.3	2.4	2.0	-	1.2	-	0.5	-	-	-	-	-	-
Aviation Cadet . .	100.0	80.4	65.7	15.0	30.8	4.6	2.9	-	0.6	-	-	-	-	-	-	-	-	-	-

Source: Personnel Statistics Division, DCS/Comptroller, Hq. USAF

TABLE 244 — ESTIMATED PERCENTAGE DISTRIBUTION OF AIRMEN BY MONTHS IN GRADE BEFORE LAST PROMOTION — 30 NOV 1953

(Table is based on Departmental Strength)

Grade	Per Cent By Months In Grade								
	1 Through 5	6 Through 11	12 Through 17	18 Through 23	24 Through 35	36 Through 47	48 Through 59	60 Through 71	72 And Over
Airman - Total	34.2	32.5	14.9	5.4	4.8	2.8	1.4	1.3	2.7
Master Sergeant	6.0	16.7	15.9	8.2	11.7	8.8	5.7	5.7	21.3
Technical Sergeant	1.9	8.5	11.6	11.3	18.7	14.3	9.9	7.7	16.1
Staff Sergeant	4.6	33.5	25.4	12.9	12.2	6.6	2.1	1.0	1.7
Airman First Class	19.9	56.3	14.4	4.7	3.0	0.8	0.2	0.4	0.3
Airman Second Class	16.2	51.2	24.2	4.8	1.8	0.6	0.4	0.8	-
Airman Third Class	85.9	9.3	2.9	0.7	0.5	0.7	-	-	-
Basic Airman				NOT APPLICABLE					
Aviation Cadet				NOT APPLICABLE					

Source: Personnel Statistics Division, DCS/Comptroller, Hq. USAF

TABLE 245 — ESTIMATED PERCENTAGE DISTRIBUTION OF USAF MILITARY PERSONNEL BY HIGHEST LEVEL OF EDUCATION — 30 NOV 1952 AND 31 MAY 1953

(Table is based on Departmental Strength)

Grade	Less Than High School Graduate		High School Graduate		College Non-Graduate		College Graduate		Post Graduate Degree a/	
	30 Nov 1952	31 May 1953	30 Nov 1952	31 May 1953	30 Nov 1952	31 May 1953	30 Nov 1952	31 May 1953	30 Nov 1952	31 May 1953
Officer - Total	1.8	1.5	17.1	17.8	37.9	37.1	32.7	33.0	10.5	10.6
Colonel	1.4	1.2	2.4	5.0	26.6	23.5	47.9	47.7	21.7	22.6
Lieutenant Colonel	3.4	2.0	8.4	10.0	38.7	36.9	34.6	34.2	14.9	16.9
Major	2.1	2.0	15.4	17.0	45.4	49.1	25.7	21.1	11.4	10.8
Captain	2.0	1.6	23.0	26.2	45.8	44.6	15.9	16.0	13.3	11.6
First Lieutenant	1.4	1.0	20.6	18.3	41.4	34.1	27.0	34.9	9.6	11.7
Second Lieutenant	0.3	0.1	3.9	3.0	17.7	21.2	73.4	70.7	4.7	5.0
Warrant Officer	8.2	8.2	57.3	56.8	32.6	32.6	1.9	2.4	-	-
Airman - Total	36.0	35.6	46.4	47.0	15.3	15.8	2.1	1.5	0.2	0.1
Master Sergeant	26.3	22.6	53.0	55.7	20.0	20.7	0.7	0.8	-	0.2
Technical Sergeant	33.4	33.2	52.6	50.5	13.3	15.7	0.7	0.6	-	-
Staff Sergeant	40.9	35.5	43.5	48.2	13.2	14.7	2.3	1.6	0.1	-
Airman First Class	27.6	25.7	50.4	51.7	19.9	20.6	2.0	1.9	0.1	0.1
Airman Second Class	30.0	34.8	49.9	49.7	17.6	14.2	2.1	1.3	0.4	-
Airman Third Class	43.0	45.3	44.7	40.9	10.6	12.2	1.6	1.4	0.1	0.2
Basic Airman	54.9	58.8	33.7	30.4	9.5	9.9	1.6	0.7	0.3	0.2
Aviation Cadet	-	0.6	13.1	27.2	60.8	58.2	25.4	13.3	0.7	0.7

a/ Includes Medical Doctors and Dentists

Source: Personnel Statistics Division, DCS/Comptroller, Hq. USAF

TABLE 246 — ESTIMATED DISTRIBUTION OF MILITARY PERSONNEL BY STATE OR TERRITORY OF PRE-SERVICE RESIDENCE — 30 NOV 1952

(Table below includes Aviation Cadets and excludes General Officers and SCARWAF.)

State Or Territory	Officer		Airman	
	Number	Per Cent	Number	Per Cent
Total	129,792	100.0	802,555	100.0
Alabama	2,726	2.1	24,077	3.0
Arizona	649	0.5	4,815	0.6
Arkansas	1,428	1.1	12,038	1.5
California	12,460	9.6	49,757	6.2
Colorado	1,298	1.0	5,618	0.7
Connecticut	1,817	1.4	9,631	1.2
Delaware	519	0.4	803	0.1
District of Columbia	1,168	0.9	3,210	0.4
Florida	2,855	2.2	17,656	2.2
Georgia	2,336	1.8	19,261	2.4
Idaho	1,038	0.8	3,210	0.4
Illinois	6,490	5.0	37,720	4.7
Indiana	2,206	1.7	21,669	2.7
Iowa	1,947	1.5	13,643	1.7
Kansas	2,466	1.9	12,038	1.5
Kentucky	1,817	1.4	16,051	2.0
Louisiana	2,596	2.0	16,051	2.0
Maine	649	0.5	7,223	0.9
Maryland	2,466	1.9	9,631	1.2
Massachusetts	3,634	2.8	28,089	3.5
Michigan	3,764	2.9	29,695	3.7
Minnesota	2,206	1.7	14,446	1.8
Mississippi	1,558	1.2	11,236	1.4
Missouri	2,985	2.3	24,077	3.0
Montana	649	0.5	4,013	0.5
Nebraska	1,558	1.2	8,828	1.1
Nevada	260	0.2	803	0.1

State Or Territory	Officer		Airman	
	Number	Per Cent	Number	Per Cent
New Hampshire	519	0.4	4,013	0.5
New Jersey	3,504	2.7	20,064	2.5
New Mexico	909	0.7	3,210	0.4
New York	10,643	8.2	60,192	7.5
North Carolina	2,077	1.6	21,669	2.7
North Dakota	649	0.5	4,013	0.5
Ohio	7,528	5.8	40,930	5.1
Oklahoma	2,726	2.1	14,446	1.8
Oregon	1,428	1.1	7,223	0.9
Pennsylvania	8,047	6.2	57,784	7.2
Rhode Island	519	0.4	4,815	0.6
South Carolina	1,168	0.9	13,643	1.7
South Dakota	519	0.4	4,013	0.5
Tennessee	2,206	1.7	19,261*	2.4
Texas	10,773	8.3	47,351	5.9
Utah	909	0.7	3,210	0.4
Vermont	519	0.4	2,408	0.3
Virginia	2,596	2.0	18,459	2.3
Washington	2,206	1.7	12,038	1.5
West Virginia	1,687	1.3	16,854	2.1
Wisconsin	2,206	1.7	18,459	2.3
Wyoming	519	0.4	803	0.1
Alaska	-	-	-	-
Canal Zone	-	-	-	-
Territory of Hawaii	260	0.2	2,408	0.3
Philippine Islands	-	-	-	-
Puerto Rico	130	0.1	-	-

Source: Personnel Statistics Division, DCS/Comptroller, Hq. USAF

TABLE 247 — ESTIMATED PERCENTAGE DISTRIBUTION OF USAF MILITARY PERSONNEL BY MARITAL STATUS 30 NOV 1952 AND 31 MAY 1953

(Table is based on Departmental Strength.)

Grade	Married		Never Married		Other a/	
	30 Nov 1952	31 May 1953	30 Nov 1952	31 May 1953	30 Nov 1952	31 May 1953
Officer - Total . .	79.2	79.0	18.7	19.1	2.1	1.9
Colonel	96.5	97.3	1.0	1.0	2.5	1.7
Lieutenant Colonel . . .	93.3	94.5	3.7	4.7	3.0	0.8
Major	92.2	94.1	5.6	4.2	2.2	1.7
Captain	90.0	90.4	7.9	7.1	2.1	2.5
First Lieutenant	78.3	75.9	19.1	22.1	2.6	2.0
Second Lieutenant . . .	43.6	42.0	55.3	57.4	1.1	0.6
Warrant Officer	94.8	90.0	3.0	3.4	2.2	6.6
Airman - Total . .	35.0	38.1	62.7	59.1	2.3	2.8
Master Sergeant	89.1	90.1	7.7	5.9	3.2	4.0
Technical Sergeant . . .	79.0	80.6	15.8	13.7	5.2	5.7
Staff Sergeant	60.7	64.4	35.7	31.5	3.6	4.1
Airman First Class . . .	34.9	34.2	62.7	63.6	2.4	2.2
Airman Second Class . .	25.9	26.6	72.5	71.2	1.6	2.2
Airman Third Class . . .	16.0	16.6	82.3	81.5	1.7	1.9
Basic Airman	12.8	16.4	85.4	80.3	1.8	3.3
Aviation Cadet	-	-	98.8	98.7	1.2	1.3

a/ Includes divorced, legally separated, and widowed personnel

Source: Personnel Statistics Division, DCS/Comptroller Hq. USAF.

TABLE 248 — ESTIMATED PERCENTAGE DISTRIBUTION OF USAF MILITARY PERSONNEL BY NUMBER OF DEPENDENTS — 30 NOV 1952

Grade	Per Cent By Number Of Dependents						
	None	1	2	3	4	5	6 Or More
Officer - Total	17.8	18.3	21.9	26.1	11.4	3.6	0.9
Colonel	1.7	12.2	21.7	32.6	21.3	8.4	2.1
Lieutenant Colonel . . .	3.5	15.8	23.9	31.8	17.0	6.2	1.8
Major	5.0	13.2	23.0	34.7	17.9	4.9	1.3
Captain	6.6	15.4	24.6	34.3	13.8	4.4	0.9
First Lieutenant	18.3	20.0	25.0	24.4	9.0	2.7	0.6
Second Lieutenant . . .	54.2	26.9	11.7	5.0	1.6	0.5	0.1
Warrant Officer	3.0	18.1	29.7	29.6	13.3	4.8	1.5
Airman - Total . .	59.0	19.7	11.3	6.3	2.2	0.9	0.6
Master Sergeant	7.0	18.2	22.5	30.3	14.4	5.3	2.3
Technical Sergeant . . .	15.9	19.1	26.2	24.1	9.0	4.1	1.6
Staff Sergeant	33.6	27.2	20.8	12.4	3.9	1.3	0.8
Airman First Class . . .	60.0	23.7	11.6	3.3	0.8	0.3	0.3
Airman Second Class . .	68.4	20.8	8.2	1.9	0.3	0.1	0.3
Airman Third Class . . .	77.0	15.5	5.5	1.4	0.3	0.1	0.2
Basic Airman	79.0	13.1	4.4	2.0	0.4	0.2	0.9
Aviation Cadet	97.5	2.5	-	-	-	-	-

Source: Personnel Statistics Division, DCS/Comptroller, Hq. USAF

TABLE 249 — AGE DISTRIBUTION OF DEPARTMENTAL STRENGTH OFFICER PERSONNEL BY GRADE IN WHICH SERVING — 30 NOV 1952 AND 31 MAY 1953

(Extreme and unknown ages were prorated in the table below.)

Age	Total	General	Colonel	Lieutenant Colonel	Major	Captain	First Lieutenant	Second Lieutenant	Warrant Officer
	30 November 1952								
Total . . .	130,158	366	3,957	8,143	19,837	37,688	30,804	25,421	3,942
Under 22	955	-	-	-	-	-	5	950	-
22	5,125	-	-	-	-	5	60	5,060	-
23	7,258	-	-	-	-	16	747	6,495	-
24	7,232	-	-	-	-	55	2,020	5,151	6
25	3,894	-	-	-	1	118	1,671	2,101	3
26	3,711	-	-	-	5	228	2,023	1,449	6
27	5,806	-	-	-	38	1,207	3,346	1,195	20
28	7,711	-	-	2	204	2,685	3,881	896	43
29	8,424	-	-	13	402	3,630	3,578	726	75
30	9,071	-	-	54	864	4,262	3,318	428	145
31	10,583	-	10	208	1,836	5,030	2,870	407	222
32	10,351	-	46	531	2,283	4,586	2,330	254	321
33	8,729	-	91	757	2,357	3,625	1,453	105	341
34	8,484	-	207	929	2,362	3,261	1,217	69	439
35	6,956	-	266	809	1,949	2,553	968	49	362
36									
36	5,522	2	303	698	1,658	1,905	628	22	306
37	4,186	1	319	625	1,325	1,286	285	52	293
38	2,526	2	300	472	673	702	138	8	231
39	1,779	4	228	313	467	528	70	2	167
40	1,723	5	207	334	468	460	65	2	182
41	1,392	9	222	296	383	332	34	-	116
42	1,348	23	212	271	401	285	28	-	128
43	1,157	21	213	239	346	218	20	-	100
44	1,118	17	189	246	355	'198	17	-	96
45	998	28	169	233	309	146	16	-	97
46	851	34	176	191	275	111	12	-	52
47	695	37	145	178	200	82	4	-	49
48	556	30	122	135	178	60	-	-	31
49	434	21	110	111	125	44	-	-	23
50	343	26	83	86	91	33	-	-	24
51	280	18	70	82	57	37	-	-	16
52	216	19	56	64	61	-	-	-	16
53	158	12	32	62	44	-	-	-	8
54	133	7	30	53	29	-	-	-	14
55	117	7	32	42	31	-	-	-	5
56	105	9	40	30	26	-	-	-	-
57	83	9	21	41	11	-	-	-	1
58	78	8	35	17	16	-	-	-	2
59	49	7	17	17	7	-	-	-	1
60 and Over . .	21	10	6	4	-	-	-	-	1
	31 May 1953								
Total . . .	128,267	363	4,168	8,162	20,791	37,156	31,300	22,522	3,805
Under 22	196	-	-	-	-	-	-	196	-
22	1,862	-	-	-	-	-	23	1,839	-
23	7,323	-	-	-	-	-	604	6,718	1
24	8,784	-	-	-	-	26	2,648	6,105	5
25	7,852	-	-	-	-	130	3,557	4,159	6

(Continued)

TABLE 249 — AGE DISTRIBUTION OF DEPARTMENTAL STRENGTH OFFICER PERSONNEL BY GRADE IN WHICH SERVING — 30 NOV 1952 AND 31 MAY 1953 (CONTINUED)

(Extreme and unknown ages were prorated in the table below.)

Age	Total	General	Colonel	Lieutenant Colonel	Major	Captain	First Lieutenant	Second Lieutenant	Warrant Officer
	31 May 1953								
26	3,805	-	-	-	-	185	2,476	1,140	4
27	3,607	-	-	-	9	333	2,541	718	6
28	5,280	-	-	4	56	1,460	3,238	503	19
29	6,983	-	-	4	286	2,818	3,459	377	39
30	7,621	-	-	22	557	3,665	3,058	259	60
31	8,352	-	2	65	1,076	4,270	2,639	168	132
32	9,889	-	10	249	2,025	5,039	2,205	144	217
33	9,770	-	62	566	2,452	4,554	1,722	104	310
34	8,221	-	120	794	2,429	3,515	995	37	331
35	7,904	-	245	945	2,375	3,125	764	26	424
36	6,496	-	295	837	1,978	2,450	587	12	337
37	5,109	2	322	698	1,669	1,733	384	5	296
38	3,943	1	344	616	1,374	1,139	171	5	293
39	2,386	3	323	442	680	609	89	3	237
40	1,694	5	231	309	473	472	39	4	161
41	1,618	4	216	321	490	375	39	-	173
42	1,329	10	226	285	399	272	28	-	109
43	1,273	23	217	277	375	238	18	-	125
44	1,116	22	228	232	348	180	9	-	97
45	1,048	18	202	222	337	167	7	-	95
46	930	30	172	211	304	121	-	-	92
47	797	33	181	183	268	81	-	-	51
48	667	39	144	172	197	68	-	-	47
49	518	29	120	127	164	49	-	-	29
50	405	22	107	103	113	38	-	-	22
51	318	26	80	86	87	19	-	-	20
52	266	19	69	81	58	25	-	-	14
53	204	19	56	64	51	-	-	-	14
54	156	11	32	60	44	-	-	-	9
55	124	6	27	50	25	-	-	-	16
56	116	7	30	43	30	-	-	-	6
57	99	8	37	27	27	-	-	-	-
58	78	6	22	37	12	-	-	-	1
59	70	6	30	16	16	-	-	-	2
60 and Over . .	58	14	18	14	7	-	-	-	5

Source: Personnel Statistics Division, DCS/Comptroller, Hq USAF

TABLE 250 — ESTIMATED DISTRIBUTION OF AIRMEN BY AGE, BY GRADE IN WHICH SERVING, BY SEX — 31 MAY 1953

(Table is based on Departmental Strength and includes Aviation Cadets)

Age	Male				Female	
	White		Negro			
	Number	Per Cent	Number	Per Cent	Number	Per Cent
Total	693,132	100.0	62,663	100.0	12,786	100.0
17	11,159	1.6	1,886	3.0	-	-
18	36,597	5.3	7,413	11.8	1,649	12.9
19	65,986	9.5	8,735	13.9	2,707	21.2
20	104,870	15.1	10,700	17.1	2,139	16.7
21	111,802	16.1	8,250	13.2	1,933	15.1
22	93,088	13.4	6,385	10.2	954	7.5
23	64,461	9.3	3,504	5.6	649	5.1
24	40,410	5.8	2,720	4.3	593	4.7
25	19,477	2.8	2,563	4.1	361	2.8
26	12,476	1.8	1,617	2.6	231	1.8
27	10,535	1.5	1,184	1.9	206	1.6
28	12,338	1.8	1,021	1.6	180	1.4
29	10,882	1.6	865	1.4	180	1.4
30	12,100	1.8	996	1.6	206	1.6
31	12,439	1.8	915	1.5	104	0.8
32	11,922	1.7	702	1.1	77	0.6
33	10,674	1.6	677	1.1	104	0.8
34	9,496	1.4	376	0.6	77	0.6

Age	Male				Female	
	White		Negro			
	Number	Per Cent	Number	Per Cent	Number	Per Cent
35	7,763	1.1	457	0.7	-	-
36	6,446	0.9	295	0.5	51	0.4
37	4,228	0.6	244	0.4	51	0.4
38	5,060	0.7	244	0.4	-	-
39	3,743	0.5	163	0.3	51	0.4
40	2,357	0.3	188	0.3	26	0.2
41	2,634	0.4	244	0.4	51	0.4
42	2,149	0.3	107	0.2	-	-
43	1,594	0.2	56	0.1	77	0.6
44	1,317	0.2	81	0.1	-	-
45	1,317	0.2	25	a/	-	-
46	901	0.1	-	-	-	-
47	693	0.1	25	a/	26	0.2
48	485	0.1	-	-	26	0.2
49	347	0.1	-	-	-	-
50	416	0.1	-	-	-	-
51 through 54 . . .	693	0.1	25	a/	26	0.2
55 and Over . .	277	a/	-	-	51	0.4

a/ Less than 0.05 Per Cent

Source: Personnel Statistics Division, DCS/Comptroller, Hq. USAF

TABLE 251 — ESTIMATED PERCENTAGE DISTRIBUTION OF AIRMEN BY AGE GROUPS, BY GRADE IN WHICH SERVING — 31 MAY 1953

(Table is based on Departmental Strength)

Grade	Per Cent By Age Group									
	18 And Under	19	20 Through 24	25 Through 29	30 Through 34	35 Through 39	40 Through 44	45 Through 49	50 And Over	Average Age
Airman - Total	6.8	10.4	59.3	10.5	7.3	3.9	1.2	0.4	0.2	24.1
Master Sergeant . .	-	-	1.5	9.2	41.0	31.9	10.7	4.0	1.7	35.5
Technical Sergeant.	-	-	14.2	26.9	36.4	15.8	4.8	1.6	0.3	31.3
Staff Sergeant. . .	-	0.2	56.9	24.6	11.2	4.9	1.6	0.4	0.2	26.1
Airman First Class.	0.3	2.5	84.0	9.6	2.1	1.1	0.3	0.1	-	23.3
Airman Second Class	3.5	10.6	77.6	6.2	1.6	0.4	0.1	-	-	22.6
Airman Third Class.	19.6	24.6	51.1	3.6	0.8	0.3	-	-	-	21.2
Basic Airman . . .	28.4	31.1	34.3	4.4	1.4	0.4	-	-	-	20.7
Aviation Cadet . .	-	5.5	89.6	4.9	-	-	-	-	-	22.6

Source: Personnel Statistics Division, DCS/Comptroller, Hq. USAF

TABLE 252 — AIRMEN (AUTHORIZED AND ASSIGNED) BY PRIMARY AFSC WITHIN CAREER FIELD - 31 JUL 1952 AND 30 JUN 1953

Career Field	Total Assigned by Primary	Permanent Party		Pipeline	
		Authorized	Assigned	Student	Transient and Patient
	31 July 1952				
Total	815,107	648,195	670,624	113,254	31,229
Intelligence	4,871	5,086	4,489	136	246
Photomapping	1,826	1,554	1,763	7	56
Photographic	5,919	5,531	5,737	39	143
Weather	6,188	6,051	5,392	531	265
Air Traffic Control and Warning	21,303	22,559	19,904	611	788
Communications-Operations	37,826	38,005	34,790	998	2,038
Radio and Radar Maintenance	38,793	27,696	36,557	986	1,250
Missile Guidance Systems	645	541	628	15	2
Armament Systems Maintenance	20,441	13,785	18,145	1,790	506
Weapons	1,029	722	969	57	3
Training Devices Maintenance	548	679	536	5	7
Wire Maintenance	10,761	9,207	9,989	317	455
Intricate Equipment Maintenance	4,120	4,496	3,918	27	175
Aircraft Accessories Maintenance	6,444	7,677	6,152	15	277
Aircraft and Engine Maintenance	105,828	100,405	97,095	5,535	3,198
Rocket Propulsion	124	170	124	-	-
Munitions and Weapons Maintenance	14,933	13,480	13,907	108	918
Vehicle Maintenance	26,402	20,597	24,870	262	1,270
Metal Working	13,318	10,555	12,650	165	503
Construction	14,345	11,607	13,530	55	760
Utilities	11,079	9,562	10,456	32	591
Fabric, Leather and Rubber	4,013	3,892	3,716	73	224
Transportation	35,611	34,737	33,987	86	1,538
Food Service	51,051	45,407	47,402	1,124	2,525
Supply	61,329	59,349	58,208	330	2,791
Procurement	481	477	457	13	11
Administrative	69,734	58,568	67,012	859	1,863
Printing	2,246	1,258	2,209	10	27
Information	1,761	1,336	1,671	52	38
Personnel	18,707	21,522	18,068	159	480
Education	4,999	3,386	4,391	501	107
Band	3,300	2,995	3,227	39	34
Entertainment	3,998	2,121	3,874	64	60
Welfare	1,295	1,017	1,238	19	38
Management Methods	674	922	644	11	19
Budgetary Accounting and Disbursing	8,044	6,129	7,658	160	226
Statistical and Machine Accounting	5,293	4,721	5,001	87	205
Medical	26,696	23,419	25,422	463	811
Rescue and Survival	451	586	443	-	8
Ground Safety	512	474	475	5	32
Marine	1,552	1,039	1,426	1	125
Firefighting	9,867	10,583	9,564	11	292
Security and Law Enforcement	39,484	42,089	37,561	62	1,861
Special Activities	8,033	9,037	7,733	27	273
Basic Airmen	95,736	32	3,379	89,512	2,845
Other Reporting Codes (AFSC 990--)	13,497	3,134	4,257	7,895	1,345
	30 June 1953				
Total	818,613	689,771	698,596	90,164	29,853
Intelligence	5,686	5,903	5,377	107	202
Photomapping	1,658	1,498	1,613	11	34
Photographic	5,953	5,833	5,790	69	94
Weather	6,143	6,520	5,736	175	232
Air Traffic Control and Warning	22,996	23,606	21,651	352	993
Communications-Operations	41,817	41,920	38,472	739	2,606
Radio and Radar Maintenance	36,060	30,747	33,924	556	1,580
Missile Guidance Systems	848	760	845	2	1
Armament Systems Maintenance	21,518	15,979	18,522	2,505	491
Weapons	1,383	1,280	1,312	46	25
Training Devices Maintenance	1,004	1,086	966	20	18
Wire Maintenance	10,271	10,248	9,747	93	431

(CONTINUED)

TABLE 252 — AIRMEN (AUTHORIZED AND ASSIGNED) BY PRIMARY AFSC WITHIN CAREER FIELD
31 JUL 1952 AND 30 JUN 1953 — CONTINUED

Career Field	Total Assigned by Primary	Permanent Party		Pipeline	
		Authorized	Assigned	Student	Transient and Patient
	30 June 1953				
Intricate Equipment Maintenance	4,407	5,376	4,071	56	280
Aircraft Accessories Maintenance	8,027	8,281	7,707	99	221
Aircraft and Engine Maintenance	119,783	112,078	111,885	5,424	2,474
Rocket Propulsion	162	90	161	1	-
Munitions and Weapons Maintenance	15,200	14,100	14,173	99	928
Vehicle Maintenance	24,998	22,553	23,108	215	1,675
Metal Working	14,125	10,392	13,449	171	505
Construction	14,049	12,563	13,231	114	704
Utilities	12,164	10,216	11,428	117	619
Fabric, Leather and Rubber	4,683	3,666	4,309	94	280
Transportation	36,164	31,541	34,592	89	1,483
Food Service	47,249	38,910	45,445	102	1,702
Supply	70,964	67,555	66,523	521	3,920
Procurement	577	583	565	-	12
Administrative	62,693	57,965	60,683	339	1,671
Printing	2,409	1,770	2,342	11	56
Information	1,562	1,244	1,519	5	38
Personnel	20,684	18,948	20,168	50	466
Education	4,308	3,662	4,119	124	65
Band	3,227	3,433	3,102	50	- 75
Entertainment	3,522	2,129	3,463	23	36
Welfare	1,240	1,017	1,223	3	14
Management Methods	875	1,334	848	2	25
Budgetary Accounting and Disbursing	7,604	6,773	7,412	40	152
Statistical and Machine Accounting	5,926	5,184	5,677	49	200
Medical	27,744	24,733	26,589	175	980
Rescue and Survival	552	667	539	1	12
Ground Safety	558	389	545	1	12
Marine	1,601	1,147	1,552	11	38
Firefighting	12,117	12,026	11,717	17	383
Security and Law Enforcement	42,388	43,845	40,687	352	1,349
Special Activities	8,608	8,454	8,404	45	159
Basic Airmen	69,780	-	2,329	66,563	888
Other Reporting Codes (AFSC 990--)	13,326	11,767	1,076	10,526	1,724

Source: Personnel Statistics Division, DCS/Comptroller, Hq USAF

TABLE 253 — PERMANENT PARTY PERSONNEL BY PERSONNEL IDENTITY — FY 1953

(WAF - Women in the Air Force; AFNC - Air Force Nurse Corps; WMSC - Women's Medical Specialist Corps).

End of Month	Total	OFFICER			WARRANT OFFICER		Aviation Cadet	ENLISTED	
		Male	WAF	AFNC and WMSC	Male	Female		Male	Female
	CONTINENTAL US								
1952									
July	561,436	79,590	692	2,143	3,031	4	-	468,444	7,532
August	556,909	80,526	716	2,086	3,015	4	-	462,762	7,800
September.	553,450	79,613	746	2,036	2,973	4	-	459,826	8,252
October.	552,586	79,511	747	2,035	2,973	3	-	458,933	8,384
November	549,636	79,580	769	2,079	2,983	3	-	455,712	8,510
December	551,400	78,698	772	2,072	2,934	3	-	458,337	8,584
1953									
January.	548,896	77,490	766	2,125	2,871	3	-	456,917	8,724
February	545,349	76,502	756	2,114	2,854	2	-	454,289	8,832
March.	548,921	75,898	764	2,144	2,836	2	-	458,452	8,825
April.	546,483	74,981	756	2,153	2,780	2	-	456,967	8,844
May.	548,842	75,136	723	2,211	2,714	2	-	459,171	8,885
June	552,004	74,651	708	2,194	2,669	2	-	462,906	8,874
	OVERSEAS								
1952									
July	250,909	28,576	132	633	993	2	-	220,096	477
August	257,198	29,045	144	668	1,006	2	-	225,781	552
September.	257,881	29,379	147	690	1,049	2	-	226,008	606
October.	262,359	28,875	146	702	1,039	2	-	230,942	653
November	266,509	29,107	151	712	1,066	3	-	234,778	692
December	268,385	28,631	160	721	1,065	3	-	237,025	780
1953									
January.	273,102	28,927	161	749	1,087	3	-	241,364	811
February	275,506	29,151	171	742	1,101	3	-	243,455	883
March.	276,841	29,215	172	729	1,094	4	-	244,678	949
April.	281,807	29,634	179	757	1,120	4	-	249,066	1,047
May.	283,048	30,017	201	779	1,120	3	-	249,850	1,078
June	284,581	30,180	228	789	1,129	3	-	251,057	1,195

Source: Personnel Statistics Division, DCS/Comptroller, Hq, USAF

TABLE 254 — FEAF AUTHORIZED AND ASSIGNED PERMANENT PARTY MILITARY PERSONNEL BY DEPARTMENTAL STATUS — FY 1953

Date	Authorized Strength	Assigned Strength a/		
	Total	Total	Air Force	SCARWAF
		TOTAL		
1952				
July	102,529	95,866	85,039	10,827
August	102,457	97,128	86,513	10,615
September	102,324	96,564	86,851	9,713
October	102,712	100,777	90,842	9,935
November	101,889	101,779	90,932	10,847
December	101,638	103,323	91,142	12,181
1953				
January	104,395	106,801	95,509	11,292
February	104,240	106,845	95,735	11,110
March	104,026	107,260	96,055	11,205
April	104,385	107,595	96,892	10,703
May	104,903	104,985	94,596	10,389
June	102,215	103,643	93,546	10,097
		OFFICER		
1952				
July	12,847	11,472	11,021	451
August	12,857	11,636	11,218	418
September	12,829	11,516	11,133	383
October	12,874	11,302	10,991	311
November	12,617	11,258	10,915	343
December	12,585	10,982	10,580	402
1953				
January	12,794	11,160	10,703	457
February	12,788	11,247	10,822	425
March	12,799	11,406	10,921	485
April	12,798	11,544	11,076	468
May	12,854	11,766	11,236	530
June	12,144	12,028	11,472	556
		ENLISTED		
1952				
July	89,682	84,394	74,018	10,376
August	89,600	85,492	75,295	10,197
September	89,495	85,048	75,718	9,330
October	89,838	89,475	79,851	9,624
November	89,272	90,521	80,017	10,504
December	89,053	92,341	80,562	11,779
1953				
January	91,601	95,641	84,806	10,835
February	91,452	95,598	84,913	10,685
March	91,227	95,854	85,134	10,720
April	91,587	96,051	85,816	10,235
May	92,049	93,219	83,360	9,859
June	90,071	91,615	82,074	9,541

a/ Includes units of Air Defense Command, Strategic Air Command and Tactical Air Command, which are under the Operational Control of Far East Air Forces for promotional and manning purposes.

Source: Personnel Statistics Division, DCS/Comptroller, Headquarters, USAF.

TABLE 255 — STUDENTS (USAF ONLY), CONTINENTAL US — FY 1953

(WAF - Women in the Air Force: AFNC - Air Force Nurse Corps; WMSC - Women's Medical Specialist Corps).

End of Month	Total	OFFICER			WARRANT OFFICER		Aviation Cadet	ENLISTED	
		Male	WAF	AFNC and WMSC	Male	Female		Male	Female
1952									
July	121,549	8,123	87	58	27	-	7,614	102,430	3,210
August	123,816	8,861	107	63	29	-	8,029	103,365	3,362
September.	118,833	9,260	66	78	32	-	7,733	98,421	3,243
October.	114,807	10,058	64	89	31	-	7,946	93,213	3,406
November	110,549	9,318	28	85	30	-	8,678	89,014	3,396
December	98,698	9,084	32	83	30	-	8,184	78,354	2,931
1953									
January.	100,176	8,787	38	80	29	-	9,280	79,226	2,736
February	105,847	9,616	39	81	29	-	9,151	84,512	2,419
March.	111,807	10,355	25	77	36	-	9,648	89,485	2,181
April.	115,127	10,609	32	55	40	-	10,467	91,939	1,985
May.	109,602	10,827	31	44	43	-	9,768	87,236	1,653
June	101,928	11,642	33	40	49	-	9,156	79,504	1,504

Source: Personnel Statistics Division DCS/Comptroller, Headquarters USAF.

TABLE 256 – USAF MILITARY DECORATIONS AND AWARDS – FY 1953

Months	Total	Air Medal			Bronze Star Medal			Commendation Ribbon		
		Total	Basic	Oak Leaf Cluster	Total	Basic	Oak Leaf Cluster	Total	Basic	Oak Leaf Cluster
Total	598	188	168	20	3	3	-	199	180	19
July (1952)	70	17	10	7	1	1	-	24	21	3
August	51	12	9	3	-	-	-	18	17	1
September	23	5	4	1	-	-	-	12	10	2
October	36	9	9	-	1	1	-	12	11	1
November	15	3	2	1	-	-	-	5	5	-
December	49	8	8	-	-	-	-	25	24	1
January (1953)	38	17	16	1	-	-	-	9	8	1
February	101	81	81	-	-	-	-	7	6	1
March	75	13	9	4	1	1	-	24	23	1
April	24	1	-	1	-	-	-	12	12	-
May	75	15	14	1	-	-	-	28	24	4
June	41	7	6	1	-	-	-	23	19	4

Months	Distinguished Flying Cross			Distinguished Service Medal			Legion of Merit		
	Total	Basic	Oak Leaf Cluster	Total	Basic	Oak Leaf Cluster	Total	Basic	Oak Leaf Cluster
Total	31	25	6	12	9	3	43	33	10
July (1952)	-	-	-	2	2	-	4	2	2
August	4	2	2	1	1	-	6	6	-
September	-	-	-	-	-	-	2	1	1
October	1	1	-	1	1	-	4	4	-
November	1	1	-	1	-	1	2	-	2
December	-	-	-	-	-	-	4	3	1
January (1953)	-	-	-	3	2	1	1	1	-
February	-	-	-	1	1	-	6	5	1
March	1	1	-	1	1	-	10	7	3
April	-	-	-	1	-	1	2	2	-
May	22	19	3	-	-	-	1	1	-
June	2	1	1	1	1	-	1	1	-

Months	Medal of Freedom			Purple Heart			Silver Medal		
	Total	Basic	Oak Leaf Cluster	Total	Basic	Oak Leaf Cluster	Total	Basic	Oak Leaf Cluster
Total	1	1	-	51	31	20	70	70	-
July (1952)	-	-	-	10	2	8	12	12	-
August	-	-	-	6	5	1	4	4	-
September	-	-	-	2	2	-	2	2	-
October	1	1	-	4	2	2	3	3	-
November	-	-	-	1	1	-	2	2	-
December	-	-	-	5	5	-	7	7	-
January (1953)	-	-	-	1	-	1	7	7	-
February	-	-	-	4	4	-	2	2	-
March	-	-	-	9	5	4	16	16	-
April	-	-	-	3	-	3	5	5	-
May	-	-	-	4	4	-	5	5	-
June	-	-	-	2	1	1	5	5	-

Source: Awards Branch, Personnel Service Division Directorate of Military Personnel, DCS/P, Hq USAF.

TABLE 257 — SUMMARY OF SAVING BONDS PURCHASED BY AIR FORCE PERSONNEL IN CONTINENTAL US AND OVERSEAS — JUN 1948 THROUGH JUN 1953

(The table below is based on the Saving Bond Committee's reports. The Committee receives its reports from Headquarters USAF Civilian Personnel, Air Force Finance Center, and Statistical Services. A table on bonds was released to the "Digest" for the first time in 1947 and covered the period June 1943 through December 1947. However, the table gives only possible resume for the captions indicated and covers FY's 1948 through 1953.)

Date	Percentage of Civilian Employees Participating in Class A Pay Reservation Plan	Civilians Participating in Class A Pay Reservations	Military Allotors Participating	Cash Purchases By Civilian Employees a/	Cash Purchases By Military Personnel a/	Average Amount Allotted By Civilian Employees	Average Amount Allotted By Military Personnel
1948							
June	26.8	33,032	28,493	$ 89,029	$ 160,968	$ 27.00	$ 22.00
December	39.2	61,250	21,780	52,548	130,314	19.00	24.00
1949							
June	40.0	68,459	17,473	$ 57,780	$ 165,100	$ 19.00	$ 25.00
December	44.5	150,468	11,178	56,639	88,786	19.00	29.00
1950							
June	43.7	154,453	9,241	$ 50,163	$ 199,714	$ 20.00	$ 36.00
December	26.5	68,107	10,540	27,713	89,275	23.00	34.00
1951							
June	24.0	63,295	11,905	$ 40,431	$ 140,388	$ 24.00	$ 36.00
December	b/ 28.7	b/ 74,831	36,043	25,638	119,513	22.80	26.74
1952							
June	33.9	97,193	63,425	$ 53,362	$ 125,338	$ 22.45	$ 24.67
December	37.46	108,695	64,119	$ 54,738	$ 114,256	$ 22.68	$ 26.44
1953							
June.	46.86	130,650	70,443	$ 49,031	$ 162,426	$ 22.83	$ 26.30

a/ Cash purchases as listed in this column represent only the cash amounts received from USAF personnel and released by the disbursing offices to the Treasury Department.

b/ Non-Citizens of US were included, July 1951 through November 1951.

Source: Personnel Services Division, Directorate of Military Personnel, DCS/P, Headquarters USAF.

TABLE 258 — SAVING BOND PURCHASES BY AIR FORCE PERSONNEL IN CONTINENTAL US AND OVERSEAS — FY 1953

(Data below is taken from the inter-departmental Savings Bond Committee Reports which are prepared monthly for the Committee and are based on reports from Headquarters USAF Civilian Personnel, Air Force Finance Center, and Statistical Services

Item	July (1952)	August	September	October	November	December
Bond Sales (Allotments and Cash Purchases) - Total a/	$ 3,795,886	$ 3,724,879	$ 3,863,219	$ 4,688,714	$ 3,629,155	$ 4,329,141
Civilian Allotments and Cash Purchases a/	$ 2,023,643	$ 2,115,687	$ 2,148,839	$ 2,548,601	$ 2,074,529	$ 2,519,520
Military Allotments and Cash Purchases a/	$ 1,772,243	$ 1,609,192	$ 1,714,380	$ 2,140,113	$ 1,554,626	$ 1,809,621
Civilian Personnel						
Civilian Employees on Payroll	287,796	286,811	286,043	287,630	288,999	290,168
Civilians Participating in Pay Reservation Plan	88,504	91,499	90,547	109,897	87,021	108,695
Percentage of Civilians Participating	30.75	31.94	31.60	38.21	30.11	37.46
Gross Payroll	$83,460,840	$84,314,068	$83,216,137	$83,668,410	$84,096,087	$84,443,925
Amount Allotted on Payroll	$ 1,997,675	$ 2,081,444	$ 2,108,496	$ 2,498,466	$ 1,976,854	$ 2,464,782
Percentage of Total Pay Allotted by Civilians	2.39	2.47	2.53	2.99	2.35	2.92
Average Allotment by Civilians	$22.57	$22.75	$23.29	$22.73	$22.72	$22.68
Cash Purchases by Civilians a/	$25,968	$34,243	$40,343	$50,135	$97,675	$54,738
Military Personnel						
Number of Military Personnel Allotments	66,352	58,058	63,537	79,348	58,242	64,119
Amount Allotted by Military Personnel	$ 1,668,812	$ 1,504,885	$ 1,608,649	$ 2,008,528	$ 1,504,326	$ 1,695,365
Average Allotment by Military Personnel	$25.15	$25.92	$25.32	$25.31	$25.83	$26.44
Cash Purchases by Military Personnel a/	$103,431	$104,307	$105,731	$131,585	$50,300	$114,256
	January (1953)	**February**	**March**	**April**	**May**	**June**
Bond Sales (Allotments and Cash Purchases - Total a/	$ 4,213,858	$ 3,876,193	$ 4,634,489	$ 5,051,471	$ 4,574,307	$ 5,046,516
Civilian Allotments and Cash Purchases a/	$ 2,417,307	$ 2,218,858	$ 2,625,117	$ 2,985,746	$ 2,797,805	$ 3,031,546
Military Allotments and Cash Purchases a/	$ 1,796,551	$ 1,657,335	$ 2,009,372	$ 2,065,725	$ 1,776,502	$ 2,014,970
Civilian Personnel						
Civilian Employees on Payroll	290,864	289,070	286,078	281,116	277,354	278,807
Civilians Participating in the Pay Reservation Plan	105,228	94,415	114,125	130,087	118,976	130,650
Percentage of Civilians Participating	36.18	32.66	39.89	46.28	42.9	46.86
Gross Payroll	$85,508,085	$84,133,105	$83,268,674	$81,844,134	$80,764,079	$81,184,095
Amount Allotted on Payroll	$ 2,373,789	$ 2,183,970	$ 2,554,473	$ 2,931,227	$ 2,760,761	$ 2,982,515
Percentage of Total Pay Allotted by Civilians	2.78	2.60	3.06	3.58	3.4	3.67
Average Allotment by Civilians	$22.56	$23.13	$22.38	$22.53	$23.20	$22.83
Cash Purchases by Civilians a/	$43,518	$34,888	$70,644	$54,519	$37,044	$49,031
Military Personnel						
Number of Military Personnel Allotments	65,113	58,851	70,267	73,082	62,013	70,443
Amount Allotted by Military Personnel	$ 1,665,576	$ 1,521,575	$ 1,858,409	$ 1,913,700	$ 1,649,453	$ 1,852,544
Average Allotments by Military Personnel	$25.58	$25.85	$22.44	$26.19	$26.60	$26.30
Cash Purchases by Military Personnel a/	$130,975	$135,760	$150,963	$152,025	$127,049	$162,426

a/ Cash purchases represent only the cash amounts received from USAP Personnel and released by the disbursing office to the Treasury Department.

Note: All of the following statements are based on end of six month period comparisons, beginning with June 1948:
Highest percentage of Civilian participation was indicated, June 1953 - 46.86%
Lowest percentage of Civilian participation was indicated July 1951- 23.5%
June 1953 showed an increase of 13.0% in Civilian personnel participation over June 1952.
Highest average allotments by Civilian personnel were indicated in June 1948 with an average of $27.00 each.
The lowest average of $19.00 was held December 1948, June 1949, and December 1949.
June 1953 showed an average of $22.83 allotted per month by Civilian personnel as compared to $22.45 for June 1952.
A general average for Civilians for FY '53 was $22.78.
The highest monthly average allotment ($36.00) by the Military was indicated in June 1950; the lowest in June 1952 with an average of $24.67 per month. The highest monthly average for Military personnel during FY 1953 was $ 26.60 for the month of May 1953. The monthly average for Military personnel allotments for FY 1953 was $25.58.

Source: Personnel Services Division, Directorate of Military Personnel, DCS/P, Headquarters USAF.

TABLE 259 — COST OF TRAINING USAF MILITARY STUDENTS BY COURSE — 15 APR 1953 THROUGH 30 JUN 1953

(Official costs of training USAF military students were developed in accordance with the uniform principles set forth by course in the table below. The data used to develop the training costs were obtained from reports prepared under the provisions of AFR 170-13. The official costs of training are set forth by career fields. The career fields are arranged numerically, and the courses in each career field are arranged numerically by Officer and Airman Courses. The assumption has been made that Air Training Command and Air University Bases have the single major mission of training, and consequently, the total operating costs of bases, including student pay plus major and intermediate command Headquarters cost, are chargeable against the end product, namely: student graduates. Since costs generated by students eliminated from a course represent a part of the cost of the finished product, eliminee costs are included in the total course cost figures. All costs specifically identified with a particular course or department were costed directly to the course. Other base costs were distributed on an equitable basis to the course being conducted. "Costs of Training USAF Military Students By Course" as published in "USAF Statistical Digest - FY 1952" were in effect, 1 July 1952 through 14 April 1953 of FY 1953.)

Course Number	Course Title	Calendar Days	Course Cost
	BASIC MILITARY TRAINING COURSES		
00010	Basic Military Training (Male)	56	$ 760
00011	Basic Military Training (Female)	56	635
00100	Officer Candidate Training	168	2,505
	INTELLIGENCE COURSES		
OFFICERS			
2011	Advanced Intelligence Officer (Technician)	87	1,955
2044	Intelligence Photo-Radar Officer	181	4,190
2054	Intelligence Officer	70	1,575
AIRMEN			
20450	Intelligence Operations Specialist	64	850
20451	Photo Interpretation Specialist	76	1,035
20470	Intelligence Operations Technician	58	765
20471	Photo Interpretation Technician	88	1,200
20570	Technical Intelligence Technician	53	700
	PHOTOGRAPHIC COURSES		
OFFICERS			
2334	Still Photographic Officer	93	2,095
AIRMEN			
23150	Aerial Photographer	180	6,325
23250	Photo and Laboratory Technician	99	1,480
23350	Motion Picture Photographer	117	1,075
	WEATHER COURSES		
OFFICERS			
2524	High Altitude Forecaster Officer	70	1,040
AIRMEN			
25100	Advanced Weather Equipment	152	2,350
25150	Basic Weather Service (Equipment Channel)	134	2,055
25171	Intermediate Weather Equipment (Keesler Phase)	99	1,375
25171	Intermediate Weather Equipment (Chanute Phase)	117	1,865
25200	Advanced Meteorological	187	2,785
25250	Basic Weather Service (Observer Channel)	99	1,435
25270	Intermediate Meteorological	233	3,325
25271	Climatological - Phase I	233	3,400
25271	Climatological - Phase II	105	1,575
	AIR TRAFFIC CONTROL AND WARNING COURSES		
AIRMEN			
27150	Air Operations Specialist	47	580
27250	Air Traffic Control Operator	82	1,010
27270	Air Traffic Control Technician	70	865
27271	Airport Control Technician	72	1,055
27272	A/C Landing Control Technician	96	1,405
27350	AC&W Operator	35	455

(Continued)

TABLE 259 — COST OF TRAINING USAF MILITARY STUDENTS BY COURSE — 15 APR 1953 THROUGH 30 JUN 1953 — (CONTINUED)

(See headnote on first page)

Course Number	Course Title	Calendar Days	Course Cost
	COMMUNICATIONS COURSES		
AIRMEN			
29150	Communications Center Specialist	82	$ 970
29250	Cryptographic Operator	53	735
29320	Radio Operator Fundamentals	88	985
29351	Radio Operator - Ground	82	920
29352	Radio Intercept Operator	117	1,370
29353	Airborne Radio Operator	93	1,090
	COMMUNICATIONS AND ELECTRONICS COURSES		
OFFICERS			
3000	Staff Officer ECM Indoctrination	5	145
3011	Advanced Communications Electronics Officer	144	3,540
3034	Communications Officer	252	6,195
3044	Electronics Officer Ground AN/CPN-4	315	7,000
3054	Electronics Officer Air	246	5,620
	RADIO-RADAR SYSTEMS MAINTENANCE COURSES		
AIRMEN			
30120	Radio Fundamentals	134	1,845
30150	Radio Mechanic Airborne Equipment	88	1,380
30151	Airborne Electronic Navigational Equipment Repairman	102	1,540
30171A	Communications and Electronic Maintenance Technician-Airborne	204	3,430
30171B	Electronic Navigational Equipment Maintenance Technician-Airborne	111	1,675
30220	Airmen Electronic Fundamentals	134	1,490
30250	ECM Repairman	82	1,240
30270	ECM Maintenance Technician	102	1,435
30351	Air Traffic Control Radar Repairman	128	1,960
30352	AC&W Radar Repairman	82	1,255
30353	Auto Tracking Radar Repairman	82	1,250
30371	Air Traffic Control Radar Maintenance Technician	134	3,335
30372	AC&W Radar Maintenance Technician	134	2,305
30373	Auto Tracking Maintenance Technician	93	1,660
30450	Radio Repairman-Ground Equipment	88	1,480
30471-A	Ground Maintenance Technician	111	1,890
30471-B	Ground Radio Maintenance Technician-Navigational Aids Communications	70	945
30570	Airman ECM Reconnaissance Equipment Operator Technician	47	660
	ARMAMENT COURSES		
OFFICERS			
3211	Advanced Armament Officer	72	1,855
3224R	Guided Missile Guidance and Control Officer	122	2,900
3234A	Armament System Officer (Fighter)	198	4,490
3234B	Armament System Officer (Bomber)	222	5,030
3244	Weapons Officer	82	1,780
3254	Munitions Officer	93	2,285
	ARMAMENT SYSTEMS MAINTENANCE COURSES		
AIRMEN			
32020	Armament Systems Fundamentals	122	1,595
32150-A	"M" Series Bombsight Mechanic	35	470
32150-B	"K" Series Stabilization and Optics Specialist	82	1,440
32150-C	"K" Series Radar and Interconnection Specialist	82	1,315
32150-D	"K" Series Computer Specialist	82	1,490
32150-E	"K" Series System Mechanic	117	1,620

(Continued)

TABLE 259 — COST OF TRAINING USAF MILITARY STUDENTS BY COURSE — 15 APR 1953 THROUGH 30 JUN 1953 — (CONTINUED)

(See headnote on first page)

Course Number	Course Title	Calendar Days	Course Cost
	ARMAMENT SYSTEMS MAINTENANCE COURSES (CONTINUED)		
AIRMEN			
32150-P	AN/APQ-24 System Mechanic	82	$1,575
32150-H	Shoran System Mechanic	82	1,185
32171-E	"K" Series System Technician	157	2,540
32171-F	AN/APQ-24 System Technician	87	1,560
32250-A	"E" Series System Mechanic	76	1,000
32250-B	AN/APG-30 Sighting System Mechanic	64	860
32250-C	A&K Series Gun-Bombsight Mechanic	29	495
32250-D	E4, 5&6 Fire Control System Mechanic	105	2,935
32271-A	E-1 Fire Control System Technician	93	3,225
32271-B	AN/APG-30 Sighting Systems Technician	82	2,705
32271-D	E4, 5&6 Series System Technician	157	5,165
32350-A	Turret System Mechanic, B-36	58	740
32350-B	Gunlaying System Mechanic, B-36	87	1,185
32350-C	Gunlaying System Mechanic, B-47	105	2,145
32350-F	Turret System Mechanic, B-26 & B-50	111	1,370
32351-A	Turret System Mechanic Gunner, B-36	42	440
32351-B	Gunlaying System Mechanic Gunner, B-36	42	440
32351-F	Turret System Mechanic Gunner, B-29	56	1,510
32351-P	Turret System Mechanic Gunner, B-26	14	200
32371-A	Turret System Technician, B-36	105	2,610
32371-F	Turret System Technician, B-26, B-29 & B-50	41	550
	TRAINING DEVICES MAINTENANCE COURSES		
AIRMEN			
34150-A	Instrument Trainer Repairman-ANT 18 & C8	99	1,645
34150-B	Instrument Trainer Repairman-Z Type	150	2,495
34150-C	Instrument Trainer Repairman-C-11	174	2,475
	WIRE MAINTENANCE COURSES		
AIRMEN			
36150	Installer Cableman	140	1,810
36250	Central Office Equipment Mechanic	152	2,235
36251	Carrier Repeater Mechanic	111	1,680
36350	Communication Machine Repairman	158	2,045
36351	Cryptographic Machine Repairman	76	3,730
	INTRICATE EQUIPMENT MAINTENANCE COURSES		
AIRMEN			
40350	Camera Repairman	169	2,605
40452	Mechanical Instrument Repairman	93	1,385
40453	Electrical Instrument Repairman	122	1,820
	AIRCRAFT ACCESSORIES MAINTENANCE COURSES		
AIRMEN			
42350	Aircraft Propeller Mechanic	111	1,655
42450	Aircraft Mechanical Accessories and Equipment Repairman	99	1,620
42550	Aircraft Hydraulic Mechanic	105	1,520
42650	Electrical Accessories Repairman	117	1,745
	MAINTENANCE ENGINEERING COURSES		
OFFICERS			
4311	Aircraft Maintenance Management	52	805
4324-I	Aircraft Performance Engineer (Pre) (Interim)	99	1,530
4344	Aircraft Maintenance Officer	187	4,660
4384	Ground Equipment Maintenance Officer	84	2,090

(Continued)

TABLE 259 — COST OF TRAINING USAF MILITARY STUDENTS BY COURSE — 15 APR 1953 THROUGH 30 JUN 1953 — (Continued)

(See headnote on first page)

Course Number	Course Title	Calendar Days	Course Cost
	AIRCRAFT AND ENGINE MAINTENANCE COURSES		
AIRMEN			
43151-A	Aircraft Mechanic-Heavy Bomber	175	$2,200
43151-B	Aircraft Mechanic-Medium Bomber	146	1,640
43151-D	Aircraft Mechanic-Transport	158	1,775
43151-E	Aircraft Mechanic-Liaison Trainer	140	1,470
43151-G	Aircraft Mechanic-Special B-26	35	660
43151-H	Aircraft Mechanic-Jet Fighter	117	2,040
43151-J	Aircraft Mechanic-Special B-47 (SAC)	47	905
43151-J	Aircraft Mechanic-Medium Bomber	93	1,790
43151-W	Aircraft Mechanic-B-26 Ground Phase	12	190
43152-A	Aircraft Reciprocating Engine Mechanic (R-4360)	99	1,485
43152-B	Aircraft Reciprocating Engine Mechanic (R-3350)	99	1,650
43152-E	Aircraft Reciprocating Engine Mechanic (R-2800)	99	1,150
43153	Aircraft Jet Engine Mechanic	111	1,650
43154-A	Aircraft Electricians (A. C. Systems)	146	2,250
43154-B	Aircraft Electrician (General)	117	1,695
43156	Aircraft Instrument Mechanic	117	1,705
43158	Aircraft Electrician Gunner, B-36	49	615
43171	Aircraft Maintenance Technician	111	1,170
43171	Pilotless Aircraft, Airframe Systems and Power Plant Mechanic (B-61)	47	785
43271-D	Flight Engineer Technician (A&D)	140	2,045
	ROCKET PROPULSION COURSES		
AIRMEN			
44170-I	Rocket Propulsion Technician (Interim)	29	475
	MUNITIONS AND WEAPONS MAINTENANCE COURSES		
AIRMEN			
46150	Munitions Specialist	122	1,560
46250	Weapons Mechanic	76	1,060
	VEHICLE MAINTENANCE COURSES		
AIRMEN			
47151	Automotive Mechanic	122	1,645
47152	Special Vehicle Mechanic	87	1,200
47154	Vehicle and Motorized Equipment Engine Mechanic	168	2,875
47155	Vehicle and Motorized Equipment Electrician	175	3,170
47171	Vehicle Maintenance Technician	111	1,500
	METAL WORKING COURSES		
AIRMEN			
53150	Machinist	128	1,955
53250	Welder	122	1,820
53271	Metals Technician	58	1,040
53450	Airframe Repairman	111	2,005
	CONSTRUCTION COURSES		
AIRMEN			
55250	Woodworker	87	2,450
	UTILITIES COURSES		
AIRMEN			
56250	Gas Generating Plant Operator	64	1,805
56550	Heating Specialist	76	1,880

(Continued)

TABLE 259 — COST OF TRAINING USAF MILITARY STUDENTS BY COURSE — 15 APR 1953 THROUGH 30 JUN 1953 — (CONTINUED)

(See headnote on first page)

Course Number	Course Title	Calendar Days	Course Cost
	FABRIC, LEATHER, AND RUBBER COURSES		
AIRMEN			
58150	Parachute Rigger	64	$1,000
58151	Fabric and Leather Worker	64	1,010
58250	Rubber Products Repairman	41	645
	TRANSPORTATION COURSES		
OFFICERS			
6024	Air Transportation Officer	70	2,070
AIRMEN			
60250	Transportation Specialist	76	1,050
60370	Motor Transportation Supervisor	76	1,325
	SUPPLY COURSES		
OFFICERS			
6424	Supply Officer	76	1,700
6434	Supply Services Officer	82	1,830
AIRMEN			
64150	Warehousing Supervisor	53	615
64151	Organizational Supply Specialist	53	615
64152	Supply Records Specialist	64	740
64171	Warehousing Supervisor	53	610
64172	Supply Inspection Technician	53	610
64173	Organizational Supply Supervisor	47	555
64174	Supply Records Supervisor	47	555
64175	Stock Control Technician	35	415
	COMPTROLLER COURSES		
OFFICERS			
6731	Budget Officer	52	1,115
6741	Management Analysis Officer	70	1,495
6744	Disbursing Officer	76	1,625
	COMPTROLLER COURSES (STATISTICAL SERVICES)		
OFFICERS			
6811	Advanced Statistical Services Officer	42	900
6834	Statistical Service Officer	70	1,515
6861	Advanced Accounting/Auditing Officer	60	1,285
6874	Auditor Officer	117	2,500
	ADMINISTRATION COURSES		
AIRMEN			
70250	Basic Clerical	76	900
70270	Administrative Supervisor	47	570
	PERSONNEL COURSES		
OFFICERS			
7324	Personnel Officer	70	1,720
7344	Personnel Services Officer	35	860
7354	Ground Safety Officer	47	1,155

(Continued)

TABLE 259 — COST OF TRAINING USAF MILITARY STUDENTS BY COURSE — 15 APR 1953 THROUGH 30 JUN 1953 — (CONTINUED)

(See headnote of first page)

Course Number	Course Title	Calendar Days	Course Cost
	PERSONNEL COURSES (CONTINUED)		
AIRMEN			
73250	Personnel Specialist	35	$ 495
73270	Advanced Personnel Specialist	35	490
	EDUCATION COURSES		
AIRMEN			
75100	Technical Instructor - Sheppard	47	625
75100	Technical Instructor - Keesler	47	630
75100	Technical Instructor - Lowery	47	1,155
75100	Technical Instructor - Amarillo	47	1,050
75100	Technical Instructor - Warren	47	650
75100	Technical Instructor - Scott	47	920
75100	Technical Instructor - Chanute	47	675
75101	Flexible Gunnery Instructor (Air)	86	1,605
	SECURITY, INVESTIGATION AND LAW ENFORCEMENT COURSES		
OFFICERS			
7711	Air Police - Provost Marshal	63	1,575
7724	Air Police Officer	84	1,850
	DISBURSING, ACCOUNTING AND AUDITING COURSES		
AIRMEN			
81150	Disbursing Clerk	64	890
81170	Disbursing Supervisor	82	1,135
81250	Accounting Clerk	76	1,055
81270	Accounting Technician	93	1,290
81370	Auditing Technician	117	1,605
	STATISTICAL AND MACHINE ACCOUNTING COURSES		
AIRMEN			
83150	Statistical Specialist	76	1,050
83170	Statistical Services Supervisor	70	970
83250	Machine Accountant	76	1,040
83251	Key Punch Machine Operator	24	335
83270	Machine Accounting Supervisor	70	970
	FIREFIGHTING COURSES		
AIRMEN			
95170	Fire and Crash Rescue Supervisor	30	1,295
	SECURITY AND LAW ENFORCEMENT COURSES		
AIRMEN			
96150	Air Policeman	84	1,260
96170	Air Policeman (NCO)	84	1,510
	COMBAT AND OPERATIONS (PILOT AND CREW) COURSES		
OFFICERS			
102401	Advanced Flying School-Medium Bomb Conventional	84	4,955

(Continued)

TABLE 259 — COST OF TRAINING USAF MILITARY STUDENTS BY COURSE — 15 APR 1953 THROUGH 30 JUN 1953 — (CONTINUED)

(See headnote on first page)

Course Number	Course Title	Calendar Days	Course Cost
	COMBAT AND OPERATIONS (TRAINING) COURSES		
OFFICERS			
112100	Pilot Training - Preflight	84	$ 1,250
G112100A	Fighter Gunnery Instructor School	70	30,505
I112100Q	Instrument Pilot Instructor - Jet	56	7,295
112101	Primary - Cadets and Student Officers	180	13,795
112101-A	Advanced Flying School - Jet Fighter	70	28,080
112101-B	Advanced Flying School - F 94	56	6,700
112101-C	Advanced Flying School - Interceptor (F-86D)	56	6,700
112102	Pilot Training Basic - Single Engine (Jet)	161	20,130
112102B	Advanced Flying School - Interceptor (F 89)	56	6,700
F112103P	Primary Instructor School (T-6)	56	4,610
F112108Q	Instrument Pilot Instructor (Jet)	56	7,295
112109	Jet Indoctrination	21	8,400
	COMBAT AND OPERATIONS (PILOT AOB) COURSES		
OFFICERS			
122100	Pilot Training Basic - Multi - Engine	161	11,810
122100C	Advanced Flying School - Lt/Bomb Conventional (B-26)	56	13,075
I122100P	Instrument Pilot Instructor (Conventional)	56	8,725
123100C	Advanced Flying School - M/Bomb Conventional (B-29)	84	4,955
124100	Basic Observer, B-47	140	13,540
	COMBAT AND OPERATIONS (A/C OBSERVER AND ALLIED SPECIALTIES) COURSES		
OFFICERS AND CADETS			
150000	Primary Observer (Cadet)	211	7,270
150000	Primary Observer (Officer)	211	9,440
150001	Primary Observer - Upgrading (Bomb)	169	7,425
150002	Primary Observer - Pilot	183	8,040
152000	Radar Target Prediction and Simulation	12	660
152001	Commanders Radar Bombing Indoctrination	6	330
152002	Observer Instructor - Technical Upgrading	85	3,885
152003	Radar Equipment Air Maintenance Upgrading	28	505
152100A	Basic Observer B-36, B-52, and B-47	154	13,490
152100B	Basic Observer B-47x (Experienced Observers)	85	10,015
152100D	Basic Observer B-50	154	13,235
152100E	Basic Observer B-26	113	9,790
152100F	Basic Observer - Strategic Reconnaissance RB-36, RB-47 and RB-52	183	19,295
153100C	Basic Observer, B-29 Navigator	112	10,820
154100	Basic Observer, B-29 Special	49	3,765
154101	Basic Observer, B-29	57	5,300
15440	Bombardment Defense Officer	35	810
155100	Basic Observer, B-29 Radar Operator	85	3,730
156102	Basic Observer, E-S-Fes Upgrading	28	1,960
	COMBAT AND OPERATIONS (CONTROLLER) COURSES		
OFFICERS			
16310	Aircraft Controller	56	5,320

(Continued)

TABLE 259 — COST OF TRAINING USAF MILITARY STUDENTS BY COURSE — 15 APR 1953 THROUGH 30 JUN 1953 — (CONTINUED)

(See headnote on first page)

Personnel by Type	Course Title	Calendar Days	Course Cost
	AIR UNIVERSITY SCHOOLS		
	AIR COMMAND AND STAFF SCHOOL COURSES		
	Field Officer's Course	151	$ 8,425
	Logistics Staff Officer Course	151	8,125
	Communications and Electronics Staff Officer Course	151	8,125
	Intelligence Staff Officer Course	151	8,125
	Comptroller Staff Officer	102	5,490
	Squadron Officer Course	70	3,490
	Judge Advocate General Course	67	3,805
	Academic Instructor Course	39	1,825
	Air Weapons Course	38	2,120
	Air Weapons Orientation Course	5	300
	Inspector Course	60	3,290
	Air War College	306	20,135
	AIR FORCE INSTITUTE OF TECHNOLOGY COURSES		
	Engineering Science - 2 years Undergraduate	704	31,055
	Engineering Science - 1 year Post Graduate	353	15,220
	Industrial Administration (Graduate)	550	23,160
	Armament Engineering (Graduate)	431	18,580
	Aeronautical Engineering (Graduate)	347	13,920
	Electronics Course (Graduate)	347	14,610
	Armament and Automatic Control Engineer (Graduate)	347	14,610
	Installation Engineer	144	6,065
	Aircraft Structural Repair	67	2,755
	SCHOOL OF AVIATION MEDICINE COURSES		
OFFICERS			
	Flight Nurse	40	1,260
	Physiological Training	54	1,920
	Primary Aviation Medicine	75	3,555
	Advanced Aviation Medicine	305	14,965
	Indoctrination Medical Service Officer	28	885
	Basic Medical Administration	105	3,210
	Clinical Laboratory Officer	112	3,425
	Medical Supply Officer	49	1,500
AIRMEN			
	Aero Medical Apprentice	54	1,330
	Medical Administration Supervisor	82	2,180
	Medical Service Supervisor	136	3,615
	Medical Laboratory Technician	217	5,985
	Preventative Medicine Supervisor	82	3,000
	Veterinary Technician - Advanced	82	2,015
	Aero Medical Technician - Advanced	75	1,995
	Dental Laboratory Technician - Advanced	110	2,925
	Dental Technician - Advanced	82	2,215
	Physiological Training - Apprentice	42	1,115
	Medical Laboratory - Apprentice	140	3,720
	Air Rescue Specialist	28	745

Source: Personnel Statistics Division, DCS/Comptroller, Hq USAF

TABLE 260 — USAF FLYING TRAINING OF USAF PERSONNEL — FY 1953

(To standardize the terminology with the Pilot Training program, Basic and Advanced Observer designations have been changed to Primary and Basic Observer, respectively.)

Type Of Training By Course	Total	First Quarter	Second Quarter	Third Quarter	Fourth Quarter
	NEW STUDENTS				
Total	55,981	13,391	10,515	16,338	15,737
Officer - Total	26,510	7,034	5,188	7,030	7,258
Pilot Training - Total	8,271	2,170	1,183	2,794	2,124
Undergraduate Pilot Training - Total	3,022	828	544	1,069	581
Primary	1,755	597	394	717	47
Basic - Total	1,267	231	150	352	534
Single Engine	826	145	85	229	367
Multi Engine	441	86	65	123	167
Miscellaneous Pilot Training - Total	5,249	1,342	639	1,725	1,543
Helicopter	135	28	24	30	53
Transition - Total	1,370	576	312	230	252
Jet	584	354	81	29	120
Multi Engine, Conventional	786	222	231	201	132
Instructor - Total	1,980	738	303	607	332
Fighter Gunnery	48	19	5	17	7
Fighter Gunnery, Familiarization	2	2	-	-	-
Instrument Pilot, Jet	483	114	96	175	98
Jet, Upgrading	336	117	43	176	-
Multi Engine, Upgrading	130	41	35	34	20
Medium Bombardment, B-47	15	15	-	-	-
Pilot Instructor School	630	430	124	61	15
Basic Instructor School	336	-	-	144	192
Pilot Refresher Training	1,764	-	-	858	906
Diversified Training - Total	1,063	324	248	198	293
Aircraft Controller	766	161	216	166	223
Tactical Air Controller	176	92	15	32	37
Flying Training AF Supervisory School	33	-	-	-	33
Ground Observer Training	88	71	17	-	-
Close Support, Radar Control	-	-	-	-	-
Aircraft Observer and Flexible Gunnery Training - Total	7,447	2,054	1,629	1,711	2,053
Basic Observer (New Production) - Total	680	190	224	108	158
B-26 1521 Navigator-Bombardier	195	91	43	41	20
B-29N 1531 Navigator	119	12	43	38	26
B-29R 1551 Radar Operator	56	4	22	19	11
BO1 1561 Interceptor	3	2	-	-	1
Electronic Countermeasure 3021	307	81	116	10	100
Primary Observer, Non-Rated Officer	499	196	161	70	72
Primary Observer, Navigator-Bombardier	966	346	52	192	376
Primary Observer, Pilot	638	165	146	162	165
Armament Operations Officer	45	8	-	8	29
Navigation Refresher	9	9	-	-	-
Aircraft Observer-Bombardment (1037)	1	1	-	-	-
Basic Observer, B-29 Radar Special	57	41	16	-	-
Basic Observer, B-26 Special	94	84	10	-	-
Basic Observer, B-29X	305	120	103	59	23
Basic Observer, B-29B	89	-	-	-	89
Basic Observer, RB-29	10	-	-	-	10
Basic Observer, B-36	287	59	67	100	61
Basic Observer, B-47 Pilot	529	149	115	137	128
Basic Observer, B-47X	523	53	103	141	226
Basic Observer, B-50	304	150	59	71	24
Basic Observer, Reconnaissance (AOR)	416	116	85	111	104
Commanders Radar Bomb Indoctrination Course	286	67	47	80	92
Primary Observer, Instructor School	371	69	76	146	80
Basic Observer, Instructor School	247	42	78	50	77
Bombardier Gunnery Training, Officer	378	164	116	49	49

(Continued)

TABLE 260 — USAF FLYING TRAINING OF USAF PERSONNEL — FY 1953 (CONTINUED)

(See headnote on first page of the table.)

Type Of Training By Course	Total	First Quarter	Second Quarter	Third Quarter	Fourth Quarter
	NEW STUDENTS (Continued)				
Aircraft Observer and Flexible Gunnery Training (Cont'd)					
Staff Officer ECM Indoctrination	615	-	152	214	249
K System In-Flight Maintenance Upgrading	28	-	-	5	23
Radar Target Prediction and Simulation Course	70	25	19	8	18
Advanced Flying Training (Individual) - Total	9,729	2,486	2,128	2,327	2,788
Fighter Bomber Escort, F-51	33	33	-	-	-
Fighter Bomber Escort, Jet F-80	283	185	98	-	-
Fighter Bomber Escort, Jet F-84	858	105	273	218	262
Fighter Bomber Escort, Jet F-86	414	-	121	126	167
Day Fighter, Jet F-86	536	71	110	183	172
Tactical Air Coordinator, T-6	36	-	-	-	36
Medium Bombardment, B-29	2,690	817	602	601	670
Medium Bombardment, B-47 - Total	1,273	155	181	305	632
Transition Phase	956	44	117	219	576
Crew Phase	317	111	64	86	56
Fighter Interceptor - Total	3,606	1,120	743	894	849
Instrument Phase	1,863	506	384	509	464
Application Phase, F-86D	386	24	116	122	124
Application Phase, F-89	215	215	-	-	-
Application Phase, F-94C	616	375	94	50	97
Fighter Gunnery Indoctrination, T-33	526	-	149	213	164
Airman - Total	29,471	6,357	5,327	9,308	8,479
Undergraduate Pilot Training - Total	13,899	2,767	1,926	5,023	4,183
Preflight	4,613	-	663	2,893	1,057
Primary	5,152	1,432	681	919	2,120
Basic - Total	4,134	1,335	582	1,211	1,006
Single Engine	3,016	968	422	886	740
Multi Engine	1,118	367	160	325	266
Aircraft Observer and Flexible Gunnery Training - Total	11,886	2,533	2,541	3,497	3,315
Basic Observer (New Production) - Total	2,716	774	629	622	691
B-26 1521 Navigator-Bombardier	862	151	229	210	272
Reconnaissance 1521 Navigator-Bombardier	29	-	-	-	29
B-36 1521 Navigator-Bombardier	31	-	-	-	31
B-29N 1531 Navigator	395	75	80	123	117
B-29R 1551 Radar Operator	486	53	34	188	211
B01 1561 Interceptor	860	495	286	79	-
Armament Operations Officer 3241	53	-	-	22	31
Preflight Observer (Cadets)	1,930	-	-	723	1,207
Primary Observer (Cadets)	3,779	871	1,098	1,137	673
Flexible Gunnery, B-26	545	234	115	157	39
Flexible Gunnery, B-29	1,622	612	457	389	164
Flexible Gunnery, Instructor	125	40	12	43	30
Gunlaying System Mechanic Gunner, B-36	129	-	32	42	55
Turret System Mechanic Gunner, B-36	423	-	88	166	169
Electronic Countermeasure Spot Jammer	42	-	-	-	42
Aircraft Electrician Gunner, B-36	166	-	35	53	78
Primary Observer Instructor School	43	-	1	4	38
Basic Observer Instructor School	7	2	2	1	2
Airman ECM Operator	357	-	72	158	127
Radar Target Prediction and Simulation Course	2	-	-	2	-
Advanced Flying Training (Individual) - Total	3,686	1,057	860	788	981
Medium Bombardment, B-29	3,686	1,057	860	788	981

(CONTINUED)

TABLE 260 — USAF FLYING TRAINING OF USAF PERSONNEL — FY 1953 (Continued)

(See headnote on first page of the table.)

Type Of Training By Course	Total	First Quarter	Second Quarter	Third Quarter	Fourth Quarter
	ATTRITION				
Total	6,053	1,544	1,259	1,514	1,736
Officer - Total	1,934	656	526	424	328
Pilot Training - Total	817	258	173	187	199
Undergraduate Pilot Training - Total	625	179	134	156	156
Primary	463	127	98	124	114
Basic - Total	162	52	36	32	42
Single Engine	136	44	31	26	35
Multi Engine	26	8	5	6	7
Miscellaneous Pilot Training - Total	192	79	39	31	43
Helicopter	19	4	8	3	4
Transition - Total	55	32	14	4	5
Jet	33	20	8	-	5
Multi Engine, Conventional	22	12	6	4	-
Instructor - Total	94	43	17	15	19
Fighter Gunnery	18	16	-	-	2
Fighter Gunnery, Familiarization	-	-	-	-	-
Instrument Pilot, Jet	15	1	6	4	4
Jet, Upgrading	10	5	1	4	-
Multi Engine, Upgrading	4	1	1	1	1
Medium Bombardment, B-47	3	3	-	-	-
Pilot Instructor School	32	17	9	5	1
Basic Instructor School	12	-	-	1	11
Pilot Refresher Training	24	-	-	9	15
Diversified Training - Total	10	2	3	2	3
Aircraft Controller	10	2	3	2	3
Tactical Air Controller	-	-	-	-	-
Flying Training AF Supervisory School	-	-	-	-	-
Ground Observer Training	-	-	-	-	-
Close Support, Radar Control	-	-	-	-	-
Aircraft Observer and Flexible Gunnery Training - Total	329	105	76	103	45
Basic Observer (New Production) - Total	71	26	19	16	10
B-26 1521 Navigator-Bombardier	2	-	-	1	1
B-29N 1531 Navigator	5	1	1	2	1
B-29R 1551 Radar Operator	5	-	2	2	1
BO1 1561 Interceptor	13	12	1	-	-
Electronic Countermeasure 3021	46	13	15	11	7
Primary Observer, Non-Rated Officer	71	18	20	21	12
Primary Observer, Navigator-Bombardier	38	16	11	10	1
Primary Observer, Pilot	29	8	8	10	3
Armament Operations Officer	-	-	-	-	-
Navigation Refresher	3	3	-	-	-
Aircraft Observer-Bombardment (1037)	5	5	-	-	-
Basic Observer, B-29 Radar Special	17	11	6	-	-
Basic Observer, B-26 Special	13	8	3	2	-
Basic Observer, B-29X	11	3	1	6	1
Basic Observer, B-29B	-	-	-	-	-
Basic Observer, RB-29	-	-	-	-	-
Basic Observer, B-36	9	-	1	4	4
Basic Observer, B-47 Pilot	7	-	1	5	1
Basic Observer, B-47X	3	1	1	-	1
Basic Observer, B-50	17	-	4	10	3
Basic Observer Reconnaissance (AOR)	10	-	-	8	2
Commanders Radar Bomb Indoctrination Course	-	-	-	-	-
Primary Observer, Instructor School	3	1	-	2	-
Basic Observer, Instructor School	13	2	-	4	7
Bombardier Gunnery Training, Officer	9	3	1	5	-

(Continued)

TABLE 260 — USAF FLYING TRAINING OF USAF PERSONNEL — FY 1953 (CONTINUED)

(See headnote on first page of the table.)

Type Of Training By Course	Total	First Quarter	Second Quarter	Third Quarter	Fourth Quarter
	ATTRITION (Continued)				
Aircraft Observer and Flexible Gunnery Training (Cont'd)					
Staff Officer ECM Indoctrination	-	-	-	-	-
X System In-Flight Maintenance Upgrading	-	-	-	-	-
Radar Target Prediction and Simulation Course	-	-	-	-	-
Advanced Flying Training (Individual) - Total	778	291	274	132	81
Fighter Bomber Escort, F-51	26	21	3	2	-
Fighter Bomber Escort, Jet F-80	105	100	5	-	-
Fighter Bomber Escort, Jet F-84	49	6	13	17	13
Fighter Bomber Escort, Jet F-86	24	-	7	11	6
Day Fighter, Jet F-86	34	4	11	14	5
Tactical Air Coordinator, T-6	1	-	-	-	1
Medium Bombardment, B-29	231	72	75	48	36
Medium Bombardment, B-47 - Total	49	7	20	15	7
Transition Phase	21	2	3	10	6
Crew Phase	28	5	17	5	1
Fighter Interceptor - Total	259	81	140	25	13
Instrument Phase	31	6	14	4	7
Application Phase, F-86D	58	1	44	10	3
Application Phase, F-89	71	71	-	-	-
Application Phase, F-94C	16	3	5	7	1
Fighter Gunnery Indoctrination, T-33	83	-	77	4	2
Airman - Total	4,119	888	733	1,090	1,408
Undergraduate Pilot Training - Total	2,421	584	433	590	814
Preflight	650	-	17	224	409
Primary	1,386	504	335	258	289
Basic - Total	385	80	81	108	116
Single Engine	340	77	73	96	94
Multi Engine	45	3	8	12	22
Aircraft Observer and Flexible Gunnery Training - Total	1,430	206	239	429	556
Basic Observer (New Production) - Total	415	74	118	145	78
B-26 1521 Navigator-Bombardier	6	-	-	5	1
Reconnaissance 1521 Navigator-Bombardier	-	-	-	-	-
B-36 1521 Navigator-Bombardier	-	-	-	-	-
B-29N 1531 Navigator	11	4	3	1	3
B-29R 1551 Radar Operator	8	2	1	-	5
B01 1561 Interceptor	369	68	114	139	48
Armament Operations Officer 3241	21	-	-	-	21
Preflight Observer (Cadets)	227	-	-	-	227
Primary Observer (Cadets)	681	116	94	254	217
Flexible Gunnery, B-26	1	-	-	-	1
Flexible Gunnery, B-29	72	14	21	21	16
Flexible Gunnery Instructor	8	2	-	3	3
Gunlaying System Mechanic Gunner, B-36	4	-	-	1	3
Turret System Mechanic Gunner, B-36	11	-	1	1	9
Electronic Countermeasure Spot Jammer	-	-	-	-	-
Aircraft Electrician Gunner, B-36	4	-	-	3	1
Primary Observer Instructor School	1	-	-	-	1
Basic Observer Instructor School	-	-	-	-	-
Airman ECM Operator	6	-	5	1	-
Radar Target Prediction and Simulation Course	-	-	-	-	-
Advanced Flying Training (Individual) - Total	268	98	61	71	38
Medium Bombardment, B-29	268	98	61	71	38

(CONTINUED)

TABLE 260 — USAF FLYING TRAINING OF USAF PERSONNEL — FY 1953 (Continued)

(See headnote on first page of the table.)

Type Of Training By Course	Total	First Quarter	Second Quarter	Third Quarter	Fourth Quarter
	GRADUATES				
Total	47,394	10,427	10,317	11,648	15,002
Officer - Total	24,697	6,089	5,609	5,633	7,366
Pilot Training - Total	7,513	1,874	1,544	1,551	2,544
Undergraduate Pilot Training - Total	2,461	683	621	650	507
Primary	1,275	230	258	479	308
Basic - Total	1,186	453	363	171	199
Single Engine	694	255	229	104	106
Multi Engine	492	198	134	67	93
Miscellaneous Pilot Training - Total	5,052	1,191	923	901	2,037
Helicopter	84	22	19	22	21
Transition - Total	1,405	566	352	245	242
Jet	646	387	133	27	99
Multi Engine, Conventional	759	179	219	218	143
Instructor - Total	1,832	603	552	430	247
Fighter Gunnery	37	12	8	5	12
Fighter Gunnery, Familiarization	5	5	-	-	-
Instrument Pilot, Jet	465	103	118	138	106
Jet, Upgrading	395	141	85	169	-
Multi Engine, Upgrading	127	33	54	25	15
Medium Bombardment, B-47	9	9	-	-	-
Pilot Instructor School	687	300	287	93	7
Basic Instructor School	107	-	-	-	107
Pilot Refresher Training	1,731	-	-	204	1,527
Diversified Training - Total	1,133	390	201	272	270
Aircraft Controller	825	199	176	240	210
Tactical Air Controller	195	110	8	32	45
Flying Training AF Supervisory School	15	-	-	-	15
Ground Observer Training	98	81	17	-	-
Close Support, Radar Control	-	-	-	-	-
Aircraft Observer and Flexible Gunnery Training - Total	7,196	1,855	1,826	1,696	1,819
Basic Observer (New Production) - Total	762	258	206	140	158
B-26 1521 Navigator-Bombardier	266	87	61	46	72
B-29N 1531 Navigator	101	10	20	43	28
B-29R 1551 Radar Operator	77	7	35	14	21
B01 1561 Interceptor	69	67	1	-	1
Electronic Countermeasure 3021	249	87	89	37	36
Primary Observer, Non-Rated Officer	510	101	84	132	193
Primary Observer, Navigator-Bombardier	930	322	273	288	47
Primary Observer, Pilot	534	155	143	134	102
Armament Operations Officer	18	5	7	-	* 6
Navigation Refresher	42	38	4	-	-
Aircraft Observer-Bombardment (1037)	216	184	32	-	-
Basic Observer, B-29 Radar Special	151	77	74	-	-
Basic Observer, B-26 Special	143	85	58	-	-
Basic Observer, B-29X	380	163	106	64	47
Basic Observer, B-29B	43	-	-	-	43
Basic Observer, RB-29	-	-	-	-	-
Basic Observer, B-36	170	15	22	18	115
Basic Observer, B-47 Pilot	412	33	113	88	178
Basic Observer, B-47X	370	13	59	130	168
Basic Observer, B-50	272	20	97	87	68
Basic Observer, Reconnaissance (AOR)	225	-	61	63	101
Commanders Radar Bomb Indoctrination Course	292	71	49	80	92
Primary Observer Instructor School	364	50	78	114	122
Basic Observer Instructor School	230	36	68	68	58
Bombardier Gunnery Training, Officer	430	200	118	63	49

(Continued)

*Officer graduates in the last quarter are New Production.

TABLE 260 — USAF FLYING TRAINING OF USAF PERSONNEL — FY 1953 (CONTINUED)

(See headnote on first page of the table.)

Type Of Training By Course	Total	First Quarter	Second Quarter	Third Quarter	Fourth Quarter
	GRADUATES (Continued)				
Aircraft Observer and Flexible Gunnery Training (Cont'd)					
Staff Officer ECM Indoctrination Course	604	-	152	214	238
K System In-Flight Maintenance Upgrading	21	-	-	5	16
Radar Target Prediction and Simulation Course	77	29	22	8	18
Advanced Flying Training (Individual) - Total	8,855	1,970	2,038	2,114	2,733
Fighter Bomber Escort, F-51	81	65	16	-	-
Fighter Bomber Escort, Jet F-80	68	44	24	-	-
Fighter Bomber Escort, Jet F-84	792	139	147	212	294
Fighter Bomber Escort, Jet F-86	354	8	78	101	167
Day Fighter Jet, F-86	549	57	152	162	178
Tactical Air Coordinator, T-6	26	-	-	-	26
Medium Bombardment, B-29	2,557	565	630	678	684
Medium Bombardment, B-47 - Total	958	46	207	225	480
Transition Phase	685	15	96	164	410
Crew Phase	273	31	111	61	70
Fighter Interceptor - Total	3,470	1,046	784	736	904
Instrument Phase	1,903	457	478	412	556
Application Phase, F-86D	241	-	46	88	107
Application Phase, F-89	210	210	-	-	-
Application Phase, F-94C	733	379	260	5	89
Fighter Gunnery Indoctrination, T-33	383	-	-	231	152
Airman - Total	22,697	4,338	4,708	6,015	7,636
Undergraduate Pilot Training - Total	10,750	1,816	2,206	3,017	3,711
Preflight	3,220	-	-	1,251	1,969
Primary	4,121	1,324	1,220	1,056	521
Basic - Total	3,409	492	986	710	1,221
Single Engine	2,357	363	622	495	877
Multi Engine	1,052	129	364	215	344
Aircraft Observer and Flexible Gunnery Training - Total	8,614	1,771	1,667	2,137	3,039
Basic Observer (New Production) - Total	2,392	425	549	594	824
B-26 1521 Navigator-Bombardier	588	47	89	180	272
Reconnaissance 1521 Navigator-Bombardier	-	-	-	-	-
B-36 1521 Navigator-Bombardier	-	-	-	-	-
B-29N 1531 Navigator	344	66	71	93	114
B-29R 1551 Radar Operator	367	71	40	33	223
E01 1561 Interceptor	1,093	241	349	288	215
Armament Operations Officer 3241	-	-	-	-	-
Preflight Observer (Cadets)	605	-	-	-	605
Primary Observer (Cadets)	2,041	332	369	573	767
Flexible Gunnery, B-26	564	261	91	145	67
Flexible Gunnery, B-29	2,029	703	519	399	408
Flexible Gunnery, Instructor	136	49	38	16	33
Gunlaying System Mechanic Gunner, B-36	86	-	8	53	25
Turret System Mechanic Gunner, B-36	305	-	20	158	127
Electronic Countermeasure Spot Jammer	-	-	-	-	-
Aircraft Electrician Gunner, B-36	109	-	4	57	48
Primary Observer Instructor School	6	-	1	3	2
Basic Observer Instructor School	6	1	3	2	-
Airman ECM Operator	333	-	65	135	133
Radar Target Prediction and Simulation Course	2	-	-	2	-
Advanced Flying Training (Individual) - Total	3,333	751	835	861	886
Medium Bombardment, B-29	3,333	751	835	861	886

NOTE: In addition to USAF Military Personnel trained, the following courses were completed by Civilian Personnel: 319, Pilot Instructor School; 73, Staff Officer ECM Indoctrination; 12, Radar Target Prediction and Simulation Course; 11, Commanders Radar Bombing Indoctrination, and 19 in Flying Training Air Force Supervisory School.

(Continued)

TABLE 260 — USAF FLYING TRAINING OF USAF PERSONNEL — FY 1953 (Continued)

(See headnote on first page of the table.)

Type Of Training By Course	Total	30 September (1952)	31 December (1952)	31 March (1953)	30 June (1953)
		STUDENTS UNDER INSTRUCTION			
Total	NOT APPLICABLE	15,267	14,253	17,428	16,439
Officer - Total		6,238	5,283	6,262	5,830
Pilot Training - Total		2,054	1,509	2,566	1,948
Undergraduate Pilot Training - Total		1,500	1,278	1,542	1,461
Primary		a/ 868	906	1,020	645
Basic - Total		632	372	522	816
Single Engine		b/ 409	g/ 223	322	r/ 549
Multi Engine		b/ 223	149	m/ 200	267
Miscellaneous Pilot Training - Total		554	231	1,024	487
Helicopter		21	18	23	51
Transition - Total		169	115	96	101
Jet		75	15	17	33
Multi Engine, Conventional		94	100	79	68
Instructor - Total		364	98	260	326
Fighter Gunnery		c/ 3	-	12	5
Fighter Gunnery, Familiarization		-	-	-	-
Instrument Pilot, Jet		81	53	86	74
Jet, Upgrading		43	-	n/ -	-
Multi Engine, Upgrading		20	-	8	12
Medium Bombardment, B-47		-	h/ -	-	-
Pilot Instructor School		217	45	8	15
Basic Instructor School		-	-	n/ 146	220
Pilot Refresher Training		-	-	645	9
Diversified Training - Total		d/ 98	142	66	86
Aircraft Controller		97	134	58	68
Tactical Air Controller		1	8	8	-
Flying Training AF Supervisory School		-	-	-	18
Ground Observer Training		d/ -	-	-	-
Close Support, Radar Control		-	-	-	-
Aircraft Observer and Flexible Gunnery Training - Total		d/ 2,507	2,237	2,154	s/ 2,346
Basic Observer (New Production) - Total		331	351	320	313
B-26 1521 Navigator-Bombardier		92	74	80	27
B-29N 1531 Navigator		17	36	29	26
B-29R 1551 Radar Operator		5	11	14	3
BOI 1561 Interceptor		2	-	-	-
Electronic Countermeasure 3021		e/ 215	i/ 230	o/ 197	t/ 257
Primary Observer, Non-Rated Officer		318	375	292	159
Primary Observer, Navigator-Bombardier		550	307	192	606
Primary Observer, Pilot		293	299	326	300
Armament Operations Officer		7	-	8	u/ 31
Navigation Refresher		-	-	-	-
Aircraft Observer-Bombardment (1037)		36	-	-	-
Basic Observer, B-29 Radar Special		86	-	-	-
Basic Observer, B-26 Special		65	14	-	-
Basic Observer, B-29X		40	36	25	-
Basic Observer, B-29B		-	-	-	46
Basic Observer, RB-29		-	-	-	10
Basic Observer, B-36		63	108	185	126
Basic Observer, B-47 Pilot		203	205	249	197
Basic Observer, B-47X		39	83	94	150
Basic Observer, B-50		198	157	131	84
Basic Observer Reconnaissance		158	182	223	226
Commanders Radar Bomb Indoctrination Course		2	-	-	-
Primary Observer, Instructor School		41	39	69	27
Basic Observer, Instructor School		31	41	19	31
Bombardier Gunnery Training Officer		43	40	21	21

(Continued)

TABLE 260 — USAF FLYING TRAINING OF USAF PERSONNEL — FY 1953 (Continued)

(See headnote on first page of the table.)

Type Of Training By Course	Total	30 September (1952)	31 December (1952)	31 March (1953)	30 June (1953)
		STUDENTS UNDER INSTRUCTION (Continued)			
Aircraft Observer and Flexible Gunnery Training (Cont'd)	NOT APPLICABLE				
Staff Officer ECM Indoctrination Course		-	-	-	11
K System In-Flight Maintenance Upgrading		-	-	-	8
Radar Target Prediction and Simulation Course		3	-	-	-
Advanced Flying Training (Individual) - Total		1,579	1,395	1,476	s/ 1,450
Fighter Bomber Escort, F-51		21	2	-	-
Fighter Bomber Escort, Jet F-80		91	-	-	-
Fighter Bomber Escort, Jet F-84		81	194	183	138
Fighter Bomber Escort, Jet F-86		-	119	119	113
Day Fighter, Jet F-86		81	105	126	115
Tactical Air Coordinator, T-6		-	-	-	9
Medium Bombardment, B-29		698	595	470	420
Medium Bombardment, B-47 - Total		154	108	173	318
Transition Phase		44	h/ 62	101	302
Crew Phase		110	h/ 46	72	16
Fighter Interceptor - Total		453	272	405	337
Instrument Phase		252	144	237	138
Application Phase, F-86D		23	49	73	87
Application Phase, F-89		-	-	-	-
Application Phase, F-94C		178	7	45	52
Fighter Gunnery Indoctrination, T-33		-	72	50	50
Airman - Total		9,029	8,970	11,166	10,609
Undergraduate Pilot Training - Total		5,082	4,369	5,778	5,435
Preflight		-	646	2,064	v/ 742
Primary		f/ 2,720	1,846	1,451	2,761
Basic - Total		2,362	1,877	2,263	1,932
Single Engine		1,629	j/ 1,355	p/ 1,644	1,413
Multi Engine		733	j/ 522	m/ 619	519
Aircraft Observer and Flexible Gunnery Training - Total		3,038	3,728	4,659	4,388
Basic Observer (New Production) - Total		1,207	1,169	917	706
B-26 1521 Navigator-Bombardier		153	293	318	317
Reconnaissance 1521 Navigator-Bombardier		-	-	-	29
B-36 1521 Navigator-Bombardier		-	-	-	31
B-29N 1531 Navigator		76	k/ 95	124	124
B-29R 1551 Radar Operator		54	k/ 34	189	172
B01 1561 Interceptor		924	747	q/ 264	1
Armament Operations Officer 3241		-	-	22	32
Preflight Observer (Cadets)		-	-	723	w/ 1,107
Primary Observer (Cadets)		1,363	1,998	q/ 2,443	2,132
Flexible Gunnery, B-26		-	24	36	7
Flexible Gunnery, B-29		427	344	313	53
Flexible Gunnery, Instructor		39	13	37	31
Gunlaying System Mechanic Gunner, B-36		-	24	12	39
Turret System Mechanic Gunner, B-36		-	67	74	107
Electronic Countermeasure Spot Jammer		-	-	-	42
Aircraft Electrician Gunner, B-36		-	31	24	53
Primary Observer Instructor School		-	-	1	36
Basic Observer Instructor School		2	1	-	2
Airman ECM Operator		-	l/ 57	79	73
Radar Target Prediction and Simulation Course		-	-	-	-
Advanced Flying Training (Individual) - Total		909	873	729	786
Medium Bombardment, B-29		909	873	729	786

(CONTINUED)

TABLE 260 – USAF FLYING TRAINING OF USAF PERSONNEL – FY 1953 (Continued)

a/ One officer erroneously reported as graduate on May report.

b/ One officer transferred from Single Engine to Multi Engine.

c/ One USN officer reported in June as USAF.

d/ Ground Observer Course included with Aircraft Observer and Flexible Gunnery Training in FY 1952 with 10 enrolled at the end of the reporting period.

e/ Seven officers transferred to Technical Training Air Force.

f/ One cadet reinstated after attending Olympic Primaries.

g/ Eleven ANG officers previously reported as USAF.

h/ Fifty two students transferred to Advanced Flying Training Course Medium Bombardment, B-47, with 25 students enrolled in the Transition Phase; 27 enrolled in the Crew Phase.

i/ Three officers transferred from Technical Training Air Force.

j/ One cadet transferred from Multi Engine to Single Engine Pilot.

k/ Thirteen cadets transferred from B-29R to B-29N.

l/ Formerly reported by Technical Training Air Force. Transferred to Flying Training Air Force with 55 Airmen enrolled.

m/ One cadet commissioned 2nd Lieutenant and held over to another class.

n/ Three officers transferred to Basic Instructor School from Jet, Upgrading.

o/ Five officers transferred from Technical Training Air Force.

p/ Six ANG cadets previously reported as USAF.

q/ One hundred and thirty five cadets transferred from Basic Observer, Interceptor to Primary Observer, Cadets.

r/ One officer previously eliminated reinstated during June.

s/ Students were transferred from one course to another to complete Advanced Training.

t/ Three officers transferred from Technical Training Air Force.

u/ Formerly reported as Flexible Gunnery Officer.

v/ Includes three cadets previously eliminated and reinstated.

w/ Includes four cadets transferred from Preflight Pilot, and five Preflight Pilot cadets previously eliminated and reinstated as Preflight Observer students.

Source: Personnel Statistics Division, DCS/Comptroller, Hq USAF.

TABLE 261 – USAF FLYING TRAINING FATALITIES OF USAF PERSONNEL – FY 1953

(Other fatalities reported in Flying Training during FY 1953 but not included in the figures below were: 1 Army officer fatality under Army Primary Flight Training, 30 fatalities in Undergraduate Pilot Training, the 30 foreign personnel fatalities were reported as follows: 1 French officer, 2 French cadets, 1 Netherlander cadet, and 1 Italian cadet under Primary Pilot Training; 1 French officer, 11 French cadets, 4 English officers, 3 Netherlander cadets, 1 Norwegian cadet, 2 Danish cadets, 2 Belgian cadets, and 1 Italian cadet under Basic Single Engine Pilot Training; 1 Italian officer under Instructor, Fighter Gunnery Training; 1 French officer under Instructor, Instrument Pilot Course; 2 Netherlander officers, 2 Belgian officers, 1 Italian officer, 1 Norwegian officer, and 4 French officers under Advanced Flying Training.)

Type of Training	Total	First Quarter	Second Quarter	Third Quarter	Fourth Quarter
	FATALITIES				
Total	155	43	35	30	47
Officer - Total	98	29	24	17	28
Undergraduate Pilot Training - Total	18	6	3	1	8
Primary	5	1	1	1	2
Basic - Total	13	5	2	-	6
Single Engine	13	5	2	-	6
Twin Engine	-	-	-	-	-
Miscellaneous Pilot Training - Total	4	2	2	-	-
Transition, Jet Pilot	2	1	1	-	-
Instructor - Total	2	1	1	-	-
Instrument Pilot	1	-	1	-	-
Jet Upgrading	1	1	-	-	-
Aircraft Observer and Flexible Gunnery Training - Total	1	1	-	-	-
Primary Observer, Navigator-Bombardier	1	1	-	-	-
Advanced Flying Training (Individual) - Total	75	20	19	16	20
Fighter Bomber Escort, F-51	3	3	-	-	-
Fighter Bomber Escort, F-80	8	6	2	-	-
Fighter Bomber Escort, F-84	20	2	5	7	6
Fighter Bomber Escort, F-86D	3	-	-	1	2
Fighter Bomber Escort, F-86	6	-	-	4	2
Fighter Bomber Escort, F-94C	1	1	-	-	-
Tactical Air Coordinator, T-6	1	-	-	-	1
Tactical Reconnaissance, RB-26	1	-	1	-	-
Tactical Reconnaissance, RF-80	1	-	1	-	-
Light Bomber, B-26	6	2	2	2	-
Medium Bomber, B-29	3	-	-	-	3
Medium Bomber, B-47	4	1	-	2	1
Fighter Interceptor - Total	18	5	8	-	5
Application Phase, T-33	6	3	2	-	1
Application Phase, F-86	9	2	6	-	1
Application Phase, F-94	1	-	-	-	1
Fighter Gunnery Indoctrination, T-33	2	-	-	-	2
Airman - Total	57	14	11	13	19
Undergraduate Pilot Training - Total	48	13	11	12	12
Primary	8	2	1	3	2
Basic - Total	40	11	10	9	10
Single Engine	40	11	10	9	10
Twin Engine	-	-	-	-	-
Aircraft Observer and Flexible Gunnery Training - Total	1	-	-	-	1
Flexible Gunnery Instructor	1	-	-	-	1
Advanced Flying Training (Individual) - Total	8	1	-	1	6
Light Bomber, B-26	2	1	-	1	-
Medium Bomber, B-29	6	-	-	-	6

Source: Personnel Statistics Division, DCS/Comptroller, Headquarters USAF.

TABLE 262 — USAF FLYING TRAINING OF ARMY AND NAVY PERSONNEL — FY 1953

Type Of Training By Course	Total		First Quarter		Second Quarter		Third Quarter		Fourth Quarter	
	Army	Navy	Army	Navy	Army	Navy	Army	Navy	Army	Navy
	NEW STUDENTS									
Total	1,408	16	430	4	249	3	363	4	366	5
Officer - Total	1,408	16	430	4	249	3	363	4	366	5
Miscellaneous Pilot Training - Total	1,370	8	430	4	249	1	363	1	328	2
Helicopter	241	-	57	-	50	-	75	-	59	-
Liaison (Army Primary Flight Training)	1,129	-	373	-	199	-	288	-	269	-
Instructor - Total	-	8	-	4	-	1	-	1	-	2
Fighter Gunnery	-	2	-	2	-	-	-	-	-	-
Instrument Pilot	-	6	-	2	-	1	-	1	-	2
Aircraft Observer and Flexible Gunnery Training - Total	38	4	-	-	-	2	-	-	38	2
Radar Target Prediction and Simulation	-	2	-	-	-	2	-	-	-	-
Staff Officer ECM Indoctrination Course	38	2	-	-	-	-	-	-	38	2
Advanced Flying Training (Individual)-Total	-	4	-	-	-	-	-	3	-	1
Fighter Interceptor - Total	-	3	-	-	-	-	-	2	-	1
Instrument Phase	-	3	-	-	-	-	-	2	-	1
Day Fighter, F-86D	-	1	-	-	-	-	-	1	-	-
	ATTRITION									
Total	394	-	99	-	68	-	98	-	129	-
Officer - Total	394	-	99	-	68	-	98	-	129	-
Miscellaneous Pilot Training - Total	394	-	99	-	68	-	98	-	129	-
Helicopter	8	-	2	-	3	-	2	-	1	-
Liaison (Army Primary Flight Training)	386	-	97	-	65	-	96	-	128	-
Instructor - Total	-	-	-	-	-	-	-	-	-	-
Fighter Gunnery	-	-	-	-	-	-	-	-	-	-
Instrument Pilot	-	-	-	-	-	-	-	-	-	-
Aircraft Observer and Flexible Gunnery Training - Total	-	-	-	-	-	-	-	-	-	-
Radar Target Prediction and Simulation	-	-	-	-	-	-	-	-	-	-
Staff Officer ECM Indoctrination Course	-	-	-	-	-	-	-	-	-	-
Advanced Flying Training (Individual)-Total	-	-	-	-	-	-	-	-	-	-
Fighter Interceptor - Total	-	-	-	-	-	-	-	-	-	-
Instrument Phase	-	-	-	-	-	-	-	-	-	-
Day Fighter, F-86D	-	-	-	-	-	-	-	-	-	-
	GRADUATES									
Total	956	16	245	3	167	7	270	2	274	4
Officer - Total	956	16	245	3	167	7	270	2	274	4
Miscellaneous Pilot Training - Total	936	9	245	3	167	5	270	-	254	1
Helicopter	234	-	54	-	57	-	62	-	61	-
Liaison (Army Primary Flight Training)	702	-	191	-	110	-	208	-	193	-
Instructor - Total	-	9	-	3	-	5	-	-	-	1
Fighter Gunnery	-	5	-	3	-	2	-	-	-	-
Instrument Pilot	-	4	-	-	-	3	-	-	-	1
Aircraft Observer and Flexible Gunnery Training - Total	20	4	-	-	-	2	-	-	20	2
Radar Target Prediction and Simulation	-	2	-	-	-	2	-	-	-	-
Staff Officer ECM Indoctrination Course	20	2	-	-	-	-	-	-	20	2
Advanced Flying Training (Individual)-Total	-	3	-	-	-	-	-	2	-	1
Fighter Interceptor - Total	-	2	-	-	-	-	-	2	-	-
Instrument Phase	-	2	-	-	-	-	-	2	-	-
Day Fighter, F-86D	-	1	-	-	-	-	-	-	-	1

(Continued)

TABLE 262 — USAF FLYING TRAINING OF ARMY AND NAVY PERSONNEL — FY 1953 (CONTINUED)

Type Of Training By Course	Total		30 September (1952)		31 December (1952)		31 March (1953)		30 June (1953)	
	Army	Navy	Army	Navy	Army	Navy	Army	Navy	Army	Navy
	STUDENTS UNDER INSTRUCTION									
Total	NOT APPLICABLE	NOT APPLICABLE	345	4	359	-	354	2	317	3
Officer - Total			345	4	359	-	354	2	317	3
Miscellaneous Pilot Training - Total			345	4	359	-	354	1	299	2
Helicopter			23	-	13	-	24	-	21	-
Liaison (Army Primary Flight Training)			322	-	346	-	330	-	278	-
Instructor - Total			-	4	-	-	-	1	-	2
Fighter Gunnery			-	2	-	-	-	-	-	-
Instrument Pilot			-	2	-	-	-	1	-	2
Aircraft Observer and Flexible Gunnery Training - Total			-	-	-	-	-	-	18	-
Radar Target Prediction and Simulation			-	-	-	-	-	-	-	-
Staff Officer ECM Indoctrination Course			-	-	-	-	-	-	18	-
Advanced Flying Training (Individual) - Total			-	-	-	-	-	1	-	1
Fighter Interceptor - Total			-	-	-	-	-	-	-	1
Instrument Phase			-	-	-	-	-	-	-	1
Day Fighter, F-86D			-	-	-	-	-	1	-	-

Source: Personnel Statistics Division, DCS/Comptroller, Headquarters USAF.

TABLE 263 — USAF FLYING TRAINING OF FOREIGN PERSONNEL — FY 1953

(Table includes MDAP Students)

Type Of Training By Course	Total	First Quarter	Second Quarter	Third Quarter	Fourth Quarter
	NEW STUDENTS				
Total	4,733	1,012	849	1,362	1,510
Officer - Total	1,632	314	321	513	484
Pilot Training - Total	808	138	74	259	337
Undergraduate Pilot Training - Total	571	111	48	160	252
Preflight	233	-	6	45	182
Primary	109	59	5	13	32
Basic - Total	229	52	37	102	38
Single Engine	219	52	37	102	28
Twin Engine	10	-	-	-	10
Miscellaneous Pilot Training - Total	237	27	26	99	85
Helicopter	13	-	4	5	4
Liaison (Army Primary Pilot Training)	6	-	6	-	-
Transition, Jet	16	14	-	-	2
Instructor - Total	202	13	16	94	79
Fighter Gunnery	19	4	4	7	4
Instrument Pilot, Jet	86	3	4	28	51
Jet, Upgrading	15	5	1	9	-
Pilot Instructor School	43	1	7	17	18
Basic Instructor School	39	-	-	33	6
Diversified Training - Total	227	79	63	85	-
Aircraft Controller	183	47	51	85	-
Tactical Air Controller	23	14	9	-	-
Ground Observer Training	21	18	3	-	-
Aircraft Observer and Flexible Gunnery Training - Total	13	5	-	3	5
Basic Observer (New Production) - Total	5	5	-	-	-
B-29N	1	1	-	-	-
Electronic Countermeasure	4	4	-	-	-
Primary Observer Non-Rated Officer	-	-	-	-	-
Staff Officer ECM Indoctrination	6	-	-	1	5
Radar Target Prediction and Simulation	1	-	-	1	-
Commanders Radar Bomb and Indoctrination	1	-	-	1	-
Advanced Flying Training (Individual) - Total	584	92	184	166	142
Fighter Bomber Escort, F-51	198	41	97	60	-
Fighter Bomber Escort, F-80	144	1	-	94	49
Fighter Bomber Escort, F-84	223	48	82	-	93
Fighter Bomber Escort, F-86	17	1	4	12	-
Fighter Interceptor - Total	2	1	1	-	-
Instrument Phase, T-33	1	-	1	-	-
Application Phase, F-89	1	1	-	-	-
Airman - Total	3,101	698	528	849	1,026
Pilot Training - Total	3,098	695	528	849	1,026
Undergraduate Pilot Training - Total	3,093	690	528	849	1,026
Preflight	928	-	205	306	417
Primary	1,162	469	195	255	243
Basic - Total	1,003	221	128	288	366
Single Engine	1,003	221	128	288	366
Twin Engine	-	-	-	-	-
Miscellaneous Pilot Training - Total	5	5	-	-	-
Pilot Instructor School	5	5	-	-	-
Aircraft Observer and Flexible Gunnery Training - Total	3	3	-	-	-
Basic Observer (New Production) - Total	3	3	-	-	-
B-29N	3	3	-	-	-
Primary Observer (Cadets)	-	-	-	-	-

(CONTINUED)

TABLE 263 -- USAF FLYING TRAINING OF FOREIGN PERSONNEL -- FY 1953 (CONTINUED)

(Table includes MDAP Students)

Type Of Training By Course	Total	First Quarter	Second Quarter	Third Quarter	Fourth Quarter
	GRADUATES				
Total	3,618	614	818	1,209	977
Officer - Total	1,285	126	334	409	416
Pilot Training - Total	568	62	132	168	206
Undergraduate Pilot Training - Total	392	42	100	109	141
Preflight	93	-	-	16	77
Primary	159	22	74	58	5
Basic - Total	140	20	26	35	59
Single Engine	130	20	16	35	59
Twin Engine	10	-	10	-	-
Miscellaneous Pilot Training - Total	176	20	32	59	65
Helicopter	10	2	-	8	-
Liaison (Army Primary Pilot Training)	5	-	-	3	2
Transition, Jet	16	-	14	-	2
Instructor - Total	145	18	18	48	61
Fighter Gunnery	18	5	7	4	2
Instrument Pilot, Jet	69	13	4	14	38
Jet, Upgrading	15	-	6	9	-
Pilot Instructor School	25	-	1	21	3
Basic Instructor School	18	-	-	-	18
Diversified Training - Total	246	62	62	77	45
Aircraft Controller	199	32	45	77	45
Tactical Air Controller	23	9	14	-	-
Ground Observer Training	24	21	3	-	-
Aircraft Observer and Flexible Gunnery Training - Total	9	-	2	4	3
Basic Observer (New Production) - Total	6	-	2	1	3
B-29N	2	-	2	-	-
Electronic Countermeasure	4	-	-	1	3
Primary Observer Non-Rated Officer	-	-	-	-	-
Staff Officer ECM Indoctrination	1	-	-	1	-
Radar Target Prediction and Simulation	1	-	-	1	-
Commanders Radar Bomb and Indoctrination	1	-	-	1	-
Advanced Flying Training (Individual) - Total	462	2	138	160	162
Fighter Bomber Escort, F-51	187	-	80	74	33
Fighter Bomber Escort, F-80	103	-	-	73	30
Fighter Bomber Escort, F-84	153	-	54	-	99
Fighter Bomber Escort, F-86	17	1	4	12	-
Fighter Interceptor - Total	2	1	-	1	-
Instrument Phase, T-33	1	-	-	1	-
Application Phase, F-89	1	1	-	-	-
Airman - Total	2,333	488	484	800	561
Pilot Training - Total	2,319	475	483	800	561
Undergraduate Pilot Training - Total	2,240	427	483	800	530
Preflight	537	-	-	329	208
Primary	1,041	251	296	346	148
Basic - Total	662	176	187	125	174
Single Engine	662	176	187	125	174
Twin Engine	-	-	-	-	-
Miscellaneous Pilot Training - Total	79	48	-	-	31
Pilot Instructor School	79	48	-	-	31
Aircraft Observer and Flexible Gunnery Training - Total	14	13	1	-	-
Basic Observer (New Production) - Total	11	10	1	-	-
B-29N	11	10	1	-	-
Primary Observer (Cadets)	3	3	-	-	-

TABLE 263 — USAF FLYING TRAINING OF FOREIGN PERSONNEL — FY 1953 (CONTINUED)

(Table includes MDAP Students.)

Type Of Training By Course	Total	First Quarter	Second Quarter	Third Quarter	Fourth Quarter
	ATTRITION				
Total	652	134	176	168	174
Officer - Total	96	13	20	28	35
Pilot Training - Total	56	8	11	13	24
Undergraduate Pilot Training - Total	48	8	10	11	19
Preflight	7	-	-	2	5
Primary	19	6	7	1	5
Basic - Total	22	2	3	8	9
Single Engine	22	2	3	8	9
Twin Engine	-	-	-	-	-
Miscellaneous Pilot Training - Total	8	-	1	2	5
Helicopter	1	-	-	-	1
Liaison (Army Primary Pilot Training)	1	-	-	1	-
Transition, Jet	-	-	-	-	-
Instructor - Total	6	-	1	1	4
Fighter Gunnery	2	-	1	1	-
Instrument Pilot, Jet	1	-	-	-	1
Jet, Upgrading	-	-	-	-	-
Pilot Instructor School	-	-	-	-	-
Basic Instructor School	3	-	-	-	3
Diversified Training - Total	1	-	-	1	-
Aircraft Controller	1	-	-	1	-
Tactical Air Controller	-	-	-	-	-
Ground Observer Training	-	-	-	-	-
Aircraft Observer and Flexible Gunnery Training - Total	1	1	-	-	-
Basic Observer (New Production) - Total	-	-	-	-	-
B-29N	-	-	-	-	-
Electronic Countermeasure	-	-	-	-	-
Primary Observer Non-Rated Officer	1	1	-	-	-
Staff Officer ECM Indoctrination	-	-	-	-	-
Radar Target Prediction and Simulation	-	-	-	-	-
Commanders Radar Bomb and Indoctrination	-	-	-	-	-
Advanced Flying Training (Individual) - Total	38	4	9	14	11
Fighter Bomber Escort, F-51	11	-	4	6	1
Fighter Bomber Escort, F-80	11	1	-	8	2
Fighter Bomber Escort, F-84	16	3	5	-	8
Fighter Bomber Escort, F-86	-	-	-	-	-
Fighter Interceptor - Total	-	-	-	-	-
Instrument Phase, T-33	-	-	-	-	-
Application Phase, F-89	-	-	-	-	-
Airman - Total	556	121	156	140	139
Pilot Training - Total	555	121	155	140	139
Undergraduate Pilot Training - Total	555	121	155	140	139
Preflight	15	-	3	6	6
Primary	345	97	111	94	43
Basic - Total	195	24	41	40	90
Single Engine	195	24	41	40	90
Twin Engine	-	-	-	-	-
Miscellaneous Pilot Training - Total	-	-	-	-	-
Pilot Instructor School	-	-	-	-	-
Aircraft Observer and Flexible Gunnery Training - Total	1	-	1	-	-
Basic Observer (New Production) - Total	1	-	1	-	-
B-29N	1	-	1	-	-
Primary Observer (Cadets)	-	-	-	-	-

(CONTINUED)

TABLE 263 — USAF FLYING TRAINING OF FOREIGN PERSONNEL — FY 1953 (CONTINUED)

(Table includes MDAP Students.)

Type Of Training By Course	Total	30 September (1952)	31 December (1952)	31 March (1953)	30 June (1953)
		STUDENTS UNDER INSTRUCTION			
Total	NOT APPLICABLE	1,600	1,455	1,440	1,799
Officer - Total		373	i/ 369	j/ 413	l/ 447
Pilot Training - Total		244	i/ 204	j/ 250	l/ 358
Undergraduate Pilot Training - Total		218	i/ 185	j/ 193	l/ 286
Preflight		-	6	33	133
Primary		a/ 140	64	18	40
Basic - Total		78	i/ 115	j/ 142	l/ 113
Single Engine		b/ 68	i/ 115	j/ 142	103
Twin Engine		b/c/ 10	-	-	10
Miscellaneous Pilot Training - Total		26	19	57	72
Helicopter		-	4	1	4
Liaison (Army Primary Pilot Training)		-	6	2	-
Transition, Jet		14	-	-	-
Instructor - Total		12	9	54	68
Fighter Gunnery		d/ 4	-	2	4
Instrument Pilot, Jet		e/ 2	2	16	28
Jet, Upgrading		5	-	-	-
Pilot Instructor School		1	7	3	18
Basic Instructor School		-	-	33	18
Diversified Training - Total		f/ 37	38	45	-
Aircraft Controller		32	38	45	-
Tactical Air Controller		5	-	-	-
Ground Observer Training		-	-	-	-
Aircraft Observer and Flexible Gunnery Training - Total		g/ 6	4	3	5
Basic Observer (New Production) - Total		6	4	3	-
B-29N		a/h/ 2	-	-	-
Electronic Countermeasure		4	4	3	-
Primary Observer Non-Rated Officer		-	-	-	-
Staff Officer ECM Indoctrination		-	-	-	5
Radar Target Prediction and Simulation		-	-	-	-
Commanders Radar Bomb and Indoctrination		-	-	-	-
Advanced Flying Training (Individual) - Total		86	123	115	84
Fighter Bomber Escort, F-51		41	54	34	-
Fighter Bomber Escort, F-80		-	-	-	-
Fighter Bomber Escort, F-84		45	68	81	84
Fighter Bomber Escort, F-86		-	-	-	-
Fighter Interceptor - Total		-	1	-	-
Instrument Phase, T-33		-	1	-	-
Application Phase, F-89		-	-	-	-
Airman - Total		1,227	i/ 1,086	j/ 1,027	l/ 1,352
Pilot Training - Total		1,225	i/ 1,086	j/ 1,027	l/ 1,352
Undergraduate Pilot Training - Total		1,225	i/ 1,086	j/ 996	l/ 1,352
Preflight		-	202	173	376
Primary		a/ 805	593	408	460
Basic - Total		420	i/ 291	j/k/ 415	l/ 516
Single Engine		g/ 420	i/ 291	j/k/ 415	l/ 516
Twin Engine		-	-	-	-
Miscellaneous Pilot Training - Total		-	-	k/ 31	-
Pilot Instructor School		g/ -	-	31	-
Aircraft Observer and Flexible Gunnery Training - Total		2	-	-	-
Basic Observer (New Production) - Total		2	-	-	-
B-29N		a/h/ 2	-	-	-
Primary Observer (Cadets)		h/ -	-	-	-

a/ One officer previously reported as a Cadet.
b/ Two officers transferred from Basic Twin Engine to Basic Single Engine.
c/ Two officers erroneously reported as New Students in Basic, Twin Engine.
d/ One USAF officer previously reported as Foreign.
e/ One officer omitted on previous report.
f/ Ground Observer Course included with Aircraft Observer and Flexible Gunnery Training during FY 1952.
g/ Forty three French cadets reinstated in Basic, Single Engine Pilot Training after graduating from the Pilot Instructor School in July; five cadets were erroneously reported as New Students on previous report under Basic, Single Engine.
h/ Four cadets transferred from Primary Observer to Basic Observer B-29N; one cadet omitted from Course B-29N on previous report.
i/ Twenty eight cadets promoted to officer status; 1 French officer previously reported as Cadet.
j/ Thirty two Norwegian cadets previously reported as officers.
k/ Thirty one cadets transferred to Pilot Instructor School.
l/ One cadet promoted to officer status.

Source: Personnel Statistics Division, DCS/Comptroller, Hq USAF.

TABLE 264 — TRAINING OF USAF MILITARY PERSONNEL AT TACTICAL AIR COMMAND — FY 1953

(In addition to Tactical Air Command Training in table below, there were 39 USAF Civilians and 26 ANG Students graduated from Air-Ground Operations School.)

Type Of Training By Course	Total	First Quarter	Second Quarter	Third Quarter	Fourth Quarter
	NEW STUDENTS				
Total	4,250	1,036	1,000	1,151	1,063
Officer - Total	3,579	832	852	1,000	895
Air-Ground Operations School - Total	1,844	467	472	518	387
Advanced Flying Training (Individual) - Total	1,735	365	380	482	508
B-26 Night Intruder, Pilot	929	365	254	156	154
B-26 Night Intruder, Observer	368	-	55	151	162
RB-26 Pilot, Reconnaissance	114	-	27	45	42
RB-26 Observer, Reconnaissance (Nav-Bomb)	218	-	30	85	103
RF-80 Pilot, Reconnaissance	106	-	14	45	47
Airman - Total	671	204	148	151	168
Advanced Flying Training (Individual) - Total	671	204	148	151	168
B-26 Night Intruder (Gunner)	612	204	148	151	109
B-26 Night Intruder (Engineer)	59	-	-	-	59
	ATTRITION				
Total	134	35	50	30	19
Officer - Total	92	24	35	21	12
Air-Ground Operations School - Total	3	3	-	-	-
Advanced Flying Training (Individual) - Total	89	21	35	21	12
B-26 Night Intruder, Pilot	50	21	16	8	5
B-26 Night Intruder, Observer	20	-	8	9	3
RB-26, Pilot, Reconnaissance	8	-	8	-	-
RB-26 Observer, Reconnaissance (Nav-Bomb)	7	-	1	2	4
RF-80 Pilot, Reconnaissance	4	-	2	2	-
Airman - Total	42	11	15	9	7
Advanced Flying Training (Individual) - Total	42	11	15	9	7
B-26 Night Intruder (Gunner)	41	11	15	9	6
B-26 Night Intruder (Engineer)	1	-	-	-	1
	GRADUATES				
Total	4,107	941	1,096	1,057	1,013
Officer - Total	3,487	765	937	928	857
Air-Ground Operations School - Total	1,841	413	523	518	387
Advanced Flying Training (Individual) - Total	1,646	352	414	410	470
B-26 Night Intruder, Pilot	909	352	279	129	149
B-26 Night Intruder, Observer	317	-	39	129	149
RB-26 Pilot, Reconnaissance	107	-	26	39	42
RB-26 Observer, Reconnaissance (Nav-Bomb)	214	-	52	78	84
RF-80 Pilot, Reconnaissance	99	-	18	35	46
Airman - Total	620	176	159	129	156
Advanced Flying Training (Individual) - Total	620	176	159	129	156
B-26 Night Intruder (Gunner)	599	176	159	129	135
B-26 Night Intruder (Engineer)	21	-	-	-	21

(Continued)

TABLE 264 — TRAINING OF USAF MILITARY PERSONNEL AT TACTICAL AIR COMMAND — FY 1953 (CONTINUED)

(In addition to Tactical Air Command Training in table below, there were 39 USAF Civilians and 26 ANG Students graduated from Air-Ground Operations School.)

Type Of Training By Course	Total	30 September (1952)	31 December (1952)	31 March (1953)	30 June (1953)
		STUDENTS UNDER INSTRUCTION			
Total	NOT APPLICABLE	305	277	341	373
Officer - Total		206	204	255	282
Air-Ground Operations School - Total		51	-	-	-
Advanced Flying Training (Individual) - Total		155	204	255	282
B-26 Night Intruder, Pilot		155	a/ 41	60	60
B-26 Night Intruder, Observer		-	73	86	96
RB-26 Pilot, Reconnaissance		-	b/ 18	24	24
RB-26 Observer, Reconnaissance (Nav-Bomb)		-	c/ 48	53	e/ 68
RF-80 Pilot, Reconnaissance		-	d/ 24	32	34
Airman - Total		99	73	86	91
Advanced Flying Training (Individual) - Total		99	73	86	91
B-26 Night Intruder (Gunner)		99	73	86	54
B-26 Night Intruder (Engineer)		-	-	-	37

a/ B-26 Night Intruder now reported B-26, Pilot; B-26 Observer.
b/ Initial reporting with 31 Students enrolled at the beginning of the month.
c/ Initial reporting with 57 Students enrolled at the beginning of the month.
d/ Initial reporting with 30 Students enrolled at the beginning of the month.
e/ Error in omitting 1 Officer on previous report.

Source: Personnel Statistics Division, DCS/Comptroller, Hq USAF.

TABLE 265 — TECHNICAL TRAINING OF USAF PERSONNEL BY AIR TRAINING COMMAND — FY 1953

Nomenclature	Total	First Quarter	Second Quarter	Third Quarter	Fourth Quarter
Officer					
In-Put	6,990	1,861	1,303	1,558	2,268
Attrition.	199	55	59	53	32
Graduates.	6,087	1,932	1,360	1,220	1,575
Under Instruction a/	b/-	1,865	1,749	2,034	2,695
Airman					
In-Put	168,592	47,772	30,916	42,055	47,849
Attrition.	12,057	3,281	2,804	2,663	3,309
Graduates.	158,912	44,764	41,310	37,055	35,783
Under Instruction a/	b/-	51,244	38,046	40,383	49,140

a/ Number of students at the end of the quarter.
b/ Not applicable.

Source: Personnel Statistics Division, DCS/Comptroller Hq USAF

TABLE 266 — TECHNICAL TRAINING OF WAF PERSONNEL BY AIR TRAINING COMMAND — FY 1953

(Comparable table in FY 1952 "USAF Statistical Digest" found on page 445 was in error. Compensating error detected was between Male and Female Personnel. The correct number for "Under Instruction" at the end of FY 1952 should have been 698)

Type of Training	Total	First Quarter	Second Quarter	Third Quarter	Fourth Quarter	Total	First Quarter	Second Quarter	Third Quarter	Fourth Quarter
	NEW STUDENTS					ATTRITION				
Total	4,077	1,067	919	1,241	850	412	97	90	99	126
Officer - Total	109	31	22	20	36	6	3	1	-	2
Intelligence-Psychological	28	17	2	1	8	3	2	-	-	1
Communications-Electronics	11	2	2	1	6	2	1	1	-	-
Supply	17	6	6	4	1	-	-	-	-	-
Comptroller	6	2	-	-	4	-	-	-	-	-
Personnel	39	4	9	12	14	1	-	-	-	1
Education-Training	7	-	3	2	2	-	-	-	-	-
Photography-Cartography	1	-	-	-	1	-	-	-	-	-
Airman - Total	3,968	1,036	897	1,221	814	406	94	89	99	124
Combat Support	1,975	482	562	547	384	242	49	58	58	77
Electronics-Engineering	840	209	136	287	208	101	22	23	20	36
Maintenance Engineering	8	-	-	7	1	-	-	-	-	-
Crafts and Trades	74	23	8	43	-	4	-	-	3	1
Logistics	263	117	25	81	40	12	8	-	2	2
Personnel-Administration	535	132	133	163	107	25	11	3	8	3
Comptroller	273	73	33	93	74	22	4	5	8	5
	GRADUATES					STUDENTS UNDER INSTRUCTION				
Total	3,615	733	800	1,050	1,032	NOT APPLICABLE	946	975	1,067	759
Officer - Total	94	18	23	17	36		21	19	22	20
Intelligence-Psychological	25	5	8	7	5		13	7	1	3
Communications-Electronics	5	1	-	-	4		3	4	5	8
Supply	18	6	4	4	4		2	4	4	1
Comptroller	5	1	1	-	3		1	-	-	1
Personnel	36	5	7	5	19		2	4	11	5
Education-Training	5	-	3	1	1		-	-	1	1
Photography-Cartography	-	-	-	-	-		-	-	-	1
Airman - Total	3,521	715	777	1,033	996		925	956	1,045	739
Combat Support	1,776	323	464	551	438		488	528	466	335
Electronics Engineering	562	38	86	176	262		236	263	354	264
Maintenance Engineering	-	-	-	-	-		-	-	7	8
Crafts and Trades	70	14	11	30	15		11	8	18	2
Logistics	346	178	44	52	72		50	31	58	24
Personnel-Administration	529	145	113	147	124		69	86	94	74
Comptroller	238	17	59	77	85		71	40	48	32

Source: Personnel Statistics Division, DCS/Comptroller, Hq USAF

TABLE 267 – TECHNICAL TRAINING OF U S ARMY PERSONNEL BY AIR TRAINING COMMAND – FY 1953

Type of Personnel	Total	First Quarter	Second Quarter	Third Quarter	Fourth Quarter	Total	First Quarter	Second Quarter	Third Quarter	Fourth Quarter
	NEW STUDENTS					ATTRITION				
Total	2,286	451	477	603	755	112	30	18	21	43
Officer - Total	1	-	-	-	1	-	-	-	-	-
Enlisted - Total	2,285	451	477	603	754	112	30	18	21	43
	Total	First Quarter	Second Quarter	Third Quarter	Fourth Quarter	Total	30 Sep (1952)	31 Dec	31 Mar (1953)	30 Jun
	GRADUATES					STUDENTS UNDER INSTRUCTION				
Total	2,161	514	389	529	729	NOT APPLICABLE	474	544	597	580
Officer - Total	-	-	-	-	-		-	-	-	1
Enlisted - Total	2,161	514	389	529	729		474	544	597	579

Source: Personnel Statistics Division, DCS/Comptroller, Hq USAF

TABLE 268 – TECHNICAL TRAINING OF U S NAVY PERSONNEL BY AIR TRAINING COMMAND – FY 1953

Type of Personnel	Total	First Quarter	Second Quarter	Third Quarter	Fourth Quarter	Total	First Quarter	Second Quarter	Third Quarter	Fourth Quarter
	NEW STUDENTS					ATTRITION				
Total	77	29	16	15	17	8	-	5	1	2
Officer - Total	-	-	-	-	-	-	-	-	-	-
Enlisted - Total	77	29	16	15	17	8	-	5	1	2
	Total	First Quarter	Second Quarter	Third Quarter	Fourth Quarter	Total	30 Sep (1952)	31 Dec	31 Mar (1953)	30 Jun
	GRADUATES					STUDENTS UNDER INSTRUCTION				
Total	82	29	21	15	17	NOT APPLICABLE	20	10	9	7
Officer - Total	-	-	-	-	-		-	-	-	-
Enlisted - Total	82	29	21	15	17		20	10	9	7

Source: Personnel Statistics Division, DCS/Comptroller, Hq USAF

TABLE 269 — TACTICAL AIR COMMAND TRAINING OF ARMY AND NAVY PERSONNEL — FY 1953

Type Of Training By Course	Total		First Quarter		Second Quarter		Third Quarter		Fourth Quarter	
	Army	Navy	Army	Navy	Army	Navy	Army	Navy	Army	Navy
	NEW STUDENTS									
Total	1,907	36	507	-	412	-	473	6	515	30
Officer - Total	1,907	36	507	-	412	-	473	6	515	30
Air-Ground Operations School	1,907	36	507	-	412	-	473	6	515	30
	ATTRITION									
Total	1	-	-	-	1	-	-	-	-	-
Officer - Total	1	-	-	-	1	-	-	-	-	-
Air-Ground Operations School	1	-	-	-	1	-	-	-	-	-
	GRADUATES									
Total	1,906	36	448	-	470	-	473	6	515	30
Officer - Total	1,906	36	448	-	470	-	473	6	515	30
Air-Ground Operations School	1,906	36	448	-	470	-	473	6	515	30
	Total		30 September (1952)		31 December		31 March (1953)		30 June	
	STUDENTS UNDER INSTRUCTION									
Total	NOT APPLICABLE	NOT APPLICABLE	59	-	-	-	-	-	-	-
Officer - Total			59	-	-	-	-	-	-	-
Air-Ground Operations School			59	-	-	-	-	-	-	-

TABLE 270 — TACTICAL AIR COMMAND TRAINING OF FOREIGN PERSONNEL — FY 1953

(No Attrition Reported for this Period.)

Type of Training By Course	Total	First Quarter	Second Quarter	Third Quarter	Fourth Quarter
	NEW STUDENTS				
Total	63	-	2	25	36
Officer - Total	63	-	2	25	36
Air-Ground Operations School	63	-	2	25	36
	GRADUATES				
Total	63	-	2	25	36
Officer - Total	63	-	2	25	36
Air-Ground Operations School	63	-	2	25	36

Source: Personnel Statistics Division, DCS/Comptroller, Hq USAF.

TABLE 271 — TECHNICAL TRAINING OF U S CIVILIAN PERSONNEL BY AIR TRAINING COMMAND — FY 1953

(The revised total for "Under Instruction" at the end of FY 1952 was 125. "Students Under Instruction" data in the table below are as of the last day of each quarter)

Type of Personnel	Total	First Quarter	Second Quarter	Third Quarter	Fourth Quarter	Total	First Quarter	Second Quarter	Third Quarter	Fourth Quarter
	NEW STUDENTS					ATTRITION				
Total	1,431	428	216	247	540	37	9	11	1	16
Officer Courses	315	108	9	5	193	1	-	1	-	-
Enlisted Courses	1,116	320	207	242	347	36	9	10	1	16
	GRADUATES					STUDENTS UNDER INSTRUCTION				
Total	1,293	353	331	214	395	NOT APPLICABLE	193	67	99	228
Officer Courses	246	97	24	4	121		18	2	3	75
Enlisted Courses	1,047	256	307	210	274		175	65	96	153

Source: Personnel Statistics Division, DCS Comptroller, Hq USAF

TABLE 272 — TECHNICAL TRAINING OF FOREIGN NATIONALS BY AIR TRAINING COMMAND — FY 1953

(Students Under Instruction in the table below are as of the last day of each quarter)

Type of Personnel	Total	First Quarter	Second Quarter	Third Quarter	Fourth Quarter	Total	First Quarter	Second Quarter	Third Quarter	Fourth Quarter
	NEW STUDENTS					ATTRITION				
Total	3,060	533	859	981	687	74	7	11	22	34
Officer - Total	787	136	229	312	110	11	2	2	7	-
Enlisted - Total	2,273	397	630	669	577	63	5	9	15	34
	GRADUATES					STUDENTS UNDER INSTRUCTION				
Total	2,976	615	743	785	833	NOT APPLICABLE	619	724	898	718
Officer - Total	828	174	193	249	212		231	265	321	219
Enlisted - Total	2,148	441	550	536	621		388	459	577	499

Source: Personnel Statistics Division, DCS/Comptroller, Hq USAF

TABLE 273 – USAF PROFESSIONAL AND TECHNOLOGICAL MILITARY TRAINING OF USAF PERSONNEL, FY 1953

Type of Training by Course	Total	First Quarter	Second Quarter	Third Quarter	Fourth Quarter
	NEW STUDENTS				
Total	12,837	3,921	2,451	4,394	2,071
Officer - Total	10,639	3,295	1,972	3,697	1,675
USAF Institute of Technology - Total	306	215	7	79	5
Aeronautical Engineer	29	28	-	-	1
Automatic Control Engineer	19	19	-	-	-
Electronics	19	19	-	-	-
Engineering Administration	24	22	-	-	2
Engineering Science - 1 Year Postgraduate	21	20	-	1	-
Engineering Science - 2 Year Postgraduate	48	46	1	-	1
Industrial Administration	-	-	-	-	-
Industrial Mobilization Training	12	12	-	-	-
Industrial Production Engineering	29	-	-	29	-
Installation Engineering	83	41	-	42	-
Training In Industry	22	8	6	7	1
Air Command and Staff School - Total	6,432	1,959	1,186	2,592	695
Academic Instructor Course	745	268	67	138	272
Air Communication and Electronics Staff Officer	133	71	-	61	1
Air Weapons Course	156	51	27	51	27
Air Weapons Orientation	864	141	337	231	155
Comptroller Course	218	78	-	78	62
Field Officer Course	837	414	-	423	-
Inspector Course	119	35	35	49	-
Intelligence Course	106	45	-	61	-
Judge Advocate General Course	257	65	69	64	59
Logistics Staff Officer Course	220	106	-	114	-
Pilotless Aircraft	162	-	-	44	118
Squadron Officer Course	2,615	685	651	1,278	1
Air War College - Total	124	124	-	-	-
USAF School of Aviation Medicine - Total	3,777	997	779	1,026	975
Aviation Medicine, Basic	11	-	11	-	-
Aviation Medicine, Primary Course	385	91	68	113	113
Clinical Laboratory Officer	49	22	15	12	-
Flight Nurse	189	95	-	40	54
Medical Administration, Basic	70	34	-	19	17
Medical Course	-	-	-	-	-
Medical Services, Indoctrination	3,013	738	668	832	775
Medical Services, Supervisor	-	-	-	-	-
Medical Supply Officer	27	-	17	10	-
Physical Training Officer	25	9	-	-	16
Veterinary Officer, Basic	8	8	-	-	-
Airman - Total	2,198	626	479	697	396
Air Command and Staff School - Total	352	116	62	124	50
Academic Instructor Course	280	44	62	124	50
Inspector Course	72	72	-	-	-
USAF School of Aviation Medicine - Total	1,846	510	417	573	346
Aeromedical Apprentice	535	160	180	195	-
Aeromedical Technician	67	-	-	-	67
Air Rescue Specialist	36	-	26	-	10
Dental Laboratory	39	-	-	39	-
Dental Technician	221	41	88	47	45
Medical Administrative Supervisor	391	93	101	97	100
Medical Laboratory	113	38	-	23	52
Medical Services Supervisor	107	53	-	54	-
Pharmacy Technician	28	28	-	-	-
Physical Training	143	45	22	42	34
Preventive Medicine	102	52	-	50	-
Veterinary Apprentice	-	-	-	-	-
Veterinary Technician	64	-	-	26	38

(Continued)

TABLE 273 – USAF PROFESSIONAL AND TECHNOLOGICAL MILITARY TRAINING OF USAF PERSONNEL
FY 1953 – (CONTINUED)

Type of Training by Course	Total	First Quarter	Second Quarter	Third Quarter	Fourth Quarter
	ATTRITION				
Total	332	108	93	42	89
Officer - Total	166	48	39	25	54
USAF Institute of Technology - Total	20	3	4	9	4
Aeronautical Engineer	1	-	-	-	1
Automatic Control Engineer	-	-	-	-	-
Electronics	4	1	-	3	-
Engineering Administration	-	-	-	-	-
Engineering Science - 1 Year Postgraduate	2	1	1	-	-
Engineering Science - 2 Year Postgraduate	5	-	2	3	-
Industrial Administration	1	-	-	1	-
Industrial Mobilization Training	-	-	-	-	-
Industrial Production Engineering	1	-	-	-	1
Installation Engineering	4	1	1	-	2
Training In Industry	2	-	-	2	-
Air Command and Staff School - Total	89	20	22	10	37
Academic Instructor Course	8	2	1	2	3
Air Communication and Electronics Staff Officer	4	-	1	1	2
Air Weapons Course	7	1	2	2	2
Air Weapons Orientation	2	-	1	1	-
Comptroller Course	3	2	-	-	1
Field Officer Course	8	-	2	-	6
Inspector Course	-	-	-	-	-
Intelligence Course	6	2	-	1	3
Judge Advocate General Course	-	-	-	-	-
Logistics Staff Officer Course	8	1	4	-	3
Pilotless Aircraft	1	-	-	-	1
Squadron Officer Course	42	12	11	3	16
Air War College - Total	-	-	-	-	-
USAF School of Aviation Medicine - Total	57	25	13	6	13
Aviation Medicine, Basic	2	1	-	-	1
Aviation Medicine, Primary Course	14	7	2	-	5
Clinical Laboratory Officer	2	2	-	-	-
Flight Nurse	4	3	-	1	-
Medical Administration, Basic	8	-	6	-	2
Medical Course	10	10	-	-	-
Medical Services, Indoctrination	14	1	4	5	4
Medical Services, Supervisor	1	1	-	-	-
Medical Supply Officer	1	-	1	-	-
Physical Training Officer	1	-	-	-	1
Veterinary Officer, Basic	-	-	-	-	-
Airman - Total	166	60	54	17	35
Air Command and Staff School - Total	19	2	7	3	7
Academic Instructor Course	19	2	7	3	7
Inspector Course	-	-	-	-	-
USAF School of Aviation Medicine - Total	147	58	47	14	28
Aeromedical Apprentice	37	17	14	4	2
Aeromedical Technician	2	-	-	-	2
Air Rescue Specialist	3	-	-	-	3
Dental Laboratory	5	-	2	1	2
Dental Technician	12	4	4	2	2
Medical Administrative Supervisor	23	10	5	2	6
Medical Laboratory	6	-	1	-	5
Medical Services Supervisor	24	14	5	4	1
Pharmacy Technician	9	1	8	-	-
Physical Training	15	6	4	1	4
Preventive Medicine	-	5	-	-	-
Veterinary Apprentice	9	-	4	-	-
Veterinary Technician	2	1	-	-	1

(Continued)

TABLE 273 — USAF PROFESSIONAL AND TECHNOLOGICAL MILITARY TRAINING OF USAF PERSONNEL
FY 1953 — (CONTINUED)

Type of Training by Course	Total	First Quarter	Second Quarter	Third Quarter	Fourth Quarter
	GRADUATES				
Total	13,549	3,168	4,485	2,188	3,708
Officer - Total	11,062	2,286	3,857	1,848	3,071
USAF Institute of Technology - Total	218	78	44	48	48
Aeronautical Engineer	15	15	-	-	-
Automatic Control Engineer	22	16	5	-	1
Electronics	16	16	-	-	-
Engineering Administration	-	-	-	-	-
Engineering Science - 1 Year Postgraduate	24	24	-	-	-
Engineering Science - 2 Year Postgraduate	-	-	-	-	-
Industrial Administration	36	-	-	36	-
Industrial Mobilization Training	6	-	-	6	-
Industrial Production Engineering	40	-	-	-	40
Installation Engineering	39	-	39	-	-
Training In Industry	20	7	-	6	7
Air Command and Staff School - Total	7,085	1,355	2,725	1,107	1,898
Academic Instructor Course	749	377	140	70	162
Air Communication and Electronics Staff Officer	129	-	70	-	59
Air Weapons Course	176	50	52	17	57
Air Weapons Orientation	862	105	372	230	155
Comptroller Course	236	82	77	-	77
Field Officer Course	829	-	412	-	417
Inspector Course	119	-	70	29	20
Intelligence Course	144	42	45	-	57
Judge Advocate General Course	257	65	69	64	59
Logistics Staff Officer Course	212	-	101	-	111
Pilotless Aircraft	161	-	-	44	117
Squadron Officer Course	3,211	634	1,317	653	607
Air War College - Total	124	-	-	-	124
USAF School of Aviation Medicine - Total	3,635	853	1,088	693	1,001
Aviation Medicine, Basic	22	22	-	-	-
Aviation Medicine, Primary Course	345	171	66	-	108
Clinical Laboratory Officer	35	-	20	15	-
Flight Nurse	209	112	38	19	40
Medical Administration, Basic	45	-	28	-	17
Medical Course	45	45	-	-	-
Medical Services, Indoctrination	2,871	490	911	659	811
Medical Services, Supervisor	5	5	-	-	-
Medical Supply Officer	26	-	16	-	10
Physical Training Officer	24	-	9	-	15
Veterinary Officer, Basic	8	8	-	-	-
Airman - Total	2,487	882	628	340	637
Air Command and Staff School - Total	409	147	99	47	116
Academic Instructor Course	262	-	99	47	116
Inspector Course	147	147	-	-	-
USAF School of Aviation Medicine - Total	2,078	735	529	293	521
Aeromedical Apprentice	759	344	226	90	99
Aeromedical Technician	65	-	-	-	65
Air Rescue Specialist	93	-	26	10	57
Dental Laboratory	116	37	-	42	37
Dental Technician	169	46	38	40	45
Medical Administrative Supervisor	367	87	88	99	93
Medical Laboratory	44	25	-	-	19
Medical Services Supervisor	179	82	48	-	49
Pharmacy Technician	19	-	19	-	-
Physical Training	121	37	40	12	32
Preventive Medicine	-	38	-	-	-
Veterinary Apprentice	82	-	44	-	-
Veterinary Technician	64	39	-	-	25

(Continued)

TABLE 273 — USAF PROFESSIONAL AND TECHNOLOGICAL MILITARY TRAINING OF USAF PERSONNEL FY 1953 — (Continued)

Type of Training by Course	Total	30 September 1952	31 December	31 March 1953	30 June
	STUDENTS UNDER INSTRUCTION				
Total	NOT APPLICABLE	2,838	711	2,875	1,149
Officer - Total		2,412	488	2,312	862
USAF Institute of Technology - Total		379	338	360	313
Aeronautical Engineer		28	28	28	27
Automatic Control Engineer		24	19	19	19
Electronics		19	19	16	16
Engineering Administration		22	22	22	24
Engineering Science - 1 Year Postgraduate		20	19	20	20
Engineering Science - 2 Year Postgraduate		150	149	146	147
Industrial Administration		37	37	-	-
Industrial Mobilization Training		17	17	11	11
Industrial Production Engineering		-	-	29	28
Installation Engineering		40	-	42	-
Training In Industry		22	28	27	21
Air Command and Staff School - Total		1,561	-	1,475	235
Academic Instructor Course		74	-	66	173
Air Communication and Electronics Staff Officer		71	-	60	-
Air Weapons Course		27	-	32	-
Air Weapons Orientation		36	-	-	-
Comptroller Course		77	-	78	62
Field Officer Course		414	-	423	-
Inspector Course		35	-	20	-
Intelligence Course		45	-	60	-
Judge Advocate General Course		-	-	-	-
Logistics Staff Officer Course		105	-	114	-
Pilotless Aircraft		-	-	-	-
Squadron Officer Course		677	-	622	-
Air War College - Total		124	124	124	-
USAF School of Aviation Medicine - Total		348	26	353	314
Aviation Medicine, Basic		-	11	11	10
Aviation Medicine, Primary Course		-	-	113	113
Clinical Laboratory Officer		20	15	12	12
Flight Nurse		38	-	20	34
Medical Administration, Basic		34	-	19	17
Medical Course		-	-	-	-
Medical Services, Indoctrination		247	-	168	128
Medical Services, Supervisor		-	-	-	-
Medical Supply Officer		-	-	10	-
Physical Training Officer		9	-	-	-
Veterinary Officer, Basic		-	-	-	-
Airman - Total		426	223	563	287
Air Command and Staff School - Total		44	-	74	1
Academic Instructor Course		44	-	74	1
Inspector Course		-	-	-	-
USAF School of Aviation Medicine - Total		382	223	489	286
Aeromedical Apprentice		60	-	101	-
Aeromedical Technician		-	-	-	-
Air Rescue Specialist		-	-	-	-
Dental Laboratory		-	43	39	-
Dental Technician		41	42	47	45
Medical Administrative Supervisor		93	101	97	98
Medical Laboratory		38	37	60	88
Medical Services Supervisor		53	-	50	-
Pharmacy Technician		27	-	-	-
Physical Training		22	-	19	17
Preventive Medicine		48	-	50	-
Veterinary Apprentice		-	-	-	-
Veterinary Technician		-	-	26	38

Source: Personnel Statistics Division, DCS/Comptroller, Headquarters USAF.

TABLE 274 — PROFESSIONAL AND TECHNOLOGICAL TRAINING OF WAF PERSONNEL — FY 1953

Type of Training by Course	Total		First Quarter		Second Quarter		Third Quarter		Fourth Quarter	
	Officer	Airman	Officer	Airman	Officer	Airman	Officer	Airman	Officer	Airman
	NEW STUDENTS									
Total	1,170	20	350	2	234	3	305	10	281	5
Air Command and Staff School - Total	70	-	10	-	17	-	41	-	2	-
Academic Instructor Course	8	-	2	-	3	-	2	-	1	-
Comptroller Staff Officer Course	2	-	-	-	-	-	1	-	1	-
Field Officer Course	2	-	1	-	-	-	1	-	-	-
Inspector Course	1	-	-	-	-	-	1	-	-	-
Intelligence Course	3	-	2	-	-	-	1	-	-	-
Judge Advocate General Course	5	-	2	-	2	-	1	-	-	-
Squadron Officer Course	49	-	3	-	12	-	34	-	-	-
USAF School of Aviation Medicine - Total	1,038	20	316	2	196	3	251	10	275	5
Basic Medical Administration	2	-	1	-	-	-	-	-	1	-
Clinic Laboratory Officer	3	-	1	-	1	-	1	-	-	-
Dental Technician	-	9	-	-	-	2	-	4	-	3
Flight Nurse Course	191	-	97	-	-	-	40	-	54	-
Indoctrination Course Medical Services	842	-	217	-	195	-	210	-	220	-
Medical Administration Supervisor Course	-	5	-	2	-	1	-	-	-	2
Medical laboratory Apprentice	-	5	-	-	-	-	-	5	-	-
Preventive Medicine Course	-	1	-	-	-	-	-	1	-	-
Civilian Schools and Hospitals - Total	24	-	6	-	10	-	4	-	4	-
Business Administration	1	-	1	-	-	-	-	-	-	-
Chemistry, Biological	2	-	1	-	1	-	-	-	-	-
Education, Teacher Training	5	-	1	-	2	-	2	-	-	-
Engineering, Nuclear	1	-	-	-	-	-	-	-	1	-
International Relations	1	-	-	-	1	-	-	-	-	-
Language, Foreign	4	-	-	-	3	-	1	-	-	-
Meteorology, General	8	-	3	-	2	-	1	-	2	-
Radiology, Biological	2	-	-	-	1	-	-	-	1	-
Medical - Total	38	-	18	-	11	-	9	-	-	-
Medical, Anaesthesia	7	-	7	-	-	-	-	-	-	-
Medical, Dental, Prosthetics	1	-	-	-	1	-	-	-	-	-
Medical, Dietetics	5	-	3	-	-	-	2	-	-	-
Medical, Interns	3	-	3	-	-	-	-	-	-	-
Medical, Nurse, Anaesthesia	1	-	-	-	1	-	-	-	-	-
Medical, Opthamology	1	-	1	-	-	-	-	-	-	-
Medical, Physical Medicine	4	-	2	-	-	-	2	-	-	-
Medical, Physiotherapy	16	-	2	-	9	-	5	-	-	-
	ATTRITION									
Total	22	3	7	-	7	-	6	1	2	2
Air Command and Staff School - Total	1	-	-	-	-	-	-	-	1	-
Field Officer Course	1	-	-	-	-	-	-	-	1	-
USAF School of Aviation Medicine - Total	8	3	3	-	3	-	1	1	1	2
Dental Technician	-	1	-	-	-	-	-	1	-	-
Flight Nurse Course	4	-	3	-	-	-	1	-	-	-
Indoctrination Course Medical Services	4	-	-	-	3	-	-	-	1	-
Medical Laboratory Apprentice	-	2	-	-	-	-	-	-	-	2
Civilian Schools and Hospitals - Total	2	-	-	-	1	-	1	-	-	-
Chemistry, Biological	1	-	-	-	1	-	-	-	-	-
Meteorology, General	1	-	-	-	-	-	1	-	-	-
Medical - Total	11	-	4	-	3	-	4	-	-	-
Medical, Dental, Prosthetics	1	-	-	-	-	-	1	-	-	-
Medical, Interns	2	-	-	-	-	-	2	-	-	-
Medical, Nurse, Anaesthesia	4	-	4	-	-	-	-	-	-	-
Medical, Opthamology	1	-	-	-	1	-	-	-	-	-
Medical, Physical Medicine	2	-	-	-	2	-	-	-	-	-
Medical, Physiotherapy	1	-	-	-	-	-	1	-	-	-

(Continued)

TABLE 274 – PROFESSIONAL AND TECHNOLOGICAL TRAINING OF WAF PERSONNEL – FY 1953 – (CONTINUED)

Type of Training by Course	Total		First Quarter		Second Quarter		Third Quarter		Fourth Quarter	
	Offi-cer	Air-man	Offi-cer	Air-man	Offi-cer	Air-man	Offi-cer	Air-man	Offi-cer	Air-man
	GRADUATES									
Total	1,150	20	306	6	318	4	205	2	321	8
Air Command and Staff School - Total	75	-	9	-	25	-	22	-	19	-
Academic Instructor Course	8	-	-	-	5	-	-	-	3	-
Air Weapons Course	1	-	1	-	-	-	-	-	-	-
Comptroller Staff Officer Course	2	-	1	-	-	-	-	-	1	-
Field Officer Course	1	-	-	-	1	-	-	-	-	-
Inspector Course	1	-	-	-	-	-	-	-	1	-
Intelligence Course	3	-	-	-	2	-	-	-	1	-
Judge Advocate General Course	5	-	2	-	2	-	1	-	-	-
Squadron Officer Course	54	-	5	-	15	-	21	-	13	-
USAF School of Aviation Medicine - Total	1,017	18	278	6	285	2	164	2	290	8
Basic Medical Administration	1	-	-	-	1	-	-	-	-	-
Clinic Laboratory Officer	2	-	-	-	1	-	1	-	-	-
Dental Technician	-	5	-	-	-	-	-	1	-	4
Flight Nurse Course	210	-	111	-	40	-	19	-	40	-
Indoctrination Course Medical Services	803	-	166	-	243	-	144	-	250	-
Medical Administration Supervisor Course	-	5	-	2	-	2	-	1	-	-
Medical Laboratory	-	4	-	4	-	-	-	-	-	-
Medical Laboratory Apprentice	-	3	-	-	-	-	-	-	-	3
Medical Services Supervisor Course	1	-	1	-	-	-	-	-	-	-
Preventive Medicine Course	-	1	-	-	-	-	-	-	-	1
Civilian Schools and Hospitals - Total	10	2	2	-	1	2	5	-	2	-
Education, Teacher Training	1	-	-	-	-	-	-	-	1	-
Electrical Engineering	1	-	1	-	-	-	-	-	-	-
Language, Foreign	3	2	-	-	1	2	1	-	1	-
Meteorology, General	5	-	1	-	-	-	4	-	-	-
Medical - Total	48	-	17	-	7	-	14	-	10	-
Medical, Anaesthesia	3	-	-	-	-	-	-	-	3	-
Medical, Dietetics	2	-	-	-	-	-	2	-	-	-
Medical, Nurse, Anaesthesia	30	-	9	-	5	-	12	-	4	-
Medical, Physical Medicine	2	-	-	-	-	-	-	-	2	-
Medical, Physiotherapy	10	-	7	-	2	-	-	-	1	-
Miscellaneous	1	-	1	-	-	-	-	-	-	-
	Total		30 Sep (1952)		31 Dec		31 Mar (1953)		30 Jun	
	Offi-cer	Air-man	Offi-cer	Air-man	Offi-cer	Air-man	Offi-cer	Air-man	Offi-cer	Air-man
	STUDENTS UNDER INSTRUCTION									
Total	NOT APPLICABLE	NOT APPLICABLE	153	4	62	3	156	10	114	5
Air Command and Staff School - Total			8	-	-	-	19	-	1	-
Academic Instructor Course			2	-	-	-	2	-	-	-
Comptroller Staff Officer Course			-	-	-	-	1	-	1	-
Field Officer Course			1	-	-	-	1	-	-	-
Inspector Course			-	-	-	-	1	-	-	-
Intelligence Course			2	-	-	-	1	-	-	-
Squadron Officer Course			3	-	-	-	13	-	-	-
USAF School of Aviation Medicine - Total			93	2	1	3	87	10	71	5
Basic Medical Administration			1	-	-	-	-	-	1	-
Clinic Laboratory Officer			1	-	1	-	1	-	1	-
Dental Technician			-	-	-	2	-	4	-	3
Flight Nurse Course			40	-	-	-	20	-	34	-
Indoctrination Course Medical Services			51	-	-	-	66	-	35	-
Medical Administration Supervisors Course			-	2	-	1	-	-	-	2
Medical Laboratory Apprentice			-	-	-	-	-	5	-	-

(Continued)

TABLE 274 - PROFESSIONAL AND TECHNOLOGICAL TRAINING OF WAF PERSONNEL - FY 1953 - (Continued)

Type of Training by Course	Total		30 Sep (1952)		31 Dec		31 Mar (1953)		30 Jun	
	Officer	Airman	Officer	Airman	Officer	Airman	Officer	Airman	Officer	Airman
	STUDENTS UNDER INSTRUCTION -- Continued									
USAF School of Aviation Medicine (Cont'd)										
Preventive Medicine Course			-	-	-	-	-	1	-	-
Civilian Schools and Hospitals - Total	NOT APPLICABLE	NOT APPLICABLE	11	2	19	-	17	-	19	-
Business Administration			1	-	1	-	1	-	1	-
Chemistry, Biological			1	-	1	-	1	-	1	-
Education, Teacher Training			1	-	3	-	5	-	4	-
Engineering, Nuclear			-	-	-	-	-	-	1	-
International Relations			-	-	1	-	1	-	1	-
Language, Foreign			1	2	3	-	3	-	2	-
Meteorology, General			7	-	9	-	5	-	7	-
Radiology, Biological			-	-	1	-	1	-	2	-
Medical - Total			41	-	42	-	33	-	23	-
Medical, Anaesthesia			7	-	7	-	7	-	4	-
Medical, Dental, Prosthetics			-	-	1	-	-	-	-	-
Medical, Dietetics			3	-	3	-	3	-	3	-
Medical, Interns			3	-	3	-	1	-	1	-
Medical, Nurse, Anaesthesia			21	-	17	-	5	-	1	-
Medical, Opthamology			1	-	-	-	-	-	-	-
Medical, Physical Medicine			2	-	-	-	2	-	-	-
Medical, Physiotherapy			4	-	11	-	15	-	14	-

Source: Personnel Statistics Division, DCS/Comptroller, Hq USAF

TABLE 275 — USAF PROFESSIONAL AND TECHNOLOGICAL TRAINING OF ARMY AND NAVY PERSONNEL BY AIR UNIVERSITY — FY 1953

Type of Training by Course	Total		First Quarter		Second Quarter		Third Quarter		Fourth Quarter	
	Army	Navy	Army	Navy	Army	Navy	Army	Navy	Army	Navy
NEW STUDENTS										
Officer - Total	86	54	44	35	6	5	29	11	7	3
USAF Institute of Technology - Total	-	1	-	-	-	-	-	-	-	1
Aeronautical Engineer	-	1	-	-	-	-	-	-	-	1
Air Command and Staff School - Total	68	39	31	21	1	5	29	11	7	2
Air Weapons Orientation Course	-	1	-	1	-	-	-	-	-	-
Comptroller Staff Officer Course	35	2	19	-	-	-	9	-	7	2
Field Officer Course	16	20	8	10	-	-	8	10	-	-
Logistics Course	8	6	4	5	-	-	4	1	-	-
Squadron Officer Course	9	10	-	5	1	5	8	-	-	-
Air War College - Total	13	14	13	14	-	-	-	-	-	-
USAF School of Aviation Medicine - Total	5	-	-	-	5	-	-	-	-	-
Primary Course in Aviation Medicine	5	-	-	-	5	-	-	-	-	-
ATTRITION										
Officer - Total	2	1	1	-	-	-	-	1	1	-
Air Command and Staff School - Total	2	1	1	-	-	-	-	1	1	-
Comptroller Staff Officer Course	2	-	1	-	-	-	-	-	1	-
Field Officer Course	-	1	-	-	-	-	-	1	-	-
GRADUATES										
Officer - Total	90	57	12	8	37	25	-	-	41	24
USAF Institute of Technology - Total	-	1	-	1	-	-	-	-	-	-
Aeronautical Engineer	-	1	-	1	-	-	-	-	-	-
Air Command and Staff School - Total	72	42	12	7	32	25	-	-	28	10
Air Weapons Orientation Course	-	1	-	1	-	-	-	-	-	-
Comptroller Staff Officer Course	37	1	10	1	19	-	-	-	8	-
Field Officer Course	16	19	-	-	8	10	-	-	8	9
Logistics Course	8	6	-	-	4	5	-	-	4	1
Squadron Officer Course	11	15	2	5	1	10	-	-	8	-
Air War College - Total	13	14	-	-	-	-	-	-	13	14
USAF School of Aviation Medicine - Total	5	-	-	-	5	-	-	-	-	-
Primary Course in Aviation Medicine	5	-	-	-	5	-	-	-	-	-
	Total		30 Sep (1952)		31 Dec		31 Mar (1953)		30 Jun	
	Army	Navy	Army	Navy	Army	Navy	Army	Navy	Army	Navy
STUDENTS UNDER INSTRUCTION										
Officer - Total	NOT APPLICABLE	NOT APPLICABLE	44	34	13	14	42	24	7	3
USAF Institute of Technology - Total			-	-	-	-	-	-	-	1
Aeronautical Engineer			-	-	-	-	-	-	-	1
Air Command and Staff School - Total			31	20	-	-	29	10	7	2
Comptroller Staff Officer Course			19	-	-	-	9	-	7	2
Field Officer Course			8	10	-	-	8	9	-	-
Logistics Course			4	5	-	-	4	1	-	-
Squadron Officer Course			-	5	-	-	8	-	-	-
Air War College - Total			13	14	13	14	13	14	-	-

Source: Personnel Statistics Division, DCS/Comptroller, Hq USAF

TABLE 276 — USAF PROFESSIONAL AND TECHNOLOGICAL TRAINING OF FOREIGN NATIONALS — FY 1953

Type of Training by Course	Total	First Quarter	Second Quarter	Third Quarter	Fourth Quarter
	NEW STUDENTS				
Total	207	59	41	90	17
Officer - Total	205	59	41	90	15
USAF Institute of Technology - Total	20	15	-	5	-
Aeronautical Engineer	2	2	-	-	-
Armament Automatic Control	2	2	-	-	-
Engineering Science, 1 Year Postgraduate	1	1	-	-	-
Installation Engineer	15	10	-	5	-
Air Command and Staff School - Total	150	31	36	78	5
Academic Instructor Course	9	3	2	-	4
Field Officer Course	55	22	-	33	-
Inspector Course	8	3	2	3	-
Intelligence Course	1	1	-	-	-
Judge Advocate General Course	1	-	-	1	-
Squadron Officer Course	76	2	32	41	1
Air War College - Total	4	4	-	-	-
USAF School of Aviation Medicine - Total	31	9	5	7	10
Aviation Medicine, Primary Course	20	5	5	7	3
Flight Nurse	8	4	-	-	4
Physical Training Officer Course	3	-	-	-	3
Airman - Total	2	-	-	-	2
USAF School of Aviation Medicine - Total	2	-	-	-	2
Physical Training Apprentice Course	2	-	-	-	2
	ATTRITION				
Total	1	-	1	-	-
Officer - Total	1	-	1	-	-
USAF Institute of Technology - Total	1	-	1	-	-
Engineering Science, 2 Year Postgraduate	1	-	1	-	-
	GRADUATES				
Total	206	23	83	26	74
Officer - Total	206	23	83	26	74
USAF Institute of Technology - Total	17	-	12	-	5
Aeronautical Engineer	-	-	-	-	-
Armament Automatic Control	2	-	2	-	-
Installation Engineer	15	-	10	-	5
Air Command and Staff School - Total	157	14	64	26	53
Academic Instructor Course	8	6	2	-	-
Comptroller Staff Course	1	1	-	-	-
Field Officer Course	55	-	22	-	33
Inspector Course	8	-	5	1	2
Intelligence Course	1	-	1	-	-
Judge Advocate General Course	1	-	-	1	-
Squadron Officer Course	83	7	34	24	18
Air War College - Total	4	-	-	-	4
USAF School of Aviation Medicine - Total	28	9	7	-	12
Aviation Medicine, Primary Course	19	7	5	-	7
Flight Nurse	6	2	2	-	2
Physical Training Officer Course	3	-	-	-	3

(Continued)

TABLE 276 — USAF PROFESSIONAL AND TECHNOLOGICAL TRAINING OF FOREIGN NATIONALS FY 1953 — (CONTINUED)

Type of Training by Course	Total	30 September 1952	31 December	31 March 1953	30 June
		STUDENTS UNDER INSTRUCTION			
Total	NOT APPLICABLE	51	8	72	15
Officer - Total		51	8	72	13
USAF Institute of Technology - Total		17	4	9	4
Aeronautical Engineer		2	2	2	2
Armament Automatic Control		3	1	1	1
Engineering Science, 1 Year Postgraduate		1	1	1	1
Engineering Science, 2 Year Postgraduate		1	-	-	-
Installation Engineer		10	-	5	-
Air Command and Staff School - Total		28	-	52	4
Academic Instructor Course		-	-	-	4
Field Officer Course		22	-	33	-
Inspector Course		3	-	2	-
Intelligence Course		1	-	-	-
Squadron Officer Course		2	-	17	-
Air War College - Total		4	4	4	-
USAF School of Aviation Medicine - Total		2	-	7	5
Aviation Medicine, Primary Course		-	-	7	3
Flight Nurse		2	-	-	2
Airman - Total		-	-	-	2
USAF School of Aviation Medicine - Total		-	-	-	2
Physical Training Apprentice Course		-	-	-	2

Source: Personnel Statistics Division, DCS/Comptroller, Hq USAF

TABLE 277 – TRAINING OF USAF PERSONNEL IN OTHER MILITARY SCHOOLS – FY 1953

Type of Training	Total	First Quarter	Second Quarter	Third Quarter	Fourth Quarter
	NEW STUDENTS				
Officer - Total	323	249	8	62	4
Department of Defense - Total	322	248	8	62	4
Air War College	124	124	-	-	-
Armed Forces Staff College	120	51	7	62	-
Industrial College of Armed Forces	46	45	-	-	1
National War College	32	28	1	-	3
USAF in Foreign Military Schools - Total	1	1	-	-	-
	ATTRITION				
Officer - Total	2	-	1	1	-
Department of Defense - Total	1	-	1	-	-
Air War College	-	-	-	-	-
Armed Forces Staff College	-	-	-	-	-
Industrial College of Armed Forces	-	-	-	-	-
National War College	1	-	1	-	-
USAF in Foreign Military Schools - Total	1	-	-	1	-
	GRADUATES				
Officer - Total	306	76	1	63	166
Department of Defense - Total	293	63	1	63	166
Air War College	124	-	-	-	124
Armed Forces Staff College	121	63	-	58	-
Industrial College of Armed Forces	28	-	1	3	24
National War College	20	-	-	2	18
USAF in Foreign Military Schools - Total	13	13	-	-	-
	Total	30 Sep (1952)	31 Dec	31 Mar (1953)	30 Jun
	STUDENTS UNDER INSTRUCTION				
Officer - Total	NOT APPLICABLE	256	262	260	98
Department of Defense - Total		255	261	260	98
Air War College		124	124	124	-
Armed Forces Staff College		56	63	67	67
Industrial College of Armed Forces		47	46	43	20
National War College		28	28	26	11
USAF in Foreign Military Schools - Total		1	1	-	-

Source: Personnel Statistics Division, DCS/Comptroller, Hq USAF

308700 O - 54 - 32

TABLE 278 — TRAINING OF USAF PERSONNEL IN ARMY SCHOOLS — FY 1953

Type of Training	Total	First Quarter	Second Quarter	Third Quarter	Fourth Quarter	Total	First Quarter	Second Quarter	Third Quarter	Fourth Quarter
	NEW STUDENTS					ATTRITION				
Total	9,073	3,556	2,105	1,833	1,579	1,072	479	256	181	156
Officer - Total	1,274	295	306	370	303	55	7	11	12	25
Adjutant General School	53	20	28	5	-	-	-	-	-	-
Armed Forces Information School	200	28	4	89	79	-	-	-	-	-
Army General School	8	-	-	-	8	-	-	-	-	-
Army Language School	24	7	7	3	7	4	2	1	1	-
Army Medical Graduate School	88	3	27	43	15	-	-	-	-	-
Army Security School	4	2	-	1	1	1	-	-	-	1
Army War College	4	4	-	-	-	-	-	-	-	-
Artillery	36	-	-	-	36	2	-	-	-	2
Censorship Officer	7	-	4	3	-	-	-	-	-	-
Chaplain School	166	41	64	61	-	-	-	-	-	-
Chemical	41	2	9	18	12	1	-	-	1	-
Command and General Staff	9	9	-	-	-	1	-	-	1	-
Counterintelligence	17	-	17	-	-	1	-	1	-	-
Engineer	131	2	25	45	59	5	-	-	2	3
Finance	53	51	-	1	1	1	1	-	-	-
Food Services	14	14	-	-	-	1	1	-	-	-
Infantry	87	4	56	7	20	11	1	1	3	6
Meat and Dairy Hygiene	17	5	3	4	5	5	-	5	-	-
Medical Field Services	58	40	11	7	-	2	1	-	1	-
Medical Equipment Maintenance	6	-	-	4	2	-	-	-	-	-
Military Police	15	8	7	-	-	1	-	1	-	-
Ordnance Automotive	2	-	-	-	2	-	-	-	-	-
Packaging Course (Joint Military)	19	-	3	10	6	-	-	-	-	-
Personnel (Administration)	3	-	-	-	3	-	-	-	-	-
Physical Training	1	-	-	-	1	-	-	-	-	-
Provost Marshal General Staff	12	-	-	12	-	1	-	-	1	-
Psychological Warfare	15	15	-	-	-	-	-	-	-	-
Quartermaster	33	3	6	14	10	-	-	-	-	-
Quartermaster Subsistence	21	4	6	5	6	-	-	-	-	-
Signal	18	1	2	8	7	9	-	-	-	9
Strategic Intelligence	111	32	26	30	23	9	1	2	2	4
Transportation	1	-	1	-	-	-	-	-	-	-
Airman - Total	7,799	3,261	1,799	1,463	1,276	1,017	472	245	169	131
Adjutant General School	236	135	44	32	25	14	7	3	3	1
Armed Forces Information School	174	25	6	34	109	-	-	-	-	-
Army Area Food Service School	1	-	-	1	-	-	-	-	-	-
Army Language School	302	61	109	71	61	37	3	10	14	10
Army Medical Graduate School	74	-	-	-	74	-	-	-	-	-
Army Security School	153	50	26	60	17	18	8	2	5	3
Chaplain Assistant	176	82	51	43	-	-	-	-	-	-
Chemical	34	6	12	8	8	2	-	2	-	-
Counterintelligence	19	-	-	-	19	-	-	-	-	-
Columbus General Depot	10	-	-	10	-	4	-	-	4	-
Engineer	1,408	458	284	346	320	421	169	122	74	56
Finance	36	36	-	-	-	2	2	-	-	-
Food Services	841	835	6	-	-	156	144	12	-	-
Infantry	226	33	61	77	55	83	6	15	34	28
Meat and Dairy Hygiene	10	5	4	-	1	5	4	1	-	-
Medical Field Services	670	306	170	104	90	177	86	54	22	15
Medical Equipment Maintenance	25	5	9	7	4	10	2	4	2	2
Military Police	805	417	388	-	-	-	-	-	-	-
Opticians	9	6	3	-	-	-	-	-	-	-
Ordnance	367	175	121	61	10	20	2	15	3	-
Packaging Course (Joint Military)	215	-	24	96	95	5	-	-	3	2
Physical Training	8	2	1	3	2	-	-	-	-	-

(Continued)

TABLE 278 – TRAINING OF USAF PERSONNEL IN ARMY SCHOOLS – FY 1953 – (CONTINUED)

Type of Training	NEW STUDENTS -- Continued					ATTRITION -- Continued				
	Total	First Quarter	Second Quarter	Third Quarter	Fourth Quarter	Total	First Quarter	Second Quarter	Third Quarter	Fourth Quarter
Airman (Cont'd)										
Provost Marshal General Staff	14	-	-	10	4	1	-	-	-	1
Quartermaster	227	115	45	36	31	48	35	5	5	3
Signal	8	2	1	5	-	1	1	-	-	-
Strategic Intelligence	27	9	5	10	3	6	-	-	-	6
Transportation	10	-	-	9	1	4	3	-	-	1
Utilities Miscellaneous	1,714	498	429	440	347	3	-	-	-	3

Type of Training	GRADUATES					STUDENTS UNDER INSTRUCTION				
	Total	First Quarter	Second Quarter	Third Quarter	Fourth Quarter	Total	30 Sep (1952)	31 Dec	31 Mar (1953)	30 Jun
Total	12,534	6,140	3,146	1,359	1,889	NOT APPLICABLE	2,199	902	1,195	729
Officer - Total	1,278	243	379	303	353		253	169	224	149
Adjutant General School	65	32	28	2	3		-	-	3	-
Armed Forces Information School	181	44	4	75	58		4	4	18	39
Army General School	4	-	-	-	4		-	-	-	4
Army Language School	51	26	5	14	6		21	22	10	11
Army Medical Graduate School	88	-	28	35	25		3	2	10	-
Army Security School	15	13	-	2	-		2	2	1	1
Army War College	4	-	-	-	4		4	4	4	-
Artillery	11	-	-	-	11		-	-	-	23
Censorship Officer	7	-	4	3	-		-	-	-	-
Chaplain School	166	-	105	31	30		41	-	30	-
Chemical	40	1	10	12	17		1	-	5	-
Command and General Staff	8	-	-	-	8		9	9	8	-
Counterintelligence	15	-	15	-	-		-	1	-	-
Engineer	114	-	27	43	44		2	-	-	12
Finance	52	-	50	1	1		50	-	-	-
Food Services	24	24	-	-	-		-	-	-	-
Infantry	84	13	5	4	62		-	50	50	2
Meat and Dairy Hygiene	8	1	-	3	4		5	3	4	5
Medical Field Services	63	10	14	25	14		43	40	21	7
Medical Equipment Maintenance	3	-	3	-	-		3	-	4	6
Military Police	14	-	14	-	-		8	-	-	-
Opticians	4	-	4	-	-		4	-	-	-
Ordnance Automotive	-	-	-	-	-		-	-	-	2
Packaging Course (Joint Military)	19	-	3	10	6		-	-	-	-
Personnel (Administration)	3	-	-	-	3		-	-	-	-
Physical Training	-	-	-	-	-		-	-	-	1
Provost Marshal General Staff	11	-	-	6	5		-	-	5	-
Psychological Warfare	15	-	15	-	-		15	-	-	-
Quartermaster	60	25	10	11	14		6	2	10	6
Quartermaster Subsistence	18	8	8	-	2		6	4	5	9
Signal	7	-	2	1	4		1	1	6	-
Strategic Intelligence	119	42	25	24	28		25	24	30	21
Transportation	5	4	-	1	-		-	1	-	-
Airman - Total	11,256	5,897	2,767	1,056	1,536		1,946	733	971	580
Adjutant General School	286	194	42	15	35		1	-	14	3
Armed Forces Information School	93	22	15	16	40		15	6	24	93
Army Area Food Services	1	-	-	1	-		-	-	-	-
Army Language School	236	-	96	51	89		157	160	166	128
Army Security School	196	63	28	36	69		67	63	82	27
Chaplain Assistant	250	82	51	43	74		-	-	-	-
Chemical	33	1	16	8	8		6	-	-	-
Counterintelligence	19	-	-	-	19		-	-	-	-

(Continued)

TABLE 278 — TRAINING OF USAF PERSONNEL IN ARMY SCHOOLS — FY 1953 — (CONTINUED)

Type of Training	Total	First Quarter	Second Quarter	Third Quarter	Fourth Quarter	Total	30 Sep (1952)	31 Dec	31 Mar (1953)	30 Jun
	GRADUATES -- Continued					STUDENTS UNDER INSTRUCTION -- Continued				
Airman (Cont'd)						NOT APPLICABLE				
Columbus General Depot . .	6	-	-	-	6		-	-	6	-
Engineer	1,503	660	326	193	324		331	167	246	186
Finance.	106	106	-	-	-		-	-	-	-
Food Services.	2,293	2,176	117	-	-		123	-	-	-
Infantry	155	34	46	42	33		9	9	10	4
Meat and Dairy Hygiene . .	8	5	3	-	-		-	-	-	1
Medical Field Services . .	1,079	697	248	51	83		160	28	59	51
Medical Equipment Maintenance.	12	-	7	-	5		14	12	17	14
Military Police.	2,160	1,150	1,010	-	-		622	-	-	-
Opticians.	9	-	6	-	3		6	3	3	-
Ordnance	383	64	182	66	71		145	69	61	-
Packaging Course (Joint Military).	210	-	24	93	93		-	-	-	-
Physical Training.	8	1	2	3	2		1	-	-	-
Provost Marshal General Staff.	11	-	-	6	5		-	-	4	2
Quartermaster.	255	123	68	29	35		87	59	61	54
Quartermaster Subsistence.	-	-	-	-	-		-	-	-	-
Signal	11	6	-	4	1		2	3	4	3
Strategic Intelligence . .	31	19	6	6	-		5	4	8	5
Transportation	16	8	-	-	8		-	-	9	1
Utilities Miscellaneous. .	1,880	480	474	393	533		195	150	197	8
Watch Repairing.	6	6	-	-	-		-	-	-	-

Source: Personnel Statistics Division, DCS/Comptroller, Hq USAF

TABLE 279 — TRAINING OF USAF PERSONNEL IN U S NAVY SCHOOLS — FY 1953

Type of Training	Total		First Quarter		Second Quarter		Third Quarter		Fourth Quarter	
	Officer	Airman	Officer	Airman	Officer	Airman	Officer	Airman	Officer	Airman
NEW STUDENTS										
Total	244	821	77	159	47	87	80	478	40	97
Technical Training - Total	215	803	50	158	46	77	79	471	40	97
Atomic Defense	7	-	3	-	-	-	-	-	4	-
Communications Technician	-	10	-	7	-	1	-	2	-	-
Damage Control Training Center	-	9	-	9	-	-	-	-	-	-
Disaster Relief	5	-	4	-	1	-	-	-	-	-
Electronics Technician	-	5	-	-	-	3	-	2	-	-
Engineman	-	99	-	10	-	28	-	35	-	26
Freight Transportation	6	-	-	-	1	-	5	-	-	-
Instructor Course	1	3	-	2	-	-	1	1	-	-
Lithographers School	-	14	-	-	-	5	-	9	-	-
Naval Photo Interpretation Center	1	1	1	-	-	-	-	-	-	1
Naval School, CECOS	1	-	-	-	-	-	1	-	-	-
Naval School, Mine Warfare	29	52	6	44	21	8	1	-	1	-
Naval School, Naval Justice	-	5	-	-	-	-	-	5	-	-
Naval Unit, ABCD Course	5	-	-	-	-	-	2	-	3	-
Naval Unit, Chemical Corps	1	-	-	-	-	-	-	-	1	-
Passive Defense	1	-	-	-	-	-	-	-	1	-
Radiac Maintenance	4	23	-	9	1	2	3	7	-	5
US Fleet Training Center	38	69	3	46	10	1	9	-	16	22
USN Amphibious Training Base	79	377	19	-	3	-	53	377	4	-
USN Explosive Ordnance Disposal	37	136	14	31	9	29	4	33	10	43
Professional Training - Total	17	14	17	-	-	7	-	7	-	-
Naval War College	17	-	17	-	-	-	-	-	-	-
USN Preparatory School	-	14	-	-	-	7	-	7	-	-
Educational Training - Total	12	4	10	1	1	3	1	-	-	-
Naval Intelligence	11	4	9	1	1	3	1	-	-	-
USN Postgraduate School	1	-	1	-	-	-	-	-	-	-
ATTRITION										
Total	5	68	-	11	3	19	1	17	1	21
Technical Training - Total	4	56	-	11	3	17	1	14	-	14
Engineman	-	16	-	-	-	10	-	4	-	2
Naval School, Mine Warfare	-	8	-	6	-	2	-	-	-	-
Naval Unit, ABCD Course	1	-	-	-	-	-	1	-	-	-
USN Explosive Ordnance Disposal	3	32	-	5	3	5	-	10	-	12
Professional Training - Total	-	11	-	-	-	1	-	3	-	7
USN Preparatory School	-	11	-	-	-	1	-	3	-	7
Educational Training - Total	1	1	-	-	-	1	-	-	1	-
Naval Intelligence	1	1	-	-	-	1	-	-	1	-
GRADUATES										
Total	245	788	65	204	50	58	75	429	55	97
Technical Training - Total	213	782	61	203	42	58	73	427	37	94
Atomic Defense	5	-	4	-	-	-	-	-	1	-
Camera and Plate Making Course	-	33	-	33	-	-	-	-	-	-
Camera School	-	2	-	-	-	2	-	-	-	-
Communications Technician	-	10	-	7	-	1	-	1	-	1
Damage Control Training Center	-	9	-	6	-	3	-	-	-	-
Disaster Relief	5	-	4	-	1	-	-	-	-	-
Electronics Technician	-	5	-	-	-	3	-	-	-	2
Engineman	-	63	-	6	-	6	-	18	-	33
Freight Transportation	6	-	-	-	-	-	-	-	6	-
Instructor Course	1	3	-	2	-	-	1	-	-	1
Lithographers School	-	14	-	-	-	5	-	5	-	4
Naval School, CECOS	1	-	-	-	-	-	1	-	-	-
Naval School, Mine Warfare	43	44	20	38	21	6	-	-	2	-
Naval School, Naval Justice	-	5	-	-	-	-	-	1	-	4

(Continued)

TABLE 279 — TRAINING OF USAF PERSONNEL IN U S NAVY SCHOOLS — FY 1953 — (CONTINUED)

Type of Training	Total		First Quarter		Second Quarter		Third Quarter		Fourth Quarter	
	Officer	Airman	Officer	Airman	Officer	Airman	Officer	Airman	Officer	Airman
	GRADUATES -- Continued									
Technical Training (Cont'd)										
Naval Unit, ABCD Course . . .	4	-	-	-	-	-	1	-	3	-
Naval Unit, Chemical Corps . .	1	-	-	-	-	-	-	-	1	-
Printers Class.	-	20	-	20	-	-	-	-	-	-
Radiac Maintenance.	4	23	-	6	1	5	2	5	1	7
US Fleet Training Center. . .	38	69	3	46	10	1	9	-	16	22
USN Amphibious Training Base.	79	377	19	-	3	-	53	377	4	-
USN Explosive Ordnance Disposal	26	105	11	39	6	26	6	20	3	20
Professional Training - Total .	17	3	-	-	-	-	-	-	17	3
Naval War College	17	-	-	-	-	-	-	-	17	-
USN Preparatory School. . . .	-	3	-	-	-	-	-	-	-	3
Educational Training - Total. .	15	3	4	1	8	-	2	2	1	-
Naval Intelligence.	15	3	4	1	8	-	2	2	1	-

Type of Training	Total	30 September 1952		31 December		31 March 1952		30 June	
	Officer and Airman	Officer	Airman	Officer	Airman	Officer	Airman	Officer	Airman
	STUDENTS UNDER INSTRUCTION								
Total.	NOT APPLICABLE	a/34	b/37	28	47	32	79	16	58
Technical Training - Total. . .		5	37	6	39	11	69	14	58
Atomic Defense.		-	-	-	-	-	-	3	-
Camera and Plate Making Course		-	-	-	-	-	-	-	-
Camera School		-	2	-	-	-	-	-	-
Communications Technician . .		-	-	-	-	-	1	-	-
Damage Control Training Center		-	3	-	-	-	-	-	-
Electronics Technician. . . .		-	-	-	-	-	2	-	-
Engineman		-	10	-	22	-	35	-	26
Freight Transportation. . . .		-	-	1	-	6	-	-	-
Instructor Course		-	-	-	-	-	1	-	-
Lithographers School.		-	-	-	-	-	4	-	-
Naval Photo Interpretation Center		1	-	1	-	1	-	1	1
Naval School, Mine Warfare. .		-	-	-	-	1	-	-	-
Naval School, Naval Justice .		-	-	-	-	-	4	-	-
Passive Defense		-	-	-	-	-	-	1	-
Radiac Maintenance.		-	3	-	-	1	2	-	-
USN Explosive Ordnance Disposal		4	19	4	17	2	20	9	31
Professional Training - Total .		17	-	17	6	17	10	-	-
Naval War College		17	-	17	-	17	-	-	-
USN Preparatory School. . . .		-	-	-	6	-	10	-	-
Educational Training - Total. .		12	-	5	2	4	-	2	-
Naval Intelligence (Languages)		11	-	4	2	3	-	1	-
USN Postgraduate School . . .		1	-	1	-	1	-	1	-

a/ One Officer was erroneously reflected in Damage Control Training Center in FY 1952 "Digest - Students Under Instruction" at the end of the fiscal year; therefore, the total of 34 at the end of first quarter of FY 1953 is correct.

b/ Dental Technician Course was transferred to Headquarters Command during the first quarter of FY 1953. The 258 Airmen reported under "Students Under Instruction" at the end of FY 1952 were involved; therefore, the total of 37 as reported for the first quarter of FY 1953 is correct.

Source: Personnel Statistics Division, DCS/Comptroller, Hq USAF

TABLE 280 - USAF PROFESSIONAL AND TECHNOLOGICAL TRAINING OF AIR FORCE PERSONNEL AT CIVILIAN SCHOOLS AND HOSPITALS - FY 1953

(Figures in parentheses under New Students represent personnel transferred from courses indicated by figures in parentheses under Attrition. These figures are included in open figures. Actual number of New Students and Attrition is the difference between figures in parentheses and open figures). (Students Under Instruction 30 June 1953).

Type of Training by Course	New Students	Attrition	Graduates	Students Under Instruction
Total	(230) 2,168	(230) 425	1,467	1,505
Officer - Total	(230) 1,672	(230) 353	1,087	a/ 1,158
Administration, Business	20	-	20	20
Administration, Public	1	-	-	1
Ceramics	2	-	-	4
Chemistry, Biological	11	(2) 4	1	9
Chemistry, Engineering	8	(2) 2	1	7
Chemistry, Engineering Plastics	(1) 1	-	-	1
Chemistry, General	(4) 15	2	2	11
Chemistry, Nuclear	18	(2) 2	6	21
Cost Statistical Management Analysis	6	-	-	6
Dental	50	-	55	-
Economics	(1) 2	-	-	2
Education, Administration	1	-	-	1
Education, General	4	-	-	4
Education, Physical	1	-	-	1
Education, Teacher Training	6	(1) 1	1	4
Engineering, Aeronautical A/C Structural	(9) 9	-	1	8
Engineering, Aeronautical Compress	(1) 1	-	-	1
Engineering, Aeronautical Dynamics	(4) 5	-	4	2
Engineering, Aeronautical General	17	(25) 25	1	1
Engineering, Aeronautical Instruments	20	(1) 1	12	26
Engineering, Aeronautical Jet Ram	(3) 7	-	2	5
Engineering, Aeronautical Jet Rocket	(11) 14	-	7	9
Engineering, Aeronautical Rotary Wing	(3) 3	-	1	2
Engineering, Architecture	(2) 4	-	2	2
Engineering, Civil	39	(33) 33	13	9
Engineering, Civil Soil	(2) 2	-	1	1
Engineering, Electrical Armament	5	(1) 1	-	4
Engineering, Electrical Communications	(3) 4	-	-	4
Engineering, Electrical Electronics	(16) 21	-	10	19
Engineering, Electrical General	14	(22) 23	6	3
Engineering, Electrical Servomotor Mech.	(5) 5	-	2	3
Engineering, Industrial Production	6	(1) 1	-	5
Engineering, Mechanical Engine Diesel	(3) 4	-	1	3
Engineering, Mechanical General	19	(18) 21	5	5
Engineering, Mechanical Hydro	1	-	-	1
Engineering, Mechanical Thermodynamics	(9) 10	-	5	5
Engineering, Nuclear	18	-	29	27
Engineering, Power	(3) 4	-	1	3
Engineering, Structural	(15) 16	-	2	14
Engineering, Structural Highway	(14) 14	-	5	9
Food Service Technician	1	-	-	1
Geophysics	(3) 7	1	1	10
Guided Missiles	39	2	24	53
International Relations	(2) 8	-	2	8
Interns	-	(15) 15	74	-
Language	316	50	252	154
Law, Legislative	2	-	2	-
Management, Advanced	50	-	82	15
Mathematics	4	-	1	4
Medical, Anaesthesia	(6) 13	-	4	9
Medical, Dental, Oral Surgery	2	-	1	2
Medical, Dental, Periodontics	3	-	4	-
Medical, Dental, Prosthetics	6	1	6	1
Medical, Dental, Research	(1) 1	-	2	-
Medical, Dermatology	(1) 2	-	1	1
Medical, Dietetics	4	-	2	3
Medical, Intern, Cardiography	2	(1) 1	-	1
Medical, Intern, Medicine	(9) 20	-	3	17
Medical, Intern, Pediatrics	(1) 5	-	2	3
Medical, Interns	(21) 103	5	77	21
Medical, Miscellaneous	9	-	1	8
Medical, Neurology	(2) 2	-	1	1
Medical, Neuro Surgery	(1) 2	-	-	2
Medical, Nurse, Anaesthesia	1	(3) 4	30	1
Medical, Nurse, Preventive Medicine	7	-	8	-
Medical, Obstetrics	2	-	-	2

(Continued)

TABLE 280 — USAF PROFESSIONAL AND TECHNOLOGICAL TRAINING OF AIR FORCE PERSONNEL AT CIVILIAN SCHOOLS AND HOSPITALS — FY 1953 — (CONTINUED)

(Figures in parentheses under New Students represent personnel transferred from courses indicated by figures in parentheses under Attrition. These figures are included in open figures. Actual number of New Students and Attrition is the difference between figures in parentheses and open figures). (Students Under Instruction 30 June 1953).

Type of Training by Course	New Students		Attrition		Graduates	Students Under Instruction
Officer (Continued)						
Medical, Obstetrics Gynecology	(1)	10		-	2	8
Medical, Ophthamology	(4)	5		-	1	4
Medical, Orthopedic	(13)	17		-	4	13
Medical, Path Bacteriol		2		-	-	2
Medical, Physical Medicine		2	(2)	2	-	-
Medical, Physiology		6		2	2	2
Medical, Physiotherapy		20	(1)	2	11	16
Medical, Plastic Surgery		1		-	-	1
Medical, Radiology	(6)	14		-	3	11
Medical, Residence		-	(64)	64	8	-
Medical, Surgery	(21)	43		3	2	38
Medical, Thoracic	(1)	3		-	-	3
Medical, Urology	(3)	3		-	1	2
Medical, Veterinary, General		1		-	-	1
Medicine, Aviation		21	(10)	10	7	12
Medicine, Preventive, Public Health		3	(1)	1	3	-
Medicine, Psychiatry	(5)	10		-	2	8
Metallurgy		3		-	1	4
Meteorology, Climatology	(3)	7		-	1	6
Meteorology, General		394	(12)	57	221	354
Meteorology, Micro	(2)	5		-	3	4
Meteorology, Oceanography	(1)	2		-	-	2
Meteorology, Seismology		-		-	1	-
Military Science, Biological Warfare	(1)	4		-	-	5
Photography		6		1	3	8
Physics, Atmospheric		-		-	1	-
Physics, Biological		1		1	-	-
Physics, Electronics		3	(2)	2	-	2
Physics, General		7	(1)	1	1	6
Physics, Nuclear		28		1	14	34
Physics, Propulsion, Thermodynamics	(1)	1		-	1	-
Psychology, General		3	(1)	1	3	6
Psychology, General Clinical	(2)	4		-	-	4
Psychology, General Education		3		1	1	2
Psychology, General Experimental		1	(1)	1	1	3
Psychology, General Social		2		-	-	3
Radiological Defense		1	(7)	7	2	-
Radiology, Biological	(8)	13		-	5	9
Reactor Technician		1		-	2	1
Social Science, Sociology		2	(1)	1	4	3
Others	(1)	1		-	-	1
Airman - Total		496		72	380	b/ 347
Languages		496		72	380	347

a/ The following errors appeared in Table 76, page 465 of the FY 1952 "Digest - Students Under Instruction:"

One Officer erroneously reported under Medical, Anaesthesia Course,
Two Officers erroneously reported under Medical, Operating Room Management Course,
Nine Officers erroneously reported under Medical, Physical Medicine Course,
Eight Officers erroneously omitted from Medical, Physiotherapy Course; therefore, the Officer total of 1,158 "Students Under Instruction" at the end of FY 1953 is correct.

b/ The Advanced Instrument Course was erroneously reported under Table 76, page 465 of FY 1952 "Digest:" Forty-three Airmen were involved; therefore, the 347 Airmen reported as "Students Under Instruction" at the end of FY 1953 is correct.

CIVILIAN PERSONNEL

DEFINITIONS

CIVILIAN EMPLOYMENT
Includes all civilian personnel paid from appropriated funds who are under the jurisdiction of the Department of the Air Force.

CPC PERSONNEL
The Crafts, Protective, and Custodial Schedules under Classification Act 1949 and amendments thereto.

DEPARTMENTAL CIVILIAN EMPLOYMENT
Employee designation indicating appointment to Headquarters, USAF.

FULL TIME EMPLOYEES
Full time employees are those who are regularly required to work, as a minimum, the number of hours and days required by the administrative work week for their employment group or class regardless of the nature of employment.

GENERAL SCHEDULE (GS)
A schedule of Civilian Personnel which includes former Professional and Scientific Service (P Service), Clerical, Administrative, and Fiscal Service (CAF), and the Sub-professional Service (SP Service) established by Classification Act 1949 (PL 429, 81st Congress) replacing Classification Act of 1923, as amended.

INDEFINITE APPOINTMENT EMPLOYEES
Indefinite Appointment Personnel are those employees who are affected by the following: On and after December 1, 1950, all new appointments shall be indefinite appointments, except those of postmasters in all classes of post offices, and, in unusual circumstances, appointments to positions for which the Civil Service Commission determines that probational appointments are in the interest of the service.

INTERMITTENT EMPLOYEES
Intermittent employees are those employed on an irregular or occasional basis whose hours or days of work are not based on a pre-arranged schedule and who are compensated only for the time when actually employed or for service actually rendered. (WAE-Special Consultants and Other than Special Consultants).

PART TIME EMPLOYEES
Part time employees are those regularly employed on a prearranged schedule whose working time is less than that prescribed for full time employees in the same group or class.

PERMANENT AND PROBATIONAL
Appointments which give or will give permanent civil service status upon satisfactory completion of the probationary period.

PRESIDENTIAL APPOINTEES
Employees whose compensation is fixed in accordance with Public Law 359, 81st Congress.

REMOVAL AND SEPARATION FOR CAUSE (DURING) OR (OTHER THAN DURING) PROBATIONARY PERIODS
Separations because of disqualification, inefficiency, disability, and charges of misconduct, delinquency, or other serious cause which occurred during or after the employee's probationary period.

SALARIED EMPLOYEES
Those personnel whose wage rates are established by law under the Classification Act of 1949 and amendments thereto.

TEMPORARY EMPLOYEES
Civilians serving under temporary appointments for definite limited periods (one year or less).

TERMINATION, DISPLACEMENT
Separations required by the Civil Service Commission under its program of displacement of Indefinite and Temporary appointees.

TERRITORIAL GROUP
Refers to the categorization of the Overseas areas in which Air Force Civilian Personnel may be employed according to governing country. It is comprised of: (a) US Territories and Possessions, and (b) Foreign countries and their Territories and Possessions.

CIVILIAN PERSONNEL — CONTINUED

DEFINITIONS

VETERAN PREFERENCE PERSONNEL

1. Veterans (Male and Female) - Civilians employed as of the end of the month, who were "veterans" resulting from their own active military or naval service in or prior to World War I or World War II.

2. Wives - Civilians employed at the end of the month, who had established veterans preference as wives of disabled veterans.

3. Widows - Civilians employed at the end of the month, who had established veterans preference as the unremarried widows of deceased veterans.

4. Mothers - Civilians employed at the end of the month, who had established veterans preference as the mother of a deceased "veteran" son or daughter who served on honorable duty in the US Service or the mother of a permanently disabled "veteran" providing the mother is widowed, divorced, or the wife of a permanently disabled husband (living husband may be either or not the father of the "veteran").

WAGE BOARD EMPLOYEES

Wage Board Personnel are those whose basic rates of compensation are fixed and adjusted, from time to time, in accordance with prevailing rates in the locality where the employee works, by wage board or similar administrative authority serving the same purpose.

"WHEN ACTUALLY EMPLOYED" (WAE) EMPLOYEES

See Intermittent Employees (Civilian Personnel).

TABLE 281 – CIVILIAN EMPLOYMENT BY DUTY LOCATION WITHIN CONTINENTAL US – FY 1953

(The distribution of civilian employment is by duty location rather than the location of the unit of assignment. Personnel who are stationed outside the Continental US, but who are assigned to units within the Continental US are excluded; personnel who are stationed in the Continental US, but who are assigned to units outside the Continental US are included.)

State	September (1952)	December	March (1953)	June
Total	273,733	277,767	273,723	266,721
Alabama	17,501	17,893	17,618	17,031
Arizona	2,613	2,637	2,581	2,437
Arkansas	2	2	2	2
California	38,236	39,409	37,708	36,233
Colorado	6,141	6,097	5,921	5,553
Connecticut	15	15	16	16
Delaware	351	367	383	393
District of Columbia	7,372	7,339	6,990	7,057
Florida	7,296	7,517	7,507	7,392
Georgia	16,116	16,708	16,527	16,976
Idaho	438	560	516	497
Illinois	5,820	5,788	5,638	5,414
Indiana	566	614	643	605
Iowa	141	168	145	152
Kansas	4,566	4,733	4,642	4,571
Kentucky	218	212	238	219
Louisiana	1,652	1,707	1,635	1,646
Maine	881	981	945	962
Maryland	2,190	2,196	2,214	2,160
Massachusetts	3,747	4,063	4,469	4,242
Michigan	1,873	1,952	1,964	2,017
Minnesota	431	510	511	533
Mississippi	2,414	2,332	2,404	2,480
Missouri	2,256	2,341	2,328	2,260
Montana	545	556	556	569
Nebraska	1,070	1,073	1,074	1,073
Nevada	613	739	698	691
New Hampshire	163	165	167	158
New Jersey	2,966	3,087	3,055	2,938
New Mexico	2,787	2,763	2,760	2,793
New York	10,805	10,934	10,958	11,023
North Carolina	505	495	483	489
North Dakota	26	31	32	36
Ohio	30,961	29,797	29,933	29,074
Oklahoma	24,751	24,598	24,185	23,046
Oregon	249	257	204	180
Pennsylvania	11,263	11,507	11,636	10,764
Rhode Island	1	1	1	1
South Carolina	837	831	826	903
South Dakota	484	520	516	529
Tennessee	3,857	3,853	3,819	3,793
Texas	40,856	41,558	41,093	40,094
Utah	11,712	12,199	11,529	11,245
Vermont	191	194	194	194
Virginia	1,459	1,488	1,601	1,626
Washington	3,043	3,226	3,138	2,945
West Virginia	14	16	12	12
Wisconsin	347	365	370	424
Wyoming	1,392	1,373	1,338	1,273

Source: Personnel Statistics Division, DCS/Comptroller, Hq. USAF

TABLE 282 – CIVILIAN EMPLOYMENT BY DUTY LOCATION OUTSIDE CONTINENTAL US – FY 1953

(The distribution of civilian employment is by duty location rather than the location of the unit of assignment. Personnel who are stationed outside the Continental US, but who are assigned to units within the Continental US are included; personnel who are stationed in the Continental US, but who are assigned to units outside the Continental US are excluded.)

Country	September (1952)	December	March (1953)	June
Total	36,523	37,355	36,701	35,586
Afghanistan	4	4	4	4
Alaska	2,882	2,866	2,975	3,010
Arabia	320	346	381	310
Argentina	4	6	5	4
Australia	3	2	2	2
Austria	210	204	272	282
Azores	1,315	1,277	1,235	1,253
Belgium	3	3	3	7
Bermuda	511	511	548	472
Bolivia	5	4	4	1
Brazil	41	39	41	39
British West Indies	20	14	11	-
Burma	3	4	4	3
Canada	20	25	23	23
Canal Zone	617	681	701	669
Chile	6	6	5	5
China	4	5	5	5
Colombia	1	-	-	2
Cuba	4	5	4	4
Cyprus	1	-	1	1
Czechoslovakia	1	2	2	2
Denmark	-	1	1	1
Ecuador	1	1	1	1
Egypt	6	7	8	7
El Salvador	1	1	1	1
England	3,249	3,310	3,359	3,220
Eritrea	1	1	-	-
Finland	2	3	2	2
Formosa	9	8	8	6
France	3,096	3,631	3,687	3,489
French Morocco	1,775	2,087	2,021	2,006
Germany	1,222	1,209	1,170	1,232
Greece	10	12	15	16
Greenland	367	349	313	294
Guam	1,511	1,479	1,441	1,303
Guatemala	9	8	8	6
Haiti	2	2	2	2
Hawaii	2,286	2,259	2,214	2,076
Honduras	1	1	2	-
Hungary	3	4	4	4
Iceland	627	685	688	617
India	13	13	7	5
Indo China	4	3	3	2
Indonesia	-	-	2	2
Iran	5	4	4	4
Iraq	6	7	7	6
Ireland	4	3	3	2
Israel	3	2	2	-
Italy	16	15	14	14
Japan	1,933	1,906	1,857	1,874
Java	1	-	-	-
Johnston Islands	43	40	41	36
Korea	70	86	83	79
Labrador	566	570	591	571
Lebanon	-	-	4	-
Levant States	4	4	-	-
Lybia	678	717	715	717

(CONTINUED)

TABLE 282 — CIVILIAN EMPLOYMENT BY DUTY LOCATION OUTSIDE CONTINENTAL US — FY 1953 — (CONTINUED)

(The distribution of civilian employment is by duty location rather than the location of the unit of assignment. Personnel who are stationed outside the Continental US, but who are assigned to units within the Continental US are included; personnel who are stationed in the Continental US, but who are assigned to units outside the Continental US are excluded.)

Country	September (1952)	December	March (1953)	June
Malay States	3	4	4	2
Marshall Islands	1	2	2	2
Mexico	4	5	5	4
Morocco	17	17	6	-
Netherlands	4	3	3	2
Netherlands East Indies	-	2	-	-
Newfoundland	2,714	2,841	2,760	2,654
Norway	8	7	6	6
Okinawa	737	754	754	691
Pakistan	-	-	6	6
Paraguay	1	1	1	1
Peru	8	6	7	5
Philippine Islands	8,140	7,933	7,363	7,240
Poland	5	4	4	4
Portugal	4	3	3	4
Puerto Rico	786	809	784	802
Russia	8	4	4	2
Scotland	98	110	126	128
Siam	6	8	-	-
South Africa	-	-	-	2
Spain	8	7	6	3
Sweden	8	7	8	5
Switzerland	7	7	7	5
Syria	-	-	-	5
Tangier	-	-	-	2
Thailand	-	-	10	7
Transvaal	2	2	2	-
Turkey	92	66	27	26
Uruguay	3	3	3	3
Venezuela	3	3	3	3
Wales	352	311	289	275
Yugoslavia	5	4	4	4

Source: Personnel Statistics Division, DCS/Comptroller, Hq. USAF

TABLE 283 — CIVILIAN EMPLOYMENT BY SEX, BY COMMAND — FY 1953

Command	July (1952)	August	September	October	November	December	January (1953)	February	March	April	May	June
WORLDWIDE - TOTAL	311,366	310,722	310,256	312,363	313,923	315,122	315,967	313,670	310,424	305,154	301,043	302,307
Male	222,571	222,504	222,223	224,126	225,554	226,840	227,951	225,847	223,398	219,420	216,333	217,069
Female	88,795	88,218	88,033	88,237	88,369	88,282	88,016	87,823	87,026	85,734	84,710	85,238
CONTINENTAL US - TOTAL	275,692	274,601	273,737	275,256	276,649	277,771	278,244	276,544	273,720	268,979	265,339	266,719
Male	194,523	194,241	193,693	195,131	196,509	197,726	198,319	196,812	194,700	191,175	188,545	189,328
Female	81,169	80,360	80,044	80,125	80,140	80,045	79,925	79,732	79,020	77,804	76,794	77,391
Air Defense Command - Total	8,182	8,184	8,269	8,426	8,570	8,760	9,070	9,026	8,681	8,559	8,517	8,656
Male	5,615	5,656	5,743	5,866	6,011	6,169	6,442	6,424	6,174	6,089	6,063	6,161
Female	2,567	2,528	2,526	2,560	2,559	2,591	2,628	2,602	2,507	2,470	2,454	2,495
AF Finance Division - Total	3,162	3,121	3,089	3,127	3,175	3,165	3,161	3,138	3,084	3,018	2,943	2,899
Male	832	829	830	825	829	837	840	828	818	808	791	789
Female	2,330	2,292	2,259	2,302	2,346	2,328	2,321	2,310	2,266	2,210	2,152	2,110
Air Materiel Command - Total	169,916	169,533	168,588	169,546	170,321	170,648	170,426	169,132	167,589	164,115	161,323	161,643
Male	125,584	125,447	124,652	125,563	126,420	126,825	126,646	125,430	124,052	121,432	119,484	119,512
Female	44,332	44,086	43,936	43,983	43,901	43,823	43,780	43,702	43,537	42,683	41,839	42,131
Air Proving Ground Command - Total	2,635	2,613	2,602	2,580	2,570	2,570	2,584	2,526	2,488	2,486	2,470	2,456
Male	2,138	2,119	2,102	2,095	2,095	2,093	2,101	2,056	2,016	2,003	1,990	1,985
Female	497	494	500	485	475	477	483	470	472	483	480	471
Air Research and Development Command - Total	19,116	19,188	19,175	19,071	19,191	19,375	19,556	19,532	19,424	19,692	19,760	19,867
Male	14,263	14,312	14,277	14,244	14,378	14,548	14,751	14,751	14,706	14,823	14,818	14,942
Female	4,853	4,876	4,898	4,827	4,813	4,827	4,805	4,781	4,718	4,869	4,942	4,925
Air Training Command - Total	31,961	31,514	31,569	31,608	31,737	31,826	31,715	31,503	31,083	30,138	29,694	30,023
Male	22,250	22,019	22,091	22,160	22,281	22,419	22,357	22,196	21,982	21,250	20,829	20,952
Female	9,711	9,495	9,478	9,448	9,456	9,407	9,358	9,307	9,101	8,888	8,865	9,071
Air University - Total	2,094	2,093	2,108	2,139	2,151	2,164	2,169	2,149	2,125	2,032	1,973	2,087
Male	1,172	1,202	1,222	1,251	1,257	1,260	1,260	1,251	1,236	1,189	1,152	1,253
Female	922	891	886	888	894	904	909	898	889	843	821	834
Continental Air Command - Total	5,023	5,027	5,126	5,124	5,189	5,270	5,438	5,441	5,362	5,408	5,391	5,622
Male	2,561	2,627	2,748	2,783	2,829	2,921	3,101	3,146	3,120	3,208	3,218	3,365
Female	2,462	2,400	2,378	2,341	2,360	2,349	2,337	2,295	2,242	2,200	2,173	2,257
Headquarters Command, USAF - Total	5,507	4,606	4,619	4,715	4,720	4,801	4,768	4,772	4,745	4,667	4,523	4,479
Male	3,330	2,659	2,651	2,717	2,670	2,766	2,746	2,733	2,725	2,686	2,596	2,574
Female	2,177	1,947	1,968	1,998	2,050	2,035	2,022	2,039	2,020	1,981	1,927	1,905
Headquarters, USAF - Total	4,971	4,923	4,902	4,909	4,854	4,883	4,885	4,890	4,879	4,862	4,808	4,819
Male	1,793	1,800	1,834	1,839	1,801	1,837	1,827	1,815	1,804	1,810	1,793	1,810
Female	3,178	3,123	3,068	3,070	3,053	3,046	3,058	3,075	3,075	3,052	3,015	3,009
Military Air Transport Service - Total	7,520	8,304	8,288	8,466	8,438	8,459	8,590	8,594	8,538	8,369	7,812	7,793
Male	4,879	5,502	5,477	5,607	5,575	5,599	5,756	5,691	5,664	5,568	5,160	5,169
Female	2,641	2,802	2,811	2,859	2,863	2,860	2,834	2,903	2,874	2,801	2,652	2,624

Strategic Air Command - Total	10,369	10,254	10,170	10,295	10,460	10,578	10,564	10,540	10,462	10,400	10,861	10,969
Male	6,751	6,681	6,662	6,757	6,915	7,007	7,013	7,007	6,924	6,844	7,178	7,256
Female	3,618	3,573	3,508	3,538	3,545	3,571	3,551	3,533	3,538	3,556	3,683	3,713
Tactical Air Command - Total	4,625	4,633	4,628	4,658	4,687	4,686	4,725	4,718	4,681	4,667	4,697	4,834
Male	3,097	3,133	3,140	3,169	3,193	3,188	3,220	3,227	3,219	3,210	3,216	3,307
Female	1,528	1,500	1,488	1,489	1,494	1,498	1,505	1,491	1,462	1,457	1,481	1,527
USAF Security Service - Total	611	608	604	592	586	586	593	583	579	566	567	572
Male	258	255	264	255	255	257	259	257	260	255	257	253
Female	353	353	340	337	331	329	334	326	319	311	310	319
OVERSEAS - TOTAL	35,674	36,121	36,519	37,107	37,274	37,351	37,723	37,126	36,704	36,175	35,704	35,588
Male	28,048	28,263	28,530	28,995	29,045	29,114	29,632	29,035	28,698	28,245	27,788	27,741
Female	7,626	7,858	7,989	8,112	8,229	8,237	8,091	8,091	8,006	7,930	7,916	7,847
Air Materiel Command - Total	10	10	10	10	12	12	9	9	11	10	11	13
Male	5	5	5	5	6	6	4	4	5	5	6	6
Female	5	5	5	5	6	6	5	5	6	5	5	7
Air Research and Development Command - Total	-	22	20	16	15	14	13	12	11	15	20	9
Male	-	22	20	16	15	14	13	12	11	15	20	9
Female	-	-	-	-	-	-	-	-	-	-	-	-
Alaskan Air Command - Total	2,917	2,846	2,868	2,850	2,813	2,857	3,101	3,074	2,971	2,843	2,846	2,996
Male	1,738	1,696	1,702	1,670	1,649	1,699	1,937	1,904	1,822	1,724	1,759	1,886
Female	1,179	1,150	1,166	1,180	1,164	1,158	1,164	1,170	1,149	1,119	1,087	1,110
Caribbean Air Command - Total	625	638	630	642	653	693	717	720	713	701	685	682
Male	518	530	522	531	537	569	588	590	587	577	567	564
Female	107	108	108	111	116	124	129	130	126	124	118	118
Far East Air Forces - Total	12,045	12,203	12,230	12,218	12,042	11,998	11,894	11,494	11,330	11,297	11,156	11,032
Male	10,079	10,052	10,037	10,019	9,878	9,833	9,753	9,377	9,268	9,246	9,111	9,018
Female	1,966	2,151	2,193	2,199	2,164	2,165	2,141	2,117	2,062	2,051	2,045	2,014
Headquarters Command, USAF - Total	547	535	568	585	601	562	590	539	593	620	630	564
Male	337	330	327	347	362	334	356	306	342	365	362	313
Female	210	205	241	238	239	228	234	233	251	255	268	251
Military Air Transport Service - Total	5,986	5,959	5,987	6,046	6,088	6,047	5,079	4,983	5,006	4,856	4,736	4,722
Male	5,017	4,988	5,011	5,051	5,086	5,039	4,157	4,072	4,102	3,965	3,863	3,872
Female	969	971	976	995	1,002	1,008	922	911	904	891	873	850
Northeast Air Command - Total	3,659	3,636	3,642	3,725	3,778	3,747	3,769	3,766	3,653	3,519	3,530	3,505
Male	3,043	3,032	3,028	3,104	3,137	3,113	3,139	3,113	3,003	2,876	2,889	2,860
Female	616	604	614	621	641	634	630	653	650	643	641	645
Strategic Air Command - Total	1,009	1,008	1,003	1,032	1,086	1,093	1,109	1,091	1,092	1,083	1,065	1,100
Male	802	802	810	822	857	867	892	881	878	876	861	894
Female	207	206	193	210	229	226	217	210	214	207	204	206
US Air Forces, Europe - Total	8,865	9,253	9,550	9,972	10,173	10,314	11,428	11,423	11,310	11,216	11,011	10,951
Male	6,505	6,802	7,064	7,426	7,514	7,635	8,788	8,770	8,675	8,591	8,346	8,315
Female	2,360	2,451	2,486	2,546	2,659	2,679	2,640	2,653	2,635	2,625	2,665	2,636
USAF Security Service - Total	11	11	11	11	13	14	14	15	14	15	14	14
Male	4	4	4	4	4	5	5	6	5	5	4	4
Female	7	7	7	7	9	9	9	9	9	10	10	10

Source: Personnel Statistics Division, DCS/Comptroller, Hq USAF

TABLE 284 — CIVILIAN EMPLOYMENT OF WAE (WHEN ACTUALLY EMPLOYED) AND PRESIDENTIAL APPOINTEES — FY 1953

Month	Presidential Appointees	WAE (Special Consultants) a/	WAE (Other Than Special Consultants) a/			Month	Presidential Appointees	WAE (Special Consultants) a/	WAE (Other Than Special Consultants) a/		
			Total	Salaried	Wage Board				Total	Salaried	Wage Board
Jul (1952) - Total	4	512	261	66	195	Jan (1953) - Total	2	520	203	68	135
Continental US	4	501	255	64	191	Continental US.	2	512	167	49	118
Overseas	-	11	6	2	4	Overseas	-	8	36	19	17
Aug - Total	4	483	176	63	113	Feb - Total	3	531	182	71	111
Continental US	4	482	166	58	108	Continental US.	3	516	149	44	105
Overseas	-	1	10	5	5	Overseas	-	15	33	27	6
Sep - Total	4	473	176	69	107	Mar - Total	3	535	166	83	83
Continental US	4	466	163	61	102	Continental US.	3	527	129	49	80
Overseas	-	7	13	8	5	Overseas	-	8	37	34	3
Oct - Total	4	537	174	58	116	Apr - Total	4	533	151	81	70
Continental US	4	527	147	51	96	Continental US.	4	527	114	48	66
Overseas	-	10	27	7	20	Overseas	-	6	37	33	4
Nov - Total	4	440	168	57	111	May - Total	4	446	133	77	56
Continental US	4	427	144	50	94	Continental US.	4	435	110	57	53
Overseas	-	13	24	7	17	Overseas	-	11	23	20	3
Dec - Total	4	545	183	55	128	Jun - Total	4	442	106	67	39
Continental US	4	525	160	49	111	Continental US.	4	433	80	44	36
Overseas	-	20	23	6	17	Overseas	-	9	26	23	3

a/ Figures represent personnel who worked for any length of time during the month.

Source: Personnel Statistics Division, DCS/Comptroller, Hq USAF

TABLE 285 — CIVILIAN EMPLOYEES WITH VETERANS' PREFERENCE — FY 1953

Personnel By Sex	30 September (1952)	31 December	31 March (1953)	30 June
	5 and 10 Point Preference Veterans			
WORLDWIDE - TOTAL	131,234	134,999	134,799	132,421
Male	126,308	129,918	129,600	127,372
Female (Own Service)	2,774	2,863	2,908	2,809
Mothers, Widows, Wives	2,152	2,218	2,291	2,240
CONTINENTAL US - TOTAL	126,870	130,544	130,425	128,247
Male	122,180	125,776	125,506	123,471
Female (Own Service)	2,572	2,579	2,657	2,575
Mothers, Widows, Wives	2,118	2,189	2,262	2,201
OVERSEAS - TOTAL	4,364	4,455	4,374	4,174
Male	4,128	4,142	4,094	3,901
Female (Own Service)	202	284	251	234
Mothers, Widows, Wives	34	29	29	39
	10 Point Preference Veterans			
WORLDWIDE - TOTAL	20,297	20,719	20,918	20,949
Male and Female (Own Service)	18,145	18,501	18,627	18,709
Mothers, Widows, Wives	2,152	2,218	2,291	2,240
CONTINENTAL US - TOTAL	20,064	20,468	20,659	20,661
Male and Female (Own Service)	17,946	18,279	18,397	18,460
Mothers, Widows, Wives	2,118	2,189	2,262	2,201
OVERSEAS - TOTAL	233	251	259	288
Male and Female (Own Service)	199	222	230	249
Mothers, Widows, Wives	34	29	29	39

Source: Personnel Statistics Division, DCS/Comptroller, Hq USAF

TABLE 288 — CIVILIAN EMPLOYMENT BY CATEGORY AND BY GRADE, CONTINENTAL US — FY 1953

Category and Grade	July (1952)	August	September	October	November	December	January (1953)	February	March	April	May	June
Total	275,692	274,601	273,737	275,256	276,649	277,771	278,244	276,544	273,720	268,979	265,339	266,719
Salaried - Total	115,094	114,503	113,902	113,813	113,869	114,010	114,277	114,353	113,809	112,627	112,104	113,665
General Schedule - Total	107,545	107,037	106,533	106,492	106,583	106,753	107,104	107,289	106,840	105,828	105,369	106,879
1	440	429	455	386	344	334	346	324	333	325	347	415
2	15,728	14,873	14,523	13,926	13,580	13,198	13,049	13,110	12,247	11,792	11,618	12,143
3	29,402	29,077	28,624	28,689	28,627	28,635	28,549	28,507	28,231	27,852	27,506	27,664
4	17,459	17,610	17,554	17,748	17,881	17,996	18,046	17,850	18,207	17,966	17,909	18,184
5	10,989	11,156	11,074	11,110	11,206	11,131	11,082	11,016	11,051	11,108	11,035	11,112
6	3,214	3,238	3,397	3,412	3,402	3,453	3,456	3,460	3,454	3,429	3,413	3,424
7	10,783	10,769	10,882	10,646	10,619	10,756	10,838	10,859	10,843	10,802	10,693	10,710
8	2,884	2,932	2,882	3,023	3,041	3,071	3,082	3,095	3,107	3,088	3,070	3,050
9	7,223	7,361	7,339	7,493	7,608	7,708	7,865	8,046	8,171	8,209	8,309	8,516
10	911	936	974	999	1,031	1,063	1,100	1,132	1,151	1,172	1,214	1,243
11	4,029	4,068	4,148	4,251	4,317	4,378	4,478	4,539	4,594	4,596	4,644	4,686
12	2,551	2,619	2,684	2,771	2,845	2,899	2,985	3,045	3,067	3,059	3,128	3,207
13	1,270	1,285	1,288	1,305	1,331	1,374	1,428	1,487	1,546	1,585	1,628	1,655
14	485	503	526	539	547	553	586	597	608	608	618	626
15	160	160	163	173	183	186	195	203	209	216	216	224
16	14	17	16	17	15	14	15	15	17	17	16	15
17	3	4	4	4	4	4	4	4	4	4	5	5
18	-	-	-	-	-	-	-	-	-	-	-	-
Crafts, Protective and Custodial - Total	7,538	7,455	7,358	7,308	7,273	7,244	7,162	7,052	6,957	6,785	6,721	6,772
1	-	-	-	-	-	-	-	-	-	1	-	-
2	161	145	136	126	114	122	123	111	106	93	88	84
3	383	387	372	349	336	332	326	314	300	302	294	306
4	357	329	308	311	289	282	260	231	204	185	178	184
5	2,002	1,978	1,961	1,799	1,802	1,728	1,566	1,526	1,476	1,372	1,344	1,352
6	2,405	2,356	2,326	2,440	2,419	2,449	2,552	2,505	2,462	2,436	2,443	2,433
7	1,024	1,040	1,041	1,055	1,078	1,086	1,087	1,093	1,121	1,100	1,076	1,087
8	783	793	789	797	799	801	798	816	826	836	841	859
9	160	187	165	168	170	176	184	189	220	191	189	195
10	263	240	260	263	266	268	266	267	242	269	268	272
Public Law 313 - Total	7	7	7	9	9	9	9	9	9	10	10	10
Presidential Appointees - Total	4	4	4	4	4	4	2	3	3	4	4	4
Total Wage Board - Total	160,097	159,616	159,369	160,916	162,353	163,236	163,455	161,675	159,384	155,825	152,800	152,621
Local Wage Rates	158,262	157,926	157,782	159,349	160,710	161,605	161,756	159,958	157,769	154,327	151,349	151,290
Maritime and Other	1,835	1,690	1,587	1,567	1,643	1,631	1,699	1,717	1,615	1,498	1,451	1,331
Special Consultants - Total	501	482	466	527	427	525	512	516	527	527	435	433

Source: Personnel Statistics Division, DCS/Comptroller, Hq, USAF

TABLE 287 — CIVILIAN EMPLOYMENT BY CITIZENSHIP OR NON-CITIZENSHIP STATUS, BY COMMAND, OVERSEAS — FY 1953

Command	July (1952)	August	September	October	November	December	January (1953)	February	March	April	May	June
OVERSEAS - TOTAL	35,674	36,121	36,519	37,107	37,274	37,351	37,723	37,126	36,704	36,175	35,704	35,588
US TERRITORIES AND POSSESSIONS - TOTAL	8,117	8,066	8,082	8,082	8,009	8,075	8,325	8,255	8,116	7,870	7,782	7,906
Continental US Citizens - Total	3,933	3,877	3,926	3,914	3,852	3,884	4,121	4,070	3,953	3,819	3,803	3,929
Citizens of US Territories and Possessions - Total	2,687	2,672	2,642	2,637	2,631	2,630	2,635	2,613	2,599	2,511	2,476	2,501
Non-US Citizens - Total	1,497	1,517	1,514	1,531	1,526	1,561	1,569	1,572	1,564	1,540	1,503	1,476
FOREIGN COUNTRIES - TOTAL	27,557	28,055	28,437	29,025	29,265	29,276	29,398	28,871	28,588	28,305	27,922	27,682
Continental US Citizens - Total	5,168	5,338	5,416	5,502	5,543	5,558	5,542	5,523	5,483	5,488	5,420	5,344
Citizens of US Territories and Possessions - Total	316	323	322	321	324	325	322	320	323	319	316	314
Non-US Citizens - Total	22,073	22,394	22,699	23,202	23,398	23,393	23,534	23,028	22,782	22,498	22,186	22,024
Air Materiel Command - Total	10	10	10	10	12	12	9	9	11	10	11	13
Foreign Countries - Total	10	10	10	10	12	12	9	9	11	10	11	13
Continental US Citizens	4	4	4	4	6	6	3	3	4	4	5	5
Citizens of US Territories and Possessions	-	-	-	-	-	-	-	-	-	-	-	-
Non-US Citizens	6	6	6	6	6	6	6	6	7	6	6	8
Air Research and Development Command - Total	-	22	20	16	15	14	13	12	11	15	20	9
US Territories and Possessions - Total	-	22	20	16	15	14	13	12	11	15	20	9
Continental US Citizens	-	22	20	16	15	14	13	12	11	15	15	4
Citizens of US Territories and Possessions	-	-	-	-	-	-	-	-	-	-	5	5
Non-US Citizens	-	-	-	-	-	-	-	-	-	-	-	-
Alaskan Air Command - Total	2,917	2,846	2,868	2,850	2,813	2,857	3,101	3,074	2,971	2,843	2,846	2,996
US Territories and Possessions - Total	2,917	2,846	2,868	2,850	2,813	2,857	3,101	3,074	2,971	2,843	2,846	2,996
Continental US Citizens	2,837	2,763	2,814	2,794	2,759	2,798	3,037	3,009	2,909	2,785	2,787	2,938
Citizens of US Territories and Possessions	57	59	30	31	32	37	40	41	39	39	39	38
Non-US Citizens	23	24	24	25	22	22	24	24	23	19	20	20
Caribbean Air Command - Total	625	638	630	642	653	693	717	720	713	701	685	682
US Territories and Possessions - Total	610	622	613	625	636	676	700	702	697	684	668	666
Continental US Citizens	194	195	195	196	195	196	196	195	193	191	189	187
Citizens of US Territories and Possessions	2	2	2	2	2	2	2	2	2	2	2	2
Non-US Citizens	414	425	416	427	439	478	502	505	502	491	477	477
Foreign Countries - Total	15	16	17	17	17	17	17	18	16	17	17	16
Continental US Citizens	-	-	-	-	-	-	-	-	-	-	-	-
Citizens of US Territories and Possessions	-	-	-	-	-	-	-	-	-	-	-	-
Non-US Citizens	15	16	17	17	17	17	17	18	16	17	17	16

Far East Air Forces - Total	12,045	12,203	12,230	12,218	12,042	11,998	11,894	11,494	11,330	11,297	11,156	11,032
US Territories and Possessions - Total	1,404	1,414	1,426	1,424	1,393	1,393	1,384	1,371	1,357	1,361	1,330	1,284
Continental US Citizens	297	300	306	307	291	287	289	278	268	277	257	250
Citizens of US Territories and Possessions	81	84	88	87	83	77	82	82	82	82	92	80
Non-US Citizens	1,026	1,030	1,032	1,030	1,019	1,029	1,013	1,011	1,007	1,002	981	954
Foreign Countries - Total	10,641	10,789	10,804	10,794	10,649	10,605	10,510	10,123	9,973	9,936	9,826	9,748
Continental US Citizens	2,305	2,424	2,449	2,461	2,430	2,437	2,411	2,409	2,372	2,351	2,312	2,280
Citizens of US Territories and Possessions	291	296	294	292	291	297	295	295	297	295	294	292
Non-US Citizens	8,045	8,069	8,061	8,041	7,928	7,871	7,804	7,419	7,304	7,290	7,220	7,176
Headquarters Command, USAF - Total	547	535	568	585	601	562	590	539	593	620	610	564
US Territories and Possessions - Total	29	28	27	28	26	27	26	29	26	26	27	28
Continental US Citizens	22	18	23	22	22	23	22	22	19	20	21	22
Citizens of US Territories and Possessions	7	7	4	4	4	4	4	5	5	5	5	5
Non-US Citizens	-	3	-	2	-	-	-	2	2	1	1	1
Foreign Countries - Total	518	507	541	557	575	535	564	510	567	594	603	536
Continental US Citizens	226	221	239	249	253	262	268	272	264	292	303	284
Citizens of US Territories and Possessions	3	2	2	2	7	2	3	3	5	4	2	2
Non-US Citizens	289	284	300	306	315	271	293	235	298	298	298	250
Military Air Transport Service - Total	5,986	5,959	5,987	6,046	6,088	6,047	5,079	4,983	5,006	4,856	4,736	4,722
US Territories and Possessions - Total	2,366	2,345	2,348	2,345	2,336	2,311	2,306	2,289	2,273	2,171	2,123	2,129
Continental US Citizens	486	483	479	484	480	480	482	475	470	450	446	449
Citizens of US Territories and Possessions	1,846	1,827	1,827	1,814	1,810	1,799	1,794	1,784	1,773	1,694	1,653	1,656
Non-US Citizens	34	35	42	47	46	32	30	30	30	27	24	24
Foreign Countries - Total	3,620	3,614	3,639	3,701	3,752	3,736	2,773	2,694	2,733	2,685	2,613	2,593
Continental US Citizens	527	534	529	520	539	543	452	442	456	467	456	461
Citizens of US Territories and Possessions	19	22	23	23	23	23	21	20	18	18	18	17
Non-US Citizens	3,074	3,058	3,087	3,158	3,190	3,170	2,300	2,232	2,259	2,200	2,139	2,115
Northeast Air Command - Total	3,659	3,636	3,642	3,725	3,778	3,747	3,769	3,766	3,653	3,519	3,530	3,505
Foreign Countries - Total	3,659	3,636	3,642	3,725	3,778	3,747	3,769	3,766	3,653	3,519	3,530	3,505
Continental US Citizens	60	59	71	87	87	87	95	92	92	91	91	90
Citizens of US Territories and Possessions	-	-	-	-	-	-	-	-	-	-	-	-
Non-US Citizens	3,599	3,577	3,571	3,638	3,691	3,660	3,674	3,674	3,561	3,428	3,439	3,415
Strategic Air Command - Total	1,009	1,008	1,003	1,032	1,086	1,093	1,109	1,091	1,092	1,083	1,065	1,100
US Territories and Possessions - Total	791	789	780	794	790	797	795	778	781	770	758	794
Continental US Citizens	97	96	89	95	90	86	82	79	83	81	78	79
Citizens of US Territories and Possessions	694	693	691	699	700	711	713	699	698	689	690	715
Non-US Citizens	-	-	-	-	-	-	-	-	-	-	-	-
Foreign Countries - Total	218	219	223	238	296	296	314	313	311	313	297	306
Continental US Citizens	56	56	56	59	69	70	67	63	67	65	63	70
Citizens of US Territories and Possessions	-	-	-	-	-	-	-	-	-	-	-	-
Non-US Citizens	162	163	167	179	227	226	247	250	244	248	234	236
US Air Forces, Europe - Total	8,865	9,253	9,550	9,972	10,173	10,314	11,428	11,423	11,310	11,216	11,011	10,951
Foreign Countries - Total	8,865	9,253	9,550	9,972	10,173	10,314	11,428	11,423	11,310	11,216	11,011	10,951
Continental US Citizens	1,979	2,029	2,057	2,111	2,146	2,139	2,232	2,227	2,214	2,203	2,176	2,14[illegible]
Citizens of US Territories and Possessions	3	3	3	4	3	3	3	2	3	2	2	3
Non-US Citizens	6,883	7,221	7,490	7,857	8,024	8,172	9,193	9,194	9,093	9,011	8,833	8,808
USAF Security Service - Total	11	11	11	11	13	14	14	15	14	15	14	14
Foreign Countries - Total	11	11	11	11	13	14	14	15	14	15	14	14
Continental US Citizens	11	11	11	11	13	14	14	15	14	15	14	14
Citizens of US Territories and Possessions	-	-	-	-	-	-	-	-	-	-	-	-
Non-US Citizens	-	-	-	-	-	-	-	-	-	-	-	-

Source: Personnel Statistics Division, DCS/Comptroller, Hq USAF

TABLE 288 — AUTHORIZED AND EMPLOYED CIVILIAN PERSONNEL IN FEAF — FY 1953

Personnel	Jun (1952)	Jul (1952)	Aug	Sep	Oct	Nov	Dec
	US CITIZENS, TERRITORIAL CITIZENS, NON CITIZENS a/						
Authorized Employment - Total	13,172	12,621	12,737	12,741	12,738	12,626	12,626
Employment - Total	11,813	12,045	12,203	12,230	12,218	12,042	11,998
Continental US Citizens	2,567	2,602	2,724	2,755	2,768	2,721	2,724
Citizens of US Territories and Possessions	306	372	380	382	379	374	374
Non-US Citizens	8,904	9,071	9,099	9,093	9,071	8,947	8,900
	INDIGENOUS PERSONNEL b/						
Employment - Total	47,330	46,993	46,280	45,342	45,002	44,790	46,892
Japanese	43,698	43,392	42,597	41,577	41,114	40,929	43,063
Okinawans	3,632	3,601	3,683	3,765	3,888	3,861	3,829

Personnel	Jan (1953)	Feb	Mar	Apr	May	Jun
	US CITIZENS, TERRITORIAL CITIZENS, NON CITIZENS a/					
Authorized Employment - Total	12,586	11,914	11,914	11,438	11,418	11,416
Employment - Total	11,894	11,494	11,330	11,297	11,156	11,032
Continental US Citizens	2,700	2,687	2,640	2,628	2,579	2,530
Citizens of US Territories and Possessions	377	377	379	377	376	372
Non-US Citizens	8,817	8,430	8,311	8,292	8,201	8,130
	INDIGENOUS PERSONNEL b/					
Employment - Total	47,097	48,748	48,666	48,283	48,548	48,572
Japanese	43,283	44,945	44,938	44,703	44,822	44,904
Okinawans	3,814	3,803	3,728	3,580	3,726	3,668

a/ Employees who are paid from 01, "Personal Services" funds.
b/ Employees who are paid from 07, "Other Contractual Services" funds.

Source: Personnel Statistics Division, DCS/Comptroller, Hq USAF

TABLE 289 — CIVILIAN EMPLOYMENT BY TYPE OF APPOINTMENT, BY SALARIED AND WAGE BOARD GROUPS — FY 1953

Type of Appointment	30 September (1952)	31 December	31 March (1953)	30 June
	By Employee Group			
WORLDWIDE - TOTAL	310,256	315,122	310,424	302,307
Permanent and Probational - Total	121,445	120,974	120,257	108,648
Salaried	58,016	57,703	57,578	50,508
Wage Board	63,429	63,271	62,679	58,140
Indefinite - Total	184,013	189,685	186,028	157,805
Salaried	69,362	70,408	70,420	62,852
Wage Board	114,651	119,277	115,608	94,953
Temporary - Total	4,798	4,463	4,139	1,974
Salaried a/	2,423	2,269	1,848	1,074
Wage Board	2,375	2,194	2,291	900
Excepted - Total	-	-	-	33,880
Salaried	-	-	-	14,439
Wage Board	-	-	-	19,441
CONTINENTAL US - TOTAL	273,737	277,771	273,720	266,719
Permanent and Probational - Total b/	109,060	109,008	108,714	106,892
Salaried	50,700	50,667	50,600	49,633
Wage Board	58,360	58,341	58,114	57,259
Indefinite - Total	162,497	166,419	163,126	156,443
Salaried	62,391	62,636	62,594	62,260
Wage Board	100,106	103,783	100,532	94,183
Temporary - Total	2,180	2,344	1,880	1,905
Salaried a/	1,277	1,232	1,142	1,062
Wage Board	903	1,112	738	843
Excepted - Total	-	-	-	1,479
Salaried	-	-	-	1,143
Wage Board	-	-	-	336
OVERSEAS - TOTAL	36,519	37,351	36,704	35,588
Permanent and Probational - Total	12,385	11,966	11,543	1,756
Salaried	7,316	7,036	6,978	875
Wage Board	5,069	4,930	4,565	881
Indefinite - Total	21,516	23,266	22,902	1,362
Salaried	6,971	7,772	7,826	592
Wage Board	14,545	15,494	15,076	770
Temporary - Total	2,618	2,119	2,259	69
Salaried	1,146	1,037	706	12
Wage Board	1,472	1,082	1,553	57
Excepted - Total	-	-	-	32,401
Salaried	-	-	-	13,296
Wage Board	-	-	-	19,105
	By Type of Service c/			
CONTINENTAL US - TOTAL	273,737	277,771	273,720	266,719
General Schedule	106,533	106,753	106,840	106,879
Crafts, Protective, Custodial	7,358	7,244	6,957	6,772
Public Law 313	7	9	9	10
Wage Board	159,369	163,236	159,384	152,621
Special Consultants	466	525	527	433
Presidential Appointees	4	4	3	4

a/ Includes Special Consultants.
b/ Includes Presidential Appointees.
c/ All comparable data on Overseas Personnel are not available.

Source: Personnel Statistics Division, DCS/Comptroller, Hq USAF

TABLE 290 — APPOINTMENT OF PHYSICALLY IMPAIRED CIVILIAN PERSONNEL BY COMMAND, CONTINENTAL US — FY 1953

Month	Total	Air Defense Command	Air Force Finance Division	Air Materiel Command	Air Proving Ground Command	Air Research and Development Command	Air Training Command	Air University
	All Appointments							
July (1952)	337	7	2	292	-	7	21	1
August	629	3	-	236	1	4	162	-
September	174	3	1	138	-	-	17	-
October	451	4	1	324	-	2	10	-
November	331	4	-	236	-	55	7	15
December	254	8	-	158	-	1	71	-
January (1953)	186	-	2	139	-	2	11	-
February	119	6	-	86	-	-	5	1
March	117	-	-	102	-	1	3	-
April	81	1	-	45	-	2	14	-
May	128	-	-	43	-	8	6	-
June	335	-	-	112	-	12	25	140
	Veteran Appointments							
July (1952)	208	6	-	179	-	7	13	-
August	321	3	-	147	-	2	75	-
September	104	2	1	75	-	-	13	-
October	207	2	1	184	-	-	8	-
November	189	3	-	142	-	31	5	-
December	132	8	-	89	-	-	29	-
January (1953)	116	-	1	77	-	1	9	-
February	76	5	-	47	-	-	4	-
March	65	-	-	54	-	1	1	-
April	37	1	-	18	-	2	9	-
May	63	-	-	25	-	7	6	-
June	112	-	-	38	-	4	1	62

Month	Continental Air Command	Headquarters Command USAF	Headquarters USAF	Military Air Transport Service	Strategic Air Command	Tactical Air Command	USAF Security Service
	All Appointments						
July (1952)	-	1	1	1	1	3	-
August	90	2	-	127	3	1	-
September	8	-	-	1	-	5	1
October	7	-	-	91	8	4	-
November	5	1	1	3	4	-	-
December	2	-	1	8	3	2	-
January (1953)	20	2	-	-	6	4	-
February	14	2	-	-	4	1	-
March	1	4	-	-	2	2	2
April	1	-	-	1	1	16	-
May	7	-	-	1	-	63	-
June	38	-	-	1	2	5	-
	Veteran Appointments						
July (1952)	-	1	1	-	-	1	-
August	90	1	-	-	2	1	-
September	8	-	-	-	-	4	1
October	6	-	-	1	3	2	-
November	3	-	1	2	2	-	-
December	2	-	-	3	-	1	-
January (1953)	18	1	-	-	6	3	-
February	13	2	-	-	4	1	-
March	1	3	-	-	2	2	1
April	-	-	-	1	1	5	-
May	6	-	-	1	-	18	-
June	4	-	-	-	1	2	-

Source: Personnel Statistics Division, DCS/Comptroller, Hq USAF

TABLE 291 – DEPARTMENTAL CIVILIAN EMPLOYMENT BY TYPE OF APPOINTMENT, BY EMPLOYEE GROUP – FY 1953

Type of Appointment	Salaried			
	September (1952)	December	March (1953)	June
Total	4,902	4,883	4,879	4,819
Permanent and Probational a/	2,886	2,820	2,815	2,742
Indefinite	1,858	1,920	1,960	1,911
Temporary b/	158	143	104	76
Excepted	-	-	-	90

a/ Includes Presidential Appointees.
b/ Includes Special Consultants.

Source: Personnel Statistics Division, DCS/Comptroller, Hq USAF

TABLE 292 – DEPARTMENTAL CIVILIAN EMPLOYMENT BY TYPE OF SERVICE – FY 1953

Type of Service	September (1952)	December	March (1953)	June
Total	4,902	4,883	4,879	4,819
General Schedule	4,760	4,747	4,747	4,689
Crafts, Protective, Custodial	92	87	87	85
Public Law 313	1	1	1	1
Special Consultants	45	44	41	40
Presidential Appointees	4	4	3	4

Source: Personnel Statistics Division, DCS/Comptroller, Hq USAF

TABLE 293 – DEPARTMENTAL CIVILIAN EMPLOYMENT WITH VETERANS' STATUS (INCLUDING 10 POINTS PREFERENCE) BY SEX – FY 1953

Personnel	September (1952)		December		March (1953)		June	
	Number	10 Point	Number	10 Point	Number	10 Point	Number	10 Point
Total	1,414	190	1,430	199	1,455	197	1,453	204
Male	1,276	155	1,279	164	1,283	147	1,287	156
Female	103		116		122		118	
Mothers, Widows, Wives	35	35	35	35	50	50	48	48

Source: Personnel Statistics Division, DCS/Comptroller, Hq USAF

TABLE 294 — ACCESSIONS AND SEPARATIONS OF USAF CIVILIAN PERSONNEL BY TYPE — FY 1953

(Table includes full time employees only.)

Accession or Separation by Type	Total	First Quarter	Second Quarter	Third Quarter	Fourth Quarter
	CONTINENTAL US				
Accession - Total	69,468	24,061	20,248	13,138	12,021
Original Probational Appointment	367	181	84	36	66
Excepted Appointment	605	273	129	85	118
Reemployed after Military Service	2,424	783	778	633	230
Temporary Appointment	6,174	1,412	1,621	1,267	1,874
Indefinite Appointment	54,374	19,580	16,310	9,859	8,625
Returned to Duty from Extended LWOP	1,522	453	353	363	353
Transfers from other Federal Agencies	4,002	1,379	973	895	755
Separation - Total	77,089	24,642	16,283	17,219	18,945
Resignations	57,603	19,602	12,392	12,619	12,990
Separations for Military Service	2,666	654	654	789	569
Reduction in Force	3,576	330	184	618	2,444
Discharges	3,149	933	764	802	650
Retirement, Death, Legal Incompetence	1,701	423	366	444	468
Termination	3,664	1,306	742	938	678
Extended LWOP, Furlough, Suspension	2,581	737	560	556	728
Transfers to other Federal Agencies	2,149	657	621	453	418
Net Change	-7,621	-581	3,965	-4,081	-6,924
	OVERSEAS				
Accession - Total	16,212	5,692	4,262	3,321	2,937
Separation - Total	15,933	4,391	3,536	3,964	4,042
Net Change	279	1,301	726	-643	-1,105

Source: Personnel Statistics Division, DCS/Comptroller, Hq USAF

TABLE 295 - PROMOTIONS AND DEMOTIONS OF CIVILIAN PERSONNEL BY VETERAN AND NON-VETERAN STATUS, BY COMMAND - CONTINENTAL US - FY 1953

Command	Jul (1952)	Aug	Sep	Oct	Nov	Dec	Jan (1953)	Feb	Mar	Apr	May	Jun
	Promotions											
CONTINENTAL US - TOTAL	7,452	8,987	8,317	7,764	7,818	6,783	5,930	6,798	8,652	7,012	6,350	6,567
With Preference	3,539	4,187	3,888	3,560	3,590	3,056	2,914	3,320	4,523	3,475	2,957	2,884
Without Preference	3,913	4,800	4,429	4,204	4,228	3,727	3,016	3,478	4,129	3,537	3,393	3,683
Air Defense Command - Total	57	104	40	64	65	34	55	34	34	50	59	58
With Preference	26	53	18	25	29	16	29	16	13	21	26	25
Without Preference	31	51	22	39	36	18	26	18	21	29	33	33
AF Finance Division - Total	199	276	191	153	137	93	115	89	119	40	62	121
With Preference	58	67	40	38	33	29	28	17	36	16	14	24
Without Preference	141	209	151	115	104	64	87	72	83	24	48	97
Air Materiel Command - Total	5,241	6,125	5,935	5,187	5,292	4,440	4,157	4,719	5,120	4,336	4,033	3,688
With Preference	2,545	2,835	2,840	2,454	2,371	2,038	1,981	2,247	2,524	2,079	1,826	1,721
Without Preference	2,696	3,290	3,095	2,733	2,921	2,402	2,176	2,472	2,596	2,257	2,207	1,967
Air Proving Ground Command - Total	40	6	45	28	59	49	23	85	50	31	39	85
With Preference	20	1	22	13	23	14	10	33	14	9	20	45
Without Pref.rence	20	5	23	15	36	35	13	52	36	22	19	40
Air Research and Development Command - Total	428	518	431	740	453	496	231	420	578	727	485	507
With Preference	261	373	221	320	260	265	141	246	307	378	246	270
Without Preference	167	145	210	420	193	231	90	174	271	349	239	237
Air Training Command - Total	698	862	742	744	727	689	507	696	1,207	910	802	1,381
With Preference	338	389	339	363	353	349	251	344	682	478	345	501
Without Preference	360	473	403	381	374	340	256	352	525	432	457	880
Air University - Total	57	61	48	52	25	12	19	35	29	16	27	23
With Preference	27	24	25	22	-	4	8	15	13	5	6	10
Without Preference	30	37	23	30	25	8	11	20	16	11	21	13
Continental Air Command - Total	185	207	127	127	113	119	114	169	178	184	133	164
With Preference	60	98	43	39	39	41	66	72	99	88	49	79
Without Preference	125	109	84	88	74	78	48	97	79	96	84	85
Headquarters Command, USAF - Total	6	3	26	37	61	53	68	54	100	68	73	53
With Preference	2	1	12	13	30	16	23	17	38	23	22	27
Without Preference	4	2	14	24	31	37	45	37	62	45	51	26
Headquarters, USAF - Total	130	184	136	118	94	136	132	34	168	118	125	105
With Preference	38	53	43	34	33	44	36	21	62	35	37	28
Without Preference	92	131	93	84	61	92	96	13	106	83	88	77
Military Air Transport Service - Total	45	250	292	161	187	215	183	156	241	158	145	166
With Preference	20	131	152	81	89	30	101	78	120	75	86	74
Without Preference	25	119	140	80	98	185	82	78	121	83	59	92
Strategic Air Command - Total	195	284	192	215	194	212	147	149	396	132	196	146
With Preference	81	114	76	98	93	88	147	149	396	132	196	49
Without Preference	114	170	116	117	101	124	-	-	-	-	-	97
Tactical Air Command - Total	171	106	112	138	393	208	177	117	409	207	141	49
With Preference	63	48	57	60	233	115	92	51	210	121	74	18
Without Preference	108	58	55	78	160	93	85	66	199	86	67	31
USAF Security Service - Total	-	1	-	-	18	27	2	41	23	35	30	21
With Preference	-	-	-	-	4	7	1	14	9	15	10	13
Without Preference	-	1	-	-	14	20	1	27	14	20	20	8

(CONTINUED)

TABLE 295 — PROMOTIONS AND DEMOTIONS OF CIVILIAN PERSONNEL BY VETERAN AND NON-VETERAN STATUS, BY COMMAND — CONTINENTAL US — FY 1953 — (CONTINUED)

Command	Jul (1952)	Aug	Sep	Oct	Nov	Dec	Jan (1953)	Feb	Mar	Apr	May	Jun
	Demotions											
CONTINENTAL US - TOTAL	762	668	553	1,161	634	848	617	798	990	1,173	1,535	1,122
With Preference	352	265	225	527	341	426	283	389	428	443	790	431
Without Preference	410	403	328	634	293	422	334	409	562	730	745	691
Air Defense Command - Total	13	6	9	6	4	3	10	4	5	7	7	15
With Preference	-	2	3	2	2	2	2	2	-	4	5	10
Without Preference	13	4	6	4	2	1	8	2	5	3	2	5
AF Finance Division - Total	2	2	4	1	5	1	2	-	2	1	4	1
With Preference	-	1	3	1	3	-	2	-	-	-	-	-
Without Preference	2	1	1	-	2	1	-	-	2	1	4	1
Air Materiel Command - Total	561	440	303	394	395	438	410	533	672	882	1,076	784
With Preference	269	188	126	237	181	169	184	225	266	278	509	292
Without Preference	292	252	177	157	214	269	226	308	406	604	567	492
Air Proving Ground Command - Total	2	-	9	2	1	5	-	30	22	9	2	-
With Preference	-	-	4	-	-	1	-	16	9	-	1	-
Without Preference	2	-	5	2	1	4	-	14	13	9	1	-
Air Research and Development Command - Total	19	28	36	436	30	24	11	19	40	28	53	27
With Preference	11	13	19	218	17	12	7	10	21	20	32	10
Without Preference	8	15	17	218	13	12	4	9	19	8	21	17
Air Training Command - Total	71	67	98	236	51	253	84	120	121	112	197	155
With Preference	33	21	39	38	51	164	29	65	49	52	104	63
Without Preference	38	46	59	198	-	89	55	55	72	60	93	92
Air University - Total	9	6	3	2	6	16	2	4	5	2	9	-
With Preference	3	2	-	-	5	10	-	4	2	2	6	-
Without Preference	6	4	3	2	1	6	2	-	3	-	3	-
Continental Air Command - Total	20	33	27	22	11	7	26	11	42	23	29	22
With Preference	6	10	12	13	4	2	15	4	21	7	10	12
Without Preference	14	23	15	9	7	5	11	7	21	16	19	10
Headquarters Command, USAF - Total	1	2	-	3	2	1	2	2	4	2	3	7
With Preference	-	-	-	1	1	-	1	1	1	1	1	2
Without Preference	1	2	-	2	1	1	1	1	3	1	2	5
Headquarters, USAF - Total	3	3	4	7	5	6	9	2	4	12	4	6
With Preference	1	-	-	1	1	2	1	-	1	4	2	2
Without Preference	2	3	4	6	4	4	8	2	3	8	2	4
Military Air Transport Service Total	13	17	15	22	23	53	24	15	20	28	41	47
With Preference	4	9	2	8	9	48	7	6	7	11	18	19
Without Preference	9	8	13	14	14	5	17	9	13	17	23	28
Strategic Air Command - Total	45	55	32	21	95	34	32	54	45	63	94	46
With Preference	24	17	11	6	63	12	32	54	45	63	94	12
Without Preference	21	38	21	15	32	22	-	-	-	-	-	34
Tactical Air Command - Total	3	9	13	9	6	7	5	4	8	4	16	12
With Preference	1	2	6	2	4	4	3	2	6	1	8	9
Without Preference	2	7	7	7	2	3	2	2	2	3	8	3
USAF Security Service - Total	-	-	-	-	-	-	-	-	-	-	-	-
With Preference	-	-	-	-	-	-	-	-	-	-	-	-
Without Preference	-	-	-	-	-	-	-	-	-	-	-	-

Source: Personnel Statistics Division, DCS/Comptroller, Hq. USAF

TABLE 296 - USAF CIVILIAN INCENTIVE AWARDS PROGRAM - FY 1953

(Authority for Suggestions and Honorary Awards is Public Law 600, 79th Congress. Authority for Superior Accomplishment Pay Increase Program and Management Improvements Awards are Title 7 and Title 10 of Classification Act 1949. Table includes statistics as reported to the bureau of Budget.)

Command	Suggestions Received	Suggestions Adopted	Cash Awards Paid	Estimated First Year Savings a/	Exceptional Decorations Approved b/	Meritorious Awards Approved c/	Title VII Awards Approved d/	Title X Awards Approved e/	Estimated First Year Savings f/	Cash Awards Paid
Total	33,269	8,281	$348,242.22	$11,400,421.37	9	84	277	8	$895,893.00	$2,961.90
Air Defense Command	423	81	3,109.80	65,882.38	-	5	6	-	-	-
AF Finance Division	520	70	2,305.60	126,296.77	-	-	6	1	20,298.00	325.00
Air Materiel Command	23,421	6,317	253,505.95	6,567,576.04	2	28	93	3	783,430.00	1,475.00
Air Proving Ground Command	126	42	2,433.60	119,303.99	-	-	7	-	-	-
Air Research and Development Command	2,581	325	26,608.85	1,444,258.64	-	7	11	-	-	-
Air Training Command	2,764	812	29,620.18	1,594,505.55	1	4	24	2	32,265.00	411.00
Air University	32	11	660.00	14,798.92	-	3	-	-	-	-
Alaskan Air Command	89	12	1,280.00	63,472.50	-	-	4	-	-	-
Caribbean Air Command	39	15	850.00	23,492.86	-	-	4	-	-	-
Continental Air Command	156	21	572.00	6,892.84	-	-	2	-	-	-
Far East Air Forces	108	21	762.50	49,248.86	1	13	7	1	13,900.00	294.78
Headquarters Command, USAF	53	12	247.50	1,445.13	-	1	3	1	46,000.00	456.12
Headquarters, USAF	134	6	487.00	14,898.33	4	10	51	-	-	-
Military Air Transport Service	820	128	3,877.10	72,544.61	1	5	26	-	-	-
Northeast Air Command	267	31	1,067.50	67,500.00	-	4	2	-	-	-
Strategic Air Command	528	206	13,292.22	508,549.74	-	2	20	-	-	-
Tactical Air Command	486	61	3,787.95	536,656.50	-	1	8	-	-	-
US Air Forces, Europe	687	107	3,359.47	109,251.71	-	1	3	-	-	-
USAF Security Service	35	3	415.00	13,846.00	-	-	-	-	-	-

a/ Savings are estimated for first year following adoption of suggestions. Savings from many suggestions involving safety, health, improvement of quality of work, and morale are not included as the benefits are intangible.
b/ Decorations for Exceptional Civilian Service is approved by Secretary of Air Force.
c/ Award for Meritorious Civilian Service is approved by Chief of Staff, USAF, or major air commanders.
d/ Title VII awards are additional step increases for superior accomplishment provided for in Classification Act of 1949.
e/ Title X awards are cash awards or additional step increases provided for in Classification Act of 1949.
f/ Savings are estimated for first year.

Source: Placement and Employee Relations Division, Directorate of Civilian Personnel, Hq. USAF

TABLE 297 — AIR FORCE AID SOCIETY SUMMARIES — FY 1953

(Received from and financial assistance to US Air Force personnel.)

Activity	Fiscal Year 1953	1 March 1946 through 30 June 1953
Excess Receipts over Disbursements a/	$ 666,808	$ 1,294,651
Receipts - Total	3,145,628	10,129,564
Memberships and Donations b/	786,948	2,951,047
Memorials	338	5,941
Fund Raising Activities	245,389	640,209
Loan Repayments	2,112,953	6,532,367
Disbursements - Total	2,478,820	8,834,913
Operating Expenses of Field Units	8,677	52,272
Grants	198,083	683,692
Loans	2,272,060	8,098,949
Cases Assisted - Total	33,075	130,317
Number of Loans Made	31,781	125,712
Number of Grants Made	1,294	4,605

a/ Of this amount $661,652 remained in the field for operating.
b/ Includes donations and memorials to The General Henry H. Arnold Educational Fund.

Note: The total amount of loans outstanding on June 30, 1953 was $1,097,962. During the period March 1, 1946 to June 30, 1953, a total of $468,620 was written off as uncollectible because the loans should have been grants originally or due to death or subsequent financial difficulties of the borrowers. This results in total assistance to date of $1,152,312 on which repayment cannot be expected.

Source: Headquarters Unit, Air Force Aid Society, Hq. USAF

TABLE 298 — USAF CIVILIAN EMPLOYEE TRAINING BY AREA OF TRAINING IN CONTINENTAL US — FY 1953

(This table shows the training received by civilian employees of the Air Force in the Continental United States during FY 1953. Man-hours of "On-the-Job" and "Off-the-Job" training are shown for each area of training. The total course completions for civilian employees in the Continental United States are shown for the same period.)

Area of Training	Number of Course Comple-tions a/	Per Cent of Total Comple-tions	Total Trainee Hours	On-the-Job		Off-the-Job	
				Number of Trainee Hours	Per Cent of Total Trainee Hours in Areas	Number of Trainee Hours	Per Cent of Total Trainee Hours in Areas
	1 Jul 1952 through 31 Dec 1952						
Total	224,704	100.0	5,462,053	2,784,931	51.0	2,677,122	49.0
Apprentice	348	-	261,043	90,639	34.7	170,404	65.3
Clerical	15,807	7.0	343,938	115,275	33.5	228,663	66.5
Inspecting and Testing	4,523	2.0	279,991	116,109	41.5	163,882	58.5
Orientation	48,035	21.4	152,873	13,858	9.1	139,015	90.9
Protection and Personal Services	20,963	9.3	580,611	476,478	82.1	104,133	17.9
Safety and Health	58,762	26.2	110,556	40,709	36.8	69,847	63.2
Semi-Skilled and Unskilled	9,319	4.2	142,475	49,563	34.8	92,912	65.2
Skilled Trades	22,964	10.2	2,187,135	1,295,322	59.2	891,813	40.8
Supervision and Management	28,802	12.9	483,594	38,816	8.0	444,778	92.0
Supply	9,111	4.1	510,077	360,288	70.6	149,789	29.4
Technical, Scientific and Professional	6,070	2.7	409,760	187,874	45.9	221,886	54.1
	1 Jan 1953 through 30 Jun 1953						
Total	209,523	100.0	4,713,529	2,233,458	47.4	2,480,071	52.6
Apprentice	154	-	359,932	94,112	26.1	265,820	73.9
Clerical	12,001	5.7	246,003	89,914	36.5	156,089	63.5
Inspection and Testing	3,877	1.9	211,307	64,242	30.4	147,065	69.6
Orientation	30,486	14.6	95,959	8,912	9.3	87,047	90.7
Protective and Personal Services	17,670	8.4	793,184	531,880	67.1	261,304	32.9
Safety and Health	40,174	19.2	117,035	37,437	32.0	79,598	68.0
Semi-Skilled and Unskilled	7,462	3.6	95,781	15,724	16.4	80,057	83.6
Skilled Trades	18,150	8.7	1,492,695	898,799	60.2	593,896	39.8
Supervision and Management	38,028	18.1	428,660	24,846	5.8	403,814	94.2
Supply	34,017	16.2	523,283	381,216	72.9	142,067	27.1
Technical, Scientific and Professional	7,504	3.6	349,690	86,376	24.7	263,314	75.3

a/ A course completion refers to one course satisfactorily completed by an employee. Only those employees who satisfactorily completed the courses in which they were enrolled are included.

Source: Career Development Division, Directorate of Civilian Personnel, DCS/P, Hq. USAF

Medical and Patient Transport

Part XV

MEDICAL AND PATIENT TRANSPORT

DEFINITIONS

ACTIVE DUTY MILITARY PERSONNEL

Consists of all military personnel who are on extended active duty. Excluded are military personnel who are on short tours of duty.

ADMISSIONS RATE

A measure which indicates the frequency of patients being relieved from duty because of medical reasons. Hence, the admission rate is based on admissions from duty. The conversion of number of admissions to show the number of admissions that would occur during a year if admissions occurred throughout an entire year at the same frequency as in the period of observation, per thousand average strength is termed the annual admission rate and is computed as follows:

$$\frac{\text{Number of admissions during period X number of such periods in a year X 1000}}{\text{Average daily strength during the period}}$$

HOSPITALIZATION RATIO

The proportion of strength occupying hospital and infirmary beds on an average day (of the period for which it is computed). It differs from the noneffective ratio in that quarters or dispensary patients are excluded. The ratio is computed per 100 strength as follows:

$$\frac{\text{Number of sick days in hospital and infirmary in the period X 100}}{\text{Average daily strength X number of days in the period}}$$

or:

$$\frac{\text{Daily average number of patients occupying hospital and infirmary beds}}{\text{Average daily strength for the period}}$$

NONEFFECTIVE RATIO (MEDICAL)

The proportion of strength not available for duty on an average day (of the period for which it is computed) because of medical reasons whether under treatment in hospital, infirmary, dispensary, or quarters. The ratio is computed per 100 strength as follows:

$$\frac{\text{Number of sick days in period X 100}}{\text{Average daily strength X number of days in period}}$$

or:

$$\frac{\text{Average daily number of "patients remaining" X 100}}{\text{Average daily strength}}$$

ADMISSIONS TO HOSPITALS AND INFIRMARIES

Include all patients admitted to the wards of an Air Force hospital or infirmary whether from duty or by transfer from another medical facility. Excluded are cases treated in quarters, or in a duty status, or in a nonmilitary medical facility.

AVERAGE OCCUPIED BEDS

The average daily number of patients occupying beds in hospitals and infirmaries as of midnight of a given day.

AVERAGE STRENGTH SERVED

Includes not only those U. S. active duty military personnel for whom a base holds sick call, but also those U. S. active duty military personnel reporting elsewhere (Dispensaries) for sick call but attached to the base for in-patient care.

OPERATING BEDS

Those medical treatment facility beds which are currently set up and in all respects ready for the care of patients, and which the facility is staffed and equipped to operate. Bassinets and dispensary beds are not included.

OUTPATIENT TREATMENTS

An outpatient who presents himself for medical advice or treatment at a medical facility, is counted as one outpatient treatment each time he reports to anyone of the clinic or departments; consequently, more than one treatment may be reported for each visit.

MEDICAL — CONTINUED

DEFINITIONS

COMPLETE PHYSICAL EXAMINATIONS

Include only routine physical examinations performed in accordance with USAF directives and recorded on the report of medical examinations (Standard Form 88); physical inspections of food handlers or barbers are not included nor are examinations for personnel reporting sick.

OUTPATIENT VISITS

A visit is counted for each patient (not excused from duty) who on a given day presents himself for either medical advice or treatment. On any given day, only one visit is counted regardless of the number of times the patient is seen; when the patient is seen on multiple days, one visit is counted for each day. Patients reporting for prescribed examinations and immunizations are not counted as a visit.

SPECIFIED PERIODIC EXAMINATIONS OR TESTS

Are those examinations or tests administered to personnel, military or civilian, exposed to industrial-type hazards.

FULL TIME EQUIVALENT PERSONNEL

Are total assigned and attached personnel converted into actual full-time strength; for example, 10 individuals employed on a full-time basis and 4 individuals employed on a half-time basis, are considered to be 12 full-time equivalents.

TABLE 299 — WORLDWIDE ADMISSION RATES OF USAF PERSONNEL — FY 1950 THROUGH FY 1953

(Data represent admissions from duty, treated at any medical facility, computed monthly as admissions-per-year per 1000 average strength.)

Diagnostic Category By Fiscal Year	Fiscal Year	Jul (1952)	Aug	Sep	Oct	Nov	Dec	Jan (1953)	Feb	Mar	Apr	May	Jun
All Causes a/													
1950	343	349	342	316	330	301	284	394	422	405	346	326	315
1951	408	313	348	322	316	330	339	503	661	539	443	372	346
1952	341	335	334	330	326	317	296	379	405	402	343	318	297
1953	320	283	293	280	287	288	290	546	370	340	323	293	283
Disease													
1950	293	296	290	266	280	255	240	345	375	356	299	271	260
1951	360	262	291	270	266	278	294	453	617	494	397	324	298
1952	300	288	290	287	283	276	257	340	368	364	304	275	255
1953	282	243	253	242	246	250	255	509	333	304	286	254	242
Non-battle Injury													
1950	50	53	52	50	50	46	44	49	47	49	47	55	55
1951	48	49	57	52	50	52	45	50	44	45	46	49	48
1952	41	47	44	43	43	41	39	39	37	38	39	43	42
1953	38	40	40	38	41	38	35	37	37	36	37	39	41

a/ Includes battle casualty admissions from July 1950 thru June 1953 not separately shown below.

Source: Biometrics Division, Office of the Surgeon General, Hq USAF.

TABLE 300 — WORLDWIDE NONEFFECTIVE RATIOS OF USAF PERSONNEL — FY 1950 THROUGH FY 1953

(Data represents per cent of strength not available for duty due to medical reasons, on an average day.)

Fiscal Year	Fiscal Year	Jul (1952)	Aug	Sep	Oct	Nov	Dec	Jan (1953)	Feb	Mar	Apr	May	Jun
1950	1.61	1.52	1.50	1.41	1.49	1.50	1.46	1.73	1.84	1.86	1.70	1.63	1.63
1951	1.57	1.67	1.69	1.57	1.51	1.50	1.44	1.83	1.90	1.60	1.53	1.45	1.38
1952	1.46	1.45	1.46	1.52	1.49	1.49	1.25	1.59	1.58	1.53	1.43	1.39	1.36
1953	1.28	1.35	1.32	1.30	1.28	1.23	1.12	1.54	1.34	1.28	1.26	1.19	1.17

Source: Biometrics Division, Office of the Surgeon General, Hq USAF.

TABLE 301 — WORLDWIDE HOSPITALIZATION RATIOS OF USAF PERSONNEL — FY 1950 THROUGH FY 1953

(Data represents per cent of strength occupying hospital beds, at any medical facility, on an average day.)

Fiscal Year	Fiscal Year	Jul (1952)	Aug	Sep	Oct	Nov	Dec	Jan (1953)	Feb	Mar	Apr	May	Jun
1950	1.32	1.28	1.26	1.24	1.29	1.29	0.90	1.59	1.56	1.46	1.44	1.37	1.31
1951	1.36	1.38	1.42	1.32	1.30	1.26	1.14	1.64	1.71	1.40	1.36	1.30	1.25
1952	1.24	1.20	1.25	1.25	1.27	1.27	1.17	1.21	1.34	1.31	1.24	1.22	1.15
1953	1.09	1.12	1.12	1.10	1.09	1.09	0.96	1.24	1.17	1.13	1.10	1.05	1.00

Source: Biometrics Division, Office of the Surgeon General, Hq USAF.

308700 O - 54 - 34

TABLE 302 — ADMISSIONS AND NUMBER OF PATIENTS OCCUPYING BEDS BY TYPE OF BENEFICIARY BY COMMAND — FY 1953

Command	Number of Admissions				Number of Patients Occupying Beds on an Average Day							
	Total	Active Duty Military		Other a/	Total	Active Duty Military			Dependents		Vets Adm Benef-iciaries	Other b/
		Air Force	Other			Air Force	Army	Navy	Air Force	Other		
Worldwide - Total	438,188	242,346	62,291	133,551	11,066	8,039	679	126	1,721	284	23	194
Continental U. S. - Total	335,486	178,520	47,748	109,218	8,479	6,326	295	94	1,442	221	3	98
Strategic Air Command	78,630	30,258	18,641	29,731	1,487	883	105	38	390	49	-	22
Continental Air Command	9,208	5,605	108	3,495	238	166	2	0	49	12	-	9
Tactical Air Command	15,015	9,107	371	5,537	293	202	7	3	76	4	-	1
Air Defense Command	15,512	9,821	1,406	4,285	290	209	17	1	56	5	-	2
Military Air Transport Service	17,455	6,684	6,630	4,141	259	182	13	8	46	6	-	4
Air Materiel Command	26,573	10,768	4,056	11,749	673	431	34	19	127	49	-	13
Air Research and Development Command	7,756	4,373	263	3,120	153	99	4	1	42	6	-	1
Air Training Command	141,469	91,404	11,504	38,561	4,321	3,564	91	17	537	75	2	35
Headquarters Command, USAF	11,148	3,469	4,585	3,094	168	105	16	5	36	3	-	3
Air Proving Ground Command	6,011	3,232	74	2,705	262	210	2	0	43	3	1	3
Air University	6,709	3,799	110	2,800	335	275	4	2	40	9	-	5
Overseas - Total	102,702	63,826	14,543	24,333	2,587	1,713	384	32	279	63	20	96
Far East Air Forces	28,735	21,186	3,366	4,183	873	623	142	16	47	16	-	29
U. S. Air Forces in Europe	34,541	23,039	1,895	9,607	963	699	64	9	141	15	-	35
Military Air Transport Service	9,554	3,696	3,986	1,872	113	63	18	5	13	3	-	11
Northeast Air Command	4,639	2,859	317	1,463	98	67	6	0	19	0	-	6
Alaskan Air Command	15,402	5,642	3,978	5,782	366	126	139	1	41	26	20	13
Strategic Air Command	9,831	7,404	1,001	1,426	174	135	15	1	18	3	-	2

a/ Includes Dependents, Retired, Employees, Allied Military Personnel, VA Beneficiaries, etc.
b/ Includes Allied Military Personnel, Bureau of Employee Compensation beneficiaries, employees, etc.

Source: Personnel Statistics Division, DCS/Comptroller, Hq USAF.

TABLE 303 — VOLUME OF SELECTED OUTPATIENT ACTIVITIES BY TYPE OF BENEFICIARY, BY COMMAND — FY 1953

Command	Total	Type of Beneficiary							
		Active Duty Military			Dependents		Retired	Vets Adm Benef	Other a/
		Air Force	Army	Navy-Marine	Air Force	Other			
	SUMMARY								
WORLDWIDE									
Treatments	12,057,406	6,654,783	264,151	38,446	3,628,168	223,137	15,141	197	1,233,383
Flight Physical Exams. . . .	252,357	227,125	3,811	206	-	-	-	-	21,215
Other Complete Physical Exams	606,611	431,624	13,596	1,824	9,136	1,098	182	12	149,139
Spec Periodic Exams or Tests	286,038	129,033	1,764	634	13,956	151	9	-	140,491
Immunizations.	4,715,713	3,805,433	80,544	15,403	573,830	54,630	1,165	1,427	183,281
CONTINENTAL U S									
Treatments	8,704,238	4,380,191	58,636	14,975	3,063,885	152,633	14,795	131	1,018,992
Flight Physical Exams. . . .	226,936	202,526	3,455	60	-	-	-	-	20,895
Other Complete Physical Exams	506,057	396,587	10,890	1,650	5,625	435	173	-	90,697
Spec Periodic Exams or Tests	198,176	90,683	190	199	7,571	11	9	-	99,513
Immunizations.	3,465,284	2,930,327	21,286	7,594	402,497	35,699	962	1,427	65,492
OVERSEAS									
Treatments	3,353,168	2,274,592	205,515	23,471	564,283	70,504	346	66	214,391
Flight Physical Exams. . . .	25,421	24,599	356	146	-	-	-	-	320
Other Complete Physical Exams	100,554	35,037	2,706	174	3,511	663	9	12	58,442
Spec Periodic Exams or Tests	87,862	38,350	1,574	435	6,385	140	-	-	40,978
Immunizations.	1,250,429	875,106	59,258	7,809	171,333	18,931	203	-	117,789
	CONTINENTAL U S								
Strategic Air Command									
Treatments	2,031,136	988,482	8,139	2,345	969,421	42,117	7,148	7	13,477
Flight Physical Exams. . . .	35,720	33,791	104	15	-	-	-	-	1,810
Other Complete Physical Exams	67,906	61,613	1,047	909	399	22	49	-	3,867
Spec Periodic Exams or Tests	19,341	16,505	2	6	1,256	-	-	-	1,572
Immunizations.	954,291	851,059	1,147	1,378	93,603	5,044	82	-	1,978
Continental Air Command									
Treatments	264,116	153,311	1,447	275	88,450	9,748	1,732	5	9,148
Flight Physical Exams. . . .	9,311	5,509	81	4	-	-	-	-	3,717
Other Complete Physical Exams	29,728	25,050	397	5	348	-	40	-	3,888
Spec Periodic Exams or Tests	1,630	988	13	166	4	-	-	-	459
Immunizations.	132,459	105,847	420	189	16,118	3,785	334	-	5,766
Tactical Air Command									
Treatments	436,697	248,156	2,185	296	178,812	2,896	550	-	3,802
Flight Physical Exams. . . .	12,731	11,829	306	6	-	-	-	-	590
Other Complete Physical Exams	29,527	27,689	293	10	168	-	-	-	1,367
Spec Periodic Exams or Tests	3,135	3,048	-	-	8	-	-	-	79
Immunizations.	189,776	147,377	764	28	39,756	1,624	9	-	218
Military Air Transport Sv									
Treatments	249,649	134,743	1,759	1,896	92,457	5,455	350	-	12,989
Flight Physical Exams. . . .	4,956	4,948	8	-	-	-	-	-	-
Other Complete Physical Exams	12,297	11,398	142	64	9	-	1	-	683
Spec Periodic Exams or Tests	2,806	2,116	-	1	17	-	-	-	672
Immunizations	76,199	42,926	3,220	2,602	11,995	6,249	502	1,427	7,278
Air Defense Command									
Treatments	604,662	402,894	5,683	992	181,235	7,374	395	9	6,080
Flight Physical Exams. . . .	15,418	13,734	146	17	-	-	-	-	1,521
Other Complete Physical Exams	43,475	36,919	772	72	155	-	7	-	5,550
Spec Periodic Exams or Tests	9,143	8,260	2	5	85	-	-	-	791
Immunizations.	179,775	145,283	962	192	28,494	2,064	6	-	2,774

TABLE 303 – VOLUME OF SELECTED OUTPATIENT ACTIVITIES BY TYPE OF BENEFICIARY, BY COMMAND – FY 1953 CONTINUED

Command	Total	Type of Beneficiary								
		Active Duty Military			Dependents		Retired	Vets Adm Benef	Other a/
		Air Force	Army	Navy-Marine	Air Force	Other			
	CONTINENTAL U S (Continued)								
Air Materiel Command									
Treatments	1,399,055	258,653	4,978	4,279	248,202	33,396	1,205	10	848,332
Flight Physical Exams	12,725	8,462	84	2	-	-	-	-	4,177
Other Complete Physical Exams	76,485	17,960	782	57	561	19	1	-	57,105
Spec Periodic Exams or Tests	143,660	45,943	13	1	5,903	-	2	-	91,798
Immunizations	219,093	118,116	3,160	1,621	50,972	8,078	8	-	37,138
Air Training Command									
Treatments	3,014,782	1,885,176	23,315	2,993	1,006,968	33,730	2,143	94	60,363
Flight Physical Exams	121,621	112,639	1,515	3	-	-	-	-	7,464
Other Complete Physical Exams	205,776	190,617	1,177	94	3,773	375	8	-	9,732
Spec Periodic Exams or Tests	8,415	7,102	69	9	152	3	1	-	1,079
Immunizations	1,570,865	1,426,526	10,435	647	120,570	7,193	2	-	5,492
Air Research & Dev Comd									
Treatments	243,858	104,150	3,279	1,365	86,707	7,651	286	-	40,420
Flight Physical Exams	4,626	3,977	61	-	-	-	-	-	588
Other Complete Physical Exams	12,237	8,165	55	14	84	-	13	-	3,906
Spec Periodic Exams or Tests	7,842	5,169	9	1	146	8	6	-	2,503
Immunizations	43,145	27,756	253	90	10,967	290	-	-	3,789
Air University									
Treatments	158,484	71,050	653	280	77,813	3,968	698	-	4,022
Flight Physical Exams	3,387	2,300	1,064	12	-	-	-	-	11
Other Complete Physical Exams	13,974	7,122	6,202	420	4	-	9	-	217
Spec Periodic Exams or Tests	1,624	1,364	33	10	-	-	-	-	217
Immunizations	29,563	12,191	378	760	15,824	240	-	-	170
Air Proving Ground									
Treatments	128,736	53,794	1,549	35	71,572	956	125	6	699
Flight Physical Exams	890	884	-	1	-	-	-	-	5
Other Complete Physical Exams	3,832	3,018	11	-	-	-	1	-	802
Spec Periodic Exams or Tests	88	86	-	-	-	-	-	-	2
Immunizations	22,505	16,304	82	-	6,012	100	-	-	7
Air Force Finance Div									
Treatments	16,347	625	-	-	-	-	-	-	15,722
Flight Physical Exams	-	-	-	-	-	-	-	-	-
Other Complete Physical Exams	705	-	-	-	-	-	-	-	705
Spec Periodic Exams or Tests	167	-	-	-	-	-	-	-	167
Immunizations	219	203	-	-	-	-	-	-	16
Headquarters Command, USAF									
Treatments	156,716	79,157	5,649	219	62,248	5,342	163	-	3,938
Flight Physical Exams	5,551	4,453	86	-	-	-	-	-	1,012
Other Complete Physical Exams	10,115	7,036	12	5	124	19	44	-	2,875
Spec Periodic Exams or Tests	325	102	49	-	-	-	-	-	174
Immunizations	47,394	36,739	465	87	8,166	1,032	19	-	866

TABLE 303 — VOLUME OF SELECTED OUTPATIENT ACTIVITIES BY TYPE OF BENEFICIARY, BY COMMAND — FY 1953 CONTINUED

Command	Total	Type of Beneficiary							
		Active Duty Military			Dependents		Retired	Vets Adm Benef	Other a/
		Air Force	Army	Navy-Marine	Air Force	Other			
	OVERSEAS								
Far East Air Forces									
Treatments	1,596,819	1,243,602	108,103	10,656	123,359	15,333	310	62	95,394
Flight Physical Exams	10,309	10,073	187	16	-	-	-	-	33
Other Complete Physical Exams	42,393	11,008	811	29	1,239	462	9	3	28,832
Spec Periodic Exams or Tests	18,649	4,317	40	9	1	-	-	-	14,282
Immunizations	514,282	381,986	31,854	520	33,248	6,057	203	-	60,414
U S. Air Forces, Europe									
Treatments	927,062	588,302	26,749	1,021	217,946	12,914	11	1	80,118
Flight Physical Exams	6,592	6,373	148	5	-	-	-	-	66
Other Complete Physical Exams	33,605	11,884	599	20	1,340	69	-	8	19,685
Spec Periodic Exams or Tests	36,408	18,055	297	31	5,726	17	-	-	12,282
Immunizations	420,711	293,879	8,977	274	74,301	4,956	-	-	38,324
Military Air Transport Sv									
Treatments	182,119	92,468	6,024	11,592	47,400	2,540	-	-	22,095
Flight Physical Exams	3,194	2,929	7	122	-	-	-	-	136
Other Complete Physical Exams	6,063	2,510	84	116	233	-	-	1	3,119
Spec Periodic Exams or Tests	18,616	7,320	345	395	129	21	-	-	10,406
Immunizations	86,167	50,125	2,514	7,006	15,225	1,666	-	-	9,631
Northeast Air Command									
Treatments	84,569	49,921	4,008	99	23,643	278	-	-	6,620
Flight Physical Exams	864	860	3	1	-	-	-	-	-
Other Complete Physical Exams	3,636	1,437	69	2	115	-	-	-	2,013
Spec Periodic Exams or Tests	4,182	2,360	33	-	-	-	-	-	1,789
Immunizations	19,897	12,843	265	9	6,568	106	-	-	106
Alaskan Air Command									
Treatments	240,154	96,134	38,735	85	72,660	28,728	15	1	3,796
Flight Physical Exams	1,724	1,713	9	2	-	-	-	-	-
Other Complete Physical Exams	8,510	4,222	448	6	477	128	-	-	3,229
Spec Periodic Exams or Tests	2,458	714	218	-	167	90	-	-	1,269
Immunizations	50,216	22,851	3,696	-	15,118	2,618	-	-	5,933
Caribbean Air Command									
Treatments	19,822	10,250	3	-	8,577	-	-	-	992
Flight Physical Exams	379	379	-	-	-	-	-	-	-
Other Complete Physical Exams	380	380	-	-	-	-	-	-	-
Spec Periodic Exams or Tests	1,351	1,351	-	-	-	-	-	-	-
Immunizations	11,421	4,050	-	-	4,538	-	-	-	2,833
Strategic Air Command									
Treatments	302,623	193,915	21,893	18	70,698	10,711	10	2	5,376
Flight Physical Exams	2,359	2,272	2	-	-	-	-	-	85
Other Complete Physical Exams	5,967	3,596	695	1	107	4	-	-	1,564
Spec Periodic Exams or Tests	6,198	4,233	641	-	362	12	-	-	950
Immunizations	147,735	109,372	11,952	-	22,335	3,528	-	-	548

a/ Includes short tour active duty military, Allied military personnel, Coast Guard, USPHS, other U. S. employees, etc.

Source: Personnel Statistics Division, DCS/Comptroller, Hq USAF.

TABLE 304 – STAFFING RATIOS OF USAF HOSPITALS AND INFIRMARIES, CONTINENTAL US – FY 1953

Type of Facility By Month	Work Units				Personnel a/											
					Currently Authorized		Full Time Equivalents Assigned To									
							Total			Inpatient Service			Dispensary and Clinic (Outpatient) Services		Other Services	
	Average Strength Served	Operating Beds	Average Beds Occupied	Daily Work Load b/	Number	Per 1,000 Strength Served	Number	Per 1,000 Strength Served	Per Cent of Authorization	Number	Per 100 Operating Beds	Per 100 Occupied Beds	Number	Daily Work Load Per Full Time Equivalents	Number	Per cent of Total Full Time Equivalents
Hospitals FY Average	538,515	12,987	8,257	21,790	23,733	44	24,455.9	45	103	15,890.7	122	192	5,578.8	3.9	2,986.4	12
July (1952)	555,713	13,980	8,452	19,873	23,803	43	24,381.5	44	102	16,213.7	116	192	5,392.2	3.7	2,775.6	11
August	550,463	13,980	8,404	21,932	23,427	43	24,171.0	44	103	16,230.0	116	193	5,329.7	4.1	2,611.3	11
September	544,565	13,902	8,066	21,338	26,648	49	24,124.5	50	103	16,324.8	117	202	5,361.0	4.0	2,438.7	9
October	544,070	13,000	7,960	20,283	23,665	43	24,341.9	45	103	16,230.9	125	204	5,514.8	3.7	2,596.2	11
November	534,693	13,017	8,101	21,315	23,686	44	24,542.8	46	104	16,433.2	126	203	5,505.2	3.9	2,604.4	11
December	518,518	13,042	6,959	17,276	23,701	46	24,665.3	48	104	16,317.5	125	234	5,590.1	3.1	2,737.7	11
January (1953)	522,877	12,437	9,022	24,031	22,767	44	24,650.0	47	108	16,305.8	131	181	5,624.0	4.3	2,720.2	11
February	528,655	12,372	8,813	22,918	23,073	44	24,502.1	46	106	15,919.0	129	181	5,666.6	4.0	2,916.5	12
March	540,954	12,572	8,772	23,813	23,276	43	24,471.8	45	105	15,790.5	126	180	5,676.0	4.2	3,005.3	12
April	547,670	12,522	8,514	22,069	23,486	43	24,574.7	45	105	15,600.6	125	183	5,651.0	3.9	3,323.1	14
May	541,717	12,497	8,316	23,152	23,582	44	24,729.8	46	105	15,237.4	122	183	5,593.5	4.2	3,938.9	16
June	532,284	12,522	7,701	23,476	23,686	44	24,316.5	46	103	14,085.5	112	183	6,081.6	3.9	4,149.4	17
Infirmaries FY Average	63,812	582	246	2,300	2,442	38	2,148.8	34	88	809.2	139	329	954.8	2.4	384.8	18
July (1952)	58,636	538	186	1,929	2,018	34	1,746.0	30	87	740.4	138	398	754.8	2.6	250.8	14
August	58,628	549	188	2,056	2,109	36	1,887.8	32	90	736.5	134	392	852.6	2.4	298.7	16
September	62,071	599	190	2,151	2,650	43	2,045.6	39	90	791.4	132	417	925.6	2.3	328.6	14
October	65,104	609	228	2,259	2,416	37	2,100.6	32	87	838.9	138	368	937.9	2.4	323.8	15
November	65,321	609	240	2,296	2,437	37	2,128.7	33	87	803.0	132	335	983.0	2.3	342.7	16
December	63,074	631	214	2,005	2,585	41	2,216.0	35	86	856.6	136	400	988.8	2.0	370.6	17
January (1953)	65,734	586	393	3,199	2,421	37	2,291.1	35	95	903.1	154	230	966.9	3.3	421.1	18
February	64,371	581	316	2,592	2,519	39	2,266.0	35	90	895.3	154	283	931.6	2.8	439.1	19
March	65,806	581	264	2,465	2,600	40	2,255.2	34	87	828.6	143	314	988.6	2.5	448.3	20
April	65,686	583	258	2,196	2,555	39	2,293.5	35	90	827.5	142	321	1,024.0	2.1	442.0	19
May	65,239	561	250	2,230	2,525	39	2,312.1	35	92	796.6	142	319	1,034.6	2.2	480.9	21
June	66,078	556	223	2,217	2,465	37	2,233.3	34	91	692.8	125	311	1,069.2	2.1	471.3	21

a/ Excludes Dental Personnel.
b/ Includes Outpatient Treatments and Complete Physical Examinations.

Source: Personnel Statistics Division, DCS/Comptroller, Hq USAF.

TABLE 305 — USAF DENTAL HEALTH AND DENTAL ACTIVITIES AT USAF INSTALLATIONS, WORLDWIDE. — FY 1953

Class I - No Dental Defects.
Class II - Minor Caries or Other Deficiencies.
Class III - Extensive Caries or Other Extensive Dental Diseases.
Class IV - Insufficient Teeth (Require Prosthesis).
Class V - Emergency.

Month	Dental Officers and Civilian Dentists a/	USAF Military Personnel Dentally Classified											Total Dental Sittings	Total Fillings (Restorations)	Total Dentures
		Total	Class V		Class IV		Class III		Class II		Class I				
			Number	Per Cent	Number	Per Cent	Number	Per Cent	Number	Per Cent	Number	Per Cent			
July (1952)	1,541	813,014	5,665	0.7	19,944	2.1	230,126	28.3	265,371	32.6	291,908	36.0	383,182	171,065	5,542
August.	1,553	823,611	4,191	0.5	18,602	2.2	236,091	28.7	264,956	32.2	299,971	36.4	376,460	174,095	5,629
September	1,626	822,900	4,017	0.5	18,076	2.2	233,540	28.4	262,861	31.9	304,406	37.0	378,524	174,744	5,772
October	1,647	822,271	2,779	0.3	17,796	2.2	233,077	28.3	258,841	31.5	309,778	37.7	394,094	200,622	5,955
November.	1,719	824,862	2,136	0.3	16,863	2.0	229,278	27.8	259,453	31.5	317,132	38.4	355,768	172,439	5,277
December.	1,602	804,979	1,833	0.2	16,805	2.1	219,963	27.3	250,693	31.2	315,685	39.2	319,090	162,200	5,688
January (1953). . . .	1,552	815,265	1,710	0.2	16,379	2.0	222,800	27.3	254,420	31.2	319,956	39.3	319,090	162,200	5,688
February.	1,505	838,792	1,603	0.2	16,846	2.0	229,018	27.3	263,033	31.4	328,292	39.1	367,127	166,984	4,886
March	1,549	820,527	1,344	0.2	16,647	2.0	222,231	27.1	257,228	31.3	323,077	39.4	420,540	190,884	6,056
April	1,581	858,558	1,251	0.1	16,736	2.0	233,207	27.2	270,662	31.5	336,702	39.2	398,311	189,542	6,097
May	1,567	869,127	1,001	0.1	17,211	2.0	227,181	26.1	274,641	31.6	349,093	40.2	382,389	194,236	6,079
June.	1,511	857,666	989	0.1	17,655	2.1	222,105	25.9	269,806	31.4	347,111	40.5	384,380	176,815	5,862

a/ Includes only those rendering dental service at Air Force Installations.

Source: Assistant for Dental Services, Office of the Surgeon General, Hq USAF.

TABLE 306 – USAF VETERINARY FOOD INSPECTION SERVICE INCIDENT TO PROCUREMENT – FY 1953

(In inspecting all foods of animal origin for the US Air Force, the Veterinary Service conducts the following classes of inspection:

Class 1 Antemortem

Class 2 Postmortem

Class 3 Prior to Purchase

Class 4 On Delivery at Purchase

Class 5 Any receipt except Purchase

Class 6 Prior to Shipment

Class 7 At time of Issue

Class 8 Purchase by Air Forces Exchange

Class 9 In Storage

This table reflects the pounds of foods of animal origin inspected by the Veterinary Service incident to procurement, 1 July 1952 through 30 June 1953. These inspections represent an estimated savings of $817,438.32 for the fiscal year 1953. However, food inspection must not be evaluated merely in terms of economy but more especially in terms of health of the Air Force.)

Food Inspected	FISCAL YEAR 1953				
	Total	First Quarter	Second Quarter	Third Quarter	Fourth Quarter
	WORLDWIDE				
CLASSES 3, 4, and 8					
Accepted - Total	480,180,118	118,320,253	116,773,803	113,411,725	131,674,337
Rejected - Total	4,159,883	913,098	1,261,702	764,849	1,220,234
Not Type, Class, or Grade	3,107,762	612,950	944,123	664,313	886,376
Insanitary or Unsound	1,052,121	300,148	317,579	100,536	333,858
CLASS 3					
Accepted - Total	69,602,037	17,047,321	15,693,104	16,221,249	20,640,363
Rejected - Total	2,709,929	550,937	794,229	610,892	753,871
Not Type, Class, or Grade	2,352,344	432,269	657,946	590,728	671,401
Insanitary or Unsound	357,585	118,668	136,283	20,164	82,470
CLASS 4					
Accepted - Total	335,555,783	81,534,901	83,797,672	79,429,795	90,793,415
Rejected - Total	1,312,829	328,861	440,139	125,990	417,839
Not Type, Class, or Grade	713,167	172,721	272,043	64,432	203,971
Insanitary or Unsound	599,662	156,140	168,096	61,558	213,868
CLASS 8					
Accepted - Total	75,022,298	19,738,031	17,283,027	17,760,681	20,240,559
Rejected - Total	137,125	33,300	27,334	27,967	48,524
Not Type, Class, or Grade	42,251	7,960	14,134	9,153	11,004
Insanitary or Unsound	94,874	25,340	13,200	18,814	37,520

TABLE 306 — USAF VETERINARY FOOD INSPECTION SERVICE INCIDENT TO PROCUREMENT — FY 1953 — Continued

(See headnote on first page of this table.)

Food Inspected	FISCAL YEAR 1953				
	Total	First Quarter	Second Quarter	Third Quarter	Fourth Quarter
	CONTINENTAL US				
CLASSES 3, 4, and 8					
Accepted - Total	386,151,051	99,168,889	94,712,054	89,008,929	103,261,179
Rejected - Total	3,409,100	833,041	859,615	705,762	1,010,682
Not Type, Class, or Grade	2,659,401	572,446	660,592	639,495	786,868
Insanitary or Unsound	749,699	260,595	199,023	66,267	223,814
CLASS 3					
Accepted - Total	59,167,814	14,849,305	13,358,968	13,570,601	17,388,940
Rejected - Total	2,546,910	538,663	733,005	589,875	685,367
Not Type, Class, or Grade	2,199,720	420,495	597,222	579,048	602,955
Insanitary or Unsound	347,190	118,168	135,783	10,827	82,412
CLASS 4					
Accepted - Total	283,947,848	71,941,143	71,210,583	65,610,960	75,185,162
Rejected - Total	766,415	265,643	110,199	102,037	288,536
Not Type, Class, or Grade	427,205	144,909	54,110	53,249	174,937
Insanitary or Unsound	339,210	120,734	56,089	48,788	113,599
CLASS 8					
Accepted - Total	43,035,389	12,378,441	10,142,503	9,827,368	10,687,077
Rejected - Total	95,775	28,735	16,411	13,850	36,779
Not Type, Class, or Grade	32,476	7,042	9,260	7,198	8,976
Insanitary or Unsound	63,299	21,693	7,151	6,652	27,803
	OVERSEAS				
CLASSES 3, 4, and 8					
Accepted - Total	94,029,067	19,151,364	22,061,749	24,402,796	28,413,158
Rejected - Total	750,783	80,057	402,087	59,087	209,552
Not Type, Class, or Grade	448,361	40,504	283,531	24,818	99,508
Insanitary or Unsound	302,422	39,553	118,556	34.269	110,044
CLASS 3					
Accepted - Total	10,434,223	2,198,016	2,334,136	2,650,648	3,251,423
Rejected - Total	163,019	12,274	61,224	21,017	68,504
Not Type, Class, or Grade	152,624	11,774	60,724	11,680	68,446
Insanitary or Unsound	10,395	500	500	9,337	58
CLASS 4					
Accepted - Total	51,607,935	9,593,758	12,587,089	13,818,835	15,608,253
Rejected - Total	546,414	63,218	329,940	23,953	129,303
Not Type, Class, or Grade	285,962	27,812	217,933	11,183	29,034
Insanitary or Unsound	260,452	35,406	112,007	12,770	100,269
CLASS 8					
Accepted - Total	31,986,909	7,359,590	7,140,524	7,933,313	9,553,482
Rejected - Total	41,350	4,565	10,923	14,117	11,745
Not Type, Class, or Grade	9,775	918	4,874	1,955	2,028
Insanitary or Unsound	31,575	3,647	6,049	12,162	9,717

Source: Veterinary Service, Office of the Surgeon General, Hq USAF.

TABLE 307 – USAF VETERINARY FOOD INSPECTION SERVICE INCIDENT TO SURVEILLANCE – FY 1953

(This table reflects the pounds of food of animal origin inspected as issued or otherwise disposed of and the percent rejected from 1 July 1952 through 30 June 1953. Although all Air Force owned subsistence items are reinspected many times as received, stored, shipped, and issued, each pound is included but once in this table. Subsistence is disposed of in one of two ways: i.e., by rejection and salvage incident to surveillance inspection or by issue or sale)

Food Inspected	FISCAL YEAR 1953				
	Total	First Quarter	Second Quarter	Third Quarter	Fourth Quarter
	WORLDWIDE				
Inspected - Total a/	582,969,436	139,727,825	145,586,385	145,820,489	151,834,737
Issued b/	581,903,680	139,400,875	145,413,156	145,460,299	151,629,350
Rejected c/	1,065,756	326,950	173,229	360,190	205,387
Percent Rejected	.180	.230	.110	.247	.135
	CONTINENTAL US				
Inspected - Total a/	368,621,023	91,140,251	90,669,044	92,572,046	94,239,682
Issued b/	368,385,518	91,065,480	90,666,455	92,456,702	94,196,881
Rejected c/	235,505	74,771	2,589	115,344	42,801
Percent Rejected	.063	.082	.003	.125	.045
	OVERSEAS				
Inspected - Total a/	214,348,413	48,587,574	54,917,341	53,248,443	57,595,055
Issued b/	213,518,162	48,335,395	54,746,701	53,003,597	57,432,469
Rejected c/	830,251	252,179	170,640	244,846	162,586
Percent Rejected	.387	.519	.311	.460	.282

a/ Total Class 7 passed plus rejections in Classes 5, 6, 7, and 9 inspections.
b/ Total Class 7 inspected and passed.
c/ Total rejections in Classes 5, 6, 7, and 9.

Source: Veterinary Service, Office of the Surgeon General, Hq USAF.

TABLE 308 — USAF VETERINARY ANIMAL SERVICES SUMMARY — FY 1953

ANIMAL SERVICES	FISCAL YEAR 1953				
	Total	First Quarter	Second Quarter	Third Quarter	Fourth Quarter
	WORLDWIDE				
Rabies Control					
Vaccinations - Total	31,436	7,864	6,463	7,733	9,376
Public Animals	544	54	103	102	285
Private Animals	30,892	7,810	6,360	7,631	9,091
Positive Cases Reported	27	-	4	15	8
Admission for Other Causes					
Public Animals	1,878	419	382	369	708
	CONTINENTAL US				
Rabies Control					
Vaccinations - Total	22,470	5,581	4,349	5,780	6,760
Public Animals	4	-	3	1	-
Private Animals	22,466	5,581	4,346	5,779	6,760
Positive Cases Reported	27	-	4	15	8
Admission for Other Causes					
Public Animals	8	-	-	-	8
	OVERSEAS				
Rabies Control					
Vaccinations - Total	8,966	2,283	2,114	1,953	2,616
Public Animals	540	54	100	101	285
Private Animals	8,426	2,229	2,014	1,852	2,331
Positive Cases Reported	-	-	-	-	-
Admission for Other Causes					
Public Animals	1,870	419	382	369	700

Source: Veterinary Service, Office of the Surgeon General, Hq USAF.

TABLE 309 — MILITARY AIR TRANSPORT SERVICE ACTIVITY IN THE AIR EVACUATION OF KOREAN WAR CASUALTIES (BODIES ONLY) — FY 1953

(Data prior to July 1952 included casualties departing from Japan whereas subsequent data were revised to include only those casualties off-loaded in the ZI. As a result of this revision, the information shown prior to July 1952 was revised to conform with current reporting requirements.)

Evacuations by Date	Total Korean Casu-alties	Type Patient		Type Patient		By Arm of Service			
		Mental	Physical	Litter	Ambu-latory	Air Force	Army	Navy-Marine	Other
TOTAL TO DATE	45,471	3,963	41,508	28,020	17,451	790	32,281	11,283	1,117
26 June '50 through 30 June '51	21,957	2,045	19,912	14,510	7,447	179	15,773	6,002	5
1 July '51 through 30 June '52	11,753	1,247	10,506	6,915	4,838	220	8,629	2,489	415
1 July '52 through 30 June '53	8,895	521	8,374	5,256	3,639	250	5,735	2,364	546
1 July '53 through 30 Dec '53	2,866	150	2,716	1,339	1,527	141	2,146	428	151
FISCAL YEAR 1953									
July (1952)	750	67	683	445	295	24	545	146	35
August	950	76	874	631	319	25	559	295	71
September	678	46	632	416	262	16	396	238	28
October	972	46	926	64[illegible]	328	29	645	258	40
November	1,064	52	1,012	618	446	20	726	279	39
December	933	65	68	514	419	28	661	197	47
January (1953)	682	47	635	389	293	27	453	169	33
February	470	36	434	282	188	21	321	94	34
March	452	15	437	236	216	15	275	108	54
April	606	15	591	354	252	15	325	233	33
May	841	34	807	447	394	20	463	293	65
June	497	22	475	270	227	10	336	54	67
FISCAL YEAR 1954									
July (1953)	591	20	571	251	340	16	461	78	36
August	973	44	929	570	403	37	722	183	31
September	846	41	805	312	534	71	680	70	25
October	248	27	221	121	127	7	159	32	50
November	97	16	81	36	61	0	59	32	6
December	111	2	109	49	62	10	65	33	3

Source: Statistical Services Division, DCS/Comptroller, Military Air Transport Service.

TABLE 310 — AEROMEDICAL EVACUATION OF CASUALTIES FROM JAPAN BY TYPE OF WAR AND NON-WAR CASUALTY — FY 1953

Date	Patients from Japan		War Patients	
	Non-War	War	Litter	Ambulatory
1952				
July	509	750	455	295
August	466	950	631	319
September	365	678	416	262
October	425	972	644	328
November	376	1,064	618	446
December	406	933	514	419
1953				
January	422	682	389	293
February	356	470	282	188
March	629	452	236	216
April	496	606	354	252
May	437	841	447	394
June	449	497	270	227

Source: Statistical Services Division, DCS/Comptroller, Military Air Transport Service

TABLE 311 — PATIENT AEROMEDICAL EVACUATIONS — FY 1953

Date	Patient Movements			Average Miles Per Patient Flown	Nautical Patient Miles Flown		
	Total	CONTINENTAL US	OVERSEAS		Total	CONTINENTAL US	OVERSEAS
1952							
July	9,458	6,227	3,231	1,509	14,275,256	4,999,554	9,275,702
August	9,314	5,980	3,334	1,516	14,118,653	4,731,003	9,387,650
September. . .	8,043	5,455	2,588	1,419	11,415,218	4,105,381	7,309,837
October. . . .	9,491	6,087	3,404	1,456	13,821,353	4,595,561	9,225,792
November . . .	8,870	5,519	3,351	1,579	14,002,286	4,530,706	9,471,580
December . . .	9,212	6,092	3,120	1,497	13,786,297	5,050,646	8,735,651
1953							
January. . . .	8,201	5,405	2,796	1,159	9,508,967	2,656,958	6,852,009
February . . .	6,948	4,637	2,311	1,465	10,182,191	3,540,490	6,641,701
March.	8,120	5,541	2,579	1,391	11,297,705	4,106,478	7,191,227
April.	8,325	5,442	2,883	1,475	12,276,400	4,106,478	7,191,227
May.	9,180	5,949	3,231	1,450	13,311,900	4,489,082	8,822,818
June	7,826	5,300	2,526	1,392	10,890,337	3,970,936	6,919,401

Source: Statistical Services Division, DCS/Comptroller, Military Air Transport Service.

TABLE 312 — AEROMEDICAL EVACUATION OF PATIENTS THROUGH U.S. PORTS — FY 1953

Date	Westover	Brookley	Travis	McChord
1952				
July	365	14	1,273	55
August	443	36	1,478	72
September.	380	58	1,044	90
October.	439	16	1,397	113
November	414	19	1,438	60
December	410	28	1,339	74
1953				
January.	405	33	1,104	73
February	461	31	826	50
March.	343	23	1,081	32
April.	481	34	1,102	63
May.	432	56	1,278	56
June	388	30	946	79

Source: Statistical Services Division, DCS/Comptroller, Military Air Transport Service.

MORALE

This area of the publication was organized as such under the title of Morale for the FY 1951 "USAF Statistical Digest." The Study of OSI "Caseload Activities on Special Investigations" appeared for the first time in the FY 1951 publication. Tables on offenses, as reported by the Air Provost Marshal, have been running since 1947 but prior to FY 1951 this information was reported under Military Personnel.

OFFICE OF SPECIAL INVESTIGATIONS

The Office of Special Investigations, Headquarters USAF, is an activity of The Inspector General, USAF, and an instrumentality of the Chief of Staff, USAF. The mission of the office is to provide a centrally directed criminal, counter intelligence, and special investigative service to all Air Force activities. The Director of Special Investigations is charged with the operational and administrative control of all Office of Special Investigations activities within the continental limits of the United States. An Office of Special Investigations activity functions within each oversea command but the operational control thereof is the responsibility of the oversea commander concerned. (For that reason no oversea summaries were included in the table.) Oversea commands, initiating cases which require Air Force investigative action in the Zone of Interior, direct all requests for Personnel Security Investigations authorized under the provisions of AFR 205-6 to the 4th OSI District Office, Bolling Air Force Base, Washington 25, D. C. All other requests are referred to the Director of Special Investigations, Hq. USAF, Washington 25, D. C.

The administrative and operational structure of the Office of Special Investigations within the continental limits of the United States during FY 1953 consisted of the Directorate of Special Investigations, Washington 25, D. C.; the 1005th IG Special Investigations Group, Bolling Air Force Base, Washington 25, D. C.; and 25 districts, numbered one to twenty-five inclusive. Each district was commanded by an officer of the district headquarters designated the District Commander. Within the various districts, detachments existed under the command of a military person designated the Detachment Commander. The area of jurisdiction for each of the twenty-five districts may be found in AFR 124-6, dated 14 Dec 1949. The map on the following page indicates districts and district headquarters.

The Office of Special Investigations initiates investigation of matters which come within its investigative responsibility under the following circumstances:

(1) Upon the direction of the Director of Special Investigations or higher authority.

(2) Upon receipt of a request from any Air Force commander responsible for the security, discipline and law enforcement of a command or installation, or from higher authority.

(3) Upon receipt of information indicating a reasonable need for investigation of matters clearly within the investigative jurisdiction of the Office of Special Investigations with the commander indicated above concurring. When an appropriate commander requests that a matter which comes within the investigative jurisdiction and responsibility of the Office of Special Investigations, not be investigated, the District Office will comply with the request but will fully advise the Director of Special Investigations of the circumstances. All reports of assigned investigations are given the appropriate security classifications.

Summaries have been compiled for the period, 1 August 1948 through 30 June 1953, covering the period since the inception of the Office of Special Investigations. For the convenience of the recipients statistics have been set up for both calendar year 1952 and fiscal year 1953. "Pending Investigations" as of 30 June 1953 are also shown.

The following definitions arranged in alphabetical order will clarify the data shown in the table - "Special Investigations Conducted by the Office of Special Investigations in Continental US":

DEFINITIONS

AUXILIARY OFFICE OF INVESTIGATIONS - (short terminology - "Auxiliary")

Investigations of any nature conducted by the Directorate of Special Investigations or a District Office, in which, in accordance with OSI policy, that office acts as an assistant to the controlling office (the office of origin) within its territorial investigative jurisdiction.

CLASSIFICATION

The numerical designation and descriptive character assigned to each investigation which indicates the principal nature of the purpose of the investigation.

COUNTER INTELLIGENCE INVESTIGATIONS

Investigations conducted to determine facts related to security control measures designed to insure the safeguarding of information, personnel, equipment and installations against the sabotage, espionage or subversive activities of foreign powers and of disaffected or dissident groups or individuals which may constitute a threat to the internal security of the Air Force.

GENERAL INVESTIGATIONS

Investigations conducted to determine facts and circumstances pertaining to alleged major violations of the Articles of the Uniform Code of Military Justice, Federal Statutes and/or other applicable directives, by USAF personnel, excluding incidents of a counter intelligence or procurement nature.

INVESTIGATIONS CLOSED

Investigations terminated by offices of origin and auxiliary offices after all relevant facts have been determined and reported to the requesting commander through proper OSI channels.

INVESTIGATIONS OPENED

Investigations initiated by offices of origin or auxiliary offices pursuant to requests from the proper commander or the Chief of Staff, USAF.

INVESTIGATIONS PENDING

Investigations opened by offices of origin or auxiliary offices on which, as of the date such investigations are inventoried, there remains further investigative work and reporting to be done before they may be considered investigations closed.

MORALE — Continued

OFFICE OF SPECIAL INVESTIGATIONS — Continued

OFFICE OF ORIGIN INVESTIGATIONS - (short terminology - "Origin")

Investigations of any nature conducted by the Directorate of Special Investigations or a District Office in which, in accordance with OSI policy, that office assumes the control of the entire investigation.

PERSONNEL SECURITY INVESTIGATIONS

Investigations conducted to determine facts upon which the requesting commander can decide whether to grant or deny to the subjects of the investigations access to restricted areas and/or classified information. The loyalty and security program within the executive departments established the requirement for such investigations, and they are governed by law, OSD directives and Air Force policies.

PROCUREMENT INVESTIGATIONS

Investigations conducted to determine facts surrounding incidents of alleged breaches of the public trust and violations of law in connection with Air Force procurement, disposal, nonappropriated funds, commissary, and pay and allowance matters.

SECURITY

Safeguarding military information - This regulation prescribes policies and procedures for the safeguarding of military information which requires protection and to achieve uniformity in the grading and assignment of classification. Ref: AFR 205-1.

The Inspector General, USAF, Office of Special Investigations District Map, under AFR 124-6, dated: 14 Dec 1949 and printed below is still in effect.

MORALE – CONTINUED

AIR PROVOST MARSHAL

Provost Marshal Statistics are a collection of selected data concerning corrections, security violations, and delinquencies charged to Worldwide Military Personnel on active duty. The statistics reported in this section are derived from AF Form 511, "Report of Air Provost Marshal Activities."

The following definitions affect this portion of the Morale Reports:

DEFINITIONS

ABSENCE WITHOUT LEAVE (AWOL)

The status or the offense of any member of the Armed Forces, who without proper authority:

(1) Fails to go to his appointed place of duty at the time prescribed, or

(2) Goes from that place, or

(3) Absents himself or remains absent from his unit, organization, or other place of duty which he is required to be at the time prescribed (Uniform Code of Military Justice, Article 86) (See AFR 35-73 1-4 dated: 19 May 1953.)

APPREHENSION

a. Cooperation of State and Local Police Forces. Commanders of zone of interior major air commands will take steps to secure the active cooperation of all State and local police forces and such other officials and organizations as they may consider useful to insure the person's prompt return to military control. Such agencies will be informed that they should not take action to apprehend an absentee or deserter unless they are in receipt of either DD Form 553 or information from an officer of the Air Force that the person is an absentee or deserter whose return to military control is desired. Commanders of major air commands overseas will take such action as the local situation may warrant.

b. Personnel Authorized to Apprehend:

(1) Military. Members of the Armed Forces are authorized to apprehend absentees and deserters in the circumstances described in MCM, 1951, paragraphs 17, 18, and 19.

(2) Civilians. Any civil officer having authority to apprehend offenders under the laws of the United States or any State, district, Territory, or Possession of the United States may summarily apprehend a deserter from the Armed Forces of the United States and deliver him into the custody of the Armed Forces of the United States (Uniform Code of Military Justice, Article 8). Generally, a private citizen does not have any authority to apprehend a deserter unless authorized to do so by a military officer (distribution of DD Form 553 has been held to be sufficient authorization).

CUSTODY GRADE

Prisoners will be classified as being in a minimum, medium or maximum custody grade in accordance with the criteria outlined in (1), (2), and (3) below. The initial classification will be determined by the confinement officer based upon the nature of the offense, demeanor of the prisoner upon admission, and any other pertinent information available.

(1) Minimum custody. This custody grade will include those prisoners who are determined to be sufficiently stable, dependable, and trustworthy as to require little or no custodial supervision.

(2) Medium custody. This custody grade will include those prisoners who require immediate and continuous custodial supervision, but who are considered not to possess characteristics of a dangerous, violent, or trouble-making nature which would require special custodial control.

(3) Maximum custody. This custody grade will include those prisoners who require close supervision, special custodial controls and handling because of their conduct or known characteristics of a dangerous, violent, or trouble-making nature, or other circumstances which make such controls necessary. Their movements within the confinement facility should be limited and under supervision.

The abbreviations used in connection with the Offense tables are explained below:

CONTINENTAL U S

ADC - Air Defense Command

AFFC - Air Force Finance Center

AMC - Air Materiel Command

APG - Air Proving Ground Command

ARDC - Air Research and Development Command

ATRC - Air Training Command

AU - Air University

CONAC - Continental Air Command

HQC - Headquarters Command

MATS - Military Air Transport Service

SAC - Strategic Air Command

SWC - Special Weapons Command

TAC - Tactical Air Command

OVERSEAS

AAC - Alaskan Air Command

CairC - Caribbean Air Command

FEAF - Far East Air Forces

MATS - Military Air Transport Service

NEAC - Northeast Air Command

SAC - Strategic Air Command

USAFE - U S Air Forces in Europe

TABLE 313 — SPECIAL INVESTIGATIONS CONDUCTED BY THE OFFICE

LINE NUMBER		Classification	Total - 1 Aug 1948 Through 30 Jun 1953					
			Opened			Closed		
			Total	Origin	Aux-iliary	Total	Origin	Aux-iliary
		Grand Total	1,618,330	980,488	637,842	1,579,440	951,428	628,012
1		Personnel Security Investigations - Total	1,541,058	935,922	605,136	1,504,793	908,601	596,192
2	36	Personnel Security Investigations - General	3,377	1,203	2,174	3,200	1,069	2,131
3	37	Atomic Energy "M" Investigations	79,738	27,825	51,913	79,657	27,778	51,879
4	38	Integrated Reg AF Officers	55,891	19,329	36,562	55,791	19,247	36,544
5	39	Cryptographic Personnel	139,993	42,723	97,270	135,871	40,573	95,298
6	40	Air Force Civilian Employees	137,300	74,011	63,289	134,971	72,325	62,646
7	41	Air Force Military Personnel	813,423	573,066	240,357	791,316	555,830	235,486
8	42	Facilities Employees	56,130	44,192	11,938	55,779	43,890	11,889
9	43	Contractor Employees	145,582	110,086	35,496	140,584	105,678	34,906
10	44	Aliens	9,886	4,403	5,483	8,719	3,714	5,005
11	45	Cadet Trainees and Officer Candidates	38,940	11,893	27,047	38,871	11,848	27,023
12	46	OSI Personnel	30,512	8,430	22,082	30,285	8,285	22,000
13	48	Munitions Board Matters	4	1	3	4	1	3
14	51	Air National Guard	10,856	8,587	2,269	10,700	8,447	2,253
15	52	Air Force Inactive Reserve	10,624	6,559	4,065	10,387	6,397	3,990
16	54	National Security Agency Matters	8,282	3,354	4,928	8,176	3,278	4,898
17	57	Atomic Energy "Q" Investigations	520	260	260	482	241	241
18		General Investigations - Total	50,014	31,843	18,171	49,006	31,063	17,943
19	5	Bribery	224	115	109	223	114	109
20	6	Homicide	1,222	898	324	1,205	883	322
21	7	Sex Offenses	10,542	6,441	4,101	10,276	6,244	4,032
22	8	Assault	936	804	132	926	794	132
23	9	Impersonation	704	436	268	694	427	267
24	10	Fraudulent Enlistment	4,766	1,996	2,770	4,744	1,983	2,761
25	11	Embezzlement	295	163	132	295	163	132
26	12	Forgery	1,587	921	666	1,534	879	655
27	13	Larceny	6,733	5,068	1,665	6,585	4,939	1,646
28	14	Theft of Government Property	6,312	4,486	1,826	6,137	4,349	1,788
29	15	Robbery	354	274	80	346	267	79
30	16	Housebreaking	1,153	911	242	1,122	882	240
31	17	Narcotics Violations	1,801	1,222	579	1,756	1,182	574
32	18	Customs Violations	231	108	123	227	107	120
33	19	Blackmarket Activities	421	140	281	395	128	267
34	20	Property Destruction	377	275	102	366	267	99
35	21	Discrimination	37	26	11	35	24	11
36	22	Intimidation	31	16	15	29	15	14
37	23	Perjury	28	17	11	28	17	11
38	24	Special Inquiry	4,576	2,384	2,192	4,535	2,356	2,179
39	25	Improper Use, Etc.	404	260	144	401	257	144
40	26	Misconduct	3,155	1,794	1,361	3,106	1,756	1,350
41	47	Postal Violations	1,087	639	448	1,043	603	440
42	50	Counterfeiting	58	36	22	57	35	22
43	53	Reciprocal Investigations	2,429	2,119	310	2,408	2,111	297
44	55	War Crimes	-	-	-	-	-	-
45	62	Bad Checks	551	294	257	533	281	252
46		Counter Intelligence - Total	21,790	10,625	11,165	20,919	10,063	10,856
47	27	Espionage	839	520	319	827	511	316
48	28	Sabotage	2,314	1,548	766	2,269	1,514	755
49	29	Treason	9	2	7	9	2	7
50	30	Sedition	12	6	6	12	6	6
51	31	Disaffection	758	272	486	741	259	482
52	32	Subversive Activities	1,355	564	791	1,316	542	774
53	33	Communist Matters	12,698	5,386	7,312	12,026	4,973	7,053
54	34	Violations AFR 205-1	3,428	1,994	1,434	3,351	1,931	1,420
55	35	Vulnerability Tests	329	300	29	320	292	28
56	49	Positive Intelligence	45	31	14	45	31	14
57	56	Essential Elements of Information	3	2	1	3	2	1
58		Procurement Investigations - Total	5,468	2,098	3,370	4,722	1,701	3,021
59	58	Procurement Matters	2,077	710	1,367	1,888	619	1,269
60	59	Disposal Matters	77	33	44	65	27	38
61	60	Non-Appropriated Funds Matters	287	158	129	262	139	123
62	61	Pay and Allowance Matters	3,027	1,197	1,830	2,507	916	1,591

Source: Directorate of Special Investigations, The Inspector General, Headquarters USAF.

OF SPECIAL INVESTIGATIONS, CONTINENTAL US – FY 1953

FISCAL YEAR 1953						CALENDAR YEAR 1952						LINE NUMBER
Opened			Closed			Opened			Closed			
Total	Origin	Aux-iliary	Total	Origin	Aux-iliary	Total	Origin	Aux-iliary	Total	Origin	Aux-iliary	
397,359	271,359	126,000	434,758	301,213	133,545	427,208	298,242	128,966	512,824	363,494	149,330	
374,729	258,410	116,319	412,503	288,478	124,025	405,890	286,070	119,820	491,246	351,072	140,174	1
2,229	785	1,444	2,222	766	1,456	1,969	662	1,307	1,911	613	1,298	2
668	255	413	763	322	441	804	328	476	1,173	557	616	3
1,877	1,367	510	2,592	1,889	703	3,930	1,982	1,948	6,869	4,133	2,736	4
35,449	11,313	24,136	37,466	12,339	25,127	36,650	12,005	24,645	44,584	14,616	29,968	5
22,678	12,108	10,570	25,222	13,700	11,522	23,960	12,354	11,606	30,171	16,244	13,927	6
246,549	185,527	61,022	273,919	208,326	65,593	273,698	212,824	60,874	328,915	256,989	71,926	7
4,695	4,058	637	6,311	5,463	848	8,952	7,574	1,378	14,634	13,152	1,482	8
42,893	36,202	6,691	45,233	38,024	7,209	37,348	30,567	6,781	41,530	34,524	7,006	9
4,932	2,185	2,747	4,683	2,057	2,626	3,894	1,963	1,931	4,001	1,934	2,067	10
419	236	183	465	276	189	443	250	193	1,253	968	285	11
6,853	1,648	5,205	7,002	1,707	5,295	7,046	1,804	5,242	7,267	1,922	5,345	12
-	-	-	-	-	-	-	-	-	-	-	-	13
1,140	778	362	1,215	820	395	1,109	796	313	1,836	1,503	333	14
1,894	1,032	862	2,450	1,489	961	2,348	1,529	819	2,777	1,902	875	15
2,089	734	1,355	2,628	1,134	1,494	3,539	1,332	2,207	4,111	1,908	2,203	16
364	182	182	332	166	166	200	100	100	214	107	107	17
12,290	8,266	4,024	12,332	8,295	4,037	12,273	7,996	4,277	12,842	8,449	4,393	18
72	46	26	78	52	26	64	43	21	66	43	23	19
361	272	89	374	279	95	359	260	99	364	259	105	20
3,313	2,143	1,170	3,358	2,191	1,167	3,568	2,241	1,327	3,647	2,301	1,346	21
268	244	24	278	251	27	296	256	40	296	260	36	22
162	125	37	163	122	41	151	103	48	158	106	52	23
316	125	191	364	154	210	421	102	319	804	402	402	24
-	-	-	2	2	-	2	2	-	4	4	-	25
466	298	168	455	285	170	418	251	167	413	253	160	26
1,894	1,474	420	1,849	1,431	418	1,671	1,271	400	1,654	1,256	398	27
1,839	1,264	575	1,796	1,243	553	1,617	1,171	446	1,600	1,159	441	28
101	85	16	97	82	15	92	76	16	96	78	18	29
314	263	51	310	260	50	321	250	71	336	264	72	30
574	393	181	608	416	192	683	450	233	707	473	234	31
42	24	18	44	28	16	38	28	10	36	25	11	32
155	70	85	143	65	78	122	56	66	119	52	67	33
84	66	18	74	59	15	69	55	14	62	48	14	34
3	3	-	1	1	-	1	1	-	1	1	-	35
5	2	3	3	1	2	9	2	7	10	3	7	36
7	6	1	8	6	2	4	2	2	4	2	2	37
775	409	366	777	409	368	732	404	328	761	428	333	38
108	66	42	116	70	46	109	64	45	106	66	40	39
657	399	258	664	403	261	643	376	267	669	396	273	40
360	226	134	345	216	129	359	227	132	357	232	125	41
23	16	7	22	15	7	7	7	-	8	8	-	42
139	109	30	135	113	22	156	110	46	194	137	57	43
-	-	-	-	-	-	-	-	-	-	-	-	44
252	138	114	268	141	127	361	188	173	370	193	177	45
6,811	3,374	3,437	6,553	3,200	3,353	6,103	3,023	3,080	6,034	2,996	3,038	46
241	153	88	244	153	91	309	192	117	318	196	122	47
505	366	139	506	370	136	508	358	150	523	370	153	48
-	-	-	-	-	-	-	-	-	-	-	-	49
3	3	-	3	3	-	3	3	-	3	3	-	50
119	50	69	114	49	65	142	51	91	157	66	91	51
313	127	186	307	125	182	288	115	173	286	121	165	52
4,509	1,977	2,532	4,231	1,792	2,439	3,725	1,632	2,093	3,626	1,565	2,061	53
967	551	416	993	560	433	1,027	577	450	1,030	589	441	54
144	140	4	144	140	4	90	88	2	80	79	1	55
9	6	3	10	7	3	10	6	4	10	6	4	56
1	1	-	1	1	-	1	1	-	1	1	-	57
3,529	1,309	2,220	3,370	1,240	2,130	2,942	1,153	1,789	2,702	977	1,725	58
1,104	355	749	1,218	411	807	1,300	485	815	1,206	400	806	59
62	22	40	52	17	35	24	15	9	25	15	10	60
158	79	79	157	84	73	188	103	85	167	90	77	61
2,205	853	1,352	1,943	728	1,215	1,430	550	880	1,304	472	832	62

TABLE 313 -- SPECIAL INVESTIGATIONS CONDUCTED BY THE OFFICE

LINE NUMBER		Classification	1 Jan 1952 Through 30 Jun 1952						1 Jul 1952	
			Opened			Closed			Open-	
			Total	Origin	Aux-iliary	Total	Origin	Aux-iliary	Total	Origin
		Grand Total	229,763	163,029	66,734	274,481	194,175	80,306	197,445	135,213
1		Personnel Security Investigations - Total	219,055	157,030	62,025	263,613	187,972	75,641	186,835	129,040
2	36	Personnel Security Investigations - General	1,044	365	679	950	300	650	925	297
3	37	Atomic Energy "M" Investigations	473	205	268	728	351	377	331	123
4	38	Integrated Reg AF Officer	2,657	1,063	1,594	4,935	2,726	2,209	1,273	919
5	39	Cryptographic Personnel	18,797	6,236	12,561	24,333	7,746	16,587	17,853	5,769
6	40	Air Force Civilian Employees	12,506	6,398	6,108	16,407	8,538	7,869	11,454	5,956
7	41	Air Force Military Personnel	150,063	119,160	30,903	176,414	138,145	38,269	123,635	93,664
8	42	Facilities Employees	6,427	5,458	969	10,646	9,752	894	2,525	2,116
9	43	Contractor Employees	17,620	13,897	3,723	18,185	14,727	3,458	19,728	16,670
10	44	Aliens	1,560	856	704	1,551	763	788	2,334	1,107
11	45	Cadet Trainees and Officer Candidates	237	132	105	970	790	180	206	118
12	46	OSI Personnel	3,721	981	2,740	3,938	1,139	2,799	3,325	823
13	51	Air National Guard	605	485	120	1,227	1,101	126	504	311
14	52	Air Force Inactive Reserve	1,354	980	374	1,193	865	328	994	549
15	54	National Security Agency Matters	1,891	764	1,127	2,024	973	1,051	1,648	568
16	57	Atomic Energy "Q" Investigations	100	50	50	112	56	56	100	50
17		General Investigations - Total	6,186	3,850	2,336	6,738	4,310	2,428	6,087	4,146
18	5	Bribery	30	20	10	28	16	12	34	23
19	6	Homicide	176	118	58	175	118	57	183	142
20	7	Sex Offenses	1,792	1,095	697	1,829	1,121	708	1,776	1,146
21	8	Assault	150	125	25	148	126	22	146	131
22	9	Impersonation	75	43	32	78	46	32	76	60
23	10	Fraudulent Enlistment	229	29	200	576	313	263	192	73
24	11	Embezzlement	2	2	-	2	2	-	-	-
25	12	Forgery	221	121	100	219	125	94	197	130
26	13	Larceny	774	571	203	835	627	208	897	700
27	14	Theft of Government Property	765	534	231	801	563	238	852	637
28	15	Robbery	49	39	10	52	40	12	43	37
29	16	Housebreaking	174	134	40	182	139	43	147	116
30	17	Narcotics Violations	383	239	144	373	234	139	300	211
31	18	Customs Violations	21	15	6	17	10	7	17	13
32	19	Blackmarket Activities	54	21	33	54	21	33	68	35
33	20	Property Destruction	39	30	9	42	32	10	30	25
34	21	Discrimination	1	1	-	1	1	-	-	-
35	22	Intimidation	7	1	6	8	2	6	2	1
36	23	Perjury	3	1	2	2	1	1	1	1
37	24	Special Inquiry	375	210	165	413	240	173	357	194
38	25	Improper Use, Etc	53	31	22	48	30	18	56	33
39	26	Misconduct	330	182	148	350	194	156	313	194
40	47	Postal Violations	185	125	60	188	126	62	174	102
41	50	Counterfeiting	2	2	-	3	3	-	5	5
42	53	Reciprocal Investigations	88	52	36	113	71	42	68	58
43	55	War Crimes	-	-	-	-	-	-	-	-
44	62	Bad Checks	208	109	99	201	109	92	153	79
45		Counter Intelligence - Total	2,972	1,459	1,513	2,966	1,478	1,488	3,131	1,564
46	27	Espionage	182	118	64	186	120	66	127	74
47	28	Sabotage	270	182	88	284	193	91	238	176
48	29	Treason	-	-	-	-	-	-	-	-
49	30	Sedition	1	1	-	1	1	-	2	2
50	31	Disaffection	88	32	56	104	42	62	54	19
51	32	Subversive Activities	146	61	85	151	64	87	142	54
52	33	Communist Matters	1,732	740	992	1,703	733	970	1,993	892
53	34	Violations AFR 205-1	517	291	226	509	298	211	510	286
54	35	Vulnerability Tests	33	32	1	25	25	-	57	56
55	49	Positive Intelligence	3	2	1	3	2	1	7	4
56	56	Essential Elements of Information	-	-	-	-	-	-	1	1
57		Procurement Investigations - Total	1,550	690	860	1,164	415	749	1,392	463
58	58	Procurement Matters	779	334	445	594	197	397	521	151
59	59	Disposal Matters	12	9	3	12	9	3	12	6
60	60	Non-Appropriated Funds Matters	109	67	42	90	47	43	79	36
61	61	Pay and Allowance Matters	650	280	370	468	162	306	780	270

Source: Directorate of Special Investigations, The Inspector General, Headquarters USAF.

OF SPECIAL INVESTIGATIONS, CONTINENTAL US — FY 1953 CONTINUED

Through 31 Dec 1952				1 Jan 53 Through 30 Jun 1953						Pending			LINE NUMBER
ed	Closed			Opened			Closed			30 June 1953			
Aux-iliary	Total	Origin	Aux-iliary	Total	Origin	Aux-iliary	Total	Origin	Aux-iliary	Origin	Aux-iliary	Total	
62,232	238,343	169,319	69,024	199,914	136,146	63,768	196,415	131,894	64,521	29,060	9,830	38,890	
57,795	227,633	163,100	64,533	187,894	129,370	58,524	184,870	125,378	59,492	27,321	8,944	36,265	1
628	961	313	648	1,304	488	816	1,261	453	808	134	43	177	2
208	445	206	239	337	132	205	318	116	202	47	34	81	3
354	1,934	1,407	527	604	448	156	658	482	176	82	18	100	4
12,084	20,251	6,870	13,381	17,596	5,544	12,052	17,215	5,469	11,746	2,150	1,972	4,122	5
5,498	13,764	7,706	6,058	11,224	6,152	5,072	11,458	5,994	5,464	1,686	643	2,329	6
29,971	152,501	118,844	33,657	122,914	91,863	31,051	121,418	89,482	31,936	17,236	4,871	22,107	7
409	3,988	3,400	588	2,170	1,942	228	2,323	2,063	260	302	49	351	8
3,058	23,345	19,797	3,548	23,165	19,532	3,633	21,888	18,227	3,661	4,408	590	4,998	9
1,227	2,450	1,171	1,279	2,598	1,078	1,520	2,233	886	1,347	689	478	1,167	10
88	283	178	105	213	118	95	182	98	84	45	24	69	11
2,502	3,329	783	2,546	3,528	825	2,703	3,673	924	2,749	145	82	227	12
193	609	402	207	636	467	169	605	418	188	140	16	156	13
445	1,584	1,037	547	900	483	417	866	452	414	162	75	237	14
1,080	2,087	935	1,152	441	166	275	541	199	342	76	30	106	15
50	102	51	51	264	132	132	230	115	115	19	19	38	16
1,941	6,104	4,139	1,965	6,203	4,120	2,083	6,228	4,156	2,072	780	228	1,008	17
11	38	27	11	38	23	15	40	25	15	1	-	1	18
41	189	141	48	178	130	48	185	138	47	15	2	17	19
630	1,818	1,180	638	1,537	997	540	1,540	1,011	529	197	69	266	20
15	148	134	14	122	113	9	130	117	13	10	-	10	21
16	80	60	20	86	65	21	83	62	21	9	1	10	22
119	228	89	139	124	52	72	136	65	71	13	9	22	23
-	2	2	-	-	-	-	-	-	-	-	-	-	24
67	194	128	66	269	168	101	261	157	104	42	11	53	25
197	819	629	190	997	774	223	1,030	802	228	129	19	148	26
215	799	596	203	987	627	360	997	647	350	137	38	175	27
6	44	38	6	58	48	10	53	44	9	7	1	8	28
31	154	125	29	167	147	20	156	135	21	29	2	31	29
89	334	239	95	274	182	92	274	177	97	40	5	45	30
4	19	15	4	25	11	14	25	13	12	1	3	4	31
33	65	31	34	87	35	52	78	34	44	12	14	26	32
5	20	16	4	54	41	13	54	43	11	8	3	11	33
-	-	-	-	3	3	-	1	1	-	2	-	2	34
1	2	1	1	3	1	2	1	-	1	1	1	2	35
-	2	1	1	6	5	1	6	5	1	-	-	-	36
163	348	188	160	418	215	203	429	221	208	28	13	41	37
23	58	36	22	52	33	19	58	34	24	3	-	3	38
119	319	202	117	344	205	139	345	201	144	38	11	49	39
72	169	106	63	186	124	62	176	110	66	36	8	44	40
-	5	5	-	18	11	7	17	10	7	1	-	1	41
10	81	66	15	71	51	20	54	47	7	8	13	21	42
-	-	-	-	-	-	-	-	-	-	-	-	-	43
74	169	84	85	99	59	- 40	99	57	42	13	5	18	44
1,567	3,068	1,518	1,550	3,680	1,810	1,870	3,485	1,682	1,803	562	309	871	45
53	132	76	56	114	79	35	112	77	35	9	3	12	46
62	239	177	62	267	190	77	267	193	74	34	11	45	47
-	-	-	-	-	-	-	-	-	-	-	-	-	48
-	2	2	-	1	1	-	1	1	-	-	-	-	49
35	53	24	29	65	31	34	61	25	36	13	4	17	50
88	135	57	78	171	73	98	172	68	104	22	17	39	51
1,101	1,923	832	1,091	2,516	1,085	1,431	2,308	960	1,348	413	259	672	52
224	521	291	230	457	265	192	472	269	203	63	14	77	53
1	55	54	1	87	84	3	89	86	3	8	1	9	54
3	7	4	3	2	2	-	3	3	-	-	-	-	55
-	1	1	-	-	-	-	-	-	-	-	-	-	56
929	1,538	562	976	2,137	846	1,291	1,832	678	1,154	397	349	746	57
370	612	203	409	583	204	379	606	208	398	91	98	189	58
6	13	6	7	50	16	34	39	11	28	6	6	12	59
43	77	43	34	79	43	36	80	41	39	19	6	25	60
510	836	310	526	1,425	583	842	1,107	418	689	281	239	520	61

TABLE 314 — OSI OPERATIONS IN FEAF — FY 1953

Type	Jul (1952)	Aug	Sep	Oct	Nov	Dec	Jan (1953)	Feb	Mar	Apr	May	Jun
	Background Investigations											
Opened	1,644	1,767	2,147	2,116	1,814	1,802	1,472	1,694	2,482	1,688	2,050	426
Closed	2,006	1,453	3,156	1,931	2,380	2,117	2,005	1,736	1,789	1,874	1,794	2,458
Pending	7,489	7,803	6,794	6,979	6,413	6,098	5,565	5,523	5,716	5,530	5,856	3,864
	Counter Intelligence Complaint Investigations											
Opened	24	19	26	28	23	23	23	28	22	14	20	17
Closed	20	19	18	27	23	21	16	24	31	15	25	25
Pending	21	21	29	30	30	31	38	42	33	32	33	25
	Criminal Investigations											
Opened	197	158	152	168	163	186	177	170	175	149	212	172
Closed	197	167	171	161	169	197	173	164	191	150	183	175
Pending	203	194	173	180	174	162	168	174	158	155	181	169

Source: Personnel Statistics Division, Directorate of Statistical Services, DCS/C

TABLE 315 — COURT MARTIAL RATES IN FEAF — FY 1953

(The following formula was used in determining rates: $\frac{\text{Number of trials X 1000}}{\text{Mean strength}}$ = rate).

Command Unit and Type Rate	Jul (1952)	Aug	Sep	Oct	Nov	Dec	Jan (1953)	Feb	Mar	Apr	May	Jun
FEAF - Overall												
Trials												
Summary - Total	321	280	378	407	395	360	349	294	378	411	386	341
Special - Total	96	97	106	109	95	131	134	111	129	111	178	134
General - Total	13	13	27	10	17	18	14	13	14	14	33	18
Rates - Total												
Summary - Total	2.9	2.8	3.3	3.5	3.3	3.0	2.9	2.2	2.3	3.1	2.8	2.7
Special - Total	.9	.9	.9	.9	.8	1.1	1.1	.8	.8	.8	1.3	1.1
General - Total	.1	.1	.2	.1	.1	.2	.1	.1	.1	.1	.2	.1
5th Air Force												
Trials												
Summary	121	91	128	140	125	101	97	98	137	134	124	140
Special	31	33	35	40	25	34	29	21	35	35	42	43
General	4	2	7	3	4	2	3	1	4	2	6	4
Rates												
Summary	3.8	2.7	3.8	4.0	3.6	2.8	2.6	2.2	3.1	3.0	2.7	3.2
Special	1.0	1.0	1.0	1.1	.7	1.0	.8	.5	.8	.8	.9	1.0
General	.1	.1	.2	.1	.1	.1	.1	.02	.1	.04	.1	.1
13th Air Force												
Trials												
Summary	34	37	25	29	44	27	59	19	11	64	63	17
Special	4	6	4	5	7	5	15	13	2	1	38	16
General	3	1	4	1	-	3	1	2	1	3	1	2
Rates												
Summary	6.5	5.4	3.6	4.1	5.7	3.3	7.5	2.4	1.4	8.1	8.4	2.3
Special	.8	.9	.6	.7	.9	.6	1.8	1.6	.3	.1	5.1	2.2
General	.6	.1	.6	.1		.4	.1	.3	.1	.4	.1	.3
20th Air Force												
Trials												
Summary	34	23	26	29	24	29	41	20	22	35	33	31
Special	4	12	11	12	5	13	14	18	19	14	33	16
General	1	2	4	1	7	5	5	6	3	3	9	
Rates												
Summary	2.8	1.7	1.9	2.0	1.7	2.1	3.0	1.4	1.6	2.5	2.5	2.5
Special	.3	.9	.8	.8	.4	.9	1.0	1.3	1.3	1.0	2.5	1.3
General	.1	.2	.4	.1	.5	.4	.4	.4	.2	.2	.7	
FEALOGFOR												
Trials												
Summary	22	24	40	44	33	33	31	31	41	43	20	24
Special	14	7	13	10	16	12	17	9	19	10	12	10
General	-	-	-	-	-	-	-	-	-	-	-	-
Rates												
Summary	2.5	2.6	4.4	4.2	3.2	3.3	2.4	2.4	3.2	3.3	1.6	1.9
Special	1.6	.8	1.4	1.0	1.5	1.2	1.3	.7	1.5	.8	.9	.8
General	-	-	-	-	-	-	-	-	-	-	-	-

TABLE 315 — COURT MARTIAL RATES IN FEAF — FY 1953 — (Continued)

(The following formula was used in determining rates: $\frac{\text{Number of Trials X 1000}}{\text{Mean strength}}$ = rate).

Command Unit and Type Rate	Jul (1952)	Aug	Sep	Oct	Nov	Dec	Jan (1953)	Feb	Mar	Apr	May	Jun
JADF b/												
Trials												
Summary	72	63	107	111	108	114	75	82	132	86	112	92
Special	31	30	18	20	26	41	27	33	37	27	31	34
General	3	4	9	4	5	8	4	3	5	6	13	12
Rates												
Summary	2.2	2.0	3.2	3.3	3.2	3.3	2.4	2.4	3.7	2.7	3.3	2.8
Special	.9	.9	.5	.6	.8	1.2	.8	1.0	1.0	.8	.9	.6
General	.05	.07	.17	.07	.09	.14	.07	.05	.08	.1	.2	.2
315th Air Division a/												
Trials												
Summary	30	31	38	46	43	38	30	21	22	23	18	26
Special	7	6	20	17	15	23	30	13	10	22	14	12
General	-	-	-	-	-	-	-	-	-	-	-	-
Rates												
Summary	2.3	2.4	2.9	3.8	3.3	3.0	2.3	1.5	1.5	1.7	1.3	2.4
Special	.5	.5	1.5	1.6	1.1	1.8	2.3	.9	.7	1.6	1.0	1.1
General	-	-	-	-	-	-	-	-	-	-	-	-
19th Bomb Wing												
Trials												
Summary	8	11	14	8	18	18	16	23	13	26	16	11
Special	5	3	5	5	1	3	2	4	7	2	8	3
General	2	4	3	1	1	-	1	1	1		4	-
Rates												
Summary	1.5	2.1	2.6	1.5	3.3	3.3	3.0	2.8	1.6	3.0	1.8	2.1
Special	.9	.6	.9	.9	.2	.6	.4	.5	.8	.2	.9	.6
General	.4	.8	.6	.2	.2		.2	.1	.1		.4	

a/ FEALOGFOR and 315 Air Division under JADF for general court martial jurisdiction.
b/ 6000 B Sv. Gp under JADF for all courts martial jurisdiction.

Source: Personnel Statistics Division, Directorate of Statistical Services, DCS/C

TABLE 316 — AWOL AND MAN DAYS LOST FROM GOING AWOL IN FEAF — FY 1953

By Area	Jul (1952)	Aug	Sep	Oct	Nov	Dec	Jan (1953)	Feb	Mar	Apr	May	Jun
FEAF Overall												
Number going AWOL	131	131	124	139	160	126	135	136	175	158	150	146
Man Days Lost	505	561	580	455	624	496	556	424	765	714	808	421
AWOL Rate	1.3	1.1	1.1	1.1	1.3	.9	1.1	1.1	1.4	1.2	1.2	1.2
FEAF Base												
Number going AWOL	7	3	1	1	1	3	1	1	3	2	3	4
Man Days Lost	34	16	2	4	19	9	6	1	9	5	18	9
AWOL Rate	2.3	1.0	.3	.3	.3	1.0	.3	.3	1.0	.7	1.0	1.3
5th Air Force												
Number going AWOL	20	8	7	9	16	14	19	21	16	35	16	12
Man Days Lost	43	39	17	51	72	62	62	81	78	125	32	67
AWOL Rate	.5	.2	.2	.2	.4	.3	.4	.5	.4	.8	.4	.3
13th Air Force												
Number going AWOL	13	14	8	6	13	20	11	11	27	13	9	17
Man Days Lost	87	48	34	35	33	63	108	24	136	48	44	60
AWOL Rate	2.6	1.8	1.1	1.2	1.9	2.9	1.6	1.6	3.9	1.6	1.3	2.4
20th Air Force												
Number going AWOL	18	23	32	29	30	15	17	22	35	40	59	30
Man Days Lost	43	90	74	75	100	63	74	76	116	150	398	102
AWOL Rate	1.4	1.4	1.9	1.7	1.7	.9	1.0	1.3	1.9	2.3	3.3	1.8
JADF a/												
Number going AWOL	20	28	27	27	32	22	28	24	36	23	32	32
Man Days Lost	44	54	89	62	89	91	69	62	194	128	83	75
AWOL Rate	.8	1.1	.9	.9	1.1	.7	.9	.9	1.2	.7	1.1	1.0
315th Air Division												
Number going AWOL	22	23	27	34	34	25	35	24	24	17	11	16
Man Days Lost	82	82	69	132	159	90	88	73	85	51	19	43
AWOL Rate	2.0	2.1	2.7	3.1	3.4	2.3	3.2	2.1	2.2	1.5	1.0	1.4
FEALOGFOR												
Number going AWOL	31	32	22	33	34	27	24	33	34	28	20	35
Man Days Lost	172	232	295	96	152	118	149	107	147	207	214	65
AWOL Rate	2.8	2.3	1.6	2.4	2.1	1.7	1.3	2.4	2.6	2.3	1.7	3.5

a/ Includes BONCOM

Source: Personnel Statistics Division, Directorate of Statistical Services, DCS/C

TABLE 317 — OFFENSES COMMITTED BY MILITARY PERSONNEL BY MONTH, BY COMMAND, CONTINENTAL US — FY 1953

Offense and Date	USAF - TOTAL		CONT'L-TOTAL		CONTINENTAL US											
	Number	Rate Per 1,000	Number	Rate Per 1,000	ADC	AFFC	AMC	APG	ARDC	ATRC	AU	CONAC	HQC	MATS	SAC	TAC
Going Absent Without Leave (AWOL) (this month)																
July (1952)	5,967	6.59	5,564	8.40	446	-	271	65	83	2,669	62	634	88	180	703	363
August	5,443	5.88	5,050	5.10	406	-	265	60	85	2,449	52	530	45	216	623	319
September	5,428	5.87	5,060	7.72	426	-	221	55	97	2,469	43	542	42	275	604	286
October	4,677	5.03	4,340	6.59	387	-	200	39	98	1,903	47	487	50	236	587	306
November	4,112	4.38	3,742	5.75	363	-	176	35	92	1,620	28	406	42	201	538	241
December	4,544	4.93	4,205	5.60	444	-	201	29	123	1,560	38	580	32	277	595	326
January (1953)	4,978	5.37	4,547	7.14	404	-	228	63	128	1,994	48	587	29	217	538	311
February	3,420	3.70	3,083	4.87	297	-	94	33	82	1,261	38	404	28	150	403	293
March	3,818	4.11	3,465	5.43	326	-	141	33	106	1,429	34	460	29	176	459	272
April	3,753	4.00	3,448	5.40	354	-	106	32	100	1,438	34	420	27	105	526	306
May	3,748	4.04	3,426	5.41	388	-	117	22	95	1,428	29	443	22	131	496	255
June	4,098	4.46	3,749	5.89	374	-	119	51	82	1,607	29	401	14	131	594	347
Voluntarily Returned (this Month)																
July (1952)	3,945	4.36	3,603	5.44	296	-	198	49	64	1,671	50	375	81	132	422	265
August	3,623	3.91	3,312	5.09	253	-	176	51	60	1,614	39	271	32	167	408	241
September	4,019	4.34	3,689	5.62	297	-	169	57	71	1,801	35	355	41	208	430	225
October	3,409	3.66	3,151	4.78	270	-	150	32	67	1,389	35	366	29	168	417	228
November	2,821	4.38	2,522	3.87	251	-	126	25	73	1,054	31	292	30	155	346	139
December	2,772	3.00	2,496	3.91	306	-	139	28	73	917	26	320	19	170	324	174
January (1953)	4,048	4.35	3,652	5.73	329	-	190	49	123	1,543	45	452	24	201	443	253
February	2,411	2.60	2,126	3.36	195	-	76	26	52	875	33	266	18	108	271	206
March	2,605	2.80	2,334	3.65	216	-	104	30	69	978	27	290	21	122	278	199
April	2,574	2.74	2,330	3.64	236	-	79	22	66	1,020	25	253	17	81	317	214
May	2,551	2.74	2,264	3.57	298	-	83	14	58	1,022	24	224	17	84	281	159
June	2,612	2.84	2,336	3.66	275	-	88	33	59	1,027	9	221	12	88	342	132
Apprehended (this Month)																
July (1952)	1,104	1.20	1,056	1.56	81	-	62	4	12	595	8	104	8	21	100	61
August	944	1.00	881	1.34	71	-	40	-	12	405	6	194	4	18	74	57
September	756	4.90	717	1.09	93	-	25	4	11	300	11	80	10	56	85	42
October	765	.82	694	1.05	58	-	24	-	18	308	6	82	12	56	85	45
November	681	.72	625	.95	52	-	24	-	14	293	5	49	12	45	84	47
December	586	.63	531	.83	63	-	26	-	13	213	3	59	10	44	62	38
January (1953)	786	.84	745	1.16	82	-	27	4	14	354	2	86	7	44	79	46
February	591	.63	548	.86	47	-	14	3	20	237	3	69	8	49	54	44
March	668	.71	598	.93	59	-	23	3	18	245	4	72	7	26	96	45
April	622	.66	570	.89	63	-	13	-	28	223	2	63	6	32	94	46
May	576	.62	539	.85	59	-	13	2	9	194	1	65	3	30	101	62
June	771	.83	720	1.13	51	-	19	5	14	330	5	76	2	31	96	91

A. By Military Authority																
July (1952)	710	.78	665	1.00	57	-	31	4	9	346	5	98	5	10	63	37
August	682	.74	621	.96	41	-	30	-	9	242	5	185	3	11	48	47
September	523	.57	487	.74	59	-	16	3	6	188	8	69	9	43	59	27
October	510	.56	441	.67	33	-	11	-	10	189	5	61	6	35	60	31
November	446	.48	392	.60	31	-	13	-	11	172	4	38	6	37	55	25
December	410	.44	356	.56	45	-	16	-	9	131	1	51	9	33	31	30
January (1953)	514	.55	473	.74	48	-	14	3	8	220	2	65	5	34	44	30
February	386	.42	346	.55	27	-	8	1	9	153	2	57	6	32	26	25
March	460	.49	394	.62	35	-	17	1	7	174	3	38	7	20	61	31
April	385	.41	336	.53	31	-	8	-	23	125	1	48	2	16	57	25
May	382	.41	347	.55	30	-	9	1	5	133	1	42	2	12	65	47
June	514	.56	465	.73	23	-	8	3	9	214	5	55	1	21	68	58
B. By Civilian Authority																
July (1952)	376	.42	373	.56	24	-	31	-	5	229	3	6	3	11	37	24
August	252	.27	250	.38	20	-	10	-	3	163	1	9	1	7	26	10
September	243	.26	240	.37	34	-	9	1	5	122	3	11	1	13	26	15
October	255	.28	253	.38	25	-	13	-	8	119	1	21	6	21	25	14
November	235	.25	233	.36	21	-	11	-	3	121	1	11	6	8	29	22
December	177	.19	175	.27	18	-	10	-	4	82	2	8	1	11	31	8
January (1953)	272	.29	272	.42	34	-	13	1	6	134	-	21	2	10	35	16
February	205	.22	202	.32	20	-	6	2	11	84	1	12	2	17	28	19
March	208	.22	204	.33	24	-	6	2	11	71	1	34	-	6	35	14
April	237	.25	234	.37	32	-	5	-	5	98	1	15	4	16	37	21
May	194	.20	192	.30	29	-	4	1	4	61	-	23	1	18	36	15
June	257	.28	255	.40	28	-	11	2	5	116	-	21	1	10	28	33
Dropped from Rolls After 30 Days																
July (1952)	857	.94	834	1.25	60	-	36	10	17	377	4	134	11	18	110	57
August	805	.86	783	1.20	68	-	37	6	12	355	7	98	5	25	138	32
September	737	.79	727	1.10	71	-	32	6	17	309	-	99	4	34	126	29
October	851	.91	840	1.27	55	-	27	6	9	451	6	102	4	25	119	36
November	626	.66	616	.94	56	-	32	3	19	263	3	74	8	17	102	39
December	607	.65	592	.92	49	-	33	3	16	243	2	79	5	31	106	25
January (1953)	700	.75	682	.73	57	-	22	4	15	284	3	122	7	33	98	37
February	532	.57	522	.82	53	-	23	3	7	214	5	88	2	11	87	29
March	462	.49	455	.71	43	-	14	3	13	190	2	66	4	18	73	29
April	476	.50	465	.72	36	-	12	5	19	187	10	70	2	14	81	29
May	469	.50	465	.73	34	-	14	-	18	200	3	62	3	18	75	38
June	522	.56	514	.80	51	-	12	4	16	200	8	65	2	16	103	37
Man Days Lost Absent Without Leave (AWOL)																
July (1952)	64,206	70.96	61,912	93.46	4,616	-	2,982	617	1,201	29,514	494	7,176	738	2,017	9,526	3,031
August	59,900	64.71	57,826	88.97	4,881	-	3,013	525	1,001	26,605	386	6,262	437	2,307	9,526	2,883
September	59,966	64.90	58,045	88.55	4,660	-	2,159	688	1,023	28,153	240	5,542	559	2,645	8,341	4,035
October	54,989	59.08	53,088	80.60	4,410	-	2,414	461	1,285	24,469	279	5,102	461	2,438	8,604	3,165
November	43,829	46.73	41,854	64.26	3,892	-	1,690	340	1,187	17,957	243	3,648	585	2,306	6,984	3,020
December	47,338	51.34	45,524	71.41	4,106	-	2,032	372	1,292	17,883	299	6,369	372	2,151	7,190	3,418
January (1953)	52,835	56.98	50,708	79.63	4,374	-	2,196	638	1,500	21,375	369	6,618	275	2,497	6,850	4,016
February	36,958	39.93	35,617	56.29	3,463	-	1,090	466	1,241	14,820	273	4,578	219	1,937	4,392	3,138
March	37,302	40.19	35,490	55.60	3,373	-	1,475	548	1,234	14,955	218	3,982	310	1,358	4,467	3,570
April	36,531	38.91	34,911	54.64	3,201	-	1,023	337	1,082	15,058	336	4,129	245	761	5,606	3,133
May	39,978	43.06	38,268	60.48	3,929	-	1,202	224	1,115	15,462	353	4,819	235	1,570	6,238	3,121
June	43,634	47.48	42,126	66.14	4,378	-	1,070	727	963	17,955	308	4,405	203	1,433	6,856	3,828

TABLE 317 — OFFENSES COMMITTED BY MILITARY PERSONNEL BY MONTH, BY COMMAND, CONTINENTAL U S — FY 1953 (Continued)

Offense and Date	USAF - TOTAL		CONT'L-TOTAL		CONTINENTAL US											
	Number	Rate Per 1,000	Number	Rate Per 1,000	ADC	AFFC	AMC	APG	ARDC	ATRC	AU	CONAC	HQC	MATS	SAC	TAC
Drunkeness																
July (1952)	2,580	2.85	1,756	2.65	104	-	104	38	41	632	17	116	34	77	429	164
August	2,787	3.01	1,838	2.83	115	-	103	35	44	606	22	122	23	212	473	183
September	2,877	3.11	1,947	2.97	82	-	151	63	74	649	32	163	26	110	406	191
October	2,452	2.64	1,624	2.47	107	-	107	33	72	516	15	150	25	87	391	121
November	2,271	2.42	1,359	2.09	111	-	84	16	29	490	18	105	14	55	324	113
December	2,543	2.76	1,600	2.51	89	-	92	11	64	596	27	132	23	100	348	118
January (1953)	2,236	2.41	1,375	2.16	82	-	75	14	52	546	10	87	16	48	375	70
February	2,253	2.43	1,431	2.26	86	-	63	23	55	537	19	106	18	63	396	65
March	2,685	2.89	1,717	2.69	92	-	60	19	63	657	25	134	6	65	491	105
April	2,476	2.64	1,520	2.38	89	-	53	17	33	661	36	74	12	88	373	84
May	2,439	2.63	1,491	2.36	81	-	45	17	42	618	25	99	11	56	394	103
June	2,554	2.78	1,519	2.38	93	-	53	33	40	562	40	76	13	103	387	119
Serious Crimes																
July (1952)	414	.46	294	.44	12	-	1	1	3	223	2	2	3	8	33	6
August	355	.38	223	.34	10	-	4	-	8	150	2	1	1	9	27	11
September	358	.36	239	.36	5	-	1	-	3	182	1	7	-	5	27	8
October	410	.44	261	.40	19	-	2	1	3	156	-	2	1	6	68	3
Nobember	365	.39	265	.41	16	-	6	-	3	171	1	4	2	3	53	6
December	366	.40	226	.35	9	-	5	1	-	141	3	3	-	7	48	9
January (1953)	375	.40	262	.41	15	-	5	3	4	140	-	6	2	12	68	7
February	314	.33	230	.36	4	-	-	2	3	182	-	3	1	1	29	5
March	400	.43	298	.47	7	-	2	1	7	211	-	2	1	7	56	4
April	320	.33	257	.40	7	-	3	4	2	153	-	6	2	7	61	12
May	314	.34	247	.39	16	-	3	6	8	118	-	4	-	4	80	8
June	345	.38	270	.42	13	-	-	-	1	197	-	12	-	2	40	5
Offenders this Month																
July (1952)	22,370	24.72	16,513	24.93	1,725	-	769	201	364	6,923	137	1,461	282	442	2,936	1,273
August	22,475	24.28	15,941	24.53	1,593	-	733	234	463	7,086	147	1,160	201	691	2,394	1,239
September	23,200	25.09	16,950	25.86	1,635	-	700	234	543	6,820	140	1,260	201	772	2,103	1,542
October	21,723	23.36	14,937	22.68	1,175	-	674	161	490	5,875	114	1,480	133	744	2,933	1,158
November	19,253	20.53	13,075	20.07	1,170		485	149	306	5,378	109	971	149	779	2,721	858
December	18,509	20.07	12,554	19.69	1,030	-	530	112	380	5,256	122	967	181	569	2,549	867
January (1953)	19,232	20.74	13,439	21.10	1,051	-	530	170	492	6,004	77	873	107	641	2,602	892
February	18,543	20.04	12,346	19.51	974	-	386	112	469	5,348	84	802	140	597	2,422	1,012
March	21,167	22.81	14,722	23.06	1,118	-	500	125	466	6,121	110	946	322	770	2,961	1,283
April	19,209	20.46	13,288	20.80	1,086	-	383	148	407	6,132	106	1,007	326	100	2,559	1,034
May	19,715	21.23	13,421	21.21	1,068	-	367	127	361	5,640	103	1,083	117	768	2,634	1,153
June	20,248	22.03	13,526	21.24	834	-	380	162	391	5,742	104	792	60	684	3,111	1,266

Insubordinate Conduct																
July (1952)	1,250	1.38	426	.64	54	-	44	16	57	159	2	10	5	26	50	3
August	1,324	1.43	376	.58	28	-	54	26	52	165	2	4	-	15	19	11
September	1,422	1.54	408	.62	48	-	102	17	46	102	-	18	7	8	53	7
October	1,373	1.48	423	.64	42	-	157	20	15	109	1	13	3	3	43	17
November	1,093	1.17	323	.50	62	-	42	19	39	99	1	6	1	13	31	8
December	1,121	1.22	396	.62	43	-	47	11	72	152	-	9	3	12	36	11
January (1953)	1,266	1.37	411	.65	50	-	37	6	111	147	-	13	-	8	24	15
February	1,015	1.10	386	.61	54	-	55	-	82	129	-	9	1	9	30	17
March	1,005	1.08	432	.68	53	-	54	-	33	147	-	13	4	6	24	98
April	920	.98	407	.64	72	-	74	3	28	154	-	6	3	10	24	33
May	993	1.07	380	.60	52	-	51	-	38	170	-	16	8	4	32	9
June	1,026	1.12	333	.52	70	-	42	1	27	121	0	11	7	3	37	14
Larceny, House Breaking, Burglary, and Robbery																
July (1952)	968	1.07	816	1.23	24	-	5	1	22	690	1	2	11	4	33	23
August	872	.94	742	1.14	37	-	6	-	29	558	-	7	-	20	46	39
September	744	.81	616	.94	50	-	6	2	16	496	-	2	-	7	18	19
October	721	.78	597	.91	33	-	8	-	21	459	-	11	-	14	25	26
November	747	.80	628	.96	30	-	16	1	47	450	-	3	-	6	57	18
December	788	.85	599	.94	32	-	13	1	34	425	-	3	-	26	41	24
January (1953)	761	.82	641	1.01	59	-	9	-	18	410	3	10	-	37	57	38
February	821	.89	648	1.02	42	-	6	-	34	419	-	2	-	30	80	35
March	977	1.05	868	1.36	63	-	11	-	24	596	-	3	43	36	50	42
April	936	1.00	777	1.22	47	-	1	-	21	567	-	5	40	8	46	42
May	848	.91	701	1.11	35	-	5	5	7	567	-	8	5	5	40	30
June	791	.86	647	1.02	45	-	4	-	9	498	-	2	14	5	26	44
Selling, Disposing, or Destroying Military Property of USAF																
July (1952)	31	.03	19	.03	4	-	-	-	2	4	-	1	1	2	4	1
August	55	.06	26	.04	2	-	-	1	-	14	1	-	-	4	4	-
September	70	.08	37	.06	4	-	3	1	-	22	2	1	1	-	2	1
October	65	.07	40	.06	2	-	-	-	-	34	-	-	-	2	2	-
November	74	.08	46	.07	3	-	1	1	-	25	1	-	-	5	9	1
December	73	.08	39	.06	2	-	-	2	1	21	-	-	-	4	8	1
January (1953)	93	.10	54	.08	7	-	2	1	1	30	-	4	-	3	4	2
February	82	.09	40	.06	7	-	-	-	-	26	-	1	-	1	3	2
March	68	.07	50	.08	3	-	-	-	-	31	-	6	1	1	5	3
April	67	.07	43	.07	1	-	-	-	-	33	-	1	1	4	2	1
May	57	.06	37	.06	5	-	-	-	-	23	-	-	-	2	3	4
June	63	.07	36	.06	-	-	1	1	-	22	-	2	-	2	3	5
Sentenced Prisoners a/																
July (1952)	2,431	2.68	1,983	2.97	190	-	109	21	56	704	35	119	29	66	478	176
August	2,542	2.75	2,109	3.21	184	-	128	18	63	836	23	155	7	70	468	157
September	2,620	2.84	2,198	3.35	182	-	143	19	64	853	31	94	16	96	535	165
October	2,792	2.74	2,370	3.54	195	-	119	14	51	1,027	29	135	12	70	555	163
November	2,617	2.79	2,155	3.30	195	-	93	17	69	830	25	85	15	81	590	155
December	2,438	2.80	1,997	2.75	175	-	80	18	67	731	8	103	21	55	590	149
January (1953)	2,992	3.23	2,547	4.00	252	-	103	25	90	1,053	13	139	25	103	566	178
February	2,655	2.88	2,141	3.38	249	-	116	12	85	866	14	108	23	109	377	182
March	2,857	3.08	2,339	3.66	247	-	113	18	74	834	10	104	22	101	618	198
April	3,036	3.23	2,503	3.91	268	-	117	13	75	881	19	111	27	106	692	194
May	2,956	3.18	2,423	3.88	243	-	69	16	98	843	22	122	23	91	701	195
June	2,809	3.05	2,285	3.59	187	-	76	18	91	841	13	111	9	95	653	191

TABLE 317 – OFFENSES COMMITTED BY MILITARY PERSONNEL BY MONTH, BY COMMAND, CONTINENTAL U S – FY 1953 (Continued)

Offense and Date	USAF-TOTAL		CONT'L-TOTAL		CONTINENTAL US											
	Number	Rate Per 1,000	Number	Rate Per 1,000	ADC	AFFC	AMC	APG	ARDC	ATRC	AU	CONAC	HQC	MATS	SAC	TAC
Unsentenced Prisoners a/																
July (1952)	2,214	2.45	2,005	3.03	148	-	137	29	33	970	11	90	54	49	331	153
August	2,339	2.53	2,082	3.20	212	-	124	29	34	986	16	87	28	103	312	151
September	2,365	2.56	2,081	3.17	172	-	130	29	42	1,006	15	82	34	82	366	123
October	2,243	2.27	1,977	3.00	196	-	130	31	47	858	10	79	28	130	331	137
November	2,347	2.50	2,082	3.21	180	-	128	34	55	868	21	97	35	102	392	170
December	2,134	2.16	1,810	2.47	176	-	115	25	44	725	26	98	34	98	334	135
January (1953)	2,486	2.68	2,135	3.35	233	-	115	29	42	933	13	105	32	84	382	167
February	2,308	2.60	2,084	4.43	154	-	141	16	77	808	4	93	45	79	462	205
March	2,374	2.55	2,044	3.20	183	-	116	22	52	847	11	107	30	72	442	162
April	2,151	2.29	1,844	2.88	159	-	89	30	55	749	11	57	47	82	390	175
May	2,280	2.45	1,908	3.02	172	-	94	38	43	744	11	141	23	57	402	183
June	2,322	2.53	1,982	3.11	210	-	91	23	51	802	13	120	24	49	406	193
Number of Prisoners Detained From Other Services End-of-Month																
July (1952)	1,030	.	837	.	102	-	57	5	7	173	35	6	-	52	282	118
August	1,062	.	893	.	132	-	63	4	16	197	36	19	-	38	301	87
September	999	.	847	.	78	-	58	2	10	222	28	46	-	34	321	48
October	1,098	.	921	.	132	-	68	5	16	212	25	48	-	45	278	92
November	936	.	788	.	83	-	48	4	12	186	23	23	-	39	317	53
December	1,031	.	874	.	90	-	58	3	23	208	27	-	-	53	349	63
January (1953)	1,191	.	1,029	.	102	-	84	3	48	259	34	11	1	53	385	49
February	1,033	.	952	.	105	-	51	7	38	240	19	62	-	27	349	54
March	1,025	.	973	.	83	-	53	4	6	302	15	58	-	28	351	73
April	972	.	896	.	104	-	57	10	15	251	12	50	-	21	295	81
May	1,006	.	939	.	105	-	57	9	6	285	21	75	-	27	300	54
June	1,091	.	990	.	91	-	47	11	21	319	18	49	-	65	313	56
Number of Prisoners in Minimum Custody at End-of-Month																
July (1952)	1,787	1.98	1,486	2.24	154	-	79	15	38	635	5	83	20	29	302	126
August	1,864	2.01	1,559	2.40	129	-	81	8	43	725	4	148	13	34	276	98
September	2,124	2.30	1,778	2.71	138	-	99	11	54	775	10	117	19	72	367	116
October	2,066	2.22	1,826	2.77	157	-	97	16	41	721	7	163	13	56	427	128
November	2,230	2.37	1,931	2.96	159	-	83	13	49	770	14	97	18	92	499	137
December	1,854	2.01	1,575	2.47	110	-	75	18	30	567	16	111	19	61	448	120
January (1953)	2,259	2.44	1,996	3.13	184	-	82	27	39	870	8	142	20	63	446	115
February	2,040	2.20	1,723	2.72	158	-	119	21	35	625	10	117	23	59	445	111
March	2,169	2.34	1,845	2.89	171	-	112	14	56	715	3	134	25	74	415	126
April	2,153	2.29	1,843	2.88	160	-	95	11	47	676	21	133	23	82	456	139
May	2,098	2.26	1,780	2.81	159	-	89	29	52	694	8	138	13	53	404	141
June	2,055	2.21	1,706	2.70	152	-	82	13	56	636	8	122	15	72	423	127

Number of Prisoners in Medium Custody at End-of-Month																
July (1952)	2,562	2.83	2,167	3.27	208	-	133	32	49	868	38	96	61	92	419	171
August	2,660	2.87	2,303	3.54	213	-	167	36	55	935	32	77	22	111	485	170
September	2,635	2.85	2,244	3.42	163	-	147	35	51	933	32	64	34	90	533	162
October	2,599	2.79	2,194	3.33	184	-	101	20	49	903	25	72	42	83	514	201
November	2,473	2.64	2,057	3.15	176	-	121	33	62	788	30	70	41	73	468	195
December	2,417	2.62	1,983	3.11	208	-	94	19	63	704	13	72	41	63	568	138
January (1953)	2,924	3.15	2,411	3.78	251	-	99	24	81	923	14	92	54	66	600	207
February	2,803	3.02	2,321	3.67	220	-	108	10	114	811	11	76	45	101	584	241
March	2,756	2.97	2,271	3.56	226	-	110	19	59	740	8	65	29	81	706	228
April	2,806	2.99	2,301	3.60	234	-	104	30	72	753	14	85	50	96	653	210
May	2,780	2.99	2,234	3.53	221	-	64	23	73	660	20	99	32	86	720	236
June	2,832	3.08	2,326	3.65	221	-	72	25	63	800	24	101	18	70	685	247
Number of Prisoners in Maximum Custody at End-of-Month																
July (1952)	570	.63	469	.71	25	-	38	3	2	214	3	30	2	10	120	22
August	587	.63	456	.70	21	-	31	3	1	176	3	17	-	14	168	22
September	729	.79	631	.96	33	-	56	2	1	209	4	24	-	12	267	23
October	683	.73	605	.91	26	-	50	10	7	210	4	22	-	10	261	5
November	683	.73	610	.93	24	-	34	7	15	180	2	18	-	9	311	10
December	708	.76	620	.97	27	-	39	8	24	209	3	18	-	17	249	26
January (1953)	759	.82	666	1.04	33	-	49	4	14	187	7	10	-	6	312	44
February	840	.91	749	1.18	22	-	43	4	16	253	16	9	-	6	333	47
March	778	.84	683	1.00	29	-	17	7	11	231	26	12	-	10	320	20
April	704	.74	599	.94	19	-	17	12	15	201	7	23	1	4	271	29
May	826	.89	739	1.17	29	-	24	8	16	238	9	20	1	15	364	15
June	698	.76	613	.96	28	-	25	12	26	218	-	14	-	13	264	13
Security Violations (Safe Guarding)																
July (1952)	501	.55	414	.62	35	-	88	-	46	20	1	27	-	3	183	11
August	446	.48	362	.55	16	5	68	-	62	11	-	26	-	6	159	9
September	551	.59	433	.66	29	3	117	-	57	25	-	24	1	6	168	3
October	547	.58	467	.70	33	32	114	-	55	17	1	30	2	10	168	5
November	496	.52	430	.66	39	2	94	-	58	20	-	21	8	12	176	-
December	540	.58	487	.76	53	3	123	3	40	36	-	26	4	19	180	-
January (1953)	600	.64	417	.65	30	2	91	3	58	23	-	21	20	17	151	1
February	423	.45	317	.50	-	49	86	-	27	60	-	39	10	-	14	32
March	433	.46	354	.55	24	5	71	-	81	49	-	15	11	22	68	8
April	337	.35	270	.42	34	2	87	2	44	29	-	20	3	13	35	1
May	358	.38	264	.41	23	-	92	1	54	21	-	26	5	6	32	4
June	334	.36	263	.41	27	-	74	-	57	27	-	26	2	14	34	2
Security Violations (Military Areas)																
July (1952)	126	.13	74	.11	24	-	1	-	1	3	-	-	-	5	26	14
August	185	.23	131	.20	6	-	3	-	2	6	-	-	-	4	108	2
September	184	.19	121	.18	8	-	2	-	4	3	-	-	-	-	104	-
October	209	.22	140	.21	6	-	3	-	6	4	-	2	-	2	117	-
November	137	.14	85	.13	13	-	2	-	-	4	-	-	-	1	65	-
December	189	.20	135	.21	10	-	1	-	-	6	-	-	-	2	116	-
January (1953)	103	.11	81	.12	7	-	-	-	1	8	-	-	-	-	64	1
February	123	.13	85	.13	5	-	-	-	2	5	-	-	-	4	69	-
March	172	.18	128	.20	24	-	5	-	2	9	-	2	-	2	84	-
April	165	.17	68	.10	4	-	-	-	5	24	-	-	-	-	35	-
May	169	.18	50	.07	8	-	-	-	5	7	-	-	-	1	28	1
June	156	.24	44	.06	1	-	-	-	10	7	-	-	-	2	24	-

TABLE 317 — OFFENSES COMMITTED BY MILITARY PERSONNEL BY MONTH, BY COMMAND, CONTINENTAL U S — FY 1953 (Continued)

Offense Date	USAF-TOTAL		CONT'L-TOTAL		CONTINENTAL US											
	Number	Rate Per 1,000	Number	Rate Per 1,000	ADC	AFFC	AMC	APG	ARDC	ATRC	AU	CONAC	HQC	MATS	SAC	TAC
Total AF Personnel Punished Under Article 15																
July (1952)	8,740	9.66	6,078	9.18	544	-	260	55	139	2,825	40	444	125	237	942	447
August	9,259	10.00	6,459	9.94	586	-	376	69	104	2,801	75	395	58	305	889	801
September	9,161	9.91	6,338	9.67	617	-	311	81	177	2,767	62	463	92	315	880	573
October	8,932	9.61	5,849	8.88	521	-	290	69	174	2,581	50	491	81	261	957	374
November	7,938	8.46	5,068	7.78	551	-	213	37	145	2,349	51	234	64	283	797	344
December	7,079	7.68	4,107	6.44	444	-	237	24	203	1,835	85	344	52	227	365	291
January (1953)	7,896	8.52	5,182	8.14	432	-	246	24	214	2,183	73	389	46	311	937	327
February	7,580	8.19	4,824	7.62	375	-	201	22	175	2,253	32	338	51	209	873	295
March	8,289	8.93	5,241	8.21	509	-	202	33	170	2,457	82	287	46	221	910	324
April	7,981	8.50	4,940	7.73	491	-	204	34	152	2,257	7	348	30	230	877	310
May	8,162	8.79	5,155	8.15	514	-	187	36	182	2,339	48	321	55	204	957	312
June	8,120	8.85	5,203	8.18	559	-	197	32	143	2,293	48	252	63	234	1,046	336

a/ Previously reported under General Prisoners.
b/ Previously reported under Garrison Prisoners.

Source: Executive Office, Director, Air Provost Marshal, Hq, USAF

TABLE 318 – OFFENSES COMMITTED BY MILITARY PERSONNEL BY MONTH, BY COMMAND, OVERSEAS – FY 1953

Offense and Date	TOTAL		OVERSEAS						
	Number	Rate Per 1,000	AAC	CairC	FEAF	MATS	NEAC	SAC	USAFE
Going Absent Without Leave (AWOL) (this month)									
July (1952)	403	1.66	61	1	131	40	22	20	128
August	393	1.43	65	1	131	29	11	21	135
September	368	1.37	46	2	124	32	15	20	129
October	337	1.24	41	-	139	13	14	15	115
November	370	1.29	38	-	160	11	12	13	136
December	339	1.19	45	1	126	14	13	31	109
January (1953)	431	1.48	70	1	135	14	13	27	171
February	337	1.15	31	2	136	10	10	21	127
March	353	1.22	33	1	175	5	15	21	103
April	305	1.02	21	3	158	11	5	18	89
May	322	1.09	29	2	150	15	9	25	92
June	349	1.24	25	1	146	9	16	10	142
Voluntarily Returned (this month)									
July (1952)	342	1.41	46	-	100	34	19	17	126
August	311	1.13	53	1	108	25	5	17	102
September	330	1.23	52	1	104	30	9	19	115
October	258	1.95	35	1	88	15	14	13	92
November	299	1.04	25	-	117	9	11	12	125
December	276	1.19	33	1	99	9	8	24	102
January (1953)	396	1.32	71	1	111	14	12	35	152
February	285	.97	26	2	112	9	7	19	110
March	271	.93	29	1	116	5	15	15	90
April	244	.81	15	2	120	7	7	14	79
May	287	.97	30	2	133	12	8	23	79
June	276	.97	24	1	113	5	8	7	118
Apprehended (this month)									
July (1952)	48	1.19	3	1	20	5	3	6	10
August	63	.25	2	-	23	5	7	3	23
September	39	.13	4	-	14	2	2	1	16
October	71	.25	1	-	45	3	3	1	18
November	56	.19	2	-	34	3	2	1	14
December	55	.19	2	-	29	7	2	3	12
January (1953)	41	.14	1	-	25	-	1	4	10
February	43	.15	2	-	26	-	-	2	13
March	70	.24	4	-	47	-	2	6	11
April	52	.17	1	1	28	3	1	4	14
May	37	.16	1	-	21	3	3	-	9
June	51	.18	2	-	24	3	4	3	13
A. By Military Authorities									
July (1952)	45	.19	3	-	20	5	2	5	10
August	61	.22	1	-	22	5	7	3	23
September	36	.13	4	-	14	2	2	1	13
October	69	.25	1	-	45	3	3	-	17
November	54	.19	2	-	34	3	2	1	12
December	54	.22	2	-	29	6	2	3	12
January (1953)	41	.14	1	-	25	-	1	4	10
February	40	.13	-	-	26	-	-	1	13
March	66	.22	3	-	47	-	2	5	9
April	49	.16	1	-	28	3	1	3	13
May	35	.12	1	-	21	3	3	-	7
June	49	.17	2	-	26	3	4	1	13
B. By Civilian Authorities									
July (1952)	3	.01	-	1	-	-	1	1	-
August	2	.01	1	-	1	-	-	-	-
September	3	.01	-	-	-	-	-	-	3
October	2	.01	-	-	-	-	-	1	1
November	2	.01	-	-	-	-	-	-	2
December	2	.01	1	-	-	1	-	-	-
January (1953)	-	-	-	-	-	-	-	-	-
February	3	.01	2	-	-	-	-	1	-
March	4	.01	1	-	-	-	-	1	2
April	3	.01	-	1	-	-	-	1	1
May	2	.01	-	-	-	-	-	-	2
June	2	.01	-	-	-	-	-	2	-
Dropped From Rolls After 30 Days									
July (1952)	23	.09	10	-	9	2	1	1	-
August	22	.08	11	-	2	1	1	-	7
September	10	.08	3	-	3	1	1	-	2
October	11	.04	1	-	4	1	2	-	3
November	10	.03	4	-	2	-	1	2	1
December	15	.05	9	-	3	-	1	-	2

308700 O - 54 - 36

TABLE 318 — OFFENSES COMMITTED BY MILITARY PERSONNEL BY MONTH, BY COMMAND, OVERSEAS — FY 1953 (Continued)

Offense and Date	TOTAL		OVERSEAS						
	Number	Rate Per 1,000	AAC	CairC	FEAF	MATS	NEAC	SAC	USAFE
Dropped From Rolls After 30 Days (Continued)									
January (1953)	18	.06	8	-	5	1	2	2	-
February	10	.03	4	-	2	-	3	1	-
March	7	.03	-	-	3	1	1	1	1
April	11	.04	2	-	2	-	3	-	4
May	4	.01	-	-	-	-	1	1	2
June	8	.03	1	-	2	-	1	2	2
Man Days Lost Absent Without Leave (AWOL)									
July (1952)	2,294	9.46	745	9	505	112	157	186	580
August	2,074	7.52	575	2	561	128	74	108	626
September	1,921	7.15	287	11	580	116	153	54	720
October	1,851	6 83	413	6	455	60	257	101	559
November	1,975	6.89	458	-	624	59	108	95	631
December	1,814	6.37	535	-	496	45	132	143	463
January (1953)	2,127	7.32	567	1	556	56	201	150	596
February	1,341	4.58	223	8	424	33	118	183	352
March	1,812	6.25	150	3	765	26	143	165	560
April	1,620	5.40	162	12	722	65	108	86	465
May	1,710	5.78	129	3	808	45	40	139	546
June	1,508	5.35	192	-	421	39	127	121	608
Drunkenness									
July (1952)	824	3.40	64	20	57	409	179	47	48
August	949	3.44	32	11	82	423	305	57	39
September	930	3.46	35	12	67	381	331	50	54
October	828	3.05	25	6	71	339	319	32	36
November	912	3.18	39	11	84	411	260	55	52
December	943	3.31	41	7	95	360	380	54	6
January (1953)	861	2.96	38	5	48	356	333	47	34
February	822	2.81	38	8	40	368	269	43	56
March	968	3.34	53	8	50	448	317	30	62
April	956	3.19	39	5	42	396	326	68	80
May	948	3.21	38	6	71	470	251	45	67
June	1,035	3.62	57	8	101	490	255	52	72
Serious Crimes									
July (1952)	120	.49	10	-	41	25	7	8	29
August	132	.47	13	-	68	16	1	1	33
September	119	.44	10	-	41	12	10	5	41
October	149	.54	12	-	69	23	-	4	41
November	100	.34	8	-	41	4	-	11	36
December	140	.49	4	-	68	22	5	6	35
January (1953)	113	.39	4	-	38	21	2	4	44
February	84	.29	5	1	28	17	2	6	25
March	102	.35	16	-	30	24	2	6	24
April	63	.21	4	-	16	27	1	9	6
May	67	.23	8	-	22	10	7	10	10
June	75	.27	6	-	29	5	8	14	13
Offenders this Month									
July (1952)	5,857	24.15	426	84	2,379	477	339	300	1,852
August	6,534	22.70	474	67	2,811	1,046	226	187	1,723
September	6,250	23.20	445	54	2,973	648	325	180	1,625
October	6,786	25.02	466	32	3,131	755	225	141	2,036
November	6,178	21.56	413	41	2,599	635	321	220	1,949
December	5,955	20.92	341	39	2,363	509	284	189	2,230
January (1953)	5,793	19.95	272	40	2,623	415	246	228	1,969
February	6,197	21.16	335	47	2,295	290	489	272	2,453
March	6,445	22.24	360	53	2,713	353	327	267	2,372
April	5,921	19.75	314	42	2,589	316	345	335	1,980
May	6,294	21.29	330	35	2,493	425	231	377	2,405
June	6,722	23.83	373	57	2,620	433	316	340	2,583
Insubordinate Conduct									
July (1952)	824	3.40	5	29	618	28	1	2	141
August	948	3.44	13	28	714	11	8	2	172
September	1,014	3.78	16	15	776	13	5	5	184
October	950	3.50	5	9	838	8	4	5	81
November	770	2.69	2	9	591	53	7	4	104
December	725	2.55	6	15	593	35	4	3	69
January (1953)	855	2.94	4	17	772	12	5	1	44
February	629	2.15	16	15	528	25	7	4	34
March	573	1.98	4	8	453	31	4	9	64
April	513	1.71	3	14	421	17	4	16	38
May	613	2.07	2	14	439	21	7	5	125
June	693	2.46	6	10	531	52	8	8	78

TABLE 318 — OFFENSES COMMITTED BY MILITARY PERSONNEL BY MONTH, BY COMMAND, OVERSEAS — FY 1953 (Continued)

Offense and Date	TOTAL		OVERSEAS						
	Number	Rate Per 1,000	AAC	CairC	FEAF	MATS	NEAC	SAC	USAFE
Larceny, House Breaking, Burglary, and Robbery									
July (1952)	152	.63	5	-	97	2	6	1	41
August	130	.47	15	1	65	8	4	2	35
September	128	.48	9	-	57	12	13	3	34
October	124	.46	8	-	66	7	10	3	30
November	119	.42	3	-	45	4	17	11	39
December	189	.66	4	-	87	9	49	4	36
January (1953)	120	.41	10	-	65	6	4	3	32
February	173	.59	15	-	85	10	29	6	28
March	109	.38	19	1	63	3	1	-	22
April	159	.53	15	-	96	1	6	3	38
May	147	.50	13	-	96	2	2	2	32
June	144	.51	9	-	39	7	26	3	60
Selling, Disposing or Destroying Military Property of USAF									
July (1952)	12	.05	1	-	3	-	-	-	8
August	29	.11	8	-	12	1	-	4	4
September	33	.12	5	-	15	3	-	2	8
October	25	.09	1	-	14	-	-	-	10
November	28	.10	2	-	12	2	3	-	9
December	34	.12	10	-	11	3	1	1	8
January (1953)	39	.13	3	-	5	3	3	4	21
February	42	.14	8	-	20	-	3	-	11
March	18	.06	2	-	13	-	2	-	1
April	24	.08	2	-	6	-	3	3	10
May	20	.07	-	-	12	2	-	2	4
June	27	.10	-	-	9	-	6	3	9
Sentenced Prisoners a/									
July (1952)	448	1.84	36	4	174	19	16	28	171
August	433	1.57	33	6	168	19	16	32	159
September	422	1.57	46	2	175	21	14	22	142
October	422	1.58	38	1	167	16	9	46	145
November	462	1.61	39	1	144	17	4	93	164
December	441	1.54	25	1	194	25	3	59	134
January (1953)	445	1.53	24	2	166	14	6	67	166
February	514	1.75	30	3	199	18	8	83	173
March	518	1.78	35	1	198	11	15	77	181
April	533	1.77	16	3	249	7	11	74	173
May	533	1.80	27	1	213	14	18	106	154
June	524	1.85	14	1	246	20	14	71	158
Unsentenced Prisoners b/									
July (1952)	209	.86	19	6	82	21	12	11	58
August	257	.93	29	4	104	28	16	5	71
September	284	1.05	19	-	120	38	16	7	84
October	266	.98	30	1	92	36	15	7	85
November	265	.92	18	1	95	30	11	12	98
December	324	1.13	19	-	171	16	8	12	98
January (1953)	351	1.20	22	4	219	16	8	6	76
February	224	.76	22	1	57	16	10	16	102
March	330	1.13	24	2	172	9	7	19	97
April	307	1.02	28	-	146	8	13	14	98
May	372	1.25	23	1	198	8	11	11	120
June	340	1.20	26	3	148	5	12	19	127
Number of Prisoners Detained From Other Services End-of-Month									
July (1952)	193	.80	11	-	131	1	1	8	41
August	169	.61	18	-	98	-	3	7	43
September	152	.57	17	-	89	1	2	7	36
October	177	.65	34	-	82	2	2	5	52
November	148	.52	18	-	68	1	7	15	39
December	157	.55	14	-	88	1	8	22	24
January (1953)	162	.56	25	-	62	7	1	36	31
February	81	.28	12	-	3	-	3	29	34
March	52	.18	7	-	3	2	5	10	25
April	76	.25	12	-	-	2	7	24	31
May	67	.23	14	-	2	1	3	35	12
June	101	.36	20	-	7	2	15	29	28
Number of Prisoners in Minimum Custody at End-of-Month									
July (1952)	301	1.24	17	2	156	15	14	21	76
August	305	1.11	21	4	160	20	17	24	59

TABLE 318 – OFFENSES COMMITTED BY MILITARY PERSONNEL BY MONTH, BY COMMAND, OVERSEAS – FY 1953 (Continued)

Offense and Date	TOTAL		OVERSEAS						
	Number	Rate Per 1,000	AAC	CairC	FEAF	MATS	NEAC	SAC	USAFE
Number of Prisoners in Minimum Custody at End-of-Month (Continued)									
September	346	1.29	20	2	170	21	21	16	96
October	240	.88	25	2	112	16	13	13	59
November	299	1.04	19	2	114	23	11	46	84
December	279	.98	16	1	154	12	7	44	45
January (1953)	263	.56	22	6	122	13	3	32	65
February	317	1.08	18	3	146	12	11	55	72
March	324	1.18	36	2	149	8	-	38	91
April	310	1.03	15	3	147	5	14	48	78
May	318	1.07	11	2	186	4	16	48	51
June	349	1.24	6	4	189	9	22	49	70
Number of Prisoners in Medium Custody at End-of-Month									
July (1952)	395	1.62	13	8	163	21	14	13	163
August	357	1.30	18	6	144	23	18	11	137
September	391	1.46	26	-	151	36	8	13	157
October	405	1.49	23	-	124	34	10	33	181
November	416	1.45	20	-	111	20	8	62	195
December	434	1.52	20	-	171	17	4	57	165
January (1953)	513	1.77	38	-	207	14	12	78	164
February	482	1.65	30	1	165	18	9	79	180
March	485	1.67	33	1	174	10	13	75	179
April	505	1.68	34	-	184	8	15	83	181
May	546	1.84	32	-	173	14	14	102	211
June	506	1.79	47	-	149	15	17	64	214
Number of Prisoners in Maximum Custody at End-of-Month									
July (1952)	101	.41	36	-	31	-	-	7	27
August	131	.48	41	-	40	3	-	9	38
September	98	.36	29	-	43	4	-	3	19
October	78	.28	24	-	23	2	-	4	25
November	73	.25	24	-	14	4	-	3	28
December	88	.30	12	-	38	4	-	1	33
January (1953)	93	.32	9	-	56	2	-	1	25
February	91	.31	5	-	45	3	-	4	34
March	95	.33	7	-	47	2	10	3	26
April	105	.36	3	-	64	2	-	3	33
May	87	.29	9	-	52	3	-	4	19
June	85	.30	-	-	56	2	-	6	21
Security Violations (Safeguarding)									
July (1952)	87	.35	2	-	3	28	43	11	-
August	84	.30	5	-	6	40	25	5	3
September	118	.43	2	-	10	50	46	7	3
October	80	.29	4	-	10	36	12	11	7
November	66	.23	1	-	1	28	27	5	4
December	53	.18	5	-	9	17	18	4	-
January (1953)	183	.63	8	-	12	105	45	11	2
February	106	.36	1	-	6	51	25	20	3
March	79	.27	12	-	9	23	27	6	2
April	67	.22	5	1	2	28	13	16	2
May	94	.31	25	-	1	33	30	3	2
June	71	.25	6	-	4	20	34	7	-
Security Violations (Military Areas)									
July (1952)	52	.21	7	-	-	10	22	12	1
August	54	.19	1	-	4	3	41	5	-
September	63	.23	3	-	2	35	22	1	-
October	69	.25	1	-	2	41	22	3	-
November	52	.18	4	-	-	25	14	9	-
December	54	.18	-	-	-	45	9	-	-
January (1953)	22	.07	2	-	-	11	9	-	-
February	38	.12	1	-	-	27	8	2	-
March	44	.15	4	-	2	32	5	-	1
April	97	.32	5	-	2	37	49	4	-
May	119	.40	12	-	-	61	38	8	-
June	112	.39	11	-	-	55	36	10	-

TABLE 318 — OFFENSES COMMITTED BY MILITARY PERSONNEL BY MONTH, BY COMMAND, OVERSEAS — FY 1953 (Continued)

Offense and Date	TOTAL		OVERSEAS						
	Number	Rate Per 1,000	AAC	CairC	FEAF	MATS	NEAC	SAC	USAFE
Air Force Personnel Punished Under Article 15									
July (1952)	2,662	10.98	286	36	1,185	153	72	126	804
August	2,800	10.16	269	30	1,343	269	73	99	717
September	2,823	10.51	239	17	1,415	244	79	87	742
October	3,083	11.37	274	12	1,491	196	95	92	923
November	2,870	10.02	244	11	1,330	193	85	142	865
December	2,972	10.44	239	19	1,259	176	106	148	1,025
January (1953)	2,714	9.35	222	21	1,306	101	79	126	859
February	2,756	9.41	305	18	1,105	84	96	177	971
March	3,048	10.52	284	16	1,262	87	96	166	1,137
April	3,041	10.14	225	13	1,434	118	101	204	946
May	3,007	10.17	233	9	1,394	127	89	146	1,009
June	2,917	10.34	231	17	1,312	107	92	184	974

a/ Previously reported under General Prisoners.
b/ Previously reported under Garrison Prisoners.

Source: Executive Office, Director, Air Provost Marshal, Hq USAF.

TABLE 319 —GOING AWOL AND MAN DAYS LOST (AWOL) SUMMARY – LAST HALF FY 1947 THROUGH FY 1953

(FY 1947 through April 1952 rates are based on the number of AWOL cases and Man-Days Lost against the average command strength chargeable to the Commanding General as of the end of the month. May and June (1952) rates are based on daily strengths as defined in the introduction of this area. A few civilians are included in FY 1947 data, but so few that they make no significant difference in the rates.)

Date	Number	Rate per 1,000 per Quarter	Date	Number	Rate per 1,000 per Quarter
GOING AWOL			MAN DAYS LOST (AWOL)		
CONTINENTAL US					
FY 1947 (Last Half) a/					
Third Quarter	6,929	32.7			
Fourth Quarter	5,789	28.7			
FY 1948			FY 1948		
First Quarter	6,543	30.3	First Quarter	99,992	463.1
Second Quarter	6,628	29.0	Second Quarter	97,910	428.8
Third Quarter	7,452	30.4	Third Quarter	90,401	368.4
Fourth Quarter	8,579	34.8	Fourth Quarter	103,717	420.5
FY 1949			FY 1949		
First Quarter	8,471	33.4	First Quarter	107,329	423.0
Second Quarter b/	6,303	24.3	Second Quarter b/	85,593	329.9
Third Quarter	5,861	20.4	Third Quarter	69,797	243.3
Fourth Quarter	5,550	19.2	Fourth Quarter	62,143	215.1
FY 1950			FY 1950		
First Quarter	7,929	25.6	First Quarter	79,089	255.0
Second Quarter	7,421	23.0	Second Quarter	84,368	261.4
Third Quarter	7,323	22.8	Third Quarter	77,008	239.6
Fourth Quarter	6,920	21.9	Fourth Quarter	77,722	245.6
FY 1951			FY 1951		
First Quarter	6,658	19.5	First Quarter	92,096	270.1
Second Quarter	6,335	15.5	Second Quarter	81,122	199.2
Third Quarter	6,530	12.8	Third Quarter	76,985	150.7
Fourth Quarter	8,014	13.4	Fourth Quarter	90,911	152.3
OVERSEAS c/					
FY 1950			FY 1950		
Third Quarter	826	9.0	Third Quarter	4,194	45.9
Fourth Quarter	755	10.4	Fourth Quarter	4,291	46.7
FY 1951			FY 1951		
First Quarter	815	7.7	First Quarter	3,748	35.3
Second Quarter	959	7.6	Second Quarter	4,556	35.9
Third Quarter	1,148	8.2	Third Quarter	5,241	37.5
Fourth Quarter	842	5.8	Fourth Quarter	4,250	29.5
WORLDWIDE					
FY 1952			FY 1952		
First Quarter	11,104	14.2	First Quarter	111,841	142.8
Second Quarter	12,199	14.7	Second Quarter	128,157	154.7
Third Quarter	13,442	15.5	Third Quarter	143,418	165.0
Fourth Quarter d/	14,887	17.5	Fourth Quarter d/	157,602	185.6
CONTINENTAL US					
FY 1952			FY 1952		
First Quarter	10,215	16.4	First Quarter	107,233	172.0
Second Quarter	11,159	17.5	Second Quarter	121,731	191.4
Third Quarter	12,426	18.6	Third Quarter	137,935	206.2
Fourth Quarter	12,381	19.1	Fourth Quarter	152,301	235.6
OVERSEAS					
FY 1952			FY 1952		
First Quarter	889	5.6	First Quarter	4,608	28.9
Second Quarter	1,040	5.4	Second Quarter	5,886	30.7
Third Quarter	1,016	4.9	Third Quarter	5,482	26.7
Fourth Quarter d/	854	4.2	Fourth Quarter d/	5,301	26.1

TABLE 319 – GOING AWOL AND MAN DAYS LOST (AWOL) SUMMARY – LAST HALF FY 1947 THROUGH FY 1953 (CONTINUED)

Date	Number	Rate per 1,000 per Quarter	Date	Number	Rate per 1,000 per Quarter
GOING AWOL			MAN DAYS LOST (AWOL)		
WORLDWIDE					
FY 1953					
Total	54,086	-	Total	577,389	-
First Quarter.	16,938	6.15	First Quarter	184,072	66.82
Second Quarter	13,332	4.78	Second Quarter.	146,106	52.37
Third Quarter.	12,216	4.39	Third Quarter	127,068	44.61
Fourth Quarter	11,600	4.16	Fourth Quarter.	120,143	43.12
CONTINENTAL US					
FY 1953					
Total	49,779	-	Total	555,369	-
First Quarter.	15,774	8.02	First Quarter	177,783	90.35
Second Quarter	12,287	6.29	Second Quarter.	140,466	72.12
Third Quarter.	11,095	5.82	Third Quarter	121,815	63.85
Fourth Quarter	10,623	5.56	Fourth Quarter.	115,305	60.41
OVERSEAS					
FY 1953					
Total	4,307	-	Total	22,020	-
First Quarter.	1,164	1.48	First Quarter	6,289	7.99
Second Quarter	1,045	1.24	Second Quarter.	5,640	6.54
Third Quarter.	1,121	1.21	Third Quarter	5,253	6.01
Fourth Quarter	977	1.11	Fourth Quarter.	4,838	5.51

a/ First and Second Quarters of FY 1947 were not available.
b/ November 1948 Tactical Air Command Report was not received.
c/ Information for Overseas was not available prior to Third Quarter 1950.
d/ June 1952 report for FEAF was not received.

Source: Executive Office, Director, Air Provost Marshal, Hq, USAF.

TABLE 320 — GOVERNMENT PROPERTY LOST OR STOLEN BY MILITARY PERSONNEL - FY 1953

Date	Total USAF	CONTINENTAL US					
		Total	Air Defense Command	Air Force Finance Center	Air Materiel Command	Air Proving Ground Command	Air Research and Development Command
Total . . .	$1,132,248.09	$525,214.90	$31,394.69	-	$84,670.50	$5,740.28	$15,883.31
July (1952). . .	101,513.01	39,341.85	1,655.78	-	10,031.38	22.50	1,831.71
August	98,411.54	38,880.70	4,274.29	-	2,572.30	66.17	725.51
September. . . .	132,637.03	39,986.34	4,323.16	-	5,664.12	385.21	1,436.99
October.	87,958.37	41,367.96	3,802.36	-	4,322.64	463.00	707.31
November	106,543.20	47,716.11	5,186.75	-	8,444.49	50.00	3,336.04
December	77,448.31	34,682.80	1,689.42	-	3,222.88	290.24	744.04
January (1953) .	83,314.73	45,712.02	1,448.96	-	6,230.85	237.25	1,293.00
February	69,343.35	27,989.85	1,273.46	-	2,160.11	74.69	635.00
March.	105,081.11	55,695.01	1,339.92	-	27,691.64	184.00	941.00
April.	122,180.93	79,340.35	1,384.33	-	2,844.08	2,600.00	1,085.09
May.	73,316.89	32,361.95	834.86	-	8,344.76	965.22	507.00
June	74,499.62	42,539.96	4,181.40	-	3,141.25	402.00	2,640.62

Date	CONTINENTAL US (Continued)						
	Air Training Command	Air University	Continental Air Command	Headquarters Command USAF	Military Air Transport Service	Strategic Air Command	Tactical Air Command
Total . . .	$178,824.82	$3,192.35	$9,498.33	$5,991.89	$10,753.46	$142,156.90	$37,108.37
July (1952). . .	10,091.24	119.50	2,482.89	266.50	1,176.08	8,385.85	3,278.42
August	8,523.98	126.36	464.69	-	1,161.72	17,548.22	3,417.46
September. . . .	8,961.27	426.20	215.14	-	976.73	12,902.40	4,695.12
October.	12,881.87	463.00	753.19	32.00	951.30	14,971.30	2,019.99
November	9,830.19	230.08	650.94	-	560.14	12,119.59	7,307.89
December	12,359.75	92.00	751.09	-	827.40	12,198.94	2,507.04
January (1953) .	15,166.88	684.29	1,669.18	-	866.17	14,801.32	3,314.12
February	8,611.42	273.32	300.55	176.00	525.27	11,795.94	1,764.09
March.	13,977.09	250.08	1,014.91	200.00	1,803.59	6,027.54	2,265.24
April.	59,500.31	241.91	416.88	137.39	946.60	8,187.60	1,996.16
May.	6,724.91	184.92	393.23	5,000.00	611.00	7,159.28	1,636.77
June	12,195.91	100.69	385.64	180.00	347.46	16,058.92	2,906.07

Date	Total USAF	OVERSEAS						
		Alaskan Air Command	Caribbean Air Command	Far East Air Forces	Military Air Transport Service	Northeast Air Command	Strategic Air Command	US Air Forces, Europe
Total . . .	$607,033.19	$35,495.88	$565.20	$363,592.02	$29,479.07	$13,400.80	$28,034.85	$136,465.37
July (1952). . .	62,171.16	2,178.63	57.52	31,731.84	3,122.40	5,268.00	2,278.77	17,534.00
August	59,530.84	6,513.12	59.40	28,803.88	2,805.04	1,287.88	3,362.52	16,699.00
September. . . .	92,650.69	2,275.77	96.08	60,005.04	3,364.00	38.00	2,446.80	24,425.00
October.	46,590.41	1,960.84	35.00	33,454.19	2,932.36	60.00	961.00	7,187.02
November	58,827.09	8,073.55	-	26,441.44	2,568.53	275.01	4,098.06	17,370.50
December	42,765.51	2,553.38	-	31,574.80	1,385.58	1,268.42	307.50	5,675.83
January (1953) .	37,602.71	664.30	31.06	20,304.24	1,012.97	1,209.00	791.14	13,590.00
February	41,753.50	1,194.55	20.00	22,826.14	5,843.95	964.69	454.17	10,450.00
March.	49,386.10	2,742.08	241.54	23,501.67	2,207.10	1,003.02	9,404.69	10,286.00
April.	42,840.58	4,423.59	-	28,653.88	1,042.70	510.44	1,458.95	6,751.02
May.	40,954.94	610.30	24.60	33,597.95	1,344.84	548.70	1,370.55	3,458.00
June	31,959.66	2,305.77	-	22,696.95	1,849.60	967.64	1,100.70	3,039.00

Source: Executive Office, Director, Air Provost Marshal, Hq USAF

TABLE 321 – LOST OR STOLEN GOVERNMENT PROPERTY RECOVERED – FY 1953

(Table represents government property that was lost or stolen by military personnel.)

Date	Total USAF	CONTINENTAL US					
		Total	Air Defense Command	Air Force Finance Center	Air Materiel Command	Air Proving Ground Command	Air Research and Development Command
Total . . .	$691,808.70	$260,887.52	$12,654.63	-	$73,284.59	$4,336.84	$6,763.32
July (1952). . .	53,421.58	12,235.40	415.15	-	3,349.70	22.50	13.40
August	62,776.42	24,046.80	1,938.31	-	5,334.54	20.17	32.92
September. . . .	61,899.24	19,384.23	1,781.51	-	6,209.49	1,935.32	595.42
October.	52,673.90	16,907.00	1,953.17	-	2,514.55	-	269.26
November	70,090.72	23,441.65	3,126.76	-	7,290.05	-	1,327.06
December	47,094.39	13,869.11	506.51	-	994.93	19.30	942.76
January (1953) .	40,182.06	19,159.62	244.64	-	6,345.30	77.25	488.00
February	54,861.56	12,779.50	736.42	-	2,195.47	-	178.00
March.	74,126.08	40,276.54	223.00	-	28,743.89	-	299.00
April.	78,139.83	46,636.81	512.86	-	2,647.26	2,055.30	196.74
May.	50,390.33	16,248.48	374.67	-	3,432.72	-	100.00
June	46,152.59	15,902.38	841.63	-	4,226.69	207.00	2,320.76

Date	CONTINENTAL US (Continued)						
	Air Training Command	Air University	Continental Air Command	Headquarters Command USAF	Military Air Transport Service	Strategic Air Command	Tactical Air Command
Total . . .	$89,440.69	$576.22	$3,344.33	$5,200.00	$2,366.87	$47,374.90	$15,545.13
July (1952). . .	3,300.90	27.50	639.58	-	-	2,814.72	1,651.95
August	5,706.44	46.00	122.00	-	35.00	10,305.42	506.00
September. . . .	4,526.63	138.00	43.02	-	299.60	3,160.49	694.75
October.	6,188,96	168.00	291.50	-	90.00	3,048.57	2,382.99
November	2,541.40	2.00	232.00	-	325.64	3,467.22	5,129.52
December	5,778.48	-	545.00	-	73.00	4,214.77	794.36
January (1953) .	7,573.21	11.50	568.10	-	84.10	3,517.42	250.10
February	4,604.28	34.96	6.87	-	100.00	3,584.12	1,339.38
March.	5,513.23	68.26	261.13	200.00	691.30	2,804.81	1,471.92
April.	37,788.68	80.00	346.26	-	275.00	2,433.73	300.98
May.	3,308.85	-	245.94	5,000.00	320.00	2,902.04	564.26
June	2,609.63	-	42.93	-	73.23	5,121.59	458.92

Date	Total	OVERSEAS					
		Alaskan Air Command	Caribbean Air Command	Far East Air Forces	Military Air Transport Service	Northeast Air Command	Strategic Air Command	US Air Forces, Europe
Total . . .	$430,921.18	$20,521.69	$60.00	$274,098.25	$10,825.80	$8,521.50	$21,269.31	$95,624.63
July (1952). . .	41,186.18	727.35	40.00	19,635.35	135.00	5,203.00	1,771.56	13,673.92
August	38,729.62	566.12	-	14,495.38	362.00	501.60	2,812.52	19,992.00
September. . . .	42,515.01	1,665.80	-	21,137.83	937.70	38.00	1,360.68	17,375.00
October.	35,766.90	446.20	-	28,407.28	309.20	-	1,573.38	5,030.84
November	46,649.07	3,657.94	-	25,096.09	1,456.80	20.00	3,319.24	13,099.00
December	33,225.28	1,280.56	-	28,126.00	31.40	603.38	367.01	2,816.93
January (1953) .	21,022.44	338.22	-	15,275.03	688.89	273.44	134.86	4,312.00
February	42,082.06	153.40	20.00	32,536.33	5,699.00	812.83	144.50	2,716.00
March.	33,849.54	654.58	-	14,681.95	221.10	297.91	8,297.00	9,697.00
April.	31,503.02	3,434.26	-	23,541.42	426.00	280.54	874.86	2,945.94
May.	34,141.85	582.20	-	30,679.51	520.48	240.66	25.00	2,094.00
June	30,250.21	7,015.06	-	20,486.08	38.23	250.14	588.70	1,872.00

Source: Executive Office, Director, Air Provost Marshal, Hq USAF

Components Etc

Part XVII

COMPONENTS

DEFINITIONS

AF RESERVE

ACTIVE DUTY FOR TRAINING
Full-time duty with the active establishment for the purpose of training. All tours accomplished under the provisions of AFR 35-76 are included in this definition.

AIR FORCE RESERVE SPECIALIST TRAINING CENTER UNIT
A non-Table of Organization, composite type unit composed of persons who will be required in the event of full and/or partial mobilization, and who may possess either Ready Reserve of Standby Reserve status.

AIR FORCE RESERVE TRAINING CENTER
A Table of Distribution unit of the regular Air Force, comprising such equipment, facilities and permanent party personnel as are necessary to conduct the training and administration of the Reserve T/O&E units assigned to it and to conduct the administration of unassigned Reservists.

COROLLARY UNIT (Discontinued in November 1952)
A unit of the Air Force Reserve organized on the same T/O&E or T/D as its parent regular Air Force unit. Each Corollary unit is located at the same location as its parent unit and is trained with the facilities and equipment available to the parent unit. A Corollary unit is activated at each location where the personnel of the regular Air Force unit can be duplicated with similar Reservists.

INACTIVE STATUS LIST RESERVE SECTION (Comparable to category designated Inactive Air Reserve prior to January 1953)
All personnel within the Standby Reserve of the Air Force Reserve who have completed their total obligated Reserve service as required by law, who are unable, or unwilling, to participate in prescribed training, who request such status and whose continued retention in the Air Force Reserve is determined to be in the best interest of the Air Force.

INACTIVE DUTY TRAINING
Training performed by members of the Air Force Reserve not on active duty. This inactive duty training includes training for pay and/or non-pay through participation in training periods and unit training assemblies or the performance of equivalent duties in place of attendance at a unit training assembly.

MOBILIZATION ASSIGNEE
An Air Force Reserve officer or airman not on extended active duty who requires regular and frequent training to attain or retain proficiency in his mobilization position. Such persons possess Ready Reserve status and are eligible for inactive duty training pay and authorized active duty training.

MOBILIZATION DESIGNEE
An Air Force Reserve officer or airman not on extended active duty who, by virtue of previous military experience and/or the similarity of his civilian occupation to his duty AFSC, is capable of filling a mobilization position with a minimum of training. Such persons may possess Ready or Standby Reserve status. A mobilization designee is not eligible for inactive duty training pay, but is eligible for active duty training subject to the availability of funds.

RESERVISTS IN PAY STATUS ASSIGNMENTS (Comparable to category designated Organized Air Reserve prior to January 1953)
All personnel of the Air Force Reserve who are physically and professionally qualified for active duty, who fulfill the age-in-grade requirements, availability requirements, and who are in the following types of assignments, comprise Pay Status Assignments: mobilization assignments; combat training centers; flying training centers; combat support training centers; and specialist training center units.

READY RESERVE (Established January 1953)
All Air Force Reserve units and personnel who are liable for active duty either in time of war, national emergency declared by the President or the Congress, or as otherwise authorized by law. All members of the Ready Reserve are in an active status.

AF RESERVE — CONTINUED

DEFINITIONS

RESERVISTS IN NON-PAY STATUS ASSIGNMENTS (Comparable to category designated Volunteer Air Reserve prior to January 1953)

All personnel of the Air Force Reserve who are physically and professionally qualified for active duty, but for whom no position vacancy exists in Pay Status Assignments, or who, for personal reasons, do not participate in the Air Force reserve training program to the extent required for retention in Pay Status Assignments comprise Reservists in Non-Pay Status assignments. Except for the maximum age of 60, there are no age-in-grade or availability requirements for Reservists in Non-Pay Status Assignments.

RETIRED RESERVE (Comparable to category designated Honorary Air Reserve prior to January 1953)

All Air Force Reserve personnel whose service has been honorable and who have completed 20 years of satisfactory Federal service on active or inactive status or combination thereof in any component or components of the armed services, or who have reached the statutory age for retirement, and who have applied for and received transfer to the Reserve Retired List comprise the Retired Reserve.

STANDBY RESERVE (Established January 1953)

All Air Force Reserve units and personnel who are liable for active duty in time of war or national emergency declared by the Congress or as may be otherwise authorized by law. All members of the Standby Reserve, except those persons on the Inactive Status List Reserve Section and the Retired Reserve List, are in an active status.

TRAINING ATTACHMENT

The attachment, for training purposes only, of an Air Force Reserve officer or airman having a mobilization assignment or designation, to an appropriate unit or activity of the regular Air Force, Air Force Reserve, or the Air National Guard of the United States (subject to the approval of the Air National Guard of the United States unit commander concerned), other than the unit or activity with which mobilization position is held.

AIR NATIONAL GUARD

AIR NATIONAL GUARD STRENGTH

The assigned strength of Air National Guard Units not on active Military Service. This strength may include Army personnel known as SCARWANG. However, no SCARWANG were included throughout fiscal year 1952.

CURRENT AUTHORIZED STRENGTH (AIR NATIONAL GUARD)

The authorized strength which is applicable to Federally recognized Air National Guard Units as of the specified date. Such authorized strengths as are issued in appropriate Air Force table of organization with the current reduction in strength by the National Guard Bureau.

SCARWANG PERSONNEL (NO SCARWANG INCLUDED THROUGHOUT FY 1952)

Special category Army type National Guard personnel who have or are awaiting Federal recognition and who are assigned to an Air National Guard Unit provided their assignment on "M" Day would be with the US Air Force. These personnel are charged to the Air National Guard Troop ceiling.

TROOP PROGRAM - AIR NATIONAL GUARD

Authorized strength of all Air National Guard Units allotted to the States, Territories and possessions as issued in appropriate Tables of Organization and Tables of Distribution currently augmented and/or reduced by the National Guard Bureau.

AIR FORCE RESERVE OFFICERS TRAINING CORPS (AF ROTC)

AFROTC STRENGTH

This is the inventory of all Air Force Reserve Officers' Training Corps (AFROTC) students in active participation of ROTC training, in conjunction with academic curriculum at civilian educational institutions.

CONDITIONAL ENROLLMENT

This type of enrollment is a tentative enrollment which will not become absolute unless and until the proper authority determines that the student concerned is fully qualified for formal enrollment in the advanced course of the Air Force ROTC.

ENROLLED STUDENTS

This group included both conditionally and formally enrolled students.

FORMAL ENROLLMENT

This type of enrollment is an absolute advanced enrollment where a condition does not exist that would question a student's qualification for enrollment. Such enrollment entitled the student concerned to receive all benefits, financial and otherwise, provided by law and regulations. (Tables in this publication are based on this type of enrollment).

EXPLORERS

NOTE: Data for FY 1953 tables on Explorers were not available at the time this section was released; therefore, no definitions for that area are included.

TABLE 322 — AF RESERVE STRENGTH BY CATEGORY OF PERSONNEL ASSIGNMENT — FY 1953

Type of Personnel By Category of Assignment	Jul (1952)	Aug	Sep	Oct	Nov	Dec
TOTAL	321,630	324,001	323,762	322,588	325,232	325,590
OFFICER - TOTAL	227,054	229,004	228,473	227,798	230,024	231,248
AIRMAN - TOTAL	94,576	94,997	95,289	94,790	95,208	94,342
Reservists in Pay Status Assignment - Total	8,922	9,421	10,010	10,242	10,621	11,262
Officer - Total	4,822	5,135	5,537	5,680	5,882	6,161
Airman - Total	4,100	4,286	4,473	4,562	4,739	5,101
Mobilization Assignee - Total	3,281	3,327	3,325	3,158	3,125	3,127
Officer	2,558	2,645	2,675	2,571	2,585	2,606
Airman	723	682	650	587	540	521
Corollary - Total	240	232	225	208	-	-
Officer	66	60	57	56	-	-
Airman	174	172	168	152	-	-
Air Force Reserve Combat Training Center - Total	3,528	3,742	4,175	4,438	4,679	5,063
Officer	1,364	1,475	1,787	1,963	2,054	2,202
Airman	2,164	2,267	2,388	2,475	2,625	2,861
Air Force Reserve Flying Training Center - Total	1,521	1,647	1,787	1,893	2,002	2,146
Officer	541	566	613	652	707	755
Airman	980	1,081	1,174	1,241	1,295	1,391
Air Force Reserve Combat Support Training Center-Total	-	-	-	-	223	228
Officer	-	-	-	-	68	78
Airman	-	-	-	-	155	150
Air Force Reserve Specialist Training Center - Total	352	473	498	545	592	698
Officer	293	389	405	438	468	520
Airman	59	84	93	107	124	178
Reservists in Non-Pay Status Assignment - Total	309,395	311,210	310,329	308,840	311,018	310,647
Officer - Total	218,957	220,543	219,561	218,670	220,613	221,476
Airman - Total	90,438	90,667	90,768	90,170	90,405	89,171
Mobilization Designee - Total	2,616	2,665	2,750	2,763	2,801	2,834
Officer	2,330	2,366	2,443	2,457	2,503	2,542
Airman	286	299	307	306	298	292
Voluntary Air Reserve Training Unit - Total	41,339	40,924	40,223	40,308	39,874	39,653
Officer	32,958	32,692	32,115	32,079	31,710	31,467
Airman	8,381	8,232	8,108	8,229	8,164	8,186
Non-Affiliated Reserve Section - Total	260,465	262,628	262,418	260,737	263,357	263,114
Officer	179,677	181,461	180,995	179,999	182,290	183,281
Airman	80,788	81,167	81,423	80,738	81,067	79,833
Inactive Status List Reserve Section - Total	4,975	4,993	4,938	5,032	4,986	5,046
Officer	3,992	4,024	4,008	4,135	4,110	4,186
Airman	983	969	930	897	876	860
Ineligible Reserve Section - Total	-	-	-	-	-	-
Officer	-	-	-	-	-	-
Airman	-	-	-	-	-	-
Reserve Retired List - Total	3,313	3,370	3,423	3,506	3,593	3,681
Officer	3,275	3,326	3,375	3,448	3,529	3,611
Airman	38	44	48	58	64	70

TABLE 323 – AF RESERVE STRENGTH BY CATEGORY OF

Line No	Type of Personnel By Type of Assignment	Jan (1954)			Feb		
		Total	Ready	Standby	Total	Ready	Standby
1	TOTAL	325,389	316,714	4,826	324,708	315,018	5,830
2	OFFICER - TOTAL	232,161	224,138	4,246	231,995	223,245	4,962
3	AIRMAN - TOTAL	93,228	92,576	580	92,713	91,773	868
4	Reservists in Pay Status Assignment - Total	11,603	11,534	69	11,824	11,714	110
5	Officer - Total	6,337	6,272	65	6,399	6,313	86
6	Airman - Total	5,266	5,262	4	5,425	5,401	24
7	Mobilization Assignee - Total	3,111	3,111	-	3,103	3,103	-
8	Officer	2,617	2,617	-	2,635	2,635	-
9	Airman	494	494	-	468	468	-
10	Corollary - Total	-	-	-	-	-	-
11	Officer	-	-	-	-	-	-
12	Airman	-	-	-	-	-	-
13	Air Force Reserve Combat Training Center - Total	5,289	5,289	-	5,351	5,351	-
14	Officer	2,301	2,301	-	2,283	2,283	-
15	Airman	2,988	2,988	-	3,068	3,068	-
16	Air Force Reserve Flying Training Center - Total	2,237	2,237	-	2,328	2,328	-
17	Officer	796	796	-	814	814	-
18	Airman	1,441	1,441	-	1,514	1,514	-
19	Air Force Reserve Combat Support Tng Center-Total	236	236	-	234	234	-
20	Officer	83	83	-	93	93	-
21	Airman	153	153	-	141	141	-
22	Air Force Reserve Specialist Tng Center - Total	730	661	69	808	698	110
23	Officer	540	475	65	574	488	86
24	Airman	190	186	4	234	210	24
25	Reservists in Non-Pay Status Assignment - Total	309,937	305,180	4,757	309,024	303,304	5,720
26	Officer - Total	222,047	217,866	4,181	221,808	216,932	4,876
27	Airman - Total	87,890	87,314	576	87,216	86,372	844
28	Mobilization Designee - Total	2,829	2,799	30	2,776	2,726	50
29	Officer	2,536	2,508	28	2,486	2,441	45
30	Airman	293	291	2	290	285	5
31	Voluntary Air Reserve Training Unit - Total	39,874	39,577	297	39,649	38,774	875
32	Officer	31,648	31,429	219	31,431	30,688	743
33	Airman	8,226	8,148	78	8,218	8,086	132
34	Non-Affiliated Reserve Section - Total	262,914	262,804	110	262,286	261,804	482
35	Officer	184,037	183,929	108	184,212	183,803	409
36	Airman	78,877	78,875	2	78,074	78,001	73
37	Inactive Status List Reserve Section - Total	4,310	-	4,310	4,298	-	4,298
38	Officer	3,817	-	3,817	3,666	-	3,666
39	Airman	493	-	493	632	-	632
40	Ineligible Reserve Section - Total	10	-	10	15	-	15
41	Officer	9	-	9	13	-	13
42	Airman	1	-	1	2	-	2
43	Reserve Retired List - Total	3,849	b/	b/	3,860	b/	b/
44	Officer	3,777	b/	b/	3,788	b/	b/
45	Airman	72	b	b/	72	b/	b/

a/ Category of Liability (Ready and Standby Reserve) was introduced with January (1953) report.
b/ Ready and Standby are not applicable to the Reserve Retired List.
Source: Personnel Statistics Division, DCS/Comptroller, Hq. USAF.

PERSONNEL ASSIGNMENT - FY 1953

Mar Total	Mar Ready	Mar Standby	Apr Total	Apr Ready	Apr Standby	May Total	May Ready	May Standby	Jun Total	Jun Ready	Jun Standby	LINE NO
323,752	308,026	11,884	248,910	229,639	15,825	243,400	222,876	17,096	240,626	219,222	18,278	1
232,813	218,155	10,887	167,222	149,299	14,544	163,913	144,922	15,630	163,645	143,814	16,770	2
90,939	89,871	997	81,688	80,340	1,281	79,487	77,954	1,466	76,981	75,408	1,508	3
12,684	12,553	131	12,777	12,687	90	13,519	13,435	84	13,817	13,733	84	4
6,859	6,752	107	7,051	6,967	84	7,352	7,274	78	7,601	7,519	82	5
5,825	5,801	24	5,726	5,720	6	6,167	6,161	6	6,216	6,214	2	6
3,089	3,089	-	2,936	2,936	-	2,975	2,975	-	2,974	2,974	-	7
2,654	2,654	-	2,636	2,636	-	2,680	2,680	-	2,701	2,701	-	8
435	435	-	300	300	-	295	295	-	273	273	-	9
-	-	-	-	-	-	-	-	-	-	-	-	10
-	-	-	-	-	-	-	-	-	-	-	-	11
-	-	-	-	-	-	-	-	-	-	-	-	12
5,764	5,764	-	5,735	5,735	-	6,028	6,208	-	6,110	6,110	-	13
2,420	2,420	-	2,414	2,414	-	2,474	2,474	-	2,534	2,534	-	14
3,344	3,344	-	3,321	3,321	-	3,554	3,554	-	3,576	3,576	-	15
2,425	2,425	-	2,448	2,448	-	2,597	2,597	-	2,589	2,589	-	16
848	848	-	851	851	-	890	890	-	898	898	-	17
1,577	1,577	-	1,597	1,597	-	1,707	1,707	-	1,691	1,691	-	18
311	311	-	360	360	-	433	433	-	473	473	-	19
131	131	-	168	168	-	212	212	-	227	227	-	20
180	180	-	192	192	-	221	221	-	246	246	-	21
1,095	964	131	1,298	1,208	90	1,486	1,402	84	1,671	1,587	84	22
806	699	107	982	898	84	1,096	1,018	78	1,241	1,159	82	23
289	265	24	316	310	6	390	384	6	430	428	2	24
307,226	295,473	11,753	232,687	216,952	15,735	226,453	209,441	17,012	223,683	205,489	18,194	25
222,183	211,403	10,780	156,792	142,332	14,460	153,200	137,648	15,552	152,983	136,295	16,688	26
85,043	84,070	973	75,895	74,620	1,275	73,253	71,793	1,460	70,700	69,194	1,506	27
2,804	2,588	216	2,748	2,464	284	2,602	2,280	322	2,617	2,253	364	28
2,527	2,325	202	2,473	2,203	270	2,415	2,101	314	2,450	2,102	348	29
277	263	14	275	261	14	187	179	8	167	151	16	30
39,741	36,349	3,392	38,220	32,876	5,344	37,810	30,919	6,891	36,963	29,539	7,424	31
31,334	28,224	3,110	30,015	25,054	4,961	29,559	23,185	6,374	28,857	21,931	6,926	32
8,407	8,125	282	8,205	7,822	383	8,251	7,734	517	8,106	7,608	498	33
260,328	256,529	3,799	188,773	181,559	7,214	183,274	176,170	7,104	181,351	173,579	7,772	34
184,553	180,849	3,704	121,971	115,041	6,930	119,047	112,316	6,731	119,508	112,172	7,336	35
75,775	75,680	95	66,802	66,518	284	64,227	63,854	373	61,843	61,407	436	36
4,331	-	4,331	2,890	-	2,890	2,687	-	2,687	2,623	-	2,623	37
3,753	-	3,753	2,296	-	2,296	2,125	-	2,125	2,067	-	2,067	38
578	-	578	594	-	594	562	-	562	556	-	556	39
22	7	15	56	53	3	80	72	8	129	118	11	40
16	5	11	37	34	3	54	46	8	101	90	11	41
6	2	4	19	19	-	26	26	-	28	28	-	42
3,842	b/	b/	3,446	b/	b/	3,428	b/	b/	3,126	b/	b/	43
3,771	b/	b/	3,379	b/	b/	3,361	b/	b/	3,061	b/	b/	44
71	b/	b/	67	b/	b/	67	b/	b/	65	b/	b/	45

TABLE 323 – AF RESERVE OFFICER STRENGTH BY GRADE, BY CATEGORY OF ASSIGNMENT – FY 1953

Grade and Category of Assignment	September (1952) a/	December a/	March (1953) b/			June		
			Total	Ready	Standby	Total	Ready	Standby
Reserve Strength - Total	228,473	231,248	232,813	218,155	10,887	163,645	143,814	16,770
General	40	38	37	31	-	37	33	-
Colonel	1,786	1,814	1,925	1,638	122	1,932	1,567	211
Lt Colonel	7,041	7,128	7,408	6,487	532	6,686	5,424	896
Major	18,931	19,325	19,885	17,804	1,558	16,118	13,232	2,435
Captain	51,497	52,845	54,708	50,356	3,391	40,158	34,263	5,121
First Lieutenant	86,519	87,418	89,585	84,656	3,714	57,569	51,100	5,651
Second Lieutenant	58,651	58,494	59,265	57,183	1,570	41,045	38,195	2,456
Pay Status Assignments - Total	5,537	6,161	6,859	6,752	107	7,601	7,519	82
General	29	25	24	24	-	22	22	-
Colonel	244	258	285	282	3	325	323	2
Lt Colonel	568	582	597	590	7	669	666	3
Major	1,030	1,072	1,121	1,099	22	1,241	1,220	21
Captain	1,566	1,718	1,963	1,931	32	2,174	2,141	33
First Lieutenant	1,399	1,627	1,878	1,853	25	2,147	2,125	22
Second Lieutenant	701	879	991	973	18	1,023	1,022	1
Mobilization Assignee - Total	2,675	2,606	2,654	2,654	-	2,701	2,701	-
General	29	25	24	24	-	22	22	-
Colonel	199	206	220	220	-	235	235	-
Lt Colonel	418	404	405	405	-	425	425	-
Major	591	567	589	589	-	608	608	-
Captain	727	717	754	754	-	750	750	-
First Lieutenant	490	452	444	444	-	454	454	-
Second Lieutenant	221	235	218	218	-	207	207	-
Corollary - Total c/	57	-	-	-	-	-	-	-
General	-	-	-	-	-	-	-	-
Colonel	2	-	-	-	-	-	-	-
Lt Colonel	2	-	-	-	-	-	-	-
Major	5	-	-	-	-	-	-	-
Captain	15	-	-	-	-	-	-	-
First Lieutenant	23	-	-	-	-	-	-	-
Second Lieutenant	10	-	-	-	-	-	-	-
Air Force Reserve Combat Training Center - Total	1,787	2,202	2,420	2,420	-	2,534	2,534	-
General	-	-	-	-	-	-	-	-
Colonel	23	26	30	30	-	40	40	-
Lt Colonel	95	111	116	116	-	120	120	-
Major	279	315	318	318	-	314	314	-
Captain	531	610	666	666	-	700	700	-
First Lieutenant	560	732	832	832	-	924	924	-
Second Lieutenant	299	408	458	458	-	436	436	-
Air Force Reserve Flying Training Center - Total	613	755	848	848	-	898	898	-
General	-	-	-	-	-	-	-	-
Colonel	16	15	16	16	-	17	17	-
Lt Colonel	31	34	31	31	-	34	34	-
Major	90	96	100	100	-	107	107	-
Captain	173	224	268	268	-	288	288	-
First Lieutenant	201	248	274	274	-	310	310	-
Second Lieutenant	102	138	159	159	-	142	142	-
Air Force Combat Support Training Center - Total	-	78	131	131	-	227	227	-
General	-	-	-	-	-	-	-	-
Colonel	-	3	5	5	-	9	9	-
Lt Colonel	-	3	4	4	-	15	15	-
Major	-	7	9	9	-	27	27	-
Captain	-	23	37	37	-	67	67	-
First Lieutenant	-	27	55	55	-	68	68	-
Second Lieutenant	-	15	21	21	-	41	41	-
Air Force Reserve Specialist Training Center - Total	405	520	806	699	107	1,241	1,159	82
General	-	-	-	-	-	-	-	-
Colonel	4	8	14	11	3	24	22	2
Lt Colonel	22	30	41	34	7	75	72	3
Major	65	87	105	83	22	185	164	21
Captain	120	144	238	206	32	369	336	33
First Lieutenant	125	168	273	248	25	391	369	22
Second Lieutenant	69	83	135	117	18	197	196	1

TABLE 323 – AF RESERVE OFFICER STRENGTH BY GRADE, BY CATEGORY OF ASSIGNMENT – FY 1953
(CONTINUED)

Grade and Category of Assignment	September (1952) a/	December a/	March (1953) b/			June		
			Total	Ready	Standby	Total	Ready	Standby
Non-Pay Status Assignments - Total . .	219,561	221,476	222,183	211,403	10,780	152,983	136,295	16,688
General	3	6	7	7	-	11	11	-
Colonel	1,411	1,414	1,475	1,356	119	1,453	1,244	209
Lt Colonel	6,133	6,184	6,422	5,897	525	5,651	4,758	893
Major	17,455	17,771	18,241	16,705	1,536	14,426	12,012	2,414
Captain	49,048	50,187	51,784	48,425	3,359	37,210	32,122	5,088
First Lieutenant	84,008	84,611	86,492	82,803	3,689	54,604	48,975	5,629
Second Lieutenant	57,495	57,117	57,762	56,210	1,552	39,628	37,173	2,455
Mobilization Designee - Total	2,443	2,542	2,527	2,325	202	2,450	2,102	348
General	-	2	2	2	-	3	3	-
Colonel	141	152	160	158	2	174	160	14
Lt Colonel	250	249	258	240	18	284	241	43
Major	420	444	463	414	49	453	373	80
Captain	718	751	743	656	87	726	605	121
First Lieutenant	663	677	645	606	39	576	502	74
Second Lieutenant	251	267	256	249	7	234	218	16
Voluntary Air Reserve Training Unit - Total	32,115	31,467	31,334	28,224	3,110	28,857	21,931	6,926
General	-	-	-	-	-	-	-	-
Colonel	290	311	342	296	46	362	283	79
Lt Colonel	1,228	1,286	1,339	1,193	146	1,368	1,015	349
Major	3,908	3,892	3,958	3,413	545	3,982	2,818	1,164
Captain	9,670	9,613	9,624	8,539	1,085	8,993	6,651	2,342
First Lieutenant	11,162	10,746	10,503	9,525	978	9,473	7,234	2,239
Second Lieutenant	5,857	5,619	5,568	5,258	310	4,679	3,926	753
Non-Affiliated Reserve Section - Total	180,995	183,281	184,553	180,849	3,704	119,508	112,172	7,336
General	3	4	5	5	-	8	8	-
Colonel	980	951	956	902	54	902	800	102
Lt Colonel	4,655	4,649	4,707	4,464	243	3,912	3,494	418
Major	13,127	13,435	13,424	12,878	546	9,736	8,812	924
Captain	38,660	39,823	40,314	39,227	1,087	26,861	24,847	2,014
First Lieutenant	72,183	73,188	73,898	72,672	1,226	43,747	41,208	2,539
Second Lieutenant	51,387	51,231	51,249	50,701	548	34,342	33,003	1,339
Ineligible Reserve Section - Total	-	-	16	5	11	101	90	11
General	-	-	-	-	-	-	-	-
Colonel	-	-	-	-	-	1	1	-
Lt Colonel	-	-	-	-	-	5	4	1
Major	-	-	2	-	2	9	9	-
Captain	-	-	10	3	7	24	19	5
First Lieutenant	-	-	2	-	2	34	31	3
Second Lieutenant	-	-	2	2	-	28	26	2
Inactive Status List Reserve Section - Total	4,008	4,186	3,753	-	3,753	2,067	-	2,067
General	d/	d/	-	-	-	-	-	-
Colonel	d/	d/	17	-	17	14	-	14
Lt Colonel	d/	d/	118	-	118	82	-	82
Major	d/	d/	394	-	394	246	-	246
Captain	d/	d/	1,093	-	1,093	606	-	606
First Lieutenant	d/	d/	1,444	-	1,444	774	-	774
Second Lieutenant	d/	d/	687	-	687	345	-	345
Retired Reserve List - Total	3,375	3,611	3,771	-	-	3,061	-	-
General	8	7	6	-	-	4	-	-
Colonel	131	142	165	-	-	154	-	-
Lt Colonel	340	362	389	-	-	366	-	-
Major	446	482	523	-	-	451	-	-
Captain	883	940	961	-	-	774	-	-
First Lieutenant	1,112	1,180	1,215	-	-	918	-	-
Second Lieutenant	455	498	512	-	-	394	-	-

a/ Grade breaks for Reserve Strength Total and Non-Pay Status Assignment Total exclude Inactive Status List Reserve section for which such breaks were not available.
b/ Beginning with the Third Quarter FY 1953 Categories of Liability (Ready and Standby Reserve Status) are shown.
c/ Discontinued November 1952.
d/ Grade Spread not available.

Source: Personnel Statistics Division, DCS/Comptroller, Hq. USAF.

TABLE 324 — AF RESERVE AIRMAN STRENGTH BY GRADE, BY CATEGORY OF ASSIGNMENT — FY 1953

Grade and Category of Assignment	September (1952) a/	December a/	March (1953) b/			June		
			Total	Ready	Standby	Total	Ready	Standby
Reserve Strength - Total	95,289	94,342	90,939	89,871	997	76,981	75,408	1,508
Grade Seven	4,464	4,628	4,565	4,371	186	3,997	3,730	260
Grade Six	8,851	8,527	8,207	8,040	164	6,813	6,561	249
Grade Five	22,166	22,330	21,908	21,677	210	17,782	17,403	359
Grade Four	24,525	23,972	22,950	22,712	220	18,728	18,405	308
Grade Three	18,019	17,820	17,307	17,162	135	15,097	14,880	205
Grade Two	10,157	10,358	10,534	10,468	57	9,947	9,857	83
Grade One	6,129	5,777	5,468	5,441	25	4,617	4,572	44
Pay Status Assignment - Total	4,473	5,101	5,825	5,801	24	6,216	6,214	2
Grade Seven	152	228	268	266	2	360	360	-
Grade Six	268	384	490	487	3	601	601	-
Grade Five	554	812	1,092	1,088	4	1,276	1,274	2
Grade Four	577	716	932	926	6	1,042	1,042	-
Grade Three	580	629	691	683	8	754	754	-
Grade Two	775	1,040	1,038	1,037	1	923	923	-
Grade One	1,567	1,292	1,314	1,314	-	1,260	1,260	-
Mobilization Assignee - Total	650	521	435	435	-	273	273	-
Grade Seven	24	21	16	16	-	14	14	-
Grade Six	30	36	27	27	-	29	29	-
Grade Five	80	71	64	64	-	46	46	-
Grade Four	102	81	73	73	-	41	41	-
Grade Three	103	78	64	64	-	29	29	-
Grade Two	143	115	90	90	-	51	51	-
Grade One	168	119	101	101	-	63	63	-
Corollary - Total c/	168	-	-	-	-	-	-	-
Grade Seven	9	-	-	-	-	-	-	-
Grade Six	3	-	-	-	-	-	-	-
Grade Five	10	-	-	-	-	-	-	-
Grade Four	7	-	-	-	-	-	-	-
Grade Three	13	-	-	-	-	-	-	-
Grade Two	17	-	-	-	-	-	-	-
Grade One	109	-	-	-	-	-	-	-
Air Force Reserve Combat Training Center - Total	2,388	2,861	3,344	3,344	-	3,576	3,576	-
Grade Seven	88	127	159	159	-	199	199	-
Grade Six	147	223	299	299	-	347	347	-
Grade Five	308	469	665	665	-	753	753	-
Grade Four	310	403	525	525	-	582	582	-
Grade Three	290	336	371	371	-	396	396	-
Grade Two	370	559	569	569	-	501	501	-
Grade One	875	744	756	756	-	798	798	-
Air Force Reserve Flying Training Center - Total	1,174	1,391	1,577	1,577	-	1,691	1,691	-
Grade Seven	26	60	64	64	-	96	96	-
Grade Six	75	98	117	117	-	146	146	-
Grade Five	131	200	250	250	-	301	301	-
Grade Four	136	178	242	242	-	274	274	-
Grade Three	158	176	197	197	-	236	236	-
Grade Two	237	315	291	291	-	280	280	-
Grade One	411	364	416	416	-	358	358	-
Air Force Reserve Combat Support Training Center - Total	-	150	180	180	-	246	246	-
Grade Seven	-	9	10	10	-	14	14	-
Grade Six	-	4	11	11	-	20	20	-
Grade Five	-	18	24	24	-	51	51	-
Grade Four	-	12	25	25	-	52	52	-
Grade Three	-	11	20	20	-	24	24	-
Grade Two	-	36	62	62	-	54	54	-
Grade One	-	60	28	28	-	31	31	-
Air Force Reserve Specialist Training Center - Total	93	178	289	265	24	430	428	2
Grade Seven	5	11	19	17	2	37	37	-
Grade Six	13	23	36	33	3	59	59	-
Grade Five	25	54	89	85	4	125	123	2
Grade Four	22	42	67	61	6	93	93	-
Grade Three	16	28	39	31	8	69	69	-
Grade Two	8	15	26	25	1	37	37	-
Grade One	4	5	13	13	-	10	10	-

TABLE 324 — AF RESERVE AIRMAN STRENGTH BY GRADE, BY CATEGORY OF ASSIGNMENT — FY 1953 (CONTINUED)

Grade and Category of Assignment	September (1952) a/	December a/	March (1953) b/			June		
			Total	Ready	Standby	Total	Ready	Standby
Non-Pay Status Assignment - Total	90,768	89,171	85,043	84,070	973	70,700	69,194	1,506
Grade Seven	4,312	4,400	4,289	4,105	184	3,630	3,370	260
Grade Six	8,583	8,143	7,714	7,553	161	6,209	5,960	249
Grade Five	21,612	21,518	20,795	20,589	206	16,486	16,129	357
Grade Four	23,948	23,256	22,000	21,786	214	17,671	17,363	308
Grade Three	17,439	17,191	16,606	16,479	127	14,331	14,126	205
Grade Two	9,382	9,318	9,487	9,431	56	9,017	8,934	83
Grade One	4,562	4,485	4,152	4,127	25	3,356	3,312	44
Mobilization Designee - Total	307	292	277	263	14	167	151	16
Grade Seven	12	10	13	12	1	16	14	2
Grade Six	27	23	19	17	2	12	11	1
Grade Five	58	49	44	40	4	29	25	4
Grade Four	56	51	45	42	3	26	21	5
Grade Three	59	57	60	56	4	33	30	3
Grade Two	51	52	52	52	-	23	22	1
Grade One	44	50	44	44	-	28	28	-
Voluntary Air Reserve Training Unit - Total	8,108	8,186	8,407	8,125	282	8,106	7,608	498
Grade Seven	457	455	481	444	37	512	455	57
Grade Six	902	893	898	851	47	953	859	94
Grade Five	1,811	1,921	2,050	1,972	78	2,171	2,021	150
Grade Four	2,083	2,099	2,037	1,956	81	1,957	1,851	106
Grade Three	1,579	1,550	1,537	1,511	26	1,454	1,395	59
Grade Two	976	984	977	965	12	865	836	29
Grade One	300	284	427	426	1	194	191	3
Non-Affiliated Reserve Section - Total	81,423	79,833	75,775	75,680	95	61,843	61,407	436
Grade Seven	3,843	3,935	3,655	3,649	6	2,924	2,901	23
Grade Six	7,654	7,227	6,704	6,685	19	5,152	5,085	67
Grade Five	19,743	19,548	18,615	18,577	38	14,203	14,075	128
Grade Four	21,809	21,106	19,807	19,788	19	15,589	15,486	103
Grade Three	15,801	15,584	14,919	14,911	8	12,766	12,697	69
Grade Two	8,355	8,282	8,417	8,414	3	8,099	8,073	26
Grade One	4,218	4,151	3,658	3,656	2	3,110	3,090	20
Ineligible Reserve Section - Total	-	-	6	2	4	28	28	-
Grade Seven	-	-	-	-	-	-	-	-
Grade Six	-	-	3	-	3	5	5	-
Grade Five	-	-	-	-	-	8	8	-
Grade Four	-	-	1	-	1	5	5	-
Grade Three	-	-	1	1	-	4	4	-
Grade Two	-	-	-	-	-	3	3	-
Grade One	-	-	1	1	-	3	3	-
Inactive Status List Reserve Section - Total	930	860	578	-	578	556	-	556
Grade Seven	d/	d/	140	-	140	178	-	178
Grade Six	d/	d/	90	-	90	87	-	87
Grade Five	d/	d/	86	-	86	75	-	75
Grade Four	d/	d/	110	-	110	94	-	94
Grade Three	d/	d/	89	-	89	74	-	74
Grade Two	d/	d/	41	-	41	27	-	27
Grade One	d/	d/	22	-	22	21	-	21
Reserve Retired List - Total b/	48	70	71	-	-	65	-	-
Grade Seven	d/	d/	8	-	-	7	-	-
Grade Six	d/	d/	3	-	-	3	-	-
Grade Five	d/	d/	21	-	-	20	-	-
Grade Four	d/	d/	18	-	-	15	-	-
Grade Three	d/	d/	10	-	-	12	-	-
Grade Two	d/	d/	9	-	-	7	-	-
Grade One	d/	d/	2	-	-	1	-	-

a/ Grade breaks for Reserve Strength Total exclude Inactive Status List Reserve Section and Reserve Retired List for which such breaks were not available. Likewise, grade breaks for Non-Pay Status assignment-Total exclude Inactive Status List Reserve Section.
b/ Beginning with the third quarter FY 1953 Categories of liability (Ready and Standby Reserve Status) are shown.
c/ Discontinued November 1952.
d/ Grade Breakdown not available.

Source: Personnel Statistics Division, DCS/Comptroller, Hq. USAF.

TABLE 325 — AF RESERVE STRENGTH BY TYPE OF PERSONNEL, BY LOCATION OF RESIDENCE — FY 1953

State, Territory, or Possession	December (1952) a/			June (1953) b/					
	Total	Officer	Enlisted	Total		Officer		Enlisted	
				Ready	Standby	Ready	Standby	Ready	Standby
WORLDWIDE - Total	321,909	227,637	94,272	219,221	18,278	143,814	16,770	75,407	1,508
CONTINENTAL U S - Total	316,277	223,782	92,495	213,273	18,083	139,267	16,611	74,006	1,472
Alabama	4,237	2,692	1,545	2,852	546	1,589	535	1,263	11
Arizona	2,075	1,599	476	1,531	24	1,134	19	397	5
Arkansas	2,694	1,625	1,069	1,691	278	993	270	698	8
California	35,978	26,815	9,163	25,585	1,122	16,905	978	8,680	144
Colorado	4,325	3,304	1,021	3,854	143	2,951	110	903	33
Connecticut	4,072	3,159	913	2,658	289	1,898	275	760	14
Delaware	589	465	124	383	24	291	22	92	2
District of Columbia	2,334	1,837	497	1,494	84	1,218	75	276	9
Florida	7,734	5,502	2,232	5,526	977	3,483	939	2,043	38
Georgia	5,753	3,651	2,102	4,123	656	2,142	641	1,981	15
Idaho	1,509	1,112	397	973	90	714	78	259	12
Illinois	17,307	12,712	4,595	11,353	816	6,976	705	4,377	111
Indiana	7,068	5,257	1,811	4,781	807	2,952	693	1,829	114
Iowa	4,687	3,442	1,245	3,369	119	2,282	100	1,087	19
Kansas	5,250	3,844	1,406	3,736	118	2,591	89	1,145	29
Kentucky	4,405	2,254	2,151	3,051	85	1,615	75	1,436	10
Louisiana	4,656	3,290	1,366	2,781	610	1,800	600	981	10
Maine	1,226	738	488	807	87	456	77	351	10
Maryland	4,183	2,965	1,218	2,920	171	2,179	167	741	4
Massachusetts	9,056	6,233	2,823	5,986	406	3,852	383	2,134	23
Michigan	12,220	8,970	3,250	8,047	690	5,158	557	2,889	133
Minnesota	5,878	4,344	1,534	4,058	216	2,604	194	1,454	22
Mississippi	2,775	1,983	792	1,904	315	1,227	308	677	7
Missouri	7,816	5,013	2,803	5,585	220	3,202	164	2,383	56
Montana	1,409	1,067	342	943	29	664	25	279	4
Nebraska	3,052	2,180	872	2,055	132	1,285	114	770	18
Nevada	428	329	99	326	7	239	6	87	1
New Hampshire	1,014	668	346	709	68	469	61	240	7
New Jersey	9,809	7,529	2,280	5,959	567	4,575	531	1,384	36
New Mexico	1,880	1,414	466	1,146	201	846	179	300	22
New York	28,714	21,412	7,302	18,649	1,019	13,168	953	5,481	66
North Carolina	4,822	3,454	1,368	3,088	661	1,921	658	1,167	3
North Dakota	773	598	175	496	75	337	63	159	12
Ohio	16,535	12,771	3,764	10,206	489	7,589	472	2,617	17
Oklahoma	6,390	3,829	2,561	3,968	681	2,079	649	1,889	32
Oregon	4,140	2,729	1,411	2,882	156	1,840	144	1,042	12
Pennsylvania	21,283	13,179	8,104	14,519	409	9,227	378	5,292	31
Rhode Island	1,211	778	433	816	23	506	19	310	4
South Carolina	2,499	1,803	696	1,697	355	1,135	347	562	8
South Dakota	1,068	721	347	715	51	446	46	269	5
Tennessee	5,338	3,285	2,053	3,453	597	1,742	593	1,711	4
Texas	24,309	16,656	7,653	15,976	2,483	10,042	2,271	5,934	212
Utah	2,382	1,774	608	1,640	62	1,137	58	503	4
Vermont	557	356	201	370	71	215	66	155	5
Virginia	5,128	3,476	1,652	3,960	189	2,876	180	1,084	9
Washington	5,422	4,154	1,268	3,954	285	2,699	228	1,255	57
West Virginia	2,980	1,563	1,417	1,837	109	985	106	852	3
Wisconsin	6,562	4,629	1,933	4,346	421	2,643	365	1,703	56
Wyoming	745	622	123	515	50	390	45	125	5

TABLE 325 — AF RESERVE STRENGTH BY TYPE OF PERSONNEL, BY LOCATION OF RESIDENCE — FY 1953 (CONTINUED)

State, Territory, or Possession	December (1952) a/			June (1953) b/					
	Total	Officer	Enlisted	Total		Officer		Enlisted	
				Ready	Standby	Ready	Standby	Ready	Standby
OVERSEAS - Total	855	666	189	722	32	554	29	168	3
Alaska	252	215	37	204	4	173	4	31	-
Canal Zone	23	19	4	20	1	16	1	4	-
England	2	1	1	1	-	-	-	1	-
Hawaiian Islands	351	247	104	294	15	192	12	102	3
Philippine Islands	6	5	1	2	1	2	1	-	-
Puerto Rico	34	24	10	48	-	43	-	5	-
Other	187	155	32	153	11	128	11	25	-
Unknown - Total	4,777	3,189	1,588	5,226	163	3,993	130	1,233	33

a/ Excludes 3,611 Officers and 70 Airmen on the Reserve Retired List.
b/ Excludes 3,061 Officers and 65 Airmen on the Reserve Retired List.

Source: Personnel Statistics Division, DCS/Comptroller, Hq. USAF.

TABLE 326 — AF RESERVE STRENGTH IN TRAINING WINGS

(TCW - Troop Carrier Wing; FBW - Fighter Bomber Wing; TRW - Tactical

LINE NO	Unit Designation and Location	As of 25 September 1952			As of 25 December 1952		
		Total	Officer	Airman	Total	Officer	Airman
1	Total	6,460	2,805	3,655	7,907	3,477	4,430
2	Combat Training Center - Total	4,175	1,787	2,388	5,063	2,202	2,861
3	Troop Carrier Wing - Total	2,055	913	1,142	2,538	1,162	1,376
4	2233 514 TCW - Mitchel AFB, New York	208	112	96	274	142	132
5	2237 512 TCW - New Castle, Delaware	282	96	186	381	136	245
6	2252 302 TCW - Clinton Air Force Base, Ohio	221	98	123	252	128	124
7	2253 375 TCW - Pittsburgh, Pennsylvania	85	50	35	222	129	93
8	2343 403 TCW - Portland, Oregon	186	78	108	185	91	94
9	2466 434 TCW - Atterbury, Indiana	346	153	193	324	152	172
10	2471 437 TCW - O'Hare Field, Chicago, Illinois.	289	122	167	354	143	211
11	2472 442 TCW - Olathe Naval Air Station, Kansas	254	115	139	283	127	156
12	2585 435 TCW - Miami International Airport, Fla	184	89	95	263	114	149
13	Fighter Bomber Wing - Total	1,546	675	871	1,885	808	1,077
14	2234 89 FBW - Hanscom Field, Massachusetts	234	115	119	291	126	165
15	2242 439 FBW - Selfridge Air Force Base, Mich	408	136	272	422	140	282
16	2256 445 FBW - Buffalo, New York	104	83	21	198	148	50
17	2346 349 FBW - Hamilton Air Force Base, Calif	180	114	66	191	121	70
18	2465 440 FBW - Mpls-St Paul Airport, Minnesota.	255	97	158	269	125	144
19	2473 459 FBW - Milwaukee, Wisconsin	365	130	235	514	148	366
20	Tactical Reconnaissance Wing - Total	574	199	375	640	232	408
21	2347 452 TRW - Long Beach, California	229	121	108	225	123	102
22	2589 94 TRW - Dobbins Air Force Base, Georgia.	345	78	267	415	109	306
23	Combat Support Training Center - Total	-	-	-	-	-	-
24	2260 88 ADW - New York, New York	-	-	-	-	-	-
25	2375 77 ADW - Long Beach, California	-	-	-	-	-	-
26	Flying Training Center - Total	1,787	613	1,174	2,146	755	1,391
27	Single Engine Pilot Training Wing - Total	1,096	408	688	1,385	519	866
28	2230 8709 PTW - New York, New York	302	106	196	397	137	260
29	2469 8711 PTW - Scott Air Force Base, Illinois.	257	98	159	298	114	184
30	2577 8707 PTW - Brooks Air Force Base, Texas	209	86	123	282	106	176
31	2596 8708 PTW - Hensley Naval Air Station, Texas	328	118	210	408	162	246
32	Multi-Engine Pilot Training Wing - Total	691	205	486	761	236	525
33	2578 8706 PTW - Ellington Air Force Base, Texas	287	115	172	348	139	209
34	2584 8710 PTW - Memphis, Tennessee	404	90	314	413	97	316
35	Specialist Training Center - Total	498	405	93	698	520	178
36	2281 . . . . . Cleveland, Ohio	-	-	-	2	2	-
37	2285 . . . . . New York, New York	85	72	13	107	82	25
38	2286 . . . . . Baltimore, Maryland	90	61	29	117	69	48
39	2287 . . . . . Louisville, Kentucky	27	19	8	54	32	22
40	2288 . . . . . Philadelphia, Pennsylvania	-	-	-	-	-	-
41	2290 . . . . . Buffalo, New York	-	-	-	2	2	-
42	2296 . . . . . Columbus, Ohio	-	-	-	2	2	-
43	2298 . . . . . Richmond, Virginia	-	-	-	2	2	-
44	2360 . . . . . San Francisco, California	63	61	2	74	68	6
45	2361 . . . . . Los Angeles, California	-	-	-	10	10	-
46	2368 . . . . . Seattle, Washington	-	-	-	-	-	-
47	2400 . . . . . Chicago, Illinois	98	79	19	154	130	24
48	2401 . . . . . Detroit, Michigan	-	-	-	2	1	1
49	2402 . . . . . Denver, Colorado	-	-	-	2	1	1
50	2403 . . . . . Omaha, Nebraska	-	-	-	-	-	-
51	2406 . . . . . St Louis, Missouri	-	-	-	-	-	-
52	2510 . . . . . Birmingham, Alabama	130	109	21	152	113	39
53	2511 . . . . . Fort Worth, Texas	5	4	1	18	6	12
54	2512 . . . . . Tampa, Florida	-	-	-	-	-	-
55	2514 . . . . . Oklahoma City, Oklahoma	-	-	-	-	-	-

Source: Personnel Statistics Division, DCS/Comptroller, Hq. USAF.

AND SPECIALIST CENTERS BY LOCATION — FY 1953

Reconnaissance Wing; ADW - Air Depot Wing; and PTW - Pilot Training Wing)

As of 25 March 1953							As of 25 June 1953							LINE NO
Total	Total		Officer		Airman		Total	Total		Officer		Airman		
	Ready	Standby	Ready	Standby	Ready	Standby		Ready	Standby	Ready	Standby	Ready	Standby	
9,595	9,464	131	4,098	107	5,366	24	10,843	10,759	84	4,818	82	5,941	2	1
5,764	5,764	-	2,420	-	3,344	-	6,110	6,110	-	2,534	-	3,576	-	2
2,979	2,979	-	1,301	-	1,678	-	3,197	3,197	-	1,391	-	1,806	-	3
314	314	-	148	-	166	-	368	368	-	170	-	198	-	4
419	419	-	142	-	277	-	466	466	-	156	-	310	-	5
284	284	-	150	-	134	-	289	289	-	152	-	137	-	6
363	363	-	138	-	225	-	472	472	-	165	-	307	-	7
180	180	-	89	-	91	-	197	197	-	118	-	79	-	8
279	279	-	134	-	145	-	253	253	-	130	-	123	-	9
420	420	-	174	-	246	-	411	411	-	187	-	224	-	10
404	404	-	183	-	221	-	414	414	-	180	-	234	-	11
316	316	-	143	-	173	-	327	327	-	133	-	194	-	12
2,057	2,057	-	868	-	1,189	-	2,085	2,085	-	861	-	1,224	-	13
334	334	-	134	-	200	-	336	336	-	136	-	200	-	14
434	434	-	136	-	298	-	468	468	-	142	-	326	-	15
290	290	-	192	-	98	-	297	297	-	160	-	137	-	16
202	202	-	122	-	80	-	230	230	-	137	-	93	-	17
308	308	-	144	-	164	-	307	307	-	150	-	157	-	18
489	489	-	140	-	349	-	447	447	-	136	-	311	-	19
728	728	-	251	-	477	-	828	828	-	282	-	546	-	20
243	243	-	126	-	117	-	281	281	-	150	-	131	-	21
485	485	-	125	-	360	-	547	547	-	132	-	415	-	22
311	311	-	131	-	180	-	47	47	-	227	-	246	-	23
111	111	-	56	-	55	-	205	205	-	96	-	109	-	24
200	200	-	75	-	125	-	268	268	-	131	-	137	-	25
2,425	2,425	-	848	-	1,577	-	2,589	2,589	-	898	-	1,691	-	26
1,593	1,593	-	592	-	1,001	-	1,769	1,769	-	624	-	1,145	-	27
465	465	-	138	-	327	-	566	566	-	167	-	399	-	28
347	347	-	152	-	195	-	349	349	-	162	-	187	-	29
335	335	-	116	-	219	-	405	405	-	123	-	282	-	30
446	446	-	186	-	260	-	449	449	-	172	-	277	-	31
832	832	-	256	-	576	-	820	820	-	274	-	546	-	32
401	401	-	147	-	254	-	436	436	-	147	-	289	-	33
431	431	-	109	-	322	-	384	384	-	127	-	257	-	34
1,095	964	131	699	107	265	24	1,671	1,587	84	1,159	82	428	2	35
29	28	1	23	1	5	-	47	47	-	39	-	8	-	36
132	126	6	104	6	22	-	149	149	-	121	-	28	-	37
123	123	-	69	-	54	-	179	179	-	107	-	72	-	38
93	93	-	32	-	61	-	129	129	-	50	-	79	-	39
-	-	-	-	-	-	-	2	2	-	2	-	-	-	40
2	2	-	2	-	-	-	34	34	-	31	-	3	-	41
36	36	-	31	-	5	-	118	118	-	93	-	25	-	42
2	2	-	2	-	-	-	105	105	-	71	-	34	-	43
99	99	-	88	-	11	-	114	111	3	92	3	19	-	44
71	71	-	66	-	5	-	135	135	-	124	-	11	-	45
112	112	-	105	-	7	-	197	189	8	168	8	21	-	46
186	160	26	125	26	35	-	195	170	25	134	25	36	-	47
3	3	-	2	-	1	-	3	3	-	2	-	1	-	48
2	2	-	1	-	1	-	47	47	-	43	-	4	-	49
-	-	-	-	-	-	-	3	3	-	1	-	2	-	50
-	-	-	-	-	-	-	7	7	-	4	-	3	-	51
170	79	91	36	72	43	19	151	114	37	55	35	59	2	52
35	28	7	13	2	15	5	34	25	9	7	9	18	-	53
-	-	-	-	-	-	-	20	19	1	14	1	5	-	54
-	-	-	-	-	-	-	2	1	1	1	1	-	-	55

TABLE 327 — AF RESERVE MOBILIZATION ASSIGNEE STRENGTH BY COMMAND — FY 1953

(Personnel after Jan 1953 have Ready Reserve status)

Type Assignee By Command	Jul (1952)	Aug	Sep	Oct	Nov	Dec	Jan (1953)	Feb	Mar	Apr	May	Jun
WORLDWIDE - TOTAL . . .	3,281	3,327	3,325	3,158	3,125	3,127	3,111	3,103	3,089	2,936	2,975	2,974
OFFICER - TOTAL.	2,558	2,645	2,675	2,571	2,585	2,606	2,617	2,635	2,654	2,636	2,680	2,701
AIRMAN - TOTAL	723	682	650	587	540	521	494	468	435	300	295	273
CONTINENTAL U. S. TOTAL . .	3,163	3,212	3,211	3,055	3,022	3,020	2,999	2,995	2,982	2,824	2,860	2,863
Officer.	2,461	2,548	2,579	2,485	2,498	2,515	2,523	2,546	2,566	2,543	2,584	2,605
Airman	702	664	632	570	524	505	476	449	416	281	276	258
Headquarters USAF - Total.	311	317	317	312	321	310	316	311	337	348	357	360
Officer.	311	317	317	312	321	310	316	311	337	348	357	360
Airman	-	-	-	-	-	-	-	-	-	-	-	-
Strategic Air Command-Total	280	282	300	264	266	266	262	267	268	262	263	266
Officer.	228	229	244	222	226	229	230	234	236	226	224	227
Airman	52	53	56	42	40	37	32	33	32	36	39	39
Continental Air Comd - Total	730	786	785	694	655	617	600	605	606	567	556	561
Officer.	669	717	716	624	591	561	558	568	569	530	521	526
Airman	61	69	69	70	64	56	42	37	37	37	35	35
Mil Air Transport Sv - Total	1,138	1,102	1,077	1,041	1,011	1,012	1,005	978	880	741	741	694
Officer.	616	617	619	610	614	626	628	623	563	566	568	541
Airman	522	485	458	431	397	386	377	355	317	175	173	153
Air Proving Ground - Total	8	9	8	9	10	11	14	12	8	8	8	8
Officer.	8	9	8	9	10	11	14	12	8	8	8	8
Airman	-	-	-	-	-	-	-	-	-	-	-	-
Air Materiel Command - Total	62	70	74	76	81	94	91	104	115	125	152	178
Officer.	62	70	74	76	81	94	91	104	115	125	152	178
Airman	-	-	-	-	-	-	-	-	-	-	-	-
Air Training Command - Total	299	293	289	275	270	275	265	272	279	278	291	301
Officer.	256	256	258	266	265	270	261	269	273	271	285	294
Airman	43	37	31	9	5	5	4	3	6	7	6	7
Air University - Total . .	38	39	45	51	55	59	59	62	64	62	64	64
Officer.	38	39	45	51	55	59	59	62	64	62	64	64
Airman	-	-	-	-	-	-	-	-	-	-	-	-
Headquarters Command -Total	61	56	55	64	68	74	75	72	76	75	71	74
Officer.	38	38	39	48	52	55	56	54	55	52	50	52
Airman	23	18	16	16	16	19	19	18	21	23	21	22
Air Defense Command - Total	171	184	184	184	194	202	197	189	194	186	179	176
Officer.	171	184	184	184	194	202	197	188	193	185	178	175
Airman	-	-	-	-	-	-	-	1	1	1	1	1
Tactical Air Command - Total	38	46	48	49	51	55	69	80	110	129	136	138
Officer.	38	46	48	49	51	55	69	80	110	129	136	138
Airman	-	-	-	-	-	-	-	-	-	-	-	-
Air R & D Command - Total.	26	27	28	29	30	32	31	32	30	29	28	29
Officer.	25	25	26	27	28	30	29	30	28	27	27	28
Airman	1	2	2	2	2	2	2	2	2	2	1	1
USAF Security Service -Total	1	1	1	1	1	1	1	1	2	2	2	2
Officer.	1	1	1	1	1	1	1	1	2	2	2	2
Airman	-	-	-	-	-	-	-	-	-	-	-	-
Air Finance Division - Total	-	-	-	6	9	12	14	10	13	12	12	12
Officer.	-	-	-	6	9	12	14	10	13	12	12	12
Airman	-	-	-	-	-	-	-	-	-	-	-	-
OVERSEAS - TOTAL	118	115	114	103	103	107	112	108	107	112	115	[illegible]
Officer.	97	97	96	86	87	91	94	89	88	93	96	95
Airman	21	18	18	17	16	16	18	19	19	19	19	15
Caribbean Air Command-Total	31	32	32	34	35	35	35	35	35	34	34	30
Officer.	22	23	23	24	24	24	22	22	23	23	23	22
Airman	9	9	9	10	11	11	13	13	12	11	11	8
Far East Air Forces - Total	-	-	-	-	-	-	-	-	-	-	-	-
Officer.	-	-	-	-	-	-	-	-	-	-	-	-
Airman	-	-	-	-	-	-	-	-	-	-	-	-
Mil Air Transport Sv - Total	61	60	59	53	52	52	55	50	47	48	48	48
Officer.	49	51	50	46	47	47	50	44	41	41	41	41
Airman	12	9	9	7	5	5	5	6	6	7	7	7
U.S. Air Forces,Europe-Total	26	23	23	16	16	20	22	23	25	30	33	33
Officer.	26	23	23	16	16	20	22	23	24	29	32	33
Airman	-	-	-	-	-	-	-	-	1	1	1	-

Source: Personnel Statistics Division, DCS/Comptroller, Hq. USAF.

TABLE 328 — AF RESERVE MOBILIZATION DESIGNEE STRENGTH BY COMMAND OF ASSIGNMENT — FY 1953

Command of Assignment	Jul (1952)	Aug	Sep	Oct	N:v	Dec	Jan (1953)		Feb		Mar		Apr		May		Jun	
							Ready	Standby	Ready	Standby	Ready	Standby	Ready	Standby	Ready	Standby	Ready	Standby
WORLDWIDE - TOTAL . .	2,616	2,665	2,750	2,763	2,801	2,834	2,799	30	2,726	50	2,588	216	2,464	284	2,280	322	2,253	364
OFFICER - TOTAL.	2,330	2,366	2,443	2,457	2,503	2,542	2,508	28	2,441	45	2,325	202	2,203	270	2,101	314	2,102	348
AIRMAN - TOTAL	286	299	307	306	298	292	291	2	285	5	263	14	261	14	179	8	151	16
CONTINENTAL US - TOTAL . .	2,546	2,590	2,677	2,691	2,729	2,763	2,728	29	2,673	34	2,519	214	2,398	283	2,215	320	2,191	357
Officer.	2,269	2,300	2,380	2,396	2,442	2,482	2,446	27	2,394	32	2,265	200	2,146	269	2,046	312	2,050	341
Airman	277	290	297	295	287	281	282	2	279	2	254	14	252	14	169	8	141	16
Headquarters USAF - Total.	591	604	618	629	650	668	674	-	666	-	674	-	653	14	657	24	676	26
Officer.	565	574	591	603	629	650	656	-	655	-	663	-	647	14	648	24	667	26
Airman	26	30	27	26	21	18	18	-	11	-	11	-	11	-	9	-	9	-
Strategic Air Command-Total	18	20	20	20	23	23	23	-	24	-	26	-	26	-	25	-	28	-
Officer.	18	20	20	20	23	23	23	23	24	-	26	-	26	-	25	-	28	-
Airman	-	-	-	-	-	-	-	-	-	-	-	-	-	-	-	-	-	-
Continental Air Command -																		
Total.	43	43	50	44	49	50	51	-	64	-	57	3	67	3	65	5	64	4
Officer.	43	43	50	44	49	50	49	-	51	-	48	1	56	1	53	3	52	2
Airman	-	-	-	-	-	-	2	-	13	-	9	2	11	2	12	2	12	2
Military Air Transport																		
Service - Total.	1,158	1,172	1,183	1,176	1,174	1,166	1,151	8	1,083	8	898	191	827	209	684	202	636	220
Officer.	923	928	931	926	926	922	908	6	847	6	683	179	619	197	562	196	543	206
Airman	235	244	252	250	248	244	243	2	236	2	215	12	208	12	122	6	93	14
Air Proving Ground - Total	10	10	10	8	8	9	9	-	9	-	12	-	11	-	9	-	8	-
Officer.	10	10	10	8	8	9	9	-	9	-	12	-	11	-	9	-	8	-
Airman	-	-	-	-	-	-	-	-	-	-	-	-	-	-	-	-	-	-
Air Materiel Command-Total	36	36	38	40	48	56	61	-	66	-	78	-	53	32	73	33	88	43
Officer.	36	36	38	40	48	56	61	-	66	-	78	-	53	32	73	33	88	43
Airman	-	-	-	-	-	-	-	-	-	-	-	-	-	-	-	-	-	-
Air Training Command -Total	370	374	376	377	372	378	347	18	343	17	339	15	330	13	313	13	291	17
Officer.	370	374	376	376	372	377	346	18	342	17	338	15	329	13	312	13	290	17
Airman	-	-	-	1	-	1	1	-	1	-	1	-	1	-	1	-	1	-
Air University - Total . .	93	93	94	94	93	96	96	-	95	-	95	-	78	-	75	-	69	-
Officer.	93	93	94	94	93	96	96	-	95	-	95	-	78	-	75	-	69	-
Airmen	-	-	-	-	-	-	-	-	-	-	-	-	-	-	-	-	-	-

TABLE 328 — AF RESERVE MOBILIZATION DESIGNEE STRENGTH BY COMMAND OF ASSIGNMENT — FY 1953 — Continued

Command of Assignment	Jul (1952)	Aug	Sep	Oct	Nov	Dec	Jan (1953)		Feb		Mar		Apr		May		Jun	
							Ready	Standby	Ready	Standby	Ready	Standby	Ready	Standby	Ready	Standby	Ready	Standby
Headquarters Command - Total	26	25	26	23	23	23	23	-	23	-	25	-	21	2	19	2	22	2
Officer.	26	25	26	23	23	23	23	-	23	-	25	-	21	2	19	2	22	2
Airman	-	-	-	-	-	-	-	-	-	-	-	-	-	-	-	-	-	-
Air Defense Command - Total	19	21	20	19	19	19	15	3	19	-	19	-	16	3	16	4	14	4
Officer.	19	21	20	19	19	19	15	3	19	-	19	-	16	3	16	4	14	4
Airman	-	-	-	-	-	-	-	-	-	-	-	-	-	-	-	-	-	-
Tactical Air Command -Total	29	35	35	37	38	42	42	-	42	-	46	-	66	-	64	-	65	-
Officer.	29	35	35	37	38	42	42	-	42	-	46	-	63	-	58	-	58	-
Airman	-	-	-	-	-	-	-	-	-	-	-	-	3	-	6	-	7	-
Air Research and Development Command - Total . . .	153	157	207	219	226	227	230	-	236	-	246	-	240	4	208	36	224	40
Officer.	137	141	189	201	208	209	212	-	218	-	228	-	222	4	189	36	205	40
Airman	16	16	18	18	18	18	18	-	18	-	18	-	18	-	19	-	19	-
USAF Security Service-Total	-	-	-	-	-	-	-	-	-	-	-	-	-	-	-	-	-	-
Officer.	-	-	-	-	-	-	-	-	-	-	-	-	-	-	-	-	-	-
Airman	-	-	-	-	-	-	-	-	-	-	-	-	-	-	-	-	-	-
Air Force Finance Division-Total.	-	-	-	5	6	6	6	-	3	9	4	5	5	3	7	1	6	1
Officer.	-	-	-	5	6	6	6	-	3	9	4	5	5	3	7	1	6	1
Airman	-	-	-	-	-	-	-	-	-	-	-	-	-	-	-	-	-	-
OVERSEAS - TOTAL	70	75	73	72	72	71	71	1	53	16	69	2	66	1	65	2	62	7
Officer.	61	66	63	61	61	60	62	1	47	13	60	2	57	1	55	2	52	7
Airman	9	9	10	11	11	11	9	-	6	3	9	-	9	-	10	-	10	-
Caribbean Air Command-Total	16	17	17	15	15	14	15	-	-	15	16	-	16	-	16	-	14	1
Officer.	12	13	13	12	12	11	12	-	-	12	13	-	13	-	13	-	11	1
Airman	4	4	4	3	3	3	3	-	-	3	3	-	3	-	3	-	3	-
Far East Air Forces - Total	19	26	23	22	22	22	22	1	21	1	20	1	21	-	22	-	20	4
Officer.	19	25	23	22	22	22	22	1	21	1	20	1	21	-	22	-	20	4
Airman	-	-	-	-	-	-	-	-	-	-	-	-	-	-	-	-	-	-
Military Air Transport Service - Total.	13	14	15	18	18	18	17	-	17	-	18	1	17	1	16	2	17	2
Officer.	8	9	9	10	10	10	11	-	11	-	12	1	11	1	9	2	10	2
Airman	5	5	6	8	8	8	6	-	6	-	6	-	6	-	7	-	7	-
US Air Forces in Europe - Total.	22	18	18	17	17	17	17	-	15	-	15	-	12	-	11	-	11	4
Officer.	22	18	18	17	17	17	17	-	15	-	15	-	12	-	11	-	11	4
Airman	-	-	-	-	-	-	-	-	-	-	-	-	-	-	-	-	-	-

Source: Personnel Statistics Division, DCS/Comptroller, Hq USAF.

TABLE 329 — AF RESERVE PERSONNEL IN PAY STATUS ASSIGNMENTS BY PROGRAM ELEMENT, PAY GRADE — FY 1953

Grade	Jul (1952)	Aug	Sep	Oct	Nov	Dec	Jan (1953)		Feb		Mar		Apr		May		Jun	
							Ready	Standby	Ready	Standby	Ready	Standby	Ready	Standby	Ready	Standby	Ready	Standby
TOTAL	8,922	9,421	10,010	10,242	10,621	11,262	11,534	69	11,714	110	12,553	131	12,687	90	13,435	84	13,733	84
OFFICER - TOTAL	4,822	5,135	5,537	5,680	5,882	6,161	6,272	65	6,313	86	6,752	107	6,967	84	7,274	78	7,519	82
General	30	31	29	29	25	25	25	-	22	-	24	-	23	-	22	-	22	-
Colonel	234	240	244	246	255	258	269	-	274	1	282	3	306	1	316	2	323	2
Lt Colonel	552	557	568	567	574	582	575	7	570	7	590	7	614	5	644	3	666	3
Major	946	991	1,030	1,028	1,045	1,072	1,072	12	1,077	19	1,099	22	1,114	18	1,164	20	1,220	21
Captain	1,358	1,439	1,566	1,605	1,656	1,718	1,751	20	1,820	27	1,931	32	2,006	27	2,100	29	2,141	33
First Lieutenant	1,126	1,252	1,399	1,449	1,508	1,627	1,681	13	1,662	18	1,853	25	1,912	24	2,019	22	2,125	22
Second Lieutenant	576	625	701	756	819	879	899	13	888	14	973	18	992	9	1,009	2	1,022	1
AIRMAN - TOTAL	4,100	4,286	4,473	4,562	4,739	5,101	5,262	4	5,401	24	5,801	24	5,720	6	6,161	6	6,214	2
Grade Seven	114	136	152	159	206	228	237	-	245	2	266	2	283	1	337	1	360	-
Grade Six	224	246	268	293	325	384	418	-	431	2	487	3	475	-	544	-	601	-
Grade Five	448	506	554	597	687	812	895	2	962	5	1,088	4	1,126	3	1,253	3	1,274	2
Grade Four	508	545	577	615	661	716	765	1	835	6	926	6	929	2	1,009	1	1,042	-
Grade Three	538	551	580	588	590	629	654	1	632	7	683	8	674	-	730	1	754	-
Grade Two	714	737	775	867	1,017	1,040	1,030	-	1,017	2	1,037	1	941	-	974	-	923	-
Grade One	1,554	1,565	1,567	1,443	1,253	1,292	1,263	-	1,279	-	1,314	-	1,292	-	1,314	-	1,260	-
Mobilization Assignee-Total	3,281	3,327	3,325	3,158	3,125	3,127	3,111	-	3,103	-	3,089	-	2,936	-	2,975	-	2,974	-
Officer - Total	2,558	2,645	2,675	2,571	2,585	2,606	2,617	-	2,635	-	2,654	-	2,636	-	2,680	-	2,701	-
General	30	31	29	29	25	25	25	-	22	-	24	-	23	-	22	-	22	-
Colonel	190	196	199	199	206	206	214	-	216	-	220	-	225	-	230	-	235	-
Lt Colonel	407	409	418	406	403	404	405	-	399	-	405	-	411	-	423	-	425	-
Major	569	593	591	565	570	567	575	-	591	-	589	-	582	-	579	-	608	-
Captain	688	706	727	703	708	717	728	-	755	-	754	-	743	-	771	-	750	-
First Lieutenant	461	492	490	452	449	452	442	-	438	-	444	-	441	-	454	-	454	-
Second Lieutenant	213	218	221	217	224	235	228	-	214	-	218	-	211	-	201	-	207	-
Airman - Total	723	682	650	587	540	521	494	-	468	-	435	-	300	-	295	-	273	-
Grade Seven	21	22	24	21	20	21	18	-	17	-	16	-	17	-	14	-	14	-
Grade Six	34	31	30	29	34	36	31	-	27	-	27	-	25	-	29	-	29	-
Grade Five	72	77	80	73	72	71	69	-	69	-	64	-	54	-	51	-	46	-
Grade Four	112	107	102	91	.85	81	85	-	82	-	73	-	51	-	44	-	41	-
Grade Three	115	110	103	98	85	78	69	-	63	-	64	-	27	-	32	-	29	-
Grade Two	165	153	143	134	118	115	108	-	99	-	90	-	54	-	56	-	51	-
Grade One	204	182	168	141	126	119	114	-	111	-	101	-	72	-	69	-	63	-
Corollary - Total a/	240	232	225	208	-	-	-	-	-	-	-	-	-	-	-	-	-	-
Officer - Total	66	60	57	56	-	-	-	-	-	-	-	-	-	-	-	-	-	-
General	-	-	-	-	-	-	-	-	-	-	-	-	-	-	-	-	-	-
Colonel	2	2	2	2	-	-	-	-	-	-	-	-	-	-	-	-	-	-
Lt Colonel	3	2	2	2	-	-	-	-	-	-	-	-	-	-	-	-	-	-
Major	6	5	5	5	-	-	-	-	-	-	-	-	-	-	-	-	-	-
Captain	18	16	15	15	-	-	-	-	-	-	-	-	-	-	-	-	-	-
First Lieutenant	24	23	23	24	-	-	-	-	-	-	-	-	-	-	-	-	-	-
Second Lieutenant	13	12	10	8	-	-	-	-	-	-	-	-	-	-	-	-	-	-

TABLE 329 — AF RESERVE PERSONNEL IN PAY STATUS ASSIGNMENTS BY PROGRAM ELEMENT, PAY GRADE — FY 1953 (Continued)

Grade	Jul (1952)	Aug	Sep	Oct	Nov	Dec	Jan (1953)		Feb		Mar		Apr		May		Jun	
							Ready	Standby	Ready	Standby	Ready	Standby	Ready	Standby	Ready	Standby	Ready	Standby
Airman - Total	174	172	168	152	-	-	-	-	-	-	-	-	-	-	-	-	-	-
Grade Seven	8	9	9	9	-	-	-	-	-	-	-	-	-	-	-	-	-	-
Grade Six	6	3	3	3	-	-	-	-	-	-	-	-	-	-	-	-	-	-
Grade Five	10	9	10	16	-	-	-	-	-	-	-	-	-	-	-	-	-	-
Grade Four	7	7	7	9	-	-	-	-	-	-	-	-	-	-	-	-	-	-
Grade Three	15	14	13	9	-	-	-	-	-	-	-	-	-	-	-	-	-	-
Grade Two	18	18	17	14	-	-	-	-	-	-	-	-	-	-	-	-	-	-
Grade One	110	112	109	92	-	-	-	-	-	-	-	-	-	-	-	-	-	-
AF Reserve Combat Training Center - Total	3,528	3,742	4,175	4,438	4,679	5,063	5,289	-	5,351	-	5,764	-	5,735	-	6,028	-	6,110	-
Officer - Total	1,364	1,475	1,787	1,963	2,054	2,202	2,301	-	2,283	-	2,420	-	2,414	-	2,474	-	2,534	-
General	-	-	-	-	-	-	-	-	-	-	-	-	-	-	-	-	-	-
Colonel	23	23	23	26	26	26	27	-	27	-	30	-	39	-	42	-	40	-
Lt Colonel	93	93	95	102	108	111	112	-	114	-	116	-	112	-	116	-	120	-
Major	242	246	279	298	304	315	317	-	310	-	318	-	307	-	308	-	314	-
Captain	411	436	531	573	591	610	619	-	639	-	666	-	680	-	687	-	700	-
First Lieutenant	374	428	560	620	656	732	794	-	764	-	832	-	835	-	873	-	924	-
Second Lieutenant	221	249	299	344	369	408	432	-	429	-	458	-	441	-	448	-	436	-
Airman - Total	2,164	2,267	2,388	2,475	2,625	2,861	2,988	-	3,068	-	3,344	-	3,321	-	3,554	-	3,576	-
Grade Seven	61	75	88	90	115	127	135	-	141	-	159	-	160	-	190	-	199	-
Grade Six	119	135	147	165	182	223	257	-	261	-	299	-	287	-	316	-	347	-
Grade Five	237	275	308	349	400	469	526	-	573	-	665	-	680	-	753	-	753	-
Grade Four	270	287	310	334	377	403	431	-	470	-	525	-	527	-	567	-	582	-
Grade Three	260	269	290	299	311	336	353	-	344	-	371	-	367	-	394	-	396	-
Grade Two	333	331	370	434	543	559	551	-	543	-	569	-	527	-	523	-	501	-
Grade One	884	895	875	804	697	744	735	-	736	-	756	-	773	-	811	-	798	-
AF Reserve Flying Training Center - Total	1,521	1,647	1,787	1,893	2,002	2,146	2,237	-	2,328	-	2,425	-	2,448	-	2,597	-	2,589	-
Officer - Total	541	566	613	652	707	755	796	-	814	-	848	-	851	-	890	-	898	-
General	-	-	-	-	-	-	-	-	-	-	-	-	-	-	-	-	-	-
Colonel	15	15	16	15	15	15	16	-	16	-	16	-	15	-	15	-	17	-
Lt Colonel	30	31	31	32	34	34	31	-	31	-	31	-	33	-	34	-	34	-
Major	81	84	90	91	92	96	95	-	98	-	100	-	96	-	108	-	107	-
Captain	159	164	173	182	205	224	242	-	254	-	268	-	281	-	294	-	288	-
First Lieutenant	177	188	201	220	229	248	259	-	263	-	274	-	286	-	298	-	310	-
Second Lieutenant	79	84	102	112	132	138	153	-	152	-	159	-	140	-	141	-	142	-
Airman - Total	980	1,081	1,174	1,241	1,295	1,391	1,441	-	1,514	-	1,577	-	1,597	-	1,707	-	1,691	-
Grade Seven	22	27	26	31	53	60	65	-	67	-	64	-	72	-	86	-	96	-
Grade Six	58	66	75	85	89	98	101	-	112	-	117	-	110	-	129	-	146	-
Grade Five	112	123	131	133	164	200	226	-	236	-	250	-	270	-	291	-	301	-
Grade Four	108	123	136	156	158	178	187	-	215	-	242	-	248	-	268	-	274	-
Grade Three	135	143	158	166	163	176	191	-	189	-	197	-	210	-	228	-	236	-
Grade Two	192	227	237	271	308	315	308	-	305	-	291	-	280	-	309	-	280	-
Grade One	353	372	411	399	360	364	363	-	390	-	416	-	407	-	396	-	358	-

AF Reserve Combat Support Training Center - Total	-	-	-	-	223	228	236	-	234	-	311	-	360	-	433	-	473	-
Officer - Total	-	-	-	-	68	78	83	-	23	-	131	-	168	-	212	-	227	-
General	-	-	-	-	-	-	-	-	-	-	-	-	-	-	-	-	-	-
Colonel	-	-	-	-	2	3	4	-	4	-	5	-	8	-	9	-	9	-
Lt Colonel	-	-	-	-	3	3	3	-	4	-	4	-	8	-	14	-	15	-
Major	-	-	-	-	7	7	8	-	7	-	9	-	20	-	26	-	27	-
Captain	-	-	-	-	16	23	27	-	30	-	37	-	43	-	64	-	67	-
First Lieutenant	-	-	-	-	27	27	26	-	32	-	55	-	59	-	61	-	68	-
Second Lieutenant	-	-	-	-	13	15	15	-	16	-	21	-	30	-	38	-	41	-
Airman - Total	-	-	-	-	155	150	153	-	141	-	180	-	192	-	221	-	246	-
Grade Seven	-	-	-	-	10	9	8	-	8	-	10	-	12	-	14	-	14	-
Grade Six	-	-	-	-	4	4	5	-	5	-	11	-	14	-	16	-	20	-
Grade Five	-	-	-	-	18	18	18	-	17	-	24	-	30	-	44	-	51	-
Grade Four	-	-	-	-	12	12	15	-	13	-	25	-	31	-	43	-	52	-
Grade Three	-	-	-	-	12	11	14	-	15	-	20	-	22	-	23	-	24	-
Grade Two	-	-	-	-	34	36	48	-	50	-	62	-	55	-	53	-	54	-
Grade One	-	-	-	-	65	60	45	-	33	-	28	-	28	-	28	-	31	-
AF Reserve Specialist Training Center - Total	352	473	498	545	592	698	661	69	698	110	964	131	1,208	90	1,402	84	1,587	84
Officers - Total	293	389	405	438	468	520	475	65	488	86	699	107	898	84	1,018	78	1,159	82
General	-	-	-	-	-	-	-	-	-	-	-	-	-	-	-	-	-	-
Colonel	4	4	4	4	6	8	8	-	11	1	11	3	19	1	20	2	22	2
Lt Colonel	19	22	22	25	26	30	24	7	22	7	34	7	50	5	57	3	72	3
Major	48	63	65	69	72	87	77	12	71	19	83	22	109	18	143	20	164	21
Captain	82	117	120	132	136	144	135	20	142	27	206	32	259	27	284	29	336	33
First Lieutenant	90	121	125	133	147	168	160	13	165	18	248	25	291	24	333	22	369	22
Second Lieutenant	50	62	69	75	81	83	71	13	77	14	117	18	170	9	181	2	196	1
Airman - Total	59	84	93	107	124	178	186	4	210	24	265	24	310	6	384	6	428	2
Grade Seven	2	3	5	8	8	11	11	-	12	2	17	2	22	1	33	1	37	-
Grade Six	7	11	13	11	16	23	24	-	26	2	33	3	39	-	54	-	59	-
Grade Five	17	22	25	26	33	54	56	2	67	5	85	4	92	3	114	3	123	2
Grade Four	11	21	22	25	29	42	47	1	55	6	61	6	72	2	87	1	93	-
Grade Three	13	15	16	16	19	28	27	1	21	7	31	8	48	-	53	1	69	-
Grade Two	6	8	8	14	14	15	15	-	20	2	25	1	25	-	33	-	37	-
Grade One	3	4	4	7	5	5	6	-	9	-	13	-	12	-	10	-	10	-

a/ Discontinued November 1952.

Source: Personnel Statistics Division, DCS/Comptroller, Hq USAF.

TABLE 330 - AF RESERVE OFFICERS IN PAY STATUS ASSIGNMENTS BY FLYING STATUS, BY CATEGORY OF ASSIGNMENT, BY GRADE - FY 1953

Grade and Category of Assignment	Total	On Flying Status				Not on Flying Status				Flying Status Unknown
		Total	Pilot	Other Rated	Non-Rated	Total	Pilot	Other Rated	Non-Rated	
	As of 25 September 1952									
Total	5,242	2,092	1,770	268	54	2,976	461	175	2,340	174
General	29	13	13	-	-	15	2	1	12	1
Colonel	242	56	51	1	4	180	9	1	170	6
Lieutenant Colonel	542	100	87	4	9	429	14	2	413	13
Major	959	264	225	30	9	673	58	22	593	22
Captain	1,473	643	537	92	14	785	141	56	588	45
First Lieutenant	1,316	761	633	117	11	498	179	71	248	57
Second Lieutenant	681	255	224	24	7	396	58	22	316	30
Mobilization Assignee - Total	2,571	640	522	92	26	1,803	202	80	1,521	128
General	29	13	13	-	-	15	2	1	12	1
Colonel	199	39	34	1	4	154	8	-	146	6
Lieutenant Colonel	406	53	46	3	4	341	7	1	333	12
Major	565	99	82	13	4	450	32	14	404	16
Captain	703	211	168	35	8	459	69	28	362	33
First Lieutenant	452	181	146	31	4	234	70	29	135	37
Second Lieutenant	217	44	33	9	2	150	14	7	129	23
Corollary - Total a/	56	21	16	5	-	35	8	2	25	-
General	-	-	-	-	-	-	-	-	-	-
Colonel	2	-	-	-	-	2	-	-	2	-
Lieutenant Colonel	2	-	-	-	-	2	-	-	2	-
Major	5	1	-	1	-	4	2	-	2	-
Captain	15	7	6	1	-	8	-	-	8	-
First Lieutenant	24	12	10	2	-	12	6	1	5	-
Second Lieutenant	8	1	-	1	-	7	-	1	6	-
Combat Training Center - Total	1,963	1,190	1,027	148	15	754	104	40	610	19
General	-	-	-	-	-	-	-	-	-	-
Colonel	26	12	12	-	-	14	-	1	13	-
Lieutenant Colonel	102	32	28	-	4	69	5	-	64	1
Major	298	134	116	13	5	160	8	2	150	4
Captain	573	364	312	50	2	202	29	12	161	7
First Lieutenant	620	471	394	75	2	145	45	20	80	4
Second Lieutenant	344	177	165	10	2	164	17	5	142	3
Flying Training Center - Total	652	241	205	23	13	384	147	53	184	27
General	-	-	-	-	-	-	-	-	-	-
Colonel	15	5	5	-	-	10	1	-	9	-
Lieutenant Colonel	32	15	13	1	1	17	2	1	14	-
Major	91	30	27	3	-	59	16	6	37	2
Captain	182	61	51	6	4	116	43	16	57	5
First Lieutenant	220	97	83	9	5	107	58	21	28	16
Second Lieutenant	112	33	26	4	3	75	27	9	39	4
	As of 25 December 1952									
Total	5,641	2,309	1,947	310	52	3,096	473	174	2,449	236
General	25	9	7	1	1	15	4	-	11	1
Colonel	250	64	60	1	3	178	7	1	170	8
Lieutenant Colonel	552	104	93	4	7	434	14	2	418	14
Major	985	285	241	34	10	667	49	22	596	33
Captain	1,574	711	586	111	14	806	134	59	613	57
First Lieutenant	1,459	856	715	127	14	522	188	68	266	81
Second Lieutenant	796	280	245	32	3	474	77	22	375	42
Mobilization Assignee - Total	2,606	664	532	103	29	1,798	177	71	1,550	144
General	25	9	7	1	1	15	4	-	11	1
Colonel	206	46	42	1	3	154	7	-	147	6
Lieutenant Colonel	404	51	45	3	3	342	9	1	332	11
Major	567	95	77	13	5	445	29	14	402	27
Captain	717	224	175	40	9	456	57	27	372	37
First Lieutenant	452	194	154	33	7	218	62	23	133	40
Second Lieutenant	235	45	32	12	1	168	9	6	153	22
Combat Training Center - Total	2,202	1,249	1,079	153	17	904	198	52	647	49
General	-	-	-	-	-	-	-	-	-	-
Colonel	26	12	12	-	-	13	-	1	12	1
Lieutenant Colonel	111	36	32	-	4	73	4	-	69	2
Major	315	144	124	16	4	169	14	2	153	2
Captain	610	370	315	53	2	227	44	18	165	13
First Lieutenant	732	498	425	68	5	213	88	31	94	21
Second Lieutenant	408	189	171	16	2	209	48	7	154	10

TABLE 330 — AF RESERVE OFFICERS IN PAY STATUS ASSIGNMENTS BY FLYING STATUS BY CATEGORY OF ASSIGNMENT, BY GRADE – FY 1953 (CONTINUED)

Grade and Category of Assignment	Total	On Flying Status				Not on Flying Status				Flying Status Unknown
		Total	Pilot	Other Rated	Non-Rated	Total	Pilot	Other Rated	Non-Rated	
	As of 25 December 1952 (Continued)									
Combat Support Training Center - Total b/	78	19	16	3	-	35	6	1	28	24
General	-	-	-	-	-	-	-	-	-	-
Colonel	3	-	-	-	-	2	-	-	2	1
Lieutenant Colonel	3	-	-	-	-	2	-	-	2	1
Major	7	1	-	1	-	4	1	-	3	2
Captain	23	10	9	1	-	10	1	-	9	3
First Lieutenant	27	8	7	1	-	9	4	1	4	10
Second Lieutenant	15	-	-	-	-	8	-	-	8	7
Flying Training Center - Total	755	377	320	51	6	359	92	43	224	19
General	-	-	-	-	-	-	-	-	-	-
Colonel	15	6	6	-	-	9	-	-	9	-
Lieutenant Colonel	34	17	16	1	-	17	1	1	15	-
Major	96	45	40	4	1	49	5	6	38	2
Captain	224	107	87	17	3	113	32	14	57	4
First Lieutenant	248	156	129	25	2	82	34	13	35	10
Second Lieutenant	138	46	42	4	-	89	20	9	60	3
	As of 25 March 1953									
Total	6,053	2,667	2,238	398	31	3,187	391	186	2,610	199
General	24	9	8	1	-	14	3	-	11	1
Colonel	271	58	56	-	2	207	7	1	199	6
Lieutenant Colonel	556	118	106	7	5	432	7	2	423	6
Major	1,016	326	273	43	10	665	33	20	612	25
Captain	1,725	808	662	139	7	866	118	64	684	51
First Lieutenant	1,605	1,013	840	170	3	515	162	82	271	77
Second Lieutenant	856	335	293	38	4	488	61	17	410	33
Mobilization Assignee - Total	2,654	715	575	122	18	1,835	162	70	1,603	104
General	24	9	8	1	-	14	3	-	11	1
Colonel	220	40	38	-	2	177	6	1	170	3
Lieutenant Colonel	405	61	54	3	4	338	5	1	332	6
Major	589	129	103	21	5	442	15	11	416	18
Captain	754	240	188	48	4	488	64	29	395	26
First Lieutenant	444	197	157	38	2	210	58	24	128	37
Second Lieutenant	218	39	27	11	1	166	11	4	151	13
Combat Training Center - Total	2,420	1,470	1,269	198	3	883	124	58	701	67
General	-	-	-	-	-	-	-	-	-	-
Colonel	30	13	13	-	-	15	1	-	14	2
Lieutenant Colonel	116	42	38	3	1	74	1	-	73	-
Major	318	146	128	16	2	169	11	5	153	3
Captain	666	417	352	65	-	232	22	18	192	17
First Lieutenant	832	621	527	94	-	180	60	29	91	31
Second Lieutenant	458	231	211	20	-	213	29	6	178	14
Flying Training Center - Total	848	437	369	61	7	392	95	51	246	19
General	-	-	-	-	-	-	-	-	-	-
Colonel	16	5	5	-	-	11	-	-	11	-
Lieutenant Colonel	31	15	14	1	-	16	1	1	14	-
Major	100	48	42	4	2	48	6	4	38	4
Captain	268	136	111	23	2	126	28	15	83	6
First Lieutenant	274	170	143	27	-	98	40	25	33	6
Second Lieutenant	159	63	54	6	3	93	20	6	67	3
Combat Support Training Center - Total	131	45	25	17	3	77	10	7	60	9
General	-	-	-	-	-	-	-	-	-	-
Colonel	5	-	-	-	-	4	-	-	4	1
Lieutenant Colonel	4	-	-	-	-	4	-	-	4	-
Major	9	3	-	2	1	6	1	-	5	-
Captain	37	15	11	3	1	20	4	2	14	2
First Lieutenant	55	25	13	11	1	27	4	4	19	3
Second Lieutenant	21	2	1	1	-	16	1	1	14	3

308700 O - 54 - 38

TABLE 330 — AF RESERVE OFFICERS IN PAY STATUS ASSIGNMENTS BY FLYING STATUS BY CATEGORY OF ASSIGNMENT, BY GRADE — FY 1953 (CONTINUED)

Grade and Category of Assignment	Total	On Flying Status				Not on Flying Status				Flying Status Unknown
		Total	Pilot	Other Rated	Non-Rated	Total	Pilot	Other Rated	Non-Rated	
	As of 25 June 1953									
Total	6,360	2,916	2,409	465	42	3,204	312	166	2,726	240
General	22	10	8	1	1	11	3	-	8	1
Colonel	301	69	66	-	3	222	7	1	214	10
Lieutenant Colonel	594	120	106	8	6	455	14	6	435	19
Major	1,056	329	262	57	10	699	21	14	664	28
Captain	1,805	927	755	162	10	819	92	56	671	59
First Lieutenant	1,756	1,113	907	200	6	546	134	69	343	97
Second Lieutenant	826	348	305	37	6	452	41	20	391	25
Mobilization Assignee - Total	2,701	702	559	125	18	1,884	150	71	1,663	115
General	22	10	8	1	1	11	3	-	8	1
Colonel	235	44	41	-	3	183	5	1	177	8
Lieutenant Colonel	425	59	51	4	4	352	8	3	341	14
Major	608	124	92	28	4	469	14	9	446	15
Captain	750	251	203	46	2	468	55	28	285	31
First Lieutenant	454	177	137	38	2	243	56	26	161	34
Second Lieutenant	207	37	27	8	2	158	9	4	145	12
Combat Training Center - Total	2,534	1,597	1,342	242	13	848	91	43	714	89
General	-	-	-	-	-	-	-	-	-	-
Colonel	40	18	18	-	-	20	1	-	19	2
Lieutenant Colonel	120	46	42	3	1	72	4	1	67	2
Major	314	144	121	21	2	159	4	-	155	11
Captain	700	471	381	85	5	211	20	10	181	18
First Lieutenant	924	688	575	110	3	189	50	23	116	47
Second Lieutenant	436	230	205	23	2	197	12	9	176	9
Flying Training Center - Total	898	521	449	63	9	359	66	51	242	18
General	-	-	-	-	-	-	-	-	-	-
Colonel	17	6	6	-	-	11	1	-	10	-
Lieutenant Colonel	34	14	13	1	-	19	1	2	16	1
Major	107	52	45	4	3	54	2	5	47	1
Captain	288	175	148	24	3	108	15	17	76	5
First Lieutenant	310	208	177	30	1	92	27	20	45	10
Second Lieutenant	142	66	60	4	2	75	20	7	48	1
Combat Support Training Center - Total	227	96	59	35	2	113	5	1	107	18
General	-	-	-	-	-	-	-	-	-	-
Colonel	9	1	1	-	-	8	-	-	8	-
Lieutenant Colonel	15	1	-	-	1	12	1	-	11	2
Major	27	9	4	4	1	17	1	-	16	1
Captain	67	30	23	7	-	32	2	1	29	5
First Lieutenant	68	40	18	22	-	22	1	-	21	6
Second Lieutenant	41	15	13	2	-	22	-	-	22	4

a/ Discontinued, November 1952.
b/ Activated, November 1952.

Source: Personnel Statistics Division, DCS/Comptroller, Hq. USAF.

TABLE 331 — AF RESERVE GAINS AND LOSSES — FY 1953

By Cause	Jul (1952)	Aug	Sep	Oct	Nov	Dec	Jan (1953)	Feb	Mar	Apr	May	Jun
						OFFICER						
Gain - Total	5,215	4,385	1,422	2,177	3,233	1,791	1,816	2,059	2,645	5,415	4,765	5,105
Commissioned from Civil Life	225	207	177	185	135	150	88	122	141	284	342	416
Reappointment	1	3	-	8	3	-	-	1	2	3	122	591
Commissioned from ROTC	3,696	2,994	433	236	113	137	72	213	616	342	160	632
Commissioned from Reserve Status	32	71	75	94	19	-	2	1	1	11	17	12
Commissioned from Enlisted Status (Regular Air Force)	-	-	-	-	-	12	19	16	23	33	82	65
On Relief from Extended Active Duty	370	682	720	1,609	1,345	1,307	1,632	1,700	1,851	3,162	1,288	1,825
From Reserve Retired List	-	4	-	3	2	1	-	-	-	40	544	488
Rescission/Revocation of Orders	17	23	17	42	15	6	3	6	11	26	73	18
Gain from Air National Guard	-	-	-	-	-	-	-	-	-	-	-	52
Net Gain from Survey of Reserve Resources	874	401	-	-	1,601	178	-	-	-	1,514	2,137	1,006
Loss - Total	1,524	2,486	2,002	2,925	1,088	649	1,069	2,236	1,810	70,614	8,056	5,073
Resignation, Term of Commission	137	118	150	169	162	138	139	119	131	87	78	168
Term of Commission/for Cause	7	-	1	3	6	-	-	-	1	4	2	1
Retirement	16	12	12	14	12	8	7	18	14	10	7	15
Decease	25	15	19	31	23	23	28	52	49	32	27	56
Ordered to Extended Active Duty	1,273	2,289	1,642	1,413	797	387	587	711	927	1,323	858	1,080
Losses to Reserve Retired List	59	43	62	44	85	87	62	25	32	15	8	13
Rescission/Revocation of Orders	7	9	8	4	3	4	2	6	5	11	60	11
Declined Indefinite Appointment	-	-	-	-	-	2	-	-	-	41,691	1,673	1,684
Non-Response to Indefinite Appointment	-	-	-	-	-	-	-	-	-	24,814	4,228	1,444
Failure to Locate for Indefinite Appointment	-	-	-	-	-	-	-	-	-	2,627	1,105	572
Loss to Air National Guard	-	-	-	-	-	-	-	-	-	-	-	29
Net Loss from Survey of Reserve Resources	-	-	108	1,247	-	-	244	1,305	651	-	10	-
NET GAIN OR LOSS	+3,691	+1,899	-580	-748	+2,145	+1,142	+747	-177	+835	-65,199	-3,291	+32
						AIRMAN						
Gain - Total	2,089	2,234	2,616	4,205	4,272	3,228	3,055	3,353	4,218	3,696	2,262	2,159
Enlisted from Civil Life	512	925	767	1,373	1,202	997	826	1,182	1,416	1,415	1,141	958
Reenlistment within 30 days of Separation from Air Force Reserve	37	41	101	161	76	46	52	56	32	75	84	64
On Relief from Extended Active Duty	1,104	1,186	1,740	2,658	2,637	2,175	2,171	2,105	2,656	1,774	745	843
From Reserve Retired List	-	-	-	1	-	-	-	2	-	-	-	-
Rescission/Revocation of Orders	8	14	8	12	6	10	3	8	13	8	5	1
Gain from Air National Guard	-	-	-	-	-	-	-	-	-	-	-	293
Net Gain from Survey of Reserve Resources	428	68	-	-	351	-	3	-	101	424	287	-
Loss - Total	1,148	1,819	2,328	4,714	3,860	4,100	4,171	3,868	5,991	12,943	4,463	4,611
Discharge for Other Than Cause	774	1,508	1,831	3,034	3,628	3,808	3,914	3,430	5,719	11,755	3,965	4,083
Discharge for Cause	-	2	2	12	9	11	5	5	5	9	2	9
Retirement	3	-	1	-	-	-	1	8	-	1	1	1
Deceased	10	6	3	7	11	18	3	12	8	8	2	7
Enlisted in Regular Establishment	39	71	40	-	53	54	51	47	51	110	136	61
Commissioned from Reserve Enlisted Status	5	4	6	44	-	8	3	7	1	2	8	6
Ordered to Extended Active Duty	295	210	159	199	152	154	185	186	203	244	342	265
Losses to Reserve Retired List	18	7	6	5	3	6	3	-	1	1	-	-
Rescission/Revocation of Orders	4	11	4	3	4	10	6	12	3	21	7	2
Loss to Air National Guard	-	-	-	-	-	-	-	-	-	-	-	8
Net Loss from Survey of Reserve Resources	-	-	276	1,410	-	31	-	161	-	792	-	169
NET GAIN OR LOSS	+ 937	+415	+288	-509	+412	-872	-1,116	-515	-1,773	-9,247	-2,201	-2,504

Source: Personnel Statistics Division, DCS/Comptroller, Hq. USAF.

TABLE 332 — AF RESERVE PERSONNEL PARTICIPATING IN INACTIVE DUTY TRAINING FOR PAY — FY 1953

Category of Personnel Assignment	Jul (1952)	Aug	Sep	Oct	Nov	Dec	Jan (1953)	Feb	Mar	Apr	May	Jun
TOTAL	5,795	5,805	6,740	7,185	7,768	8,018	8,448	8,746	9,399	9,904	9,954	10,284
OFFICER - TOTAL	3,542	3,460	4,097	4,364	4,599	4,708	4,885	4,982	5,271	5,569	5,557	5,868
AIRMAN - TOTAL	2,253	2,345	2,643	2,821	3,169	3,310	3,563	3,764	4,128	4,335	4,397	4,416
Assigned Mobilization Assignment - Total	1,547	1,282	1,492	1,506	1,524	1,546	1,581	1,593	1,636	1,553	1,461	1,530
Officer	1,450	1,218	1,403	1,430	1,443	1,438	1,507	1,521	1,490	1,471	1,367	1,396
Airman	97	64	89	76	81	108	74	72	146	82	94	134
Attached Mobilization Assignment - Total	298	271	244	267	263	271	286	330	180	287	275	186
Officer	172	169	166	179	176	188	202	244	176	230	215	182
Airmen	126	102	78	88	87	83	84	86	4	57	60	4
Mobilization Assignment with Training Attachment - Total	221	191	212	219	229	223	70	58	62	56	50	50
Officer	219	190	211	219	229	223	68	58	62	56	50	50
Airman	2	1	1	-	-	-	2	-	-	-	-	-
Air Force Reserve Combat Training Center - Total	2,191	2,650	3,092	3,320	3,567	3,856	4,182	4,230	4,637	4,778	4,783	4,735
Officer	1,025	1,238	1,534	1,693	1,817	1,876	2,016	1,978	2,111	2,138	2,147	2,167
Airman	1,166	1,412	1,558	1,627	1,750	1,980	2,166	2,252	2,526	2,640	2,636	2,568
Air Force Reserve Flying Training Center - Total	1,199	1,207	1,297	1,442	1,592	1,606	1,705	1,814	1,827	1,903	1,938	2,016
Officer	490	476	528	575	614	658	696	705	703	745	750	790
Airman	709	731	769	867	978	948	1,009	1,109	1,124	1,158	1,188	1,226
Air Force Reserve Combat Support Training Center-Total	-	-	-	-	234	144	185	193	265	299	355	408
Officer	-	-	-	-	47	50	72	93	122	148	190	215
Airman	-	-	-	-	187	94	113	100	143	151	165	193
Air Force Reserve Specialist Training Center-Total	131	204	252	303	359	372	439	528	792	1,028	1,092	1,359
Officer	113	169	208	236	273	275	324	383	607	781	838	1,068
Airman	18	35	44	67	86	97	115	145	185	247	254	291
Corollary - Total a/	208	-	151	128	-	-	-	-	-	-	-	-
Officer	73	-	47	32	-	-	-	-	-	-	-	-
Airman	135	-	104	96	-	-	-	-	-	-	-	-

a/ Discontinued November 1952.

Source: Personnel Statistics Division, DCS/Comptroller, Hq USAF.

TABLE 333 — AF RESERVE INACTIVE DUTY TRAINING PERIODS ACCOMPLISHED FOR PAY — FY 1953

Category of Assignment	Jul (1952)	Aug	Sep	Oct	Nov	Dec	Jan (1953)	Feb	Mar	Apr	May	Jun
TOTAL	18,976	19,315	22,932	23,951	25,382	26,719	29,284	30,607	32,862	33,577	33,008	34,215
OFFICER - TOTAL	10,757	11,097	13,167	13,751	14,413	14,938	15,820	16,232	17,372	17,624	17,127	18,187
AIRMAN - TOTAL	8,219	8,218	9,765	10,200	10,969	11,781	13,464	14,375	15,490	15,953	15,881	16,028
Assigned Mobilization Assignment - Total	3,336	3,101	3,405	3,329	3,231	3,373	3,566	3,394	4,055	3,466	3,012	3,697
Officer	3,172	2,944	3,197	3,136	3,043	3,127	3,379	3,236	3,703	3,300	2,860	3,338
Airman	164	157	208	193	188	246	187	158	352	166	152	359
Attached Mobilization Assignment - Total	843	742	686	685	738	729	759	892	486	820	728	525
Officer	473	450	487	469	495	515	543	674	468	665	558	517
Airman	370	292	199	216	243	214	216	218	18	155	170	8
Mobilization Assignment with Training Attachment- Total	731	610	828	730	736	796	162	132	160	151	125	142
Officer	727	609	827	730	736	796	150	132	160	151	125	142
Airman	4	1	1	-	-	-	12	-	-	-	-	-
Corollary - Total a/	734	-	583	510	-	-	-	-	-	-	-	-
Officer	234	-	187	148	-	-	-	-	-	-	-	-
Airman	500	-	396	362	-	-	-	-	-	-	-	-
AF Reserve Combat Training Center - Total	8,285	10,297	11,915	12,561	13,486	14,502	16,871	17,324	18,293	18,469	18,353	17,862
Officer	3,946	5,016	5,947	6,538	7,067	7,172	8,109	8,221	8,386	8,319	8,341	8,140
Airman	4,339	5,281	5,968	6,023	6,419	7,330	8,762	9,103	9,907	10,150	10,012	9,722
AF Reserve Flying Training Center - Total	4,720	4,110	4,919	5,422	5,926	5,940	6,211	6,843	6,970	7,255	7,309	7,590
Officer	1,923	1,700	2,033	2,170	2,365	2,517	2,588	2,716	2,754	2,901	2,885	2,998
Airman	2,797	2,410	2,886	3,252	3,561	3,423	3,623	4,127	4,216	4,354	4,424	4,592
AF Reserve Combat Support Training Center - Total	-	-	-	-	502	553	662	719	1,003	1,114	1,358	1,529
Officer	-	-	-	-	105	193	276	337	484	572	744	811
Airman	-	-	-	-	397	360	386	382	519	542	614	718
AF Reserve Specialist Training Center - Total	327	455	596	714	763	826	1,053	1,303	1,895	2,302	2,123	2,870
Officer	282	378	489	560	602	618	775	916	1,417	1,716	1,614	2,241
Airman	45	77	107	154	161	208	278	387	478	586	509	629

a/ Discontinued November 1952.

Source: Personnel Statistics Division, DCS/Comptroller, Hq USAF.

TABLE 334 — AF RESERVE PERSONNEL PARTICIPATING IN UNPAID INACTIVE DUTY TRAINING — FY 1953

Program Element	Jul (1952)	Aug	Sep	Oct	Nov	Dec	Jan (1953)		Feb		Mar		Apr		May		Jun	
							Ready	Standby	Ready	Standby	Ready	Standby	Ready	Standby	Ready	Standby	Ready	Standby
TOTAL	53,410	51,963	66,558	68,977	65,276	63,400	74,571	1,250	76,172	3,349	76,232	12,493	68,011	18,945	62,794	21,700	56,499	22,261
OFFICER - TOTAL	45,293	43,885	56,027	57,848	54,318	52,911	60,656	1,040	63,637	2,991	62,835	11,483	54,432	17,429	50,023	20,028	45,141	20,408
AIRMAN - TOTAL	8,117	8,078	10,531	11,129	10,958	10,489	13,915	210	12,535	358	13,397	1,010	13,579	1,516	12,771	1,672	11,358	1,853
Assigned Mobilization Assignment - Total	447	447	750	272	386	567	371	-	611	-	1,223	-	851	-	693	-	1,230	-
Officer	437	423	739	259	345	519	352	-	584	-	1,072	-	822	-	678	-	1,057	-
Airman	10	24	11	13	41	48	19	-	27	-	151	-	29	-	15	-	173	-
Attached Mobilization Assignment - Total	22	36	71	19	38	94	72	-	156	-	61	-	138	-	190	-	68	-
Officer	7	18	40	13	17	43	27	-	87	-	60	-	52	-	98	-	68	-
Airman	15	18	31	6	21	51	45	-	69	-	1	-	86	-	92	-	-	-
Mobilization Assignee with Training Attachment-Total	63	62	132	134	138	92	2	-	16	-	39	-	47	-	51	-	112	-
Officer	63	62	132	134	138	92	2	-	16	-	39	-	47	-	51	-	112	-
Airman	-	-	-	-	-	-	-	-	-	-	-	-	-	-	-	-	-	-
Corollary - Total a/	4	-	-	64	-	-	-	-	-	-	-	-	-	-	-	-	-	-
Officer	4	-	-	64	-	-	-	-	-	-	-	-	-	-	-	-	-	-
Airman	-	-	-	-	-	-	-	-	-	-	-	-	-	-	-	-	-	-
AF Reserve Combat Training Center - Total	173	267	235	446	402	256	241	-	364	-	241	-	260	-	250	-	289	-
Officer	144	215	143	323	292	220	213	-	287	-	198	-	185	-	192	-	227	-
Airman	29	52	92	123	110	36	28	-	77	-	43	-	75	-	58	-	62	-
AF Reserve Flying Training Center - Total	42	91	188	207	230	156	155	-	196	-	200	-	251	-	168	-	205	-
Officer	40	88	176	193	126	136	148	-	166	-	155	-	179	-	107	-	146	-
Airman	2	3	12	14	104	20	7	-	30	-	45	-	72	-	61	-	59	-
AF Reserve Combat Support Training Center - Total	-	-	-	-	-	-	22	-	52	-	81	-	25	-	39	-	41	-
Officer	-	-	-	-	-	-	22	-	50	-	63	-	24	-	39	-	36	-
Airman	-	-	-	-	-	-	-	-	2	-	18	-	1	-	-	-	5	-
AF Reserve Specialist Training Center - Total	284	327	356	382	354	317	192	238	502	71	637	192	545	162	659	146	785	196
Officer	241	284	307	331	317	256	162	200	407	71	535	191	431	162	551	146	700	192
Airman	43	43	49	51	37	61	30	38	95	-	102	1	114	-	108	-	85	4
Mobilization Designee-Total	669	663	1,156	960	865	928	839	37	1,168	10	1,277	22	1,088	37	924	246	861	214
Officer	644	646	1,138	921	837	894	806	37	1,075	10	1,191	22	1,023	37	865	243	781	214
Airman	25	17	18	39	28	34	33	-	93	-	86	-	65	-	59	3	80	-
Voluntary Air Reserve-Total	47,154	45,798	57,881	61,230	57,447	54,062	64,909	781	66,042	3,188	64,756	12,113	57,778	18,438	53,511	20,926	48,095	21,564
Officer	39,957	38,652	48,665	51,474	48,090	45,334	53,030	653	55,173	2,830	52,980	11,109	46,284	16,954	42,502	19,276	38,330	19,724
Airman	7,197	7,146	9,216	9,756	9,357	8,728	11,879	128	10,869	358	11,776	1,004	11,494	1,484	11,009	1,650	9,765	1,840
Non-Affiliated Reserve Section - Total	4,552	4,272	5,789	5,263	5,416	6,928	7,768	194	7,065	80	7,717	166	7,028	308	6,309	382	4,813	287
Officer	3,756	3,497	4,687	4,136	4,156	5,417	5,894	150	5,792	80	6,542	161	5,385	276	4,940	363	3,684	278
Airman	796	775	1,102	1,127	1,260	1,511	1,874	44	1,273	-	1,175	5	1,643	32	1,369	19	1,129	9

a/ Discontinued November 1952.
Source: Personnel Statistics Division, DCS/Comptroller, Hq USAF.

TABLE 335 — AF RESERVE UNPAID INACTIVE DUTY TRAINING PERIODS ACCOMPLISHED — FY 1953

Program Element	Jul (1952)	Aug	Sep	Oct	Nov	Dec	Jan (1953)		Feb		Mar		Apr		May		Jun	
							Ready	Standby	Ready	Standby	Ready	Standby	Ready	Standby	Ready	Standby	Ready	Standby
TOTAL	21,288	21,238	25,320	25,131	25,920	26,937	27,753	404	27,990	1,226	27,014	4,042	23,368	6,011	22,597	7,253	20,170	7,555
OFFICER - TOTAL	17,775	17,733	20,772	20,449	21,054	22,048	22,339	338	22,968	1,088	21,661	3,694	18,133	5,515	17,535	6,649	15,505	6,905
AIRMAN - TOTAL	3,513	3,505	4,548	4,682	4,866	4,889	5,414	66	5,022	138	5,353	348	5,235	496	5,062	604	4,665	650
Assigned Mobilization Assignment - Total	89	127	244	110	161	217	156	-	231	-	341	-	265	-	177	-	391	-
Officer	86	122	241	103	155	202	150	-	223	-	308	-	254	-	170	-	344	-
Airman	3	5	3	7	6	15	6	-	8	-	33	-	11	-	7	-	47	-
Attached Mobilization Assignment - Total	11	16	29	11	23	43	33	-	47	-	16	-	49	-	55	-	15	-
Officer	3	7	15	9	11	22	13	-	22	-	15	-	17	-	27	-	15	-
Airman	8	9	14	2	12	21	20	-	25	-	1	-	32	-	28	-	-	-
Mobilization Assignee with Training Attachment-Total	41	46	58	63	73	52	1	-	5	-	7	-	5	-	12	-	26	-
Officer	41	46	58	63	73	52	1	-	5	-	7	-	5	-	12	-	26	-
Airman	-	-	-	-	-	-	-	-	-	-	-	-	-	-	-	-	-	-
Corollary - Total a/	3	-	-	19	-	-	-	-	-	-	-	-	-	-	-	-	-	-
Officer	3	-	-	19	-	-	-	-	-	-	-	-	-	-	-	-	-	-
Airman	-	-	-	-	-	-	-	-	-	-	-	-	-	-	-	-	-	-
AF Reserve Combat Training Center - Total	43	48	17	87	211	46	61	-	104	-	32	-	69	-	72	-	37	-
Officer	26	36	13	65	134	44	52	-	80	-	22	-	42	-	45	-	22	-
Airman	17	12	4	22	77	2	9	-	24	-	10	-	27	-	27	-	15	-
AF Reserve Flying Training Center - Total	14	20	60	31	34	29	44	-	37	-	48	-	63	-	46	-	69	-
Officer	13	19	56	27	26	26	40	-	31	-	47	-	58	-	28	-	53	-
Airman	1	1	4	4	8	3	4	-	6	-	1	-	5	-	18	-	16	-
AF Reserve Combat Support Training Center - Total	-	-	-	-	-	-	3	-	14	-	43	-	21	-	24	-	22	-
Officer	-	-	-	-	-	-	3	-	13	-	30	-	20	-	24	-	17	-
Airman	-	-	-	-	-	-	-	-	1	-	13	-	1	-	-	-	5	-
AF Reserve Specialist Training Center - Total	115	129	147	153	134	131	67	77	185	27	156	76	107	66	119	58	140	86
Officer	99	112	126	133	121	108	54	64	146	27	126	75	87	66	97	58	126	84
Airman	16	17	21	20	13	23	13	13	39	-	30	1	20	-	22	-	14	2
Mobilization Designee-Total	458	411	567	648	561	650	565	12	777	5	940	10	761	18	703	111	577	100
Officer	445	405	560	628	549	638	550	12	745	5	919	10	737	18	683	108	553	100
Airman	13	6	7	20	12	12	15	-	32	-	21	-	24	-	20	3	24	-
Voluntary Air Reserve-Total	18,293	18,320	21,385	31,597	22,039	21,540	22,506	228	23,250	1,157	21,630	3,901	18,955	5,814	18,702	6,952	16,910	7,254
Officer	15,328	15,347	17,524	17,589	18,052	17,810	18,354	194	18,981	1,019	17,190	3,555	14,538	5,331	14,394	6,361	12,857	6,609
Airman	2,965	2,973	3,861	4,008	3,987	3,730	4,152	34	4,269	138	4,440	346	4,417	483	4,308	591	4,053	645
Non-Affiliated Reserve Section - Total	2,221	2,121	2,813	2,412	2,684	1,229	4,317	87	3,340	37	3,801	55	3,073	113	2,687	132	1,983	115
Officer - Total	1,731	1,639	2,179	1,813	1,951	3,146	3,122	68	2,722	37	2,997	54	2,375	100	2,055	122	1,492	112
Airman - Total	490	482	634	599	733	1,083	1,195	19	618	-	804	1	698	13	632	10	491	3

a/ Discontinued November 1952.

Source: Personnel Statistics Division, DCS/Comptroller, Hq USAF.

TABLE 336 — AF RESERVE ACTIVE DUTY TRAINING MAN-DAYS COMPLETED FOR SCHOOL AND OTHER THAN SCHOOL TRAINING - FY 1953

Category of Assignment	Jul (1952)	Aug	Sep	Oct	Nov	Dec	Jan (1953) Ready	Jan (1953) Standby	Feb Ready	Feb Standby	Mar Ready	Mar Standby	Apr Ready	Apr Standby	May Ready	May Standby	Jun Ready	Jun Standby
TOTAL	12,363	29,024	8,371	5,539	6,190	16,589	11,989	54	11,950	44	12,537	260	12,008	379	15,455	733	24,458	2,510
OFFICER - TOTAL	9,363	17,138	7,511	5,054	5,545	15,049	10,419	45	10,398	44	11,171	236	9,933	313	13,206	700	21,018	2,444
AIRMAN - TOTAL	3,000	11,886	860	485	645	1,540	1,570	9	1,552	-	1,366	24	2,075	66	2,249	33	3,440	66
Assigned Mobilization																		
Assignment - Total	2,076	2,205	2,003	839	1,149	3,502	1,484	-	1,422	-	2,237	-	2,406	-	3,034	-	6,586	-
Officer	1,944	2,151	1,919	824	1,090	3,323	1,398	-	1,352	-	2,213	-	2,320	-	2,980	-	6,113	-
Airman	132	54	84	15	59	179	86	-	70	-	24	-	86	-	54	-	473	-
Attached Mobilization																		
Assignment - Total	180	398	349	94	106	809	342	-	309	-	261	-	461	-	791	-	1,104	-
Officer	180	361	334	94	106	794	312	-	238	-	231	-	420	-	697	-	942	-
Airman	-	37	15	-	-	15	30	-	71	-	30	-	41	-	94	-	162	-
Mobilization Assignment with																		
Training Attachment-Total	1,219	1,385	249	229	103	1,404	448	-	620	-	687	-	780	-	797	-	669	-
Officer	1,219	1,368	249	229	103	1,404	448	-	620	-	687	-	780	-	797	-	654	-
Airman	-	17	-	-	-	-	-	-	-	-	-	-	-	-	-	-	15	-
Corollary - Total a/	-	2,503	-	-	-	-	-	-	-	-	-	-	-	-	-	-	-	-
Officer	-	778	-	-	-	-	-	-	-	-	-	-	-	-	-	-	-	-
Airman	-	1,725	-	-	-	-	-	-	-	-	-	-	-	-	-	-	-	-
AF Reserve Combat Training																		
Center - Total	4,601	17,844	1,420	1,055	1,158	2,174	2,706	-	2,941	-	1,847	-	1,884	-	2,067	-	2,826	-
Officer	2,078	8,121	966	797	738	1,574	1,989	-	2,233	-	1,356	-	1,209	-	1,547	-	1,777	-
Airman	2,523	9,723	454	258	420	600	717	-	708	-	491	-	675	-	520	-	1,049	-
AF Reserve Flying Training																		
Center - Total	322	116	449	227	573	863	1,483	-	1,244	-	1,791	-	1,746	-	1,912	-	2,297	-
Officer	218	89	438	136	429	614	797	-	711	-	1,225	-	756	-	975	-	1,269	-
Airman	114	27	11	91	144	249	686	-	533	-	566	-	990	-	937	-	1,028	-
AF Reserve Combat Support																		
Training Center - Total	-	-	-	-	-	15	6	-	9	-	65	-	123	-	103	-	65	-
Officer	-	-	-	-	-	15	6	-	9	-	65	-	96	-	103	-	65	-
Airman	-	-	-	-	-	-	-	-	-	-	-	-	27	-	-	-	-	-
AF Reserve Specialist																		
Training Center - Total	-	137	103	25	461	291	213	9	240	-	239	38	198	-	1,781	9	2,772	53
Officer	-	137	88	25	461	201	213	-	222	-	176	38	184	-	1,283	9	2,309	53
Airman	-	-	15	-	-	90	-	9	18	-	63	-	14	-	498	-	463	-
Mobilization Designee-Total	195	381	139	60	30	230	414	30	393	5	570	25	623	21	1,062	173	1,480	456
Officer	195	351	139	60	30	230	414	30	393	5	570	25	608	21	1,055	173	1,444	456
Airman	-	30	-	-	-	-	-	-	-	-	-	-	15	-	7	-	36	-
Voluntary Air Reserve-Total	3,309	3,351	3,232	2,580	2,321	6,607	3,978	15	3,987	39	3,945	173	3,384	-	3,118	542	6,004	1,988
Officer	3,078	3,078	2,966	2,459	2,299	6,200	3,935	15	3,835	39	3,753	173	3,157	-	2,979	509	5,805	1,922
Airman	231	273	266	121	22	407	43	-	152	-	192	-	227	-	139	33	199	66
Non-Affiliated Reserve																		
Section - Total	451	704	427	430	289	694	915	-	785	-	895	24	403	358	790	9	655	13
Officer	451	704	412	430	289	694	907	-	785	-	895	-	403	292	790	9	640	13
Airman	-	-	15	-	-	-	8	-	-	-	-	24	-	66	-	-	15	-

a/ Discontinued November 1952.

Source: Personnel Statistics Division, DCS/Comptroller, Hq USAF.

TABLE 337 – AF RESERVE PERSONNEL WHO COMPLETED ACTIVE DUTY SCHOOL AND OTHER THAN SCHOOL TRAINING – FY 1953

Category of Personnel Assignment	Jul (1952)	Aug	Sep	Oct	Nov	Dec	Jan (1953) Ready	Jan (1953) Stand-by	Feb Ready	Feb Stand-by	Mar Ready	Mar Stand-by	Apr Ready	Apr Stand-by	May Ready	May Stand-by	Jun Ready	Jun Stand-by
TOTAL	749	1,945	626	362	362	760	821	4	790	4	919	25	938	33	1,266	60	2,032	201
OFFICER - TOTAL	546	1,116	559	330	311	673	702	3	670	4	792	23	778	29	1,088	58	1,786	197
AIRMAN - TOTAL	203	829	67	32	51	87	119	1	120	-	127	2	160	4	178	2	246	4
Assigned Mobilization Assignment - Total	144	155	130	56	72	198	130	-	118	-	189	-	212	-	250	-	485	-
Officer	134	151	123	55	69	186	123	-	112	-	182	-	205	-	244	-	451	-
Airman	10	4	7	1	3	12	7	-	6	-	7	-	7	-	6	-	34	-
Attached Mobilization Assignment - Total	12	27	24	8	8	17	16	-	23	-	19	-	33	-	66	-	81	-
Officer	12	24	23	8	8	16	14	-	18	-	16	-	31	-	59	-	71	-
Airman	-	3	1	-	-	1	2	-	5	-	3	-	2	-	7	-	10	-
Mobilization Assignment with Training Attachment - Total	46	69	9	10	6	46	22	-	25	-	31	-	32	-	34	-	43	-
Officer	46	68	9	10	6	46	22	-	25	-	31	-	32	-	34	-	42	-
Airman	-	1	-	-	-	-	-	-	-	-	-	-	-	-	-	-	1	-
Air Force Reserve Combat Training Center-Total	310	1,209	91	73	78	108	196	-	188	-	155	-	163	-	192	-	232	-
Officer	138	544	61	55	50	77	143	-	139	-	109	-	104	-	142	-	150	-
Airman	172	665	30	18	28	31	53	-	49	-	46	-	59	-	50	-	82	-
Air Force Reserve Flying Training Center-Total	20	9	43	20	59	70	114	-	128	-	160	-	156	-	160	-	170	-
Officer	15	5	35	14	42	47	63	-	77	-	105	-	81	-	98	-	107	-
Airman	5	4	8	6	17	23	51	-	51	-	55	-	75	-	62	-	63	-
Air Force Reserve Combat Support Training Center - Total	-	-	-	-	-	1	1	-	1	-	6	-	7	-	7	-	6	4
Officer	-	-	-	-	-	1	1	-	1	-	6	-	6	-	7	-	6	4
Airman	-	-	-	-	-	-	-	-	-	-	-	-	1	-	-	-	-	-
Air Force Reserve Specialist Training Center - Total	-	8	8	2	8	9	10	1	17	-	16	2	21	-	147	1	203	37
Officer	-	8	7	2	8	8	10	-	16	-	13	2	20	-	109	1	169	37
Airman	-	-	1	-	-	1	-	1	1	-	3	-	1	-	38	-	34	-
Corollary - Total a/	-	165	-	-	-	-	-	-	-	-	-	-	-	-	-	-	-	-
Officer	-	50	-	-	-	-	-	-	-	-	-	-	-	-	-	-	-	-
Airman	-	115	-	-	-	-	-	-	-	-	-	-	-	-	-	-	-	-
Mobilization Designee - Total	14	26	9	4	2	23	24	2	25	1	40	2	47	1	86	17	112	-
Officer	14	24	9	4	2	23	24	2	25	1	40	2	46	1	85	17	109	-
Airman	-	2	-	-	-	-	-	-	-	-	-	-	1	-	1	-	3	-
Voluntary Air Reserve Training Unit - Total	169	227	256	160	117	278	241	1	230	3	244	21	240	32	263	41	653	158
Officer	153	192	237	153	114	259	237	1	222	3	231	19	226	28	249	39	635	154
Airman	16	35	19	7	3	19	4	-	8	-	13	2	14	4	14	2	18	4
Non-Affiliated Reserve Section - Total	34	50	56	29	12	10	67	-	35	-	59	-	27	-	61	1	47	2
Officer	34	50	55	29	12	10	65	-	35	-	59	-	27	-	61	1	46	2
Airman	-	-	1	-	-	-	2	-	-	-	-	-	-	-	-	-	1	-

a/ Discontinued November 1952

Source: Personnel Statistics Division, DCS/Comptroller, Hq. USAF

TABLE 338 — AF RESERVE OFFICERS SENT TO ACTIVE MILITARY SERVICE (AMS) BY GRADE, BY CATEGORY OF PERSONNEL ASSIGNMENT — FY 1953

Grade and Category of Assignment	Jul (1952)	Aug	Sep	Oct	Nov	Dec	Jan (1953)	Feb	Mar	Apr	May	Jun
Total	1,470	5,041	6,721	7,942	8,813	9,211	10,273	11,697	13,237	14,758	15,804	17,138
General	-	-	-	-	-	-	-	-	-	-	-	-
Colonel	-	-	-	-	-	1	1	1	1	2	2	2
Lt Colonel	8	10	11	16	20	20	23	31	38	53	70	107
Major	24	47	56	62	67	74	110	159	211	288	324	394
Captain	158	242	297	360	447	500	695	820	1,018	1,241	1,321	1,447
First Lieutenant	276	447	611	765	949	1,064	1,284	1,531	1,827	2,151	2,271	2,450
Second Lieutenant	683	3,792	5,174	5,802	5,994	6,203	6,468	7,072	7,662	8,346	8,812	9,319
Mobilization Assignee - Total	11	12	17	21	21	25	39	58	81	100	132	156
General	-	-	-	-	-	-	-	-	-	-	-	-
Colonel	-	-	-	-	-	-	-	-	-	-	-	-
Lt Colonel	-	-	-	1	2	2	3	7	9	11	15	19
Major	-	-	-	-	1	4	5	6	10	12	15	25
Captain	4	4	9	9	9	9	15	20	31	41	57	66
First Lieutenant	6	7	7	9	8	8	13	18	22	24	32	31
Second Lieutenant	1	1	1	2	1	2	3	7	9	12	13	15
Air Force Reserve Combat Training Center - Total	10	19	25	35	54	60	128	163	187	219	232	257
General	-	-	-	-	-	-	-	-	-	-	-	-
Colonel	-	-	-	-	-	-	-	-	-	-	-	-
Lt Colonel	-	-	-	-	1	1	1	1	2	2	[illegible]	6
Major	-	1	1	1	1	1	7	13	16	22	23	26
Captain	5	11	13	19	28	32	51	57	63	72	80	85
First Lieutenant	5	7	11	15	24	26	38	55	68	81	84	92
Second Lieutenant	-	-	-	-	-	-	31	37	38	42	43	48
Air Force Reserve Flying Training Center - Total	-	-	2	2	7	12	26	37	56	77	78	86
General	-	-	-	-	-	-	-	-	-	-	-	-
Colonel	-	-	-	-	-	-	-	-	-	-	-	-
Lt Colonel	-	-	-	-	-	-	1	1	1	2	2	2
Major	-	-	-	-	-	-	3	4	5	9	9	10
Captain	-	-	-	-	3	5	10	10	16	22	22	25
First Lieutenant	-	-	2	2	4	7	12	19	27	32	33	33
Second Lieutenant	-	-	-	-	-	-	-	3	7	12	12	16
Air Force Reserve Combat Support Training Center-Total	-	-	-	-	-	-	-	-	-	-	-	2
General	-	-	-	-	-	-	-	-	-	-	-	-
Colonel	-	-	-	-	-	-	-	-	-	-	-	-
Lt Colonel	-	-	-	-	-	-	-	-	-	-	-	1
Major	-	-	-	-	-	-	-	-	-	-	-	-
Captain	-	-	-	-	-	-	-	-	-	-	-	-
First Lieutenant	-	-	-	-	-	-	-	-	-	-	-	-
Second Lieutenant	-	-	-	-	-	-	-	-	-	-	-	1

TABLE 338 — AF RESERVE OFFICERS SENT TO ACTIVE MILITARY SERVICE (AMS) BY GRADE BY CATEGORY OF PERSONNEL ASSIGNMENT — FY 1953 (CONTINUED)

Grade and Category of Assignment	Jul (1952)	Aug	Sep	Oct	Nov	Dec	Jan (1953)	Feb	Mar	Apr	May	Jun
Air Force Reserve Specialist Training Center - Total	2	2	2	2	2	4	6	8	10	10	12	13
General	-	-	-	-	-	-	-	-	-	-	-	-
Colonel	-	-	-	-	-	-	-	-	-	-	-	-
Lt Colonel	-	-	-	-	-	-	-	-	-	-	-	-
Major	-	-	-	-	-	-	-	1	1	1	2	2
Captain	1	1	1	1	1	2	2	2	3	3	3	3
First Lieutenant	1	1	1	1	1	2	2	3	3	3	3	4
Second Lieutenant	-	-	-	-	-	-	2	2	3	3	4	4
Mobilization Designee - Total	-	1	1	1	4	6	7	17	23	29	35	39
General	-	-	-	-	-	-	-	-	-	-	-	-
Colonel	-	-	-	-	-	1	1	1	1	1	1	1
Lt Colonel	-	-	-	-	-	-	-	1	1	3	4	3
Major	-	-	-	-	2	2	2	5	6	9	10	13
Captain	-	1	1	1	1	1	1	4	7	8	9	10
First Lieutenant	-	-	-	-	-	1	2	2	4	4	5	6
Second Lieutenant	-	-	-	-	1	1	2	4	4	4	6	6
Volunteer Air Reserve Training Unit and Non-Affiliated Reserve Section - Total	1,447	5,007	6,674	7,881	8,725	9,104	10,066	11,414	12,880	14,322	15,314	16,583
General	-	-	-	-	-	-	-	-	-	-	-	-
Colonel	-	-	-	-	-	-	-	-	-	1	1	1
Lt Colonel	8	10	11	15	17	17	18	21	25	35	47	76
Major	24	46	55	61	63	67	93	130	173	235	265	316
Captain	148	225	273	330	405	451	616	727	898	1,093	1,148	1,256
First Lieutenant	264	432	590	738	912	1,020	1,217	1,434	1,703	2,007	2,114	2,284
Second Lieutenant - Total	682	3,791	5,173	5,800	5,992	6,200	6,430	7,019	7,601	8,273	8,734	9,229
AF Reserve Officers Training Corps	554	3,138	4,196	4,629	4,719	4,779	4,857	5,127	5,518	5,908	6,187	6,454
Direct Appointments	94	585	880	1,049	1,132	1,253	1,253	1,253	1,253	1,253	1,253	1,253
Other	34	68	97	122	141	168	320	639	830	1,112	1,294	1,522
Medical Services a/	321	503	572	937	1,308	1,321	1,664	2,055	2,452	2,650	2,977	3,393
Seminary Graduates a/	-	-	-	-	28	28	28	28	28	28	28	28
Ineligible Reserve Section	-	-	-	-	-	-	-	-	-	b/ 1	b/ 1	c/ 2

a/ Grade spread is not available for Medical Services and Seminary Graduates.
b/ Indicates 1 Captain.
c/ Indicates 1 Captain and 1 Major.

Source: Personnel Statistics Division, DCS/Comptroller, Hq. USAF.

TABLE 339 — AF RESERVE AIRMEN SENT TO ACTIVE MILITARY SERVICE (AMS) BY CATEGORY OF ASSIGNMENT, BY GRADE - FY 1953

Grade and Category of Assignment	Jul (1952)	Aug	Sep	Oct	Nov	Dec	Jan (1953)	Feb	Mar	Apr	May	Jun
TOTAL	205	423	573	744	953	1,139	1,343	1,614	1,895	2,211	2,666	3,069
Grade Seven	15	33	56	87	112	129	161	188	233	277	346	399
Grade Six	44	88	117	155	199	238	271	320	388	450	539	632
Grade Five	59	141	205	266	361	433	511	628	748	876	1,089	1,264
Grade Four	55	97	116	140	172	198	233	276	301	342	409	463
Grade Three	17	37	47	54	63	79	88	105	118	136	145	160
Grade Two	11	21	25	33	36	51	65	83	90	107	118	131
Grade One	4	6	7	9	10	11	14	14	17	23	20	20
Mobilization Assignee - Total	2	4	4	8	10	11	12	12	14	16	21	23
Grade Seven	-	-	-	2	2	2	2	2	2	2	3	4
Grade Six	2	3	3	4	4	4	4	4	5	5	6	6
Grade Five	-	-	-	1	3	4	5	5	5	7	10	11
Grade Four	-	-	-	-	-	-	-	-	-	-	-	-
Grade Three	-	-	1	1	1	1	1	1	2	2	2	2
Grade Two	-	1	-	-	-	-	-	-	-	-	-	-
Grade One	-	-	-	-	-	-	-	-	-	-	-	-
Air Force Reserve Combat Training Center - Total	7	11	17	27	32	32	44	57	70	78	101	133
Grade Seven	-	-	-	1	2	2	4	6	7	4	14	20
Grade Six	1	3	6	7	7	7	8	10	12	12	19	24
Grade Five	1	3	5	11	13	13	16	19	26	19	34	46
Grade Four	3	3	3	4	5	5	7	9	10	10	12	17
Grade Three	-	-	-	-	1	1	3	6	7	16	12	14
Grade Two	-	-	1	2	2	2	4	5	6	10	8	10
Grade One	2	2	2	2	2	2	2	2	2	7	2	2
Air Force Reserve Flying Training Center - Total	-	-	1	3	4	6	10	18	37	43	57	67
Grade Seven	-	-	1	1	1	1	1	1	6	6	7	8
Grade Six	-	-	-	-	-	-	1	2	7	9	9	10
Grade Five	-	-	-	2	2	2	5	10	14	15	23	29
Grade Four	-	-	-	-	-	2	2	2	3	5	9	10
Grade Three	-	-	-	-	1	1	1	1	3	3	3	3
Grade Two	-	-	-	-	-	-	-	2	3	4	5	6
Grade One	-	-	-	-	-	-	-	-	1	1	1	1
Air Force Reserve Combat Support Training Center - Total	-	-	-	-	-	-	1	3	3	3	3	3
Grade Seven	-	-	-	-	-	-	1	1	1	1	1	1
Grade Six	-	-	-	-	-	-	-	2	2	2	2	2
Grade Five	-	-	-	-	-	-	-	-	-	-	-	-
Grade Four	-	-	-	-	-	-	-	-	-	-	-	-
Grade Three	-	-	-	-	-	-	-	-	-	-	-	-
Grade Two	-	-	-	-	-	-	-	-	-	-	-	-
Grade One	-	-	-	-	-	-	-	-	-	-	-	-
Air Force Reserve Specialist Training Center - Total	1	1	1	2	2	2	4	4	6	9	13	17
Grade Seven	-	-	-	-	-	-	-	-	1	1	1	2
Grade Six	-	-	-	1	1	1	1	1	2	2	2	3
Grade Five	-	-	-	-	-	-	1	1	1	3	6	8
Grade Four	-	-	-	-	-	-	-	-	-	1	2	2
Grade Three	1	1	1	1	1	1	2	2	2	2	2	2
Grade Two	-	-	-	-	-	-	-	-	-	-	-	-
Grade One	-	-	-	-	-	-	-	-	-	-	-	-
Mobilization Designee - Total	-	-	-	2	2	2	2	2	2	2	2	3
Grade Seven	-	-	-	1	1	1	1	1	1	1	1	1
Grade Six	-	-	-	1	1	1	1	1	1	1	1	2
Grade Five	-	-	-	-	-	-	-	-	-	-	-	-
Grade Four	-	-	-	-	-	-	-	-	-	-	-	-
Grade Three	-	-	-	-	-	-	-	-	-	-	-	-
Grade Two	-	-	-	-	-	-	-	-	-	-	-	-
Grade One	-	-	-	-	-	-	-	-	-	-	-	-
Volunteer Air Reserve Training Unit and Non-Affiliated Reserve Section-Total	195	407	550	702	903	1,086	1,270	1,518	1,763	2,060	2,469	2,823
Grade Seven	15	33	55	82	106	123	152	177	215	262	319	363
Grade Six	41	82	108	142	186	225	256	300	359	419	500	585
Grade Five	58	138	200	252	343	414	484	593	702	832	1,016	1,170
Grade Four	52	94	113	136	167	191	224	265	288	326	386	434
Grade Three	16	36	45	52	59	75	81	95	104	113	126	139
Grade Two	11	20	24	31	34	49	61	76	81	93	105	115
Grade One	2	4	5	7	8	9	12	12	14	15	17	17

Source: Personnel Statistics Division, DCS/Comptroller, Hq. USAF.

TABLE 340 — AF RESERVE PERSONNEL REJECTED FOR ACTIVE MILITARY SERVICE (AMS) BY CATEGORY OF PERSONNEL ASSIGNMENT — FY 1953

(Table below is not applicable to April, May, and June)

Type of Rejection	Jul (1952)	Aug	Sep	Oct	Nov	Dec	Jan (1953)	Feb	Mar
Total	13	21	22	27	29	26	26	26	33
Disqualified Permanently	8	9	11	13	13	11	11	11	11
Disqualified Temporarily	1	2	2	4	5	5	5	5	12
Security	-	-	-	-	-	-	-	-	-
Other Administrative	4	10	9	10	11	10	10	10	10
OFFICER - Total	6	11	11	14	16	15	15	15	18
Disqualified Permanently	3	4	4	5	5	5	5	5	5
Disqualified Temporarily	-	1	1	3	4	4	4	4	7
Security	-	-	-	-	-	-	-	-	-
Other Administrative	3	6	6	6	7	6	6	6	6
AIRMAN - Total	7	10	11	13	13	11	11	11	15
Disqualified Permanently	5	5	7	8	8	6	6	6	6
Disqualified Temporarily	1	1	1	1	1	1	1	1	5
Security	-	-	-	-	-	-	-	-	-
Other Administrative	1	4	3	4	4	4	4	4	4
Mobilization Assignee Officer - Total	1	1	1	1	1	1	1	1	4
Disqualified Permanently	-	-	-	-	-	-	-	-	-
Disqualified Temporarily	-	-	-	-	-	-	-	-	3
Security	-	-	-	-	-	-	-	-	-
Other Administrative	1	1	1	1	1	1	1	1	1
Mobilization Assignee Airman - Total	-	-	-	-	-	-	-	-	-
Disqualified Permanently	-	-	-	-	-	-	-	-	-
Disqualified Temporarily	-	-	-	-	-	-	-	-	-
Security	-	-	-	-	-	-	-	-	-
Other Administrative	-	-	-	-	-	-	-	-	-
Mobilization Designee Officer - Total	-	-	-	-	-	-	-	-	-
Disqualified Permanently	-	-	-	-	-	-	-	-	-
Disqualified Temporarily	-	-	-	-	-	-	-	-	-
Security	-	-	-	-	-	-	-	-	-
Other Administrative	-	-	-	-	-	-	-	-	-
Mobilization Designee Airman - Total	-	-	-	-	-	-	-	-	3
Disqualified Permanently	-	-	-	-	-	-	-	-	-
Disqualified Temporarily	-	-	-	-	-	-	-	-	3
Security	-	-	-	-	-	-	-	-	-
Other Administrative	-	-	-	-	-	-	-	-	-
Voluntary Air Reserve Training Unit and Non-Affiliated Reserve Section Officer - Total	4	4	4	4	5	4	4	4	4
Disqualified Permanently	2	2	2	2	2	2	2	2	2
Disqualified Temporarily	-	-	-	-	-	-	-	-	-
Security	-	-	-	-	-	-	-	-	-
Other Administrative	2	2	2	2	3	2	2	2	2
Voluntary Air Reserve Training Unit and Non-Affiliated Reserve Section Airman - Total	7	10	11	13	13	11	11	11	12
Disqualified Permanently	5	5	7	8	8	6	6	6	6
Disqualified Temporarily	1	1	1	1	1	1	1	1	2
Security	-	-	-	-	-	-	-	-	-
Other Administrative	1	4	3	4	4	4	4	4	4
Second Lieutenants - Total a/	2	6	6	9	10	10	10	10	10
Disqualified Permanently	1	2	2	3	3	3	3	3	3
Disqualified Temporarily	-	1	1	3	4	4	4	4	4
Security	-	-	-	-	-	-	-	-	-
Other Administrative	1	3	3	3	3	3	3	3	3

a/ Second Lieutenants falling within scope of "Program to Secure 12,000 Second Lieutenants."

Source: Personnel Statistics Division, DCS/Comptroller, Hq. USAF.

TABLE 341 — AF RESERVE OFFICER PROMOTIONS BY GRADE TO WHICH PROMOTED — FY 1953

Category of Assignment	Total	Major General	Brigadier General	Colonel	Lieutenant Colonel	Major	Captain	First Lieutenant
Total	3,752	-	-	103	190	601	1,588	1,270
Reserves in Pay Status Assignments -Total	732	-	-	52	64	138	301	177
Mobilization Assignees	226	-	-	28	33	48	82	35
Corollary.	2	-	-	-	-	-	2	-
Air Force Reserve Training Wing. . . .	405	-	-	22	21	62	185	115
Specialist Training Center	99	-	-	2	10	28	32	27
Reserves in Non-Pay Status Assignments - Total.	3,020	-	-	51	126	463	1,287	1,093
Mobilization Designees	67	-	-	11	8	16	20	12
Voluntary Air Reserve Training Unit. .	2,318	-	-	38	107	398	1,011	764
Voluntary Reserve Section (NARS) . . .	635	-	-	2	11	49	256	317

Source: Personnel Statistics Division, DCS/Comptroller, Hq. USAF.

TABLE 342 — FUNCTIONAL DISTRIBUTION OF AIR FORCE RESERVE AIRPLANE INVENTORY — BY TYPE, QUARTERLY - FISCAL YEAR 1953

TYPE	TOTAL INVENTORY	ACTIVE				INACTIVE		
		TOTAL	TACTICAL AND TRANSPORT	TRAINING	MAINTENANCE	TOTAL	MODIFICATION	OTHER
30 September 1952								
TOTAL	143	143	143	-	-	-	-	-
Cargo	80	80	80	-	-	-	-	-
Trainer	63	63	63	-	-	-	-	-
31 December 1952								
TOTAL	178	175	174		1	3	3	-
Fighter	8	8	8	-	-	-	-	-
Cargo	107	107	106	-	1	-	-	-
Trainer	63	60	60	-	-	3	3	-
31 March 1953								
TOTAL	267	264	233	2	29	3	3	-
Fighter	40	40	34	2	4	-	-	-
Cargo	112	112	104	-	8	-	-	-
Trainer	115	112	95	-	17	3	3	-
30 June 1953								
TOTAL	321	315	285	-	30	6	5	1
Fighter	67	65	61	-	4	2	2	-
Cargo	113	113	103	-	10	-	-	-
Trainer	141	137	121	-	16	4	3	1

SOURCE: Materiel Statistics Division, Directorate of Statistical Services, DCS/C

TABLE 343 — CALENDAR AGE DISTRIBUTION OF THE AIR FORCE RESERVE AIRPLANE INVENTORY — 30 JUN 1953

AGE IN MONTHS			NUMBER OF AIRPLANES
0	Through	2.9	26
3.0	"	5.9	23
6.0	"	8.9	-
9.0	"	11.9	-
12.0	"	14.9	-
15.0	"	17.9	-
18.0	"	20.9	-
21.0	"	23.9	-
24.0	"	26.9	-
27.0	"	29.9	-
30.0	"	32.9	-
33.0	"	35.9	-
36.0	"	38.9	-
39.0	"	41.9	-
42.0	"	44.9	-
45.0	"	47.9	-
48.0	"	50.9	-
51.0	"	53.9	-
54.0	"	56.9	-
57.0	"	59.9	-
60.0	"	62.9	-
63.0	"	65.9	-
66.0	"	68.9	-
69.0	"	71.9	-
72.0	"	74.9	-
75.0	"	77.9	-
78.0	"	80.9	-
81.0	"	83.9	-
84.0	"	86.9	-
87.0	"	89.9	-
90.0	"	92.9	-
93.0	"	95.9	24
96.0	"	98.9	54
99.0	"	101.9	48
102.0	"	104.9	27
105.0	"	107.9	55
108.0	"	110.9	28
111.0	"	113.9	8
114.0	"	116.9	7
117.0	"	119.9	8
120.0	"	122.9	7
123.0	"	125.9	5
126.0	"	128.9	1
Average Age in Months 88.7			

SOURCE: Materiel Statistics Division, Directorate of Statistical Services, DCS/C

TABLE 344 — AIR FORCE RESERVE AIRPLANE PROGRAM — QUARTERLY — FY 1953

TYPE AND MODEL	PROGRAM	INVENTORY	DIFFERENCES	
			OVERAGES	SHORTAGES
31 July 1952 a/				
TOTAL	81	72	30	39
C-46	81	42	-	39
T-6	-	30	30	-
30 September 1952				
TOTAL	111	143	32	-
C-46	81	81	-	-
T-6	30	62	32	-
31 December 1952				
TOTAL	301	178	-	123
F-51	101	8	-	93
C-46	138	108	-	30
T-6	62	62	-	-
31 March 1953				
TOTAL	266	267	2	1
F-51	68	70	2	-
C-46	114	113	-	1
T-6	61	61	-	-
T-28	23	23	-	-
30 June 1953				
TOTAL	366	321	1	46
B-26	10	-	-	10
F-51	132	97	-	35
C-46	113	114	1	-
T-6	62	61	-	1
T-28	49	49	-	-

a/ Program resumed.

SOURCE: Materiel Statistics Division, Directorate of Statistical Services, DCS/C

308700 O - 54 - 39

TABLE 345 — STATUS AND LINE CLASSIFICATION OF AIR FORCE RESERVE AIRPLANE INVENTORY BY TYPE AND MODEL — QUARTERLY — FY 1953

TYPE AND MODEL	TOTAL			ACTIVE			INACTIVE		
	TOTAL	FIRST LINE	SECOND LINE	TOTAL	FIRST LINE	SECOND LINE	TOTAL	FIRST LINE	SECOND LINE
	30 SEPTEMBER 1952								
TOTAL	143	-	143	143	-	143	-	-	-
C-46	80	-	80	80	-	80	-	-	-
T-6	62	-	62	62	-	62	-	-	-
TC-46	1	-	1	1	-	1	-	-	-
	31 DECEMBER 1952								
TOTAL	178	-	178	175	-	175	3	-	3
F-51	8	-	8	8	-	8	-	-	-
C-46	107	-	107	107	-	107	-	-	-
T-6	62	-	62	59	-	59	3	-	3
TC-46	1	-	1	1	-	1	-	-	-
	31 MARCH 1953								
TOTAL	267	23	244	264	23	241	3	-	3
F-51	40	-	40	40	-	40	-	-	-
C-46	112	-	112	112	-	112	-	-	-
T-6	61	-	61	58	-	58	3	-	3
T-28	23	23	-	23	23	-	-	-	-
TC-46	1	-	1	1	-	1	-	-	-
TF-51	30	-	30	30	-	30	-	-	-
	30 JUNE 1953								
TOTAL	321	49	272	315	48	267	6	1	5
F-51	67	-	67	65	-	65	2	-	2
C-46	113	-	113	113	-	113	-	-	-
T-6	61	-	61	58	-	58	3	-	3
T-28	49	49	-	48	48	-	1	1	-
TC-46	1	-	1	1	-	1	-	-	-
TF-51	30	-	30	30	-	30	-	-	-

SOURCE: Materiel Statistics Division, Directorate of Statistical Services, DCS/C

TABLE 346 — SUMMARY OF AF RESERVE AIRPLANE ACTIVITIES — FY 1953

MONTH AND YEAR	TOTAL HOURS FLOWN	AVERAGE AIRPLANES ON HAND	PER CENT OF A/P IN COM	AV. HRS. FLOWN PER A/P		TOTAL FUEL CONSUMPTION
				On Hand	In Com	
1952						
July	2,142	71	75	30	40	216,851
August	3,082	94	68	33	48	317,684
September	3,774	129	64	29	46	391,372
October	4,814	144	73	33	46	465,550
November	4,711	148	72	32	44	413,967
December	4,760	160	73	30	41	447,978
1953						
January	5,170	174	77	30	39	493,753
February	6,621	195	73	34	48	604,878
March	8,017	237	73	34	46	698,659
April	8,274	265	72	31	43	700,349
May	9,690	286	72	34	47	796,890
June	11,843	304	71	39	55	953,605

SOURCE: Materiel Statistics Division, D/Statistical Services, DCS/C

TABLE 347 — NET OBLIGATIONS DURING FY 1953 AGAINST FUNDS AVAILABLE FOR RESERVE PERSONNEL REQUIREMENTS

(Excludes reimbursements. Figures in parentheses indicate minus amounts.)

SOURCE OF FUNDS	TOTAL	PROJECT 520 PAY AND ALLOWANCES RESERVE AND ROTC	PROJECT 540 TRAVEL RESERVE AND ROTC	PROJECT 550 SUBSISTENCE	PROJECT 560 INDIVIDUAL CLOTHING
Against Funds Appropriated in FY 1953.	11,901,754	8,377,942	761,811	82,000	2,680,001
Against Funds Appropriated in FY 1952.	8,272,045	5,926,769	-	-	2,345,276
Total For FY 1953 Program.	$20,173,799	$14,304,711	$761,811	$82,000	$5,025,277
For FY 1952 Program Against Funds Appropriated in FY 1952 a/	963,226	694,687	370,297	158,116	(259,874)
Total Obligated During FY 1953 . . .	$21,137,025	$14,999,398	$1,132,108	$240,116	$4,765,403

a/ Includes that portion of the FY 1952 summer camp program occurring in FY 1953.

Source: Financial Management Division, Directorate of Budget, DCS/C.

TABLE 348 – AIR NATIONAL GUARD STRENGTH (AUTHORIZED AND ASSIGNED) IN FEDERALLY RECOGNIZED UNITS BY STATE OR TERRITORY – FY 1953

State or Territory	30 September (1952)			31 December			31 March (1953)			30 June		
	Units	Auth	Asgd	Units	Auth	Asgd	Units	Auth	Asgd	Units	Auth	Asgd
WORLDWIDE - Total	298	33,504	20,314	440	50,564	26,942	547	63,952	32,275	557	63,968	35,556
CONTINENTAL U.S. - Total	290	32,112	19,227	432	49,160	25,851	539	62,543	31,106	549	62,485	34,292
First Air Force -Total	126	13,820	10,339	187	20,421	12,286	206	21,984	13,292	210	22,286	14,107
Connecticut	2	251	463	14	1,139	723	15	1,205	704	15	1,204	681
Delaware	2	129	224	2	457	233	2	457	228	2	454	213
District of Columbia	3	290	252	15	1,178	296	15	1,178	379	15	1,179	469
Kentucky	14	1,113	318	14	1,126	380	14	1,126	475	15	1,140	546
Maine	2	246	135	14	1,134	268	14	1,134	327	14	1,133	345
Maryland	2	511	450	2	456	457	2	456	456	2	453	450
Massachusetts	20	1,833	1,723	20	1,852	1,764	20	1,852	1,799	21	1,878	1,835
New Hampshire	2	129	101	2	457	195	2	457	227	2	464	242
New Jersey	5	790	808	16	1,602	992	16	1,602	1,103	17	1,764	1,193
New York	23	3,055	2,185	33	4,113	2,732	36	4,338	2,746	36	4,329	3,072
Ohio	22	2,424	1,489	24	2,935	1,664	25	3,011	1,780	24	2,993	1,830
Pennsylvania	22	2,002	1,523	24	2,585	1,823	37	3,626	2,166	38	3,696	2,204
Rhode Island	3	463	436	3	469	437	4	624	490	5	687	559
Vermont	2	129	53	2	457	131	2	457	176	2	454	196
Virginia	-	-	-	-	-	-	-	-	-	-	-	-
West Virginia	2	455	179	2	461	191	2	461	236	2	458	272
Fourth Air Force-Total	36	3,696	2,217	55	5,779	3,296	77	9,670	4,366	80	9,632	5,152
Arizona	2	135	105	2	457	138	2	457	177	2	454	330
California	21	2,524	1,440	24	2,365	1,648	42	4,337	2,031	43	4,297	2,279
Idaho	2	145	88	2	145	223	2	468	281	2	475	362
Montana	2	133	96	2	133	178	2	461	255	2	458	268
Nevada	1	13	74	2	461	194	2	461	196	2	458	223
Oregon	3	406	223	14	1,193	343	15	1,504	467	15	1,500	664
Utah	2	133	106	3	196	235	3	772	524	3	766	598
Washington	3	207	85	6	829	337	9	1,210	435	11	1,224	428
Tenth Air Force -Total	37	4,640	2,612	93	11,017	5,157	139	16,100	7,016	137	15,588	7,758
Colorado	3	413	181	4	533	343	19	1,685	663	19	1,657	627
Illinois	5	896	749	5	1,411	936	19	2,487	966	8	1,507	1,141
Indiana	3	371	94	8	937	369	11	1,187	469	12	1,197	554
Iowa	3	371	62	3	371	253	10	1,345	556	10	1,339	580
Kansas	2	451	102	2	457	106	2	457	143	6	660	197
Michigan	3	378	371	16	1,747	547	16	1,747	689	18	1,921	830
Minnesota	3	371	68	16	1,625	453	16	1,625	793	16	1,621	864
Missouri	4	479	396	16	1,482	659	17	1,810	829	18	1,931	1,044
Nebraska	2	133	29	2	133	240	7	703	353	7	702	335
North Dakota	2	133	74	2	133	171	2	461	267	2	458	265
South Dakota	2	133	122	2	461	327	2	461	352	2	458	346
Wisconsin	3	378	334	15	1,594	656	16	1,660	779	17	1,668	802
Wyoming	2	133	30	2	133	97	2	472	157	2	469	173
Fourteenth Air Force - Total	91	9,956	4,059	97	11,943	5,112	117	14,789	6,432	122	14,979	7,275
Alabama	16	1,353	364	18	1,710	620	21	2,419	908	22	2,565	1,098
Arkansas	4	523	181	4	476	217	10	1,126	459	12	1,292	575
Florida	2	455	179	2	461	220	2	461	267	2	458	311
Georgia	19	1,958	873	20	2,393	917	21	2,506	986	21	2,482	1,046
Louisiana	2	135	212	3	290	249	3	581	296	3	578	343
Mississippi	3	279	152	3	602	225	5	837	349	5	834	370
New Mexico	2	129	100	2	457	123	2	457	159	2	454	182
North Carolina	2	455	111	3	562	175	4	577	269	4	574	326
Oklahoma	15	1,535	282	15	1,554	392	15	1,587	521	12	1,396	591
South Carolina	3	493	224	3	499	237	3	499	272	4	515	310
Tennessee	4	416	416	5	689	646	11	1,454	734	14	1,533	872
Texas	19	2,225	965	19	2,250	1,091	20	2,285	1,212	21	2,298	1,251
OVERSEAS - Total	8	1,392	1,087	8	1,404	1,091	8	1,409	1,169	8	1,483	1,264
Alaska	2	84		2	84	-	2	89	39	4	854	62
Hawaii	4	858	701	4	864	704	4	864	753	2	453	809
Puerto Rico	2	450	386	2	456	387	2	456	377	2	176	393

Source: Personnel Statistics Division, DCS/Comptroller, Hq. USAF.

TABLE 349 — AUTHORIZED AND ASSIGNED AIR NATIONAL

State or Territory	30 September 1952				31 December 1952			
	Officer		Airman		Officer		Airman	
	Authorized	Assigned	Authorized	Assigned	Authorized	Assigned	Authorized	Assigned
WORLDWIDE - TOTAL	3,510	1,892	29,994	18,422	5,663	2,613	44,901	24,329
CONTINENTAL U.S.-TOTAL	3,359	1,814	28,753	17,413	5,512	2,542	43,648	23,309
First Air Force - Total . .	1,548	994	12,272	9,345	2,370	1,226	18,051	11,060
Connecticut	20	19	231	444	150	52	989	671
Delaware.	6	10	123	214	43	17	414	216
District of Columbia. . .	21	11	269	241	151	30	1,027	266
Kentucky.	145	35	968	283	145	48	981	332
Maine	19	8	227	127	149	20	985	248
Maryland.	60	50	451	400	43	50	413	407
Massachusetts	214	203	1,619	1,520	214	198	1,638	1,566
New Hampshire	6	3	123	98	43	5	414	190
New Jersey.	70	53	720	755	197	93	1,405	899
New York.	335	210	2,720	1,975	494	251	3,619	2,481
Ohio.	294	167	2,130	1,322	317	183	2,618	1,481
Pennsylvania.	255	155	1,747	1,368	284	196	2,301	1,627
Rhode Island.	50	42	413	394	50	40	419	397
Vermont	6	10	123	43	43	23	414	108
Virginia.	-	-	-	-	-	-	-	-
West Virginia	47	18	408	161	47	20	414	171
Fourth Air Force - Total. . .	392	241	3,304	1,976	626	357	5,153	2,939
Arizona	12	5	123	100	43	10	414	128
California.	298	176	2,226	1,264	280	210	2,085	1,438
Idaho	15	8	130	80	15	23	130	200
Montana	10	11	123	85	10	16	123	162
Nevada.	7	4	6	70	47	15	414	179
Oregon.	24	15	382	208	121	27	1,072	316
Utah.	10	11	123	95	18	24	178	211
Washington.	16	11	191	74	92	32	737	305
Tenth Air Force - Total	331	137	4,309	2,475	1,249	331	9,768	4,826
Colorado.	28	10	385	171	38	23	495	320
Illinois.	62	47	834	702	113	60	1,298	876
Indiana	23	8	348	86	157	31	780	338
Iowa.	23	7	348	55	23	6	348	247
Kansas.	43	8	408	94	43	13	414	93
Michigan.	27	12	351	359	224	39	1,523	508
Minnesota	23	8	348	60	192	30	1,433	423
Missouri.	35	12	444	384	188	33	1,294	626
Nebraska.	10	6	123	23	10	10	123	230
North Dakota.	10	5	123	69	10	12	123	159
South Dakota.	10	4	123	118	47	28	414	299
Wisconsin	27	6	351	328	194	36	1,400	620
Wyoming	10	4	123	26	10	10	123	87
Fourteenth Air Force - Total	1,088	442	8,868	3,617	1,267	628	10,676	4,484
Alabama	191	57	1,162	307	212	80	1,498	540
Arkansas.	53	21	470	160	51	26	425	191
Florida	47	26	408	153	47	28	414	192
Georgia	212	124	1,746	749	257	146	2,136	771
Louisiana	12	13	123	199	16	24	274	225
Mississippi	30	6	249	146	64	23	538	202
New Mexico.	6	5	123	95	43	16	414	107
North Carolina.	47	14	408	97	55	20	507	155
Oklahoma.	163	27	1,372	255	163	68	1,391	324
South Carolina.	49	14	444	210	49	17	450	220
Tennessee	29	33	387	383	61	71	628	575
Texas	249	102	1,976	963	249	109	2,001	982
OVERSEAS - TOTAL . . .	151	78	1,241	1,009	151	71	1,253	1,020
Alaska.	18	-	66	-	18	-	66	-
Hawaii.	90	59	768	642	90	52	774	652
Puerto Rico	43	19	407	367	43	19	413	368

Source: Personnel Statistics Division, DCS/Comptroller, Hq. USAF

GUARD STRENGTH BY STATE OR TERRITORY – FY 1953

throughout FY 1953)

31 March 1953				30 June 1953				State or Territory
Officer		Airman		Officer		Airman		
Authorized	Assigned	Authorized	Assigned	Authorized	Assigned	Authorized	Assigned	
7,314	3,266	56,638	29,009	7,340	3,839	56,628	31,717	WORLDWIDE - TOTAL
7,158	3,160	55,385	27,946	7,171	3,730	55,314	30,562	CONTINENTAL U.S. - TOTAL
2,569	1,346	19,415	11,946	2,588	1,468	19,698	12,639	First Air Force - Total
152	61	1,053	643	151	81	1,053	600	Connecticut
43	14	414	214	43	17	411	196	Delaware
151	38	1,027	341	150	50	1,029	419	District of Columbia
145	67	981	408	149	73	991	473	Kentucky
149	32	985	295	148	42	985	303	Maine
43	48	413	408	42	49	411	401	Maryland
214	202	1,638	1,597	225	204	1,653	1,631	Massachusetts
43	7	414	220	44	9	420	233	New Hampshire
197	106	1,405	997	202	118	1,562	1,075	New Jersey
524	267	3,814	2,479	523	307	3,806	2,765	New York
320	195	2,691	1,585	315	198	2,678	1,632	Ohio
444	219	3,182	1,947	451	222	3,245	1,982	Pennsylvania
54	41	570	449	55	46	632	513	Rhode Island
43	27	414	149	43	25	411	171	Vermont
-	-	-	-	-	-	-		Virginia
47	22	414	214	47	27	411	245	West Virginia
1,085	461	8,585	3,905	1,103	549	8,529	4,603	Fourth Air Force - Total
43	19	414	158	43	30	411	300	Arizona
545	255	3,792	1,776	545	288	3,752	1,991	California
47	27	421	254	48	35	427	327	Idaho
47	27	414	228	47	26	411	242	Montana
47	18	414	178	47	25	411	198	Nevada
153	37	1,351	430	153	52	1,347	612	Oregon
79	34	693	490	80	45	686	553	Utah
124	44	1,086	391	140	48	1,084	380	Washington
1,893	582	14,207	6,434	1,848	817	13,740	6,941	Tenth Air Force - Total
186	77	1,499	586	185	89	1,472	538	Colorado
274	70	2,213	896	183	142	1,324	999	Illinois
166	41	1,021	428	169	63	1,028	491	Indiana
171	41	1,174	515	171	50	1,168	530	Iowa
43	20	414	123	61	34	599	163	Kansas
224	55	1,523	634	231	85	1,690	745	Michigan
192	73	1,433	720	191	84	1,430	780	Minnesota
233	59	1,577	770	253	92	1,678	952	Missouri
66	21	637	332	65	32	637	303	Nebraska
47	15	414	252	47	22	411	243	North Dakota
47	35	414	317	47	33	411	313	South Dakota
196	51	1,464	728	197	66	1,471	736	Wisconsin
48	24	424	133	48	25	421	148	Wyoming
1,611	771	13,178	5,661	1,632	896	13,347	6,379	Fourteenth Air Force - Total
257	110	2,162	798	263	141	2,302	957	Alabama
108	40	1,018	419	113	59	1,179	516	Arkansas
47	36	414	231	47	38	411	273	Florida
268	165	2,238	821	269	177	2,213	869	Georgia
58	22	523	274	58	22	520	321	Louisiana
71	27	766	322	71	32	763	338	Mississippi
43	19	414	140	43	21	411	161	New Mexico
60	24	517	245	60	29	514	297	North Carolina
190	78	1,397	443	176	88	1,220	503	Oklahoma
49	33	450	239	54	34	461	276	South Carolina
210	102	1,244	632	224	122	1,309	750	Tennessee
250	115	2,035	1,097	254	133	2,044	1,118	Texas
156	106	1,253	1,063	169	109	1,314	1,155	OVERSEAS - TOTAL
23	13	66	26	92	17	762	45	Alaska
90	74	774	679	42	72	411	737	Hawaii
43	19	413	358	35	20	141	373	Puerto Rico

TABLE 350 – AIR NATIONAL GUARD WARRANT OFFICER STRENGTH (AUTHORIZED AND ASSIGNED) BY STATE OR TERRITORY – FY 1953

(Data in the table below are included in the preceding table).

State or Territory	30 September 1952		31 December 1952		31 March 1953		30 June 1953	
	Authorized	Assigned	Authorized	Assigned	Authorized	Assigned	Authorized	Assigned
WORLDWIDE - TOTAL	94	35	184	49	238	62	252	94
CONTINENTAL U. S. - TOTAL	89	33	179	48	233	60	246	90
First Air Force - Total	26	16	70	20	74	22	77	34
Connecticut	1	1	3	1	3	1	3	3
Delaware	-	-	2	-	2	-	2	-
District of Columbia	1	-	3	1	3	1	3	1
Kentucky	3	1	3	1	3	1	4	1
Maine	1	-	3	1	3	1	3	3
Maryland	-	-	2	-	2	-	2	-
Massachusetts	6	4	6	4	6	5	6	6
New Hampshire	-	-	2	-	2	-	2	-
New Jersey	3	3	5	4	5	4	7	5
New York	1	3	11	3	12	4	12	4
Ohio	2	2	11	2	11	2	11	5
Pennsylvania	2	1	11	2	13	2	13	3
Rhode Island	3	1	3	1	4	1	4	1
Vermont	-	-	2	-	2	-	2	-
Virginia	-	-	-	-	-	-	-	-
West Virginia	3	-	3	-	3	-	3	2
Fourth Air Force - Total	11	7	22	14	36	17	39	14
Arizona	-	-	2	-	2	-	2	-
California	4	5	6	9	12	11	13	9
Idaho	1	-	1	-	3	-	3	-
Montana	1	-	1	-	3	1	3	1
Nevada	1	-	3	-	3	-	3	-
Oregon	2	-	4	1	4	2	5	1
Utah	1	1	1	1	3	1	4	1
Washington	1	1	4	3	6	2	6	2
Tenth Air Force - Total	16	4	40	6	60	9	59	21
Colorado	2	1	2	1	6	4	6	4
Illinois	2	-	8	1	11	1	9	3
Indiana	1	1	3	1	4	1	4	1
Iowa	1	-	1	-	5	-	5	2
Kansas	2	-	2	-	2	-	2	1
Michigan	1	-	5	-	5	-	6	1
Minnesota	1	-	5	1	5	1	5	2
Missouri	1	1	3	1	5	1	5	1
Nebraska	1	-	1	-	3	-	3	1
North Dakota	1	-	1	-	3	-	3	1
South Dakota	1	-	3	-	3	1	3	2
Wisconsin	1	-	5	-	5	-	5	2
Wyoming	1	1	1	1	3	-	3	-
Fourteenth Air Force-Total	36	6	47	8	63	12	71	21
Alabama	3	-	8	-	12	-	15	6
Arkansas	3	1	1	1	7	3	8	2
Florida	3	1	3	1	3	1	3	1
Georgia	6	2	7	2	8	4	9	2
Louisiana	1	-	2	-	3	-	3	-
Mississippi	1	-	3	1	4	1	4	1
New Mexico	-	-	2	-	2	-	2	-
North Carolina	3	1	3	1	3	1	4	1
Oklahoma	5	-	5	1	5	1	6	1
South Carolina	3	-	3	-	3	-	4	-
Tennessee	1	-	3	-	5	-	5	1
Texas	7	1	7	1	8	1	8	6
OVERSEAS - TOTAL	5	2	5	1	5	2	6	4
Alaska	-	-	-	-	-	-	-	-
Hawaii	3	2	3	1	3	2	4	4
Puerto Rico	2	-	2	-	2	-	2	-

Source: Personnel Statistics Division, DCS/Comptroller, Hq USAF

TABLE 351 — AIR NATIONAL GUARD PARTICIPATION IN TRAINING ASSEMBLIES — FY 1953

End of Month	Potential Drill	Actual Drill	Per Cent of Partici- pation	Potential Drill	Actual Drill	Per Cent of Partici- pation
	Officer			Airman		
1952						
July	5,831	5,122	87.8	54,602	45,629	83.5
August	5,628	4,925	87.5	55,300	44,179	79.8
September.	7,429	6,538	88.0	74,380	59,066	79.4
October.	7,996	6,953	87.0	81,414	66,145	81.2
November	8,947	7,858	87.8	85,706	69,438	81.0
December	9,989	8,759	87.8	94,416	76,215	80.7
1953						
January.	11,373	9,934	87.3	104,184	85,976	82.5
February	11,771	10,458	88.8	109,056	89,537	82.1
March.	12,697	11,464	90.2	117,085	98,019	83.7
April.	13,635	12,350	90.5	122,957	103,411	84.1
May.	14,213	12,802	90.1	126,936	105,398	83.3
June	14,071	12,521	89.0	120,955	99,460	82.2

Source: Personnel Statistics Division, DCS/Comptroller, Hq. USAF

TABLE 352 — AIR NATIONAL GUARD PARTICIPATION IN FIELD TRAINING — FY 1953

End of Quarter	Number Completing 15 Day Field Training		Cumulative Number Completing 15 Day Field Training	
	Officer	Airman	Officer	Airman
FY 1953				
First Quarter . . .	1,124	8,566	1,124	8,566
Second Quarter. . .	0	0	1,124	8,566
Third Quarter . . .	0	0	1,124	8,566
Fourth Quarter. . .	631	5,261	1,755	13,827

Source: Personnel Statistics Division, DCS/Comptroller, Hq. USAF

TABLE 353 — AIR NATIONAL GUARD PILOT TRAINING — FY 1953

End Of Month	Input This Month Into Pilot Training Replacement Program		Attrition in Pilot Training Replacement Program		Number in Pilot Training Replacement Program		Graduates From Pilot Training	
	Officer	Airman	Officer	Airman	Officer	Airman	Officer	Airman
1952								
July. . . .	11	8	-	-	40	40	2	10
August. . .	3	9	1	-	42	49	-	-
September .	18	14	1	2	49	56	10	5
October . .	20	30	2	-	57	84	10	2
November. .	-	-	3	2	54	82	-	-
December. .	-	-	-	3	a/ 33	75	3	4
1953								
January . .	21	27	-	-	54	102	-	-
February. .	18	24	-	2	70	115	2	9
March . . .	10	16	-	6	80	120	-	5
April . . .	11	16	-	-	91	136	-	-
May	14	7	1	2	102	125	2	16
June. . . .	14	27	9	12	99	136	8	4

a/ Large decrease in Officers in Pilot Training Replacement Program due to Transfer of 18 Officers to a Class Reporting on a Later Date.

Source: Personnel Statistics Division, DCS/Comptroller, Hq. USAF.

TABLE 354 — AIR NATIONAL GUARD SCHOOL TRAINING — FY 1953

(Data exclude pilot trainees and pilot training.)

End Of Month	Number of ANG Completing School Training		Cumulative Number Completing School Training This Date		Average Days Per Man In School Training		Number Now In School Training	
	Officer	Airman	Officer	Airman	Officer	Airman	Officer	Airman
1952								
July. . . .	12	50	12	50	84.85	71.75	16	162
August. . .	4	39	16	89	99.69	49.05	26	162
September .	6	71	22	160	98.19	83.68	24	132
October . .	10	44	32	204	107.50	90.86	14	147
November. .	4	78	36	282	101.33	96.59	12	117
December. .	10	21	46	303	101.33	103.63	13	154
1953								
January . .	6	46	52	349	103.28	103.95	26	181
February. .	3	58	55	407	103.04	102.82	35	222
March . . .	37	46	92	453	77.29	105.06	70	256
April . . .	19	65	95	518	73.18	102.23	73	280
May	25	164	114	782	70.57	99.30	80	240
June. . . .	47	116	139	898	68.64	89.81	57	384

Source: Personnel Statistics Division, DCS/Comptroller, Hq. USAF.

TABLE 355 — AIR NATIONAL GUARD AIRPLANE PROGRAM — QUARTERLY — FY 1953

TYPE AND MODEL	PROGRAM	INVENTORY	DIFFERENCES	
			OVERAGES	SHORTAGES
	30 SEPTEMBER 1952			
TOTAL	476	473	5	8
B-26	7	7	-	-
F-47	38	43	5	-
F-51	252	249	-	3
C-47	76	76	-	-
C-53	1	1	-	-
T-6	102	97	-	5
	31 DECEMBER 1952			
TOTAL	492	513	27	6
B-26	7	18	11	-
F-47	35	37	2	-
F-51	252	246	-	6
C-46	-	10	10	-
C-47	76	76	-	-
C-53	1	1	-	-
T-6	121	125	4	-
	31 MARCH 1953			
TOTAL	589	741	165	13
B-26	42	33	-	9
F-47	39	35	-	4
F-51	236	279	43	-
F-84	-	4	4	-
C-46	10	10	-	-
C-47	76	76	-	-
C-53	1	1	-	-
T-6	185	302	117	-
L-16	-	1	1	-
	30 JUNE 1953			
TOTAL	975	1,020	186	141
B-26	48	44	-	4
F-47	37	35	-	2
F-51	566	431	-	135
F-80	-	11	11	-
C-46	10	10	-	-
C-47	75	76	1	-
C-53	1	1	-	-
T-6	232	404	172	-
T-33	6	6	-	-
L-16	-	2	2	-

SOURCE: Materiel Statistics Division, Directorate of Statistical Services, DCS/C.

TABLE 356 — FUNCTIONAL DISTRIBUTION OF AIR NATIONAL GUARD AIRPLANE INVENTORY BY TYPE - QUARTERLY — FY 1953

TYPE	TOTAL AIRPLANE INVENTORY	ACTIVE								INACTIVE				
		TOTAL	TACTICAL AND TRANSPORT	TRAINING	MINIMUM INDIV. TRAINING	ADMINISTRATIVE	SPECIAL MISSION	MAINTENANCE	PROJECT	TOTAL	MODIFICATION	BAILMENT AND X-MODEL	OTHER	EXCESS AND REC. RECL.
	30 SEPTEMBER 1952													
TOTAL	473	470	421	-	-	35	-	14	-	3	1	-	-	2
FIGHTER	292	290	281	-	-	1	-	8	-	2	-	-	-	2
CARGO	77	76	38	-	-	32	-	6	-	1	1	-	-	-
TRAINER	104	104	102	-	-	2	-	-	-	-	-	-	-	-
	31 DECEMBER 1952													
TOTAL	513	496	447	-	-	21	7	20	1	17	2	12	2	1
BOMBER	9	8	8	-	-	-	-	-	-	1	1	-	-	-
FIGHTER	283	282	273	-	-	-	1	8	-	1	-	-	-	1
RECONNAISSANCE	2	2	1	-	-	-	-	-	1	-	-	-	-	-
CARGO	87	86	51	-	-	21	4	10	-	1	1	-	-	-
TRAINER	132	118	114	-	-	-	2	2	-	14	-	12	2	-
	31 MARCH 1953													
TOTAL	741	687	630	1	-	13	6	32	5	54	-	1	53	-
BOMBER	18	18	10	-	-	-	-	8	-	-	-	-	-	-
FIGHTER	318	318	305	-	-	-	1	12	-	-	-	-	-	-
RECONNAISSANCE	8	8	3	-	-	-	-	-	5	-	-	-	-	-
CARGO	87	87	63	-	-	13	4	7	-	-	-	-	-	-
TRAINER	309	255	249	-	-	-	1	5	-	54	-	1	53	-
COMMUNICATION .	1	1	-	1	-	-	-	-	-	-	-	-	-	-
	30 JUNE 1953													
TOTAL	1,020	989	916	8	5	-	9	52	-	31	12	-	18	1
BOMBER	27	27	23	-	-	-	-	4	-	-	-	-	-	-
FIGHTER	450	438	395	6	1	-	1	35	-	12	6	-	5	1
RECONNAISSANCE	14	12	12	-	-	-	-	-	-	2	-	-	2	-
CARGO	86	86	80	-	-	-	4	2	-	-	-	-	-	-
TRAINER	441	424	406	2	4	-	2	10	-	17	6	-	11	-
COMMUNICATION .	2	2	-	-	-	-	2	-	-	-	-	-	-	-

SOURCE: Materiel Statistics Division, Directorate of Statistical Services, DCS/C.

TABLE 357 — CALENDAR AGE DISTRIBUTION OF AIR NATIONAL GUARD AIRPLANE INVENTORY — QUARTERLY. — FY 1953

AGE IN MONTHS			NUMBER OF AIRPLANES			
			30 SEPTEMBER 1952	31 DECEMBER 1952	31 MARCH 1953	30 JUNE 1953
0	Through	2.9	9	2	41	-
3.0	"	5.9	-	10	4	41
6.0	"	8.9	-	-	10	4
9.0	"	11.9	-	-	-	10
12.0	"	14.9	8	-	5	-
15.0	"	17.9	32	8	-	5
18.0	"	20.9	-	32	8	-
21.0	"	23.9	-	-	25	8
24.0	"	26.9	-	-	7	25
27.0	"	29.9	-	-	-	8
30.0	"	32.9	-	-	-	1
33.0	"	35.9	-	-	-	-
36.0	"	38.9	-	-	-	-
39.0	"	41.9	-	-	-	-
42.0	"	44.9	-	-	-	-
45.0	"	47.9	-	-	-	1
48.0	"	50.9	-	-	-	-
51.0	"	53.9	-	-	-	-
54.0	"	56.9	-	-	-	3
57.0	"	59.9	-	-	1	-
60.0	"	62.9	-	-	1	-
63.0	"	65.9	-	-	2	1
66.0	"	68.9	-	-	1	2
69.0	"	71.9	-	-	-	5
72.0	"	74.9	-	-	-	1
75.0	"	77.9	-	-	-	-
78.0	"	80.9	-	-	-	3
81.0	"	83.9	50	-	-	-
84.0	"	86.9	178	49	-	-
87.0	"	89.9	57	175	49	-
90.0	"	92.9	25	58	184	56
93.0	"	95.9	12	38	76	235
96.0	"	98.9	25	17	96	131
99.0	"	101.9	38	34	43	194
102.0	"	104.9	11	44	69	75
105.0	"	107.9	12	15	55	74
108.0	"	110.9	7	13	20	62
111.0	"	113.9	7	9	22	22
114.0	"	116.9	1	7	13	25
117.0	"	119.9	-	1	7	19
120.0	"	122.9	1	-	1	7
123.0	"	125.9		-	-	1
126.0	"	128.9		-	-	-
129.0	"	131.9		1	-	-
132.0	"	134.9			1	-
135.0	"	137.9				1
Average Age in Months			82.3	86.0	86.0	91.5

SOURCE: Materiel Statistics Division, Directorate of Statistical Services, DCS/C

TABLE 358 — STATUS AND LINE CLASSIFICATION OF AIR NATIONAL GUARD AIRPLANE INVENTORY BY MODEL — QUARTERLY — FY 1953

TYPE AND MODEL	TOTAL			ACTIVE			INACTIVE		
	TOTAL	FIRST LINE	SECOND LINE	TOTAL	FIRST LINE	SECOND LINE	TOTAL	FIRST LINE	SECOND LINE
	30 SEPTEMBER 1952								
TOTAL	473	49	424	470	49	421	3	-	3
F-47	43	-	43	42	-	42	1	-	1
F-51	249	-	249	248	-	248	1	-	1
C-47	76	-	76	75	-	75	1	-	1
C-53	1	-	1	1	-	1	-	-	-
T-6	97	49	48	97	49	48	-	-	-
TB-26	7	-	7	7	-	7	-	-	-
	31 DECEMBER 1952								
TOTAL	513	52	461	496	50	446	17	2	15
B-26	9	-	9	8	-	8	1	-	1
F-47	37	-	37	36	-	36	1	-	1
F-51	246	-	246	246	-	246	-	-	-
RB-26	2	-	2	2	-	2	-	-	-
C-46	10	-	10	10	-	10	-	-	-
C-47	76	-	76	75	-	75	1	-	1
C-53	1	-	1	1	-	1	-	-	-
T-6	125	52	73	111	50	61	14	2	12
TB-26	7	-	7	7	-	7	-	-	-
	31 MARCH 1953								
TOTAL	741	100	641	687	85	602	54	15	39
B-26	18	-	18	18	-	18	-	-	-
F-47	35	-	35	35	-	35	-	-	-
F-51	279	-	279	279	-	279	-	-	-
F-84	4	-	4	4	-	4	-	-	-
RB-26	8	-	8	8	-	8	-	-	-
C-46	10	-	10	10	-	10	-	-	-
C-47	76	-	76	76	-	76	-	-	-
C-53	1	-	1	1	-	1	-	-	-
T-6	302	100	202	248	85	163	54	15	39
TB-26	7	-	7	7	-	7	-	-	-
L-16	1	-	1	1	-	1	-	-	-
	30 JUNE 1953								
TOTAL	1,020	106	914	989	106	883	31	-	31
B-26	27	-	27	27	-	27	-	-	-
F-47	35	-	35	35	-	35	-	-	-
F-51	406	-	406	395	-	395	11	-	11
F-80	9	-	9	8	-	8	1	-	1
RB-26	10	-	10	10	-	10	-	-	-
RF-51	4	-	4	2	-	2	2	-	2
C-46	9	-	9	9	-	9	-	-	-
C-47	76	-	76	76	-	76	-	-	-
C-53	1	-	1	1	-	1	-	-	-
T-6	404	100	304	391	100	291	13	-	13
TB-26	7	-	7	7	-	7	-	-	-
TC-46	1	-	1	1	-	1	-	-	-
TF-51	20	-	20	18	-	18	2	-	2
TRF-51	1	-	1	1	-	1	-	-	-
T-33	6	6	-	6	6	-	-	-	-
TF-80	2	-	2	-	-	-	2	-	2
L-16	2	-	2	2	-	2	-	-	-

SOURCE: Materiel Statistics Division, Directorate of Statistical Services, DCS/C.

TABLE 359 — AIR NATIONAL GUARD FLIGHT OPERATIONS BY TYPE AND MODEL OF AIRPLANE — FY 1953

TYPE AND MODEL	TOTAL HOURS FLOWN	AVERAGE AIRPLANES			AV. HOURS FLOWN PER A/P ON HAND	AVIATION FUEL ISSUED (GALS)	TOTAL HOURS FLOWN	AVERAGE AIRPLANES			AV. HOURS FLOWN PER A/P ON HAND	AVIATION FUEL ISSUED (GALS)
		On Hand	In Com	Percent In Com				On Hand	In Com	Percent In Com		
	JULY 1952						AUGUST 1952					
TOTAL. .	13,821	442	354	80	31	1,040,054	11,734	414	340	82	28	856,147
F-47. . . .	260	40	22	55	7	29,747	332	42	21	50	8	37,028
F-51. . . .	8,483	271	218	80	31	602,135	6,496	245	207	84	27	452,410
C-47/53 . .	3,299	83	71	86	40	336,541	3,116	76	67	88	41	297,758
TB-26 . . .	126	7	5	71	18	20,910	126	7	4	57	18	21,568
T-6	1,653	41	38	93	40	50,721	1,664	44	41	93	38	47,383
	SEPTEMBER 1952						OCTOBER 1952					
TOTAL. .	8,987	464	350	75	19	651,239	8,853	463	351	76	19	658,378
F-47. . . .	211	42	25	60	5	22,750	193	40	24	60	5	22,093
F-51. . . .	4,294	247	193	78	17	306,790	3,910	247	185	75	16	284,725
C-47/53 . .	2,342	73	55	75	32	238,170	2,558	73	59	81	35	252,181
TB-26 . . .	154	7	6	86	22	24,668	128	7	5	71	18	20,131
T-6	1,986	95	71	75	21	58,861	2,064	96	78	81	22	79,248
	NOVEMBER 1952						DECEMBER 1952					
TOTAL. .	7,173	467	351	75	15	504,761	6,997	481	292	61	15	488,201
B-26. . . .	48	3	3	100	16	7,773	71	8	7	88	9	10,840
F-47. . . .	155	36	25	69	4	18,125	162	36	23	64	5	19,557
F-51. . . .	3,140	245	174	71	13	212,045	2,257	244	125	51	9	156,260
RB-26 . . .	-	1	-	-	-	-	33	1	1	100	33	5,352
C-46. . . .	-	-	-	-	-	-	14	7	3	43	2	1,612
C-47. . . .	2,018	75	57	76	27	195,987	2,206	75	50	67	29	208,239
C-53. . . .	26	1	1	100	26	2,178	46	1	1	100	46	5,592
TB-26 . . .	124	7	4	57	18	19,659	143	7	5	71	20	23,512
T-6	1,662	99	87	88	17	48,994	2,065	102	77	75	20	57,237
	JANUARY 1953						FEBRUARY 1953					
TOTAL. .	6,994	497	312	63	14	502,635	9,988	516	358	69	19	711,786
B-26. . . .	40	7	6	86	6	6,181	123	10	6	60	12	17,377
F-47. . . .	219	36	20	56	6	27,212	279	35	23	66	8	36,319
F-51. . . .	2,287	246	128	52	9	167,009	4,066	245	152	62	17	280,806
RB-26 . . .	41	2	1	50	21	6,818	70	3	2	67	23	11,552
C-46. . . .	90	10	5	50	9	14,007	156	10	6	60	16	26,395
C-47. . . .	2,092	73	57	78	29	199,712	2,452	74	59	80	33	239,251
C-53. . . .	16	-	-	-	-	1,512	35	1	1	100	35	3,257
TB-26 . . .	120	7	4	57	17	21,051	139	7	6	86	20	21,094
T-6	2,089	116	91	78	18	59,133	2,668	131	103	79	20	75,735
	MARCH 1953						APRIL 1953					
TOTAL. .	13,660	591	402	68	23	897,153	14,529	730	525	72	20	910,568
B-26. . . .	175	10	6	60	18	28,240	227	10	8	80	23	36,792
F-47. . . .	283	35	24	69	8	35,659	155	35	24	69	4	18,442
F-51. . . .	4,741	249	155	62	19	329,054	5,416	281	193	69	19	359,557
RB-26 . . .	110	3	3	100	37	15,334	173	6	6	100	29	25,577
C-46. . . .	84	10	4	40	8	15,749	150	10	4	40	15	23,704
C-47. . . .	3,200	76	62	82	42	300,098	2,683	76	63	83	35	257,988
C-53. . . .	55	1	1	100	55	5,316	45	1	1	100	45	3,089
TB-26 . . .	168	7	5	71	24	30,599	179	7	5	71	26	28,275
TF-51 . . .	-	-	-	-	-	-	7	-	-	-	-	309
T-6	4,844	200	142	71	24	137,104	5,484	303	220	73	18	156,773
L-16. . . .	-	-	-	-	-	-	10	1	1	100	10	62

TABLE 359 — AIR NATIONAL GUARD FLIGHT OPERATIONS BY TYPE AND MODEL OF AIRPLANE — FY 1953 — CONTINUED

TYPE AND MODEL	TOTAL HOURS FLOWN	AVERAGE AIRPLANES			AV. HOURS FLOWN PER A/P ON HAND	AVIATION FUEL ISSUED (GALS)	TOTAL HOURS FLOWN	AVERAGE AIRPLANES			AV. HOURS FLOWN PER A/P ON HAND	AVIATION FUEL ISSUED (GALS)
		On Hand	In Com	Percent In Com				On Hand	In Com	Percent In Com		
	MAY 1953						JUNE 1953					
TOTAL. .	17,850	820	597	73	22	1,084,220	26,074	930	725	78	28	1,624,380
B-26. . . .	292	15	8	53	19	42,246	428	23	17	74	19	66,736
F-47. . . .	227	35	25	71	6	21,812	886	35	28	80	25	104,193
F-51. . . .	6,193	323	214	66	19	413,347	9,308	369	258	70	25	624,766
RB-26 . . .	273	10	7	70	27	44,494	327	10	9	90	33	47,826
RF-51 . . .	17	-	-	-	-	986	25	2	-	-	12	2,020
C-46. . . .	132	10	3	30	13	25,480	214	9	7	78	24	32,511
C-47. . . .	3,147	74	67	91	43	297,655	4,224	76	70	92	56	394,780
C-53. . . .	48	1	1	100	48	5,323	60	1	1	100	60	5,933
TB-26 . . .	121	7	5	71	17	22,204	213	7	5	71	30	32,836
TC-46 . . .	-	-	-	-	-	-	64	1	1	100	64	9,553
TF-51 . . .	88	4	2	50	22	5,703	180	9	4	50	22	10,756
T-6	7,303	339	263	78	22	204,935	10,102	382	321	84	26	283,374
T-33. . . .	-	-	-	-	-	-	40	4	2	50	10	9,077
L-16. . . .	9	2	2	100	4	35	3	2	2	100	2	19

SOURCE: Materiel Statistics Division, D/Statistical Services, DCS/C

TABLE 360 — SUMMARY OF AIR NATIONAL GUARD AIRPLANE ACTIVITIES — FY 1953

MONTH AND YEAR	OPERATING ACTIVE			Accident Rate Per 100,000 Hrs. Flown	TOTAL HOURS FLOWN	TOTAL FUEL CONSUMPTION
	Hours Flown	Av. A/P On Hand	Av. Hours Flown Per Airplane On Hand			
1952						
July.	13,821	444	31	65	13,821	1,040,054
August.	11,734	409	29	51	11,734	856,147
September	8,981	449	20	33	8,987	651,239
October	8,853	449	20	45	8,853	658,378
November.	7,173	451	16	28	7,173	504,761
December.	6,997	460	15	43	6,997	488,201
1953						
January	6,976	483	14	43	6,994	502,635
February.	9,988	497	20	40	9,988	711,786
March	13,656	570	24	15	13,660	897,153
April	14,522	714	20	21	14,529	910,568
May	17,849	806	22	17	17,850	1,084,220
June.	26,074	912	29	27	26,074	1,624,380

SOURCE: Materiel Statistics Division, D/Statistical Services, DCS/C

TABLE 361 — OBLIGATIONS DURING FISCAL YEAR 1953 FROM FUNDS APPROPRIATED FOR AIR NATIONAL GUARD

PROGRAM SYMBOL	BUDGET PROGRAM TITLE	ACTUAL OBLIGATIONS DURING FY 1953 AS OF 30 JUNE 1953		
		NET OBLIGATIONS	REIMBURSEMENTS COLLECTED	GROSS OBLIGATIONS
	Total	$ 93,847,572	$ 265,929	$ 94,113,452
210	Weapons and Ammunition.	1,242,142	-	1,242,142
220	Ground Powered and Marine Equipment	5,798,244	-	5,798,244
230	Electronics and Communications Equipment.	3,162,391	-	3,162,391
250	Training Equipment.	5,293	-	5,293
270	Other Major Equipment	4,299,562	-	4,299,562
320	Acquisition and Construction, Continental U. S.	13,003,633	696	13,004,329
410	Operation of Aircraft	12,817,395	242,586	13,059,981
420	Organization, Base and Maintenance Equipment and Supplies	13,024,551	164	13,024,715
430	Logistical Support.	6,536,351	-	6,536,351
440	Training Support.	23,011,563	11	23,011,574
470	Medical Support	600,538	-	600,538
480	Service-Wide Support.	216,736	-	216,736
520	Pay and Allowances, Air National Guard.	8,119,517	-	8,119,517
550	Subsistence	377,258	22,450	399,708
560	Individual Clothing	1,632,349	22	1,632,371

Source: Financial Management Division, Directorate of Budget, DCS/C.

308700 O - 54 - 40

TABLE 362 – FORMALLY ENROLLED AF RESERVE OFFICER TRAINING CORPS (ROTC) STUDENTS BY INSTITUTION, BY YEAR OF COURSE – FY 1953

Institution	Total			Basic		Advanced	
	Total	Basic	Advanced	First Year	Second Year	First Year	Second Year
	15 November 1952 a/						
Total	144,139	113,178	30,961	64,432	48,746	17,103	13,858
ALABAMA							
Alabama Polytechnic Institute	1,103	864	239	554	310	98	141
Alabama University	859	591	268	359	232	131	137
Tuskegee Institute	349	220	129	140	80	67	62
ARIZONA							
Arizona University	965	721	244	412	309	122	122
Arizona State College	632	501	131	293	208	68	63
ARKANSAS							
Arkansas University	676	452	224	253	199	134	90
CALIFORNIA							
Fresno State College	604	474	130	309	165	102	28
Loyola University of Los Angeles	747	465	282	263	202	138	144
San Jose State College	464	375	89	241	134	45	44
Stanford University	759	612	147	305	307	86	61
California University (Los Angeles)	1,230	960	270	515	445	140	130
Southern California, University of	662	436	226	247	189	143	83
California Institute of Technology	259	259	-	118	141	-	-
Occidental College	444	376	68	192	184	50	18
San Diego State College	580	527	53	317	210	21	32
San Francisco State College	438	395	43	262	133	30	13
California University (Berkely	945	820	125	491	329	75	50
COLORADO							
Colorado A & M College	893	655	238	395	260	110	128
Denver University	372	287	85	156	131	44	41
Colorado State College of Education	301	285	16	166	119	9	7
Colorado University	863	690	173	401	289	95	78
CONNECTICUT							
Trinity College	550	382	168	180	202	127	41
Connecticut University	1,235	915	320	439	476	172	148
Yale University	817	562	255	223	339	179	76
DISTRICT OF COLUMBIA							
Georgetown University	471	367	104	235	132	66	38
Howard University	452	282	170	143	139	91	79
Catholic University	203	186	17	90	96	17	-
George Washington University	235	219	16	140	79	15	1
FLORIDA							
Florida State University	515	399	116	225	174	59	57
Florida, University of	1,879	1,499	380	849	650	183	197
Miami University	941	691	250	383	308	149	101
GEORGIA							
Georgia University	668	417	251	243	174	118	133
Georgia Institute of Technology	908	651	257	431	220	121	136
Emory University	556	476	80	275	201	48	32
HAWAII							
Hawaii University	560	403	157	255	148	81	76
IDAHO							
Idaho University	656	431	225	254	177	82	143
ILLINOIS							
Bradley University	1,164	880	284	534	346	170	114
Illinois University	2,122	1,677	445	1,030	647	212	233
Illinois Institute of Technology	217	193	24	99	94	13	11
Northwestern University	642	553	89	251	302	64	25
Southern Illinois University	1,060	1,031	29	658	373	12	17
INDIANA							
Butler University	615	497	118	304	193	64	54
Indiana University	1,559	1,142	417	636	506	215	202
Purdue University	1,582	1,364	218	827	537	123	95
Notre Dame University	954	724	230	394	330	156	74
Ball State Teachers College	657	513	144	329	184	100	44
DePauw University	418	406	12	200	206	5	7
Evansville College	331	272	59	133	139	48	11
IOWA							
Coe College	366	267	99	174	93	50	49
Iowa State College	1,757	1,358	399	840	518	225	174
Iowa State University	1,047	759	288	422	337	162	126
Drake University	651	574	77	351	223	58	19
Grinnell College	325	301	24	162	139	18	6
KANSAS							
Kansas State College	1,311	946	365	574	372	185	180
Wichita Muncipal University	421	323	98	220	103	56	42

TABLE 362 — FORMALLY ENROLLED AF RESERVE OFFICER TRAINING CORPS (ROTC) STUDENTS BY INSTITUTION, BY YEAR OF COURSE — FY 1953 (CONTINUED)

Institution	Total			Basic		Advanced	
	Total	Basic	Advanced	First Year	Second Year	First Year	Second Year
	15 November 1952 a/						
KANSAS (Continued)							
Kansas University	1,182	819	363	400	419	207	156
Washburn University	414	310	104	178	132	51	53
KENTUCKY							
Kentucky University	1,045	715	330	430	285	164	166
Louisville University	436	305	131	157	148	76	55
Western Kentucky State College	469	322	147	150	172	83	64
LOUISIANA							
Louisiana Polytechnic Institute	706	551	155	345	206	85	70
Louisiana State University	1,190	879	311	512	367	170	141
Southwestern Louisiana Institute	947	763	184	464	299	131	53
Tulane University	551	360	191	218	142	111	80
MAINE							
Colby College	280	277	3	148	129	3	-
MARYLAND							
Maryland University	3,141	2,361	780	1,363	998	399	381
MASSACHUSETTS							
Amherst College	451	451	-	166	285	-	-
Holy Cross College	580	580	-	335	245	-	-
Lowell Textile Institute	238	204	34	108	96	34	-
Tufts College	472	454	18	218	236	9	9
Boston University	980	771	209	438	333	118	91
Harvard University	472	349	123	148	201	83	40
Massachusetts Institute of Technology	793	568	225	349	219	131	94
Massachusetts University	815	602	213	348	254	113	100
Williams College	448	348	100	162	186	71	29
MICHIGAN							
Michigan State College	1,999	1,406	593	828	578	315	278
Detroit University	834	698	136	414	284	80	56
Michigan University	1,021	868	153	488	380	85	68
Wayne University	470	374	96	222	152	57	39
Michigan College of M & T	339	235	104	134	101	59	45
MINNESOTA							
St Olaf College	479	459	20	254	205	20	-
St Thomas College	935	660	275	352	308	112	163
Minnesota University (Minneapolis)	1,251	896	355	401	495	229	126
Minnesota University (Duluth)	242	205	37	109	96	31	6
MISSISSIPPI							
Mississippi State College	609	437	172	283	154	77	95
Mississippi University	335	211	124	124	87	74	50
MISSOURI							
St Louis University	1,311	988	323	549	439	170	153
Missouri, University of	1,401	1,056	345	551	505	148	197
Washington University	452	449	3	263	186	1	2
MONTANA							
Montana College	437	333	104	202	131	46	58
Montana State University	394	260	134	156	104	60	74
Montana School of Mines	167	139	28	95	44	11	17
NEBRASKA							
Nebraska University	1,031	759	272	420	339	130	142
Omaha Municipal University	543	433	110	272	161	69	41
NEW HAMPSHIRE							
New Hampshire University	744	515	229	266	249	101	128
Dartmouth College	699	686	13	267	419	9	4
NEW JERSEY							
Rutgers University	1,050	726	324	388	338	158	166
Newark College of Engineering	777	680	97	368	312	62	35
Stevens Institute of Technology	412	314	98	187	127	49	49
Princeton University	399	399	-	148	251	-	-
NEW MEXICO							
New Mexico College of A & MA	347	251	96	158	93	41	55
New Mexico, University of	614	466	148	278	188	77	71
NEW YORK							
Colgate University	765	577	188	302	275	153	35
Cornell University	1,714	1,286	428	667	619	230	198
Fordham University	935	703	232	387	316	144	88
New York University	1,780	1,547	233	857	690	157	76
Syracuse University	1,067	820	247	450	370	164	83
Columbia University	402	371	31	197	174	23	8
Union College	509	394	115	238	156	78	37
Rensselaer Polytechnic Institute	428	294	134	145	149	85	49
Brooklyn College	775	748	27	447	301	27	-
Manhattan College	1,321	1,268	53	648	620	53	-
Queens College of New York	419	388	31	234	154	28	3

TABLE 362 — FORMALLY ENROLLED AF RESERVE OFFICER TRAINING CORPS (ROTC) STUDENTS BY INSTITUTION, BY YEAR OF COURSE — FY 1953 (CONTINUED)

Institution	Total			Basic		Advanced	
	Total	Basic	Advanced	First Year	Second Year	First Year	Second Year
	15 November 1952 a/						
NEW YORK (Continued)							
Hobart College	341	311	30	196	115	30	-
Buffalo University	1,168	1,149	19	713	436	19	-
Rochester University	280	271	9	143	128	9	-
NORTH CAROLINA							
Duke University	668	460	208	282	178	123	85
North Carolina University	847	613	234	335	278	135	99
North Carolina State College of Agriculture	920	744	176	449	295	71	105
East Carolina Teachers College	549	411	138	276	135	86	52
Agri. & Tech. College of North Carolina	428	363	65	222	141	35	30
NORTH DAKOTA							
North Dakota Agricultural College	627	476	151	289	187	138	13
North Dakota University	479	367	112	179	188	50	62
OHIO							
Bowling Green State University	349	304	45	182	122	45	-
Case Institute of Technology	415	398	17	262	136	10	7
Kent State University	463	431	32	255	176	15	17
Western Reserve University	376	327	49	136	191	38	11
Miami University (Ohio)	1,288	1,048	240	573	475	183	57
Ohio State University	3,200	2,313	887	1,397	916	413	474
Ohio University	1,032	725	307	407	318	135	172
Ohio Wesleyan University	1,162	939	223	607	332	123	100
Akron, University of	465	329	136	224	105	47	89
Cincinnati, University of	898	603	295	315	288	132	163
OKLAHOMA							
Oklahoma A & M College	2,074	1,747	327	1,113	634	174	153
Oklahoma University	1,273	907	366	556	351	174	192
Tulsa University	619	468	151	229	239	77	74
OREGON							
Oregon State College	962	661	301	417	244	131	170
Oregon, University of	714	495	219	300	195	98	121
Portland, University of	435	399	36	200	199	15	21
Willamette University	402	369	33	186	183	27	6
PENNSYLVANIA							
Duquesne University	407	265	142	158	107	67	75
Gettysburg College	339	213	126	118	95	83	43
Lehigh University	828	651	177	365	286	89	88
Pennsylvania State College	2,739	2,294	445	1,284	1,010	272	173
Pennsylvania, University of	715	522	193	252	270	131	62
Pittsburgh, University of	855	621	234	354	267	139	95
Allegheny College	280	235	45	128	107	45	-
Franklin and Marshall College	485	406	79	218	188	68	11
Grove City College	380	344	36	190	154	36	-
St Joseph's College	652	652	-	333	319	-	-
PUERTO RICO							
Puerto Rico, University of	776	757	19	453	304	19	-
RHODE ISLAND							
Brown University	466	466	-	280	186	-	-
SOUTH CAROLINA							
Citadel, The	453	345	108	185	160	55	53
Clemson Agricultural College	783	610	173	391	219	78	95
South Carolina, University of	940	713	227	407	306	207	20
SOUTH DAKOTA							
South Dakota State College of A & M	361	318	43	236	82	14	29
TENNESSEE							
Memphis State College	732	668	64	396	272	43	21
Tennessee Agri. & Ind. State College	507	494	13	303	191	3	10
South, University of the	318	278	40	148	130	30	10
Tennessee, University of	684	543	141	343	200	54	87
TEXAS							
Texas A & M College	2,051	1,313	738	740	573	348	390
Baylor University	835	641	194	323	318	118	76
Southern Methodist University	907	563	344	276	287	180	164
Texas Tech. College	784	590	194	304	286	108	86
Texas, University of	1,150	871	279	376	495	164	115
East Texas State College	523	328	195	162	166	74	121
North Texas State College	799	666	133	361	305	73	60
Southwest Texas State Teachers College	233	210	23	123	87	10	13
Texas Christian University	290	247	43	145	102	31	12
UTAH							
Utah University	1,316	1,081	235	582	499	162	73
Brigham Young University	1,826	1,745	81	1,058	687	51	30
Utah State Agricultural College	1,022	685	337	404	281	160	177

TABLE 362 — FORMALLY ENROLLED AF RESERVE OFFICER TRAINING CORPS (ROTC) STUDENTS BY INSTITUTION, BY YEAR OF COURSE — FY 1953 (CONTINUED)

Institution	Total			Basic		Advanced	
	Total	Basic	Advanced	First Year	Second Year	First Year	Second Year
	15 November 1952 a/						
VERMONT							
St Michael's College	447	383	64	203	180	60	4
Vermont, University of	563	452	111	263	189	46	65
VIRGINIA							
Virginia Polytechnic Institute	663	477	186	290	187	81	105
Virginia Military Instititute	421	273	148	121	152	81	67
Richmond University	145	138	7	74	64	1	6
Virginia University	301	271	30	145	126	9	21
WASHINGTON							
Central Washington College of Education	441	388	53	233	155	46	7
Puget Sound, College of	265	238	27	145	93	21	6
Washington State College	1,156	878	278	535	343	121	157
Washington University	1,833	1,347	486	762	585	245	241
WEST VIRGINIA							
West Virginia University	765	557	208	341	216	112	96
Davis and Elkins College	283	256	27	162	94	27	-
WISCONSIN							
Lawrence College	314	269	45	128	141	45	-
Wisconsin University	1,129	909	220	548	361	121	99
Wisconsin State College	336	277	59	176	101	27	32
WYOMING							
Wyoming, University of	200	189	11	189	-	11	-
	15 February 1953 b/						
Total	133,224	102,660	30,564	57,434	45,226	17,213	13,351
ALABAMA							
Alabama Polytechnic Institute	954	738	216	480	258	91	125
Alabama University	756	509	247	307	202	121	126
Tuskegee Institute	362	229	133	124	105	71	62
ARIZONA							
Arizona University	916	671	245	379	292	127	118
Arizona State College	589	457	132	235	222	68	64
ARKANSAS							
Arkansas University	631	405	226	229	176	134	92
CALIFORNIA							
Fresno State College	508	384	124	232	152	101	23
Loyola University of Los Angeles	724	453	271	255	198	137	134
San Jose State College	400	309	91	175	134	46	45
Stanford University	716	540	176	281	259	113	63
California University (Los Angeles)	1,196	950	246	513	437	135	111
Southern California, University of	588	372	216	177	195	143	73
California Institute of Technology	244	244	-	114	130	-	-
Occidental College	429	363	66	203	160	50	16
San Diego State College	551	503	48	299	204	20	28
San Francisco State College	440	369	71	224	145	46	25
California University (Berkeley)	900	765	135	417	348	74	61
COLORADO							
Colorado A & M College	803	593	210	337	256	89	121
Denver University	344	256	88	144	112	49	39
Colorado State College of Education	283	265	18	157	108	9	9
Colorado University	792	621	171	358	263	96	75
CONNECTICUT							
Trinity College	523	354	169	175	179	127	42
Connecticut University	1,138	827	311	388	439	175	136
Yale University	805	551	254	219	332	178	76
DISTRICT OF COLUMBIA							
Georgetown University	412	317	95	208	109	54	41
Howard University	415	248	167	150	98	69	98
Catholic University	197	178	19	91	87	18	1
George Washington University	233	218	15	130	88	15	-
FLORIDA							
Florida State University	401	299	102	164	135	51	51
Florida, University of	1,581	1,213	368	706	507	176	192
Miami University	794	543	251	284	259	153	98
GEORGIA							
Georgia University	633	374	259	217	157	135	124
Georgia Institute of Technology	867	620	247	421	199	127	120
Emory University	541	458	83	267	191	46	37
HAWAII							
Hawaii University	524	374	150	229	145	77	73

TABLE 362 – FORMALLY ENROLLED AF RESERVE OFFICER TRAINING CORPS (ROTC) STUDENTS BY INSTITUTION, BY YEAR OF COURSE – FY 1953 (CONTINUED)

Institution	Total			Basic		Advanced	
	Total	Basic	Advanced	First Year	Second Year	First Year	Second Year
	15 February 1953 b/						
IDAHO							
Idaho University	611	399	212	223	176	81	131
ILLINOIS							
Bradley University	1,072	791	281	449	342	168	113
Illinois University	2,013	1,595	418	959	636	199	219
Illinois Institute of Technology	227	197	30	80	117	16	14
Northwestern University	600	515	85	240	275	59	26
Southern Illinois University	928	902	26	555	347	10	16
INDIANA							
Butler University	583	452	131	263	189	80	51
Indiana University	1,395	993	402	560	433	215	187
Purdue University	1,478	1,259	219	770	489	127	92
Notre Dame University	839	608	231	304	304	164	67
Ball State Teachers College	594	461	133	299	162	90	43
DePauw University	408	396	12	194	202	6	6
Evansville College	276	215	61	112	103	49	12
IOWA							
Coe College	354	251	103	154	97	55	48
Iowa State College	1,641	1,257	384	783	474	224	160
Iowa State University	984	713	271	374	339	152	119
Drake University	616	529	87	300	229	64	23
Grinnell College	312	289	23	152	137	17	6
KANSAS							
Kansas State College	1,171	819	352	476	343	164	188
Wichita Municipal University	369	265	104	161	104	62	42
Kansas University	1,063	724	339	336	388	209	130
Washburn University	354	240	114	124	116	63	51
KENTUCKY							
Kentucky University	995	690	305	415	275	163	142
Louisville University	394	270	124	135	135	83	41
Western Kentucky State College	431	295	136	137	158	77	59
LOUISIANA							
Louisiana Polytechnic Institute	618	431	187	280	151	114	73
Louisiana State University	1,120	824	296	472	352	176	120
Southwestern Louisiana Institute	801	577	224	309	268	177	47
Tulane University	536	353	183	190	163	110	73
MAINE							
Colby College	258	253	5	143	110	5	-
MARYLAND							
Maryland University	2,852	2,091	761	1,203	888	398	363
MASSACHUSETTS							
Amherst College	437	437	-	156	281	-	-
Holy Cross College	554	554	-	315	239	-	-
Lowell Textile Institute	226	194	32	99	95	32	-
Tufts College	431	411	20	173	238	11	9
Boston University	894	693	201	375	318	112	89
Harvard University	454	331	123	139	192	82	41
Massachusetts Institute of Technology	779	559	220	338	221	128	92
Massachusetts University	781	568	213	319	249	113	100
Williams College	432	335	97	156	179	70	27
MICHIGAN							
Michigan State College	1,897	1,330	567	764	566	305	262
Detroit University	779	583	196	322	261	124	72
Michigan University	1,000	819	181	446	373	120	61
Wayne University	433	331	102	178	153	70	32
Michigan College of M & T.	312	217	95	122	95	54	41
MINNESOTA							
St Olaf College	438	418	20	228	190	20	-
St Thomas College	838	599	239	313	286	97	142
Minnesota University (Minneapolis)	1,098	780	318	321	459	218	100
Minnesota University (Duluth)	198	168	30	87	81	23	7
MISSISSIPPI							
Mississippi State College	575	399	176	250	149	93	83
Mississippi University	330	205	125	123	82	76	49
MISSOURI							
St Louis University	1,221	861	360	504	357	216	144
Missouri, University of	1,310	993	317	516	477	138	179
Washington University	411	408	3	239	169	1	2
MONTANA							
Montana College	399	301	98	178	123	43	55
Montana State University	385	250	135	140	110	61	74
Montana School of Mines	145	117	28	77	40	10	18

TABLE 362 — FORMALLY ENROLLED AF RESERVE OFFICER TRAINING CORPS (ROTC) STUDENTS BY INSTITUTION, BY YEAR OF COURSE — FY 1953 (CONTINUED)

Institution	Total			Basic		Advanced	
	Total	Basic	Advanced	First Year	Second Year	First Year	Second Year
	15 February 1953 b/						
NEBRASKA							
Nebraska University.	977	724	253	406	318	122	131
Omaha Municipal University	474	367	107	225	142	65	42
NEW HAMPSHIRE							
New Hampshire University	697	473	224	240	233	101	123
Dartmouth College.	659	647	12	249	398	8	4
NEW JERSEY							
Rutgers University	997	678	319	358	320	177	142
Newark College of Engineering.	717	630	87	352	278	53	34
Stevens Institute of Technology.	383	286	97	172	114	48	49
Princeton University	392	392	-	146	246	-	-
NEW MEXICO							
New Mexico College of A & MA	343	264	79	172	92	37	42
New Mexico, University of.	569	414	155	229	185	85	70
NEW YORK							
Colgate University	717	496	221	271	225	182	39
Cornell University	1,674	1,249	425	650	599	225	200
Fordham University	910	680	230	371	309	143	87
New York University.	1,833	1,599	234	856	743	157	77
Syracuse University.	1,033	779	254	432	347	179	75
Columbia University.	360	330	30	175	155	21	9
Union College.	459	347	112	211	136	75	37
Rensselaer Polytechnic Institute	403	287	116	155	132	73	43
Brooklyn College	741	714	27	423	291	27	-
Manhattan College.	1,270	1,217	53	616	601	53	-
Queens College of New York	439	370	69	203	167	62	7
Hobart College	322	292	30	184	108	30	-
Buffalo University	978	960	18	568	392	18	-
Rochester University	253	244	9	132	112	9	-
NORTH CAROLINA							
Duke University.	606	404	202	252	152	115	87
North Carolina University.	797	573	224	306	267	131	93
North Carolina State College of Agriculture. . .	884	705	179	423	282	77	102
East Carolina Teachers College	487	350	137	213	137	50	87
Agri. & Tech. College of North Carolina.	414	351	63	208	143	34	29
NORTH DAKOTA							
North Dakota Agricultural College.	546	404	142	229	175	70	72
North Dakota University.	451	348	103	176	172	48	55
OHIO							
Bowling Green State University	353	299	54	166	133	27	27
Case Institute of Technology	392	375	17	251	124	10	7
Kent State University.	410	380	30	205	175	12	18
Western Reserve University	386	309	77	165	144	67	10
Miami University (Ohio).	1,144	924	220	524	400	174	46
Ohio State University.	2,981	2,157	824	1,281	876	415	409
Ohio University.	1,020	680	340	405	275	161	179
Ohio Wesleyan University	1,072	858	214	559	299	115	99
Akron, University of	435	302	133	184	118	60	73
Cincinnati, University of.	861	568	293	278	290	131	162
OKLAHOMA							
Oklahoma A & M College	1,820	1,499	321	933	566	170	151
Oklahoma University.	1,146	823	323	514	309	156	167
Tulsa University	477	341	136	186	155	67	69
OREGON							
Oregon State College	904	621	283	388	233	122	161
Oregon, University of.	653	448	205	266	182	105	100
Portland, University of.	424	391	33	186	205	14	19
Willamette University.	374	341	33	171	170	27	6
PENNSYLVANIA							
Duquesne University.	390	254	136	147	107	60	76
Gettysburg College	319	203	116	110	93	75	41
Lehigh University.	767	598	169	341	257	87	82
Pennsylvania State College	2,594	2,165	429	1,218	947	273	156
Pennsylvania, University of.	631	443	188	218	225	129	59
Pittsburgh, University of.	859	586	273	342	244	167	106
Allegheny College.	267	222	45	122	100	45	-
Franklin and Marshall College.	426	343	83	175	168	64	19
Grove City College	366	333	33	181	152	33	-
St Joseph's College.	609	503	106	314	189	106	-
PUERTO RICO							
Puerto Rico, University of	739	721	18	427	294	18	-
RHODE ISLAND							
Brown University	357	357	-	194	163	-	-

TABLE 362 – FORMALLY ENROLLED AF RESERVE OFFICER TRAINING CORPS (ROTC) STUDENTS BY INSTITUTION, BY YEAR OF COURSE – FY 1953 (CONTINUED)

Institution	Total			Basic		Advanced	
	Total	Basic	Advanced	First Year	Second Year	First Year	Second Year
	15 February 1953 b/						
SOUTH CAROLINA							
Citadel, The	417	313	104	166	147	51	53
Clemson Agricultural College	712	549	163	345	204	76	87
South Carolina, University of	859	600	259	329	271	162	97
SOUTH DAKOTA							
South Dakota State College of A & M	347	304	43	221	83	15	28
TENNESSEE							
Memphis State College	645	578	67	327	251	47	20
Tennessee Agri. & Ind. State College	436	427	9	255	172	1	8
South, University of the	260	228	32	130	98	21	11
Tennessee, University of	629	495	134	306	189	50	84
TEXAS							
Texas A & M College	1,780	1,067	713	591	476	347	366
Baylor University	771	545	226	275	270	142	84
Southern Methodist University	838	496	342	251	245	173	169
Texas Tech. College	662	478	184	252	226	106	78
Texas, University of	936	682	254	317	365	159	95
East Texas State College	509	304	205	144	160	79	126
North Texas State College	728	592	136	324	268	76	60
Southwest Texas State Teachers College	206	183	23	107	76	10	13
Texas Christian University	278	235	43	126	109	31	12
UTAH							
Utah University	1,235	1,009	226	501	508	150	76
Brigham Young University	1,769	1,670	99	902	768	65	34
Utah State Agricultural College	972	644	328	357	287	151	177
VERMONT							
St Michael's College	351	290	61	179	111	57	4
Vermont, University of	494	387	107	223	164	44	63
VIRGINIA							
Virginia Polytechnic Institute	650	455	195	276	179	91	104
Virginia Military Institute	402	258	144	111	147	78	66
Richmond University	124	117	7	59	58	1	6
Virginia University	261	229	32	116	113	9	23
WASHINGTON							
Central Washington College of Education	411	362	49	212	150	42	7
Puget Sound, College of	262	236	26	140	96	21	5
Washington State College	977	736	241	429	307	105	136
Washington University	1,674	1,199	475	655	544	248	227
WEST VIRGINIA							
West Virginia University	709	514	195	311	203	105	90
Davis and Elkins College	261	235	26	145	90	26	-
WISCONSIN							
Lawrence College	294	253	41	121	132	41	-
Wisconsin University	1,081	879	202	537	342	114	88
Wisconsin State College	297	233	64	146	87	28	36
WYOMING							
Wyoming, University of	186	175	11	175	-	11	-
	15 June 1953 c/						
Total	116,447	92,962	23,485	52,552	40,410	16,434	7,051
ALABAMA							
Alabama Polytechnic Institute	773	587	186	475	112	101	85
Alabama University	695	500	195	306	194	117	78
Tuskegee Institute	323	214	109	117	97	69	40
ARIZONA							
Arizona University	834	630	204	354	276	123	81
Arizona State College	543	441	102	226	215	68	34
ARKANSAS							
Arkansas University	562	382	180	214	168	128	52
CALIFORNIA							
Fresno State College	433	331	102	226	105	90	12
Loyola University of Los Angeles	628	409	219	224	185	123	96
San Jose State College	335	269	66	152	117	43	23
Stanford University	587	432	155	250	182	117	38
California University (Los Angeles)	1,185	923	262	481	442	128	134
Southern California, University of	558	382	176	186	196	136	40
California Institute of Technology	214	214	-	97	117	-	-
Occidental College	348	335	13	191	144	8	5
San Diego State College	454	399	55	235	164	26	29
San Francisco State College	385	326	59	195	131	37	22

TABLE 362 — FORMALLY ENROLLED AF RESERVE OFFICER TRAINING CORPS (ROTC) STUDENTS BY INSTITUTION, BY YEAR OF COURSE — FY 1953 (Continued)

Institution	Total			Basic		Advanced	
	Total	Basic	Advanced	First Year	Second Year	First Year	Second Year
	15 June 1953 c/						
CALIFORNIA (Continued)							
California University (Berkeley)	917	786	131	420	366	69	62
COLORADO							
Colorado A & M College	660	511	149	298	213	96	53
Denver University.	246	177	69	104	73	49	20
Colorado State College of Education.	259	241	18	138	103	-	18
Colorado University.	671	547	124	346	201	90	34
CONNECTICUT							
Trinity College.	485	346	139	167	179	126	13
Connecticut University	997	770	227	330	440	164	63
Yale University.	727	534	193	211	323	174	19
DISTRICT OF COLUMBIA							
Georgetown University.	370	293	77	198	95	42	35
Howard University.	397	274	123	153	121	68	55
Catholic University.	187	171	16	88	83	15	1
George Washington University	211	199	12	118	81	12	-
FLORIDA							
Florida State University	346	277	69	145	132	46	23
Florida, University of	1,448	1,195	253	694	501	165	88
Miami University	620	447	173	230	217	118	55
GEORGIA							
Georgia University	551	346	205	198	148	131	74
Georgia Institute of Technology.	734	531	203	374	157	136	67
Emory University	391	335	56	231	104	42	14
HAWAII							
Hawaii University.	464	366	98	223	143	76	22
IDAHO							
Idaho University	523	379	144	214	165	77	67
ILLINOIS							
Bradley University	967	780	187	444	336	149	38
Illinois University.	1,959	1,554	405	925	629	187	218
Illinois Institute of Techology.	186	164	22	81	83	16	6
Northwestern University.	383	316	67	182	134	52	15
Southern Illinois University	813	792	21	475	317	11	10
INDIANA							
Butler University.	526	427	99	241	186	67	32
Indiana University	1,239	975	264	543	432	211	53
Purdue University.	1,398	1,229	169	750	479	124	45
Notre Dame University.	798	605	193	299	306	162	31
Ball State Teachers College.	409	312	97	220	92	76	21
DePauw University.	320	310	10	192	118	6	4
Evansville College	170	114	56	5	109	47	9
IOWA							
Coe College.	306	245	61	150	95	45	16
Iowa State College	1,453	1,164	289	721	443	222	67
Iowa State University.	710	539	171	353	186	136	35
Drake University	586	508	78	285	223	60	18
Grinnell College	277	256	21	147	109	18	3
KANSAS							
Kansas State College	1,033	790	243	467	323	148	95
Wichita Municipal University	337	252	85	150	102	61	24
Kansas University.	856	599	257	315	284	166	91
Washburn University.	316	225	91	115	110	61	30
KENTUCKY							
Kentucky University.	883	659	224	395	264	154	70
Louisville University.	299	208	91	125	83	59	32
Western Kentucky State College	390	279	111	129	150	66	45
LOUISIANA							
Louisiana Polytechnic Institute.	570	404	166	265	139	112	54
Louisiana State University	1,057	799	258	455	344	167	91
Southwestern Louisiana Institute	687	482	205	280	202	173	32
Tulane University.	448	308	140	179	129	98	42
MAINE							
Colby College.	243	238	5	140	98	5	-
MARYLAND							
Maryland University.	2,563	2,008	555	1,126	882	346	209
MASSACHUSETTS							
Amherst College.	147	147	-	-	147	-	-
Holy Cross College	448	448	-	311	137	-	-
Lowell Textile Institute	217	185	32	94	91	32	-
Tufts College.	398	384	14	166	218	10	4
Boston University.	724	598	126	295	303	106	20
Harvard University	387	302	85	137	165	77	8

TABLE 362 — FORMALLY ENROLLED AF RESERVE OFFICER TRAINING CORPS (ROTC) STUDENTS BY INSTITUTION, BY YEAR OF COURSE — FY 1953 (CONTINUED)

Institution	Total			Basic		Advanced	
	Total	Basic	Advanced	First Year	Second Year	First Year	Second Year
	15 June 1953 c/						
MASSACHUSETTS (Continued)							
Massachusetts Institute of Technology	611	436	175	322	114	131	44
Massachusetts University	679	559	120	313	246	112	8
Williams College	401	330	71	155	175	69	2
MICHIGAN							
Michigan State College	1,661	1,212	449	724	488	310	139
Detroit University	719	551	168	291	260	116	52
Michigan University	960	804	156	441	363	117	39
Wayne University	355	263	92	143	120	60	32
Michigan College of M & T	262	194	68	111	83	52	16
MINNESOTA							
St Olaf College	400	382	18	222	160	18	-
St Thomas College	722	569	153	297	272	91	62
Minnesota University (Minneapolis)	912	652	260	258	394	204	56
Minnesota University (Duluth)	174	148	26	74	74	24	2
MISSISSIPPI							
Mississippi State College	469	361	108	237	124	76	32
Mississippi University	282	185	97	106	79	74	23
MISSOURI							
St. Louis University	1,119	822	297	427	395	193	104
Missouri, University of	1,199	968	231	517	451	146	85
Washington University	330	328	2	219	109	-	2
MONTANA							
Montana College	314	260	54	147	113	38	16
Montana State University	323	229	94	128	101	63	31
Montana School of Mines	138	117	21	76	41	9	12
NEBRASKA							
Nebraska University	865	694	171	390	304	116	55
Omaha Municipal University	419	334	85	217	117	65	20
NEW HAMPSHIRE							
New Hampshire University	590	454	136	236	218	99	37
Dartmouth College	404	397	7	241	156	7	-
NEW JERSEY							
Rutgers University	888	669	219	353	316	155	64
Newark College of Engineering	691	627	64	350	277	52	12
Stevens Institute of Technology	281	231	50	157	74	48	2
Princeton University	387	387	-	144	243	-	-
NEW MEXICO							
New Mexico College of A & MA	286	228	58	169	59	33	25
New Mexico, University of	454	330	124	219	111	83	41
NEW YORK							
Colgate University	664	475	189	252	223	174	15
Cornell University	1,485	1,202	283	623	579	217	66
Fordham University	719	568	151	309	259	125	26
New York University	1,600	1,437	163	764	673	153	10
Syracuse University	905	687	218	362	325	183	35
Columbia University	323	306	17	-	306	16	1
Union College	323	256	67	191	65	64	3
Rensselaer Polytechnic Institute	380	286	94	153	133	73	21
Brooklyn College	828	767	61	439	328	61	-
Manhattan College	1,156	1,108	48	564	544	48	-
Queens College of New York	388	320	68	181	139	61	7
Hobart College	314	284	30	180	104	30	-
Buffalo University	753	735	18	547	188	18	-
Rochester University	170	163	7	122	41	1	6
NORTH CAROLINA							
Duke University	523	368	155	221	147	110	45
North Carolina University	679	498	181	282	216	127	54
North Carolina State College of Agriculture	786	662	124	392	270	75	49
East Carolina Teachers College	427	303	124	175	128	47	77
Agri. & Tech. College of North Carolina	348	308	40	180	128	31	9
NORTH DAKOTA							
North Dakota Agricultural College	453	352	101	194	158	63	38
North Dakota University	392	328	64	161	167	47	17
OHIO							
Bowling Green State University	278	247	31	158	89	15	16
Case Institute of Technology	364	351	13	233	118	10	3
Kent State University	368	345	23	176	169	11	12
Western Reserve University	330	258	72	151	107	65	7
Miami University (Ohio)	1,102	909	193	504	405	172	21
Ohio State University	2,582	1,978	604	1,174	804	435	169
Ohio University	905	658	247	397	261	159	88
Ohio Wesleyan University	917	794	123	539	255	109	14
Akron, University of	424	291	133	178	113	55	78

TABLE 362 — FORMALLY ENROLLED AF RESERVE OFFICER TRAINING CORPS (ROTC) STUDENTS BY INSTITUTION, BY YEAR OF COURSE — FY 1953 (CONTINUED)

Institution	Total			Basic		Advanced	
	Total	Basic	Advanced	First Year	Second Year	First Year	Second Year
	15 June 1953 c/						
OHIO (Continued)							
Cincinnati, University of.	735	488	247	252	236	193	54
OKLAHOMA							
Oklahoma A & M College	1,686	1,443	243	893	550	165	78
Oklahoma University.	1,019	767	252	478	289	144	108
Tulsa University	470	335	135	181	154	65	70
OREGON							
Oregon State College	708	523	185	342	181	116	69
Oregon, University of.	510	403	107	235	168	102	5
Portland, University of.	360	334	26	179	155	13	13
Willamette University.	310	307	3	162	145	3	-
PENNSYLVANIA							
Duquesne University.	342	248	94	142	106	66	28
Gettysburg College	281	202	79	109	93	75	4
Lehigh University.	692	588	104	333	255	81	23
Pennsylvania State College	2,418	2,097	321	1,174	923	268	53
Pennsylvania, University of.	566	423	143	211	212	126	17
Pittsburgh, University of.	780	560	220	326	234	164	56
Allegheny College.	210	189	21	114	75	21	-
Franklin and Marshall College.	406	329	77	170	159	63	14
Grove City College	347	329	18	178	151	18	-
St Joseph's College.	592	486	106	300	186	106	-
PUERTO RICO							
Puerto Rico, University of	709	695	14	412	283	14	-
RHODE ISLAND							
Brown University	355	355	-	191	164	-	-
SOUTH CAROLINA							
Citadel, The	360	296	64	158	138	53	11
Clemson Agricultural College	687	558	129	353	205	73	56
South Carolina, University of.	777	559	218	300	259	148	70
SOUTH DAKOTA							
South Dakota State College of A & M	300	277	23	198	79	13	10
TENNESSEE							
Memphis State College.	522	464	58	261	203	45	13
Tennessee Agri. & Ind. State College	232	231	1	18	213	1	-
South, University of the	181	159	22	118	41	19	3
Tennessee, University of	553	440	113	270	170	45	68
TEXAS							
Texas A & M College.	1,587	1,031	556	562	469	341	215
Baylor University.	684	448	236	265	183	156	80
Southern Methodist University.	774	486	288	246	240	171	117
Texas Tech. College.	605	458	147	240	218	94	53
Texas, University of	874	662	212	311	351	158	54
East Texas State College	446	296	150	139	157	76	74
North Texas State College.	561	453	108	295	158	79	29
Southwest Texas State Teachers College	167	150	17	97	53	10	7
Texas Christian University	261	222	39	121	101	31	8
UTAH							
Utah University.	1,031	778	253	360	418	206	47
Brigham Young University	1,487	1,341	146	809	532	98	48
Utah State Agricultural College.	781	557	224	304	253	136	88
VERMONT							
St Michael's College	337	278	59	169	109	57	2
Vermont, University of	435	379	56	216	163	41	15
VIRGINIA							
Virginia Polytechnic Institute	541	401	140	257	144	89	51
Virginia Military Institute.	323	244	79	108	136	76	3
Richmond University.	120	114	6	57	57	1	5
Virginia University.	253	222	31	114	108	9	22
WASHINGTON							
Central Washington College of Education.	332	325	7	182	143	2	5
Puget Sound, College of.	206	183	23	133	50	21	2
Washington State College	917	738	179	428	310	103	76
Washington University.	1,449	1,056	393	579	477	245	148
WEST VIRGINIA							
West Virginia University	457	309	148	-	309	101	47
Davis and Elkins College	254	229	25	143	86	25	-
WISCONSIN							
Lawrence College	257	243	14	112	131	14	-
Wisconsin University	1,017	827	190	502	325	103	87
Wisconsin State College.	276	224	52	139	85	27	25
WYOMING							
Wyoming, University of	162	154	8	154	-	8	-

a/ Includes 16 First Year Advanced and 2 Second Year Advanced Conditionally Enrolled Students.
b/ Includes 1,130 First Year Advanced and 66 Second Year Advanced Conditionally Enrolled Students.
c/ Includes 277 First Year Advanced and 17 Second Year Advanced Conditionally Enrolled Students.

Source: Personnel Statistics Division, DCS/Comptroller, Hq. USAF.

TABLE 363 — USAF ROTC COMMISSIONS GRANTED BY FISCAL YEAR — FY 1947 THROUGH FY 1953

FY 1947	FY 1948	FY 1949	FY 1950	FY 1951	FY 1952	FY 1953
2	1,470	2,960	4,395	7,031	8,244	8,143

Source: Personnel Statistics Division, DCS/Comptroller, Hq. USAF

TABLE 364 — USAF ROTC COMMISSIONS GRANTED BY MONTH — FY 1953

Total	Jul (1952)	Aug	Sep	Oct	Nov	Dec	Jul (1953)	Feb	Mar	Apr	May	Jun
8,143	370	44	57	35	11	-	305	900	121	193	113	5,994

Source: Personnel Statistics Division, DCS/Comptroller, Hq USAF.

TABLE 365 — USAF COMMISSIONED ROTC OFFICERS SENT TO ACTIVE MILITARY SERVICE (AMS) BY TYPE OF TRAINING — FY 1953

Month	Total	Number Entering Pilot Training	Number Entering Observer Training	Other Training and On-the-Job Training
TOTAL	6,454	922	55	5,477
July (1952).	554	66	7	481
August	2,584	316	25	2,243
September.	1,058	269	4	785
October.	433	94	2	337
November	90	a/ - 13	a/ - 6	109
December	60	28	1	31
January (1953)	78	8	-	70
February	270	36	2	232
March.	391	16	15	360
April.	390	19	1	370
May.	279	10	2	267
June	267	73	2	192

a/ The minus (-) figures for November (1952) are due to revocation of orders.

Source: Personnel Statistics Division, DCS/Comptroller, Hq USAF.

TABLE 366 — FORMALLY ENROLLED ADVANCED AF RESERVE OFFICER TRAINING CORPS (ROTC) STUDENTS BY ROTC SPECIALTY — FY 1953

ROTC Specialty	Total	First Year	Second Year
15 November - 1952			
Total	30,961	17,103	13,858
Administrative and Logistics	13,331	7,231	6,100
Aircraft Maintenance and Engineering	2,396	1,009	1,387
Air Installation	486	215	271
Armament	1,077	547	530
Communications	1,131	520	611
Comptrollership	1,939	1,116	823
Flight Operations	7,950	4,802	3,148
General Technical	2,363	1,399	964
Other Courses	288	264	24
15 February - 1953			
Total	30,564	17,213	13,351
Administration and Logistics	13,144	7,296	5,848
Aircraft Maintenance and Engineering	2,176	1,039	1,137
Air Installation	443	175	268
Armament	1,030	523	507
Communications	1,072	511	561
Comptrollership	1,817	1,063	754
Flight Operations	8,238	4,992	3,246
General Technical	2,411	1,405	1,006
Other Courses	233	209	24
15 June - 1953			
Total	23,485	16,434	7,051
Administration and Logistics	9,819	6,864	2,955
Aircraft Maintenance and Engineering	1,717	1,068	649
Air Installation	308	161	147
Armament	754	490	264
Communications	777	467	310
Comptrollership	1,367	1,059	308
Flight Operations	6,606	4,828	1,778
General Technical	1,948	1,326	622
Other Courses	189	171	18

Source: Personnel Statistics Division, DCS/Comptroller, Hq. USAF.

TABLE 367 – PARTICIPATION IN CIVIL AIR PATROL (CAP) ACTIVITIES BY WING – FY 1953

Wings	31 December 1952							30 June 1953						
	Total	Officer		Senior		Cadet		Total	Officer		Senior		Cadet	
		Male	Female	Male	Female	Male	Female		Male	Female	Male	Female	Male	Female
WORLDWIDE-TOTAL . . .	79,426	9,144	898	19,487	3201	37,150	9546	79,592	9,106	855	19,962	3070	37,222	9377
CONTINENTAL US-TOTAL	76,120	8,862	864	18,913	3044	35,692	8745	75,627	8,848	826	19,390	2904	35,173	8486
Alabama	1,063	118	11	202	27	617	88	826	154	11	152	22	446	41
Arizona	1,409	207	21	458	108	495	120	1,134	165	26	452	90	326	75
Arkansas.	1,131	114	11	336	34	590	46	777	166	8	177	29	369	28
California. . . .	5,176	608	72	2,079	506	1,559	352	4,836	654	92	1,647	437	1,634	372
Colorado.	2,562	254	30	342	72	1,224	640	2,641	196	15	325	87	1,348	670
Connecticut . . .	1,270	140	20	175	58	695	182	860	153	18	201	38	358	92
Delaware.	211	47	8	28	7	104	17	234	61	6	44	12	96	15
Dist. of Columbia	550	92	16	169	20	213	40	555	78	10	116	40	252	59
Florida	2,965	439	45	637	111	1,324	409	3,316	321	41	870	120	1,502	462
Georgia	1,139	85	3	334	36	647	34	1,125	98	7	291	34	648	47
Idaho	493	76	2	135	4	232	44	658	112	5	216	21	259	45
Illinois.	1,987	422	37	1,047	123	251	107	2,631	387	46	1,050	124	779	245
Indiana	1,784	263	23	469	53	791	185	1,316	311	24	557	67	301	56
Iowa.	902	158	7	145	5	485	102	1,164	184	4	174	18	666	118
Kansas.	1,202	107	13	250	32	692	108	1,494	125	10	347	46	827	139
Kentucky.	450	65	7	105	11	238	24	462	76	2	171	22	173	18
Louisiana	1,066	179	17	358	76	352	84	895	184	18	269	27	337	60
Maine	912	119	17	187	33	526	30	803	138	21	188	37	367	52
Maryland.	962	104	13	207	22	522	94	673	133	9	187	32	273	39
Massachusetts . .	3,777	212	28	403	64	2,234	836	3,799	227	30	382	69	2,279	812
Michigan.	3,422	510	47	802	145	1,436	482	3,409	470	37	1,034	173	1,322	373
Minnesota	1,374	194	10	218	34	747	171	1,448	122	9	268	19	866	164
Mississippi . . .	557	101	1	189	23	230	13	527	109	7	168	19	212	12
Missouri.	755	160	20	213	40	286	36	771	157	14	255	34	290	41
Montana	811	59	2	76	2	446	226	619	67	3	119	7	296	127
Nebraska.	859	109	13	211	13	410	103	715	116	10	263	27	224	75
Nevada.	698	91	7	253	55	217	75	624	87	12	211	39	200	75
New Hampshire . .	1,062	91	11	241	28	541	150	1,041	110	11	158	22	582	158
New Jersey. . . .	1,819	148	14	519	73	853	212	1,821	173	17	456	82	887	206
New Mexico. . . .	993	126	17	201	43	483	123	1,075	119	22	280	50	460	144
New York.	5,782	541	56	904	182	3,142	957	5,774	382	27	1,100	166	3,142	957
North Carolina. .	1,846	295	13	555	63	793	127	1,672	285	15	520	40	705	107
North Dakota. . .	891	68	3	317	10	420	73	1,129	66	6	397	15	559	86
Ohio.	2,413	184	9	622	140	1,193	265	2,498	336	40	570	92	1,195	265
Oklahoma.	1,242	136	15	326	30	637	98	1,443	157	14	356	46	773	97
Oregon.	1,045	116	20	248	41	489	131	1,382	141	17	243	38	734	209
Pennsylvania. . .	3,938	349	33	926	148	2,051	431	3,801	241	24	906	102	2,111	417
Rhode Island. . .	757	69	5	186	32	348	117	719	49	2	177	15	346	130
South Carolina. .	1,027	131	4	250	28	572	42	793	126	6	240	14	389	18
South Dakota. . .	414	58	2	109	7	212	26	567	66	1	213	21	225	41
Tennessee	1,198	134	5	307	35	655	62	1,357	148	13	240	32	822	102
Texas	4,136	572	76	1,376	198	1,611	303	4,015	538	34	1,280	193	1,619	351
Utah.	1,080	114	10	127	24	695	110	999	92	9	195	21	614	68
Vermont	863	42	7	189	36	454	135	886	76	13	124	17	496	160
Virginia.	1,571	134	10	404	43	844	136	1,133	168	13	412	60	419	61
Washington. . . .	1,596	186	12	561	67	598	172	1,726	173	10	597	79	683	184
West Virginia . .	772	112	11	171	29	414	35	1,042	134	9	266	37	536	60
Wisconsin	1,450	136	21	247	50	745	251	1,797	125	15	421	53	918	265
Wyoming	738	87	9	99	23	379	141	645	92	13	125	19	308	88
OVERSEAS-TOTAL.	3,306	282	34	574	157	1,458	801	3,965	258	29	572	166	2,049	891
Alaska.	364	67	10	132	20	81	54	381	56	8	112	24	118	63
Hawaii.	1,546	30	6	170	78	762	500	1,397	22	4	254	102	629	386
Puerto Rico . . .	1,396	185	18	272	59	615	247	2,187	180	17	206	40	1,302	442

Source: Personnel Statistics Division, DCS/Comptroller, Hq. USAF.

TABLE 368 — CIVIL AIR PATROL UNITS BY TYPE — FY 1953

Date	Units By Type			
	Total	Wings	Groups	Squadrons
30 September 1952	2,002	52	196	1,754
31 December 1952.	1,984	52	210	1,722
31 March 1953	2,112	52	214	1,846
30 June 1953.	2,200	52	218	1,930

Source: Director of CAP Personnel, DCS/Personnel, Hq CAP, USAF

TABLE 369 — CIVIL AIR PATROL WING HEADQUARTERS BY LOCATION — AS OF 30 JUN 1953

Wing and City	Wing and City	Wing and City
	CONTINENTAL US	
Alabama - Birmingham	Maine - Fort Williams	North Dakota - Fargo
Arizona - Tucson	Maryland - Friendship	Ohio - Cincinnati
Arkansas - Little Rock	Massachusetts - Bedford	Oklahoma - Oklahoma City
California - San Francisco	Michigan - Detroit	Oregon - Portland
Colorado - Denver	Minnesota - Minneapolis	Pennsylvania - Allentown
Connecticut - New Haven	Mississippi - Jackson	Rhode Island - Providence
Delaware - Wilmington	Missouri - Joplin	South Carolina - Rock Hill
Florida - Orlando	Montana - Helena	South Dakota - Sioux Falls
Georgia - Marietta	National Capital - Washington, D. C.	Tennessee - Memphis
Idaho - Boise	Nebraska - Omaha	Texas - Dallas
Illinois - Chicago	Nevada - Sparks	Utah - Salt Lake City
Indiana - Indianapolis	New Hampshire - Keene	Vermont - Rutland
Iowa - Des Moines	New Jersey - Newark	Virginia - Richmond
Kansas - Wichita	New Mexico - Albuquerque	Washington - Seattle
Kentucky - Louisville	New York - New York	West Virginia - Martinsburg
Louisiana - New Orleans	North Carolina - Charlotte	Wisconsin - Racine Wyoming Cheyenne
	OUTSIDE CONTINENTAL US	
Alaska - Anchorage	Hawaii - Honolulu	Puerto Rico - San Juan

Source: Headquarters, Civil Air Patrol, USAF.

TABLE 370 — CIVIL AIR PATROL TRAINING BY STATE OR TERRITORY — FY 1953

State and Territory	FIRST HALF FY 1953 (Jul 1952 through 31 Dec 1952)								SECOND HALF FY 1953 (1 Jan 1953 through 30 Jun 1953)							
	AF Reserve Participation		Classroom Training by CAP		Other Training By CAP		Cadet Orientation Flights		AF Reserve Participation		Classroom Training by CAP		Other Training By CAP		Cadet Orientation Flights	
	Persons	Man-Hours	Persons	Man-Hours	Persons	Man-Hours	Persons	Flying Hours	Persons	Man-Hours	Persons	Man-Hours	Persons	Man-Hours	Persons	Flying Hours
USAF - TOTAL	4,287	34,422	91,050	537,671	34,341	213,582	16,032	37,060:48	1,072	15,817	161,297	4583952	62,694	1897,193	12,441	13,805:00
CONTINENTAL - TOTAL	4,272	34,285	82,674	467,723	34,291	213,482	15,497	36,479:30	1,042	15,705	153,306	4510891	60,920	1884,736	11,562	13,499:00
Alabama	12	70	2,133	8,100	838	3,224	220	1,011:00	8	73	5,051	22,205	2,775	11,147	244	340:00
Arizona	6	46	2,520	9,100	600	2,200	61	204:00	3	258	2,432	9,374	435	3,221	109	99:00
Arkansas	43	224	1,639	11,085	534	6,628	655	1,198:00	8	112	438	15,224	157	2,837	97	16:00
California	870	10,673	5,892	42,231	2,360	21,758	1,066	4,354:45	77	994	12,437	327,459	3,683	215,122	661	745:00
Colorado	66	108	4,150	31,200	2,000	6,420	336	211:20	13	229	3,075	13,369	1,496	6,575	319	356:00
Connecticut	15	174	575	5,436	339	1,828	182	974:00	59	499	1,716	6,175	1,101	6,077	31	18:00
Delaware	69	248	398	1,547	105	1,136	128	134:55	31	318	209	1,206	30	132	26	22:00
Florida	84	288	1,717	10,571	1,000	7,649	39	796:45	10	134	3,352	19,618	1,526	23,117	271	82:00
Georgia	13	0	498	1,813	633	2,734	807	1,645:00	8	90	3,409	69,707	811	15,010	349	216:00
Idaho	44	419	75	610	18	1,572	34	242:00	4	156	202	1,140	49	372	0	0:00
Illinois	461	1,813	3,956	23,498	1,170	7,266	1,179	1,695:40	67	655	3,048	28,132	2,286	30,983	1,349	2,546:00
Indiana	75	456	316	2,873	271	2,065	82	170:00	48	405	6,677	269,022	958	142,048	196	326:00
Iowa	21	1,464	772	3,155	433	20,510	211	281:00	6	156	2,423	5,218	710	3,040	144	185:00
Kansas	110	439	678	4,325	300	600	93	223:00	57	246	300	3,000	162	658	109	360:00
Kentucky	57	123	348	3,046	39	104	116	150:25	17	289	687	4,219	148	749	24	19:00
Louisiana	36	10	3,306	10,422	2,960	16,271	322	575:30	16	227	4,600	15,687	1,525	5,079	201	91:00
Maine	33	196	1,195	7,463	656	4,616	156	738:00	17	313	2,546	13,936	660	6,812	108	256:00
Maryland	20	75	911	5,740	382	1,909	355	723:40	14	126	2,840	7,010	1,029	2,214	128	35:00
Massachusetts	63	716	2,604	19,109	1,153	7,255	735	783:00	30	389	3,379	28,836	2,426	14,372	621	694:00
Michigan	140	993	8,457	57,675	1,408	8,084	989	1,462:50	44	924	11,973	78,870	4,075	21,840	699	477:00
Minnesota	16	115	1,154	6,513	559	2,519	360	404:25	44	1,179	1,418	18,507	533	5,066	333	1,039:00
Mississipp	13	100	178	1,458	61	347	51	191:15	5	42	388	2,929	136	1,250	55	32:00
Missouri	8	79	912	4,413	85	77	133	619:00	5	102	3,064	17,551	912	4,107	112	15:00
Montana	0	0	247	877	23	32	58	85:00	0	0	466	2,027	101	316	0	0:00
National Capital (DC)	62	514	1,295	9,582	246	573	187	308:00	31	120	983	7,183	543	4,835	133	519:00
Nebraska	46	318	2,466	10,562	337	1,063	286	351:16	23	564	1,100	203,495	603	134,645	180	122:00
Nevada	108	648	386	1,651	95	726	161	102:30	0	0	2,735	9,972	892	8,448	285	74:00
New Hampshire	7	276	227	3,689	52	410	101	208:30	3	120	480	7,211	178	4,901	65	14:00
New Jersey	96	0	2,269	17,006	1,323	9,489	818	1,075:55	12	0	4,951	1530080	2,898	14,490	712	978:00
New Mexico	102	1,557	5,883	13,855	3,513	9,116	170	1,252:00	47	347	5,347	12,120	4,311	12,411	147	116:00

New York.	16	82	3,058	8,170	585	1,678	614	560:00	46	506	5,791	131,449	3,350	105,889	288	222:00
North Carolina.	201	601	1,448	5,542	847	2,058	446	1,229:15	27	660	6,593	26,427	1,605	5,895	336	206:00
North Dakota.	105	104	499	776	156	257	87	63:00	2	32	819	15,202	449	1,128	82	16:00
Ohio.	393	5,952	2,346	12,096	1,547	8,424	719	2,355:00	24	422	8,664	385,934	2,521	143,305	479	985:00
Oklahoma.	70	591	1,912	7,792	1,616	4,604	504	552:00	13	277	2,193	7,306	558	6,507	176	201:00
Oregon.	98	585	441	1,978	143	406	32	305:10	69	663	2,540	12,685	1,335	6,456	99	246:00
Pennsylvania.	119	406	2,664	22,624	436	2,858	324	661:15	30	1,923	7,373	800,468	3,584	621,244	281	130:00
Rhode Island.	7	48	580	2,025	233	18,502	418	518:55	4	112	5,867	10,452	2,200	3,232	593	457:00
South Carolina.	28	288	1,631	7,991	893	5,163	76	136:20	10	101	2,115	62,821	795	102,783	202	96:00
South Dakota.	24	180	608	10,830	652	6,472	10	9:25	8	408	991	8,786	530	3,595	42	6:00
Tennessee	0	0	121	780	111	138	234	255:00	0	0	235	2,250	210	1,890	105	3:00
Texas	150	235	2,144	12,622	1,621	7,178	816	4,836:00	3	116	6,414	51,097	1,119	8,705	379	433:00
Utah.	32	537	384	2,246	101	325	83	228:30	17	999	976	8,710	185	5,440	29	226:00
Vermont	34	64	2,859	11,436	0	0	100	90:55	0	0	1,276	10,292	439	2,634	126	16:00
Virginia.	0	0	85	226	56	260	127	513:15	0	0	3,063	25,766	679	11,271	122	113:00
Washington.	83	1,205	1,150	12,977	870	2,226	336	418:45	37	205	3,451	139,262	2,108	89,376	271	108:00
West Virginia	47	111	613	9,073	430	3,337	141	283:40	36	147	1,257	46,757	582	60,101	97	120:00
Wisconsin	167	1,146	2,854	9,889	501	1,415	316	1,181:00	4	32	1,400	9,555	1,327	2,644	117	90:00
Wyoming	2	8	120	45	0	0	23	109:24	5	35	562	5,190	195	767	30	33:00
OUTSIDE CONTINENTAL US-TOTAL	15	137	8,376	69,948	50	100	535	581:18	30	112	7,991	73,061	1,774	12,457	879	306:00
Alaska.	0	0	283	3,000	50	100	22	40:55	0	0	549	6,303	339	4,333	68	7:00
Hawaii.	6	100	8,014	60,512	0	0	197	261:53	30	112	5,781	36,512	1,190	2,724	471	298:00
Puerto Rico	9	37	79	6,436	0	0	316	278:30	0	0	1,661	30,246	245	5,400	340	1:00

Source: Headquarters Civil Air Patrol, USAF.

TABLE 371 — FLYING ACTIVITY OF CIVIL AIR PATROL ON ACTUAL MISSIONS (SEARCH, RESCUE, AND MERCY) — FY 1953

Requesting Agency	Missions	Personnel Participating		Number Aircraft Flown	Number Hours Flown
		Seniors	Cadets		
TOTAL	282	10,479	2,423	4,007	15,884:49
Air Rescue Service	134	6,594	1,518	2,462	11,010:26
American Red Cross	0	0	0	0	0:00
City and State Officials	4	184	73	29	50:59
Ground Observer Corps.	110	2,827	503	1,293	3,922:59
Others	34	871	329	223	900:25

Source: Headquarters, Civil Air Patrol, USAF

TABLE 372 — FLYING ACTIVITY OF CIVIL AIR PATROL ON PRACTICE MISSIONS (SEARCH AND RESCUE — SCARCAP) — CY 1953

Missions-Aircraft-Hours Participants	Total	Missions-Aircraft-Hours Participants	Total
Missions	65	Number Seniors Participating	7,337
Number Aircraft Flown.	1,703	Number Cadets Participating.	4,078
Number Hours Flown	7,249:19		

Source: Headquarters, Civil Air Patrol, USAF

TABLE 373 — CIVIL AIR PATROL CADET ENCAMPMENT BY CALENDAR YEAR — 1947 THROUGH 1953

Calendar Year	Air Force Bases Used As Sites	Encampments			Attendance				
		Total	Number of Air Force Bases	Number of Other Sites	Total	Cadets		Seniors	
						Male	Female	Male	Female
TOTAL . . .	179	202	193	9	26,454	18,269	3,249	1,814	499
1947	25	25	25	-	2,623	a/	a/	a/	a/
1948	14	14	14	-	1,923	1,574	202	116	31
1949	21	22	22	-	2,401	1,918	229	207	47
1950	21	26	24	2	3,244	2,486	336	362	60
1951	20	33	26	7	4,534	3,542	572	344	76
1952	39	42	42	-	5,383	3,939	939	368	137
1953	39	40	40	-	6,346	4,810	971	417	148

a/ Not Available.

Source: Headquarters, Civil Air Patrol, USAF

TABLE 374 — CIVIL AIR PATROL (CAP) — HIGH SCHOOL AVIATION EDUCATION PROGRAM — 1949 (FALL) THROUGH 1953 (SPRING)

The Coordinated CAP-High School Aviation Education Program is an aviation education plan which may be described as general education in regard to aviation.

The course, as a one-year program for high school instruction, is taught by regular members of the school faculty. (It is also designed as a two-year course for use at CAP squadron level with CAP and Air Force Reserve personnel serving as instructors.) Any student is eligible to participate in the high school course of instruction, and CAP membership, though desirable, is not necessary.

The data below reflect a 153 per cent increase in the number of high schools offering coordinated CAP aviation education with corresponding increase of 101 per cent in the number of students between the Fall Semester 1949 and Fall Semester 1952. This gradual build up attained its maximum peak in both number of participating schools and number of students in Spring Semester 1952 with increases to 157 per cent, and 144 per cent, respectively.

Date	Number of High Schools	Number of Students
Fall Semester 1949	89	2,780
Spring Semester 1950	119	3,531
Fall Semester 1950	192	5,475
Spring Semester 1951	228	6,115
Fall Semester 1951	225	6,633
Spring Semester 1952	229	6,771
Fall Semester 1952	225	5,595
Spring Semester 1953	189	5,002

Source: Headquarters Civil Air Patrol, USAF.

TABLE 375 — CIVIL AIR PATROL CADET SUMMER ENCAMPMENT — 1952

1. Forty-two (42) cadet encampments were held during 1952 at thirty-nine (39) Air Force Bases. All Wings participated with the exception of the Louisiana Wing which did not participate due to a polio outbreak in their State.

2. Cadet Participation:

   a. Enrollment: 4,878 (3,939 boys and 939 girls)

   b. Satisfactorily completed course of instruction: 4,737

      Did not satisfactorily complete course of instruction: 39

      Early departures for various reasons: 102

3. Senior Participation:

   a. Enrollment: 505 (368 men and 137 women)

   b. 5,112 man-days served by the seniors for an average of 10 days service per senior.

4. Direct Manpower Assistance from Encampment Site:

   a. USAF Personnel: 496 Officers and 506 Airmen

   b. Air Reservists: 184 Officers and 11 Airmen

   c. Civilians: 81

TABLE 375 — CIVIL AIR PATROL CADET SUMMER ENCAMPMENT — 1952 — Continued

5. Aerial transportation to and/or from Encampment Sites (as part of routine training flights without additional expense to the Government):

Source	Planes	Number Transported	Flying Time
TOTAL	251	4,191	1,027:50
USAF	217	3,831	900:20
Air National Guard	13	282	67:00
Civil Air Patrol	21	78	60:30

6. Orientation flights at Encampment Sites (as part of routine training flights without additional expense to the Government) 68.8% of the total Cadet attendance (excluding early departures) were flown on orientation flights:

Source	Planes	Number Cadets Flown	Flying Time
TOTAL	276	3,284	812:35
USAF	274	3,206	800:40
Air National Guard	1	75	4:00
Civil Air Patrol	1	3	7:55

7. Familiarization firing of small arms (this firing was conducted strictly on an individual, volunteer basis, and was scheduled only where adequate range supervisory personnel were available):

Type of Weapon	Number Cadets Firing	Rounds Fired
TOTAL	2,564	72,667
Carbine	2,509	72,392
12 Guage "Skeet"	55	275

Source: Headquarters, Civil Air Patrol, USAF.

TABLE 376 — STATUS AND LINE CLASSIFICATION OF CIVIL AIR PATROL AIRPLANE INVENTORY BY MODEL — QUARTERLY — FY 1953

MODEL	TOTAL			ACTIVE			INACTIVE		
	TOTAL	FIRST LINE	SECOND LINE	TOTAL	FIRST LINE	SECOND LINE	TOTAL	FIRST LINE	SECOND LINE
	30 SEPTEMBER 1952								
TOTAL	359	123	236	358	123	235	1	-	1
L-4	125	-	125	124	-	124	1	-	1
L-5	51	-	51	51	-	51	-	-	-
L-16	183	123	60	183	123	60	-	-	-
	31 DECEMBER 1952								
TOTAL	474	25	449	472	25	447	2	-	2
L-4	139	-	139	138	-	138	1	-	1
L-5	68	-	68	68	-	68	-	-	-
L-16	267	25	242	266	25	241	1	-	1
	31 MARCH 1953								
TOTAL	521	-	521	519	-	519	2	-	2
L-4	133	-	133	131	-	131	2	-	2
L-5	66	-	66	66	-	66	-	-	-
L-16	322	-	322	322	-	322	-	-	-
	30 JUNE 1953								
TOTAL	519	-	519	519	-	519	-	-	-
L-4	127	-	127	127	-	127	-	-	-
L-5	66	-	66	66	-	66	-	-	-
L-16	326	-	326	326	-	326	-	-	-

SOURCE: Materiel Statistics Division, Directorate of Statistical Services, DCS/C.

TABLE 377 — FUNCTIONAL DISTRIBUTION OF CIVIL AIR PATROL AIRPLANE INVENTORY — QUARTERLY — FY 1953

TYPE	TOTAL AIRPLANES	ACTIVE						INACTIVE	
		TOTAL	TRAINING	MINIMUM INDIVIDUAL TRAINING	SPECIAL MISSION	MAINTE- NANCE	PROJECT	TOTAL	EXCESS AND RECOMMENDED RECLAMATION
	30 SEPTEMBER 1952								
TOTAL . . .	359	358	-	358	-	-	-	1	1
Communication . .	359	358	-	358	-	-	-	1	1
	31 DECEMBER 1952								
TOTAL . . .	474	472	-	406	-	64	2	2	2
Communication . .	474	472	-	406	-	64	2	2	2
	31 MARCH 1953								
TOTAL . . .	521	519	-	433	-	85	1	2	2
Communication . .	521	519	-	433	-	85	1	2	2
	30 JUNE 1953								
TOTAL . . .	519	519	3	447	1	68	-	-	-
Communication . .	519	519	3	447	1	68	-	-	-

SOURCE: Materiel Statistics Division, Directorate of Statistical Services, DCS/C.

Printed in Great Britain
by Amazon